Deep Learning

Adaptive Computation and Machine Learning

Thomas Dietterich, Editor

Christopher Bishop, David Heckerman, Michael Jordan, and
Michael Kearns, Associate Editors

A complete list of books published in The Adaptive Computation and
Machine Learning series appears at the back of this book.

Deep Learning

Ian Goodfellow
Yoshua Bengio and
Aaron Courville

The MIT Press
Cambridge, Massachusetts
London, England

This book was set in SFRM1095 by diacriTech, Chennai.

Printed and bound in the United States of America.

Library of Congress Cataloging-in-Publication Data

Names: Goodfellow, Ian, author. | Bengio, Yoshua, author. | Courville, Aaron, author.
Title: Deep learning / Ian Goodfellow, Yoshua Bengio, and Aaron Courville.
Description: Cambridge, MA : MIT Press, [2017] | Series: Adaptive computation and machine learning series | Includes bibliographical references and index.
Identifiers: LCCN 2016022992 | ISBN 9780262035613 (hardcover : alk. paper)
Subjects: LCSH: Machine learning,
Classification: LCC Q325.5 .G66 2017 | DDC 006.3/1–dc23 LC record available at https://lccn.loc.gov/2016022992

10 9 8 7 6 5

Contents

Website

www.deeplearningbook.org

This book is accompanied by the above website. The website provides a variety of supplementary material, including exercises, lecture slides, corrections of mistakes, and other resources that should be useful to both readers and instructors.

Acknowledgments

This book would not have been possible without the contributions of many people.

We would like to thank those who commented on our proposal for the book and helped plan its contents and organization: Guillaume Alain, Kyunghyun Cho, Çağlar Gülçehre, David Krueger, Hugo Larochelle, Razvan Pascanu and Thomas Rohée.

We would like to thank the people who offered feedback on the content of the book itself. Some offered feedback on many chapters: Martín Abadi, Guillaume Alain, Ion Androutsopoulos, Fred Bertsch, Olexa Bilaniuk, Ufuk Can Biçici, Matko Bošnjak, John Boersma, Greg Brockman, Alexandre de Brébisson, Pierre Luc Carrier, Sarath Chandar, Pawel Chilinski, Mark Daoust, Oleg Dashevskii, Laurent Dinh, Stephan Dreseitl, Jim Fan, Miao Fan, Meire Fortunato, Frédéric Francis, Nando de Freitas, Çağlar Gülçehre, Jurgen Van Gael, Javier Alonso García, Jonathan Hunt, Gopi Jeyaram, Chingiz Kabytayev, Lukasz Kaiser, Varun Kanade, Asifullah Khan, Akiel Khan, John King, Diederik P. Kingma, Yann LeCun, Rudolf Mathey, Matías Mattamala, Abhinav Maurya, Kevin Murphy, Oleg Mürk, Roman Novak, Augustus Q. Odena, Simon Pavlik, Karl Pichotta, Eddie Pierce, Kari Pulli, Roussel Rahman, Tapani Raiko, Anurag Ranjan, Johannes Roith, Mihaela Rosca, Halis Sak, César Salgado, Grigory Sapunov, Yoshinori Sasaki, Mike Schuster, Julian Serban, Nir Shabat, Ken Shirriff, Andre Simpelo, David Slate, Scott Stanley, David Sussillo, Ilya Sutskever, Carles Gelada Sáez, Graham Taylor, Valentin Tolmer, Massimiliano Tomassoli, An Tran, Shubhendu Trivedi, Alexey Umnov, Vincent Vanhoucke, Marco Visentini-Scarzanella, Martin Vita, David Warde-Farley, Dustin Webb, Kelvin Xu, Wei Xue, Ke Yang, Li Yao, Zygmunt Zając and Ozan Çağlayan.

We would also like to thank those who provided us with useful feedback on individual chapters:

- Notation: Zhang Yuanhang.

- Chapter 1, Introduction: Yusuf Akgul, Sebastien Bratieres, Samira Ebrahimi,

Charlie Gorichanaz, Brendan Loudermilk, Eric Morris, Cosmin Pârvulescu and Alfredo Solano.

- Chapter 2, Linear Algebra: Amjad Almahairi, Nikola Banić, Kevin Bennett, Philippe Castonguay, Oscar Chang, Eric Fosler-Lussier, Andrey Khalyavin, Sergey Oreshkov, István Petrás, Dennis Prangle, Thomas Rohée, Gitanjali Gulve Sehgal, Colby Toland, Alessandro Vitale and Bob Welland.

- Chapter 3, Probability and Information Theory: John Philip Anderson, Kai Arulkumaran, Vincent Dumoulin, Rui Fa, Stephan Gouws, Artem Oboturov, Antti Rasmus, Alexey Surkov and Volker Tresp.

- Chapter 4, Numerical Computation: Tran Lam AnIan Fischer and Hu Yuhuang.

- Chapter 5, Machine Learning Basics: Dzmitry Bahdanau, Justin Domingue, Nikhil Garg, Makoto Otsuka, Bob Pepin, Philip Popien, Bharat Prabhakar, Emmanuel Rayner, Peter Shepard, Kee-Bong Song, Zheng Sun and Andy Wu.

- Chapter 6, Deep Feedforward Networks: Uriel Berdugo, Fabrizio Bottarel, Elizabeth Burl, Ishan Durugkar, Jeff Hlywa, Jong Wook Kim, David Krueger, Aditya Kumar Praharaj and Sten Sootla.

- Chapter 7, Regularization for Deep Learning: Morten Kolbæk, Kshitij Lauria, Inkyu Lee, Sunil Mohan, Hai Phong Phan and Joshua Salisbury.

- Chapter 8, Optimization for Training Deep Models: Marcel Ackermann, Peter Armitage, Rowel Atienza, Andrew Brock, Tegan Maharaj, James Martens, Mostafa Nategh, Kashif Rasul, Klaus Strobl and Nicholas Turner.

- Chapter 9, Convolutional Networks: Martín Arjovsky, Eugene Brevdo, Konstantin Divilov, Eric Jensen, Mehdi Mirza, Alex Paino, Marjorie Sayer, Ryan Stout and Wentao Wu.

- Chapter 10, Sequence Modeling: Recurrent and Recursive Nets: Gökçen Eraslan, Steven Hickson, Razvan Pascanu, Lorenzo von Ritter, Rui Rodrigues, Dmitriy Serdyuk, Dongyu Shi and Kaiyu Yang.

- Chapter 11, Practical Methodology: Daniel Beckstein.

- Chapter 12, Applications: George Dahl, Vladimir Nekrasov and Ribana Roscher.

- Chapter 13, Linear Factor Models: Jayanth Koushik.

- Chapter 15, Representation Learning: Kunal Ghosh.

- Chapter 16, Structured Probabilistic Models for Deep Learning: Minh Lê and Anton Varfolom.

- Chapter 18, Confronting the Partition Function: Sam Bowman.

- Chapter 19, Approximate Inference: Yujia Bao.

- Chapter 20, Deep Generative Models: Nicolas Chapados, Daniel Galvez, Wenming Ma, Fady Medhat, Shakir Mohamed and Grégoire Montavon.

- Bibliography: Lukas Michelbacher and Leslie N. Smith.

We also want to thank those who allowed us to reproduce images, figures or data from their publications. We indicate their contributions in the figure captions throughout the text.

We would like to thank Lu Wang for writing pdf2htmlEX, which we used to make the web version of the book, and for offering support to improve the quality of the resulting HTML.

We would like to thank Ian's wife Daniela Flori Goodfellow for patiently supporting Ian during the writing of the book as well as for help with proofreading.

We would like to thank the Google Brain team for providing an intellectual environment where Ian could devote a tremendous amount of time to writing this book and receive feedback and guidance from colleagues. We would especially like to thank Ian's former manager, Greg Corrado, and his current manager, Samy Bengio, for their support of this project. Finally, we would like to thank Geoffrey Hinton for encouragement when writing was difficult.

Notation

This section provides a concise reference describing the notation used throughout this book. If you are unfamiliar with any of the corresponding mathematical concepts, we describe most of these ideas in chapters 2–4.

Numbers and Arrays

a	A scalar (integer or real)
$\boldsymbol{a}$	A vector
$\boldsymbol{A}$	A matrix
A	A tensor
$\boldsymbol{I}_n$	Identity matrix with n rows and n columns
$\boldsymbol{I}$	Identity matrix with dimensionality implied by context
$\boldsymbol{e}^{(i)}$	Standard basis vector $[0, \ldots, 0, 1, 0, \ldots, 0]$ with a 1 at position i
$\mathrm{diag}(\boldsymbol{a})$	A square, diagonal matrix with diagonal entries given by $\boldsymbol{a}$
a	A scalar random variable
$\mathbf{a}$	A vector-valued random variable
$\mathbf{A}$	A matrix-valued random variable

Sets and Graphs

$\mathbb{A}$	A set
$\mathbb{R}$	The set of real numbers
$\{0, 1\}$	The set containing 0 and 1
$\{0, 1, \ldots, n\}$	The set of all integers between 0 and n
$[a, b]$	The real interval including a and b
$(a, b]$	The real interval excluding a but including b
$\mathbb{A} \backslash \mathbb{B}$	Set subtraction, i.e., the set containing the elements of $\mathbb{A}$ that are not in $\mathbb{B}$
$\mathcal{G}$	A graph
$Pa_{\mathcal{G}}(\mathrm{x}_i)$	The parents of x_i in $\mathcal{G}$

Indexing

a_i	Element i of vector $\boldsymbol{a}$, with indexing starting at 1
a_{-i}	All elements of vector $\boldsymbol{a}$ except for element i
$A_{i,j}$	Element i, j of matrix $\boldsymbol{A}$
$\boldsymbol{A}_{i,:}$	Row i of matrix $\boldsymbol{A}$
$\boldsymbol{A}_{:,i}$	Column i of matrix $\boldsymbol{A}$
$A_{i,j,k}$	Element (i, j, k) of a 3-D tensor A
$\mathsf{A}_{:,:,i}$	2-D slice of a 3-D tensor
a_i	Element i of the random vector $\mathbf{a}$

Linear Algebra Operations

$\boldsymbol{A}^{\top}$	Transpose of matrix $\boldsymbol{A}$
$\boldsymbol{A}^{+}$	Moore-Penrose pseudoinverse of $\boldsymbol{A}$
$\boldsymbol{A} \odot \boldsymbol{B}$	Element-wise (Hadamard) product of $\boldsymbol{A}$ and $\boldsymbol{B}$
$\det(\boldsymbol{A})$	Determinant of $\boldsymbol{A}$

Calculus

$\dfrac{dy}{dx}$ Derivative of y with respect to x

$\dfrac{\partial y}{\partial x}$ Partial derivative of y with respect to x

$\nabla_{\boldsymbol{x}} y$ Gradient of y with respect to $\boldsymbol{x}$

$\nabla_{\boldsymbol{X}} y$ Matrix derivatives of y with respect to $\boldsymbol{X}$

$\nabla_{\mathsf{X}} y$ Tensor containing derivatives of y with respect to X

$\dfrac{\partial f}{\partial \boldsymbol{x}}$ Jacobian matrix $\boldsymbol{J} \in \mathbb{R}^{m \times n}$ of $f : \mathbb{R}^n \to \mathbb{R}^m$

$\nabla_{\boldsymbol{x}}^2 f(\boldsymbol{x})$ or $\boldsymbol{H}(f)(\boldsymbol{x})$ The Hessian matrix of f at input point $\boldsymbol{x}$

$\displaystyle\int f(\boldsymbol{x}) d\boldsymbol{x}$ Definite integral over the entire domain of $\boldsymbol{x}$

$\displaystyle\int_{\mathbb{S}} f(\boldsymbol{x}) d\boldsymbol{x}$ Definite integral with respect to $\boldsymbol{x}$ over the set $\mathbb{S}$

Probability and Information Theory

$\mathrm{a} \perp \mathrm{b}$ The random variables a and b are independent

$\mathrm{a} \perp \mathrm{b} \mid \mathrm{c}$ They are conditionally independent given c

$P(\mathrm{a})$ A probability distribution over a discrete variable

$p(\mathrm{a})$ A probability distribution over a continuous variable, or over a variable whose type has not been specified

$\mathrm{a} \sim P$ Random variable a has distribution P

$\mathbb{E}_{\mathrm{x} \sim P}[f(x)]$ or $\mathbb{E}f(x)$ Expectation of $f(x)$ with respect to $P(\mathrm{x})$

$\mathrm{Var}(f(x))$ Variance of $f(x)$ under $P(\mathrm{x})$

$\mathrm{Cov}(f(x), g(x))$ Covariance of $f(x)$ and $g(x)$ under $P(\mathrm{x})$

$H(\mathrm{x})$ Shannon entropy of the random variable x

$D_{\mathrm{KL}}(P\|Q)$ Kullback-Leibler divergence of P and Q

$\mathcal{N}(\boldsymbol{x}; \boldsymbol{\mu}, \boldsymbol{\Sigma})$ Gaussian distribution over $\boldsymbol{x}$ with mean $\boldsymbol{\mu}$ and covariance $\boldsymbol{\Sigma}$

Functions

$f : \mathbb{A} \to \mathbb{B}$	The function f with domain $\mathbb{A}$ and range $\mathbb{B}$
$f \circ g$	Composition of the functions f and g
$f(\boldsymbol{x}; \boldsymbol{\theta})$	A function of $\boldsymbol{x}$ parametrized by $\boldsymbol{\theta}$. (Sometimes we write $f(\boldsymbol{x})$ and omit the argument $\boldsymbol{\theta}$ to lighten notation)
$\log x$	Natural logarithm of x
$\sigma(x)$	Logistic sigmoid, $\dfrac{1}{1 + \exp(-x)}$
$\zeta(x)$	Softplus, $\log(1 + \exp(x))$
$||\boldsymbol{x}||_p$	L^p norm of $\boldsymbol{x}$
$||\boldsymbol{x}||$	L^2 norm of $\boldsymbol{x}$
x^+	Positive part of x, i.e., $\max(0, x)$
$\mathbf{1}_{\text{condition}}$	is 1 if the condition is true, 0 otherwise

Sometimes we use a function f whose argument is a scalar but apply it to a vector, matrix, or tensor: $f(\boldsymbol{x})$, $f(\boldsymbol{X})$, or $f(\mathbf{X})$. This denotes the application of f to the array element-wise. For example, if $\mathbf{C} = \sigma(\mathbf{X})$, then $C_{i,j,k} = \sigma(X_{i,j,k})$ for all valid values of i, j and k.

Datasets and Distributions

p_{data}	The data generating distribution
$\hat{p}_{\text{data}}$	The empirical distribution defined by the training set
$\mathbb{X}$	A set of training examples
$\boldsymbol{x}^{(i)}$	The i-th example (input) from a dataset
$y^{(i)}$ or $\boldsymbol{y}^{(i)}$	The target associated with $\boldsymbol{x}^{(i)}$ for supervised learning
$\boldsymbol{X}$	The $m \times n$ matrix with input example $\boldsymbol{x}^{(i)}$ in row $\boldsymbol{X}_{i,:}$

1

Introduction

Inventors have long dreamed of creating machines that think. This desire dates back to at least the time of ancient Greece. The mythical figures Pygmalion, Daedalus, and Hephaestus may all be interpreted as legendary inventors, and Galatea, Talos, and Pandora may all be regarded as artificial life (Ovid and Martin, 2004; Sparkes, 1996; Tandy, 1997).

When programmable computers were first conceived, people wondered whether such machines might become intelligent, over a hundred years before one was built (Lovelace, 1842). Today, **artificial intelligence** (AI) is a thriving field with many practical applications and active research topics. We look to intelligent software to automate routine labor, understand speech or images, make diagnoses in medicine and support basic scientific research.

In the early days of artificial intelligence, the field rapidly tackled and solved problems that are intellectually difficult for human beings but relatively straightforward for computers—problems that can be described by a list of formal, mathematical rules. The true challenge to artificial intelligence proved to be solving the tasks that are easy for people to perform but hard for people to describe formally—problems that we solve intuitively, that feel automatic, like recognizing spoken words or faces in images.

This book is about a solution to these more intuitive problems. This solution is to allow computers to learn from experience and understand the world in terms of a hierarchy of concepts, with each concept defined through its relation to simpler concepts. By gathering knowledge from experience, this approach avoids the need for human operators to formally specify all the knowledge that the computer needs. The hierarchy of concepts enables the computer to learn complicated concepts by building them out of simpler ones. If we draw a graph showing how these concepts are built on top of each other, the graph is deep, with many layers. For this reason, we call this approach to AI **deep learning**.

Many of the early successes of AI took place in relatively sterile and formal environments and did not require computers to have much knowledge about the world. For example, IBM's Deep Blue chess-playing system defeated world champion Garry Kasparov in 1997 (Hsu, 2002). Chess is of course a very simple world, containing only sixty-four locations and thirty-two pieces that can move in only rigidly circumscribed ways. Devising a successful chess strategy is a tremendous accomplishment, but the challenge is not due to the difficulty of describing the set of chess pieces and allowable moves to the computer. Chess can be completely described by a very brief list of completely formal rules, easily provided ahead of time by the programmer.

Ironically, abstract and formal tasks that are among the most difficult mental undertakings for a human being are among the easiest for a computer. Computers have long been able to defeat even the best human chess player but only recently have begun matching some of the abilities of average human beings to recognize objects or speech. A person's everyday life requires an immense amount of knowledge about the world. Much of this knowledge is subjective and intuitive, and therefore difficult to articulate in a formal way. Computers need to capture this same knowledge in order to behave in an intelligent way. One of the key challenges in artificial intelligence is how to get this informal knowledge into a computer.

Several artificial intelligence projects have sought to hard-code knowledge about the world in formal languages. A computer can reason automatically about statements in these formal languages using logical inference rules. This is known as the **knowledge base** approach to artificial intelligence. None of these projects has led to a major success. One of the most famous such projects is Cyc (Lenat and Guha, 1989). Cyc is an inference engine and a database of statements in a language called CycL. These statements are entered by a staff of human supervisors. It is an unwieldy process. People struggle to devise formal rules with enough complexity to accurately describe the world. For example, Cyc failed to understand a story about a person named Fred shaving in the morning (Linde, 1992). Its inference engine detected an inconsistency in the story: it knew that people do not have electrical parts, but because Fred was holding an electric razor, it believed the entity "FredWhileShaving" contained electrical parts. It therefore asked whether Fred was still a person while he was shaving.

The difficulties faced by systems relying on hard-coded knowledge suggest that AI systems need the ability to acquire their own knowledge, by extracting patterns from raw data. This capability is known as **machine learning**. The introduction of machine learning enabled computers to tackle problems involving knowledge of the real world and make decisions that appear subjective. A simple machine learning algorithm called **logistic regression** can determine whether to recommend cesarean delivery (Mor-Yosef et al., 1990). A simple machine learning algorithm called **naive Bayes** can separate legitimate e-mail from spam e-mail.

The performance of these simple machine learning algorithms depends heavily on the **representation** of the data they are given. For example, when logistic regression is used to recommend cesarean delivery, the AI system does not examine the patient directly. Instead, the doctor tells the system several pieces of relevant information, such as the presence or absence of a uterine scar. Each piece of information included in the representation of the patient is known as a **feature**. Logistic regression learns how each of these features of the patient correlates with various outcomes. However, it cannot influence how features are defined in any way. If logistic regression were given an MRI scan of the patient, rather than the doctor's formalized report, it would not be able to make useful predictions. Individual pixels in an MRI scan have negligible correlation with any complications that might occur during delivery.

This dependence on representations is a general phenomenon that appears throughout computer science and even daily life. In computer science, operations such as searching a collection of data can proceed exponentially faster if the collection is structured and indexed intelligently. People can easily perform arithmetic on Arabic numerals but find arithmetic on Roman numerals much more time consuming. It is not surprising that the choice of representation has an enormous effect on the performance of machine learning algorithms. For a simple visual example, see figure 1.1.

Many artificial intelligence tasks can be solved by designing the right set of features to extract for that task, then providing these features to a simple machine learning algorithm. For example, a useful feature for speaker identification from sound is an estimate of the size of the speaker's vocal tract. This feature gives a strong clue as to whether the speaker is a man, woman, or child.

For many tasks, however, it is difficult to know what features should be extracted. For example, suppose that we would like to write a program to detect cars in photographs. We know that cars have wheels, so we might like to use the presence of a wheel as a feature. Unfortunately, it is difficult to describe exactly what a wheel looks like in terms of pixel values. A wheel has a simple geometric shape, but its image may be complicated by shadows falling on the wheel, the sun glaring off the metal parts of the wheel, the fender of the car or an object in the foreground obscuring part of the wheel, and so on.

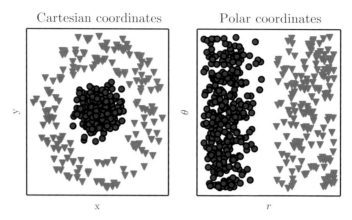

Figure 1.1: Example of different representations: suppose we want to separate two categories of data by drawing a line between them in a scatterplot. In the plot on the left, we represent some data using Cartesian coordinates, and the task is impossible. In the plot on the right, we represent the data with polar coordinates and the task becomes simple to solve with a vertical line. (Figure produced in collaboration with David Warde-Farley.)

One solution to this problem is to use machine learning to discover not only the mapping from representation to output but also the representation itself. This approach is known as **representation learning**. Learned representations often result in much better performance than can be obtained with hand-designed representations. They also enable AI systems to rapidly adapt to new tasks, with minimal human intervention. A representation learning algorithm can discover a good set of features for a simple task in minutes, or for a complex task in hours to months. Manually designing features for a complex task requires a great deal of human time and effort; it can take decades for an entire community of researchers.

The quintessential example of a representation learning algorithm is the **autoencoder**. An autoencoder is the combination of an **encoder** function, which converts the input data into a different representation, and a **decoder** function, which converts the new representation back into the original format. Autoencoders are trained to preserve as much information as possible when an input is run through the encoder and then the decoder, but they are also trained to make the new representation have various nice properties. Different kinds of autoencoders aim to achieve different kinds of properties.

When designing features or algorithms for learning features, our goal is usually to separate the **factors of variation** that explain the observed data. In this context, we use the word "factors" simply to refer to separate sources of influence; the factors are usually not combined by multiplication. Such factors are often not quantities that are directly observed. Instead, they may exist as either unobserved objects or unobserved forces in the physical world that affect observable quantities. They may also exist as constructs in the human mind that provide useful simplifying explanations or inferred causes of the observed data. They can be thought of as concepts or abstractions that help us make sense of the rich variability in the data. When analyzing a speech recording, the factors of variation include the speaker's age, their sex, their accent and the words they are speaking. When analyzing an image of a car, the factors of variation include the position of the car, its color, and the angle and brightness of the sun.

A major source of difficulty in many real-world artificial intelligence applications is that many of the factors of variation influence every single piece of data we are able to observe. The individual pixels in an image of a red car might be very close to black at night. The shape of the car's silhouette depends on the viewing angle. Most applications require us to *disentangle* the factors of variation and discard the ones that we do not care about.

Of course, it can be very difficult to extract such high-level, abstract features from raw data. Many of these factors of variation, such as a speaker's accent, can be identified only using sophisticated, nearly human-level understanding of the data. When it is nearly as difficult to obtain a representation as to solve the original problem, representation learning does not, at first glance, seem to help us.

Deep learning solves this central problem in representation learning by introducing representations that are expressed in terms of other, simpler representations. Deep learning enables the computer to build complex concepts out of simpler concepts. Figure 1.2 shows how a deep learning system can represent the concept of an image of a person by combining simpler concepts, such as corners and contours, which are in turn defined in terms of edges.

The quintessential example of a deep learning model is the feedforward deep network, or **multilayer perceptron** (MLP). A multilayer perceptron is just a mathematical function mapping some set of input values to output values. The function is formed by composing many simpler functions. We can think of each application of a different mathematical function as providing a new representation of the input.

The idea of learning the right representation for the data provides one perspective on deep learning. Another perspective on deep learning is that depth enables the computer to learn a multistep computer program. Each layer of the representation can be thought of as the state of the computer's memory after executing another set of instructions in parallel. Networks with greater depth can execute more instructions in sequence. Sequential instructions offer great power because later instructions can refer back to the results of earlier instructions.

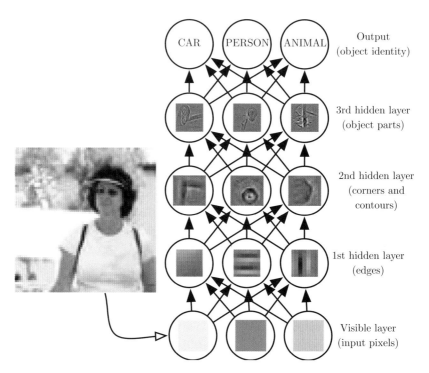

Figure 1.2: Illustration of a deep learning model. It is difficult for a computer to understand the meaning of raw sensory input data, such as this image represented as a collection of pixel values. The function mapping from a set of pixels to an object identity is very complicated. Learning or evaluating this mapping seems insurmountable if tackled directly. Deep learning resolves this difficulty by breaking the desired complicated mapping into a series of nested simple mappings, each described by a different layer of the model. The input is presented at the **visible layer**, so named because it contains the variables that we are able to observe. Then a series of **hidden layers** extracts increasingly abstract features from the image. These layers are called "hidden" because their values are not given in the data; instead the model must determine which concepts are useful for explaining the relationships in the observed data. The images here are visualizations of the kind of feature represented by each hidden unit. Given the pixels, the first layer can easily identify edges, by comparing the brightness of neighboring pixels. Given the first hidden layer's description of the edges, the second hidden layer can easily search for corners and extended contours, which are recognizable as collections of edges. Given the second hidden layer's description of the image in terms of corners and contours, the third hidden layer can detect entire parts of specific objects, by finding specific collections of contours and corners. Finally, this description of the image in terms of the object parts it contains can be used to recognize the objects present in the image. Images reproduced with permission from Zeiler and Fergus (2014).

According to this view of deep learning, not all the information in a layer's activations necessarily encodes factors of variation that explain the input. The representation also stores state information that helps to execute a program that can make sense of the input. This state information could be analogous to a counter or pointer in a traditional computer program. It has nothing to do with the content of the input specifically, but it helps the model to organize its processing.

There are two main ways of measuring the depth of a model. The first view is based on the number of sequential instructions that must be executed to evaluate the architecture. We can think of this as the length of the longest path through a flow chart that describes how to compute each of the model's outputs given its inputs. Just as two equivalent computer programs will have different lengths depending on which language the program is written in, the same function may be drawn as a flowchart with different depths depending on which functions we allow to be used as individual steps in the flowchart. Figure 1.3 illustrates how this choice of language can give two different measurements for the same architecture.

Another approach, used by deep probabilistic models, regards the depth of a model as being not the depth of the computational graph but the depth of the graph describing how concepts are related to each other. In this case, the depth

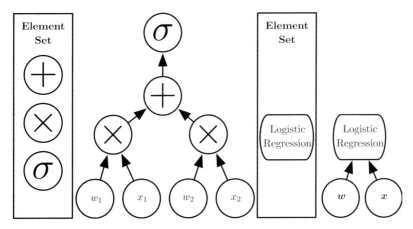

Figure 1.3: Illustration of computational graphs mapping an input to an output where each node performs an operation. Depth is the length of the longest path from input to output but depends on the definition of what constitutes a possible computational step. The computation depicted in these graphs is the output of a logistic regression model, $\sigma(\boldsymbol{w}^T \boldsymbol{x})$, where σ is the logistic sigmoid function. If we use addition, multiplication and logistic sigmoids as the elements of our computer language, then this model has depth three. If we view logistic regression as an element itself, then this model has depth one.

of the flowchart of the computations needed to compute the representation of each concept may be much deeper than the graph of the concepts themselves. This is because the system's understanding of the simpler concepts can be refined given information about the more complex concepts. For example, an AI system observing an image of a face with one eye in shadow may initially see only one eye. After detecting that a face is present, the system can then infer that a second eye is probably present as well. In this case, the graph of concepts includes only two layers—a layer for eyes and a layer for faces—but the graph of computations includes $2n$ layers if we refine our estimate of each concept given the other n times.

Because it is not always clear which of these two views—the depth of the computational graph, or the depth of the probabilistic modeling graph—is most relevant, and because different people choose different sets of smallest elements from which to construct their graphs, there is no single correct value for the depth of an architecture, just as there is no single correct value for the length of a computer program. Nor is there a consensus about how much depth a model requires to qualify as "deep." However, deep learning can be safely regarded as the study of models that involve a greater amount of composition of either learned functions or learned concepts than traditional machine learning does.

To summarize, deep learning, the subject of this book, is an approach to AI. Specifically, it is a type of machine learning, a technique that enables computer systems to improve with experience and data. We contend that machine learning is the only viable approach to building AI systems that can operate in complicated real-world environments. Deep learning is a particular kind of machine learning that achieves great power and flexibility by representing the world as a nested hierarchy of concepts, with each concept defined in relation to simpler concepts, and more abstract representations computed in terms of less abstract ones. Figure 1.4 illustrates the relationship between these different AI disciplines. Figure 1.5 gives a high-level schematic of how each works.

1.1 Who Should Read This Book?

This book can be useful for a variety of readers, but we wrote it with two target audiences in mind. One of these target audiences is university students (undergraduate or graduate) learning about machine learning, including those who are beginning a career in deep learning and artificial intelligence research. The other target audience is software engineers who do not have a machine learning or statistics background but want to rapidly acquire one and begin using deep learning in their product or platform. Deep learning has already proved useful in many soft-

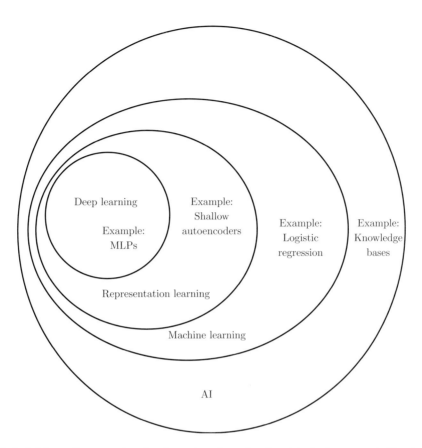

Figure 1.4: A Venn diagram showing how deep learning is a kind of representation learning, which is in turn a kind of machine learning, which is used for many but not all approaches to AI. Each section of the Venn diagram includes an example of an AI technology.

ware disciplines, including computer vision, speech and audio processing, natural language processing, robotics, bioinformatics and chemistry, video games, search engines, online advertising and finance.

This book has been organized into three parts to best accommodate a variety of readers. Part I introduces basic mathematical tools and machine learning concepts. Part II describes the most established deep learning algorithms, which are essentially solved technologies. Part III describes more speculative ideas that are widely believed to be important for future research in deep learning.

Readers should feel free to skip parts that are not relevant given their interests or background. Readers familiar with linear algebra, probability, and fundamental machine learning concepts can skip part I, for example, while those who just want

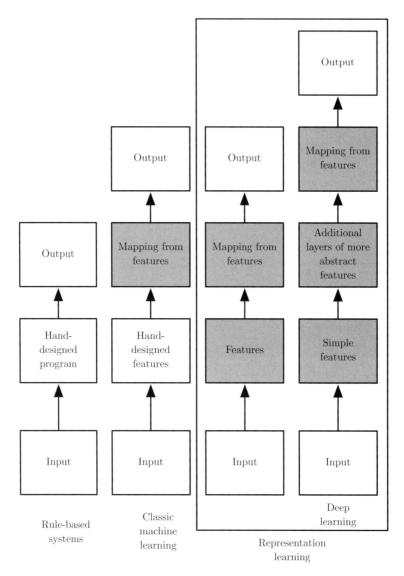

Figure 1.5: Flowcharts showing how the different parts of an AI system relate to each other within different AI disciplines. Shaded boxes indicate components that are able to learn from data.

to implement a working system need not read beyond part II. To help choose which chapters to read, figure 1.6 provides a flowchart showing the high-level organization of the book.

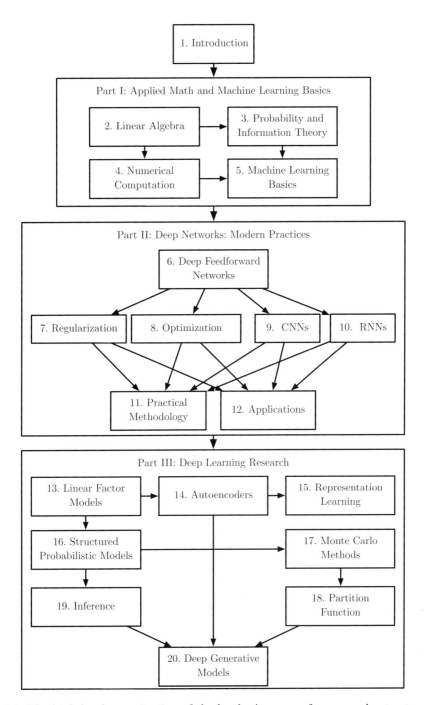

Figure 1.6: The high-level organization of the book. An arrow from one chapter to another indicates that the former chapter is prerequisite material for understanding the latter.

We do assume that all readers come from a computer science background. We assume familiarity with programming, a basic understanding of computational performance issues, complexity theory, introductory level calculus and some of the terminology of graph theory.

1.2 Historical Trends in Deep Learning

It is easiest to understand deep learning with some historical context. Rather than providing a detailed history of deep learning, we identify a few key trends:

- Deep learning has had a long and rich history, but has gone by many names, reflecting different philosophical viewpoints, and has waxed and waned in popularity.

- Deep learning has become more useful as the amount of available training data has increased.

- Deep learning models have grown in size over time as computer infrastructure (both hardware and software) for deep learning has improved.

- Deep learning has solved increasingly complicated applications with increasing accuracy over time.

1.2.1 The Many Names and Changing Fortunes of Neural Networks

We expect that many readers of this book have heard of deep learning as an exciting new technology, and are surprised to see a mention of "history" in a book about an emerging field. In fact, deep learning dates back to the 1940s. Deep learning only *appears* to be new, because it was relatively unpopular for several years preceding its current popularity, and because it has gone through many different names, only recently being called "deep learning." The field has been rebranded many times, reflecting the influence of different researchers and different perspectives.

A comprehensive history of deep learning is beyond the scope of this textbook. Some basic context, however, is useful for understanding deep learning. Broadly speaking, there have been three waves of development: deep learning known as **cybernetics** in the 1940s–1960s, deep learning known as **connectionism** in the 1980s–1990s, and the current resurgence under the name deep learning beginning in 2006. This is quantitatively illustrated in figure 1.7.

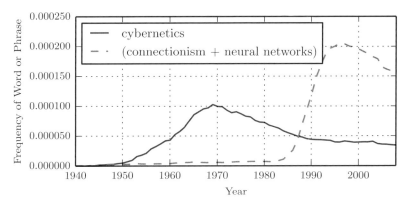

Figure 1.7: Two of the three historical waves of artificial neural nets research, as measured by the frequency of the phrases "cybernetics" and "connectionism" or "neural networks," according to Google Books (the third wave is too recent to appear). The first wave started with cybernetics in the 1940s–1960s, with the development of theories of biological learning (McCulloch and Pitts, 1943; Hebb, 1949) and implementations of the first models, such as the perceptron (Rosenblatt, 1958), enabling the training of a single neuron. The second wave started with the connectionist approach of the 1980–1995 period, with back-propagation (Rumelhart et al., 1986a) to train a neural network with one or two hidden layers. The current and third wave, deep learning, started around 2006 (Hinton et al., 2006; Bengio et al., 2007; Ranzato et al., 2007a) and is just now appearing in book form as of 2016. The other two waves similarly appeared in book form much later than the corresponding scientific activity occurred.

Some of the earliest learning algorithms we recognize today were intended to be computational models of biological learning, that is, models of how learning happens or could happen in the brain. As a result, one of the names that deep learning has gone by is **artificial neural networks** (ANNs). The corresponding perspective on deep learning models is that they are engineered systems inspired by the biological brain (whether the human brain or the brain of another animal). While the kinds of neural networks used for machine learning have sometimes been used to understand brain function (Hinton and Shallice, 1991), they are generally not designed to be realistic models of biological function. The neural perspective on deep learning is motivated by two main ideas. One idea is that the brain provides a proof by example that intelligent behavior is possible, and a conceptually straightforward path to building intelligence is to reverse engineer the computational principles behind the brain and duplicate its functionality. Another perspective is that it would be deeply interesting to understand the brain and the principles that underlie human intelligence, so machine learning models that shed light on these basic scientific questions are useful apart from their ability to solve engineering applications.

The modern term "deep learning" goes beyond the neuroscientific perspective on the current breed of machine learning models. It appeals to a more general principle of learning *multiple levels of composition*, which can be applied in machine learning frameworks that are not necessarily neurally inspired.

The earliest predecessors of modern deep learning were simple linear models motivated from a neuroscientific perspective. These models were designed to take a set of n input values $x_1, \ldots, x_n$ and associate them with an output y. These models would learn a set of weights $w_1, \ldots, w_n$ and compute their output $f(\boldsymbol{x}, \boldsymbol{w}) = x_1 w_1 + \cdots + x_n w_n$. This first wave of neural networks research was known as cybernetics, as illustrated in figure 1.7.

The McCulloch-Pitts neuron (McCulloch and Pitts, 1943) was an early model of brain function. This linear model could recognize two different categories of inputs by testing whether $f(\boldsymbol{x}, \boldsymbol{w})$ is positive or negative. Of course, for the model to correspond to the desired definition of the categories, the weights needed to be set correctly. These weights could be set by the human operator. In the 1950s, the perceptron (Rosenblatt, 1958, 1962) became the first model that could learn the weights that defined the categories given examples of inputs from each category. The **adaptive linear element** (ADALINE), which dates from about the same time, simply returned the value of $f(\boldsymbol{x})$ itself to predict a real number (Widrow and Hoff, 1960) and could also learn to predict these numbers from data.

These simple learning algorithms greatly affected the modern landscape of machine learning. The training algorithm used to adapt the weights of the ADALINE was a special case of an algorithm called **stochastic gradient descent**. Slightly modified versions of the stochastic gradient descent algorithm remain the dominant training algorithms for deep learning models today.

Models based on the $f(\boldsymbol{x}, \boldsymbol{w})$ used by the perceptron and ADALINE are called **linear models**. These models remain some of the most widely used machine learning models, though in many cases they are *trained* in different ways than the original models were trained.

Linear models have many limitations. Most famously, they cannot learn the XOR function, where $f([0, 1], \boldsymbol{w}) = 1$ and $f([1, 0], \boldsymbol{w}) = 1$ but $f([1, 1], \boldsymbol{w}) = 0$ and $f([0, 0], \boldsymbol{w}) = 0$. Critics who observed these flaws in linear models caused a backlash against biologically inspired learning in general (Minsky and Papert, 1969). This was the first major dip in the popularity of neural networks.

Today, neuroscience is regarded as an important source of inspiration for deep learning researchers, but it is no longer the predominant guide for the field.

The main reason for the diminished role of neuroscience in deep learning research today is that we simply do not have enough information about the brain to use it as a guide. To obtain a deep understanding of the actual algorithms used by the brain, we would need to be able to monitor the activity of (at the very least) thousands of interconnected neurons simultaneously. Because we are not able to do this, we are far from understanding even some of the most simple and well-studied parts of the brain (Olshausen and Field, 2005).

Neuroscience has given us a reason to hope that a single deep learning algorithm can solve many different tasks. Neuroscientists have found that ferrets can learn to "see" with the auditory processing region of their brain if their brains are rewired to send visual signals to that area (Von Melchner et al., 2000). This suggests that much of the mammalian brain might use a single algorithm to solve most of the different tasks that the brain solves. Before this hypothesis, machine learning research was more fragmented, with different communities of researchers studying natural language processing, vision, motion planning and speech recognition. Today, these application communities are still separate, but it is common for deep learning research groups to study many or even all these application areas simultaneously.

We are able to draw some rough guidelines from neuroscience. The basic idea of having many computational units that become intelligent only via their interactions with each other is inspired by the brain. The neocognitron (Fukushima, 1980) introduced a powerful model architecture for processing images that was inspired by the structure of the mammalian visual system and later became the basis for the modern convolutional network (LeCun et al., 1998b), as we will see in section 9.10. Most neural networks today are based on a model neuron called the **rectified linear unit**. The original cognitron (Fukushima, 1975) introduced a more complicated version that was highly inspired by our knowledge of brain function. The simplified modern version was developed incorporating ideas from many viewpoints, with Nair and Hinton (2010) and Glorot et al. (2011a) citing neuroscience as an influence, and Jarrett et al. (2009) citing more engineering-oriented influences. While neuroscience is an important source of inspiration, it need not be taken as a rigid guide. We know that actual neurons compute very different functions than modern rectified linear units, but greater neural realism has not yet led to an improvement in machine learning performance. Also, while neuroscience has successfully inspired several neural network *architectures*, we do not yet know enough about biological learning for neuroscience to offer much guidance for the *learning algorithms* we use to train these architectures.

Media accounts often emphasize the similarity of deep learning to the brain. While it is true that deep learning researchers are more likely to cite the brain as an influence than researchers working in other machine learning fields, such as kernel machines or Bayesian statistics, one should not view deep learning as an attempt to simulate the brain. Modern deep learning draws inspiration from many fields, especially applied math fundamentals like linear algebra, probability, information theory, and numerical optimization. While some deep learning researchers cite neuroscience as an important source of inspiration, others are not concerned with neuroscience at all.

It is worth noting that the effort to understand how the brain works on an algorithmic level is alive and well. This endeavor is primarily known as "computational neuroscience" and is a separate field of study from deep learning. It is common for researchers to move back and forth between both fields. The field of deep learning is primarily concerned with how to build computer systems that are able to successfully solve tasks requiring intelligence, while the field of computational neuroscience is primarily concerned with building more accurate models of how the brain actually works.

In the 1980s, the second wave of neural network research emerged in great part via a movement called **connectionism**, or **parallel distributed processing** (Rumelhart et al., 1986c; McClelland et al., 1995). Connectionism arose in the context of cognitive science. Cognitive science is an interdisciplinary approach to understanding the mind, combining multiple different levels of analysis. During the early 1980s, most cognitive scientists studied models of symbolic reasoning. Despite their popularity, symbolic models were difficult to explain in terms of how the brain could actually implement them using neurons. The connectionists began to study models of cognition that could actually be grounded in neural implementations (Touretzky and Minton, 1985), reviving many ideas dating back to the work of psychologist Donald Hebb in the 1940s (Hebb, 1949).

The central idea in connectionism is that a large number of simple computational units can achieve intelligent behavior when networked together. This insight applies equally to neurons in biological nervous systems as it does to hidden units in computational models.

Several key concepts arose during the connectionism movement of the 1980s that remain central to today's deep learning.

One of these concepts is that of **distributed representation** (Hinton et al., 1986). This is the idea that each input to a system should be represented by many features, and each feature should be involved in the representation of many possible inputs. For example, suppose we have a vision system that can recognize cars, trucks, and birds, and these objects can each be red, green, or blue. One way of representing these inputs would be to have a separate neuron or hidden unit that activates for each of the nine possible combinations: red truck, red car, red bird, green truck, and so on. This requires nine different neurons, and each neuron must independently learn the concept of color and object identity. One way to improve on this situation is to use a distributed representation, with three neurons describing the color and three neurons describing the object identity. This requires only six neurons total instead of nine, and the neuron describing redness is able to learn about redness from images of cars, trucks and birds, not just from images of one specific category of objects. The concept of distributed representation is central to this book and is described in greater detail in chapter 15.

Another major accomplishment of the connectionist movement was the successful use of back-propagation to train deep neural networks with internal representations and the popularization of the back-propagation algorithm (Rumelhart et al., 1986a; LeCun, 1987). This algorithm has waxed and waned in popularity but, as of this writing, is the dominant approach to training deep models.

During the 1990s, researchers made important advances in modeling sequences with neural networks. Hochreiter (1991) and Bengio et al. (1994) identified some of the fundamental mathematical difficulties in modeling long sequences, described in section 10.7. Hochreiter and Schmidhuber (1997) introduced the long short-term memory (LSTM) network to resolve some of these difficulties. Today, the LSTM is widely used for many sequence modeling tasks, including many natural language processing tasks at Google.

The second wave of neural networks research lasted until the mid-1990s. Ventures based on neural networks and other AI technologies began to make unrealistically ambitious claims while seeking investments. When AI research did not fulfill these unreasonable expectations, investors were disappointed. Simultaneously, other fields of machine learning made advances. Kernel machines (Boser et al., 1992; Cortes and Vapnik, 1995; Schölkopf et al., 1999) and graphical models (Jordan, 1998) both achieved good results on many important tasks. These two factors led to a decline in the popularity of neural networks that lasted until 2007.

During this time, neural networks continued to obtain impressive performance on some tasks (LeCun et al., 1998b; Bengio et al., 2001). The Canadian Institute for Advanced Research (CIFAR) helped to keep neural networks research alive via its Neural Computation and Adaptive Perception (NCAP) research initiative. This program united machine learning research groups led by Geoffrey Hinton at University of Toronto, Yoshua Bengio at University of Montreal, and Yann LeCun at New York University. The multidisciplinary CIFAR NCAP research initiative was also included neuroscientists and experts in human and computer vision.

At this point, deep networks were generally believed to be very difficult to train. We now know that algorithms that have existed since the 1980s work quite well, but this was not apparent circa 2006. The issue is perhaps simply that these algorithms were too computationally costly to allow much experimentation with the hardware available at the time.

The third wave of neural networks research began with a breakthrough in 2006. Geoffrey Hinton showed that a kind of neural network called a deep belief network could be efficiently trained using a strategy called greedy layer-wise pretraining (Hinton et al., 2006), which we describe in more detail in section 15.1. The other CIFAR-affiliated research groups quickly showed that the same strategy could be used to train many other kinds of deep networks (Bengio et al., 2007; Ranzato et al., 2007a) and systematically helped to improve generalization on test examples. This wave of neural networks research popularized the use of the term "deep learning" to emphasize that researchers were now able to train deeper neural networks than had been possible before, and to focus attention on the theoretical importance of depth (Bengio and LeCun, 2007; Delalleau and Bengio, 2011; Pascanu et al., 2014a; Montufar et al., 2014). At this time, deep neural networks outperformed competing AI systems based on other machine learning technologies as well as hand-designed functionality. This third wave of popularity of neural networks continues to the time of this writing, though the focus of deep learning research has changed dramatically within the time of this wave. The third wave began with a focus on new unsupervised learning techniques and the ability of deep models to generalize well from small datasets, but today there is more interest in much older supervised learning algorithms and the ability of deep models to leverage large labeled datasets.

1.2.2 Increasing Dataset Sizes

One may wonder why deep learning has only recently become recognized as a crucial technology even though the first experiments with artificial neural networks were conducted in the 1950s. Deep learning has been successfully used in commercial applications since the 1990s but was often regarded as being more of an art than a technology and something that only an expert could use, until recently. It is true that some skill is required to get good performance from a deep learning algorithm. Fortunately, the amount of skill required reduces as the amount of training data increases. The learning algorithms reaching human performance on complex tasks today are nearly identical to the learning algorithms that struggled to solve toy problems in the 1980s, though the models we train with these algorithms have undergone changes that simplify the training of very deep architectures. The most important new development is that today we can provide these algorithms with the resources they need to succeed. Figure 1.8 shows how the size of benchmark datasets has expanded remarkably over time. This trend is driven by the increasing digitization of society. As more and more of our activities take place on computers, more and more of what we do is recorded. As our computers are increasingly networked together, it becomes easier to centralize these records and curate them into a dataset appropriate for machine learning applications. The age of "Big Data" has made machine learning much easier because the key burden of statistical estimation—generalizing well to new data after observing only a small amount

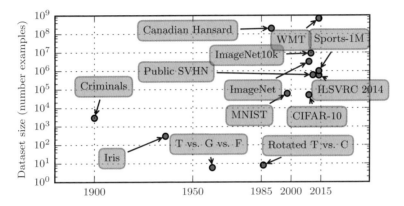

Figure 1.8: Increasing dataset size over time. In the early 1900s, statisticians studied datasets using hundreds or thousands of manually compiled measurements (Garson, 1900; Gosset, 1908; Anderson, 1935; Fisher, 1936). In the 1950s through the 1980s, the pioneers of biologically inspired machine learning often worked with small synthetic datasets, such as low-resolution bitmaps of letters, that were designed to incur low computational cost and demonstrate that neural networks were able to learn specific kinds of functions (Widrow and Hoff, 1960; Rumelhart et al., 1986b). In the 1980s and 1990s, machine learning became more statistical and began to leverage larger datasets containing tens of thousands of examples, such as the MNIST dataset (shown in figure 1.9) of scans of handwritten numbers (LeCun et al., 1998b). In the first decade of the 2000s, more sophisticated datasets of this same size, such as the CIFAR-10 dataset (Krizhevsky and Hinton, 2009), continued to be produced. Toward the end of that decade and throughout the first half of the 2010s, significantly larger datasets, containing hundreds of thousands to tens of millions of examples, completely changed what was possible with deep learning. These datasets included the public Street View House Numbers dataset (Netzer et al., 2011), various versions of the ImageNet dataset (Deng et al., 2009, 2010a; Russakovsky et al., 2014a), and the Sports-1M dataset (Karpathy et al., 2014). At the top of the graph, we see that datasets of translated sentences, such as IBM's dataset constructed from the Canadian Hansard (Brown et al., 1990) and the WMT 2014 English to French dataset (Schwenk, 2014), are typically far ahead of other dataset sizes.

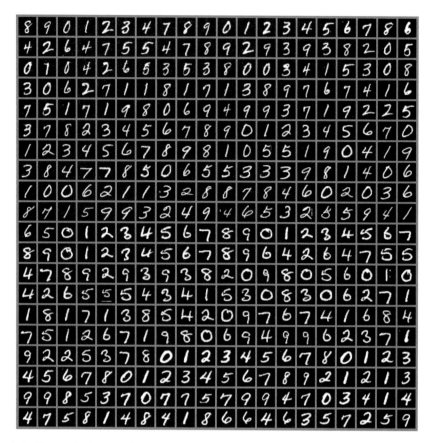

Figure 1.9: Example inputs from the MNIST dataset. The "NIST" stands for National Institute of Standards and Technology, the agency that originally collected this data. The "M" stands for "modified," since the data has been preprocessed for easier use with machine learning algorithms. The MNIST dataset consists of scans of handwritten digits and associated labels describing which digit 0–9 is contained in each image. This simple classification problem is one of the simplest and most widely used tests in deep learning research. It remains popular despite being quite easy for modern techniques to solve. Geoffrey Hinton has described it as "the *drosophila* of machine learning," meaning that it enables machine learning researchers to study their algorithms in controlled laboratory conditions, much as biologists often study fruit flies.

of data—has been considerably lightened. As of 2016, a rough rule of thumb is that a supervised deep learning algorithm will generally achieve acceptable performance with around 5,000 labeled examples per category and will match or exceed human performance when trained with a dataset containing at least 10 million labeled examples. Working successfully with datasets smaller than this is an important research area, focusing in particular on how we can take advantage of large quantities of unlabeled examples, with unsupervised or semi-supervised learning.

1.2.3 Increasing Model Sizes

Another key reason that neural networks are wildly successful today after enjoying comparatively little success since the 1980s is that we have the computational resources to run much larger models today. One of the main insights of connectionism is that animals become intelligent when many of their neurons work together. An individual neuron or small collection of neurons is not particularly useful.

Biological neurons are not especially densely connected. As seen in figure 1.10, our machine learning models have had a number of connections per neuron within an order of magnitude of even mammalian brains for decades.

In terms of the total number of neurons, neural networks have been astonishingly small until quite recently, as shown in figure 1.11. Increasing neural network size over time. Since the introduction of hidden units, artificial neural networks have doubled in size roughly every 2.4 years. This growth is driven by faster computers with larger memory and by the availability of larger datasets. Larger networks are able to achieve higher accuracy on more complex tasks. This trend looks set to continue for decades. Unless new technologies enable faster scaling, artificial neural networks will not have the same number of neurons as the human brain until at least the 2050s. Biological neurons may represent more complicated functions than current artificial neurons, so biological neural networks may be even larger than this plot portrays.

In retrospect, it is not particularly surprising that neural networks with fewer neurons than a leech were unable to solve sophisticated artificial intelligence problems. Even today's networks, which we consider quite large from a computational systems point of view, are smaller than the nervous system of even relatively primitive vertebrate animals like frogs.

The increase in model size over time, due to the availability of faster CPUs, the advent of general purpose GPUs (described in section 12.1.2), faster network connectivity and better software infrastructure for distributed computing, is one of the most important trends in the history of deep learning. This trend is generally expected to continue well into the future.

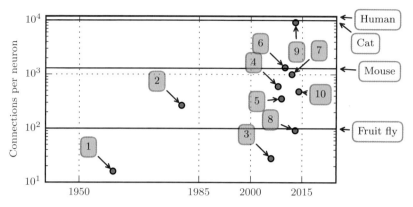

Figure 1.10: Number of connections per neuron over time. Initially, the number of connections between neurons in artificial neural networks was limited by hardware capabilities. Today, the number of connections between neurons is mostly a design consideration. Some artificial neural networks have nearly as many connections per neuron as a cat, and it is quite common for other neural networks to have as many connections per neuron as smaller mammals like mice. Even the human brain does not have an exorbitant amount of connections per neuron. Biological neural network sizes from Wikipedia (2015).

1. Adaptive linear element (Widrow and Hoff, 1960)

2. Neocognitron (Fukushima, 1980)

3. GPU-accelerated convolutional network (Chellapilla et al., 2006)

4. Deep Boltzmann machine (Salakhutdinov and Hinton, 2009a)

5. Unsupervised convolutional network (Jarrett et al., 2009)

6. GPU-accelerated multilayer perceptron (Ciresan et al., 2010)

7. Distributed autoencoder (Le et al., 2012)

8. Multi-GPU convolutional network (Krizhevsky et al., 2012)

9. COTS HPC unsupervised convolutional network (Coates et al., 2013)

10. GoogLeNet (Szegedy et al., 2014a)

1.2.4 Increasing Accuracy, Complexity and Real-World Impact

Since the 1980s, deep learning has consistently improved in its ability to provide accurate recognition and prediction. Moreover, deep learning has consistently been applied with success to broader and broader sets of applications.

The earliest deep models were used to recognize individual objects in tightly cropped, extremely small images (Rumelhart et al., 1986a). Since then there has been a gradual increase in the size of images neural networks could process. Modern object recognition networks process rich high-resolution photographs and do not have a requirement that the photo be cropped near the object to be recognized

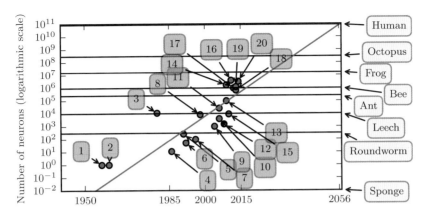

Figure 1.11: Increasing neural network size over time. Since the introduction of hidden units, artificial neural networks have doubled in size roughly every 2.4 years. Biological neural network sizes from Wikipedia (2015).

1. Perceptron (Rosenblatt, 1958, 1962)

2. Adaptive linear element (Widrow and Hoff, 1960)

3. Neocognitron (Fukushima, 1980)

4. Early back-propagation network (Rumelhart et al., 1986b)

5. Recurrent neural network for speech recognition (Robinson and Fallside, 1991)

6. Multilayer perceptron for speech recognition (Bengio et al., 1991)

7. Mean field sigmoid belief network (Saul et al., 1996)

8. LeNet-5 (LeCun et al., 1998b)

9. Echo state network (Jaeger and Haas, 2004)

10. Deep belief network (Hinton et al., 2006)

11. GPU-accelerated convolutional network (Chellapilla et al., 2006)

12. Deep Boltzmann machine (Salakhutdinov and Hinton, 2009a)

13. GPU-accelerated deep belief network (Raina et al., 2009)

14. Unsupervised convolutional network (Jarrett et al., 2009)

15. GPU-accelerated multilayer perceptron (Ciresan et al., 2010)

16. OMP-1 network (Coates and Ng, 2011)

17. Distributed autoencoder (Le et al., 2012)

18. Multi-GPU convolutional network (Krizhevsky et al., 2012)

19. COTS HPC unsupervised convolutional network (Coates et al., 2013)

20. GoogLeNet (Szegedy et al., 2014a)

(Krizhevsky et al., 2012). Similarly, the earliest networks could recognize only two kinds of objects (or in some cases, the absence or presence of a single kind of object), while these modern networks typically recognize at least 1,000 different categories of objects. The largest contest in object recognition is the ImageNet Large Scale Visual Recognition Challenge (ILSVRC) held each year. A dramatic moment in the meteoric rise of deep learning came when a convolutional network won this challenge for the first time and by a wide margin, bringing down the state-of-the-art top-5 error rate from 26.1 percent to 15.3 percent (Krizhevsky et al., 2012), meaning that the convolutional network produces a ranked list of possible categories for each image, and the correct category appeared in the first five entries of this list for all but 15.3 percent of the test examples. Since then, these competitions are consistently won by deep convolutional nets, and as of this writing, advances in deep learning have brought the latest top-5 error rate in this contest down to 3.6 percent, as shown in figure 1.12.

Deep learning has also had a dramatic impact on speech recognition. After improving throughout the 1990s, the error rates for speech recognition stagnated starting in about 2000. The introduction of deep learning (Dahl et al., 2010; Deng et al., 2010b; Seide et al., 2011; Hinton et al., 2012a) to speech recognition resulted in a sudden drop in error rates, with some error rates cut in half. We explore this history in more detail in section 12.3.

Deep networks have also had spectacular successes for pedestrian detection and image segmentation (Sermanet et al., 2013; Farabet et al., 2013; Couprie et al., 2013) and yielded superhuman performance in traffic sign classification (Ciresan et al., 2012).

At the same time that the scale and accuracy of deep networks have increased, so has the complexity of the tasks that they can solve. Goodfellow et al. (2014d) showed that neural networks could learn to output an entire sequence of characters transcribed from an image, rather than just identifying a single object. Previously,

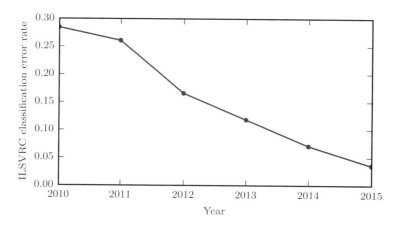

Figure 1.12: Decreasing error rate over time. Since deep networks reached the scale necessary to compete in the ImageNet Large Scale Visual Recognition Challenge, they have consistently won the competition every year, yielding lower and lower error rates each time. Data from Russakovsky et al. (2014b) and He et al. (2015).

it was widely believed that this kind of learning required labeling of the individual elements of the sequence (Gülçehre and Bengio, 2013). Recurrent neural networks, such as the LSTM sequence model mentioned above, are now used to model relationships between *sequences* and other *sequences* rather than just fixed inputs. This sequence-to-sequence learning seems to be on the cusp of revolutionizing another application: machine translation (Sutskever et al., 2014; Bahdanau et al., 2015).

This trend of increasing complexity has been pushed to its logical conclusion with the introduction of neural Turing machines (Graves et al., 2014a) that learn to read from memory cells and write arbitrary content to memory cells. Such neural networks can learn simple programs from examples of desired behavior. For example, they can learn to sort lists of numbers given examples of scrambled and sorted sequences. This self-programming technology is in its infancy, but in the future it could in principle be applied to nearly any task.

Another crowning achievement of deep learning is its extension to the domain of **reinforcement learning**. In the context of reinforcement learning, an autonomous agent must learn to perform a task by trial and error, without any guidance from the human operator. DeepMind demonstrated that a reinforcement learning system based on deep learning is capable of learning to play Atari video games, reaching human-level performance on many tasks (Mnih et al., 2015). Deep learning has also significantly improved the performance of reinforcement learning for robotics (Finn et al., 2015).

Many of these applications of deep learning are highly profitable. Deep learning is now used by many top technology companies, including Google, Microsoft, Facebook, IBM, Baidu, Apple, Adobe, Netflix, NVIDIA, and NEC.

Advances in deep learning have also depended heavily on advances in software infrastructure. Software libraries such as Theano (Bergstra et al., 2010; Bastien et al., 2012), PyLearn2 (Goodfellow et al., 2013c), Torch (Collobert et al., 2011b), DistBelief (Dean et al., 2012), Caffe (Jia, 2013), MXNet (Chen et al., 2015), and TensorFlow (Abadi et al., 2015) have all supported important research projects or commercial products.

Deep learning has also made contributions to other sciences. Modern convolutional networks for object recognition provide a model of visual processing that neuroscientists can study (DiCarlo, 2013). Deep learning also provides useful tools for processing massive amounts of data and making useful predictions in scientific fields. It has been successfully used to predict how molecules will interact in order to help pharmaceutical companies design new drugs (Dahl et al., 2014), to search for subatomic particles (Baldi et al., 2014), and to automatically parse microscope images used to construct a 3-D map of the human brain (Knowles-Barley et al., 2014). We expect deep learning to appear in more and more scientific fields in the future.

In summary, deep learning is an approach to machine learning that has drawn heavily on our knowledge of the human brain, statistics and applied math as it developed over the past several decades. In recent years, deep learning has seen tremendous growth in its popularity and usefulness, largely as the result of more powerful computers, larger datasets and techniques to train deeper networks. The years ahead are full of challenges and opportunities to improve deep learning even further and to bring it to new frontiers.

I

Applied Math and Machine Learning Basics

This part of the book introduces the basic mathematical concepts needed to understand deep learning. We begin with general ideas from applied math that enable us to define functions of many variables, find the highest and lowest points on these functions, and quantify degrees of belief.

Next, we describe the fundamental goals of machine learning. We describe how to accomplish these goals by specifying a model that represents certain beliefs, designing a cost function that measures how well those beliefs correspond with reality, and using a training algorithm to minimize that cost function.

This elementary framework is the basis for a broad variety of machine learning algorithms, including approaches to machine learning that are not deep. In the subsequent parts of the book, we develop deep learning algorithms within this framework.

2

Linear Algebra

Linear algebra is a branch of mathematics that is widely used throughout science and engineering. Yet because linear algebra is a form of continuous rather than discrete mathematics, many computer scientists have little experience with it. A good understanding of linear algebra is essential for understanding and working with many machine learning algorithms, especially deep learning algorithms. We therefore precede our introduction to deep learning with a focused presentation of the key linear algebra prerequisites.

If you are already familiar with linear algebra, feel free to skip this chapter. If you have previous experience with these concepts but need a detailed reference sheet to review key formulas, we recommend *The Matrix Cookbook* (Petersen and Pedersen, 2006). If you have had no exposure at all to linear algebra, this chapter will teach you enough to read this book, but we highly recommend that you also consult another resource focused exclusively on teaching linear algebra, such as Shilov (1977). This chapter completely omits many important linear algebra topics that are not essential for understanding deep learning.

2.1 Scalars, Vectors, Matrices and Tensors

The study of linear algebra involves several types of mathematical objects:

- **Scalars**: A scalar is just a single number, in contrast to most of the other objects studied in linear algebra, which are usually arrays of multiple numbers. We write scalars in italics. We usually give scalars lowercase variable names. When we introduce them, we specify what kind of number they are. For example, we might say "Let $s \in \mathbb{R}$ be the slope of the line," while defining a real-valued scalar, or "Let $n \in \mathbb{N}$ be the number of units," while defining a natural number scalar.

- **Vectors**: A vector is an array of numbers. The numbers are arranged in order. We can identify each individual number by its index in that ordering. Typically we give vectors lowercase names in bold typeface, such as $\boldsymbol{x}$. The elements of the vector are identified by writing its name in italic typeface, with a subscript. The first element of $\boldsymbol{x}$ is x_1, the second element is x_2, and so on. We also need to say what kind of numbers are stored in the vector. If each element is in $\mathbb{R}$, and the vector has n elements, then the vector lies in the set formed by taking the Cartesian product of $\mathbb{R}$ n times, denoted as $\mathbb{R}^n$. When we need to explicitly identify the elements of a vector, we write them as a column enclosed in square brackets:

$$\boldsymbol{x} = \begin{bmatrix} x_1 \\ x_2 \\ \vdots \\ x_n \end{bmatrix}. \tag{2.1}$$

We can think of vectors as identifying points in space, with each element giving the coordinate along a different axis.

Sometimes we need to index a set of elements of a vector. In this case, we define a set containing the indices and write the set as a subscript. For example, to access x_1, x_3 and x_6, we define the set $S = \{1, 3, 6\}$ and write $\boldsymbol{x}_S$. We use the $-$ sign to index the complement of a set. For example $\boldsymbol{x}_{-1}$ is the vector containing all elements of $\boldsymbol{x}$ except for x_1, and $\boldsymbol{x}_{-S}$ is the vector containing all elements of $\boldsymbol{x}$ except for x_1, x_3 and x_6.

- **Matrices**: A matrix is a 2-D array of numbers, so each element is identified by two indices instead of just one. We usually give matrices uppercase variable names with bold typeface, such as $\boldsymbol{A}$. If a real-valued matrix $\boldsymbol{A}$ has a height of m and a width of n, then we say that $\boldsymbol{A} \in \mathbb{R}^{m \times n}$. We usually identify the elements of a matrix using its name in italic but not bold font, and the indices are listed with separating commas. For example, $A_{1,1}$ is the upper left entry of $\boldsymbol{A}$ and $A_{m,n}$ is the bottom right entry. We can identify all the numbers with vertical coordinate i by writing a ":" for the horizontal coordinate. For example, $\boldsymbol{A}_{i,:}$ denotes the horizontal cross section of $\boldsymbol{A}$ with vertical coordinate i. This is known as the i-th **row** of $\boldsymbol{A}$. Likewise, $\boldsymbol{A}_{:,i}$ is the i-th **column** of $\boldsymbol{A}$. When we need to explicitly identify the elements of a matrix, we write them as an array enclosed in square brackets:

$$\begin{bmatrix} A_{1,1} & A_{1,2} \\ A_{2,1} & A_{2,2} \end{bmatrix}. \tag{2.2}$$

Sometimes we may need to index matrix-valued expressions that are not just a single letter. In this case, we use subscripts after the expression but do not convert anything to lowercase. For example, $f(\boldsymbol{A})_{i,j}$ gives element (i,j) of the matrix computed by applying the function f to $\boldsymbol{A}$.

- **Tensors**: In some cases we will need an array with more than two axes. In the general case, an array of numbers arranged on a regular grid with a variable number of axes is known as a tensor. We denote a tensor named "A" with this typeface: **A**. We identify the element of **A** at coordinates (i,j,k) by writing $\mathsf{A}_{i,j,k}$.

One important operation on matrices is the **transpose**. The transpose of a matrix is the mirror image of the matrix across a diagonal line, called the **main diagonal**, running down and to the right, starting from its upper left corner. See figure 2.1 for a graphical depiction of this operation. We denote the transpose of a matrix $\boldsymbol{A}$ as $\boldsymbol{A}^\top$, and it is defined such that

$$(\boldsymbol{A}^\top)_{i,j} = A_{j,i}. \tag{2.3}$$

Vectors can be thought of as matrices that contain only one column. The transpose of a vector is therefore a matrix with only one row. Sometimes we define a vector by writing out its elements in the text inline as a row matrix, then using the transpose operator to turn it into a standard column vector, for example $\boldsymbol{x} = [x_1, x_2, x_3]^\top$.

A scalar can be thought of as a matrix with only a single entry. From this, we can see that a scalar is its own transpose: $a = a^\top$.

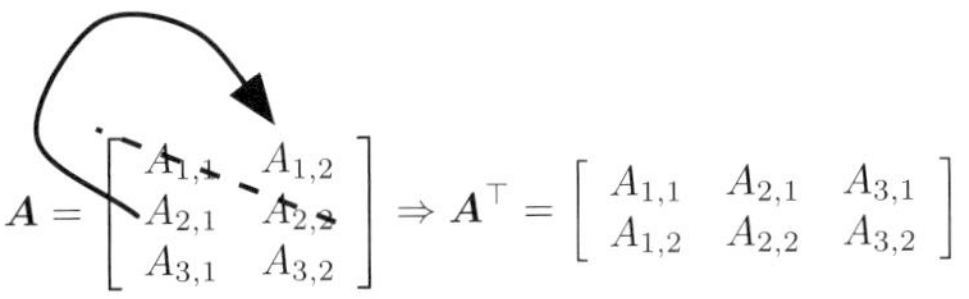

$$\boldsymbol{A} = \begin{bmatrix} A_{1,1} & A_{1,2} \\ A_{2,1} & A_{2,2} \\ A_{3,1} & A_{3,2} \end{bmatrix} \Rightarrow \boldsymbol{A}^\top = \begin{bmatrix} A_{1,1} & A_{2,1} & A_{3,1} \\ A_{1,2} & A_{2,2} & A_{3,2} \end{bmatrix}$$

Figure 2.1: The transpose of the matrix can be thought of as a mirror image across the main diagonal.

We can add matrices to each other, as long as they have the same shape, just by adding their corresponding elements: $\boldsymbol{C} = \boldsymbol{A} + \boldsymbol{B}$ where $C_{i,j} = A_{i,j} + B_{i,j}$.

We can also add a scalar to a matrix or multiply a matrix by a scalar, just by performing that operation on each element of a matrix: $\boldsymbol{D} = a \cdot \boldsymbol{B} + c$ where $D_{i,j} = a \cdot B_{i,j} + c$.

In the context of deep learning, we also use some less conventional notation. We allow the addition of matrix and a vector, yielding another matrix: $\boldsymbol{C} = \boldsymbol{A} + \boldsymbol{b}$, where $C_{i,j} = A_{i,j} + b_j$. In other words, the vector $\boldsymbol{b}$ is added to each row of the matrix. This shorthand eliminates the need to define a matrix with $\boldsymbol{b}$ copied into each row before doing the addition. This implicit copying of $\boldsymbol{b}$ to many locations is called **broadcasting**.

2.2 Multiplying Matrices and Vectors

One of the most important operations involving matrices is multiplication of two matrices. The **matrix product** of matrices $\boldsymbol{A}$ and $\boldsymbol{B}$ is a third matrix $\boldsymbol{C}$. In order for this product to be defined, $\boldsymbol{A}$ must have the same number of columns as $\boldsymbol{B}$ has rows. If $\boldsymbol{A}$ is of shape $m \times n$ and $\boldsymbol{B}$ is of shape $n \times p$, then $\boldsymbol{C}$ is of shape $m \times p$. We can write the matrix product just by placing two or more matrices together, for example,

$$\boldsymbol{C} = \boldsymbol{A}\boldsymbol{B}. \tag{2.4}$$

The product operation is defined by

$$C_{i,j} = \sum_k A_{i,k} B_{k,j}. \tag{2.5}$$

Note that the standard product of two matrices is *not* just a matrix containing the product of the individual elements. Such an operation exists and is called the **element-wise product**, or **Hadamard product**, and is denoted as $\boldsymbol{A} \odot \boldsymbol{B}$.

The **dot product** between two vectors $\boldsymbol{x}$ and $\boldsymbol{y}$ of the same dimensionality is the matrix product $\boldsymbol{x}^\top \boldsymbol{y}$. We can think of the matrix product $\boldsymbol{C} = \boldsymbol{A}\boldsymbol{B}$ as computing $C_{i,j}$ as the dot product between row i of $\boldsymbol{A}$ and column j of $\boldsymbol{B}$.

Matrix product operations have many useful properties that make mathematical analysis of matrices more convenient. For example, matrix multiplication is distributive:

$$\boldsymbol{A}(\boldsymbol{B} + \boldsymbol{C}) = \boldsymbol{A}\boldsymbol{B} + \boldsymbol{A}\boldsymbol{C}. \tag{2.6}$$

It is also associative:

$$\boldsymbol{A}(\boldsymbol{B}\boldsymbol{C}) = (\boldsymbol{A}\boldsymbol{B})\boldsymbol{C}. \tag{2.7}$$

Matrix multiplication is *not* commutative (the condition $\boldsymbol{AB} = \boldsymbol{BA}$ does not always hold), unlike scalar multiplication. However, the dot product between two vectors is commutative:

$$\boldsymbol{x}^\top \boldsymbol{y} = \boldsymbol{y}^\top \boldsymbol{x}. \tag{2.8}$$

The transpose of a matrix product has a simple form:

$$(\boldsymbol{AB})^\top = \boldsymbol{B}^\top \boldsymbol{A}^\top. \tag{2.9}$$

This enables us to demonstrate equation 2.8 by exploiting the fact that the value of such a product is a scalar and therefore equal to its own transpose:

$$\boldsymbol{x}^\top \boldsymbol{y} = \left(\boldsymbol{x}^\top \boldsymbol{y}\right)^\top = \boldsymbol{y}^\top \boldsymbol{x}. \tag{2.10}$$

Since the focus of this textbook is not linear algebra, we do not attempt to develop a comprehensive list of useful properties of the matrix product here, but the reader should be aware that many more exist.

We now know enough linear algebra notation to write down a system of linear equations:

$$\boldsymbol{Ax} = \boldsymbol{b} \tag{2.11}$$

where $\boldsymbol{A} \in \mathbb{R}^{m \times n}$ is a known matrix, $\boldsymbol{b} \in \mathbb{R}^m$ is a known vector, and $\boldsymbol{x} \in \mathbb{R}^n$ is a vector of unknown variables we would like to solve for. Each element x_i of $\boldsymbol{x}$ is one of these unknown variables. Each row of $\boldsymbol{A}$ and each element of $\boldsymbol{b}$ provide another constraint. We can rewrite equation 2.11 as

$$\boldsymbol{A}_{1,:}\boldsymbol{x} = b_1 \tag{2.12}$$

$$\boldsymbol{A}_{2,:}\boldsymbol{x} = b_2 \tag{2.13}$$

$$\ldots \tag{2.14}$$

$$\boldsymbol{A}_{m,:}\boldsymbol{x} = b_m \tag{2.15}$$

or even more explicitly as

$$\boldsymbol{A}_{1,1}x_1 + \boldsymbol{A}_{1,2}x_2 + \cdots + \boldsymbol{A}_{1,n}x_n = b_1 \tag{2.16}$$

$$\boldsymbol{A}_{2,1}x_1 + \boldsymbol{A}_{2,2}x_2 + \cdots + \boldsymbol{A}_{2,n}x_n = b_2 \tag{2.17}$$

$$\ldots \tag{2.18}$$

$$\boldsymbol{A}_{m,1}x_1 + \boldsymbol{A}_{m,2}x_2 + \cdots + \boldsymbol{A}_{m,n}x_n = b_m. \tag{2.19}$$

Matrix-vector product notation provides a more compact representation for equations of this form.

2.3   Identity and Inverse Matrices

Linear algebra offers a powerful tool called **matrix inversion** that enables us to analytically solve equation 2.11 for many values of $\boldsymbol{A}$.

To describe matrix inversion, we first need to define the concept of an **identity matrix**. An identity matrix is a matrix that does not change any vector when we multiply that vector by that matrix. We denote the identity matrix that preserves n-dimensional vectors as $\boldsymbol{I}_n$. Formally, $\boldsymbol{I}_n \in \mathbb{R}^{n \times n}$, and

$$\forall \boldsymbol{x} \in \mathbb{R}^n, \boldsymbol{I}_n \boldsymbol{x} = \boldsymbol{x}. \tag{2.20}$$

The structure of the identity matrix is simple: all the entries along the main diagonal are 1, while all the other entries are zero. See figure 2.2 for an example.

The **matrix inverse** of $\boldsymbol{A}$ is denoted as $\boldsymbol{A}^{-1}$, and it is defined as the matrix such that

$$\boldsymbol{A}^{-1} \boldsymbol{A} = \boldsymbol{I}_n. \tag{2.21}$$

We can now solve equation 2.11 using the following steps:

$$\boldsymbol{A}\boldsymbol{x} = \boldsymbol{b} \tag{2.22}$$

$$\boldsymbol{A}^{-1}\boldsymbol{A}\boldsymbol{x} = \boldsymbol{A}^{-1}\boldsymbol{b} \tag{2.23}$$

$$\boldsymbol{I}_n\boldsymbol{x} = \boldsymbol{A}^{-1}\boldsymbol{b} \tag{2.24}$$

$$\boldsymbol{x} = \boldsymbol{A}^{-1}\boldsymbol{b}. \tag{2.25}$$

Of course, this process depends on it being possible to find $\boldsymbol{A}^{-1}$. We discuss the conditions for the existence of $\boldsymbol{A}^{-1}$ in the following section.

When $\boldsymbol{A}^{-1}$ exists, several different algorithms can find it in closed form. In theory, the same inverse matrix can then be used to solve the equation many times for different values of $\boldsymbol{b}$. $\boldsymbol{A}^{-1}$ is primarily useful as a theoretical tool, however, and should not actually be used in practice for most software applications. Because $\boldsymbol{A}^{-1}$ can be represented with only limited precision on a digital computer, algorithms that make use of the value of $\boldsymbol{b}$ can usually obtain more accurate estimates of $\boldsymbol{x}$.

$$\begin{bmatrix} 1 & 0 & 0 \\ 0 & 1 & 0 \\ 0 & 0 & 1 \end{bmatrix}$$

Figure 2.2: Example identity matrix: This is $\boldsymbol{I}_3$.

2.4 Linear Dependence and Span

For A^{-1} to exist, equation 2.11 must have exactly one solution for every value of b. It is also possible for the system of equations to have no solutions or infinitely many solutions for some values of b. It is not possible, however, to have more than one but less than infinitely many solutions for a particular b; if both x and y are solutions, then

$$z = \alpha x + (1 - \alpha)y \tag{2.26}$$

is also a solution for any real α.

To analyze how many solutions the equation has, think of the columns of A as specifying different directions we can travel in from the **origin** (the point specified by the vector of all zeros), then determine how many ways there are of reaching b. In this view, each element of x specifies how far we should travel in each of these directions, with x_i specifying how far to move in the direction of column i:

$$Ax = \sum_i x_i A_{:,i}. \tag{2.27}$$

In general, this kind of operation is called a **linear combination**. Formally, a linear combination of some set of vectors $\{v^{(1)}, \ldots, v^{(n)}\}$ is given by multiplying each vector $v^{(i)}$ by a corresponding scalar coefficient and adding the results:

$$\sum_i c_i v^{(i)}. \tag{2.28}$$

The **span** of a set of vectors is the set of all points obtainable by linear combination of the original vectors.

Determining whether $Ax = b$ has a solution thus amounts to testing whether b is in the span of the columns of A. This particular span is known as the **column space**, or the **range**, of A.

In order for the system $Ax = b$ to have a solution for all values of $b \in \mathbb{R}^m$, we therefore require that the column space of A be all of $\mathbb{R}^m$. If any point in $\mathbb{R}^m$ is excluded from the column space, that point is a potential value of b that has no solution. The requirement that the column space of A be all of $\mathbb{R}^m$ implies immediately that A must have at least m columns, that is, $n \geq m$. Otherwise, the dimensionality of the column space would be less than m. For example, consider a 3×2 matrix. The target b is 3-D, but x is only 2-D, so modifying the value of x at best enables us to trace out a 2-D plane within $\mathbb{R}^3$. The equation has a solution if and only if b lies on that plane.

Having $n \geq m$ is only a necessary condition for every point to have a solution. It is not a sufficient condition, because it is possible for some of the columns to be redundant. Consider a 2×2 matrix where both of the columns are identical. This has the same column space as a 2×1 matrix containing only one copy of the replicated column. In other words, the column space is still just a line and fails to encompass all of $\mathbb{R}^2$, even though there are two columns.

Formally, this kind of redundancy is known as **linear dependence**. A set of vectors is **linearly independent** if no vector in the set is a linear combination of the other vectors. If we add a vector to a set that is a linear combination of the other vectors in the set, the new vector does not add any points to the set's span. This means that for the column space of the matrix to encompass all of $\mathbb{R}^m$, the matrix must contain at least one set of m linearly independent columns. This condition is both necessary and sufficient for equation 2.11 to have a solution for every value of $\boldsymbol{b}$. Note that the requirement is for a set to have exactly m linear independent columns, not at least m. No set of m-dimensional vectors can have more than m mutually linearly independent columns, but a matrix with more than m columns may have more than one such set.

For the matrix to have an inverse, we additionally need to ensure that equation 2.11 has *at most* one solution for each value of $\boldsymbol{b}$. To do so, we need to make certain that the matrix has at most m columns. Otherwise there is more than one way of parametrizing each solution.

Together, this means that the matrix must be **square**, that is, we require that $m = n$ and that all the columns be linearly independent. A square matrix with linearly dependent columns is known as **singular**.

If $\boldsymbol{A}$ is not square or is square but singular, solving the equation is still possible, but we cannot use the method of matrix inversion to find the solution.

So far we have discussed matrix inverses as being multiplied on the left. It is also possible to define an inverse that is multiplied on the right:

$$\boldsymbol{A}\boldsymbol{A}^{-1} = \boldsymbol{I}. \tag{2.29}$$

For square matrices, the left inverse and right inverse are equal.

2.5 Norms

Sometimes we need to measure the size of a vector. In machine learning, we usually measure the size of vectors using a function called a **norm**. Formally, the L^p norm is given by

$$||\boldsymbol{x}||_p = \left(\sum_i |x_i|^p \right)^{\frac{1}{p}} \tag{2.30}$$

for $p \in \mathbb{R}, p \geq 1$.

Norms, including the L^p norm, are functions mapping vectors to non-negative values. On an intuitive level, the norm of a vector $\boldsymbol{x}$ measures the distance from the origin to the point $\boldsymbol{x}$. More rigorously, a norm is any function f that satisfies the following properties:

- $f(\boldsymbol{x}) = 0 \Rightarrow \boldsymbol{x} = \boldsymbol{0}$

- $f(\boldsymbol{x} + \boldsymbol{y}) \leq f(\boldsymbol{x}) + f(\boldsymbol{y})$ (the **triangle inequality**)

- $\forall \alpha \in \mathbb{R}, f(\alpha\boldsymbol{x}) = |\alpha| f(\boldsymbol{x})$

The L^2 norm, with $p = 2$, is known as the **Euclidean norm**, which is simply the Euclidean distance from the origin to the point identified by $\boldsymbol{x}$. The L^2 norm is used so frequently in machine learning that it is often denoted simply as $||\boldsymbol{x}||$, with the subscript 2 omitted. It is also common to measure the size of a vector using the squared L^2 norm, which can be calculated simply as $\boldsymbol{x}^\top \boldsymbol{x}$.

The squared L^2 norm is more convenient to work with mathematically and computationally than the L^2 norm itself. For example, each derivative of the squared L^2 norm with respect to each element of $\boldsymbol{x}$ depends only on the corresponding element of $\boldsymbol{x}$, while all the derivatives of the L^2 norm depend on the entire vector. In many contexts, the squared L^2 norm may be undesirable because it increases very slowly near the origin. In several machine learning applications, it is important to discriminate between elements that are exactly zero and elements that are small but nonzero. In these cases, we turn to a function that grows at the same rate in all locations, but that retains mathematical simplicity: the L^1 norm. The L^1 norm may be simplified to

$$||\boldsymbol{x}||_1 = \sum_i |x_i|. \tag{2.31}$$

The L^1 norm is commonly used in machine learning when the difference between zero and nonzero elements is very important. Every time an element of $\boldsymbol{x}$ moves away from 0 by ϵ, the L^1 norm increases by ϵ.

We sometimes measure the size of the vector by counting its number of nonzero elements. Some authors refer to this function as the "L^0 norm," but this is incorrect terminology. The number of nonzero entries in a vector is not a norm, because scaling the vector by α does not change the number of nonzero entries. The L^1 norm is often used as a substitute for the number of nonzero entries.

One other norm that commonly arises in machine learning is the L^∞ norm, also known as the **max norm**. This norm simplifies to the absolute value of the element with the largest magnitude in the vector,

$$||\boldsymbol{x}||_\infty = \max_i |x_i|. \tag{2.32}$$

Sometimes we may also wish to measure the size of a matrix. In the context of deep learning, the most common way to do this is with the otherwise obscure **Frobenius norm**:

$$||A||_F = \sqrt{\sum_{i,j} A_{i,j}^2}, \tag{2.33}$$

which is analogous to the L^2 norm of a vector.

The dot product of two vectors can be rewritten in terms of norms. Specifically,

$$\boldsymbol{x}^\top \boldsymbol{y} = ||\boldsymbol{x}||_2 ||\boldsymbol{y}||_2 \cos \theta, \tag{2.34}$$

where θ is the angle between $\boldsymbol{x}$ and $\boldsymbol{y}$.

2.6   Special Kinds of Matrices and Vectors

Some special kinds of matrices and vectors are particularly useful.

Diagonal matrices consist mostly of zeros and have nonzero entries only along the main diagonal. Formally, a matrix $\boldsymbol{D}$ is diagonal if and only if $D_{i,j} = 0$ for all $i \neq j$. We have already seen one example of a diagonal matrix: the identity matrix, where all the diagonal entries are 1. We write diag($\boldsymbol{v}$) to denote a square diagonal matrix whose diagonal entries are given by the entries of the vector $\boldsymbol{v}$. Diagonal matrices are of interest in part because multiplying by a diagonal matrix is computationally efficient. To compute diag($\boldsymbol{v}$)$\boldsymbol{x}$, we only need to scale each element x_i by v_i. In other words, diag($\boldsymbol{v}$)$\boldsymbol{x} = \boldsymbol{v} \odot \boldsymbol{x}$. Inverting a square diagonal matrix is also efficient. The inverse exists only if every diagonal entry is nonzero, and in that case, diag($\boldsymbol{v}$)$^{-1}$ = diag($[1/v_1, \ldots, 1/v_n]^\top$). In many cases, we may derive some general machine learning algorithm in terms of arbitrary matrices but obtain a less expensive (and less descriptive) algorithm by restricting some matrices to be diagonal.

Not all diagonal matrices need be square. It is possible to construct a rectangular diagonal matrix. Nonsquare diagonal matrices do not have inverses, but we can still multiply by them cheaply. For a nonsquare diagonal matrix $\boldsymbol{D}$, the product $\boldsymbol{Dx}$ will involve scaling each element of $\boldsymbol{x}$ and either concatenating some zeros to the result, if $\boldsymbol{D}$ is taller than it is wide, or discarding some of the last elements of the vector, if $\boldsymbol{D}$ is wider than it is tall.

A **symmetric** matrix is any matrix that is equal to its own transpose:

$$\boldsymbol{A} = \boldsymbol{A}^\top. \tag{2.35}$$

Symmetric matrices often arise when the entries are generated by some function of two arguments that does not depend on the order of the arguments. For example, if $\boldsymbol{A}$ is a matrix of distance measurements, with $\boldsymbol{A}_{i,j}$ giving the distance from point i to point j, then $\boldsymbol{A}_{i,j} = \boldsymbol{A}_{j,i}$ because distance functions are symmetric.

A **unit vector** is a vector with **unit norm**:

$$||\boldsymbol{x}||_2 = 1. \tag{2.36}$$

A vector $\boldsymbol{x}$ and a vector $\boldsymbol{y}$ are **orthogonal** to each other if $\boldsymbol{x}^\top \boldsymbol{y} = 0$. If both vectors have nonzero norm, this means that they are at a 90 degree angle to each other. In $\mathbb{R}^n$, at most n vectors may be mutually orthogonal with nonzero norm. If the vectors not only are orthogonal but also have unit norm, we call them **orthonormal**.

An **orthogonal matrix** is a square matrix whose rows are mutually orthonormal and whose columns are mutually orthonormal:

$$\boldsymbol{A}^\top \boldsymbol{A} = \boldsymbol{A}\boldsymbol{A}^\top = \boldsymbol{I}. \tag{2.37}$$

This implies that

$$\boldsymbol{A}^{-1} = \boldsymbol{A}^\top, \tag{2.38}$$

so orthogonal matrices are of interest because their inverse is very cheap to compute. Pay careful attention to the definition of orthogonal matrices. Counterintuitively, their rows are not merely orthogonal but fully orthonormal. There is no special term for a matrix whose rows or columns are orthogonal but not orthonormal.

2.7   Eigendecomposition

Many mathematical objects can be understood better by breaking them into constituent parts, or finding some properties of them that are universal, not caused by the way we choose to represent them.

For example, integers can be decomposed into prime factors. The way we represent the number 12 will change depending on whether we write it in base ten or in binary, but it will always be true that $12 = 2 \times 2 \times 3$. From this representation we can conclude useful properties, for example, that 12 is not divisible by 5, and that any integer multiple of 12 will be divisible by 3.

Much as we can discover something about the true nature of an integer by decomposing it into prime factors, we can also decompose matrices in ways that show us information about their functional properties that is not obvious from the representation of the matrix as an array of elements.

One of the most widely used kinds of matrix decomposition is called **eigendecomposition**, in which we decompose a matrix into a set of eigenvectors and eigenvalues.

An **eigenvector** of a square matrix $\boldsymbol{A}$ is a nonzero vector $\boldsymbol{v}$ such that multiplication by $\boldsymbol{A}$ alters only the scale of $\boldsymbol{v}$:

$$\boldsymbol{A}\boldsymbol{v} = \lambda\boldsymbol{v}. \tag{2.39}$$

The scalar λ is known as the **eigenvalue** corresponding to this eigenvector. (One can also find a **left eigenvector** such that $\boldsymbol{v}^\top \boldsymbol{A} = \lambda \boldsymbol{v}^\top$, but we are usually concerned with right eigenvectors.)

If $\boldsymbol{v}$ is an eigenvector of $\boldsymbol{A}$, then so is any rescaled vector $s\boldsymbol{v}$ for $s \in \mathbb{R}, s \neq 0$. Moreover, $s\boldsymbol{v}$ still has the same eigenvalue. For this reason, we usually look only for unit eigenvectors.

Suppose that a matrix $\boldsymbol{A}$ has n linearly independent eigenvectors $\{\boldsymbol{v}^{(1)}, \ldots, \boldsymbol{v}^{(n)}\}$ with corresponding eigenvalues $\{\lambda_1, \ldots, \lambda_n\}$. We may concatenate all the eigenvectors to form a matrix $\boldsymbol{V}$ with one eigenvector per column: $\boldsymbol{V} = [\boldsymbol{v}^{(1)}, \ldots, \boldsymbol{v}^{(n)}]$. Likewise, we can concatenate the eigenvalues to form a vector $\boldsymbol{\lambda} = [\lambda_1, \ldots, \lambda_n]^\top$. The **eigendecomposition** of $\boldsymbol{A}$ is then given by

$$\boldsymbol{A} = \boldsymbol{V}\mathrm{diag}(\boldsymbol{\lambda})\boldsymbol{V}^{-1}. \tag{2.40}$$

We have seen that *constructing* matrices with specific eigenvalues and eigenvectors enables us to stretch space in desired directions. Yet we often want to **decompose** matrices into their eigenvalues and eigenvectors. Doing so can help us analyze certain properties of the matrix, much as decomposing an integer into its prime factors can help us understand the behavior of that integer.

Not every matrix can be decomposed into eigenvalues and eigenvectors. In some cases, the decomposition exists but involves complex rather than real numbers.

Fortunately, in this book, we usually need to decompose only a specific class of matrices that have a simple decomposition. Specifically, every real symmetric matrix can be decomposed into an expression using only real-valued eigenvectors and eigenvalues:

$$\boldsymbol{A} = \boldsymbol{Q}\boldsymbol{\Lambda}\boldsymbol{Q}^{\top}, \tag{2.41}$$

where $\boldsymbol{Q}$ is an orthogonal matrix composed of eigenvectors of $\boldsymbol{A}$, and $\boldsymbol{\Lambda}$ is a diagonal matrix. The eigenvalue $\Lambda_{i,i}$ is associated with the eigenvector in column i of $\boldsymbol{Q}$, denoted as $\boldsymbol{Q}_{:,i}$. Because $\boldsymbol{Q}$ is an orthogonal matrix, we can think of $\boldsymbol{A}$ as scaling space by λ_i in direction $\boldsymbol{v}^{(i)}$. See figure 2.3 for an example.

While any real symmetric matrix $\boldsymbol{A}$ is guaranteed to have an eigendecomposition, the eigendecomposition may not be unique. If any two or more eigenvectors share the same eigenvalue, then any set of orthogonal vectors lying in their span are also eigenvectors with that eigenvalue, and we could equivalently choose a $\boldsymbol{Q}$ using those eigenvectors instead. By convention, we usually sort the entries of $\boldsymbol{\Lambda}$ in descending order. Under this convention, the eigendecomposition is unique only if all the eigenvalues are unique.

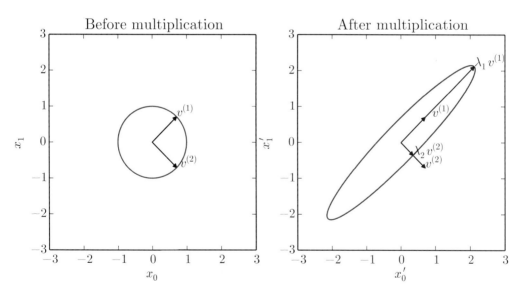

Figure 2.3: Effect of eigenvectors and eigenvalues. An example of the effect of eigenvectors and eigenvalues. Here, we have a matrix $\boldsymbol{A}$ with two orthonormal eigenvectors, $\boldsymbol{v}^{(1)}$ with eigenvalue λ_1 and $\boldsymbol{v}^{(2)}$ with eigenvalue λ_2. *(Left)*We plot the set of all unit vectors $\boldsymbol{u} \in \mathbb{R}^2$ as a unit circle. *(Right)*We plot the set of all points $\boldsymbol{A}\boldsymbol{u}$. By observing the way that $\boldsymbol{A}$ distorts the unit circle, we can see that it scales space in direction $\boldsymbol{v}^{(i)}$ by λ_i.

The eigendecomposition of a matrix tells us many useful facts about the matrix. The matrix is singular if and only if any of the eigenvalues are zero. The eigendecomposition of a real symmetric matrix can also be used to optimize quadratic expressions of the form $f(\boldsymbol{x}) = \boldsymbol{x}^\top \boldsymbol{A}\boldsymbol{x}$ subject to $||\boldsymbol{x}||_2 = 1$. Whenever $\boldsymbol{x}$ is equal to an eigenvector of $\boldsymbol{A}$, f takes on the value of the corresponding eigenvalue. The maximum value of f within the constraint region is the maximum eigenvalue and its minimum value within the constraint region is the minimum eigenvalue.

A matrix whose eigenvalues are all positive is called **positive definite**. A matrix whose eigenvalues are all positive or zero valued is called **positive semidefinite**. Likewise, if all eigenvalues are negative, the matrix is **negative definite**, and if all eigenvalues are negative or zero valued, it is **negative semidefinite**. Positive semidefinite matrices are interesting because they guarantee that $\forall \boldsymbol{x}$, $\boldsymbol{x}^\top \boldsymbol{A}\boldsymbol{x} \geq 0$. Positive definite matrices additionally guarantee that $\boldsymbol{x}^\top \boldsymbol{A}\boldsymbol{x} = 0 \Rightarrow \boldsymbol{x} = \boldsymbol{0}$.

2.8   Singular Value Decomposition

In section 2.7, we saw how to decompose a matrix into eigenvectors and eigenvalues. The **singular value decomposition** (SVD) provides another way to factorize a matrix, into **singular vectors** and **singular values**. The SVD enables us to discover some of the same kind of information as the eigendecomposition reveals; however, the SVD is more generally applicable. Every real matrix has a singular value decomposition, but the same is not true of the eigenvalue decomposition. For example, if a matrix is not square, the eigendecomposition is not defined, and we must use a singular value decomposition instead.

Recall that the eigendecomposition involves analyzing a matrix $\boldsymbol{A}$ to discover a matrix $\boldsymbol{V}$ of eigenvectors and a vector of eigenvalues $\boldsymbol{\lambda}$ such that we can rewrite $\boldsymbol{A}$ as

$$\boldsymbol{A} = \boldsymbol{V}\mathrm{diag}(\boldsymbol{\lambda})\boldsymbol{V}^{-1}. \tag{2.42}$$

The singular value decomposition is similar, except this time we will write $\boldsymbol{A}$ as a product of three matrices:

$$\boldsymbol{A} = \boldsymbol{U}\boldsymbol{D}\boldsymbol{V}^\top. \tag{2.43}$$

Suppose that $\boldsymbol{A}$ is an $m \times n$ matrix. Then $\boldsymbol{U}$ is defined to be an $m \times m$ matrix, $\boldsymbol{D}$ to be an $m \times n$ matrix, and $\boldsymbol{V}$ to be an $n \times n$ matrix.

Each of these matrices is defined to have a special structure. The matrices $\boldsymbol{U}$ and $\boldsymbol{V}$ are both defined to be orthogonal matrices. The matrix $\boldsymbol{D}$ is defined to be a diagonal matrix. Note that $\boldsymbol{D}$ is not necessarily square.

The elements along the diagonal of $\boldsymbol{D}$ are known as the **singular values** of the matrix $\boldsymbol{A}$. The columns of $\boldsymbol{U}$ are known as the **left-singular vectors**. The columns of $\boldsymbol{V}$ are known as as the **right-singular vectors**.

We can actually interpret the singular value decomposition of $\boldsymbol{A}$ in terms of the eigendecomposition of functions of $\boldsymbol{A}$. The left-singular vectors of $\boldsymbol{A}$ are the eigenvectors of $\boldsymbol{A}\boldsymbol{A}^{\top}$. The right-singular vectors of $\boldsymbol{A}$ are the eigenvectors of $\boldsymbol{A}^{\top}\boldsymbol{A}$. The nonzero singular values of $\boldsymbol{A}$ are the square roots of the eigenvalues of $\boldsymbol{A}^{\top}\boldsymbol{A}$. The same is true for $\boldsymbol{A}\boldsymbol{A}^{\top}$.

Perhaps the most useful feature of the SVD is that we can use it to partially generalize matrix inversion to nonsquare matrices, as we will see in the next section.

2.9   The Moore-Penrose Pseudoinverse

Matrix inversion is not defined for matrices that are not square. Suppose we want to make a left-inverse $\boldsymbol{B}$ of a matrix $\boldsymbol{A}$ so that we can solve a linear equation

$$\boldsymbol{A}\boldsymbol{x} = \boldsymbol{y} \tag{2.44}$$

by left-multiplying each side to obtain

$$\boldsymbol{x} = \boldsymbol{B}\boldsymbol{y}. \tag{2.45}$$

Depending on the structure of the problem, it may not be possible to design a unique mapping from $\boldsymbol{A}$ to $\boldsymbol{B}$.

If $\boldsymbol{A}$ is taller than it is wide, then it is possible for this equation to have no solution. If $\boldsymbol{A}$ is wider than it is tall, then there could be multiple possible solutions.

The **Moore-Penrose pseudoinverse** enables us to make some headway in these cases. The pseudoinverse of $\boldsymbol{A}$ is defined as a matrix

$$\boldsymbol{A}^{+} = \lim_{\alpha \searrow 0} (\boldsymbol{A}^{\top}\boldsymbol{A} + \alpha\boldsymbol{I})^{-1}\boldsymbol{A}^{\top}. \tag{2.46}$$

Practical algorithms for computing the pseudoinverse are based not on this definition, but rather on the formula

$$\boldsymbol{A}^{+} = \boldsymbol{V}\boldsymbol{D}^{+}\boldsymbol{U}^{\top}, \tag{2.47}$$

where U, D and V are the singular value decomposition of A, and the pseudoinverse D^+ of a diagonal matrix D is obtained by taking the reciprocal of its nonzero elements then taking the transpose of the resulting matrix.

When A has more columns than rows, then solving a linear equation using the pseudoinverse provides one of the many possible solutions. Specifically, it provides the solution $x = A^+ y$ with minimal Euclidean norm $||x||_2$ among all possible solutions.

When A has more rows than columns, it is possible for there to be no solution. In this case, using the pseudoinverse gives us the x for which Ax is as close as possible to y in terms of Euclidean norm $||Ax - y||_2$.

2.10   The Trace Operator

The trace operator gives the sum of all the diagonal entries of a matrix:

$$\mathrm{Tr}(A) = \sum_i A_{i,i}. \tag{2.48}$$

The trace operator is useful for a variety of reasons. Some operations that are difficult to specify without resorting to summation notation can be specified using matrix products and the trace operator. For example, the trace operator provides an alternative way of writing the Frobenius norm of a matrix:

$$||A||_F = \sqrt{\mathrm{Tr}(AA^\top)}. \tag{2.49}$$

Writing an expression in terms of the trace operator opens up opportunities to manipulate the expression using many useful identities. For example, the trace operator is invariant to the transpose operator:

$$\mathrm{Tr}(A) = \mathrm{Tr}(A^\top). \tag{2.50}$$

The trace of a square matrix composed of many factors is also invariant to moving the last factor into the first position, if the shapes of the corresponding matrices allow the resulting product to be defined:

$$\mathrm{Tr}(ABC) = \mathrm{Tr}(CAB) = \mathrm{Tr}(BCA) \tag{2.51}$$

or more generally,

$$\mathrm{Tr}\left(\prod_{i=1}^{n} F^{(i)}\right) = \mathrm{Tr}\left(F^{(n)} \prod_{i=1}^{n-1} F^{(i)}\right). \tag{2.52}$$

This invariance to cyclic permutation holds even if the resulting product has a different shape. For example, for $\boldsymbol{A} \in \mathbb{R}^{m \times n}$ and $\boldsymbol{B} \in \mathbb{R}^{n \times m}$, we have

$$\mathrm{Tr}(\boldsymbol{A}\boldsymbol{B}) = \mathrm{Tr}(\boldsymbol{B}\boldsymbol{A}) \tag{2.53}$$

even though $\boldsymbol{A}\boldsymbol{B} \in \mathbb{R}^{m \times m}$ and $\boldsymbol{B}\boldsymbol{A} \in \mathbb{R}^{n \times n}$.

Another useful fact to keep in mind is that a scalar is its own trace: $a = \mathrm{Tr}(a)$.

2.11 The Determinant

The determinant of a square matrix, denoted $\det(\boldsymbol{A})$, is a function that maps matrices to real scalars. The determinant is equal to the product of all the eigenvalues of the matrix. The absolute value of the determinant can be thought of as a measure of how much multiplication by the matrix expands or contracts space. If the determinant is 0, then space is contracted completely along at least one dimension, causing it to lose all its volume. If the determinant is 1, then the transformation preserves volume.

2.12 Example: Principal Components Analysis

One simple machine learning algorithm, **principal components analysis** (PCA), can be derived using only knowledge of basic linear algebra.

Suppose we have a collection of m points $\{\boldsymbol{x}^{(1)}, \ldots, \boldsymbol{x}^{(m)}\}$ in $\mathbb{R}^n$ and we want to apply lossy compression to these points. Lossy compression means storing the points in a way that requires less memory but may lose some precision. We want to lose as little precision as possible.

One way we can encode these points is to represent a lower-dimensional version of them. For each point $\boldsymbol{x}^{(i)} \in \mathbb{R}^n$ we will find a corresponding code vector $\boldsymbol{c}^{(i)} \in \mathbb{R}^l$. If l is smaller than n, storing the code points will take less memory than storing the original data. We will want to find some encoding function that produces the code for an input, $f(\boldsymbol{x}) = \boldsymbol{c}$, and a decoding function that produces the reconstructed input given its code, $\boldsymbol{x} \approx g(f(\boldsymbol{x}))$.

PCA is defined by our choice of the decoding function. Specifically, to make the decoder very simple, we choose to use matrix multiplication to map the code back into $\mathbb{R}^n$. Let $g(\boldsymbol{c}) = \boldsymbol{D}\boldsymbol{c}$, where $\boldsymbol{D} \in \mathbb{R}^{n \times l}$ is the matrix defining the decoding.

Computing the optimal code for this decoder could be a difficult problem. To keep the encoding problem easy, PCA constrains the columns of $\boldsymbol{D}$ to be orthogonal to each other. (Note that $\boldsymbol{D}$ is still not technically "an orthogonal matrix" unless $l = n$.)

With the problem as described so far, many solutions are possible, because we can increase the scale of $\boldsymbol{D}_{:,i}$ if we decrease c_i proportionally for all points. To give the problem a unique solution, we constrain all the columns of $\boldsymbol{D}$ to have unit norm.

In order to turn this basic idea into an algorithm we can implement, the first thing we need to do is figure out how to generate the optimal code point $\boldsymbol{c}^*$ for each input point $\boldsymbol{x}$. One way to do this is to minimize the distance between the input point $\boldsymbol{x}$ and its reconstruction, $g(\boldsymbol{c}^*)$. We can measure this distance using a norm. In the principal components algorithm, we use the L^2 norm:

$$\boldsymbol{c}^* = \arg\min_{\boldsymbol{c}} ||\boldsymbol{x} - g(\boldsymbol{c})||_2. \tag{2.54}$$

We can switch to the squared L^2 norm instead of using the L^2 norm itself because both are minimized by the same value of $\boldsymbol{c}$. Both are minimized by the same value of $\boldsymbol{c}$ because the L^2 norm is non-negative and the squaring operation is monotonically increasing for non-negative arguments.

$$\boldsymbol{c}^* = \arg\min_{\boldsymbol{c}} ||\boldsymbol{x} - g(\boldsymbol{c})||_2^2. \tag{2.55}$$

The function being minimized simplifies to

$$(\boldsymbol{x} - g(\boldsymbol{c}))^\top (\boldsymbol{x} - g(\boldsymbol{c})) \tag{2.56}$$

(by the definition of the L^2 norm, equation 2.30)

$$= \boldsymbol{x}^\top \boldsymbol{x} - \boldsymbol{x}^\top g(\boldsymbol{c}) - g(\boldsymbol{c})^\top \boldsymbol{x} + g(\boldsymbol{c})^\top g(\boldsymbol{c}) \tag{2.57}$$

(by the distributive property)

$$= \boldsymbol{x}^\top \boldsymbol{x} - 2\boldsymbol{x}^\top g(\boldsymbol{c}) + g(\boldsymbol{c})^\top g(\boldsymbol{c}) \tag{2.58}$$

(because the scalar $g(\boldsymbol{c})^\top \boldsymbol{x}$ is equal to the transpose of itself).

We can now change the function being minimized again, to omit the first term, since this term does not depend on $\boldsymbol{c}$:

$$\boldsymbol{c}^* = \arg\min_{\boldsymbol{c}} -2\boldsymbol{x}^\top g(\boldsymbol{c}) + g(\boldsymbol{c})^\top g(\boldsymbol{c}). \tag{2.59}$$

To make further progress, we must substitute in the definition of $g(\boldsymbol{c})$:

$$\boldsymbol{c}^* = \arg\min_{\boldsymbol{c}} -2\boldsymbol{x}^\top \boldsymbol{D}\boldsymbol{c} + \boldsymbol{c}^\top \boldsymbol{D}^\top \boldsymbol{D}\boldsymbol{c} \tag{2.60}$$

$$= \arg\min_{\boldsymbol{c}} -2\boldsymbol{x}^\top \boldsymbol{D}\boldsymbol{c} + \boldsymbol{c}^\top \boldsymbol{I}_l \boldsymbol{c} \tag{2.61}$$

(by the orthogonality and unit norm constraints on $\boldsymbol{D}$)

$$= \arg\min_{\boldsymbol{c}} -2\boldsymbol{x}^\top \boldsymbol{D}\boldsymbol{c} + \boldsymbol{c}^\top \boldsymbol{c}. \tag{2.62}$$

We can solve this optimization problem using vector calculus (see section 4.3 if you do not know how to do this):

$$\nabla_{\boldsymbol{c}}(-2\boldsymbol{x}^\top \boldsymbol{D}\boldsymbol{c} + \boldsymbol{c}^\top \boldsymbol{c}) = \boldsymbol{0} \tag{2.63}$$

$$-2\boldsymbol{D}^\top \boldsymbol{x} + 2\boldsymbol{c} = \boldsymbol{0} \tag{2.64}$$

$$\boldsymbol{c} = \boldsymbol{D}^\top \boldsymbol{x}. \tag{2.65}$$

This makes the algorithm efficient: we can optimally encode $\boldsymbol{x}$ using just a matrix-vector operation. To encode a vector, we apply the encoder function

$$f(\boldsymbol{x}) = \boldsymbol{D}^\top \boldsymbol{x}. \tag{2.66}$$

Using a further matrix multiplication, we can also define the PCA reconstruction operation:

$$r(\boldsymbol{x}) = g(f(\boldsymbol{x})) = \boldsymbol{D}\boldsymbol{D}^\top \boldsymbol{x}. \tag{2.67}$$

Next, we need to choose the encoding matrix $\boldsymbol{D}$. To do so, we revisit the idea of minimizing the L^2 distance between inputs and reconstructions. Since we will use the same matrix $\boldsymbol{D}$ to decode all the points, we can no longer consider the points in isolation. Instead, we must minimize the Frobenius norm of the matrix of errors computed over all dimensions and all points:

$$\boldsymbol{D}^* = \arg\min_{\boldsymbol{D}} \sqrt{\sum_{i,j} \left(x_j^{(i)} - r(\boldsymbol{x}^{(i)})_j \right)^2} \text{ subject to } \boldsymbol{D}^\top \boldsymbol{D} = \boldsymbol{I}_l. \tag{2.68}$$

To derive the algorithm for finding $\boldsymbol{D}^*$, we start by considering the case where $l = 1$. In this case, $\boldsymbol{D}$ is just a single vector, $\boldsymbol{d}$. Substituting equation 2.67 into equation 2.68 and simplifying $\boldsymbol{D}$ into $\boldsymbol{d}$, the problem reduces to

$$\boldsymbol{d}^* = \arg\min_{\boldsymbol{d}} \sum_i ||\boldsymbol{x}^{(i)} - \boldsymbol{d}\boldsymbol{d}^\top \boldsymbol{x}^{(i)}||_2^2 \text{ subject to } ||\boldsymbol{d}||_2 = 1. \tag{2.69}$$

The above formulation is the most direct way of performing the substitution but is not the most stylistically pleasing way to write the equation. It places the scalar value $\boldsymbol{d}^\top \boldsymbol{x}^{(i)}$ on the right of the vector $\boldsymbol{d}$. Scalar coefficients are conventionally written on the left of vector they operate on. We therefore usually write such a formula as

$$\boldsymbol{d}^* = \arg\min_{\boldsymbol{d}} \sum_i ||\boldsymbol{x}^{(i)} - \boldsymbol{d}^\top \boldsymbol{x}^{(i)} \boldsymbol{d}||_2^2 \text{ subject to } ||\boldsymbol{d}||_2 = 1, \qquad (2.70)$$

or, exploiting the fact that a scalar is its own transpose, as

$$\boldsymbol{d}^* = \arg\min_{\boldsymbol{d}} \sum_i ||\boldsymbol{x}^{(i)} - \boldsymbol{x}^{(i)\top} \boldsymbol{d}\boldsymbol{d}||_2^2 \text{ subject to } ||\boldsymbol{d}||_2 = 1. \qquad (2.71)$$

The reader should aim to become familiar with such cosmetic rearrangements.

At this point, it can be helpful to rewrite the problem in terms of a single design matrix of examples, rather than as a sum over separate example vectors. This will enable us to use more compact notation. Let $\boldsymbol{X} \in \mathbb{R}^{m \times n}$ be the matrix defined by stacking all the vectors describing the points, such that $\boldsymbol{X}_{i,:} = \boldsymbol{x}^{(i)\top}$. We can now rewrite the problem as

$$\boldsymbol{d}^* = \arg\min_{\boldsymbol{d}} ||\boldsymbol{X} - \boldsymbol{X}\boldsymbol{d}\boldsymbol{d}^\top||_F^2 \text{ subject to } \boldsymbol{d}^\top \boldsymbol{d} = 1. \qquad (2.72)$$

Disregarding the constraint for the moment, we can simplify the Frobenius norm portion as follows:

$$\arg\min_{\boldsymbol{d}} ||\boldsymbol{X} - \boldsymbol{X}\boldsymbol{d}\boldsymbol{d}^\top||_F^2 \qquad (2.73)$$

$$= \arg\min_{\boldsymbol{d}} \text{Tr}\left(\left(\boldsymbol{X} - \boldsymbol{X}\boldsymbol{d}\boldsymbol{d}^\top \right)^\top \left(\boldsymbol{X} - \boldsymbol{X}\boldsymbol{d}\boldsymbol{d}^\top \right) \right) \qquad (2.74)$$

(by equation 2.49)

$$= \arg\min_{\boldsymbol{d}} \text{Tr}(\boldsymbol{X}^\top \boldsymbol{X} - \boldsymbol{X}^\top \boldsymbol{X}\boldsymbol{d}\boldsymbol{d}^\top - \boldsymbol{d}\boldsymbol{d}^\top \boldsymbol{X}^\top \boldsymbol{X} + \boldsymbol{d}\boldsymbol{d}^\top \boldsymbol{X}^\top \boldsymbol{X}\boldsymbol{d}\boldsymbol{d}^\top) \qquad (2.75)$$

$$= \arg\min_{\boldsymbol{d}} \text{Tr}(\boldsymbol{X}^\top \boldsymbol{X}) - \text{Tr}(\boldsymbol{X}^\top \boldsymbol{X}\boldsymbol{d}\boldsymbol{d}^\top) - \text{Tr}(\boldsymbol{d}\boldsymbol{d}^\top \boldsymbol{X}^\top \boldsymbol{X}) + \text{Tr}(\boldsymbol{d}\boldsymbol{d}^\top \boldsymbol{X}^\top \boldsymbol{X}\boldsymbol{d}\boldsymbol{d}^\top)$$
$$\qquad (2.76)$$

$$= \arg\min_{\boldsymbol{d}} - \text{Tr}(\boldsymbol{X}^\top \boldsymbol{X}\boldsymbol{d}\boldsymbol{d}^\top) - \text{Tr}(\boldsymbol{d}\boldsymbol{d}^\top \boldsymbol{X}^\top \boldsymbol{X}) + \text{Tr}(\boldsymbol{d}\boldsymbol{d}^\top \boldsymbol{X}^\top \boldsymbol{X}\boldsymbol{d}\boldsymbol{d}^\top) \qquad (2.77)$$

(because terms not involving $\boldsymbol{d}$ do not affect the arg min)

$$= \arg\min_{\boldsymbol{d}} -2 \text{Tr}(\boldsymbol{X}^\top \boldsymbol{X}\boldsymbol{d}\boldsymbol{d}^\top) + \text{Tr}(\boldsymbol{d}\boldsymbol{d}^\top \boldsymbol{X}^\top \boldsymbol{X}\boldsymbol{d}\boldsymbol{d}^\top) \qquad (2.78)$$

(because we can cycle the order of the matrices inside a trace, equation 2.52)

$$= \arg\min_{\boldsymbol{d}} -2\operatorname{Tr}(\boldsymbol{X}^\top \boldsymbol{X} \boldsymbol{d}\boldsymbol{d}^\top) + \operatorname{Tr}(\boldsymbol{X}^\top \boldsymbol{X} \boldsymbol{d}\boldsymbol{d}^\top \boldsymbol{d}\boldsymbol{d}^\top) \qquad (2.79)$$

(using the same property again).

At this point, we reintroduce the constraint:

$$\arg\min_{\boldsymbol{d}} -2\operatorname{Tr}(\boldsymbol{X}^\top \boldsymbol{X} \boldsymbol{d}\boldsymbol{d}^\top) + \operatorname{Tr}(\boldsymbol{X}^\top \boldsymbol{X} \boldsymbol{d}\boldsymbol{d}^\top \boldsymbol{d}\boldsymbol{d}^\top) \text{ subject to } \boldsymbol{d}^\top \boldsymbol{d} = 1 \qquad (2.80)$$

$$= \arg\min_{\boldsymbol{d}} -2\operatorname{Tr}(\boldsymbol{X}^\top \boldsymbol{X} \boldsymbol{d}\boldsymbol{d}^\top) + \operatorname{Tr}(\boldsymbol{X}^\top \boldsymbol{X} \boldsymbol{d}\boldsymbol{d}^\top) \text{ subject to } \boldsymbol{d}^\top \boldsymbol{d} = 1 \qquad (2.81)$$

(due to the constraint)

$$= \arg\min_{\boldsymbol{d}} -\operatorname{Tr}(\boldsymbol{X}^\top \boldsymbol{X} \boldsymbol{d}\boldsymbol{d}^\top) \text{ subject to } \boldsymbol{d}^\top \boldsymbol{d} = 1 \qquad (2.82)$$

$$= \arg\max_{\boldsymbol{d}} \operatorname{Tr}(\boldsymbol{X}^\top \boldsymbol{X} \boldsymbol{d}\boldsymbol{d}^\top) \text{ subject to } \boldsymbol{d}^\top \boldsymbol{d} = 1 \qquad (2.83)$$

$$= \arg\max_{\boldsymbol{d}} \operatorname{Tr}(\boldsymbol{d}^\top \boldsymbol{X}^\top \boldsymbol{X} \boldsymbol{d}) \text{ subject to } \boldsymbol{d}^\top \boldsymbol{d} = 1. \qquad (2.84)$$

This optimization problem may be solved using eigendecomposition. Specifically, the optimal $\boldsymbol{d}$ is given by the eigenvector of $\boldsymbol{X}^\top \boldsymbol{X}$ corresponding to the largest eigenvalue.

This derivation is specific to the case of $l = 1$ and recovers only the first principal component. More generally, when we wish to recover a basis of principal components, the matrix $\boldsymbol{D}$ is given by the l eigenvectors corresponding to the largest eigenvalues. This may be shown using proof by induction. We recommend writing this proof as an exercise.

Linear algebra is one of the fundamental mathematical disciplines necessary to understanding deep learning. Another key area of mathematics that is ubiquitous in machine learning is probability theory, presented next.

3

Probability and Information Theory

In this chapter, we describe probability theory and information theory.

Probability theory is a mathematical framework for representing uncertain statements. It provides a means of quantifying uncertainty as well as axioms for deriving new uncertain statements. In artificial intelligence applications, we use probability theory in two major ways. First, the laws of probability tell us how AI systems should reason, so we design our algorithms to compute or approximate various expressions derived using probability theory. Second, we can use probability and statistics to theoretically analyze the behavior of proposed AI systems.

Probability theory is a fundamental tool of many disciplines of science and engineering. We provide this chapter to ensure that readers whose background is primarily in software engineering, with limited exposure to probability theory, can understand the material in this book.

While probability theory allows us to make uncertain statements and to reason in the presence of uncertainty, information theory enables us to quantify the amount of uncertainty in a probability distribution.

If you are already familiar with probability theory and information theory, you may wish to skip this chapter except for section 3.14, which describes the graphs we use to describe structured probabilistic models for machine learning. If you have absolutely no prior experience with these subjects, this chapter should be sufficient to successfully carry out deep learning research projects, but we do suggest that you consult an additional resource, such as Jaynes (2003).

3.1 Why Probability?

Many branches of computer science deal mostly with entities that are entirely deterministic and certain. A programmer can usually safely assume that a CPU will execute each machine instruction flawlessly. Errors in hardware do occur but are rare enough that most software applications do not need to be designed to account for them. Given that many computer scientists and software engineers work in a relatively clean and certain environment, it can be surprising that machine learning makes heavy use of probability theory.

Machine learning must always deal with uncertain quantities and sometimes stochastic (nondeterministic) quantities. Uncertainty and stochasticity can arise from many sources. Researchers have made compelling arguments for quantifying uncertainty using probability since at least the 1980s. Many of the arguments presented here are summarized from or inspired by Pearl (1988).

Nearly all activities require some ability to reason in the presence of uncertainty. In fact, beyond mathematical statements that are true by definition, it is difficult to think of any proposition that is absolutely true or any event that is absolutely guaranteed to occur.

There are three possible sources of uncertainty:

1. Inherent stochasticity in the system being modeled. For example, most interpretations of quantum mechanics describe the dynamics of subatomic particles as being probabilistic. We can also create theoretical scenarios that we postulate to have random dynamics, such as a hypothetical card game where we assume that the cards are truly shuffled into a random order.

2. Incomplete observability. Even deterministic systems can appear stochastic when we cannot observe all the variables that drive the behavior of the system. For example, in the Monty Hall problem, a game show contestant is asked to choose between three doors and wins a prize held behind the chosen door. Two doors lead to a goat while a third leads to a car. The outcome given the contestant's choice is deterministic, but from the contestant's point of view, the outcome is uncertain.

3. Incomplete modeling. When we use a model that must discard some of the information we have observed, the discarded information results in uncertainty in the model's predictions. For example, suppose we build a robot that can exactly observe the location of every object around it. If the robot discretizes space when predicting the future location of these objects,

then the discretization makes the robot immediately become uncertain about the precise position of objects: each object could be anywhere within the discrete cell that it was observed to occupy.

In many cases, it is more practical to use a simple but uncertain rule rather than a complex but certain one, even if the true rule is deterministic and our modeling system has the fidelity to accommodate a complex rule. For example, the simple rule "Most birds fly" is cheap to develop and is broadly useful, while a rule of the form, "Birds fly, except for very young birds that have not yet learned to fly, sick or injured birds that have lost the ability to fly, flightless species of birds including the cassowary, ostrich and kiwi. . ." is expensive to develop, maintain and communicate and, after all this effort, is still brittle and prone to failure.

While it should be clear that we need a means of representing and reasoning about uncertainty, it is not immediately obvious that probability theory can provide all the tools we want for artificial intelligence applications. Probability theory was originally developed to analyze the frequencies of events. It is easy to see how probability theory can be used to study events like drawing a certain hand of cards in a poker game. These kinds of events are often repeatable. When we say that an outcome has a probability p of occurring, it means that if we repeated the experiment (e.g., drawing a hand of cards) infinitely many times, then proportion p of the repetitions would result in that outcome. This kind of reasoning does not seem immediately applicable to propositions that are not repeatable. If a doctor analyzes a patient and says that the patient has a 40 percent chance of having the flu, this means something very different—we cannot make infinitely many replicas of the patient, nor is there any reason to believe that different replicas of the patient would present with the same symptoms yet have varying underlying conditions. In the case of the doctor diagnosing the patient, we use probability to represent a **degree of belief**, with 1 indicating absolute certainty that the patient has the flu and 0 indicating absolute certainty that the patient does not have the flu. The former kind of probability, related directly to the rates at which events occur, is known as **frequentist probability**, while the latter, related to qualitative levels of certainty, is known as **Bayesian probability**.

If we list several properties that we expect common sense reasoning about uncertainty to have, then the only way to satisfy those properties is to treat Bayesian probabilities as behaving exactly the same as frequentist probabilities. For example, if we want to compute the probability that a player will win a poker game given that she has a certain set of cards, we use exactly the same formulas as when we compute the probability that a patient has a disease given that she has certain symptoms. For more details about why a small set of common sense assumptions implies that the same axioms must control both kinds of probability, see Ramsey (1926).

Probability can be seen as the extension of logic to deal with uncertainty. Logic provides a set of formal rules for determining what propositions are implied to be true or false given the assumption that some other set of propositions is true or false. Probability theory provides a set of formal rules for determining the likelihood of a proposition being true given the likelihood of other propositions.

3.2 Random Variables

A **random variable** is a variable that can take on different values randomly. We typically denote the random variable itself with a lowercase letter in plain typeface, and the values it can take on with lowercase script letters. For example, x_1 and x_2 are both possible values that the random variable x can take on. For vector-valued variables, we would write the random variable as $\mathbf{x}$ and one of its values as $\boldsymbol{x}$. On its own, a random variable is just a description of the states that are possible; it must be coupled with a probability distribution that specifies how likely each of these states are.

Random variables may be discrete or continuous. A discrete random variable is one that has a finite or countably infinite number of states. Note that these states are not necessarily the integers; they can also just be named states that are not considered to have any numerical value. A continuous random variable is associated with a real value.

3.3 Probability Distributions

A **probability distribution** is a description of how likely a random variable or set of random variables is to take on each of its possible states. The way we describe probability distributions depends on whether the variables are discrete or continuous.

3.3.1 Discrete Variables and Probability Mass Functions

A probability distribution over discrete variables may be described using a **probability mass function** (PMF). We typically denote probability mass functions with a capital P. Often we associate each random variable with a different probability mass function and the reader must infer which PMF to use based on the identity of the random variable, rather than on the name of the function; $P(\mathrm{x})$ is usually not the same as $P(\mathrm{y})$.

The probability mass function maps from a state of a random variable to the probability of that random variable taking on that state. The probability that $\mathrm{x} = x$ is denoted as $P(x)$, with a probability of 1 indicating that $\mathrm{x} = x$ is certain and a probability of 0 indicating that $\mathrm{x} = x$ is impossible. Sometimes to disambiguate which PMF to use, we write the name of the random variable explicitly: $P(\mathrm{x} = x)$. Sometimes we define a variable first, then use $\sim$ notation to specify which distribution it follows later: $\mathrm{x} \sim P(\mathrm{x})$.

Probability mass functions can act on many variables at the same time. Such a probability distribution over many variables is known as a **joint probability distribution**. $P(\mathrm{x} = x, \mathrm{y} = y)$ denotes the probability that $\mathrm{x} = x$ and $\mathrm{y} = y$ simultaneously. We may also write $P(x, y)$ for brevity.

To be a PMF on a random variable x, a function P must satisfy the following properties:

- The domain of P must be the set of all possible states of x.

- $\forall x \in \mathrm{x}, 0 \leq P(x) \leq 1$. An impossible event has probability 0, and no state can be less probable than that. Likewise, an event that is guaranteed to happen has probability 1, and no state can have a greater chance of occurring.

- $\sum_{x \in \mathrm{x}} P(x) = 1$. We refer to this property as being **normalized**. Without this property, we could obtain probabilities greater than one by computing the probability of one of many events occurring.

For example, consider a single discrete random variable x with k different states. We can place a **uniform distribution** on x—that is, make each of its states equally likely—by setting its PMF to

$$P(\mathrm{x} = x_i) = \frac{1}{k} \tag{3.1}$$

for all i. We can see that this fits the requirements for a probability mass function. The value $\frac{1}{k}$ is positive because k is a positive integer. We also see that

$$\sum_i P(\mathrm{x} = x_i) = \sum_i \frac{1}{k} = \frac{k}{k} = 1, \tag{3.2}$$

so the distribution is properly normalized.

3.3.2 Continuous Variables and Probability Density Functions

When working with continuous random variables, we describe probability distributions using a **probability density function** (PDF) rather than a probability mass function. To be a probability density function, a function p must satisfy the following properties:

- The domain of p must be the set of all possible states of x.

- $\forall x \in \text{x}, p(x) \geq 0$. Note that we do not require $p(x) \leq 1$.

- $\int p(x)dx = 1$.

A probability density function $p(x)$ does not give the probability of a specific state directly; instead the probability of landing inside an infinitesimal region with volume δx is given by $p(x)\delta x$.

We can integrate the density function to find the actual probability mass of a set of points. Specifically, the probability that x lies in some set $\mathbb{S}$ is given by the integral of $p(x)$ over that set. In the univariate example, the probability that x lies in the interval $[a, b]$ is given by $\int_{[a,b]} p(x)dx$.

For an example of a PDF corresponding to a specific probability density over a continuous random variable, consider a uniform distribution on an interval of the real numbers. We can do this with a function $u(x; a, b)$, where a and b are the endpoints of the interval, with $b > a$. The ";" notation means "parametrized by"; we consider x to be the argument of the function, while a and b are parameters that define the function. To ensure that there is no probability mass outside the interval, we say $u(x; a, b) = 0$ for all $x \notin [a, b]$. Within $[a, b]$, $u(x; a, b) = \frac{1}{b-a}$. We can see that this is non-negative everywhere. Additionally, it integrates to 1. We often denote that x follows the uniform distribution on $[a, b]$ by writing $\text{x} \sim U(a, b)$.

3.4 Marginal Probability

Sometimes we know the probability distribution over a set of variables and we want to know the probability distribution over just a subset of them. The probability distribution over the subset is known as the **marginal probability distribution.**

For example, suppose we have discrete random variables x and y, and we know $P(\text{x}, \text{y})$. We can find $P(\text{x})$ with the **sum rule**:

$$\forall x \in \text{x}, P(\text{x} = x) = \sum_{y} P(\text{x} = x, \text{y} = y). \tag{3.3}$$

The name "marginal probability" comes from the process of computing marginal probabilities on paper. When the values of $P(\mathrm{x}, \mathrm{y})$ are written in a grid with different values of x in rows and different values of y in columns, it is natural to sum across a row of the grid, then write $P(x)$ in the margin of the paper just to the right of the row.

For continuous variables, we need to use integration instead of summation:

$$p(x) = \int p(x, y) dy. \tag{3.4}$$

3.5 Conditional Probability

In many cases, we are interested in the probability of some event, given that some other event has happened. This is called a **conditional probability**. We denote the conditional probability that $\mathrm{y} = y$ given $\mathrm{x} = x$ as $P(\mathrm{y} = y \mid \mathrm{x} = x)$. This conditional probability can be computed with the formula

$$P(\mathrm{y} = y \mid \mathrm{x} = x) = \frac{P(\mathrm{y} = y, \mathrm{x} = x)}{P(\mathrm{x} = x)}. \tag{3.5}$$

The conditional probability is only defined when $P(\mathrm{x} = x) > 0$. We cannot compute the conditional probability conditioned on an event that never happens.

It is important not to confuse conditional probability with computing what would happen if some action were undertaken. The conditional probability that a person is from Germany given that they speak German is quite high, but if a randomly selected person is taught to speak German, their country of origin does not change. Computing the consequences of an action is called making an **intervention query**. Intervention queries are the domain of **causal modeling**, which we do not explore in this book.

3.6 The Chain Rule of Conditional Probabilities

Any joint probability distribution over many random variables may be decomposed into conditional distributions over only one variable:

$$P(\mathrm{x}^{(1)}, \ldots, \mathrm{x}^{(n)}) = P(\mathrm{x}^{(1)})\Pi_{i=2}^{n}P(\mathrm{x}^{(i)} \mid \mathrm{x}^{(1)}, \ldots, \mathrm{x}^{(i-1)}). \tag{3.6}$$

This observation is known as the **chain rule**, or **product rule**, of probability. It follows immediately from the definition of conditional probability in equation 3.5.

For example, applying the definition twice, we get

$$
\begin{aligned}
P(\mathrm{a},\mathrm{b},\mathrm{c}) &= P(\mathrm{a} \mid \mathrm{b},\mathrm{c})P(\mathrm{b},\mathrm{c}) \\
P(\mathrm{b},\mathrm{c}) &= P(\mathrm{b} \mid \mathrm{c})P(\mathrm{c}) \\
P(\mathrm{a},\mathrm{b},\mathrm{c}) &= P(\mathrm{a} \mid \mathrm{b},\mathrm{c})P(\mathrm{b} \mid \mathrm{c})P(\mathrm{c}).
\end{aligned}
$$

3.7 Independence and Conditional Independence

Two random variables x and y are **independent** if their probability distribution can be expressed as a product of two factors, one involving only x and one involving only y:

$$
\forall x \in \mathrm{x}, y \in \mathrm{y}, \ p(\mathrm{x} = x, \mathrm{y} = y) = p(\mathrm{x} = x)p(\mathrm{y} = y). \tag{3.7}
$$

Two random variables x and y are **conditionally independent** given a random variable z if the conditional probability distribution over x and y factorizes in this way for every value of z:

$$
\forall x \in \mathrm{x}, y \in \mathrm{y}, z \in \mathrm{z}, \ p(\mathrm{x} = x, \mathrm{y} = y \mid \mathrm{z} = z) = p(\mathrm{x} = x \mid \mathrm{z} = z)p(\mathrm{y} = y \mid \mathrm{z} = z). \tag{3.8}
$$

We can denote independence and conditional independence with compact notation: $\mathrm{x} \perp \mathrm{y}$ means that x and y are independent, while $\mathrm{x} \perp \mathrm{y} \mid \mathrm{z}$ means that x and y are conditionally independent given z.

3.8 Expectation, Variance and Covariance

The **expectation**, or **expected value**, of some function $f(x)$ with respect to a probability distribution $P(\mathrm{x})$ is the average, or mean value, that f takes on when x is drawn from P. For discrete variables this can be computed with a summation:

$$
\mathbb{E}_{\mathrm{x} \sim P}[f(x)] = \sum_x P(x)f(x), \tag{3.9}
$$

while for continuous variables, it is computed with an integral:

$$
\mathbb{E}_{\mathrm{x} \sim p}[f(x)] = \int p(x)f(x)dx. \tag{3.10}
$$

When the identity of the distribution is clear from the context, we may simply write the name of the random variable that the expectation is over, as in $\mathbb{E}_{\mathrm{x}}[f(x)]$. If it is clear which random variable the expectation is over, we may omit the subscript entirely, as in $\mathbb{E}[f(x)]$. By default, we can assume that $\mathbb{E}[\cdot]$ averages over the values of all the random variables inside the brackets. Likewise, when there is no ambiguity, we may omit the square brackets.

Expectations are linear, for example,

$$\mathbb{E}_{\mathrm{x}}[\alpha f(x) + \beta g(x)] = \alpha \mathbb{E}_{\mathrm{x}}[f(x)] + \beta \mathbb{E}_{\mathrm{x}}[g(x)], \tag{3.11}$$

when α and β are not dependent on x.

The **variance** gives a measure of how much the values of a function of a random variable x vary as we sample different values of x from its probability distribution:

$$\mathrm{Var}(f(x)) = \mathbb{E}\left[(f(x) - \mathbb{E}[f(x)])^2\right]. \tag{3.12}$$

When the variance is low, the values of $f(x)$ cluster near their expected value. The square root of the variance is known as the **standard deviation**.

The **covariance** gives some sense of how much two values are linearly related to each other, as well as the scale of these variables:

$$\mathrm{Cov}(f(x), g(y)) = \mathbb{E}\left[(f(x) - \mathbb{E}\left[f(x)\right])(g(y) - \mathbb{E}\left[g(y)\right])\right]. \tag{3.13}$$

High absolute values of the covariance mean that the values change very much and are both far from their respective means at the same time. If the sign of the covariance is positive, then both variables tend to take on relatively high values simultaneously. If the sign of the covariance is negative, then one variable tends to take on a relatively high value at the times that the other takes on a relatively low value and vice versa. Other measures such as **correlation** normalize the contribution of each variable in order to measure only how much the variables are related, rather than also being affected by the scale of the separate variables.

The notions of covariance and dependence are related but distinct concepts. They are related because two variables that are independent have zero covariance, and two variables that have nonzero covariance are dependent. Independence, however, is a distinct property from covariance. For two variables to have zero covariance, there must be no linear dependence between them. Independence is a stronger requirement than zero covariance, because independence also excludes nonlinear relationships. It is possible for two variables to be dependent but have zero covariance. For example, suppose we first sample a real number x from a uniform distribution over the interval $[-1, 1]$. We next sample a random variable s.

With probability $\frac{1}{2}$, we choose the value of s to be 1. Otherwise, we choose the value of s to be -1. We can then generate a random variable y by assigning $y = sx$. Clearly, x and y are not independent, because x completely determines the magnitude of y. However, $\mathrm{Cov}(x, y) = 0$.

The **covariance matrix** of a random vector $\boldsymbol{x} \in \mathbb{R}^n$ is an $n \times n$ matrix, such that

$$\mathrm{Cov}(\mathbf{x})_{i,j} = \mathrm{Cov}(\mathrm{x}_i, \mathrm{x}_j). \tag{3.14}$$

The diagonal elements of the covariance give the variance:

$$\mathrm{Cov}(\mathrm{x}_i, \mathrm{x}_i) = \mathrm{Var}(\mathrm{x}_i). \tag{3.15}$$

3.9   Common Probability Distributions

Several simple probability distributions are useful in many contexts in machine learning.

3.9.1   Bernoulli Distribution

The **Bernoulli distribution** is a distribution over a single binary random variable. It is controlled by a single parameter $\phi \in [0, 1]$, which gives the probability of the random variable being equal to 1. It has the following properties:

$$P(\mathrm{x} = 1) = \phi \tag{3.16}$$

$$P(\mathrm{x} = 0) = 1 - \phi \tag{3.17}$$

$$P(\mathrm{x} = x) = \phi^x (1 - \phi)^{1-x} \tag{3.18}$$

$$\mathbb{E}_{\mathrm{x}}[\mathrm{x}] = \phi \tag{3.19}$$

$$\mathrm{Var}_{\mathrm{x}}(\mathrm{x}) = \phi(1 - \phi) \tag{3.20}$$

3.9.2   Multinoulli Distribution

The **multinoulli**, or **categorical**, **distribution** is a distribution over a single discrete variable with k different states, where k is finite.[1] The multinoulli distribution

---

[1] "Multinoulli" is a term that was recently coined by Gustavo Lacerdo and popularized by Murphy (2012). The multinoulli distribution is a special case of the **multinomial distribution**. A multinomial distribution is the distribution over vectors in $\{0, \dots, n\}^k$ representing how many times each of the k categories is visited when n samples are drawn from a multinoulli distribution. Many texts use the term "multinomial" to refer to multinoulli distributions without clarifying that they are referring only to the $n = 1$ case.

is parametrized by a vector $\boldsymbol{p} \in [0, 1]^{k-1}$, where p_i gives the probability of the i-th state. The final, k-th state's probability is given by $1 - \mathbf{1}^\top \boldsymbol{p}$. Note that we must constrain $\mathbf{1}^\top \boldsymbol{p} \leq 1$. Multinoulli distributions are often used to refer to distributions over categories of objects, so we do not usually assume that state 1 has numerical value 1, and so on. For this reason, we do not usually need to compute the expectation or variance of multinoulli-distributed random variables.

The Bernoulli and multinoulli distributions are sufficient to describe any distribution over their domain. They are able to describe any distribution over their domain not so much because they are particularly powerful but rather because their domain is simple; they model discrete variables for which it is feasible to enumerate all the states. When dealing with continuous variables, there are uncountably many states, so any distribution described by a small number of parameters must impose strict limits on the distribution.

3.9.3 Gaussian Distribution

The most commonly used distribution over real numbers is the **normal distribution**, also known as the **Gaussian distribution**:

$$\mathcal{N}(x; \mu, \sigma^2) = \sqrt{\frac{1}{2\pi\sigma^2}} \exp\left(-\frac{1}{2\sigma^2}(x-\mu)^2\right). \tag{3.21}$$

See figure 3.1 for a plot of the normal distribution density function.

The two parameters $\mu \in \mathbb{R}$ and $\sigma \in (0, \infty)$ control the normal distribution. The parameter μ gives the coordinate of the central peak. This is also the mean of the distribution: $\mathbb{E}[\mathrm{x}] = \mu$. The standard deviation of the distribution is given by σ, and the variance by σ^2.

When we evaluate the PDF, we need to square and invert σ. When we need to frequently evaluate the PDF with different parameter values, a more efficient way of parametrizing the distribution is to use a parameter $\beta \in (0, \infty)$ to control the **precision**, or inverse variance, of the distribution:

$$\mathcal{N}(x; \mu, \beta^{-1}) = \sqrt{\frac{\beta}{2\pi}} \exp\left(-\frac{1}{2}\beta(x-\mu)^2\right). \tag{3.22}$$

Normal distributions are a sensible choice for many applications. In the absence of prior knowledge about what form a distribution over the real numbers should take, the normal distribution is a good default choice for two major reasons.

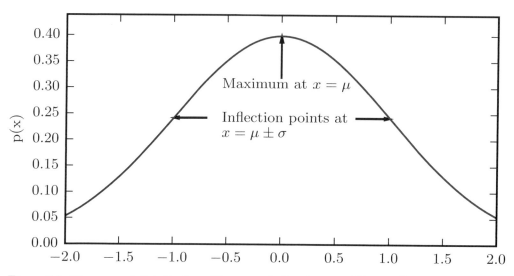

Figure 3.1: The normal distribution. The normal distribution $\mathcal{N}(x; \mu, \sigma^2)$ exhibits a classic "bell curve" shape, with the x coordinate of its central peak given by μ, and the width of its peak controlled by σ. In this example, we depict the **standard normal distribution**, with $\mu = 0$ and $\sigma = 1$.

First, many distributions we wish to model are truly close to being normal distributions. The **central limit theorem** shows that the sum of many independent random variables is approximately normally distributed. This means that in practice, many complicated systems can be modeled successfully as normally distributed noise, even if the system can be decomposed into parts with more structured behavior.

Second, out of all possible probability distributions with the same variance, the normal distribution encodes the maximum amount of uncertainty over the real numbers. We can thus think of the normal distribution as being the one that inserts the least amount of prior knowledge into a model. Fully developing and justifying this idea requires more mathematical tools and is postponed to section 19.4.2.

The normal distribution generalizes to $\mathbb{R}^n$, in which case it is known as the **multivariate normal distribution**. It may be parametrized with a positive definite symmetric matrix $\boldsymbol{\Sigma}$:

$$\mathcal{N}(\boldsymbol{x}; \boldsymbol{\mu}, \boldsymbol{\Sigma}) = \sqrt{\frac{1}{(2\pi)^n \det(\boldsymbol{\Sigma})}} \exp\left(-\frac{1}{2}(\boldsymbol{x} - \boldsymbol{\mu})^\top \boldsymbol{\Sigma}^{-1}(\boldsymbol{x} - \boldsymbol{\mu})\right). \qquad (3.23)$$

The parameter $\boldsymbol{\mu}$ still gives the mean of the distribution, though now it is vector valued. The parameter $\boldsymbol{\Sigma}$ gives the covariance matrix of the distribution.

As in the univariate case, when we wish to evaluate the PDF several times for many different values of the parameters, the covariance is not a computationally efficient way to parametrize the distribution, since we need to invert $\boldsymbol{\Sigma}$ to evaluate the PDF. We can instead use a **precision matrix** $\boldsymbol{\beta}$:

$$\mathcal{N}(\boldsymbol{x}; \boldsymbol{\mu}, \boldsymbol{\beta}^{-1}) = \sqrt{\frac{\det(\boldsymbol{\beta})}{(2\pi)^n}} \exp\left(-\frac{1}{2}(\boldsymbol{x} - \boldsymbol{\mu})^\top \boldsymbol{\beta}(\boldsymbol{x} - \boldsymbol{\mu})\right). \tag{3.24}$$

We often fix the covariance matrix to be a diagonal matrix. An even simpler version is the **isotropic** Gaussian distribution, whose covariance matrix is a scalar times the identity matrix.

3.9.4 Exponential and Laplace Distributions

In the context of deep learning, we often want to have a probability distribution with a sharp point at $x = 0$. To accomplish this, we can use the **exponential distribution**:

$$p(x; \lambda) = \lambda \mathbf{1}_{x \geq 0} \exp\left(-\lambda x\right). \tag{3.25}$$

The exponential distribution uses the indicator function $\mathbf{1}_{x \geq 0}$ to assign probability zero to all negative values of x.

A closely related probability distribution that allows us to place a sharp peak of probability mass at an arbitrary point μ is the **Laplace distribution**

$$\text{Laplace}(x; \mu, \gamma) = \frac{1}{2\gamma} \exp\left(-\frac{|x - \mu|}{\gamma}\right). \tag{3.26}$$

3.9.5 The Dirac Distribution and Empirical Distribution

In some cases, we wish to specify that all the mass in a probability distribution clusters around a single point. This can be accomplished by defining a PDF using the **Dirac delta function**, $\delta(x)$:

$$p(x) = \delta(x - \mu). \tag{3.27}$$

The Dirac delta function is defined such that it is zero valued everywhere except 0, yet integrates to 1. The Dirac delta function is not an ordinary function that associates each value x with a real-valued output; instead it is a different kind of mathematical object called a **generalized function** that is defined in terms of its properties when integrated. We can think of the Dirac delta function as being the limit point of a series of functions that put less and less mass on all points other than zero.

By defining $p(x)$ to be δ shifted by $-\mu$ we obtain an infinitely narrow and infinitely high peak of probability mass where $x = \mu$.

A common use of the Dirac delta distribution is as a component of an **empirical distribution**,

$$\hat{p}(\boldsymbol{x}) = \frac{1}{m} \sum_{i=1}^{m} \delta(\boldsymbol{x} - \boldsymbol{x}^{(i)}) \tag{3.28}$$

which puts probability mass $\frac{1}{m}$ on each of the m points $\boldsymbol{x}^{(1)}, \ldots, \boldsymbol{x}^{(m)}$, forming a given data set or collection of samples. The Dirac delta distribution is only necessary to define the empirical distribution over continuous variables. For discrete variables, the situation is simpler: an empirical distribution can be conceptualized as a multinoulli distribution, with a probability associated with each possible input value that is simply equal to the **empirical frequency** of that value in the training set.

We can view the empirical distribution formed from a dataset of training examples as specifying the distribution that we sample from when we train a model on this dataset. Another important perspective on the empirical distribution is that it is the probability density that maximizes the likelihood of the training data (see section 5.5).

3.9.6 Mixtures of Distributions

It is also common to define probability distributions by combining other simpler probability distributions. One common way of combining distributions is to construct a **mixture distribution**. A mixture distribution is made up of several component distributions. On each trial, the choice of which component distribution should generate the sample is determined by sampling a component identity from a multinoulli distribution:

$$P(\mathrm{x}) = \sum_{i} P(\mathrm{c} = i) P(\mathrm{x} \mid \mathrm{c} = i), \tag{3.29}$$

where $P(\mathrm{c})$ is the multinoulli distribution over component identities.

We have already seen one example of a mixture distribution: the empirical distribution over real-valued variables is a mixture distribution with one Dirac component for each training example.

The mixture model is one simple strategy for combining probability distributions to create a richer distribution. In chapter 16, we explore the art of building complex probability distributions from simple ones in more detail.

The mixture model allows us to briefly glimpse a concept that will be of paramount importance later—the **latent variable**. A latent variable is a random variable that we cannot observe directly. The component identity variable c of the mixture model provides an example. Latent variables may be related to x through the joint distribution, in this case, $P(\mathrm{x}, \mathrm{c}) = P(\mathrm{x} \mid \mathrm{c})P(\mathrm{c})$. The distribution $P(\mathrm{c})$ over the latent variable and the distribution $P(\mathrm{x} \mid \mathrm{c})$ relating the latent variables to the visible variables determines the shape of the distribution $P(\mathrm{x})$, even though it is possible to describe $P(\mathrm{x})$ without reference to the latent variable. Latent variables are discussed further in section 16.5.

A very powerful and common type of mixture model is the **Gaussian mixture model**, in which the components $p(\mathbf{x} \mid \mathrm{c} = i)$ are Gaussians. Each component has a separately parametrized mean $\boldsymbol{\mu}^{(i)}$ and covariance $\boldsymbol{\Sigma}^{(i)}$. Some mixtures can have more constraints. For example, the covariances could be shared across components via the constraint $\boldsymbol{\Sigma}^{(i)} = \boldsymbol{\Sigma}, \forall i$. As with a single Gaussian distribution, the mixture of Gaussians might constrain the covariance matrix for each component to be diagonal or isotropic.

In addition to the means and covariances, the parameters of a Gaussian mixture specify the **prior probability** $\alpha_i = P(\mathrm{c} = i)$ given to each component i. The word "prior" indicates that it expresses the model's beliefs about c *before* it has observed **x**. By comparison, $P(\mathrm{c} \mid \boldsymbol{x})$ is a **posterior probability**, because it is computed *after* observation of **x**. A Gaussian mixture model is a **universal approximator** of densities, in the sense that any smooth density can be approximated with any specific nonzero amount of error by a Gaussian mixture model with enough components.

Figure 3.2 shows samples from a Gaussian mixture model.

3.10   Useful Properties of Common Functions

Certain functions arise often while working with probability distributions, especially the probability distributions used in deep learning models.

One of these functions is the **logistic sigmoid**:

$$\sigma(x) = \frac{1}{1 + \exp(-x)}. \tag{3.30}$$

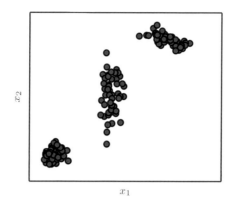

Figure 3.2: Samples from a Gaussian mixture model. In this example, there are three components. From left to right, the first component has an isotropic covariance matrix, meaning it has the same amount of variance in each direction. The second has a diagonal covariance matrix, meaning it can control the variance separately along each axis-aligned direction. This example has more variance along the x_2 axis than along the x_1 axis. The third component has a full-rank covariance matrix, enabling it to control the variance separately along an arbitrary basis of directions.

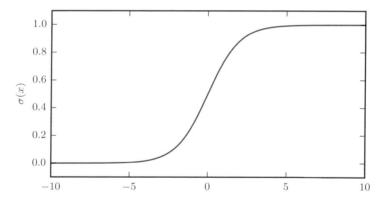

Figure 3.3: The logistic sigmoid function.

The logistic sigmoid is commonly used to produce the ϕ parameter of a Bernoulli distribution because its range is $(0, 1)$, which lies within the valid range of values for the ϕ parameter. See figure 3.3 for a graph of the sigmoid function. The sigmoid function **saturates** when its argument is very positive or very negative, meaning that the function becomes very flat and insensitive to small changes in its input.

Another commonly encountered function is the **softplus function** (Dugas et al., 2001):

$$\zeta(x) = \log\left(1 + \exp(x)\right).\tag{3.31}$$

The softplus function can be useful for producing the β or σ parameter of a normal distribution because its range is $(0, \infty)$. It also arises commonly when manipulating expressions involving sigmoids. The name of the softplus function comes from the fact that it is a smoothed, or "softened," version of

$$x^+ = \max(0, x). \tag{3.32}$$

See figure 3.4 for a graph of the softplus function.

The following properties are all useful enough that you may wish to memorize them:

$$\sigma(x) = \frac{\exp(x)}{\exp(x) + \exp(0)} \tag{3.33}$$

$$\frac{d}{dx}\sigma(x) = \sigma(x)(1 - \sigma(x)) \tag{3.34}$$

$$1 - \sigma(x) = \sigma(-x) \tag{3.35}$$

$$\log \sigma(x) = -\zeta(-x) \tag{3.36}$$

$$\frac{d}{dx}\zeta(x) = \sigma(x) \tag{3.37}$$

$$\forall x \in (0, 1), \ \sigma^{-1}(x) = \log\left(\frac{x}{1 - x}\right) \tag{3.38}$$

$$\forall x > 0, \ \zeta^{-1}(x) = \log\left(\exp(x) - 1\right) \tag{3.39}$$

$$\zeta(x) = \int_{-\infty}^{x} \sigma(y)dy \tag{3.40}$$

$$\zeta(x) - \zeta(-x) = x \tag{3.41}$$

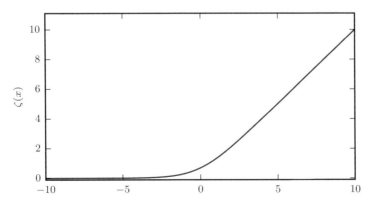

Figure 3.4: The softplus function.

The function $\sigma^{-1}(x)$ is called the **logit** in statistics, but this term is rarely used in machine learning.

Equation 3.41 provides extra justification for the name "softplus." The softplus function is intended as a smoothed version of the **positive part function**, $x^+ = \max\{0, x\}$. The positive part function is the counterpart of the **negative part function**, $x^- = \max\{0, -x\}$. To obtain a smooth function that is analogous to the negative part, one can use $\zeta(-x)$. Just as x can be recovered from its positive part and its negative part via the identity $x^+ - x^- = x$, it is also possible to recover x using the same relationship between $\zeta(x)$ and $\zeta(-x)$, as shown in equation 3.41.

3.11 Bayes' Rule

We often find ourselves in a situation where we know $P(\mathrm{y} \mid \mathrm{x})$ and need to know $P(\mathrm{x} \mid \mathrm{y})$. Fortunately, if we also know $P(\mathrm{x})$, we can compute the desired quantity using **Bayes' rule**:

$$P(\mathrm{x} \mid \mathrm{y}) = \frac{P(\mathrm{x})P(\mathrm{y} \mid \mathrm{x})}{P(\mathrm{y})}. \tag{3.42}$$

Note that while $P(\mathrm{y})$ appears in the formula, it is usually feasible to compute $P(\mathrm{y}) = \sum_x P(\mathrm{y} \mid x)P(x)$, so we do not need to begin with knowledge of $P(\mathrm{y})$.

Bayes' rule is straightforward to derive from the definition of conditional probability, but it is useful to know the name of this formula since many texts refer to it by name. It is named after the Reverend Thomas Bayes, who first discovered a special case of the formula. The general version presented here was independently discovered by Pierre-Simon Laplace.

3.12 Technical Details of Continuous Variables

A proper formal understanding of continuous random variables and probability density functions requires developing probability theory in terms of a branch of mathematics known as **measure theory**. Measure theory is beyond the scope of this textbook, but we can briefly sketch some of the issues that measure theory is employed to resolve.

In section 3.3.2, we saw that the probability of a continuous vector-valued $\mathbf{x}$ lying in some set $\mathbb{S}$ is given by the integral of $p(\boldsymbol{x})$ over the set $\mathbb{S}$. Some choices of set $\mathbb{S}$ can produce paradoxes. For example, it is possible to construct two sets $\mathbb{S}_1$ and $\mathbb{S}_2$ such that $p(\boldsymbol{x} \in \mathbb{S}_1) + p(\boldsymbol{x} \in \mathbb{S}_2) > 1$ but $\mathbb{S}_1 \cap \mathbb{S}_2 = \emptyset$. These sets are generally constructed making very heavy use of the infinite precision of real numbers, for example by making fractal-shaped sets or sets that are defined by transforming the set of rational numbers.[2] One of the key contributions of measure theory is to provide a characterization of the set of sets we can compute the probability of without encountering paradoxes. In this book, we integrate only over sets with relatively simple descriptions, so this aspect of measure theory never becomes a relevant concern.

For our purposes, measure theory is more useful for describing theorems that apply to most points in $\mathbb{R}^n$ but do not apply to some corner cases. Measure theory provides a rigorous way of describing that a set of points is negligibly small. Such a set is said to have **measure zero**. We do not formally define this concept in this textbook. For our purposes, it is sufficient to understand the intuition that a set of measure zero occupies no volume in the space we are measuring. For example, within $\mathbb{R}^2$, a line has measure zero, while a filled polygon has positive measure. Likewise, an individual point has measure zero. Any union of countably many sets that each have measure zero also has measure zero (so the set of all the rational numbers has measure zero, for instance).

Another useful term from measure theory is **almost everywhere**. A property that holds almost everywhere holds throughout all space except for on a set of measure zero. Because the exceptions occupy a negligible amount of space, they can be safely ignored for many applications. Some important results in probability theory hold for all discrete values but hold "almost everywhere" only for continuous values.

Another technical detail of continuous variables relates to handling continuous random variables that are deterministic functions of one another. Suppose we have two random variables, $\mathbf{x}$ and $\mathbf{y}$, such that $\boldsymbol{y} = g(\boldsymbol{x})$, where g is an invertible, continuous, differentiable transformation. One might expect that $p_y(\boldsymbol{y}) = p_x(g^{-1}(\boldsymbol{y}))$. This is actually not the case.

As a simple example, suppose we have scalar random variables x and y. Suppose $y = \frac{x}{2}$ and $x \sim U(0, 1)$. If we use the rule $p_y(y) = p_x(2y)$ then p_y will be 0 everywhere except the interval $[0, \frac{1}{2}]$, and it will be 1 on this interval. This means

$$\int p_y(y)dy = \frac{1}{2},$$

(3.43)

which violates the definition of a probability distribution. This is a common mistake. The problem with this approach is that it fails to account for the distortion of space introduced by the function g. Recall that the probability of $\boldsymbol{x}$ lying in an infinitesimally small region with volume $\delta\boldsymbol{x}$ is given by $p(\boldsymbol{x})\delta\boldsymbol{x}$. Since g can expand

---

[2]The Banach-Tarski theorem provides a fun example of such sets.

or contract space, the infinitesimal volume surrounding $\boldsymbol{x}$ in $\boldsymbol{x}$ space may have different volume in $\boldsymbol{y}$ space.

To see how to correct the problem, we return to the scalar case. We need to preserve the property

$$|p_y(g(x))dy| = |p_x(x)dx|. \tag{3.44}$$

Solving from this, we obtain

$$p_y(y) = p_x(g^{-1}(y)) \left| \frac{\partial x}{\partial y} \right| \tag{3.45}$$

or equivalently

$$p_x(x) = p_y(g(x)) \left| \frac{\partial g(x)}{\partial x} \right|. \tag{3.46}$$

In higher dimensions, the derivative generalizes to the determinant of the **Jacobian matrix**—the matrix with $J_{i,j} = \frac{\partial x_i}{\partial y_j}$. Thus, for real-valued vectors $\boldsymbol{x}$ and $\boldsymbol{y}$,

$$p_x(\boldsymbol{x}) = p_y(g(\boldsymbol{x})) \left| \det \left(\frac{\partial g(\boldsymbol{x})}{\partial \boldsymbol{x}} \right) \right|. \tag{3.47}$$

3.13 Information Theory

Information theory is a branch of applied mathematics that revolves around quantifying how much information is present in a signal. It was originally invented to study sending messages from discrete alphabets over a noisy channel, such as communication via radio transmission. In this context, information theory tells how to design optimal codes and calculate the expected length of messages sampled from specific probability distributions using various encoding schemes. In the context of machine learning, we can also apply information theory to continuous variables where some of these message length interpretations do not apply. This field is fundamental to many areas of electrical engineering and computer science. In this textbook, we mostly use a few key ideas from information theory to characterize probability distributions or to quantify similarity between probability distributions. For more detail on information theory, see Cover and Thomas (2006) or MacKay (2003).

The basic intuition behind information theory is that learning that an unlikely event has occurred is more informative than learning that a likely event has occurred. A message saying "the sun rose this morning" is so uninformative as to be unnecessary to send, but a message saying "there was a solar eclipse this morning" is very informative.

We would like to quantify information in a way that formalizes this intuition.

- Likely events should have low information content, and in the extreme case, events that are guaranteed to happen should have no information content whatsoever.

- Less likely events should have higher information content.

- Independent events should have additive information. For example, finding out that a tossed coin has come up as heads twice should convey twice as much information as finding out that a tossed coin has come up as heads once.

To satisfy all three of these properties, we define the **self-information** of an event x = x to be

$$I(x) = -\log P(x). \tag{3.48}$$

In this book, we always use log to mean the natural logarithm, with base e. Our definition of $I(x)$ is therefore written in units of **nats**. One nat is the amount of information gained by observing an event of probability $\frac{1}{e}$. Other texts use base-2 logarithms and units called **bits** or **shannons**; information measured in bits is just a rescaling of information measured in nats.

When x is continuous, we use the same definition of information by analogy, but some of the properties from the discrete case are lost. For example, an event with unit density still has zero information, despite not being an event that is guaranteed to occur.

Self-information deals only with a single outcome. We can quantify the amount of uncertainty in an entire probability distribution using the **Shannon entropy**,

$$H(x) = \mathbb{E}_{x \sim P}[I(x)] = -\mathbb{E}_{x \sim P}[\log P(x)], \tag{3.49}$$

also denoted $H(P)$. In other words, the Shannon entropy of a distribution is the expected amount of information in an event drawn from that distribution. It gives a lower bound on the number of bits (if the logarithm is base 2, otherwise the units are different) needed on average to encode symbols drawn from a distribution P. Distributions that are nearly deterministic (where the outcome is nearly certain) have low entropy; distributions that are closer to uniform have high entropy. See figure 3.5 for a demonstration. When x is continuous, the Shannon entropy is known as the **differential entropy**.

If we have two separate probability distributions $P(x)$ and $Q(x)$ over the same random variable x, we can measure how different these two distributions are using

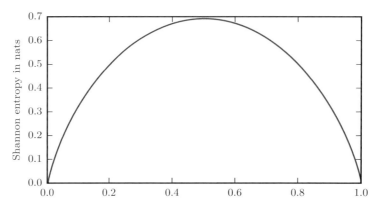

Figure 3.5: Shannon entropy of a binary random variable. This plot shows how distributions that are closer to deterministic have low Shannon entropy while distributions that are close to uniform have high Shannon entropy. On the horizontal axis, we plot p, the probability of a binary random variable being equal to 1. The entropy is given by $(p-1)\log(1-p)-p\log p$. When p is near 0, the distribution is nearly deterministic, because the random variable is nearly always 0. When p is near 1, the distribution is nearly deterministic, because the random variable is nearly always 1. When $p = 0.5$, the entropy is maximal, because the distribution is uniform over the two outcomes.

the **Kullback-Leibler (KL) divergence**:

$$D_{\mathrm{KL}}(P\|Q) = \mathbb{E}_{\mathrm{x}\sim P}\left[\log\frac{P(x)}{Q(x)}\right] = \mathbb{E}_{\mathrm{x}\sim P}\left[\log P(x) - \log Q(x)\right]. \qquad (3.50)$$

In the case of discrete variables, it is the extra amount of information (measured in bits if we use the base-2 logarithm, but in machine learning we usually use nats and the natural logarithm) needed to send a message containing symbols drawn from probability distribution P, when we use a code that was designed to minimize the length of messages drawn from probability distribution Q.

The KL divergence has many useful properties, most notably being non-negative. The KL divergence is 0 if and only if P and Q are the same distribution in the case of discrete variables, or equal "almost everywhere" in the case of continuous variables. Because the KL divergence is non-negative and measures the difference between two distributions, it is often conceptualized as measuring some sort of distance between these distributions. It is not a true distance measure because it is not symmetric: $D_{\mathrm{KL}}(P\|Q) \neq D_{\mathrm{KL}}(Q\|P)$ for some P and Q. This asymmetry means that there are important consequences to the choice of whether to use $D_{\mathrm{KL}}(P\|Q)$ or $D_{\mathrm{KL}}(Q\|P)$. See figure 3.6 for more detail.

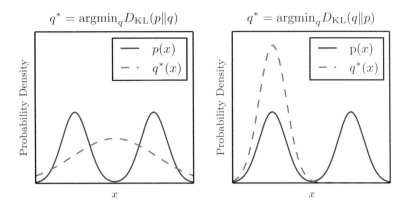

Figure 3.6: The KL divergence is asymmetric. Suppose we have a distribution $p(x)$ and wish to approximate it with another distribution $q(x)$. We have the choice of minimizing either $D_{\mathrm{KL}}(p\|q)$ or $D_{\mathrm{KL}}(q\|p)$. We illustrate the effect of this choice using a mixture of two Gaussians for p, and a single Gaussian for q. The choice of which direction of the KL divergence to use is problem dependent. Some applications require an approximation that usually places high probability anywhere that the true distribution places high probability, while other applications require an approximation that rarely places high probability anywhere that the true distribution places low probability. The choice of the direction of the KL divergence reflects which of these considerations takes priority for each application. *(Left)*The effect of minimizing $D_{\mathrm{KL}}(p\|q)$. In this case, we select a q that has high probability where p has high probability. When p has multiple modes, q chooses to blur the modes together, in order to put high probability mass on all of them. *(Right)*The effect of minimizing $D_{\mathrm{KL}}(q\|p)$. In this case, we select a q that has low probability where p has low probability. When p has multiple modes that are sufficiently widely separated, as in this figure, the KL divergence is minimized by choosing a single mode, to avoid putting probability mass in the low-probability areas between modes of p. Here, we illustrate the outcome when q is chosen to emphasize the left mode. We could also have achieved an equal value of the KL divergence by choosing the right mode. If the modes are not separated by a sufficiently strong low-probability region, then this direction of the KL divergence can still choose to blur the modes.

A quantity that is closely related to the KL divergence is the **cross-entropy** $H(P,Q) = H(P) + D_{\mathrm{KL}}(P\|Q)$, which is similar to the KL divergence but lacking the term on the left:

$$H(P,Q) = -\mathbb{E}_{\mathrm{x}\sim P}\log Q(x). \tag{3.51}$$

Minimizing the cross-entropy with respect to Q is equivalent to minimizing the KL divergence, because Q does not participate in the omitted term.

When computing many of these quantities, it is common to encounter expressions of the form $0\log 0$. By convention, in the context of information theory, we treat these expressions as $\lim_{x\to 0} x\log x = 0$.

3.14   Structured Probabilistic Models

Machine learning algorithms often involve probability distributions over a very large number of random variables. Often, these probability distributions involve direct interactions between relatively few variables. Using a single function to describe the entire joint probability distribution can be very inefficient (both computationally and statistically).

Instead of using a single function to represent a probability distribution, we can split a probability distribution into many factors that we multiply together. For example, suppose we have three random variables: a, b and c. Suppose that a influences the value of b, and b influences the value of c, but that a and c are independent given b. We can represent the probability distribution over all three variables as a product of probability distributions over two variables:

$$p(\mathrm{a}, \mathrm{b}, \mathrm{c}) = p(\mathrm{a})p(\mathrm{b} \mid \mathrm{a})p(\mathrm{c} \mid \mathrm{b}). \tag{3.52}$$

These factorizations can greatly reduce the number of parameters needed to describe the distribution. Each factor uses a number of parameters that is exponential in the number of variables in the factor. This means that we can greatly reduce the cost of representing a distribution if we are able to find a factorization into distributions over fewer variables.

We can describe these kinds of factorizations using graphs. Here, we use the word "graph" in the sense of graph theory: a set of vertices that may be connected to each other with edges. When we represent the factorization of a probability distribution with a graph, we call it a **structured probabilistic model**, or **graphical model**.

There are two main kinds of structured probabilistic models: directed and undirected. Both kinds of graphical models use a graph $\mathcal{G}$ in which each node in the graph corresponds to a random variable, and an edge connecting two random variables means that the probability distribution is able to represent direct interactions between those two random variables.

Directed models use graphs with directed edges, and they represent factorizations into conditional probability distributions, as in the example above. Specifically, a directed model contains one factor for every random variable x_i in the distribution, and that factor consists of the conditional distribution over x_i given the parents of x_i, denoted $Pa_{\mathcal{G}}(\mathrm{x}_i)$:

$$p(\mathbf{x}) = \prod_i p\left(\mathrm{x}_i \mid Pa_{\mathcal{G}}(\mathrm{x}_i)\right). \tag{3.53}$$

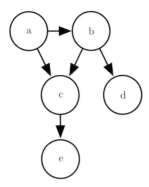

Figure 3.7: A directed graphical model over random variables a, b, c, d and e. This graph corresponds to probability distributions that can be factored as

$$p(\mathrm{a}, \mathrm{b}, \mathrm{c}, \mathrm{d}, \mathrm{e}) = p(\mathrm{a})p(\mathrm{b} \mid \mathrm{a})p(\mathrm{c} \mid \mathrm{a}, \mathrm{b})p(\mathrm{d} \mid \mathrm{b})p(\mathrm{e} \mid \mathrm{c}). \tag{3.54}$$

This graphical model enables us to quickly see some properties of the distribution. For example, a and c interact directly, but a and e interact only indirectly via c.

See figure 3.7 for an example of a directed graph and the factorization of probability distributions it represents.

Undirected models use graphs with undirected edges, and they represent factorizations into a set of functions; unlike in the directed case, these functions are usually not probability distributions of any kind. Any set of nodes that are all connected to each other in $\mathcal{G}$ is called a clique. Each clique $\mathcal{C}^{(i)}$ in an undirected model is associated with a factor $\phi^{(i)}(\mathcal{C}^{(i)})$. These factors are just functions, not probability distributions. The output of each factor must be non-negative, but there is no constraint that the factor must sum or integrate to 1 like a probability distribution.

The probability of a configuration of random variables is **proportional** to the product of all these factors—assignments that result in larger factor values are more likely. Of course, there is no guarantee that this product will sum to 1. We therefore divide by a normalizing constant Z, defined to be the sum or integral over all states of the product of the ϕ functions, in order to obtain a normalized probability distribution:

$$p(\mathbf{x}) = \frac{1}{Z} \prod_i \phi^{(i)}\left(\mathcal{C}^{(i)}\right). \tag{3.55}$$

See figure 3.8 for an example of an undirected graph and the factorization of probability distributions it represents.

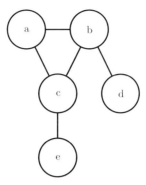

Figure 3.8: An undirected graphical model over random variables a, b, c, d and e. This graph corresponds to probability distributions that can be factored as

$$p(\mathrm{a}, \mathrm{b}, \mathrm{c}, \mathrm{d}, \mathrm{e}) = \frac{1}{Z}\phi^{(1)}(\mathrm{a}, \mathrm{b}, \mathrm{c})\phi^{(2)}(\mathrm{b}, \mathrm{d})\phi^{(3)}(\mathrm{c}, \mathrm{e}). \tag{3.56}$$

This graphical model enables us to quickly see some properties of the distribution. For example, a and c interact directly, but a and e interact only indirectly via c.

Keep in mind that these graphical representations of factorizations are a language for describing probability distributions. They are not mutually exclusive families of probability distributions. Being directed or undirected is not a property of a probability distribution; it is a property of a particular **description** of a probability distribution, but any probability distribution may be described in both ways.

Throughout parts I and II of this book, we use structured probabilistic models merely as a language to describe which direct probabilistic relationships different machine learning algorithms choose to represent. No further understanding of structured probabilistic models is needed until the discussion of research topics, in part III, where we explore structured probabilistic models in much greater detail.

This chapter has reviewed the basic concepts of probability theory that are most relevant to deep learning. One more set of fundamental mathematical tools remains: numerical methods.

4

Numerical Computation

Machine learning algorithms usually require a high amount of numerical computation. This typically refers to algorithms that solve mathematical problems by methods that update estimates of the solution via an iterative process, rather than analytically deriving a formula to provide a symbolic expression for the correct solution. Common operations include optimization (finding the value of an argument that minimizes or maximizes a function) and solving systems of linear equations. Even just evaluating a mathematical function on a digital computer can be difficult when the function involves real numbers, which cannot be represented precisely using a finite amount of memory.

4.1 Overflow and Underflow

The fundamental difficulty in performing continuous math on a digital computer is that we need to represent infinitely many real numbers with a finite number of bit patterns. This means that for almost all real numbers, we incur some approximation error when we represent the number in the computer. In many cases, this is just rounding error. Rounding error is problematic, especially when it compounds across many operations, and can cause algorithms that work in theory to fail in practice if they are not designed to minimize the accumulation of rounding error.

One form of rounding error that is particularly devastating is **underflow**. Underflow occurs when numbers near zero are rounded to zero. Many functions behave qualitatively differently when their argument is zero rather than a small positive number. For example, we usually want to avoid division by zero (some software environments will raise exceptions when this occurs, others will return a result with a placeholder not-a-number value) or taking the logarithm of zero (this is usually treated as $-\infty$, which then becomes not-a-number if it is used for many further arithmetic operations).

Another highly damaging form of numerical error is **overflow**. Overflow occurs when numbers with large magnitude are approximated as ∞ or $-\infty$. Further arithmetic will usually change these infinite values into not-a-number values.

One example of a function that must be stabilized against underflow and overflow is the **softmax function**. The softmax function is often used to predict the probabilities associated with a multinoulli distribution. The softmax function is defined to be

$$\text{softmax}(\boldsymbol{x})_i = \frac{\exp(x_i)}{\sum_{j=1}^{n} \exp(x_j)}. \tag{4.1}$$

Consider what happens when all the x_i are equal to some constant c. Analytically, we can see that all the outputs should be equal to $\frac{1}{n}$. Numerically, this may not occur when c has large magnitude. If c is very negative, then $\exp(c)$ will underflow. This means the denominator of the softmax will become 0, so the final result is undefined. When c is very large and positive, $\exp(c)$ will overflow, again resulting in the expression as a whole being undefined. Both of these difficulties can be resolved by instead evaluating softmax($\boldsymbol{z}$) where $\boldsymbol{z} = \boldsymbol{x} - \max_i x_i$. Simple algebra shows that the value of the softmax function is not changed analytically by adding or subtracting a scalar from the input vector. Subtracting $\max_i x_i$ results in the largest argument to exp being 0, which rules out the possibility of overflow. Likewise, at least one term in the denominator has a value of 1, which rules out the possibility of underflow in the denominator leading to a division by zero.

There is still one small problem. Underflow in the numerator can still cause the expression as a whole to evaluate to zero. This means that if we implement $\log \text{softmax}(\boldsymbol{x})$ by first running the softmax subroutine then passing the result to the log function, we could erroneously obtain $-\infty$. Instead, we must implement a separate function that calculates $\log \text{softmax}$ in a numerically stable way. The $\log \text{softmax}$ function can be stabilized using the same trick as we used to stabilize the softmax function.

For the most part, we do not explicitly detail all the numerical considerations involved in implementing the various algorithms described in this book. Developers of low-level libraries should keep numerical issues in mind when implementing deep learning algorithms. Most readers of this book can simply rely on low-level libraries that provide stable implementations. In some cases, it is possible to implement a new algorithm and have the new implementation automatically stabilized. Theano (Bergstra et al., 2010; Bastien et al., 2012) is an example of a software package that automatically detects and stabilizes many common numerically unstable expressions that arise in the context of deep learning.

4.2 Poor Conditioning

Conditioning refers to how rapidly a function changes with respect to small changes in its inputs. Functions that change rapidly when their inputs are perturbed slightly can be problematic for scientific computation because rounding errors in the inputs can result in large changes in the output.

Consider the function $f(\boldsymbol{x}) = \boldsymbol{A}^{-1}\boldsymbol{x}$. When $\boldsymbol{A} \in \mathbb{R}^{n \times n}$ has an eigenvalue decomposition, its **condition number** is

$$\max_{i,j} \left| \frac{\lambda_i}{\lambda_j} \right|. \tag{4.2}$$

This is the ratio of the magnitude of the largest and smallest eigenvalue. When this number is large, matrix inversion is particularly sensitive to error in the input.

This sensitivity is an intrinsic property of the matrix itself, not the result of rounding error during matrix inversion. Poorly conditioned matrices amplify pre-existing errors when we multiply by the true matrix inverse. In practice, the error will be compounded further by numerical errors in the inversion process itself.

4.3 Gradient-Based Optimization

Most deep learning algorithms involve optimization of some sort. Optimization refers to the task of either minimizing or maximizing some function $f(\boldsymbol{x})$ by altering $\boldsymbol{x}$. We usually phrase most optimization problems in terms of minimizing $f(\boldsymbol{x})$. Maximization may be accomplished via a minimization algorithm by minimizing $-f(\boldsymbol{x})$.

The function we want to minimize or maximize is called the **objective function**, or **criterion**. When we are minimizing it, we may also call it the **cost function**, **loss function**, or **error function**. In this book, we use these terms interchangeably, though some machine learning publications assign special meaning to some of these terms.

We often denote the value that minimizes or maximizes a function with a superscript $*$. For example, we might say $\boldsymbol{x}^* = \arg\min f(\boldsymbol{x})$.

We assume the reader is already familiar with calculus but provide a brief review of how calculus concepts relate to optimization here.

Suppose we have a function $y = f(x)$, where both x and y are real numbers. The **derivative** of this function is denoted as $f'(x)$ or as $\frac{dy}{dx}$. The derivative $f'(x)$ gives the slope of $f(x)$ at the point x. In other words, it specifies how to scale a small change in the input to obtain the corresponding change in the output: $f(x + \epsilon) \approx f(x) + \epsilon f'(x)$.

The derivative is therefore useful for minimizing a function because it tells us how to change x in order to make a small improvement in y. For example, we know that $f(x - \epsilon \operatorname{sign}(f'(x)))$ is less than $f(x)$ for small enough ϵ. We can thus reduce $f(x)$ by moving x in small steps with the opposite sign of the derivative. This technique is called **gradient descent** (Cauchy, 1847). See figure 4.1 for an example of this technique.

When $f'(x) = 0$, the derivative provides no information about which direction to move. Points where $f'(x) = 0$ are known as **critical points**, or **stationary points**. A **local minimum** is a point where $f(x)$ is lower than at all neighboring points, so it is no longer possible to decrease $f(x)$ by making infinitesimal steps. A **local maximum** is a point where $f(x)$ is higher than at all neighboring points, so it is not possible to increase $f(x)$ by making infinitesimal steps. Some critical points are neither maxima nor minima. These are known as **saddle points**. See figure 4.2 for examples of each type of critical point.

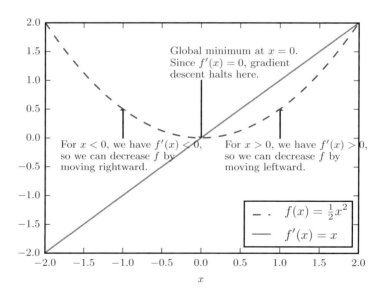

Figure 4.1: Gradient descent. An illustration of how the gradient descent algorithm uses the derivatives of a function can be used to follow the function downhill to a minimum.

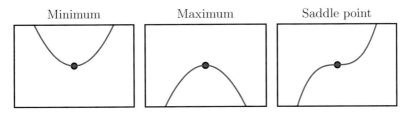

Figure 4.2: Types of critical points. Examples of the three types of critical points in one dimension. A critical point is a point with zero slope. Such a point can either be a local minimum, which is lower than the neighboring points; a local maximum, which is higher than the neighboring points; or a saddle point, which has neighbors that are both higher and lower than the point itself.

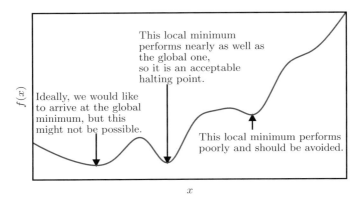

Figure 4.3: Approximate minimization. Optimization algorithms may fail to find a global minimum when there are multiple local minima or plateaus present. In the context of deep learning, we generally accept such solutions even though they are not truly minimal, so long as they correspond to significantly low values of the cost function.

A point that obtains the absolute lowest value of $f(x)$ is a **global minimum**. There can be only one global minimum or multiple global minima of the function. It is also possible for there to be local minima that are not globally optimal. In the context of deep learning, we optimize functions that may have many local minima that are not optimal and many saddle points surrounded by very flat regions. All of this makes optimization difficult, especially when the input to the function is multidimensional. We therefore usually settle for finding a value of f that is very low but not necessarily minimal in any formal sense. See figure 4.3 for an example.

We often minimize functions that have multiple inputs: $f : \mathbb{R}^n \to \mathbb{R}$. For the concept of "minimization" to make sense, there must still be only one (scalar) output.

For functions with multiple inputs, we must make use of the concept of **partial derivatives**. The partial derivative $\frac{\partial}{\partial x_i} f(\boldsymbol{x})$ measures how f changes as only the variable x_i increases at point $\boldsymbol{x}$. The **gradient** generalizes the notion of derivative to the case where the derivative is with respect to a vector: the gradient of f is the vector containing all the partial derivatives, denoted $\nabla_{\boldsymbol{x}} f(\boldsymbol{x})$. Element i of the gradient is the partial derivative of f with respect to x_i. In multiple dimensions, critical points are points where every element of the gradient is equal to zero.

The **directional derivative** in direction $\boldsymbol{u}$ (a unit vector) is the slope of the function f in direction u. In other words, the directional derivative is the derivative of the function $f(\boldsymbol{x} + \alpha \boldsymbol{u})$ with respect to α, evaluated at $\alpha = 0$. Using the chain rule, we can see that $\frac{\partial}{\partial \alpha} f(\boldsymbol{x} + \alpha \boldsymbol{u})$ evaluates to $\boldsymbol{u}^\top \nabla_{\boldsymbol{x}} f(\boldsymbol{x})$ when $\alpha = 0$.

To minimize f, we would like to find the direction in which f decreases the fastest. We can do this using the directional derivative:

$$\min_{\boldsymbol{u},\,\boldsymbol{u}^\top \boldsymbol{u}=1} \boldsymbol{u}^\top \nabla_{\boldsymbol{x}} f(\boldsymbol{x}) \tag{4.3}$$

$$= \min_{\boldsymbol{u},\,\boldsymbol{u}^\top \boldsymbol{u}=1} ||\boldsymbol{u}||_2 ||\nabla_{\boldsymbol{x}} f(\boldsymbol{x})||_2 \cos \theta \tag{4.4}$$

where θ is the angle between $\boldsymbol{u}$ and the gradient. Substituting in $||\boldsymbol{u}||_2 = 1$ and ignoring factors that do not depend on $\boldsymbol{u}$, this simplifies to $\min_{\boldsymbol{u}} \cos \theta$. This is minimized when $\boldsymbol{u}$ points in the opposite direction as the gradient. In other words, the gradient points directly uphill, and the negative gradient points directly downhill. We can decrease f by moving in the direction of the negative gradient. This is known as the **method of steepest descent**, or **gradient descent**.

Steepest descent proposes a new point

$$\boldsymbol{x}' = \boldsymbol{x} - \epsilon \nabla_{\boldsymbol{x}} f(\boldsymbol{x}) \tag{4.5}$$

where ϵ is the **learning rate**, a positive scalar determining the size of the step. We can choose ϵ in several different ways. A popular approach is to set ϵ to a small constant. Sometimes, we can solve for the step size that makes the directional derivative vanish. Another approach is to evaluate $f(\boldsymbol{x} - \epsilon \nabla_{\boldsymbol{x}} f(\boldsymbol{x}))$ for several values of ϵ and choose the one that results in the smallest objective function value. This last strategy is called a **line search**.

Steepest descent converges when every element of the gradient is zero (or, in practice, very close to zero). In some cases, we may be able to avoid running this iterative algorithm and just jump directly to the critical point by solving the equation $\nabla_{\boldsymbol{x}} f(\boldsymbol{x}) = 0$ for $\boldsymbol{x}$.

Although gradient descent is limited to optimization in continuous spaces, the general concept of repeatedly making a small move (that is approximately the best small move) toward better configurations can be generalized to discrete spaces. Ascending an objective function of discrete parameters is called **hill climbing** (Russel and Norvig, 2003).

4.3.1 Beyond the Gradient: Jacobian and Hessian Matrices

Sometimes we need to find all the partial derivatives of a function whose input and output are both vectors. The matrix containing all such partial derivatives is known as a **Jacobian matrix**. Specifically, if we have a function $\boldsymbol{f} : \mathbb{R}^m \to \mathbb{R}^n$, then the Jacobian matrix $\boldsymbol{J} \in \mathbb{R}^{n \times m}$ of $\boldsymbol{f}$ is defined such that $J_{i,j} = \frac{\partial}{\partial x_j} f(\boldsymbol{x})_i$.

We are also sometimes interested in a derivative of a derivative. This is known as a **second derivative**. For example, for a function $f : \mathbb{R}^n \to \mathbb{R}$, the derivative with respect to x_i of the derivative of f with respect to x_j is denoted as $\frac{\partial^2}{\partial x_i \partial x_j} f$. In a single dimension, we can denote $\frac{d^2}{dx^2} f$ by $f''(x)$. The second derivative tells us how the first derivative will change as we vary the input. This is important because it tells us whether a gradient step will cause as much of an improvement as we would expect based on the gradient alone. We can think of the second derivative as measuring **curvature**. Suppose we have a quadratic function (many functions that arise in practice are not quadratic but can be approximated well as quadratic, at least locally). If such a function has a second derivative of zero, then there is no curvature. It is a perfectly flat line, and its value can be predicted using only the gradient. If the gradient is 1, then we can make a step of size ϵ along the negative gradient, and the cost function will decrease by ϵ. If the second derivative is negative, the function curves downward, so the cost function will actually decrease by more than ϵ. Finally, if the second derivative is positive, the function curves upward, so the cost function can decrease by less than ϵ. See figure 4.4 to see how different forms of curvature affect the relationship between the value of the cost function predicted by the gradient and the true value.

When our function has multiple input dimensions, there are many second derivatives. These derivatives can be collected together into a matrix called the **Hessian matrix**. The Hessian matrix $\boldsymbol{H}(f)(\boldsymbol{x})$ is defined such that

$$\boldsymbol{H}(f)(\boldsymbol{x})_{i,j} = \frac{\partial^2}{\partial x_i \partial x_j} f(\boldsymbol{x}). \tag{4.6}$$

Equivalently, the Hessian is the Jacobian of the gradient.

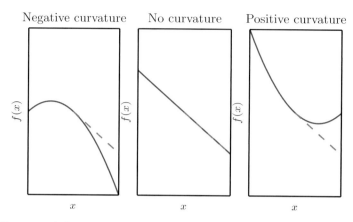

Figure 4.4: The second derivative determines the curvature of a function. Here we show quadratic functions with various curvature. The dashed line indicates the value of the cost function we would expect based on the gradient information alone as we make a gradient step downhill. With negative curvature, the cost function actually decreases faster than the gradient predicts. With no curvature, the gradient predicts the decrease correctly. With positive curvature, the function decreases more slowly than expected and eventually begins to increase, so steps that are too large can actually increase the function inadvertently.

Anywhere that the second partial derivatives are continuous, the differential operators are commutative; that is, their order can be swapped:

$$\frac{\partial^2}{\partial x_i \partial x_j} f(\boldsymbol{x}) = \frac{\partial^2}{\partial x_j \partial x_i} f(\boldsymbol{x}). \tag{4.7}$$

This implies that $H_{i,j} = H_{j,i}$, so the Hessian matrix is symmetric at such points. Most of the functions we encounter in the context of deep learning have a symmetric Hessian almost everywhere. Because the Hessian matrix is real and symmetric, we can decompose it into a set of real eigenvalues and an orthogonal basis of eigenvectors. The second derivative in a specific direction represented by a unit vector $\boldsymbol{d}$ is given by $\boldsymbol{d}^\top \boldsymbol{H} \boldsymbol{d}$. When $\boldsymbol{d}$ is an eigenvector of $\boldsymbol{H}$, the second derivative in that direction is given by the corresponding eigenvalue. For other directions of $\boldsymbol{d}$, the directional second derivative is a weighted average of all the eigenvalues, with weights between 0 and 1, and eigenvectors that have a smaller angle with $\boldsymbol{d}$ receiving more weight. The maximum eigenvalue determines the maximum second derivative, and the minimum eigenvalue determines the minimum second derivative.

The (directional) second derivative tells us how well we can expect a gradient descent step to perform. We can make a second-order Taylor series approximation to the function $f(\boldsymbol{x})$ around the current point $\boldsymbol{x}^{(0)}$:

$$f(\boldsymbol{x}) \approx f(\boldsymbol{x}^{(0)}) + (\boldsymbol{x} - \boldsymbol{x}^{(0)})^\top \boldsymbol{g} + \frac{1}{2}(\boldsymbol{x} - \boldsymbol{x}^{(0)})^\top \boldsymbol{H}(\boldsymbol{x} - \boldsymbol{x}^{(0)}), \qquad (4.8)$$

where $\boldsymbol{g}$ is the gradient and $\boldsymbol{H}$ is the Hessian at $\boldsymbol{x}^{(0)}$. If we use a learning rate of ϵ, then the new point $\boldsymbol{x}$ will be given by $\boldsymbol{x}^{(0)} - \epsilon\boldsymbol{g}$. Substituting this into our approximation, we obtain

$$f(\boldsymbol{x}^{(0)} - \epsilon\boldsymbol{g}) \approx f(\boldsymbol{x}^{(0)}) - \epsilon\boldsymbol{g}^\top \boldsymbol{g} + \frac{1}{2}\epsilon^2 \boldsymbol{g}^\top \boldsymbol{H}\boldsymbol{g}. \qquad (4.9)$$

There are three terms here: the original value of the function, the expected improvement due to the slope of the function, and the correction we must apply to account for the curvature of the function. When this last term is too large, the gradient descent step can actually move uphill. When $\boldsymbol{g}^\top \boldsymbol{H}\boldsymbol{g}$ is zero or negative, the Taylor series approximation predicts that increasing ϵ forever will decrease f forever. In practice, the Taylor series is unlikely to remain accurate for large ϵ, so one must resort to more heuristic choices of ϵ in this case. When $\boldsymbol{g}^\top \boldsymbol{H}\boldsymbol{g}$ is positive, solving for the optimal step size that decreases the Taylor series approximation of the function the most yields

$$\epsilon^* = \frac{\boldsymbol{g}^\top \boldsymbol{g}}{\boldsymbol{g}^\top \boldsymbol{H}\boldsymbol{g}}. \qquad (4.10)$$

In the worst case, when $\boldsymbol{g}$ aligns with the eigenvector of $\boldsymbol{H}$ corresponding to the maximal eigenvalue $\lambda_{\max}$, then this optimal step size is given by $\frac{1}{\lambda_{\max}}$. To the extent that the function we minimize can be approximated well by a quadratic function, the eigenvalues of the Hessian thus determine the scale of the learning rate.

The second derivative can be used to determine whether a critical point is a local maximum, a local minimum, or a saddle point. Recall that on a critical point, $f'(x) = 0$. When the second derivative $f''(x) > 0$, the first derivative $f'(x)$ increases as we move to the right and decreases as we move to the left. This means $f'(x - \epsilon) < 0$ and $f'(x + \epsilon) > 0$ for small enough ϵ. In other words, as we move right, the slope begins to point uphill to the right, and as we move left, the slope begins to point uphill to the left. Thus, when $f'(x) = 0$ and $f''(x) > 0$, we can conclude that x is a local minimum. Similarly, when $f'(x) = 0$ and $f''(x) < 0$, we can conclude that x is a local maximum. This is known as the **second derivative test**. Unfortunately, when $f''(x) = 0$, the test is inconclusive. In this case x may be a saddle point or a part of a flat region.

In multiple dimensions, we need to examine all the second derivatives of the function. Using the eigendecomposition of the Hessian matrix, we can generalize the second derivative test to multiple dimensions. At a critical point, where $\nabla_{\boldsymbol{x}} f(\boldsymbol{x}) = 0$, we can examine the eigenvalues of the Hessian to determine whether the critical point is a local maximum, local minimum, or saddle point. When the Hessian is positive definite (all its eigenvalues are positive), the point is a local minimum. This can be seen by observing that the directional second derivative in any direction must be positive, and making reference to the univariate second derivative test. Likewise, when the Hessian is negative definite (all its eigenvalues are negative), the point is a local maximum. In multiple dimensions, it is actually possible to find positive evidence of saddle points in some cases. When at least one eigenvalue is positive and at least one eigenvalue is negative, we know that $\boldsymbol{x}$ is a local maximum on one cross section of f but a local minimum on another cross section. See figure 4.5 for an example. Finally, the multidimensional second derivative test can be inconclusive, just as the univariate version can. The test is inconclusive whenever all the nonzero eigenvalues have the same sign but at least one eigenvalue is zero. This is because the univariate second derivative test is inconclusive in the cross section corresponding to the zero eigenvalue.

In multiple dimensions, there is a different second derivative for each direction at a single point. The condition number of the Hessian at this point measures how much the second derivatives differ from each other. When the Hessian has a poor condition number, gradient descent performs poorly. This is because in one

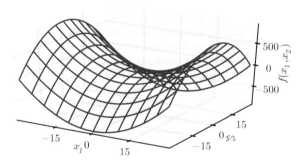

Figure 4.5: A saddle point containing both positive and negative curvature. The function in this example is $f(\boldsymbol{x}) = x_1^2 - x_2^2$. Along the axis corresponding to x_1, the function curves upward. This axis is an eigenvector of the Hessian and has a positive eigenvalue. Along the axis corresponding to x_2, the function curves downward. This direction is an eigenvector of the Hessian with negative eigenvalue. The name "saddle point" derives from the saddle-like shape of this function. This is the quintessential example of a function with a saddle point. In more than one dimension, it is not necessary to have an eigenvalue of 0 to get a saddle point: it is only necessary to have both positive and negative eigenvalues. We can think of a saddle point with both signs of eigenvalues as being a local maximum within one cross section and a local minimum within another cross section.

direction, the derivative increases rapidly, while in another direction, it increases slowly. Gradient descent is unaware of this change in the derivative, so it does not know that it needs to explore preferentially in the direction where the derivative remains negative for longer. Poor condition number also makes choosing a good step size difficult. The step size must be small enough to avoid overshooting the minimum and going uphill in directions with strong positive curvature. This usually means that the step size is too small to make significant progress in other directions with less curvature. See figure 4.6 for an example.

This issue can be resolved by using information from the Hessian matrix to guide the search. The simplest method for doing so is known as **Newton's method**. Newton's method is based on using a second-order Taylor series expansion to approximate $f(\boldsymbol{x})$ near some point $\boldsymbol{x}^{(0)}$:

$$f(\boldsymbol{x}) \approx f(\boldsymbol{x}^{(0)}) + (\boldsymbol{x} - \boldsymbol{x}^{(0)})^\top \nabla_{\boldsymbol{x}} f(\boldsymbol{x}^{(0)}) + \frac{1}{2}(\boldsymbol{x} - \boldsymbol{x}^{(0)})^\top \boldsymbol{H}(f)(\boldsymbol{x}^{(0)})(\boldsymbol{x} - \boldsymbol{x}^{(0)}). \quad (4.11)$$

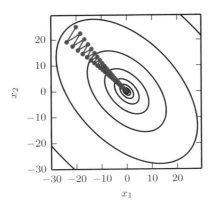

Figure 4.6: Gradient descent fails to exploit the curvature information contained in the Hessian matrix. Here we use gradient descent to minimize a quadratic function $f(\boldsymbol{x})$ whose Hessian matrix has condition number 5. This means that the direction of most curvature has five times more curvature than the direction of least curvature. In this case, the most curvature is in the direction $[1, 1]^\top$, and the least curvature is in the direction $[1, -1]^\top$. The red lines indicate the path followed by gradient descent. This very elongated quadratic function resembles a long canyon. Gradient descent wastes time repeatedly descending canyon walls because they are the steepest feature. Since the step size is somewhat too large, it has a tendency to overshoot the bottom of the function and thus needs to descend the opposite canyon wall on the next iteration. The large positive eigenvalue of the Hessian corresponding to the eigenvector pointed in this direction indicates that this directional derivative is rapidly increasing, so an optimization algorithm based on the Hessian could predict that the steepest direction is not actually a promising search direction in this context.

If we then solve for the critical point of this function, we obtain

$$\boldsymbol{x}^* = \boldsymbol{x}^{(0)} - \boldsymbol{H}(f)(\boldsymbol{x}^{(0)})^{-1}\nabla_{\boldsymbol{x}}f(\boldsymbol{x}^{(0)}). \tag{4.12}$$

When f is a positive definite quadratic function, Newton's method consists of applying equation 4.12 once to jump to the minimum of the function directly. When f is not truly quadratic but can be locally approximated as a positive definite quadratic, Newton's method consists of applying equation 4.12 multiple times. Iteratively updating the approximation and jumping to the minimum of the approximation can reach the critical point much faster than gradient descent would. This is a useful property near a local minimum, but it can be a harmful property near a saddle point. As discussed in section 8.2.3, Newton's method is only appropriate when the nearby critical point is a minimum (all the eigenvalues of the Hessian are positive), whereas gradient descent is not attracted to saddle points unless the gradient points toward them.

Optimization algorithms that use only the gradient, such as gradient descent, are called **first-order optimization algorithms**. Optimization algorithms that also use the Hessian matrix, such as Newton's method, are called **second-order optimization algorithms** (Nocedal and Wright, 2006).

The optimization algorithms employed in most contexts in this book are applicable to a wide variety of functions but come with almost no guarantees. Deep learning algorithms tend to lack guarantees because the family of functions used in deep learning is quite complicated. In many other fields, the dominant approach to optimization is to design optimization algorithms for a limited family of functions.

In the context of deep learning, we sometimes gain some guarantees by restricting ourselves to functions that are either **Lipschitz continuous** or have Lipschitz continuous derivatives. A Lipschitz continuous function is a function f whose rate of change is bounded by a **Lipschitz constant** $\mathcal{L}$:

$$\forall \boldsymbol{x}, \forall \boldsymbol{y}, |f(\boldsymbol{x}) - f(\boldsymbol{y})| \leq \mathcal{L}\|\boldsymbol{x} - \boldsymbol{y}\|_2. \tag{4.13}$$

This property is useful because it enables us to quantify our assumption that a small change in the input made by an algorithm such as gradient descent will have a small change in the output. Lipschitz continuity is also a fairly weak constraint, and many optimization problems in deep learning can be made Lipschitz continuous with relatively minor modifications.

Perhaps the most successful field of specialized optimization is **convex optimization**. Convex optimization algorithms are able to provide many more guarantees by making stronger restrictions. These algorithms are applicable only to convex functions—functions for which the Hessian is positive semidefinite everywhere. Such functions are well-behaved because they lack saddle points, and all their local minima are necessarily global minima. However, most problems in deep learning are difficult to express in terms of convex optimization. Convex optimization is used only as a subroutine of some deep learning algorithms. Ideas from the analysis of convex optimization algorithms can be useful for proving the convergence of deep learning algorithms, but in general, the importance of convex optimization is greatly diminished in the context of deep learning. For more information about convex optimization, see Boyd and Vandenberghe (2004) or Rockafellar (1997).

4.4 Constrained Optimization

Sometimes we wish not only to maximize or minimize a function $f(\boldsymbol{x})$ over all possible values of $\boldsymbol{x}$. Instead we may wish to find the maximal or minimal value of $f(\boldsymbol{x})$ for values of $\boldsymbol{x}$ in some set $\mathbb{S}$. This is known as **constrained optimization**. Points $\boldsymbol{x}$ that lie within the set $\mathbb{S}$ are called **feasible** points in constrained optimization terminology.

We often wish to find a solution that is small in some sense. A common approach in such situations is to impose a norm constraint, such as $||\boldsymbol{x}|| \leq 1$.

One simple approach to constrained optimization is simply to modify gradient descent taking the constraint into account. If we use a small constant step size ϵ, we can make gradient descent steps, then project the result back into $\mathbb{S}$. If we use a line search, we can search only over step sizes ϵ that yield new $\boldsymbol{x}$ points that are feasible, or we can project each point on the line back into the constraint region. When possible, this method can be made more efficient by projecting the gradient into the tangent space of the feasible region before taking the step or beginning the line search (Rosen, 1960).

A more sophisticated approach is to design a different, unconstrained optimization problem whose solution can be converted into a solution to the original, constrained optimization problem. For example, if we want to minimize $f(\boldsymbol{x})$ for $\boldsymbol{x} \in \mathbb{R}^2$ with $\boldsymbol{x}$ constrained to have exactly unit L^2 norm, we can instead minimize $g(\theta) = f([\cos\theta, \sin\theta]^\top)$ with respect to θ, then return $[\cos\theta, \sin\theta]$ as the solution to the original problem. This approach requires creativity; the transformation between optimization problems must be designed specifically for each case we encounter.

The **Karush–Kuhn–Tucker** (KKT) approach[1] provides a very general solution to constrained optimization. With the KKT approach, we introduce a new function called the **generalized Lagrangian** or **generalized Lagrange function**.

To define the Lagrangian, we first need to describe $\mathbb{S}$ in terms of equations and inequalities. We want a description of $\mathbb{S}$ in terms of m functions $g^{(i)}$ and n functions $h^{(j)}$ so that $\mathbb{S} = \{\boldsymbol{x} \mid \forall i, g^{(i)}(\boldsymbol{x}) = 0 \text{ and } \forall j, h^{(j)}(\boldsymbol{x}) \leq 0\}$. The equations involving $g^{(i)}$ are called the **equality constraints**, and the inequalities involving $h^{(j)}$ are called **inequality constraints**.

We introduce new variables λ_i and α_j for each constraint, these are called the KKT multipliers. The generalized Lagrangian is then defined as

$$L(\boldsymbol{x}, \boldsymbol{\lambda}, \boldsymbol{\alpha}) = f(\boldsymbol{x}) + \sum_i \lambda_i g^{(i)}(\boldsymbol{x}) + \sum_j \alpha_j h^{(j)}(\boldsymbol{x}). \tag{4.14}$$

We can now solve a constrained minimization problem using unconstrained optimization of the generalized Lagrangian. As long as at least one feasible point exists and $f(\boldsymbol{x})$ is not permitted to have value ∞, then

$$\min_{\boldsymbol{x}} \max_{\boldsymbol{\lambda}} \max_{\boldsymbol{\alpha}, \boldsymbol{\alpha} \geq 0} L(\boldsymbol{x}, \boldsymbol{\lambda}, \boldsymbol{\alpha}) \tag{4.15}$$

has the same optimal objective function value and set of optimal points $\boldsymbol{x}$ as

$$\min_{\boldsymbol{x} \in \mathbb{S}} f(\boldsymbol{x}). \tag{4.16}$$

This follows because any time the constraints are satisfied,

$$\max_{\boldsymbol{\lambda}} \max_{\boldsymbol{\alpha}, \boldsymbol{\alpha} \geq 0} L(\boldsymbol{x}, \boldsymbol{\lambda}, \boldsymbol{\alpha}) = f(\boldsymbol{x}), \tag{4.17}$$

while any time a constraint is violated,

$$\max_{\boldsymbol{\lambda}} \max_{\boldsymbol{\alpha}, \boldsymbol{\alpha} \geq 0} L(\boldsymbol{x}, \boldsymbol{\lambda}, \boldsymbol{\alpha}) = \infty. \tag{4.18}$$

These properties guarantee that no infeasible point can be optimal, and that the optimum within the feasible points is unchanged.

---

[1] The KKT approach generalizes the method of **Lagrange multipliers**, which allows equality constraints but not inequality constraints.

To perform constrained maximization, we can construct the generalized Lagrange function of $-f(\boldsymbol{x})$, which leads to this optimization problem:

$$\min_{\boldsymbol{x}} \max_{\boldsymbol{\lambda}} \max_{\boldsymbol{\alpha}, \boldsymbol{\alpha} \geq 0} -f(\boldsymbol{x}) + \sum_i \lambda_i g^{(i)}(\boldsymbol{x}) + \sum_j \alpha_j h^{(j)}(\boldsymbol{x}). \qquad (4.19)$$

We may also convert this to a problem with maximization in the outer loop:

$$\max_{\boldsymbol{x}} \min_{\boldsymbol{\lambda}} \min_{\boldsymbol{\alpha}, \boldsymbol{\alpha} \geq 0} f(\boldsymbol{x}) + \sum_i \lambda_i g^{(i)}(\boldsymbol{x}) - \sum_j \alpha_j h^{(j)}(\boldsymbol{x}). \qquad (4.20)$$

The sign of the term for the equality constraints does not matter; we may define it with addition or subtraction as we wish, because the optimization is free to choose any sign for each λ_i.

The inequality constraints are particularly interesting. We say that a constraint $h^{(i)}(\boldsymbol{x})$ is **active** if $h^{(i)}(\boldsymbol{x}^*) = 0$. If a constraint is not active, then the solution to the problem found using that constraint would remain at least a local solution if that constraint were removed. It is possible that an inactive constraint excludes other solutions. For example, a convex problem with an entire region of globally optimal points (a wide, flat region of equal cost) could have a subset of this region eliminated by constraints, or a nonconvex problem could have better local stationary points excluded by a constraint that is inactive at convergence. Yet the point found at convergence remains a stationary point whether or not the inactive constraints are included. Because an inactive $h^{(i)}$ has negative value, then the solution to $\min_{\boldsymbol{x}} \max_{\boldsymbol{\lambda}} \max_{\boldsymbol{\alpha}, \boldsymbol{\alpha} \geq 0} L(\boldsymbol{x}, \boldsymbol{\lambda}, \boldsymbol{\alpha})$ will have $\alpha_i = 0$. We can thus observe that at the solution, $\boldsymbol{\alpha} \odot \boldsymbol{h}(\boldsymbol{x}) = \boldsymbol{0}$. In other words, for all i, we know that at least one of the constraints $\alpha_i \geq 0$ or $h^{(i)}(\boldsymbol{x}) \leq 0$ must be active at the solution. To gain some intuition for this idea, we can say that either the solution is on the boundary imposed by the inequality and we must use its KKT multiplier to influence the solution to $\boldsymbol{x}$, or the inequality has no influence on the solution and we represent this by zeroing out its KKT multiplier.

A simple set of properties describe the optimal points of constrained optimization problems. These properties are called the Karush-Kuhn-Tucker (KKT) conditions (Karush, 1939; Kuhn and Tucker, 1951). They are necessary conditions, but not always sufficient conditions, for a point to be optimal. The conditions are:

- The gradient of the generalized Lagrangian is zero.

- All constraints on both $\boldsymbol{x}$ and the KKT multipliers are satisfied.

- The inequality constraints exhibit "complementary slackness": $\boldsymbol{\alpha} \odot \boldsymbol{h}(\boldsymbol{x}) = \boldsymbol{0}$.

For more information about the KKT approach, see Nocedal and Wright (2006).

4.5   Example: Linear Least Squares

Suppose we want to find the value of $\boldsymbol{x}$ that minimizes

$$f(\boldsymbol{x}) = \frac{1}{2}\|\boldsymbol{A}\boldsymbol{x} - \boldsymbol{b}\|_2^2. \tag{4.21}$$

Specialized linear algebra algorithms can solve this problem efficiently; however, we can also explore how to solve it using gradient-based optimization as a simple example of how these techniques work.

First, we need to obtain the gradient:

$$\nabla_{\boldsymbol{x}} f(\boldsymbol{x}) = \boldsymbol{A}^\top (\boldsymbol{A}\boldsymbol{x} - \boldsymbol{b}) = \boldsymbol{A}^\top \boldsymbol{A}\boldsymbol{x} - \boldsymbol{A}^\top \boldsymbol{b}. \tag{4.22}$$

We can then follow this gradient downhill, taking small steps. See algorithm 4.1 for details.

Algorithm 4.1 An algorithm to minimize $f(\boldsymbol{x}) = \frac{1}{2}\|\boldsymbol{A}\boldsymbol{x} - \boldsymbol{b}\|_2^2$ with respect to $\boldsymbol{x}$ using gradient descent, starting from an arbitrary value of $\boldsymbol{x}$.

Set the step size (ϵ) and tolerance (δ) to small, positive numbers.
while $\|\boldsymbol{A}^\top \boldsymbol{A}\boldsymbol{x} - \boldsymbol{A}^\top \boldsymbol{b}\|_2 > \delta$ **do**
$\quad \boldsymbol{x} \leftarrow \boldsymbol{x} - \epsilon \left(\boldsymbol{A}^\top \boldsymbol{A}\boldsymbol{x} - \boldsymbol{A}^\top \boldsymbol{b} \right)$
end while

One can also solve this problem using Newton's method. In this case, because the true function is quadratic, the quadratic approximation employed by Newton's method is exact, and the algorithm converges to the global minimum in a single step.

Now suppose we wish to minimize the same function, but subject to the constraint $\boldsymbol{x}^\top \boldsymbol{x} \leq 1$. To do so, we introduce the Lagrangian

$$L(\boldsymbol{x}, \lambda) = f(\boldsymbol{x}) + \lambda \left(\boldsymbol{x}^\top \boldsymbol{x} - 1 \right). \tag{4.23}$$

We can now solve the problem

$$\min_{\boldsymbol{x}} \max_{\lambda, \lambda \geq 0} L(\boldsymbol{x}, \lambda). \tag{4.24}$$

The smallest-norm solution to the unconstrained least-squares problem may be found using the Moore-Penrose pseudoinverse: $\boldsymbol{x} = \boldsymbol{A}^+ \boldsymbol{b}$. If this point is feasible, then it is the solution to the constrained problem. Otherwise, we must find a solution where the constraint is active. By differentiating the Lagrangian with respect to $\boldsymbol{x}$, we obtain the equation

$$\boldsymbol{A}^\top \boldsymbol{A}\boldsymbol{x} - \boldsymbol{A}^\top \boldsymbol{b} + 2\lambda\boldsymbol{x} = 0. \qquad (4.25)$$

This tells us that the solution will take the form

$$\boldsymbol{x} = (\boldsymbol{A}^\top \boldsymbol{A} + 2\lambda \boldsymbol{I})^{-1}\boldsymbol{A}^\top \boldsymbol{b}. \qquad (4.26)$$

The magnitude of λ must be chosen such that the result obeys the constraint. We can find this value by performing gradient ascent on λ. To do so, observe

$$\frac{\partial}{\partial \lambda} L(\boldsymbol{x}, \lambda) = \boldsymbol{x}^\top \boldsymbol{x} - 1. \qquad (4.27)$$

When the norm of $\boldsymbol{x}$ exceeds 1, this derivative is positive, so to follow the derivative uphill and increase the Lagrangian with respect to λ, we increase λ. Because the coefficient on the $\boldsymbol{x}^\top \boldsymbol{x}$ penalty has increased, solving the linear equation for $\boldsymbol{x}$ will now yield a solution with a smaller norm. The process of solving the linear equation and adjusting λ continues until $\boldsymbol{x}$ has the correct norm and the derivative on λ is 0.

This concludes the mathematical preliminaries that we use to develop machine learning algorithms. We are now ready to build and analyze some full-fledged learning systems.

5

Machine Learning Basics

Deep learning is a specific kind of machine learning. To understand deep learning well, one must have a solid understanding of the basic principles of machine learning. This chapter provides a brief course in the most important general principles that are applied throughout the rest of the book. Novice readers or those who want a wider perspective are encouraged to consider machine learning textbooks with a more comprehensive coverage of the fundamentals, such as Murphy (2012) or Bishop (2006). If you are already familiar with machine learning basics, feel free to skip ahead to section 5.11. That section covers some perspectives on traditional machine learning techniques that have strongly influenced the development of deep learning algorithms.

We begin with a definition of what a learning algorithm is and present an example: the linear regression algorithm. We then proceed to describe how the challenge of fitting the training data differs from the challenge of finding patterns that generalize to new data. Most machine learning algorithms have settings called *hyperparameters*, which must be determined outside the learning algorithm itself; we discuss how to set these using additional data. Machine learning is essentially a form of applied statistics with increased emphasis on the use of computers to statistically estimate complicated functions and a decreased emphasis on proving confidence intervals around these functions; we therefore present the two central approaches to statistics: frequentist estimators and Bayesian inference. Most machine learning algorithms can be divided into the categories of supervised learning and unsupervised learning; we describe these categories and give some examples of simple learning algorithms from each category. Most deep learning algorithms are based on an optimization algorithm called stochastic gradient descent. We describe how to combine various algorithm components, such as an optimization algorithm, a cost function, a model, and a dataset, to build a machine learning algorithm. Finally, in section 5.11, we describe some of the factors that have limited the ability of traditional machine learning to generalize. These challenges have motivated the development of deep learning algorithms that overcome these obstacles.

5.1 Learning Algorithms

A machine learning algorithm is an algorithm that is able to learn from data. But what do we mean by learning? Mitchell (1997) provides a succinct definition: "A computer program is said to learn from experience E with respect to some class of tasks T and performance measure P, if its performance at tasks in T, as measured by P, improves with experience E." One can imagine a wide variety of experiences E, tasks T, and performance measures P, and we do not attempt in this book to formally define what may be used for each of these entities. Instead, in the following sections, we provide intuitive descriptions and examples of the different kinds of tasks, performance measures, and experiences that can be used to construct machine learning algorithms.

5.1.1 The Task, T

Machine learning enables us to tackle tasks that are too difficult to solve with fixed programs written and designed by human beings. From a scientific and philosophical point of view, machine learning is interesting because developing our understanding of it entails developing our understanding of the principles that underlie intelligence.

In this relatively formal definition of the word "task," the process of learning itself is not the task. Learning is our means of attaining the ability to perform the task. For example, if we want a robot to be able to walk, then walking is the task. We could program the robot to learn to walk, or we could attempt to directly write a program that specifies how to walk manually.

Machine learning tasks are usually described in terms of how the machine learning system should process an **example**. An example is a collection of **features** that have been quantitatively measured from some object or event that we want the machine learning system to process. We typically represent an example as a vector $\boldsymbol{x} \in \mathbb{R}^n$ where each entry x_i of the vector is another feature. For example, the features of an image are usually the values of the pixels in the image.

Many kinds of tasks can be solved with machine learning. Some of the most common machine learning tasks include the following:

- **Classification**: In this type of task, the computer program is asked to specify which of k categories some input belongs to. To solve this task, the learning algorithm is usually asked to produce a function $f : \mathbb{R}^n \to \{1, \ldots, k\}$. When $y = f(\boldsymbol{x})$, the model assigns an input described by vector $\boldsymbol{x}$ to a category identified by numeric code y. There are other variants of the classification task, for example, where f outputs a probability distribution over classes. An example of a classification task is object recognition, where the input is an image (usually described as a set of pixel brightness values), and the output is a numeric code identifying the object in the image. For example, the Willow Garage PR2 robot is able to act as a waiter that can recognize different kinds of drinks and deliver them to people on command (Goodfellow et al., 2010). Modern object recognition is best accomplished with deep learning (Krizhevsky et al., 2012; Ioffe and Szegedy, 2015). Object recognition is the same basic technology that enables computers to recognize faces (Taigman et al., 2014), which can be used to automatically tag people in photo collections and for computers to interact more naturally with their users.

- **Classification with missing inputs**: Classification becomes more challenging if the computer program is not guaranteed that every measurement in its input vector will always be provided. To solve the classification task, the learning algorithm only has to define a *single* function mapping from a vector input to a categorical output. When some of the inputs may be missing, rather than providing a single classification function, the learning algorithm must learn a *set* of functions. Each function corresponds to classifying $\boldsymbol{x}$ with a different subset of its inputs missing. This kind of situation arises frequently in medical diagnosis, because many kinds of medical tests are expensive or invasive. One way to efficiently define such a large set of functions is to learn a probability distribution over all the relevant variables, then solve the classification task by marginalizing out the missing variables. With n input variables, we can now obtain all 2^n different classification functions needed for each possible set of missing inputs, but the computer program needs to learn only a single function describing the joint probability distribution. See Goodfellow et al. (2013b) for an example of a deep probabilistic model applied to such a task in this way. Many of the other tasks described in this section can also be generalized to work with missing inputs; classification with missing inputs is just one example of what machine learning can do.

- **Regression**: In this type of task, the computer program is asked to predict a numerical value given some input. To solve this task, the learning algorithm is asked to output a function $f : \mathbb{R}^n \to \mathbb{R}$. This type of task is similar to classification, except that the format of output is different. An example of a regression task is the prediction of the expected claim amount that an insured person will make (used to set insurance premiums), or the prediction of future prices of securities. These kinds of predictions are also used for algorithmic trading.

- **Transcription**: In this type of task, the machine learning system is asked to observe a relatively unstructured representation of some kind of data and transcribe the information into discrete textual form. For example, in optical character recognition, the computer program is shown a photograph containing an image of text and is asked to return this text in the form of a sequence of characters (e.g., in ASCII or Unicode format). Google Street View uses deep learning to process address numbers in this way (Goodfellow et al., 2014d). Another example is speech recognition, where the computer program is provided an audio waveform and emits a sequence of characters or word ID codes describing the words that were spoken in the audio recording. Deep learning is a crucial component of modern speech recognition systems used at major companies, including Microsoft, IBM and Google (Hinton et al., 2012b).

- **Machine translation**: In a machine translation task, the input already consists of a sequence of symbols in some language, and the computer program must convert this into a sequence of symbols in another language. This is commonly applied to natural languages, such as translating from English to French. Deep learning has recently begun to have an important impact on this kind of task (Sutskever et al., 2014; Bahdanau et al., 2015).

- **Structured output**: Structured output tasks involve any task where the output is a vector (or other data structure containing multiple values) with important relationships between the different elements. This is a broad category and subsumes the transcription and translation tasks described above, as well as many other tasks. One example is parsing—mapping a natural language sentence into a tree that describes its grammatical structure by tagging nodes of the trees as being verbs, nouns, adverbs, and so on. See Collobert (2011) for an example of deep learning applied to a parsing task. Another example is pixel-wise segmentation of images, where the computer program assigns every pixel in an image to a specific category.

For example, deep learning can be used to annotate the locations of roads in aerial photographs (Mnih and Hinton, 2010). The output form need not mirror the structure of the input as closely as in these annotation-style tasks. For example, in image captioning, the computer program observes an image and outputs a natural language sentence describing the image (Kiros et al., 2014a,b; Mao et al., 2015; Vinyals et al., 2015b; Donahue et al., 2014; Karpathy and Li, 2015; Fang et al., 2015; Xu et al., 2015). These tasks are called *structured output tasks* because the program must output several values that are all tightly interrelated. For example, the words produced by an image captioning program must form a valid sentence.

- **Anomaly detection**: In this type of task, the computer program sifts through a set of events or objects and flags some of them as being unusual or atypical. An example of an anomaly detection task is credit card fraud detection. By modeling your purchasing habits, a credit card company can detect misuse of your cards. If a thief steals your credit card or credit card information, the thief's purchases will often come from a different probability distribution over purchase types than your own. The credit card company can prevent fraud by placing a hold on an account as soon as that card has been used for an uncharacteristic purchase. See Chandola et al. (2009) for a survey of anomaly detection methods.

- **Synthesis and sampling**: In this type of task, the machine learning algorithm is asked to generate new examples that are similar to those in the training data. Synthesis and sampling via machine learning can be useful for media applications when generating large volumes of content by hand would be expensive, boring, or require too much time. For example, video games can automatically generate textures for large objects or landscapes, rather than requiring an artist to manually label each pixel (Luo et al., 2013). In some cases, we want the sampling or synthesis procedure to generate a specific kind of output given the input. For example, in a speech synthesis task, we provide a written sentence and ask the program to emit an audio waveform containing a spoken version of that sentence. This is a kind of structured output task, but with the added qualification that there is no single correct output for each input, and we explicitly desire a large amount of variation in the output, in order for the output to seem more natural and realistic.

- **Imputation of missing values**: In this type of task, the machine learning algorithm is given a new example $x \in \mathbb{R}^n$, but with some entries x_i of x missing. The algorithm must provide a prediction of the values of the missing entries.

- **Denoising**: In this type of task, the machine learning algorithm is given in input a *corrupted example* $\tilde{x} \in \mathbb{R}^n$ obtained by an unknown corruption process from a *clean example* $x \in \mathbb{R}^n$. The learner must predict the clean example x from its corrupted version $\tilde{x}$, or more generally predict the conditional probability distribution $p(x \mid \tilde{x})$.

- **Density estimation** or **probability mass function estimation**: In the density estimation problem, the machine learning algorithm is asked to learn a function $p_{\text{model}} : \mathbb{R}^n \to \mathbb{R}$, where $p_{\text{model}}(x)$ can be interpreted as a probability density function (if $\mathbf{x}$ is continuous) or a probability mass function (if $\mathbf{x}$ is discrete) on the space that the examples were drawn from. To do such a task well (we will specify exactly what that means when we discuss performance measures P), the algorithm needs to learn the structure of the data it has seen. It must know where examples cluster tightly and where they are unlikely to occur. Most of the tasks described above require the learning algorithm to at least implicitly capture the structure of the probability distribution. Density estimation enables us to explicitly capture that distribution. In principle, we can then perform computations on that distribution to solve the other tasks as well. For example, if we have performed density estimation to obtain a probability distribution $p(x)$, we can use that distribution to solve the missing value imputation task. If a value x_i is missing, and all the other values, denoted x_{-i}, are given, then we know the distribution over it is given by $p(x_i \mid x_{-i})$. In practice, density estimation does not always enable us to solve all these related tasks, because in many cases the required operations on $p(x)$ are computationally intractable.

Of course, many other tasks and types of tasks are possible. The types of tasks we list here are intended only to provide examples of what machine learning can do, not to define a rigid taxonomy of tasks.

5.1.2 The Performance Measure, P

To evaluate the abilities of a machine learning algorithm, we must design a quantitative measure of its performance. Usually this performance measure P is specific to the task T being carried out by the system.

For tasks such as classification, classification with missing inputs, and transcription, we often measure the **accuracy** of the model. Accuracy is just the proportion of examples for which the model produces the correct output. We can also obtain equivalent information by measuring the **error rate**, the proportion of examples for which the model produces an incorrect output. We often refer to the error rate as the expected 0-1 loss. The 0-1 loss on a particular example is 0 if it is correctly classified and 1 if it is not. For tasks such as density estimation, it does not make sense to measure accuracy, error rate, or any other kind of 0-1 loss. Instead, we must use a different performance metric that gives the model a continuous-valued score for each example. The most common approach is to report the average log-probability the model assigns to some examples.

Usually we are interested in how well the machine learning algorithm performs on data that it has not seen before, since this determines how well it will work when deployed in the real world. We therefore evaluate these performance measures using a **test set** of data that is separate from the data used for training the machine learning system.

The choice of performance measure may seem straightforward and objective, but it is often difficult to choose a performance measure that corresponds well to the desired behavior of the system.

In some cases, this is because it is difficult to decide what should be measured. For example, when performing a transcription task, should we measure the accuracy of the system at transcribing entire sequences, or should we use a more fine-grained performance measure that gives partial credit for getting some elements of the sequence correct? When performing a regression task, should we penalize the system more if it frequently makes medium-sized mistakes or if it rarely makes very large mistakes? These kinds of design choices depend on the application.

In other cases, we know what quantity we would ideally like to measure, but measuring it is impractical. For example, this arises frequently in the context of density estimation. Many of the best probabilistic models represent probability distributions only implicitly. Computing the actual probability value assigned to a specific point in space in many such models is intractable. In these cases, one must design an alternative criterion that still corresponds to the design objectives, or design a good approximation to the desired criterion.

5.1.3 The Experience, E

Machine learning algorithms can be broadly categorized as **unsupervised** or **supervised** by what kind of experience they are allowed to have during the learning process.

Most of the learning algorithms in this book can be understood as being allowed to experience an entire **dataset**. A dataset is a collection of many examples, as defined in section 5.1.1. Sometimes we call examples **data points**.

One of the oldest datasets studied by statisticians and machine learning researchers is the Iris dataset (Fisher, 1936). It is a collection of measurements of different parts of 150 iris plants. Each individual plant corresponds to one example. The features within each example are the measurements of each part of the plant: the sepal length, sepal width, petal length and petal width. The dataset also records which species each plant belonged to. Three different species are represented in the dataset.

Unsupervised learning algorithms experience a dataset containing many features, then learn useful properties of the structure of this dataset. In the context of deep learning, we usually want to learn the entire probability distribution that generated a dataset, whether explicitly, as in density estimation, or implicitly, for tasks like synthesis or denoising. Some other unsupervised learning algorithms perform other roles, like clustering, which consists of dividing the dataset into clusters of similar examples.

Supervised learning algorithms experience a dataset containing features, but each example is also associated with a **label** or **target**. For example, the Iris dataset is annotated with the species of each iris plant. A supervised learning algorithm can study the Iris dataset and learn to classify iris plants into three different species based on their measurements.

Roughly speaking, unsupervised learning involves observing several examples of a random vector $\mathbf{x}$ and attempting to implicitly or explicitly learn the probability distribution $p(\mathbf{x})$, or some interesting properties of that distribution; while supervised learning involves observing several examples of a random vector $\mathbf{x}$ and an associated value or vector $\mathbf{y}$, then learning to predict $\mathbf{y}$ from $\mathbf{x}$, usually by estimating $p(\mathbf{y} \mid \mathbf{x})$. The term **supervised learning** originates from the view of the target $\mathbf{y}$ being provided by an instructor or teacher who shows the machine learning system what to do. In unsupervised learning, there is no instructor or teacher, and the algorithm must learn to make sense of the data without this guide.

Unsupervised learning and supervised learning are not formally defined terms. The lines between them are often blurred. Many machine learning technologies can be used to perform both tasks. For example, the chain rule of probability states that for a vector $\mathbf{x} \in \mathbb{R}^n$, the joint distribution can be decomposed as

$$p(\mathbf{x}) = \prod_{i=1}^{n} p(\mathbf{x}_i \mid \mathbf{x}_1, \dots, \mathbf{x}_{i-1}). \tag{5.1}$$

This decomposition means that we can solve the ostensibly unsupervised problem of modeling $p(\mathbf{x})$ by splitting it into n supervised learning problems. Alternatively, we can solve the supervised learning problem of learning $p(y \mid \mathbf{x})$ by using traditional unsupervised learning technologies to learn the joint distribution $p(\mathbf{x}, y)$, then inferring

$$p(y \mid \mathbf{x}) = \frac{p(\mathbf{x}, y)}{\sum_{y'} p(\mathbf{x}, y')}. \tag{5.2}$$

Though unsupervised learning and supervised learning are not completely formal or distinct concepts, they do help roughly categorize some of the things we do with machine learning algorithms. Traditionally, people refer to regression, classification and structured output problems as supervised learning. Density estimation in support of other tasks is usually considered unsupervised learning.

Other variants of the learning paradigm are possible. For example, in semi-supervised learning, some examples include a supervision target but others do not. In multi-instance learning, an entire collection of examples is labeled as containing or not containing an example of a class, but the individual members of the collection are not labeled. For a recent example of multi-instance learning with deep models, see Kotzias et al. (2015).

Some machine learning algorithms do not just experience a fixed dataset. For example, **reinforcement learning** algorithms interact with an environment, so there is a feedback loop between the learning system and its experiences. Such algorithms are beyond the scope of this book. Please see Sutton and Barto (1998) or Bertsekas and Tsitsiklis (1996) for information about reinforcement learning, and Mnih et al. (2013) for the deep learning approach to reinforcement learning.

Most machine learning algorithms simply experience a dataset. A dataset can be described in many ways. In all cases, a dataset is a collection of examples, which are in turn collections of features.

One common way of describing a dataset is with a **design matrix**. A design matrix is a matrix containing a different example in each row. Each column of the matrix corresponds to a different feature. For instance, the Iris dataset contains 150 examples with four features for each example. This means we can represent the dataset with a design matrix $\boldsymbol{X} \in \mathbb{R}^{150 \times 4}$, where $X_{i,1}$ is the sepal length of plant i, $X_{i,2}$ is the sepal width of plant i, etc. We describe most of the learning algorithms in this book in terms of how they operate on design matrix datasets.

Of course, to describe a dataset as a design matrix, it must be possible to describe each example as a vector, and each of these vectors must be the same size. This is not always possible. For example, if you have a collection of photographs with different widths and heights, then different photographs will contain different numbers of pixels, so not all the photographs may be described with the same length of vector. In Section 9.7 and chapter 10, we describe how to handle different types of such heterogeneous data. In cases like these, rather than describing the dataset as a matrix with m rows, we describe it as a set containing m elements: $\{\boldsymbol{x}^{(1)}, \boldsymbol{x}^{(2)}, \ldots, \boldsymbol{x}^{(m)}\}$. This notation does not imply that any two example vectors $\boldsymbol{x}^{(i)}$ and $\boldsymbol{x}^{(j)}$ have the same size.

In the case of supervised learning, the example contains a label or target as well as a collection of features. For example, if we want to use a learning algorithm to perform object recognition from photographs, we need to specify which object appears in each of the photos. We might do this with a numeric code, with 0 signifying a person, 1 signifying a car, 2 signifying a cat, and so forth. Often when working with a dataset containing a design matrix of feature observations $\boldsymbol{X}$, we also provide a vector of labels $\boldsymbol{y}$, with y_i providing the label for example i.

Of course, sometimes the label may be more than just a single number. For example, if we want to train a speech recognition system to transcribe entire sentences, then the label for each example sentence is a sequence of words.

Just as there is no formal definition of supervised and unsupervised learning, there is no rigid taxonomy of datasets or experiences. The structures described here cover most cases, but it is always possible to design new ones for new applications.

5.1.4 Example: Linear Regression

Our definition of a machine learning algorithm as an algorithm that is capable of improving a computer program's performance at some task via experience is somewhat abstract. To make this more concrete, we present an example of a simple machine learning algorithm: **linear regression**. We will return to this example repeatedly as we introduce more machine learning concepts that help to understand the algorithm's behavior.

As the name implies, linear regression solves a regression problem. In other words, the goal is to build a system that can take a vector $\boldsymbol{x} \in \mathbb{R}^n$ as input and predict the value of a scalar $y \in \mathbb{R}$ as its output. The output of linear regression is a linear function of the input. Let $\hat{y}$ be the value that our model predicts y should take on. We define the output to be

$$\hat{y} = \boldsymbol{w}^\top \boldsymbol{x}, \tag{5.3}$$

where $\boldsymbol{w} \in \mathbb{R}^n$ is a vector of **parameters**.

Parameters are values that control the behavior of the system. In this case, w_i is the coefficient that we multiply by feature x_i before summing up the contributions from all the features. We can think of $\boldsymbol{w}$ as a set of **weights** that determine how each feature affects the prediction. If a feature x_i receives a positive weight w_i, then increasing the value of that feature increases the value of our prediction $\hat{y}$.

If a feature receives a negative weight, then increasing the value of that feature decreases the value of our prediction. If a feature's weight is large in magnitude, then it has a large effect on the prediction. If a feature's weight is zero, it has no effect on the prediction.

We thus have a definition of our task T: to predict y from $\boldsymbol{x}$ by outputting $\hat{y} = \boldsymbol{w}^\top \boldsymbol{x}$. Next we need a definition of our performance measure, P.

Suppose that we have a design matrix of m example inputs that we will not use for training, only for evaluating how well the model performs. We also have a vector of regression targets providing the correct value of y for each of these examples. Because this dataset will only be used for evaluation, we call it the test set. We refer to the design matrix of inputs as $\boldsymbol{X}^{(\text{test})}$ and the vector of regression targets as $\boldsymbol{y}^{(\text{test})}$.

One way of measuring the performance of the model is to compute the **mean squared error** of the model on the test set. If $\hat{\boldsymbol{y}}^{(\text{test})}$ gives the predictions of the model on the test set, then the mean squared error is given by

$$\text{MSE}_{\text{test}} = \frac{1}{m} \sum_i (\hat{\boldsymbol{y}}^{(\text{test})} - \boldsymbol{y}^{(\text{test})})_i^2. \tag{5.4}$$

Intuitively, one can see that this error measure decreases to 0 when $\hat{\boldsymbol{y}}^{(\text{test})} = \boldsymbol{y}^{(\text{test})}$. We can also see that

$$\text{MSE}_{\text{test}} = \frac{1}{m} ||\hat{\boldsymbol{y}}^{(\text{test})} - \boldsymbol{y}^{(\text{test})}||_2^2, \tag{5.5}$$

so the error increases whenever the Euclidean distance between the predictions and the targets increases.

To make a machine learning algorithm, we need to design an algorithm that will improve the weights $\boldsymbol{w}$ in a way that reduces MSE_{test} when the algorithm is allowed to gain experience by observing a training set $(\boldsymbol{X}^{(\text{train})}, \boldsymbol{y}^{(\text{train})})$. One intuitive way of doing this (which we justify later, in section 5.5.1) is just to minimize the mean squared error on the training set, $\text{MSE}_{\text{train}}$.

To minimize $\text{MSE}_{\text{train}}$, we can simply solve for where its gradient is $\boldsymbol{0}$:

$$\nabla_{\boldsymbol{w}} \text{MSE}_{\text{train}} = 0 \tag{5.6}$$

$$\Rightarrow \nabla_{\boldsymbol{w}} \frac{1}{m} ||\hat{\boldsymbol{y}}^{(\text{train})} - \boldsymbol{y}^{(\text{train})}||_2^2 = 0 \tag{5.7}$$

$$\Rightarrow \frac{1}{m} \nabla_{\boldsymbol{w}} ||\boldsymbol{X}^{(\text{train})} \boldsymbol{w} - \boldsymbol{y}^{(\text{train})}||_2^2 = 0 \tag{5.8}$$

$$\Rightarrow \nabla_{\boldsymbol{w}} \left(\boldsymbol{X}^{(\text{train})} \boldsymbol{w} - \boldsymbol{y}^{(\text{train})} \right)^{\top} \left(\boldsymbol{X}^{(\text{train})} \boldsymbol{w} - \boldsymbol{y}^{(\text{train})} \right) = 0 \tag{5.9}$$

$$\Rightarrow \nabla_{\boldsymbol{w}} \left(\boldsymbol{w}^{\top} \boldsymbol{X}^{(\text{train})\top} \boldsymbol{X}^{(\text{train})} \boldsymbol{w} - 2\boldsymbol{w}^{\top} \boldsymbol{X}^{(\text{train})\top} \boldsymbol{y}^{(\text{train})} + \boldsymbol{y}^{(\text{train})\top} \boldsymbol{y}^{(\text{train})} \right) = 0 \tag{5.10}$$

$$\Rightarrow 2\boldsymbol{X}^{(\text{train})\top} \boldsymbol{X}^{(\text{train})} \boldsymbol{w} - 2\boldsymbol{X}^{(\text{train})\top} \boldsymbol{y}^{(\text{train})} = 0 \tag{5.11}$$

$$\Rightarrow \boldsymbol{w} = \left(\boldsymbol{X}^{(\text{train})\top} \boldsymbol{X}^{(\text{train})} \right)^{-1} \boldsymbol{X}^{(\text{train})\top} \boldsymbol{y}^{(\text{train})} \tag{5.12}$$

The system of equations whose solution is given by equation 5.12 is known as the **normal equations**. Evaluating equation 5.12 constitutes a simple learning algorithm. For an example of the linear regression learning algorithm in action, see figure 5.1.

It is worth noting that the term **linear regression** is often used to refer to a slightly more sophisticated model with one additional parameter—an intercept term b. In this model

$$\hat{y} = \boldsymbol{w}^{\top} \boldsymbol{x} + b, \tag{5.13}$$

so the mapping from parameters to predictions is still a linear function but the mapping from features to predictions is now an affine function. This extension to affine functions means that the plot of the model's predictions still looks like a line, but it need not pass through the origin. Instead of adding the bias parameter b, one can continue to use the model with only weights but augment $\boldsymbol{x}$ with an

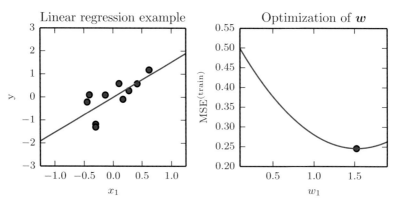

Figure 5.1: A linear regression problem, with a training set consisting of ten data points, each containing one feature. Because there is only one feature, the weight vector $\boldsymbol{w}$ contains only a single parameter to learn, w_1. *(Left)*Observe that linear regression learns to set w_1 such that the line $y = w_1 x$ comes as close as possible to passing through all the training points. *(Right)*The plotted point indicates the value of w_1 found by the normal equations, which we can see minimizes the mean squared error on the training set.

extra entry that is always set to 1. The weight corresponding to the extra 1 entry plays the role of the bias parameter. We frequently use the term "linear" when referring to affine functions throughout this book.

The intercept term b is often called the **bias** parameter of the affine transformation. This terminology derives from the point of view that the output of the transformation is biased toward being b in the absence of any input. This term is different from the idea of a statistical bias, in which a statistical estimation algorithm's expected estimate of a quantity is not equal to the true quantity.

Linear regression is of course an extremely simple and limited learning algorithm, but it provides an example of how a learning algorithm can work. In subsequent sections we describe some of the basic principles underlying learning algorithm design and demonstrate how these principles can be used to build more complicated learning algorithms.

5.2 Capacity, Overfitting and Underfitting

The central challenge in machine learning is that our algorithm must perform well on *new, previously unseen* inputs—not just those on which our model was trained. The ability to perform well on previously unobserved inputs is called **generalization**.

Typically, when training a machine learning model, we have access to a training set; we can compute some error measure on the training set, called the **training error**; and we reduce this training error. So far, what we have described is simply an optimization problem. What separates machine learning from optimization is that we want the **generalization error**, also called the **test error**, to be low as well. The generalization error is defined as the expected value of the error on a new input. Here the expectation is taken across different possible inputs, drawn from the distribution of inputs we expect the system to encounter in practice.

We typically estimate the generalization error of a machine learning model by measuring its performance on a **test set** of examples that were collected separately from the training set.

In our linear regression example, we trained the model by minimizing the training error,

$$\frac{1}{m^{(\text{train})}} ||\boldsymbol{X}^{(\text{train})} \boldsymbol{w} - \boldsymbol{y}^{(\text{train})}||_2^2, \tag{5.14}$$

but we actually care about the test error, $\frac{1}{m^{(\text{test})}} ||\boldsymbol{X}^{(\text{test})} \boldsymbol{w} - \boldsymbol{y}^{(\text{test})}||_2^2$.

How can we affect performance on the test set when we can observe only the training set? The field of **statistical learning theory** provides some answers. If the training and the test set are collected arbitrarily, there is indeed little we can do. If we are allowed to make some assumptions about how the training and test set are collected, then we can make some progress.

The training and test data are generated by a probability distribution over datasets called the **data-generating process**. We typically make a set of assumptions known collectively as the **i.i.d. assumptions**. These assumptions are that the examples in each dataset are **independent** from each other, and that the training set and test set are **identically distributed**, drawn from the same probability distribution as each other. This assumption enables us to describe the data-generating process with a probability distribution over a single example. The same distribution is then used to generate every train example and every test example. We call that shared underlying distribution the **data-generating distribution**, denoted p_{data}. This probabilistic framework and the i.i.d. assumptions enables us to mathematically study the relationship between training error and test error.

One immediate connection we can observe between training error and test error is that the expected training error of a randomly selected model is equal to the expected test error of that model. Suppose we have a probability distribution $p(x, y)$ and we sample from it repeatedly to generate the training set and the test set. For some fixed value w, the expected training set error is exactly the same as the expected test set error, because both expectations are formed using the same dataset sampling process. The only difference between the two conditions is the name we assign to the dataset we sample.

Of course, when we use a machine learning algorithm, we do not fix the parameters ahead of time, then sample both datasets. We sample the training set, then use it to choose the parameters to reduce training set error, then sample the test set. Under this process, the expected test error is greater than or equal to the expected value of training error. The factors determining how well a machine learning algorithm will perform are its ability to

1. Make the training error small.

2. Make the gap between training and test error small.

These two factors correspond to the two central challenges in machine learning: **underfitting** and **overfitting**. Underfitting occurs when the model is not able to obtain a sufficiently low error value on the training set. Overfitting occurs when the gap between the training error and test error is too large.

We can control whether a model is more likely to overfit or underfit by altering its **capacity**. Informally, a model's capacity is its ability to fit a wide variety of functions. Models with low capacity may struggle to fit the training set. Models with high capacity can overfit by memorizing properties of the training set that do not serve them well on the test set.

One way to control the capacity of a learning algorithm is by choosing its **hypothesis space**, the set of functions that the learning algorithm is allowed to select as being the solution. For example, the linear regression algorithm has the set of all linear functions of its input as its hypothesis space. We can generalize linear regression to include polynomials, rather than just linear functions, in its hypothesis space. Doing so increases the model's capacity.

A polynomial of degree 1 gives us the linear regression model with which we are already familiar, with the prediction

$$\hat{y} = b + wx. \tag{5.15}$$

By introducing x^2 as another feature provided to the linear regression model, we can learn a model that is quadratic as a function of x:

$$\hat{y} = b + w_1 x + w_2 x^2. \tag{5.16}$$

Though this model implements a quadratic function of its *input*, the output is still a linear function of the *parameters*, so we can still use the normal equations to train the model in closed form. We can continue to add more powers of x as additional features, for example, to obtain a polynomial of degree 9:

$$\hat{y} = b + \sum_{i=1}^{9} w_i x^i. \tag{5.17}$$

Machine learning algorithms will generally perform best when their capacity is appropriate for the true complexity of the task they need to perform and the amount of training data they are provided with. Models with insufficient capacity are unable to solve complex tasks. Models with high capacity can solve complex tasks, but when their capacity is higher than needed to solve the present task, they may overfit.

Figure 5.2 shows this principle in action. We compare a linear, quadratic and degree-9 predictor attempting to fit a problem where the true underlying function is quadratic. The linear function is unable to capture the curvature in the true underlying problem, so it underfits. The degree-9 predictor is capable of representing the correct function, but it is also capable of representing infinitely

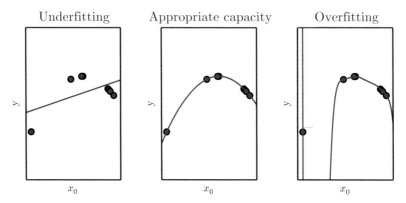

Figure 5.2: We fit three models to this example training set. The training data was generated synthetically, by randomly sampling x values and choosing y deterministically by evaluating a quadratic function. *(Left)*A linear function fit to the data suffers from underfitting—it cannot capture the curvature that is present in the data. *(Center)*A quadratic function fit to the data generalizes well to unseen points. It does not suffer from a significant amount of overfitting or underfitting. *(Right)*A polynomial of degree 9 fit to the data suffers from overfitting. Here we used the Moore-Penrose pseudoinverse to solve the underdetermined normal equations. The solution passes through all the training points exactly, but we have not been lucky enough for it to extract the correct structure. It now has a deep valley between two training points that does not appear in the true underlying function. It also increases sharply on the left side of the data, while the true function decreases in this area.

many other functions that pass exactly through the training points, because we have more parameters than training examples. We have little chance of choosing a solution that generalizes well when so many wildly different solutions exist. In this example, the quadratic model is perfectly matched to the true structure of the task, so it generalizes well to new data.

So far we have described only one way of changing a model's capacity: by changing the number of input features it has, and simultaneously adding new parameters associated with those features. There are in fact many ways to change a model's capacity. Capacity is not determined only by the choice of model. The model specifies which family of functions the learning algorithm can choose from when varying the parameters in order to reduce a training objective. This is called the **representational capacity** of the model. In many cases, finding the best function within this family is a difficult optimization problem. In practice, the learning algorithm does not actually find the best function, but merely one that significantly reduces the training error. These additional limitations, such as the imperfection of the optimization algorithm, mean that the learning algorithm's

effective capacity may be less than the representational capacity of the model family.

Our modern ideas about improving the generalization of machine learning models are refinements of thought dating back to philosophers at least as early as Ptolemy. Many early scholars invoke a principle of parsimony that is now most widely known as **Occam's razor** (c. 1287–1347). This principle states that among competing hypotheses that explain known observations equally well, we should choose the "simplest" one. This idea was formalized and made more precise in the twentieth century by the founders of statistical learning theory (Vapnik and Chervonenkis, 1971; Vapnik, 1982; Blumer et al., 1989; Vapnik, 1995).

Statistical learning theory provides various means of quantifying model capacity. Among these, the most well known is the **Vapnik-Chervonenkis dimension**, or VC dimension. The VC dimension measures the capacity of a binary classifier. The VC dimension is defined as being the largest possible value of m for which there exists a training set of m different x points that the classifier can label arbitrarily.

Quantifying the capacity of the model enables statistical learning theory to make quantitative predictions. The most important results in statistical learning theory show that the discrepancy between training error and generalization error is bounded from above by a quantity that grows as the model capacity grows but shrinks as the number of training examples increases (Vapnik and Chervonenkis, 1971; Vapnik, 1982; Blumer et al., 1989; Vapnik, 1995). These bounds provide intellectual justification that machine learning algorithms can work, but they are rarely used in practice when working with deep learning algorithms. This is in part because the bounds are often quite loose and in part because it can be quite difficult to determine the capacity of deep learning algorithms. The problem of determining the capacity of a deep learning model is especially difficult because the effective capacity is limited by the capabilities of the optimization algorithm, and we have little theoretical understanding of the general nonconvex optimization problems involved in deep learning.

We must remember that while simpler functions are more likely to generalize (to have a small gap between training and test error), we must still choose a sufficiently complex hypothesis to achieve low training error. Typically, training error decreases until it asymptotes to the minimum possible error value as model capacity increases (assuming the error measure has a minimum value). Typically, generalization error has a U-shaped curve as a function of model capacity. This is illustrated in figure 5.3.

To reach the most extreme case of arbitrarily high capacity, we introduce the concept of **nonparametric** *models*. So far, we have seen only parametric

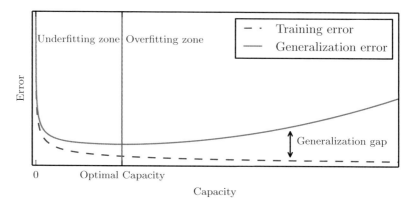

Figure 5.3: Typical relationship between capacity and error. Training and test error behave differently. At the left end of the graph, training error and generalization error are both high. This is the **underfitting regime**. As we increase capacity, training error decreases, but the gap between training and generalization error increases. Eventually, the size of this gap outweighs the decrease in training error, and we enter the **overfitting regime**, where capacity is too large, above the **optimal capacity**.

models, such as linear regression. Parametric models learn a function described by a parameter vector whose size is finite and fixed before any data is observed. Nonparametric models have no such limitation.

Sometimes, nonparametric models are just theoretical abstractions (such as an algorithm that searches over all possible probability distributions) that cannot be implemented in practice. However, we can also design practical nonparametric models by making their complexity a function of the training set size. One example of such an algorithm is **nearest neighbor regression**. Unlike linear regression, which has a fixed-length vector of weights, the nearest neighbor regression model simply stores the X and y from the training set. When asked to classify a test point x, the model looks up the nearest entry in the training set and returns the associated regression target. In other words, $\hat{y} = y_i$ where $i = \arg\min ||X_{i,:} - x||_2^2$. The algorithm can also be generalized to distance metrics other than the L^2 norm, such as learned distance metrics (Goldberger et al., 2005). If the algorithm is allowed to break ties by averaging the y_i values for all $X_{i,:}$ that are tied for nearest, then this algorithm is able to achieve the minimum possible training error (which might be greater than zero, if two identical inputs are associated with different outputs) on any regression dataset.

Finally, we can also create a nonparametric learning algorithm by wrapping a parametric learning algorithm inside another algorithm that increases the number of parameters as needed. For example, we could imagine an outer loop of learning that changes the degree of the polynomial learned by linear regression on top of a polynomial expansion of the input.

The ideal model is an oracle that simply knows the true probability distribution that generates the data. Even such a model will still incur some error on many problems, because there may still be some noise in the distribution. In the case of supervised learning, the mapping from x to y may be inherently stochastic, or y may be a deterministic function that involves other variables besides those included in x. The error incurred by an oracle making predictions from the true distribution $p(x, y)$ is called the **Bayes error**.

Training and generalization error vary as the size of the training set varies. Expected generalization error can never increase as the number of training examples increases. For nonparametric models, more data yield better generalization until the best possible error is achieved. Any fixed parametric model with less than optimal capacity will asymptote to an error value that exceeds the Bayes error. See figure 5.4 for an illustration. Note that it is possible for the model to have optimal capacity and yet still have a large gap between training and generalization errors. In this situation, we may be able to reduce this gap by gathering more training examples.

5.2.1 The No Free Lunch Theorem

Learning theory claims that a machine learning algorithm can generalize well from a finite training set of examples. This seems to contradict some basic principles of logic. Inductive reasoning, or inferring general rules from a limited set of examples, is not logically valid. To logically infer a rule describing every member of a set, one must have information about every member of that set.

In part, machine learning avoids this problem by offering only probabilistic rules, rather than the entirely certain rules used in purely logical reasoning. Machine learning promises to find rules that are *probably* correct about *most* members of the set they concern.

Unfortunately, even this does not resolve the entire problem. The **no free lunch theorem** for machine learning (Wolpert, 1996) states that, averaged over all possible data-generating distributions, every classification algorithm has the same error rate when classifying previously unobserved points. In other words, in some sense, no machine learning algorithm is universally any better than any other. The most sophisticated algorithm we can conceive of has the same average performance (over all possible tasks) as merely predicting that every point belongs to the same class.

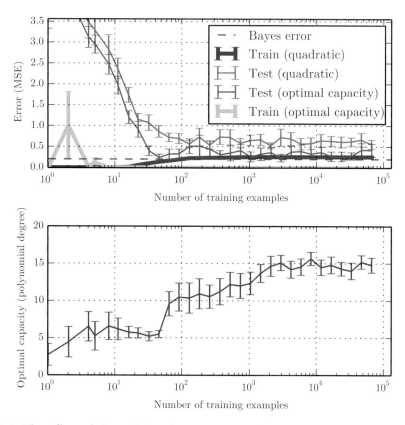

Figure 5.4: The effect of the training dataset size on the train and test error, as well as on the optimal model capacity. We constructed a synthetic regression problem based on adding a moderate amount of noise to a degree-5 polynomial, generated a single test set, and then generated several different sizes of training set. For each size, we generated 40 different training sets in order to plot error bars showing 95 percent confidence intervals. *(Top)*The MSE on the training and test set for two different models: a quadratic model, and a model with degree chosen to minimize the test error. Both are fit in closed form. For the quadratic model, the training error increases as the size of the training set increases. This is because larger datasets are harder to fit. Simultaneously, the test error decreases, because fewer incorrect hypotheses are consistent with the training data. The quadratic model does not have enough capacity to solve the task, so its test error asymptotes to a high value. The test error at optimal capacity asymptotes to the Bayes error. The training error can fall below the Bayes error, due to the ability of the training algorithm to memorize specific instances of the training set. As the training size increases to infinity, the training error of any fixed-capacity model (here, the quadratic model) must rise to at least the Bayes error. *(Bottom)*As the training set size increases, the optimal capacity (shown here as the degree of the optimal polynomial regressor) increases. The optimal capacity plateaus after reaching sufficient complexity to solve the task.

Fortunately, these results hold only when we average over *all* possible data-generating distributions. If we make assumptions about the kinds of probability distributions we encounter in real-world applications, then we can design learning algorithms that perform well on these distributions.

This means that the goal of machine learning research is not to seek a universal learning algorithm or the absolute best learning algorithm. Instead, our goal is to understand what kinds of distributions are relevant to the "real world" that an AI agent experiences, and what kinds of machine learning algorithms perform well on data drawn from the kinds of data-generating distributions we care about.

5.2.2 Regularization

The no free lunch theorem implies that we must design our machine learning algorithms to perform well on a specific task. We do so by building a set of preferences into the learning algorithm. When these preferences are aligned with the learning problems that we ask the algorithm to solve, it performs better.

So far, the only method of modifying a learning algorithm that we have discussed concretely is to increase or decrease the model's representational capacity by adding or removing functions from the hypothesis space of solutions the learning algorithm is able to choose from. We gave the specific example of increasing or decreasing the degree of a polynomial for a regression problem. The view we have described so far is oversimplified.

The behavior of our algorithm is strongly affected not just by how large we make the set of functions allowed in its hypothesis space, but by the specific identity of those functions. The learning algorithm we have studied so far, linear regression, has a hypothesis space consisting of the set of linear functions of its input. These linear functions can be useful for problems where the relationship between inputs and outputs truly is close to linear. They are less useful for problems that behave in a very nonlinear fashion. For example, linear regression would not perform well if we tried to use it to predict $\sin(x)$ from x. We can thus control the performance of our algorithms by choosing what kind of functions we allow them to draw solutions from, as well as by controlling the amount of these functions.

We can also give a learning algorithm a preference for one solution over another in its hypothesis space. This means that both functions are eligible, but one is preferred. The unpreferred solution will be chosen only if it fits the training data significantly better than the preferred solution.

For example, we can modify the training criterion for linear regression to include **weight decay**. To perform linear regression with weight decay, we minimize a sum comprising both the mean squared error on the training and a criterion $J(\boldsymbol{w})$ that expresses a preference for the weights to have smaller squared L^2 norm. Specifically,

$$J(\boldsymbol{w}) = \text{MSE}_{\text{train}} + \lambda \boldsymbol{w}^\top \boldsymbol{w}, \tag{5.18}$$

where λ is a value chosen ahead of time that controls the strength of our preference for smaller weights. When $\lambda = 0$, we impose no preference, and larger λ forces the weights to become smaller. Minimizing $J(\boldsymbol{w})$ results in a choice of weights that make a tradeoff between fitting the training data and being small. This gives us solutions that have a smaller slope, or that put weight on fewer of the features. As an example of how we can control a model's tendency to overfit or underfit via weight decay, we can train a high-degree polynomial regression model with different values of λ. See figure 5.5 for the results.

More generally, we can regularize a model that learns a function $f(\boldsymbol{x}; \boldsymbol{\theta})$ by adding a penalty called a **regularizer** to the cost function. In the case of weight decay, the regularizer is $\Omega(\boldsymbol{w}) = \boldsymbol{w}^\top \boldsymbol{w}$. In chapter 7, we will see that many other regularizers are possible.

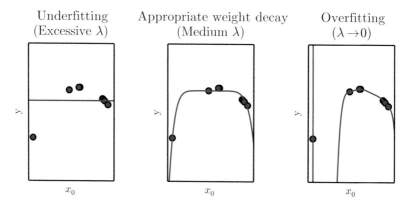

Figure 5.5: We fit a high-degree polynomial regression model to our example training set from figure 5.2. The true function is quadratic, but here we use only models with degree 9. We vary the amount of weight decay to prevent these high-degree models from overfitting. *(Left)*With very large λ, we can force the model to learn a function with no slope at all. This underfits because it can only represent a constant function. *(Center)*With a medium value of λ, the learning algorithm recovers a curve with the right general shape. Even though the model is capable of representing functions with much more complicated shapes, weight decay has encouraged it to use a simpler function described by smaller coefficients. *(Right)*With weight decay approaching zero (i.e., using the Moore-Penrose pseudoinverse to solve the underdetermined problem with minimal regularization), the degree-9 polynomial overfits significantly, as we saw in figure 5.2.

Expressing preferences for one function over another is a more general way of controlling a model's capacity than including or excluding members from the hypothesis space. We can think of excluding a function from a hypothesis space as expressing an infinitely strong preference against that function.

In our weight decay example, we expressed our preference for linear functions defined with smaller weights explicitly, via an extra term in the criterion we minimize. There are many other ways of expressing preferences for different solutions, both implicitly and explicitly. Together, these different approaches are known as **regularization**. *Regularization is any modification we make to a learning algorithm that is intended to reduce its generalization error but not its training error.* Regularization is one of the central concerns of the field of machine learning, rivaled in its importance only by optimization.

The no free lunch theorem has made it clear that there is no best machine learning algorithm, and, in particular, no best form of regularization. Instead we must choose a form of regularization that is well suited to the particular task we want to solve. The philosophy of deep learning in general and this book in particular is that a wide range of tasks (such as all the intellectual tasks that people can do) may all be solved effectively using very general-purpose forms of regularization.

5.3 Hyperparameters and Validation Sets

Most machine learning algorithms have hyperparameters, settings that we can use to control the algorithm's behavior. The values of hyperparameters are not adapted by the learning algorithm itself (though we can design a nested learning procedure in which one learning algorithm learns the best hyperparameters for another learning algorithm).

The polynomial regression example in figure 5.2 has a single hyperparameter: the degree of the polynomial, which acts as a **capacity** hyperparameter. The λ value used to control the strength of weight decay is another example of a hyperparameter.

Sometimes a setting is chosen to be a hyperparameter that the learning algorithm does not learn because the setting is difficult to optimize. More frequently, the setting must be a hyperparameter because it is not appropriate to learn that hyperparameter on the training set. This applies to all hyperparameters that control model capacity. If learned on the training set, such hyperparameters would always choose the maximum possible model capacity, resulting in overfitting (refer to figure 5.3). For example, we can always fit the training set better with a higher-degree polynomial and a weight decay setting of $\lambda = 0$ than we could with a lower-degree polynomial and a positive weight decay setting.

To solve this problem, we need a **validation set** of examples that the training algorithm does not observe.

Earlier we discussed how a held-out test set, composed of examples coming from the same distribution as the training set, can be used to estimate the generalization error of a learner, after the learning process has completed. It is important that the test examples are not used in any way to make choices about the model, including its hyperparameters. For this reason, no example from the test set can be used in the validation set. Therefore, we always construct the validation set from the *training* data. Specifically, we split the training data into two disjoint subsets. One of these subsets is used to learn the parameters. The other subset is our validation set, used to estimate the generalization error during or after training, allowing for the hyperparameters to be updated accordingly. The subset of data used to learn the parameters is still typically called the training set, even though this may be confused with the larger pool of data used for the entire training process. The subset of data used to guide the selection of hyperparameters is called the validation set. Typically, one uses about 80 percent of the training data for training and 20 percent for validation. Since the validation set is used to "train" the hyperparameters, the validation set error will underestimate the generalization error, though typically by a smaller amount than the training error does. After all hyperparameter optimization is complete, the generalization error may be estimated using the test set.

In practice, when the same test set has been used repeatedly to evaluate performance of different algorithms over many years, and especially if we consider all the attempts from the scientific community at beating the reported state-of-the-art performance on that test set, we end up having optimistic evaluations with the test set as well. Benchmarks can thus become stale and then do not reflect the true field performance of a trained system. Thankfully, the community tends to move on to new (and usually more ambitious and larger) benchmark datasets.

5.3.1 Cross-Validation

Dividing the dataset into a fixed training set and a fixed test set can be problematic if it results in the test set being small. A small test set implies statistical uncertainty around the estimated average test error, making it difficult to claim that algorithm A works better than algorithm B on the given task.

When the dataset has hundreds of thousands of examples or more, this is not a serious issue. When the dataset is too small, are alternative procedures enable one to use all the examples in the estimation of the mean test error, at the price of increased computational cost. These procedures are based on the idea of repeating the training and testing computation on different randomly chosen subsets or splits of the original dataset. The most common of these is the k-fold cross-validation procedure, shown in algorithm 5.1, in which a partition of the dataset is formed by splitting it into k nonoverlapping subsets. The test error may then be estimated by taking the average test error across k trials. On trial i, the i-th subset of the data is used as the test set, and the rest of the data is used as the training set. One problem is that no unbiased estimators of the variance of such average error estimators exist (Bengio and Grandvalet, 2004), but approximations are typically used.

5.4   Estimators, Bias and Variance

The field of statistics gives us many tools to achieve the machine learning goal of solving a task not only on the training set but also to generalize. Foundational concepts such as parameter estimation, bias and variance are useful to formally characterize notions of generalization, underfitting and overfitting.

5.4.1   Point Estimation

Point estimation is the attempt to provide the single "best" prediction of some quantity of interest. In general the quantity of interest can be a single parameter or a vector of parameters in some parametric model, such as the weights in our linear regression example in section 5.1.4, but it can also be a whole function.

To distinguish estimates of parameters from their true value, our convention will be to denote a point estimate of a parameter $\boldsymbol{\theta}$ by $\hat{\boldsymbol{\theta}}$.

Let $\{\boldsymbol{x}^{(1)}, \ldots, \boldsymbol{x}^{(m)}\}$ be a set of m independent and identically distributed (i.i.d.) data points. A **point estimator** or **statistic** is any function of the data:

$$\hat{\boldsymbol{\theta}}_m = g(\boldsymbol{x}^{(1)}, \ldots, \boldsymbol{x}^{(m)}). \tag{5.19}$$

The definition does not require that g return a value that is close to the true $\boldsymbol{\theta}$ or even that the range of g be the same as the set of allowable values of $\boldsymbol{\theta}$. This definition of a point estimator is very general and would enable the designer of an

Algorithm 5.1 The k-fold cross-validation algorithm. It can be used to estimate generalization error of a learning algorithm A when the given dataset $\mathbb{D}$ is too small for a simple train/test or train/valid split to yield accurate estimation of generalization error, because the mean of a loss L on a small test set may have too high a variance. The dataset $\mathbb{D}$ contains as elements the abstract examples $\boldsymbol{z}^{(i)}$ (for the i-th example), which could stand for an (input,target) pair $\boldsymbol{z}^{(i)} = (\boldsymbol{x}^{(i)}, y^{(i)})$ in the case of supervised learning, or for just an input $\boldsymbol{z}^{(i)} = \boldsymbol{x}^{(i)}$ in the case of unsupervised learning. The algorithm returns the vector of errors $\boldsymbol{e}$ for each example in $\mathbb{D}$, whose mean is the estimated generalization error. The errors on individual examples can be used to compute a confidence interval around the mean (equation 5.47). Though these confidence intervals are not well justified after the use of cross-validation, it is still common practice to use them to declare that algorithm A is better than algorithm B only if the confidence interval of the error of algorithm A lies below and does not intersect the confidence interval of algorithm B.

Define KFoldXV($\mathbb{D}, A, L, k$):
Require: $\mathbb{D}$, the given dataset, with elements $\boldsymbol{z}^{(i)}$
Require: A, the learning algorithm, seen as a function that takes a dataset as input and outputs a learned function
Require: L, the loss function, seen as a function from a learned function f and an example $\boldsymbol{z}^{(i)} \in \mathbb{D}$ to a scalar $\in \mathbb{R}$
Require: k, the number of folds
  Split $\mathbb{D}$ into k mutually exclusive subsets $\mathbb{D}_i$, whose union is $\mathbb{D}$
  for i from 1 to k **do**
    $f_i = A(\mathbb{D} \backslash \mathbb{D}_i)$
    for $\boldsymbol{z}^{(j)}$ in $\mathbb{D}_i$ **do**
      $e_j = L(f_i, \boldsymbol{z}^{(j)})$
    end for
  end for
  Return $\boldsymbol{e}$

---

estimator great flexibility. While almost any function thus qualifies as an estimator, a good estimator is a function whose output is close to the true underlying $\boldsymbol{\theta}$ that generated the training data.

For now, we take the frequentist perspective on statistics. That is, we assume that the true parameter value $\boldsymbol{\theta}$ is fixed but unknown, while the point estimate $\hat{\boldsymbol{\theta}}$ is a function of the data. Since the data is drawn from a random process, any function of the data is random. Therefore $\hat{\boldsymbol{\theta}}$ is a random variable.

Point estimation can also refer to the estimation of the relationship between input and target variables. We refer to these types of point estimates as function estimators.

Function Estimation Sometimes we are interested in performing function estimation (or function approximation). Here, we are trying to predict a variable y given an input vector x. We assume that there is a function $f(x)$ that describes the approximate relationship between y and x. For example, we may assume that $y = f(x) + \epsilon$, where ϵ stands for the part of y that is not predictable from x. In function estimation, we are interested in approximating f with a model or estimate $\hat{f}$. Function estimation is really just the same as estimating a parameter θ; the function estimator $\hat{f}$ is simply a point estimator in function space. The linear regression example (discussed in section 5.1.4) and the polynomial regression example (discussed in section 5.2) both illustrate scenarios that may be interpreted as either estimating a parameter w or estimating a function $\hat{f}$ mapping from x to y.

We now review the most commonly studied properties of point estimators and discuss what they tell us about these estimators.

5.4.2 Bias

The bias of an estimator is defined as

$$\text{bias}(\hat{\boldsymbol{\theta}}_m) = \mathbb{E}(\hat{\boldsymbol{\theta}}_m) - \boldsymbol{\theta}, \tag{5.20}$$

where the expectation is over the data (seen as samples from a random variable) and $\boldsymbol{\theta}$ is the true underlying value of $\boldsymbol{\theta}$ used to define the data-generating distribution. An estimator $\hat{\boldsymbol{\theta}}_m$ is said to be **unbiased** if $\text{bias}(\hat{\boldsymbol{\theta}}_m) = \mathbf{0}$, which implies that $\mathbb{E}(\hat{\boldsymbol{\theta}}_m) = \boldsymbol{\theta}$. An estimator $\hat{\boldsymbol{\theta}}_m$ is said to be **asymptotically unbiased** if $\lim_{m \to \infty} \text{bias}(\hat{\boldsymbol{\theta}}_m) = \mathbf{0}$, which implies that $\lim_{m \to \infty} \mathbb{E}(\hat{\boldsymbol{\theta}}_m) = \boldsymbol{\theta}$.

Example: Bernoulli Distribution Consider a set of samples $\{x^{(1)}, \ldots, x^{(m)}\}$ that are independently and identically distributed according to a Bernoulli distribution with mean θ:

$$P(x^{(i)}; \theta) = \theta^{x^{(i)}} (1 - \theta)^{(1 - x^{(i)})}. \tag{5.21}$$

A common estimator for the θ parameter of this distribution is the mean of the training samples:

$$\hat{\theta}_m = \frac{1}{m} \sum_{i=1}^{m} x^{(i)}. \tag{5.22}$$

To determine whether this estimator is biased, we can substitute equation 5.22 into equation 5.20:

$$\text{bias}(\hat{\theta}_m) = \mathbb{E}[\hat{\theta}_m] - \theta \tag{5.23}$$

$$= \mathbb{E}\left[\frac{1}{m}\sum_{i=1}^{m} x^{(i)}\right] - \theta \tag{5.24}$$

$$= \frac{1}{m}\sum_{i=1}^{m} \mathbb{E}\left[x^{(i)}\right] - \theta \tag{5.25}$$

$$= \frac{1}{m}\sum_{i=1}^{m} \sum_{x^{(i)}=0}^{1} \left(x^{(i)}\theta^{x^{(i)}}(1-\theta)^{(1-x^{(i)})}\right) - \theta \tag{5.26}$$

$$= \frac{1}{m}\sum_{i=1}^{m} (\theta) - \theta \tag{5.27}$$

$$= \theta - \theta = 0 \tag{5.28}$$

Since $\text{bias}(\hat{\theta}) = 0$, we say that our estimator $\hat{\theta}$ is unbiased.

Example: Gaussian Distribution Estimator of the Mean Now, consider a set of samples $\{x^{(1)}, \ldots, x^{(m)}\}$ that are independently and identically distributed according to a Gaussian distribution $p(x^{(i)}) = \mathcal{N}(x^{(i)}; \mu, \sigma^2)$, where $i \in \{1, \ldots, m\}$. Recall that the Gaussian probability density function is given by

$$p(x^{(i)}; \mu, \sigma^2) = \frac{1}{\sqrt{2\pi\sigma^2}} \exp\left(-\frac{1}{2}\frac{(x^{(i)} - \mu)^2}{\sigma^2}\right). \tag{5.29}$$

A common estimator of the Gaussian mean parameter is known as the **sample mean**:

$$\hat{\mu}_m = \frac{1}{m}\sum_{i=1}^{m} x^{(i)} \tag{5.30}$$

To determine the bias of the sample mean, we are again interested in calculating its expectation:

$$\text{bias}(\hat{\mu}_m) = \mathbb{E}[\hat{\mu}_m] - \mu \tag{5.31}$$

$$= \mathbb{E}\left[\frac{1}{m}\sum_{i=1}^{m} x^{(i)}\right] - \mu \tag{5.32}$$

$$= \left(\frac{1}{m} \sum_{i=1}^{m} \mathbb{E}\left[x^{(i)}\right] \right) - \mu \tag{5.33}$$

$$= \left(\frac{1}{m} \sum_{i=1}^{m} \mu \right) - \mu \tag{5.34}$$

$$= \mu - \mu = 0 \tag{5.35}$$

Thus we find that the sample mean is an unbiased estimator of Gaussian mean parameter.

Example: Estimators of the Variance of a Gaussian Distribution For this example, we compare two different estimators of the variance parameter σ^2 of a Gaussian distribution. We are interested in knowing if either estimator is biased.

The first estimator of σ^2 we consider is known as the **sample variance**

$$\hat{\sigma}_m^2 = \frac{1}{m} \sum_{i=1}^{m} \left(x^{(i)} - \hat{\mu}_m \right)^2, \tag{5.36}$$

where $\hat{\mu}_m$ is the sample mean. More formally, we are interested in computing

$$\text{bias}(\hat{\sigma}_m^2) = \mathbb{E}[\hat{\sigma}_m^2] - \sigma^2. \tag{5.37}$$

We begin by evaluating the term $\mathbb{E}[\hat{\sigma}_m^2]$:

$$\mathbb{E}[\hat{\sigma}_m^2] = \mathbb{E}\left[\frac{1}{m} \sum_{i=1}^{m} \left(x^{(i)} - \hat{\mu}_m \right)^2 \right] \tag{5.38}$$

$$= \frac{m-1}{m} \sigma^2 \tag{5.39}$$

Returning to equation 5.37, we conclude that the bias of $\hat{\sigma}_m^2$ is $-\sigma^2/m$. Therefore, the sample variance is a biased estimator.

The **unbiased sample variance** estimator

$$\tilde{\sigma}_m^2 = \frac{1}{m-1} \sum_{i=1}^{m} \left(x^{(i)} - \hat{\mu}_m \right)^2 \tag{5.40}$$

provides an alternative approach. As the name suggests this estimator is unbiased. That is, we find that $\mathbb{E}[\tilde{\sigma}_m^2] = \sigma^2$:

$$\mathbb{E}[\tilde{\sigma}_m^2] = \mathbb{E}\left[\frac{1}{m-1} \sum_{i=1}^{m} \left(x^{(i)} - \hat{\mu}_m \right)^2 \right] \tag{5.41}$$

$$= \frac{m}{m-1} \mathbb{E}[\hat{\sigma}_m^2] \tag{5.42}$$

$$= \frac{m}{m-1} \left(\frac{m-1}{m} \sigma^2 \right) \tag{5.43}$$

$$= \sigma^2. \tag{5.44}$$

We have two estimators: one is biased, and the other is not. While unbiased estimators are clearly desirable, they are not always the "best" estimators. As we will see we often use biased estimators that possess other important properties.

5.4.3 Variance and Standard Error

Another property of the estimator that we might want to consider is how much we expect it to vary as a function of the data sample. Just as we computed the expectation of the estimator to determine its bias, we can compute its variance. The **variance** of an estimator is simply the variance

$$\text{Var}(\hat{\theta}) \tag{5.45}$$

where the random variable is the training set. Alternately, the square root of the variance is called the **standard error**, denoted $\text{SE}(\hat{\theta})$.

The variance, or the standard error, of an estimator provides a measure of how we would expect the estimate we compute from data to vary as we independently resample the dataset from the underlying data-generating process. Just as we might like an estimator to exhibit low bias, we would also like it to have relatively low variance.

When we compute any statistic using a finite number of samples, our estimate of the true underlying parameter is uncertain, in the sense that we could have obtained other samples from the same distribution and their statistics would have been different. The expected degree of variation in any estimator is a source of error that we want to quantify.

The standard error of the mean is given by

$$\text{SE}(\hat{\mu}_m) = \sqrt{\text{Var}\left[\frac{1}{m} \sum_{i=1}^{m} x^{(i)} \right]} = \frac{\sigma}{\sqrt{m}}, \tag{5.46}$$

where σ^2 is the true variance of the samples x^i. The standard error is often estimated by using an estimate of σ. Unfortunately, neither the square root of the sample variance nor the square root of the unbiased estimator of the variance provide an unbiased estimate of the standard deviation. Both approaches tend to underestimate the true standard deviation but are still used in practice. The square root of the unbiased estimator of the variance is less of an underestimate. For large m, the approximation is quite reasonable.

The standard error of the mean is very useful in machine learning experiments. We often estimate the generalization error by computing the sample mean of the error on the test set. The number of examples in the test set determines the accuracy of this estimate. Taking advantage of the central limit theorem, which tells us that the mean will be approximately distributed with a normal distribution, we can use the standard error to compute the probability that the true expectation falls in any chosen interval. For example, the 95 percent confidence interval centered on the mean $\hat{\mu}_m$ is

$$(\hat{\mu}_m - 1.96\text{SE}(\hat{\mu}_m), \hat{\mu}_m + 1.96\text{SE}(\hat{\mu}_m)), \tag{5.47}$$

under the normal distribution with mean $\hat{\mu}_m$ and variance $\text{SE}(\hat{\mu}_m)^2$. In machine learning experiments, it is common to say that algorithm A is better than algorithm B if the upper bound of the 95 percent confidence interval for the error of algorithm A is less than the lower bound of the 95 percent confidence interval for the error of algorithm B.

Example: Bernoulli Distribution We once again consider a set of samples $\{x^{(1)}, \ldots, x^{(m)}\}$ drawn independently and identically from a Bernoulli distribution (recall $P(x^{(i)}; \theta) = \theta^{x^{(i)}}(1-\theta)^{(1-x^{(i)})}$). This time we are interested in computing the variance of the estimator $\hat{\theta}_m = \frac{1}{m}\sum_{i=1}^m x^{(i)}$.

$$\text{Var}\left(\hat{\theta}_m\right) = \text{Var}\left(\frac{1}{m}\sum_{i=1}^m x^{(i)}\right) \tag{5.48}$$

$$= \frac{1}{m^2}\sum_{i=1}^m \text{Var}\left(x^{(i)}\right) \tag{5.49}$$

$$= \frac{1}{m^2}\sum_{i=1}^m \theta(1-\theta) \tag{5.50}$$

$$= \frac{1}{m^2}m\theta(1-\theta) \tag{5.51}$$

$$= \frac{1}{m}\theta(1-\theta) \tag{5.52}$$

The variance of the estimator decreases as a function of m, the number of examples in the dataset. This is a common property of popular estimators that we will return to when we discuss consistency (see section 5.4.5).

5.4.4 Trading Off Bias and Variance to Minimize Mean Squared Error

Bias and variance measure two different sources of error in an estimator. Bias measures the expected deviation from the true value of the function or parameter. Variance on the other hand, provides a measure of the deviation from the expected estimator value that any particular sampling of the data is likely to cause.

What happens when we are given a choice between two estimators, one with more bias and one with more variance? How do we choose between them? For example, imagine that we are interested in approximating the function shown in figure 5.2 and we are only offered the choice between a model with large bias and one that suffers from large variance. How do we choose between them?

The most common way to negotiate this trade-off is to use cross-validation. Empirically, cross-validation is highly successful on many real-world tasks. Alternatively, we can also compare the **mean squared error** (MSE) of the estimates:

$$\text{MSE} = \mathbb{E}[(\hat{\theta}_m - \theta)^2] \tag{5.53}$$

$$= \text{Bias}(\hat{\theta}_m)^2 + \text{Var}(\hat{\theta}_m) \tag{5.54}$$

The MSE measures the overall expected deviation—in a squared error sense—between the estimator and the true value of the parameter θ. As is clear from equation 5.54, evaluating the MSE incorporates both the bias and the variance. Desirable estimators are those with small MSE and these are estimators that manage to keep both their bias and variance somewhat in check.

The relationship between bias and variance is tightly linked to the machine learning concepts of capacity, underfitting and overfitting. When generalization error is measured by the MSE (where bias and variance are meaningful components of generalization error), increasing capacity tends to increase variance and decrease bias. This is illustrated in figure 5.6, where we see again the U-shaped curve of generalization error as a function of capacity.

5.4.5 Consistency

So far we have discussed the properties of various estimators for a training set of fixed size. Usually, we are also concerned with the behavior of an estimator as the

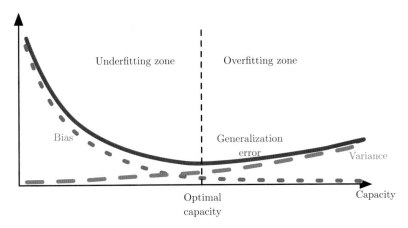

Figure 5.6: As capacity increases (x-axis), bias (dotted) tends to decrease and variance (dashed) tends to increase, yielding another U-shaped curve for generalization error (bold curve). If we vary capacity along one axis, there is an optimal capacity, with underfitting when the capacity is below this optimum and overfitting when it is above. This relationship is similar to the relationship between capacity, underfitting, and overfitting, discussed in section 5.2 and figure 5.3.

amount of training data grows. In particular, we usually wish that, as the number of data points m in our dataset increases, our point estimates converge to the true value of the corresponding parameters. More formally, we would like that

$$\text{plim}_{m \to \infty} \hat{\theta}_m = \theta. \tag{5.55}$$

The symbol plim indicates convergence in probability, meaning that for any $\epsilon > 0$, $P(|\hat{\theta}_m - \theta| > \epsilon) \to 0$ as $m \to \infty$. The condition described by equation 5.55 is known as **consistency**. It is sometimes referred to as weak consistency, with strong consistency referring to the **almost sure** convergence of $\hat{\theta}$ to θ. **Almost sure convergence** of a sequence of random variables $\mathbf{x}^{(1)}, \mathbf{x}^{(2)}, \ldots$ to a value $\boldsymbol{x}$ occurs when $p(\lim_{m \to \infty} \mathbf{x}^{(m)} = \boldsymbol{x}) = 1$.

Consistency ensures that the bias induced by the estimator diminishes as the number of data examples grows. However, the reverse is not true—asymptotic unbiasedness does not imply consistency. For example, consider estimating the mean parameter μ of a normal distribution $\mathcal{N}(x; \mu, \sigma^2)$, with a dataset consisting of m samples: $\{x^{(1)}, \ldots, x^{(m)}\}$. We could use the first sample $x^{(1)}$ of the dataset as an unbiased estimator: $\hat{\theta} = x^{(1)}$. In that case, $\mathbb{E}(\hat{\theta}_m) = \theta$, so the estimator is unbiased no matter how many data points are seen. This, of course, implies that the estimate is asymptotically unbiased. However, this is not a consistent estimator as it is *not* the case that $\hat{\theta}_m \to \theta$ as $m \to \infty$.

5.5 Maximum Likelihood Estimation

We have seen some definitions of common estimators and analyzed their properties. But where did these estimators come from? Rather than guessing that some function might make a good estimator and then analyzing its bias and variance, we would like to have some principle from which we can derive specific functions that are good estimators for different models.

The most common such principle is the maximum likelihood principle.

Consider a set of m examples $\mathbb{X} = \{\boldsymbol{x}^{(1)}, \ldots, \boldsymbol{x}^{(m)}\}$ drawn independently from the true but unknown data-generating distribution $p_{\text{data}}(\mathbf{x})$.

Let $p_{\text{model}}(\mathbf{x}; \boldsymbol{\theta})$ be a parametric family of probability distributions over the same space indexed by $\boldsymbol{\theta}$. In other words, $p_{\text{model}}(\boldsymbol{x}; \boldsymbol{\theta})$ maps any configuration $\boldsymbol{x}$ to a real number estimating the true probability $p_{\text{data}}(\boldsymbol{x})$.

The maximum likelihood estimator for $\boldsymbol{\theta}$ is then defined as

$$\boldsymbol{\theta}_{\text{ML}} = \arg\max_{\boldsymbol{\theta}} p_{\text{model}}(\mathbb{X}; \boldsymbol{\theta}), \tag{5.56}$$

$$= \arg\max_{\boldsymbol{\theta}} \prod_{i=1}^{m} p_{\text{model}}(\boldsymbol{x}^{(i)}; \boldsymbol{\theta}). \tag{5.57}$$

This product over many probabilities can be inconvenient for various reasons. For example, it is prone to numerical underflow. To obtain a more convenient but equivalent optimization problem, we observe that taking the logarithm of the likelihood does not change its $\arg\max$ but does conveniently transform a product into a sum:

$$\boldsymbol{\theta}_{\text{ML}} = \arg\max_{\boldsymbol{\theta}} \sum_{i=1}^{m} \log p_{\text{model}}(\boldsymbol{x}^{(i)}; \boldsymbol{\theta}). \tag{5.58}$$

Because the $\arg\max$ does not change when we rescale the cost function, we can divide by m to obtain a version of the criterion that is expressed as an expectation with respect to the empirical distribution $\hat{p}_{\text{data}}$ defined by the training data:

$$\boldsymbol{\theta}_{\text{ML}} = \arg\max_{\boldsymbol{\theta}} \mathbb{E}_{\mathbf{x} \sim \hat{p}_{\text{data}}} \log p_{\text{model}}(\boldsymbol{x}; \boldsymbol{\theta}). \tag{5.59}$$

One way to interpret maximum likelihood estimation is to view it as minimizing the dissimilarity between the empirical distribution $\hat{p}_{\text{data}}$, defined by the training set and the model distribution, with the degree of dissimilarity between the two measured by the KL divergence. The KL divergence is given by

$$D_{\text{KL}}(\hat{p}_{\text{data}} \| p_{\text{model}}) = \mathbb{E}_{\mathbf{x} \sim \hat{p}_{\text{data}}} [\log \hat{p}_{\text{data}}(\boldsymbol{x}) - \log p_{\text{model}}(\boldsymbol{x})]. \tag{5.60}$$

The term on the left is a function only of the data-generating process, not the model. This means when we train the model to minimize the KL divergence, we need only minimize

$$- \mathbb{E}_{\mathbf{x} \sim \hat{p}_{\text{data}}} \left[\log p_{\text{model}}(\boldsymbol{x}) \right], \tag{5.61}$$

which is of course the same as the maximization in equation 5.59.

Minimizing this KL divergence corresponds exactly to minimizing the cross-entropy between the distributions. Many authors use the term "cross-entropy" to identify specifically the negative log-likelihood of a Bernoulli or softmax distribution, but that is a misnomer. Any loss consisting of a negative log-likelihood is a cross-entropy between the empirical distribution defined by the training set and the probability distribution defined by model. For example, mean squared error is the cross-entropy between the empirical distribution and a Gaussian model.

We can thus see maximum likelihood as an attempt to make the model distribution match the empirical distribution $\hat{p}_{\text{data}}$. Ideally, we would like to match the true data-generating distribution p_{data}, but we have no direct access to this distribution.

While the optimal $\boldsymbol{\theta}$ is the same regardless of whether we are maximizing the likelihood or minimizing the KL divergence, the values of the objective functions are different. In software, we often phrase both as minimizing a cost function. Maximum likelihood thus becomes minimization of the negative log-likelihood (NLL), or equivalently, minimization of the cross-entropy. The perspective of maximum likelihood as minimum KL divergence becomes helpful in this case because the KL divergence has a known minimum value of zero. The negative log-likelihood can actually become negative when $\boldsymbol{x}$ is real-valued.

5.5.1 Conditional Log-Likelihood and Mean Squared Error

The maximum likelihood estimator can readily be generalized to estimate a conditional probability $P(\mathbf{y} \mid \mathbf{x}; \boldsymbol{\theta})$ in order to predict $\mathbf{y}$ given $\mathbf{x}$. This is actually the most common situation because it forms the basis for most supervised learning. If $\boldsymbol{X}$ represents all our inputs and $\boldsymbol{Y}$ all our observed targets, then the conditional maximum likelihood estimator is

$$\boldsymbol{\theta}_{\text{ML}} = \arg\max_{\boldsymbol{\theta}} P(\boldsymbol{Y} \mid \boldsymbol{X}; \boldsymbol{\theta}). \tag{5.62}$$

If the examples are assumed to be i.i.d., then this can be decomposed into

$$\boldsymbol{\theta}_{\text{ML}} = \arg\max_{\boldsymbol{\theta}} \sum_{i=1}^{m} \log P(\boldsymbol{y}^{(i)} \mid \boldsymbol{x}^{(i)}; \boldsymbol{\theta}). \tag{5.63}$$

Example: Linear Regression as Maximum Likelihood Linear regression, introduced in section 5.1.4, may be justified as a maximum likelihood procedure. Previously, we motivated linear regression as an algorithm that learns to take an input x and produce an output value $\hat{y}$. The mapping from x to $\hat{y}$ is chosen to minimize mean squared error, a criterion that we introduced more or less arbitrarily. We now revisit linear regression from the point of view of maximum likelihood estimation. Instead of producing a single prediction $\hat{y}$, we now think of the model as producing a conditional distribution $p(y \mid x)$. We can imagine that with an infinitely large training set, we might see several training examples with the same input value x but different values of y. The goal of the learning algorithm is now to fit the distribution $p(y \mid x)$ to all those different y values that are all compatible with x. To derive the same linear regression algorithm we obtained before, we define $p(y \mid x) = \mathcal{N}(y; \hat{y}(x; w), \sigma^2)$. The function $\hat{y}(x; w)$ gives the prediction of the mean of the Gaussian. In this example, we assume that the variance is fixed to some constant σ^2 chosen by the user. We will see that this choice of the functional form of $p(y \mid x)$ causes the maximum likelihood estimation procedure to yield the same learning algorithm as we developed before. Since the examples are assumed to be i.i.d., the conditional log-likelihood (equation 5.63) is given by

$$\sum_{i=1}^{m} \log p(y^{(i)} \mid x^{(i)}; \boldsymbol{\theta}) \tag{5.64}$$

$$= -m \log \sigma - \frac{m}{2} \log(2\pi) - \sum_{i=1}^{m} \frac{\left\| \hat{y}^{(i)} - y^{(i)} \right\|^2}{2\sigma^2}, \tag{5.65}$$

where $\hat{y}^{(i)}$ is the output of the linear regression on the i-th input $x^{(i)}$ and m is the number of the training examples. Comparing the log-likelihood with the mean squared error,

$$\mathrm{MSE}_{\mathrm{train}} = \frac{1}{m} \sum_{i=1}^{m} ||\hat{y}^{(i)} - y^{(i)}||^2, \tag{5.66}$$

we immediately see that maximizing the log-likelihood with respect to w yields the same estimate of the parameters w as does minimizing the mean squared error. The two criteria have different values but the same location of the optimum. This justifies the use of the MSE as a maximum likelihood estimation procedure. As we will see, the maximum likelihood estimator has several desirable properties.

5.5.2 Properties of Maximum Likelihood

The main appeal of the maximum likelihood estimator is that it can be shown to be the best estimator asymptotically, as the number of examples $m \to \infty$, in terms of its rate of convergence as m increases.

Under appropriate conditions, the maximum likelihood estimator has the property of consistency (see section 5.4.5), meaning that as the number of training examples approaches infinity, the maximum likelihood estimate of a parameter converges to the true value of the parameter. These conditions are as follows:

- The true distribution p_{data} must lie within the model family $p_{\text{model}}(\cdot; \boldsymbol{\theta})$. Otherwise, no estimator can recover p_{data}.

- The true distribution p_{data} must correspond to exactly one value of $\boldsymbol{\theta}$. Otherwise, maximum likelihood can recover the correct p_{data} but will not be able to determine which value of $\boldsymbol{\theta}$ was used by the data-generating process.

There are other inductive principles besides the maximum likelihood estimator, many of which share the property of being consistent estimators. Consistent estimators can differ, however, in their **statistical efficiency**, meaning that one consistent estimator may obtain lower generalization error for a fixed number of samples m, or equivalently, may require fewer examples to obtain a fixed level of generalization error.

Statistical efficiency is typically studied in the **parametric case** (as in linear regression), where our goal is to estimate the value of a parameter (assuming it is possible to identify the true parameter), not the value of a function. A way to measure how close we are to the true parameter is by the expected mean squared error, computing the squared difference between the estimated and true parameter values, where the expectation is over m training samples from the data-generating distribution. That parametric mean squared error decreases as m increases, and for m large, the Cramér-Rao lower bound (Rao, 1945; Cramér, 1946) shows that no consistent estimator has a lower MSE than the maximum likelihood estimator.

For these reasons (consistency and efficiency), maximum likelihood is often considered the preferred estimator to use for machine learning. When the number of examples is small enough to yield overfitting behavior, regularization strategies such as weight decay may be used to obtain a biased version of maximum likelihood that has less variance when training data is limited.

5.6 Bayesian Statistics

So far we have discussed **frequentist statistics** and approaches based on estimating a single value of $\boldsymbol{\theta}$, then making all predictions thereafter based on that one estimate. Another approach is to consider all possible values of $\boldsymbol{\theta}$ when making a prediction. The latter is the domain of **Bayesian statistics**.

As discussed in section 5.4.1, the frequentist perspective is that the true parameter value $\boldsymbol{\theta}$ is fixed but unknown, while the point estimate $\hat{\boldsymbol{\theta}}$ is a random variable on account of it being a function of the dataset (which is seen as random).

The Bayesian perspective on statistics is quite different. The Bayesian uses probability to reflect degrees of certainty in states of knowledge. The dataset is directly observed and so is not random. On the other hand, the true parameter $\boldsymbol{\theta}$ is unknown or uncertain and thus is represented as a random variable.

Before observing the data, we represent our knowledge of $\boldsymbol{\theta}$ using the **prior probability distribution**, $p(\boldsymbol{\theta})$ (sometimes referred to as simply "the prior"). Generally, the machine learning practitioner selects a prior distribution that is quite broad (i.e., with high entropy) to reflect a high degree of uncertainty in the value of $\boldsymbol{\theta}$ before observing any data. For example, one might assume a priori that $\boldsymbol{\theta}$ lies in some finite range or volume, with a uniform distribution. Many priors instead reflect a preference for "simpler" solutions (such as smaller magnitude coefficients, or a function that is closer to being constant).

Now consider that we have a set of data samples $\{x^{(1)}, \ldots, x^{(m)}\}$. We can recover the effect of data on our belief about $\boldsymbol{\theta}$ by combining the data likelihood $p(x^{(1)}, \ldots, x^{(m)} \mid \boldsymbol{\theta})$ with the prior via Bayes' rule:

$$p(\boldsymbol{\theta} \mid x^{(1)}, \ldots, x^{(m)}) = \frac{p(x^{(1)}, \ldots, x^{(m)} \mid \boldsymbol{\theta})p(\boldsymbol{\theta})}{p(x^{(1)}, \ldots, x^{(m)})} \tag{5.67}$$

In the scenarios where Bayesian estimation is typically used, the prior begins as a relatively uniform or Gaussian distribution with high entropy, and the observation of the data usually causes the posterior to lose entropy and concentrate around a few highly likely values of the parameters.

Relative to maximum likelihood estimation, Bayesian estimation offers two important differences. First, unlike the maximum likelihood approach that makes predictions using a point estimate of $\boldsymbol{\theta}$, the Bayesian approach is to make predictions using a full distribution over $\boldsymbol{\theta}$. For example, after observing m examples, the predicted distribution over the next data sample, $x^{(m+1)}$, is given by

$$p(x^{(m+1)} \mid x^{(1)}, \ldots, x^{(m)}) = \int p(x^{(m+1)} \mid \boldsymbol{\theta})p(\boldsymbol{\theta} \mid x^{(1)}, \ldots, x^{(m)}) \, d\boldsymbol{\theta}. \tag{5.68}$$

Here each value of $\boldsymbol{\theta}$ with positive probability density contributes to the prediction of the next example, with the contribution weighted by the posterior density itself. After having observed $\{x^{(1)}, \ldots, x^{(m)}\}$, if we are still quite uncertain about the value of $\boldsymbol{\theta}$, then this uncertainty is incorporated directly into any predictions we might make.

In section 5.4, we discussed how the frequentist approach addresses the uncertainty in a given point estimate of $\boldsymbol{\theta}$ by evaluating its variance. The variance of the estimator is an assessment of how the estimate might change with alternative samplings of the observed data. The Bayesian answer to the question of how to deal with the uncertainty in the estimator is to simply integrate over it, which tends to protect well against overfitting. This integral is of course just an application of the laws of probability, making the Bayesian approach simple to justify, while the frequentist machinery for constructing an estimator is based on the rather ad hoc decision to summarize all knowledge contained in the dataset with a single point estimate.

The second important difference between the Bayesian approach to estimation and the maximum likelihood approach is due to the contribution of the Bayesian prior distribution. The prior has an influence by shifting probability mass density towards regions of the parameter space that are preferred a priori. In practice, the prior often expresses a preference for models that are simpler or more smooth. Critics of the Bayesian approach identify the prior as a source of subjective human judgment affecting the predictions.

Bayesian methods typically generalize much better when limited training data is available but typically suffer from high computational cost when the number of training examples is large.

Example: Bayesian Linear Regression Here we consider the Bayesian estimation approach to learning the linear regression parameters. In linear regression, we learn a linear mapping from an input vector $\boldsymbol{x} \in \mathbb{R}^n$ to predict the value of a scalar $y \in \mathbb{R}$. The prediction is parametrized by the vector $\boldsymbol{w} \in \mathbb{R}^n$:

$$\hat{y} = \boldsymbol{w}^\top \boldsymbol{x}. \tag{5.69}$$

Given a set of m training samples $(\boldsymbol{X}^{(\text{train})}, \boldsymbol{y}^{(\text{train})})$, we can express the prediction of y over the entire training set as

$$\hat{\boldsymbol{y}}^{(\text{train})} = \boldsymbol{X}^{(\text{train})} \boldsymbol{w}. \tag{5.70}$$

Expressed as a Gaussian conditional distribution on $\boldsymbol{y}^{(\text{train})}$, we have

$$p(\boldsymbol{y}^{(\text{train})} \mid \boldsymbol{X}^{(\text{train})}, \boldsymbol{w}) = \mathcal{N}(\boldsymbol{y}^{(\text{train})}; \boldsymbol{X}^{(\text{train})}\boldsymbol{w}, \boldsymbol{I}) \tag{5.71}$$

$$\propto \exp\left(-\frac{1}{2}(\boldsymbol{y}^{(\text{train})} - \boldsymbol{X}^{(\text{train})}\boldsymbol{w})^\top (\boldsymbol{y}^{(\text{train})} - \boldsymbol{X}^{(\text{train})}\boldsymbol{w})\right), \tag{5.72}$$

where we follow the standard MSE formulation in assuming that the Gaussian variance on y is one. In what follows, to reduce the notational burden, we refer to $(\boldsymbol{X}^{(\text{train})}, \boldsymbol{y}^{(\text{train})})$ as simply $(\boldsymbol{X}, \boldsymbol{y})$.

To determine the posterior distribution over the model parameter vector $\boldsymbol{w}$, we first need to specify a prior distribution. The prior should reflect our naive belief about the value of these parameters. While it is sometimes difficult or unnatural to express our prior beliefs in terms of the parameters of the model, in practice we typically assume a fairly broad distribution, expressing a high degree of uncertainty about $\boldsymbol{\theta}$. For real-valued parameters it is common to use a Gaussian as a prior distribution,

$$p(\boldsymbol{w}) = \mathcal{N}(\boldsymbol{w}; \boldsymbol{\mu}_0, \boldsymbol{\Lambda}_0) \propto \exp\left(-\frac{1}{2}(\boldsymbol{w} - \boldsymbol{\mu}_0)^\top \boldsymbol{\Lambda}_0^{-1}(\boldsymbol{w} - \boldsymbol{\mu}_0)\right), \tag{5.73}$$

where $\boldsymbol{\mu}_0$ and $\boldsymbol{\Lambda}_0$ are the prior distribution mean vector and covariance matrix respectively.[1]

With the prior thus specified, we can now proceed in determining the **posterior distribution** over the model parameters:

$$p(\boldsymbol{w} \mid \boldsymbol{X}, \boldsymbol{y}) \propto p(\boldsymbol{y} \mid \boldsymbol{X}, \boldsymbol{w})p(\boldsymbol{w}) \tag{5.74}$$

$$\propto \exp\left(-\frac{1}{2}(\boldsymbol{y} - \boldsymbol{X}\boldsymbol{w})^\top (\boldsymbol{y} - \boldsymbol{X}\boldsymbol{w})\right) \exp\left(-\frac{1}{2}(\boldsymbol{w} - \boldsymbol{\mu}_0)^\top \boldsymbol{\Lambda}_0^{-1}(\boldsymbol{w} - \boldsymbol{\mu}_0)\right) \tag{5.75}$$

$$\propto \exp\left(-\frac{1}{2}\left(-2\boldsymbol{y}^\top \boldsymbol{X}\boldsymbol{w} + \boldsymbol{w}^\top \boldsymbol{X}^\top \boldsymbol{X}\boldsymbol{w} + \boldsymbol{w}^\top \boldsymbol{\Lambda}_0^{-1}\boldsymbol{w} - 2\boldsymbol{\mu}_0^\top \boldsymbol{\Lambda}_0^{-1}\boldsymbol{w}\right)\right). \tag{5.76}$$

---

[1] Unless there is a reason to use a particular covariance structure, we typically assume a diagonal covariance matrix $\boldsymbol{\Lambda}_0 = \text{diag}(\boldsymbol{\lambda}_0)$.

We now define $\boldsymbol{\Lambda}_m = \left(\boldsymbol{X}^\top \boldsymbol{X} + \boldsymbol{\Lambda}_0^{-1}\right)^{-1}$ and $\boldsymbol{\mu}_m = \boldsymbol{\Lambda}_m \left(\boldsymbol{X}^\top \boldsymbol{y} + \boldsymbol{\Lambda}_0^{-1}\boldsymbol{\mu}_0\right)$. Using these new variables, we find that the posterior may be rewritten as a Gaussian distribution:

$$p(\boldsymbol{w} \mid \boldsymbol{X}, \boldsymbol{y}) \propto \exp\left(-\frac{1}{2}(\boldsymbol{w} - \boldsymbol{\mu}_m)^\top \boldsymbol{\Lambda}_m^{-1}(\boldsymbol{w} - \boldsymbol{\mu}_m) + \frac{1}{2}\boldsymbol{\mu}_m^\top \boldsymbol{\Lambda}_m^{-1}\boldsymbol{\mu}_m\right) \quad (5.77)$$

$$\propto \exp\left(-\frac{1}{2}(\boldsymbol{w} - \boldsymbol{\mu}_m)^\top \boldsymbol{\Lambda}_m^{-1}(\boldsymbol{w} - \boldsymbol{\mu}_m)\right). \quad (5.78)$$

All terms that do not include the parameter vector $\boldsymbol{w}$ have been omitted; they are implied by the fact that the distribution must be normalized to integrate to 1. Equation 3.23 shows how to normalize a multivariate Gaussian distribution.

Examining this posterior distribution enables us to gain some intuition for the effect of Bayesian inference. In most situations, we set $\boldsymbol{\mu}_0$ to $\boldsymbol{0}$. If we set $\boldsymbol{\Lambda}_0 = \frac{1}{\alpha}\boldsymbol{I}$, then $\boldsymbol{\mu}_m$ gives the same estimate of $\boldsymbol{w}$ as does frequentist linear regression with a weight decay penalty of $\alpha \boldsymbol{w}^\top \boldsymbol{w}$. One difference is that the Bayesian estimate is undefined if α is set to zero—we are not allowed to begin the Bayesian learning process with an infinitely wide prior on $\boldsymbol{w}$. The more important difference is that the Bayesian estimate provides a covariance matrix, showing how likely all the different values of $\boldsymbol{w}$ are, rather than providing only the estimate $\boldsymbol{\mu}_m$.

5.6.1 Maximum A Posteriori (MAP) Estimation

While the most principled approach is to make predictions using the full Bayesian posterior distribution over the parameter $\boldsymbol{\theta}$, it is still often desirable to have a single point estimate. One common reason for desiring a point estimate is that most operations involving the Bayesian posterior for most interesting models are intractable, and a point estimate offers a tractable approximation. Rather than simply returning to the maximum likelihood estimate, we can still gain some of the benefit of the Bayesian approach by allowing the prior to influence the choice of the point estimate. One rational way to do this is to choose the **maximum a posteriori** (MAP) point estimate. The MAP estimate chooses the point of maximal posterior probability (or maximal probability density in the more common case of continuous $\boldsymbol{\theta}$):

$$\boldsymbol{\theta}_{\text{MAP}} = \arg\max_{\boldsymbol{\theta}} p(\boldsymbol{\theta} \mid \boldsymbol{x}) = \arg\max_{\boldsymbol{\theta}} \log p(\boldsymbol{x} \mid \boldsymbol{\theta}) + \log p(\boldsymbol{\theta}). \quad (5.79)$$

We recognize, on the righthand side, $\log p(\boldsymbol{x} \mid \boldsymbol{\theta})$, that is, the standard log-likelihood term, and $\log p(\boldsymbol{\theta})$, corresponding to the prior distribution.

As an example, consider a linear regression model with a Gaussian prior on the weights $\boldsymbol{w}$. If this prior is given by $\mathcal{N}(\boldsymbol{w}; \boldsymbol{0}, \frac{1}{\lambda}\boldsymbol{I}^2)$, then the log-prior term in equation 5.79 is proportional to the familiar $\lambda \boldsymbol{w}^\top \boldsymbol{w}$ weight decay penalty, plus a term that does not depend on $\boldsymbol{w}$ and does not affect the learning process. MAP Bayesian inference with a Gaussian prior on the weights thus corresponds to weight decay.

As with full Bayesian inference, MAP Bayesian inference has the advantage of leveraging information that is brought by the prior and cannot be found in the training data. This additional information helps to reduce the variance in the MAP point estimate (in comparison to the ML estimate). However, it does so at the price of increased bias.

Many regularized estimation strategies, such as maximum likelihood learning regularized with weight decay, can be interpreted as making the MAP approximation to Bayesian inference. This view applies when the regularization consists of adding an extra term to the objective function that corresponds to $\log p(\boldsymbol{\theta})$. Not all regularization penalties correspond to MAP Bayesian inference. For example, some regularizer terms may not be the logarithm of a probability distribution. Other regularization terms depend on the data, which of course a prior probability distribution is not allowed to do.

MAP Bayesian inference provides a straightforward way to design complicated yet interpretable regularization terms. For example, a more complicated penalty term can be derived by using a mixture of Gaussians, rather than a single Gaussian distribution, as the prior (Nowlan and Hinton, 1992).

5.7 Supervised Learning Algorithms

Recall from section 5.1.3 that supervised learning algorithms are, roughly speaking, learning algorithms that learn to associate some input with some output, given a training set of examples of inputs $\boldsymbol{x}$ and outputs $\boldsymbol{y}$. In many cases the outputs $\boldsymbol{y}$ may be difficult to collect automatically and must be provided by a human "supervisor," but the term still applies even when the training set targets were collected automatically.

5.7.1 Probabilistic Supervised Learning

Most supervised learning algorithms in this book are based on estimating a probability distribution $p(y \mid \boldsymbol{x})$. We can do this simply by using maximum likelihood estimation to find the best parameter vector $\boldsymbol{\theta}$ for a parametric family of distributions $p(y \mid \boldsymbol{x}; \boldsymbol{\theta})$.

We have already seen that linear regression corresponds to the family

$$p(y \mid \boldsymbol{x}; \boldsymbol{\theta}) = \mathcal{N}(y; \boldsymbol{\theta}^\top \boldsymbol{x}, \boldsymbol{I}). \tag{5.80}$$

We can generalize linear regression to the classification scenario by defining a different family of probability distributions. If we have two classes, class 0 and class 1, then we need only specify the probability of one of these classes. The probability of class 1 determines the probability of class 0, because these two values must add up to 1.

The normal distribution over real-valued numbers that we used for linear regression is parametrized in terms of a mean. Any value we supply for this mean is valid. A distribution over a binary variable is slightly more complicated, because its mean must always be between 0 and 1. One way to solve this problem is to use the logistic sigmoid function to squash the output of the linear function into the interval (0, 1) and interpret that value as a probability:

$$p(y = 1 \mid \boldsymbol{x}; \boldsymbol{\theta}) = \sigma(\boldsymbol{\theta}^\top \boldsymbol{x}). \tag{5.81}$$

This approach is known as **logistic regression** (a somewhat strange name since we use the model for classification rather than regression).

In the case of linear regression, we were able to find the optimal weights by solving the normal equations. Logistic regression is somewhat more difficult. There is no closed-form solution for its optimal weights. Instead, we must search for them by maximizing the log-likelihood. We can do this by minimizing the negative log-likelihood using gradient descent.

This same strategy can be applied to essentially any supervised learning problem, by writing down a parametric family of conditional probability distributions over the right kind of input and output variables.

5.7.2 Support Vector Machines

One of the most influential approaches to supervised learning is the support vector machine (Boser et al., 1992; Cortes and Vapnik, 1995). This model is similar to logistic regression in that it is driven by a linear function $\boldsymbol{w}^\top \boldsymbol{x} + b$. Unlike logistic regression, the support vector machine does not provide probabilities, but only outputs a class identity. The SVM predicts that the positive class is present when $\boldsymbol{w}^\top \boldsymbol{x} + b$ is positive. Likewise, it predicts that the negative class is present when $\boldsymbol{w}^\top \boldsymbol{x} + b$ is negative.

One key innovation associated with support vector machines is the **kernel trick**. The kernel trick consists of observing that many machine learning algorithms can be written exclusively in terms of dot products between examples. For example, it can be shown that the linear function used by the support vector machine can be re-written as

$$\boldsymbol{w}^\top \boldsymbol{x} + b = b + \sum_{i=1}^{m} \alpha_i \boldsymbol{x}^\top \boldsymbol{x}^{(i)}, \qquad (5.82)$$

where $\boldsymbol{x}^{(i)}$ is a training example, and $\boldsymbol{\alpha}$ is a vector of coefficients. Rewriting the learning algorithm this way enables us to replace $\boldsymbol{x}$ with the output of a given feature function $\phi(\boldsymbol{x})$ and the dot product with a function $k(\boldsymbol{x}, \boldsymbol{x}^{(i)}) = \phi(\boldsymbol{x}) \cdot \phi(\boldsymbol{x}^{(i)})$ called a **kernel**. The $\cdot$ operator represents an inner product analogous to $\phi(\boldsymbol{x})^\top \phi(\boldsymbol{x}^{(i)})$. For some feature spaces, we may not use literally the vector inner product. In some infinite dimensional spaces, we need to use other kinds of inner products, for example, inner products based on integration rather than summation. A complete development of these kinds of inner products is beyond the scope of this book.

After replacing dot products with kernel evaluations, we can make predictions using the function

$$f(\boldsymbol{x}) = b + \sum_{i} \alpha_i k(\boldsymbol{x}, \boldsymbol{x}^{(i)}). \qquad (5.83)$$

This function is nonlinear with respect to $\boldsymbol{x}$, but the relationship between $\phi(\boldsymbol{x})$ and $f(\boldsymbol{x})$ is linear. Also, the relationship between $\boldsymbol{\alpha}$ and $f(\boldsymbol{x})$ is linear. The kernel-based function is exactly equivalent to preprocessing the data by applying $\phi(\boldsymbol{x})$ to all inputs, then learning a linear model in the new transformed space.

The kernel trick is powerful for two reasons. First, it enables us to learn models that are nonlinear as a function of $\boldsymbol{x}$ using convex optimization techniques that are guaranteed to converge efficiently. This is possible because we consider ϕ fixed and optimize only $\boldsymbol{\alpha}$, that is, the optimization algorithm can view the decision function as being linear in a different space. Second, the kernel function k often admits an implementation that is significantly more computationally efficient than naively constructing two $\phi(\boldsymbol{x})$ vectors and explicitly taking their dot product.

In some cases, $\phi(\boldsymbol{x})$ can even be infinite dimensional, which would result in an infinite computational cost for the naive, explicit approach. In many cases, $k(\boldsymbol{x}, \boldsymbol{x}')$ is a nonlinear, tractable function of $\boldsymbol{x}$ even when $\phi(\boldsymbol{x})$ is intractable. As an example of an infinite-dimensional feature space with a tractable kernel, we construct a feature mapping $\phi(x)$ over the nonnegative integers x. Suppose that this mapping returns a vector containing x ones followed by infinitely many zeros. We can write a kernel function $k(x, x^{(i)}) = \min(x, x^{(i)})$ that is exactly equivalent to the corresponding infinite-dimensional dot product.

The most commonly used kernel is the **Gaussian kernel**,

$$k(\boldsymbol{u}, \boldsymbol{v}) = \mathcal{N}(\boldsymbol{u} - \boldsymbol{v}; 0, \sigma^2 \boldsymbol{I}), \tag{5.84}$$

where $\mathcal{N}(\boldsymbol{x}; \boldsymbol{\mu}, \boldsymbol{\Sigma})$ is the standard normal density. This kernel is also known as the **radial basis function** (RBF) kernel, because its value decreases along lines in $\boldsymbol{v}$ space radiating outward from $\boldsymbol{u}$. The Gaussian kernel corresponds to a dot product in an infinite-dimensional space, but the derivation of this space is less straightforward than in our example of the min kernel over the integers.

We can think of the Gaussian kernel as performing a kind of **template matching**. A training example $\boldsymbol{x}$ associated with training label y becomes a template for class y. When a test point $\boldsymbol{x}'$ is near $\boldsymbol{x}$ according to Euclidean distance, the Gaussian kernel has a large response, indicating that $\boldsymbol{x}'$ is very similar to the $\boldsymbol{x}$ template. The model then puts a large weight on the associated training label y. Overall, the prediction will combine many such training labels weighted by the similarity of the corresponding training examples.

Support vector machines are not the only algorithm that can be enhanced using the kernel trick. Many other linear models can be enhanced in this way. The category of algorithms that employ the kernel trick is known as **kernel machines**, or **kernel methods** (Williams and Rasmussen, 1996; Schölkopf et al., 1999).

A major drawback to kernel machines is that the cost of evaluating the decision function is linear in the number of training examples, because the i-th example contributes a term $\alpha_i k(\boldsymbol{x}, \boldsymbol{x}^{(i)})$ to the decision function. Support vector machines are able to mitigate this by learning an $\boldsymbol{\alpha}$ vector that contains mostly zeros. Classifying a new example then requires evaluating the kernel function only for the training examples that have nonzero α_i. These training examples are known as **support vectors**.

Kernel machines also suffer from a high computational cost of training when the dataset is large. We revisit this idea in section 5.9. Kernel machines with generic kernels struggle to generalize well. We explain why in section 5.11. The modern incarnation of deep learning was designed to overcome these limitations of kernel machines. The current deep learning renaissance began when Hinton et al. (2006) demonstrated that a neural network could outperform the RBF kernel SVM on the MNIST benchmark.

5.7.3 Other Simple Supervised Learning Algorithms

We have already briefly encountered another nonprobabilistic supervised learning algorithm, nearest neighbor regression. More generally, k-nearest neighbors is a family of techniques that can be used for classification or regression. As a nonparametric learning algorithm, k-nearest neighbors is not restricted to a fixed number of parameters. We usually think of the k-nearest neighbors algorithm as not having any parameters but rather implementing a simple function of the training data. In fact, there is not even really a training stage or learning process. Instead, at test time, when we want to produce an output y for a new test input x, we find the k-nearest neighbors to x in the training data X. We then return the average of the corresponding y values in the training set. This works for essentially any kind of supervised learning where we can define an average over y values. In the case of classification, we can average over one-hot code vectors c with $c_y = 1$ and $c_i = 0$ for all other values of i. We can then interpret the average over these one-hot codes as giving a probability distribution over classes. As a nonparametric learning algorithm, k-nearest neighbor can achieve very high capacity. For example, suppose we have a multiclass classification task and measure performance with 0-1 loss. In this setting, 1-nearest neighbor converges to double the Bayes error as the number of training examples approaches infinity. The error in excess of the Bayes error results from choosing a single neighbor by breaking ties between equally distant neighbors randomly. When there is infinite training data, all test points x will have infinitely many training set neighbors at distance zero. If we allow the algorithm to use all these neighbors to vote, rather than randomly choosing one of them, the procedure converges to the Bayes error rate. The high capacity of k-nearest neighbors enables it to obtain high accuracy given a large training set. It does so at high computational cost, however, and it may generalize very badly given a small finite training set. One weakness of k-nearest neighbors is that it cannot learn that one feature is more discriminative than another. For example, imagine we have a regression task with $x \in \mathbb{R}^{100}$ drawn from an isotropic Gaussian distribution, but only a single variable x_1 is relevant to the output. Suppose further that this feature simply encodes the output directly, that $y = x_1$ in all cases. Nearest neighbor regression will not be able to detect this simple pattern. The nearest neighbor of most points x will be determined by the large number of features x_2 through x_{100}, not by the lone feature x_1. Thus the output on small training sets will essentially be random.

Another type of learning algorithm that also breaks the input space into regions and has separate parameters for each region is the **decision tree** (Breiman et al., 1984) and its many variants. As shown in figure 5.7, each node of the decision tree is associated with a region in the input space, and internal nodes break that region into one subregion for each child of the node (typically using an axis-aligned cut). Space is thus subdivided into nonoverlapping regions, with a one-to-one correspondence between leaf nodes and input regions. Each leaf node usually maps

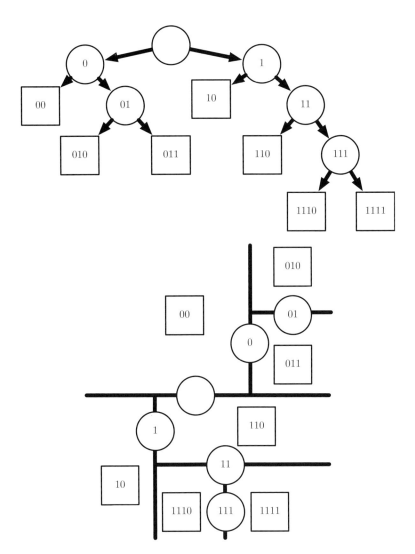

Figure 5.7: Diagrams describing how a decision tree works. *(Top)*Each node of the tree chooses to send the input example to the child node on the left (0) or to the child node on the right (1). Internal nodes are drawn as circles and leaf nodes as squares. Each node is displayed with a binary string identifier corresponding to its position in the tree, obtained by appending a bit to its parent identifier (0 = choose left or top, 1 = choose right or bottom). *(Bottom)*The tree divides space into regions. The 2-D plane shows how a decision tree might divide $\mathbb{R}^2$. The nodes of the tree are plotted in this plane, with each internal node drawn along the dividing line it uses to categorize examples, and leaf nodes drawn in the center of the region of examples they receive. The result is a piecewise-constant function, with one piece per leaf. Each leaf requires at least one training example to define, so it is not possible for the decision tree to learn a function that has more local maxima than the number of training examples.

every point in its input region to the same output. Decision trees are usually trained with specialized algorithms that are beyond the scope of this book. The learning algorithm can be considered nonparametric if it is allowed to learn a tree of arbitrary size, though decision trees are usually regularized with size constraints that turn them into parametric models in practice. Decision trees as they are typically used, with axis-aligned splits and constant outputs within each node, struggle to solve some problems that are easy even for logistic regression. For example, if we have a two-class problem, and the positive class occurs wherever $x_2 > x_1$, the decision boundary is not axis aligned. The decision tree will thus need to approximate the decision boundary with many nodes, implementing a step function that constantly walks back and forth across the true decision function with axis-aligned steps.

As we have seen, nearest neighbor predictors and decision trees have many limitations. Nonetheless, they are useful learning algorithms when computational resources are constrained. We can also build intuition for more sophisticated learning algorithms by thinking about the similarities and differences between sophisticated algorithms and k-nearest neighbors or decision tree baselines.

See Murphy (2012), Bishop (2006), Hastie et al. (2001) or other machine learning textbooks for more material on traditional supervised learning algorithms.

5.8 Unsupervised Learning Algorithms

Recall from section 5.1.3 that unsupervised algorithms are those that experience only "features" but not a supervision signal. The distinction between supervised and unsupervised algorithms is not formally and rigidly defined because there is no objective test for distinguishing whether a value is a feature or a target provided by a supervisor. Informally, unsupervised learning refers to most attempts to extract information from a distribution that do not require human labor to annotate examples. The term is usually associated with density estimation, learning to draw samples from a distribution, learning to denoise data from some distribution, finding a manifold that the data lies near, or clustering the data into groups of related examples.

A classic unsupervised learning task is to find the "best" representation of the data. By "best" we can mean different things, but generally speaking we are looking for a representation that preserves as much information about x as possible while obeying some penalty or constraint aimed at keeping the representation *simpler* or more accessible than x itself.

There are multiple ways of defining a simpler representation. Three of the most common include lower-dimensional representations, sparse representations, and independent representations. Low-dimensional representations attempt to compress as much information about x as possible in a smaller representation. Sparse representations (Barlow, 1989; Olshausen and Field, 1996; Hinton and Ghahramani, 1997) embed the dataset into a representation whose entries are mostly zeros for most inputs. The use of sparse representations typically requires increasing the dimensionality of the representation, so that the representation becoming mostly zeros does not discard too much information. This results in an overall structure of the representation that tends to distribute data along the axes of the representation space. Independent representations attempt to *disentangle* the sources of variation underlying the data distribution such that the dimensions of the representation are statistically independent.

Of course these three criteria are certainly not mutually exclusive. Low-dimensional representations often yield elements that have fewer or weaker dependencies than the original high-dimensional data. This is because one way to reduce the size of a representation is to find and remove redundancies. Identifying and removing more redundancy enables the dimensionality reduction algorithm to achieve more compression while discarding less information.

The notion of representation is one of the central themes of deep learning and therefore one of the central themes in this book. In this section, we develop some simple examples of representation learning algorithms. Together, these example algorithms show how to operationalize all three of the criteria above. Most of the remaining chapters introduce additional representation learning algorithms that develop these criteria in different ways or introduce other criteria.

5.8.1 Principal Components Analysis

In section 2.12, we saw that the principal components analysis algorithm provides a means of compressing data. We can also view PCA as an unsupervised learning algorithm that learns a representation of data. This representation is based on two of the criteria for a simple representation described above. PCA learns a representation that has lower dimensionality than the original input. It also learns a representation whose elements have no linear correlation with each other. This is a first step toward the criterion of learning representations whose elements are statistically independent. To achieve full independence, a representation learning algorithm must also remove the nonlinear relationships between variables.

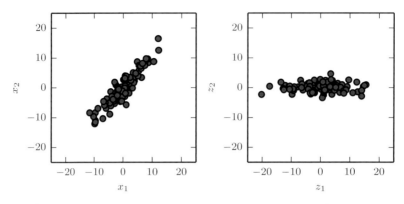

Figure 5.8: PCA learns a linear projection that aligns the direction of greatest variance with the axes of the new space. *(Left)*The original data consist of samples of $\boldsymbol{x}$. In this space, the variance might occur along directions that are not axis aligned. *(Right)*The transformed data $\boldsymbol{z} = \boldsymbol{x}^\top \boldsymbol{W}$ now varies most along the axis z_1. The direction of second-most variance is now along z_2.

PCA learns an orthogonal, linear transformation of the data that projects an input $\boldsymbol{x}$ to a representation $\boldsymbol{z}$ as shown in figure 5.8. In section 2.12, we saw that we could learn a one-dimensional representation that best reconstructs the original data (in the sense of mean squared error) and that this representation actually corresponds to the first principal component of the data. Thus we can use PCA as a simple and effective dimensionality reduction method that preserves as much of the information in the data as possible (again, as measured by least-squares reconstruction error). In the following, we will study how the PCA representation decorrelates the original data representation $\boldsymbol{X}$.

Let us consider the $m \times n$ design matrix $\boldsymbol{X}$. We will assume that the data has a mean of zero, $\mathbb{E}[\boldsymbol{x}] = \boldsymbol{0}$. If this is not the case, the data can easily be centered by subtracting the mean from all examples in a preprocessing step.

The unbiased sample covariance matrix associated with $\boldsymbol{X}$ is given by

$$\text{Var}[\boldsymbol{x}] = \frac{1}{m-1}\boldsymbol{X}^\top\boldsymbol{X}. \tag{5.85}$$

PCA finds a representation (through linear transformation) $\boldsymbol{z} = \boldsymbol{W}^\top x$, where $\text{Var}[\boldsymbol{z}]$ is diagonal.

In section 2.12, we saw that the principal components of a design matrix $\boldsymbol{X}$ are given by the eigenvectors of $\boldsymbol{X}^\top\boldsymbol{X}$. From this view,

$$\boldsymbol{X}^\top\boldsymbol{X} = \boldsymbol{W}\boldsymbol{\Lambda}\boldsymbol{W}^\top. \tag{5.86}$$

In this section, we exploit an alternative derivation of the principal components. The principal components may also be obtained via singular value decomposition (SVD). Specifically, they are the right singular vectors of $\boldsymbol{X}$. To see this, let $\boldsymbol{W}$ be the right singular vectors in the decomposition $\boldsymbol{X} = \boldsymbol{U\Sigma W}^\top$. We then recover the original eigenvector equation with $\boldsymbol{W}$ as the eigenvector basis:

$$\boldsymbol{X}^\top\boldsymbol{X} = \left(\boldsymbol{U\Sigma W}^\top\right)^\top \boldsymbol{U\Sigma W}^\top = \boldsymbol{W\Sigma}^2\boldsymbol{W}^\top. \tag{5.87}$$

The SVD is helpful to show that PCA results in a diagonal $\mathrm{Var}[z]$. Using the SVD of $\boldsymbol{X}$, we can express the variance of $\boldsymbol{X}$ as:

$$\mathrm{Var}[\boldsymbol{x}] = \frac{1}{m-1}\boldsymbol{X}^\top\boldsymbol{X} \tag{5.88}$$

$$= \frac{1}{m-1}(\boldsymbol{U\Sigma W}^\top)^\top\boldsymbol{U\Sigma W}^\top \tag{5.89}$$

$$= \frac{1}{m-1}\boldsymbol{W\Sigma}^\top\boldsymbol{U}^\top\boldsymbol{U\Sigma W}^\top \tag{5.90}$$

$$= \frac{1}{m-1}\boldsymbol{W\Sigma}^2\boldsymbol{W}^\top, \tag{5.91}$$

where we use the fact that $\boldsymbol{U}^\top\boldsymbol{U} = \boldsymbol{I}$ because the $\boldsymbol{U}$ matrix of the singular value decomposition is defined to be orthogonal. This shows that the covariance of $\boldsymbol{z}$ is diagonal as required:

$$\mathrm{Var}[\boldsymbol{z}] = \frac{1}{m-1}\boldsymbol{Z}^\top\boldsymbol{Z} \tag{5.92}$$

$$= \frac{1}{m-1}\boldsymbol{W}^\top\boldsymbol{X}^\top\boldsymbol{X}\boldsymbol{W} \tag{5.93}$$

$$= \frac{1}{m-1}\boldsymbol{W}^\top\boldsymbol{W\Sigma}^2\boldsymbol{W}^\top\boldsymbol{W} \tag{5.94}$$

$$= \frac{1}{m-1}\boldsymbol{\Sigma}^2, \tag{5.95}$$

where this time we use the fact that $\boldsymbol{W}^\top\boldsymbol{W} = \boldsymbol{I}$, again from the definition of the SVD.

The above analysis shows that when we project the data $\boldsymbol{x}$ to $\boldsymbol{z}$, via the linear transformation $\boldsymbol{W}$, the resulting representation has a diagonal covariance matrix (as given by $\boldsymbol{\Sigma}^2$), which immediately implies that the individual elements of $\boldsymbol{z}$ are mutually uncorrelated.

This ability of PCA to transform data into a representation where the elements are mutually uncorrelated is a very important property of PCA. It is a simple example of a representation that attempts to *disentangle the unknown factors of variation* underlying the data. In the case of PCA, this disentangling takes the form of finding a rotation of the input space (described by $\boldsymbol{W}$) that aligns the principal axes of variance with the basis of the new representation space associated with $\boldsymbol{z}$.

While correlation is an important category of dependency between elements of the data, we are also interested in learning representations that disentangle more complicated forms of feature dependencies. For this, we will need more than what can be done with a simple linear transformation.

5.8.2 k-means Clustering

Another example of a simple representation learning algorithm is k-means clustering. The k-means clustering algorithm divides the training set into k different clusters of examples that are near each other. We can thus think of the algorithm as providing a k-dimensional one-hot code vector $\boldsymbol{h}$ representing an input $\boldsymbol{x}$. If $\boldsymbol{x}$ belongs to cluster i, then $h_i = 1$, and all other entries of the representation $\boldsymbol{h}$ are zero.

The one-hot code provided by k-means clustering is an example of a sparse representation, because the majority of its entries are zero for every input. Later, we develop other algorithms that learn more flexible sparse representations, where more than one entry can be nonzero for each input $\boldsymbol{x}$. One-hot codes are an extreme example of sparse representations that lose many of the benefits of a distributed representation. The one-hot code still confers some statistical advantages (it naturally conveys the idea that all examples in the same cluster are similar to each other), and it confers the computational advantage that the entire representation may be captured by a single integer.

The k-means algorithm works by initializing k different centroids $\{\boldsymbol{\mu}^{(1)}, \ldots, \boldsymbol{\mu}^{(k)}\}$ to different values, then alternating between two different steps until convergence. In one step, each training example is assigned to cluster i, where i is the index of the nearest centroid $\boldsymbol{\mu}^{(i)}$. In the other step, each centroid $\boldsymbol{\mu}^{(i)}$ is updated to the mean of all training examples $\boldsymbol{x}^{(j)}$ assigned to cluster i.

One difficulty pertaining to clustering is that the clustering problem is inherently ill posed, in the sense that there is no single criterion that measures how well a clustering of the data corresponds to the real world. We can measure properties of the clustering, such as the average Euclidean distance from a cluster centroid to the members of the cluster. This enables us to tell how well we are able to reconstruct the training data from the cluster assignments. We do not know how well the cluster assignments correspond to properties of the real world. Moreover, there may be many different clusterings that all correspond well to some property of the real world. We may hope to find a clustering that relates to one feature but obtain a different, equally valid clustering that is not relevant to our task. For example, suppose that we run two clustering algorithms on a dataset consisting of images of red trucks, images of red cars, images of gray trucks, and images of gray cars. If we ask each clustering algorithm to find two clusters, one algorithm may find a cluster of cars and a cluster of trucks, while another may find a cluster of red vehicles and a cluster of gray vehicles. Suppose we also run a third clustering algorithm, which is allowed to determine the number of clusters. This may assign the examples to four clusters, red cars, red trucks, gray cars, and gray trucks. This new clustering now at least captures information about both attributes, but it has lost information about similarity. Red cars are in a different cluster from gray cars, just as they are in a different cluster from gray trucks. The output of the clustering algorithm does not tell us that red cars are more similar to gray cars than they are to gray trucks. They are different from both things, and that is all we know.

These issues illustrate some of the reasons that we may prefer a distributed representation to a one-hot representation. A distributed representation could have two attributes for each vehicle—one representing its color and one representing whether it is a car or a truck. It is still not entirely clear what the optimal distributed representation is (how can the learning algorithm know whether the two attributes we are interested in are color and car-versus-truck rather than manufacturer and age?), but having many attributes reduces the burden on the algorithm to guess which single attribute we care about, and gives us the ability to measure similarity between objects in a fine-grained way by comparing many attributes instead of just testing whether one attribute matches.

5.9 Stochastic Gradient Descent

Nearly all of deep learning is powered by one very important algorithm: **stochastic gradient descent** (SGD). Stochastic gradient descent is an extension of the gradient descent algorithm introduced in section 4.3.

A recurring problem in machine learning is that large training sets are necessary for good generalization, but large training sets are also more computationally expensive.

The cost function used by a machine learning algorithm often decomposes as a sum over training examples of some per-example loss function. For example, the negative conditional log-likelihood of the training data can be written as

$$J(\boldsymbol{\theta}) = \mathbb{E}_{\mathbf{x},\mathbf{y} \sim \hat{p}_{\text{data}}} L(\boldsymbol{x}, y, \boldsymbol{\theta}) = \frac{1}{m} \sum_{i=1}^{m} L(\boldsymbol{x}^{(i)}, y^{(i)}, \boldsymbol{\theta}), \qquad (5.96)$$

where L is the per-example loss $L(\boldsymbol{x}, y, \boldsymbol{\theta}) = -\log p(y \mid \boldsymbol{x}; \boldsymbol{\theta})$.

For these additive cost functions, gradient descent requires computing

$$\nabla_{\boldsymbol{\theta}} J(\boldsymbol{\theta}) = \frac{1}{m} \sum_{i=1}^{m} \nabla_{\boldsymbol{\theta}} L(\boldsymbol{x}^{(i)}, y^{(i)}, \boldsymbol{\theta}). \qquad (5.97)$$

The computational cost of this operation is $O(m)$. As the training set size grows to billions of examples, the time to take a single gradient step becomes prohibitively long.

The insight of SGD is that the gradient is an expectation. The expectation may be approximately estimated using a small set of samples. Specifically, on each step of the algorithm, we can sample a **minibatch** of examples $\mathbb{B} = \{\boldsymbol{x}^{(1)}, \ldots, \boldsymbol{x}^{(m')}\}$ drawn uniformly from the training set. The minibatch size m' is typically chosen to be a relatively small number of examples, ranging from one to a few hundred. Crucially, m' is usually held fixed as the training set size m grows. We may fit a training set with billions of examples using updates computed on only a hundred examples.

The estimate of the gradient is formed as

$$\boldsymbol{g} = \frac{1}{m'} \nabla_{\boldsymbol{\theta}} \sum_{i=1}^{m'} L(\boldsymbol{x}^{(i)}, y^{(i)}, \boldsymbol{\theta}) \qquad (5.98)$$

using examples from the minibatch $\mathbb{B}$. The stochastic gradient descent algorithm then follows the estimated gradient downhill:

$$\boldsymbol{\theta} \leftarrow \boldsymbol{\theta} - \epsilon \boldsymbol{g}, \qquad (5.99)$$

where ϵ is the learning rate.

Gradient descent in general has often been regarded as slow or unreliable. In the past, the application of gradient descent to nonconvex optimization problems was regarded as foolhardy or unprincipled. Today, we know that the machine learning models described in part II work very well when trained with gradient descent. The optimization algorithm may not be guaranteed to arrive at even a local minimum in a reasonable amount of time, but it often finds a very low value of the cost function quickly enough to be useful.

Stochastic gradient descent has many important uses outside the context of deep learning. It is the main way to train large linear models on very large datasets. For a fixed model size, the cost per SGD update does not depend on the training set size m. In practice, we often use a larger model as the training set size increases, but we are not forced to do so. The number of updates required to reach convergence usually increases with training set size. However, as m approaches infinity, the model will eventually converge to its best possible test error before SGD has sampled every example in the training set. Increasing m further will not extend the amount of training time needed to reach the model's best possible test error. From this point of view, one can argue that the asymptotic cost of training a model with SGD is $O(1)$ as a function of m.

Prior to the advent of deep learning, the main way to learn nonlinear models was to use the kernel trick in combination with a linear model. Many kernel learning algorithms require constructing an $m \times m$ matrix $G_{i,j} = k(\boldsymbol{x}^{(i)}, \boldsymbol{x}^{(j)})$. Constructing this matrix has computational cost $O(m^2)$, which is clearly undesirable for datasets with billions of examples. In academia, starting in 2006, deep learning was initially interesting because it was able to generalize to new examples better than competing algorithms when trained on medium-sized datasets with tens of thousands of examples. Soon after, deep learning garnered additional interest in industry because it provided a scalable way of training nonlinear models on large datasets.

Stochastic gradient descent and many enhancements to it are described further in chapter 8.

5.10 Building a Machine Learning Algorithm

Nearly all deep learning algorithms can be described as particular instances of a fairly simple recipe: combine a specification of a dataset, a cost function, an optimization procedure and a model.

For example, the linear regression algorithm combines a dataset consisting of $\boldsymbol{X}$ and $\boldsymbol{y}$, the cost function

$$J(\boldsymbol{w}, b) = -\mathbb{E}_{\mathbf{x}, \mathbf{y} \sim \hat{p}_{\text{data}}} \log p_{\text{model}}(y \mid \boldsymbol{x}), \qquad (5.100)$$

the model specification $p_{\text{model}}(y \mid \boldsymbol{x}) = \mathcal{N}(y; \boldsymbol{x}^\top \boldsymbol{w} + b, 1)$, and, in most cases, the optimization algorithm defined by solving for where the gradient of the cost is zero using the normal equations.

By realizing that we can replace any of these components mostly independently from the others, we can obtain a wide range of algorithms.

The cost function typically includes at least one term that causes the learning process to perform statistical estimation. The most common cost function is the negative log-likelihood, so that minimizing the cost function causes maximum likelihood estimation.

The cost function may also include additional terms, such as regularization terms. For example, we can add weight decay to the linear regression cost function to obtain

$$J(\boldsymbol{w}, b) = \lambda ||\boldsymbol{w}||_2^2 - \mathbb{E}_{\mathrm{x,y} \sim \hat{p}_{\mathrm{data}}} \log p_{\mathrm{model}}(y \mid \boldsymbol{x}).$$ (5.101)

This still allows closed form optimization.

If we change the model to be nonlinear, then most cost functions can no longer be optimized in closed form. This requires us to choose an iterative numerical optimization procedure, such as gradient descent.

The recipe for constructing a learning algorithm by combining models, costs, and optimization algorithms supports both supervised and unsupervised learning. The linear regression example shows how to support supervised learning. Unsupervised learning can be supported by defining a dataset that contains only $\boldsymbol{X}$ and providing an appropriate unsupervised cost and model. For example, we can obtain the first PCA vector by specifying that our loss function is

$$J(\boldsymbol{w}) = \mathbb{E}_{\mathrm{x} \sim \hat{p}_{\mathrm{data}}} ||\boldsymbol{x} - r(\boldsymbol{x}; \boldsymbol{w})||_2^2$$ (5.102)

while our model is defined to have $\boldsymbol{w}$ with norm one and reconstruction function $r(\boldsymbol{x}) = \boldsymbol{w}^\top \boldsymbol{x} \boldsymbol{w}$.

In some cases, the cost function may be a function that we cannot actually evaluate, for computational reasons. In these cases, we can still approximately minimize it using iterative numerical optimization, as long as we have some way of approximating its gradients.

Most machine learning algorithms make use of this recipe, though it may not be immediately obvious. If a machine learning algorithm seems especially unique or hand designed, it can usually be understood as using a special-case optimizer. Some models, such as decision trees and k-means, require special-case optimizers because their cost functions have flat regions that make them inappropriate for minimization by gradient-based optimizers. Recognizing that most machine learning algorithms can be described using this recipe helps to see the different algorithms as part of a taxonomy of methods for doing related tasks that work for similar reasons, rather than as a long list of algorithms that each have separate justifications.

5.11 Challenges Motivating Deep Learning

The simple machine learning algorithms described in this chapter work well on a wide variety of important problems. They have not succeeded, however, in solving the central problems in AI, such as recognizing speech or recognizing objects.

The development of deep learning was motivated in part by the failure of traditional algorithms to generalize well on such AI tasks.

This section is about how the challenge of generalizing to new examples becomes exponentially more difficult when working with high-dimensional data, and how the mechanisms used to achieve generalization in traditional machine learning are insufficient to learn complicated functions in high-dimensional spaces. Such spaces also often impose high computational costs. Deep learning was designed to overcome these and other obstacles.

5.11.1 The Curse of Dimensionality

Many machine learning problems become exceedingly difficult when the number of dimensions in the data is high. This phenomenon is known as the **curse of dimensionality**. Of particular concern is that the number of possible distinct configurations of a set of variables increases exponentially as the number of variables increases.

The curse of dimensionality arises in many places in computer science, especially in machine learning.

One challenge posed by the curse of dimensionality is a statistical challenge. As illustrated in figure 5.9, a statistical challenge arises because the number of possible configurations of x is much larger than the number of training examples. To understand the issue, let us consider that the input space is organized into a grid, as in the figure. We can describe low-dimensional space with a small number of grid cells that are mostly occupied by the data. When generalizing to a new data point, we can usually tell what to do simply by inspecting the training examples that lie in the same cell as the new input. For example, if estimating the probability density at some point x, we can just return the number of training examples in the same unit volume cell as x, divided by the total number of training examples. If we wish to classify an example, we can return the most common class of training examples in the same cell. If we are doing regression, we can average the target values observed over the examples in that cell. But what about the cells for which we have seen no example? Because in high-dimensional spaces, the number of configurations is huge, much larger than our number of examples, a typical grid cell

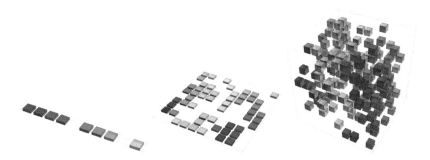

Figure 5.9: As the number of relevant dimensions of the data increases (from left to right), the number of configurations of interest may grow exponentially. *(Left)*In this one-dimensional example, we have one variable for which we only care to distinguish 10 regions of interest. With enough examples falling within each of these regions (each region corresponds to a cell in the illustration), learning algorithms can easily generalize correctly. A straightforward way to generalize is to estimate the value of the target function within each region (and possibly interpolate between neighboring regions). *(Center)*With two dimensions, it is more difficult to distinguish 10 different values of each variable. We need to keep track of up to $10 \times 10 = 100$ regions, and we need at least that many examples to cover all those regions. *(Right)*With three dimensions, this grows to $10^3 = 1,000$ regions and at least that many examples. For d dimensions and v values to be distinguished along each axis, we seem to need $O(v^d)$ regions and examples. This is an instance of the curse of dimensionality. Figure graciously provided by Nicolas Chapados.

has no training example associated with it. How could we possibly say something meaningful about these new configurations? Many traditional machine learning algorithms simply assume that the output at a new point should be approximately the same as the output at the nearest training point.

5.11.2 Local Constancy and Smoothness Regularization

To generalize well, machine learning algorithms need to be guided by prior beliefs about what kind of function they should learn. We have seen these priors incorporated as explicit beliefs in the form of probability distributions over parameters of the model. More informally, we may also discuss prior beliefs as directly influencing the *function* itself and influencing the parameters only indirectly, as a result of the relationship between the parameters and the function. Additionally, we informally discuss prior beliefs as being expressed implicitly by choosing algorithms that are biased toward choosing some class of functions over another, even though these biases may not be expressed (or even be possible to express) in terms of a probability distribution representing our degree of belief in various functions.

Among the most widely used of these implicit "priors" is the **smoothness prior**, or **local constancy prior**. This prior states that the function we learn should not change very much within a small region.

Many simpler algorithms rely exclusively on this prior to generalize well, and as a result, they fail to scale to the statistical challenges involved in solving AI-level tasks. Throughout this book, we describe how deep learning introduces additional (explicit and implicit) priors in order to reduce the generalization error on sophisticated tasks. Here, we explain why the smoothness prior alone is insufficient for these tasks.

There are many different ways to implicitly or explicitly express a prior belief that the learned function should be smooth or locally constant. All these different methods are designed to encourage the learning process to learn a function f^* that satisfies the condition

$$f^*(\boldsymbol{x}) \approx f^*(\boldsymbol{x} + \epsilon) \tag{5.103}$$

for most configurations $\boldsymbol{x}$ and small change ϵ. In other words, if we know a good answer for an input $\boldsymbol{x}$ (for example, if $\boldsymbol{x}$ is a labeled training example), then that answer is probably good in the neighborhood of $\boldsymbol{x}$. If we have several good answers in some neighborhood, we would combine them (by some form of averaging or interpolation) to produce an answer that agrees with as many of them as much as possible.

An extreme example of the local constancy approach is the k-nearest neighbors family of learning algorithms. These predictors are literally constant over each region containing all the points $\boldsymbol{x}$ that have the same set of k nearest neighbors in the training set. For $k = 1$, the number of distinguishable regions cannot be more than the number of training examples.

While the k-nearest neighbors algorithm copies the output from nearby training examples, most kernel machines interpolate between training set outputs associated with nearby training examples. An important class of kernels is the family of **local kernels**, where $k(\boldsymbol{u}, \boldsymbol{v})$ is large when $\boldsymbol{u} = \boldsymbol{v}$ and decreases as $\boldsymbol{u}$ and $\boldsymbol{v}$ grow further apart from each other. A local kernel can be thought of as a similarity function that performs template matching, by measuring how closely a test example $\boldsymbol{x}$ resembles each training example $\boldsymbol{x}^{(i)}$. Much of the modern motivation for deep learning is derived from studying the limitations of local template matching and how deep models are able to succeed in cases where local template matching fails (Bengio et al., 2006b).

Decision trees also suffer from the limitations of exclusively smoothness-based learning, because they break the input space into as many regions as there are leaves and use a separate parameter (or sometimes many parameters for extensions of decision trees) in each region. If the target function requires a tree with at least n leaves to be represented accurately, then at least n training examples are required to fit the tree. A multiple of n is needed to achieve some level of statistical confidence in the predicted output.

In general, to distinguish $O(k)$ regions in input space, all these methods require $O(k)$ examples. Typically there are $O(k)$ parameters, with $O(1)$ parameters associated with each of the $O(k)$ regions. The nearest neighbor scenario, in which each training example can be used to define at most one region, is illustrated in figure 5.10.

Is there a way to represent a complex function that has many more regions to be distinguished than the number of training examples? Clearly, assuming only smoothness of the underlying function will not allow a learner to do that. For example, imagine that the target function is a kind of checkerboard. A checkerboard contains many variations, but there is a simple structure to them. Imagine what happens when the number of training examples is substantially smaller than the number of black and white squares on the checkerboard. Based on only local generalization and the smoothness or local constancy prior, the learner would be

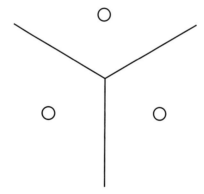

Figure 5.10: Illustration of how the nearest neighbor algorithm breaks up the input space into regions. An example (represented here by a circle) within each region defines the region boundary (represented here by the lines). The y value associated with each example defines what the output should be for all points within the corresponding region. The regions defined by nearest neighbor matching form a geometric pattern called a Voronoi diagram. The number of these contiguous regions cannot grow faster than the number of training examples. While this figure illustrates the behavior of the nearest neighbor algorithm specifically, other machine learning algorithms that rely exclusively on the local smoothness prior for generalization exhibit similar behaviors: each training example only informs the learner about how to generalize in some neighborhood immediately surrounding that example.

guaranteed to correctly guess the color of a new point if it lay within the same checkerboard square as a training example. There is no guarantee, however, that the learner could correctly extend the checkerboard pattern to points lying in squares that do not contain training examples. With this prior alone, the only information that an example tells us is the color of its square, and the only way to get the colors of the entire checkerboard right is to cover each of its cells with at least one example.

The smoothness assumption and the associated nonparametric learning algorithms work extremely well as long as there are enough examples for the learning algorithm to observe high points on most peaks and low points on most valleys of the true underlying function to be learned. This is generally true when the function to be learned is smooth enough and varies in few enough dimensions. In high dimensions, even a very smooth function can change smoothly but in a different way along each dimension. If the function additionally behaves differently in various regions, it can become extremely complicated to describe with a set of training examples. If the function is complicated (we want to distinguish a huge number of regions compared to the number of examples), is there any hope to generalize well?

The answer to both of these questions—whether it is possible to represent a complicated function efficiently, and whether it is possible for the estimated function to generalize well to new inputs—is yes. The key insight is that a very large number of regions, such as $O(2^k)$, can be defined with $O(k)$ examples, so long as we introduce some dependencies between the regions through additional assumptions about the underlying data-generating distribution. In this way, we can actually generalize nonlocally (Bengio and Monperrus, 2005; Bengio et al., 2006c). Many different deep learning algorithms provide implicit or explicit assumptions that are reasonable for a broad range of AI tasks in order to capture these advantages.

Other approaches to machine learning often make stronger, task-specific assumptions. For example, we could easily solve the checkerboard task by providing the assumption that the target function is periodic. Usually we do not include such strong, task-specific assumptions in neural networks so that they can generalize to a much wider variety of structures. AI tasks have structure that is much too complex to be limited to simple, manually specified properties such as periodicity, so we want learning algorithms that embody more general-purpose assumptions. The core idea in deep learning is that we assume that the data was generated by the *composition of factors*, or features, potentially at multiple levels in a hierarchy. Many other similarly generic assumptions can further improve deep learning algorithms. These apparently mild assumptions allow an exponential gain in the relationship between the number of examples and the number of regions that can be distinguished. We describe these exponential gains more precisely in sections 6.4.1, 15.4 and 15.5. The exponential advantages conferred by the use of deep distributed representations counter the exponential challenges posed by the curse of dimensionality.

5.11.3 Manifold Learning

An important concept underlying many ideas in machine learning is that of a manifold.

A **manifold** is a connected region. Mathematically, it is a set of points associated with a neighborhood around each point. From any given point, the manifold locally appears to be a Euclidean space. In everyday life, we experience the surface of the world as a 2-D plane, but it is in fact a spherical manifold in 3-D space.

The concept of a neighborhood surrounding each point implies the existence of transformations that can be applied to move on the manifold from one position to a neighboring one. In the example of the world's surface as a manifold, one can walk north, south, east, or west.

Although there is a formal mathematical meaning to the term "manifold," in machine learning it tends to be used more loosely to designate a connected set of points that can be approximated well by considering only a small number of degrees of freedom, or dimensions, embedded in a higher-dimensional space. Each dimension corresponds to a local direction of variation. See figure 5.11 for an example of training data lying near a one-dimensional manifold embedded in two-dimensional space. In the context of machine learning, we allow the dimensionality of the manifold to vary from one point to another. This often happens when a manifold intersects itself. For example, a figure eight is a manifold that has a single dimension in most places but two dimensions at the intersection at the center.

Many machine learning problems seem hopeless if we expect the machine learning algorithm to learn functions with interesting variations across all of $\mathbb{R}^n$. **Manifold learning** algorithms surmount this obstacle by assuming that most of $\mathbb{R}^n$ consists of invalid inputs, and that interesting inputs occur only along a collection of manifolds containing a small subset of points, with interesting variations in the output of the learned function occurring only along directions that lie on the manifold, or with interesting variations happening only when we move from one manifold to another. Manifold learning was introduced in the case of continuous-valued data and in the unsupervised learning setting, although this probability concentration idea can be generalized to both discrete data and the

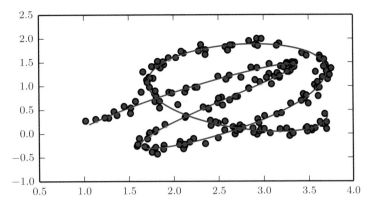

Figure 5.11: Data sampled from a distribution in a two-dimensional space that is actually concentrated near a one-dimensional manifold, like a twisted string. The solid line indicates the underlying manifold that the learner should infer.

supervised learning setting: the key assumption remains that probability mass is highly concentrated.

The assumption that the data lies along a low-dimensional manifold may not always be correct or useful. We argue that in the context of AI tasks, such as those that involve processing images, sounds, or text, the manifold assumption is at least approximately correct. The evidence in favor of this assumption consists of two categories of observations.

The first observation in favor of the **manifold hypothesis** is that the probability distribution over images, text strings, and sounds that occur in real life is highly concentrated. Uniform noise essentially never resembles structured inputs from these domains. Figure 5.12 shows how, instead, uniformly sampled points look like the patterns of static that appear on analog television sets when no signal is available. Similarly, if you generate a document by picking letters uniformly at random, what is the probability that you will get a meaningful English-language text? Almost zero, again, because most of the long sequences of letters do not correspond to a natural language sequence: the distribution of natural language sequences occupies a very little volume in the total space of sequences of letters.

Of course, concentrated probability distributions are not sufficient to show that the data lies on a reasonably small number of manifolds. We must also establish that the examples we encounter are connected to each other by other examples, with each example surrounded by other highly similar examples that can be reached by applying transformations to traverse the manifold. The second argument in favor of the manifold hypothesis is that we can imagine such neighborhoods and

Figure 5.12: Sampling images uniformly at random (by randomly picking each pixel according to a uniform distribution) gives rise to noisy images. Although there is a nonzero probability of generating an image of a face or of any other object frequently encountered in AI applications, we never actually observe this happening in practice. This suggests that the images encountered in AI applications occupy a negligible proportion of the volume of image space.

transformations, at least informally. In the case of images, we can certainly think of many possible transformations that allow us to trace out a manifold in image space: we can gradually dim or brighten the lights, gradually move or rotate objects in the image, gradually alter the colors on the surfaces of objects, and so forth. Multiple manifolds are likely involved in most applications. For example, the manifold of human face images may not be connected to the manifold of cat face images.

These thought experiments convey some intuitive reasons supporting the manifold hypothesis. More rigorous experiments (Cayton, 2005; Narayanan and Mitter, 2010; Schölkopf et al., 1998; Roweis and Saul, 2000; Tenenbaum et al., 2000; Brand, 2003; Belkin and Niyogi, 2003; Donoho and Grimes, 2003; Weinberger and Saul, 2004) clearly support the hypothesis for a large class of datasets of interest in AI.

When the data lies on a low-dimensional manifold, it can be most natural for machine learning algorithms to represent the data in terms of coordinates on the manifold, rather than in terms of coordinates in $\mathbb{R}^n$. In everyday life, we can think of roads as 1-D manifolds embedded in 3-D space. We give directions to specific addresses in terms of address numbers along these 1-D roads, not in terms of coordinates in 3-D space. Extracting these manifold coordinates is challenging but holds the promise of improving many machine learning algorithms. This general principle is applied in many contexts. Figure 5.13 shows the manifold structure of a dataset consisting of faces. By the end of this book, we will have developed the methods necessary to learn such a manifold structure. In figure 20.6, we will see how a machine learning algorithm can successfully accomplish this goal.

This concludes part I, which has provided the basic concepts in mathematics and machine learning that are employed throughout the remaining parts of the book. You are now prepared to embark on your study of deep learning.

Figure 5.13: Training examples from the QMUL Multiview Face Dataset (Gong et al., 2000), for which the subjects were asked to move in such a way as to cover the two-dimensional manifold corresponding to two angles of rotation. We would like learning algorithms to be able to discover and disentangle such manifold coordinates. Figure 20.6 illustrates such a feat.

II

Deep Networks: Modern Practices

This part of the book summarizes the state of modern deep learning as it is used to solve practical applications.

Deep learning has a long history and many aspirations. Several proposed approaches have yet to entirely bear fruit. Several ambitious goals have yet to be realized. These less-developed branches of deep learning appear in the final part of the book.

This part focuses only on those approaches that are essentially working technologies that are already used heavily in industry.

Modern deep learning provides a powerful framework for supervised learning. By adding more layers and more units within a layer, a deep network can represent functions of increasing complexity. Most tasks that consist of mapping an input vector to an output vector, and that are easy for a person to do rapidly, can be accomplished via deep learning, given sufficiently large models and sufficiently large datasets of labeled training examples. Other tasks, that cannot be described as associating one vector to another, or that are difficult enough that a person would require time to think and reflect in order to accomplish the task, remain beyond the scope of deep learning for now.

This part of the book describes the core parametric function approximation technology that is behind nearly all modern practical applications of deep learning. We begin by describing the feedforward deep network model that is used to represent these functions. Next, we present advanced techniques for regularization and optimization of such models. Scaling these models to large inputs such as high-resolution images or long temporal sequences requires specialization. We introduce the convolutional network for scaling to large images and the recurrent neural network for processing temporal sequences. Finally, we present general guidelines for the practical methodology involved in designing, building, and configuring an application involving deep learning and review some of its applications.

These chapters are the most important for a practitioner—someone who wants to begin implementing and using deep learning algorithms to solve real-world problems today.

6

Deep Feedforward Networks

Deep feedforward networks, also called **feedforward neural networks**, or **multilayer perceptrons** (MLPs), are the quintessential deep learning models. The goal of a feedforward network is to approximate some function f^*. For example, for a classifier, $y = f^*(\boldsymbol{x})$ maps an input $\boldsymbol{x}$ to a category y. A feedforward network defines a mapping $\boldsymbol{y} = f(\boldsymbol{x}; \boldsymbol{\theta})$ and learns the value of the parameters $\boldsymbol{\theta}$ that result in the best function approximation.

These models are called **feedforward** because information flows through the function being evaluated from $\boldsymbol{x}$, through the intermediate computations used to define f, and finally to the output $\boldsymbol{y}$. There are no **feedback** connections in which outputs of the model are fed back into itself. When feedforward neural networks are extended to include feedback connections, they are called **recurrent neural networks**, as presented in chapter 10.

Feedforward networks are of extreme importance to machine learning practitioners. They form the basis of many important commercial applications. For example, the convolutional networks used for object recognition from photos are a specialized kind of feedforward network. Feedforward networks are a conceptual stepping stone on the path to recurrent networks, which power many natural language applications.

Feedforward neural networks are called **networks** because they are typically represented by composing together many different functions. The model is associated with a directed acyclic graph describing how the functions are composed together. For example, we might have three functions $f^{(1)}$, $f^{(2)}$, and $f^{(3)}$ connected in a chain, to form $f(\boldsymbol{x}) = f^{(3)}(f^{(2)}(f^{(1)}(\boldsymbol{x})))$. These chain structures are the most commonly used structures of neural networks. In this case, $f^{(1)}$ is called the **first layer** of the network, $f^{(2)}$ is called the **second layer**, and so on. The overall length of the chain gives the **depth** of the model. The name "deep learning" arose from this terminology. The final layer of a feedforward network is called the **output layer**. During neural network training, we drive $f(\boldsymbol{x})$ to match $f^*(\boldsymbol{x})$. The training data provides us with noisy, approximate examples of $f^*(\boldsymbol{x})$ evaluated at different training points. Each example $\boldsymbol{x}$ is accompanied by a label $y \approx f^*(\boldsymbol{x})$. The training examples specify directly what the output layer must do at each point $\boldsymbol{x}$; it must produce a value that is close to y. The behavior of the other layers is not directly specified by the training data. The learning algorithm must decide how to use those layers to produce the desired output, but the training data do not say what each individual layer should do. Instead, the learning algorithm must decide how to use these layers to best implement an approximation of f^*. Because the training data does not show the desired output for each of these layers, they are called **hidden layers**.

Finally, these networks are called *neural* because they are loosely inspired by neuroscience. Each hidden layer of the network is typically vector valued. The dimensionality of these hidden layers determines the **width** of the model. Each element of the vector may be interpreted as playing a role analogous to a neuron. Rather than thinking of the layer as representing a single vector-to-vector function, we can also think of the layer as consisting of many **units** that act in parallel, each representing a vector-to-scalar function. Each unit resembles a neuron in the sense that it receives input from many other units and computes its own activation value. The idea of using many layers of vector-valued representations is drawn from neuroscience. The choice of the functions $f^{(i)}(\boldsymbol{x})$ used to compute these representations is also loosely guided by neuroscientific observations about the functions that biological neurons compute. Modern neural network research, however, is guided by many mathematical and engineering disciplines, and the goal of neural networks is not to perfectly model the brain. It is best to think of feedforward networks as function approximation machines that are designed to achieve statistical generalization, occasionally drawing some insights from what we know about the brain, rather than as models of brain function.

One way to understand feedforward networks is to begin with linear models and consider how to overcome their limitations. Linear models, such as logistic regression and linear regression, are appealing because they can be fit efficiently and reliably, either in closed form or with convex optimization. Linear models also have the obvious defect that the model capacity is limited to linear functions, so the model cannot understand the interaction between any two input variables.

To extend linear models to represent nonlinear functions of $\boldsymbol{x}$, we can apply the linear model not to $\boldsymbol{x}$ itself but to a transformed input $\phi(\boldsymbol{x})$, where ϕ is a nonlinear transformation. Equivalently, we can apply the kernel trick described in section 5.7.2, to obtain a nonlinear learning algorithm based on implicitly applying the ϕ mapping. We can think of ϕ as providing a set of features describing $\boldsymbol{x}$, or as providing a new representation for $\boldsymbol{x}$.

The question is then how to choose the mapping ϕ.

1. One option is to use a very generic ϕ, such as the infinite-dimensional ϕ that is implicitly used by kernel machines based on the RBF kernel. If $\phi(\boldsymbol{x})$ is of high enough dimension, we can always have enough capacity to fit the training set, but generalization to the test set often remains poor. Very generic feature mappings are usually based only on the principle of local smoothness and do not encode enough prior information to solve advanced problems.

2. Another option is to manually engineer ϕ. Until the advent of deep learning, this was the dominant approach. It requires decades of human effort for each separate task, with practitioners specializing in different domains, such as speech recognition or computer vision, and with little transfer between domains.

3. The strategy of deep learning is to learn ϕ. In this approach, we have a model $y = f(\boldsymbol{x}; \boldsymbol{\theta}, \boldsymbol{w}) = \phi(\boldsymbol{x}; \boldsymbol{\theta})^\top \boldsymbol{w}$. We now have parameters $\boldsymbol{\theta}$ that we use to learn ϕ from a broad class of functions, and parameters $\boldsymbol{w}$ that map from $\phi(\boldsymbol{x})$ to the desired output. This is an example of a deep feedforward network, with ϕ defining a hidden layer. This approach is the only one of the three that gives up on the convexity of the training problem, but the benefits outweigh the harms. In this approach, we parametrize the representation as $\phi(\boldsymbol{x}; \boldsymbol{\theta})$ and use the optimization algorithm to find the $\boldsymbol{\theta}$ that corresponds to a good representation. If we wish, this approach can capture the benefit of the first approach by being highly generic—we do so by using a very broad family $\phi(\boldsymbol{x}; \boldsymbol{\theta})$. Deep learning can also capture the benefit of the second approach. Human practitioners can encode their knowledge to help generalization by designing families $\phi(\boldsymbol{x}; \boldsymbol{\theta})$ that they expect will perform well. The advantage is that the human designer only needs to find the right general function family rather than finding precisely the right function.

This general principle of improving models by learning features extends beyond the feedforward networks described in this chapter. It is a recurring theme of deep learning that applies to all the kinds of models described throughout this book. Feedforward networks are the application of this principle to learning deterministic mappings from $\boldsymbol{x}$ to $\boldsymbol{y}$ that lack feedback connections. Other models, presented later, apply these principles to learning stochastic mappings, functions with feedback, and probability distributions over a single vector.

We begin this chapter with a simple example of a feedforward network. Next, we address each of the design decisions needed to deploy a feedforward network. First, training a feedforward network requires making many of the same design decisions as are necessary for a linear model: choosing the optimizer, the cost function, and the form of the output units. We review these basics of gradient-based learning, then proceed to confront some of the design decisions that are unique to feedforward networks. Feedforward networks have introduced the concept of a hidden layer, and this requires us to choose the **activation functions** that will be used to compute the hidden layer values. We must also design the architecture of the network, including how many layers the network should contain, how these layers should be connected to each other, and how many units should be in each layer. Learning in deep neural networks requires computing the gradients of complicated functions. We present the **back-propagation** algorithm and its modern generalizations, which can be used to efficiently compute these gradients. Finally, we close with some historical perspective.

6.1 Example: Learning XOR

To make the idea of a feedforward network more concrete, we begin with an example of a fully functioning feedforward network on a very simple task: learning the XOR function.

The XOR function ("exclusive or") is an operation on two binary values, x_1 and x_2. When exactly one of these binary values is equal to 1, the XOR function returns 1. Otherwise, it returns 0. The XOR function provides the target function $y = f^*(\boldsymbol{x})$ that we want to learn. Our model provides a function $y = f(\boldsymbol{x}; \boldsymbol{\theta})$, and our learning algorithm will adapt the parameters $\boldsymbol{\theta}$ to make f as similar as possible to f^*.

In this simple example, we will not be concerned with statistical generalization. We want our network to perform correctly on the four points $\mathbb{X} = \{[0,0]^\top, [0,1]^\top, [1,0]^\top, \text{and } [1,1]^\top\}$. We will train the network on all four of these points. The only challenge is to fit the training set.

We can treat this problem as a regression problem and use a mean squared error loss function. We have chosen this loss function to simplify the math for this example as much as possible. In practical applications, MSE is usually not an appropriate cost function for modeling binary data. More appropriate approaches are described in section 6.2.2.2.

Evaluated on our whole training set, the MSE loss function is

$$J(\boldsymbol{\theta}) = \frac{1}{4} \sum_{\boldsymbol{x} \in \mathbb{X}} (f^*(\boldsymbol{x}) - f(\boldsymbol{x}; \boldsymbol{\theta}))^2 . \tag{6.1}$$

Now we must choose the form of our model, $f(\boldsymbol{x}; \boldsymbol{\theta})$. Suppose that we choose a linear model, with $\boldsymbol{\theta}$ consisting of $\boldsymbol{w}$ and b. Our model is defined to be

$$f(\boldsymbol{x}; \boldsymbol{w}, b) = \boldsymbol{x}^\top \boldsymbol{w} + b. \tag{6.2}$$

We can minimize $J(\boldsymbol{\theta})$ in closed form with respect to $\boldsymbol{w}$ and b using the normal equations.

After solving the normal equations, we obtain $\boldsymbol{w} = \boldsymbol{0}$ and $b = \frac{1}{2}$. The linear model simply outputs 0.5 everywhere. Why does this happen? Figure 6.1 shows how a linear model is not able to represent the XOR function. One way to solve this problem is to use a model that learns a different feature space in which a linear model is able to represent the solution.

Specifically, we will introduce a simple feedforward network with one hidden layer containing two hidden units. See figure 6.2 for an illustration of this model. This feedforward network has a vector of hidden units $\boldsymbol{h}$ that are computed by a function $f^{(1)}(\boldsymbol{x}; \boldsymbol{W}, \boldsymbol{c})$. The values of these hidden units are then used as the input for a second layer. The second layer is the output layer of the network. The output layer is still just a linear regression model, but now it is applied to $\boldsymbol{h}$ rather than to $\boldsymbol{x}$. The network now contains two functions chained together, $\boldsymbol{h} = f^{(1)}(\boldsymbol{x}; \boldsymbol{W}, \boldsymbol{c})$ and $y = f^{(2)}(\boldsymbol{h}; \boldsymbol{w}, b)$, with the complete model being $f(\boldsymbol{x}; \boldsymbol{W}, \boldsymbol{c}, \boldsymbol{w}, b) = f^{(2)}(f^{(1)}(\boldsymbol{x}))$.

What function should $f^{(1)}$ compute? Linear models have served us well so far, and it may be tempting to make $f^{(1)}$ linear as well. Unfortunately, if $f^{(1)}$ were linear, then the feedforward network as a whole would remain a linear function of its input. Ignoring the intercept terms for the moment, suppose $f^{(1)}(\boldsymbol{x}) = \boldsymbol{W}^\top \boldsymbol{x}$ and $f^{(2)}(\boldsymbol{h}) = \boldsymbol{h}^\top \boldsymbol{w}$. Then $f(\boldsymbol{x}) = \boldsymbol{w}^\top \boldsymbol{W}^\top \boldsymbol{x}$. We could represent this function as $f(\boldsymbol{x}) = \boldsymbol{x}^\top \boldsymbol{w}'$ where $\boldsymbol{w}' = \boldsymbol{W} \boldsymbol{w}$.

Clearly, we must use a nonlinear function to describe the features. Most neural networks do so using an affine transformation controlled by learned parameters, followed by a fixed nonlinear function called an activation function. We use that strategy here, by defining $\boldsymbol{h} = g(\boldsymbol{W}^\top \boldsymbol{x} + \boldsymbol{c})$, where $\boldsymbol{W}$ provides the weights of a

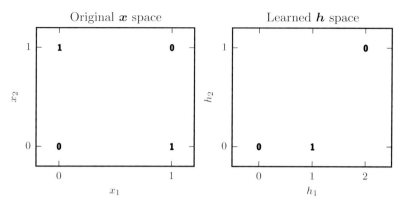

Figure 6.1: Solving the XOR problem by learning a representation. The bold numbers printed on the plot indicate the value that the learned function must output at each point. *(Left)* A linear model applied directly to the original input cannot implement the XOR function. When $x_1 = 0$, the model's output must increase as x_2 increases. When $x_1 = 1$, the model's output must decrease as x_2 increases. A linear model must apply a fixed coefficient w_2 to x_2. The linear model therefore cannot use the value of x_1 to change the coefficient on x_2 and cannot solve this problem. *(Right)* In the transformed space represented by the features extracted by a neural network, a linear model can now solve the problem. In our example solution, the two points that must have output 1 have been collapsed into a single point in feature space. In other words, the nonlinear features have mapped both $\boldsymbol{x} = [1, 0]^\top$ and $\boldsymbol{x} = [0, 1]^\top$ to a single point in feature space, $\boldsymbol{h} = [1, 0]^\top$. The linear model can now describe the function as increasing in h_1 and decreasing in h_2. In this example, the motivation for learning the feature space is only to make the model capacity greater so that it can fit the training set. In more realistic applications, learned representations can also help the model to generalize.

linear transformation and $\boldsymbol{c}$ the biases. Previously, to describe a linear regression model, we used a vector of weights and a scalar bias parameter to describe an affine transformation from an input vector to an output scalar. Now, we describe an affine transformation from a vector $\boldsymbol{x}$ to a vector $\boldsymbol{h}$, so an entire vector of bias parameters is needed. The activation function g is typically chosen to be a function that is applied element-wise, with $h_i = g(\boldsymbol{x}^\top \boldsymbol{W}_{:,i} + c_i)$. In modern neural networks, the default recommendation is to use the **rectified linear unit**, or ReLU (Jarrett et al., 2009; Nair and Hinton, 2010; Glorot et al., 2011a), defined by the activation function $g(z) = \max\{0, z\}$, depicted in figure 6.3.

We can now specify our complete network as

$$f(\boldsymbol{x}; \boldsymbol{W}, \boldsymbol{c}, \boldsymbol{w}, b) = \boldsymbol{w}^\top \max\{0, \boldsymbol{W}^\top \boldsymbol{x} + \boldsymbol{c}\} + b. \tag{6.3}$$

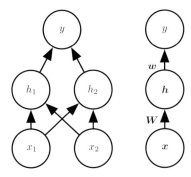

Figure 6.2: An example of a feedforward network, drawn in two different styles. Specifically, this is the feedforward network we use to solve the XOR example. It has a single hidden layer containing two units. *(Left)* In this style, we draw every unit as a node in the graph. This style is explicit and unambiguous, but for networks larger than this example, it can consume too much space. *(Right)* In this style, we draw a node in the graph for each entire vector representing a layer's activations. This style is much more compact. Sometimes we annotate the edges in this graph with the name of the parameters that describe the relationship between two layers. Here, we indicate that a matrix W describes the mapping from x to h, and a vector w describes the mapping from h to y. We typically omit the intercept parameters associated with each layer when labeling this kind of drawing.

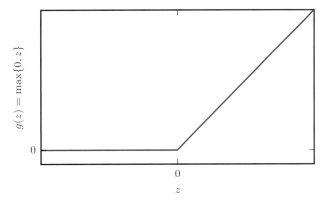

Figure 6.3: The rectified linear activation function. This activation function is the default activation function recommended for use with most feedforward neural networks. Applying this function to the output of a linear transformation yields a nonlinear transformation. The function remains very close to linear, however, in the sense that is a piecewise linear function with two linear pieces. Because rectified linear units are nearly linear, they preserve many of the properties that make linear models easy to optimize with gradient-based methods. They also preserve many of the properties that make linear models generalize well. A common principle throughout computer science is that we can build complicated systems from minimal components. Much as a Turing machine's memory needs only to be able to store 0 or 1 states, we can build a universal function approximator from rectified linear functions.

We can then specify a solution to the XOR problem. Let

$$W = \begin{bmatrix} 1 & 1 \\ 1 & 1 \end{bmatrix}, \tag{6.4}$$

$$c = \begin{bmatrix} 0 \\ -1 \end{bmatrix}, \tag{6.5}$$

$$w = \begin{bmatrix} 1 \\ -2 \end{bmatrix}, \tag{6.6}$$

and $b = 0$.

We can now walk through how the model processes a batch of inputs. Let X be the design matrix containing all four points in the binary input space, with one example per row:

$$X = \begin{bmatrix} 0 & 0 \\ 0 & 1 \\ 1 & 0 \\ 1 & 1 \end{bmatrix}. \tag{6.7}$$

The first step in the neural network is to multiply the input matrix by the first layer's weight matrix:

$$XW = \begin{bmatrix} 0 & 0 \\ 1 & 1 \\ 1 & 1 \\ 2 & 2 \end{bmatrix}. \tag{6.8}$$

Next, we add the bias vector c, to obtain

$$\begin{bmatrix} 0 & -1 \\ 1 & 0 \\ 1 & 0 \\ 2 & 1 \end{bmatrix}. \tag{6.9}$$

In this space, all the examples lie along a line with slope 1. As we move along this line, the output needs to begin at 0, then rise to 1, then drop back down to 0. A linear model cannot implement such a function. To finish computing the value of h for each example, we apply the rectified linear transformation:

$$\begin{bmatrix} 0 & 0 \\ 1 & 0 \\ 1 & 0 \\ 2 & 1 \end{bmatrix}. \tag{6.10}$$

This transformation has changed the relationship between the examples. They no longer lie on a single line. As shown in figure 6.1, they now lie in a space where a linear model can solve the problem.

We finish with multiplying by the weight vector $\boldsymbol{w}$:

$$
\begin{bmatrix} 0 \\ 1 \\ 1 \\ 0 \end{bmatrix}.
\tag{6.11}
$$

The neural network has obtained the correct answer for every example in the batch.

In this example, we simply specified the solution, then showed that it obtained zero error. In a real situation, there might be billions of model parameters and billions of training examples, so one cannot simply guess the solution as we did here. Instead, a gradient-based optimization algorithm can find parameters that produce very little error. The solution we described to the XOR problem is at a global minimum of the loss function, so gradient descent could converge to this point. There are other equivalent solutions to the XOR problem that gradient descent could also find. The convergence point of gradient descent depends on the initial values of the parameters. In practice, gradient descent would usually not find clean, easily understood, integer-valued solutions like the one we presented here.

6.2 Gradient-Based Learning

Designing and training a neural network is not much different from training any other machine learning model with gradient descent. In section 5.10, we described how to build a machine learning algorithm by specifying an optimization procedure, a cost function, and a model family.

The largest difference between the linear models we have seen so far and neural networks is that the nonlinearity of a neural network causes most interesting loss functions to become nonconvex. This means that neural networks are usually trained by using iterative, gradient-based optimizers that merely drive the cost function to a very low value, rather than the linear equation solvers used to train linear regression models or the convex optimization algorithms with global convergence guarantees used to train logistic regression or SVMs. Convex optimization converges starting from any initial parameters (in theory—in practice it is robust but can encounter numerical problems). Stochastic gradient descent applied to nonconvex loss functions has no such convergence guarantee and is sensitive to the values of the initial parameters. For feedforward neural networks, it is important to initialize all weights to small random values. The biases may be initialized to zero or to small positive values. The iterative gradient-based optimization algorithms used to train feedforward networks and almost all other deep models are described in detail in chapter 8, with parameter initialization in particular discussed in section 8.4. For the moment, it suffices to understand that the training algorithm is almost always based on using the gradient to descend the cost function in one way or another. The specific algorithms are improvements and refinements on the ideas of gradient descent, introduced in section 4.3, and, more specifically, are most often improvements of the stochastic gradient descent algorithm, introduced in section 5.9.

We can of course train models such as linear regression and support vector machines with gradient descent too, and in fact this is common when the training set is extremely large. From this point of view, training a neural network is not much different from training any other model. Computing the gradient is slightly more complicated for a neural network but can still be done efficiently and exactly. In Section 6.5 we describe how to obtain the gradient using the back-propagation algorithm and modern generalizations of the back-propagation algorithm.

As with other machine learning models, to apply gradient-based learning we must choose a cost function, and we must choose how to represent the output of the model. We now revisit these design considerations with special emphasis on the neural networks scenario.

6.2.1 Cost Functions

An important aspect of the design of a deep neural network is the choice of the cost function. Fortunately, the cost functions for neural networks are more or less the same as those for other parametric models, such as linear models.

In most cases, our parametric model defines a distribution $p(y \mid x; \theta)$ and we simply use the principle of maximum likelihood. This means we use the cross-entropy between the training data and the model's predictions as the cost function.

Sometimes, we take a simpler approach, where rather than predicting a complete probability distribution over y, we merely predict some statistic of y conditioned on x. Specialized loss functions enable us to train a predictor of these estimates.

The total cost function used to train a neural network will often combine one of the primary cost functions described here with a regularization term. We have already seen some simple examples of regularization applied to linear models in section 5.2.2. The weight decay approach used for linear models is also directly applicable to deep neural networks and is among the most popular regularization strategies. More advanced regularization strategies for neural networks are described in chapter 7.

6.2.1.1 Learning Conditional Distributions with Maximum Likelihood

Most modern neural networks are trained using maximum likelihood. This means that the cost function is simply the negative log-likelihood, equivalently described as the cross-entropy between the training data and the model distribution. This cost function is given by

$$J(\boldsymbol{\theta}) = -\mathbb{E}_{\mathbf{x},\mathbf{y} \sim \hat{p}_{\text{data}}} \log p_{\text{model}}(\boldsymbol{y} \mid \boldsymbol{x}). \tag{6.12}$$

The specific form of the cost function changes from model to model, depending on the specific form of $\log p_{\text{model}}$. The expansion of the above equation typically yields some terms that do not depend on the model parameters and may be discarded. For example, as we saw in section 5.5.1, if $p_{\text{model}}(\boldsymbol{y} \mid \boldsymbol{x}) = \mathcal{N}(\boldsymbol{y}; f(\boldsymbol{x}; \boldsymbol{\theta}), \boldsymbol{I})$, then we recover the mean squared error cost,

$$J(\theta) = \frac{1}{2} \mathbb{E}_{\mathbf{x},\mathbf{y} \sim \hat{p}_{\text{data}}} ||\boldsymbol{y} - f(\boldsymbol{x}; \boldsymbol{\theta})||^2 + \text{const}, \tag{6.13}$$

up to a scaling factor of $\frac{1}{2}$ and a term that does not depend on $\boldsymbol{\theta}$. The discarded constant is based on the variance of the Gaussian distribution, which in this case we chose not to parametrize. Previously, we saw that the equivalence between maximum likelihood estimation with an output distribution and minimization of mean squared error holds for a linear model, but in fact, the equivalence holds regardless of the $f(\boldsymbol{x}; \boldsymbol{\theta})$ used to predict the mean of the Gaussian.

An advantage of this approach of deriving the cost function from maximum likelihood is that it removes the burden of designing cost functions for each model. Specifying a model $p(\boldsymbol{y} \mid \boldsymbol{x})$ automatically determines a cost function $\log p(\boldsymbol{y} \mid \boldsymbol{x})$.

One recurring theme throughout neural network design is that the gradient of the cost function must be large and predictable enough to serve as a good guide for the learning algorithm. Functions that saturate (become very flat) undermine this objective because they make the gradient become very small. In many cases this happens because the activation functions used to produce the output of the hidden units or the output units saturate. The negative log-likelihood helps to avoid this problem for many models. Several output units involve an exp function that can saturate when its argument is very negative. The log function in the negative log-likelihood cost function undoes the exp of some output units. We will discuss the interaction between the cost function and the choice of output unit in section 6.2.2.

One unusual property of the cross-entropy cost used to perform maximum likelihood estimation is that it usually does not have a minimum value when applied to the models commonly used in practice. For discrete output variables, most models are parametrized in such a way that they cannot represent a probability of zero or one, but can come arbitrarily close to doing so. Logistic regression is an example of such a model. For real-valued output variables, if the model can control the density of the output distribution (for example, by learning the variance parameter of a Gaussian output distribution) then it becomes possible to assign extremely high density to the correct training set outputs, resulting in cross-entropy approaching negative infinity. Regularization techniques described in chapter 7 provide several different ways of modifying the learning problem so that the model cannot reap unlimited reward in this way.

6.2.1.2 Learning Conditional Statistics

Instead of learning a full probability distribution $p(\boldsymbol{y} \mid \boldsymbol{x}; \boldsymbol{\theta})$, we often want to learn just one conditional statistic of $\boldsymbol{y}$ given $\boldsymbol{x}$.

For example, we may have a predictor $f(\boldsymbol{x}; \boldsymbol{\theta})$ that we wish to employ to predict the mean of $\boldsymbol{y}$.

If we use a sufficiently powerful neural network, we can think of the neural network as being able to represent any function f from a wide class of functions, with this class being limited only by features such as continuity and boundedness rather than by having a specific parametric form. From this point of view, we can view the cost function as being a **functional** rather than just a function. A functional is a mapping from functions to real numbers. We can thus think of learning as choosing a function rather than merely choosing a set of parameters. We can design our cost functional to have its minimum occur at some specific function we desire. For example, we can design the cost functional to have its minimum lie on the function that maps $\boldsymbol{x}$ to the expected value of $\boldsymbol{y}$ given $\boldsymbol{x}$. Solving an optimization problem with respect to a function requires a mathematical tool called **calculus of variations**, described in section 19.4.2. It is not necessary to understand calculus of variations to understand the content of this chapter. At the moment, it is only necessary to understand that calculus of variations may be used to derive the following two results.

Our first result derived using calculus of variations is that solving the optimization problem

$$f^* = \arg\min_f \mathbb{E}_{\mathbf{x},\mathbf{y}\sim p_{\text{data}}}||\boldsymbol{y} - f(\boldsymbol{x})||^2 \tag{6.14}$$

yields

$$f^*(\boldsymbol{x}) = \mathbb{E}_{\mathbf{y}\sim p_{\text{data}}(\boldsymbol{y}|\boldsymbol{x})}[\boldsymbol{y}], \tag{6.15}$$

so long as this function lies within the class we optimize over. In other words, if we could train on infinitely many samples from the true data generating distribution, minimizing the mean squared error cost function would give a function that predicts the mean of $\boldsymbol{y}$ for each value of $\boldsymbol{x}$.

Different cost functions give different statistics. A second result derived using calculus of variations is that

$$f^* = \arg\min_f \mathbb{E}_{\mathbf{x},\mathbf{y}\sim p_{\text{data}}}||\boldsymbol{y} - f(\boldsymbol{x})||_1 \tag{6.16}$$

yields a function that predicts the *median* value of $\boldsymbol{y}$ for each $\boldsymbol{x}$, as long as such a function may be described by the family of functions we optimize over. This cost function is commonly called **mean absolute error**.

Unfortunately, mean squared error and mean absolute error often lead to poor results when used with gradient-based optimization. Some output units that saturate produce very small gradients when combined with these cost functions. This is one reason that the cross-entropy cost function is more popular than mean squared error or mean absolute error, even when it is not necessary to estimate an entire distribution $p(\boldsymbol{y} \mid \boldsymbol{x})$.

6.2.2   Output Units

The choice of cost function is tightly coupled with the choice of output unit. Most of the time, we simply use the cross-entropy between the data distribution and the model distribution. The choice of how to represent the output then determines the form of the cross-entropy function.

Any kind of neural network unit that may be used as an output can also be used as a hidden unit. Here, we focus on the use of these units as outputs of the model, but in principle they can be used internally as well. We revisit these units with additional detail about their use as hidden units in section 6.3.

Throughout this section, we suppose that the feedforward network provides a set of hidden features defined by $\boldsymbol{h} = f(\boldsymbol{x}; \boldsymbol{\theta})$. The role of the output layer is then to provide some additional transformation from the features to complete the task that the network must perform.

6.2.2.1 Linear Units for Gaussian Output Distributions

One simple kind of output unit is based on an affine transformation with no nonlinearity. These are often just called linear units.

Given features $\boldsymbol{h}$, a layer of linear output units produces a vector $\hat{\boldsymbol{y}} = \boldsymbol{W}^\top \boldsymbol{h} + \boldsymbol{b}$.

Linear output layers are often used to produce the mean of a conditional Gaussian distribution:

$$p(\boldsymbol{y} \mid \boldsymbol{x}) = \mathcal{N}(\boldsymbol{y}; \hat{\boldsymbol{y}}, \boldsymbol{I}). \tag{6.17}$$

Maximizing the log-likelihood is then equivalent to minimizing the mean squared error.

The maximum likelihood framework makes it straightforward to learn the covariance of the Gaussian too, or to make the covariance of the Gaussian be a function of the input. However, the covariance must be constrained to be a positive definite matrix for all inputs. It is difficult to satisfy such constraints with a linear output layer, so typically other output units are used to parametrize the covariance. Approaches to modeling the covariance are described shortly, in section 6.2.2.4.

Because linear units do not saturate, they pose little difficulty for gradient-based optimization algorithms and may be used with a wide variety of optimization algorithms.

6.2.2.2 Sigmoid Units for Bernoulli Output Distributions

Many tasks require predicting the value of a binary variable y. Classification problems with two classes can be cast in this form.

The maximum likelihood approach is to define a Bernoulli distribution over y conditioned on $\boldsymbol{x}$.

A Bernoulli distribution is defined by just a single number. The neural net needs to predict only $P(y = 1 \mid \boldsymbol{x})$. For this number to be a valid probability, it must lie in the interval $[0, 1]$.

Satisfying this constraint requires some careful design effort. Suppose we were to use a linear unit and threshold its value to obtain a valid probability:

$$P(y = 1 \mid \boldsymbol{x}) = \max \left\{ 0, \min \left\{ 1, \boldsymbol{w}^\top \boldsymbol{h} + b \right\} \right\}. \tag{6.18}$$

This would indeed define a valid conditional distribution, but we would not be able to train it very effectively with gradient descent. Any time that $\boldsymbol{w}^\top \boldsymbol{h} + b$ strayed outside the unit interval, the gradient of the output of the model with respect to its parameters would be $\mathbf{0}$. A gradient of $\mathbf{0}$ is typically problematic because the learning algorithm no longer has a guide for how to improve the corresponding parameters.

Instead, it is better to use a different approach that ensures there is always a strong gradient whenever the model has the wrong answer. This approach is based on using sigmoid output units combined with maximum likelihood.

A sigmoid output unit is defined by

$$\hat{y} = \sigma \left(\boldsymbol{w}^\top \boldsymbol{h} + b \right), \tag{6.19}$$

where σ is the logistic sigmoid function described in section 3.10.

We can think of the sigmoid output unit as having two components. First, it uses a linear layer to compute $z = \boldsymbol{w}^\top \boldsymbol{h} + b$. Next, it uses the sigmoid activation function to convert z into a probability.

We omit the dependence on $\boldsymbol{x}$ for the moment to discuss how to define a probability distribution over y using the value z. The sigmoid can be motivated by constructing an unnormalized probability distribution $\tilde{P}(y)$, which does not sum to 1. We can then divide by an appropriate constant to obtain a valid probability distribution. If we begin with the assumption that the unnormalized log probabilities are linear in y and z, we can exponentiate to obtain the unnormalized probabilities. We then normalize to see that this yields a Bernoulli distribution controlled by a sigmoidal transformation of z:

$$\log \tilde{P}(y) = yz, \tag{6.20}$$

$$\tilde{P}(y) = \exp(yz), \tag{6.21}$$

$$P(y) = \frac{\exp(yz)}{\sum_{y'=0}^{1} \exp(y'z)}, \tag{6.22}$$

$$P(y) = \sigma \left((2y - 1)z \right). \tag{6.23}$$

Probability distributions based on exponentiation and normalization are common throughout the statistical modeling literature. The z variable defining such a distribution over binary variables is called a **logit**.

This approach to predicting the probabilities in log space is natural to use with maximum likelihood learning. Because the cost function used with maximum likelihood is $- \log P(y \mid \boldsymbol{x})$, the log in the cost function undoes the exp of the sigmoid. Without this effect, the saturation of the sigmoid could prevent gradient-based learning from making good progress. The loss function for maximum likelihood learning of a Bernoulli parametrized by a sigmoid is

$$J(\boldsymbol{\theta}) = -\log P(y \mid \boldsymbol{x}) \tag{6.24}$$

$$= -\log \sigma \left((2y - 1)z \right) \tag{6.25}$$

$$= \zeta \left((1 - 2y)z \right). \tag{6.26}$$

This derivation makes use of some properties from section 3.10. By rewriting the loss in terms of the softplus function, we can see that it saturates only when $(1 - 2y)z$ is very negative. Saturation thus occurs only when the model already has the right answer—when $y = 1$ and z is very positive, or $y = 0$ and z is very negative. When z has the wrong sign, the argument to the softplus function, $(1 - 2y)z$, may be simplified to $|z|$. As $|z|$ becomes large while z has the wrong sign, the softplus function asymptotes toward simply returning its argument $|z|$. The derivative with respect to z asymptotes to $\text{sign}(z)$, so, in the limit of extremely incorrect z, the softplus function does not shrink the gradient at all. This property is useful because it means that gradient-based learning can act to quickly correct a mistaken z.

When we use other loss functions, such as mean squared error, the loss can saturate anytime $\sigma(z)$ saturates. The sigmoid activation function saturates to 0 when z becomes very negative and saturates to 1 when z becomes very positive. The gradient can shrink too small to be useful for learning when this happens, whether the model has the correct answer or the incorrect answer. For this reason, maximum likelihood is almost always the preferred approach to training sigmoid output units.

Analytically, the logarithm of the sigmoid is always defined and finite, because the sigmoid returns values restricted to the open interval $(0, 1)$, rather than using the entire closed interval of valid probabilities $[0, 1]$. In software implementations, to avoid numerical problems, it is best to write the negative log-likelihood as a function of z, rather than as a function of $\hat{y} = \sigma(z)$. If the sigmoid function underflows to zero, then taking the logarithm of $\hat{y}$ yields negative infinity.

6.2.2.3 Softmax Units for Multinoulli Output Distributions

Any time we wish to represent a probability distribution over a discrete variable with n possible values, we may use the softmax function. This can be seen as a generalization of the sigmoid function, which was used to represent a probability distribution over a binary variable.

Softmax functions are most often used as the output of a classifier, to represent the probability distribution over n different classes. More rarely, softmax functions can be used inside the model itself, if we wish the model to choose between one of n different options for some internal variable.

In the case of binary variables, we wished to produce a single number

$$\hat{y} = P(y = 1 \mid \boldsymbol{x}). \tag{6.27}$$

Because this number needed to lie between 0 and 1, and because we wanted the logarithm of the number to be well behaved for gradient-based optimization of the log-likelihood, we chose to instead predict a number $z = \log \tilde{P}(y = 1 \mid \boldsymbol{x})$. Exponentiating and normalizing gave us a Bernoulli distribution controlled by the sigmoid function.

To generalize to the case of a discrete variable with n values, we now need to produce a vector $\hat{\boldsymbol{y}}$, with $\hat{y}_i = P(y = i \mid \boldsymbol{x})$. We require not only that each element of $\hat{y}_i$ be between 0 and 1, but also that the entire vector sums to 1 so that it represents a valid probability distribution. The same approach that worked for the Bernoulli distribution generalizes to the multinoulli distribution. First, a linear layer predicts unnormalized log probabilities:

$$\boldsymbol{z} = \boldsymbol{W}^\top \boldsymbol{h} + \boldsymbol{b}, \tag{6.28}$$

where $z_i = \log \tilde{P}(y = i \mid \boldsymbol{x})$. The softmax function can then exponentiate and normalize $\boldsymbol{z}$ to obtain the desired $\hat{\boldsymbol{y}}$. Formally, the softmax function is given by

$$\text{softmax}(\boldsymbol{z})_i = \frac{\exp(z_i)}{\sum_j \exp(z_j)}. \tag{6.29}$$

As with the logistic sigmoid, the use of the exp function works well when training the softmax to output a target value y using maximum log-likelihood. In this case, we wish to maximize $\log P(\text{y} = i; \boldsymbol{z}) = \log \text{softmax}(\boldsymbol{z})_i$. Defining the softmax in terms of exp is natural because the log in the log-likelihood can undo the exp of the softmax:

$$\log \text{softmax}(\boldsymbol{z})_i = z_i - \log \sum_j \exp(z_j). \tag{6.30}$$

The first term of equation 6.30 shows that the input z_i always has a direct contribution to the cost function. Because this term cannot saturate, we know that learning can proceed, even if the contribution of z_i to the second term of equation 6.30 becomes very small. When maximizing the log-likelihood, the first term encourages z_i to be pushed up, while the second term encourages all of $\boldsymbol{z}$ to be pushed down. To gain some intuition for the second term, $\log \sum_j \exp(z_j)$, observe that this term can be roughly approximated by $\max_j z_j$. This approximation is based on the idea that $\exp(z_k)$ is insignificant for any z_k that is noticeably less than $\max_j z_j$. The intuition we can gain from this approximation is that the negative log-likelihood cost function always strongly penalizes the most active incorrect prediction. If the correct answer already has the largest input to the softmax, then the $-z_i$ term and the $\log \sum_j \exp(z_j) \approx \max_j z_j = z_i$ terms will roughly cancel. This example will then contribute little to the overall training cost, which will be dominated by other examples that are not yet correctly classified.

So far we have discussed only a single example. Overall, unregularized maximum likelihood will drive the model to learn parameters that drive the softmax to predict the fraction of counts of each outcome observed in the training set:

$$\text{softmax}(\boldsymbol{z}(\boldsymbol{x}; \boldsymbol{\theta}))_i \approx \frac{\sum_{j=1}^{m} \mathbf{1}_{y^{(j)}=i, \boldsymbol{x}^{(j)}=\boldsymbol{x}}}{\sum_{j=1}^{m} \mathbf{1}_{\boldsymbol{x}^{(j)}=\boldsymbol{x}}}. \tag{6.31}$$

Because maximum likelihood is a consistent estimator, this is guaranteed to happen as long as the model family is capable of representing the training distribution. In practice, limited model capacity and imperfect optimization will mean that the model is only able to approximate these fractions.

Many objective functions other than the log-likelihood do not work as well with the softmax function. Specifically, objective functions that do not use a log to undo the exp of the softmax fail to learn when the argument to the exp becomes very negative, causing the gradient to vanish. In particular, squared error is a poor loss function for softmax units and can fail to train the model to change its output, even when the model makes highly confident incorrect predictions (Bridle, 1990). To understand why these other loss functions can fail, we need to examine the softmax function itself.

Like the sigmoid, the softmax activation can saturate. The sigmoid function has a single output that saturates when its input is extremely negative or extremely positive. The softmax has multiple output values. These output values can saturate when the differences between input values become extreme. When the softmax saturates, many cost functions based on the softmax also saturate, unless they are able to invert the saturating activating function.

To see that the softmax function responds to the difference between its inputs, observe that the softmax output is invariant to adding the same scalar to all its inputs:

$$\text{softmax}(\boldsymbol{z}) = \text{softmax}(\boldsymbol{z} + c). \tag{6.32}$$

Using this property, we can derive a numerically stable variant of the softmax:

$$\text{softmax}(\boldsymbol{z}) = \text{softmax}(\boldsymbol{z} - \max_i z_i). \qquad (6.33)$$

The reformulated version enables us to evaluate softmax with only small numerical errors, even when $\boldsymbol{z}$ contains extremely large or extremely negative numbers. Examining the numerically stable variant, we see that the softmax function is driven by the amount that its arguments deviate from $\max_i z_i$.

An output $\text{softmax}(\boldsymbol{z})_i$ saturates to 1 when the corresponding input is maximal $(z_i = \max_i z_i)$ and z_i is much greater than all the other inputs. The output $\text{softmax}(\boldsymbol{z})_i$ can also saturate to 0 when z_i is not maximal and the maximum is much greater. This is a generalization of the way that sigmoid units saturate and can cause similar difficulties for learning if the loss function is not designed to compensate for it.

The argument $\boldsymbol{z}$ to the softmax function can be produced in two different ways. The most common is simply to have an earlier layer of the neural network output every element of $\boldsymbol{z}$, as described above using the linear layer $\boldsymbol{z} = \boldsymbol{W}^\top \boldsymbol{h} + \boldsymbol{b}$. While straightforward, this approach actually overparametrizes the distribution. The constraint that the n outputs must sum to 1 means that only $n-1$ parameters are necessary; the probability of the n-th value may be obtained by subtracting the first $n-1$ probabilities from 1. We can thus impose a requirement that one element of $\boldsymbol{z}$ be fixed. For example, we can require that $z_n = 0$. Indeed, this is exactly what the sigmoid unit does. Defining $P(y = 1 \mid \boldsymbol{x}) = \sigma(z)$ is equivalent to defining $P(y = 1 \mid \boldsymbol{x}) = \text{softmax}(\boldsymbol{z})_1$ with a two-dimensional $\boldsymbol{z}$ and $z_1 = 0$. Both the $n-1$ argument and the n argument approaches to the softmax can describe the same set of probability distributions but have different learning dynamics. In practice, there is rarely much difference between using the overparametrized version or the restricted version, and it is simpler to implement the overparametrized version.

From a neuroscientific point of view, it is interesting to think of the softmax as a way to create a form of competition between the units that participate in it: the softmax outputs always sum to 1 so an increase in the value of one unit necessarily corresponds to a decrease in the value of others. This is analogous to the lateral inhibition that is believed to exist between nearby neurons in the cortex. At the extreme (when the difference between the maximal a_i and the others is large in magnitude) it becomes a form of **winner-take-all** (one of the outputs is nearly 1, and the others are nearly 0).

The name "softmax" can be somewhat confusing. The function is more closely related to the arg max function than the max function. The term "soft" derives from the fact that the softmax function is continuous and differentiable. The arg max function, with its result represented as a one-hot vector, is not continuous or differentiable. The softmax function thus provides a "softened" version of the arg max. The corresponding soft version of the maximum function is $\text{softmax}(\boldsymbol{z})^\top \boldsymbol{z}$. It would perhaps be better to call the softmax function "softargmax," but the current name is an entrenched convention.

6.2.2.4 Other Output Types

The linear, sigmoid, and softmax output units described above are the most common. Neural networks can generalize to almost any kind of output layer that we wish. The principle of maximum likelihood provides a guide for how to design a good cost function for nearly any kind of output layer.

In general, if we define a conditional distribution $p(\boldsymbol{y} \mid \boldsymbol{x}; \boldsymbol{\theta})$, the principle of maximum likelihood suggests we use $-\log p(\boldsymbol{y} \mid \boldsymbol{x}; \boldsymbol{\theta})$ as our cost function.

In general, we can think of the neural network as representing a function $f(\boldsymbol{x}; \boldsymbol{\theta})$. The outputs of this function are not direct predictions of the value $\boldsymbol{y}$. Instead, $f(\boldsymbol{x}; \boldsymbol{\theta}) = \boldsymbol{\omega}$ provides the parameters for a distribution over y. Our loss function can then be interpreted as $-\log p(\mathbf{y}; \boldsymbol{\omega}(\boldsymbol{x}))$.

For example, we may wish to learn the variance of a conditional Gaussian for $\mathbf{y}$, given $\mathbf{x}$. In the simple case, where the variance σ^2 is a constant, there is a closed form expression because the maximum likelihood estimator of variance is simply the empirical mean of the squared difference between observations $\mathbf{y}$ and their expected value. A computationally more expensive approach that does not require writing special-case code is to simply include the variance as one of the properties of the distribution $p(\mathbf{y} \mid \boldsymbol{x})$ that is controlled by $\boldsymbol{\omega} = f(\boldsymbol{x}; \boldsymbol{\theta})$. The negative log-likelihood $-\log p(\boldsymbol{y}; \boldsymbol{\omega}(\boldsymbol{x}))$ will then provide a cost function with the appropriate terms necessary to make our optimization procedure incrementally learn the variance. In the simple case where the standard deviation does not depend on the input, we can make a new parameter in the network that is copied directly into $\boldsymbol{\omega}$. This new parameter might be σ itself or could be a parameter v representing σ^2 or it could be a parameter β representing $\frac{1}{\sigma^2}$, depending on how we choose to parametrize the distribution. We may wish our model to predict a different amount of variance in $\mathbf{y}$ for different values of $\mathbf{x}$. This is called a **heteroscedastic** model. In the heteroscedastic case, we simply make the specification of the variance be one of the values output by $f(\mathbf{x}; \boldsymbol{\theta})$. A typical way to do this is to formulate the Gaussian distribution using precision, rather than variance, as described in equation 3.22. In the multivariate case, it is most common to use a diagonal precision matrix

$$\text{diag}(\boldsymbol{\beta}). \tag{6.34}$$

This formulation works well with gradient descent because the formula for the log-likelihood of the Gaussian distribution parametrized by $\boldsymbol{\beta}$ involves only multiplication by β_i and addition of $\log \beta_i$. The gradient of multiplication, addition, and logarithm operations is well behaved. By comparison, if we parametrized the output in terms of variance, we would need to use division. The division function becomes arbitrarily steep near zero. While large gradients can help learning, arbitrarily large gradients usually result in instability. If we parametrized the output in terms of standard deviation, the log-likelihood would still involve division as well as squaring. The gradient through the squaring operation can vanish near zero, making it difficult to learn parameters that are squared. Regardless of whether we use standard deviation, variance, or precision, we must ensure that the covariance matrix of the Gaussian is positive definite. Because the eigenvalues of the precision matrix are the reciprocals of the eigenvalues of the covariance matrix, this is equivalent to ensuring that the precision matrix is positive definite. If we use a diagonal matrix, or a scalar times the diagonal matrix, then the only condition we need to enforce on the output of the model is positivity. If we suppose that $\boldsymbol{a}$ is the raw activation of the model used to determine the diagonal precision, we can use the softplus function to obtain a positive precision vector: $\boldsymbol{\beta} = \zeta(\boldsymbol{a})$. This same strategy applies equally if using variance or standard deviation rather than precision or if using a scalar times identity rather than diagonal matrix.

It is rare to learn a covariance or precision matrix with richer structure than diagonal. If the covariance is full and conditional, then a parametrization must be chosen that guarantees positive definiteness of the predicted covariance matrix. This can be achieved by writing $\boldsymbol{\Sigma}(\boldsymbol{x}) = \boldsymbol{B}(\boldsymbol{x})\boldsymbol{B}^{\top}(\boldsymbol{x})$, where $\boldsymbol{B}$ is an unconstrained square matrix. One practical issue if the matrix is full rank is that computing the likelihood is expensive, with a $d \times d$ matrix requiring $O(d^3)$ computation for the determinant and inverse of $\boldsymbol{\Sigma}(\boldsymbol{x})$ (or equivalently, and more commonly done, its eigendecomposition or that of $\boldsymbol{B}(\boldsymbol{x})$).

We often want to perform multimodal regression, that is, to predict real values from a conditional distribution $p(\boldsymbol{y} \mid \boldsymbol{x})$ that can have several different peaks in $\boldsymbol{y}$ space for the same value of $\boldsymbol{x}$. In this case, a Gaussian mixture is a natural representation for the output (Jacobs et al., 1991; Bishop, 1994). Neural networks with Gaussian mixtures as their output are often called **mixture density networks**. A Gaussian mixture output with n components is defined by the conditional probability distribution:

$$p(\boldsymbol{y} \mid \boldsymbol{x}) = \sum_{i=1}^{n} p(\mathrm{c} = i \mid \boldsymbol{x}) \mathcal{N}(\boldsymbol{y}; \boldsymbol{\mu}^{(i)}(\boldsymbol{x}), \boldsymbol{\Sigma}^{(i)}(\boldsymbol{x})). \qquad (6.35)$$

The neural network must have three outputs: a vector defining $p(\mathrm{c} = i \mid \boldsymbol{x})$, a matrix providing $\boldsymbol{\mu}^{(i)}(\boldsymbol{x})$ for all i, and a tensor providing $\boldsymbol{\Sigma}^{(i)}(\boldsymbol{x})$ for all i. These outputs must satisfy different constraints:

1. Mixture components $p(\mathrm{c} = i \mid \boldsymbol{x})$: these form a multinoulli distribution over the n different components associated with latent variable[1] c, and can typically be obtained by a softmax over an n-dimensional vector, to guarantee that these outputs are positive and sum to 1.

2. Means $\boldsymbol{\mu}^{(i)}(\boldsymbol{x})$: these indicate the center or mean associated with the i-th Gaussian component and are unconstrained (typically with no nonlinearity at all for these output units). If $\mathbf{y}$ is a d-vector, then the network must output an $n \times d$ matrix containing all n of these d-dimensional vectors. Learning these means with maximum likelihood is slightly more complicated than learning the means of a distribution with only one output mode. We only want to update the mean for the component that actually produced the observation. In practice, we do not know which component produced each observation. The expression for the negative log-likelihood naturally weights each example's contribution to the loss for each component by the probability that the component produced the example.

3. Covariances $\boldsymbol{\Sigma}^{(i)}(\boldsymbol{x})$: these specify the covariance matrix for each component i. As when learning a single Gaussian component, we typically use a diagonal matrix to avoid needing to compute determinants. As with learning the means of the mixture, maximum likelihood is complicated by needing to assign partial responsibility for each point to each mixture component. Gradient descent will automatically follow the correct process if given the correct specification of the negative log-likelihood under the mixture model.

It has been reported that gradient-based optimization of conditional Gaussian mixtures (on the output of neural networks) can be unreliable, in part because one gets divisions (by the variance) which can be numerically unstable (when some variance gets to be small for a particular example, yielding very large gradients). One solution is to **clip gradients** (see section 10.11.1), while another is to scale the gradients heuristically (Murray and Larochelle, 2014).

Gaussian mixture outputs are particularly effective in generative models of speech (Schuster, 1999) and movements of physical objects (Graves, 2013). The

---

[1] We consider c to be latent because we do not observe it in the data: given input $\mathbf{x}$ and target $\mathbf{y}$, it is not possible to know with certainty which Gaussian component was responsible for $\mathbf{y}$, but we can imagine that $\mathbf{y}$ was generated by picking one of them, and we can make that unobserved choice a random variable.

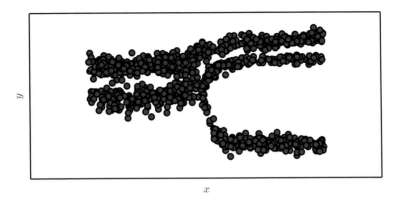

Figure 6.4: Samples drawn from a neural network with a mixture density output layer. The input x is sampled from a uniform distribution, and the output y is sampled from $p_{\text{model}}(y \mid x)$. The neural network is able to learn nonlinear mappings from the input to the parameters of the output distribution. These parameters include the probabilities governing which of three mixture components will generate the output as well as the parameters for each mixture component. Each mixture component is Gaussian with predicted mean and variance. All these aspects of the output distribution are able to vary with respect to the input x, and to do so in nonlinear ways.

mixture density strategy gives a way for the network to represent multiple output modes and to control the variance of its output, which is crucial for obtaining a high degree of quality in these real-valued domains. An example of a mixture density network is shown in figure 6.4.

In general, we may wish to continue to model larger vectors $\boldsymbol{y}$ containing more variables, and to impose richer and richer structures on these output variables. For example, if we want our neural network to output a sequence of characters that forms a sentence, we might continue to use the principle of maximum likelihood applied to our model $p(\boldsymbol{y}; \boldsymbol{\omega}(\boldsymbol{x}))$. In this case, the model we use to describe $\boldsymbol{y}$ would become complex enough to be beyond the scope of this chapter. In Chapter 10 we describe how to use recurrent neural networks to define such models over sequences, and in part III we describe advanced techniques for modeling arbitrary probability distributions.

6.3 Hidden Units

So far we have focused our discussion on design choices for neural networks that are common to most parametric machine learning models trained with gradient-based optimization. Now we turn to an issue that is unique to feedforward neural networks: how to choose the type of hidden unit to use in the hidden layers of the model.

The design of hidden units is an extremely active area of research and does not yet have many definitive guiding theoretical principles.

Rectified linear units are an excellent default choice of hidden unit. Many other types of hidden units are available. It can be difficult to determine when to use which kind (though rectified linear units are usually an acceptable choice). We describe here some of the basic intuitions motivating each type of hidden unit. These intuitions can help decide when to try out which unit. Predicting in advance which will work best is usually impossible. The design process consists of trial and error, intuiting that a kind of hidden unit may work well, and then training a network with that kind of hidden unit and evaluating its performance on a validation set.

Some of the hidden units included in this list are not actually differentiable at all input points. For example, the rectified linear function $g(z) = \max\{0, z\}$ is not differentiable at $z = 0$. This may seem like it invalidates g for use with a gradient-based learning algorithm. In practice, gradient descent still performs well enough for these models to be used for machine learning tasks. This is in part because neural network training algorithms do not usually arrive at a local minimum of the cost function, but instead merely reduce its value significantly, as shown in figure 4.3. (These ideas are described further in chapter 8.) Because we do not expect training to actually reach a point where the gradient is $\mathbf{0}$, it is acceptable for the minima of the cost function to correspond to points with undefined gradient. Hidden units that are not differentiable are usually nondifferentiable at only a small number of points. In general, a function $g(z)$ has a left derivative defined by the slope of the function immediately to the left of z and a right derivative defined by the slope of the function immediately to the right of z. A function is differentiable at z only if both the left derivative and the right derivative are defined and equal to each other. The functions used in the context of neural networks usually have defined left derivatives and defined right derivatives. In the case of $g(z) = \max\{0, z\}$, the left derivative at $z = 0$ is 0, and the right derivative is 1. Software implementations of neural network training usually return one of the one-sided derivatives rather than reporting that the derivative is undefined or raising an error. This may be heuristically justified by observing that gradient-based optimization on a digital computer is subject to numerical error anyway. When a function is asked to evaluate $g(0)$, it is very unlikely that the underlying value truly was 0. Instead, it was likely to be some small value ϵ that was rounded to 0. In some contexts, more theoretically pleasing justifications are available, but these usually do not apply to neural network training. The important point is that in practice one can safely disregard the nondifferentiability of the hidden unit activation functions described below.

Unless indicated otherwise, most hidden units can be described as accepting a vector of inputs $\boldsymbol{x}$, computing an affine transformation $\boldsymbol{z} = \boldsymbol{W}^\top \boldsymbol{x} + \boldsymbol{b}$, and then applying an element-wise nonlinear function $g(\boldsymbol{z})$. Most hidden units are distinguished from each other only by the choice of the form of the activation function $g(\boldsymbol{z})$.

6.3.1 Rectified Linear Units and Their Generalizations

Rectified linear units use the activation function $g(z) = \max\{0, z\}$.

These units are easy to optimize because they are so similar to linear units. The only difference between a linear unit and a rectified linear unit is that a rectified linear unit outputs zero across half its domain. This makes the derivatives through a rectified linear unit remain large whenever the unit is active. The gradients are not only large but also consistent. The second derivative of the rectifying operation is 0 almost everywhere, and the derivative of the rectifying operation is 1 everywhere that the unit is active. This means that the gradient direction is far more useful for learning than it would be with activation functions that introduce second-order effects.

Rectified linear units are typically used on top of an affine transformation:

$$\boldsymbol{h} = g(\boldsymbol{W}^\top \boldsymbol{x} + \boldsymbol{b}). \tag{6.36}$$

When initializing the parameters of the affine transformation, it can be a good practice to set all elements of $\boldsymbol{b}$ to a small positive value, such as 0.1. Doing so makes it very likely that the rectified linear units will be initially active for most inputs in the training set and allow the derivatives to pass through.

Several generalizations of rectified linear units exist. Most of these generalizations perform comparably to rectified linear units and occasionally perform better.

One drawback to rectified linear units is that they cannot learn via gradient-based methods on examples for which their activation is zero. Various generalizations of rectified linear units guarantee that they receive gradient everywhere.

Three generalizations of rectified linear units are based on using a nonzero slope α_i when $z_i < 0$: $h_i = g(\boldsymbol{z}, \boldsymbol{\alpha})_i = \max(0, z_i) + \alpha_i \min(0, z_i)$. **Absolute value rectification** fixes $\alpha_i = -1$ to obtain $g(z) = |z|$. It is used for object recognition from images (Jarrett et al., 2009), where it makes sense to seek features that are invariant under a polarity reversal of the input illumination. Other generalizations of rectified linear units are more broadly applicable. A **leaky ReLU** (Maas et al., 2013) fixes α_i to a small value like 0.01, while a **parametric ReLU**, or **PReLU**, treats α_i as a learnable parameter (He et al., 2015).

Maxout units (Goodfellow et al., 2013a) generalize rectified linear units further. Instead of applying an element-wise function $g(z)$, maxout units divide $\boldsymbol{z}$ into groups of k values. Each maxout unit then outputs the maximum element of one of these groups:

$$g(\boldsymbol{z})_i = \max_{j \in \mathbb{G}^{(i)}} z_j, \tag{6.37}$$

where $\mathbb{G}^{(i)}$ is the set of indices into the inputs for group i, $\{(i-1)k+1, \ldots, ik\}$. This provides a way of learning a piecewise linear function that responds to multiple directions in the input $\boldsymbol{x}$ space.

A maxout unit can learn a piecewise linear, convex function with up to k pieces. Maxout units can thus be seen as *learning the activation function* itself rather than just the relationship between units. With large enough k, a maxout unit can learn to approximate any convex function with arbitrary fidelity. In particular, a maxout layer with two pieces can learn to implement the same function of the input $\boldsymbol{x}$ as a traditional layer using the rectified linear activation function, the absolute value rectification function, or the leaky or parametric ReLU, or it can learn to implement a totally different function altogether. The maxout layer will of course be parametrized differently from any of these other layer types, so the learning dynamics will be different even in the cases where maxout learns to implement the same function of $\boldsymbol{x}$ as one of the other layer types.

Each maxout unit is now parametrized by k weight vectors instead of just one, so maxout units typically need more regularization than rectified linear units. They can work well without regularization if the training set is large and the number of pieces per unit is kept low (Cai et al., 2013).

Maxout units have a few other benefits. In some cases, one can gain some statistical and computational advantages by requiring fewer parameters. Specifically, if the features captured by n different linear filters can be summarized without losing information by taking the max over each group of k features, then the next layer can get by with k times fewer weights.

Because each unit is driven by multiple filters, maxout units have some redundancy that helps them resist a phenomenon called **catastrophic forgetting**, in which neural networks forget how to perform tasks that they were trained on in the past (Goodfellow et al., 2014a).

Rectified linear units and all these generalizations of them are based on the principle that models are easier to optimize if their behavior is closer to linear.

This same general principle of using linear behavior to obtain easier optimization also applies in other contexts besides deep linear networks. Recurrent networks can learn from sequences and produce a sequence of states and outputs. When training them, one needs to propagate information through several time steps, which is much easier when some linear computations (with some directional derivatives being of magnitude near 1) are involved. One of the best-performing recurrent network architectures, the LSTM, propagates information through time via summation—a particular straightforward kind of linear activation. This is discussed further in section 10.10.

6.3.2 Logistic Sigmoid and Hyperbolic Tangent

Prior to the introduction of rectified linear units, most neural networks used the logistic sigmoid activation function

$$g(z) = \sigma(z) \tag{6.38}$$

or the hyperbolic tangent activation function

$$g(z) = \tanh(z). \tag{6.39}$$

These activation functions are closely related because $\tanh(z) = 2\sigma(2z) - 1$.

We have already seen sigmoid units as output units, used to predict the probability that a binary variable is 1. Unlike piecewise linear units, sigmoidal units saturate across most of their domain—they saturate to a high value when z is very positive, saturate to a low value when z is very negative, and are only strongly sensitive to their input when z is near 0. The widespread saturation of sigmoidal units can make gradient-based learning very difficult. For this reason, their use as hidden units in feedforward networks is now discouraged. Their use as output units is compatible with the use of gradient-based learning when an appropriate cost function can undo the saturation of the sigmoid in the output layer.

When a sigmoidal activation function must be used, the hyperbolic tangent activation function typically performs better than the logistic sigmoid. It resembles the identity function more closely, in the sense that $\tanh(0) = 0$ while $\sigma(0) = \frac{1}{2}$. Because tanh is similar to the identity function near 0, training a deep neural network $\hat{y} = \boldsymbol{w}^\top \tanh(\boldsymbol{U}^\top \tanh(\boldsymbol{V}^\top \boldsymbol{x}))$ resembles training a linear model $\hat{y} = \boldsymbol{w}^\top \boldsymbol{U}^\top \boldsymbol{V}^\top \boldsymbol{x}$ as long as the activations of the network can be kept small. This makes training the tanh network easier.

Sigmoidal activation functions are more common in settings other than feed-forward networks. Recurrent networks, many probabilistic models, and some autoencoders have additional requirements that rule out the use of piecewise linear activation functions and make sigmoidal units more appealing despite the drawbacks of saturation.

6.3.3 Other Hidden Units

Many other types of hidden units are possible but are used less frequently.

In general, a wide variety of differentiable functions perform perfectly well. Many unpublished activation functions perform just as well as the popular ones. To provide a concrete example, we tested a feedforward network using $h = \cos(Wx+b)$ on the MNIST dataset and obtained an error rate of less than 1 percent, which is competitive with results obtained using more conventional activation functions. During research and development of new techniques, it is common to test many different activation functions and find that several variations on standard practice perform comparably. This means that usually new hidden unit types are published only if they are clearly demonstrated to provide a significant improvement. New hidden unit types that perform roughly comparably to known types are so common as to be uninteresting.

It would be impractical to list all the hidden unit types that have appeared in the literature. We highlight a few especially useful and distinctive ones.

One possibility is to not have an activation $g(z)$ at all. One can also think of this as using the identity function as the activation function. We have already seen that a linear unit can be useful as the output of a neural network. It may also be used as a hidden unit. If every layer of the neural network consists of only linear transformations, then the network as a whole will be linear. However, it is acceptable for some layers of the neural network to be purely linear. Consider a neural network layer with n inputs and p outputs, $h = g(W^\top x + b)$. We may replace this with two layers, with one layer using weight matrix U and the other using weight matrix V. If the first layer has no activation function, then we have essentially factored the weight matrix of the original layer based on W. The factored approach is to compute $h = g(V^\top U^\top x + b)$. If U produces q outputs, then U and V together contain only $(n + p)q$ parameters, while W contains np parameters. For small q, this can be a considerable saving in parameters. It comes at the cost of constraining the linear transformation to be low rank, but these low-rank relationships are often sufficient. Linear hidden units thus offer an effective way of reducing the number of parameters in a network.

Softmax units are another kind of unit that is usually used as an output (as described in section 6.2.2.3) but may sometimes be used as a hidden unit. Softmax units naturally represent a probability distribution over a discrete variable with k possible values, so they may be used as a kind of switch. These kinds of hidden units are usually only used in more advanced architectures that explicitly learn to manipulate memory, as described in section 10.12.

A few other reasonably common hidden unit types include

- **Radial basis function** (RBF), unit: $h_i = \exp\left(-\frac{1}{\sigma_i^2}||\boldsymbol{W}_{:,i} - \boldsymbol{x}||^2\right)$. This function becomes more active as $\boldsymbol{x}$ approaches a template $\boldsymbol{W}_{:,i}$. Because it saturates to 0 for most $\boldsymbol{x}$, it can be difficult to optimize.

- **Softplus**: $g(a) = \zeta(a) = \log(1 + e^a)$. This is a smooth version of the rectifier, introduced by Dugas et al. (2001) for function approximation and by Nair and Hinton (2010) for the conditional distributions of undirected probabilistic models. Glorot et al. (2011a) compared the softplus and rectifier and found better results with the latter. The use of the softplus is generally discouraged. The softplus demonstrates that the performance of hidden unit types can be very counterintuitive—one might expect it to have an advantage over the rectifier due to being differentiable everywhere or due to saturating less completely, but empirically it does not.

- **Hard tanh**. This is shaped similarly to the tanh and the rectifier, but unlike the latter, it is bounded, $g(a) = \max(-1, \min(1, a))$. It was introduced by Collobert (2004).

Hidden unit design remains an active area of research, and many useful hidden unit types remain to be discovered.

6.4 Architecture Design

Another key design consideration for neural networks is determining the architecture. The word **architecture** refers to the overall structure of the network: how many units it should have and how these units should be connected to each other.

Most neural networks are organized into groups of units called layers. Most neural network architectures arrange these layers in a chain structure, with each layer being a function of the layer that preceded it. In this structure, the first layer is given by

$$\boldsymbol{h}^{(1)} = g^{(1)}\left(\boldsymbol{W}^{(1)\top}\boldsymbol{x} + \boldsymbol{b}^{(1)}\right);$$ (6.40)

the second layer is given by

$$\boldsymbol{h}^{(2)} = g^{(2)} \left(\boldsymbol{W}^{(2)\top} \boldsymbol{h}^{(1)} + \boldsymbol{b}^{(2)} \right) ; \qquad (6.41)$$

and so on.

In these chain-based architectures, the main architectural considerations are choosing the depth of the network and the width of each layer. As we will see, a network with even one hidden layer is sufficient to fit the training set. Deeper networks are often able to use far fewer units per layer and far fewer parameters, as well as frequently generalizing to the test set, but they also tend to be harder to optimize. The ideal network architecture for a task must be found via experimentation guided by monitoring the validation set error.

6.4.1 Universal Approximation Properties and Depth

A linear model, mapping from features to outputs via matrix multiplication, can by definition represent only linear functions. It has the advantage of being easy to train because many loss functions result in convex optimization problems when applied to linear models. Unfortunately, we often want our systems to learn nonlinear functions.

At first glance, we might presume that learning a nonlinear function requires designing a specialized model family for the kind of nonlinearity we want to learn. Fortunately, feedforward networks with hidden layers provide a universal approximation framework. Specifically, the **universal approximation theorem** (Hornik et al., 1989; Cybenko, 1989) states that a feedforward network with a linear output layer and at least one hidden layer with any "squashing" activation function (such as the logistic sigmoid activation function) can approximate any Borel measurable function from one finite-dimensional space to another with any desired nonzero amount of error, provided that the network is given enough hidden units. The derivatives of the feedforward network can also approximate the derivatives of the function arbitrarily well (Hornik et al., 1990). The concept of Borel measurability is beyond the scope of this book; for our purposes it suffices to say that any continuous function on a closed and bounded subset of $\mathbb{R}^n$ is Borel measurable and therefore may be approximated by a neural network. A neural network may also approximate any function mapping from any finite dimensional discrete space to another. While the original theorems were first stated in terms of units with activation functions that saturate for both very negative and very positive arguments, universal approximation theorems have also been proved for a wider class of activation functions, which includes the now commonly used rectified linear unit (Leshno et al., 1993).

The universal approximation theorem means that regardless of what function we are trying to learn, we know that a large MLP will be able to *represent* this function. We are not guaranteed, however, that the training algorithm will be able to *learn* that function. Even if the MLP is able to represent the function, learning can fail for two different reasons. First, the optimization algorithm used for training may not be able to find the value of the parameters that corresponds to the desired function. Second, the training algorithm might choose the wrong function as a result of overfitting. Recall from section 5.2.1 that the no free lunch theorem shows that there is no universally superior machine learning algorithm. Feedforward networks provide a universal system for representing functions in the sense that, given a function, there exists a feedforward network that approximates the function. There is no universal procedure for examining a training set of specific examples and choosing a function that will generalize to points not in the training set.

According to the universal approximation theorem, there exists a network large enough to achieve any degree of accuracy we desire, but the theorem does not say how large this network will be. Barron (1993) provides some bounds on the size of a single-layer network needed to approximate a broad class of functions. Unfortunately, in the worst case, an exponential number of hidden units (possibly with one hidden unit corresponding to each input configuration that needs to be distinguished) may be required. This is easiest to see in the binary case: the number of possible binary functions on vectors $v \in \{0, 1\}^n$ is 2^{2^n} and selecting one such function requires 2^n bits, which will in general require $O(2^n)$ degrees of freedom.

In summary, a feedforward network with a single layer is sufficient to represent any function, but the layer may be infeasibly large and may fail to learn and generalize correctly. In many circumstances, using deeper models can reduce the number of units required to represent the desired function and can reduce the amount of generalization error.

Various families of functions can be approximated efficiently by an architecture with depth greater than some value d, but they require a much larger model if depth is restricted to be less than or equal to d. In many cases, the number of hidden units required by the shallow model is exponential in n. Such results were first proved for models that do not resemble the continuous, differentiable neural networks used for machine learning but have since been extended to these models. The first results were for circuits of logic gates (Håstad, 1986). Later work extended these results to linear threshold units with nonnegative weights (Håstad and Goldmann, 1991; Hajnal et al., 1993), and then to networks with continuous-valued activations (Maass, 1992; Maass et al., 1994). Many modern neural networks use rectified linear units. Leshno et al. (1993) demonstrated that shallow networks with a broad family of nonpolynomial activation functions, including rectified linear units, have universal approximation properties, but these results do not address the questions of depth or efficiency—they specify only that a sufficiently wide rectifier network could represent any function. Montufar et al. (2014) showed that functions representable with a deep rectifier net can require an exponential number of hidden units with a shallow (one hidden layer) network. More precisely, they showed that piecewise linear networks (which can be obtained from rectifier nonlinearities or maxout units) can represent functions with a number of regions that is exponential in the depth of the network. Figure 6.5 illustrates how a network with absolute value rectification creates mirror images of the function computed on top of some hidden unit, with respect to the input of that hidden unit. Each hidden unit specifies where to fold the input space in order to create mirror responses (on both sides of the absolute value nonlinearity). By composing these folding operations, we obtain an exponentially large number of piecewise linear regions that can capture all kinds of regular (e.g., repeating) patterns.

The main theorem in Montufar et al. (2014) states that the number of linear regions carved out by a deep rectifier network with d inputs, depth l, and n units per hidden layer is

$$O\left(\binom{n}{d}^{d(l-1)} n^d\right), \tag{6.42}$$

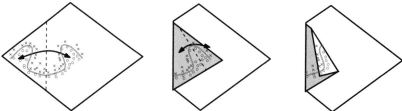

Figure 6.5: An intuitive, geometric explanation of the exponential advantage of deeper rectifier networks formally by Montufar et al. (2014). *(Left)* An absolute value rectification unit has the same output for every pair of mirror points in its input. The mirror axis of symmetry is given by the hyperplane defined by the weights and bias of the unit. A function computed on top of that unit (the green decision surface) will be a mirror image of a simpler pattern across that axis of symmetry. *(Center)* The function can be obtained by folding the space around the axis of symmetry. *(Right)* Another repeating pattern can be folded on top of the first (by another downstream unit) to obtain another symmetry (which is now repeated four times, with two hidden layers). Figure reproduced with permission from Montufar et al. (2014).

that is, exponential in depth l. In the case of maxout networks with k filters per unit, the number of linear regions is

$$O\left(k^{(l-1)+d}\right). \tag{6.43}$$

Of course, there is no guarantee that the kinds of functions we want to learn in applications of machine learning (and in particular for AI) share such a property.

We may also want to choose a deep model for statistical reasons. Any time we choose a specific machine learning algorithm, we are implicitly stating some set of prior beliefs we have about what kind of function the algorithm should learn. Choosing a deep model encodes a very general belief that the function we want to learn should involve composition of several simpler functions. This can be interpreted from a representation learning point of view as saying that we believe the learning problem consists of discovering a set of underlying factors of variation that can in turn be described in terms of other, simpler underlying factors of variation. Alternately, we can interpret the use of a deep architecture as expressing a belief that the function we want to learn is a computer program consisting of multiple steps, where each step makes use of the previous step's output. These intermediate outputs are not necessarily factors of variation but can instead be analogous to counters or pointers that the network uses to organize its internal processing. Empirically, greater depth does seem to result in better generalization for a wide variety of tasks (Bengio et al., 2007; Erhan et al., 2009; Bengio, 2009; Mesnil et al., 2011; Ciresan et al., 2012; Krizhevsky et al., 2012; Sermanet et al., 2013; Farabet et al., 2013; Couprie et al., 2013; Kahou et al., 2013; Goodfellow et al., 2014d; Szegedy et al., 2014a). See figure 6.6 and figure 6.7 for examples of some of these empirical results. These results suggest that using deep architectures does indeed express a useful prior over the space of functions the model learns.

6.4.2 Other Architectural Considerations

So far we have described neural networks as being simple chains of layers, with the main considerations being the depth of the network and the width of each layer. In practice, neural networks show considerably more diversity.

Many neural network architectures have been developed for specific tasks. Specialized architectures for computer vision called convolutional networks are described in chapter 9. Feedforward networks may also be generalized to the recurrent neural networks for sequence processing, described in chapter 10, which have their own architectural considerations.

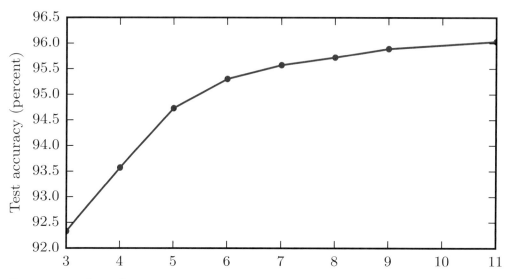

Figure 6.6: Effect of depth. Empirical results showing that deeper networks generalize better when used to transcribe multidigit numbers from photographs of addresses. Data from Goodfellow et al. (2014d). The test set accuracy consistently increases with increasing depth. See figure 6.7 for a control experiment demonstrating that other increases to the model size do not yield the same effect.

In general, the layers need not be connected in a chain, even though this is the most common practice. Many architectures build a main chain but then add extra architectural features to it, such as skip connections going from layer i to layer $i + 2$ or higher. These skip connections make it easier for the gradient to flow from output layers to layers nearer the input.

Another key consideration of architecture design is exactly how to connect a pair of layers to each other. In the default neural network layer described by a linear transformation via a matrix $\boldsymbol{W}$, every input unit is connected to every output unit. Many specialized networks in the chapters ahead have fewer connections, so that each unit in the input layer is connected to only a small subset of units in the output layer. These strategies for decreasing the number of connections reduce the number of parameters and the amount of computation required to evaluate the network but are often highly problem dependent. For example, convolutional networks, described in chapter 9, use specialized patterns of sparse connections that are very effective for computer vision problems. In this chapter, it is difficult to give more specific advice concerning the architecture of a generic neural network. In subsequent chapters we develop the particular architectural strategies that have been found to work well for different application domains.

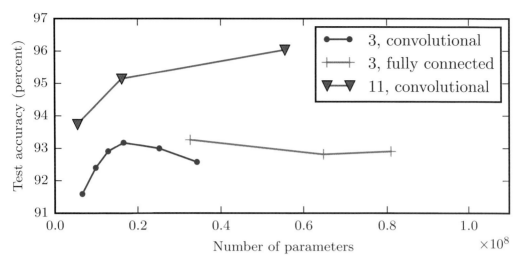

Figure 6.7: Effect of number of parameters. Deeper models tend to perform better. This is not merely because the model is larger. This experiment from Goodfellow et al. (2014d) shows that increasing the number of parameters in layers of convolutional networks without increasing their depth is not nearly as effective at increasing test set performance, as illustrated in this figure. The legend indicates the depth of network used to make each curve and whether the curve represents variation in the size of the convolutional or the fully connected layers. We observe that shallow models in this context overfit at around 20 million parameters while deep ones can benefit from having over 60 million. This suggests that using a deep model expresses a useful preference over the space of functions the model can learn. Specifically, it expresses a belief that the function should consist of many simpler functions composed together. This could result either in learning a representation that is composed in turn of simpler representations (e.g., corners defined in terms of edges) or in learning a program with sequentially dependent steps (e.g., first locate a set of objects, then segment them from each other, then recognize them).

6.5 Back-Propagation and Other Differentiation Algorithms

When we use a feedforward neural network to accept an input x and produce an output $\hat{y}$, information flows forward through the network. The input x provides the initial information that then propagates up to the hidden units at each layer and finally produces $\hat{y}$. This is called **forward propagation**. During training, forward propagation can continue onward until it produces a scalar cost $J(\boldsymbol{\theta})$. The **back-propagation** algorithm (Rumelhart et al., 1986a), often simply called **backprop**, allows the information from the cost to then flow backward through the network in order to compute the gradient.

Computing an analytical expression for the gradient is straightforward, but numerically evaluating such an expression can be computationally expensive. The back-propagation algorithm does so using a simple and inexpensive procedure.

The term back-propagation is often misunderstood as meaning the whole learning algorithm for multi layer neural networks. Actually, back-propagation refers only to the method for computing the gradient, while another algorithm, such as stochastic gradient descent, is used to perform learning using this gradient. Furthermore, back-propagation is often misunderstood as being specific to multi-layer neural networks, but in principle it can compute derivatives of any function (for some functions, the correct response is to report that the derivative of the function is undefined). Specifically, we will describe how to compute the gradient $\nabla_{\boldsymbol{x}} f(\boldsymbol{x}, \boldsymbol{y})$ for an arbitrary function f, where $\boldsymbol{x}$ is a set of variables whose derivatives are desired, and $\boldsymbol{y}$ is an additional set of variables that are inputs to the function but whose derivatives are not required. In learning algorithms, the gradient we most often require is the gradient of the cost function with respect to the parameters, $\nabla_{\boldsymbol{\theta}} J(\boldsymbol{\theta})$. Many machine learning tasks involve computing other derivatives, either as part of the learning process, or to analyze the learned model. The back-propagation algorithm can be applied to these tasks as well and is not restricted to computing the gradient of the cost function with respect to the parameters. The idea of computing derivatives by propagating information through a network is very general and can be used to compute values such as the Jacobian of a function f with multiple outputs. We restrict our description here to the most commonly used case, where f has a single output.

6.5.1 Computational Graphs

So far we have discussed neural networks with a relatively informal graph language. To describe the back-propagation algorithm more precisely, it is helpful to have a more precise **computational graph** language.

Many ways of formalizing computation as graphs are possible.

Here, we use each node in the graph to indicate a variable. The variable may be a scalar, vector, matrix, tensor, or even a variable of another type.

To formalize our graphs, we also need to introduce the idea of an **operation**. An operation is a simple function of one or more variables. Our graph language is accompanied by a set of allowable operations. Functions more complicated than the operations in this set may be described by composing many operations together.

Without loss of generality, we define an operation to return only a single output variable. This does not lose generality because the output variable can have multiple entries, such as a vector. Software implementations of back-propagation usually support operations with multiple outputs, but we avoid this case in our description because it introduces many extra details that are not important to conceptual understanding.

If a variable y is computed by applying an operation to a variable x, then we draw a directed edge from x to y. We sometimes annotate the output node with the name of the operation applied, and other times omit this label when the operation is clear from context.

Examples of computational graphs are shown in figure 6.8.

6.5.2 Chain Rule of Calculus

The chain rule of calculus (not to be confused with the chain rule of probability) is used to compute the derivatives of functions formed by composing other functions whose derivatives are known. Back-propagation is an algorithm that computes the chain rule, with a specific order of operations that is highly efficient.

Let x be a real number, and let f and g both be functions mapping from a real number to a real number. Suppose that $y = g(x)$ and $z = f(g(x)) = f(y)$. Then the chain rule states that

$$\frac{dz}{dx} = \frac{dz}{dy}\frac{dy}{dx}. \tag{6.44}$$

We can generalize this beyond the scalar case. Suppose that $\boldsymbol{x} \in \mathbb{R}^m$, $\boldsymbol{y} \in \mathbb{R}^n$, g maps from $\mathbb{R}^m$ to $\mathbb{R}^n$, and f maps from $\mathbb{R}^n$ to $\mathbb{R}$. If $\boldsymbol{y} = g(\boldsymbol{x})$ and $z = f(\boldsymbol{y})$, then

$$\frac{\partial z}{\partial x_i} = \sum_j \frac{\partial z}{\partial y_j}\frac{\partial y_j}{\partial x_i}. \tag{6.45}$$

In vector notation, this may be equivalently written as

$$\nabla_{\boldsymbol{x}} z = \left(\frac{\partial \boldsymbol{y}}{\partial \boldsymbol{x}}\right)^{\top} \nabla_{\boldsymbol{y}} z, \tag{6.46}$$

where $\frac{\partial \boldsymbol{y}}{\partial \boldsymbol{x}}$ is the $n \times m$ Jacobian matrix of g.

From this we see that the gradient of a variable $\boldsymbol{x}$ can be obtained by multiplying a Jacobian matrix $\frac{\partial \boldsymbol{y}}{\partial \boldsymbol{x}}$ by a gradient $\nabla_{\boldsymbol{y}} z$. The back-propagation algorithm consists of performing such a Jacobian-gradient product for each operation in the graph.

Usually we apply the back-propagation algorithm to tensors of arbitrary dimensionality, not merely to vectors. Conceptually, this is exactly the same as

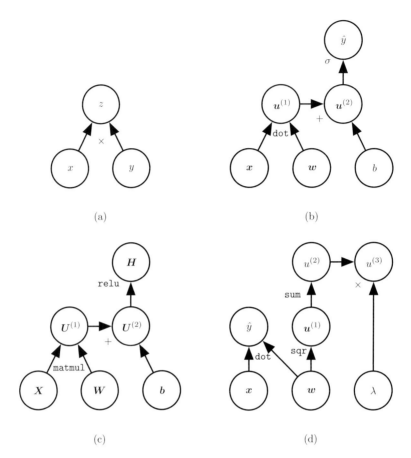

Figure 6.8: Examples of computational graphs. *(a)* The graph using the $\times$ operation to compute $z = xy$. *(b)* The graph for the logistic regression prediction $\hat{y} = \sigma\left(\boldsymbol{x}^{\top}\boldsymbol{w} + b\right)$. Some of the intermediate expressions do not have names in the algebraic expression but need names in the graph. We simply name the i-th such variable $\boldsymbol{u}^{(i)}$. *(c)* The computational graph for the expression $\boldsymbol{H} = \max\{0, \boldsymbol{XW} + \boldsymbol{b}\}$, which computes a design matrix of rectified linear unit activations $\boldsymbol{H}$ given a design matrix containing a minibatch of inputs $\boldsymbol{X}$. *(d)* Examples a–c applied at most one operation to each variable, but it is possible to apply more than one operation. Here we show a computation graph that applies more than one operation to the weights $\boldsymbol{w}$ of a linear regression model. The weights are used to make both the prediction $\hat{y}$ and the weight decay penalty $\lambda \sum_i w_i^2$.

back-propagation with vectors. The only difference is how the numbers are arranged in a grid to form a tensor. We could imagine flattening each tensor into a vector before we run back-propagation, computing a vector-valued gradient, and then reshaping the gradient back into a tensor. In this rearranged view, back-propagation is still just multiplying Jacobians by gradients.

To denote the gradient of a value z with respect to a tensor $\mathbf{X}$, we write $\nabla_{\mathbf{X}} z$, just as if $\mathbf{X}$ were a vector. The indices into $\mathbf{X}$ now have multiple coordinates—for example, a 3-D tensor is indexed by three coordinates. We can abstract this away by using a single variable i to represent the complete tuple of indices. For all possible index tuples i, $(\nabla_{\mathbf{X}} z)_i$ gives $\frac{\partial z}{\partial \mathsf{X}_i}$. This is exactly the same as how for all possible integer indices i into a vector, $(\nabla_{\boldsymbol{x}} z)_i$ gives $\frac{\partial z}{\partial x_i}$. Using this notation, we can write the chain rule as it applies to tensors. If $\mathbf{Y} = g(\mathbf{X})$ and $z = f(\mathbf{Y})$, then

$$\nabla_{\mathbf{X}} z = \sum_j (\nabla_{\mathbf{X}} \mathsf{Y}_j) \frac{\partial z}{\partial \mathsf{Y}_j}. \tag{6.47}$$

6.5.3 Recursively Applying the Chain Rule to Obtain Backprop

Using the chain rule, it is straightforward to write down an algebraic expression for the gradient of a scalar with respect to any node in the computational graph that produced that scalar. Actually evaluating that expression in a computer, however, introduces some extra considerations.

Specifically, many subexpressions may be repeated several times within the overall expression for the gradient. Any procedure that computes the gradient will need to choose whether to store these subexpressions or to recompute them several times. An example of how these repeated subexpressions arise is given in figure 6.9. In some cases, computing the same subexpression twice would simply be wasteful. For complicated graphs, there can be exponentially many of these wasted computations, making a naive implementation of the chain rule infeasible. In other cases, computing the same subexpression twice could be a valid way to reduce memory consumption at the cost of higher runtime.

We begin with a version of the back-propagation algorithm that specifies the actual gradient computation directly (algorithm 6.2 along with algorithm 6.1 for the associated forward computation), in the order it will actually be done and according to the recursive application of chain rule. One could either directly perform these computations or view the description of the algorithm as a symbolic specification of the computational graph for computing the back-propagation. However, this formulation does not make explicit the manipulation and the construction of the symbolic graph that performs the gradient computation. Such a formulation is presented in section 6.5.6, with algorithm 6.5, where we also generalize to nodes that contain arbitrary tensors.

First consider a computational graph describing how to compute a single scalar $u^{(n)}$ (say, the loss on a training example). This scalar is the quantity whose gradient we want to obtain, with respect to the n_i input nodes $u^{(1)}$ to $u^{(n_i)}$. In other words, we wish to compute $\frac{\partial u^{(n)}}{\partial u^{(i)}}$ for all $i \in \{1, 2, \ldots, n_i\}$. In the application of back-propagation to computing gradients for gradient descent over parameters, $u^{(n)}$ will be the cost associated with an example or a minibatch, while $u^{(1)}$ to $u^{(n_i)}$ correspond to the parameters of the model.

We will assume that the nodes of the graph have been ordered in such a way that we can compute their output one after the other, starting at $u^{(n_i+1)}$ and going up to $u^{(n)}$. As defined in algorithm 6.1, each node $u^{(i)}$ is associated with an operation $f^{(i)}$ and is computed by evaluating the function

$$u^{(i)} = f(\mathbb{A}^{(i)}), \tag{6.48}$$

where $\mathbb{A}^{(i)}$ is the set of all nodes that are parents of $u^{(i)}$.

That algorithm specifies the forward propagation computation, which we could put in a graph $\mathcal{G}$. To perform back-propagation, we can construct a computational graph that depends on $\mathcal{G}$ and adds to it an extra set of nodes. These form a subgraph $\mathcal{B}$ with one node per node of $\mathcal{G}$. Computation in $\mathcal{B}$ proceeds in exactly the reverse of the order of computation in $\mathcal{G}$, and each node of $\mathcal{B}$ computes the derivative $\frac{\partial u^{(n)}}{\partial u^{(i)}}$ associated with the forward graph node $u^{(i)}$. This is done using the chain rule with respect to scalar output $u^{(n)}$:

$$\frac{\partial u^{(n)}}{\partial u^{(j)}} = \sum_{i:j \in Pa(u^{(i)})} \frac{\partial u^{(n)}}{\partial u^{(i)}} \frac{\partial u^{(i)}}{\partial u^{(j)}} \tag{6.49}$$

Algorithm 6.1 A procedure that performs the computations mapping n_i inputs $u^{(1)}$ to $u^{(n_i)}$ to an output $u^{(n)}$. This defines a computational graph where each node computes numerical value $u^{(i)}$ by applying a function $f^{(i)}$ to the set of arguments $\mathbb{A}^{(i)}$ that comprises the values of previous nodes $u^{(j)}$, $j < i$, with $j \in Pa(u^{(i)})$. The input to the computational graph is the vector $\boldsymbol{x}$, and is set into the first n_i nodes $u^{(1)}$ to $u^{(n_i)}$. The output of the computational graph is read off the last (output) node $u^{(n)}$.

---

    for $i = 1, \ldots, n_i$ **do**
       $u^{(i)} \leftarrow x_i$
    end for
    for $i = n_i + 1, \ldots, n$ **do**
       $\mathbb{A}^{(i)} \leftarrow \{u^{(j)} \mid j \in Pa(u^{(i)})\}$
       $u^{(i)} \leftarrow f^{(i)}(\mathbb{A}^{(i)})$
    end for
    return $u^{(n)}$

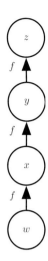

Figure 6.9: A computational graph that results in repeated subexpressions when computing the gradient. Let $w \in \mathbb{R}$ be the input to the graph. We use the same function $f : \mathbb{R} \to \mathbb{R}$ as the operation that we apply at every step of a chain: $x = f(w)$, $y = f(x)$, $z = f(y)$. To compute $\frac{\partial z}{\partial w}$, we apply equation 6.44 and obtain:

$$\frac{\partial z}{\partial w} \tag{6.50}$$

$$= \frac{\partial z}{\partial y} \frac{\partial y}{\partial x} \frac{\partial x}{\partial w} \tag{6.51}$$

$$= f'(y) f'(x) f'(w) \tag{6.52}$$

$$= f'(f(f(w))) f'(f(w)) f'(w). \tag{6.53}$$

Equation 6.52 suggests an implementation in which we compute the value of $f(w)$ only once and store it in the variable x. This is the approach taken by the back-propagation algorithm. An alternative approach is suggested by equation 6.53, where the subexpression $f(w)$ appears more than once. In the alternative approach, $f(w)$ is recomputed each time it is needed. When the memory required to store the value of these expressions is low, the back-propagation approach of equation 6.52 is clearly preferable because of its reduced runtime. However, equation 6.53 is also a valid implementation of the chain rule and is useful when memory is limited.

as specified by algorithm 6.2. The subgraph $\mathcal{B}$ contains exactly one edge for each edge from node $u^{(j)}$ to node $u^{(i)}$ of $\mathcal{G}$. The edge from $u^{(j)}$ to $u^{(i)}$ is associated with the computation of $\frac{\partial u^{(i)}}{\partial u^{(j)}}$. In addition, a dot product is performed for each node, between the gradient already computed with respect to nodes $u^{(i)}$ that are children of $u^{(j)}$ and the vector containing the partial derivatives $\frac{\partial u^{(i)}}{\partial u^{(j)}}$ for the same children nodes $u^{(i)}$. To summarize, the amount of computation required for performing the back-propagation scales linearly with the number of edges in $\mathcal{G}$, where the computation for each edge corresponds to computing a partial derivative (of one node with respect to one of its parents) as well as performing one multiplication and one addition. Below, we generalize this analysis to tensor-valued nodes, which is just a way to group multiple scalar values in the same node and enable more efficient implementations.

The back-propagation algorithm is designed to reduce the number of common subexpressions without regard to memory. Specifically, it performs on the order of one Jacobian product per node in the graph. This can be seen from the fact that backprop (algorithm 6.2) visits each edge from node $u^{(j)}$ to node $u^{(i)}$ of the graph exactly once in order to obtain the associated partial derivative $\frac{\partial u^{(i)}}{\partial u^{(j)}}$. Back-propagation thus avoids the exponential explosion in repeated subexpressions. Other algorithms may be able to avoid more subexpressions by performing simplifications

---

Algorithm 6.2 Simplified version of the back-propagation algorithm for computing the derivatives of $u^{(n)}$ with respect to the variables in the graph. This example is intended to further understanding by showing a simplified case where all variables are scalars, and we wish to compute the derivatives with respect to $u^{(1)}, \ldots, u^{(n_i)}$. This simplified version computes the derivatives of all nodes in the graph. The computational cost of this algorithm is proportional to the number of edges in the graph, assuming that the partial derivative associated with each edge requires a constant time. This is of the same order as the number of computations for the forward propagation. Each $\frac{\partial u^{(i)}}{\partial u^{(j)}}$ is a function of the parents $u^{(j)}$ of $u^{(i)}$, thus linking the nodes of the forward graph to those added for the back-propagation graph.

Run forward propagation (algorithm 6.1 for this example) to obtain the activations of the network.

Initialize `grad_table`, a data structure that will store the derivatives that have been computed. The entry `grad_table`$[u^{(i)}]$ will store the computed value of $\frac{\partial u^{(n)}}{\partial u^{(i)}}$.

`grad_table`$[u^{(n)}] \leftarrow 1$

for $j = n - 1$ down to 1 **do**

  The next line computes $\frac{\partial u^{(n)}}{\partial u^{(j)}} = \sum_{i:j \in Pa(u^{(i)})} \frac{\partial u^{(n)}}{\partial u^{(i)}} \frac{\partial u^{(i)}}{\partial u^{(j)}}$ using stored values:

  `grad_table`$[u^{(j)}] \leftarrow \sum_{i:j \in Pa(u^{(i)})}$ `grad_table`$[u^{(i)}] \frac{\partial u^{(i)}}{\partial u^{(j)}}$

end for

return $\{$`grad_table`$[u^{(i)}] \mid i = 1, \ldots, n_i\}$

---

on the computational graph, or may be able to conserve memory by recomputing rather than storing some subexpressions. We revisit these ideas after describing the back-propagation algorithm itself.

6.5.4 Back-Propagation Computation in Fully Connected MLP

To clarify the above definition of the back-propagation computation, let us consider the specific graph associated with a fully-connected multi layer MLP.

Algorithm 6.3 first shows the forward propagation, which maps parameters to the supervised loss $L(\hat{y}, y)$ associated with a single (input,target) training example (x, y), with $\hat{y}$ the output of the neural network when x is provided in input.

Algorithm 6.4 then shows the corresponding computation to be done for applying the back-propagation algorithm to this graph.

Algorithms 6.3 and 6.4 are demonstrations chosen to be simple and straight-forward to understand. However, they are specialized to one specific problem.

Modern software implementations are based on the generalized form of back-propagation described in section 6.5.6 below, which can accommodate any

---

Algorithm 6.3 Forward propagation through a typical deep neural network and the computation of the cost function. The loss $L(\hat{y}, y)$ depends on the output $\hat{y}$ and on the target y (see section 6.2.1.1 for examples of loss functions). To obtain the total cost J, the loss may be added to a regularizer $\Omega(\theta)$, where θ contains all the parameters (weights and biases). Algorithm 6.4 shows how to compute gradients of J with respect to parameters W and b. For simplicity, this demonstration uses only a single input example x. Practical applications should use a minibatch. See section 6.5.7 for a more realistic demonstration.

Require: Network depth, l
Require: $W^{(i)}, i \in \{1, \ldots, l\}$, the weight matrices of the model
Require: $b^{(i)}, i \in \{1, \ldots, l\}$, the bias parameters of the model
Require: x, the input to process
Require: y, the target output
  $h^{(0)} = x$
  for $k = 1, \ldots, l$ **do**
    $a^{(k)} = b^{(k)} + W^{(k)} h^{(k-1)}$
    $h^{(k)} = f(a^{(k)})$
  end for
  $\hat{y} = h^{(l)}$
  $J = L(\hat{y}, y) + \lambda \Omega(\theta)$

Algorithm 6.4 Backward computation for the deep neural network of algorithm 6.3, which uses, in addition to the input $\boldsymbol{x}$, a target $\boldsymbol{y}$. This computation yields the gradients on the activations $\boldsymbol{a}^{(k)}$ for each layer k, starting from the output layer and going backwards to the first hidden layer. From these gradients, which can be interpreted as an indication of how each layer's output should change to reduce error, one can obtain the gradient on the parameters of each layer. The gradients on weights and biases can be immediately used as part of a stochastic gradient update (performing the update right after the gradients have been computed) or used with other gradient-based optimization methods.

After the forward computation, compute the gradient on the output layer:
$\boldsymbol{g} \leftarrow \nabla_{\hat{\boldsymbol{y}}} J = \nabla_{\hat{\boldsymbol{y}}} L(\hat{\boldsymbol{y}}, \boldsymbol{y})$
for $k = l, l - 1, \ldots, 1$ **do**
    Convert the gradient on the layer's output into a gradient into the pre-nonlinearity activation (element-wise multiplication if f is element-wise):

    $\boldsymbol{g} \leftarrow \nabla_{\boldsymbol{a}^{(k)}} J = \boldsymbol{g} \odot f'(\boldsymbol{a}^{(k)})$
    Compute gradients on weights and biases (including the regularization term, where needed):
    $\nabla_{\boldsymbol{b}^{(k)}} J = \boldsymbol{g} + \lambda \nabla_{\boldsymbol{b}^{(k)}} \Omega(\theta)$
    $\nabla_{\boldsymbol{W}^{(k)}} J = \boldsymbol{g} \, \boldsymbol{h}^{(k-1)\top} + \lambda \nabla_{\boldsymbol{W}^{(k)}} \Omega(\theta)$
    Propagate the gradients w.r.t. the next lower-level hidden layer's activations:
    $\boldsymbol{g} \leftarrow \nabla_{\boldsymbol{h}^{(k-1)}} J = \boldsymbol{W}^{(k)\top} \boldsymbol{g}$
end for

---

computational graph by explicitly manipulating a data structure for representing symbolic computation.

6.5.5 Symbol-to-Symbol Derivatives

Algebraic expressions and computational graphs both operate on **symbols**, or variables that do not have specific values. These algebraic and graph-based representations are called **symbolic representations**. When we actually use or train a neural network, we must assign specific values to these symbols. We replace a symbolic input to the network $\boldsymbol{x}$ with a specific **numeric** value, such as $[1.2, 3.765, -1.8]^\top$.

Some approaches to back-propagation take a computational graph and a set of numerical values for the inputs to the graph, then return a set of numerical values describing the gradient at those input values. We call this approach

symbol-to-number differentiation. This is the approach used by libraries such as Torch (Collobert et al., 2011b) and Caffe (Jia, 2013).

Another approach is to take a computational graph and add additional nodes to the graph that provide a symbolic description of the desired derivatives. This is the approach taken by Theano (Bergstra et al., 2010; Bastien et al., 2012) and TensorFlow (Abadi et al., 2015). An example of how it works is illustrated in figure 6.10. The primary advantage of this approach is that the derivatives are described in the same language as the original expression. Because the derivatives are just another computational graph, it is possible to run back-propagation again, differentiating the derivatives to obtain higher derivatives. (Computation of higher-order derivatives is described in section 6.5.10.)

We will use the latter approach and describe the back-propagation algorithm in terms of constructing a computational graph for the derivatives. Any subset of the graph may then be evaluated using specific numerical values at a later time. This allows us to avoid specifying exactly when each operation should be computed.

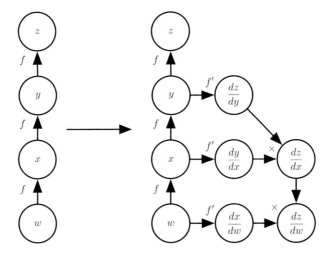

Figure 6.10: An example of the symbol-to-symbol approach to computing derivatives. In this approach, the back-propagation algorithm does not need to ever access any actual specific numeric values. Instead, it adds nodes to a computational graph describing how to compute these derivatives. A generic graph evaluation engine can later compute the derivatives for any specific numeric values. *(Left)* In this example, we begin with a graph representing $z = f(f(f(w)))$. *(Right)* We run the back-propagation algorithm, instructing it to construct the graph for the expression corresponding to $\frac{dz}{dw}$. In this example, we do not explain how the back-propagation algorithm works. The purpose is only to illustrate what the desired result is: a computational graph with a symbolic description of the derivative.

Instead, a generic graph evaluation engine can evaluate every node as soon as its parents' values are available.

The description of the symbol-to-symbol based approach subsumes the symbol-to-number approach. The symbol-to-number approach can be understood as performing exactly the same computations as are done in the graph built by the symbol-to-symbol approach. The key difference is that the symbol-to-number approach does not expose the graph.

6.5.6 General Back-Propagation

The back-propagation algorithm is very simple. To compute the gradient of some scalar z with respect to one of its ancestors x in the graph, we begin by observing that the gradient with respect to z is given by $\frac{dz}{dz} = 1$. We can then compute the gradient with respect to each parent of z in the graph by multiplying the current gradient by the Jacobian of the operation that produced z. We continue multiplying by Jacobians, traveling backward through the graph in this way until we reach x. For any node that may be reached by going backward from z through two or more paths, we simply sum the gradients arriving from different paths at that node.

More formally, each node in the graph $\mathcal{G}$ corresponds to a variable. To achieve maximum generality, we describe this variable as being a tensor $\mathbf{V}$. Tensors in general can have any number of dimensions. They subsume scalars, vectors, and matrices.

We assume that each variable $\mathbf{V}$ is associated with the following subroutines:

- `get_operation(V)`: This returns the operation that computes $\mathbf{V}$, represented by the edges coming into $\mathbf{V}$ in the computational graph. For example, there may be a Python or C++ class representing the matrix multiplication operation, and the `get_operation` function. Suppose we have a variable that is created by matrix multiplication, $\boldsymbol{C} = \boldsymbol{A}\boldsymbol{B}$. Then `get_operation(V)` returns a pointer to an instance of the corresponding C++ class.

- `get_consumers(V, `$\mathcal{G}$`)`: This returns the list of variables that are children of $\mathbf{V}$ in the computational graph $\mathcal{G}$.

- `get_inputs(V, `$\mathcal{G}$`)`: This returns the list of variables that are parents of $\mathbf{V}$ in the computational graph $\mathcal{G}$.

Each operation `op` is also associated with a `bprop` operation. This `bprop` operation can compute a Jacobian-vector product as described by equation 6.47.

This is how the back-propagation algorithm is able to achieve great generality. Each operation is responsible for knowing how to back-propagate through the edges in the graph that it participates in. For example, we might use a matrix multiplication operation to create a variable $C = AB$. Suppose that the gradient of a scalar z with respect to C is given by G. The matrix multiplication operation is responsible for defining two back-propagation rules, one for each of its input arguments. If we call the `bprop` method to request the gradient with respect to A given that the gradient on the output is G, then the `bprop` method of the matrix multiplication operation must state that the gradient with respect to A is given by $GB^\top$. Likewise, if we call the `bprop` method to request the gradient with respect to B, then the matrix operation is responsible for implementing the `bprop` method and specifying that the desired gradient is given by $A^\top G$. The back-propagation algorithm itself does not need to know any differentiation rules. It only needs to call each operation's `bprop` rules with the right arguments. Formally, `op.bprop(inputs, X, G)` must return

$$\sum_i (\nabla_{\mathsf{X}} \mathrm{op.f(inputs)}_i)\, \mathsf{G}_i, \qquad (6.54)$$

which is just an implementation of the chain rule as expressed in equation 6.47. Here, `inputs` is a list of inputs that are supplied to the operation, `op.f` is the mathematical function that the operation implements, X is the input whose gradient we wish to compute, and G is the gradient on the output of the operation.

The `op.bprop` method should always pretend that all its inputs are distinct from each other, even if they are not. For example, if the `mul` operator is passed two copies of x to compute x^2, the `op.bprop` method should still return x as the derivative with respect to both inputs. The back-propagation algorithm will later add both of these arguments together to obtain $2x$, which is the correct total derivative on x.

Software implementations of back-propagation usually provide both the operations and their `bprop` methods, so that users of deep learning software libraries are able to back-propagate through graphs built using common operations like matrix multiplication, exponents, logarithms, and so on. Software engineers who build a new implementation of back-propagation or advanced users who need to add their own operation to an existing library must usually derive the `op.bprop` method for any new operations manually.

The back-propagation algorithm is formally described in algorithm 6.5.

In section 6.5.2, we explained that back-propagation was developed in order to avoid computing the same subexpression in the chain rule multiple times. The naive

---

Algorithm 6.5 The outermost skeleton of the back-propagation algorithm. This portion does simple setup and cleanup work. Most of the important work happens in the `build_grad` subroutine of algorithm 6.6

Require: $\mathbb{T}$, the target set of variables whose gradients must be computed.
Require: $\mathcal{G}$, the computational graph
Require: z, the variable to be differentiated
  Let $\mathcal{G}'$ be $\mathcal{G}$ pruned to contain only nodes that are ancestors of z and descendents of nodes in $\mathbb{T}$.
  Initialize `grad_table`, a data structure associating tensors to their gradients
  grad_table[z] $\leftarrow 1$
  for $\mathbf{V}$ in $\mathbb{T}$ **do**
    build_grad($\mathbf{V}, \mathcal{G}, \mathcal{G}',$ grad_table)
  end for
  Return `grad_table` restricted to $\mathbb{T}$

Algorithm 6.6 The inner loop subroutine build_grad($\mathbf{V}, \mathcal{G}, \mathcal{G}',$ grad_table) of the back-propagation algorithm, called by the back-propagation algorithm defined in algorithm 6.5.

Require: $\mathbf{V}$, the variable whose gradient should be added to $\mathcal{G}$ and `grad_table`
Require: $\mathcal{G}$, the graph to modify
Require: $\mathcal{G}'$, the restriction of $\mathcal{G}$ to nodes that participate in the gradient
Require: `grad_table`, a data structure mapping nodes to their gradients
  if $\mathbf{V}$ is in `grad_table` **then**
    Return grad_table[$\mathbf{V}$]
  end if
  $i \leftarrow 1$
  for $\mathbf{C}$ in get_consumers($\mathbf{V}, \mathcal{G}'$) **do**
    op $\leftarrow$ get_operation($\mathbf{C}$)
    $\mathbf{D} \leftarrow$ build_grad($\mathbf{C}, \mathcal{G}, \mathcal{G}',$ grad_table)
    $\mathbf{G}^{(i)} \leftarrow$ op.bprop(get_inputs($\mathbf{C}, \mathcal{G}'$), $\mathbf{V}, \mathbf{D}$)
    $i \leftarrow i + 1$
  end for
  $\mathbf{G} \leftarrow \sum_i \mathbf{G}^{(i)}$
  grad_table[$\mathbf{V}$] $= \mathbf{G}$
  Insert $\mathbf{G}$ and the operations creating it into $\mathcal{G}$
  Return $\mathbf{G}$

---

algorithm could have exponential runtime due to these repeated subexpressions. Now that we have specified the back-propagation algorithm, we can understand its computational cost. If we assume that each operation evaluation has roughly the same cost, then we may analyze the computational cost in terms of the number of operations executed. Keep in mind here that we refer to an operation as the fundamental unit of our computational graph, which might actually consist of several arithmetic operations (for example, we might have a graph that treats matrix multiplication as a single operation). Computing a gradient in a graph with n nodes will never execute more than $O(n^2)$ operations or store the output of more than $O(n^2)$ operations. Here we are counting operations in the computational graph, not individual operations executed by the underlying hardware, so it is important to remember that the runtime of each operation may be highly variable. For example, multiplying two matrices that each contain millions of entries might correspond to a single operation in the graph. We can see that computing the gradient requires at most $O(n^2)$ operations because the forward propagation stage will at worst execute all n nodes in the original graph (depending on which values we want to compute, we may not need to execute the entire graph). The back-propagation algorithm adds one Jacobian-vector product, which should be expressed with $O(1)$ nodes, per edge in the original graph. Because the computational graph is a directed acyclic graph it has at most $O(n^2)$ edges. For the kinds of graphs that are commonly used in practice, the situation is even better. Most neural network cost functions are roughly chain-structured, causing back-propagation to have $O(n)$ cost. This is far better than the naive approach, which might need to execute exponentially many nodes. This potentially exponential cost can be seen by expanding and rewriting the recursive chain rule (equation 6.49) nonrecursively:

$$\frac{\partial u^{(n)}}{\partial u^{(j)}} = \sum_{\substack{\text{path } (u^{(\pi_1)}, u^{(\pi_2)}, \dots, u^{(\pi_t)}), \\ \text{from } \pi_1 = j \text{ to } \pi_t = n}} \prod_{k=2}^{t} \frac{\partial u^{(\pi_k)}}{\partial u^{(\pi_{k-1})}}. \tag{6.55}$$

Since the number of paths from node j to node n can grow exponentially in the length of these paths, the number of terms in the above sum, which is the number of such paths, can grow exponentially with the depth of the forward propagation graph. This large cost would be incurred because the same computation for $\frac{\partial u^{(i)}}{\partial u^{(j)}}$ would be redone many times. To avoid such recomputation, we can think of back-propagation as a table-filling algorithm that takes advantage of storing intermediate results $\frac{\partial u^{(n)}}{\partial u^{(i)}}$. Each node in the graph has a corresponding slot in a table to store the gradient for that node. By filling in these table entries in order, back-propagation avoids repeating many common subexpressions. This table-filling strategy is sometimes called **dynamic programming**.

6.5.7 Example: Back-Propagation for MLP Training

As an example, we walk through the back-propagation algorithm as it is used to train a multilayer perceptron.

Here we develop a very simple multilayer perceptron with a single hidden layer. To train this model, we will use minibatch stochastic gradient descent. The back-propagation algorithm is used to compute the gradient of the cost on a single minibatch. Specifically, we use a minibatch of examples from the training set formatted as a design matrix $\boldsymbol{X}$ and a vector of associated class labels $\boldsymbol{y}$. The network computes a layer of hidden features $\boldsymbol{H} = \max\{0, \boldsymbol{X}\boldsymbol{W}^{(1)}\}$. To simplify the presentation we do not use biases in this model. We assume that our graph language includes a `relu` operation that can compute $\max\{0, \boldsymbol{Z}\}$ element-wise. The predictions of the unnormalized log probabilities over classes are then given by $\boldsymbol{H}\boldsymbol{W}^{(2)}$. We assume that our graph language includes a `cross_entropy` operation that computes the cross-entropy between the targets $\boldsymbol{y}$ and the probability distribution defined by these unnormalized log probabilities. The resulting cross-entropy defines the cost J_{MLE}. Minimizing this cross-entropy performs maximum likelihood estimation of the classifier. However, to make this example more realistic, we also include a regularization term. The total cost

$$J = J_{\mathrm{MLE}} + \lambda \left(\sum_{i,j} \left(W_{i,j}^{(1)}\right)^2 + \sum_{i,j} \left(W_{i,j}^{(2)}\right)^2 \right) \tag{6.56}$$

consists of the cross-entropy and a weight decay term with coefficient λ. The computational graph is illustrated in figure 6.11.

The computational graph for the gradient of this example is large enough that it would be tedious to draw or to read. This demonstrates one of the benefits of the back-propagation algorithm, which is that it can automatically generate gradients that would be straightforward but tedious for a software engineer to derive manually.

We can roughly trace out the behavior of the back-propagation algorithm by looking at the forward propagation graph in figure 6.11. To train, we wish to compute both $\nabla_{\boldsymbol{W}^{(1)}} J$ and $\nabla_{\boldsymbol{W}^{(2)}} J$. There are two different paths leading backward from J to the weights: one through the cross-entropy cost, and one through the weight decay cost. The weight decay cost is relatively simple; it will always contribute $2\lambda \boldsymbol{W}^{(i)}$ to the gradient on $\boldsymbol{W}^{(i)}$.

The other path through the cross-entropy cost is slightly more complicated. Let $\boldsymbol{G}$ be the gradient on the unnormalized log probabilities $\boldsymbol{U}^{(2)}$ provided by the `cross_entropy` operation. The back-propagation algorithm now needs to

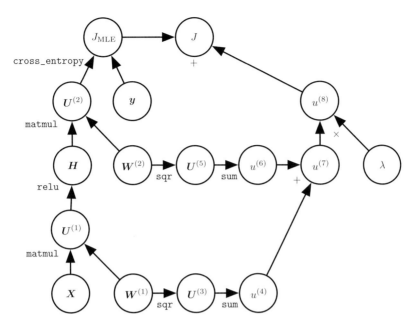

Figure 6.11: The computational graph used to compute the cost to train our example of a single-layer MLP using the cross-entropy loss and weight decay.

explore two different branches. On the shorter branch, it adds $\boldsymbol{H}^\top \boldsymbol{G}$ to the gradient on $\boldsymbol{W}^{(2)}$, using the back-propagation rule for the second argument to the matrix multiplication operation. The other branch corresponds to the longer chain descending further along the network. First, the back-propagation algorithm computes $\nabla_{\boldsymbol{H}} J = \boldsymbol{G} \boldsymbol{W}^{(2)\top}$ using the back-propagation rule for the first argument to the matrix multiplication operation. Next, the `relu` operation uses its back-propagation rule to zero out components of the gradient corresponding to entries of $\boldsymbol{U}^{(1)}$ that are less than 0. Let the result be called $\boldsymbol{G}'$. The last step of the back-propagation algorithm is to use the back-propagation rule for the second argument of the `matmul` operation to add $\boldsymbol{X}^\top \boldsymbol{G}'$ to the gradient on $\boldsymbol{W}^{(1)}$.

After these gradients have been computed, the gradient descent algorithm, or another optimization algorithm, uses these gradients to update the parameters.

For the MLP, the computational cost is dominated by the cost of matrix multiplication. During the forward propagation stage, we multiply by each weight matrix, resulting in $O(w)$ multiply-adds, where w is the number of weights. During the backward propagation stage, we multiply by the transpose of each weight matrix, which has the same computational cost. The main memory cost of the algorithm is that we need to store the input to the nonlinearity of the hidden layer. This value is stored from the time it is computed until the backward pass has returned to the same point. The memory cost is thus $O(mn_h)$, where m is the number of examples in the minibatch and n_h is the number of hidden units.

6.5.8 Complications

Our description of the back-propagation algorithm here is simpler than the implementations actually used in practice.

As noted above, we have restricted the definition of an operation to be a function that returns a single tensor. Most software implementations need to support operations that can return more than one tensor. For example, if we wish to compute both the maximum value in a tensor and the index of that value, it is best to compute both in a single pass through memory, so it is most efficient to implement this procedure as a single operation with two outputs.

We have not described how to control the memory consumption of back-propagation. Back-propagation often involves summation of many tensors together. In the naive approach, each of these tensors would be computed separately, then all of them would be added in a second step. The naive approach has an overly high memory bottleneck that can be avoided by maintaining a single buffer and adding each value to that buffer as it is computed.

Real-world implementations of back-propagation also need to handle various data types, such as 32-bit floating point, 64-bit floating point, and integer values. The policy for handling each of these types takes special care to design.

Some operations have undefined gradients, and it is important to track these cases and determine whether the gradient requested by the user is undefined.

Various other technicalities make real-world differentiation more complicated. These technicalities are not insurmountable, and this chapter has described the key intellectual tools needed to compute derivatives, but it is important to be aware that many more subtleties exist.

6.5.9 Differentiation outside the Deep Learning Community

The deep learning community has been somewhat isolated from the broader computer science community and has largely developed its own cultural attitudes concerning how to perform differentiation. More generally, the field of **automatic differentiation** is concerned with how to compute derivatives algorithmically. The back-propagation algorithm described here is only one approach to automatic differentiation. It is a special case of a broader class of techniques called **reverse**

mode accumulation. Other approaches evaluate the subexpressions of the chain rule in different orders. In general, determining the order of evaluation that results in the lowest computational cost is a difficult problem. Finding the optimal sequence of operations to compute the gradient is NP-complete (Naumann, 2008), in the sense that it may require simplifying algebraic expressions into their least expensive form.

For example, suppose we have variables $p_1, p_2, \ldots, p_n$ representing probabilities, and variables $z_1, z_2, \ldots, z_n$ representing unnormalized log probabilities. Suppose we define

$$q_i = \frac{\exp(z_i)}{\sum_i \exp(z_i)}, \tag{6.57}$$

where we build the softmax function out of exponentiation, summation and division operations, and construct a cross-entropy loss $J = -\sum_i p_i \log q_i$. A human mathematician can observe that the derivative of J with respect to z_i takes a very simple form: $q_i - p_i$. The back-propagation algorithm is not capable of simplifying the gradient this way and will instead explicitly propagate gradients through all the logarithm and exponentiation operations in the original graph. Some software libraries such as Theano (Bergstra et al., 2010; Bastien et al., 2012) are able to perform some kinds of algebraic substitution to improve over the graph proposed by the pure back-propagation algorithm.

When the forward graph $\mathcal{G}$ has a single output node and each partial derivative $\frac{\partial u^{(i)}}{\partial u^{(j)}}$ can be computed with a constant amount of computation, back-propagation guarantees that the number of computations for the gradient computation is of the same order as the number of computations for the forward computation: this can be seen in algorithm 6.2, because each local partial derivative $\frac{\partial u^{(i)}}{\partial u^{(j)}}$ needs to be computed only once along with an associated multiplication and addition for the recursive chain-rule formulation (equation 6.49). The overall computation is therefore $O(\#\ \text{edges})$. It can potentially be reduced, however, by simplifying the computational graph constructed by back-propagation, and this is an NP-complete task. Implementations such as Theano and TensorFlow use heuristics based on matching known simplification patterns to iteratively attempt to simplify the graph. We defined back-propagation only for computing a scalar output gradient, but back-propagation can be extended to compute a Jacobian (either of k different scalar nodes in the graph, or of a tensor-valued node containing k values). A naive implementation may then need k times more computation: for each scalar internal node in the original forward graph, the naive implementation computes k gradients instead of a single gradient. When the number of outputs of the graph is larger than the number of inputs, it is sometimes preferable to use another form of automatic differentiation called **forward mode accumulation**. Forward mode accumulation has been proposed for obtaining real-time computation of gradients in recurrent networks, for example (Williams and Zipser, 1989). This approach also avoids the need to store the values and gradients for the whole graph, trading off computational efficiency for memory. The relationship between forward mode and backward mode is analogous to the relationship between left-multiplying versus right-multiplying a sequence of matrices, such as

$$\boldsymbol{ABCD}, \tag{6.58}$$

where the matrices can be thought of as Jacobian. For example, if $\boldsymbol{D}$ is a column vector while $\boldsymbol{A}$ has many rows, the graph will have a single output and many inputs, and starting the multiplications from the end and going backward requires only matrix-vector products. This order corresponds to the backward mode. Instead, starting to multiply from the left would involve a series of matrix-matrix products, which makes the whole computation much more expensive. If $\boldsymbol{A}$ has fewer rows than $\boldsymbol{D}$ has columns, however, it is cheaper to run the multiplications left-to-right, corresponding to the forward mode.

In many communities outside machine learning, it is more common to implement differentiation software that acts directly on traditional programming language code, such as Python or C code, and automatically generates programs that differentiate functions written in these languages. In the deep learning community, computational graphs are usually represented by explicit data structures created by specialized libraries. The specialized approach has the drawback of requiring the library developer to define the `bprop` methods for every operation and limiting the user of the library to only those operations that have been defined. Yet the specialized approach also has the benefit of allowing customized back-propagation rules to be developed for each operation, enabling the developer to improve speed or stability in nonobvious ways that an automatic procedure would presumably be unable to replicate.

Back-propagation is therefore not the only way or the optimal way of computing the gradient, but it is a practical method that continues to serve the deep learning community well. In the future, differentiation technology for deep networks may improve as deep learning practitioners become more aware of advances in the broader field of automatic differentiation.

6.5.10 Higher-Order Derivatives

Some software frameworks support the use of higher-order derivatives. Among the deep learning software frameworks, this includes at least Theano and TensorFlow.

These libraries use the same kind of data structure to describe the expressions for derivatives as they use to describe the original function being differentiated. This means that the symbolic differentiation machinery can be applied to derivatives.

In the context of deep learning, it is rare to compute a single second derivative of a scalar function. Instead, we are usually interested in properties of the Hessian matrix. If we have a function $f : \mathbb{R}^n \to \mathbb{R}$, then the Hessian matrix is of size $n \times n$. In typical deep learning applications, n will be the number of parameters in the model, which could easily number in the billions. The entire Hessian matrix is thus infeasible to even represent.

Instead of explicitly computing the Hessian, the typical deep learning approach is to use **Krylov methods**. Krylov methods are a set of iterative techniques for performing various operations, such as approximately inverting a matrix or finding approximations to its eigenvectors or eigenvalues, without using any operation other than matrix-vector products.

To use Krylov methods on the Hessian, we only need to be able to compute the product between the Hessian matrix $\boldsymbol{H}$ and an arbitrary vector $\boldsymbol{v}$. A straightforward technique (Christianson, 1992) for doing so is to compute

$$\boldsymbol{H}\boldsymbol{v} = \nabla_{\boldsymbol{x}} \left[\left(\nabla_{\boldsymbol{x}} f(x) \right)^{\top} \boldsymbol{v} \right]. \tag{6.59}$$

Both gradient computations in this expression may be computed automatically by the appropriate software library. Note that the outer gradient expression takes the gradient of a function of the inner gradient expression.

If $\boldsymbol{v}$ is itself a vector produced by a computational graph, it is important to specify that the automatic differentiation software should not differentiate through the graph that produced $\boldsymbol{v}$.

While computing the Hessian is usually not advisable, it is possible to do with Hessian vector products. One simply computes $\boldsymbol{H}\boldsymbol{e}^{(i)}$ for all $i = 1, \ldots, n$, where $\boldsymbol{e}^{(i)}$ is the one-hot vector with $e_i^{(i)} = 1$ and all other entries are equal to 0.

6.6 Historical Notes

Feedforward networks can be seen as efficient nonlinear function approximators based on using gradient descent to minimize the error in a function approximation. From this point of view, the modern feedforward network is the culmination of centuries of progress on the general function approximation task.

The chain rule that underlies the back-propagation algorithm was invented in the seventeenth century (Leibniz, 1676; L'Hôpital, 1696). Calculus and algebra have long been used to solve optimization problems in closed form, but gradient descent was not introduced as a technique for iteratively approximating the solution to optimization problems until the nineteenth century (Cauchy, 1847).

Beginning in the 1940s, these function approximation techniques were used to motivate machine learning models such as the perceptron. However, the earliest models were based on linear models. Critics including Marvin Minsky pointed out several of the flaws of the linear model family, such as its inability to learn the XOR function, which led to a backlash against the entire neural network approach.

Learning nonlinear functions required the development of a multilayer perceptron and a means of computing the gradient through such a model. Efficient applications of the chain rule based on dynamic programming began to appear in the 1960s and 1970s, mostly for control applications (Kelley, 1960; Bryson and Denham, 1961; Dreyfus, 1962; Bryson and Ho, 1969; Dreyfus, 1973) but also for sensitivity analysis (Linnainmaa, 1976). Werbos (1981) proposed applying these techniques to training artificial neural networks. The idea was finally developed in practice after being independently rediscovered in different ways (LeCun, 1985; Parker, 1985; Rumelhart et al., 1986a). The book **Parallel Distributed Processing** presented the results of some of the first successful experiments with back-propagation in a chapter (Rumelhart et al., 1986b) that contributed greatly to the popularization of back-propagation and initiated a very active period of research in multilayer neural networks. The ideas put forward by the authors of that book, particularly by Rumelhart and Hinton, go much beyond back-propagation. They include crucial ideas about the possible computational implementation of several central aspects of cognition and learning, which came under the name "connectionism" because of the importance this school of thought places on the connections between neurons as the locus of learning and memory. In particular, these ideas include the notion of distributed representation (Hinton et al., 1986).

Following the success of back-propagation, neural network research gained popularity and reached a peak in the early 1990s. Afterwards, other machine learning techniques became more popular until the modern deep learning renaissance that began in 2006.

The core ideas behind modern feedforward networks have not changed substantially since the 1980s. The same back-propagation algorithm and the same approaches to gradient descent are still in use. Most of the improvement in neural network performance from 1986 to 2015 can be attributed to two factors. First, larger datasets have reduced the degree to which statistical generalization is a challenge for neural networks. Second, neural networks have become much larger, because of more powerful computers and better software infrastructure. A small number of algorithmic changes have also improved the performance of neural networks noticeably.

One of these algorithmic changes was the replacement of mean squared error with the cross-entropy family of loss functions. Mean squared error was popular in the 1980s and 1990s but was gradually replaced by cross-entropy losses and the principle of maximum likelihood as ideas spread between the statistics community and the machine learning community. The use of cross-entropy losses greatly improved the performance of models with sigmoid and softmax outputs, which had previously suffered from saturation and slow learning when using the mean squared error loss.

The other major algorithmic change that has greatly improved the performance of feedforward networks was the replacement of sigmoid hidden units with piecewise linear hidden units, such as rectified linear units. Rectification using the $\max\{0, z\}$ function was introduced in early neural network models and dates back at least as far as the cognitron and neocognitron (Fukushima, 1975, 1980). These early models did not use rectified linear units but instead applied rectification to nonlinear functions. Despite the early popularity of rectification, it was largely replaced by sigmoids in the 1980s, perhaps because sigmoids perform better when neural networks are very small. As of the early 2000s, rectified linear units were avoided because of a somewhat superstitious belief that activation functions with nondifferentiable points must be avoided. This began to change in about 2009. Jarrett et al. (2009) observed that "using a rectifying nonlinearity is the single most important factor in improving the performance of a recognition system," among several different factors of neural network architecture design.

For small datasets, Jarrett et al. (2009) observed that using rectifying non-linearities is even more important than learning the weights of the hidden layers. Random weights are sufficient to propagate useful information through a rectified linear network, enabling the classifier layer at the top to learn how to map different feature vectors to class identities.

When more data is available, learning begins to extract enough useful knowledge to exceed the performance of randomly chosen parameters. Glorot et al. (2011a) showed that learning is far easier in deep rectified linear networks than in deep networks that have curvature or two-sided saturation in their activation functions.

Rectified linear units are also of historical interest because they show that neuroscience has continued to have an influence on the development of deep learning algorithms. Glorot et al. (2011a) motivated rectified linear units from biological considerations. The half-rectifying nonlinearity was intended to capture these properties of biological neurons: (1) For some inputs, biological neurons are completely inactive. (2) For some inputs, a biological neuron's output is proportional to its input. (3) Most of the time, biological neurons operate in the regime where they are inactive (i.e., they should have **sparse activations**).

When the modern resurgence of deep learning began in 2006, feedforward networks continued to have a bad reputation. From about 2006 to 2012, it was widely believed that feedforward networks would not perform well unless they were assisted by other models, such as probabilistic models. Today, it is now known that with the right resources and engineering practices, feedforward networks perform very well. Today, gradient-based learning in feedforward networks is used as a tool to develop probabilistic models, such as the variational autoencoder and generative adversarial networks, described in chapter 20. Rather than being viewed as an unreliable technology that must be supported by other techniques, gradient-based learning in feedforward networks has been viewed since 2012 as a powerful technology that can be applied to many other machine learning tasks. In 2006, the community used unsupervised learning to support supervised learning, and now, ironically, it is more common to use supervised learning to support unsupervised learning.

Feedforward networks continue to have unfulfilled potential. In the future, we expect they will be applied to many more tasks, and that advances in optimization algorithms and model design will improve their performance even further. This chapter has primarily described the neural network family of models. In the subsequent chapters, we turn to how to use these models—how to regularize and train them.

7

Regularization for Deep Learning

A central problem in machine learning is how to make an algorithm that will perform well not just on the training data, but also on new inputs. Many strategies used in machine learning are explicitly designed to reduce the test error, possibly at the expense of increased training error. These strategies are known collectively as regularization. A great many forms of regularization are available to the deep learning practitioner. In fact, developing more effective regularization strategies has been one of the major research efforts in the field.

Chapter 5 introduced the basic concepts of generalization, underfitting, overfitting, bias, variance and regularization. If you are not already familiar with these notions, please refer to that chapter before continuing with this one.

In this chapter, we describe regularization in more detail, focusing on regularization strategies for deep models or models that may be used as building blocks to form deep models.

Some sections of this chapter deal with standard concepts in machine learning. If you are already familiar with these concepts, feel free to skip the relevant sections. However, most of this chapter is concerned with the extension of these basic concepts to the particular case of neural networks.

In section 5.2.2, we defined regularization as "any modification we make to a learning algorithm that is intended to reduce its generalization error but not its training error." There are many regularization strategies. Some put extra constraints on a machine learning model, such as adding restrictions on the parameter values. Some add extra terms in the objective function that can be thought of as corresponding to a soft constraint on the parameter values. If chosen carefully, these extra constraints and penalties can lead to improved performance on the test set. Sometimes these constraints and penalties are designed to encode specific kinds of prior knowledge. Other times, these constraints and penalties are designed to express a generic preference for a simpler model class in order to promote generalization. Sometimes penalties and constraints are necessary to make an underdetermined problem determined. Other forms of regularization, known as ensemble methods, combine multiple hypotheses that explain the training data.

In the context of deep learning, most regularization strategies are based on regularizing estimators. Regularization of an estimator works by trading increased bias for reduced variance. An effective regularizer is one that makes a profitable trade, reducing variance significantly while not overly increasing the bias. When we discussed generalization and overfitting in chapter 5, we focused on three situations, where the model family being trained either (1) excluded the true data-generating process—corresponding to underfitting and inducing bias, or (2) matched the true data-generating process, or (3) included the generating process but also many other possible generating processes—the overfitting regime where variance rather than bias dominates the estimation error. The goal of regularization is to take a model from the third regime into the second regime.

In practice, an overly complex model family does not necessarily include the target function or the true data-generating process, or even a close approximation of either. We almost never have access to the true data-generating process so we can never know for sure if the model family being estimated includes the generating process or not. Most applications of deep learning algorithms, however, are to domains where the true data-generating process is almost certainly outside the model family. Deep learning algorithms are typically applied to extremely complicated domains such as images, audio sequences and text, for which the true generation process essentially involves simulating the entire universe. To some extent, we are always trying to fit a square peg (the data-generating process) into a round hole (our model family).

What this means is that controlling the complexity of the model is not a simple matter of finding the model of the right size, with the right number of parameters. Instead, we might find—and indeed in practical deep learning scenarios, we almost always do find—that the best fitting model (in the sense of minimizing generalization error) is a large model that has been regularized appropriately.

We now review several strategies for how to create such a large, deep regularized model.

7.1 Parameter Norm Penalties

Regularization has been used for decades prior to the advent of deep learning. Linear models such as linear regression and logistic regression allow simple, straightforward, and effective regularization strategies.

Many regularization approaches are based on limiting the capacity of models, such as neural networks, linear regression, or logistic regression, by adding a parameter norm penalty $\Omega(\boldsymbol{\theta})$ to the objective function J. We denote the regularized objective function by $\tilde{J}$:

$$\tilde{J}(\boldsymbol{\theta}; \boldsymbol{X}, \boldsymbol{y}) = J(\boldsymbol{\theta}; \boldsymbol{X}, \boldsymbol{y}) + \alpha\Omega(\boldsymbol{\theta}), \qquad (7.1)$$

where $\alpha \in [0, \infty)$ is a hyperparameter that weights the relative contribution of the norm penalty term, Ω, relative to the standard objective function J. Setting α to 0 results in no regularization. Larger values of α correspond to more regularization.

When our training algorithm minimizes the regularized objective function $\tilde{J}$ it will decrease both the original objective J on the training data and some measure of the size of the parameters $\boldsymbol{\theta}$ (or some subset of the parameters). Different choices for the parameter norm Ω can result in different solutions being preferred. In this section, we discuss the effects of the various norms when used as penalties on the model parameters.

Before delving into the regularization behavior of different norms, we note that for neural networks, we typically choose to use a parameter norm penalty Ω that penalizes *only the weights* of the affine transformation at each layer and leaves the biases unregularized. The biases typically require less data than the weights to fit accurately. Each weight specifies how two variables interact. Fitting the weight well requires observing both variables in a variety of conditions. Each bias controls only a single variable. This means that we do not induce too much variance by leaving the biases unregularized. Also, regularizing the bias parameters can introduce a significant amount of underfitting. We therefore use the vector $\boldsymbol{w}$ to indicate all the weights that should be affected by a norm penalty, while the vector $\boldsymbol{\theta}$ denotes all the parameters, including both $\boldsymbol{w}$ and the unregularized parameters.

In the context of neural networks, it is sometimes desirable to use a separate penalty with a different α coefficient for each layer of the network. Because it can be expensive to search for the correct value of multiple hyperparameters, it is still reasonable to use the same weight decay at all layers just to reduce the size of search space.

7.1.1 L^2 Parameter Regularization

We have already seen, in section 5.2.2, one of the simplest and most common kinds of parameter norm penalty: the L^2 parameter norm penalty commonly known as **weight decay**. This regularization strategy drives the weights closer to the origin[1] by adding a regularization term $\Omega(\boldsymbol{\theta}) = \frac{1}{2}\|\boldsymbol{w}\|_2^2$ to the objective function. In other academic communities, L^2 regularization is also known as **ridge regression** or **Tikhonov regularization**.

We can gain some insight into the behavior of weight decay regularization by studying the gradient of the regularized objective function. To simplify the presentation, we assume no bias parameter, so $\boldsymbol{\theta}$ is just $\boldsymbol{w}$. Such a model has the following total objective function:

$$\tilde{J}(\boldsymbol{w}; \boldsymbol{X}, \boldsymbol{y}) = \frac{\alpha}{2}\boldsymbol{w}^\top \boldsymbol{w} + J(\boldsymbol{w}; \boldsymbol{X}, \boldsymbol{y}), \tag{7.2}$$

with the corresponding parameter gradient

$$\nabla_{\boldsymbol{w}}\tilde{J}(\boldsymbol{w}; \boldsymbol{X}, \boldsymbol{y}) = \alpha\boldsymbol{w} + \nabla_{\boldsymbol{w}}J(\boldsymbol{w}; \boldsymbol{X}, \boldsymbol{y}). \tag{7.3}$$

To take a single gradient step to update the weights, we perform this update:

$$\boldsymbol{w} \leftarrow \boldsymbol{w} - \epsilon\left(\alpha\boldsymbol{w} + \nabla_{\boldsymbol{w}}J(\boldsymbol{w}; \boldsymbol{X}, \boldsymbol{y})\right). \tag{7.4}$$

Written another way, the update is

$$\boldsymbol{w} \leftarrow (1 - \epsilon\alpha)\boldsymbol{w} - \epsilon\nabla_{\boldsymbol{w}}J(\boldsymbol{w}; \boldsymbol{X}, \boldsymbol{y}). \tag{7.5}$$

We can see that the addition of the weight decay term has modified the learning rule to multiplicatively shrink the weight vector by a constant factor on each step, just before performing the usual gradient update. This describes what happens in a single step. But what happens over the entire course of training?

We will further simplify the analysis by making a quadratic approximation to the objective function in the neighborhood of the value of the weights that obtains minimal unregularized training cost, $\boldsymbol{w}^* = \arg\min_{\boldsymbol{w}} J(\boldsymbol{w})$. If the objective function is truly quadratic, as in the case of fitting a linear regression model with

---

[1]More generally, we could regularize the parameters to be near any specific point in space and, surprisingly, still get a regularization effect, but better results will be obtained for a value closer to the true one, with zero being a default value that makes sense when we do not know if the correct value should be positive or negative. Since it is far more common to regularize the model parameters toward zero, we will focus on this special case in our exposition.

mean squared error, then the approximation is perfect. The approximation $\hat{J}$ is given by

$$\hat{J}(\boldsymbol{\theta}) = J(\boldsymbol{w}^*) + \frac{1}{2}(\boldsymbol{w} - \boldsymbol{w}^*)^\top \boldsymbol{H}(\boldsymbol{w} - \boldsymbol{w}^*), \qquad (7.6)$$

where $\boldsymbol{H}$ is the Hessian matrix of J with respect to $\boldsymbol{w}$ evaluated at $\boldsymbol{w}^*$. There is no first-order term in this quadratic approximation, because $\boldsymbol{w}^*$ is defined to be a minimum, where the gradient vanishes. Likewise, because $\boldsymbol{w}^*$ is the location of a minimum of J, we can conclude that $\boldsymbol{H}$ is positive semidefinite.

The minimum of $\hat{J}$ occurs where its gradient

$$\nabla_{\boldsymbol{w}}\hat{J}(\boldsymbol{w}) = \boldsymbol{H}(\boldsymbol{w} - \boldsymbol{w}^*) \qquad (7.7)$$

is equal to $\boldsymbol{0}$.

To study the effect of weight decay, we modify equation 7.7 by adding the weight decay gradient. We can now solve for the minimum of the regularized version of $\hat{J}$. We use the variable $\tilde{\boldsymbol{w}}$ to represent the location of the minimum.

$$\alpha\tilde{\boldsymbol{w}} + \boldsymbol{H}(\tilde{\boldsymbol{w}} - \boldsymbol{w}^*) = 0 \qquad (7.8)$$

$$(\boldsymbol{H} + \alpha\boldsymbol{I})\tilde{\boldsymbol{w}} = \boldsymbol{H}\boldsymbol{w}^* \qquad (7.9)$$

$$\tilde{\boldsymbol{w}} = (\boldsymbol{H} + \alpha\boldsymbol{I})^{-1}\boldsymbol{H}\boldsymbol{w}^* \qquad (7.10)$$

As α approaches 0, the regularized solution $\tilde{\boldsymbol{w}}$ approaches $\boldsymbol{w}^*$. But what happens as α grows? Because $\boldsymbol{H}$ is real and symmetric, we can decompose it into a diagonal matrix $\boldsymbol{\Lambda}$ and an orthonormal basis of eigenvectors, $\boldsymbol{Q}$, such that $\boldsymbol{H} = \boldsymbol{Q}\boldsymbol{\Lambda}\boldsymbol{Q}^\top$. Applying the decomposition to equation 7.10, we obtain

$$\tilde{\boldsymbol{w}} = (\boldsymbol{Q}\boldsymbol{\Lambda}\boldsymbol{Q}^\top + \alpha\boldsymbol{I})^{-1}\boldsymbol{Q}\boldsymbol{\Lambda}\boldsymbol{Q}^\top\boldsymbol{w}^* \qquad (7.11)$$

$$= \left[\boldsymbol{Q}(\boldsymbol{\Lambda} + \alpha\boldsymbol{I})\boldsymbol{Q}^\top\right]^{-1}\boldsymbol{Q}\boldsymbol{\Lambda}\boldsymbol{Q}^\top\boldsymbol{w}^* \qquad (7.12)$$

$$= \boldsymbol{Q}(\boldsymbol{\Lambda} + \alpha\boldsymbol{I})^{-1}\boldsymbol{\Lambda}\boldsymbol{Q}^\top\boldsymbol{w}^*. \qquad (7.13)$$

We see that the effect of weight decay is to rescale $\boldsymbol{w}^*$ along the axes defined by the eigenvectors of $\boldsymbol{H}$. Specifically, the component of $\boldsymbol{w}^*$ that is aligned with the i-th eigenvector of $\boldsymbol{H}$ is rescaled by a factor of $\frac{\lambda_i}{\lambda_i + \alpha}$. (You may wish to review how this kind of scaling works, first explained in figure 2.3).

Along the directions where the eigenvalues of $\boldsymbol{H}$ are relatively large, for example, where $\lambda_i \gg \alpha$, the effect of regularization is relatively small. Yet components with $\lambda_i \ll \alpha$ will be shrunk to have nearly zero magnitude. This effect is illustrated in figure 7.1.

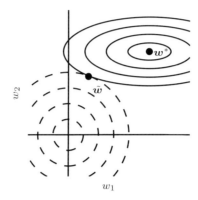

Figure 7.1: An illustration of the effect of L^2 (or weight decay) regularization on the value of the optimal $\boldsymbol{w}$. The solid ellipses represent contours of equal value of the unregularized objective. The dotted circles represent contours of equal value of the L^2 regularizer. At the point $\tilde{\boldsymbol{w}}$, these competing objectives reach an equilibrium. In the first dimension, the eigenvalue of the Hessian of J is small. The objective function does not increase much when moving horizontally away from $\boldsymbol{w}^*$. Because the objective function does not express a strong preference along this direction, the regularizer has a strong effect on this axis. The regularizer pulls w_1 close to zero. In the second dimension, the objective function is very sensitive to movements away from $\boldsymbol{w}^*$. The corresponding eigenvalue is large, indicating high curvature. As a result, weight decay affects the position of w_2 relatively little.

Only directions along which the parameters contribute significantly to reducing the objective function are preserved relatively intact. In directions that do not contribute to reducing the objective function, a small eigenvalue of the Hessian tells us that movement in this direction will not significantly increase the gradient. Components of the weight vector corresponding to such unimportant directions are decayed away through the use of the regularization throughout training.

So far we have discussed weight decay in terms of its effect on the optimization of an abstract, general quadratic cost function. How do these effects relate to machine learning in particular? We can find out by studying linear regression, a model for which the true cost function is quadratic and therefore amenable to the same kind of analysis we have used so far. Applying the analysis again, we will be able to obtain a special case of the same results, but with the solution now phrased in terms of the training data. For linear regression, the cost function is the sum of squared errors:

$$(\boldsymbol{X}\boldsymbol{w} - \boldsymbol{y})^{\top}(\boldsymbol{X}\boldsymbol{w} - \boldsymbol{y}). \tag{7.14}$$

When we add L^2 regularization, the objective function changes to

$$(\boldsymbol{Xw} - \boldsymbol{y})^\top (\boldsymbol{Xw} - \boldsymbol{y}) + \frac{1}{2}\alpha \boldsymbol{w}^\top \boldsymbol{w}. \tag{7.15}$$

This changes the normal equations for the solution from

$$\boldsymbol{w} = (\boldsymbol{X}^\top \boldsymbol{X})^{-1}\boldsymbol{X}^\top \boldsymbol{y} \tag{7.16}$$

to

$$\boldsymbol{w} = (\boldsymbol{X}^\top \boldsymbol{X} + \alpha \boldsymbol{I})^{-1}\boldsymbol{X}^\top \boldsymbol{y}. \tag{7.17}$$

The matrix $\boldsymbol{X}^\top \boldsymbol{X}$ in equation 7.16 is proportional to the covariance matrix $\frac{1}{m}\boldsymbol{X}^\top \boldsymbol{X}$. Using L^2 regularization replaces this matrix with $(\boldsymbol{X}^\top \boldsymbol{X} + \alpha \boldsymbol{I})^{-1}$ in equation 7.17. The new matrix is the same as the original one, but with the addition of α to the diagonal. The diagonal entries of this matrix correspond to the variance of each input feature. We can see that L^2 regularization causes the learning algorithm to "perceive" the input $\boldsymbol{X}$ as having higher variance, which makes it shrink the weights on features whose covariance with the output target is low compared to this added variance.

7.1.2 L^1 Regularization

While L^2 weight decay is the most common form of weight decay, there are other ways to penalize the size of the model parameters. Another option is to use L^1 regularization.

Formally, L^1 regularization on the model parameter $\boldsymbol{w}$ is defined as

$$\Omega(\boldsymbol{\theta}) = ||\boldsymbol{w}||_1 = \sum_i |w_i|, \tag{7.18}$$

that is, as the sum of absolute values of the individual parameters.[2] We will now discuss the effect of L^1 regularization on the simple linear regression model, with no bias parameter, that we studied in our analysis of L^2 regularization. In particular, we are interested in delineating the differences between L^1 and L^2 forms of regularization. As with L^2 weight decay, L^1 weight decay controls the strength of the regularization by scaling the penalty Ω using a positive hyperparameter α. Thus, the regularized objective function $\tilde{J}(\boldsymbol{w}; \boldsymbol{X}, \boldsymbol{y})$ is given by

$$\tilde{J}(\boldsymbol{w}; \boldsymbol{X}, \boldsymbol{y}) = \alpha ||\boldsymbol{w}||_1 + J(\boldsymbol{w}; \boldsymbol{X}, \boldsymbol{y}), \tag{7.19}$$

---

[2]As with L^2 regularization, we could regularize the parameters toward a value that is not zero, but instead toward some parameter value $\boldsymbol{w}^{(o)}$. In that case the L^1 regularization would introduce the term $\Omega(\boldsymbol{\theta}) = ||\boldsymbol{w} - \boldsymbol{w}^{(o)}||_1 = \sum_i |w_i - w_i^{(o)}|$.

with the corresponding gradient (actually, sub gradient)

$$\nabla_{\boldsymbol{w}} \tilde{J}(\boldsymbol{w}; \boldsymbol{X}, \boldsymbol{y}) = \alpha \text{sign}(\boldsymbol{w}) + \nabla_{\boldsymbol{w}} J(\boldsymbol{X}, \boldsymbol{y}; \boldsymbol{w}), \tag{7.20}$$

where $\text{sign}(\boldsymbol{w})$ is simply the sign of $\boldsymbol{w}$ applied element-wise.

By inspecting equation 7.20, we can see immediately that the effect of L^1 regularization is quite different from that of L^2 regularization. Specifically, we can see that the regularization contribution to the gradient no longer scales linearly with each w_i; instead it is a constant factor with a sign equal to $\text{sign}(w_i)$. One consequence of this form of the gradient is that we will not necessarily see clean algebraic solutions to quadratic approximations of $J(\boldsymbol{X}, \boldsymbol{y}; \boldsymbol{w})$ as we did for L^2 regularization.

Our simple linear model has a quadratic cost function that we can represent via its Taylor series. Alternately, we could imagine that this is a truncated Taylor series approximating the cost function of a more sophisticated model. The gradient in this setting is given by

$$\nabla_{\boldsymbol{w}} \hat{J}(\boldsymbol{w}) = \boldsymbol{H}(\boldsymbol{w} - \boldsymbol{w}^*), \tag{7.21}$$

where, again, $\boldsymbol{H}$ is the Hessian matrix of J with respect to $\boldsymbol{w}$ evaluated at $\boldsymbol{w}^*$.

Because the L^1 penalty does not admit clean algebraic expressions in the case of a fully general Hessian, we will also make the further simplifying assumption that the Hessian is diagonal, $\boldsymbol{H} = \text{diag}([H_{1,1}, \ldots, H_{n,n}])$, where each $H_{i,i} > 0$. This assumption holds if the data for the linear regression problem has been preprocessed to remove all correlation between the input features, which may be accomplished using PCA.

Our quadratic approximation of the L^1 regularized objective function decomposes into a sum over the parameters:

$$\hat{J}(\boldsymbol{w}; \boldsymbol{X}, \boldsymbol{y}) = J(\boldsymbol{w}^*; \boldsymbol{X}, \boldsymbol{y}) + \sum_i \left[\frac{1}{2} H_{i,i}(w_i - w_i^*)^2 + \alpha |w_i| \right]. \tag{7.22}$$

The problem of minimizing this approximate cost function has an analytical solution (for each dimension i), with the following form:

$$w_i = \text{sign}(w_i^*) \max \left\{ |w_i^*| - \frac{\alpha}{H_{i,i}}, 0 \right\}. \tag{7.23}$$

Consider the situation where $w_i^* > 0$ for all i. There are two possible outcomes:

1. The case where $w_i^* \leq \frac{\alpha}{H_{i,i}}$. Here the optimal value of w_i under the regularized objective is simply $w_i = 0$. This occurs because the contribution of $J(\boldsymbol{w}; \boldsymbol{X}, \boldsymbol{y})$ to the regularized objective $\tilde{J}(\boldsymbol{w}; \boldsymbol{X}, \boldsymbol{y})$ is overwhelmed—in direction i—by the L^1 regularization, which pushes the value of w_i to zero.

2. The case where $w_i^* > \frac{\alpha}{H_{i,i}}$. In this case, the regularization does not move the optimal value of w_i to zero but instead just shifts it in that direction by a distance equal to $\frac{\alpha}{H_{i,i}}$.

A similar process happens when $w_i^* < 0$, but with the L^1 penalty making w_i less negative by $\frac{\alpha}{H_{i,i}}$, or 0.

In comparison to L^2 regularization, L^1 regularization results in a solution that is more **sparse**. Sparsity in this context refers to the fact that some parameters have an optimal value of zero. The sparsity of L^1 regularization is a qualitatively different behavior than arises with L^2 regularization. Equation 7.13 gave the solution $\tilde{w}$ for L^2 regularization. If we revisit that equation using the assumption of a diagonal and positive definite Hessian $\boldsymbol{H}$ that we introduced for our analysis of L^1 regularization, we find that $\tilde{w}_i = \frac{H_{i,i}}{H_{i,i} + \alpha} w_i^*$. If w_i^* was nonzero, then $\tilde{w}_i$ remains nonzero. This demonstrates that L^2 regularization does not cause the parameters to become sparse, while L^1 regularization may do so for large enough α.

The sparsity property induced by L^1 regularization has been used extensively as a **feature selection** mechanism. Feature selection simplifies a machine learning problem by choosing which subset of the available features should be used. In particular, the well known LASSO (Tibshirani, 1995) (least absolute shrinkage and selection operator) model integrates an L^1 penalty with a linear model and a least-squares cost function. The L^1 penalty causes a subset of the weights to become zero, suggesting that the corresponding features may safely be discarded.

In section 5.6.1, we saw that many regularization strategies can be interpreted as MAP Bayesian inference, and that in particular, L^2 regularization is equivalent to MAP Bayesian inference with a Gaussian prior on the weights. For L^1 regularization, the penalty $\alpha \Omega(\boldsymbol{w}) = \alpha \sum_i |w_i|$ used to regularize a cost function is equivalent to the log-prior term that is maximized by MAP Bayesian inference when the prior is an isotropic Laplace distribution (equation 3.26) over $\boldsymbol{w} \in \mathbb{R}^n$:

$$\log p(\boldsymbol{w}) = \sum_i \log \text{Laplace}(w_i; 0, \frac{1}{\alpha}) = -\alpha ||\boldsymbol{w}||_1 + n \log \alpha - n \log 2. \quad (7.24)$$

From the point of view of learning via maximization with respect to $\boldsymbol{w}$, we can ignore the $\log \alpha - \log 2$ terms because they do not depend on $\boldsymbol{w}$.

7.2 Norm Penalties as Constrained Optimization

Consider the cost function regularized by a parameter norm penalty:

$$\tilde{J}(\boldsymbol{\theta}; \boldsymbol{X}, \boldsymbol{y}) = J(\boldsymbol{\theta}; \boldsymbol{X}, \boldsymbol{y}) + \alpha \Omega(\boldsymbol{\theta}). \tag{7.25}$$

Recall from section 4.4 that we can minimize a function subject to constraints by constructing a generalized Lagrange function, consisting of the original objective function plus a set of penalties. Each penalty is a product between a coefficient, called a Karush–Kuhn–Tucker (KKT) multiplier, and a function representing whether the constraint is satisfied. If we wanted to constrain $\Omega(\boldsymbol{\theta})$ to be less than some constant k, we could construct a generalized Lagrange function

$$\mathcal{L}(\boldsymbol{\theta}, \alpha; \boldsymbol{X}, \boldsymbol{y}) = J(\boldsymbol{\theta}; \boldsymbol{X}, \boldsymbol{y}) + \alpha(\Omega(\boldsymbol{\theta}) - k). \tag{7.26}$$

The solution to the constrained problem is given by

$$\boldsymbol{\theta}^* = \arg\min_{\boldsymbol{\theta}} \max_{\alpha, \alpha \geq 0} \mathcal{L}(\boldsymbol{\theta}, \alpha). \tag{7.27}$$

As described in section 4.4, solving this problem requires modifying both $\boldsymbol{\theta}$ and α. Section 4.5 provides a worked example of linear regression with an L^2 constraint. Many different procedures are possible—some may use gradient descent, while others may use analytical solutions for where the gradient is zero—but in all procedures α must increase whenever $\Omega(\boldsymbol{\theta}) > k$ and decrease whenever $\Omega(\boldsymbol{\theta}) < k$. All positive α encourage $\Omega(\boldsymbol{\theta})$ to shrink. The optimal value α^* will encourage $\Omega(\boldsymbol{\theta})$ to shrink, but not so strongly to make $\Omega(\boldsymbol{\theta})$ become less than k.

To gain some insight into the effect of the constraint, we can fix α^* and view the problem as just a function of $\boldsymbol{\theta}$:

$$\boldsymbol{\theta}^* = \arg\min_{\boldsymbol{\theta}} \mathcal{L}(\boldsymbol{\theta}, \alpha^*) = \arg\min_{\boldsymbol{\theta}} J(\boldsymbol{\theta}; \boldsymbol{X}, \boldsymbol{y}) + \alpha^* \Omega(\boldsymbol{\theta}). \tag{7.28}$$

This is exactly the same as the regularized training problem of minimizing $\tilde{J}$. We can thus think of a parameter norm penalty as imposing a constraint on the weights. If Ω is the L^2 norm, then the weights are constrained to lie in an L^2 ball. If Ω is the L^1 norm, then the weights are constrained to lie in a region of limited

L^1 norm. Usually we do not know the size of the constraint region that we impose by using weight decay with coefficient α^* because the value of α^* does not directly tell us the value of k. In principle, one can solve for k, but the relationship between k and α^* depends on the form of J. While we do not know the exact size of the constraint region, we can control it roughly by increasing or decreasing α in order to grow or shrink the constraint region. Larger α will result in a smaller constraint region. Smaller α will result in a larger constraint region.

Sometimes we may wish to use explicit constraints rather than penalties. As described in section 4.4, we can modify algorithms such as stochastic gradient descent to take a step downhill on $J(\boldsymbol{\theta})$ and then project $\boldsymbol{\theta}$ back to the nearest point that satisfies $\Omega(\boldsymbol{\theta}) < k$. This can be useful if we have an idea of what value of k is appropriate and do not want to spend time searching for the value of α that corresponds to this k.

Another reason to use explicit constraints and reprojection rather than enforcing constraints with penalties is that penalties can cause nonconvex optimization procedures to get stuck in local minima corresponding to small $\boldsymbol{\theta}$. When training neural networks, this usually manifests as neural networks that train with several "dead units." These are units that do not contribute much to the behavior of the function learned by the network because the weights going into or out of them are all very small. When training with a penalty on the norm of the weights, these configurations can be locally optimal, even if it is possible to significantly reduce J by making the weights larger. Explicit constraints implemented by reprojection can work much better in these cases because they do not encourage the weights to approach the origin. Explicit constraints implemented by reprojection have an effect only when the weights become large and attempt to leave the constraint region.

Finally, explicit constraints with reprojection can be useful because they impose some stability on the optimization procedure. When using high learning rates, it is possible to encounter a positive feedback loop in which large weights induce large gradients, which then induce a large update to the weights. If these updates consistently increase the size of the weights, then $\boldsymbol{\theta}$ rapidly moves away from the origin until numerical overflow occurs. Explicit constraints with reprojection prevent this feedback loop from continuing to increase the magnitude of the weights without bound. Hinton et al. (2012c) recommend using constraints combined with a high learning rate to enable rapid exploration of parameter space while maintaining some stability.

In particular, Hinton et al. (2012c) recommend a strategy introduced by Srebro and Shraibman (2005): constraining the norm of each *column* of the weight matrix of a neural net layer, rather than constraining the Frobenius norm of the entire weight matrix. Constraining the norm of each column separately prevents any one hidden unit from having very large weights. If we converted this constraint into a penalty in a Lagrange function, it would be similar to L^2 weight decay but with a separate KKT multiplier for the weights of each hidden unit. Each of these KKT multipliers would be dynamically updated separately to make each hidden unit obey the constraint. In practice, column norm limitation is always implemented as an explicit constraint with reprojection.

7.3 Regularization and Under-Constrained Problems

In some cases, regularization is necessary for machine learning problems to be properly defined. Many linear models in machine learning, including linear regression and PCA, depend on inverting the matrix $X^\top X$. This is not possible when $X^\top X$ is singular. This matrix can be singular whenever the data-generating distribution truly has no variance in some direction, or when no variance is *observed* in some direction because there are fewer examples (rows of X) than input features (columns of X). In this case, many forms of regularization correspond to inverting $X^\top X + \alpha I$ instead. This regularized matrix is guaranteed to be invertible.

These linear problems have closed form solutions when the relevant matrix is invertible. It is also possible for a problem with no closed form solution to be underdetermined. An example is logistic regression applied to a problem where the classes are linearly separable. If a weight vector w is able to achieve perfect classification, then $2w$ will also achieve perfect classification and higher likelihood. An iterative optimization procedure like stochastic gradient descent will continually increase the magnitude of w and, in theory, will never halt. In practice, a numerical implementation of gradient descent will eventually reach sufficiently large weights to cause numerical overflow, at which point its behavior will depend on how the programmer has decided to handle values that are not real numbers.

Most forms of regularization are able to guarantee the convergence of iterative methods applied to underdetermined problems. For example, weight decay will cause gradient descent to quit increasing the magnitude of the weights when the slope of the likelihood is equal to the weight decay coefficient.

The idea of using regularization to solve underdetermined problems extends beyond machine learning. The same idea is useful for several basic linear algebra problems.

As we saw in section 2.9, we can solve underdetermined linear equations using the Moore-Penrose pseudoinverse. Recall that one definition of the pseudoinverse $\boldsymbol{X}^+$ of a matrix $\boldsymbol{X}$ is

$$\boldsymbol{X}^+ = \lim_{\alpha \searrow 0} (\boldsymbol{X}^\top \boldsymbol{X} + \alpha \boldsymbol{I})^{-1} \boldsymbol{X}^\top. \tag{7.29}$$

We can now recognize equation 7.29 as performing linear regression with weight decay. Specifically, equation 7.29 is the limit of equation 7.17 as the regularization coefficient shrinks to zero. We can thus interpret the pseudoinverse as stabilizing underdetermined problems using regularization.

7.4 Dataset Augmentation

The best way to make a machine learning model generalize better is to train it on more data. Of course, in practice, the amount of data we have is limited. One way to get around this problem is to create fake data and add it to the training set. For some machine learning tasks, it is reasonably straightforward to create new fake data.

This approach is easiest for classification. A classifier needs to take a complicated, high-dimensional input $\boldsymbol{x}$ and summarize it with a single category identity y. This means that the main task facing a classifier is to be invariant to a wide variety of transformations. We can generate new $(\boldsymbol{x}, y)$ pairs easily just by transforming the $\boldsymbol{x}$ inputs in our training set.

This approach is not as readily applicable to many other tasks. For example, it is difficult to generate new fake data for a density estimation task unless we have already solved the density estimation problem.

Dataset augmentation has been a particularly effective technique for a specific classification problem: object recognition. Images are high dimensional and include an enormous range of factors of variation, many of which can be easily simulated. Operations like translating the training images a few pixels in each direction can often greatly improve generalization, even if the model has already been designed to be partially translation invariant by using the convolution and pooling techniques described in chapter 9. Many other operations, such as rotating the image or scaling the image, have also proved quite effective.

One must be careful not to apply transformations that would change the correct class. For example, optical character recognition tasks require recognizing the difference between "b" and "d" and the difference between "6" and "9", so horizontal flips and 180° rotations are not appropriate ways of augmenting datasets for these tasks.

There are also transformations that we would like our classifiers to be invariant to but that are not easy to perform. For example, out-of-plane rotation cannot be implemented as a simple geometric operation on the input pixels.

Dataset augmentation is effective for speech recognition tasks as well (Jaitly and Hinton, 2013).

Injecting noise in the input to a neural network (Sietsma and Dow, 1991) can also be seen as a form of data augmentation. For many classification and even some regression tasks, the task should still be possible to solve even if small random noise is added to the input. Neural networks prove not to be very robust to noise, however (Tang and Eliasmith, 2010). One way to improve the robustness of neural networks is simply to train them with random noise applied to their inputs. Input noise injection is part of some unsupervised learning algorithms, such as the denoising autoencoder (Vincent et al., 2008). Noise injection also works when the noise is applied to the hidden units, which can be seen as doing dataset augmentation at multiple levels of abstraction. Poole et al. (2014) recently showed that this approach can be highly effective provided that the magnitude of the noise is carefully tuned. Dropout, a powerful regularization strategy that will be described in section 7.12, can be seen as a process of constructing new inputs by *multiplying* by noise.

When comparing machine learning benchmark results, taking the effect of dataset augmentation into account is important. Often, hand-designed dataset augmentation schemes can dramatically reduce the generalization error of a machine learning technique. To compare the performance of one machine learning algorithm to another, it is necessary to perform controlled experiments. When comparing machine learning algorithm A and machine learning algorithm B, make sure that both algorithms are evaluated using the same hand-designed dataset augmentation schemes. Suppose that algorithm A performs poorly with no dataset augmentation, and algorithm B performs well when combined with numerous synthetic transformations of the input. In such a case the synthetic transformations likely caused the improved performance, rather than the use of machine learning algorithm B. Sometimes deciding whether an experiment has been properly controlled requires subjective judgment. For example, machine learning algorithms that inject noise into the input are performing a form of dataset augmentation. Usually, operations that are generally applicable (such as adding Gaussian noise to the input) are considered part of the machine learning algorithm, while operations that are specific to one application domain (such as randomly cropping an image) are considered to be separate preprocessing steps.

7.5   Noise Robustness

Section 7.4 has motivated the use of noise applied to the inputs as a dataset augmentation strategy. For some models, the addition of noise with infinitesimal variance at the input of the model is equivalent to imposing a penalty on the norm of the weights (Bishop, 1995a,b). In the general case, it is important to remember that noise injection can be much more powerful than simply shrinking the parameters, especially when the noise is added to the hidden units. Noise applied to the hidden units is such an important topic that it merits its own separate discussion; the dropout algorithm described in section 7.12 is the main development of that approach.

Another way that noise has been used in the service of regularizing models is by adding it to the weights. This technique has been used primarily in the context of recurrent neural networks (Jim et al., 1996; Graves, 2011). This can be interpreted as a stochastic implementation of Bayesian inference over the weights. The Bayesian treatment of learning would consider the model weights to be uncertain and representable via a probability distribution that reflects this uncertainty. Adding noise to the weights is a practical, stochastic way to reflect this uncertainty.

Noise applied to the weights can also be interpreted as equivalent (under some assumptions) to a more traditional form of regularization, encouraging stability of the function to be learned. Consider the regression setting, where we wish to train a function $\hat{y}(\boldsymbol{x})$ that maps a set of features $\boldsymbol{x}$ to a scalar using the least-squares cost function between the model predictions $\hat{y}(\boldsymbol{x})$ and the true values y:

$$J = \mathbb{E}_{p(x,y)}\left[(\hat{y}(\boldsymbol{x}) - y)^2\right]. \tag{7.30}$$

The training set consists of m labeled examples $\{(\boldsymbol{x}^{(1)}, y^{(1)}), \ldots, (\boldsymbol{x}^{(m)}, y^{(m)})\}$.

We now assume that with each input presentation we also include a random perturbation $\epsilon_{\boldsymbol{W}} \sim \mathcal{N}(\boldsymbol{\epsilon}; \boldsymbol{0}, \eta \boldsymbol{I})$ of the network weights. Let us imagine that we have a standard l-layer MLP. We denote the perturbed model as $\hat{y}_{\epsilon_{\boldsymbol{W}}}(\boldsymbol{x})$. Despite the injection of noise, we are still interested in minimizing the squared error of the output of the network. The objective function thus becomes

$$\tilde{J}_{\boldsymbol{W}} = \mathbb{E}_{p(\boldsymbol{x},y,\epsilon_{\boldsymbol{W}})}\left[(\hat{y}_{\epsilon_{\boldsymbol{W}}}(\boldsymbol{x}) - y)^2\right] \tag{7.31}$$

$$= \mathbb{E}_{p(\boldsymbol{x},y,\epsilon_{\boldsymbol{W}})}\left[\hat{y}_{\epsilon_{\boldsymbol{W}}}^2(\boldsymbol{x}) - 2y\hat{y}_{\epsilon_{\boldsymbol{W}}}(\boldsymbol{x}) + y^2\right]. \tag{7.32}$$

For small η, the minimization of J with added weight noise (with covariance $\eta \boldsymbol{I}$) is equivalent to minimization of J with an additional regularization term: $\eta \mathbb{E}_{p(\boldsymbol{x},y)}\left[\|\nabla_{\boldsymbol{W}}\hat{y}(\boldsymbol{x})\|^2\right]$. This form of regularization encourages the parameters to go to regions of parameter space where small perturbations of the weights have a relatively small influence on the output. In other words, it pushes the model into regions where the model is relatively insensitive to small variations in the weights, finding points that are not merely minima, but minima surrounded by flat regions (Hochreiter and Schmidhuber, 1995). In the simplified case of linear regression (where, for instance, $\hat{y}(\boldsymbol{x}) = \boldsymbol{w}^\top \boldsymbol{x} + b$), this regularization term collapses into $\eta \mathbb{E}_{p(\boldsymbol{x})} \left[\|\boldsymbol{x}\|^2 \right]$, which is not a function of parameters and therefore does not contribute to the gradient of $\tilde{J}_{\boldsymbol{W}}$ with respect to the model parameters.

7.5.1 Injecting Noise at the Output Targets

Most datasets have some number of mistakes in the y labels. It can be harmful to maximize $\log p(y \mid \boldsymbol{x})$ when y is a mistake. One way to prevent this is to explicitly model the noise on the labels. For example, we can assume that for some small constant ϵ, the training set label y is correct with probability $1 - \epsilon$, and otherwise any of the other possible labels might be correct. This assumption is easy to incorporate into the cost function analytically, rather than by explicitly drawing noise samples. For example, **label smoothing** regularizes a model based on a softmax with k output values by replacing the hard 0 and 1 classification targets with targets of $\frac{\epsilon}{k-1}$ and $1 - \epsilon$, respectively. The standard cross-entropy loss may then be used with these soft targets. Maximum likelihood learning with a softmax classifier and hard targets may actually never converge—the softmax can never predict a probability of exactly 0 or exactly 1, so it will continue to learn larger and larger weights, making more extreme predictions forever. It is possible to prevent this scenario using other regularization strategies like weight decay. Label smoothing has the advantage of preventing the pursuit of hard probabilities without discouraging correct classification. This strategy has been used since the 1980s and continues to be featured prominently in modern neural networks (Szegedy et al., 2015).

7.6 Semi-Supervised Learning

In the paradigm of semi-supervised learning, both unlabeled examples from $P(\mathbf{x})$ and labeled examples from $P(\mathbf{x}, \mathbf{y})$ are used to estimate $P(\mathbf{y} \mid \mathbf{x})$ or predict $\mathbf{y}$ from $\mathbf{x}$.

In the context of deep learning, semi-supervised learning usually refers to learning a representation $\boldsymbol{h} = f(\boldsymbol{x})$. The goal is to learn a representation so that examples from the same class have similar representations. Unsupervised learning can provide useful clues for how to group examples in representation space. Examples that cluster tightly in the input space should be mapped to similar representations. A linear classifier in the new space may achieve better generalization in many cases (Belkin and Niyogi, 2002; Chapelle et al., 2003). A long-standing variant of this approach is the application of principal components analysis as a preprocessing step before applying a classifier (on the projected data).

Instead of having separate unsupervised and supervised components in the model, one can construct models in which a generative model of either $P(\mathbf{x})$ or $P(\mathbf{x}, \mathbf{y})$ shares parameters with a discriminative model of $P(\mathbf{y} \mid \mathbf{x})$. One can then trade off the supervised criterion $-\log P(\mathbf{y} \mid \mathbf{x})$ with the unsupervised or generative one (such as $-\log P(\mathbf{x})$ or $-\log P(\mathbf{x}, \mathbf{y})$). The generative criterion then expresses a particular form of prior belief about the solution to the supervised learning problem (Lasserre et al., 2006), namely that the structure of $P(\mathbf{x})$ is connected to the structure of $P(\mathbf{y} \mid \mathbf{x})$ in a way that is captured by the shared parametrization. By controlling how much of the generative criterion is included in the total criterion, one can find a better trade-off than with a purely generative or a purely discriminative training criterion (Lasserre et al., 2006; Larochelle and Bengio, 2008).

Salakhutdinov and Hinton (2008) describe a method for learning the kernel function of a kernel machine used for regression, in which the usage of unlabeled examples for modeling $P(\mathbf{x})$ improves $P(\mathbf{y} \mid \mathbf{x})$ quite significantly.

See Chapelle et al. (2006) for more information about semi-supervised learning.

7.7 Multitask Learning

Multitask learning (Caruana, 1993) is a way to improve generalization by pooling the examples (which can be seen as soft constraints imposed on the parameters) arising out of several tasks. In the same way that additional training examples put more pressure on the parameters of the model toward values that generalize well, when part of a model is shared across tasks, that part of the model is more constrained toward good values (assuming the sharing is justified), often yielding better generalization.

Figure 7.2 illustrates a very common form of multitask learning, in which different supervised tasks (predicting $\mathbf{y}^{(i)}$ given $\mathbf{x}$) share the same input $\mathbf{x}$, as well as some intermediate-level representation $\boldsymbol{h}^{(\text{shared})}$, capturing a common pool of

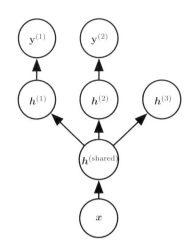

Figure 7.2: Multitask learning can be cast in several ways in deep learning frameworks, and this figure illustrates the common situation where the tasks share a common input but involve different target random variables. The lower layers of a deep network (whether it is supervised and feedforward or includes a generative component with downward arrows) can be shared across such tasks, while task-specific parameters (associated respectively with the weights into and from $\boldsymbol{h}^{(1)}$ and $\boldsymbol{h}^{(2)}$) can be learned on top of those yielding a shared representation $\boldsymbol{h}^{(\text{shared})}$. The underlying assumption is that there exists a common pool of factors that explain the variations in the input $\mathbf{x}$, while each task is associated with a subset of these factors. In this example, it is additionally assumed that top-level hidden units $\boldsymbol{h}^{(1)}$ and $\boldsymbol{h}^{(2)}$ are specialized to each task (respectively predicting $\mathbf{y}^{(1)}$ and $\mathbf{y}^{(2)}$), while some intermediate-level representation $\boldsymbol{h}^{(\text{shared})}$ is shared across all tasks. In the unsupervised learning context, it makes sense for some of the top-level factors to be associated with none of the output tasks ($\boldsymbol{h}^{(3)}$): these are the factors that explain some of the input variations but are not relevant for predicting $\mathbf{y}^{(1)}$ or $\mathbf{y}^{(2)}$.

factors. The model can generally be divided into two kinds of parts and associated parameters:

1. Task-specific parameters (which only benefit from the examples of their task to achieve good generalization). These are the upper layers of the neural network in figure 7.2.

2. Generic parameters, shared across all the tasks (which benefit from the pooled data of all the tasks). These are the lower layers of the neural network in figure 7.2.

Improved generalization and generalization error bounds (Baxter, 1995) can be achieved because of the shared parameters, for which statistical strength can be greatly improved (in proportion with the increased number of examples for the shared parameters, compared to the scenario of single-task models). Of course this will happen only if some assumptions about the statistical relationship between the different tasks are valid, meaning that there is something shared across some of the tasks.

From the point of view of deep learning, the underlying prior belief is the following: *among the factors that explain the variations observed in the data associated with the different tasks, some are shared across two or more tasks.*

7.8 Early Stopping

When training large models with sufficient representational capacity to overfit the task, we often observe that training error decreases steadily over time, but validation set error begins to rise again. See figure 7.3 for an example of this behavior, which occurs reliably.

This means we can obtain a model with better validation set error (and thus, hopefully better test set error) by returning to the parameter setting at the point in time with the lowest validation set error. Every time the error on the validation set improves, we store a copy of the model parameters. When the training algorithm terminates, we return these parameters, rather than the latest parameters. The algorithm terminates when no parameters have improved over the best recorded

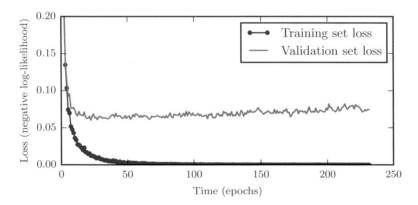

Figure 7.3: Learning curves showing how the negative log-likelihood loss changes over time (indicated as number of training iterations over the dataset, or **epochs**). In this example, we train a maxout network on MNIST. Observe that the training objective decreases consistently over time, but the validation set average loss eventually begins to increase again, forming an asymmetric U-shaped curve.

validation error for some pre-specified number of iterations. This procedure is specified more formally in algorithm 7.1.

This strategy is known as **early stopping**. It is probably the most commonly used form of regularization in deep learning. Its popularity is due to both its effectiveness and its simplicity.

One way to think of early stopping is as a very efficient hyperparameter selection algorithm. In this view, the number of training steps is just another hyperparameter. We can see in figure 7.3 that this hyperparameter has a U-shaped validation set performance curve. Most hyperparameters that control model capacity have such a

---

Algorithm 7.1 The early stopping meta-algorithm for determining the best amount of time to train. This meta-algorithm is a general strategy that works well with a variety of training algorithms and ways of quantifying error on the validation set.

Let n be the number of steps between evaluations.

Let p be the "patience," the number of times to observe worsening validation set error before giving up.

Let $\boldsymbol{\theta}_o$ be the initial parameters.

$\boldsymbol{\theta} \leftarrow \boldsymbol{\theta}_o$

$i \leftarrow 0$

$j \leftarrow 0$

$v \leftarrow \infty$

$\boldsymbol{\theta}^* \leftarrow \boldsymbol{\theta}$

$i^* \leftarrow i$

while $j < p$ **do**

    Update $\boldsymbol{\theta}$ by running the training algorithm for n steps.

    $i \leftarrow i + n$

    $v' \leftarrow \text{ValidationSetError}(\boldsymbol{\theta})$

    if $v' < v$ **then**

        $j \leftarrow 0$

        $\boldsymbol{\theta}^* \leftarrow \boldsymbol{\theta}$

        $i^* \leftarrow i$

        $v \leftarrow v'$

    else

        $j \leftarrow j + 1$

    end if

end while

Best parameters are $\boldsymbol{\theta}^*$, best number of training steps is i^*.

U-shaped validation set performance curve, as illustrated in figure 5.3. In the case of early stopping, we are controlling the effective capacity of the model by determining how many steps it can take to fit the training set. Most hyperparameters must be chosen using an expensive guess and check process, where we set a hyperparameter at the start of training, then run training for several steps to see its effect. The "training time" hyperparameter is unique in that by definition, a single run of training tries out many values of the hyperparameter. The only significant cost to choosing this hyperparameter automatically via early stopping is running the validation set evaluation periodically during training. Ideally, this is done in parallel to the training process on a separate machine, separate CPU, or separate GPU from the main training process. If such resources are not available, then the cost of these periodic evaluations may be reduced by using a validation set that is small compared to the training set or by evaluating the validation set error less frequently and obtaining a lower-resolution estimate of the optimal training time.

An additional cost to early stopping is the need to maintain a copy of the best parameters. This cost is generally negligible, because it is acceptable to store these parameters in a slower and larger form of memory (for example, training in GPU memory, but storing the optimal parameters in host memory or on a disk drive). Since the best parameters are written to infrequently and never read during training, these occasional slow writes have little effect on the total training time.

Early stopping is an unobtrusive form of regularization, in that it requires almost no change in the underlying training procedure, the objective function, or the set of allowable parameter values. This means that it is easy to use early stopping without damaging the learning dynamics. This is in contrast to weight decay, where one must be careful not to use too much weight decay and trap the network in a bad local minimum corresponding to a solution with pathologically small weights.

Early stopping may be used either alone or in conjunction with other regularization strategies. Even when using regularization strategies that modify the objective function to encourage better generalization, it is rare for the best generalization to occur at a local minimum of the training objective.

Early stopping requires a validation set, which means some training data is not fed to the model. To best exploit this extra data, one can perform extra training after the initial training with early stopping has completed. In the second, extra training step, all the training data is included. There are two basic strategies one can use for this second training procedure.

One strategy (algorithm 7.2) is to initialize the model again and retrain on all the data. In this second training pass, we train for the same number of steps as

Algorithm 7.2 A meta-algorithm for using early stopping to determine how long to train, then retraining on all the data.

Let $\boldsymbol{X}^{(\text{train})}$ and $\boldsymbol{y}^{(\text{train})}$ be the training set.
Split $\boldsymbol{X}^{(\text{train})}$ and $\boldsymbol{y}^{(\text{train})}$ into $(\boldsymbol{X}^{(\text{subtrain})}, \boldsymbol{X}^{(\text{valid})})$ and $(\boldsymbol{y}^{(\text{subtrain})}, \boldsymbol{y}^{(\text{valid})})$ respectively.
Run early stopping (algorithm 7.1) starting from random $\boldsymbol{\theta}$ using $\boldsymbol{X}^{(\text{subtrain})}$ and $\boldsymbol{y}^{(\text{subtrain})}$ for training data and $\boldsymbol{X}^{(\text{valid})}$ and $\boldsymbol{y}^{(\text{valid})}$ for validation data. This returns i^*, the optimal number of steps.
Set $\boldsymbol{\theta}$ to random values again.
Train on $\boldsymbol{X}^{(\text{train})}$ and $\boldsymbol{y}^{(\text{train})}$ for i^* steps.

the early stopping procedure determined was optimal in the first pass. There are some subtleties associated with this procedure. For example, there is not a good way of knowing whether to retrain for the same number of parameter updates or the same number of passes through the dataset. On the second round of training, each pass through the dataset will require more parameter updates because the training set is bigger.

Another strategy for using all the data is to keep the parameters obtained from the first round of training and then *continue* training, but now using all the data. At this stage, we now no longer have a guide for when to stop in terms of a number of steps. Instead, we can monitor the average loss function on the validation set and continue training until it falls below the value of the training set objective at which the early stopping procedure halted. This strategy avoids the high cost of retraining the model from scratch but is not as well behaved. For example, the objective on the validation set may not ever reach the target value, so this strategy is not even guaranteed to terminate. This procedure is presented more formally in algorithm 7.3.

Early stopping is also useful because it reduces the computational cost of the training procedure. Besides the obvious reduction in cost due to limiting the number of training iterations, it also has the benefit of providing regularization without requiring the addition of penalty terms to the cost function or the computation of the gradients of such additional terms.

How early stopping acts as a regularizer: So far we have stated that early stopping *is* a regularization strategy, but we have supported this claim only by showing learning curves where the validation set error has a U-shaped curve. What is the actual mechanism by which early stopping regularizes the model?

Algorithm 7.3 Meta-algorithm using early stopping to determine at what objective value we start to overfit, then continue training until that value is reached.

Let $\boldsymbol{X}^{(\text{train})}$ and $\boldsymbol{y}^{(\text{train})}$ be the training set.
Split $\boldsymbol{X}^{(\text{train})}$ and $\boldsymbol{y}^{(\text{train})}$ into $(\boldsymbol{X}^{(\text{subtrain})}, \boldsymbol{X}^{(\text{valid})})$ and $(\boldsymbol{y}^{(\text{subtrain})}, \boldsymbol{y}^{(\text{valid})})$ respectively.
Run early stopping (algorithm 7.1) starting from random $\boldsymbol{\theta}$ using $\boldsymbol{X}^{(\text{subtrain})}$ and $\boldsymbol{y}^{(\text{subtrain})}$ for training data and $\boldsymbol{X}^{(\text{valid})}$ and $\boldsymbol{y}^{(\text{valid})}$ for validation data. This updates $\boldsymbol{\theta}$.
$\epsilon \leftarrow J(\boldsymbol{\theta}, \boldsymbol{X}^{(\text{subtrain})}, \boldsymbol{y}^{(\text{subtrain})})$
while $J(\boldsymbol{\theta}, \boldsymbol{X}^{(\text{valid})}, \boldsymbol{y}^{(\text{valid})}) > \epsilon$ **do**
    Train on $\boldsymbol{X}^{(\text{train})}$ and $\boldsymbol{y}^{(\text{train})}$ for n steps.
end while

Bishop (1995a) and Sjöberg and Ljung (1995) argued that early stopping has the effect of restricting the optimization procedure to a relatively small volume of parameter space in the neighborhood of the initial parameter value $\boldsymbol{\theta}_o$, as illustrated in figure 7.4. More specifically, imagine taking τ optimization steps (corresponding to τ training iterations) and with learning rate ϵ. We can view the product $\epsilon\tau$ as a measure of effective capacity. Assuming the gradient is bounded, restricting both the number of iterations and the learning rate limits the volume of parameter space reachable from $\boldsymbol{\theta}_o$. In this sense, $\epsilon\tau$ behaves as if it were the reciprocal of the coefficient used for weight decay.

Indeed, we can show how—in the case of a simple linear model with a quadratic error function and simple gradient descent—early stopping is equivalent to L^2 regularization.

To compare with classical L^2 regularization, we examine a simple setting where the only parameters are linear weights $(\boldsymbol{\theta} = \boldsymbol{w})$. We can model the cost function J with a quadratic approximation in the neighborhood of the empirically optimal value of the weights $\boldsymbol{w}^*$:

$$\hat{J}(\boldsymbol{\theta}) = J(\boldsymbol{w}^*) + \frac{1}{2}(\boldsymbol{w} - \boldsymbol{w}^*)^\top \boldsymbol{H}(\boldsymbol{w} - \boldsymbol{w}^*), \qquad (7.33)$$

where $\boldsymbol{H}$ is the Hessian matrix of J with respect to $\boldsymbol{w}$ evaluated at $\boldsymbol{w}^*$. Given the assumption that $\boldsymbol{w}^*$ is a minimum of $J(\boldsymbol{w})$, we know that $\boldsymbol{H}$ is positive semidefinite. Under a local Taylor series approximation, the gradient is given by

$$\nabla_{\boldsymbol{w}}\hat{J}(\boldsymbol{w}) = \boldsymbol{H}(\boldsymbol{w} - \boldsymbol{w}^*). \qquad (7.34)$$

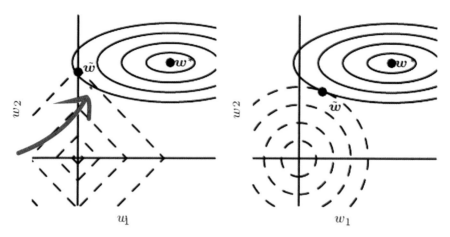

Figure 7.4: An illustration of the effect of early stopping. *(Left)*The solid contour lines indicate the contours of the negative log-likelihood. The dashed line indicates the trajectory taken by SGD beginning from the origin. Rather than stopping at the point $\boldsymbol{w}^*$ that minimizes the cost, early stopping results in the trajectory stopping at an earlier point $\tilde{\boldsymbol{w}}$. *(Right)*An illustration of the effect of L^2 regularization for comparison. The dashed circles indicate the contours of the L^2 penalty, which causes the minimum of the total cost to lie nearer the origin than the minimum of the unregularized cost.

We are going to study the trajectory followed by the parameter vector during training. For simplicity, let us set the initial parameter vector to the origin,[3] $\boldsymbol{w}^{(0)} = \boldsymbol{0}$. Let us study the approximate behavior of gradient descent on J by analyzing gradient descent on $\hat{J}$:

$$\boldsymbol{w}^{(\tau)} = \boldsymbol{w}^{(\tau-1)} - \epsilon \nabla_{\boldsymbol{w}} \hat{J}(\boldsymbol{w}^{(\tau-1)}) \tag{7.35}$$

$$= \boldsymbol{w}^{(\tau-1)} - \epsilon \boldsymbol{H}(\boldsymbol{w}^{(\tau-1)} - \boldsymbol{w}^*), \tag{7.36}$$

$$\boldsymbol{w}^{(\tau)} - \boldsymbol{w}^* = (\boldsymbol{I} - \epsilon \boldsymbol{H})(\boldsymbol{w}^{(\tau-1)} - \boldsymbol{w}^*). \tag{7.37}$$

Let us now rewrite this expression in the space of the eigenvectors of $\boldsymbol{H}$, exploiting the eigendecomposition of $\boldsymbol{H}$: $\boldsymbol{H} = \boldsymbol{Q}\boldsymbol{\Lambda}\boldsymbol{Q}^\top$, where $\boldsymbol{\Lambda}$ is a diagonal matrix and $\boldsymbol{Q}$ is an orthonormal basis of eigenvectors.

$$\boldsymbol{w}^{(\tau)} - \boldsymbol{w}^* = (\boldsymbol{I} - \epsilon \boldsymbol{Q}\boldsymbol{\Lambda}\boldsymbol{Q}^\top)(\boldsymbol{w}^{(\tau-1)} - \boldsymbol{w}^*) \tag{7.38}$$

$$\boldsymbol{Q}^\top(\boldsymbol{w}^{(\tau)} - \boldsymbol{w}^*) = (\boldsymbol{I} - \epsilon \boldsymbol{\Lambda})\boldsymbol{Q}^\top(\boldsymbol{w}^{(\tau-1)} - \boldsymbol{w}^*) \tag{7.39}$$

---

[3]For neural networks, to obtain symmetry breaking between hidden units, we cannot initialize all the parameters to $\boldsymbol{0}$, as discussed in section 6.2. However, the argument holds for any other initial value $\boldsymbol{w}_{(0)}$.

Assuming that $\boldsymbol{w}^{(0)} = 0$ and that ϵ is chosen to be small enough to guarantee $|1 - \epsilon\lambda_i| < 1$, the parameter trajectory during training after τ parameter updates is as follows:

$$\boldsymbol{Q}^\top\boldsymbol{w}^{(\tau)} = [\boldsymbol{I} - (\boldsymbol{I} - \epsilon\boldsymbol{\Lambda})^\tau]\boldsymbol{Q}^\top\boldsymbol{w}^*. \tag{7.40}$$

Now, the expression for $\boldsymbol{Q}^\top\tilde{\boldsymbol{w}}$ in equation 7.13 for L^2 regularization can be rearranged as

$$\boldsymbol{Q}^\top\tilde{\boldsymbol{w}} = (\boldsymbol{\Lambda} + \alpha\boldsymbol{I})^{-1}\boldsymbol{\Lambda}\boldsymbol{Q}^\top\boldsymbol{w}^*, \tag{7.41}$$

$$\boldsymbol{Q}^\top\tilde{\boldsymbol{w}} = [\boldsymbol{I} - (\boldsymbol{\Lambda} + \alpha\boldsymbol{I})^{-1}\alpha]\boldsymbol{Q}^\top\boldsymbol{w}^*. \tag{7.42}$$

Comparing equation 7.40 and equation 7.42, we see that if the hyperparameters ϵ, α, and τ are chosen such that

$$(\boldsymbol{I} - \epsilon\boldsymbol{\Lambda})^\tau = (\boldsymbol{\Lambda} + \alpha\boldsymbol{I})^{-1}\alpha, \tag{7.43}$$

then L^2 regularization and early stopping can be seen as equivalent (at least under the quadratic approximation of the objective function). Going even further, by taking logarithms and using the series expansion for $\log(1 + x)$, we can conclude that if all λ_i are small (that is, $\epsilon\lambda_i \ll 1$ and $\lambda_i/\alpha \ll 1$) then

$$\tau \approx \frac{1}{\epsilon\alpha}, \tag{7.44}$$

$$\alpha \approx \frac{1}{\tau\epsilon}. \tag{7.45}$$

That is, under these assumptions, the number of training iterations τ plays a role inversely proportional to the L^2 regularization parameter, and the inverse of $\tau\epsilon$ plays the role of the weight decay coefficient.

Parameter values corresponding to directions of significant curvature (of the objective function) are regularized less than directions of less curvature. Of course, in the context of early stopping, this really means that parameters that correspond to directions of significant curvature tend to learn early relative to parameters corresponding to directions of less curvature.

The derivations in this section have shown that a trajectory of length τ ends at a point that corresponds to a minimum of the L^2-regularized objective. Early stopping is of course more than the mere restriction of the trajectory length; instead, early stopping typically involves monitoring the validation set error in order to stop the trajectory at a particularly good point in space. Early stopping therefore has the advantage over weight decay in that it automatically determines the correct amount of regularization while weight decay requires many training experiments with different values of its hyperparameter.

7.9   Parameter Tying and Parameter Sharing

Thus far, in this chapter, when we have discussed adding constraints or penalties to the parameters, we have always done so with respect to a fixed region or point. For example, L^2 regularization (or weight decay) penalizes model parameters for deviating from the fixed value of zero. Sometimes, however, we may need other ways to express our prior knowledge about suitable values of the model parameters. Sometimes we might not know precisely what values the parameters should take, but we know, from knowledge of the domain and model architecture, that there should be some dependencies between the model parameters.

A common type of dependency that we often want to express is that certain parameters should be close to one another. Consider the following scenario: we have two models performing the same classification task (with the same set of classes) but with somewhat different input distributions. Formally, we have model A with parameters $\boldsymbol{w}^{(A)}$ and model B with parameters $\boldsymbol{w}^{(B)}$. The two models map the input to two different but related outputs: $\hat{y}^{(A)} = f(\boldsymbol{w}^{(A)}, \boldsymbol{x})$ and $\hat{y}^{(B)} = g(\boldsymbol{w}^{(B)}, \boldsymbol{x})$.

Let us imagine that the tasks are similar enough (perhaps with similar input and output distributions) that we believe the model parameters should be close to each other: $\forall i$, $w_i^{(A)}$ should be close to $w_i^{(B)}$. We can leverage this information through regularization. Specifically, we can use a parameter norm penalty of the form $\Omega(\boldsymbol{w}^{(A)}, \boldsymbol{w}^{(B)}) = \|\boldsymbol{w}^{(A)} - \boldsymbol{w}^{(B)}\|_2^2$. Here we used an L^2 penalty, but other choices are also possible.

This kind of approach was proposed by Lasserre et al. (2006), who regularized the parameters of one model, trained as a classifier in a supervised paradigm, to be close to the parameters of another model, trained in an unsupervised paradigm (to capture the distribution of the observed input data). The architectures were constructed such that many of the parameters in the classifier model could be paired to corresponding parameters in the unsupervised model.

While a parameter norm penalty is one way to regularize parameters to be close to one another, the more popular way is to use constraints: *to force sets of parameters to be equal*. This method of regularization is often referred to as **parameter sharing**, because we interpret the various models or model components as sharing a unique set of parameters. A significant advantage of parameter sharing over regularizing the parameters to be close (via a norm penalty) is that only a subset of the parameters (the unique set) needs to be stored in memory. In certain models—such as the convolutional neural network—this can lead to significant reduction in the memory footprint of the model.

7.9.1 Convolutional Neural Networks

By far the most popular and extensive use of parameter sharing occurs in **convolutional neural networks** (CNNs) applied to computer vision.

Natural images have many statistical properties that are invariant to translation. For example, a photo of a cat remains a photo of a cat if it is translated one pixel to the right. CNNs take this property into account by sharing parameters across multiple image locations. The same feature (a hidden unit with the same weights) is computed over different locations in the input. This means that we can find a cat with the same cat detector whether the cat appears at column i or column $i + 1$ in the image.

Parameter sharing has enabled CNNs to dramatically lower the number of unique model parameters and to significantly increase network sizes without requiring a corresponding increase in training data. It remains one of the best examples of how to effectively incorporate domain knowledge into the network architecture.

CNNs are discussed in more detail in chapter 9.

7.10 Sparse Representations

Weight decay acts by placing a penalty directly on the model parameters. Another strategy is to place a penalty on the activations of the units in a neural network, encouraging their activations to be sparse. This indirectly imposes a complicated penalty on the model parameters.

We have already discussed (in section 7.1.2) how L^1 penalization induces a sparse parametrization—meaning that many of the parameters become zero (or close to zero). Representational sparsity, on the other hand, describes a representation where many of the elements of the representation are zero (or close to zero). A simplified view of this distinction can be illustrated in the context of linear regression:

$$
\begin{array}{cc}
\begin{bmatrix} 18 \\ 5 \\ 15 \\ -9 \\ -3 \end{bmatrix} =
\begin{bmatrix} 4 & 0 & 0 & -2 & 0 & 0 \\ 0 & 0 & -1 & 0 & 3 & 0 \\ 0 & 5 & 0 & 0 & 0 & 0 \\ 1 & 0 & 0 & -1 & 0 & -4 \\ 1 & 0 & 0 & 0 & -5 & 0 \end{bmatrix}
\begin{bmatrix} 2 \\ 3 \\ -2 \\ -5 \\ 1 \\ 4 \end{bmatrix}
\end{array}
\tag{7.46}
$$

$$
\boldsymbol{y} \in \mathbb{R}^m \qquad \boldsymbol{A} \in \mathbb{R}^{m \times n} \qquad \boldsymbol{x} \in \mathbb{R}^n
$$

$$
\begin{bmatrix} -14 \\ 1 \\ 19 \\ 2 \\ 23 \end{bmatrix} = \begin{bmatrix} 3 & -1 & 2 & -5 & 4 & 1 \\ 4 & 2 & -3 & -1 & 1 & 3 \\ -1 & 5 & 4 & 2 & -3 & -2 \\ 3 & 1 & 2 & -3 & 0 & -3 \\ -5 & 4 & -2 & 2 & -5 & -1 \end{bmatrix} \begin{bmatrix} 0 \\ 2 \\ 0 \\ 0 \\ -3 \\ 0 \end{bmatrix} \tag{7.47}
$$

$$
\boldsymbol{y} \in \mathbb{R}^m \qquad\qquad \boldsymbol{B} \in \mathbb{R}^{m \times n} \qquad\qquad \boldsymbol{h} \in \mathbb{R}^n
$$

In the first expression, we have an example of a sparsely parametrized linear regression model. In the second, we have linear regression with a sparse representation $\boldsymbol{h}$ of the data $\boldsymbol{x}$. That is, $\boldsymbol{h}$ is a function of $\boldsymbol{x}$ that, in some sense, represents the information present in $\boldsymbol{x}$, but does so with a sparse vector.

Representational regularization is accomplished by the same sorts of mechanisms that we have used in parameter regularization.

Norm penalty regularization of representations is performed by adding to the loss function J a norm penalty on the *representation*. This penalty is denoted $\Omega(\boldsymbol{h})$. As before, we denote the regularized loss function by $\tilde{J}$:

$$
\tilde{J}(\boldsymbol{\theta}; \boldsymbol{X}, \boldsymbol{y}) = J(\boldsymbol{\theta}; \boldsymbol{X}, \boldsymbol{y}) + \alpha \Omega(\boldsymbol{h}), \tag{7.48}
$$

where $\alpha \in [0, \infty)$ weights the relative contribution of the norm penalty term, with larger values of α corresponding to more regularization.

Just as an L^1 penalty on the parameters induces parameter sparsity, an L^1 penalty on the elements of the representation induces representational sparsity: $\Omega(\boldsymbol{h}) = ||\boldsymbol{h}||_1 = \sum_i |h_i|$. Of course, the L^1 penalty is only one choice of penalty that can result in a sparse representation. Others include the penalty derived from a Student t prior on the representation (Olshausen and Field, 1996; Bergstra, 2011) and KL divergence penalties (Larochelle and Bengio, 2008), which are especially useful for representations with elements constrained to lie on the unit interval. Lee et al. (2008) and Goodfellow et al. (2009) both provide examples of strategies based on regularizing the average activation across several examples, $\frac{1}{m} \sum_i \boldsymbol{h}^{(i)}$, to be near some target value, such as a vector with .01 for each entry.

Other approaches obtain representational sparsity with a hard constraint on the activation values. For example, **orthogonal matching pursuit** (Pati et al., 1993) encodes an input $\boldsymbol{x}$ with the representation $\boldsymbol{h}$ that solves the constrained optimization problem

$$
\underset{\boldsymbol{h}, ||\boldsymbol{h}||_0 < k}{\arg\min} ||\boldsymbol{x} - \boldsymbol{W}\boldsymbol{h}||^2, \tag{7.49}
$$

where $||\boldsymbol{h}||_0$ is the number of nonzero entries of $\boldsymbol{h}$. This problem can be solved efficiently when $\boldsymbol{W}$ is constrained to be orthogonal. This method is often called

OMP-k, with the value of k specified to indicate the number of nonzero features allowed. Coates and Ng (2011) demonstrated that OMP-1 can be a very effective feature extractor for deep architectures.

Essentially any model that has hidden units can be made sparse. Throughout this book, we see many examples of sparsity regularization used in various contexts.

7.11 Bagging and Other Ensemble Methods

Bagging (short for **bootstrap aggregating**) is a technique for reducing generalization error by combining several models (Breiman, 1994). The idea is to train several different models separately, then have all the models vote on the output for test examples. This is an example of a general strategy in machine learning called **model averaging**. Techniques employing this strategy are known as **ensemble methods**.

The reason that model averaging works is that different models will usually not make all the same errors on the test set.

Consider for example a set of k regression models. Suppose that each model makes an error ϵ_i on each example, with the errors drawn from a zero-mean multivariate normal distribution with variances $\mathbb{E}[\epsilon_i^2] = v$ and covariances $\mathbb{E}[\epsilon_i \epsilon_j] = c$. Then the error made by the average prediction of all the ensemble models is $\frac{1}{k} \sum_i \epsilon_i$. The expected squared error of the ensemble predictor is

$$\mathbb{E}\left[\left(\frac{1}{k}\sum_i \epsilon_i\right)^2\right] = \frac{1}{k^2}\mathbb{E}\left[\sum_i \left(\epsilon_i^2 + \sum_{j \neq i}\epsilon_i\epsilon_j\right)\right], \tag{7.50}$$

$$= \frac{1}{k}v + \frac{k-1}{k}c. \tag{7.51}$$

In the case where the errors are perfectly correlated and $c = v$, the mean squared error reduces to v, so the model averaging does not help at all. In the case where the errors are perfectly uncorrelated and $c = 0$, the expected squared error of the ensemble is only $\frac{1}{k}v$. This means that the expected squared error of the ensemble decreases linearly with the ensemble size. In other words, on average, the ensemble will perform at least as well as any of its members, and if the members make independent errors, the ensemble will perform significantly better than its members.

Different ensemble methods construct the ensemble of models in different ways. For example, each member of the ensemble could be formed by training a completely different kind of model using a different algorithm or objective function. Bagging is a method that allows the same kind of model, training algorithm and objective function to be reused several times.

Specifically, bagging involves constructing k different datasets. Each dataset has the same number of examples as the original dataset, but each dataset is constructed by sampling with replacement from the original dataset. This means that, with high probability, each dataset is missing some of the examples from the original dataset and contains several duplicate examples (on average around two–thirds of the examples from the original dataset are found in the resulting training set, if it has the same size as the original). Model i is then trained on dataset i. The differences between which examples are included in each dataset result in differences between the trained models. See figure 7.5 for an example.

Neural networks reach a wide enough variety of solution points that they can often benefit from model averaging even if all the models are trained on the same dataset. Differences in random initialization, in random selection of minibatches, in hyperparameters, or in outcomes of nondeterministic implementations of neural networks are often enough to cause different members of the ensemble to make partially independent errors.

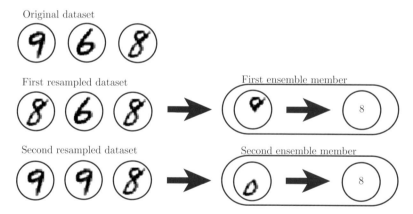

Figure 7.5: A cartoon depiction of how bagging works. Suppose we train an 8 detector on the dataset depicted above, containing an 8, a 6 and a 9. Suppose we make two different resampled datasets. The bagging training procedure is to construct each of these datasets by sampling with replacement. The first dataset omits the 9 and repeats the 8. On this dataset, the detector learns that a loop on top of the digit corresponds to an 8. On the second dataset, we repeat the 9 and omit the 6. In this case, the detector learns that a loop on the bottom of the digit corresponds to an 8. Each of these individual classification rules is brittle, but if we average their output, then the detector is robust, achieving maximal confidence only when both loops of the 8 are present.

Model averaging is an extremely powerful and reliable method for reducing generalization error. Its use is usually discouraged when benchmarking algorithms for scientific papers, because any machine learning algorithm can benefit substantially from model averaging at the price of increased computation and memory. For this reason, benchmark comparisons are usually made using a single model.

Machine learning contests are usually won by methods using model averaging over dozens of models. A recent prominent example is the Netflix Grand Prize (Koren, 2009).

Not all techniques for constructing ensembles are designed to make the ensemble more regularized than the individual models. For example, a technique called **boosting** (Freund and Schapire, 1996b,a) constructs an ensemble with higher capacity than the individual models. Boosting has been applied to build ensembles of neural networks (Schwenk and Bengio, 1998) by incrementally adding neural networks to the ensemble. Boosting has also been applied interpreting an individual neural network as an ensemble (Bengio et al., 2006a), incrementally adding hidden units to the network.

7.12 Dropout

Dropout (Srivastava et al., 2014) provides a computationally inexpensive but powerful method of regularizing a broad family of models. To a first approximation, dropout can be thought of as a method of making bagging practical for ensembles of very many large neural networks. Bagging involves training multiple models and evaluating multiple models on each test example. This seems impractical when each model is a large neural network, since training and evaluating such networks is costly in terms of runtime and memory. It is common to use ensembles of five to ten neural networks—Szegedy et al. (2014a) used six to win the ILSVRC— but more than this rapidly becomes unwieldy. Dropout provides an inexpensive approximation to training and evaluating a bagged ensemble of exponentially many neural networks.

Specifically, dropout trains the ensemble consisting of all subnetworks that can be formed by removing nonoutput units from an underlying base network, as illustrated in figure 7.6. In most modern neural networks, based on a series of affine transformations and nonlinearities, we can effectively remove a unit from a network by multiplying its output value by zero. This procedure requires some slight modification for models such as radial basis function networks, which take the difference between the unit's state and some reference value. Here, we present the dropout algorithm in terms of multiplication by zero for simplicity, but it can

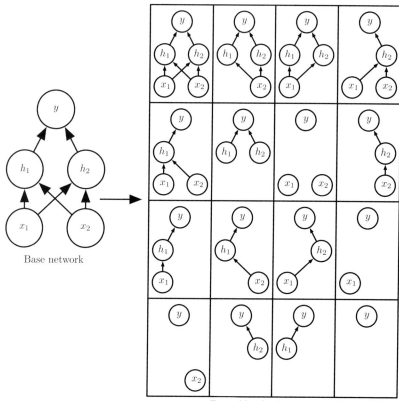

Base network

Ensemble of subnetworks

Figure 7.6: Dropout trains an ensemble consisting of all subnetworks that can be constructed by removing nonoutput units from an underlying base network. Here, we begin with a base network with two visible units and two hidden units. There are sixteen possible subsets of these four units. We show all sixteen subnetworks that may be formed by dropping out different subsets of units from the original network. In this small example, a large proportion of the resulting networks have no input units or no path connecting the input to the output. This problem becomes insignificant for networks with wider layers, where the probability of dropping all possible paths from inputs to outputs becomes smaller.

be trivially modified to work with other operations that remove a unit from the network.

Recall that to learn with bagging, we define k different models, construct k different datasets by sampling from the training set with replacement, and then train model i on dataset i. Dropout aims to approximate this process, but with an exponentially large number of neural networks. Specifically, to train with dropout, we use a minibatch-based learning algorithm that makes small steps, such as stochastic gradient descent. Each time we load an example into a minibatch, we randomly sample a different binary mask to apply to all the input and hidden units in the network. The mask for each unit is sampled independently from all the others. The probability of sampling a mask value of one (causing a unit to be included) is a hyperparameter fixed before training begins. It is not a function of the current value of the model parameters or the input example. Typically, an input unit is included with probability 0.8, and a hidden unit is included with probability 0.5. We then run forward propagation, back-propagation, and the learning update as usual. Figure 7.7 illustrates how to run forward propagation with dropout.

More formally, suppose that a mask vector $\boldsymbol{\mu}$ specifies which units to include, and $J(\boldsymbol{\theta}, \boldsymbol{\mu})$ defines the cost of the model defined by parameters $\boldsymbol{\theta}$ and mask $\boldsymbol{\mu}$. Then dropout training consists of minimizing $\mathbb{E}_{\boldsymbol{\mu}} J(\boldsymbol{\theta}, \boldsymbol{\mu})$. The expectation contains exponentially many terms, but we can obtain an unbiased estimate of its gradient by sampling values of $\boldsymbol{\mu}$.

Dropout training is not quite the same as bagging training. In the case of bagging, the models are all independent. In the case of dropout, the models share parameters, with each model inheriting a different subset of parameters from the parent neural network. This parameter sharing makes it possible to represent an exponential number of models with a tractable amount of memory. In the case of bagging, each model is trained to convergence on its respective training set. In the case of dropout, typically most models are not explicitly trained at all—usually, the model is large enough that it would be infeasible to sample all possible subnetworks within the lifetime of the universe. Instead, a tiny fraction of the possible subnetworks are each trained for a single step, and the parameter sharing causes the remaining subnetworks to arrive at good settings of the parameters. These are the only differences. Beyond these, dropout follows the bagging algorithm. For example, the training set encountered by each subnetwork is indeed a subset of the original training set sampled with replacement.

To make a prediction, a bagged ensemble must accumulate votes from all its members. We refer to this process as **inference** in this context. So far, our description of bagging and dropout has not required that the model be explicitly probabilistic. Now, we assume that the model's role is to output a probability distribution. In the case of bagging, each model i produces a probability distribution $p^{(i)}(y \mid \boldsymbol{x})$. The prediction of the ensemble is given by the arithmetic mean of all these distributions,

$$\frac{1}{k} \sum_{i=1}^{k} p^{(i)}(y \mid \boldsymbol{x}). \tag{7.52}$$

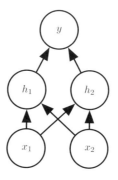

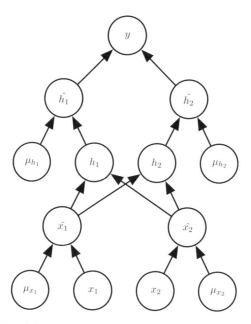

Figure 7.7: An example of forward propagation through a feedforward network using dropout. *(Top)*In this example, we use a feedforward network with two input units, one hidden layer with two hidden units, and one output unit. *(Bottom)*To perform forward propagation with dropout, we randomly sample a vector $\boldsymbol{\mu}$ with one entry for each input or hidden unit in the network. The entries of $\boldsymbol{\mu}$ are binary and are sampled independently from each other. The probability of each entry being 1 is a hyperparameter, usually 0.5 for the hidden layers and 0.8 for the input. Each unit in the network is multiplied by the corresponding mask, and then forward propagation continues through the rest of the network as usual. This is equivalent to randomly selecting one of the sub-networks from figure 7.6 and running forward propagation through it.

In the case of dropout, each submodel defined by mask vector $\boldsymbol{\mu}$ defines a probability distribution $p(y \mid \boldsymbol{x}, \boldsymbol{\mu})$. The arithmetic mean over all masks is given by

$$\sum_{\boldsymbol{\mu}} p(\boldsymbol{\mu}) p(y \mid \boldsymbol{x}, \boldsymbol{\mu}), \tag{7.53}$$

where $p(\boldsymbol{\mu})$ is the probability distribution that was used to sample $\boldsymbol{\mu}$ at training time.

Because this sum includes an exponential number of terms, it is intractable to evaluate except when the structure of the model permits some form of simplification. So far, deep neural nets are not known to permit any tractable simplification. Instead, we can approximate the inference with sampling, by averaging together the output from many masks. Even 10–20 masks are often sufficient to obtain good performance.

An even better approach, however, allows us to obtain a good approximation to the predictions of the entire ensemble, at the cost of only one forward propagation. To do so, we change to using the geometric mean rather than the arithmetic mean of the ensemble members' predicted distributions. Warde-Farley et al. (2014) present arguments and empirical evidence that the geometric mean performs comparably to the arithmetic mean in this context.

The geometric mean of multiple probability distributions is not guaranteed to be a probability distribution. To guarantee that the result is a probability distribution, we impose the requirement that none of the submodels assigns probability 0 to any event, and we renormalize the resulting distribution. The unnormalized probability distribution defined directly by the geometric mean is given by

$$\tilde{p}_{\text{ensemble}}(y \mid \boldsymbol{x}) = \sqrt[2^d]{\prod_{\boldsymbol{\mu}} p(y \mid \boldsymbol{x}, \boldsymbol{\mu})}, \tag{7.54}$$

where d is the number of units that may be dropped. Here we use a uniform distribution over $\boldsymbol{\mu}$ to simplify the presentation, but nonuniform distributions are also possible. To make predictions we must renormalize the ensemble:

$$p_{\text{ensemble}}(y \mid \boldsymbol{x}) = \frac{\tilde{p}_{\text{ensemble}}(y \mid \boldsymbol{x})}{\sum_{y'} \tilde{p}_{\text{ensemble}}(y' \mid \boldsymbol{x})}. \tag{7.55}$$

A key insight (Hinton et al., 2012c) involved in dropout is that we can approximate p_{ensemble} by evaluating $p(y \mid \boldsymbol{x})$ in one model: the model with all units, but with the weights going out of unit i multiplied by the probability of including unit i. The motivation for this modification is to capture the right expected value of the output from that unit. We call this approach the **weight scaling inference rule**. There is not yet any theoretical argument for the accuracy of this approximate inference rule in deep nonlinear networks, but empirically it performs very well.

Because we usually use an inclusion probability of $\frac{1}{2}$, the weight scaling rule usually amounts to dividing the weights by 2 at the end of training, and then using the model as usual. Another way to achieve the same result is to multiply the states of the units by 2 during training. Either way, the goal is to make sure that the expected total input to a unit at test time is roughly the same as the expected total input to that unit at train time, even though half the units at train time are missing on average.

For many classes of models that do not have nonlinear hidden units, the weight scaling inference rule is exact. For a simple example, consider a softmax regression classifier with n input variables represented by the vector $\mathbf{v}$:

$$P(\mathrm{y} = y \mid \mathbf{v}) = \mathrm{softmax}\left(\boldsymbol{W}^\top \mathbf{v} + \boldsymbol{b}\right)_y. \tag{7.56}$$

We can index into the family of submodels by element-wise multiplication of the input with a binary vector d:

$$P(\mathrm{y} = y \mid \mathbf{v}; \boldsymbol{d}) = \mathrm{softmax}\left(\boldsymbol{W}^\top (\boldsymbol{d} \odot \mathbf{v}) + \boldsymbol{b}\right)_y. \tag{7.57}$$

The ensemble predictor is defined by renormalizing the geometric mean over all ensemble members' predictions:

$$P_{\mathrm{ensemble}}(\mathrm{y} = y \mid \mathbf{v}) = \frac{\tilde{P}_{\mathrm{ensemble}}(\mathrm{y} = y \mid \mathbf{v})}{\sum_{y'} \tilde{P}_{\mathrm{ensemble}}(\mathrm{y} = y' \mid \mathbf{v})}, \tag{7.58}$$

where

$$\tilde{P}_{\mathrm{ensemble}}(\mathrm{y} = y \mid \mathbf{v}) = \sqrt[2^n]{\prod_{\boldsymbol{d} \in \{0,1\}^n} P(\mathrm{y} = y \mid \mathbf{v}; \boldsymbol{d})}. \tag{7.59}$$

To see that the weight scaling rule is exact, we can simplify $\tilde{P}_{\mathrm{ensemble}}$:

$$\tilde{P}_{\mathrm{ensemble}}(\mathrm{y} = y \mid \mathbf{v}) = \sqrt[2^n]{\prod_{\boldsymbol{d} \in \{0,1\}^n} P(\mathrm{y} = y \mid \mathbf{v}; \boldsymbol{d})} \tag{7.60}$$

$$= \sqrt[2^n]{\prod_{\boldsymbol{d} \in \{0,1\}^n} \mathrm{softmax}\left(\boldsymbol{W}^\top (\boldsymbol{d} \odot \mathbf{v}) + \boldsymbol{b}\right)_y} \tag{7.61}$$

$$= \sqrt[2^n]{\prod_{\boldsymbol{d}\in\{0,1\}^n} \frac{\exp\left(\boldsymbol{W}_{y,:}^{\top}(\boldsymbol{d}\odot\mathbf{v})+b_y\right)}{\sum_{y'}\exp\left(\boldsymbol{W}_{y',:}^{\top}(\boldsymbol{d}\odot\mathbf{v})+b_{y'}\right)}} \tag{7.62}$$

$$= \frac{\sqrt[2^n]{\prod_{\boldsymbol{d}\in\{0,1\}^n}\exp\left(\boldsymbol{W}_{y,:}^{\top}(\boldsymbol{d}\odot\mathbf{v})+b_y\right)}}{\sqrt[2^n]{\prod_{\boldsymbol{d}\in\{0,1\}^n}\sum_{y'}\exp\left(\boldsymbol{W}_{y',:}^{\top}(\boldsymbol{d}\odot\mathbf{v})+b_{y'}\right)}} \tag{7.63}$$

Because $\tilde{P}$ will be normalized, we can safely ignore multiplication by factors that are constant with respect to y:

$$\tilde{P}_{\text{ensemble}}(\mathbf{y}=y\mid\mathbf{v}) \propto \sqrt[2^n]{\prod_{\boldsymbol{d}\in\{0,1\}^n}\exp\left(\boldsymbol{W}_{y,:}^{\top}(\boldsymbol{d}\odot\mathbf{v})+b_y\right)} \tag{7.64}$$

$$= \exp\left(\frac{1}{2^n}\sum_{\boldsymbol{d}\in\{0,1\}^n}\boldsymbol{W}_{y,:}^{\top}(\boldsymbol{d}\odot\mathbf{v})+b_y\right) \tag{7.65}$$

$$= \exp\left(\frac{1}{2}\boldsymbol{W}_{y,:}^{\top}\mathbf{v}+b_y\right). \tag{7.66}$$

Substituting this back into equation 7.58, we obtain a softmax classifier with weights $\frac{1}{2}\boldsymbol{W}$.

The weight scaling rule is also exact in other settings, including regression networks with conditionally normal outputs as well as deep networks that have hidden layers without nonlinearities. However, the weight scaling rule is only an approximation for deep models that have nonlinearities. Though the approximation has not been theoretically characterized, it often works well, empirically. Goodfellow et al. (2013a) found experimentally that the weight scaling approximation can work better (in terms of classification accuracy) than Monte Carlo approximations to the ensemble predictor. This held true even when the Monte Carlo approximation was allowed to sample up to 1,000 subnetworks. Gal and Ghahramani (2015) found that some models obtain better classification accuracy using twenty samples and the Monte Carlo approximation. It appears that the optimal choice of inference approximation is problem dependent.

Srivastava et al. (2014) showed that dropout is more effective than other standard computationally inexpensive regularizers, such as weight decay, filter norm constraints, and sparse activity regularization. Dropout may also be combined with other forms of regularization to yield a further improvement.

One advantage of dropout is that it is very computationally cheap. Using dropout during training requires only $O(n)$ computation per example per update, to generate n random binary numbers and multiply them by the state. Depending on the implementation, it may also require $O(n)$ memory to store these binary numbers until the back-propagation stage. Running inference in the trained model has the same cost per example as if dropout were not used, though we must pay the cost of dividing the weights by 2 once before beginning to run inference on examples.

Another significant advantage of dropout is that it does not significantly limit the type of model or training procedure that can be used. It works well with nearly any model that uses a distributed representation and can be trained with stochastic gradient descent. This includes feedforward neural networks, probabilistic models such as restricted Boltzmann machines (Srivastava et al., 2014), and recurrent neural networks (Bayer and Osendorfer, 2014; Pascanu et al., 2014a). Many other regularization strategies of comparable power impose more severe restrictions on the architecture of the model.

Though the cost per step of applying dropout to a specific model is negligible, the cost of using dropout in a complete system can be significant. Because dropout is a regularization technique, it reduces the effective capacity of a model. To offset this effect, we must increase the size of the model. Typically the optimal validation set error is much lower when using dropout, but this comes at the cost of a much larger model and many more iterations of the training algorithm. For very large datasets, regularization confers little reduction in generalization error. In these cases, the computational cost of using dropout and larger models may outweigh the benefit of regularization.

When extremely few labeled training examples are available, dropout is less effective. Bayesian neural networks (Neal, 1996) outperform dropout on the Alternative Splicing Dataset (Xiong et al., 2011), where fewer than 5,000 examples are available (Srivastava et al., 2014). When additional unlabeled data is available, unsupervised feature learning can gain an advantage over dropout.

Wager et al. (2013) showed that, when applied to linear regression, dropout is equivalent to L^2 weight decay, with a different weight decay coefficient for each input feature. The magnitude of each feature's weight decay coefficient is determined by its variance. Similar results hold for other linear models. For deep models, dropout is not equivalent to weight decay.

The stochasticity used while training with dropout is not necessary for the approach's success. It is just a means of approximating the sum over all submodels. Wang and Manning (2013) derived analytical approximations to this marginalization. Their approximation, known as **fast dropout**, resulted in faster convergence time due to the reduced stochasticity in the computation of the gradient. This method can also be applied at test time, as a more principled (but also more computationally expensive) approximation to the average over all sub-networks than the weight scaling approximation. Fast dropout has been used to nearly match the performance of standard dropout on small neural network problems, but has not yet yielded a significant improvement or been applied to a large problem.

Just as stochasticity is not necessary to achieve the regularizing effect of dropout, it is also not sufficient. To demonstrate this, Warde-Farley et al. (2014) designed control experiments using a method called **dropout boosting**, which they designed to use exactly the same mask noise as traditional dropout but lack its regularizing effect. Dropout boosting trains the entire ensemble to jointly maximize the log-likelihood on the training set. In the same sense that traditional dropout is analogous to bagging, this approach is analogous to boosting. As intended, experiments with dropout boosting show almost no regularization effect compared to training the entire network as a single model. This demonstrates that the interpretation of dropout as bagging has value beyond the interpretation of dropout as robustness to noise. The regularization effect of the bagged ensemble is only achieved when the stochastically sampled ensemble members are trained to perform well independently of each other.

Dropout has inspired other stochastic approaches to training exponentially large ensembles of models that share weights. DropConnect is a special case of dropout where each product between a single scalar weight and a single hidden unit state is considered a unit that can be dropped (Wan et al., 2013). Stochastic pooling is a form of randomized pooling (see section 9.3) for building ensembles of convolutional networks, with each convolutional network attending to different spatial locations of each feature map. So far, dropout remains the most widely used implicit ensemble method.

One of the key insights of dropout is that training a network with stochastic behavior and making predictions by averaging over multiple stochastic decisions implements a form of bagging with parameter sharing. Earlier, we described dropout as bagging an ensemble of models formed by including or excluding units. Yet this model averaging strategy does not need to be based on inclusion and exclusion. In principle, any kind of random modification is admissible. In practice, we must choose modification families that neural networks are able to learn to resist. Ideally, we should also use model families that allow a fast approximate inference rule. We can think of any form of modification parametrized by a vector $\boldsymbol{\mu}$ as training an ensemble consisting of $p(y \mid \boldsymbol{x}, \boldsymbol{\mu})$ for all possible values of $\boldsymbol{\mu}$. There is no requirement that $\boldsymbol{\mu}$ have a finite number of values. For example, $\boldsymbol{\mu}$ can be real valued. Srivastava et al. (2014) showed that multiplying the weights by $\boldsymbol{\mu} \sim \mathcal{N}(\mathbf{1}, I)$ can outperform dropout based on binary masks. Because $\mathbb{E}[\boldsymbol{\mu}] = \mathbf{1}$, the standard network automatically implements approximate inference in the ensemble, without needing any weight scaling.

So far we have described dropout purely as a means of performing efficient, approximate bagging. Another view of dropout goes further than this. Dropout trains not just a bagged ensemble of models, but an ensemble of models that share hidden units. This means each hidden unit must be able to perform well regardless of which other hidden units are in the model. Hidden units must be prepared to be swapped and interchanged between models. Hinton et al. (2012c) were inspired by an idea from biology: sexual reproduction, which involves swapping genes between two different organisms, creates evolutionary pressure for genes to become not just good but readily swapped between different organisms. Such genes and such features are robust to changes in their environment because they are not able to incorrectly adapt to unusual features of any one organism or model. Dropout thus regularizes each hidden unit to be not merely a good feature but a feature that is good in many contexts. Warde-Farley et al. (2014) compared dropout training to training of large ensembles and concluded that dropout offers additional improvements to generalization error beyond those obtained by ensembles of independent models.

It is important to understand that a large portion of the power of dropout arises from the fact that the masking noise is applied to the hidden units. This can be seen as a form of highly intelligent, adaptive destruction of the information content of the input rather than destruction of the raw values of the input. For example, if the model learns a hidden unit h_i that detects a face by finding the nose, then dropping h_i corresponds to erasing the information that there is a nose in the image. The model must learn another h_i, that either redundantly encodes the presence of a nose or detects the face by another feature, such as the mouth. Traditional noise injection techniques that add unstructured noise at the input are not able to randomly erase the information about a nose from an image of a face unless the magnitude of the noise is so great that nearly all the information in the image is removed. Destroying extracted features rather than original values allows the destruction process to make use of all the knowledge about the input distribution that the model has acquired so far.

Another important aspect of dropout is that the noise is multiplicative. If the noise were additive with fixed scale, then a rectified linear hidden unit h_i with added noise ϵ could simply learn to have h_i become very large in order to make the added noise ϵ insignificant by comparison. Multiplicative noise does not allow such a pathological solution to the noise robustness problem.

Another deep learning algorithm, batch normalization, reparametrizes the model in a way that introduces both additive and multiplicative noise on the hidden units at training time. The primary purpose of batch normalization is to improve optimization, but the noise can have a regularizing effect, and sometimes makes dropout unnecessary. Batch normalization is described further in section 8.7.1.

7.13   Adversarial Training

In many cases, neural networks have begun to reach human performance when evaluated on an i.i.d. test set. It is natural therefore to wonder whether these models have obtained a true human-level understanding of these tasks. To probe the level of understanding a network has of the underlying task, we can search for examples that the model misclassifies. Szegedy et al. (2014b) found that even neural networks that perform at human level accuracy have a nearly 100 percent error rate on examples that are intentionally constructed by using an optimization procedure to search for an input x' near a data point x such that the model output is very different at x'. In many cases, x' can be so similar to x that a human observer cannot tell the difference between the original example and the **adversarial example**, but the network can make highly different predictions. See figure 7.8 for an example.

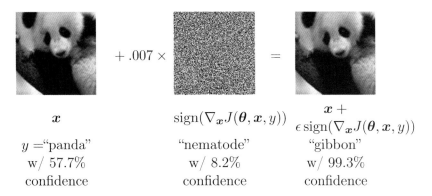

Figure 7.8: A demonstration of adversarial example generation applied to GoogLeNet (Szegedy et al., 2014a) on ImageNet. By adding an imperceptibly small vector whose elements are equal to the sign of the elements of the gradient of the cost function with respect to the input, we can change GoogLeNet's classification of the image. Reproduced with permission from Goodfellow et al. (2014b).

Adversarial examples have many implications, for example, in computer security, that are beyond the scope of this chapter. They are interesting in the context of regularization, however, because one can reduce the error rate on the original i.i.d. test set via **adversarial training**—training on adversarially perturbed examples from the training set (Szegedy et al., 2014b; Goodfellow et al., 2014b).

Goodfellow et al. (2014b) showed that one of the primary causes of these adversarial examples is excessive linearity. Neural networks are built out of primarily linear building blocks. In some experiments the overall function they implement proves to be highly linear as a result. These linear functions are easy to optimize. Unfortunately, the value of a linear function can change very rapidly if it has numerous inputs. If we change each input by ϵ, then a linear function with weights $\boldsymbol{w}$ can change by as much as $\epsilon||\boldsymbol{w}||_1$, which can be a very large amount if $\boldsymbol{w}$ is highdimensional. Adversarial training discourages this highly sensitive locally linear behavior by encouraging the network to be locally constant in the neighborhood of the training data. This can be seen as a way of explicitly introducing a local constancy prior into supervised neural nets.

Adversarial training helps to illustrate the power of using a large function family in combination with aggressive regularization. Purely linear models, like logistic regression, are not able to resist adversarial examples because they are forced to be linear. Neural networks are able to represent functions that can range from nearly linear to nearly locally constant and thus have the flexibility to capture linear trends in the training data while still learning to resist local perturbation.

Adversarial examples also provide a means of accomplishing semi-supervised learning. At a point $\boldsymbol{x}$ that is not associated with a label in the dataset, the model itself assigns some label $\hat{y}$. The model's label $\hat{y}$ may not be the true label, but if the model is high quality, then $\hat{y}$ has a high probability of providing the true label. We can seek an adversarial example $\boldsymbol{x}'$ that causes the classifier to output a label y' with $y' \neq \hat{y}$. Adversarial examples generated using not the true label but a label provided by a trained model are called **virtual adversarial examples** (Miyato et al., 2015). The classifier may then be trained to assign the same label to $\boldsymbol{x}$ and $\boldsymbol{x}'$. This encourages the classifier to learn a function that is robust to small changes anywhere along the manifold where the unlabeled data lie. The assumption motivating this approach is that different classes usually lie on disconnected manifolds, and a small perturbation should not be able to jump from one class manifold to another class manifold.

7.14 Tangent Distance, Tangent Prop and Manifold Tangent Classifier

Many machine learning algorithms aim to overcome the curse of dimensionality by assuming that the data lies near a low-dimensional manifold, as described in section 5.11.3.

One of the early attempts to take advantage of the manifold hypothesis is the **tangent distance** algorithm (Simard et al., 1993, 1998). It is a non-parametric nearest neighbor algorithm in which the metric used is not the generic Euclidean distance but one that is derived from knowledge of the manifolds near which probability concentrates. It is assumed that we are trying to classify examples, and that examples on the same manifold share the same category. Since the classifier should be invariant to the local factors of variation that correspond to movement on the manifold, it would make sense to use as nearest neighbor distance between points $\boldsymbol{x}_1$ and $\boldsymbol{x}_2$ the distance between the manifolds M_1 and M_2 to which they respectively belong. Although that may be computationally difficult (it would require solving an optimization problem, to find the nearest pair of points on M_1 and M_2), a cheap alternative that makes sense locally is to approximate M_i by its tangent plane at $\boldsymbol{x}_i$ and measure the distance between the two tangents, or between a tangent plane and a point. That can be achieved by solving a low-dimensional linear system (in the dimension of the manifolds). Of course, this algorithm requires one to specify the tangent vectors.

In a related spirit, the **tangent prop** algorithm (Simard et al., 1992) (figure 7.9) trains a neural net classifier with an extra penalty to make each output $f(\boldsymbol{x})$ of the neural net locally invariant to known factors of variation. These factors of variation correspond to movement along the manifold near which examples of the same class concentrate. Local invariance is achieved by requiring $\nabla_{\boldsymbol{x}} f(\boldsymbol{x})$ to be orthogonal to the known manifold tangent vectors $\boldsymbol{v}^{(i)}$ at $\boldsymbol{x}$, or equivalently that the directional derivative of f at $\boldsymbol{x}$ in the directions $\boldsymbol{v}^{(i)}$ be small by adding a regularization penalty Ω:

$$\Omega(f) = \sum_i \left((\nabla_{\boldsymbol{x}} f(\boldsymbol{x}))^\top \boldsymbol{v}^{(i)} \right)^2 . \tag{7.67}$$

This regularizer can of course be scaled by an appropriate hyperparameter, and for most neural networks, we would need to sum over many outputs rather than the lone output $f(\boldsymbol{x})$ described here for simplicity. As with the tangent distance algorithm, the tangent vectors are derived a priori, usually from the formal knowledge of

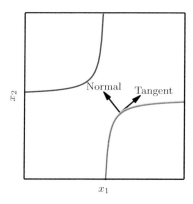

Figure 7.9: Illustration of the main idea of the tangent prop algorithm (Simard et al., 1992) and manifold tangent classifier (Rifai et al., 2011c), which both regularize the classifier output function $f(\boldsymbol{x})$. Each curve represents the manifold for a different class, illustrated here as a one-dimensional manifold embedded in a two-dimensional space. On one curve, we have chosen a single point and drawn a vector that is tangent to the class manifold (parallel to and touching the manifold) and a vector that is normal to the class manifold (orthogonal to the manifold). In multiple dimensions there may be many tangent directions and many normal directions. We expect the classification function to change rapidly as it moves in the direction normal to the manifold, and not to change as it moves along the class manifold. Both tangent propagation and the manifold tangent classifier regularize $f(\boldsymbol{x})$ to not change very much as $\boldsymbol{x}$ moves along the manifold. Tangent propagation requires the user to manually specify functions that compute the tangent directions (such as specifying that small translations of images remain in the same class manifold), while the manifold tangent classifier estimates the manifold tangent directions by training an autoencoder to fit the training data. The use of autoencoders to estimate manifolds is described in chapter 14.

the effect of transformations, such as translation, rotation, and scaling in images. Tangent prop has been used not just for supervised learning (Simard et al., 1992) but also in the context of reinforcement learning (Thrun, 1995).

Tangent propagation is closely related to dataset augmentation. In both cases, the user of the algorithm encodes his or her prior knowledge of the task by specifying a set of transformations that should not alter the output of the network. The difference is that in the case of dataset augmentation, the network is explicitly trained to correctly classify distinct inputs that were created by applying more than an infinitesimal amount of these transformations. Tangent propagation does not require explicitly visiting a new input point. Instead, it analytically regularizes the model to resist perturbation in the directions corresponding to the specified transformation. While this analytical approach is intellectually elegant, it has two major drawbacks. First, it only regularizes the model to resist infinitesimal perturbation. Explicit dataset augmentation confers resistance to larger perturbations. Second, the infinitesimal approach poses difficulties for models based on rectified linear units. These models can only shrink their derivatives by turning units off or shrinking their weights. They are not able to shrink their derivatives by saturating at a high value with large weights, as sigmoid or tanh units can. Dataset augmentation works well with rectified linear units because different subsets of rectified units can activate for different transformed versions of each original input.

Tangent propagation is also related to **double backprop** (Drucker and LeCun, 1992) and adversarial training (Szegedy et al., 2014b; Goodfellow et al., 2014b). Double backprop regularizes the Jacobian to be small, while adversarial training finds inputs near the original inputs and trains the model to produce the same output on these as on the original inputs. Tangent propagation and dataset augmentation using manually specified transformations both require that the model be invariant to certain specified directions of change in the input. Double backprop and adversarial training both require that the model should be invariant to *all* directions of change in the input as long as the change is small. Just as dataset augmentation is the non-infinitesimal version of tangent propagation, adversarial training is the non-infinitesimal version of double backprop.

The manifold tangent classifier (Rifai et al., 2011c), eliminates the need to know the tangent vectors a priori. As we will see in chapter 14, autoencoders can estimate the manifold tangent vectors. The manifold tangent classifier makes use of this technique to avoid needing user-specified tangent vectors. As illustrated in figure 14.10, these estimated tangent vectors go beyond the classical invariants that arise out of the geometry of images (such as translation, rotation, and scaling) and include factors that must be learned because they are object-specific (such as moving body parts). The algorithm proposed with the manifold tangent classifier is therefore simple: (1) use an autoencoder to learn the manifold structure by unsupervised learning, and (2) use these tangents to regularize a neural net classifier as in tangent prop (equation 7.67).

In this chapter, we have described most of the general strategies used to regularize neural networks. Regularization is a central theme of machine learning and as such will be revisited periodically in most of the remaining chapters. Another central theme of machine learning is optimization, described next.

8

Optimization for Training Deep Models

Deep learning algorithms involve optimization in many contexts. For example, performing inference in models such as PCA involves solving an optimization problem. We often use analytical optimization to write proofs or design algorithms. Of all the many optimization problems involved in deep learning, the most difficult is neural network training. It is quite common to invest days to months of time on hundreds of machines to solve even a single instance of the neural network training problem. Because this problem is so important and so expensive, a specialized set of optimization techniques have been developed for solving it. This chapter presents these optimization techniques for neural network training.

If you are unfamiliar with the basic principles of gradient-based optimization, we suggest reviewing chapter 4. That chapter includes a brief overview of numerical optimization in general.

This chapter focuses on one particular case of optimization: finding the parameters $\boldsymbol{\theta}$ of a neural network that significantly reduce a cost function $J(\boldsymbol{\theta})$, which typically includes a performance measure evaluated on the entire training set as well as additional regularization terms.

We begin with a description of how optimization used as a training algorithm for a machine learning task differs from pure optimization. Next, we present several of the concrete challenges that make optimization of neural networks difficult. We then define several practical algorithms, including both optimization algorithms themselves and strategies for initializing the parameters. More advanced algorithms adapt their learning rates during training or leverage information contained in the second derivatives of the cost function. Finally, we conclude with a review of several optimization strategies that are formed by combining simple optimization algorithms into higher-level procedures.

8.1 How Learning Differs from Pure Optimization

Optimization algorithms used for training of deep models differ from traditional optimization algorithms in several ways. Machine learning usually acts indirectly. In most machine learning scenarios, we care about some performance measure P, that is defined with respect to the test set and may also be intractable. We therefore optimize P only indirectly. We reduce a different cost function $J(\boldsymbol{\theta})$ in the hope that doing so will improve P. This is in contrast to pure optimization, where minimizing J is a goal in and of itself. Optimization algorithms for training deep models also typically include some specialization on the specific structure of machine learning objective functions.

Typically, the cost function can be written as an average over the training set, such as

$$J(\boldsymbol{\theta}) = \mathbb{E}_{(\boldsymbol{x},\mathrm{y})\sim\hat{p}_{\mathrm{data}}} L(f(\boldsymbol{x};\boldsymbol{\theta}), y), \tag{8.1}$$

where L is the per-example loss function, $f(\boldsymbol{x};\boldsymbol{\theta})$ is the predicted output when the input is $\boldsymbol{x}$, and $\hat{p}_{\mathrm{data}}$ is the empirical distribution. In the supervised learning case, y is the target output. Throughout this chapter, we develop the unregularized supervised case, where the arguments to L are $f(\boldsymbol{x};\boldsymbol{\theta})$ and y. It is trivial to extend this development, for example, to include $\boldsymbol{\theta}$ or $\boldsymbol{x}$ as arguments, or to exclude y as arguments, to develop various forms of regularization or unsupervised learning.

Equation 8.1 defines an objective function with respect to the training set. We would usually prefer to minimize the corresponding objective function where the expectation is taken across *the data-generating distribution* p_{data} rather than just over the finite training set:

$$J^*(\boldsymbol{\theta}) = \mathbb{E}_{(\boldsymbol{x},\mathrm{y})\sim p_{\mathrm{data}}} L(f(\boldsymbol{x};\boldsymbol{\theta}), y). \tag{8.2}$$

8.1.1 Empirical Risk Minimization

The goal of a machine learning algorithm is to reduce the expected generalization error given by equation 8.2. This quantity is known as the **risk**. We emphasize here that the expectation is taken over the true underlying distribution p_{data}. If we knew the true distribution $p_{\mathrm{data}}(\boldsymbol{x}, y)$, risk minimization would be an optimization task solvable by an optimization algorithm. When we do not know $p_{\text{data}}(\boldsymbol{x}, y)$ but only have a training set of samples, however, we have a machine learning problem.

The simplest way to convert a machine learning problem back into an optimization problem is to minimize the expected loss on the training set. This means replacing the true distribution $p(\boldsymbol{x}, y)$ with the empirical distribution $\hat{p}(\boldsymbol{x}, y)$ defined by the training set. We now minimize the **empirical risk**

$$\mathbb{E}_{\boldsymbol{x},\text{y} \sim \hat{p}_{\text{data}}(\boldsymbol{x},y)}[L(f(\boldsymbol{x}; \boldsymbol{\theta}), y)] = \frac{1}{m} \sum_{i=1}^{m} L(f(\boldsymbol{x}^{(i)}; \boldsymbol{\theta}), y^{(i)}), \qquad (8.3)$$

where m is the number of training examples.

The training process based on minimizing this average training error is known as **empirical risk minimization**. In this setting, machine learning is still very similar to straightforward optimization. Rather than optimizing the risk directly, we optimize the empirical risk and hope that the risk decreases significantly as well. A variety of theoretical results establish conditions under which the true risk can be expected to decrease by various amounts.

Nonetheless, empirical risk minimization is prone to overfitting. Models with high capacity can simply memorize the training set. In many cases, empirical risk minimization is not really feasible. The most effective modern optimization algorithms are based on gradient descent, but many useful loss functions, such as 0-1 loss, have no useful derivatives (the derivative is either zero or undefined everywhere). These two problems mean that, in the context of deep learning, we rarely use empirical risk minimization. Instead, we must use a slightly different approach, in which the quantity that we actually optimize is even more different from the quantity that we truly want to optimize.

8.1.2 Surrogate Loss Functions and Early Stopping

Sometimes, the loss function we actually care about (say, classification error) is not one that can be optimized efficiently. For example, exactly minimizing expected 0-1 loss is typically intractable (exponential in the input dimension), even for a linear classifier (Marcotte and Savard, 1992). In such situations, one typically optimizes a **surrogate loss function** instead, which acts as a proxy but has advantages. For example, the negative log-likelihood of the correct class is typically used as a surrogate for the 0-1 loss. The negative log-likelihood allows the model to estimate the conditional probability of the classes, given the input, and if the model can do that well, then it can pick the classes that yield the least classification error in expectation.

In some cases, a surrogate loss function actually results in being able to learn more. For example, the test set 0-1 loss often continues to decrease for a long time after the training set 0-1 loss has reached zero, when training using the log-likelihood surrogate. This is because even when the expected 0-1 loss is zero, one can improve the robustness of the classifier by further pushing the classes apart from each other, obtaining a more confident and reliable classifier, thus extracting more information from the training data than would have been possible by simply minimizing the average 0-1 loss on the training set.

A very important difference between optimization in general and optimization as we use it for training algorithms is that training algorithms do not usually halt at a local minimum. Instead, a machine learning algorithm usually minimizes a surrogate loss function but halts when a convergence criterion based on early stopping (section 7.8) is satisfied. Typically the early stopping criterion is based on the true underlying loss function, such as 0-1 loss measured on a validation set, and is designed to cause the algorithm to halt whenever overfitting begins to occur. Training often halts while the surrogate loss function still has large derivatives, which is very different from the pure optimization setting, where an optimization algorithm is considered to have converged when the gradient becomes very small.

8.1.3 Batch and Minibatch Algorithms

One aspect of machine learning algorithms that separates them from general optimization algorithms is that the objective function usually decomposes as a sum over the training examples. Optimization algorithms for machine learning typically compute each update to the parameters based on an expected value of the cost function estimated using only a subset of the terms of the full cost function.

For example, maximum likelihood estimation problems, when viewed in log space, decompose into a sum over each example:

$$\boldsymbol{\theta}_{\mathrm{ML}} = \arg\max_{\boldsymbol{\theta}} \sum_{i=1}^{m} \log p_{\mathrm{model}}(\boldsymbol{x}^{(i)}, y^{(i)}; \boldsymbol{\theta}). \tag{8.4}$$

Maximizing this sum is equivalent to maximizing the expectation over the empirical distribution defined by the training set:

$$J(\boldsymbol{\theta}) = \mathbb{E}_{\mathbf{x},\mathbf{y} \sim \hat{p}_{\mathrm{data}}} \log p_{\mathrm{model}}(\boldsymbol{x}, y; \boldsymbol{\theta}). \tag{8.5}$$

Most of the properties of the objective function J used by most of our optimization algorithms are also expectations over the training set. For example, the most commonly used property is the gradient:

$$\nabla_{\boldsymbol{\theta}} J(\boldsymbol{\theta}) = \mathbb{E}_{\mathbf{x},\mathrm{y}\sim\hat{p}_{\mathrm{data}}} \nabla_{\boldsymbol{\theta}} \log p_{\mathrm{model}}(\boldsymbol{x}, y; \boldsymbol{\theta}). \tag{8.6}$$

Computing this expectation exactly is very expensive because it requires evaluating the model on every example in the entire dataset. In practice, we can compute these expectations by randomly sampling a small number of examples from the dataset, then taking the average over only those examples.

Recall that the standard error of the mean (equation 5.46) estimated from n samples is given by $\sigma/\sqrt{n}$, where σ is the true standard deviation of the value of the samples. The denominator of $\sqrt{n}$ shows that there are less than linear returns to using more examples to estimate the gradient. Compare two hypothetical estimates of the gradient, one based on 100 examples and another based on 10,000 examples. The latter requires 100 times more computation than the former but reduces the standard error of the mean only by a factor of 10. Most optimization algorithms converge much faster (in terms of total computation, not in terms of number of updates) if they are allowed to rapidly compute approximate estimates of the gradient rather than slowly computing the exact gradient.

Another consideration motivating statistical estimation of the gradient from a small number of samples is redundancy in the training set. In the worst case, all m samples in the training set could be identical copies of each other. A sampling-based estimate of the gradient could compute the correct gradient with a single sample, using m times less computation than the naive approach. In practice, we are unlikely to encounter this worst-case situation, but we may find large numbers of examples that all make very similar contributions to the gradient.

Optimization algorithms that use the entire training set are called **batch** or **deterministic** gradient methods, because they process all the training examples simultaneously in a large batch. This terminology can be somewhat confusing because the word "batch" is also often used to describe the minibatch used by minibatch stochastic gradient descent. Typically the term "batch gradient descent" implies the use of the full training set, while the use of the term "batch" to describe a group of examples does not. For example, it is common to use the term "batch size" to describe the size of a minibatch.

Optimization algorithms that use only a single example at a time are sometimes called **stochastic** and sometimes **online** methods. The term "online" is usually reserved for when the examples are drawn from a stream of continually created examples rather than from a fixed-size training set over which several passes are made.

Most algorithms used for deep learning fall somewhere in between, using more than one but fewer than all the training examples. These were traditionally called **minibatch** or **minibatch stochastic** methods, and it is now common to call them simply **stochastic** methods.

The canonical example of a stochastic method is stochastic gradient descent, presented in detail in section 8.3.1.

Minibatch sizes are generally driven by the following factors:

- Larger batches provide a more accurate estimate of the gradient, but with less than linear returns.

- Multicore architectures are usually underutilized by extremely small batches. This motivates using some absolute minimum batch size, below which there is no reduction in the time to process a minibatch.

- If all examples in the batch are to be processed in parallel (as is typically the case), then the amount of memory scales with the batch size. For many hardware setups this is the limiting factor in batch size.

- Some kinds of hardware achieve better runtime with specific sizes of arrays. Especially when using GPUs, it is common for power of 2 batch sizes to offer better runtime. Typical power of 2 batch sizes range from 32 to 256, with 16 sometimes being attempted for large models.

- Small batches can offer a regularizing effect (Wilson and Martinez, 2003), perhaps due to the noise they add to the learning process. Generalization error is often best for a batch size of 1. Training with such a small batch size might require a small learning rate to maintain stability because of the high variance in the estimate of the gradient. The total runtime can be very high as a result of the need to make more steps, both because of the reduced learning rate and because it takes more steps to observe the entire training set.

Different kinds of algorithms use different kinds of information from the minibatch in various ways. Some algorithms are more sensitive to sampling error than others, either because they use information that is difficult to estimate accurately with few samples, or because they use information in ways that amplify sampling errors more. Methods that compute updates based only on the gradient $\boldsymbol{g}$ are usually relatively robust and can handle smaller batch sizes, like 100. Second-order methods, which also use the Hessian matrix $\boldsymbol{H}$ and compute updates such as $\boldsymbol{H}^{-1}\boldsymbol{g}$, typically require much larger batch sizes, like 10,000. These large batch sizes are required to minimize fluctuations in the estimates of $H^{-1}g$. Suppose that H is estimated perfectly but has a poor condition number. Multiplication by H or its inverse amplifies pre-existing errors, in this case, estimation errors in g. Very small changes in the estimate of g can thus cause large changes in the update $H^{-1}g$, even if H is estimated perfectly. Of course, H is estimated only approximately, so the update $H^{-1}g$ will contain even more error than we would predict from applying a poorly conditioned operation to the estimate of g.

It is also crucial that the minibatches be selected randomly. Computing an unbiased estimate of the expected gradient from a set of samples requires that those samples be independent. We also wish for two subsequent gradient estimates to be independent from each other, so two subsequent minibatches of examples should also be independent from each other. Many datasets are most naturally arranged in a way where successive examples are highly correlated. For example, we might have a dataset of medical data with a long list of blood sample test results. This list might be arranged so that first we have five blood samples taken at different times from the first patient, then we have three blood samples taken from the second patient, then the blood samples from the third patient, and so on. If we were to draw examples in order from this list, then each of our minibatches would be extremely biased, because it would represent primarily one patient out of the many patients in the dataset. In cases such as these, where the order of the dataset holds some significance, it is necessary to shuffle the examples before selecting minibatches. For very large datasets, for example, datasets containing billions of examples in a data center, it can be impractical to sample examples truly uniformly at random every time we want to construct a minibatch. Fortunately, in practice it is usually sufficient to shuffle the order of the dataset once and then store it in shuffled fashion. This will impose a fixed set of possible minibatches of consecutive examples that all models trained thereafter will use, and each individual model will be forced to reuse this ordering every time it passes through the training data. This deviation from true random selection does not seem to have a significant detrimental effect. Failing to ever shuffle the examples in any way can seriously reduce the effectiveness of the algorithm.

Many optimization problems in machine learning decompose over examples well enough that we can compute entire separate updates over different examples in parallel. In other words, we can compute the update that minimizes $J(X)$ for one minibatch of examples X at the same time that we compute the update for several other minibatches. Such asynchronous parallel distributed approaches are discussed further in section 12.1.3.

An interesting motivation for minibatch stochastic gradient descent is that it follows the gradient of the true *generalization error* (equation 8.2) as long as no examples are repeated. Most implementations of minibatch stochastic gradient descent shuffle the dataset once and then pass through it multiple times. On the first pass, each minibatch is used to compute an unbiased estimate of the true generalization error. On the second pass, the estimate becomes biased because it is formed by resampling values that have already been used, rather than obtaining new fair samples from the data-generating distribution.

The fact that stochastic gradient descent minimizes generalization error is easiest to see in online learning, where examples or minibatches are drawn from a **stream** of data. In other words, instead of receiving a fixed-size training set, the learner is similar to a living being who sees a new example at each instant, with every example $(\boldsymbol{x}, y)$ coming from the data-generating distribution $p_{\text{data}}(\boldsymbol{x}, y)$. In this scenario, examples are never repeated; every experience is a fair sample from p_{data}.

The equivalence is easiest to derive when both $\boldsymbol{x}$ and y are discrete. In this case, the generalization error (equation 8.2) can be written as a sum

$$J^*(\boldsymbol{\theta}) = \sum_{\boldsymbol{x}} \sum_{y} p_{\text{data}}(\boldsymbol{x}, y) L(f(\boldsymbol{x}; \boldsymbol{\theta}), y), \tag{8.7}$$

with the exact gradient

$$\boldsymbol{g} = \nabla_{\boldsymbol{\theta}} J^*(\boldsymbol{\theta}) = \sum_{\boldsymbol{x}} \sum_{y} p_{\text{data}}(\boldsymbol{x}, y) \nabla_{\boldsymbol{\theta}} L(f(\boldsymbol{x}; \boldsymbol{\theta}), y). \tag{8.8}$$

We have already seen the same fact demonstrated for the log-likelihood in equation 8.5 and equation 8.6; we observe now that this holds for other functions L besides the likelihood. A similar result can be derived when $\boldsymbol{x}$ and y are continuous, under mild assumptions regarding p_{data} and L.

Hence, we can obtain an unbiased estimator of the exact gradient of the generalization error by sampling a minibatch of examples $\{\boldsymbol{x}^{(1)}, \dots \boldsymbol{x}^{(m)}\}$ with corresponding targets $y^{(i)}$ from the data-generating distribution p_{data}, then computing the gradient of the loss with respect to the parameters for that minibatch:

$$\hat{\boldsymbol{g}} = \frac{1}{m} \nabla_{\boldsymbol{\theta}} \sum_{i} L(f(\boldsymbol{x}^{(i)}; \boldsymbol{\theta}), y^{(i)}). \tag{8.9}$$

Updating $\boldsymbol{\theta}$ in the direction of $\hat{\boldsymbol{g}}$ performs SGD on the generalization error.

Of course, this interpretation applies only when examples are not reused. Nonetheless, it is usually best to make several passes through the training set, unless the training set is extremely large. When multiple such epochs are used, only the first epoch follows the unbiased gradient of the generalization error, but of course, the additional epochs usually provide enough benefit due to decreased training error to offset the harm they cause by increasing the gap between training error and test error.

With some datasets growing rapidly in size, faster than computing power, it is becoming more common for machine learning applications to use each training example only once or even to make an incomplete pass through the training set. When using an extremely large training set, overfitting is not an issue, so underfitting and computational efficiency become the predominant concerns. See also Bottou and Bousquet (2008) for a discussion of the effect of computational bottlenecks on generalization error, as the number of training examples grows.

8.2 Challenges in Neural Network Optimization

Optimization in general is an extremely difficult task. Traditionally, machine learning has avoided the difficulty of general optimization by carefully designing the objective function and constraints to ensure that the optimization problem is convex. When training neural networks, we must confront the general nonconvex case. Even convex optimization is not without its complications. In this section, we summarize several of the most prominent challenges involved in optimization for training deep models.

8.2.1 Ill-Conditioning

Some challenges arise even when optimizing convex functions. Of these, the most prominent is ill-conditioning of the Hessian matrix $\boldsymbol{H}$. This is a very general problem in most numerical optimization, convex or otherwise, and is described in more detail in section 4.3.1.

The ill-conditioning problem is generally believed to be present in neural network training problems. Ill-conditioning can manifest by causing SGD to get "stuck" in the sense that even very small steps increase the cost function.

Recall from equation 4.9 that a second-order Taylor series expansion of the cost function predicts that a gradient descent step of $-\epsilon \boldsymbol{g}$ will add

$$\frac{1}{2}\epsilon^2 \boldsymbol{g}^\top \boldsymbol{H} \boldsymbol{g} - \epsilon \boldsymbol{g}^\top \boldsymbol{g} \tag{8.10}$$

to the cost. Ill-conditioning of the gradient becomes a problem when $\frac{1}{2}\epsilon^2 \boldsymbol{g}^\top \boldsymbol{H} \boldsymbol{g}$ exceeds $\epsilon \boldsymbol{g}^\top \boldsymbol{g}$. To determine whether ill-conditioning is detrimental to a neural network training task, one can monitor the squared gradient norm $g^\top g$ and the $g^\top H g$ term. In many cases, the gradient norm does not shrink significantly throughout learning, but the $g^\top H g$ term grows by more than an order of magnitude. The result is that learning becomes very slow despite the presence of a strong gradient because the learning rate must be shrunk to compensate for even stronger curvature. Figure 8.1 shows an example of the gradient increasing significantly during the successful training of a neural network.

Though ill-conditioning is present in other settings besides neural network training, some of the techniques used to combat it in other contexts are less applicable to neural networks. For example, Newton's method is an excellent tool for minimizing convex functions with poorly conditioned Hessian matrices, but as we argue in subsequent sections, Newton's method requires significant modification before it can be applied to neural networks.

8.2.2 Local Minima

One of the most prominent features of a convex optimization problem is that it can be reduced to the problem of finding a local minimum. Any local minimum is guaranteed to be a global minimum. Some convex functions have a flat region at

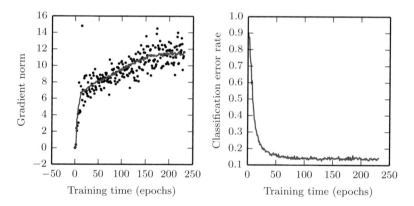

Figure 8.1: Gradient descent often does not arrive at a critical point of any kind. In this example, the gradient norm increases throughout training of a convolutional network used for object detection. *(Left)*A scatterplot showing how the norms of individual gradient evaluations are distributed over time. To improve legibility, only one gradient norm is plotted per epoch. The running average of all gradient norms is plotted as a solid curve. The gradient norm clearly increases over time, rather than decreasing as we would expect if the training process converged to a critical point. *(Right)*Despite the increasing gradient, the training process is reasonably successful. The validation set classification error decreases to a low level.

the bottom rather than a single global minimum point, but any point within such a flat region is an acceptable solution. When optimizing a convex function, we know that we have reached a good solution if we find a critical point of any kind.

With nonconvex functions, such as neural nets, it is possible to have many local minima. Indeed, nearly any deep model is essentially guaranteed to have an extremely large number of local minima. As we will see, however, this is not necessarily a major problem.

Neural networks and any models with multiple equivalently parametrized latent variables all have multiple local minima because of the **model identifiability** problem. A model is said to be identifiable if a sufficiently large training set can rule out all but one setting of the model's parameters. Models with latent variables are often not identifiable because we can obtain equivalent models by exchanging latent variables with each other. For example, we could take a neural network and modify layer 1 by swapping the incoming weight vector for unit i with the incoming weight vector for unit j, then do the same for the outgoing weight vectors. If we have m layers with n units each, then there are $n!^m$ ways of arranging the hidden units. This kind of nonidentifiability is known as **weight space symmetry**.

In addition to weight space symmetry, many kinds of neural networks have additional causes of nonidentifiability. For example, in any rectified linear or maxout network, we can scale all the incoming weights and biases of a unit by α if we also scale all its outgoing weights by $\frac{1}{\alpha}$. This means that—if the cost function does not include terms such as weight decay that depend directly on the weights rather than the models' outputs—every local minimum of a rectified linear or maxout network lies on an $(m \times n)$-dimensional hyperbola of equivalent local minima.

These model identifiability issues mean that a neural network cost function can have an extremely large or even uncountably infinite amount of local minima. However, all these local minima arising from nonidentifiability are equivalent to each other in cost function value. As a result, these local minima are not a problematic form of nonconvexity.

Local minima can be problematic if they have high cost in comparison to the global minimum. One can construct small neural networks, even without hidden units, that have local minima with higher cost than the global minimum (Sontag and Sussman, 1989; Brady et al., 1989; Gori and Tesi, 1992). If local minima with high cost are common, this could pose a serious problem for gradient-based optimization algorithms.

Whether newtons of practical interest home many local minima of high cost and whether optimization algorithms encounter them remain open questions. For many years, most practitioners believed that local minima were a common problem plaguing neural network optimization. Today, that does not appear to be the case. The problem remains an active area of research, but experts now suspect that, for sufficiently large neural networks, most local minima have a low cost function value, and that it is not important to find a true global minimum rather than to find a point in parameter space that has low but not minimal cost (Saxe et al., 2013; Dauphin et al., 2014; Goodfellow et al., 2015; Choromanska et al., 2014).

Many practitioners attribute nearly all difficulty with neural network optimization to local minima. We encourage practitioners to carefully test for specific problems. A test that can rule out local minima as the problem is plotting the norm of the gradient over time. If the norm of the gradient does not shrink to insignificant size, the problem is neither local minima nor any other kind of critical point. In high-dimensional spaces, positively establishing that local minima are the problem can be very difficult. Many structures other than local minima also have small gradients.

8.2.3   Plateaus, Saddle Points and Other Flat Regions

For many high-dimensional nonconvex functions, local minima (and maxima) are in fact rare compared to another kind of point with zero gradient: a saddle point. Some points around a saddle point have greater cost than the saddle point, while others have a lower cost. At a saddle point, the Hessian matrix has both positive and negative eigenvalues. Points lying along eigenvectors associated with positive eigenvalues have greater cost than the saddle point, while points lying along negative eigenvalues have lower value. We can think of a saddle point as being a local minimum along one cross-section of the cost function and a local maximum along another cross-section. See figure 4.5 for an illustration.

Many classes of random functions exhibit the following behavior: in low-dimensional spaces, local minima are common. In higher-dimensional spaces, local minima are rare, and saddle points are more common. For a function $f : \mathbb{R}^n \to \mathbb{R}$ of this type, the expected ratio of the number of saddle points to local minima grows exponentially with n. To understand the intuition behind this behavior, observe that the Hessian matrix at a local minimum has only positive eigenvalues. The Hessian matrix at a saddle point has a mixture of positive and negative eigenvalues. Imagine that the sign of each eigenvalue is generated by flipping a coin. In a single dimension, it is easy to obtain a local minimum by tossing a coin and getting heads once. In n-dimensional space, it is exponentially unlikely that all n coin tosses will be heads. See Dauphin et al. (2014) for a review of the relevant theoretical work.

An amazing property of many random functions is that the eigenvalues of the Hessian become more likely to be positive as we reach regions of lower cost. In our coin tossing analogy, this means we are more likely to have our coin come up heads n times if we are at a critical point with low cost. It also means that local minima are much more likely to have low cost than high cost. Critical points with high cost are far more likely to be saddle points. Critical points with extremely high cost are more likely to be local maxima.

This happens for many classes of random functions. Does it happen for neural networks? Baldi and Hornik (1989) showed theoretically that shallow autoencoders (feedforward networks trained to copy their input to their output, described in chapter 14) with no nonlinearities have global minima and saddle points but no local minima with higher cost than the global minimum. They observed without proof that these results extend to deeper networks without nonlinearities. The output of such networks is a linear function of their input, but they are useful to study as a model of nonlinear neural networks because their loss function is a nonconvex function of their parameters. Such networks are essentially just multiple matrices composed together. Saxe et al. (2013) provided exact solutions to the complete learning dynamics in such networks and showed that learning in these models captures many of the qualitative features observed in the training of deep models with nonlinear activation functions. Dauphin et al. (2014) showed experimentally that real neural networks also have loss functions that contain very many high-cost saddle points. Choromanska et al. (2014) provided additional theoretical arguments, showing that another class of high-dimensional random functions related to neural networks does so as well.

What are the implications of the proliferation of saddle points for training algorithms? For first-order optimization, algorithms that use only gradient information, the situation is unclear. The gradient can often become very small near a saddle point. On the other hand, gradient descent empirically seems able to escape saddle points in many cases. Goodfellow et al. (2015) provided visualizations of several learning trajectories of state-of-the-art neural networks, with an example given in figure 8.2. These visualizations show a flattening of the cost function near a prominent saddle point, where the weights are all zero, but they also show the gradient descent trajectory rapidly escaping this region. Goodfellow et al. (2015) also argue that continuous-time gradient descent may be shown analytically to be repelled from, rather than attracted to, a nearby saddle point, but the situation may be different for more realistic uses of gradient descent.

For Newton's method, saddle points clearly constitute a problem. Gradient descent is designed to move "downhill" and is not explicitly designed to seek a critical point. Newton's method, however, is designed to solve for a point where the gradient is zero. Without appropriate modification, it can jump to a saddle point. The proliferation of saddle points in high-dimensional spaces presumably explains

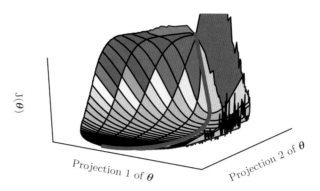

Figure 8.2: A visualization of the cost function of a neural network. These visualizations appear similar for feedforward neural networks, convolutional networks, and recurrent networks applied to real object recognition and natural language processing tasks. Surprisingly, these visualizations usually do not show many conspicuous obstacles. Prior to the success of stochastic gradient descent for training very large models beginning in roughly 2012, neural net cost function surfaces were generally believed to have much more nonconvex structure than is revealed by these projections. The primary obstacle revealed by this projection is a saddle point of high cost near where the parameters are initialized, but, as indicated by the blue path, the SGD training trajectory escapes this saddle point readily. Most of training time is spent traversing the relatively flat valley of the cost function, perhaps because of high noise in the gradient, poor conditioning of the Hessian matrix in this region, or simply the need to circumnavigate the tall "mountain" visible in the figure via an indirect arcing path. Image adapted with permission from Goodfellow et al. (2015).

why second-order methods have not succeeded in replacing gradient descent for neural network training. Dauphin et al. (2014) introduced a **saddle-free Newton method** for second-order optimization and showed that it improves significantly over the traditional version. Second-order methods remain difficult to scale to large neural networks, but this saddle-free approach holds promise if it can be scaled.

There are other kinds of points with zero gradient besides minima and saddle points. Maxima are much like saddle points from the perspective of optimization—many algorithms are not attracted to them, but unmodified Newton's method is. Maxima of many classes of random functions become exponentially rare in high-dimensional space, just as minima do.

There may also be wide, flat regions of constant value. In these locations, the gradient and the Hessian are all zero. Such degenerate locations pose major problems for all numerical optimization algorithms. In a convex problem, a wide, flat region must consist entirely of global minima, but in a general optimization problem, such a region could correspond to a high value of the objective function.

8.2.4 Cliffs and Exploding Gradients

Neural networks with many layers often have extremely steep regions resembling cliffs, as illustrated in figure 8.3. These result from the multiplication of several large weights together. On the face of an extremely steep cliff structure, the gradient update step can move the parameters extremely far, usually jumping off the cliff structure altogether.

The cliff can be dangerous whether we approach it from above or from below, but fortunately its most serious consequences can be avoided using the **gradient clipping** heuristic described in section 10.11.1. The basic idea is to recall that the gradient specifies not the optimal step size, but only the optimal direction within an infinitesimal region. When the traditional gradient descent algorithm proposes making a very large step, the gradient clipping heuristic intervenes to reduce the step size, making it less likely to go outside the region where the gradient indicates the direction of approximately steepest descent. Cliff structures are most common in the cost functions for recurrent neural networks, because such models involve a multiplication of many factors, with one factor for each time step. Long temporal sequences thus incur an extreme amount of multiplication.

8.2.5 Long-Term Dependencies

Another difficulty that neural network optimization algorithms must overcome arises when the computational graph becomes extremely deep. Feedforward networks

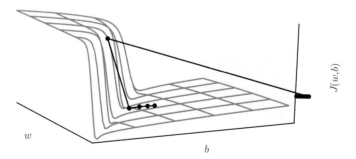

Figure 8.3: The objective function for highly nonlinear deep neural networks or for recurrent neural networks often contains sharp nonlinearities in parameter space resulting from the multiplication of several parameters. These nonlinearities give rise to very high derivatives in some places. When the parameters get close to such a cliff region, a gradient descent update can catapult the parameters very far, possibly losing most of the optimization work that has been done. Figure adapted with permission from Pascanu et al. (2013).

with many layers have such deep computational graphs. So do recurrent networks, described in chapter 10, which construct very deep computational graphs by repeatedly applying the same operation at each time step of a long temporal sequence. Repeated application of the same parameters gives rise to especially pronounced difficulties.

For example, suppose that a computational graph contains a path that consists of repeatedly multiplying by a matrix $\boldsymbol{W}$. After t steps, this is equivalent to multiplying by $\boldsymbol{W}^t$. Suppose that $\boldsymbol{W}$ has an eigendecomposition $\boldsymbol{W} = \boldsymbol{V}\operatorname{diag}(\boldsymbol{\lambda})\boldsymbol{V}^{-1}$. In this simple case, it is straightforward to see that

$$\boldsymbol{W}^t = \left(\boldsymbol{V}\operatorname{diag}(\boldsymbol{\lambda})\boldsymbol{V}^{-1}\right)^t = \boldsymbol{V}\operatorname{diag}(\boldsymbol{\lambda})^t\boldsymbol{V}^{-1}. \tag{8.11}$$

Any eigenvalues λ_i that are not near an absolute value of 1 will either explode if they are greater than 1 in magnitude or vanish if they are less than 1 in magnitude. The **vanishing and exploding gradient problem** refers to the fact that gradients through such a graph are also scaled according to $\operatorname{diag}(\boldsymbol{\lambda})^t$. Vanishing gradients make it difficult to know which direction the parameters should move to improve the cost function, while exploding gradients can make learning unstable. The cliff structures described earlier that motivate gradient clipping are an example of the exploding gradient phenomenon.

The repeated multiplication by $\boldsymbol{W}$ at each time step described here is very similar to the **power method** algorithm used to find the largest eigenvalue of a matrix $\boldsymbol{W}$ and the corresponding eigenvector. From this point of view it is not surprising that $\boldsymbol{x}^\top\boldsymbol{W}^t$ will eventually discard all components of $\boldsymbol{x}$ that are orthogonal to the principal eigenvector of $\boldsymbol{W}$.

Recurrent networks use the same matrix $\boldsymbol{W}$ at each time step, but feedforward networks do not, so even very deep feedforward networks can largely avoid the vanishing and exploding gradient problem (Sussillo, 2014).

We defer further discussion of the challenges of training recurrent networks until section 10.7, after recurrent networks have been described in more detail.

8.2.6 Inexact Gradients

Most optimization algorithms are designed with the assumption that we have access to the exact gradient or Hessian matrix. In practice, we usually have only a noisy or even biased estimate of these quantities. Nearly every deep learning algorithm relies on sampling-based estimates, at least insofar as using a minibatch of training examples to compute the gradient.

In other cases, the objective function we want to minimize is actually intractable. When the objective function is intractable, typically its gradient is intractable as well. In such cases we can only approximate the gradient. These issues mostly arise with the more advanced models we cover in part III. For example, contrastive divergence gives a technique for approximating the gradient of the intractable log-likelihood of a Boltzmann machine.

Various neural network optimization algorithms are designed to account for imperfections in the gradient estimate. One can also avoid the problem by choosing a surrogate loss function that is easier to approximate than the true loss.

8.2.7 Poor Correspondence between Local and Global Structure

Many of the problems we have discussed so far correspond to properties of the loss function at a single point—it can be difficult to make a single step if $J(\boldsymbol{\theta})$ is poorly conditioned at the current point $\boldsymbol{\theta}$, or if $\boldsymbol{\theta}$ lies on a cliff, or if $\boldsymbol{\theta}$ is a saddle point hiding the opportunity to make progress downhill from the gradient.

It is possible to overcome all these problems at a single point and still perform poorly if the direction that results in the most improvement locally does not point toward distant regions of much lower cost.

Goodfellow et al. (2015) argue that much of the runtime of training is due to the length of the trajectory needed to arrive at the solution. Figure 8.2 shows that the learning trajectory spends most of its time tracing out a wide arc around a mountain-shaped structure.

Much of research into the difficulties of optimization has focused on whether training arrives at a global minimum, a local minimum, or a saddle point, but in practice, neural networks do not arrive at a critical point of any kind. Figure 8.1 shows that neural networks often do not arrive at a region of small gradient. Indeed, such critical points do not even necessarily exist. For example, the loss function $-\log p(y \mid \boldsymbol{x}; \boldsymbol{\theta})$ can lack a global minimum point and instead asymptotically approach some value as the model becomes more confident. For a classifier with discrete y and $p(y \mid \boldsymbol{x})$ provided by a softmax, the negative log-likelihood can become arbitrarily close to zero if the model is able to correctly classify every example in the training set, but it is impossible to actually reach the value of zero. Likewise, a model of real values $p(y \mid \boldsymbol{x}) = \mathcal{N}(y; f(\boldsymbol{\theta}), \beta^{-1})$ can have negative log-likelihood that asymptotes to negative infinity—if $f(\boldsymbol{\theta})$ is able to correctly predict the value of all training set y targets, the learning algorithm will increase β without bound. See figure 8.4 for an example of a failure of local optimization to find a good cost function value even in the absence of any local minima or saddle points.

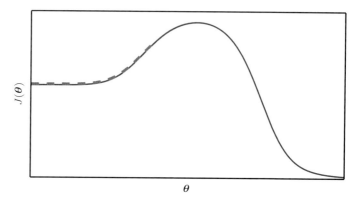

Figure 8.4: Optimization based on local downhill moves can fail if the local surface does not point toward the global solution. Here we provide an example of how this can occur, even if there are no saddle points or local minima. This example cost function contains only asymptotes toward low values, not minima. The main cause of difficulty in this case is being initialized on the wrong side of the "mountain" and not being able to traverse it. In higher-dimensional space, learning algorithms can often circumnavigate such mountains, but the trajectory associated with doing so may be long and result in excessive training time, as illustrated in figure 8.2.

Future research will need to develop further understanding of the factors that influence the length of the learning trajectory and better characterize the outcome of the process.

Many existing research directions are aimed at finding good initial points for problems that have difficult global structure, rather than at developing algorithms that use nonlocal moves.

Gradient descent and essentially all learning algorithms that are effective for training neural networks are based on making small local moves. The previous sections have primarily focused on how the correct direction of these local moves can be difficult to compute. We may be able to compute some properties of the objective function, such as its gradient, only approximately, with bias or variance in our estimate of the correct direction. In these cases, local descent may or may not define a reasonably short path to a valid solution, but we are not actually able to follow the local descent path. The objective function may have issues, such as poor conditioning or discontinuous gradients, causing the region where the gradient provides a good model of the objective function to be very small. In these cases, local descent with steps of size ϵ may define a reasonably short path to the solution, but we are only able to compute the local descent direction with steps of size $\delta \ll \epsilon$. In these cases, local descent may define a path to the solution, but the path contains many steps, so following it incurs a high computational cost. Sometimes local information provides us no guide, such as when the function has a wide flat region, or if we manage to land exactly on a critical point (usually this latter scenario only happens to methods that solve explicitly for critical points, such as Newton's method). In these cases, local descent does not define a path to a solution at all. In other cases, local moves can be too greedy and lead us along a path that moves downhill but away from any solution, as in figure 8.4, or along an unnecessarily long trajectory to the solution, as in figure 8.2. Currently, we do not understand which of these problems are most relevant to making neural network optimization difficult, and this is an active area of research.

Regardless of which of these problems are most significant, all of them might be avoided if there exists a region of space connected reasonably directly to a solution by a path that local descent can follow, and if we are able to initialize learning within that well-behaved region. This last view suggests research into choosing good initial points for traditional optimization algorithms to use.

8.2.8 Theoretical Limits of Optimization

Several theoretical results show that there are limits on the performance of any optimization algorithm we might design for neural networks (Blum and Rivest, 1992; Judd, 1989; Wolpert and MacReady, 1997). Typically these results have little bearing on the use of neural networks in practice.

Some theoretical results apply only when the units of a neural network output discrete values. Most neural network units output smoothly increasing values that make optimization via local search feasible. Some theoretical results show that there exist problem classes that are intractable, but it can be difficult to tell whether a particular problem falls into that class. Other results show that finding a solution for a network of a given size is intractable, but in practice we can find a solution easily by using a larger network for which many more parameter settings correspond to an acceptable solution. Moreover, in the context of neural network training, we usually do not care about finding the exact minimum of a function, but seek only to reduce its value sufficiently to obtain good generalization error. Theoretical analysis of whether an optimization algorithm can accomplish this goal is extremely difficult. Developing more realistic bounds on the performance of optimization algorithms therefore remains an important goal for machine learning research.

8.3 Basic Algorithms

We have previously introduced the gradient descent (section 4.3) algorithm that follows the gradient of an entire training set downhill. This may be accelerated considerably by using stochastic gradient descent to follow the gradient of randomly selected minibatches downhill, as discussed in section 5.9 and section 8.1.3.

8.3.1 Stochastic Gradient Descent

Stochastic gradient descent (SGD) and its variants are probably the most used optimization algorithms for machine learning in general and for deep learning in particular. As discussed in section 8.1.3, it is possible to obtain an unbiased estimate of the gradient by taking the average gradient on a minibatch of m examples drawn i.i.d from the data-generating distribution.

Algorithm 8.1 shows how to follow this estimate of the gradient downhill.

A crucial parameter for the SGD algorithm is the learning rate. Previously, we have described SGD as using a fixed learning rate ϵ. In practice, it is necessary to gradually decrease the learning rate over time, so we now denote the learning rate at iteration k as ϵ_k.

This is because the SGD gradient estimator introduces a source of noise (the random sampling of m training examples) that does not vanish even when we arrive at a minimum. By comparison, the true gradient of the total cost function becomes small and then $\mathbf{0}$ when we approach and reach a minimum using batch gradient descent, so batch gradient descent can use a fixed learning rate. A sufficient

---

Algorithm 8.1 Stochastic gradient descent (SGD) update at training iteration k

---

Require: Learning rate ϵ_k
Require: Initial parameter $\boldsymbol{\theta}$
  while stopping criterion not met **do**
    Sample a minibatch of m examples from the training set $\{\boldsymbol{x}^{(1)}, \ldots, \boldsymbol{x}^{(m)}\}$ with corresponding targets $\boldsymbol{y}^{(i)}$.
    Compute gradient estimate: $\hat{\boldsymbol{g}} \leftarrow +\frac{1}{m}\nabla_{\boldsymbol{\theta}}\sum_i L(f(\boldsymbol{x}^{(i)}; \boldsymbol{\theta}), \boldsymbol{y}^{(i)})$.
    Apply update: $\boldsymbol{\theta} \leftarrow \boldsymbol{\theta} - \epsilon\hat{\boldsymbol{g}}$.
  end while

---

condition to guarantee convergence of SGD is that

$$\sum_{k=1}^{\infty} \epsilon_k = \infty, \quad \text{and} \tag{8.12}$$

$$\sum_{k=1}^{\infty} \epsilon_k^2 < \infty. \tag{8.13}$$

In practice, it is common to decay the learning rate linearly until iteration τ:

$$\epsilon_k = (1 - \alpha)\epsilon_0 + \alpha \epsilon_\tau \tag{8.14}$$

with $\alpha = \frac{k}{\tau}$. After iteration τ, it is common to leave ϵ constant.

The learning rate may be chosen by trial and error, but it is usually best to choose it by monitoring learning curves that plot the objective function as a function of time. This is more of an art than a science, and most guidance on this subject should be regarded with some skepticism. When using the linear schedule, the parameters to choose are ϵ_0, ϵ_τ, and τ. Usually τ may be set to the number of iterations required to make a few hundred passes through the training set. Usually ϵ_τ should be set to roughly 1 percent the value of ϵ_0. The main question is how to set ϵ_0. If it is too large, the learning curve will show violent oscillations, with the cost function often increasing significantly. Gentle oscillations are fine, especially if training with a stochastic cost function, such as the cost function arising from the use of dropout. If the learning rate is too low, learning proceeds slowly, and if the initial learning rate is too low, learning may become stuck with a high cost value. Typically, the optimal initial learning rate, in terms of total training time and the final cost value, is higher than the learning rate that yields the best performance after the first 100 iterations or so. Therefore, it is usually best to monitor the first several iterations and use a learning rate that is higher than the best-performing learning rate at this time, but not so high that it causes severe instability.

The most important property of SGD and related minibatch or online gradient-based optimization is that computation time per update does not grow with the number of training examples. This allows convergence even when the number of training examples becomes very large. For a large enough dataset, SGD may converge to within some fixed tolerance of its final test set error before it has processed the entire training set.

To study the convergence rate of an optimization algorithm it is common to measure the **excess error** $J(\boldsymbol{\theta}) - \min_{\boldsymbol{\theta}} J(\boldsymbol{\theta})$, which is the amount by which the current cost function exceeds the minimum possible cost. When SGD is applied to a convex problem, the excess error is $O(\frac{1}{\sqrt{k}})$ after k iterations, while in the strongly convex case, it is $O(\frac{1}{k})$. These bounds cannot be improved unless extra conditions are assumed. Batch gradient descent enjoys better convergence rates than stochastic gradient descent in theory. However, the Cramér-Rao bound (Cramér, 1946; Rao, 1945) states that generalization error cannot decrease faster than $O(\frac{1}{k})$. Bottou and Bousquet (2008) argue that it therefore may not be worthwhile to pursue an optimization algorithm that converges faster than $O(\frac{1}{k})$ for machine learning tasks—faster convergence presumably corresponds to overfitting. Moreover, the asymptotic analysis obscures many advantages that stochastic gradient descent has after a small number of steps. With large datasets, the ability of SGD to make rapid initial progress while evaluating the gradient for very few examples outweighs its slow asymptotic convergence. Most of the algorithms described in the remainder of this chapter achieve benefits that matter in practice but are lost in the constant factors obscured by the $O(\frac{1}{k})$ asymptotic analysis. One can also trade off the benefits of both batch and stochastic gradient descent by gradually increasing the minibatch size during the course of learning.

For more information on SGD, see Bottou (1998).

8.3.2 Momentum

While stochastic gradient descent remains a popular optimization strategy, learning with it can sometimes be slow. The method of momentum (Polyak, 1964) is designed to accelerate learning, especially in the face of high curvature, small but consistent gradients, or noisy gradients. The momentum algorithm accumulates an exponentially decaying moving average of past gradients and continues to move in their direction. The effect of momentum is illustrated in figure 8.5.

Formally, the momentum algorithm introduces a variable $\boldsymbol{v}$ that plays the role of velocity—it is the direction and speed at which the parameters move through parameter space. The velocity is set to an exponentially decaying average of the negative gradient. The name **momentum** derives from a physical analogy, in which the negative gradient is a force moving a particle through parameter space, according to Newton's laws of motion. Momentum in physics is mass times velocity. In the momentum learning algorithm, we assume unit mass, so the velocity vector $\boldsymbol{v}$ may also be regarded as the momentum of the particle. A hyperparameter $\alpha \in [0, 1)$ determines how quickly the contributions of previous gradients exponentially decay. The update rule is given by

$$\boldsymbol{v} \leftarrow \alpha \boldsymbol{v} - \epsilon \nabla_{\boldsymbol{\theta}} \left(\frac{1}{m} \sum_{i=1}^{m} L(\boldsymbol{f}(\boldsymbol{x}^{(i)}; \boldsymbol{\theta}), \boldsymbol{y}^{(i)}) \right), \qquad (8.15)$$

$$\boldsymbol{\theta} \leftarrow \boldsymbol{\theta} + \boldsymbol{v}. \qquad (8.16)$$

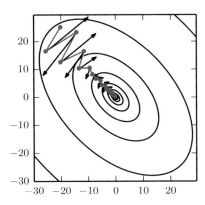

Figure 8.5: Momentum aims primarily to solve two problems: poor conditioning of the Hessian matrix and variance in the stochastic gradient. Here, we illustrate how momentum overcomes the first of these two problems. The contour lines depict a quadratic loss function with a poorly conditioned Hessian matrix. The red path cutting across the contours indicates the path followed by the momentum learning rule as it minimizes this function. At each step along the way, we draw an arrow indicating the step that gradient descent would take at that point. We can see that a poorly conditioned quadratic objective looks like a long, narrow valley or canyon with steep sides. Momentum correctly traverses the canyon lengthwise, while gradient steps waste time moving back and forth across the narrow axis of the canyon. Compare also figure 4.6, which shows the behavior of gradient descent without momentum.

Algorithm 8.2 Stochastic gradient descent (SGD) with momentum

---

Require: Learning rate ϵ, momentum parameter α
Require: Initial parameter $\boldsymbol{\theta}$, initial velocity $\boldsymbol{v}$
  while stopping criterion not met **do**
    Sample a minibatch of m examples from the training set $\{\boldsymbol{x}^{(1)}, \ldots, \boldsymbol{x}^{(m)}\}$ with corresponding targets $\boldsymbol{y}^{(i)}$.
    Compute gradient estimate: $\boldsymbol{g} \leftarrow \frac{1}{m} \nabla_{\boldsymbol{\theta}} \sum_i L(f(\boldsymbol{x}^{(i)}; \boldsymbol{\theta}), \boldsymbol{y}^{(i)})$.
    Compute velocity update: $\boldsymbol{v} \leftarrow \alpha \boldsymbol{v} - \epsilon \boldsymbol{g}$.
    Apply update: $\boldsymbol{\theta} \leftarrow \boldsymbol{\theta} + \boldsymbol{v}$.
  end while

The velocity $\boldsymbol{v}$ accumulates the gradient elements $\nabla_{\boldsymbol{\theta}} \left(\frac{1}{m} \sum_{i=1}^{m} L(\boldsymbol{f}(\boldsymbol{x}^{(i)}; \boldsymbol{\theta}), \boldsymbol{y}^{(i)}) \right)$. The larger α is relative to ϵ, the more previous gradients affect the current direction. The SGD algorithm with momentum is given in algorithm 8.2.

Previously, the size of the step was simply the norm of the gradient multiplied by the learning rate. Now, the size of the step depends on how large and how aligned a *sequence* of gradients are. The step size is largest when many successive gradients point in exactly the same direction. If the momentum algorithm always observes gradient $\boldsymbol{g}$, then it will accelerate in the direction of $-\boldsymbol{g}$, until reaching a terminal velocity where the size of each step is

$$\frac{\epsilon\|\boldsymbol{g}\|}{1-\alpha}. \tag{8.17}$$

It is thus helpful to think of the momentum hyperparameter in terms of $\frac{1}{1-\alpha}$. For example, $\alpha = 0.9$ corresponds to multiplying the maximum speed by 10 relative to the gradient descent algorithm.

Common values of α used in practice include 0.5, 0.9, and 0.99. Like the learning rate, α may also be adapted over time. Typically it begins with a small value and is later raised. Adapting α over time is less important than shrinking ϵ over time.

We can view the momentum algorithm as simulating a particle subject to continuous-time Newtonian dynamics. The physical analogy can help build intuition for how the momentum and gradient descent algorithms behave.

The position of the particle at any point in time is given by $\boldsymbol{\theta}(t)$. The particle experiences net force $\boldsymbol{f}(t)$. This force causes the particle to accelerate:

$$\boldsymbol{f}(t) = \frac{\partial^2}{\partial t^2}\boldsymbol{\theta}(t). \tag{8.18}$$

Rather than viewing this as a second-order differential equation of the position, we can introduce the variable $\boldsymbol{v}(t)$ representing the velocity of the particle at time t and rewrite the Newtonian dynamics as a first-order differential equation:

$$\boldsymbol{v}(t) = \frac{\partial}{\partial t}\boldsymbol{\theta}(t), \tag{8.19}$$

$$\boldsymbol{f}(t) = \frac{\partial}{\partial t}\boldsymbol{v}(t). \tag{8.20}$$

The momentum algorithm then consists of solving the differential equations via numerical simulation. A simple numerical method for solving differential equations is Euler's method, which simply consists of simulating the dynamics defined by the equation by taking small, finite steps in the direction of each gradient.

This explains the basic form of the momentum update, but what specifically are the forces? One force is proportional to the negative gradient of the cost function: $-\nabla_{\boldsymbol{\theta}}J(\boldsymbol{\theta})$. This force pushes the particle downhill along the cost function surface. The gradient descent algorithm would simply take a single step based on each gradient, but the Newtonian scenario used by the momentum algorithm instead uses this force to alter the velocity of the particle. We can think of the particle as being like a hockey puck sliding down an icy surface. Whenever it descends a steep part of the surface, it gathers speed and continues sliding in that direction until it begins to go uphill again.

One other force is necessary. If the only force is the gradient of the cost function, then the particle might never come to rest. Imagine a hockey puck sliding down one side of a valley and straight up the other side, oscillating back and forth forever, assuming the ice is perfectly frictionless. To resolve this problem, we add one other force, proportional to $-\boldsymbol{v}(t)$. In physics terminology, this force corresponds to viscous drag, as if the particle must push through a resistant medium such as syrup. This causes the particle to gradually lose energy over time and eventually converge to a local minimum.

Why do we use $-\boldsymbol{v}(t)$ and viscous drag in particular? Part of the reason to use $-\boldsymbol{v}(t)$ is mathematical convenience—an integer power of the velocity is easy to work with. Yet other physical systems have other kinds of drag based on other integer powers of the velocity. For example, a particle traveling through the air experiences turbulent drag, with force proportional to the square of the velocity, while a particle moving along the ground experiences dry friction, with a force of constant magnitude. We can reject each of these options. Turbulent drag, proportional to the square of the velocity, becomes very weak when the velocity is small. It is not powerful enough to force the particle to come to rest. A particle with a nonzero initial velocity that experiences only the force of turbulent drag will move away from its initial position forever, with the distance from the starting point growing like $O(\log t)$. We must therefore use a lower power of the velocity. If we use a power of zero, representing dry friction, then the force is too strong. When the force due to the gradient of the cost function is small but nonzero, the constant force due to friction can cause the particle to come to rest before reaching a local minimum. Viscous drag avoids both of these problems—it is weak enough that the gradient can continue to cause motion until a minimum is reached, but strong enough to prevent motion if the gradient does not justify moving.

8.3.3 Nesterov Momentum

Sutskever et al. (2013) introduced a variant of the momentum algorithm that was inspired by Nesterov's accelerated gradient method (Nesterov, 1983, 2004). The update rules in this case are given by

$$\boldsymbol{v} \leftarrow \alpha \boldsymbol{v} - \epsilon \nabla_{\boldsymbol{\theta}} \left[\frac{1}{m} \sum_{i=1}^{m} L\left(\boldsymbol{f}(\boldsymbol{x}^{(i)}; \boldsymbol{\theta} + \alpha \boldsymbol{v}), \boldsymbol{y}^{(i)} \right) \right], \tag{8.21}$$

$$\boldsymbol{\theta} \leftarrow \boldsymbol{\theta} + \boldsymbol{v}, \tag{8.22}$$

Algorithm 8.3 Stochastic gradient descent (SGD) with Nesterov momentum

---

Require: Learning rate ϵ, momentum parameter α
Require: Initial parameter $\boldsymbol{\theta}$, initial velocity $\boldsymbol{v}$
  while stopping criterion not met **do**
    Sample a minibatch of m examples from the training set $\{\boldsymbol{x}^{(1)}, \dots, \boldsymbol{x}^{(m)}\}$ with corresponding labels $\boldsymbol{y}^{(i)}$.
    Apply interim update: $\tilde{\boldsymbol{\theta}} \leftarrow \boldsymbol{\theta} + \alpha \boldsymbol{v}$.
    Compute gradient (at interim point): $\boldsymbol{g} \leftarrow \frac{1}{m} \nabla_{\tilde{\boldsymbol{\theta}}} \sum_i L(f(\boldsymbol{x}^{(i)}; \tilde{\boldsymbol{\theta}}), \boldsymbol{y}^{(i)})$.
    Compute velocity update: $\boldsymbol{v} \leftarrow \alpha \boldsymbol{v} - \epsilon \boldsymbol{g}$.
    Apply update: $\boldsymbol{\theta} \leftarrow \boldsymbol{\theta} + \boldsymbol{v}$.
  end while

---

where the parameters α and ϵ play a similar role as in the standard momentum method. The difference between Nesterov momentum and standard momentum is where the gradient is evaluated. With Nesterov momentum, the gradient is evaluated after the current velocity is applied. Thus one can interpret Nesterov momentum as attempting to add a *correction factor* to the standard method of momentum. The complete Nesterov momentum algorithm is presented in algorithm 8.3.

In the convex batch gradient case, Nesterov momentum brings the rate of convergence of the excess error from $O(1/k)$ (after k steps) to $O(1/k^2)$ as shown by Nesterov (1983). Unfortunately, in the stochastic gradient case, Nesterov momentum does not improve the rate of convergence.

8.4 Parameter Initialization Strategies

Some optimization algorithms are not iterative by nature and simply solve for a solution point. Other optimization algorithms are iterative by nature but, when applied to the right class of optimization problems, converge to acceptable solutions in an acceptable amount of time regardless of initialization. Deep learning training algorithms usually do not have either of these luxuries. Training algorithms for deep learning models are usually iterative and thus require the user to specify some initial point from which to begin the iterations. Moreover, training deep models is a sufficiently difficult task that most algorithms are strongly affected by the choice of initialization. The initial point can determine whether the algorithm converges at all, with some initial points being so unstable that the algorithm encounters numerical difficulties and fails altogether. When learning does converge, the initial point can determine how quickly learning converges and whether it converges to a point with high or low cost. Also, points of comparable cost can have wildly varying generalization error, and the initial point can affect the generalization as well.

Modern initialization strategies are simple and heuristic. Designing improved initialization strategies is a difficult task because neural network optimization is not yet well understood. Most initialization strategies are based on achieving some nice properties when the network is initialized. However, we do not have a good understanding of which of these properties are preserved under which circumstances after learning begins to proceed. A further difficulty is that some initial points may be beneficial from the viewpoint of optimization but detrimental from the viewpoint of generalization. Our understanding of how the initial point affects generalization is especially primitive, offering little to no guidance for how to select the initial point.

Perhaps the only property known with complete certainty is that the initial parameters need to "break symmetry" between different units. If two hidden units with the same activation function are connected to the same inputs, then these units must have different initial parameters. If they have the same initial parameters, then a deterministic learning algorithm applied to a deterministic cost and model will constantly update both of these units in the same way. Even if the model or training algorithm is capable of using stochasticity to compute different updates for different units (for example, if one trains with dropout), it is usually best to initialize each unit to compute a different function from all the other units. This may help to make sure that no input patterns are lost in the null space of forward propagation and that no gradient patterns are lost in the null space of back-propagation. The goal of having each unit compute a different function motivates random initialization of the parameters. We could explicitly search for a large set of basis functions that are all mutually different from each other, but this often incurs a noticeable computational cost. For example, if we have at most as many outputs as inputs, we could use Gram-Schmidt orthogonalization on an initial weight matrix and be guaranteed that each unit would compute a very different function from each other unit. Random initialization from a high-entropy distribution over a high-dimensional space is computationally cheaper and unlikely to assign any units to compute the same function as each other.

Typically, we set the biases for each unit to heuristically chosen constants, and initialize only the weights randomly. Extra parameters—for example, parameters encoding the conditional variance of a prediction—are usually set to heuristically chosen constants much like the biases are.

We almost always initialize all the weights in the model to values drawn randomly from a Gaussian or uniform distribution. The choice of Gaussian or uniform distribution does not seem to matter much but has not been exhaustively studied. The scale of the initial distribution, however, does have a large effect on both the outcome of the optimization procedure and the ability of the network to generalize.

Larger initial weights will yield a stronger symmetry-breaking effect, helping to avoid redundant units. They also help to avoid losing signal during forward or back-propagation through the linear component of each layer—larger values in the matrix result in larger outputs of matrix multiplication. Initial weights that are too large may, however, result in exploding values during forward propagation or back-propagation. In recurrent networks, large weights can also result in **chaos** (such extreme sensitivity to small perturbations of the input that the behavior of the deterministic forward propagation procedure appears random). To some extent, the exploding gradient problem can be mitigated by gradient clipping (thresholding the values of the gradients before performing a gradient descent step). Large weights may also result in extreme values that cause the activation function to saturate, causing complete loss of gradient through saturated units. These competing factors determine the ideal initial scale of the weights.

The perspectives of regularization and optimization can give very different insights into how we should initialize a network. The optimization perspective suggests that the weights should be large enough to propagate information successfully, but some regularization concerns encourage making them smaller. The use of an optimization algorithm, such as stochastic gradient descent, that makes small incremental changes to the weights and tends to halt in areas that are nearer to the initial parameters (whether due to getting stuck in a region of low gradient, or due to triggering some early stopping criterion based on overfitting) expresses a prior that the final parameters should be close to the initial parameters. Recall from section 7.8 that gradient descent with early stopping is equivalent to weight decay for some models. In the general case, gradient descent with early stopping is not the same as weight decay, but it does provide a loose analogy for thinking about the effect of initialization. We can think of initializing the parameters $\boldsymbol{\theta}$ to $\boldsymbol{\theta}_0$ as being similar to imposing a Gaussian prior $p(\boldsymbol{\theta})$ with mean $\boldsymbol{\theta}_0$. From this point of view, it makes sense to choose $\boldsymbol{\theta}_0$ to be near 0. This prior says that it is more likely that units do not interact with each other than that they do interact. Units interact only if the likelihood term of the objective function expresses a strong preference for them to interact. On the other hand, if we initialize $\boldsymbol{\theta}_0$ to large values, then our prior specifies which units should interact with each other, and how they should interact.

Some heuristics are available for choosing the initial scale of the weights. One heuristic is to initialize the weights of a fully connected layer with m inputs and

n outputs by sampling each weight from $U(-\frac{1}{\sqrt{m}}, \frac{1}{\sqrt{m}})$, while Glorot and Bengio (2010) suggest using the **normalized initialization**

$$\mathrm{W}_{i,j} \sim U\left(-\sqrt{\frac{6}{m+n}}, \sqrt{\frac{6}{m+n}}\right). \tag{8.23}$$

This latter heuristic is designed to compromise between the goal of initializing all layers to have the same activation variance and the goal of initializing all layers to have the same gradient variance. The formula is derived using the assumption that the network consists only of a chain of matrix multiplications, with no nonlinearities. Real neural networks obviously violate this assumption, but many strategies designed for the linear model perform reasonably well on its nonlinear counterparts.

Saxe et al. (2013) recommend initializing to random orthogonal matrices, with a carefully chosen scaling or **gain** factor g that accounts for the nonlinearity applied at each layer. They derive specific values of the scaling factor for different types of nonlinear activation functions. This initialization scheme is also motivated by a model of a deep network as a sequence of matrix multiplies without nonlinearities. Under such a model, this initialization scheme guarantees that the total number of training iterations required to reach convergence is independent of depth.

Increasing the scaling factor g pushes the network toward the regime where activations increase in norm as they propagate forward through the network and gradients increase in norm as they propagate backward. Sussillo (2014) showed that setting the gain factor correctly is sufficient to train networks as deep as 1,000 layers, without needing to use orthogonal initializations. A key insight of this approach is that in feedforward networks, activations and gradients can grow or shrink on each step of forward or back-propagation, following a random walk behavior. This is because feedforward networks use a different weight matrix at each layer. If this random walk is tuned to preserve norms, then feedforward networks can mostly avoid the vanishing and exploding gradients problem that arises when the same weight matrix is used at each step, as described in section 8.2.5.

Unfortunately, these optimal criteria for initial weights often do not lead to optimal performance. This may be for three different reasons. First, we may be using the wrong criteria—it may not actually be beneficial to preserve the norm of a signal throughout the entire network. Second, the properties imposed at initialization may not persist after learning has begun to proceed. Third, the criteria might succeed at improving the speed of optimization but inadvertently increase generalization error. In practice, we usually need to treat the scale of the weights as a hyperparameter whose optimal value lies somewhere roughly near but not exactly equal to the theoretical predictions.

One drawback to scaling rules that set all the initial weights to have the same standard deviation, such as $\frac{1}{\sqrt{m}}$, is that every individual weight becomes extremely small when the layers become large. Martens (2010) introduced an alternative initialization scheme called **sparse initialization**, in which each unit is initialized to have exactly k nonzero weights. The idea is to keep the total amount of input to the unit independent from the number of inputs m without making the magnitude of individual weight elements shrink with m. Sparse initialization helps to achieve more diversity among the units at initialization time. However, it also imposes a very strong prior on the weights that are chosen to have large Gaussian values. Because it takes a long time for gradient descent to shrink "incorrect" large values, this initialization scheme can cause problems for units, such as maxout units, that have several filters that must be carefully coordinated with each other.

When computational resources allow it, it is usually a good idea to treat the initial scale of the weights for each layer as a hyperparameter, and to choose these scales using a hyperparameter search algorithm described in section 11.4.2, such as random search. The choice of whether to use dense or sparse initialization can also be made a hyperparameter. Alternately, one can manually search for the best initial scales. A good rule of thumb for choosing the initial scales is to look at the range or standard deviation of activations or gradients on a single minibatch of data. If the weights are too small, the range of activations across the minibatch will shrink as the activations propagate forward through the network. By repeatedly identifying the first layer with unacceptably small activations and increasing its weights, it is possible to eventually obtain a network with reasonable initial activations throughout. If learning is still too slow at this point, it can be useful to look at the range or standard deviation of the gradients as well as the activations. This procedure can in principle be automated and is generally less computationally costly than hyperparameter optimization based on validation set error because it is based on feedback from the behavior of the initial model on a single batch of data, rather than on feedback from a trained model on the validation set. While long used heuristically, this protocol has recently been specified more formally and studied by Mishkin and Matas (2015).

So far we have focused on the initialization of the weights. Fortunately, initialization of other parameters is typically easier.

The approach for setting the biases must be coordinated with the approach for setting the weights. Setting the biases to zero is compatible with most weight initialization schemes. There are a few situations where we may set some biases to nonzero values:

- If a bias is for an output unit, then it is often beneficial to initialize the bias to obtain the right marginal statistics of the output. To do this, we assume that the initial weights are small enough that the output of the unit is determined only by the bias. This justifies setting the bias to the inverse of the activation function applied to the marginal statistics of the output in the training set. For example, if the output is a distribution over classes, and this distribution is a highly skewed distribution with the marginal probability of class i given by element c_i of some vector c, then we can set the bias vector b by solving the equation softmax(b) = c. This applies not only to classifiers but also to models we will encounter in Part III, such as autoencoders and Boltzmann machines. These models have layers whose output should resemble the input data x, and it can be very helpful to initialize the biases of such layers to match the marginal distribution over x.

- Sometimes we may want to choose the bias to avoid causing too much saturation at initialization. For example, we may set the bias of a ReLU hidden unit to 0.1 rather than 0 to avoid saturating the ReLU at initialization. This approach is not compatible with weight initialization schemes that do not expect strong input from the biases though. For example, it is not recommended for use with random walk initialization (Sussillo, 2014).

- Sometimes a unit controls whether other units are able to participate in a function. In such situations, we have a unit with output u and another unit $h \in [0, 1]$, and they are multiplied together to produce an output uh. We can view h as a gate that determines whether $uh \approx u$ or $uh \approx 0$. In these situations, we want to set the bias for h so that $h \approx 1$ most of the time at initialization. Otherwise u does not have a chance to learn. For example, Jozefowicz et al. (2015) advocate setting the bias to 1 for the forget gate of the LSTM model, described in section 10.10.

Another common type of parameter is a variance or precision parameter. For example, we can perform linear regression with a conditional variance estimate using the model

$$p(y \mid x) = \mathcal{N}(y \mid w^T x + b, 1/\beta), \tag{8.24}$$

where β is a precision parameter. We can usually initialize variance or precision parameters to 1 safely. Another approach is to assume the initial weights are close enough to zero that the biases may be set while ignoring the effect of the weights, then set the biases to produce the correct marginal mean of the output, and set the variance parameters to the marginal variance of the output in the training set.

Besides these simple constant or random methods of initializing model parameters, it is possible to initialize model parameters using machine learning. A common strategy discussed in part III of this book is to initialize a supervised model with the parameters learned by an unsupervised model trained on the same inputs. One can also perform supervised training on a related task. Even performing supervised training on an unrelated task can sometimes yield an initialization that offers faster convergence than a random initialization. Some of these initialization strategies may yield faster convergence and better generalization because they encode information about the distribution in the initial parameters of the model. Others apparently perform well primarily because they set the parameters to have the right scale or set different units to compute different functions from each other.

8.5 Algorithms with Adaptive Learning Rates

Neural network researchers have long realized that the learning rate is reliably one of the most difficult to set hyperparameters because it significantly affects model performance. As we discuss in sections 4.3 and 8.2, the cost is often highly sensitive to some directions in parameter space and insensitive to others. The momentum algorithm can mitigate these issues somewhat, but it does so at the expense of introducing another hyperparameter. In the face of this, it is natural to ask if there is another way. If we believe that the directions of sensitivity are somewhat axis aligned, it can make sense to use a separate learning rate for each parameter and automatically adapt these learning rates throughout the course of learning.

The **delta-bar-delta** algorithm (Jacobs, 1988) is an early heuristic approach to adapting individual learning rates for model parameters during training. The approach is based on a simple idea: if the partial derivative of the loss, with respect to a given model parameter, remains the same sign, then the learning rate should increase. If that partial derivative changes sign, then the learning rate should decrease. Of course, this kind of rule can only be applied to full batch optimization.

More recently, a number of incremental (or mini batch-based) methods have been introduced that adapt the learning rates of model parameters. In this section, we briefly review a few of these algorithms.

8.5.1 AdaGrad

The **AdaGrad** algorithm, shown in algorithm 8.4, individually adapts the learning rates of all model parameters by scaling them inversely proportional to the square root of the sum of all the historical squared values of the gradient (Duchi et al., 2011). The parameters with the largest partial derivative of the loss have a correspondingly rapid decrease in their learning rate, while parameters with small partial derivatives have a relatively small decrease in their learning rate. The net effect is greater progress in the more gently sloped directions of parameter space.

In the context of convex optimization, the AdaGrad algorithm enjoys some desirable theoretical properties. Empirically, however, for training deep neural network models, the accumulation of squared gradients *from the beginning of training* can result in a premature and excessive decrease in the effective learning rate. AdaGrad performs well for some but not all deep learning models.

8.5.2 RMSProp

The **RMSProp** algorithm (Hinton, 2012) modifies AdaGrad to perform better in the nonconvex setting by changing the gradient accumulation into an exponentially weighted moving average. AdaGrad is designed to converge rapidly when applied to a convex function. When applied to a nonconvex function to train a neural network, the learning trajectory may pass through many different structures and eventually

---

Algorithm 8.4 The AdaGrad algorithm

Require: Global learning rate ϵ
Require: Initial parameter $\boldsymbol{\theta}$
Require: Small constant δ, perhaps 10^{-7}, for numerical stability
  Initialize gradient accumulation variable $\boldsymbol{r} = \boldsymbol{0}$
  while stopping criterion not met **do**
    Sample a minibatch of m examples from the training set $\{\boldsymbol{x}^{(1)}, \dots, \boldsymbol{x}^{(m)}\}$ with corresponding targets $\boldsymbol{y}^{(i)}$.
    Compute gradient: $\boldsymbol{g} \leftarrow \frac{1}{m} \nabla_{\boldsymbol{\theta}} \sum_i L(f(\boldsymbol{x}^{(i)}; \boldsymbol{\theta}), \boldsymbol{y}^{(i)})$.
    Accumulate squared gradient: $\boldsymbol{r} \leftarrow \boldsymbol{r} + \boldsymbol{g} \odot \boldsymbol{g}$.
    Compute update: $\Delta\boldsymbol{\theta} \leftarrow -\frac{\epsilon}{\delta + \sqrt{\boldsymbol{r}}} \odot \boldsymbol{g}$. (Division and square root applied element-wise)
    Apply update: $\boldsymbol{\theta} \leftarrow \boldsymbol{\theta} + \Delta\boldsymbol{\theta}$.
  end while

---

arrive at a region that is a locally convex bowl. AdaGrad shrinks the learning rate according to the entire history of the squared gradient and may have made the learning rate too small before arriving at such a convex structure. RMSProp uses an exponentially decaying average to discard history from the extreme past so that it can converge rapidly after finding a convex bowl, as if it were an instance of the AdaGrad algorithm initialized within that bowl.

RMSProp is shown in its standard form in algorithm 8.5 and combined with Nesterov momentum in algorithm 8.6. Compared to AdaGrad, the use of the

---

Algorithm 8.5 The RMSProp algorithm

Require: Global learning rate ϵ, decay rate ρ
Require: Initial parameter $\boldsymbol{\theta}$
Require: Small constant δ, usually 10^{-6}, used to stabilize division by small numbers
  Initialize accumulation variables $\boldsymbol{r} = 0$
  while stopping criterion not met **do**
    Sample a minibatch of m examples from the training set $\{\boldsymbol{x}^{(1)}, \dots, \boldsymbol{x}^{(m)}\}$ with corresponding targets $\boldsymbol{y}^{(i)}$.
    Compute gradient: $\boldsymbol{g} \leftarrow \frac{1}{m} \nabla_{\boldsymbol{\theta}} \sum_i L(f(\boldsymbol{x}^{(i)}; \boldsymbol{\theta}), \boldsymbol{y}^{(i)})$.
    Accumulate squared gradient: $\boldsymbol{r} \leftarrow \rho \boldsymbol{r} + (1 - \rho) \boldsymbol{g} \odot \boldsymbol{g}$.
    Compute parameter update: $\Delta \boldsymbol{\theta} = -\frac{\epsilon}{\sqrt{\delta + \boldsymbol{r}}} \odot \boldsymbol{g}$.   ($\frac{1}{\sqrt{\delta + \boldsymbol{r}}}$ applied element-wise)
    Apply update: $\boldsymbol{\theta} \leftarrow \boldsymbol{\theta} + \Delta \boldsymbol{\theta}$.
  end while

Algorithm 8.6 RMSProp algorithm with Nesterov momentum

Require: Global learning rate ϵ, decay rate ρ, momentum coefficient α
Require: Initial parameter $\boldsymbol{\theta}$, initial velocity $\boldsymbol{v}$
  Initialize accumulation variable $\boldsymbol{r} = 0$
  while stopping criterion not met **do**
    Sample a minibatch of m examples from the training set $\{\boldsymbol{x}^{(1)}, \dots, \boldsymbol{x}^{(m)}\}$ with corresponding targets $\boldsymbol{y}^{(i)}$.
    Compute interim update: $\tilde{\boldsymbol{\theta}} \leftarrow \boldsymbol{\theta} + \alpha \boldsymbol{v}$.
    Compute gradient: $\boldsymbol{g} \leftarrow \frac{1}{m} \nabla_{\tilde{\boldsymbol{\theta}}} \sum_i L(f(\boldsymbol{x}^{(i)}; \tilde{\boldsymbol{\theta}}), \boldsymbol{y}^{(i)})$.
    Accumulate gradient: $\boldsymbol{r} \leftarrow \rho \boldsymbol{r} + (1 - \rho) \boldsymbol{g} \odot \boldsymbol{g}$.
    Compute velocity update: $\boldsymbol{v} \leftarrow \alpha \boldsymbol{v} - \frac{\epsilon}{\sqrt{\boldsymbol{r}}} \odot \boldsymbol{g}$.   ($\frac{1}{\sqrt{\boldsymbol{r}}}$ applied element-wise)
    Apply update: $\boldsymbol{\theta} \leftarrow \boldsymbol{\theta} + \boldsymbol{v}$.
  end while

---

moving average introduces a new hyperparameter, ρ, that controls the length scale of the moving average.

Empirically, RMSProp has been shown to be an effective and practical optimization algorithm for deep neural networks. It is currently one of the go-to optimization methods being employed routinely by deep learning practitioners.

8.5.3 Adam

Adam (Kingma and Ba, 2014) is yet another adaptive learning rate optimization algorithm and is presented in algorithm 8.7. The name "Adam" derives from the phrase "adaptive moments." In the context of the earlier algorithms, it is perhaps best seen as a variant on the combination of RMSProp and momentum with a few important distinctions. First, in Adam, momentum is incorporated directly as an estimate of the first-order moment (with exponential weighting) of the gradient. The most straightforward way to add momentum to RMSProp is to apply momentum to the rescaled gradients. The use of momentum in combination with

---

Algorithm 8.7 The Adam algorithm

Require: Step size ϵ (Suggested default: 0.001)
Require: Exponential decay rates for moment estimates, ρ_1 and ρ_2 in $[0, 1)$. (Suggested defaults: 0.9 and 0.999 respectively)
Require: Small constant δ used for numerical stabilization (Suggested default: 10^{-8})
Require: Initial parameters $\boldsymbol{\theta}$
  Initialize 1st and 2nd moment variables $\boldsymbol{s} = \boldsymbol{0}$, $\boldsymbol{r} = \boldsymbol{0}$
  Initialize time step $t = 0$
  while stopping criterion not met **do**
    Sample a minibatch of m examples from the training set $\{\boldsymbol{x}^{(1)}, \dots, \boldsymbol{x}^{(m)}\}$ with corresponding targets $\boldsymbol{y}^{(i)}$.
    Compute gradient: $\boldsymbol{g} \leftarrow \frac{1}{m} \nabla_{\boldsymbol{\theta}} \sum_i L(f(\boldsymbol{x}^{(i)}; \boldsymbol{\theta}), \boldsymbol{y}^{(i)})$
    $t \leftarrow t + 1$
    Update biased first moment estimate: $\boldsymbol{s} \leftarrow \rho_1 \boldsymbol{s} + (1 - \rho_1)\boldsymbol{g}$
    Update biased second moment estimate: $\boldsymbol{r} \leftarrow \rho_2 \boldsymbol{r} + (1 - \rho_2)\boldsymbol{g} \odot \boldsymbol{g}$
    Correct bias in first moment: $\hat{\boldsymbol{s}} \leftarrow \frac{\boldsymbol{s}}{1 - \rho_1^t}$
    Correct bias in second moment: $\hat{\boldsymbol{r}} \leftarrow \frac{\boldsymbol{r}}{1 - \rho_2^t}$
    Compute update: $\Delta\boldsymbol{\theta} = -\epsilon \frac{\hat{\boldsymbol{s}}}{\sqrt{\hat{\boldsymbol{r}}} + \delta}$ (operations applied element-wise)
    Apply update: $\boldsymbol{\theta} \leftarrow \boldsymbol{\theta} + \Delta\boldsymbol{\theta}$
  end while

---

rescaling does not have a clear theoretical motivation. Second, Adam includes bias corrections to the estimates of both the first-order moments (the momentum term) and the (uncentered) second-order moments to account for their initialization at the origin (see algorithm 8.7). RMSProp also incorporates an estimate of the (uncentered) second-order moment; however, it lacks the correction factor. Thus, unlike in Adam, the RMSProp second-order moment estimate may have high bias early in training. Adam is generally regarded as being fairly robust to the choice of hyperparameters, though the learning rate sometimes needs to be changed from the suggested default.

8.5.4 Choosing the Right Optimization Algorithm

We have discussed a series of related algorithms that each seek to address the challenge of optimizing deep models by adapting the learning rate for each model parameter. At this point, a natural question is: which algorithm should one choose?

Unfortunately, there is currently no consensus on this point. Schaul et al. (2014) presented a valuable comparison of a large number of optimization algorithms across a wide range of learning tasks. While the results suggest that the family of algorithms with adaptive learning rates (represented by RMSProp and AdaDelta) performed fairly robustly, no single best algorithm has emerged.

Currently, the most popular optimization algorithms actively in use include SGD, SGD with momentum, RMSProp, RMSProp with momentum, AdaDelta, and Adam. The choice of which algorithm to use, at this point, seems to depend largely on the user's familiarity with the algorithm (for ease of hyperparameter tuning).

8.6 Approximate Second-Order Methods

In this section we discuss the application of second-order methods to training deep networks. See LeCun et al. (1998a) for an earlier treatment of this subject. For simplicity of exposition, the only objective function we examine is the empirical risk:

$$J(\boldsymbol{\theta}) = \mathbb{E}_{\mathbf{x},\mathbf{y} \sim \hat{p}_{\text{data}}(\boldsymbol{x},y)}[L(f(\boldsymbol{x};\boldsymbol{\theta}),y)] = \frac{1}{m}\sum_{i=1}^{m} L(f(\boldsymbol{x}^{(i)};\boldsymbol{\theta}),y^{(i)}). \qquad (8.25)$$

The methods we discuss here extend readily, however, to more general objective functions, such as those that include parameter regularization terms, as discussed in chapter 7.

8.6.1 Newton's Method

In section 4.3, we introduced second-order gradient methods. In contrast to first-order methods, second-order methods make use of second derivatives to improve optimization. The most widely used second-order method is Newton's method. We now describe Newton's method in more detail, with emphasis on its application to neural network training.

Newton's method is an optimization scheme based on using a second-order Taylor series expansion to approximate $J(\boldsymbol{\theta})$ near some point $\boldsymbol{\theta}_0$, ignoring derivatives of higher order:

$$J(\boldsymbol{\theta}) \approx J(\boldsymbol{\theta}_0) + (\boldsymbol{\theta} - \boldsymbol{\theta}_0)^\top \nabla_{\boldsymbol{\theta}} J(\boldsymbol{\theta}_0) + \frac{1}{2}(\boldsymbol{\theta} - \boldsymbol{\theta}_0)^\top \boldsymbol{H}(\boldsymbol{\theta} - \boldsymbol{\theta}_0), \tag{8.26}$$

where $\boldsymbol{H}$ is the Hessian of J with respect to $\boldsymbol{\theta}$ evaluated at $\boldsymbol{\theta}_0$. If we then solve for the critical point of this function, we obtain the Newton parameter update rule:

$$\boldsymbol{\theta}^* = \boldsymbol{\theta}_0 - \boldsymbol{H}^{-1}\nabla_{\boldsymbol{\theta}} J(\boldsymbol{\theta}_0). \tag{8.27}$$

Thus for a locally quadratic function (with positive definite $\boldsymbol{H}$), by rescaling the gradient by $\boldsymbol{H}^{-1}$, Newton's method jumps directly to the minimum. If the objective function is convex but not quadratic (there are higher-order terms), this update can be iterated, yielding the training algorithm associated with Newton's method, given in algorithm 8.8.

For surfaces that are not quadratic, as long as the Hessian remains positive definite, Newton's method can be applied iteratively. This implies a two-step iterative procedure. First, update or compute the inverse Hessian (i.e., by updating the quadratic approximation). Second, update the parameters according to equation 8.27.

Algorithm 8.8 Newton's method with objective $J(\boldsymbol{\theta}) = \frac{1}{m}\sum_{i=1}^{m} L(f(\boldsymbol{x}^{(i)}; \boldsymbol{\theta}), y^{(i)})$

Require: Initial parameter $\boldsymbol{\theta}_0$
Require: Training set of m examples
    while stopping criterion not met **do**
        Compute gradient: $\boldsymbol{g} \leftarrow \frac{1}{m}\nabla_{\boldsymbol{\theta}} \sum_i L(f(\boldsymbol{x}^{(i)}; \boldsymbol{\theta}), y^{(i)})$
        Compute Hessian: $\boldsymbol{H} \leftarrow \frac{1}{m}\nabla_{\boldsymbol{\theta}}^2 \sum_i L(f(\boldsymbol{x}^{(i)}; \boldsymbol{\theta}), y^{(i)})$
        Compute Hessian inverse: $\boldsymbol{H}^{-1}$
        Compute update: $\Delta\boldsymbol{\theta} = -\boldsymbol{H}^{-1}\boldsymbol{g}$
        Apply update: $\boldsymbol{\theta} = \boldsymbol{\theta} + \Delta\boldsymbol{\theta}$
    end while

In section 8.2.3, we discuss how Newton's method is appropriate only when the Hessian is positive definite. In deep learning, the surface of the objective function is typically nonconvex, with many features, such as saddle points, that are problematic for Newton's method. If the eigenvalues of the Hessian are not all positive, for example, near a saddle point, then Newton's method can actually cause updates to move in the wrong direction. This situation can be avoided by regularizing the Hessian. Common regularization strategies include adding a constant, α, along the diagonal of the Hessian. The regularized update becomes

$$\boldsymbol{\theta}^* = \boldsymbol{\theta}_0 - [H\left(f(\boldsymbol{\theta}_0)\right) + \alpha\boldsymbol{I}]^{-1}\,\nabla_{\boldsymbol{\theta}}f(\boldsymbol{\theta}_0). \qquad (8.28)$$

This regularization strategy is used in approximations to Newton's method, such as the Levenberg-Marquardt algorithm (Levenberg, 1944; Marquardt, 1963), and works fairly well as long as the negative eigenvalues of the Hessian are still relatively close to zero. When there are more extreme directions of curvature, the value of α would have to be sufficiently large to offset the negative eigenvalues. As α increases in size, however, the Hessian becomes dominated by the $\alpha\boldsymbol{I}$ diagonal, and the direction chosen by Newton's method converges to the standard gradient divided by α. When strong negative curvature is present, α may need to be so large that Newton's method would make smaller steps than gradient descent with a properly chosen learning rate.

Beyond the challenges created by certain features of the objective function, such as saddle points, the application of Newton's method for training large neural networks is limited by the significant computational burden it imposes. The number of elements in the Hessian is squared in the number of parameters, so with k parameters (and for even very small neural networks, the number of parameters k can be in the millions), Newton's method would require the inversion of a $k \times k$ matrix—with computational complexity of $O(k^3)$. Also, since the parameters will change with every update, the inverse Hessian has to be computed *at every training iteration*. As a consequence, only networks with a very small number of parameters can be practically trained via Newton's method. In the remainder of this section, we discuss alternatives that attempt to gain some of the advantages of Newton's method while side-stepping the computational hurdles.

8.6.2 Conjugate Gradients

Conjugate gradients is a method to efficiently avoid the calculation of the inverse Hessian by iteratively descending **conjugate directions**. The inspiration for this approach follows from a careful study of the weakness of the method of steepest descent (see section 4.3 for details), where line searches are applied iteratively in

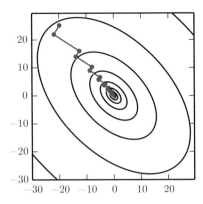

Figure 8.6: The method of steepest descent applied to a quadratic cost surface. The method of steepest descent involves jumping to the point of lowest cost along the line defined by the gradient at the initial point on each step. This resolves some of the problems seen with using a fixed learning rate in figure 4.6, but even with the optimal step size the algorithm still makes back-and-forth progress toward the optimum. By definition, at the minimum of the objective along a given direction, the gradient at the final point is orthogonal to that direction.

the direction associated with the gradient. Figure 8.6 illustrates how the method of steepest descent, when applied in a quadratic bowl, progresses in a rather ineffective back-and-forth zig-zag pattern. This happens because each line search direction, when given by the gradient, is guaranteed to be orthogonal to the previous line search direction.

Let the previous search direction be d_{t-1}. At the minimum, where the line search terminates, the directional derivative is zero in direction d_{t-1}: $\nabla_{\theta} J(\theta) \cdot d_{t-1} = 0$. Since the gradient at this point defines the current search direction, $d_t = \nabla_{\theta} J(\theta)$ will have no contribution in the direction d_{t-1}. Thus d_t is orthogonal to d_{t-1}. This relationship between d_{t-1} and d_t is illustrated in figure 8.6 for multiple iterations of steepest descent. As demonstrated in the figure, the choice of orthogonal directions of descent do not preserve the minimum along the previous search directions. This gives rise to the zig-zag pattern of progress, where by descending to the minimum in the current gradient direction, we must reminimize the objective in the previous gradient direction. Thus, by following the gradient at the end of each line search we are, in a sense, undoing progress we have already made in the direction of the previous line search. The method of conjugate gradients seeks to address this problem.

In the method of conjugate gradients, we seek to find a search direction that is **conjugate** to the previous line search direction; that is, it will not undo progress made in that direction. At training iteration t, the next search direction $\boldsymbol{d}_t$ takes the form:

$$\boldsymbol{d}_t = \nabla_{\boldsymbol{\theta}} J(\boldsymbol{\theta}) + \beta_t \boldsymbol{d}_{t-1}, \tag{8.29}$$

where β_t is a coefficient whose magnitude controls how much of the direction, $\boldsymbol{d}_{t-1}$, we should add back to the current search direction.

Two directions, $\boldsymbol{d}_t$ and $\boldsymbol{d}_{t-1}$, are defined as conjugate if $\boldsymbol{d}_t^\top \boldsymbol{H} \boldsymbol{d}_{t-1} = 0$, where $\boldsymbol{H}$ is the Hessian matrix.

The straightforward way to impose conjugacy would involve calculation of the eigenvectors of $\boldsymbol{H}$ to choose β_t, which would not satisfy our goal of developing a method that is more computationally viable than Newton's method for large problems. Can we calculate the conjugate directions without resorting to these calculations? Fortunately, the answer to that is yes.

Two popular methods for computing the β_t are

1. Fletcher-Reeves:

$$\beta_t = \frac{\nabla_{\boldsymbol{\theta}} J(\boldsymbol{\theta}_t)^\top \nabla_{\boldsymbol{\theta}} J(\boldsymbol{\theta}_t)}{\nabla_{\boldsymbol{\theta}} J(\boldsymbol{\theta}_{t-1})^\top \nabla_{\boldsymbol{\theta}} J(\boldsymbol{\theta}_{t-1})} \tag{8.30}$$

2. Polak-Ribière:

$$\beta_t = \frac{(\nabla_{\boldsymbol{\theta}} J(\boldsymbol{\theta}_t) - \nabla_{\boldsymbol{\theta}} J(\boldsymbol{\theta}_{t-1}))^\top \nabla_{\boldsymbol{\theta}} J(\boldsymbol{\theta}_t)}{\nabla_{\boldsymbol{\theta}} J(\boldsymbol{\theta}_{t-1})^\top \nabla_{\boldsymbol{\theta}} J(\boldsymbol{\theta}_{t-1})} \tag{8.31}$$

For a quadratic surface, the conjugate directions ensure that the gradient along the previous direction does not increase in magnitude. We therefore stay at the minimum along the previous directions. As a consequence, in a k-dimensional parameter space, the conjugate gradient method requires at most k line searches to achieve the minimum. The conjugate gradient algorithm is given in algorithm 8.9.

Nonlinear Conjugate Gradients: So far we have discussed the method of conjugate gradients as it is applied to quadratic objective functions. Of course, our primary interest in this chapter is to explore optimization methods for training neural networks and other related deep learning models where the corresponding objective function is far from quadratic. Perhaps surprisingly, the method of conjugate gradients is still applicable in this setting, though with some modification. Without any assurance that the objective is quadratic, the conjugate directions are no longer assured to remain at the minimum of the objective for previous directions. As a result, the **nonlinear conjugate gradients** algorithm includes

---

Algorithm 8.9 The conjugate gradient method

Require: Initial parameters $\boldsymbol{\theta}_0$
Require: Training set of m examples
    Initialize $\boldsymbol{\rho}_0 = \mathbf{0}$
    Initialize $g_0 = 0$
    Initialize $t = 1$
    while stopping criterion not met **do**
        Initialize the gradient $\boldsymbol{g}_t = \mathbf{0}$
        Compute gradient: $\boldsymbol{g}_t \leftarrow \frac{1}{m} \nabla_{\boldsymbol{\theta}} \sum_i L(f(\boldsymbol{x}^{(i)}; \boldsymbol{\theta}), \boldsymbol{y}^{(i)})$
        Compute $\beta_t = \frac{(\boldsymbol{g}_t - \boldsymbol{g}_{t-1})^\top \boldsymbol{g}_t}{\boldsymbol{g}_{t-1}^\top \boldsymbol{g}_{t-1}}$ (Polak-Ribière)
        (Nonlinear conjugate gradient: optionally reset β_t to zero, for example if t is a multiple of some constant k, such as $k = 5$)
        Compute search direction: $\boldsymbol{\rho}_t = -\boldsymbol{g}_t + \beta_t \boldsymbol{\rho}_{t-1}$
        Perform line search to find: $\epsilon^* = \arg\min_\epsilon \frac{1}{m} \sum_{i=1}^m L(f(\boldsymbol{x}^{(i)}; \boldsymbol{\theta}_t + \epsilon \boldsymbol{\rho}_t), \boldsymbol{y}^{(i)})$
        (On a truly quadratic cost function, analytically solve for ϵ^* rather than explicitly searching for it)
        Apply update: $\boldsymbol{\theta}_{t+1} = \boldsymbol{\theta}_t + \epsilon^* \boldsymbol{\rho}_t$
        $t \leftarrow t + 1$
    end while

---

occasional resets where the method of conjugate gradients is restarted with line search along the unaltered gradient.

Practitioners report reasonable results in applications of the nonlinear conjugate gradients algorithm to training neural networks, though it is often beneficial to initialize the optimization with a few iterations of stochastic gradient descent before commencing nonlinear conjugate gradients. Also, while the (nonlinear) conjugate gradients algorithm has traditionally been cast as a batch method, minibatch versions have been used successfully for training neural networks (Le et al., 2011). Adaptations of conjugate gradients specifically for neural networks have been proposed earlier, such as the scaled conjugate gradients algorithm (Moller, 1993).

8.6.3 BFGS

The **Broyden–Fletcher–Goldfarb–Shanno (BFGS) algorithm** attempts to bring some of the advantages of Newton's method without the computational burden. In that respect, BFGS is similar to the conjugate gradient method.

However, BFGS takes a more direct approach to the approximation of Newton's update. Recall that Newton's update is given by

$$\boldsymbol{\theta}^* = \boldsymbol{\theta}_0 - \boldsymbol{H}^{-1}\nabla_{\boldsymbol{\theta}}J(\boldsymbol{\theta}_0), \tag{8.32}$$

where $\boldsymbol{H}$ is the Hessian of J with respect to $\boldsymbol{\theta}$ evaluated at $\boldsymbol{\theta}_0$. The primary computational difficulty in applying Newton's update is the calculation of the inverse Hessian $\boldsymbol{H}^{-1}$. The approach adopted by quasi-Newton methods (of which the BFGS algorithm is the most prominent) is to approximate the inverse with a matrix $\boldsymbol{M}_t$ that is iteratively refined by low-rank updates to become a better approximation of $\boldsymbol{H}^{-1}$.

The specification and derivation of the BFGS approximation is given in many textbooks on optimization, including in Luenberger (1984).

Once the inverse Hessian approximation $\boldsymbol{M}_t$ is updated, the direction of descent $\boldsymbol{\rho}_t$ is determined by $\boldsymbol{\rho}_t = \boldsymbol{M}_t\boldsymbol{g}_t$. A line search is performed in this direction to determine the size of the step, ϵ^*, taken in this direction. The final update to the parameters is given by

$$\boldsymbol{\theta}_{t+1} = \boldsymbol{\theta}_t + \epsilon^*\boldsymbol{\rho}_t. \tag{8.33}$$

Like the method of conjugate gradients, the BFGS algorithm iterates a series of line searches with the direction incorporating second-order information. Unlike conjugate gradients, however, the success of the approach is not heavily dependent on the line search finding a point very close to the true minimum along the line. Thus, relative to conjugate gradients, BFGS has the advantage that it can spend less time refining each line search. On the other hand, the BFGS algorithm must store the inverse Hessian matrix, $\boldsymbol{M}$, that requires $O(n^2)$ memory, making BFGS impractical for most modern deep learning models that typically have millions of parameters.

Limited Memory BFGS (or L-BFGS)   The memory costs of the BFGS algorithm can be significantly decreased by avoiding storing the complete inverse Hessian approximation $\boldsymbol{M}$. The L-BFGS algorithm computes the approximation $\boldsymbol{M}$ using the same method as the BFGS algorithm but beginning with the assumption that $\boldsymbol{M}^{(t-1)}$ is the identity matrix, rather than storing the approximation from one step to the next. If used with exact line searches, the directions defined by L-BFGS are mutually conjugate. However, unlike the method of conjugate gradients, this procedure remains well behaved when the minimum of the line search is reached only approximately. The L-BFGS strategy with no storage described here can be generalized to include more information about the Hessian by storing some of the vectors used to update $\boldsymbol{M}$ at each time step, which costs only $O(n)$ per step.

8.7 Optimization Strategies and Meta-Algorithms

Many optimization techniques are not exactly algorithms but rather general templates that can be specialized to yield algorithms, or subroutines that can be incorporated into many different algorithms.

8.7.1 Batch Normalization

Batch normalization (Ioffe and Szegedy, 2015) is one of the most exciting recent innovations in optimizing deep neural networks, and it is actually not an optimization algorithm at all. Instead, it is a method of adaptive reparametrization, motivated by the difficulty of training very deep models.

Very deep models involve the composition of several functions, or layers. The gradient tells how to update each parameter, under the assumption that the other layers do not change. In practice, we update all the layers simultaneously. When we make the update, unexpected results can happen because many functions composed together are changed simultaneously, using updates that were computed under the assumption that the other functions remain constant. As a simple example, suppose we have a deep neural network that has only one unit per layer and does not use an activation function at each hidden layer: $\hat{y} = x w_1 w_2 w_3 \ldots w_l$. Here, w_i provides the weight used by layer i. The output of layer i is $h_i = h_{i-1} w_i$. The output $\hat{y}$ is a linear function of the input x but a nonlinear function of the weights w_i. Suppose our cost function has put a gradient of 1 on $\hat{y}$, so we wish to decrease $\hat{y}$ slightly. The back-propagation algorithm can then compute a gradient $\boldsymbol{g} = \nabla_{\boldsymbol{w}} \hat{y}$. Consider what happens when we make an update $\boldsymbol{w} \leftarrow \boldsymbol{w} - \epsilon \boldsymbol{g}$. The first-order Taylor series approximation of $\hat{y}$ predicts that the value of $\hat{y}$ will decrease by $\epsilon \boldsymbol{g}^\top \boldsymbol{g}$. If we wanted to decrease $\hat{y}$ by 0.1, this first-order information available in the gradient suggests we could set the learning rate ϵ to $\frac{0.1}{\boldsymbol{g}^\top \boldsymbol{g}}$. Yet, the actual update will include second-order and third-order effects, on up to effects of order l. The new value of $\hat{y}$ is given by

$$x(w_1 - \epsilon g_1)(w_2 - \epsilon g_2) \ldots (w_l - \epsilon g_l). \tag{8.34}$$

An example of one second-order term arising from this update is $\epsilon^2 g_1 g_2 \prod_{i=3}^{l} w_i$. This term might be negligible if $\prod_{i=3}^{l} w_i$ is small, or might be exponentially large if the weights on layers 3 through l are greater than 1. This makes it very hard to choose an appropriate learning rate, because the effects of an update to the parameters for one layer depend so strongly on all the other layers. Second-order optimization algorithms address this issue by computing an update that takes these second-order interactions into account, but we can see that in very deep networks, even higher-order interactions can be significant. Even second-order optimization algorithms are expensive and usually require numerous approximations that prevent them from truly accounting for all significant second-order interactions. Building an n-th order optimization algorithm for $n > 2$ thus seems hopeless. What can we do instead?

Batch normalization provides an elegant way of reparametrizing almost any deep network. The reparametrization significantly reduces the problem of coordinating updates across many layers. Batch normalization can be applied to any input or hidden layer in a network. Let $\boldsymbol{H}$ be a minibatch of activations of the layer to normalize, arranged as a design matrix, with the activations for each example appearing in a row of the matrix. To normalize $\boldsymbol{H}$, we replace it with

$$\boldsymbol{H}' = \frac{\boldsymbol{H} - \boldsymbol{\mu}}{\boldsymbol{\sigma}}, \tag{8.35}$$

where $\boldsymbol{\mu}$ is a vector containing the mean of each unit and $\boldsymbol{\sigma}$ is a vector containing the standard deviation of each unit. The arithmetic here is based on broadcasting the vector $\boldsymbol{\mu}$ and the vector $\boldsymbol{\sigma}$ to be applied to every row of the matrix $\boldsymbol{H}$. Within each row, the arithmetic is element-wise, so $H_{i,j}$ is normalized by subtracting μ_j and dividing by σ_j. The rest of the network then operates on $\boldsymbol{H}'$ in exactly the same way that the original network operated on $\boldsymbol{H}$.

At training time,

$$\boldsymbol{\mu} = \frac{1}{m} \sum_i \boldsymbol{H}_{i,:} \tag{8.36}$$

and

$$\boldsymbol{\sigma} = \sqrt{\delta + \frac{1}{m} \sum_i (\boldsymbol{H} - \boldsymbol{\mu})_i^2}, \tag{8.37}$$

where δ is a small positive value such as 10^{-8}, imposed to avoid encountering the undefined gradient of $\sqrt{z}$ at $z = 0$. Crucially, *we back-propagate through these operations* for computing the mean and the standard deviation, and for applying them to normalize $\boldsymbol{H}$. This means that the gradient will never propose an operation that acts simply to increase the standard deviation or mean of h_i; the normalization operations remove the effect of such an action and zero out its component in the gradient. This was a major innovation of the batch normalization approach. Previous approaches had involved adding penalties to the cost function to encourage units to have normalized activation statistics or involved intervening to renormalize unit statistics after each gradient descent step. The former approach usually resulted in imperfect normalization and the latter usually resulted in significant wasted time, as the learning algorithm repeatedly proposed changing the mean and variance, and the normalization step repeatedly undid this change. Batch normalization reparametrizes the model to make some units always be standardized by definition, deftly sidestepping both problems.

At test time, $\boldsymbol{\mu}$ and $\boldsymbol{\sigma}$ may be replaced by running averages that were collected during training time. This allows the model to be evaluated on a single example, without needing to use definitions of $\boldsymbol{\mu}$ and $\boldsymbol{\sigma}$ that depend on an entire minibatch.

Revisiting the $\hat{y} = xw_1w_2\ldots w_l$ example, we see that we can mostly resolve the difficulties in learning this model by normalizing h_{l-1}. Suppose that x is drawn from a unit Gaussian. Then h_{l-1} will also come from a Gaussian, because the transformation from x to h_l is linear. However, h_{l-1} will no longer have zero mean and unit variance. After applying batch normalization, we obtain the normalized $\hat{h}_{l-1}$ that restores the zero mean and unit variance properties. For almost any update to the lower layers, $\hat{h}_{l-1}$ will remain a unit Gaussian. The output $\hat{y}$ may then be learned as a simple linear function $\hat{y} = w_l\hat{h}_{l-1}$. Learning in this model is now very simple because the parameters at the lower layers do not have an effect in most cases; their output is always renormalized to a unit Gaussian. In some corner cases, the lower layers can have an effect. Changing one of the lower layer weights to 0 can make the output become degenerate, and changing the sign of one of the lower weights can flip the relationship between $\hat{h}_{l-1}$ and y. These situations are very rare. Without normalization, nearly every update would have an extreme effect on the statistics of h_{l-1}. Batch normalization has thus made this model significantly easier to learn. In this example, the ease of learning of course came at the cost of making the lower layers useless. In our linear example, the lower layers no longer have any harmful effect, but they also no longer have any beneficial effect. This is because we have normalized out the first- and second-order statistics, which is all that a linear network can influence. In a deep neural network with nonlinear activation functions, the lower layers can perform nonlinear transformations of the data, so they remain useful. Batch normalization acts to standardize only the mean and variance of each unit in order to stabilize learning, but it allows the relationships between units and the nonlinear statistics of a single unit to change.

Because the final layer of the network is able to learn a linear transformation, we may actually wish to remove all linear relationships between units within a layer. Indeed, this is the approach taken by Desjardins et al. (2015), who provided the inspiration for batch normalization. Unfortunately, eliminating all linear interactions is much more expensive than standardizing the mean and standard deviation of each individual unit, and so far batch normalization remains the most practical approach.

Normalizing the mean and standard deviation of a unit can reduce the expressive power of the neural network containing that unit. To maintain the expressive power of the network, it is common to replace the batch of hidden unit activations $\boldsymbol{H}$ with $\boldsymbol{\gamma} \boldsymbol{H}' + \boldsymbol{\beta}$ rather than simply the normalized $\boldsymbol{H}'$. The variables $\boldsymbol{\gamma}$ and $\boldsymbol{\beta}$ are learned parameters that allow the new variable to have any mean and standard deviation. At first glance, this may seem useless—why did we set the mean to $\boldsymbol{0}$, and then introduce a parameter that allows it to be set back to any arbitrary value $\boldsymbol{\beta}$? The answer is that the new parametrization can represent the same family of functions of the input as the old parametrization, but the new parametrization has different learning dynamics. In the old parametrization, the mean of $\boldsymbol{H}$ was determined by a complicated interaction between the parameters in the layers below $\boldsymbol{H}$. In the new parametrization, the mean of $\boldsymbol{\gamma} \boldsymbol{H}' + \boldsymbol{\beta}$ is determined solely by $\boldsymbol{\beta}$. The new parametrization is much easier to learn with gradient descent.

Most neural network layers take the form of $\phi(\boldsymbol{X}\boldsymbol{W} + \boldsymbol{b})$, where ϕ is some fixed nonlinear activation function such as the rectified linear transformation. It is natural to wonder whether we should apply batch normalization to the input $\boldsymbol{X}$, or to the transformed value $\boldsymbol{X}\boldsymbol{W} + \boldsymbol{b}$. Ioffe and Szegedy (2015) recommend the latter. More specifically, $\boldsymbol{X}\boldsymbol{W} + \boldsymbol{b}$ should be replaced by a normalized version of $\boldsymbol{X}\boldsymbol{W}$. The bias term should be omitted because it becomes redundant with the β parameter applied by the batch normalization reparametrization. The input to a layer is usually the output of a nonlinear activation function such as the rectified linear function in a previous layer. The statistics of the input are thus more non-Gaussian and less amenable to standardization by linear operations.

In convolutional networks, described in chapter 9, it is important to apply the same normalizing μ and σ at every spatial location within a feature map, so that the statistics of the feature map remain the same regardless of spatial location.

8.7.2 Coordinate Descent

In some cases, it may be possible to solve an optimization problem quickly by breaking it into separate pieces. If we minimize $f(\boldsymbol{x})$ with respect to a single variable x_i, then minimize it with respect to another variable x_j, and so on, repeatedly cycling through all variables, we are guaranteed to arrive at a (local) minimum. This practice is known as **coordinate descent**, because we optimize one coordinate at a time. More generally, **block coordinate descent** refers to minimizing with respect to a subset of the variables simultaneously. The term "coordinate descent" is often used to refer to block coordinate descent as well as the strictly individual coordinate descent.

Coordinate descent makes the most sense when the different variables in the optimization problem can be clearly separated into groups that play relatively isolated roles, or when optimization with respect to one group of variables is significantly more efficient than optimization with respect to all of the variables. For example, consider the cost function

$$J(\boldsymbol{H}, \boldsymbol{W}) = \sum_{i,j} |H_{i,j}| + \sum_{i,j} \left(\boldsymbol{X} - \boldsymbol{W}^\top \boldsymbol{H} \right)^2_{i,j}. \tag{8.38}$$

This function describes a learning problem called sparse coding, where the goal is to find a weight matrix $\boldsymbol{W}$ that can linearly decode a matrix of activation values $\boldsymbol{H}$ to reconstruct the training set $\boldsymbol{X}$. Most applications of sparse coding also involve weight decay or a constraint on the norms of the columns of $\boldsymbol{W}$, to prevent the pathological solution with extremely small $\boldsymbol{H}$ and large $\boldsymbol{W}$.

The function J is not convex. However, we can divide the inputs to the training algorithm into two sets: the dictionary parameters $\boldsymbol{W}$ and the code representations $\boldsymbol{H}$. Minimizing the objective function with respect to either one of these sets of variables is a convex problem. Block coordinate descent thus gives us an optimization strategy that allows us to use efficient convex optimization algorithms, by alternating between optimizing $\boldsymbol{W}$ with $\boldsymbol{H}$ fixed, then optimizing $\boldsymbol{H}$ with $\boldsymbol{W}$ fixed.

Coordinate descent is not a very good strategy when the value of one variable strongly influences the optimal value of another variable, as in the function $f(\boldsymbol{x}) = (x_1 - x_2)^2 + \alpha \left(x_1^2 + x_2^2 \right)$ where α is a positive constant. The first term encourages the two variables to have similar value, while the second term encourages them to be near zero. The solution is to set both to zero. Newton's method can solve the problem in a single step because it is a positive definite quadratic problem. For small α, however, coordinate descent will make very slow progress because the first term does not allow a single variable to be changed to a value that differs significantly from the current value of the other variable.

8.7.3 Polyak Averaging

Polyak averaging (Polyak and Juditsky, 1992) consists of averaging several points in the trajectory through parameter space visited by an optimization algorithm. If t iterations of gradient descent visit points $\boldsymbol{\theta}^{(1)}, \ldots, \boldsymbol{\theta}^{(t)}$, then the output of the Polyak averaging algorithm is $\hat{\boldsymbol{\theta}}^{(t)} = \frac{1}{t} \sum_i \boldsymbol{\theta}^{(i)}$. On some problem classes, such as gradient descent applied to convex problems, this approach has strong convergence guarantees. When applied to neural networks, its justification is more heuristic, but it performs well in practice. The basic idea is that the optimization algorithm may leap back and forth across a valley several times without ever visiting a point near the bottom of the valley. The average of all the locations on either side should be close to the bottom of the valley though.

In nonconvex problems, the path taken by the optimization trajectory can be very complicated and visit many different regions. Including points in parameter space from the distant past that may be separated from the current point by large barriers in the cost function does not seem like a useful behavior. As a result, when applying Polyak averaging to nonconvex problems, it is typical to use an exponentially decaying running average:

$$\hat{\boldsymbol{\theta}}^{(t)} = \alpha \hat{\boldsymbol{\theta}}^{(t-1)} + (1 - \alpha)\boldsymbol{\theta}^{(t)}. \tag{8.39}$$

The running average approach is used in numerous applications. See Szegedy et al. (2015) for a recent example.

8.7.4 Supervised Pretraining

Sometimes, directly training a model to solve a specific task can be too ambitious if the model is complex and hard to optimize or if the task is very difficult. It is sometimes more effective to train a simpler model to solve the task, then make the model more complex. It can also be more effective to train the model to solve a simpler task, then move on to confront the final task. These strategies that involve training simple models on simple tasks before confronting the challenge of training the desired model to perform the desired task are collectively known as **pretraining**.

Greedy algorithms break a problem into many components, then solve for the optimal version of each component in isolation. Unfortunately, combining the individually optimal components is not guaranteed to yield an optimal complete solution. Nonetheless, greedy algorithms can be computationally much cheaper than algorithms that solve for the best joint solution, and the quality of a greedy solution is often acceptable if not optimal. Greedy algorithms may also be followed by a **fine-tuning** stage in which a joint optimization algorithm searches for an optimal solution to the full problem. Initializing the joint optimization algorithm with a greedy solution can greatly speed it up and improve the quality of the solution it finds.

Pretraining, and especially greedy pretraining, algorithms are ubiquitous in deep learning. In this section, we describe specifically those pretraining algorithms that break supervised learning problems into other simpler supervised learning problems. This approach is known as **greedy supervised pretraining**.

In the original (Bengio et al., 2007) version of greedy supervised pretraining, each stage consists of a supervised learning training task involving only a subset of the layers in the final neural network. An example of greedy supervised pretraining is illustrated in figure 8.7, in which each added hidden layer is pretrained as part of a shallow supervised MLP, taking as input the output of the previously trained hidden layer. Instead of pretraining one layer at a time, Simonyan and Zisserman (2015) pretrain a deep convolutional network (eleven weight layers) and then use the first four and last three layers from this network to initialize even deeper networks (with up to nineteen layers of weights). The middle layers of the new, very deep network are initialized randomly. The new network is then jointly trained. Another option, explored by Yu et al. (2010), is to use the *outputs* of the previously trained MLPs, as well as the raw input, as inputs for each added stage.

Why would greedy supervised pretraining help? The hypothesis initially discussed by Bengio et al. (2007) is that it helps to provide better guidance to the intermediate levels of a deep hierarchy. In general, pretraining may help both in terms of optimization and generalization.

An approach related to supervised pretraining extends the idea to the context of transfer learning: Yosinski et al. (2014) pretrain a deep convolutional net with eight layers of weights on a set of tasks (a subset of the 1,000 ImageNet object categories) and then initialize a same-size network with the first k layers of the first net. All the layers of the second network (with the upper layers initialized randomly) are then jointly trained to perform a different set of tasks (another subset of the 1,000 ImageNet object categories), with fewer training examples than for the first set of tasks. Other approaches to transfer learning with neural networks are discussed in section 15.2.

Another related line of work is the **FitNets** (Romero et al., 2015) approach. This approach begins by training a network that has low enough depth and great enough width (number of units per layer) to be easy to train. This network then becomes a **teacher** for a second network, designated the **student**. The student network is much deeper and thinner (eleven to nineteen layers) and would be difficult to train with SGD under normal circumstances. The training of the student network is made easier by training the student network not only to predict the output for the original task, but also to predict the value of the middle layer of the teacher network. This extra task provides a set of hints about how the hidden layers should be used and can simplify the optimization problem. Additional parameters are introduced to regress the middle layer of the five layer teacher

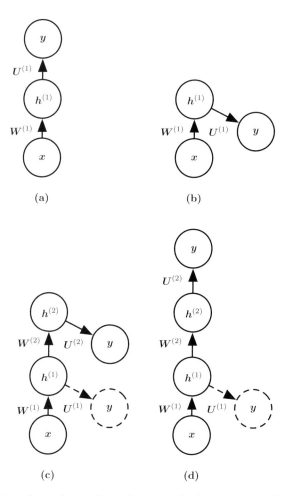

Figure 8.7: Illustration of one form of greedy supervised pretraining (Bengio et al., 2007). *(a)*We start by training a sufficiently shallow architecture. *(b)*Another drawing of the same architecture. *(c)*We keep only the input-to-hidden layer of the original network and discard the hidden-to-output layer. We send the output of the first hidden layer as input to another supervised single hidden layer MLP that is trained with the same objective as the first network was, thus adding a second hidden layer. This can be repeated for as many layers as desired. *(d)*Another drawing of the result, viewed as a feedforward network. To further improve the optimization, we can jointly fine-tune all the layers, either only at the end or at each stage of this process.

network from the middle layer of the deeper student network. Instead of predicting the final classification target, however, the objective is to predict the middle hidden layer of the teacher network. The lower layers of the student networks thus have two objectives: to help the outputs of the student network accomplish their task, as well as to predict the intermediate layer of the teacher network. Although a thin and deep network appears to be more difficult to train than a wide and shallow network, the thin and deep network may generalize better and certainly has lower computational cost if it is thin enough to have far fewer parameters. Without the hints on the hidden layer, the student network performs very poorly in the experiments, on both the training and the test set. Hints on middle layers may thus be one of the tools to help train neural networks that otherwise seem difficult to train, but other optimization techniques or changes in the architecture may also solve the problem.

8.7.5 Designing Models to Aid Optimization

To improve optimization, the best strategy is not always to improve the optimization algorithm. Instead, many improvements in the optimization of deep models have come from designing the models to be easier to optimize.

In principle, we could use activation functions that increase and decrease in jagged nonmonotonic patterns, but this would make optimization extremely difficult. In practice, *it is more important to choose a model family that is easy to optimize than to use a powerful optimization algorithm*. Most of the advances in neural network learning over the past thirty years have been obtained by changing the model family rather than changing the optimization procedure. Stochastic gradient descent with momentum, which was used to train neural networks in the 1980s, remains in use in modern state-of-the-art neural network applications.

Specifically, modern neural networks reflect a *design choice* to use linear transformations between layers and activation functions that are differentiable almost everywhere, with significant slope in large portions of their domain. In particular, model innovations like the LSTM, rectified linear units and maxout units have all moved toward using more linear functions than previous models like deep networks based on sigmoidal units. These models have nice properties that make optimization easier. The gradient flows through many layers provided that the Jacobian of the linear transformation has reasonable singular values. Moreover, linear functions consistently increase in a single direction, so even if the model's output is very far from correct, it is clear simply from computing the gradient which direction its output should move to reduce the loss function. In other words, modern neural nets have been designed so that their *local* gradient information corresponds reasonably well to moving toward a distant solution.

Other model design strategies can help to make optimization easier. For example, linear paths or skip connections between layers reduce the length of the shortest path from the lower layer's parameters to the output, and thus mitigate the vanishing gradient problem (Srivastava et al., 2015). A related idea to skip connections is adding extra copies of the output that are attached to the intermediate hidden layers of the network, as in GoogLeNet (Szegedy et al., 2014a) and deeply supervised nets (Lee et al., 2014). These "auxiliary heads" are trained to perform the same task as the primary output at the top of the network to ensure that the lower layers receive a large gradient. When training is complete, the auxiliary heads may be discarded. This is an alternative to the pretraining strategies, which were introduced in the previous section. In this way, one can train jointly all the layers in a single phase but change the architecture, so that intermediate layers (especially the lower ones) can get some hints about what they should do, via a shorter path. These hints provide an error signal to lower layers.

8.7.6 Continuation Methods and Curriculum Learning

As argued in section 8.2.7, many of the challenges in optimization arise from the global structure of the cost function and cannot be resolved merely by making better estimates of local update directions. The predominant strategy for overcoming this problem is to attempt to initialize the parameters in a region connected to the solution by a short path through parameter space that local descent can discover.

Continuation methods are a family of strategies that can make optimization easier by choosing initial points to ensure that local optimization spends most of its time in well-behaved regions of space. The idea behind continuation methods is to construct a series of objective functions over the same parameters. To minimize a cost function $J(\boldsymbol{\theta})$, we construct new cost functions $\{J^{(0)}, \ldots, J^{(n)}\}$. These cost functions are designed to be increasingly difficult, with $J^{(0)}$ being fairly easy to minimize, and $J^{(n)}$, the most difficult, being $J(\boldsymbol{\theta})$, the true cost function motivating the entire process. When we say that $J^{(i)}$ is easier than $J^{(i+1)}$, we mean that it is well behaved over more of $\boldsymbol{\theta}$ space. A random initialization is more likely to land in the region where local descent can minimize the cost function successfully because this region is larger. The series of cost functions are designed so that a solution to one is a good initial point of the next. We thus begin by solving an easy problem, then refine the solution to solve incrementally harder problems until we arrive at a solution to the true underlying problem.

Traditional continuation methods (predating the use of continuation methods for neural network training) are usually based on smoothing the objective function. See Wu (1997) for an example of such a method and a review of some related methods. Continuation methods are also closely related to simulated annealing, which adds noise to the parameters (Kirkpatrick et al., 1983). Continuation methods have been extremely successful in recent years. See Mobahi and Fisher (2015) for an overview of recent literature, especially for AI applications.

Continuation methods traditionally were mostly designed with the goal of overcoming the challenge of local minima. Specifically, they were designed to reach a global minimum despite the presence of many local minima. To do so, these continuation methods would construct easier cost functions by "blurring" the original cost function. This blurring operation can be done by approximating

$$J^{(i)}(\boldsymbol{\theta}) = \mathbb{E}_{\theta' \sim \mathcal{N}(\boldsymbol{\theta}'; \boldsymbol{\theta}, \sigma^{(i)2})} J(\boldsymbol{\theta}') \tag{8.40}$$

via sampling. The intuition for this approach is that some nonconvex functions become approximately convex when blurred. In many cases, this blurring preserves enough information about the location of a global minimum that we can find the global minimum by solving progressively less-blurred versions of the problem. This approach can break down in three different ways. First, it might successfully define a series of cost functions where the first is convex and the optimum tracks from one function to the next, arriving at the global minimum, but it might require so many incremental cost functions that the cost of the entire procedure remains high. NP-hard optimization problems remain NP-hard, even when continuation methods are applicable. The other two ways continuation methods fail both correspond to the method not being applicable. First, the function might not become convex, no matter how much it is blurred. Consider, for example, the function $J(\boldsymbol{\theta}) = -\boldsymbol{\theta}^\top \boldsymbol{\theta}$. Second, the function may become convex as a result of blurring, but the minimum of this blurred function may track to a local rather than a global minimum of the original cost function.

Though continuation methods were mostly originally designed to deal with the problem of local minima, local minima are no longer believed to be the primary problem for neural network optimization. Fortunately, continuation methods can still help. The easier objective functions introduced by the continuation method can eliminate flat regions, decrease variance in gradient estimates, improve conditioning of the Hessian matrix, or do anything else that will either make local updates easier to compute or improve the correspondence between local update directions and progress toward a global solution.

Bengio et al. (2009) observed that an approach called **curriculum learning**, or **shaping**, can be interpreted as a continuation method. Curriculum learning is based on the idea of planning a learning process to begin by learning simple concepts and progress to learning more complex concepts that depend on these simpler concepts. This basic strategy was previously known to accelerate progress in animal training (Skinner, 1958; Peterson, 2004; Krueger and Dayan, 2009) and in machine learning (Solomonoff, 1989; Elman, 1993; Sanger, 1994). Bengio et al. (2009)

justified this strategy as a continuation method, where earlier $J^{(i)}$ are made easier by increasing the influence of simpler examples (either by assigning their contributions to the cost function larger coefficients, or by sampling them more frequently), and experimentally demonstrated that better results could be obtained by following a curriculum on a large-scale neural language modeling task. Curriculum learning has been successful on a wide range of natural language (Spitkovsky et al., 2010; Collobert et al., 2011a; Mikolov et al., 2011b; Tu and Honavar, 2011) and computer vision (Kumar et al., 2010; Lee and Grauman, 2011; Supancic and Ramanan, 2013) tasks. Curriculum learning was also verified as being consistent with the way in which humans *teach* (Khan et al., 2011): teachers start by showing easier and more prototypical examples and then help the learner refine the decision surface with the less obvious cases. Curriculum-based strategies are *more effective* for teaching humans than strategies based on uniform sampling of examples and can also increase the effectiveness of other teaching strategies (Basu and Christensen, 2013).

Another important contribution to research on curriculum learning arose in the context of training recurrent neural networks to capture long-term dependencies: Zaremba and Sutskever (2014) found that much better results were obtained with a *stochastic curriculum*, in which a random mix of easy and difficult examples is always presented to the learner, but where the average proportion of the more difficult examples (here, those with longer-term dependencies) is gradually increased. With a deterministic curriculum, no improvement over the baseline (ordinary training from the full training set) was observed.

We have now described the basic family of neural network models and how to regularize and optimize them. In the chapters ahead, we turn to specializations of the neural network family that allow neural networks to scale to very large sizes and process input data that has special structure. The optimization methods discussed in this chapter are often directly applicable to these specialized architectures with little or no modification.

9

Convolutional Networks

Convolutional networks (LeCun, 1989), also known as **convolutional neural networks**, or CNNs, are a specialized kind of neural network for processing data that has a known grid-like topology. Examples include time-series data, which can be thought of as a 1-D grid taking samples at regular time intervals, and image data, which can be thought of as a 2-D grid of pixels. Convolutional networks have been tremendously successful in practical applications. The name "convolutional neural network" indicates that the network employs a mathematical operation called **convolution**. Convolution is a specialized kind of linear operation. *Convolutional networks are simply neural networks that use convolution in place of general matrix multiplication in at least one of their layers.*

In this chapter, we first describe what convolution is. Next, we explain the motivation behind using convolution in a neural network. We then describe an operation called **pooling**, which almost all convolutional networks employ. Usually, the operation used in a convolutional neural network does not correspond precisely to the definition of convolution as used in other fields, such as engineering or pure mathematics. We describe several variants on the convolution function that are widely used in practice for neural networks. We also show how convolution may be applied to many kinds of data, with different numbers of dimensions. We then discuss means of making convolution more efficient. Convolutional networks stand out as an example of neuroscientific principles influencing deep learning. We discuss these neuroscientific principles, then conclude with comments about the role convolutional networks have played in the history of deep learning. One topic this chapter does not address is how to choose the architecture of your convolutional network. The goal of this chapter is to describe the kinds of tools that convolutional networks provide, while chapter 11 describes general guidelines for choosing which tools to use in which circumstances. Research into convolutional network architectures proceeds so rapidly that a new best architecture for a given benchmark is announced every few weeks to months, rendering it impractical to describe in print the best architecture. Nonetheless, the best architectures have consistently been composed of the building blocks described here.

9.1   The Convolution Operation

In its most general form, convolution is an operation on two functions of a real-valued argument. To motivate the definition of convolution, we start with examples of two functions we might use.

Suppose we are tracking the location of a spaceship with a laser sensor. Our laser sensor provides a single output $x(t)$, the position of the spaceship at time t. Both x and t are real valued, that is, we can get a different reading from the laser sensor at any instant in time.

Now suppose that our laser sensor is somewhat noisy. To obtain a less noisy estimate of the spaceship's position, we would like to average several measurements. Of course, more recent measurements are more relevant, so we will want this to be a weighted average that gives more weight to recent measurements. We can do this with a weighting function $w(a)$, where a is the age of a measurement. If we apply such a weighted average operation at every moment, we obtain a new function s providing a smoothed estimate of the position of the spaceship:

$$s(t) = \int x(a)w(t - a)da. \tag{9.1}$$

This operation is called **convolution**. The convolution operation is typically denoted with an asterisk:

$$s(t) = (x * w)(t). \tag{9.2}$$

In our example, w needs to be a valid probability density function, or the output will not be a weighted average. Also, w needs to be 0 for all negative arguments, or it will look into the future, which is presumably beyond our capabilities. These limitations are particular to our example, though. In general, convolution is defined for any functions for which the above integral is defined and may be used for other purposes besides taking weighted averages.

In convolutional network terminology, the first argument (in this example, the function x) to the convolution is often referred to as the **input**, and the second argument (in this example, the function w) as the **kernel**. The output is sometimes referred to as the **feature map**.

In our example, the idea of a laser sensor that can provide measurements at every instant is not realistic. Usually, when we work with data on a computer, time will be discretized, and our sensor will provide data at regular intervals. In our example, it might be more realistic to assume that our laser provides a measurement once per second. The time index t can then take on only integer values. If we now assume that x and w are defined only on integer t, we can define the discrete convolution:

$$s(t) = (x * w)(t) = \sum_{a=-\infty}^{\infty} x(a)w(t-a). \tag{9.3}$$

In machine learning applications, the input is usually a multidimensional array of data, and the kernel is usually a multidimensional array of parameters that are adapted by the learning algorithm. We will refer to these multidimensional arrays as tensors. Because each element of the input and kernel must be explicitly stored separately, we usually assume that these functions are zero everywhere but in the finite set of points for which we store the values. This means that in practice, we can implement the infinite summation as a summation over a finite number of array elements.

Finally, we often use convolutions over more than one axis at a time. For example, if we use a two-dimensional image I as our input, we probably also want to use a two-dimensional kernel K:

$$S(i,j) = (I * K)(i,j) = \sum_m \sum_n I(m,n)K(i-m,j-n). \tag{9.4}$$

Convolution is commutative, meaning we can equivalently write

$$S(i,j) = (K * I)(i,j) = \sum_m \sum_n I(i-m,j-n)K(m,n). \tag{9.5}$$

Usually the latter formula is more straightforward to implement in a machine learning library, because there is less variation in the range of valid values of m and n.

The commutative property of convolution arises because we have **flipped** the kernel relative to the input, in the sense that as m increases, the index into the input increases, but the index into the kernel decreases. The only reason to flip the kernel is to obtain the commutative property. While the commutative property is useful for writing proofs, it is not usually an important property of a neural network implementation. Instead, many neural network libraries implement a related function called the **cross-correlation**, which is the same as convolution but without flipping the kernel:

$$S(i,j) = (I * K)(i,j) = \sum_m \sum_n I(i+m, j+n)K(m,n). \qquad (9.6)$$

Many machine learning libraries implement cross-correlation but call it convolution. In this text we follow this convention of calling both operations convolution and specify whether we mean to flip the kernel or not in contexts where kernel flipping is relevant. In the context of machine learning, the learning algorithm will learn the appropriate values of the kernel in the appropriate place, so an algorithm based on convolution with kernel flipping will learn a kernel that is flipped relative to the kernel learned by an algorithm without the flipping. It is also rare for convolution to be used alone in machine learning; instead convolution is used simultaneously with other functions, and the combination of these functions does not commute regardless of whether the convolution operation flips its kernel or not.

See figure 9.1 for an example of convolution (without kernel flipping) applied to a 2-D tensor.

Discrete convolution can be viewed as multiplication by a matrix, but the matrix has several entries constrained to be equal to other entries. For example, for univariate discrete convolution, each row of the matrix is constrained to be equal to the row above shifted by one element. This is known as a **Toeplitz matrix**. In two dimensions, a **doubly block circulant matrix** corresponds to convolution. In addition to these constraints that several elements be equal to each other, convolution usually corresponds to a very sparse matrix (a matrix whose entries are mostly equal to zero). This is because the kernel is usually much smaller than the input image. Any neural network algorithm that works with matrix multiplication and does not depend on specific properties of the matrix structure should work with convolution, without requiring any further changes to the neural network. Typical convolutional neural networks do make use of further specializations in order to deal with large inputs efficiently, but these are not strictly necessary from a theoretical perspective.

9.2   Motivation

Convolution leverages three important ideas that can help improve a machine learning system: **sparse interactions**, **parameter sharing** and **equivariant**

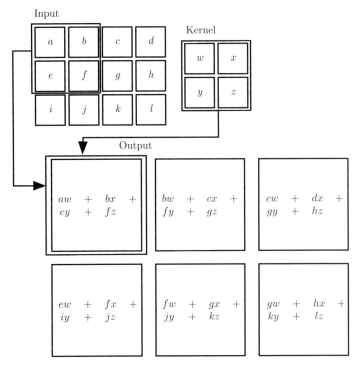

Figure 9.1: An example of 2-D convolution without kernel flipping. We restrict the output to only positions where the kernel lies entirely within the image, called "valid" convolution in some contexts. We draw boxes with arrows to indicate how the upper-left element of the output tensor is formed by applying the kernel to the corresponding upper-left region of the input tensor.

representations. Moreover, convolution provides a means for working with inputs of variable size. We now describe each of these ideas in turn.

Traditional neural network layers use matrix multiplication by a matrix of parameters with a separate parameter describing the interaction between each input unit and each output unit. This means that every output unit interacts with every input unit. Convolutional networks, however, typically have **sparse interactions** (also referred to as **sparse connectivity** or **sparse weights**). This is accomplished by making the kernel smaller than the input. For example, when processing an image, the input image might have thousands or millions of pixels, but we can detect small, meaningful features such as edges with kernels that occupy only tens or hundreds of pixels. This means that we need to store fewer parameters, which both reduces the memory requirements of the model and improves its statistical efficiency. It also means that computing the output requires fewer operations. These improvements in efficiency are usually quite large. If there are m inputs and n outputs, then matrix multiplication requires $m \times n$ parameters, and the algorithms used in practice have $O(m \times n)$ runtime (per example). If we limit the number of connections each output may have to k, then the sparsely connected approach requires only $k \times n$ parameters and $O(k \times n)$ runtime. For many practical applications, it is possible to obtain good performance on the machine learning task while keeping k several orders of magnitude smaller than m. For graphical demonstrations of sparse connectivity, see figure 9.2 and figure 9.3. In a deep convolutional network, units in the deeper layers may *indirectly* interact with a larger portion of the input, as shown in figure 9.4. This allows the network to efficiently describe complicated interactions between many variables by constructing such interactions from simple building blocks that each describe only sparse interactions.

Parameter sharing refers to using the same parameter for more than one function in a model. In a traditional neural net, each element of the weight matrix

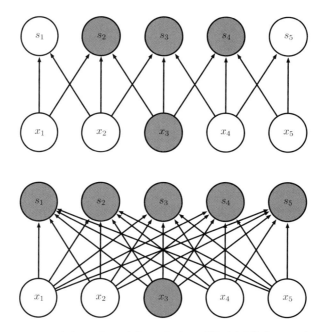

Figure 9.2: Sparse connectivity, viewed from below. We highlight one input unit, x_3, and highlight the output units in s that are affected by this unit. *(Top)*When s is formed by convolution with a kernel of width 3, only three outputs are affected by x. *(Bottom)*When s is formed by matrix multiplication, connectivity is no longer sparse, so all the outputs are affected by x_3.

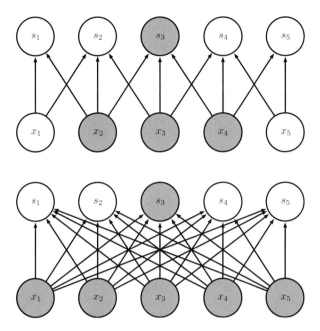

Figure 9.3: Sparse connectivity, viewed from above. We highlight one output unit, s_3, and highlight the input units in $\boldsymbol{x}$ that affect this unit. These units are known as the **receptive field** of s_3. *(Top)*When $\boldsymbol{s}$ is formed by convolution with a kernel of width 3, only three inputs affect s_3. *(Bottom)*When $\boldsymbol{s}$ is formed by matrix multiplication, connectivity is no longer sparse, so all the inputs affect s_3.

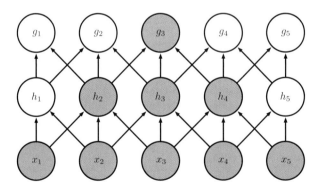

Figure 9.4: The receptive field of the units in the deeper layers of a convolutional network is larger than the receptive field of the units in the shallow layers. This effect increases if the network includes architectural features like strided convolution (figure 9.12) or pooling (section 9.3). This means that even though *direct* connections in a convolutional net are very sparse, units in the deeper layers can be *indirectly* connected to all or most of the input image.

is used exactly once when computing the output of a layer. It is multiplied by one element of the input and then never revisited. As a synonym for parameter sharing, one can say that a network has **tied weights**, because the value of the weight applied to one input is tied to the value of a weight applied elsewhere. In a convolutional neural net, each member of the kernel is used at every position of the input (except perhaps some of the boundary pixels, depending on the design decisions regarding the boundary). The parameter sharing used by the convolution operation means that rather than learning a separate set of parameters for every location, we learn only one set. This does not affect the runtime of forward propagation—it is still $O(k \times n)$—but it does further reduce the storage requirements of the model to k parameters. Recall that k is usually several orders of magnitude smaller than m. Since m and n are usually roughly the same size, k is practically insignificant compared to $m \times n$. Convolution is thus dramatically more efficient than dense matrix multiplication in terms of the memory requirements and statistical efficiency. For a graphical depiction of how parameter sharing works, see figure 9.5.

As an example of both of these first two principles in action, figure 9.6 shows how sparse connectivity and parameter sharing can dramatically improve the efficiency of a linear function for detecting edges in an image.

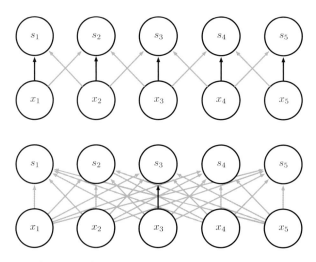

Figure 9.5: Parameter sharing. Black arrows indicate the connections that use a particular parameter in two different models. *(Top)*The black arrows indicate uses of the central element of a 3-element kernel in a convolutional model. Because of parameter sharing, this single parameter is used at all input locations. *(Bottom)*The single black arrow indicates the use of the central element of the weight matrix in a fully connected model. This model has no parameter sharing, so the parameter is used only once.

Figure 9.6: Efficiency of edge detection. The image on the right was formed by taking each pixel in the original image and subtracting the value of its neighboring pixel on the left. This shows the strength of all the vertically oriented edges in the input image, which can be a useful operation for object detection. Both images are 280 pixels tall. The input image is 320 pixels wide, while the output image is 319 pixels wide. This transformation can be described by a convolution kernel containing two elements, and requires $319 \times 280 \times 3 = 267,960$ floating-point operations (two multiplications and one addition per output pixel) to compute using convolution. To describe the same transformation with a matrix multiplication would take $320 \times 280 \times 319 \times 280$, or over eight billion, entries in the matrix, making convolution four billion times more efficient for representing this transformation. The straightforward matrix multiplication algorithm performs over sixteen billion floating point operations, making convolution roughly 60,000 times more efficient computationally. Of course, most of the entries of the matrix would be zero. If we stored only the nonzero entries of the matrix, then both matrix multiplication and convolution would require the same number of floating-point operations to compute. The matrix would still need to contain $2 \times 319 \times 280 = 178,640$ entries. Convolution is an extremely efficient way of describing transformations that apply the same linear transformation of a small local region across the entire input. Photo credit: Paula Goodfellow.

In the case of convolution, the particular form of parameter sharing causes the layer to have a property called **equivariance** to translation. To say a function is equivariant means that if the input changes, the output changes in the same way. Specifically, a function $f(x)$ is equivariant to a function g if $f(g(x)) = g(f(x))$. In the case of convolution, if we let g be any function that translates the input, that is, shifts it, then the convolution function is equivariant to g. For example, let I be a function giving image brightness at integer coordinates. Let g be a function mapping one image function to another image function, such that $I' = g(I)$ is the image function with $I'(x, y) = I(x - 1, y)$. This shifts every pixel of I one unit to the right. If we apply this transformation to I, then apply convolution, the result will be the same as if we applied convolution to I', then applied the transformation g to the output. When processing time-series data, this means that convolution produces a sort of timeline that shows when different features appear in the input.

If we move an event later in time in the input, the exact same representation of it will appear in the output, just later. Similarly with images, convolution creates a 2-D map of where certain features appear in the input. If we move the object in the input, its representation will move the same amount in the output. This is useful for when we know that some function of a small number of neighboring pixels is useful when applied to multiple input locations. For example, when processing images, it is useful to detect edges in the first layer of a convolutional network. The same edges appear more or less everywhere in the image, so it is practical to share parameters across the entire image. In some cases, we may not wish to share parameters across the entire image. For example, if we are processing images that are cropped to be centered on an individual's face, we probably want to extract different features at different locations—the part of the network processing the top of the face needs to look for eyebrows, while the part of the network processing the bottom of the face needs to look for a chin.

Convolution is not naturally equivariant to some other transformations, such as changes in the scale or rotation of an image. Other mechanisms are necessary for handling these kinds of transformations.

Finally, some kinds of data cannot be processed by neural networks defined by matrix multiplication with a fixed-shape matrix. Convolution enables processing of some of these kinds of data. We discuss this further in section 9.7.

9.3 Pooling

A typical layer of a convolutional network consists of three stages (see figure 9.7). In the first stage, the layer performs several convolutions in parallel to produce a set of linear activations. In the second stage, each linear activation is run through a nonlinear activation function, such as the rectified linear activation function. This stage is sometimes called the **detector stage**. In the third stage, we use a **pooling function** to modify the output of the layer further.

A pooling function replaces the output of the net at a certain location with a summary statistic of the nearby outputs. For example, the **max pooling** (Zhou and Chellappa, 1988) operation reports the maximum output within a rectangular neighborhood. Other popular pooling functions include the average of a rectangular neighborhood, the L^2 norm of a rectangular neighborhood, or a weighted average based on the distance from the central pixel.

In all cases, pooling helps to make the representation approximately **invariant** to small translations of the input. Invariance to translation means that if we

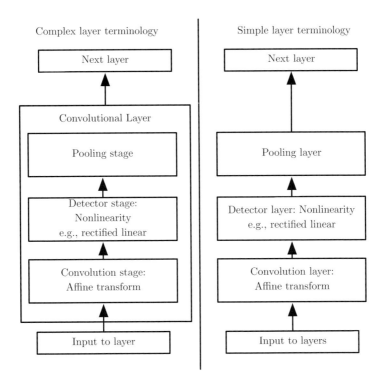

Figure 9.7: The components of a typical convolutional neural network layer. There are two commonly used sets of terminology for describing these layers. *(Left)*In this terminology, the convolutional net is viewed as a small number of relatively complex layers, with each layer having many "stages." In this terminology, there is a one-to-one mapping between kernel tensors and network layers. In this book we generally use this terminology. *(Right)*In this terminology, the convolutional net is viewed as a larger number of simple layers; every step of processing is regarded as a layer in its own right. This means that not every "layer" has parameters.

translate the input by a small amount, the values of most of the pooled outputs do not change. See figure 9.8 for an example of how this works. *Invariance to local translation can be a useful property if we care more about whether some feature is present than exactly where it is.* For example, when determining whether an image contains a face, we need not know the location of the eyes with pixel-perfect accuracy, we just need to know that there is an eye on the left side of the face and an eye on the right side of the face. In other contexts, it is more important to preserve the location of a feature. For example, if we want to find a corner defined by two edges meeting at a specific orientation, we need to preserve the location of the edges well enough to test whether they meet.

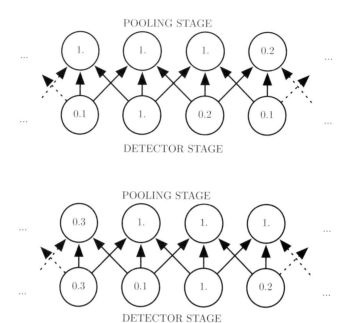

Figure 9.8: Max pooling introduces invariance. *(Top)*A view of the middle of the output of a convolutional layer. The bottom row shows outputs of the nonlinearity. The top row shows the outputs of max pooling, with a stride of one pixel between pooling regions and a pooling region width of three pixels. *(Bottom)*A view of the same network, after the input has been shifted to the right by one pixel. Every value in the bottom row has changed, but only half of the values in the top row have changed, because the max pooling units are sensitive only to the maximum value in the neighborhood, not its exact location.

The use of pooling can be viewed as adding an infinitely strong prior that the function the layer learns must be invariant to small translations. When this assumption is correct, it can greatly improve the statistical efficiency of the network.

Pooling over spatial regions produces invariance to translation, but if we pool over the outputs of separately parametrized convolutions, the features can learn which transformations to become invariant to (see figure 9.9).

Because pooling summarizes the responses over a whole neighborhood, it is possible to use fewer pooling units than detector units, by reporting summary statistics for pooling regions spaced k pixels apart rather than 1 pixel apart. See figure 9.10 for an example. This improves the computational efficiency of the network because the next layer has roughly k times fewer inputs to process. When the number of parameters in the next layer is a function of its input size (such as

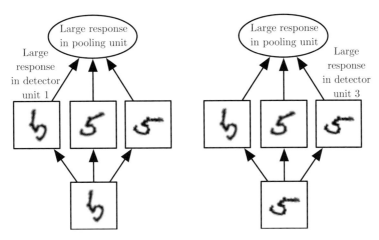

Figure 9.9: Example of learned invariances. A pooling unit that pools over multiple features that are learned with separate parameters can learn to be invariant to transformations of the input. Here we show how a set of three learned filters and a max pooling unit can learn to become invariant to rotation. All three filters are intended to detect a hand written 5. Each filter attempts to match a slightly different orientation of the 5. When a 5 appears in the input, the corresponding filter will match it and cause a large activation in a detector unit. The max pooling unit then has a large activation regardless of which detector unit was activated. We show here how the network processes two different inputs, resulting in two different detector units being activated. The effect on the pooling unit is roughly the same either way. This principle is leveraged by maxout networks (Goodfellow et al., 2013a) and other convolutional networks. Max pooling over spatial positions is naturally invariant to translation; this multichannel approach is only necessary for learning other transformations.

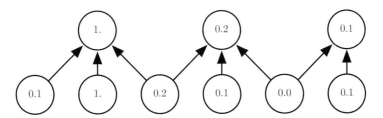

Figure 9.10: Pooling with downsampling. Here we use max pooling with a pool width of three and a stride between pools of two. This reduces the representation size by a factor of two, which reduces the computational and statistical burden on the next layer. Note that the rightmost pooling region has a smaller size but must be included if we do not want to ignore some of the detector units.

when the next layer is fully connected and based on matrix multiplication), this reduction in the input size can also result in improved statistical efficiency and reduced memory requirements for storing the parameters.

For many tasks, pooling is essential for handling inputs of varying size. For example, if we want to classify images of variable size, the input to the classification layer must have a fixed size. This is usually accomplished by varying the size of an offset between pooling regions so that the classification layer always receives the same number of summary statistics regardless of the input size. For example, the final pooling layer of the network may be defined to output four sets of summary statistics, one for each quadrant of an image, regardless of the image size.

Some theoretical work gives guidance as to which kinds of pooling one should use in various situations (Boureau et al., 2010). It is also possible to dynamically pool features together, for example, by running a clustering algorithm on the locations of interesting features (Boureau et al., 2011). This approach yields a different set of pooling regions for each image. Another approach is to *learn* a single pooling structure that is then applied to all images (Jia et al., 2012).

Pooling can complicate some kinds of neural network architectures that use top-down information, such as Boltzmann machines and autoencoders. These issues are discussed further when we present these types of networks in part III. Pooling in convolutional Boltzmann machines is presented in section 20.6. The inverse-like operations on pooling units needed in some differentiable networks are covered in section 20.10.6.

Some examples of complete convolutional network architectures for classification using convolution and pooling are shown in figure 9.11.

9.4 Convolution and Pooling as an Infinitely Strong Prior

Recall the concept of a **prior probability distribution** from section 5.2. This is a probability distribution over the parameters of a model that encodes our beliefs about what models are reasonable, before we have seen any data.

Priors can be considered weak or strong depending on how concentrated the probability density in the prior is. A weak prior is a prior distribution with high entropy, such as a Gaussian distribution with high variance. Such a prior allows the data to move the parameters more or less freely. A strong prior has very low

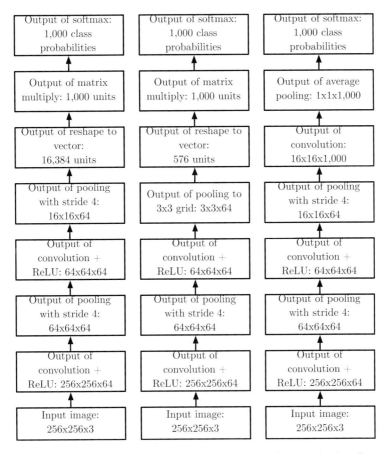

Figure 9.11: Examples of architectures for classification with convolutional networks. The specific strides and depths used in this figure are not advisable for real use; they are designed to be very shallow to fit onto the page. Real convolutional networks also often involve significant amounts of branching, unlike the chain structures used here for simplicity. *(Left)*A convolutional network that processes a fixed image size. After alternating between convolution and pooling for a few layers, the tensor for the convolutional feature map is reshaped to flatten out the spatial dimensions. The rest of the network is an ordinary feedforward network classifier, as described in chapter 6. *(Center)*A convolutional network that processes a variably sized image but still maintains a fully connected section. This network uses a pooling operation with variably sized pools but a fixed number of pools, in order to provide a fixed-size vector of 576 units to the fully connected portion of the network. *(Right)*A convolutional network that does not have any fully connected weight layer. Instead, the last convolutional layer outputs one feature map per class. The model presumably learns a map of how likely each class is to occur at each spatial location. Averaging a feature map down to a single value provides the argument to the softmax classifier at the top.

entropy, such as a Gaussian distribution with low variance. Such a prior plays a more active role in determining where the parameters end up.

An infinitely strong prior places zero probability on some parameters and says that these parameter values are completely forbidden, regardless of how much support the data give to those values.

We can imagine a convolutional net as being similar to a fully connected net, but with an infinitely strong prior over its weights. This infinitely strong prior says that the weights for one hidden unit must be identical to the weights of its neighbor but shifted in space. The prior also says that the weights must be zero, except for in the small, spatially contiguous receptive field assigned to that hidden unit. Overall, we can think of the use of convolution as introducing an infinitely strong prior probability distribution over the parameters of a layer. This prior says that the function the layer should learn contains only local interactions and is equivariant to translation. Likewise, the use of pooling is an infinitely strong prior that each unit should be invariant to small translations.

Of course, implementing a convolutional net as a fully connected net with an infinitely strong prior would be extremely wasteful computationally. But thinking of a convolutional net as a fully connected net with an infinitely strong prior can give us some insights into how convolutional nets work.

One key insight is that convolution and pooling can cause underfitting. Like any prior, convolution and pooling are only useful when the assumptions made by the prior are reasonably accurate. If a task relies on preserving precise spatial information, then using pooling on all features can increase the training error. Some convolutional network architectures (Szegedy et al., 2014a) are designed to use pooling on some channels but not on other channels, in order to get both highly invariant features and features that will not underfit when the translation invariance prior is incorrect. When a task involves incorporating information from very distant locations in the input, then the prior imposed by convolution may be inappropriate.

Another key insight from this view is that we should only compare convolutional models to other convolutional models in benchmarks of statistical learning performance. Models that do not use convolution would be able to learn even if we permuted all the pixels in the image. For many image datasets, there are separate benchmarks for models that are **permutation invariant** and must discover the concept of topology via learning and for models that have the knowledge of spatial relationships hard coded into them by their designer.

9.5 Variants of the Basic Convolution Function

When discussing convolution in the context of neural networks, we usually do not refer exactly to the standard discrete convolution operation as it is usually understood in the mathematical literature. The functions used in practice differ slightly. Here we describe these differences in detail and highlight some useful properties of the functions used in neural networks.

First, when we refer to convolution in the context of neural networks, we usually actually mean an operation that consists of many applications of convolution in parallel. This is because convolution with a single kernel can extract only one kind of feature, albeit at many spatial locations. Usually we want each layer of our network to extract many kinds of features, at many locations.

Additionally, the input is usually not just a grid of real values. Rather, it is a grid of vector-valued observations. For example, a color image has a red, green and blue intensity at each pixel. In a multilayer convolutional network, the input to the second layer is the output of the first layer, which usually has the output of many different convolutions at each position. When working with images, we usually think of the input and output of the convolution as being 3-D tensors, with one index into the different channels and two indices into the spatial coordinates of each channel. Software implementations usually work in batch mode, so they will actually use 4-D tensors, with the fourth axis indexing different examples in the batch, but we will omit the batch axis in our description here for simplicity.

Because convolutional networks usually use multichannel convolution, the linear operations they are based on are not guaranteed to be commutative, even if kernel flipping is used. These multichannel operations are only commutative if each operation has the same number of output channels as input channels.

Assume we have a 4-D kernel tensor $\mathbf{K}$ with element $K_{i,j,k,l}$ giving the connection strength between a unit in channel i of the output and a unit in channel j of the input, with an offset of k rows and l columns between the output unit and the input unit. Assume our input consists of observed data $\mathbf{V}$ with element $V_{i,j,k}$ giving the value of the input unit within channel i at row j and column k. Assume our output consists of $\mathbf{Z}$ with the same format as $\mathbf{V}$. If $\mathbf{Z}$ is produced by convolving $\mathbf{K}$ across $\mathbf{V}$ without flipping $\mathbf{K}$, then

$$Z_{i,j,k} = \sum_{l,m,n} V_{l,j+m-1,k+n-1} K_{i,l,m,n}, \tag{9.7}$$

where the summation over l, m and n is over all values for which the tensor indexing operations inside the summation are valid. In linear algebra notation, we index into arrays using a 1 for the first entry. This necessitates the -1 in the above formula. Programming languages such as C and Python index starting from 0, rendering the above expression even simpler.

We may want to skip over some positions of the kernel to reduce the computational cost (at the expense of not extracting our features as finely). We can think of this as downsampling the output of the full convolution function. If we want to sample only every s pixels in each direction in the output, then we can define a downsampled convolution function c such that

$$Z_{i,j,k} = c(\mathbf{K}, \mathbf{V}, s)_{i,j,k} = \sum_{l,m,n} \left[V_{l,(j-1)\times s+m,(k-1)\times s+n} K_{i,l,m,n} \right]. \tag{9.8}$$

We refer to s as the **stride** of this downsampled convolution. It is also possible to define a separate stride for each direction of motion. See figure 9.12 for an illustration.

One essential feature of any convolutional network implementation is the ability to implicitly zero pad the input $\mathbf{V}$ to make it wider. Without this feature, the width of the representation shrinks by one pixel less than the kernel width at each layer. Zero padding the input allows us to control the kernel width and the size of the output independently. Without zero padding, we are forced to choose between shrinking the spatial extent of the network rapidly and using small kernels—both scenarios that significantly limit the expressive power of the network. See figure 9.13 for an example.

Three special cases of the zero-padding setting are worth mentioning. One is the extreme case in which no zero padding is used whatsoever, and the convolution kernel is allowed to visit only positions where the entire kernel is contained entirely within the image. In MATLAB terminology, this is called **valid** convolution. In this case, all pixels in the output are a function of the same number of pixels in the input, so the behavior of an output pixel is somewhat more regular. However, the size of the output shrinks at each layer. If the input image has width m and the kernel has width k, the output will be of width $m - k + 1$. The rate of this shrinkage can be dramatic if the kernels used are large. Since the shrinkage is greater than 0, it limits the number of convolutional layers that can be included in the network. As layers are added, the spatial dimension of the network will eventually drop to 1×1, at which point additional layers cannot meaningfully be considered convolutional. Another special case of the zero-padding setting is when just enough zero padding is added to keep the size of the output equal to the size of the input. MATLAB calls this **same** convolution. In this case, the network

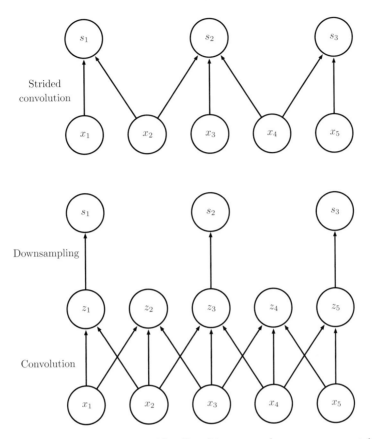

Figure 9.12: Convolution with a stride. In this example, we use a stride of two. *(Top)*Convolution with a stride length of two implemented in a single operation. *(Bottom)*Convolution with a stride greater than one pixel is mathematically equivalent to convolution with unit stride followed by downsampling. Obviously, the two-step approach involving downsampling is computationally wasteful, because it computes many values that are then discarded.

can contain as many convolutional layers as the available hardware can support, since the operation of convolution does not modify the architectural possibilities available to the next layer. The input pixels near the border, however, influence fewer output pixels than the input pixels near the center. This can make the border pixels somewhat underrepresented in the model. This motivates the other extreme case, which MATLAB refers to as **full** convolution, in which enough zeros are added for every pixel to be visited k times in each direction, resulting in an output image of width $m + k - 1$. In this case, the output pixels near the border are a function of fewer pixels than the output pixels near the center. This can make it difficult

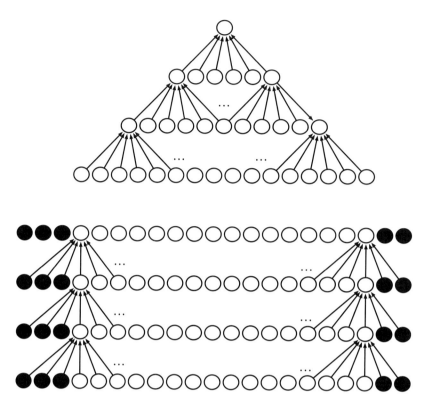

Figure 9.13: The effect of zero padding on network size. Consider a convolutional network with a kernel of width six at every layer. In this example, we do not use any pooling, so only the convolution operation itself shrinks the network size. *(Top)*In this convolutional network, we do not use any implicit zero padding. This causes the representation to shrink by five pixels at each layer. Starting from an input of sixteen pixels, we are only able to have three convolutional layers, and the last layer does not ever move the kernel, so arguably only two of the layers are truly convolutional. The rate of shrinking can be mitigated by using smaller kernels, but smaller kernels are less expressive, and some shrinking is inevitable in this kind of architecture. *(Bottom)*By adding five implicit zeros to each layer, we prevent the representation from shrinking with depth. This allows us to make an arbitrarily deep convolutional network.

to learn a single kernel that performs well at all positions in the convolutional feature map. Usually the optimal amount of zero padding (in terms of test set classification accuracy) lies somewhere between "valid" and "same" convolution.

In some cases, we do not actually want to use convolution, but want to use locally connected layers instead (LeCun, 1986, 1989). In this case, the adjacency matrix in the graph of our MLP is the same, but every connection has its own weight, specified by a 6-D tensor $\mathbf{W}$. The indices into $\mathbf{W}$ are respectively: i; the output channel; j, the output row; k, the output column; l, the input channel; m, the row offset within the input; and n, the column offset within the input. The linear part of a locally connected layer is then given by

$$Z_{i,j,k} = \sum_{l,m,n} \left[V_{l,j+m-1,k+n-1} w_{i,j,k,l,m,n} \right]. \tag{9.9}$$

This is sometimes also called **unshared convolution**, because it is a similar operation to discrete convolution with a small kernel, but without sharing parameters across locations. Figure 9.14 compares local connections, convolution, and full connections.

Locally connected layers are useful when we know that each feature should be a function of a small part of space, but there is no reason to think that the same feature should occur across all of space. For example, if we want to tell if an image is a picture of a face, we only need to look for the mouth in the bottom half of the image.

It can also be useful to make versions of convolution or locally connected layers in which the connectivity is further restricted, for example to constrain each output channel i to be a function of only a subset of the input channels l. A common way to do this is to make the first m output channels connect to only the first n input channels, the second m output channels connect to only the second n input channels, and so on. See figure 9.15 for an example. Modeling interactions between few channels allows the network to have fewer parameters, reducing memory consumption, increasing statistical efficiency, and reducing the amount of computation needed to perform forward and back-propagation. It accomplishes these goals without reducing the number of hidden units.

Tiled convolution (Gregor and LeCun, 2010a; Le et al., 2010) offers a compromise between a convolutional layer and a locally connected layer. Rather than learning a separate set of weights at *every* spatial location, we learn a set of kernels that we rotate through as we move through space. This means that immediately neighboring locations will have different filters, as in a locally connected layer, but the memory requirements for storing the parameters will increase only by a factor of the size of this set of kernels, rather than by the size of the entire output feature map. See figure 9.16 for a comparison of locally connected layers, tiled convolution, and standard convolution.

To define tiled convolution algebraically, let k be a 6-D tensor, where two of the dimensions correspond to different locations in the output map. Rather than having a separate index for each location in the output map, output locations cycle

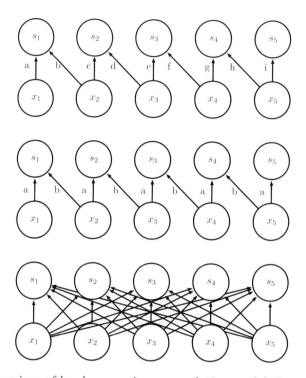

Figure 9.14: Comparison of local connections, convolution, and full connections. *(Top)*A locally connected layer with a patch size of two pixels. Each edge is labeled with a unique letter to show that each edge is associated with its own weight parameter. *(Center)*A convolutional layer with a kernel width of two pixels. This model has exactly the same connectivity as the locally connected layer. The difference lies not in which units interact with each other, but in how the parameters are shared. The locally connected layer has no parameter sharing. The convolutional layer uses the same two weights repeatedly across the entire input, as indicated by the repetition of the letters labeling each edge. *(Bottom)*A fully connected layer resembles a locally connected layer in the sense that each edge has its own parameter (there are too many to label explicitly with letters in this diagram). It does not, however, have the restricted connectivity of the locally connected layer.

through a set of t different choices of kernel stack in each direction. If t is equal to the output width, this is the same as a locally connected layer.

$$Z_{i,j,k} = \sum_{l,m,n} V_{l,j+m-1,k+n-1} K_{i,l,m,n,j\%t+1,k\%t+1}, \qquad (9.10)$$

where percent is the modulo operation, with $t\%t = 0$, $(t+1)\%t = 1$, and so on. It is straightforward to generalize this equation to use a different tiling range for each dimension.

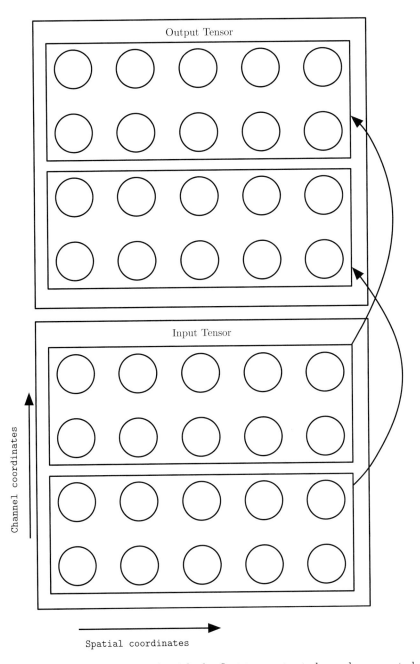

Figure 9.15: A convolutional network with the first two output channels connected to only the first two input channels, and the second two output channels connected to only the second two input channels.

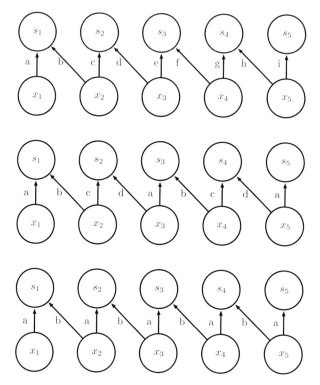

Figure 9.16: A comparison of locally connected layers, tiled convolution, and standard convolution. All three have the same sets of connections between units, when the same size of kernel is used. This diagram illustrates the use of a kernel that is two pixels wide. The differences between the methods lies in how they share parameters. *(Top)* A locally connected layer has no sharing at all. We indicate that each connection has its own weight by labeling each connection with a unique letter. *(Center)* Tiled convolution has a set of t different kernels. Here we illustrate the case of $t = 2$. One of these kernels has edges labeled "a" and "b," while the other has edges labeled "c" and "d." Each time we move one pixel to the right in the output, we move on to using a different kernel. This means that, like the locally connected layer, neighboring units in the output have different parameters. Unlike the locally connected layer, after we have gone through all t available kernels, we cycle back to the first kernel. If two output units are separated by a multiple of t steps, then they share parameters. *(Bottom)* Traditional convolution is equivalent to tiled convolution with $t = 1$. There is only one kernel, and it is applied everywhere, as indicated in the diagram by using the kernel with weights labeled "a" and "b" everywhere.

Locally connected layers and tiled convolutional layers have both an interesting interaction with max pooling: the detector units of these layers are driven by different filters. If these filters learn to detect different transformed versions of the same underlying features, then the max-pooled units become invariant to the learned transformation (see figure 9.9). Convolutional layers are hard coded to be invariant specifically to translation.

Other operations besides convolution are usually necessary to implement a convolutional network. To perform learning, one must be able to compute the gradient with respect to the kernel, given the gradient with respect to the outputs. In some simple cases, this operation can be performed using the convolution operation, but many cases of interest, including the case of stride greater than 1, do not have this property.

Recall that convolution is a linear operation and can thus be described as a matrix multiplication (if we first reshape the input tensor into a flat vector). The matrix involved is a function of the convolution kernel. The matrix is sparse, and each element of the kernel is copied to several elements of the matrix. This view helps us to derive some of the other operations needed to implement a convolutional network.

Multiplication by the transpose of the matrix defined by convolution is one such operation. This is the operation needed to back-propagate error derivatives through a convolutional layer, so it is needed to train convolutional networks that have more than one hidden layer. This same operation is also needed if we wish to reconstruct the visible units from the hidden units (Simard et al., 1992). Reconstructing the visible units is an operation commonly used in the models described in part III of this book, such as autoencoders, RBMs, and sparse coding. Transpose convolution is necessary to construct convolutional versions of those models. Like the kernel gradient operation, this input gradient operation can sometimes be implemented using a convolution but in general requires a third operation to be implemented. Care must be taken to coordinate this transpose operation with the forward propagation. The size of the output that the transpose operation should return depends on the zero-padding policy and stride of the forward propagation operation, as well as the size of the forward propagation's output map. In some cases, multiple sizes of input to forward propagation can result in the same size of output map, so the transpose operation must be explicitly told what the size of the original input was.

These three operations—convolution, backprop from output to weights, and backprop from output to inputs—are sufficient to compute all the gradients needed to train any depth of feedforward convolutional network, as well as to train convolutional networks with reconstruction functions based on the transpose of convolution. See Goodfellow (2010) for a full derivation of the equations in the fully general multidimensional, multiexample case. To give a sense of how these equations work, we present the two-dimensional, single example version here.

Suppose we want to train a convolutional network that incorporates strided convolution of kernel stack $\mathbf{K}$ applied to multichannel image $\mathbf{V}$ with stride s as defined by $c(\mathbf{K}, \mathbf{V}, s)$, as in equation 9.8. Suppose we want to minimize some loss function $J(\mathbf{V}, \mathbf{K})$. During forward propagation, we will need to use c itself to output $\mathbf{Z}$, which is then propagated through the rest of the network and used to compute the cost function J. During back-propagation, we will receive a tensor $\mathbf{G}$ such that $G_{i,j,k} = \frac{\partial}{\partial Z_{i,j,k}} J(\mathbf{V}, \mathbf{K})$.

To train the network, we need to compute the derivatives with respect to the weights in the kernel. To do so, we can use a function

$$g(\mathbf{G}, \mathbf{V}, s)_{i,j,k,l} = \frac{\partial}{\partial K_{i,j,k,l}} J(\mathbf{V}, \mathbf{K}) = \sum_{m,n} G_{i,m,n} V_{j,(m-1)\times s+k,(n-1)\times s+l}. \quad (9.11)$$

If this layer is not the bottom layer of the network, we will need to compute the gradient with respect to $\mathbf{V}$ to back-propagate the error further down. To do so, we can use a function

$$h(\mathbf{K}, \mathbf{G}, s)_{i,j,k} = \frac{\partial}{\partial V_{i,j,k}} J(\mathbf{V}, \mathbf{K}) \quad (9.12)$$

$$= \sum_{\substack{l,m \\ \text{s.t.} \\ (l-1)\times s+m=j}} \sum_{\substack{n,p \\ \text{s.t.} \\ (n-1)\times s+p=k}} \sum_{q} K_{q,i,m,p} G_{q,l,n}. \quad (9.13)$$

Autoencoder networks, described in chapter 14, are feedforward networks trained to copy their input to their output. A simple example is the PCA algorithm, which copies its input $\boldsymbol{x}$ to an approximate reconstruction $\boldsymbol{r}$ using the function $\boldsymbol{W}^\top \boldsymbol{W} \boldsymbol{x}$. It is common for more general autoencoders to use multiplication by the transpose of the weight matrix just as PCA does. To make such models convolutional, we can use the function h to perform the transpose of the convolution operation. Suppose we have hidden units $\mathbf{H}$ in the same format as $\mathbf{Z}$ and we define a reconstruction

$$\mathbf{R} = h(\mathbf{K}, \mathbf{H}, s). \quad (9.14)$$

To train the autoencoder, we will receive the gradient with respect to $\mathbf{R}$ as a tensor $\mathbf{E}$. To train the decoder, we need to obtain the gradient with respect to $\mathbf{K}$. This is given by $g(\mathbf{H}, \mathbf{E}, s)$. To train the encoder, we need to obtain the gradient with respect to $\mathbf{H}$. This is given by $c(\mathbf{K}, \mathbf{E}, s)$. It is also possible to differentiate through g using c and h, but these operations are not needed for the back-propagation algorithm on any standard network architectures.

Generally, we do not use only a linear operation to transform from the inputs to the outputs in a convolutional layer. We generally also add some bias term to each output before applying the nonlinearity. This raises the question of how to share parameters among the biases. For locally connected layers, it is natural to give each unit its own bias, and for tiled convolution, it is natural to share the biases with the same tiling pattern as the kernels. For convolutional layers, it is typical to have one bias per channel of the output and share it across all locations within each convolution map. If the input is of known, fixed size, however, it is also possible to learn a separate bias at each location of the output map. Separating the biases may slightly reduce the statistical efficiency of the model, but it allows the model to correct for differences in the image statistics at different locations. For example, when using implicit zero padding, detector units at the edge of the image receive less total input and may need larger biases.

9.6   Structured Outputs

Convolutional networks can be used to output a high-dimensional structured object, rather than just predicting a class label for a classification task or a real value for a regression task. Typically this object is just a tensor, emitted by a standard convolutional layer. For example, the model might emit a tensor $\mathbf{S}$, where $S_{i,j,k}$ is the probability that pixel (j, k) of the input to the network belongs to class i. This allows the model to label every pixel in an image and draw precise masks that follow the outlines of individual objects.

One issue that often comes up is that the output plane can be smaller than the input plane, as shown in figure 9.13. In the kinds of architectures typically used for classification of a single object in an image, the greatest reduction in the spatial dimensions of the network comes from using pooling layers with large stride. To produce an output map of similar size as the input, one can avoid pooling altogether (Jain et al., 2007). Another strategy is to simply emit a lower-resolution grid of labels (Pinheiro and Collobert, 2014, 2015). Finally, in principle, one could use a pooling operator with unit stride.

One strategy for pixel-wise labeling of images is to produce an initial guess of the image labels, then refine this initial guess using the interactions between neighboring pixels. Repeating this refinement step several times corresponds to using the same convolutions at each stage, sharing weights between the last layers of the deep net (Jain et al., 2007). This makes the sequence of computations performed by the successive convolutional layers with weights shared across layers a particular kind of recurrent network (Pinheiro and Collobert, 2014, 2015). Figure 9.17 shows the architecture of such a recurrent convolutional network.

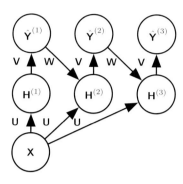

Figure 9.17: An example of a recurrent convolutional network for pixel labeling. The input is an image tensor **X**, with axes corresponding to image rows, image columns, and channels (red, green, blue). The goal is to output a tensor of labels $\hat{Y}$, with a probability distribution over labels for each pixel. This tensor has axes corresponding to image rows, image columns, and the different classes. Rather than outputting $\hat{Y}$ in a single shot, the recurrent network iteratively refines its estimate $\hat{Y}$ by using a previous estimate of $\hat{Y}$ as input for creating a new estimate. The same parameters are used for each updated estimate, and the estimate can be refined as many times as we wish. The tensor of convolution kernels **U** is used on each step to compute the hidden representation given the input image. The kernel tensor **V** is used to produce an estimate of the labels given the hidden values. On all but the first step, the kernels **W** are convolved over $\hat{Y}$ to provide input to the hidden layer. On the first time step, this term is replaced by zero. Because the same parameters are used on each step, this is an example of a recurrent network, as described in chapter 10.

Once a prediction for each pixel is made, various methods can be used to further process these predictions to obtain a segmentation of the image into regions (Briggman et al., 2009; Turaga et al., 2010; Farabet et al., 2013). The general idea is to assume that large groups of contiguous pixels tend to be associated with the same label. Graphical models can describe the probabilistic relationships between neighboring pixels. Alternatively, the convolutional network can be trained to maximize an approximation of the graphical model training objective (Ning et al., 2005; Thompson et al., 2014).

9.7 Data Types

The data used with a convolutional network usually consist of several channels, each channel being the observation of a different quantity at some point in space or time. See table 9.1 for examples of data types with different dimensionalities and number of channels.

	Single channel	Multichannel
1-D	Audio waveform: The axis we convolve over corresponds to time. We discretize time and measure the amplitude of the waveform once per time step.	Skeleton animation data: Animations of 3-D computer-rendered characters are generated by altering the pose of a "skeleton" over time. At each point in time, the pose of the character is described by a specification of the angles of each of the joints in the character's skeleton. Each channel in the data we feed to the convolutional model represents the angle about one axis of one joint.
2-D	Audio data that has been pre-processed with a Fourier transform: We can transform the audio waveform into a 2-D tensor with different rows corresponding to different frequencies and different columns corresponding to different points in time. Using convolution in the time makes the model equivariant to shifts in time. Using convolution across the frequency axis makes the model equivariant to frequency, so that the same melody played in a different octave produces the same representation but at a different height in the network's output.	Color image data: One channel contains the red pixels, one the green pixels, and one the blue pixels. The convolution kernel moves over both the horizontal and the vertical axes of the image, conferring translation equivariance in both directions.
3-D	Volumetric data: A common source of this kind of data is medical imaging technology, such as CT scans.	Color video data: One axis corresponds to time, one to the height of the video frame, and one to the width of the video frame.

Table 9.1: Examples of different formats of data that can be used with convolutional networks.

For an example of convolutional networks applied to video, see Chen et al. (2010).

So far we have discussed only the case where every example in the train and test data has the same spatial dimensions. One advantage to convolutional networks is that they can also process inputs with varying spatial extents. These kinds of input simply cannot be represented by traditional, matrix multiplication-based neural networks. This provides a compelling reason to use convolutional networks even when computational cost and overfitting are not significant issues.

For example, consider a collection of images in which each image has a different width and height. It is unclear how to model such inputs with a weight matrix of fixed size. Convolution is straightforward to apply; the kernel is simply applied a different number of times depending on the size of the input, and the output of the convolution operation scales accordingly. Convolution may be viewed as matrix multiplication; the same convolution kernel induces a different size of doubly block circulant matrix for each size of input. Sometimes the output of the network as well as the input is allowed to have variable size, for example, if we want to assign a class label to each pixel of the input. In this case, no further design work is necessary. In other cases, the network must produce some fixed-size output, for example, if we want to assign a single class label to the entire image. In this case, we must make some additional design steps, like inserting a pooling layer whose pooling regions scale in size proportional to the size of the input, to maintain a fixed number of pooled outputs. Some examples of this kind of strategy are shown in figure 9.11.

Note that the use of convolution for processing variably sized inputs makes sense only for inputs that have variable size because they contain varying amounts of observation of the same kind of thing—different lengths of recordings over time, different widths of observations over space, and so forth. Convolution does not make sense if the input has variable size because it can optionally include different kinds of observations. For example, if we are processing college applications, and our features consist of both grades and standardized test scores, but not every applicant took the standardized test, then it does not make sense to convolve the same weights over features corresponding to the grades as well as the features corresponding to the test scores.

9.8 Efficient Convolution Algorithms

Modern convolutional network applications often involve networks containing more than one million units. Powerful implementations exploiting parallel computation resources, as discussed in section 12.1, are essential. In many cases, however, it is also possible to speed up convolution by selecting an appropriate convolution algorithm.

Convolution is equivalent to converting both the input and the kernel to the frequency domain using a Fourier transform, performing point-wise multiplication of the two signals, and converting back to the time domain using an inverse Fourier transform. For some problem sizes, this can be faster than the naive implementation of discrete convolution.

When a d-dimensional kernel can be expressed as the outer product of d vectors, one vector per dimension, the kernel is called **separable**. When the kernel is separable, naive convolution is inefficient. It is equivalent to compose d one-dimensional convolutions with each of these vectors. The composed approach is significantly faster than performing one d-dimensional convolution with their outer product. The kernel also takes fewer parameters to represent as vectors. If the kernel is w elements wide in each dimension, then naive multidimensional convolution requires $O(w^d)$ runtime and parameter storage space, while separable convolution requires $O(w \times d)$ runtime and parameter storage space. Of course, not every convolution can be represented in this way.

Devising faster ways of performing convolution or approximate convolution without harming the accuracy of the model is an active area of research. Even techniques that improve the efficiency of only forward propagation are useful because in the commercial setting, it is typical to devote more resources to deployment of a network than to its training.

9.9 Random or Unsupervised Features

Typically, the most expensive part of convolutional network training is learning the features. The output layer is usually relatively inexpensive because of the small number of features provided as input to this layer after passing through several layers of pooling. When performing supervised training with gradient descent, every gradient step requires a complete run of forward propagation and backward propagation through the entire network. One way to reduce the cost of convolutional network training is to use features that are not trained in a supervised fashion.

There are three basic strategies for obtaining convolution kernels without supervised training. One is to simply initialize them randomly. Another is to design them by hand, for example, by setting each kernel to detect edges at a certain orientation or scale. Finally, one can learn the kernels with an unsupervised criterion. For example, Coates et al. (2011) apply k-means clustering to small image patches, then use each learned centroid as a convolution kernel. In Part III we describe many more unsupervised learning approaches. Learning the features with an unsupervised criterion allows them to be determined separately from the classifier layer at the top of the architecture. One can then extract the features for the entire training set just once, essentially constructing a new training set for the last layer. Learning the last layer is then typically a convex optimization problem, assuming the last layer is something like logistic regression or an SVM.

Random filters often work surprisingly well in convolutional networks (Jarrett et al., 2009; Saxe et al., 2011; Pinto et al., 2011; Cox and Pinto, 2011). Saxe et al. (2011) showed that layers consisting of convolution followed by pooling naturally become frequency selective and translation invariant when assigned random weights. They argue that this provides an inexpensive way to choose the architecture of a convolutional network: first, evaluate the performance of several convolutional network architectures by training only the last layer; then take the best of these architectures and train the entire architecture using a more expensive approach.

An intermediate approach is to learn the features, but using methods that do not require full forward and back-propagation at every gradient step. As with multilayer perceptrons, we use greedy layer-wise pretraining, to train the first layer in isolation, then extract all features from the first layer only once, then train the second layer in isolation given those features, and so on. In chapter 8 we described how to perform supervised greedy layer-wise pretraining, and in part III extend this to greedy layer-wise pretraining using an unsupervised criterion at each layer. The canonical example of greedy layer-wise pretraining of a convolutional model is the convolutional deep belief network (Lee et al., 2009). Convolutional networks offer us the opportunity to take the pretraining strategy one step further than is possible with multilayer perceptrons. Instead of training an entire convolutional layer at a time, we can train a model of a small patch, as Coates et al. (2011) do with k-means. We can then use the parameters from this patch-based model to define the kernels of a convolutional layer. This means that it is possible to use unsupervised learning to train a convolutional network *without ever using convolution during the training process*. Using this approach, we can train very large models and incur a high computational cost only at inference time (Ranzato et al., 2007b; Jarrett et al., 2009; Kavukcuoglu et al., 2010; Coates et al., 2013). This approach was popular from roughly 2007 to 2013, when labeled datasets were small and computational power was more limited. Today, most convolutional networks are trained in a purely supervised fashion, using full forward and back-propagation through the entire network on each training iteration.

As with other approaches to unsupervised pretraining, it remains difficult to tease apart the cause of some of the benefits seen with this approach. Unsupervised pretraining may offer some regularization relative to supervised training, or it may simply allow us to train much larger architectures because of the reduced computational cost of the learning rule.

9.10 The Neuroscientific Basis for Convolutional Networks

Convolutional networks are perhaps the greatest success story of biologically inspired artificial intelligence. Though convolutional networks have been guided by many other fields, some of the key design principles of neural networks were drawn from neuroscience.

The history of convolutional networks begins with neuroscientific experiments long before the relevant computational models were developed. Neurophysiologists David Hubel and Torsten Wiesel collaborated for several years to determine many of the most basic facts about how the mammalian vision system works (Hubel and Wiesel, 1959, 1962, 1968). Their accomplishments were eventually recognized with a Nobel prize. Their findings that have had the greatest influence on contemporary deep learning models were based on recording the activity of individual neurons in cats. They observed how neurons in the cat's brain responded to images projected in precise locations on a screen in front of the cat. Their great discovery was that neurons in the early visual system responded most strongly to very specific patterns of light, such as precisely oriented bars, but responded hardly at all to other patterns.

Their work helped to characterize many aspects of brain function that are beyond the scope of this book. From the point of view of deep learning, we can focus on a simplified, cartoon view of brain function.

In this simplified view, we focus on a part of the brain called V1, also known as the **primary visual cortex**. V1 is the first area of the brain that begins to perform significantly advanced processing of visual input. In this cartoon view, images are formed by light arriving in the eye and stimulating the retina, the light-sensitive tissue in the back of the eye. The neurons in the retina perform some simple preprocessing of the image but do not substantially alter the way it is represented. The image then passes through the optic nerve and a brain region called the *lateral geniculate nucleus*. The main role, as far as we are concerned here, of both anatomical regions is primarily just to carry the signal from the eye to V1, which is located at the back of the head.

A convolutional network layer is designed to capture three properties of V1:

1. V1 is arranged in a spatial map. It actually has a two-dimensional structure, mirroring the structure of the image in the retina. For example, light arriving at the lower half of the retina affects only the corresponding half of V1. Convolutional networks capture this property by having their features defined in terms of two-dimensional maps.

2. V1 contains many **simple cells**. A simple cell's activity can to some extent be characterized by a linear function of the image in a small, spatially localized receptive field. The detector units of a convolutional network are designed to emulate these properties of simple cells.

3. V1 also contains many **complex cells**. These cells respond to features that are similar to those detected by simple cells, but complex cells are invariant to small shifts in the position of the feature. This inspires the pooling units of convolutional networks. Complex cells are also invariant to some changes in lighting that cannot be captured simply by pooling over spatial locations. These invariances have inspired some of the cross-channel pooling strategies in convolutional networks, such as maxout units (Goodfellow et al., 2013a).

Though we know the most about V1, it is generally believed that the same basic principles apply to other areas of the visual system. In our cartoon view of the visual system, the basic strategy of detection followed by pooling is repeatedly applied as we move deeper into the brain. As we pass through multiple anatomical layers of the brain, we eventually find cells that respond to some specific concept and are invariant to many transformations of the input. These cells have been nicknamed "grandmother cells"—the idea is that a person could have a neuron that activates when seeing an image of their grandmother, regardless of whether she appears in the left or right side of the image, whether the image is a close-up of her face or zoomed-out shot of her entire body, whether she is brightly lit or in shadow, and so on.

These grandmother cells have been shown to actually exist in the human brain, in a region called the *medial temporal lobe* (Quiroga et al., 2005). Researchers tested whether individual neurons would respond to photos of famous individuals. They found what has come to be called the "Halle Berry neuron," an individual neuron that is activated by the concept of Halle Berry. This neuron fires when a person sees a photo of Halle Berry, a drawing of Halle Berry, or even text containing the words "Halle Berry." Of course, this has nothing to do with Halle Berry herself;

other neurons responded to the presence of Bill Clinton, Jennifer Aniston, and so forth.

These medial temporal lobe neurons are somewhat more general than modern convolutional networks, which would not automatically generalize to identifying a person or object when reading its name. The closest analog to a convolutional network's last layer of features is a brain area called the *inferotemporal cortex* (IT). When viewing an object, information flows from the retina, through the LGN, to V1, then onward to V2, then V4, then IT. This happens within the first 100ms of glimpsing an object. If a person is allowed to continue looking at the object for more time, then information will begin to flow backward as the brain uses top-down feedback to update the activations in the lower level brain areas. If we interrupt the person's gaze, however, and observe only the firing rates that result from the first 100ms of mostly feedforward activation, then IT proves to be similar to a convolutional network. Convolutional networks can predict IT firing rates and perform similarly to (time-limited) humans on object recognition tasks (DiCarlo, 2013).

That being said, there are many differences between convolutional networks and the mammalian vision system. Some of these differences are well known to computational neuroscientists but outside the scope of this book. Some of these differences are not yet known, because many basic questions about how the mammalian vision system works remain unanswered. As a brief list:

- The human eye is mostly very low resolution, except for a tiny patch called the **fovea**. The fovea only observes an area about the size of a thumbnail held at arms length. Though we feel as if we can see an entire scene in high resolution, this is an illusion created by the subconscious part of our brain, as it stitches together several glimpses of small areas. Most convolutional networks actually receive large full-resolution photographs as input. The human brain makes several eye movements called **saccades** to glimpse the most visually salient or task-relevant parts of a scene. Incorporating similar attention mechanisms into deep learning models is an active research direction. In the context of deep learning, attention mechanisms have been most successful for natural language processing, as described in section 12.4.5.1. Several visual models with foveation mechanisms have been developed but so far have not become the dominant approach (Larochelle and Hinton, 2010; Denil et al., 2012).

- The human visual system is integrated with many other senses, such as hearing, and factors like our moods and thoughts. Convolutional networks so far are purely visual.

- The human visual system does much more than just recognize objects. It is able to understand entire scenes, including many objects and relationships between objects, and it processes rich 3-D geometric information needed for our bodies to interface with the world. Convolutional networks have been applied to some of these problems, but these applications are in their infancy.

- Even simple brain areas like V1 are heavily affected by feedback from higher levels. Feedback has been explored extensively in neural network models but has not yet been shown to offer a compelling improvement.

- While feedforward IT firing rates capture much of the same information as convolutional network features, it is not clear how similar the intermediate computations are. The brain probably uses very different activation and pooling functions. An individual neuron's activation probably is not well characterized by a single linear filter response. A recent model of V1 involves multiple quadratic filters for each neuron (Rust et al., 2005). Indeed our cartoon picture of "simple cells" and "complex cells" might create a nonexistent distinction; simple cells and complex cells might both be the same kind of cell but with their "parameters" enabling a continuum of behaviors ranging from what we call "simple" to what we call "complex."

It is also worth mentioning that neuroscience has told us relatively little about how to *train* convolutional networks. Model structures with parameter sharing across multiple spatial locations date back to early connectionist models of vision (Marr and Poggio, 1976), but these models did not use the modern back-propagation algorithm and gradient descent. For example, the neocognitron (Fukushima, 1980) incorporated most of the model architecture design elements of the modern convolutional network but relied on a layer-wise unsupervised clustering algorithm.

Lang and Hinton (1988) introduced the use of back-propagation to train **time-delay neural networks** (TDNNs). To use contemporary terminology, TDNNs are one-dimensional convolutional networks applied to time series. Back-propagation applied to these models was not inspired by any neuroscientific observation and is considered by some to be biologically implausible. Following the success of back-propagation-based training of TDNNs, LeCun et al. (1989) developed the modern convolutional network by applying the same training algorithm to 2-D convolution applied to images.

So far we have described how simple cells are roughly linear and selective for certain features, complex cells are more nonlinear and become invariant to some transformations of these simple cell features, and stacks of layers that alternate between selectivity and invariance can yield grandmother cells for specific phenomena. We have not yet described precisely what these individual cells detect. In a deep nonlinear network, it can be difficult to understand the function of individual cells. Simple cells in the first layer are easier to analyze, because their responses are driven by a linear function. In an artificial neural network, we can just display an image of the convolution kernel to see what the corresponding channel of a convolutional layer responds to. In a biological neural network, we do not have access to the weights themselves. Instead, we put an electrode in the neuron, display several samples of white noise images in front of the animal's retina, and record how each of these samples causes the neuron to activate. We can then fit a linear model to these responses to obtain an approximation of the neuron's weights. This approach is known as **reverse correlation** (Ringach and Shapley, 2004).

Reverse correlation shows us that most V1 cells have weights that are described by **Gabor functions**. The Gabor function describes the weight at a 2-D point in the image. We can think of an image as being a function of 2-D coordinates, $I(x, y)$. Likewise, we can think of a simple cell as sampling the image at a set of locations, defined by a set of x coordinates $\mathbb{X}$ and a set of y coordinates $\mathbb{Y}$, then applying weights that are also a function of the location, $w(x, y)$. From this point of view, the response of a simple cell to an image is given by

$$s(I) = \sum_{x \in \mathbb{X}} \sum_{y \in \mathbb{Y}} w(x, y) I(x, y). \tag{9.15}$$

Specifically, $w(x, y)$ takes the form of a Gabor function:

$$w(x, y; \alpha, \beta_x, \beta_y, f, \phi, x_0, y_0, \tau) = \alpha \exp\left(-\beta_x x'^2 - \beta_y y'^2\right) \cos(f x' + \phi), \tag{9.16}$$

where

$$x' = (x - x_0) \cos(\tau) + (y - y_0) \sin(\tau) \tag{9.17}$$

and

$$y' = -(x - x_0) \sin(\tau) + (y - y_0) \cos(\tau). \tag{9.18}$$

Here, α, β_x, β_y, f, ϕ, x_0, y_0, and τ are parameters that control the properties of the Gabor function. Figure 9.18 shows some examples of Gabor functions with different settings of these parameters.

The parameters x_0, y_0, and τ define a coordinate system. We translate and rotate x and y to form x' and y'. Specifically, the simple cell will respond to image features centered at the point (x_0, y_0), and it will respond to changes in brightness as we move along a line rotated τ radians from the horizontal.

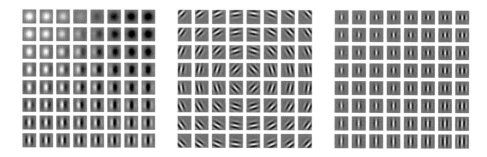

Figure 9.18: Gabor functions with a variety of parameter settings. White indicates large positive weight, black indicates large negative weight, and the background gray corresponds to zero weight. *(Left)*Gabor functions with different values of the parameters that control the coordinate system: x_0, y_0, and τ. Each Gabor function in this grid is assigned a value of x_0 and y_0 proportional to its position in its grid, and τ is chosen so that each Gabor filter is sensitive to the direction radiating out from the center of the grid. For the other two plots, x_0, y_0, and τ are fixed to zero. *(Center)*Gabor functions with different Gaussian scale parameters β_x and β_y. Gabor functions are arranged in increasing width (decreasing β_x) as we move left to right through the grid, and increasing height (decreasing β_y) as we move top to bottom. For the other two plots, the β values are fixed to 1.5 times the image width. *(Right)*Gabor functions with different sinusoid parameters f and ϕ. As we move top to bottom, f increases, and as we move left to right, ϕ increases. For the other two plots, ϕ is fixed to 0 and f is fixed to 5 times the image width.

Viewed as a function of x' and y', the function w then responds to changes in brightness as we move along the x' axis. It has two important factors: one is a Gaussian function, and the other is a cosine function.

The Gaussian factor $\alpha \exp\left(-\beta_x x'^2 - \beta_y y'^2\right)$ can be seen as a gating term that ensures that the simple cell will respond only to values near where x' and y' are both zero, in other words, near the center of the cell's receptive field. The scaling factor α adjusts the total magnitude of the simple cell's response, while β_x and β_y control how quickly its receptive field falls off.

The cosine factor $\cos(fx' + \phi)$ controls how the simple cell responds to changing brightness along the x' axis. The parameter f controls the frequency of the cosine, and ϕ controls its phase offset.

Altogether, this cartoon view of simple cells means that a simple cell responds to a specific spatial frequency of brightness in a specific direction at a specific location. Simple cells are most excited when the wave of brightness in the image has the same phase as the weights. This occurs when the image is bright where the weights are positive and dark where the weights are negative. Simple cells are most inhibited when the wave of brightness is fully out of phase with the weights—when the image is dark where the weights are positive and bright where the weights are negative.

The cartoon view of a complex cell is that it computes the L^2 norm of the 2-D vector containing two simple cells' responses: $c(I) = \sqrt{s_0(I)^2 + s_1(I)^2}$. An important special case occurs when s_1 has all the same parameters as s_0 except for ϕ, and ϕ is set such that s_1 is one quarter cycle out of phase with s_0. In this case, s_0 and s_1 form a **quadrature pair**. A complex cell defined in this way responds when the Gaussian reweighted image $I(x, y) \exp(-\beta_x x'^2 - \beta_y y'^2)$ contains a high-amplitude sinusoidal wave with frequency f in direction τ near (x_0, y_0), *regardless of the phase offset of this wave*. In other words, the complex cell is invariant to small translations of the image in direction τ, or to negating the image (replacing black with white and vice versa).

Some of the most striking correspondences between neuroscience and machine learning come from visually comparing the features learned by machine learning models with those employed by V1. Olshausen and Field (1996) showed that a simple unsupervised learning algorithm, sparse coding, learns features with receptive fields similar to those of simple cells. Since then, we have found that an extremely wide variety of statistical learning algorithms learn features with Gabor-like functions when applied to natural images. This includes most deep learning algorithms, which learn these features in their first layer. Figure 9.19 shows some examples. Because so many different learning algorithms learn edge detectors, it is difficult to conclude that any specific learning algorithm is the "right" model of the brain just based on the features it learns (though it can certainly be a bad sign if an algorithm does *not* learn some sort of edge detector when applied to natural images). These features are an important part of the statistical structure of natural images and can be recovered by many different approaches to statistical modeling. See Hyvärinen et al. (2009) for a review of the field of natural image statistics.

9.11 Convolutional Networks and the History of Deep Learning

Convolutional networks have played an important role in the history of deep learning. They are a key example of a successful application of insights obtained by studying the brain to machine learning applications. They were also some of the first deep models to perform well, long before arbitrary deep models were considered viable. Convolutional networks were also some of the first neural

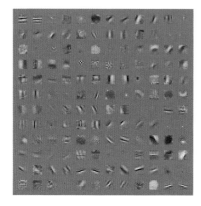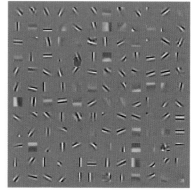

Figure 9.19: Many machine learning algorithms learn features that detect edges or specific colors of edges when applied to natural images. These feature detectors are reminiscent of the Gabor functions known to be present in primary visual cortex. *(Left)*Weights learned by an unsupervised learning algorithm (spike and slab sparse coding) applied to small image patches. *(Right)*Convolution kernels learned by the first layer of a fully supervised convolutional maxout network. Neighboring pairs of filters drive the same maxout unit.

networks to solve important commercial applications and remain at the forefront of commercial applications of deep learning today. For example, in the 1990s, the neural network research group at AT&T developed a convolutional network for reading checks (LeCun et al., 1998b). By the end of the 1990s, this system deployed by NEC was reading over 10 percent of all the checks in the United States. Later, several OCR and handwriting recognition systems based on convolutional nets were deployed by Microsoft (Simard et al., 2003). See chapter 12 for more details on such applications and more modern applications of convolutional networks. See LeCun et al. (2010) for a more in-depth history of convolutional networks up to 2010.

Convolutional networks were also used to win many contests. The current intensity of commercial interest in deep learning began when Krizhevsky et al. (2012) won the ImageNet object recognition challenge, but convolutional networks had been used to win other machine learning and computer vision contests with less impact for years earlier.

Convolutional nets were some of the first working deep networks trained with back-propagation. It is not entirely clear why convolutional networks succeeded when general back-propagation networks were considered to have failed. It may simply be that convolutional networks were more computationally efficient than fully connected networks, so it was easier to run multiple experiments with them and tune their implementation and hyperparameters. Larger networks also seem to be easier to train. With modern hardware, large fully connected networks appear to perform reasonably on many tasks, even when using datasets that were available and activation functions that were popular during the times when fully connected networks were believed not to work well. It may be that the primary barriers to the success of neural networks were psychological (practitioners did not expect neural networks to work, so they did not make a serious effort to use neural networks). Whatever the case, it is fortunate that convolutional networks performed well decades ago. In many ways, they carried the torch for the rest of deep learning and paved the way to the acceptance of neural networks in general.

Convolutional networks provide a way to specialize neural networks to work with data that has a clear grid-structured topology and to scale such models to very large size. This approach has been the most successful on a two-dimensional image topology. To process one-dimensional sequential data, we turn next to another powerful specialization of the neural networks framework: recurrent neural networks.

10

Sequence Modeling: Recurrent and Recursive Nets

Recurrent neural networks, or RNNs (Rumelhart et al., 1986a), are a family of neural networks for processing sequential data. Much as a convolutional network is a neural network that is specialized for processing a grid of values X such as an image, a recurrent neural network is a neural network that is specialized for processing a sequence of values $x^{(1)}, \ldots, x^{(\tau)}$. Just as convolutional networks can readily scale to images with large width and height, and some convolutional networks can process images of variable size, recurrent networks can scale to much longer sequences than would be practical for networks without sequence-based specialization. Most recurrent networks can also process sequences of variable length.

To go from multilayer networks to recurrent networks, we need to take advantage of one of the early ideas found in machine learning and statistical models of the 1980s: sharing parameters across different parts of a model. Parameter sharing makes it possible to extend and apply the model to examples of different forms (different lengths, here) and generalize across them. If we had separate parameters for each value of the time index, we could not generalize to sequence lengths not seen during training, nor share statistical strength across different sequence lengths and across different positions in time. Such sharing is particularly important when a specific piece of information can occur at multiple positions within the sequence. For example, consider the two sentences "I went to Nepal in 2009" and "In 2009, I went to Nepal." If we ask a machine learning model to read each sentence and extract the year in which the narrator went to Nepal, we would like it to recognize the year 2009 as the relevant piece of information, whether it appears in the sixth word or in the second word of the sentence. Suppose that we trained a feedforward network that processes sentences of fixed length. A traditional fully connected feedforward network would have separate parameters for each input feature, so it would need to learn all the rules of the language separately at each position in the sentence. By comparison, a recurrent neural network shares the same weights across several time steps.

A related idea is the use of convolution across a 1-D temporal sequence. This convolutional approach is the basis for time-delay neural networks (Lang and Hinton, 1988; Waibel et al., 1989; Lang et al., 1990). The convolution operation allows a network to share parameters across time but is shallow. The output of convolution is a sequence where each member of the output is a function of a small number of neighboring members of the input. The idea of parameter sharing manifests in the application of the same convolution kernel at each time step. Recurrent networks share parameters in a different way. Each member of the output is a function of the previous members of the output. Each member of the output is produced using the same update rule applied to the previous outputs. This recurrent formulation results in the sharing of parameters through a very deep computational graph.

For the simplicity of exposition, we refer to RNNs as operating on a sequence that contains vectors $\boldsymbol{x}^{(t)}$ with the time step index t ranging from 1 to τ. In practice, recurrent networks usually operate on minibatches of such sequences, with a different sequence length τ for each member of the minibatch. We have omitted the minibatch indices to simplify notation. Moreover, the time step index need not literally refer to the passage of time in the real world. Sometimes it refers only to the position in the sequence. RNNs may also be applied in two dimensions across spatial data such as images, and even when applied to data involving time, the network may have connections that go backward in time, provided that the entire sequence is observed before it is provided to the network.

This chapter extends the idea of a computational graph to include cycles. These cycles represent the influence of the present value of a variable on its own value at a future time step. Such computational graphs allow us to define recurrent neural networks. We then describe many different ways to construct, train, and use recurrent neural networks.

For more information on recurrent neural networks than is available in this chapter, we refer the reader to the textbook of Graves (2012).

10.1 Unfolding Computational Graphs

A computational graph is a way to formalize the structure of a set of computations, such as those involved in mapping inputs and parameters to outputs and loss. Please refer to section 6.5.1 for a general introduction. In this section we explain the idea of **unfolding** a recursive or recurrent computation into a computational graph that has a repetitive structure, typically corresponding to a chain of events. Unfolding this graph results in the sharing of parameters across a deep network structure.

For example, consider the classical form of a dynamical system:

$$s^{(t)} = f(s^{(t-1)}; \boldsymbol{\theta}), \tag{10.1}$$

where $s^{(t)}$ is called the state of the system.

Equation 10.1 is recurrent because the definition of s at time t refers back to the same definition at time $t - 1$.

For a finite number of time steps τ, the graph can be unfolded by applying the definition $\tau - 1$ times. For example, if we unfold equation 10.1 for $\tau = 3$ time steps, we obtain

$$s^{(3)} = f(s^{(2)}; \boldsymbol{\theta}) \tag{10.2}$$
$$= f(f(s^{(1)}; \boldsymbol{\theta}); \boldsymbol{\theta}). \tag{10.3}$$

Unfolding the equation by repeatedly applying the definition in this way has yielded an expression that does not involve recurrence. Such an expression can now be represented by a traditional directed acyclic computational graph. The unfolded computational graph of equation 10.1 and equation 10.3 is illustrated in figure 10.1.

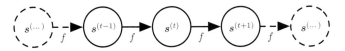

Figure 10.1: The classical dynamical system described by equation 10.1, illustrated as an unfolded computational graph. Each node represents the state at some time t, and the function f maps the state at t to the state at $t + 1$. The same parameters (the same value of $\boldsymbol{\theta}$ used to parametrize f) are used for all time steps.

As another example, let us consider a dynamical system driven by an external signal $\boldsymbol{x}^{(t)}$,

$$s^{(t)} = f(s^{(t-1)}, \boldsymbol{x}^{(t)}; \boldsymbol{\theta}), \tag{10.4}$$

where we see that the state now contains information about the whole past sequence.

Recurrent neural networks can be built in many different ways. Much as almost any function can be considered a feedforward neural network, essentially any function involving recurrence can be considered a recurrent neural network.

Many recurrent neural networks use equation 10.5 or a similar equation to define the values of their hidden units. To indicate that the state is the hidden units of the network, we now rewrite equation 10.4 using the variable $\boldsymbol{h}$ to represent the state,

$$\boldsymbol{h}^{(t)} = f(\boldsymbol{h}^{(t-1)}, \boldsymbol{x}^{(t)}; \boldsymbol{\theta}), \tag{10.5}$$

illustrated in figure 10.2; typical RNNs will add extra architectural features such as output layers that read information out of the state $\boldsymbol{h}$ to make predictions.

When the recurrent network is trained to perform a task that requires predicting the future from the past, the network typically learns to use $\boldsymbol{h}^{(t)}$ as a kind of lossy summary of the task-relevant aspects of the past sequence of inputs up to t. This summary is in general necessarily lossy, since it maps an arbitrary length sequence $(\boldsymbol{x}^{(t)}, \boldsymbol{x}^{(t-1)}, \boldsymbol{x}^{(t-2)}, \ldots, \boldsymbol{x}^{(2)}, \boldsymbol{x}^{(1)})$ to a fixed length vector $\boldsymbol{h}^{(t)}$. Depending on the training criterion, this summary might selectively keep some aspects of the past sequence with more precision than other aspects. For example, if the RNN is used in statistical language modeling, typically to predict the next word given previous words, storing all the information in the input sequence up to time t may not be necessary; storing only enough information to predict the rest of the sentence is sufficient. The most demanding situation is when we ask $\boldsymbol{h}^{(t)}$ to be rich

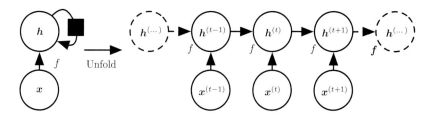

Figure 10.2: A recurrent network with no outputs. This recurrent network just processes information from the input $\boldsymbol{x}$ by incorporating it into the state $\boldsymbol{h}$ that is passed forward through time. *(Left)* Circuit diagram. The black square indicates a delay of a single time step. *(Right)* The same network seen as an unfolded computational graph, where each node is now associated with one particular time instance.

enough to allow one to approximately recover the input sequence, as in autoencoder frameworks (chapter 14).

Equation 10.5 can be drawn in two different ways. One way to draw the RNN is with a diagram containing one node for every component that might exist in a physical implementation of the model, such as a biological neural network. In this view, the network defines a circuit that operates in real time, with physical parts whose current state can influence their future state, as in the left of figure 10.2. Throughout this chapter, we use a black square in a circuit diagram to indicate that an interaction takes place with a delay of a single time step, from the state at time t to the state at time $t + 1$. The other way to draw the RNN is as an unfolded computational graph, in which each component is represented by many different variables, with one variable per time step, representing the state of the component at that point in time. Each variable for each time step is drawn as a separate node of the computational graph, as in the right of figure 10.2. What we call unfolding is the operation that maps a circuit, as in the left side of the figure, to a computational graph with repeated pieces, as in the right side. The unfolded graph now has a size that depends on the sequence length.

We can represent the unfolded recurrence after t steps with a function $g^{(t)}$:

$$\boldsymbol{h}^{(t)} = g^{(t)}(\boldsymbol{x}^{(t)}, \boldsymbol{x}^{(t-1)}, \boldsymbol{x}^{(t-2)}, \ldots, \boldsymbol{x}^{(2)}, \boldsymbol{x}^{(1)}) \tag{10.6}$$

$$= f(\boldsymbol{h}^{(t-1)}, \boldsymbol{x}^{(t)}; \boldsymbol{\theta}). \tag{10.7}$$

The function $g^{(t)}$ takes the whole past sequence $(\boldsymbol{x}^{(t)}, \boldsymbol{x}^{(t-1)}, \boldsymbol{x}^{(t-2)}, \ldots, \boldsymbol{x}^{(2)}, \boldsymbol{x}^{(1)})$ as input and produces the current state, but the unfolded recurrent structure allows us to factorize $g^{(t)}$ into repeated application of a function f. The unfolding process thus introduces two major advantages:

1. Regardless of the sequence length, the learned model always has the same input size, because it is specified in terms of transition from one state to another state, rather than specified in terms of a variable-length history of states.

2. It is possible to use the *same* transition function f with the same parameters at every time step.

These two factors make it possible to learn a single model f that operates on all time steps and all sequence lengths, rather than needing to learn a separate model $g^{(t)}$ for all possible time steps. Learning a single shared model allows generalization to sequence lengths that did not appear in the training set, and enables the model to be estimated with far fewer training examples than would be required without parameter sharing.

Both the recurrent graph and the unrolled graph have their uses. The recurrent graph is succinct. The unfolded graph provides an explicit description of which computations to perform. The unfolded graph also helps illustrate the idea of information flow forward in time (computing outputs and losses) and backward in time (computing gradients) by explicitly showing the path along which this information flows.

10.2   Recurrent Neural Networks

Armed with the graph-unrolling and parameter-sharing ideas of section 10.1, we can design a wide variety of recurrent neural networks.

Some examples of important design patterns for recurrent neural networks include the following:

- Recurrent networks that produce an output at each time step and have recurrent connections between hidden units, illustrated in figure 10.3

- Recurrent networks that produce an output at each time step and have recurrent connections only from the output at one time step to the hidden units at the next time step, illustrated in figure 10.4

- Recurrent networks with recurrent connections between hidden units, that read an entire sequence and then produce a single output, illustrated in figure 10.5

Figure 10.3 is a reasonably representative example that we return to throughout most of the chapter.

The recurrent neural network of figure 10.3 and equation 10.8 is universal in the sense that any function computable by a Turing machine can be computed by such a recurrent network of a finite size. The output can be read from the RNN after a number of time steps that is asymptotically linear in the number of time steps used by the Turing machine and asymptotically linear in the length of the input (Siegelmann and Sontag, 1991; Siegelmann, 1995; Siegelmann and Sontag, 1995; Hyotyniemi, 1996). The functions computable by a Turing machine are discrete, so these results regard exact implementation of the function, not approximations. The RNN, when used as a Turing machine, takes a binary sequence as input, and its outputs must be discretized to provide a binary output. It is possible to

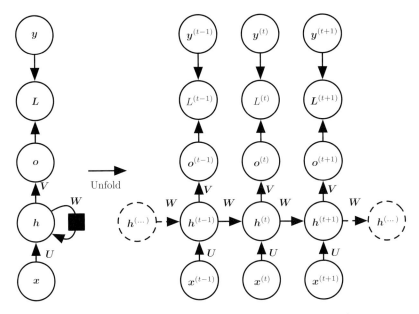

Figure 10.3: The computational graph to compute the training loss of a recurrent network that maps an input sequence of x values to a corresponding sequence of output o values. A loss L measures how far each o is from the corresponding training target y. When using softmax outputs, we assume o is the unnormalized log probabilities. The loss L internally computes $\hat{y} = \text{softmax}(o)$ and compares this to the target y. The RNN has input to hidden connections parametrized by a weight matrix U, hidden-to-hidden recurrent connections parametrized by a weight matrix W, and hidden-to-output connections parametrized by a weight matrix V. Equation 10.8 defines forward propagation in this model. *(Left)* The RNN and its loss drawn with recurrent connections. *(Right)* The same seen as a time-unfolded computational graph, where each node is now associated with one particular time instance.

compute all functions in this setting using a single specific RNN of finite size (Siegelmann and Sontag[1995] use 886 units). The "input" of the Turing machine is a specification of the function to be computed, so the same network that simulates this Turing machine is sufficient for all problems. The theoretical RNN used for the proof can simulate an unbounded stack by representing its activations and weights with rational numbers of unbounded precision.

We now develop the forward propagation equations for the RNN depicted in figure 10.3. The figure does not specify the choice of activation function for the hidden units. Here we assume the hyperbolic tangent activation function. Also, the figure does not specify exactly what form the output and loss function take. Here we assume that the output is discrete, as if the RNN is used to predict words or characters. A natural way to represent discrete variables is to regard the output o

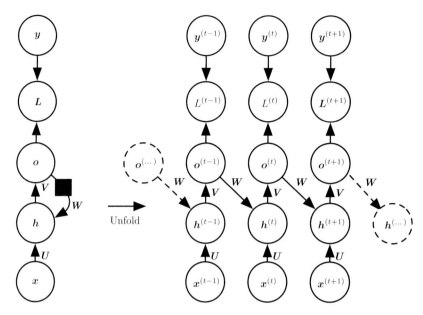

Figure 10.4: An RNN whose only recurrence is the feedback connection from the output to the hidden layer. At each time step t, the input is $\boldsymbol{x}_t$, the hidden layer activations are $\boldsymbol{h}^{(t)}$, the outputs are $\boldsymbol{o}^{(t)}$, the targets are $\boldsymbol{y}^{(t)}$, and the loss is $L^{(t)}$. *(Left)* Circuit diagram. *(Right)* Unfolded computational graph. Such an RNN is less powerful (can express a smaller set of functions) than those in the family represented by figure 10.3. The RNN in figure 10.3 can choose to put any information it wants about the past into its hidden representation $\boldsymbol{h}$ and transmit $\boldsymbol{h}$ to the future. The RNN in this figure is trained to put a specific output value into $\boldsymbol{o}$, and $\boldsymbol{o}$ is the only information it is allowed to send to the future. There are no direct connections from $\boldsymbol{h}$ going forward. The previous $\boldsymbol{h}$ is connected to the present only indirectly, via the predictions it was used to produce. Unless $\boldsymbol{o}$ is very high-dimensional and rich, it will usually lack important information from the past. This makes the RNN in this figure less powerful, but it may be easier to train because each time step can be trained in isolation from the others, allowing greater parallelization during training, as described in section 10.2.1.

as giving the unnormalized log probabilities of each possible value of the discrete variable. We can then apply the softmax operation as a post-processing step to obtain a vector $\hat{\boldsymbol{y}}$ of normalized probabilities over the output. Forward propagation begins with a specification of the initial state $\boldsymbol{h}^{(0)}$. Then, for each time step from $t = 1$ to $t = \tau$, we apply the following update equations:

$$\boldsymbol{a}^{(t)} = \boldsymbol{b} + \boldsymbol{W}\boldsymbol{h}^{(t-1)} + \boldsymbol{U}\boldsymbol{x}^{(t)}, \tag{10.8}$$
$$\boldsymbol{h}^{(t)} = \tanh(\boldsymbol{a}^{(t)}), \tag{10.9}$$
$$\boldsymbol{o}^{(t)} = \boldsymbol{c} + \boldsymbol{V}\boldsymbol{h}^{(t)}, \tag{10.10}$$

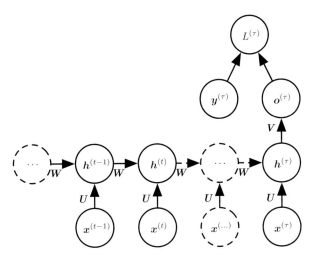

Figure 10.5: Time-unfolded recurrent neural network with a single output at the end of the sequence. Such a network can be used to summarize a sequence and produce a fixed-size representation used as input for further processing. There might be a target right at the end (as depicted here), or the gradient on the output $\boldsymbol{o}^{(t)}$ can be obtained by back-propagating from further downstream modules.

$$\hat{\boldsymbol{y}}^{(t)} \;=\; \text{softmax}(\boldsymbol{o}^{(t)}), \tag{10.11}$$

where the parameters are the bias vectors $\boldsymbol{b}$ and $\boldsymbol{c}$ along with the weight matrices $\boldsymbol{U}$, $\boldsymbol{V}$ and $\boldsymbol{W}$, respectively, for input-to-hidden, hidden-to-output and hidden-to-hidden connections. This is an example of a recurrent network that maps an input sequence to an output sequence of the same length. The total loss for a given sequence of $\boldsymbol{x}$ values paired with a sequence of $\boldsymbol{y}$ values would then be just the sum of the losses over all the time steps. For example, if $L^{(t)}$ is the negative log-likelihood of $y^{(t)}$ given $\boldsymbol{x}^{(1)}, \ldots, \boldsymbol{x}^{(t)}$, then

$$L\left(\{\boldsymbol{x}^{(1)}, \ldots, \boldsymbol{x}^{(\tau)}\}, \{\boldsymbol{y}^{(1)}, \ldots, \boldsymbol{y}^{(\tau)}\}\right) \tag{10.12}$$

$$= \sum_t L^{(t)} \tag{10.13}$$

$$= -\sum_t \log p_{\text{model}}\left(y^{(t)} \mid \{\boldsymbol{x}^{(1)}, \ldots, \boldsymbol{x}^{(t)}\}\right), \tag{10.14}$$

where $p_{\text{model}}\left(y^{(t)} \mid \{\boldsymbol{x}^{(1)}, \ldots, \boldsymbol{x}^{(t)}\}\right)$ is given by reading the entry for $y^{(t)}$ from the model's output vector $\hat{\boldsymbol{y}}^{(t)}$. Computing the gradient of this loss function with respect to the parameters is an expensive operation. The gradient computation involves performing a forward propagation pass moving left to right through our illustration of the unrolled graph in figure 10.3, followed by a backward propagation pass moving right to left through the graph. The runtime is $O(\tau)$ and cannot be reduced by parallelization because the forward propagation graph is inherently sequential; each time step may be computed only after the previous one. States computed in the forward pass must be stored until they are reused during the backward pass, so the memory cost is also $O(\tau)$. The back-propagation algorithm applied to the unrolled graph with $O(\tau)$ cost is called **back-propagation through time** (BPTT) and is discussed further in section 10.2.2. The network with recurrence between hidden units is thus very powerful but also expensive to train. Is there an alternative?

10.2.1 Teacher Forcing and Networks with Output Recurrence

The network with recurrent connections only from the output at one time step to the hidden units at the next time step (shown in figure 10.4) is strictly less powerful because it lacks hidden-to-hidden recurrent connections. For example, it cannot simulate a universal Turing machine. Because this network lacks hidden-to-hidden recurrence, it requires that the output units capture all the information about the past that the network will use to predict the future. Because the output units are explicitly trained to match the training set targets, they are unlikely to capture the necessary information about the past history of the input, unless the user knows how to describe the full state of the system and provides it as part of the training set targets. The advantage of eliminating hidden-to-hidden recurrence is that, for any loss function based on comparing the prediction at time t to the training target at time t, all the time steps are decoupled. Training can thus be parallelized, with the gradient for each step t computed in isolation. There is no need to compute the output for the previous time step first, because the training set provides the ideal value of that output.

Models that have recurrent connections from their outputs leading back into the model may be trained with **teacher forcing**. Teacher forcing is a procedure that emerges from the maximum likelihood criterion, in which during training the model receives the ground truth output $y^{(t)}$ as input at time $t + 1$. We can see this by examining a sequence with two time steps. The conditional maximum likelihood criterion is

$$\log p\left(\boldsymbol{y}^{(1)}, \boldsymbol{y}^{(2)} \mid \boldsymbol{x}^{(1)}, \boldsymbol{x}^{(2)}\right) \tag{10.15}$$

$$= \log p\left(\boldsymbol{y}^{(2)} \mid \boldsymbol{y}^{(1)}, \boldsymbol{x}^{(1)}, \boldsymbol{x}^{(2)}\right) + \log p\left(\boldsymbol{y}^{(1)} \mid \boldsymbol{x}^{(1)}, \boldsymbol{x}^{(2)}\right). \tag{10.16}$$

In this example, we see that at time $t = 2$, the model is trained to maximize the conditional probability of $\boldsymbol{y}^{(2)}$ given *both* the $\boldsymbol{x}$ sequence so far and the previous $\boldsymbol{y}$ value from the training set. Maximum likelihood thus specifies that during training, rather than feeding the model's own output back into itself, these connections should be fed with the target values specifying what the correct output should be. This is illustrated in figure 10.6.

We originally motivated teacher forcing as allowing us to avoid back-propagation through time in models that lack hidden-to-hidden connections. Teacher forcing may still be applied to models that have hidden-to-hidden connections as long as they have connections from the output at one time step to values computed in the next time step. As soon as the hidden units become a function of earlier time steps, however, the BPTT algorithm is necessary. Some models may thus be trained with both teacher forcing and BPTT.

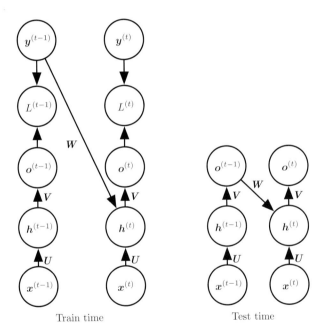

Figure 10.6: Illustration of teacher forcing. Teacher forcing is a training technique that is applicable to RNNs that have connections from their output to their hidden states at the next time step. *(Left)* At train time, we feed the *correct output* $\boldsymbol{y}^{(t)}$ drawn from the train set as input to $\boldsymbol{h}^{(t+1)}$. *(Right)* When the model is deployed, the true output is generally not known. In this case, we approximate the correct output $\boldsymbol{y}^{(t)}$ with the model's output $\boldsymbol{o}^{(t)}$, and feed the output back into the model.

The disadvantage of strict teacher forcing arises if the network is going to be later used in an **open-loop** mode, with the network outputs (or samples from the output distribution) fed back as input. In this case, the kind of inputs that the network sees during training could be quite different from the kind of inputs that it will see at test time. One way to mitigate this problem is to train with both teacher-forced inputs and free-running inputs, for example by predicting the correct target a number of steps in the future through the unfolded recurrent output-to-input paths. In this way, the network can learn to take into account input conditions (such as those it generates itself in the free-running mode) not seen during training and how to map the state back toward one that will make the network generate proper outputs after a few steps. Another approach (Bengio et al., 2015b) to mitigate the gap between the inputs seen at training time and the inputs seen at test time randomly chooses to use generated values or actual data values as input. This approach exploits a curriculum learning strategy to gradually use more of the generated values as input.

10.2.2 Computing the Gradient in a Recurrent Neural Network

Computing the gradient through a recurrent neural network is straightforward. One simply applies the generalized back-propagation algorithm of section 6.5.6 to the unrolled computational graph. No specialized algorithms are necessary. Gradients obtained by back-propagation may then be used with any general-purpose gradient-based techniques to train an RNN.

To gain some intuition for how the BPTT algorithm behaves, we provide an example of how to compute gradients by BPTT for the RNN equations above (equation 10.8 and equation 10.12). The nodes of our computational graph include the parameters $\boldsymbol{U}$, $\boldsymbol{V}$, $\boldsymbol{W}$, $\boldsymbol{b}$ and $\boldsymbol{c}$ as well as the sequence of nodes indexed by t for $\boldsymbol{x}^{(t)}$, $\boldsymbol{h}^{(t)}$, $\boldsymbol{o}^{(t)}$ and $L^{(t)}$. For each node N we need to compute the gradient $\nabla_{\mathsf{N}} L$ recursively, based on the gradient computed at nodes that follow it in the graph. We start the recursion with the nodes immediately preceding the final loss:

$$\frac{\partial L}{\partial L^{(t)}} = 1. \tag{10.17}$$

In this derivation we assume that the outputs $\boldsymbol{o}^{(t)}$ are used as the argument to the softmax function to obtain the vector $\hat{\boldsymbol{y}}$ of probabilities over the output. We also assume that the loss is the negative log-likelihood of the true target $y^{(t)}$ given the input so far. The gradient $\nabla_{\boldsymbol{o}^{(t)}} L$ on the outputs at time step t, for all i, t, is as follows:

$$(\nabla_{\boldsymbol{o}^{(t)}} L)_i = \frac{\partial L}{\partial o_i^{(t)}} = \frac{\partial L}{\partial L^{(t)}} \frac{\partial L^{(t)}}{\partial o_i^{(t)}} = \hat{y}_i^{(t)} - \mathbf{1}_{i, y^{(t)}}. \tag{10.18}$$

We work our way backward, starting from the end of the sequence. At the final time step τ, $\boldsymbol{h}^{(\tau)}$ only has $\boldsymbol{o}^{(\tau)}$ as a descendent, so its gradient is simple:

$$\nabla_{\boldsymbol{h}^{(\tau)}} L = \boldsymbol{V}^\top \nabla_{\boldsymbol{o}^{(\tau)}} L. \tag{10.19}$$

We can then iterate backward in time to back-propagate gradients through time, from $t = \tau - 1$ down to $t = 1$, noting that $\boldsymbol{h}^{(t)}$ (for $t < \tau$) has as descendents both $\boldsymbol{o}^{(t)}$ and $\boldsymbol{h}^{(t+1)}$. Its gradient is thus given by

$$\nabla_{\boldsymbol{h}^{(t)}} L = \left(\frac{\partial \boldsymbol{h}^{(t+1)}}{\partial \boldsymbol{h}^{(t)}}\right)^\top (\nabla_{\boldsymbol{h}^{(t+1)}} L) + \left(\frac{\partial \boldsymbol{o}^{(t)}}{\partial \boldsymbol{h}^{(t)}}\right)^\top (\nabla_{\boldsymbol{o}^{(t)}} L) \tag{10.20}$$

$$= \boldsymbol{W}^\top (\nabla_{\boldsymbol{h}^{(t+1)}} L) \operatorname{diag}\left(1 - \left(\boldsymbol{h}^{(t+1)}\right)^2\right) + \boldsymbol{V}^\top (\nabla_{\boldsymbol{o}^{(t)}} L), \tag{10.21}$$

where $\operatorname{diag}\left(1 - \left(\boldsymbol{h}^{(t+1)}\right)^2\right)$ indicates the diagonal matrix containing the elements $1 - (h_i^{(t+1)})^2$. This is the Jacobian of the hyperbolic tangent associated with the hidden unit i at time $t + 1$.

Once the gradients on the internal nodes of the computational graph are obtained, we can obtain the gradients on the parameter nodes. Because the parameters are shared across many time steps, we must take some care when denoting calculus operations involving these variables. The equations we wish to implement use the `bprop` method of section 6.5.6, which computes the contribution of a single edge in the computational graph to the gradient. The $\nabla_{\boldsymbol{W}} f$ operator used in calculus, however, takes into account the contribution of $\boldsymbol{W}$ to the value of f due to *all* edges in the computational graph. To resolve this ambiguity, we introduce dummy variables $\boldsymbol{W}^{(t)}$ that are defined to be copies of $\boldsymbol{W}$ but with each $\boldsymbol{W}^{(t)}$ used only at time step t. We may then use $\nabla_{\boldsymbol{W}^{(t)}}$ to denote the contribution of the weights at time step t to the gradient.

Using this notation, the gradient on the remaining parameters is given by

$$\nabla_{\boldsymbol{c}} L = \sum_t \left(\frac{\partial \boldsymbol{o}^{(t)}}{\partial \boldsymbol{c}}\right)^\top \nabla_{\boldsymbol{o}^{(t)}} L = \sum_t \nabla_{\boldsymbol{o}^{(t)}} L, \tag{10.22}$$

$$\nabla_{\boldsymbol{b}} L = \sum_t \left(\frac{\partial \boldsymbol{h}^{(t)}}{\partial \boldsymbol{b}^{(t)}}\right)^\top \nabla_{\boldsymbol{h}^{(t)}} L = \sum_t \operatorname{diag}\left(1 - \left(\boldsymbol{h}^{(t)}\right)^2\right) \nabla_{\boldsymbol{h}^{(t)}} L, \tag{10.23}$$

$$\nabla_{\boldsymbol{V}} L = \sum_t \sum_i \left(\frac{\partial L}{\partial o_i^{(t)}}\right) \nabla_{\boldsymbol{V}} o_i^{(t)} = \sum_t (\nabla_{\boldsymbol{o}^{(t)}} L) \boldsymbol{h}^{(t)\top}, \tag{10.24}$$

$$\nabla_{\boldsymbol{W}} L = \sum_t \sum_i \left(\frac{\partial L}{\partial h_i^{(t)}} \right) \nabla_{\boldsymbol{W}^{(t)}} h_i^{(t)} \tag{10.25}$$

$$= \sum_t \text{diag}\left(1 - \left(\boldsymbol{h}^{(t)} \right)^2 \right) (\nabla_{\boldsymbol{h}^{(t)}} L) \, \boldsymbol{h}^{(t-1)\top}, \tag{10.26}$$

$$\nabla_{\boldsymbol{U}} L = \sum_t \sum_i \left(\frac{\partial L}{\partial h_i^{(t)}} \right) \nabla_{\boldsymbol{U}^{(t)}} h_i^{(t)} \tag{10.27}$$

$$= \sum_t \text{diag}\left(1 - \left(\boldsymbol{h}^{(t)} \right)^2 \right) (\nabla_{\boldsymbol{h}^{(t)}} L) \, \boldsymbol{x}^{(t)\top}, \tag{10.28}$$

We do not need to compute the gradient with respect to $\boldsymbol{x}^{(t)}$ for training because it does not have any parameters as ancestors in the computational graph defining the loss.

10.2.3 Recurrent Networks as Directed Graphical Models

In the example recurrent network we have developed so far, the losses $L^{(t)}$ were cross-entropies between training targets $\boldsymbol{y}^{(t)}$ and outputs $\boldsymbol{o}^{(t)}$. As with a feedforward network, it is in principle possible to use almost any loss with a recurrent network. The loss should be chosen based on the task. As with a feedforward network, we usually wish to interpret the output of the RNN as a probability distribution, and we usually use the cross-entropy associated with that distribution to define the loss. Mean squared error is the cross-entropy loss associated with an output distribution that is a unit Gaussian, for example, just as with a feedforward network.

When we use a predictive log-likelihood training objective, such as equation 10.12, we train the RNN to estimate the conditional distribution of the next sequence element $\boldsymbol{y}^{(t)}$ given the past inputs. This may mean that we maximize the log-likelihood

$$\log p(\boldsymbol{y}^{(t)} \mid \boldsymbol{x}^{(1)}, \ldots, \boldsymbol{x}^{(t)}), \tag{10.29}$$

or, if the model includes connections from the output at one time step to the next time step,

$$\log p(\boldsymbol{y}^{(t)} \mid \boldsymbol{x}^{(1)}, \ldots, \boldsymbol{x}^{(t)}, \boldsymbol{y}^{(1)}, \ldots, \boldsymbol{y}^{(t-1)}). \tag{10.30}$$

Decomposing the joint probability over the sequence of $\boldsymbol{y}$ values as a series of one-step probabilistic predictions is one way to capture the full joint distribution across the whole sequence. When we do not feed past $\boldsymbol{y}$ values as inputs that condition the next step prediction, the directed graphical model contains no edges from any $\boldsymbol{y}^{(i)}$ in the past to the current $\boldsymbol{y}^{(t)}$. In this case, the outputs $\boldsymbol{y}$ are conditionally independent given the sequence of $\boldsymbol{x}$ values. When we do feed the actual $\boldsymbol{y}$ values (not their prediction, but the actual observed or generated values) back into the network, the directed graphical model contains edges from all $\boldsymbol{y}^{(i)}$ values in the past to the current $y^{(t)}$ value.

As a simple example, let us consider the case where the RNN models only a sequence of scalar random variables $\mathbb{Y} = \{\mathbf{y}^{(1)}, \dots, \mathbf{y}^{(\tau)}\}$, with no additional inputs x. The input at time step t is simply the output at time step $t-1$. The RNN then defines a directed graphical model over the y variables. We parametrize the joint distribution of these observations using the chain rule (equation 3.6) for conditional probabilities:

$$P(\mathbb{Y}) = P(\mathbf{y}^{(1)}, \dots, \mathbf{y}^{(\tau)}) = \prod_{t=1}^{\tau} P(\mathbf{y}^{(t)} \mid \mathbf{y}^{(t-1)}, \mathbf{y}^{(t-2)}, \dots, \mathbf{y}^{(1)}), \qquad (10.31)$$

where the righthand side of the bar is empty for $t = 1$, of course. Hence the negative log-likelihood of a set of values $\{y^{(1)}, \dots, y^{(\tau)}\}$ according to such a model is

$$L = \sum_t L^{(t)}, \qquad (10.32)$$

where

$$L^{(t)} = -\log P(\mathbf{y}^{(t)} = y^{(t)} \mid y^{(t-1)}, y^{(t-2)}, \dots, y^{(1)}). \qquad (10.33)$$

The edges in a graphical model indicate which variables depend directly on other variables. Many graphical models aim to achieve statistical and computational efficiency by omitting edges that do not correspond to strong interactions. For example, it is common to make the Markov assumption that the graphical model should contain only edges from $\{\mathbf{y}^{(t-k)}, \dots, \mathbf{y}^{(t-1)}\}$ to $\mathbf{y}^{(t)}$, rather than containing edges from the entire history. In some cases, however, we believe that all past inputs should have an influence on the next element of the sequence. RNNs are useful when we believe that the distribution over $\mathbf{y}^{(t)}$ may depend on a value of $\mathbf{y}^{(i)}$ from the distant past in a way that is not captured by the effect of $\mathbf{y}^{(i)}$ on $\mathbf{y}^{(t-1)}$.

One way to interpret an RNN as a graphical model is to view the RNN as defining a graphical model whose structure is the complete graph, able to represent direct dependencies between any pair of y values. The graphical model over the y values with the complete graph structure is shown in figure 10.7. The complete graph interpretation of the RNN is based on ignoring the hidden units $\boldsymbol{h}^{(t)}$ by marginalizing them out of the model.

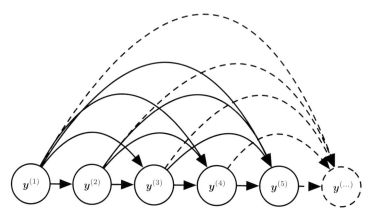

Figure 10.7: Fully connected graphical model for a sequence $y^{(1)}, y^{(2)}, \ldots, y^{(t)}, \ldots$. Every past observation $y^{(i)}$ may influence the conditional distribution of some $y^{(t)}$ (for $t > i$), given the previous values. Parametrizing the graphical model directly according to this graph (as in equation 10.6) might be very inefficient, with an ever growing number of inputs and parameters for each element of the sequence. RNNs obtain the same full connectivity but efficient parametrization, as illustrated in figure 10.8.

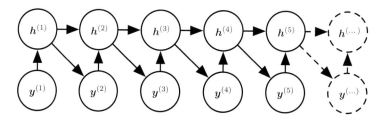

Figure 10.8: Introducing the state variable in the graphical model of the RNN, even though it is a deterministic function of its inputs, helps to see how we can obtain a very efficient parametrization, based on equation 10.5. Every stage in the sequence (for $h^{(t)}$ and $y^{(t)}$) involves the same structure (the same number of inputs for each node) and can share the same parameters with the other stages.

It is more interesting to consider the graphical model structure of RNNs that results from regarding the hidden units $h^{(t)}$ as random variables.[1] Including the hidden units in the graphical model reveals that the RNN provides an efficient parametrization of the joint distribution over the observations. Suppose that we represented an arbitrary joint distribution over discrete values with a tabular

---

[1]The conditional distribution over these variables given their parents is deterministic. This is perfectly legitimate, though it is somewhat rare to design a graphical model with such deterministic hidden units.

representation—an array containing a separate entry for each possible assignment of values, with the value of that entry giving the probability of that assignment occurring. If y can take on k different values, the tabular representation would have $O(k^\tau)$ parameters. By comparison, because of parameter sharing, the number of parameters in the RNN is $O(1)$ as a function of sequence length. The number of parameters in the RNN may be adjusted to control model capacity but is not forced to scale with sequence length. Equation 10.5 shows that the RNN parametrizes long-term relationships between variables efficiently, using recurrent applications of the same function f and the same parameters $\boldsymbol{\theta}$ at each time step. Figure 10.8 illustrates the graphical model interpretation. Incorporating the $\boldsymbol{h}^{(t)}$ nodes in the graphical model decouples the past and the future, acting as an intermediate quantity between them. A variable $y^{(i)}$ in the distant past may influence a variable $y^{(t)}$ via its effect on $\boldsymbol{h}$. The structure of this graph shows that the model can be efficiently parametrized by using the same conditional probability distributions at each time step, and that when the variables are all observed, the probability of the joint assignment of all variables can be evaluated efficiently.

Even with the efficient parametrization of the graphical model, some operations remain computationally challenging. For example, it is difficult to predict missing values in the middle of the sequence.

The price recurrent networks pay for their reduced number of parameters is that *optimizing* the parameters may be difficult.

The parameter sharing used in recurrent networks relies on the assumption that the same parameters can be used for different time steps. Equivalently, the assumption is that the conditional probability distribution over the variables at time $t+1$ given the variables at time t is **stationary**, meaning that the relationship between the previous time step and the next time step does not depend on t. In principle, it would be possible to use t as an extra input at each time step and let the learner discover any time-dependence while sharing as much as it can between different time steps. This would already be much better than using a different conditional probability distribution for each t, but the network would then have to extrapolate when faced with new values of t.

To complete our view of an RNN as a graphical model, we must describe how to draw samples from the model. The main operation that we need to perform is simply to sample from the conditional distribution at each time step. However, there is one additional complication. The RNN must have some mechanism for determining the length of the sequence. This can be achieved in various ways.

When the output is a symbol taken from a vocabulary, one can add a special symbol corresponding to the end of a sequence (Schmidhuber, 2012). When that symbol is generated, the sampling process stops. In the training set, we insert this symbol as an extra member of the sequence, immediately after $x^{(\tau)}$ in each training example.

Another option is to introduce an extra Bernoulli output to the model that represents the decision to either continue generation or halt generation at each time step. This approach is more general than the approach of adding an extra symbol to the vocabulary, because it may be applied to any RNN, rather than only RNNs that output a sequence of symbols. For example, it may be applied to an RNN that emits a sequence of real numbers. The new output unit is usually a sigmoid unit trained with the cross-entropy loss. In this approach the sigmoid is trained to maximize the log-probability of the correct prediction as to whether the sequence ends or continues at each time step.

Another way to determine the sequence length τ is to add an extra output to the model that predicts the integer τ itself. The model can sample a value of τ and then sample τ steps worth of data. This approach requires adding an extra input to the recurrent update at each time step so that the recurrent update is aware of whether it is near the end of the generated sequence. This extra input can either consist of the value of τ or can consist of $\tau - t$, the number of remaining time steps. Without this extra input, the RNN might generate sequences that end abruptly, such as a sentence that ends before it is complete. This approach is based on the decomposition

$$P(x^{(1)}, \ldots, x^{(\tau)}) = P(\tau)P(x^{(1)}, \ldots, x^{(\tau)} \mid \tau). \qquad (10.34)$$

The strategy of predicting τ directly is used, for example, by Goodfellow et al. (2014d).

10.2.4 Modeling Sequences Conditioned on Context with RNNs

In the previous section we described how an RNN could correspond to a directed graphical model over a sequence of random variables $y^{(t)}$ with no inputs x. Of course, our development of RNNs as in equation 10.8 included a sequence of inputs $x^{(1)}, x^{(2)}, \ldots, x^{(\tau)}$. In general, RNNs allow the extension of the graphical model view to represent not only a joint distribution over the y variables but also a conditional distribution over y given x. As discussed in the context of feedforward networks in section 6.2.1.1, any model representing a variable $P(y; \theta)$ can be reinterpreted as a model representing a conditional distribution $P(y|\omega)$ with $\omega = \theta$. We can extend such a model to represent a distribution $P(y \mid x)$ by using the same $P(y \mid \omega)$ as before, but making ω a function of x. In the case of an RNN, this can be achieved in different ways. We review here the most common and obvious choices.

Previously, we have discussed RNNs that take a sequence of vectors $x^{(t)}$ for $t = 1, \ldots, \tau$ as input. Another option is to take only a single vector x as input. When x is a fixed-size vector, we can simply make it an extra input of the RNN that generates the y sequence. Some common ways of providing an extra input to an RNN are

1. as an extra input at each time step, or

2. as the initial state $h^{(0)}$, or

3. both.

The first and most common approach is illustrated in figure 10.9. The interaction between the input x and each hidden unit vector $h^{(t)}$ is parametrized by a newly introduced weight matrix R that was absent from the model of only the sequence

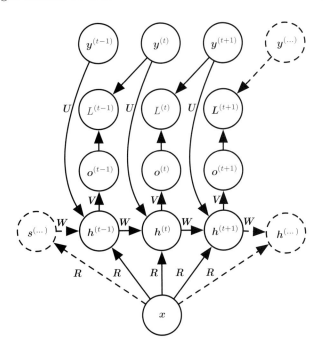

Figure 10.9: An RNN that maps a fixed-length vector x into a distribution over sequences Y. This RNN is appropriate for tasks such as image captioning, where a single image is used as input to a model that then produces a sequence of words describing the image. Each element $y^{(t)}$ of the observed output sequence serves both as input (for the current time step) and, during training, as target (for the previous time step).

of y values. The same product $x^\top R$ is added as additional input to the hidden units at every time step. We can think of the choice of x as determining the value of $x^\top R$ that is effectively a new bias parameter used for each of the hidden units. The weights remain independent of the input. We can think of this model as taking the parameters θ of the nonconditional model and turning them into ω, where the bias parameters within ω are now a function of the input.

Rather than receiving only a single vector x as input, the RNN may receive a sequence of vectors $x^{(t)}$ as input. The RNN described in equation 10.8 corresponds to a conditional distribution $P(y^{(1)}, \ldots, y^{(\tau)} \mid x^{(1)}, \ldots, x^{(\tau)})$ that makes a conditional independence assumption that this distribution factorizes as

$$\prod_t P(y^{(t)} \mid x^{(1)}, \ldots, x^{(t)}). \tag{10.35}$$

To remove the conditional independence assumption, we can add connections from the output at time t to the hidden unit at time $t+1$, as shown in figure 10.10. The

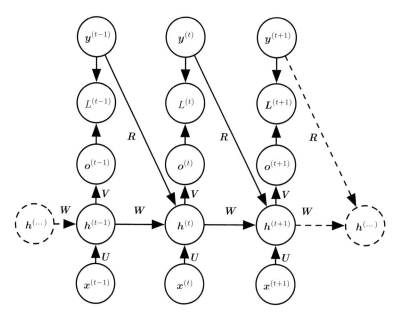

Figure 10.10: A conditional recurrent neural network mapping a variable-length sequence of x values into a distribution over sequences of y values of the same length. Compared to figure 10.3, this RNN contains connections from the previous output to the current state. These connections allow this RNN to model an arbitrary distribution over sequences of y given sequences of x of the same length. The RNN of figure 10.3 is only able to represent distributions in which the y values are conditionally independent from each other given the x values.

model can then represent arbitrary probability distributions over the y sequence. This kind of model representing a distribution over a sequence given another sequence still has one restriction, which is that the length of both sequences must be the same. We describe how to remove this restriction in section 10.4.

10.3 Bidirectional RNNs

All the recurrent networks we have considered up to now have a "causal" structure, meaning that the state at time t captures only information from the past, $x^{(1)}, \ldots, x^{(t-1)}$, and the present input $x^{(t)}$. Some of the models we have discussed also allow information from past y values to affect the current state when the y values are available.

In many applications, however, we want to output a prediction of $y^{(t)}$ that may depend on *the whole input sequence*. For example, in speech recognition, the correct interpretation of the current sound as a phoneme may depend on the next few phonemes because of co-articulation and may even depend on the next few words because of the linguistic dependencies between nearby words: if there are two interpretations of the current word that are both acoustically plausible, we may have to look far into the future (and the past) to disambiguate them. This is also true of handwriting recognition and many other sequence-to-sequence learning tasks, described in the next section.

Bidirectional recurrent neural networks (or bidirectional RNNs) were invented to address that need (Schuster and Paliwal, 1997). They have been extremely successful (Graves, 2012) in applications where that need arises, such as handwriting recognition (Graves et al., 2008; Graves and Schmidhuber, 2009), speech recognition (Graves and Schmidhuber, 2005; Graves et al., 2013), and bioinformatics (Baldi et al., 1999).

As the name suggests, bidirectional RNNs combine an RNN that moves forward through time, beginning from the start of the sequence, with another RNN that moves backward through time, beginning from the end of the sequence. Figure 10.11 illustrates the typical bidirectional RNN, with $h^{(t)}$ standing for the state of the sub-RNN that moves forward through time and $g^{(t)}$ standing for the state of the sub-RNN that moves backward through time. This allows the output units $o^{(t)}$ to compute a representation that depends on *both the past and the future* but is most sensitive to the input values around time t, without having to specify a fixed-size window around t (as one would have to do with a feedforward network, a convolutional network, or a regular RNN with a fixed-size look-ahead buffer).

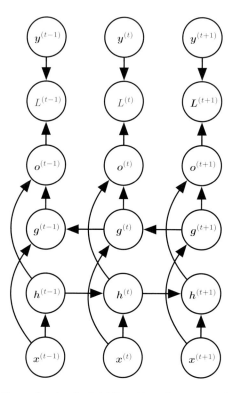

Figure 10.11: Computation of a typical bidirectional recurrent neural network, meant to learn to map input sequences x to target sequences y, with loss $L^{(t)}$ at each step t. The h recurrence propagates information forward in time (toward the right), while the g recurrence propagates information backward in time (toward the left). Thus at each point t, the output units $o^{(t)}$ can benefit from a relevant summary of the past in its $h^{(t)}$ input and from a relevant summary of the future in its $g^{(t)}$ input.

This idea can be naturally extended to two-dimensional input, such as images, by having *four* RNNs, each one going in one of the four directions: up, down, left, right. At each point (i, j) of a 2-D grid, an output $O_{i,j}$ could then compute a representation that would capture mostly local information but could also depend on long-range inputs, if the RNN is able to learn to carry that information. Compared to a convolutional network, RNNs applied to images are typically more expensive but allow for long-range lateral interactions between features in the same feature map (Visin et al., 2015; Kalchbrenner et al., 2015). Indeed, the forward propagation equations for such RNNs may be written in a form that shows they use a convolution that computes the bottom-up input to each layer, prior to the recurrent propagation across the feature map that incorporates the lateral interactions.

10.4 Encoder-Decoder Sequence-to-Sequence Architectures

We have seen in figure 10.5 how an RNN can map an input sequence to a fixed-size vector. We have seen in figure 10.9 how an RNN can map a fixed-size vector to a sequence. We have seen in figures 10.3, 10.4, 10.10 and 10.11 how an RNN can map an input sequence to an output sequence of the same length.

Here we discuss how an RNN can be trained to map an input sequence to an output sequence which is not necessarily of the same length. This comes up in many applications, such as speech recognition, machine translation and question answering, where the input and output sequences in the training set are generally not of the same length (although their lengths might be related).

We often call the input to the RNN the "context." We want to produce a representation of this context, C. The context C might be a vector or sequence of vectors that summarize the input sequence $\boldsymbol{X} = (\boldsymbol{x}^{(1)}, \ldots, \boldsymbol{x}^{(n_x)})$.

The simplest RNN architecture for mapping a variable-length sequence to another variable-length sequence was first proposed by Cho et al. (2014a) and shortly after by Sutskever et al. (2014), who independently developed that architecture and were the first to obtain state-of-the-art translation using this approach. The former system is based on scoring proposals generated by another machine translation system, while the latter uses a standalone recurrent network to generate the translations. These authors respectively called this architecture, illustrated in figure 10.12, the encoder-decoder or sequence-to-sequence architecture. The idea is very simple: (1) An **encoder** or **reader** or **input** RNN processes the input sequence. The encoder emits the context C, usually as a simple function of its final hidden state. (2) A **decoder** or **writer** or **output** RNN is conditioned on that fixed-length vector (just as in figure 10.9) to generate the output sequence $\boldsymbol{Y} = (\boldsymbol{y}^{(1)}, \ldots, \boldsymbol{y}^{(n_y)})$. The innovation of this kind of architecture over those presented in earlier sections of this chapter is that the lengths n_x and n_y can vary from each other, while previous architectures constrained $n_x = n_y = \tau$. In a sequence-to-sequence architecture, the two RNNs are trained jointly to maximize the average of $\log P(\boldsymbol{y}^{(1)}, \ldots, \boldsymbol{y}^{(n_y)} \mid \boldsymbol{x}^{(1)}, \ldots, \boldsymbol{x}^{(n_x)})$ over all the pairs of $\boldsymbol{x}$ and $\boldsymbol{y}$ sequences in the training set. The last state $\boldsymbol{h}_{n_x}$ of the encoder RNN is typically used as a representation C of the input sequence that is provided as input to the decoder RNN.

If the context C is a vector, then the decoder RNN is simply a vector-to-sequence RNN, as described in section 10.2.4. As we have seen, there are at least two ways for a vector-to-sequence RNN to receive input. The input can be provided

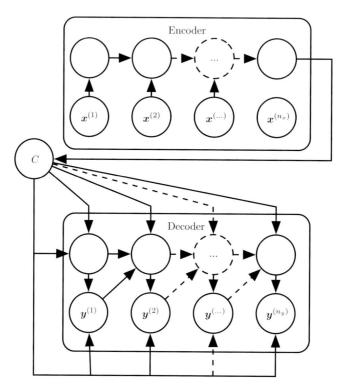

Figure 10.12: Example of an encoder-decoder or sequence-to-sequence RNN architecture, for learning to generate an output sequence $(\mathbf{y}^{(1)}, \ldots, \mathbf{y}^{(n_y)})$ given an input sequence $(\mathbf{x}^{(1)}, \mathbf{x}^{(2)}, \ldots, \mathbf{x}^{(n_x)})$. It is composed of an encoder RNN that reads the input sequence as well as a decoder RNN that generates the output sequence (or computes the probability of a given output sequence). The final hidden state of the encoder RNN is used to compute a generally fixed-size context variable C, which represents a semantic summary of the input sequence and is given as input to the decoder RNN.

as the initial state of the RNN, or the input can be connected to the hidden units at each time step. These two ways can also be combined.

There is no constraint that the encoder must have the same size of hidden layer as the decoder.

One clear limitation of this architecture is when the context C output by the encoder RNN has a dimension that is too small to properly summarize a long sequence. This phenomenon was observed by Bahdanau et al. (2015) in the context of machine translation. They proposed to make C a variable-length sequence rather than a fixed-size vector. Additionally, they introduced an **attention mechanism** that learns to associate elements of the sequence C to elements of the output sequence. See section 12.4.5.1 for more details.

10.5 Deep Recurrent Networks

The computation in most RNNs can be decomposed into three blocks of parameters and associated transformations:

1. from the input to the hidden state,

2. from the previous hidden state to the next hidden state, and

3. from the hidden state to the output.

With the RNN architecture of figure 10.3, each of these three blocks is associated with a single weight matrix. In other words, when the network is unfolded, each of these blocks corresponds to a shallow transformation. By a shallow transformation, we mean a transformation that would be represented by a single layer within a deep MLP. Typically this is a transformation represented by a learned affine transformation followed by a fixed nonlinearity.

Would it be advantageous to introduce depth in each of these operations? Experimental evidence (Graves et al., 2013; Pascanu et al., 2014a) strongly suggests so. The experimental evidence is in agreement with the idea that we need enough depth to perform the required mappings. See also Schmidhuber (1992), El Hihi and Bengio (1996), or Jaeger (2007a) for earlier work on deep RNNs.

Graves et al. (2013) were the first to show a significant benefit of decomposing the state of an RNN into multiple layers, as in figure 10.13 (left). We can think of the lower layers in the hierarchy depicted in figure 10.13a as playing a role in transforming the raw input into a representation that is more appropriate, at the higher levels of the hidden state. Pascanu et al. (2014a) go a step further and propose to have a separate MLP (possibly deep) for each of the three blocks enumerated above, as illustrated in figure 10.13b. Considerations of representational capacity suggest allocating enough capacity in each of these three steps, but doing so by adding depth may hurt learning by making optimization difficult. In general, it is easier to optimize shallower architectures, and adding the extra depth of figure 10.13b makes the shortest path from a variable in time step t to a variable in time step $t + 1$ become longer. For example, if an MLP with a single hidden layer is used for the state-to-state transition, we have doubled the length of the shortest path between variables in any two different time steps, compared with the ordinary RNN of figure 10.3. However, as argued by Pascanu et al. (2014a), this can be mitigated by introducing skip connections in the hidden-to-hidden path, as illustrated in figure 10.13c.

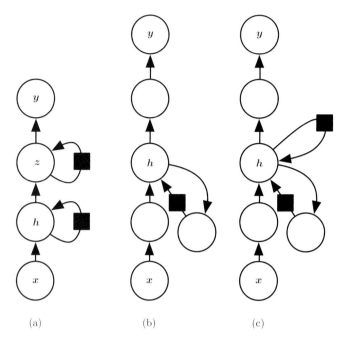

Figure 10.13: A recurrent neural network can be made deep in many ways (Pascanu et al., 2014a). *(a)* The hidden recurrent state can be broken down into groups organized hierarchically. *(b)* Deeper computation (e.g., an MLP) can be introduced in the input-to-hidden, hidden-to-hidden, and hidden-to-output parts. This may lengthen the shortest path linking different time steps. *(c)* The path-lengthening effect can be mitigated by introducing skip connections.

10.6   Recursive Neural Networks

Recursive neural networks[2] represent yet another generalization of recurrent networks, with a different kind of computational graph, which is structured as a deep tree, rather than the chain-like structure of RNNs. The typical computational graph for a recursive network is illustrated in figure 10.14. Recursive neural networks were introduced by Pollack (1990), and their potential use for learning to reason was described by Bottou (2011). Recursive networks have been successfully applied to processing *data structures* as input to neural nets (Frasconi et al., 1997, 1998), in natural language processing (Socher et al., 2011a,c, 2013a), as well as in computer vision (Socher et al., 2011b).

---

[2]We suggest not abbreviating "recursive neural network" as "RNN" to avoid confusion with "recurrent neural network."

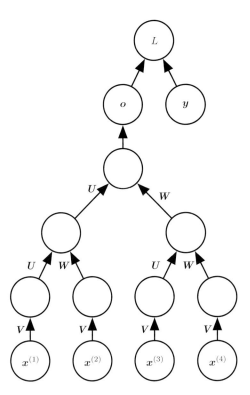

Figure 10.14: A recursive network has a computational graph that generalizes that of the recurrent network from a chain to a tree. A variable-size sequence $x^{(1)}, x^{(2)}, \ldots, x^{(t)}$ can be mapped to a fixed-size representation (the output o), with a fixed set of parameters (the weight matrices U, V, W). The figure illustrates a supervised learning case in which some target y is provided that is associated with the whole sequence.

One clear advantage of recursive nets over recurrent nets is that for a sequence of the same length τ, the depth (measured as the number of compositions of nonlinear operations) can be drastically reduced from τ to $O(\log \tau)$, which might help deal with long-term dependencies. An open question is how to best structure the tree. One option is to have a tree structure that does not depend on the data, such as a balanced binary tree. In some application domains, external methods can suggest the appropriate tree structure. For example, when processing natural language sentences, the tree structure for the recursive network can be fixed to the structure of the parse tree of the sentence provided by a natural language parser (Socher et al., 2011a, 2013a). Ideally, one would like the learner itself to discover and infer the tree structure that is appropriate for any given input, as suggested by Bottou (2011).

Many variants of the recursive net idea are possible. For example, Frasconi et al. (1997) and Frasconi et al. (1998) associate the data with a tree structure, and associate the inputs and targets with individual nodes of the tree. The computation performed by each node does not have to be the traditional artificial neuron computation (affine transformation of all inputs followed by a monotone nonlinearity). For example, Socher et al. (2013a) propose using tensor operations and bilinear forms, which have previously been found useful to model relationships between concepts (Weston et al., 2010; Bordes et al., 2012) when the concepts are represented by continuous vectors (embeddings).

10.7 The Challenge of Long-Term Dependencies

The mathematical challenge of learning long-term dependencies in recurrent networks is introduced in section 8.2.5. The basic problem is that gradients propagated over many stages tend to either vanish (most of the time) or explode (rarely, but with much damage to the optimization). Even if we assume that the parameters are such that the recurrent network is stable (can store memories, with gradients not exploding), the difficulty with long-term dependencies arises from the exponentially smaller weights given to long-term interactions (involving the multiplication of many Jacobians) compared to short-term ones. Many other sources provide a deeper treatment (Hochreiter, 1991; Doya, 1993; Bengio et al., 1994; Pascanu et al., 2013). In this section, we describe the problem in more detail. The remaining sections describe approaches to overcoming the problem.

Recurrent networks involve the composition of the same function multiple times, once per time step. These compositions can result in extremely nonlinear behavior, as illustrated in figure 10.15.

In particular, the function composition employed by recurrent neural networks somewhat resembles matrix multiplication. We can think of the recurrence relation

$$\boldsymbol{h}^{(t)} = \boldsymbol{W}^{\top} \boldsymbol{h}^{(t-1)} \tag{10.36}$$

as a very simple recurrent neural network lacking a nonlinear activation function, and lacking inputs $\boldsymbol{x}$. As described in section 8.2.5, this recurrence relation essentially describes the power method. It may be simplified to

$$\boldsymbol{h}^{(t)} = \left(\boldsymbol{W}^t\right)^{\top} \boldsymbol{h}^{(0)}, \tag{10.37}$$

and if $\boldsymbol{W}$ admits an eigendecomposition of the form

$$\boldsymbol{W} = \boldsymbol{Q}\boldsymbol{\Lambda}\boldsymbol{Q}^{\top}, \tag{10.38}$$

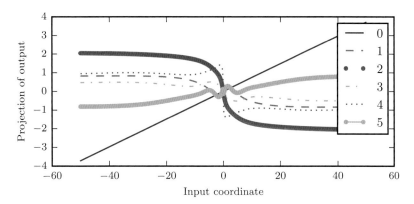

Figure 10.15: Repeated function composition. When composing many nonlinear functions (like the linear-tanh layer shown here), the result is highly nonlinear, typically with most of the values associated with a tiny derivative, some values with a large derivative, and many alternations between increasing and decreasing. Here, we plot a linear projection of a 100-dimensional hidden state down to a single dimension, plotted on the y-axis. The x-axis is the coordinate of the initial state along a random direction in the 100-dimensional space. We can thus view this plot as a linear cross-section of a high-dimensional function. The plots show the function after each time step, or equivalently, after each number of times the transition function has been composed.

with orthogonal $\boldsymbol{Q}$, the recurrence may be simplified further to

$$\boldsymbol{h}^{(t)} = \boldsymbol{Q}^{\top}\boldsymbol{\Lambda}^{t}\boldsymbol{Q}\boldsymbol{h}^{(0)}. \tag{10.39}$$

The eigenvalues are raised to the power of t, causing eigenvalues with magnitude less than one to decay to zero and eigenvalues with magnitude greater than one to explode. Any component of $\boldsymbol{h}^{(0)}$ that is not aligned with the largest eigenvector will eventually be discarded.

This problem is particular to recurrent networks. In the scalar case, imagine multiplying a weight w by itself many times. The product w^t will either vanish or explode depending on the magnitude of w. If we make a nonrecurrent network that has a different weight $w^{(t)}$ at each time step, the situation is different. If the initial state is given by 1, then the state at time t is given by $\prod_t w^{(t)}$. Suppose that the $w^{(t)}$ values are generated randomly, independently from one another, with zero mean and variance v. The variance of the product is $O(v^n)$. To obtain some desired variance v^* we may choose the individual weights with variance $v = \sqrt[n]{v^*}$. Very deep feedforward networks with carefully chosen scaling can thus avoid the vanishing and exploding gradient problem, as argued by Sussillo (2014).

The vanishing and exploding gradient problem for RNNs was independently discovered by separate researchers (Hochreiter, 1991; Bengio et al., 1993, 1994).

One may hope that the problem can be avoided simply by staying in a region of parameter space where the gradients do not vanish or explode. Unfortunately, in order to store memories in a way that is robust to small perturbations, the RNN must enter a region of parameter space where gradients vanish (Bengio et al., 1993, 1994). Specifically, whenever the model is able to represent long-term dependencies, the gradient of a long-term interaction has exponentially smaller magnitude than the gradient of a short-term interaction. This means not that it is impossible to learn, but that it might take a very long time to learn long-term dependencies, because the signal about these dependencies will tend to be hidden by the smallest fluctuations arising from short-term dependencies. In practice, the experiments in Bengio et al. (1994) show that as we increase the span of the dependencies that need to be captured, gradient-based optimization becomes increasingly difficult, with the probability of successful training of a traditional RNN via SGD rapidly reaching 0 for sequences of only length 10 or 20.

For a deeper treatment of recurrent networks as dynamical systems, see Doya (1993), Bengio et al. (1994), and Siegelmann and Sontag (1995), with a review in Pascanu et al. (2013). The remaining sections of this chapter discuss various approaches that have been proposed to reduce the difficulty of learning long-term dependencies (in some cases allowing an RNN to learn dependencies across hundreds of steps), but the problem of learning long-term dependencies remains one of the main challenges in deep learning.

10.8 Echo State Networks

The recurrent weights mapping from $h^{(t-1)}$ to $h^{(t)}$ and the input weights mapping from $x^{(t)}$ to $h^{(t)}$ are some of the most difficult parameters to learn in a recurrent network. One proposed (Jaeger, 2003; Maass et al., 2002; Jaeger and Haas, 2004; Jaeger, 2007b) approach to avoiding this difficulty is to set the recurrent weights such that the recurrent hidden units do a good job of capturing the history of past inputs, and *only learn the output weights*. This is the idea that was independently proposed for **echo state networks**, or ESNs (Jaeger and Haas, 2004; Jaeger, 2007b), and **liquid state machines** (Maass et al., 2002). The latter is similar, except that it uses spiking neurons (with binary outputs) instead of the continuous-valued hidden units used for ESNs. Both ESNs and liquid state machines are termed **reservoir computing** (Lukoševičius and Jaeger, 2009) to denote the fact that the hidden units form a reservoir of temporal features that may capture different aspects of the history of inputs.

One way to think about these reservoir computing recurrent networks is that they are similar to kernel machines: they map an arbitrary length sequence (the history of inputs up to time t) into a fixed-length vector (the recurrent state $\boldsymbol{h}^{(t)}$), on which a linear predictor (typically a linear regression) can be applied to solve the problem of interest. The training criterion may then be easily designed to be convex as a function of the output weights. For example, if the output consists of linear regression from the hidden units to the output targets, and the training criterion is mean squared error, then it is convex and may be solved reliably with simple learning algorithms (Jaeger, 2003).

The important question is therefore: how do we set the input and recurrent weights so that a rich set of histories can be represented in the recurrent neural network state? The answer proposed in the reservoir computing literature is to view the recurrent net as a dynamical system, and set the input and recurrent weights such that the dynamical system is near the edge of stability.

The original idea was to make the eigenvalues of the Jacobian of the state-to-state transition function be close to 1. As explained in section 8.2.5, an important characteristic of a recurrent network is the eigenvalue spectrum of the Jacobians $\boldsymbol{J}^{(t)} = \frac{\partial s^{(t)}}{\partial s^{(t-1)}}$. Of particular importance is the **spectral radius** of $\boldsymbol{J}^{(t)}$, defined to be the maximum of the absolute values of its eigenvalues.

To understand the effect of the spectral radius, consider the simple case of back-propagation with a Jacobian matrix $\boldsymbol{J}$ that does not change with t. This case happens, for example, when the network is purely linear. Suppose that $\boldsymbol{J}$ has an eigenvector $\boldsymbol{v}$ with corresponding eigenvalue λ. Consider what happens as we propagate a gradient vector backward through time. If we begin with a gradient vector $\boldsymbol{g}$, then after one step of back-propagation, we will have $\boldsymbol{J}\boldsymbol{g}$, and after n steps we will have $\boldsymbol{J}^n\boldsymbol{g}$. Now consider what happens if we instead back-propagate a perturbed version of $\boldsymbol{g}$. If we begin with $\boldsymbol{g} + \delta\boldsymbol{v}$, then after one step, we will have $\boldsymbol{J}(\boldsymbol{g} + \delta\boldsymbol{v})$. After n steps, we will have $\boldsymbol{J}^n(\boldsymbol{g} + \delta\boldsymbol{v})$. From this we can see that back-propagation starting from $\boldsymbol{g}$ and back-propagation starting from $\boldsymbol{g} + \delta\boldsymbol{v}$ diverge by $\delta\boldsymbol{J}^n\boldsymbol{v}$ after n steps of back-propagation. If $\boldsymbol{v}$ is chosen to be a unit eigenvector of $\boldsymbol{J}$ with eigenvalue λ, then multiplication by the Jacobian simply scales the difference at each step. The two executions of back-propagation are separated by a distance of $\delta|\lambda|^n$. When $\boldsymbol{v}$ corresponds to the largest value of $|\lambda|$, this perturbation achieves the widest possible separation of an initial perturbation of size δ.

When $|\lambda| > 1$, the deviation size $\delta|\lambda|^n$ grows exponentially large. When $|\lambda| < 1$, the deviation size becomes exponentially small.

Of course, this example assumed that the Jacobian was the same at every time step, corresponding to a recurrent network with no nonlinearity. When a nonlinearity is present, the derivative of the nonlinearity will approach zero on many time steps and help prevent the explosion resulting from a large spectral radius. Indeed, the most recent work on echo state networks advocates using a spectral radius much larger than unity (Yildiz et al., 2012; Jaeger, 2012).

Everything we have said about back-propagation via repeated matrix multiplication applies equally to forward propagation in a network with no nonlinearity, where the state $\boldsymbol{h}^{(t+1)} = \boldsymbol{h}^{(t)\top}\boldsymbol{W}$.

When a linear map $\boldsymbol{W}^{\top}$ always shrinks $\boldsymbol{h}$ as measured by the L^2 norm, then we say that the map is **contractive**. When the spectral radius is less than one, the mapping from $\boldsymbol{h}^{(t)}$ to $\boldsymbol{h}^{(t+1)}$ is contractive, so a small change becomes smaller after each time step. This necessarily makes the network forget information about the past when we use a finite level of precision (such as 32-bit integers) to store the state vector.

The Jacobian matrix tells us how a small change of $\boldsymbol{h}^{(t)}$ propagates one step forward, or equivalently, how the gradient on $\boldsymbol{h}^{(t+1)}$ propagates one step backward, during back-propagation. Note that neither $\boldsymbol{W}$ nor $\boldsymbol{J}$ need to be symmetric (although they are square and real), so they can have complex-valued eigenvalues and eigenvectors, with imaginary components corresponding to potentially oscillatory behavior (if the same Jacobian was applied iteratively). Even though $\boldsymbol{h}^{(t)}$ or a small variation of $\boldsymbol{h}^{(t)}$ of interest in back-propagation are real valued, they can be expressed in such a complex-valued basis. What matters is what happens to the magnitude (complex absolute value) of these possibly complex-valued basis coefficients when we multiply the matrix by the vector. An eigenvalue with magnitude greater than one corresponds to magnification (exponential growth, if applied iteratively) or shrinking (exponential decay, if applied iteratively).

With a nonlinear map, the Jacobian is free to change at each step. The dynamics therefore become more complicated. It remains true, however, that a small initial variation can turn into a large variation after several steps. One difference between the purely linear case and the nonlinear case is that the use of a squashing nonlinearity such as tanh can cause the recurrent dynamics to become bounded. Note that it is possible for back-propagation to retain unbounded dynamics even when forward propagation has bounded dynamics, for example, when a sequence of tanh units are all in the middle of their linear regime and are connected by weight matrices with spectral radius greater than 1. Nonetheless, it is rare for all the tanh units to simultaneously lie at their linear activation point.

The strategy of echo state networks is simply to fix the weights to have some spectral radius such as 3, where information is carried forward through time but does not explode because of the stabilizing effect of saturating nonlinearities like tanh.

More recently, it has been shown that the techniques used to set the weights in ESNs could be used to *initialize* the weights in a fully trainable recurrent network (with the hidden-to-hidden recurrent weights trained using back-propagation through time), helping to learn long-term dependencies (Sutskever, 2012; Sutskever et al., 2013). In this setting, an initial spectral radius of 1.2 performs well, combined with the sparse initialization scheme described in section 8.4.

10.9 Leaky Units and Other Strategies for Multiple Time Scales

One way to deal with long-term dependencies is to design a model that operates at multiple time scales, so that some parts of the model operate at fine-grained time scales and can handle small details, while other parts operate at coarse time scales and transfer information from the distant past to the present more efficiently. Various strategies for building both fine and coarse time scales are possible. These include the addition of skip connections across time, "leaky units" that integrate signals with different time constants, and the removal of some of the connections used to model fine-grained time scales.

10.9.1 Adding Skip Connections through Time

One way to obtain coarse time scales is to add direct connections from variables in the distant past to variables in the present. The idea of using such skip connections dates back to Lin et al. (1996) and follows from the idea of incorporating delays in feedforward neural networks (Lang and Hinton, 1988). In an ordinary recurrent network, a recurrent connection goes from a unit at time t to a unit at time $t + 1$. It is possible to construct recurrent networks with longer delays (Bengio, 1991).

As we have seen in section 8.2.5, gradients may vanish or explode exponentially *with respect to the number of time steps*. Lin et al. (1996) introduced recurrent connections with a time delay of d to mitigate this problem. Gradients now diminish exponentially as a function of $\frac{\tau}{d}$ rather than τ. Since there are both delayed and single step connections, gradients may still explode exponentially in τ. This allows the learning algorithm to capture longer dependencies, although not all long-term dependencies may be represented well in this way.

10.9.2   Leaky Units and a Spectrum of Different Time Scales

Another way to obtain paths on which the product of derivatives is close to one is to have units with *linear* self-connections and a weight near one on these connections.

When we accumulate a running average $\mu^{(t)}$ of some value $v^{(t)}$ by applying the update $\mu^{(t)} \leftarrow \alpha\mu^{(t-1)} + (1-\alpha)v^{(t)}$, the α parameter is an example of a linear self-connection from $\mu^{(t-1)}$ to $\mu^{(t)}$. When α is near one, the running average remembers information about the past for a long time, and when α is near zero, information about the past is rapidly discarded. Hidden units with linear self-connections can behave similarly to such running averages. Such hidden units are called **leaky units**.

Skip connections through d time steps are a way of ensuring that a unit can always learn to be influenced by a value from d time steps earlier. The use of a linear self-connection with a weight near one is a different way of ensuring that the unit can access values from the past. The linear self-connection approach allows this effect to be adapted more smoothly and flexibly by adjusting the real valued α rather than by adjusting the integer-valued skip length.

These ideas were proposed by Mozer (1992) and by El Hihi and Bengio (1996). Leaky units were also found to be useful in the context of echo state networks (Jaeger et al., 2007).

There are two basic strategies for setting the time constants used by leaky units. One strategy is to manually fix them to values that remain constant, for example, by sampling their values from some distribution once at initialization time. Another strategy is to make the time constants free parameters and learn them. Having such leaky units at different time scales appears to help with long-term dependencies (Mozer, 1992; Pascanu et al., 2013).

10.9.3   Removing Connections

Another approach to handling long-term dependencies is the idea of organizing the state of the RNN at multiple time scales (El Hihi and Bengio, 1996), with information flowing more easily through long distances at the slower time scales.

This idea differs from the skip connections through time discussed earlier because it involves actively *removing* length-one connections and replacing them with longer connections. Units modified in such a way are forced to operate on a long time scale. Skip connections through time *add* edges. Units receiving such new connections may learn to operate on a long time scale but may also choose to focus on their other, short-term connections.

There are different ways in which a group of recurrent units can be forced to operate at different time scales. One option is to make the recurrent units leaky, but to have different groups of units associated with different fixed time scales. This was the proposal in Mozer (1992) and has been successfully used in Pascanu et al. (2013). Another option is to have explicit and discrete updates taking place at different times, with a different frequency for different groups of units. This is the approach of El Hihi and Bengio (1996) and Koutnik et al. (2014). It worked well on a number of benchmark datasets.

10.10   The Long Short-Term Memory and Other Gated RNNs

As of this writing, the most effective sequence models used in practical applications are called **gated RNNs**. These include the **long short-term memory** and networks based on the **gated recurrent unit**.

Like leaky units, gated RNNs are based on the idea of creating paths through time that have derivatives that neither vanish nor explode. Leaky units did this with connection weights that were either manually chosen constants or were parameters. Gated RNNs generalize this to connection weights that may change at each time step.

Leaky units allow the network to *accumulate* information (such as evidence for a particular feature or category) over a long duration. Once that information has been used, however, it might be useful for the neural network to *forget* the old state. For example, if a sequence is made of subsequences and we want a leaky unit to accumulate evidence inside each sub-subsequence, we need a mechanism to forget the old state by setting it to zero. Instead of manually deciding when to clear the state, we want the neural network to learn to decide when to do it. This is what gated RNNs do.

10.10.1   LSTM

The clever idea of introducing self-loops to produce paths where the gradient can flow for long durations is a core contribution of the initial **long short-term memory** (LSTM) model (Hochreiter and Schmidhuber, 1997). A crucial addition has been to make the weight on this self-loop conditioned on the context, rather than fixed (Gers et al., 2000). By making the weight of this self-loop gated (controlled by another hidden unit), the time scale of integration can be changed dynamically. In this case, we mean that even for an LSTM with fixed parameters, the time scale of integration can change based on the input sequence, because the time constants are output by the model itself. The LSTM has been found extremely successful in many applications, such as unconstrained handwriting recognition (Graves et al., 2009), speech recognition (Graves et al., 2013; Graves and Jaitly, 2014), handwriting generation (Graves, 2013), machine translation (Sutskever et al., 2014), image captioning (Kiros et al., 2014b; Vinyals et al., 2014b; Xu et al., 2015), and parsing (Vinyals et al., 2014a).

The LSTM block diagram is illustrated in figure 10.16. The corresponding forward propagation equations are given below, for a shallow recurrent network architecture. Deeper architectures have also been successfully used (Graves et al.,

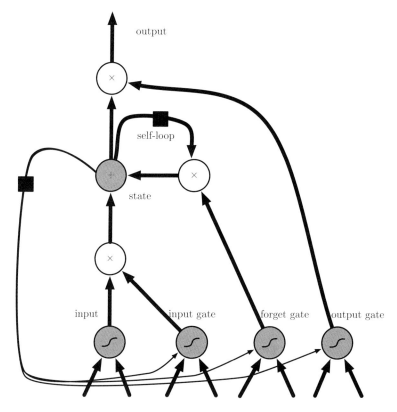

Figure 10.16: Block diagram of the LSTM recurrent network "cell." Cells are connected recurrently to each other, replacing the usual hidden units of ordinary recurrent networks. An input feature is computed with a regular artificial neuron unit. Its value can be accumulated into the state if the sigmoidal input gate allows it. The state unit has a linear self-loop whose weight is controlled by the forget gate. The output of the cell can be shut off by the output gate. All the gating units have a sigmoid nonlinearity, while the input unit can have any squashing nonlinearity. The state unit can also be used as an extra input to the gating units. The black square indicates a delay of a single time step.

2013; Pascanu et al., 2014a). Instead of a unit that simply applies an element-wise nonlinearity to the affine transformation of inputs and recurrent units, LSTM recurrent networks have "LSTM cells" that have an internal recurrence (a self-loop), in addition to the outer recurrence of the RNN. Each cell has the same inputs and outputs as an ordinary recurrent network, but also has more parameters and a system of gating units that controls the flow of information. The most important component is the state unit $s_i^{(t)}$, which has a linear self-loop similar to the leaky units described in the previous section. Here, however, the self-loop weight (or the associated time constant) is controlled by a **forget gate** unit $f_i^{(t)}$ (for time step t and cell i), which sets this weight to a value between 0 and 1 via a sigmoid unit:

$$f_i^{(t)} = \sigma \left(b_i^f + \sum_j U_{i,j}^f x_j^{(t)} + \sum_j W_{i,j}^f h_j^{(t-1)} \right), \tag{10.40}$$

where $\boldsymbol{x}^{(t)}$ is the current input vector and $\boldsymbol{h}^{(t)}$ is the current hidden layer vector, containing the outputs of all the LSTM cells, and $\boldsymbol{b}^f$, $\boldsymbol{U}^f$, $\boldsymbol{W}^f$ are respectively biases, input weights, and recurrent weights for the forget gates. The LSTM cell internal state is thus updated as follows, but with a conditional self-loop weight $f_i^{(t)}$:

$$s_i^{(t)} = f_i^{(t)} s_i^{(t-1)} + g_i^{(t)} \sigma \left(b_i + \sum_j U_{i,j} x_j^{(t)} + \sum_j W_{i,j} h_j^{(t-1)} \right), \tag{10.41}$$

where $\boldsymbol{b}$, $\boldsymbol{U}$ and $\boldsymbol{W}$ respectively denote the biases, input weights, and recurrent weights into the LSTM cell. The **external input gate** unit $g_i^{(t)}$ is computed similarly to the forget gate (with a sigmoid unit to obtain a gating value between 0 and 1), but with its own parameters:

$$g_i^{(t)} = \sigma \left(b_i^g + \sum_j U_{i,j}^g x_j^{(t)} + \sum_j W_{i,j}^g h_j^{(t-1)} \right). \tag{10.42}$$

The output $h_i^{(t)}$ of the LSTM cell can also be shut off, via the **output gate** $q_i^{(t)}$, which also uses a sigmoid unit for gating:

$$h_i^{(t)} = \tanh\left(s_i^{(t)} \right) q_i^{(t)}, \tag{10.43}$$

$$q_i^{(t)} = \sigma \left(b_i^o + \sum_j U_{i,j}^o x_j^{(t)} + \sum_j W_{i,j}^o h_j^{(t-1)} \right), \tag{10.44}$$

which has parameters $\boldsymbol{b}^o$, $\boldsymbol{U}^o$, $\boldsymbol{W}^o$ for its biases, input weights and recurrent weights, respectively. Among the variants, one can choose to use the cell state $s_i^{(t)}$ as an extra input (with its weight) into the three gates of the i-th unit, as shown in figure 10.16. This would require three additional parameters.

LSTM networks have been shown to learn long-term dependencies more easily than the simple recurrent architectures, first on artificial datasets designed for testing the ability to learn long-term dependencies (Bengio et al., 1994; Hochreiter and Schmidhuber, 1997; Hochreiter et al., 2001), then on challenging sequence processing tasks where state-of-the-art performance was obtained (Graves, 2012; Graves et al., 2013; Sutskever et al., 2014). Variants and alternatives to the LSTM that have been studied and used are discussed next.

10.10.2 Other Gated RNNs

Which pieces of the LSTM architecture are actually necessary? What other successful architectures could be designed that allow the network to dynamically control the time scale and forgetting behavior of different units?

Some answers to these questions are given with the recent work on gated RNNs, whose units are also known as gated recurrent units, or GRUs (Cho et al., 2014b; Chung et al., 2014, 2015a; Jozefowicz et al., 2015; Chrupala et al., 2015). The main difference with the LSTM is that a single gating unit simultaneously controls the forgetting factor and the decision to update the state unit. The update equations are the following:

$$
h_i^{(t)} = u_i^{(t-1)} h_i^{(t-1)} + (1 - u_i^{(t-1)}) \sigma \left(b_i + \sum_j U_{i,j} x_j^{(t-1)} + \sum_j W_{i,j} r_j^{(t-1)} h_j^{(t-1)} \right),
$$
(10.45)

where $\boldsymbol{u}$ stands for "update" gate and $\boldsymbol{r}$ for "reset" gate. Their value is defined as usual:

$$
u_i^{(t)} = \sigma \left(b_i^u + \sum_j U_{i,j}^u x_j^{(t)} + \sum_j W_{i,j}^u h_j^{(t)} \right)
$$
(10.46)

and

$$
r_i^{(t)} = \sigma \left(b_i^r + \sum_j U_{i,j}^r x_j^{(t)} + \sum_j W_{i,j}^r h_j^{(t)} \right).
$$
(10.47)

The reset and update gates can individually "ignore" parts of the state vector. The update gates act like conditional leaky integrators that can linearly gate any dimension, thus choosing to copy it (at one extreme of the sigmoid) or completely ignore it (at the other extreme) by replacing it with the new "target state" value (toward which the leaky integrator wants to converge). The reset gates control which parts of the state get used to compute the next target state, introducing an additional nonlinear effect in the relationship between past state and future state.

Many more variants around this theme can be designed. For example the reset gate (or forget gate) output could be shared across multiple hidden units. Alternately, the product of a global gate (covering a whole group of units, such as an entire layer) and a local gate (per unit) could be used to combine global control and local control. Several investigations over architectural variations of the LSTM and GRU, however, found no variant that would clearly beat both of these across a wide range of tasks (Greff et al., 2015; Jozefowicz et al., 2015). Greff et al. (2015) found that a crucial ingredient is the forget gate, while Jozefowicz et al. (2015) found that adding a bias of 1 to the LSTM forget gate, a practice advocated by Gers et al. (2000), makes the LSTM as strong as the best of the explored architectural variants.

10.11 Optimization for Long-Term Dependencies

Section 8.2.5 and section 10.7 have described the vanishing and exploding gradient problems that occur when optimizing RNNs over many time steps.

An interesting idea proposed by Martens and Sutskever (2011) is that second derivatives may vanish at the same time that first derivatives vanish. Second-order optimization algorithms may roughly be understood as dividing the first derivative by the second derivative (in higher dimension, multiplying the gradient by the inverse Hessian). If the second derivative shrinks at a similar rate to the first derivative, then the ratio of first and second derivatives may remain relatively constant. Unfortunately, second-order methods have many drawbacks, including high computational cost, the need for a large minibatch, and a tendency to be attracted to saddle points. Martens and Sutskever (2011) found promising results using second-order methods. Later, Sutskever et al. (2013) found that simpler methods such as Nesterov momentum with careful initialization could achieve similar results. See Sutskever (2012) for more detail. Both of these approaches have largely been replaced by simply using SGD (even without momentum) applied to LSTMs. This is part of a continuing theme in machine learning that it is often much easier to design a model that is easy to optimize than it is to design a more powerful optimization algorithm.

10.11.1 Clipping Gradients

As discussed in section 8.2.4, strongly nonlinear functions, such as those computed by a recurrent net over many time steps, tend to have derivatives that can be either very large or very small in magnitude. This is illustrated in figure 8.3 and in figure 10.17, in which we see that the objective function (as a function of the parameters) has a "landscape" in which one finds "cliffs": wide and rather flat regions separated by tiny regions where the objective function changes quickly, forming a kind of cliff.

The difficulty that arises is that when the parameter gradient is very large, a gradient descent parameter update could throw the parameters very far into a region where the objective function is larger, undoing much of the work that had been done to reach the current solution. The gradient tells us the direction that corresponds to the steepest descent within an infinitesimal region surrounding the current parameters. Outside this infinitesimal region, the cost function may begin to curve back upward. The update must be chosen to be small enough to

Without clipping   With clipping

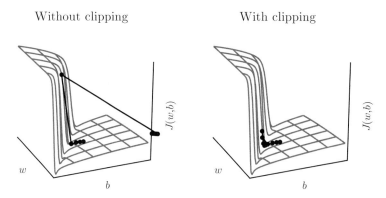

Figure 10.17: Example of the effect of gradient clipping in a recurrent network with two parameters w and b. Gradient clipping can make gradient descent perform more reasonably in the vicinity of extremely steep cliffs. These steep cliffs commonly occur in recurrent networks near where a recurrent network behaves approximately linearly. The cliff is exponentially steep in the number of time steps because the weight matrix is multiplied by itself once for each time step. *(Left)* Gradient descent without gradient clipping overshoots the bottom of this small ravine, then receives a very large gradient from the cliff face. The large gradient catastrophically propels the parameters outside the axes of the plot. *(Right)* Gradient descent with gradient clipping has a more moderate reaction to the cliff. While it does ascend the cliff face, the step size is restricted so that it cannot be propelled away from the steep region near the solution. Figure adapted with permission from Pascanu et al. (2013).

avoid traversing too much upward curvature. We typically use learning rates that decay slowly enough that consecutive steps have approximately the same learning rate. A step size that is appropriate for a relatively linear part of the landscape is often inappropriate and causes uphill motion if we enter a more curved part of the landscape on the next step.

A simple type of solution has been in use by practitioners for many years: **clipping the gradient**. There are different instances of this idea (Mikolov, 2012; Pascanu et al., 2013). One option is to clip the parameter gradient from a minibatch *element-wise* (Mikolov, 2012), just before the parameter update. Another is to *clip the norm* $||\boldsymbol{g}||$ *of the gradient* $\boldsymbol{g}$ (Pascanu et al., 2013) just before the parameter update:

$$\text{if } ||\boldsymbol{g}|| > v \tag{10.48}$$

$$\boldsymbol{g} \leftarrow \frac{\boldsymbol{g}v}{||\boldsymbol{g}||}, \tag{10.49}$$

where v is the norm threshold and $\boldsymbol{g}$ is used to update parameters. Because the gradient of all the parameters (including different groups of parameters, such as weights and biases) is renormalized jointly with a single scaling factor, the latter method has the advantage of guaranteeing that each step is still in the gradient direction, but experiments suggest that both forms work similarly. Although the parameter update has the same direction as the true gradient, with gradient norm clipping, the parameter update vector norm is now bounded. This bounded gradient avoids performing a detrimental step when the gradient explodes. In fact, even simply taking a *random step* when the gradient magnitude is above a threshold tends to work almost as well. If the explosion is so severe that the gradient is numerically `Inf` or `Nan` (considered infinite or not-a-number), then a random step of size v can be taken and will typically move away from the numerically unstable configuration. Clipping the gradient norm per minibatch will not change the direction of the gradient for an individual minibatch. Taking the average of the norm-clipped gradient from many minibatches, however, is not equivalent to clipping the norm of the true gradient (the gradient formed from using all examples). Examples that have large gradient norm, as well as examples that appear in the same minibatch as such examples, will have their contribution to the final direction diminished. This stands in contrast to traditional minibatch gradient descent, where the true gradient direction is equal to the average over all minibatch gradients. Put another way, traditional stochastic gradient descent uses an unbiased estimate of the gradient, while gradient descent with norm clipping introduces a heuristic bias that we know empirically to be useful. With element-wise clipping, the direction of the update is not aligned with the true gradient or the minibatch gradient, but it is still a descent direction. It has also been proposed (Graves, 2013) to clip the back-propagated gradient (with respect to hidden units), but no comparison has been published between these variants; we conjecture that all these methods behave similarly.

10.11.2   Regularizing to Encourage Information Flow

Gradient clipping helps to deal with exploding gradients, but it does not help with vanishing gradients. To address vanishing gradients and better capture long-term dependencies, we discussed the idea of creating paths in the computational graph of the unfolded recurrent architecture along which the product of gradients associated with arcs is near 1. One approach to achieve this is with LSTMs and other self-loops and gating mechanisms, described in section 10.10. Another idea is to regularize or constrain the parameters so as to encourage "information flow." In particular, we would like the gradient vector $\nabla_{\boldsymbol{h}^{(t)}} L$ being back-propagated to maintain its magnitude, even if the loss function only penalizes the output at the end of the sequence. Formally, we want

$$(\nabla_{\boldsymbol{h}^{(t)}} L) \frac{\partial \boldsymbol{h}^{(t)}}{\partial \boldsymbol{h}^{(t-1)}} \tag{10.50}$$

to be as large as

$$\nabla_{\boldsymbol{h}^{(t)}} L. \tag{10.51}$$

With this objective, Pascanu et al. (2013) propose the following regularizer:

$$\Omega = \sum_t \left(\frac{\left|\left| (\nabla_{\boldsymbol{h}^{(t)}} L) \frac{\partial \boldsymbol{h}^{(t)}}{\partial \boldsymbol{h}^{(t-1)}} \right|\right|}{||\nabla_{\boldsymbol{h}^{(t)}} L||} - 1 \right)^2. \tag{10.52}$$

Computing the gradient of this regularizer may appear difficult, but Pascanu et al. (2013) propose an approximation in which we consider the back-propagated vectors $\nabla_{\boldsymbol{h}^{(t)}} L$ as if they were constants (for the purpose of this regularizer, so that there is no need to back-propagate through them). The experiments with this regularizer suggest that, if combined with the norm clipping heuristic (which handles gradient explosion), the regularizer can considerably increase the span of the dependencies that an RNN can learn. Because it keeps the RNN dynamics on the edge of explosive gradients, the gradient clipping is particularly important. Without gradient clipping, gradient explosion prevents learning from succeeding.

A key weakness of this approach is that it is not as effective as the LSTM for tasks where data is abundant, such as language modeling.

10.12 Explicit Memory

Intelligence requires knowledge, and acquiring knowledge can be done via learning, which has motivated the development of large-scale deep architectures. However, there are different kinds of knowledge. Some knowledge can be implicit, subconscious, and difficult to verbalize—such as how to walk, or how a dog looks different from a cat. Other knowledge can be explicit, declarative, and relatively straightforward to put into words—everyday commonsense knowledge, like "a cat is a kind of animal," or very specific facts that you need to know to accomplish your current goals, like "the meeting with the sales team is at 3:00 PM in room 141."

Neural networks excel at storing implicit knowledge, but they struggle to memorize facts. Stochastic gradient descent requires many presentations of the same input before it can be stored in neural network parameters, and even then, that input will not be stored especially precisely. Graves et al. (2014b) hypothesized that this is because neural networks lack the equivalent of the **working memory** system that enables human beings to explicitly hold and manipulate pieces of information that are relevant to achieving some goal. Such explicit memory components would allow our systems not only to rapidly and "intentionally" store and retrieve specific facts but also to sequentially reason with them. The need for neural networks that can process information in a sequence of steps, changing the way the input is fed into the network at each step, has long been recognized as important for the ability to reason rather than to make automatic, intuitive responses to the input (Hinton, 1990).

To resolve this difficulty, Weston et al. (2014) introduced **memory networks** that include a set of memory cells that can be accessed via an addressing mechanism. Memory networks originally required a supervision signal instructing them how to use their memory cells. Graves et al. (2014b) introduced the **neural Turing machine**, which is able to learn to read from and write arbitrary content to memory cells without explicit supervision about which actions to undertake, and allowed end-to-end training without this supervision signal, via the use of a content-based soft attention mechanism (see Bahdanau et al.[2015] and section 12.4.5.1). This soft addressing mechanism has become standard with other related architectures, emulating algorithmic mechanisms in a way that still allows gradient-based optimization (Sukhbaatar et al., 2015; Joulin and Mikolov, 2015; Kumar et al., 2015; Vinyals et al., 2015a; Grefenstette et al., 2015).

Each memory cell can be thought of as an extension of the memory cells in LSTMs and GRUs. The difference is that the network outputs an internal state that chooses which cell to read from or write to, just as memory accesses in a digital computer read from or write to a specific address.

It is difficult to optimize functions that produce exact integer addresses. To alleviate this problem, NTMs actually read to or write from many memory cells simultaneously. To read, they take a weighted average of many cells. To write, they modify multiple cells by different amounts. The coefficients for these operations are chosen to be focused on a small number of cells, for example, by producing them via a softmax function. Using these weights with nonzero derivatives enables the functions controlling access to the memory to be optimized using gradient descent. The gradient on these coefficients indicates whether each of them should be increased or decreased, but the gradient will typically be large only for those memory addresses receiving a large coefficient.

These memory cells are typically augmented to contain a vector, rather than the single scalar stored by an LSTM or GRU memory cell. There are two reasons to increase the size of the memory cell. One reason is that we have increased the cost of accessing a memory cell. We pay the computational cost of producing a coefficient for many cells, but we expect these coefficients to cluster around a small number of cells. By reading a vector value, rather than a scalar value, we can offset some of this cost. Another reason to use vector valued memory cells is that they allow for **content-based addressing**, where the weight used to read to or write from a cell is a function of that cell. Vector valued cells allow us to retrieve a complete vector valued memory if we are able to produce a pattern that matches some but not all its elements. This is analogous to how people can recall the lyrics of a song based on a few words. We can think of a content-based read instruction as saying, "Retrieve the lyrics of the song that has the chorus 'We all live in a yellow submarine.'" Content-based addressing is more useful when we make the objects to be retrieved large—if every letter of the song was stored in a separate memory cell, we would not be able to find them this way. By comparison, **location-based addressing** is not allowed to refer to the content of the memory. We can think of a location-based read instruction as saying "Retrieve the lyrics of the song in slot 347." Location-based addressing can often be a perfectly sensible mechanism even when the memory cells are small.

If the content of a memory cell is copied (not forgotten) at most time steps, then the information it contains can be propagated forward in time and the gradients propagated backward in time without either vanishing or exploding.

The explicit memory approach is illustrated in figure 10.18, where we see that a "task neural network" is coupled with a memory. Although that task neural network could be feedforward or recurrent, the overall system is a recurrent network. The

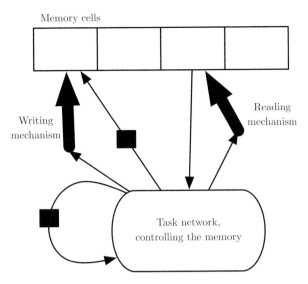

Figure 10.18: A schematic of a network with an explicit memory, capturing some of the key design elements of the neural Turing machine. In this diagram we distinguish the "representation" part of the model (the "task network," here a recurrent net in the bottom) from the "memory" part of the model (the set of cells), which can store facts. The task network learns to "control" the memory, deciding where to read from and where to write to within the memory (through the reading and writing mechanisms, indicated by bold arrows pointing at the reading and writing addresses).

task network can choose to read from or write to specific memory addresses. Explicit memory seems to allow models to learn tasks that ordinary RNNs or LSTM RNNs cannot learn. One reason for this advantage may be that information and gradients can be propagated (forward in time or backward in time, respectively) for very long durations.

As an alternative to back-propagation through weighted averages of memory cells, we can interpret the memory addressing coefficients as probabilities and stochastically read just one cell (Zaremba and Sutskever, 2015). Optimizing models that make discrete decisions requires specialized optimization algorithms, described in section 20.9.1. So far, training these stochastic architectures that make discrete decisions remains harder than training deterministic algorithms that make soft decisions.

Whether it is soft (allowing back-propagation) or stochastic and hard, the mechanism for choosing an address is in its form identical to the **attention mechanism**, which had been previously introduced in the context of machine translation (Bahdanau et al., 2015) and is discussed in section 12.4.5.1. The idea of attention mechanisms for neural networks was introduced even earlier, in the context of handwriting generation (Graves, 2013), with an attention mechanism that was constrained to move only forward in time through the sequence. In the case of machine translation and memory networks, at each step, the focus of attention can move to a completely different place, compared to the previous step.

Recurrent neural networks provide a way to extend deep learning to sequential data. They are the last major tool in our deep learning toolbox. Our discussion now moves to how to choose and use these tools and how to apply them to real-world tasks.

11

Practical Methodology

Successfully applying deep learning techniques requires more than just a good knowledge of what algorithms exist and the principles that explain how they work. A good machine learning practitioner also needs to know how to choose an algorithm for a particular application and how to monitor and respond to feedback obtained from experiments in order to improve a machine learning system. During day-to-day development of machine learning systems, practitioners need to decide whether to gather more data, increase or decrease model capacity, add or remove regularizing features, improve the optimization of a model, improve approximate inference in a model, or debug the software implementation of the model. All these operations are at the very least time consuming to try out, so it is important to be able to determine the right course of action rather than blindly guessing.

Most of this book is about different machine learning models, training algorithms, and objective functions. This may give the impression that the most important ingredient to being a machine learning expert is knowing a wide variety of machine learning techniques and being good at different kinds of math. In practice, one can usually do much better with a correct application of a commonplace algorithm than by sloppily applying an obscure algorithm. Correct application of an algorithm depends on mastering some fairly simple methodology. Many of the recommendations in this chapter are adapted from Ng (2015).

We recommend the following practical design process:

- Determine your goals—what error metric to use, and your target value for this error metric. These goals and error metrics should be driven by the problem that the application is intended to solve.

- Establish a working end-to-end pipeline as soon as possible, including the estimation of the appropriate performance metrics.

- Instrument the system well to determine bottlenecks in performance. Diagnose which components are performing worse than expected and whether poor performance is due to overfitting, underfitting, or a defect in the data or software.

- Repeatedly make incremental changes such as gathering new data, adjusting hyperparameters, or changing algorithms, based on specific findings from your instrumentation.

As a running example, we will use the Street View address number transcription system (Goodfellow et al., 2014d). The purpose of this application is to add buildings to Google Maps. Street View cars photograph the buildings and record the GPS coordinates associated with each photograph. A convolutional network recognizes the address number in each photograph, allowing the Google Maps database to add that address in the correct location. The story of how this commercial application was developed gives an example of how to follow the design methodology we advocate.

We now describe each of the steps in this process.

11.1   Performance Metrics

Determining your goals, in terms of which error metric to use, is a necessary first step because your error metric will guide all your future actions. You should also have an idea of what level of performance you desire.

Keep in mind that for most applications, it is impossible to achieve absolute zero error. The Bayes error defines the minimum error rate that you can hope to achieve, even if you have infinite training data and can recover the true probability distribution. This is because your input features may not contain complete information about the output variable, or because the system might be intrinsically stochastic. You will also be limited by having a finite amount of training data.

The amount of training data can be limited for a variety of reasons. When your goal is to build the best possible real-world product or service, you can typically collect more data but must determine the value of reducing error further and weigh this against the cost of collecting more data. Data collection can require time, money, or human suffering (for example, if your data collection process involves performing invasive medical tests). When your goal is to answer a scientific question about which algorithm performs better on a fixed benchmark, the benchmark specification usually determines the training set, and you are not allowed to collect more data.

How can one determine a reasonable level of performance to expect? Typically, in the academic setting, we have some estimate of the error rate that is attainable based on previously published benchmark results. In the real-word setting, we have some idea of the error rate that is necessary for an application to be safe, cost-effective, or appealing to consumers. Once you have determined your realistic desired error rate, your design decisions will be guided by reaching this error rate.

Another important consideration besides the target value of the performance metric is the choice of which metric to use. Several different performance metrics may be used to measure the effectiveness of a complete application that includes machine learning components. These performance metrics are usually different from the cost function used to train the model. As described in section 5.1.2, it is common to measure the accuracy, or equivalently, the error rate, of a system.

However, many applications require more advanced metrics.

Sometimes it is much more costly to make one kind of a mistake than another. For example, an e-mail spam detection system can make two kinds of mistakes: incorrectly classifying a legitimate message as spam, and incorrectly allowing a spam message to appear in the inbox. It is much worse to block a legitimate message than to allow a questionable message to pass through. Rather than measuring the error rate of a spam classifier, we may wish to measure some form of total cost, where the cost of blocking legitimate messages is higher than the cost of allowing spam messages.

Sometimes we wish to train a binary classifier that is intended to detect some rare event. For example, we might design a medical test for a rare disease. Suppose that only one in every million people has this disease. We can easily achieve 99.9999 percent accuracy on the detection task, by simply hard coding the classifier to always report that the disease is absent. Clearly, accuracy is a poor way to characterize the performance of such a system. One way to solve this problem is to instead measure **precision** and **recall**. Precision is the fraction of detections reported by the model that were correct, while recall is the fraction of true events that were detected. A detector that says no one has the disease would achieve perfect precision, but zero recall. A detector that says everyone has the disease would achieve perfect recall, but precision equal to the percentage of people who have the disease (0.0001 percent in our example of a disease that only one people in a million have). When using precision and recall, it is common to plot a **PR curve**, with precision on the y-axis and recall on the x-axis. The classifier generates a score that is higher if the event to be detected occurred. For example, a feedforward network designed to detect a disease outputs $\hat{y} = P(y = 1 \mid \boldsymbol{x})$, estimating the probability that a person whose medical results are described by features $\boldsymbol{x}$ has the disease. We choose to report a detection whenever this score exceeds some threshold. By varying the threshold, we can trade precision for recall. In many cases, we wish to summarize the performance of the classifier with a single number rather than a curve. To do so, we can convert precision p and recall r into an **F-score** given by

$$F = \frac{2pr}{p + r}. \tag{11.1}$$

Another option is to report the total area lying beneath the PR curve.

In some applications, it is possible for the machine learning system to refuse to make a decision. This is useful when the machine learning algorithm can estimate how confident it should be about a decision, especially if a wrong decision can be harmful and if a human operator is able to occasionally take over. The Street View transcription system provides an example of this situation. The task is to transcribe the address number from a photograph to associate the location where the photo was taken with the correct address in a map. Because the value of the map degrades considerably if the map is inaccurate, it is important to add an address only if the transcription is correct. If the machine learning system thinks that it is less likely than a human being to obtain the correct transcription, then the best course of action is to allow a human to transcribe the photo instead. Of course, the machine learning system is only useful if it is able to dramatically reduce the amount of photos that the human operators must process. A natural performance metric to use in this situation is **coverage**. Coverage is the fraction of examples for which the machine learning system is able to produce a response. It is possible to trade coverage for accuracy. One can always obtain 100 percent accuracy by refusing to process any example, but this reduces the coverage to 0 percent. For the Street View task, the goal for the project was to reach human-level transcription accuracy while maintaining 95 percent coverage. Human-level performance on this task is 98 percent accuracy.

Many other metrics are possible. We can, for example, measure click-through rates, collect user satisfaction surveys, and so on. Many specialized application areas have application-specific criteria as well.

What is important is to determine which performance metric to improve ahead of time, then concentrate on improving this metric. Without clearly defined goals, it can be difficult to tell whether changes to a machine learning system make progress or not.

11.2 Default Baseline Models

After choosing performance metrics and goals, the next step in any practical application is to establish a reasonable end-to-end system as soon as possible. In this section, we provide recommendations for which algorithms to use as the first baseline approach in various situations. Keep in mind that deep learning research progresses quickly, so better default algorithms are likely to become available soon after this writing.

Depending on the complexity of your problem, you may even want to begin without using deep learning. If your problem has a chance of being solved by just choosing a few linear weights correctly, you may want to begin with a simple statistical model like logistic regression.

If you know that your problem falls into an "AI-complete" category like object recognition, speech recognition, machine translation, and so on, then you are likely to do well by beginning with an appropriate deep learning model.

First, choose the general category of model based on the structure of your data. If you want to perform supervised learning with fixed-size vectors as input, use a feedforward network with fully connected layers. If the input has known topological structure (for example, if the input is an image), use a convolutional network. In these cases, you should begin by using some kind of piecewise linear unit (ReLUs or their generalizations, such as Leaky ReLUs, PreLus, or maxout). If your input or output is a sequence, use a gated recurrent net (LSTM or GRU).

A reasonable choice of optimization algorithm is SGD with momentum with a decaying learning rate (popular decay schemes that perform better or worse on different problems include decaying linearly until reaching a fixed minimum learning rate, decaying exponentially, or decreasing the learning rate by a factor of 2–10 each time validation error plateaus). Another reasonable alternative is Adam. Batch normalization can have a dramatic effect on optimization performance, especially for convolutional networks and networks with sigmoidal nonlinearities. While it is reasonable to omit batch normalization from the very first baseline, it should be introduced quickly if optimization appears to be problematic.

Unless your training set contains tens of millions of examples or more, you should include some mild forms of regularization from the start. Early stopping should be used almost universally. Dropout is an excellent regularizer that is easy to implement and compatible with many models and training algorithms. Batch normalization also sometimes reduces generalization error and allows dropout to be omitted, because of the noise in the estimate of the statistics used to normalize each variable.

If your task is similar to another task that has been studied extensively, you will probably do well by first copying the model and algorithm that is already known to perform best on the previously studied task. You may even want to copy a trained model from that task. For example, it is common to use the features from a convolutional network trained on ImageNet to solve other computer vision tasks (Girshick et al., 2015).

A common question is whether to begin by using unsupervised learning, described further in part III. This is somewhat domain specific. Some domains, such as natural language processing, are known to benefit tremendously from unsupervised learning techniques, such as learning unsupervised word embeddings. In other domains, such as computer vision, current unsupervised learning techniques do not bring a benefit, except in the semi-supervised setting, when the number of labeled examples is very small (Kingma et al., 2014; Rasmus et al., 2015). If your application is in a context where unsupervised learning is known to be important, then include it in your first end-to-end baseline. Otherwise, only use unsupervised learning in your first attempt if the task you want to solve is unsupervised. You can always try adding unsupervised learning later if you observe that your initial baseline overfits.

11.3 Determining Whether to Gather More Data

After the first end-to-end system is established, it is time to measure the performance of the algorithm and determine how to improve it. Many machine learning novices are tempted to make improvements by trying out many different algorithms. Yet, it is often much better to gather more data than to improve the learning algorithm.

How does one decide whether to gather more data? First, determine whether the performance on the training set is acceptable. If performance on the training set is poor, the learning algorithm is not using the training data that is already available, so there is no reason to gather more data. Instead, try increasing the size of the model by adding more layers or adding more hidden units to each layer. Also, try improving the learning algorithm, for example by tuning the learning rate hyperparameter. If large models and carefully tuned optimization algorithms do not work well, then the problem might be the *quality* of the training data. The data may be too noisy or may not include the right inputs needed to predict the desired outputs. This suggests starting over, collecting cleaner data, or collecting a richer set of features.

If the performance on the training set is acceptable, then measure the performance on a test set. If the performance on the test set is also acceptable, then there is nothing left to be done. If test set performance is much worse than training set performance, then gathering more data is one of the most effective solutions. The key considerations are the cost and feasibility of gathering more data, the cost and feasibility of reducing the test error by other means, and the amount of data that is expected to be necessary to improve test set performance significantly. At large internet companies with millions or billions of users, it is feasible to gather large datasets, and the expense of doing so can be considerably less than that of the alternatives, so the answer is almost always to gather more training data. For example, the development of large labeled datasets was one of the most important factors in solving object recognition. In other contexts, such as medical applications, it may be costly or infeasible to gather more data. A simple alternative to gathering more data is to reduce the size of the model or improve regularization, by adjusting hyperparameters such as weight decay coefficients, or by adding regularization strategies such as dropout. If you find that the gap between train and test performance is still unacceptable even after tuning the regularization hyperparameters, then gathering more data is advisable.

When deciding whether to gather more data, it is also necessary to decide how much to gather. It is helpful to plot curves showing the relationship between training set size and generalization error, as in figure 5.4. By extrapolating such curves, one can predict how much additional training data would be needed to achieve a certain level of performance. Usually, adding a small fraction of the total number of examples will not have a noticeable effect on generalization error. It is therefore recommended to experiment with training set sizes on a logarithmic scale, for example, doubling the number of examples between consecutive experiments.

If gathering much more data is not feasible, the only other way to improve generalization error is to improve the learning algorithm itself. This becomes the domain of research and not the domain of advice for applied practitioners.

11.4 Selecting Hyperparameters

Most deep learning algorithms come with several hyperparameters that control many aspects of the algorithm's behavior. Some of these hyperparameters affect the time and memory cost of running the algorithm. Some of these hyperparameters affect the quality of the model recovered by the training process and its ability to infer correct results when deployed on new inputs.

There are two basic approaches to choosing these hyperparameters: choosing them manually and choosing them automatically. Choosing the hyperparameters manually requires understanding what the hyperparameters do and how machine learning models achieve good generalization. Automatic hyperparameter selection algorithms greatly reduce the need to understand these ideas, but they are often much more computationally costly.

11.4.1 Manual Hyperparameter Tuning

To set hyperparameters manually, one must understand the relationship between hyperparameters, training error, generalization error and computational resources (memory and runtime). This means establishing a solid foundation on the fundamental ideas concerning the effective capacity of a learning algorithm, as described in chapter 5.

The goal of manual hyperparameter search is usually to find the lowest generalization error subject to some runtime and memory budget. We do not discuss how to determine the runtime and memory impact of various hyperparameters here because this is highly platform dependent.

The primary goal of manual hyperparameter search is to adjust the effective capacity of the model to match the complexity of the task. Effective capacity is constrained by three factors: the representational capacity of the model, the ability of the learning algorithm to successfully minimize the cost function used to train the model, and the degree to which the cost function and training procedure regularize the model. A model with more layers and more hidden units per layer has higher representational capacity—it is capable of representing more complicated functions. It cannot necessarily learn all these functions though, if the training algorithm cannot discover that certain functions do a good job of minimizing the training cost, or if regularization terms such as weight decay forbid some of these functions.

The generalization error typically follows a U-shaped curve when plotted as a function of one of the hyperparameters, as in figure 5.3. At one extreme, the hyperparameter value corresponds to low capacity, and generalization error is high because training error is high. This is the underfitting regime. At the other extreme, the hyperparameter value corresponds to high capacity, and the generalization error is high because the gap between training and test error is high. Somewhere in the middle lies the optimal model capacity, which achieves the lowest possible generalization error, by adding a medium generalization gap to a medium amount of training error.

For some hyperparameters, overfitting occurs when the value of the hyperparameter is large. The number of hidden units in a layer is one such example, because increasing the number of hidden units increases the capacity of the model. For some hyperparameters, overfitting occurs when the value of the hyperparameter is small. For example, the smallest allowable weight decay coefficient of zero corresponds to the greatest effective capacity of the learning algorithm.

Not every hyperparameter will be able to explore the entire U-shaped curve. Many hyperparameters are discrete, such as the number of units in a layer or the number of linear pieces in a maxout unit, so it is only possible to visit a few points along the curve. Some hyperparameters are binary. Usually these hyperparameters are switches that specify whether or not to use some optional component of the learning algorithm, such as a preprocessing step that normalizes the input features by subtracting their mean and dividing by their standard deviation. These hyperparameters can explore only two points on the curve. Other hyperparameters have some minimum or maximum value that prevents them from exploring some part of the curve. For example, the minimum weight decay coefficient is zero. This means that if the model is underfitting when weight decay is zero, we cannot enter the overfitting region by modifying the weight decay coefficient. In other words, some hyperparameters can only subtract capacity.

The learning rate is perhaps the most important hyperparameter. If you have time to tune only one hyperparameter, tune the learning rate. It controls the effective capacity of the model in a more complicated way than other hyperparameters— the effective capacity of the model is highest when the learning rate is *correct* for the optimization problem, not when the learning rate is especially large or especially small. The learning rate has a U-shaped curve for *training* error, illustrated in figure 11.1. When the learning rate is too large, gradient descent can inadvertently increase rather than decrease the training error. In the idealized quadratic case, this occurs if the learning rate is at least twice as large as its optimal value (LeCun et al., 1998a). When the learning rate is too small, training is not only slower but may become permanently stuck with a high training error. This effect is poorly understood (it would not happen for a convex loss function).

Tuning the parameters other than the learning rate requires monitoring both training and test error to diagnose whether your model is overfitting or underfitting, then adjusting its capacity appropriately.

If your error on the training set is higher than your target error rate, you have no choice but to increase capacity. If you are not using regularization and you are confident that your optimization algorithm is performing correctly, then you must

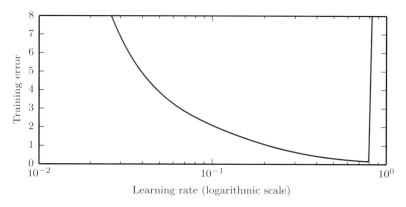

Figure 11.1: Typical relationship between the learning rate and the training error. Notice the sharp rise in error when the learning is above an optimal value. This is for a fixed training time, as a smaller learning rate may sometimes only slow down training by a factor proportional to the learning rate reduction. Generalization error can follow this curve or be complicated by regularization effects arising out of having too large or too small learning rates, since poor optimization can, to some degree, reduce or prevent overfitting, and even points with equivalent training error can have different generalization error.

add more layers to your network or add more hidden units. Unfortunately, this increases the computational costs associated with the model.

If your error on the test set is higher than than your target error rate, you can now take two kinds of actions. The test error is the sum of the training error and the gap between training and test error. The optimal test error is found by trading off these quantities. Neural networks typically perform best when the training error is very low (and thus, when capacity is high) and the test error is primarily driven by the gap between training and test error. Your goal is to reduce this gap without increasing training error faster than the gap decreases. To reduce the gap, change regularization hyperparameters to reduce effective model capacity, such as by adding dropout or weight decay. Usually the best performance comes from a large model that is regularized well, for example, by using dropout.

Most hyperparameters can be set by reasoning about whether they increase or decrease model capacity. Some examples are included in table 11.1.

While manually tuning hyperparameters, do not lose sight of your end goal: good performance on the test set. Adding regularization is only one way to achieve this goal. As long as you have low training error, you can always reduce generalization error by collecting more training data. The brute force way to practically guarantee success is to continually increase model capacity and training set size until the task is solved. This approach does of course increase the computational cost of

Hyperparameter	Increases capacity when...	Reason	Caveats
Number of hidden units	increased	Increasing the number of hidden units increases the representational capacity of the model.	Increasing the number of hidden units increases both the time and memory cost of essentially every operation on the model.
Learning rate	tuned optimally	An improper learning rate, whether too high or too low, results in a model with low effective capacity due to optimization failure.	
Convolution kernel width	increased	Increasing the kernel width increases the number of parameters in the model.	A wider kernel results in a narrower output dimension, reducing model capacity unless you use implicit zero padding to reduce this effect. Wider kernels require more memory for parameter storage and increase runtime, but a narrower output reduces memory cost.
Implicit zero padding	increased	Adding implicit zeros before convolution keeps the representation size large.	Increases time and memory cost of most operations.
Weight decay coefficient	decreased	Decreasing the weight decay coefficient frees the model parameters to become larger.	
Dropout rate	decreased	Dropping units less often gives the units more opportunities to "conspire" with each other to fit the training set.	

Table 11.1: The effect of various hyperparameters on model capacity.

training and inference, so it is only feasible given appropriate resources. In principle, this approach could fail due to optimization difficulties, but for many problems optimization does not seem to be a significant barrier, provided that the model is chosen appropriately.

11.4.2   Automatic Hyperparameter Optimization Algorithms

The ideal learning algorithm just takes a dataset and outputs a function, without requiring hand tuning of hyperparameters. The popularity of several learning algorithms such as logistic regression and SVMs stems in part from their ability to perform well with only one or two tuned hyperparameters. Neural networks can sometimes perform well with only a small number of tuned hyperparameters, but often benefit significantly from tuning of forty or more. Manual hyperparameter tuning can work very well when the user has a good starting point, such as one determined by others having worked on the same type of application and architecture, or when the user has months or years of experience in exploring hyperparameter values for neural networks applied to similar tasks. For many applications, however, these starting points are not available. In these cases, automated algorithms can find useful values of the hyperparameters.

If we think about the way in which the user of a learning algorithm searches for good values of the hyperparameters, we realize that an optimization is taking place: we are trying to find a value of the hyperparameters that optimizes an objective function, such as validation error, sometimes under constraints (such as a budget for training time, memory or recognition time). It is therefore possible, in principle, to develop **hyperparameter optimization** algorithms that wrap a learning algorithm and choose its hyperparameters, thus hiding the hyperparameters of the learning algorithm from the user. Unfortunately, hyperparameter optimization algorithms often have their own hyperparameters, such as the range of values that should be explored for each of the learning algorithm's hyperparameters. These secondary hyperparameters are usually easier to choose, however, in the sense that acceptable performance may be achieved on a wide range of tasks using the same secondary hyperparameters for all tasks.

11.4.3   Grid Search

When there are three or fewer hyperparameters, the common practice is to perform **grid search**. For each hyperparameter, the user selects a small finite set of values to explore. The grid search algorithm then trains a model for every joint specification of hyperparameter values in the Cartesian product of the set of values for each individual hyperparameter. The experiment that yields the best validation set error is then chosen as having found the best hyperparameters. See the left of figure 11.2 for an illustration of a grid of hyperparameter values.

How should the lists of values to search over be chosen? In the case of numerical (ordered) hyperparameters, the smallest and largest element of each list is chosen

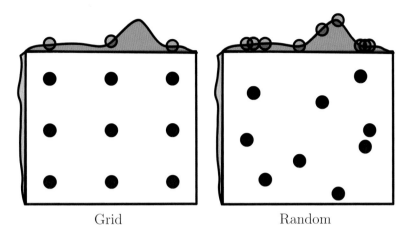

Grid   Random

Figure 11.2: Comparison of grid search and random search. For illustration purposes, we display two hyperparameters, but we are typically interested in having many more. *(Left)* To perform grid search, we provide a set of values for each hyperparameter. The search algorithm runs training for every joint hyperparameter setting in the cross product of these sets. *(Right)* To perform random search, we provide a probability distribution over joint hyperparameter configurations. Usually most of these hyperparameters are independent from each other. Common choices for the distribution over a single hyperparameter include uniform and log-uniform (to sample from a log-uniform distribution, take the exp of a sample from a uniform distribution). The search algorithm then randomly samples joint hyperparameter configurations and runs training with each of them. Both grid search and random search evaluate the validation set error and return the best configuration. The figure illustrates the typical case where only some hyperparameters have a significant influence on the result. In this illustration, only the hyperparameter on the horizontal axis has a significant effect. Grid search wastes an amount of computation that is exponential in the number of noninfluential hyperparameters, while random search tests a unique value of every influential hyperparameter on nearly every trial. Figure reproduced with permission from Bergstra and Bengio (2012).

conservatively, based on prior experience with similar experiments, to make sure that the optimal value is likely to be in the selected range. Typically, a grid search involves picking values approximately on a *logarithmic scale*, e.g., a learning rate taken within the set $\{0.1, 0.01, 10^{-3}, 10^{-4}, 10^{-5}\}$, or a number of hidden units taken with the set $\{50, 100, 200, 500, 1000, 2000\}$.

Grid search usually performs best when it is performed repeatedly. For example, suppose that we ran a grid search over a hyperparameter α using values of $\{-1, 0, 1\}$. If the best value found is 1, then we underestimated the range in which the best α lies and should shift the grid and run another search with α in, for example, $\{1, 2, 3\}$. If we find that the best value of α is 0, then we may wish to refine our estimate by zooming in and running a grid search over $\{-0.1, 0, 0.1\}$.

The obvious problem with grid search is that its computational cost grows exponentially with the number of hyperparameters. If there are m hyperparameters, each taking at most n values, then the number of training and evaluation trials required grows as $O(n^m)$. The trials may be run in parallel and exploit loose parallelism (with almost no need for communication between different machines carrying out the search). Unfortunately, because of the exponential cost of grid search, even parallelization may not provide a satisfactory size of search.

11.4.4 Random Search

Fortunately, there is an alternative to grid search that is as simple to program, more convenient to use, and converges much faster to good values of the hyperparameters: random search (Bergstra and Bengio, 2012).

A random search proceeds as follows. First we define a marginal distribution for each hyperparameter, for example, a Bernoulli or multinoulli for binary or discrete hyperparameters, or a uniform distribution on a log-scale for positive real-valued hyperparameters. For example,

$$\texttt{log\_learning\_rate} \sim u(-1, -5), \tag{11.2}$$

$$\texttt{learning\_rate} = 10^{\texttt{log\_learning\_rate}}, \tag{11.3}$$

where $u(a, b)$ indicates a sample of the uniform distribution in the interval (a, b). Similarly the $\texttt{log\_number\_of\_hidden\_units}$ may be sampled from $u(\log(50), \log(2000))$.

Unlike in a grid search, we *should not discretize* or bin the values of the hyperparameters, so that we can explore a larger set of values and avoid additional computational cost. In fact, as illustrated in figure 11.2, a random search can be exponentially more efficient than a grid search, when there are several hyperparameters that do not strongly affect the performance measure. This is studied at length in Bergstra and Bengio (2012), who found that random search reduces the validation set error much faster than grid search, in terms of the number of trials run by each method.

As with grid search, we may often want to run repeated versions of random search, to refine the search based on the results of the first run.

The main reason that random search finds good solutions faster than grid search is that it has no wasted experimental runs, unlike in the case of grid search, when two values of a hyperparameter (given values of the other hyperparameters) would give the same result. In the case of grid search, the other hyperparameters would have the same values for these two runs, whereas with random search, they would usually have different values. Hence if the change between these two values does not marginally make much difference in terms of validation set error, grid search will unnecessarily repeat two equivalent experiments while random search will still give two independent explorations of the other hyperparameters.

11.4.5   Model-Based Hyperparameter Optimization

The search for good hyperparameters can be cast as an optimization problem. The decision variables are the hyperparameters. The cost to be optimized is the validation set error that results from training using these hyperparameters. In simplified settings where it is feasible to compute the gradient of some differentiable error measure on the validation set with respect to the hyperparameters, we can simply follow this gradient (Bengio et al., 1999; Bengio, 2000; Maclaurin et al., 2015). Unfortunately, in most practical settings, this gradient is unavailable, either because of its high computation and memory cost, or because of hyperparameters that have intrinsically nondifferentiable interactions with the validation set error, as in the case of discrete-valued hyperparameters.

To compensate for this lack of a gradient, we can build a model of the validation set error, then propose new hyperparameter guesses by performing optimization within this model. Most model-based algorithms for hyperparameter search use a Bayesian regression model to estimate both the expected value of the validation set error for each hyperparameter and the uncertainty around this expectation. Optimization thus involves a trade-off between exploration (proposing hyperparameters for that there is high uncertainty, which may lead to a large improvement but may also perform poorly) and exploitation (proposing hyperparameters that the model is confident will perform as well as any hyperparameters it has seen so far—usually hyperparameters that are very similar to ones it has seen before). Contemporary approaches to hyperparameter optimization include Spearmint (Snoek et al., 2012), TPE (Bergstra et al., 2011) and SMAC (Hutter et al., 2011).

Currently, we cannot unambiguously recommend Bayesian hyperparameter optimization as an established tool for achieving better deep learning results or for obtaining those results with less effort. Bayesian hyperparameter optimization sometimes performs comparably to human experts, sometimes better, but fails catastrophically on other problems. It may be worth trying to see if it works on a particular problem but is not yet sufficiently mature or reliable. That being said, hyperparameter optimization is an important field of research that, while often driven primarily by the needs of deep learning, holds the potential to benefit not only the entire field of machine learning but also the discipline of engineering in general.

One drawback common to most hyperparameter optimization algorithms with more sophistication than random search is that they require for a training experiment to run to completion before they are able to extract any information from the experiment. This is much less efficient, in the sense of how much information can be gleaned early in an experiment, than manual search by a human practitioner, since one can usually tell early on if some set of hyperparameters is completely pathological. Swersky et al. (2014) have introduced an early version of an algorithm that maintains a set of multiple experiments. At various time points, the hyperparameter optimization algorithm can choose to begin a new experiment, to "freeze" a running experiment that is not promising, or to "thaw" and resume an experiment that was earlier frozen but now appears promising given more information.

11.5   Debugging Strategies

When a machine learning system performs poorly, it is usually difficult to tell whether the poor performance is intrinsic to the algorithm itself or whether there is a bug in the implementation of the algorithm. Machine learning systems are difficult to debug for various reasons.

In most cases, we do not know a priori what the intended behavior of the algorithm is. In fact, the entire point of using machine learning is that it will discover useful behavior that we were not able to specify ourselves. If we train a neural network on a *new* classification task and it achieves 5 percent test error, we have no straightforward way of knowing if this is the expected behavior or suboptimal behavior.

A further difficulty is that most machine learning models have multiple parts that are each adaptive. If one part is broken, the other parts can adapt and still achieve roughly acceptable performance. For example, suppose that we are training a neural net with several layers parametrized by weights $\boldsymbol{W}$ and biases $\boldsymbol{b}$. Suppose further that we have manually implemented the gradient descent rule for each parameter separately, and we made an error in the update for the biases:

$$\boldsymbol{b} \leftarrow \boldsymbol{b} - \alpha, \tag{11.4}$$

where α is the learning rate. This erroneous update does not use the gradient at all. It causes the biases to constantly become negative throughout learning, which is clearly not a correct implementation of any reasonable learning algorithm. The bug may not be apparent just from examining the output of the model though. Depending on the distribution of the input, the weights may be able to adapt to compensate for the negative biases.

Most debugging strategies for neural nets are designed to get around one or both of these two difficulties. Either we design a case that is so simple that the correct behavior actually can be predicted, or we design a test that exercises one part of the neural net implementation in isolation.

Some important debugging tests include the following.

Visualize the model in action: When training a model to detect objects in images, view some images with the detections proposed by the model displayed superimposed on the image. When training a generative model of speech, listen to some of the speech samples it produces. This may seem obvious, but it is easy to fall into the practice of looking only at quantitative performance measurements like accuracy or log-likelihood. Directly observing the machine learning model performing its task will help to determine whether the quantitative performance numbers it achieves seem reasonable. Evaluation bugs can be some of the most devastating bugs because they can mislead you into believing your system is performing well when it is not.

Visualize the worst mistakes: Most models are able to output some sort of confidence measure for the task they perform. For example, classifiers based on a softmax output layer assign a probability to each class. The probability assigned to the most likely class thus gives an estimate of the confidence the model has in its classification decision. Typically, maximum likelihood training results in these values being overestimates rather than accurate probabilities of correct prediction, but they are somewhat useful in the sense that examples that are actually less likely to be correctly labeled receive smaller probabilities under the model. By viewing the training set examples that are the hardest to model correctly, one can often discover problems with the way the data have been preprocessed or labeled. For example, the Street View transcription system originally had a problem where the address number detection system would crop the image too tightly and omit some digits. The transcription network then assigned very low probability to the correct answer on these images. Sorting the images to identify the most confident mistakes showed that there was a systematic problem with the cropping. Modifying the detection system to crop much wider images resulted in much better performance of the overall system, even though the transcription network needed to be able to process greater variation in the position and scale of the address numbers.

Reason about software using training and test error: It is often difficult to determine whether the underlying software is correctly implemented. Some clues can be obtained from the training and test errors. If training error is low but test error is high, then it is likely that that the training procedure works correctly, and the model is overfitting for fundamental algorithmic reasons. An alternative possibility is that the test error is measured incorrectly because of a problem with saving the model after training then reloading it for test set evaluation, or because the test data was prepared differently from the training data. If both training and test errors are high, then it is difficult to determine whether there is a software defect or whether the model is underfitting due to fundamental algorithmic reasons. This scenario requires further tests, described next.

Fit a tiny dataset: If you have high error on the training set, determine whether it is due to genuine underfitting or due to a software defect. Usually even small models can be guaranteed to be able fit a sufficiently small dataset. For example, a classification dataset with only one example can be fit just by setting the biases of the output layer correctly. Usually if you cannot train a classifier to correctly label a single example, an autoencoder to successfully reproduce a single example with high fidelity, or a generative model to consistently emit samples resembling a single example, there is a software defect preventing successful optimization on the training set. This test can be extended to a small dataset with few examples.

Compare back-propagated derivatives to numerical derivatives: If you are using a software framework that requires you to implement your own gradient computations, or if you are adding a new operation to a differentiation library and must define its `bprop` method, then a common source of error is implementing this gradient expression incorrectly. One way to verify that these derivatives are correct is to compare the derivatives computed by your implementation of automatic differentiation to the derivatives computed by **finite differences**. Because

$$f'(x) = \lim_{\epsilon \to 0} \frac{f(x + \epsilon) - f(x)}{\epsilon}, \tag{11.5}$$

we can approximate the derivative by using a small, finite ϵ:

$$f'(x) \approx \frac{f(x + \epsilon) - f(x)}{\epsilon}. \tag{11.6}$$

We can improve the accuracy of the approximation by using the **centered difference**:

$$f'(x) \approx \frac{f(x + \frac{1}{2}\epsilon) - f(x - \frac{1}{2}\epsilon)}{\epsilon}. \tag{11.7}$$

The perturbation size ϵ must be large enough to ensure that the perturbation is not rounded down too much by finite-precision numerical computations.

Usually, we will want to test the gradient or Jacobian of a vector-valued function $g : \mathbb{R}^m \to \mathbb{R}^n$. Unfortunately, finite differencing only allows us to take a single derivative at a time. We can either run finite differencing mn times to evaluate all the partial derivatives of g, or apply the test to a new function that uses random projections at both the input and the output of g. For example, we can apply our test of the implementation of the derivatives to $f(x)$, where $f(x) = \boldsymbol{u}^T g(\boldsymbol{v}x)$, and $\boldsymbol{u}$ and $\boldsymbol{v}$ are randomly chosen vectors. Computing $f'(x)$ correctly requires being able to back-propagate through g correctly yet is efficient to do with finite differences because f has only a single input and a single output. It is usually a good idea to repeat this test for more than one value of $\boldsymbol{u}$ and $\boldsymbol{v}$ to reduce the chance of the test overlooking mistakes that are orthogonal to the random projection.

If one has access to numerical computation on complex numbers, then there is a very efficient way to numerically estimate the gradient by using complex numbers as input to the function (Squire and Trapp, 1998). The method is based on the observation that

$$f(x + i\epsilon) = f(x) + i\epsilon f'(x) + O(\epsilon^2), \tag{11.8}$$

$$\text{real}(f(x + i\epsilon)) = f(x) + O(\epsilon^2), \quad \text{imag}(\frac{f(x + i\epsilon)}{\epsilon}) = f'(x) + O(\epsilon^2), \tag{11.9}$$

where $i = \sqrt{-1}$. Unlike in the real-valued case above, there is no cancellation effect because we take the difference between the value of f at different points. This allows the use of tiny values of ϵ, like $\epsilon = 10^{-150}$, which make the $O(\epsilon^2)$ error insignificant for all practical purposes.

Monitor histograms of activations and gradient: It is often useful to visualize statistics of neural network activations and gradients, collected over a large amount of training iterations (maybe one epoch). The preactivation value of hidden units can tell us if the units saturate, or how often they do. For example, for rectifiers, how often are they off? Are there units that are always off? For tanh units, the average of the absolute value of the preactivations tells us how saturated the unit is. In a deep network where the propagated gradients quickly grow or quickly vanish, optimization may be hampered. Finally, it is useful to compare the magnitude of parameter gradients to the magnitude of the parameters themselves. As suggested by Bottou (2015), we would like the magnitude of parameter updates over a minibatch to represent something like 1 percent of the magnitude of the parameter, not 50 percent or 0.001 percent (which would make the parameters move too slowly). It may be that some groups of parameters are moving at a good pace while others are stalled. When the data is sparse (like in natural language), some parameters may be very rarely updated, and this should be kept in mind when monitoring their evolution.

Finally, many deep learning algorithms provide some sort of guarantee about the results produced at each step. For example, in part III, we will see some approximate inference algorithms that work by using algebraic solutions to optimization problems. Typically these can be debugged by testing each of their guarantees. Some guarantees that some optimization algorithms offer include that the objective function will never increase after one step of the algorithm, that the gradient with respect to some subset of variables will be zero after each step of the algorithm, and that the gradient with respect to all variables will be zero at convergence. Usually due to rounding error, these conditions will not hold exactly in a digital computer, so the debugging test should include some tolerance parameter.

11.6   Example: Multi-Digit Number Recognition

To provide an end-to-end description of how to apply our design methodology in practice, we present a brief account of the Street View transcription system, from the point of view of designing the deep learning components. Obviously, many other components of the complete system, such as the Street View cars, the database infrastructure, and so on, were of paramount importance.

From the point of view of the machine learning task, the process began with data collection. The cars collected the raw data, and human operators provided labels. The transcription task was preceded by a significant amount of dataset curation, including using other machine learning techniques to *detect* the house numbers prior to transcribing them.

The transcription project began with a choice of performance metrics and desired values for these metrics. An important general principle is to tailor the choice of metric to the business goals for the project. Because maps are only useful if they have high accuracy, it was important to set a high accuracy requirement for this project. Specifically, the goal was to obtain human-level, 98 percent accuracy. This level of accuracy may not always be feasible to obtain. To reach this level of accuracy, the Street View transcription system sacrificed coverage. Coverage thus became the main performance metric optimized during the project, with accuracy held at 98 percent. As the convolutional network improved, it became possible to reduce the confidence threshold below which the network refused to transcribe the input, eventually exceeding the goal of 95 percent coverage.

After choosing quantitative goals, the next step in our recommended methodology is to rapidly establish a sensible baseline system. For vision tasks, this means a convolutional network with rectified linear units. The transcription project began with such a model. At the time, it was not common for a convolutional network to output a sequence of predictions. To begin with the simplest possible baseline, the first implementation of the output layer of the model consisted of n different softmax units to predict a sequence of n characters. These softmax units were trained exactly the same as if the task were classification, with each softmax unit trained independently.

Our recommended methodology is to iteratively refine the baseline and test whether each change makes an improvement. The first change to the Street View transcription system was motivated by a theoretical understanding of the coverage metric and the structure of the data. Specifically, the network refused to classify an input x whenever the probability of the output sequence $p(y \mid x) < t$ for some threshold t. Initially, the definition of $p(y \mid x)$ was ad-hoc, based on simply multiplying all the softmax outputs together. This motivated the development of a specialized output layer and cost function that actually computed a principled log-likelihood. This approach allowed the example rejection mechanism to function much more effectively.

At this point, coverage was still below 90 percent, yet there were no obvious theoretical problems with the approach. Our methodology therefore suggested instrumenting the training and test set performance to determine whether the problem was underfitting or overfitting. In this case, training and test set error were nearly identical. Indeed, the main reason this project proceeded so smoothly was the availability of a dataset with tens of millions of labeled examples. Because training and test set error were so similar, this suggested that the problem was due to either underfitting or a problem with the training data. One of the debugging strategies we recommend is to visualize the model's worst errors. In this case, that meant visualizing the incorrect training set transcriptions that the model gave the highest confidence. These proved to mostly consist of examples where the input image had been cropped too tightly, with some of the digits of the address being removed by the cropping operation. For example, a photo of an address "1849" might be cropped too tightly, with only the "849" remaining visible. This problem could have been resolved by spending weeks improving the accuracy of the address number detection system responsible for determining the cropping regions. Instead, the team made a much more practical decision, to simply expand the width of the crop region to be systematically wider than the address number detection system predicted. This single change added ten percentage points to the transcription system's coverage.

Finally, the last few percentage points of performance came from adjusting hyperparameters. This mostly consisted of making the model larger while maintaining some restrictions on its computational cost. Because train and test error remained roughly equal, it was always clear that any performance deficits were due to underfitting, as well as to a few remaining problems with the dataset itself.

Overall, the transcription project was a great success and allowed hundreds of millions of addresses to be transcribed both faster and at lower cost than would have been possible via human effort.

We hope that the design principles described in this chapter will lead to many other similar successes.

12

Applications

In this chapter, we describe how to use deep learning to solve applications in computer vision, speech recognition, natural language processing, and other areas of commercial interest. We begin by discussing the large-scale neural network implementations required for most serious AI applications. Next, we review several specific application areas that deep learning has been used to solve. While one goal of deep learning is to design algorithms that are capable of solving a broad variety of tasks, so far some degree of specialization is needed. For example, vision tasks require processing a large number of input features (pixels) per example. Language tasks require modeling a large number of possible values (words in the vocabulary) per input feature.

12.1 Large-Scale Deep Learning

Deep learning is based on the philosophy of connectionism: while an individual biological neuron or an individual feature in a machine learning model is not intelligent, a large population of these neurons or features acting together can exhibit intelligent behavior. It truly is important to emphasize the fact that the number of neurons must be *large*. One of the key factors responsible for the improvement in neural network's accuracy and the improvement of the complexity of tasks they can solve between the 1980s and today is the dramatic increase in the size of the networks we use. As we saw in section 1.2.3, network sizes have grown exponentially for the past three decades, yet artificial neural networks are only as large as the nervous systems of insects.

Because the size of neural networks is critical, deep learning requires high performance hardware and software infrastructure.

12.1.1 Fast CPU Implementations

Traditionally, neural networks were trained using the CPU of a single machine. Today, this approach is generally considered insufficient. We now mostly use GPU computing or the CPUs of many machines networked together. Before moving to these expensive setups, researchers worked hard to demonstrate that CPUs could not manage the high computational workload required by neural networks.

A description of how to implement efficient numerical CPU code is beyond the scope of this book, but we emphasize here that careful implementation for specific CPU families can yield large improvements. For example, in 2011, the best CPUs available could run neural network workloads faster when using fixed-point arithmetic rather than floating-point arithmetic. By creating a carefully tuned fixed-point implementation, Vanhoucke et al. (2011) obtained a threefold speedup over a strong floating-point system. Each new model of CPU has different performance characteristics, so sometimes floating-point implementations can be faster too. The important principle is that careful specialization of numerical computation routines can yield a large payoff. Other strategies, besides choosing whether to use fixed or floating point, include optimizing data structures to avoid cache misses and using vector instructions. Many machine learning researchers neglect these implementation details, but when the performance of an implementation restricts the size of the model, the accuracy of the model suffers.

12.1.2 GPU Implementations

Most modern neural network implementations are based on graphics processing units. Graphics processing units (GPUs) are specialized hardware components that were originally developed for graphics applications. The consumer market for video gaming systems spurred development of graphics processing hardware. The performance characteristics needed for good video gaming systems turn out to be beneficial for neural networks as well.

Video game rendering requires performing many operations in parallel quickly. Models of characters and environments are specified in lists of 3-D coordinates of vertices. Graphics cards must perform matrix multiplication and division on many vertices in parallel to convert these 3-D coordinates into 2-D on-screen coordinates. The graphics card must then perform many computations at each pixel in parallel to determine the color of each pixel. In both cases, the computations are fairly simple and do not involve much branching compared to the computational workload that a CPU usually encounters. For example, each vertex in the same rigid object will be multiplied by the same matrix; there is no need to evaluate an if statement per vertex to determine which matrix to multiply by. The computations are also entirely independent of each other, and thus may be parallelized easily. The computations also involve processing massive buffers of memory, containing bitmaps describing the texture (color pattern) of each object to be rendered. Together, this results in graphics cards having been designed to have a high degree of parallelism and high memory bandwidth, at the cost of having a lower clock speed and less branching capability relative to traditional CPUs.

Neural network algorithms require the same performance characteristics as the real-time graphics algorithms described above. Neural networks usually involve large and numerous buffers of parameters, activation values, and gradient values, each of which must be completely updated during every step of training. These buffers are large enough to fall outside the cache of a traditional desktop computer, so the memory bandwidth of the system often becomes the rate-limiting factor. GPUs offer a compelling advantage over CPUs because of their high memory bandwidth. Neural network training algorithms typically do not involve much branching or sophisticated control, so they are appropriate for GPU hardware. Since neural networks can be divided into multiple individual "neurons" that can be processed independently from the other neurons in the same layer, neural networks easily benefit from the parallelism of GPU computing.

GPU hardware was originally so specialized that it could be used only for graphics tasks. Over time, GPU hardware became more flexible, allowing custom subroutines to be used to transform the coordinates of vertices or to assign colors to pixels. In principle, there was no requirement that these pixel values actually be based on a rendering task. These GPUs could be used for scientific computing by writing the output of a computation to a buffer of pixel values. Steinkrau et al. (2005) implemented a two-layer fully connected neural network on a GPU and reported a three-times speedup over their CPU-based baseline. Shortly thereafter, Chellapilla et al. (2006) demonstrated that the same technique could be used to accelerate supervised convolutional networks.

The popularity of graphics cards for neural network training exploded after the advent of **general purpose GPUs**. These GP-GPUs could execute arbitrary code, not just rendering subroutines. NVIDIA's CUDA programming language provided a way to write this arbitrary code in a C-like language. With their relatively convenient programming model, massive parallelism, and high memory bandwidth, GP-GPUs now offer an ideal platform for neural network programming. This platform was rapidly adopted by deep learning researchers soon after it became available (Raina et al., 2009; Ciresan et al., 2010).

Writing efficient code for GP-GPUs remains a difficult task best left to specialists. The techniques required to obtain good performance on GPU are very different from those used on CPU. For example, good CPU-based code is usually designed to read information from the cache as much as possible. On GPU, most writable memory locations are not cached, so it can actually be faster to compute the same value twice, rather than compute it once and read it back from memory. GPU code is also inherently multithreaded and the different threads must be coordinated with each other carefully. For example, memory operations are faster if they can be **coalesced**. Coalesced reads or writes occur when several threads can each read or write a value that they need simultaneously, as part of a single memory transaction. Different models of GPUs are able to coalesce different kinds of read and write patterns. Typically, memory operations are easier to coalesce if among n threads, thread i accesses byte $i + j$ of memory, and j is a multiple of some power of 2. The exact specifications differ between models of GPU. Another common consideration for GPUs is making sure that each thread in a group executes the same instruction simultaneously. This means that branching can be difficult on GPU. Threads are divided into small groups called **warps**. Each thread in a warp executes the same instruction during each cycle, so if different threads within the same warp need to execute different code paths, these different code paths must be traversed sequentially rather than in parallel.

Because of the difficulty of writing high-performance GPU code, researchers should structure their workflow to avoid needing to write new GPU code to test new models or algorithms. Typically, one can do this by building a software library of high-performance operations like convolution and matrix multiplication, then specifying models in terms of calls to this library of operations. For example, the machine learning library Pylearn2 (Goodfellow et al., 2013c) specifies all its machine learning algorithms in terms of calls to Theano (Bergstra et al., 2010; Bastien et al., 2012) and cuda-convnet (Krizhevsky, 2010), which provide these high-performance operations. This factored approach can also ease support for multiple kinds of hardware. For example, the same Theano program can run on either CPU or GPU, without needing to change any of the calls to Theano itself. Other libraries like TensorFlow (Abadi et al., 2015) and Torch (Collobert et al., 2011b) provide similar features.

12.1.3 Large-Scale Distributed Implementations

In many cases, the computational resources available on a single machine are insufficient. We therefore want to distribute the workload of training and inference across many machines.

Distributing inference is simple, because each input example we want to process can be run by a separate machine. This is known as **data parallelism**.

It is also possible to get **model parallelism**, where multiple machines work together on a single data point, with each machine running a different part of the model. This is feasible for both inference and training.

Data parallelism during training is somewhat harder. We can increase the size of the minibatch used for a single SGD step, but usually we get less than linear returns in terms of optimization performance. It would be better to allow multiple machines to compute multiple gradient descent steps in parallel. Unfortunately, the standard definition of gradient descent is as a completely sequential algorithm: the gradient at step t is a function of the parameters produced by step $t-1$.

This can be solved using **asynchronous stochastic gradient descent** (Bengio et al., 2001; Recht et al., 2011). In this approach, several processor cores share the memory representing the parameters. Each core reads parameters without a lock, then computes a gradient, then increments the parameters without a lock. This reduces the average amount of improvement that each gradient descent step yields, because some of the cores overwrite each other's progress, but the increased rate of production of steps causes the learning process to be faster overall. Dean et al. (2012) pioneered the multimachine implementation of this lock-free approach to gradient descent, where the parameters are managed by a **parameter server** rather than stored in shared memory. Distributed asynchronous gradient descent remains the primary strategy for training large deep networks and is used by most major deep learning groups in industry (Chilimbi et al., 2014; Wu et al., 2015). Academic deep learning researchers typically cannot afford the same scale of distributed learning systems, but some research has focused on how to build distributed networks with relatively low-cost hardware available in the university setting (Coates et al., 2013).

12.1.4 Model Compression

In many commercial applications, it is much more important that the time and memory cost of running inference in a machine learning model be low than that the time and memory cost of training be low. For applications that do not require personalization, it is possible to train a model once, then deploy it to be used by billions of users. In many cases, the end user is more resource constrained than the developer. For example, one might train a speech recognition network with a powerful computer cluster, then deploy it on mobile phones.

A key strategy for reducing the cost of inference is **model compression** (Buciluă et al., 2006). The basic idea of model compression is to replace the original, expensive model with a smaller model that requires less memory and runtime to store and evaluate.

Model compression is applicable when the size of the original model is driven primarily by a need to prevent overfitting. In most cases, the model with the lowest generalization error is an ensemble of several independently trained models. Evaluating all n ensemble members is expensive. Sometimes, even a single model generalizes better if it is large (for example, if it is regularized with dropout).

These large models learn some function $f(x)$, but do so using many more parameters than are necessary for the task. Their size is necessary only because of the limited number of training examples. As soon as we have fit this function $f(x)$, we can generate a training set containing infinitely many examples, simply by applying f to randomly sampled points x. We then train the new, smaller model to match $f(x)$ on these points. To most efficiently use the capacity of the new, small model, it is best to sample the new x points from a distribution resembling the actual test inputs that will be supplied to the model later. This can be done by corrupting training examples or by drawing points from a generative model trained on the original training set.

Alternatively, one can train the smaller model only on the original training points, but train it to copy other features of the model, such as its posterior distribution over the incorrect classes (Hinton et al., 2014, 2015).

12.1.5 Dynamic Structure

One strategy for accelerating data-processing systems in general is to build systems that have **dynamic structure** in the graph describing the computation needed to process an input. Data-processing systems can dynamically determine which subset of many neural networks should be run on a given input. Individual neural networks can also exhibit dynamic structure internally by determining which subset of features (hidden units) to compute given information from the input. This form of dynamic structure inside neural networks is sometimes called **conditional computation** (Bengio, 2013; Bengio et al., 2013b). Since many components of the architecture may be relevant only for a small amount of possible inputs, the system can run faster by computing these features only when they are needed.

Dynamic structure of computations is a basic computer science principle applied generally throughout the software engineering discipline. The simplest versions of dynamic structure applied to neural networks are based on determining which subset of some group of neural networks (or other machine learning models) should be applied to a particular input.

A venerable strategy for accelerating inference in a classifier is to use a **cascade** of classifiers. The cascade strategy may be applied when the goal is to detect the presence of a rare object (or event). To know for sure that the object is present, we must use a sophisticated classifier with high capacity, which is expensive to run. Because the object is rare, however, we can usually use much less computation to reject inputs as not containing the object. In these situations, we can train a sequence of classifiers. The first classifiers in the sequence have low capacity and are trained to have high recall. In other words, they are trained to make sure we do not wrongly reject an input when the object is present. The final classifier is trained to have high precision. At test time, we run inference by running the classifiers in a sequence, abandoning any example as soon as any one element in the cascade rejects it. Overall, this allows us to verify the presence of objects with high confidence, using a high capacity model, but does not force us to pay the cost of full inference for every example. There are two different ways that the cascade can achieve high capacity. One way is to make the later members of the cascade individually have high capacity. In this case, the system as a whole obviously has high capacity, because some of its individual members do. It is also possible to make a cascade in which every individual model has low capacity but the system as a whole has high capacity as a result of the combination of many small models. Viola and Jones (2001) used a cascade of boosted decision trees to implement a fast and robust face detector suitable for use in handheld digital cameras. Their classifier localizes a face using essentially a sliding window approach in which many windows are examined and rejected if they do not contain faces. Another version of cascades uses the earlier models to implement a sort of hard attention mechanism: the early members of the cascade localize an object, and later members of the cascade perform further processing given the location of the object. For example, Google transcribes address numbers from Street View imagery using a two-step cascade that first locates the address number with one machine learning model and then transcribes it with another (Goodfellow et al., 2014d).

Decision trees themselves are an example of dynamic structure, because each node in the tree determines which of its subtrees should be evaluated for each input. A simple way to accomplish the union of deep learning and dynamic structure is to train a decision tree in which each node uses a neural network to make the splitting decision (Guo and Gelfand, 1992), though this has typically not been done with the primary goal of accelerating inference computations.

In the same spirit, one can use a neural network called the **gater** to select which one out of several **expert networks** will be used to compute the output, given the current input. The first version of this idea is called the **mixture of experts** (Nowlan, 1990; Jacobs et al., 1991), in which the gater outputs a set of probabilities or weights (obtained via a softmax nonlinearity), one per expert, and the final output is obtained by the weighted combination of the output of the experts. In that case, the use of the gater does not offer a reduction in computational cost, but if a single expert is chosen by the gater for each example, we obtain the **hard mixture of experts** (Collobert et al., 2001, 2002), which can considerably accelerate training and inference time. This strategy works well when the number of gating decisions is small because it is not combinatorial. But when we want to select different subsets of units or parameters, it is not possible to use a "soft switch" because it requires enumerating (and computing outputs for) all the gater configurations. To deal with this problem, several approaches have been explored to train combinatorial gaters. Bengio et al. (2013b) experiment with several estimators of the gradient on the gating probabilities, while Bacon et al. (2015) and Bengio et al. (2015a) use reinforcement learning techniques (policy gradient) to learn a form of conditional dropout on blocks of hidden units and get an actual reduction in computational cost without negatively affecting the quality of the approximation.

Another kind of dynamic structure is a switch, where a hidden unit can receive input from different units depending on the context. This dynamic routing approach can be interpreted as an attention mechanism (Olshausen et al., 1993). So far, the use of a hard switch has not proven effective on large-scale applications. Contemporary approaches instead use a weighted average over many possible inputs, and thus do not achieve all the possible computational benefits of dynamic structure. Contemporary attention mechanisms are described in section 12.4.5.1.

One major obstacle to using dynamically structured systems is the decreased degree of parallelism that results from the system following different code branches for different inputs. This means that few operations in the network can be described as matrix multiplication or batch convolution on a minibatch of examples. We can write more specialized subroutines that convolve each example with different kernels or multiply each row of a design matrix by a different set of columns of weights. Unfortunately, these more specialized subroutines are difficult to implement efficiently. CPU implementations will be slow as a result of the lack of cache coherence, and GPU implementations will be slow because of the lack of coalesced memory transactions and the need to serialize warps when members of a warp take different branches. In some cases, these issues can be mitigated by partitioning the examples into groups that all take the same branch, then processing these groups of examples simultaneously. This can be an acceptable strategy for minimizing the time required to process a fixed amount of examples in an offline setting. In a real-time setting where examples must be processed continuously, partitioning the workload can result in load-balancing issues. For example, if we assign one machine to process the first step in a cascade and another machine to process the last step in a cascade, then the first will tend to be overloaded, and the last will tend to be underloaded. Similar issues arise if each machine is assigned to implement different nodes of a neural decision tree.

12.1.6 Specialized Hardware Implementations of Deep Networks

Since the early days of neural networks research, hardware designers have worked on specialized hardware implementations that could speed up training and/or inference of neural network algorithms. See early and more recent reviews of specialized hardware for deep networks (Lindsey and Lindblad, 1994; Beiu et al., 2003; Misra and Saha, 2010).

Different forms of specialized hardware (Graf and Jackel, 1989; Mead and Ismail, 2012; Kim et al., 2009; Pham et al., 2012; Chen et al., 2014a,b) have been developed over the last decades with ASICs (application-specific integrated circuits), either with digital (based on binary representations of numbers), analog (Graf and Jackel, 1989; Mead and Ismail, 2012) (based on physical implementations of continuous values as voltages or currents), or hybrid implementations (combining digital and analog components). In recent years more flexible FPGA (field programmable gated array) implementations (where the particulars of the circuit can be written on the chip after it has been built) have been developed.

Though software implementations on general-purpose processing units (CPUs and GPUs) typically use 32 or 64 bits of precision to represent floating-point numbers, it has long been known that it was possible to use less precision, at least at inference time (Holt and Baker, 1991; Holi and Hwang, 1993; Presley and Haggard, 1994; Simard and Graf, 1994; Wawrzynek et al., 1996; Savich et al., 2007). This has become a more pressing issue in recent years as deep learning has gained in popularity in industrial products, and as the great impact of faster hardware was demonstrated with GPUs. Another factor that motivates current research on specialized hardware for deep networks is that the rate of progress of a single CPU or GPU core has slowed down, and most recent improvements in computing speed have come from parallelization across cores (either in CPUs or GPUs). This is very different from the situation of the 1990s (the previous neural network era), when the hardware implementations of neural networks (which might take two years from inception to availability of a chip) could not keep up with the rapid progress and low prices of general-purpose CPUs. Building specialized hardware is thus a way to push the envelope further, at a time when new hardware designs are being developed for low-power devices such as phones, aiming for general-public applications of deep learning (e.g., with speech, computer vision, or natural language).

Recent work on low-precision implementations of backprop-based neural nets (Vanhoucke et al., 2011; Courbariaux et al., 2015; Gupta et al., 2015) suggests that between 8 and 16 bits of precision can suffice for using or training deep neural networks with back-propagation. What is clear is that more precision is required during training than at inference time, and that some forms of dynamic fixed-point representation of numbers can be used to reduce how many bits are required per number. Traditional fixed-point numbers are restricted to a fixed range (which corresponds to a given exponent in a floating-point representation). Dynamic fixed-point representations share that range among a set of numbers (such as all the weights in one layer). Using fixed-point rather than floating-point representations and using fewer bits per number reduces the hardware surface area, power requirements, and computing time needed for performing multiplications, and multiplications are the most demanding of the operations needed to use or train a modern deep network with backprop.

12.2 Computer Vision

Computer vision has traditionally been one of the most active research areas for deep learning applications, because vision is a task that is effortless for humans and many animals but challenging for computers (Ballard et al., 1983). Many of the most popular standard benchmark tasks for deep learning algorithms are forms of object recognition or optical character recognition.

Computer vision is a very broad field encompassing a wide variety of ways to process images and an amazing diversity of applications. Applications of computer vision range from reproducing human visual abilities, such as recognizing faces, to creating entirely new categories of visual abilities. As an example of the latter category, one recent computer vision application is to recognize sound waves from the vibrations they induce in objects visible in a video (Davis et al., 2014). Most deep learning research on computer vision has focused not on such exotic applications that expand the realm of what is possible with imagery but rather on a small core of AI goals aimed at replicating human abilities. Most deep learning for computer vision is used for object recognition or detection of some form, whether this means reporting which object is present in an image, annotating an image with bounding boxes around each object, transcribing a sequence of symbols from an image, or labeling each pixel in an image with the identity of the object it belongs to. Because generative modeling has been a guiding principle of deep learning research, there is also a large body of work on image synthesis using deep models. While image synthesis *ex nihilo* is usually not considered a computer vision endeavor, models capable of image synthesis are usually useful for image restoration, a computer vision task involving repairing defects in images or removing objects from images.

12.2.1   Preprocessing

Many application areas require sophisticated preprocessing because the original input comes in a form that is difficult for many deep learning architectures to represent. Computer vision usually requires relatively little of this kind of preprocessing. The images should be standardized so that their pixels all lie in the same reasonable range, like [0,1] or [-1, 1]. Mixing images that lie in [0,1] with images that lie in [0, 255] will usually result in failure. Formatting images to have the same scale is the only kind of preprocessing that is strictly necessary. Many computer vision architectures require images of a standard size, so images must be cropped or scaled to fit that size. Even this rescaling is not always strictly necessary. Some convolutional models accept variably sized inputs and dynamically adjust the size of their pooling regions to keep the output size constant (Waibel et al., 1989). Other convolutional models have variably sized output that automatically scales in size with the input, such as models that denoise or label each pixel in an image (Hadsell et al., 2007).

Dataset augmentation may be seen as a way of preprocessing the training set only. Dataset augmentation is an excellent way to reduce the generalization error of most computer vision models. A related idea applicable at test time is to show the model many different versions of the same input (for example, the same image cropped at slightly different locations) and have the different instantiations of the model vote to determine the output. This latter idea can be interpreted as an ensemble approach, and it helps to reduce generalization error.

Other kinds of preprocessing are applied to both the training and the test set with the goal of putting each example into a more canonical form to reduce the amount of variation that the model needs to account for. Reducing the amount of variation in the data can reduce both generalization error and the size of the model needed to fit the training set. Simpler tasks may be solved by smaller models, and simpler solutions are more likely to generalize well. Preprocessing of this kind is usually designed to remove some kind of variability in the input data that is easy for a human designer to describe and that the human designer is confident has no relevance to the task. When training with large datasets and large models, this kind of preprocessing is often unnecessary, and it is best to just let the model learn which kinds of variability it should become invariant to. For example, the AlexNet system for classifying ImageNet has only one preprocessing step: subtracting the mean across training examples of each pixel (Krizhevsky et al., 2012).

12.2.1.1 Contrast Normalization

One of the most obvious sources of variation that can be safely removed for many tasks is the amount of contrast in the image. Contrast simply refers to the magnitude of the difference between the bright and the dark pixels in an image. There are many ways of quantifying the contrast of an image. In the context of deep learning, contrast usually refers to the standard deviation of the pixels in an image or region of an image. Suppose we have an image represented by a tensor $\mathbf{X} \in \mathbb{R}^{r \times c \times 3}$, with $X_{i,j,1}$ being the red intensity at row i, and column j, $X_{i,j,2}$ giving the green intensity, and $X_{i,j,3}$ giving the blue intensity. Then the contrast of the entire image is given by

$$\sqrt{\frac{1}{3rc} \sum_{i=1}^{r} \sum_{j=1}^{c} \sum_{k=1}^{3} \left(X_{i,j,k} - \bar{\mathbf{X}} \right)^2}, \tag{12.1}$$

where $\bar{\mathbf{X}}$ is the mean intensity of the entire image:

$$\bar{\mathbf{X}} = \frac{1}{3rc} \sum_{i=1}^{r} \sum_{j=1}^{c} \sum_{k=1}^{3} X_{i,j,k}. \tag{12.2}$$

Global contrast normalization (GCN) aims to prevent images from having varying amounts of contrast by subtracting the mean from each image, then rescaling it so that the standard deviation across its pixels is equal to some constant s. This approach is complicated by the fact that no scaling factor can change the contrast of a zero-contrast image (one whose pixels all have equal intensity). Images with very low but nonzero contrast often have little information content. Dividing by the true standard deviation usually accomplishes nothing more than amplifying sensor noise or compression artifacts in such cases. This motivates introducing a small positive regularization parameter λ to bias the estimate of the standard deviation. Alternately, one can constrain the denominator to be at least ϵ. Given an input image $\mathbf{X}$, GCN produces an output image $\mathbf{X}'$, defined such that

$$X'_{i,j,k} = s \frac{X_{i,j,k} - \bar{X}}{\max \left\{ \epsilon, \sqrt{\lambda + \frac{1}{3rc} \sum_{i=1}^{r} \sum_{j=1}^{c} \sum_{k=1}^{3} \left(X_{i,j,k} - \bar{X} \right)^2} \right\}}. \tag{12.3}$$

Datasets consisting of large images cropped to interesting objects are unlikely to contain any images with nearly constant intensity. In these cases, it is safe to practically ignore the small denominator problem by setting $\lambda = 0$ and avoid division by 0 in extremely rare cases by setting ϵ to an extremely low value like 10^{-8}. This is the approach used by Goodfellow et al. (2013a) on the CIFAR-10 dataset. Small images cropped randomly are more likely to have nearly constant intensity, making aggressive regularization more useful. Coates et al. (2011) used $\epsilon = 0$ and $\lambda = 10$ on small, randomly selected patches drawn from CIFAR-10.

The scale parameter s can usually be set to 1, as done by Coates et al. (2011), or chosen to make each individual pixel have standard deviation across examples close to 1, as done by Goodfellow et al. (2013a).

The standard deviation in equation 12.3 is just a rescaling of the L^2 norm of the image (assuming the mean of the image has already been removed). It is preferable to define GCN in terms of standard deviation rather than L^2 norm because the standard deviation includes division by the number of pixels, so GCN based on standard deviation allows the same s to be used regardless of image size. However, the observation that the L^2 norm is proportional to the standard deviation can help build a useful intuition. One can understand GCN as mapping examples to a spherical shell. See figure 12.1 for an illustration. This can be a useful property because neural networks are often better at responding to directions in space rather than to exact locations. Responding to multiple distances in the same direction requires hidden units with collinear weight vectors but different biases. Such coordination can be difficult for the learning algorithm to discover.

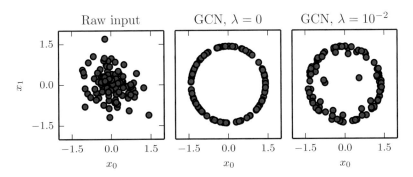

Figure 12.1: GCN maps examples onto a sphere. *(Left)*Raw input data may have any norm. *(Center)*GCN with $\lambda = 0$ maps all nonzero examples perfectly onto a sphere. Here we use $s = 1$ and $\epsilon = 10^{-8}$. Because we use GCN based on normalizing the standard deviation rather than the L^2 norm, the resulting sphere is not the unit sphere. *(Right)*Regularized GCN, with $\lambda > 0$, draws examples toward the sphere but does not completely discard the variation in their norm. We leave s and ϵ the same as before.

Additionally, many shallow graphical models have problems with representing multiple separated modes along the same line. GCN avoids these problems by reducing each example to a direction rather than a direction and a distance.

Counterintuitively, there is a preprocessing operation known as **sphering** that is not the same operation as GCN. Sphering does not refer to making the data lie on a spherical shell, but rather refers to rescaling the principal components to have equal variance, so that the multivariate normal distribution used by PCA has spherical contours. Sphering is more commonly known as **whitening**.

Global contrast normalization will often fail to highlight image features we would like to have stand out, such as edges and corners. If we have a scene with a large dark area and a large bright area (such as a city square with half the image in the shadow of a building), then global contrast normalization will ensure that there is a large difference between the brightness of the dark area and the brightness of the light area. It will not, however, ensure that edges within the dark region stand out.

This motivates **local contrast normalization**. Local contrast normalization ensures that the contrast is normalized across each small window, rather than over the image as a whole. See figure 12.2 for a comparison of global and local contrast normalization.

Various definitions of local contrast normalization are possible. In all cases, one modifies each pixel by subtracting a mean of nearby pixels and dividing by a standard deviation of nearby pixels. In some cases, this is literally the mean and standard deviation of all pixels in a rectangular window centered on the pixel to be modified (Pinto et al., 2008). In other cases, this is a weighted mean and weighted standard deviation using Gaussian weights centered on the pixel to be modified. In the case of color images, some strategies process different color channels separately while others combine information from different channels to normalize each pixel (Sermanet et al., 2012).

Local contrast normalization can usually be implemented efficiently by using separable convolution (see section 9.8) to compute feature maps of local means and local standard deviations, then using element-wise subtraction and element-wise division on different feature maps.

Local contrast normalization is a differentiable operation and can also be used as a nonlinearity applied to the hidden layers of a network, as well as a preprocessing operation applied to the input.

As with global contrast normalization, we typically need to regularize local contrast normalization to avoid division by zero. In fact, because local contrast

Input image   GCN   LCN

Figure 12.2: A comparison of global and local contrast normalization. Visually, the effects of global contrast normalization are subtle. It places all images on roughly the same scale, which reduces the burden on the learning algorithm to handle multiple scales. Local contrast normalization modifies the image much more, discarding all regions of constant intensity. This allows the model to focus on just the edges. Regions of fine texture, such as the houses in the second row, may lose some detail due to the bandwidth of the normalization kernel being too high.

normalization typically acts on smaller windows, it is even more important to regularize. Smaller windows are more likely to contain values that are all nearly the same as each other, and thus more likely to have zero standard deviation.

12.2.1.2   Dataset Augmentation

As described in section 7.4, it is easy to improve the generalization of a classifier by increasing the size of the training set by adding extra copies of the training examples that have been modified with transformations that do not change the class. Object recognition is a classification task that is especially amenable to this form of dataset augmentation because the class is invariant to so many transformations and the input can be easily transformed with many geometric operations. As described before, classifiers can benefit from random translations, rotations, and in some cases, flips of the input to augment the dataset. In specialized computer vision applications, more advanced transformations are commonly used for dataset augmentation. These schemes include random perturbation of the colors in an image (Krizhevsky et al., 2012) and nonlinear geometric distortions of the input (LeCun et al., 1998b).

12.3 Speech Recognition

The task of speech recognition is to map an acoustic signal containing a spoken natural language utterance into the corresponding sequence of words intended by the speaker. Let $\boldsymbol{X} = (\boldsymbol{x}^{(1)}, \boldsymbol{x}^{(2)}, \ldots, \boldsymbol{x}^{(T)})$ denote the sequence of acoustic input vectors (traditionally produced by splitting the audio into 20ms frames). Most speech recognition systems preprocess the input using specialized hand-designed features, but some (Jaitly and Hinton, 2011) deep learning systems learn features from raw input. Let $\boldsymbol{y} = (y_1, y_2, \ldots, y_N)$ denote the target output sequence (usually a sequence of words or characters). The **automatic speech recognition** (ASR) task consists of creating a function f_{ASR}^* that computes the most probable linguistic sequence $\boldsymbol{y}$ given the acoustic sequence $\boldsymbol{X}$:

$$f_{\mathrm{ASR}}^*(\boldsymbol{X}) = \arg\max_{\boldsymbol{y}} P^*(\mathbf{y} \mid \mathbf{X} = \boldsymbol{X}), \tag{12.4}$$

where P^* is the true conditional distribution relating the inputs $\boldsymbol{X}$ to the targets $\boldsymbol{y}$.

Since the 1980s and until about 2009–2012, state-of-the-art speech recognition systems primarily combined hidden Markov models (HMMs) and Gaussian mixture models (GMMs). GMMs modeled the association between acoustic features and phonemes (Bahl et al., 1987), while HMMs modeled the sequence of phonemes. The GMM-HMM model family treats acoustic waveforms as being generated by the following process: first an HMM generates a sequence of phonemes and discrete subphonemic states (such as the beginning, middle, and end of each phoneme), then a GMM transforms each discrete symbol into a brief segment of audio waveform. Although GMM-HMM systems dominated ASR until recently, speech recognition was actually one of the first areas where neural networks were applied, and numerous ASR systems from the late 1980s and early 1990s used neural nets (Bourlard and Wellekens, 1989; Waibel et al., 1989; Robinson and Fallside, 1991; Bengio et al., 1991, 1992; Konig et al., 1996). At the time, the performance of ASR based on neural nets approximately matched the performance of GMM-HMM systems. For example, Robinson and Fallside (1991) achieved 26 percent phoneme error rate on the TIMIT (Garofolo et al., 1993) corpus (with 39 phonemes to discriminate among), which was better than or comparable to HMM-based systems. Since then, TIMIT has been a benchmark for phoneme recognition, playing a role similar to the role MNIST plays for object recognition. Nonetheless, because of the complex engineering involved in software systems for speech recognition and the effort that had been invested in building these systems on the basis of GMM-HMMs, the industry did not see a compelling argument for switching to neural networks. As a consequence, until the late 2000s, both academic and industrial research in using neural nets for speech recognition mostly focused on using neural nets to learn extra features for GMM-HMM systems.

Later, with *much larger and deeper models* and much larger datasets, recognition accuracy was dramatically improved by using neural networks to replace GMMs for the task of associating acoustic features to phonemes (or subphonemic states). Starting in 2009, speech researchers applied a form of deep learning based on unsupervised learning to speech recognition. This approach to deep learning was based on training undirected probabilistic models called restricted Boltzmann machines (RBMs) to model the input data. RBMs are described in part III. To solve speech recognition tasks, unsupervised pretraining was used to build deep feedforward networks whose layers were each initialized by training an RBM. These networks take spectral acoustic representations in a fixed-size input window (around a center frame) and predict the conditional probabilities of HMM states for that center frame. Training such deep networks helped to significantly improve the recognition rate on TIMIT (Mohamed et al., 2009, 2012a), bringing down the phoneme error rate from about 26 percent to 20.7 percent. See Mohamed et al. (2012b) for an analysis of reasons for the success of these models. Extensions to the basic phone recognition pipeline included the addition of speaker-adaptive features (Mohamed et al., 2011) that further reduced the error rate. This was quickly followed up by work to expand the architecture from phoneme recognition (which is what TIMIT is focused on) to large-vocabulary speech recognition (Dahl et al., 2012), which involves not just recognizing phonemes but also recognizing sequences of words from a large vocabulary. Deep networks for speech recognition eventually shifted from being based on pretraining and Boltzmann machines to being based on techniques such as rectified linear units and dropout (Zeiler et al., 2013; Dahl et al., 2013). By that time, several of the major speech groups in industry had started exploring deep learning in collaboration with academic researchers. Hinton et al. (2012a) describe the breakthroughs achieved by these collaborators, which are now deployed in products such as mobile phones.

Later, as these groups explored larger and larger labeled datasets and incorporated some of the methods for initializing, training, and setting up the architecture of deep nets, they realized that the unsupervised pretraining phase was either unnecessary or did not bring any significant improvement.

These breakthroughs in recognition performance for word error rate in speech recognition were unprecedented (around 30 percent improvement) and were following a long period, of about ten years, during which error rates did not improve much with the traditional GMM-HMM technology, in spite of the continuously growing size of training sets (see figure 2.4 of Deng and Yu [2014]). This created

447

a rapid shift in the speech recognition community toward deep learning. In a matter of roughly two years, most of the industrial products for speech recognition incorporated deep neural networks, and this success spurred a new wave of research into deep learning algorithms and architectures for ASR, which is ongoing today.

One of these innovations was the use of convolutional networks (Sainath et al., 2013) that replicate weights across time and frequency, improving over the earlier time-delay neural networks that replicated weights only across time. The new two-dimensional convolutional models regard the input spectrogram not as one long vector but as an image, with one axis corresponding to time and the other to frequency of spectral components.

Another important push, still ongoing, has been toward end-to-end deep learning speech recognition systems that completely remove the HMM. The first major breakthrough in this direction came from Graves et al. (2013), who trained a deep LSTM RNN (see section 10.10), using MAP inference over the frame-to-phoneme alignment, as in LeCun et al. (1998b) and in the CTC framework (Graves et al., 2006; Graves, 2012). A deep RNN (Graves et al., 2013) has state variables from several layers at each time step, giving the unfolded graph two kinds of depth: ordinary depth due to a stack of layers, and depth due to time unfolding. This work brought the phoneme error rate on TIMIT to a record low of 17.7 percent. See Pascanu et al. (2014a) and Chung et al. (2014) for other variants of deep RNNs, applied in other settings.

Another contemporary step toward end-to-end deep learning ASR is to let the system learn how to "align" the acoustic-level information with the phonetic-level information (Chorowski et al., 2014; Lu et al., 2015).

12.4 Natural Language Processing

Natural language processing (NLP) is the use of human languages, such as English or French, by a computer. Computer programs typically read and emit specialized languages designed to allow efficient and unambiguous parsing by simple programs. More naturally occurring languages are often ambiguous and defy formal description. Natural language processing includes applications such as machine translation, in which the learner must read a sentence in one human language and emit an equivalent sentence in another human language. Many NLP applications are based on language models that define a probability distribution over sequences of words, characters, or bytes in a natural language.

As with the other applications discussed in this chapter, very generic neural network techniques can be successfully applied to natural language processing. To achieve excellent performance and to scale well to large applications, however, some domain-specific strategies become important. To build an efficient model of natural language, we must usually use techniques that are specialized for processing sequential data. In many cases, we choose to regard natural language as a sequence of words, rather than a sequence of individual characters or bytes. Because the total number of possible words is so large, word-based language models must operate on an extremely high-dimensional and sparse discrete space. Several strategies have been developed to make models of such a space efficient, in both a computational and a statistical sense.

12.4.1 n-grams

A **language model** defines a probability distribution over sequences of tokens in a natural language. Depending on how the model is designed, a token may be a word, a character, or even a byte. Tokens are always discrete entities. The earliest successful language models were based on models of fixed-length sequences of tokens called n-grams. An n-gram is a sequence of n tokens.

Models based on n-grams define the conditional probability of the n-th token given the preceding $n - 1$ tokens. The model uses products of these conditional distributions to define the probability distribution over longer sequences:

$$P(x_1, \ldots, x_\tau) = P(x_1, \ldots, x_{n-1}) \prod_{t=n}^{\tau} P(x_t \mid x_{t-n+1}, \ldots, x_{t-1}). \qquad (12.5)$$

This decomposition is justified by the chain rule of probability. The probability distribution over the initial sequence $P(x_1, \ldots, x_{n-1})$ may be modeled by a different model with a smaller value of n.

Training n-gram models is straightforward because the maximum likelihood estimate can be computed simply by counting how many times each possible n-gram occurs in the training set. Models based on n-grams have been the core building block of statistical language modeling for many decades (Jelinek and Mercer, 1980; Katz, 1987; Chen and Goodman, 1999).

For small values of n, models have particular names: **unigram** for $n = 1$, **bigram** for $n = 2$, and **trigram** for $n = 3$. These names derive from the Latin prefixes for the corresponding numbers and the Greek suffix "-gram," denoting something that is written.

Usually we train both an n-gram model and an $n-1$ gram model simultaneously. This makes it easy to compute

$$P(x_t \mid x_{t-n+1}, \ldots, x_{t-1}) = \frac{P_n(x_{t-n+1}, \ldots, x_t)}{P_{n-1}(x_{t-n+1}, \ldots, x_{t-1})} \tag{12.6}$$

simply by looking up two stored probabilities. For this to exactly reproduce inference in P_n, we must omit the final character from each sequence when we train P_{n-1}.

As an example, we demonstrate how a trigram model computes the probability of the sentence "THE DOG RAN AWAY." The first words of the sentence cannot be handled by the default formula based on conditional probability because there is no context at the beginning of the sentence. Instead, we must use the marginal probability over words at the start of the sentence. We thus evaluate P_3(THE DOG RAN). Finally, the last word may be predicted using the typical case, of using the conditional distribution $P(\text{AWAY} \mid \text{DOG RAN})$. Putting this together with equation 12.6, we obtain:

$$P(\text{THE DOG RAN AWAY}) = P_3(\text{THE DOG RAN})P_3(\text{DOG RAN AWAY})/P_2(\text{DOG RAN}). \tag{12.7}$$

A fundamental limitation of maximum likelihood for n-gram models is that P_n as estimated from training set counts is very likely to be zero in many cases, even though the tuple $(x_{t-n+1}, \ldots, x_t)$ may appear in the test set. This can cause two different kinds of catastrophic outcomes. When P_{n-1} is zero, the ratio is undefined, so the model does not even produce a sensible output. When P_{n-1} is nonzero but P_n is zero, the test log-likelihood is $-\infty$. To avoid such catastrophic outcomes, most n-gram models employ some form of **smoothing**. Smoothing techniques shift probability mass from the observed tuples to unobserved ones that are similar. See Chen and Goodman (1999) for a review and empirical comparisons. One basic technique consists of adding nonzero probability mass to all the possible next symbol values. This method can be justified as Bayesian inference with a uniform or Dirichlet prior over the count parameters. Another very popular idea is to form a mixture model containing higher-order and lower-order n-gram models, with the higher-order models providing more capacity and the lower-order models being more likely to avoid counts of zero. **Back-off methods** look up the lower-order n-grams if the frequency of the context $x_{t-1}, \ldots, x_{t-n+1}$ is too small to use the higher-order model. More formally, they estimate the distribution over x_t by using contexts $x_{t-n+k}, \ldots, x_{t-1}$, for increasing k, until a sufficiently reliable estimate is found.

Classical n-gram models are particularly vulnerable to the curse of dimensionality. There are $|\mathbb{V}|^n$ possible n-grams and $|\mathbb{V}|$ is often very large. Even with a massive training set and modest n, most n-grams will not occur in the training set. One way to view a classical n-gram model is that it is performing nearest neighbor lookup. In other words, it can be viewed as a local nonparametric predictor, similar to k-nearest neighbors. The statistical problems facing these extremely local predictors are described in section 5.11.2. The problem for a language model is even more severe than usual, because any two different words have the same distance from each other in one-hot vector space. It is thus difficult to leverage much information from any "neighbors"—only training examples that repeat literally the same context are useful for local generalization. To overcome these problems, a language model must be able to share knowledge between one word and other semantically similar words.

To improve the statistical efficiency of n-gram models, **class-based language models** (Brown et al., 1992; Ney and Kneser, 1993; Niesler et al., 1998) introduce the notion of word categories and then share statistical strength between words that are in the same category. The idea is to use a clustering algorithm to partition the set of words into clusters or classes, based on their co-occurrence frequencies with other words. The model can then use word class IDs rather than individual word IDs to represent the context on the right side of the conditioning bar. Composite models combining word-based and class-based models via mixing or back-off are also possible. Although word classes provide a way to generalize between sequences in which some word is replaced by another of the same class, much information is lost in this representation.

12.4.2 Neural Language Models

Neural language models, or NLMs, are a class of language model designed to overcome the curse of dimensionality problem for modeling natural language sequences by using a distributed representation of words (Bengio et al., 2001). Unlike class-based n-gram models, neural language models are able to recognize that two words are similar without losing the ability to encode each word as distinct from the other. Neural language models share statistical strength between one word (and its context) and other similar words and contexts. The distributed representation the model learns for each word enables this sharing by allowing the model to treat words that have features in common similarly. For example, if the word `dog` and the word `cat` map to representations that share many attributes, then sentences that contain the word `cat` can inform the predictions that will be made by the model for sentences that contain the word `dog`, and vice versa. Because there are many such attributes, there are many ways in which generalization can happen, transferring information from each training sentence to an exponentially large number of semantically related sentences. The curse of dimensionality requires the model to generalize to a number of sentences that is exponential in the sentence length. The model counters this curse by relating each training sentence to an exponential number of similar sentences.

We sometimes call these word representations **word embeddings**. In this interpretation, we view the raw symbols as points in a space of dimension equal to the vocabulary size. The word representations embed those points in a feature space of lower dimension. In the original space, every word is represented by a one-hot vector, so every pair of words is at Euclidean distance $\sqrt{2}$ from each other. In the embedding space, words that frequently appear in similar contexts (or any pair of words sharing some "features" learned by the model) are close to each other. This often results in words with similar meanings being neighbors. Figure 12.3 zooms in on specific areas of a learned word embedding space to show how semantically similar words map to representations that are close to each other.

Neural networks in other domains also define embeddings. For example, a hidden layer of a convolutional network provides an "image embedding." Usually NLP practitioners are much more interested in this idea of embeddings because natural language does not originally lie in a real-valued vector space. The hidden layer has provided a more qualitatively dramatic change in the way the data is represented.

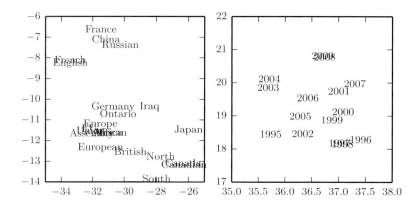

Figure 12.3: Two-dimensional visualizations of word embeddings obtained from a neural machine translation model (Bahdanau et al., 2015), zooming in on specific areas where semantically related words have embedding vectors that are close to each other. Countries appear on the left and numbers on the right. Keep in mind that these embeddings are 2-D for the purpose of visualization. In real applications, embeddings typically have higher dimensionality and can simultaneously capture many kinds of similarity between words.

The basic idea of using distributed representations to improve models for natural language processing is not restricted to neural networks. It may also be used with graphical models that have distributed representations in the form of multiple latent variables (Mnih and Hinton, 2007).

12.4.3 High-Dimensional Outputs

In many natural language applications, we often want our models to produce words (rather than characters) as the fundamental unit of the output. For large vocabularies, it can be very computationally expensive to represent an output distribution over the choice of a word, because the vocabulary size is large. In many applications, $\mathbb{V}$ contains hundreds of thousands of words. The naive approach to representing such a distribution is to apply an affine transformation from a hidden representation to the output space, then apply the softmax function. Suppose we have a vocabulary $\mathbb{V}$ with size $|\mathbb{V}|$. The weight matrix describing the linear component of this affine transformation is very large, because its output dimension is $|\mathbb{V}|$. This imposes a high memory cost to represent the matrix, and a high computational cost to multiply by it. Because the softmax is normalized across all $|\mathbb{V}|$ outputs, it is necessary to perform the full matrix multiplication at training time as well as test time—we cannot calculate only the dot product with the weight vector for the correct output. The high computational costs of the output layer thus arise both at training time (to compute the likelihood and its gradient) and at test time (to compute probabilities for all or selected words). For specialized loss functions, the gradient can be computed efficiently (Vincent et al., 2015), but the standard cross-entropy loss applied to a traditional softmax output layer poses many difficulties.

Suppose that h is the top hidden layer used to predict the output probabilities $\hat{y}$. If we parametrize the transformation from h to $\hat{y}$ with learned weights W and learned biases b, then the affine-softmax output layer performs the following computations:

$$a_i = b_i + \sum_j W_{ij} h_j \quad \forall i \in \{1, \dots, |\mathbb{V}|\}, \tag{12.8}$$

$$\hat{y}_i = \frac{e^{a_i}}{\sum_{i'=1}^{|\mathbb{V}|} e^{a_{i'}}}. \tag{12.9}$$

If h contains n_h elements, then the above operation is $O(|\mathbb{V}|n_h)$. With n_h in the thousands and $|\mathbb{V}|$ in the hundreds of thousands, this operation dominates the computation of most neural language models.

12.4.3.1 Use of a Short List

The first neural language models (Bengio et al., 2001, 2003) dealt with the high cost of using a softmax over a large number of output words by limiting the vocabulary size to 10,000 or 20,000 words. Schwenk and Gauvain (2002) and Schwenk (2007) built upon this approach by splitting the vocabulary $\mathbb{V}$ into a **shortlist** $\mathbb{L}$ of most frequent words (handled by the neural net) and a tail $\mathbb{T} = \mathbb{V} \backslash \mathbb{L}$ of more rare words (handled by an n-gram model). To be able to combine the two predictions, the neural net also has to predict the probability that a word appearing after context C belongs to the tail list. This may be achieved by adding an extra sigmoid output unit to provide an estimate of $P(i \in \mathbb{T} \mid C)$. The extra output can then be used to achieve an estimate of the probability distribution over all words in $\mathbb{V}$ as follows:

$$\begin{aligned} P(y = i \mid C) = &1_{i \in \mathbb{L}} P(y = i \mid C, i \in \mathbb{L})(1 - P(i \in \mathbb{T} \mid C)) \\ &+ 1_{i \in \mathbb{T}} P(y = i \mid C, i \in \mathbb{T}) P(i \in \mathbb{T} \mid C), \end{aligned} \qquad (12.10)$$

where $P(y = i \mid C, i \in \mathbb{L})$ is provided by the neural language model and $P(y = i \mid C, i \in \mathbb{T})$ is provided by the n-gram model. With slight modification, this approach can also work using an extra output value in the neural language model's softmax layer, rather than a separate sigmoid unit.

An obvious disadvantage of the short list approach is that the potential generalization advantage of the neural language models is limited to the most frequent words, where, arguably, it is the least useful. This disadvantage has stimulated the exploration of alternative methods to deal with high-dimensional outputs, described below.

12.4.3.2 Hierarchical Softmax

A classical approach (Goodman, 2001) to reducing the computational burden of high-dimensional output layers over large vocabulary sets $\mathbb{V}$ is to decompose probabilities hierarchically. Instead of necessitating a number of computations proportional to $|\mathbb{V}|$ (and also proportional to the number of hidden units, n_h), the $|\mathbb{V}|$ factor can be reduced to as low as $\log |\mathbb{V}|$. Bengio (2002) and Morin and Bengio (2005) introduced this factorized approach to the context of neural language models.

One can think of this hierarchy as building categories of words, then categories of categories of words, then categories of categories of categories of words, and so on. These nested categories form a tree, with words at the leaves. In a balanced tree, the tree has depth $O(\log |\mathbb{V}|)$. The probability of choosing a word is given by the product of the probabilities of choosing the branch leading to that word at every node on a path from the root of the tree to the leaf containing the word. Figure 12.4 illustrates a simple example. Mnih and Hinton (2009) also describe how to use multiple paths to identify a single word in order to better model words that have multiple meanings. Computing the probability of a word then involves summation over all the paths that lead to that word.

To predict the conditional probabilities required at each node of the tree, we typically use a logistic regression model at each node of the tree, and provide the same context C as input to all these models. Because the correct output is encoded in the training set, we can use supervised learning to train the logistic regression models. This is typically done using a standard cross-entropy loss, corresponding to maximizing the log-likelihood of the correct sequence of decisions.

Because the output log-likelihood can be computed efficiently (as low as $\log |\mathbb{V}|$ rather than $|\mathbb{V}|$), its gradients may also be computed efficiently. This includes not only the gradient with respect to the output parameters but also the gradients with respect to the hidden layer activations.

It is possible but usually not practical to optimize the tree structure to minimize the expected number of computations. Tools from information theory specify how to choose the optimal binary code given the relative frequencies of the words. To do so, we could structure the tree so that the number of bits associated with a word is approximately equal to the logarithm of the frequency of that word. In practice, however, the computational savings are typically not worth the effort because the computation of the output probabilities is only one part of the total computation in the neural language model. For example, suppose there are l fully connected hidden layers of width n_h. Let n_b be the weighted average of the number of bits required to identify a word, with the weighting given by the frequency of these words. In this example, the number of operations needed to compute the hidden activations grows as $O(ln_h^2)$, while the output computations grow as $O(n_h n_b)$. As long as $n_b \leq ln_h$, we can reduce computation more by shrinking n_h than by shrinking n_b. Indeed, n_b is often small. Because the size of the vocabulary rarely exceeds a million words and $\log_2(10^6) \approx 20$, it is possible to reduce n_b to about 20, but n_h is often much larger, around 10^3 or more. Rather than carefully optimizing a tree with a branching factor of 2, one can instead define a tree with depth two and a branching factor of $\sqrt{|\mathbb{V}|}$. Such a tree corresponds to simply defining a set of mutually exclusive word classes. The simple approach based on a tree of depth two captures most of the computational benefit of the hierarchical strategy.

One question that remains somewhat open is how to best define these word classes, or how to define the word hierarchy in general. Early work used existing

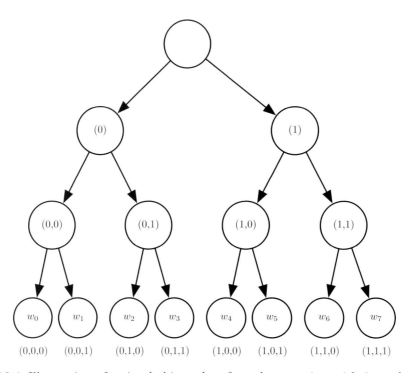

Figure 12.4: Illustration of a simple hierarchy of word categories, with 8 words $w_0, \ldots,$ w_7 organized into a three-level hierarchy. The leaves of the tree represent actual specific words. Internal nodes represent groups of words. Any node can be indexed by the sequence of binary decisions $(0 = \text{left}, 1 = \text{right})$ to reach the node from the root. Super-class (0) contains the classes $(0, 0)$ and $(0, 1)$, which respectively contain the sets of words $\{w_0, w_1\}$ and $\{w_2, w_3\}$, and similarly super-class (1) contains the classes $(1, 0)$ and $(1, 1)$, which respectively contain the words (w_4, w_5) and (w_6, w_7). If the tree is sufficiently balanced, the maximum depth (number of binary decisions) is on the order of the logarithm of the number of words $|\mathbb{V}|$: the choice of one out of $|\mathbb{V}|$ words can be obtained by doing $O(\log |\mathbb{V}|)$ operations (one for each of the nodes on the path from the root). In this example, computing the probability of a word y can be done by multiplying three probabilities, associated with the binary decisions to move left or right at each node on the path from the root to a node y. Let $b_i(y)$ be the i-th binary decision when traversing the tree toward the value y. The probability of sampling an output y decomposes into a product of conditional probabilities, using the chain rule for conditional probabilities, with each node indexed by the prefix of these bits. For example, node $(1, 0)$ corresponds to the prefix $(b_0(w_4) = 1, b_1(w_4) = 0)$, and the probability of w_4 can be decomposed as follows:

$$P(\mathrm{y} = w_4) = P(\mathrm{b}_0 = 1, \mathrm{b}_1 = 0, \mathrm{b}_2 = 0) \tag{12.11}$$
$$= P(\mathrm{b}_0 = 1)P(\mathrm{b}_1 = 0 \mid \mathrm{b}_0 = 1)P(\mathrm{b}_2 = 0 \mid \mathrm{b}_0 = 1, \mathrm{b}_1 = 0). \tag{12.12}$$

hierarchies (Morin and Bengio, 2005), but the hierarchy can also be learned, ideally jointly with the neural language model. Learning the hierarchy is difficult. An exact optimization of the log-likelihood appears intractable because the choice of a word hierarchy is a discrete one, not amenable to gradient-based optimization. However, one could use discrete optimization to approximately optimize the partition of words into word classes.

An important advantage of the hierarchical softmax is that it brings computational benefits both at training time and at test time, if at test time we want to compute the probability of specific words.

Of course, computing the probability of all $|\mathbb{V}|$ words will remain expensive even with the hierarchical softmax. Another important operation is selecting the most likely word in a given context. Unfortunately the tree structure does not provide an efficient and exact solution to this problem.

A disadvantage is that in practice the hierarchical softmax tends to give worse test results than sampling-based methods, which we describe next. This may be due to a poor choice of word classes.

12.4.3.3 Importance Sampling

One way to speed up the training of neural language models is to avoid explicitly computing the contribution of the gradient from all the words that do not appear in the next position. Every incorrect word should have low probability under the model. It can be computationally costly to enumerate all these words. Instead, it is possible to sample only a subset of the words. Using the notation introduced in equation 12.8, the gradient can be written as follows:

$$\frac{\partial \log P(y \mid C)}{\partial \theta} = \frac{\partial \log \operatorname{softmax}_y(\boldsymbol{a})}{\partial \theta} \tag{12.13}$$

$$= \frac{\partial}{\partial \theta} \log \frac{e^{a_y}}{\sum_i e^{a_i}} \tag{12.14}$$

$$= \frac{\partial}{\partial \theta} \left(a_y - \log \sum_i e^{a_i} \right) \tag{12.15}$$

$$= \frac{\partial a_y}{\partial \theta} - \sum_i P(y = i \mid C) \frac{\partial a_i}{\partial \theta}, \tag{12.16}$$

where $\boldsymbol{a}$ is the vector of presoftmax activations (or scores), with one element per word. The first term is the **positive phase** term, pushing a_y up, while the second term is the **negative phase** term, pushing a_i down for all i, with weight

$P(i \mid C)$. Since the negative phase term is an expectation, we can estimate it with a Monte Carlo sample. However, that would require sampling from the model itself. Sampling from the model requires computing $P(i \mid C)$ for all i in the vocabulary, which is precisely what we are trying to avoid.

Instead of sampling from the model, we can sample from another distribution, called the proposal distribution (denoted q), and use appropriate weights to correct for the bias introduced by sampling from the wrong distribution (Bengio and Sénécal, 2003; Bengio and Sénécal, 2008). This is an application of a more general technique called **importance sampling**, which we describe in more detail in section 17.2. Unfortunately, even exact importance sampling is not efficient because it requires computing weights p_i/q_i, where $p_i = P(i \mid C)$, which can only be computed if all the scores a_i are computed. The solution adopted for this application is called **biased importance sampling**, where the importance weights are normalized to sum to 1. When negative word n_i is sampled, the associated gradient is weighted by

$$w_i = \frac{p_{n_i}/q_{n_i}}{\sum_{j=1}^{N} p_{n_j}/q_{n_j}}. \tag{12.17}$$

These weights are used to give the appropriate importance to the m negative samples from q used to form the estimated negative phase contribution to the gradient:

$$\sum_{i=1}^{|\mathbb{V}|} P(i \mid C)\frac{\partial a_i}{\partial \theta} \approx \frac{1}{m}\sum_{i=1}^{m} w_i \frac{\partial a_{n_i}}{\partial \theta}. \tag{12.18}$$

A unigram or a bigram distribution works well as the proposal distribution q. It is easy to estimate the parameters of such a distribution from data. After estimating the parameters, it is also possible to sample from such a distribution very efficiently.

Importance sampling is not only useful for speeding up models with large softmax outputs. More generally, it is useful for accelerating training with large sparse output layers, where the output is a sparse vector rather than a 1-of-n choice. An example is a **bag of words**. A bag of words is a sparse vector $\boldsymbol{v}$ where v_i indicates the presence or absence of word i from the vocabulary in the document. Alternately, v_i can indicate the number of times that word i appears. Machine learning models that emit such sparse vectors can be expensive to train for a variety of reasons. Early in learning, the model may not actually choose to make the output truly sparse. Moreover, the loss function we use for training might most naturally be described in terms of comparing every element of the output to every element of the target. This means that it is not always clear that there is a computational benefit to using sparse outputs, because the model may choose to make the majority of the output nonzero, and all these non-zero values need to be compared to the corresponding training target, even if the training target is zero. Dauphin et al. (2011) demonstrated that such models can be accelerated using importance sampling. The efficient algorithm minimizes the loss reconstruction for the "positive words" (those that are nonzero in the target) and an equal number of "negative words." The negative words are chosen randomly, using a heuristic to sample words that are more likely to be mistaken. The bias introduced by this heuristic oversampling can then be corrected using importance weights.

In all these cases, the computational complexity of gradient estimation for the output layer is reduced to be proportional to the number of negative samples rather than proportional to the size of the output vector.

12.4.3.4 Noise-Contrastive Estimation and Ranking Loss

Other approaches based on sampling have been proposed to reduce the computational cost of training neural language models with large vocabularies. An early example is the ranking loss proposed by Collobert and Weston (2008a), which views the output of the neural language model for each word as a score and tries to make the score of the correct word a_y be ranked high in comparison to the other scores a_i. The ranking loss proposed then is

$$L = \sum_i \max(0, 1 - a_y + a_i). \qquad (12.19)$$

The gradient is zero for the i-th term if the score of the observed word, a_y, is greater than the score of the negative word a_i by a margin of 1. One issue with this criterion is that it does not provide estimated conditional probabilities, which are useful in some applications, including speech recognition and text generation (including conditional text generation tasks such as translation).

A more recently used training objective for neural language models is noise-contrastive estimation, which is introduced in section 18.6. This approach has been successfully applied to neural language models (Mnih and Teh, 2012; Mnih and Kavukcuoglu, 2013).

12.4.4 Combining Neural Language Models with n-grams

A major advantage of n-gram models over neural networks is that n-gram models achieve high model capacity (by storing the frequencies of very many tuples), while requiring very little computation to process an example (by looking up only a few tuples that match the current context). If we use hash tables or trees to access the counts, the computation used for n-grams is almost independent of capacity. In comparison, doubling a neural network's number of parameters typically also roughly doubles its computation time. Exceptions include models that avoid using all parameters on each pass. Embedding layers index only a single embedding in each pass, so we can increase the vocabulary size without increasing the computation time per example. Some other models, such as tiled convolutional networks, can add parameters while reducing the degree of parameter sharing to maintain the same amount of computation. Typical neural network layers based on matrix multiplication, however, use an amount of computation proportional to the number of parameters.

One easy way to add capacity is thus to combine both approaches in an ensemble consisting of a neural language model and an n-gram language model (Bengio et al., 2001, 2003). As with any ensemble, this technique can reduce test error if the ensemble members make independent mistakes. The field of ensemble learning provides many ways of combining the ensemble members' predictions, including uniform weighting and weights chosen on a validation set. Mikolov et al. (2011a) extended the ensemble to include not just two models but a large array of models. It is also possible to pair a neural network with a maximum entropy model and train both jointly (Mikolov et al., 2011b). This approach can be viewed as training a neural network with an extra set of inputs that are connected directly to the output and not connected to any other part of the model. The extra inputs are indicators for the presence of particular n-grams in the input context, so these variables are very high dimensional and very sparse. The increase in model capacity is huge—the new portion of the architecture contains up to $|sV|^n$ parameters—but the amount of added computation needed to process an input is minimal because the extra inputs are very sparse.

12.4.5   Neural Machine Translation

Machine translation is the task of reading a sentence in one natural language and emitting a sentence with the equivalent meaning in another language. Machine translation systems often involve many components. At a high level, there is often one component that proposes many candidate translations. Many of these translations will not be grammatical due to differences between the languages. For example, many languages put adjectives after nouns, so when translated to English directly they yield phrases such as "apple red." The proposal mechanism suggests many variants of the suggested translation, ideally including "red apple." A second component of the translation system, a language model, evaluates the proposed translations and can score "red apple" as better than "apple red."

The earliest exploration of neural networks for machine translation already incorporated the idea of encoder and decoder (Allen 1987; Chrisman 1991; Forcada and Ñeco 1997), while the first large-scale competitive use of neural networks in translation was to upgrade the language model of a translation system by using a neural language model (Schwenk et al., 2006; Schwenk, 2010). Previously, most machine translation systems had used an n-gram model for this component. The n-gram-based models used for machine translation include not just traditional back-off n-gram models (Jelinek and Mercer, 1980; Katz, 1987; Chen and Goodman, 1999) but also **maximum entropy language models** (Berger et al., 1996), in which an affine-softmax layer predicts the next word given the presence of frequent n-grams in the context.

Traditional language models simply report the probability of a natural language sentence. Because machine translation involves producing an output sentence given an input sentence, it makes sense to extend the natural language model to be conditional. As described in section 6.2.1.1, it is straightforward to extend a model that defines a marginal distribution over some variable to define a conditional distribution over that variable given a context C, where C might be a single variable or a list of variables. Devlin et al. (2014) beat the state-of-the-art in some statistical machine translation benchmarks by using an MLP to score a phrase $t_1, t_2, \ldots, t_k$ in the target language given a phrase $s_1, s_2, \ldots, s_n$ in the source language. The MLP estimates $P(t_1, t_2, \ldots, t_k \mid s_1, s_2, \ldots, s_n)$. The estimate formed by this MLP replaces the estimate provided by conditional n-gram models.

A drawback of the MLP-based approach is that it requires the sequences to be preprocessed to be of fixed length. To make the translation more flexible, we would like to use a model that can accommodate variable length inputs and variable length outputs. An RNN provides this ability. Section 10.2.4 describes several ways of constructing an RNN that represents a conditional distribution over a sequence given some input, and section 10.4 describes how to accomplish this conditioning when the input is a sequence. In all cases, one model first reads the input sequence and emits a data structure that summarizes the input sequence. We call this summary the "context" C. The context C may be a list of vectors, or it may be a vector or tensor. The model that reads the input to produce C may be an RNN (Cho et al., 2014a; Sutskever et al., 2014; Jean et al., 2014) or a convolutional network (Kalchbrenner and Blunsom, 2013). A second model, usually an RNN, then reads the context C and generates a sentence in the target language. This general idea of an encoder-decoder framework for machine translation is illustrated in figure 12.5.

To generate an entire sentence conditioned on the source sentence, the model must have a way to represent the entire source sentence. Earlier models were able

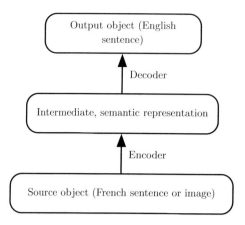

Figure 12.5: The encoder-decoder architecture to map back and forth between a surface representation (such as a sequence of words or an image) and a semantic representation. By using the output of an encoder of data from one modality (such as the encoder mapping from French sentences to hidden representations capturing the meaning of sentences) as the input to a decoder for another modality (such as the decoder mapping from hidden representations capturing the meaning of sentences to English), we can train systems that translate from one modality to another. This idea has been applied successfully not just to machine translation but also to caption generation from images.

to represent only individual words or phrases. From a representation learning point of view, it can be useful to learn a representation in which sentences that have the same meaning have similar representations regardless of whether they were written in the source language or in the target language. This strategy was explored first using a combination of convolutions and RNNs (Kalchbrenner and Blunsom, 2013). Later work introduced the use of an RNN for scoring proposed translations (Cho et al., 2014a) and for generating translated sentences (Sutskever et al., 2014). Jean et al. (2014) scaled these models to larger vocabularies.

12.4.5.1   Using an Attention Mechanism and Aligning Pieces of Data

Using a fixed-size representation to capture all the semantic details of a very long sentence of, say, 60 words is very difficult. It can be achieved by training a sufficiently large RNN well enough and for long enough, as demonstrated by Cho et al. (2014a) and Sutskever et al. (2014). A more efficient approach, however, is to read the whole sentence or paragraph (to get the context and the gist of what is being expressed), then produce the translated words one at a time, each time focusing on a different part of the input sentence to gather the semantic details required to produce the next output word. That is exactly the idea that Bahdanau

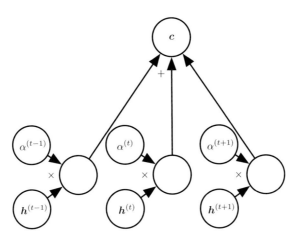

Figure 12.6: A modern attention mechanism, as introduced by Bahdanau et al. (2015), is essentially a weighted average. A context vector c is formed by taking a weighted average of feature vectors $\boldsymbol{h}^{(t)}$ with weights $\alpha^{(t)}$. In some applications, the feature vectors $\boldsymbol{h}$ are hidden units of a neural network, but they may also be raw input to the model. The weights $\alpha^{(t)}$ are produced by the model itself. They are usually values in the interval $[0, 1]$ and are intended to concentrate around just one $\boldsymbol{h}^{(t)}$ so that the weighted average approximates reading that one specific time step precisely. The weights $\alpha^{(t)}$ are usually produced by applying a softmax function to relevance scores emitted by another portion of the model. The attention mechanism is more expensive computationally than directly indexing the desired $\boldsymbol{h}^{(t)}$, but direct indexing cannot be trained with gradient descent. The attention mechanism based on weighted averages is a smooth, differentiable approximation that can be trained with existing optimization algorithms.

et al. (2015) first introduced. The attention mechanism used to focus on specific parts of the input sequence at each time step is illustrated in figure 12.6.

We can think of an attention-based system as having three components:

1. A process that *reads* raw data (such as source words in a source sentence) and converts them into distributed representations, with one feature vector associated with each word position.

2. A list of feature vectors storing the output of the reader. This can be understood as a *memory* containing a sequence of facts, which can be retrieved later, not necessarily in the same order, without having to visit all of them.

3. A process that *exploits* the content of the memory to sequentially perform a task, at each time step having the ability put attention on the content of one memory element (or a few, with a different weight).

The third component generates the translated sentence.

When words in a sentence written in one language are aligned with corresponding words in a translated sentence in another language, it becomes possible to relate the corresponding word embeddings. Earlier work showed that one could learn a kind of translation matrix relating the word embeddings in one language with the word embeddings in another (Kočiský et al., 2014), yielding lower alignment error rates than traditional approaches based on the frequency counts in the phrase table. There is even earlier work on learning cross-lingual word vectors (Klementiev et al., 2012). Many extensions to this approach are possible. For example, more efficient cross-lingual alignment (Gouws et al., 2014) allows training on larger datasets.

12.4.6 Historical Perspective

The idea of distributed representations for symbols was introduced by Rumelhart et al. (1986a) in one of the first explorations of back-propagation, with symbols corresponding to the identity of family members, and the neural network capturing the relationships between family members, with training examples forming triplets such as (Colin, Mother, Victoria). The first layer of the neural network learned a representation of each family member. For example, the features for Colin might represent which family tree Colin was in, what branch of that tree he was in, what generation he was from, and so on. One can think of the neural network as computing learned rules relating these attributes together to obtain the desired predictions. The model can then make predictions such as inferring who is the mother of Colin.

The idea of forming an embedding for a symbol was extended to the idea of an embedding for a word by Deerwester et al. (1990). These embeddings were learned using the SVD. Later, embeddings would be learned by neural networks.

The history of natural language processing is marked by transitions in the popularity of different ways of representing the input to the model. Following this early work on symbols and words, some of the earliest applications of neural networks to NLP (Miikkulainen and Dyer, 1991; Schmidhuber, 1996) represented the input as a sequence of characters.

Bengio et al. (2001) returned the focus to modeling words and introduced neural language models, which produce interpretable word embeddings. These neural models have scaled up from defining representations of a small set of symbols in the 1980s to millions of words (including proper nouns and misspellings) in modern applications. This computational scaling effort led to the invention of the techniques described in section 12.4.3.

Initially, the use of words as the fundamental units of language models yielded improved language modeling performance (Bengio et al., 2001). To this day, new techniques continually push both character-based models (Sutskever et al., 2011) and word-based models forward, with recent work (Gillick et al., 2015) even modeling individual bytes of Unicode characters.

The ideas behind neural language models have been extended into several natural language processing applications, such as parsing (Henderson, 2003, 2004; Collobert, 2011), part-of-speech tagging, semantic role labeling, chunking, and so on, sometimes using a single multitask learning architecture (Collobert and Weston, 2008a; Collobert et al., 2011a) in which the word embeddings are shared across tasks.

Two-dimensional visualizations of embeddings became a popular tool for analyzing language models following the development of the t-SNE dimensionality reduction algorithm (van der Maaten and Hinton, 2008) and its high-profile application to visualization word embeddings by Joseph Turian in 2009.

12.5 Other Applications

In this section we cover a few other types of applications of deep learning that are different from the standard object recognition, speech recognition, and natural language processing tasks discussed above. Part III of this book will expand that scope even further to tasks that remain primarily research areas.

12.5.1 Recommender Systems

One of the major families of applications of machine learning in the information technology sector is the ability to make recommendations of items to potential users or customers. Two major types of applications can be distinguished: online advertising and item recommendations (often these recommendations are still for the purpose of selling a product). Both rely on predicting the association between a user and an item, either to predict the probability of some action (the user buying the product, or some proxy for this action) or the expected gain (which may depend on the value of the product) if an ad is shown or a recommendation is made regarding that product to that user. The internet is currently financed in great part by various forms of online advertising. Major parts of the economy rely on online shopping. Companies including Amazon and eBay use machine learning, including deep learning, for their product recommendations. Sometimes, the items are not products that are actually for sale. Examples include selecting posts to display on social network news feeds, recommending movies to watch, recommending jokes, recommending advice from experts, matching players for video games, or matching people in dating services.

Often, this association problem is handled like a supervised learning problem: given some information about the item and about the user, predict the proxy of interest (user clicks on ad, user enters a rating, user clicks on a "like" button, user buys product, user spends some amount of money on the product, user spends time visiting a page for the product, and so forth). This often ends up being either a regression problem (predicting some conditional expected value) or a probabilistic classification problem (predicting the conditional probability of some discrete event).

The early work on recommender systems relied on minimal information as inputs for these predictions: the user ID and the item ID. In this context, the only way to generalize is to rely on the similarity between the patterns of values of the target variable for different users or for different items. Suppose that user 1 and user 2 both like items A, B and C. From this, we may infer that user 1 and user 2 have similar tastes. If user 1 likes item D, then this should be a strong cue that user 2 will also like D. Algorithms based on this principle come under the name of **collaborative filtering**. Both nonparametric approaches (such as nearest neighbor methods based on the estimated similarity between patterns of preferences) and parametric methods are possible. Parametric methods often rely on learning a distributed representation (also called an embedding) for each user and for each item. Bilinear prediction of the target variable (such as a rating) is a simple parametric method that is highly successful and often found as a component of state-of-the-art systems. The prediction is obtained by the dot product between the user embedding and the item embedding (possibly corrected by constants that depend only on either the user ID or the item ID). Let $\hat{R}$ be the matrix containing our predictions, A a matrix with user embeddings in its rows, and B a matrix with item embeddings in its columns. Let b and c be vectors that contain respectively a kind of bias for each user (representing how grumpy or positive that user is in general) and for each item (representing its general popularity). The bilinear prediction is thus obtained as follows:

$$\hat{R}_{u,i} = b_u + c_i + \sum_j A_{u,j} B_{j,i}. \tag{12.20}$$

Typically one wants to minimize the squared error between predicted ratings $\hat{R}_{u,i}$ and actual ratings $R_{u,i}$. User embeddings and item embeddings can then be conveniently visualized when they are first reduced to a low dimension (two or three), or they can be used to compare users or items against each other, just like word embeddings. One way to obtain these embeddings is by performing a singular value decomposition of the matrix $\boldsymbol{R}$ of actual targets (such as ratings). This corresponds to factorizing $\boldsymbol{R} = \boldsymbol{U}\boldsymbol{D}\boldsymbol{V}'$ (or a normalized variant) into the product of two factors, the lower rank matrices $\boldsymbol{A} = \boldsymbol{U}\boldsymbol{D}$ and $\boldsymbol{B} = \boldsymbol{V}'$. One problem with the SVD is that it treats the missing entries in an arbitrary way, as if they corresponded to a target value of 0. Instead we would like to avoid paying any cost for the predictions made on missing entries. Fortunately, the sum of squared errors on the observed ratings can also be easily minimized by gradient-based optimization. The SVD and the bilinear prediction of equation 12.20 both performed very well in the competition for the Netflix prize (Bennett and Lanning, 2007), aiming at predicting ratings for films, based only on previous ratings by a large set of anonymous users. Many machine learning experts participated in this competition, which took place between 2006 and 2009. It raised the level of research in recommender systems using advanced machine learning and yielded improvements in recommender systems. Even though the simple bilinear prediction, or SVD, did not win by itself, it was a component of the ensemble models presented by most of the competitors, including the winners (Töscher et al., 2009; Koren, 2009).

Beyond these bilinear models with distributed representations, one of the first uses of neural networks for collaborative filtering is based on the RBM undirected probabilistic model (Salakhutdinov et al., 2007). RBMs were an important element of the ensemble of methods that won the Netflix competition (Töscher et al., 2009; Koren, 2009). More advanced variants on the idea of factorizing the ratings matrix have also been explored in the neural networks community (Salakhutdinov and Mnih, 2008).

Collaborative filtering systems have a basic limitation, however: when a new item or a new user is introduced, its lack of rating history means that there is no way to evaluate its similarity with other items or users, or the degree of association between, say, that new user and existing items. This is called the problem of cold-start recommendations. A general way of solving the cold-start recommendation problem is to introduce extra information about the individual users and items. For example, this extra information could be user profile information or features of each item. Systems that use such information are called **content-based recommender systems**. The mapping from a rich set of user features or item features to an embedding can be learned through a deep learning architecture (Huang et al., 2013; Elkahky et al., 2015).

Specialized deep learning architectures, such as convolutional networks, have also been applied to learn to extract features from rich content, such as from musical audio tracks for music recommendation (van den Oörd et al., 2013). In that work, the convolutional net takes acoustic features as input and computes an embedding for the associated song. The dot product between this song embedding and the embedding for a user is then used to predict whether a user will listen to the song.

12.5.1.1 Exploration versus Exploitation

When making recommendations to users, an issue arises that goes beyond ordinary supervised learning and into the realm of reinforcement learning. Many recommendation problems are most accurately described theoretically as **contextual bandits** (Langford and Zhang, 2008; Lu et al., 2010). The issue is that when we use the recommendation system to collect data, we get a biased and incomplete view of the preferences of users: we see the responses of users only to the items recommended to them and not to the other items. In addition, in some cases we may not get any information on users for whom no recommendation has been made (for example, with ad auctions, it may be that the price proposed for an ad was below a minimum price threshold, or does not win the auction, so the ad is not shown at all). More importantly, we get no information about what outcome would have resulted from recommending any of the other items. This would be like training a classifier by picking one class $\hat{y}$ for each training example $\boldsymbol{x}$ (typically the class with the highest probability according to the model) and then only getting as feedback whether this was the correct class or not. Clearly, each example conveys less information than in the supervised case, where the true label y is directly accessible, so more examples are necessary. Worse, if we are not careful, we could end up with a system that continues picking the wrong decisions even as more and more data is collected, because the correct decision initially had a very low probability: until the learner picks that correct decision, it does not learn about the correct decision. This is similar to the situation in reinforcement learning where only the reward for the selected action is observed. In general, reinforcement learning can involve a sequence of many actions and many rewards. The bandits scenario is a special case of reinforcement learning, in which the learner takes only a single action and receives a single reward. The bandit problem is easier in the sense that the learner knows which reward is associated with which action. In the general reinforcement learning scenario, a high reward or a low reward might have been caused by a recent action or by an action in the distant past. The term **contextual bandits** refers to the case where the action is taken in the context of some input variable that can inform the decision. For example, we at least know the user identity, and we want to pick an item.

The mapping from context to action is also called a **policy**. The feedback loop between the learner and the data distribution (which now depends on the actions of the learner) is a central research issue in the reinforcement learning and bandits literature.

Reinforcement learning requires choosing a trade-off between **exploration** and **exploitation**. Exploitation refers to taking actions that come from the current, best version of the learned policy—actions that we know will achieve a high reward. Exploration refers to taking actions specifically to obtain more training data. If we know that given context x, action a gives us a reward of 1, we do not know whether that is the best possible reward. We may want to exploit our current policy and continue taking action a to be relatively sure of obtaining a reward of 1. However, we may also want to explore by trying action a'. We do not know what will happen if we try action a'. We hope to get a reward of 2, but we run the risk of getting a reward of 0. Either way, we at least gain some knowledge.

Exploration can be implemented in many ways, ranging from occasionally taking random actions intended to cover the entire space of possible actions, to model-based approaches that compute a choice of action based on its expected reward and the model's amount of uncertainty about that reward.

Many factors determine the extent to which we prefer exploration or exploitation. One of the most prominent factors is the time scale we are interested in. If the agent has only a short amount of time to accrue reward, then we prefer more exploitation. If the agent has a long time to accrue reward, then we begin with more exploration so that future actions can be planned more effectively with more knowledge. As time progresses and our learned policy improves, we move toward more exploitation.

Supervised learning has no trade-off between exploration and exploitation because the supervision signal always specifies which output is correct for each input. There is no need to try out different outputs to determine if one is better than the model's current output—we always know that the label is the best output.

Another difficulty arising in the context of reinforcement learning, besides the exploration-exploitation trade-off, is the difficulty of evaluating and comparing different policies. Reinforcement learning involves interaction between the learner and the environment. This feedback loop means that it is not straightforward to evaluate the learner's performance using a fixed set of test set input values. The policy itself determines which inputs will be seen. Dudik et al. (2011) present techniques for evaluating contextual bandits.

12.5.2 Knowledge Representation, Reasoning and Question Answering

Deep learning approaches have been very successful in language modeling, machine translation and natural language processing because of the use of embeddings for symbols (Rumelhart et al., 1986a) and words (Deerwester et al., 1990; Bengio et al., 2001). These embeddings represent semantic knowledge about individual words and concepts. A research frontier is to develop embeddings for phrases and for relations between words and facts. Search engines already use machine learning for this purpose, but much more remains to be done to improve these more advanced representations.

12.5.2.1 Knowledge, Relations and Question Answering

One interesting research direction is determining how distributed representations can be trained to capture the **relations** between two entities. These relations allow us to formalize facts about objects and how objects interact with each other.

In mathematics, a **binary relation** is a set of ordered pairs of objects. Pairs that are in the set are said to have the relation while those not in the set do not. For example, we can define the relation "is less than" on the set of entities $\{1, 2, 3\}$ by defining the set of ordered pairs $\mathbb{S} = \{(1, 2), (1, 3), (2, 3)\}$. Once this relation is defined, we can use it like a verb. Because $(1, 2) \in \mathbb{S}$, we say that 1 is less than 2. Because $(2, 1) \notin \mathbb{S}$, we cannot say that 2 is less than 1. Of course, the entities that are related to one another need not be numbers. We could define a relation `is_a_type_of` containing tuples like (`dog`, `mammal`).

In the context of AI, we think of a relation as a sentence in a syntactically simple and highly structured language. The relation plays the role of a verb, while two arguments to the relation play the role of its subject and object. These sentences take the form of a triplet of tokens

$$(\text{subject}, \text{verb}, \text{object}) \tag{12.21}$$

with values

$$(\text{entity}_i, \text{relation}_j, \text{entity}_k). \tag{12.22}$$

We can also define an **attribute**, a concept analogous to a relation, but taking only one argument:

$$(\text{entity}_i, \text{attribute}_j). \tag{12.23}$$

For example, we could define the `has_fur` attribute, and apply it to entities like `dog`.

Many applications require representing relations and reasoning about them. How should we best do this within the context of neural networks?

Machine learning models of course require training data. We can infer relations between entities from training datasets consisting of unstructured natural language. There are also structured databases that identify relations explicitly. A common structure for these databases is the **relational database**, which stores this same kind of information, albeit not formatted as three token sentences. When a database is intended to convey commonsense knowledge about everyday life or expert knowledge about an application area to an artificial intelligence system, we call the database a **knowledge base**. Knowledge bases range from general ones like `Freebase`, `OpenCyc`, `WordNet`, `Wikibase`,[1] and so forth, to more specialized knowledge bases like `GeneOntology`.[2] Representations for entities and relations can be learned by considering each triplet in a knowledge base as a training example and maximizing a training objective that captures their joint distribution (Bordes et al., 2013a).

In addition to training data, we also need to define a model family to train. A common approach is to extend neural language models to model entities and relations. Neural language models learn a vector that provides a distributed representation of each word. They also learn about interactions between words, such as which word is likely to come after a sequence of words, by learning functions of these vectors. We can extend this approach to entities and relations by learning an embedding vector for each relation. In fact, the parallel between modeling language and modeling knowledge encoded as relations is so close that researchers have trained representations of such entities by using *both* knowledge bases *and* natural language sentences (Bordes et al., 2011, 2012; Wang et al., 2014a), or by combining data from multiple relational databases (Bordes et al., 2013b). Many possibilities exist for the particular parametrization associated with such a model. Early work on learning about relations between entities (Paccanaro and Hinton, 2000) posited highly constrained parametric forms ("linear relational embeddings"), often using a different form of representation for the relation than for the entities. For example, Paccanaro and Hinton (2000) and Bordes et al. (2011) used vectors for entities and matrices for relations, with the idea that a relation acts like an operator on entities. Alternatively, relations can be considered as any other entity (Bordes et al., 2012), allowing us to make statements about relations, but more flexibility is put in the machinery that combines them in order to model their joint distribution.

---

[1] Respectively available from these web sites: `freebase.com`, `cyc.com/opencyc`, `wordnet.princeton.edu`, `wikiba.se`

[2] `geneontology.org`

A practical short-term application of such models is **link prediction**: predicting missing arcs in the knowledge graph. This is a form of generalization to new facts based on old facts. Most of the knowledge bases that currently exist have been constructed through manual labor, which tends to leave many and probably the majority of true relations absent from the knowledge base. See Wang et al. (2014b), Lin et al. (2015), and Garcia-Duran et al. (2015) for examples of such an application.

Evaluating the performance of a model on a link prediction task is difficult because we have only a dataset of positive examples (facts that are known to be true). If the model proposes a fact that is not in the dataset, we are unsure whether the model has made a mistake or discovered a new, previously unknown fact. The metrics are thus somewhat imprecise and are based on testing how the model ranks a held-out set of known true positive facts compared to other facts that are less likely to be true. A common way to construct interesting examples that are probably negative (facts that are probably false) is to begin with a true fact and create corrupted versions of that fact, for example, by replacing one entity in the relation with a different entity selected at random. The popular precision at 10 percent metric counts how many times the model ranks a "correct" fact among the top 10 percent of all corrupted versions of that fact.

Another application of knowledge bases and distributed representations for them is **word-sense disambiguation** (Navigli and Velardi, 2005; Bordes et al., 2012), which is the task of deciding which sense of a word is the appropriate one in some context.

Eventually, knowledge of relations combined with a reasoning process and an understanding of natural language could allow us to build a general question-answering system. A general question-answering system must be able to process input information and remember important facts, organized in a way that enables it to retrieve and reason about them later. This remains a difficult open problem that can only be solved in restricted "toy" environments. Currently, the best approach to remembering and retrieving specific declarative facts is to use an explicit memory mechanism, as described in section 10.12. Memory networks were first proposed to solve a toy question-answering task (Weston et al., 2014). Kumar et al. (2015) have proposed an extension that uses GRU recurrent nets to read the input into the memory and to produce the answer given the contents of the memory.

Deep learning has been applied to many other applications besides the ones described here, and will surely be applied to even more after this writing. It would be impossible to describe anything remotely resembling a comprehensive coverage of such a topic. This survey provides a representative sample of what is possible as of this writing.

This concludes part II, which has described modern practices involving deep networks, comprising all the most successful methods. Generally speaking, these methods involve using the gradient of a cost function to find the parameters of a model that approximates some desired function. With enough training data, this approach is extremely powerful. We now turn to part III, in which we step into the territory of research—methods that are designed to work with less training data or to perform a greater variety of tasks, where the challenges are more difficult and not as close to being solved as the situations we have described so far.

III

Deep Learning Research

This part of the book describes the more ambitious and advanced approaches to deep learning, currently pursued by the research community.

In the previous parts of the book, we have shown how to solve supervised learning problems—how to learn to map one vector to another, given enough examples of the mapping.

Not all problems we might want to solve fall into this category. We may wish to generate new examples, or determine how likely some point is, or handle missing values and take advantage of a large set of unlabeled examples or examples from related tasks. A shortcoming of the current state of the art for industrial applications is that our learning algorithms require large amounts of supervised data to achieve good accuracy. In this part of the book, we discuss some of the speculative approaches to reducing the amount of labeled data necessary for existing models to work well and be applicable across a broader range of tasks. Accomplishing these goals usually requires some form of unsupervised or semi-supervised learning.

Many deep learning algorithms have been designed to tackle unsupervised learning problems, but none has truly solved the problem in the same way that deep learning has largely solved the supervised learning problem for a wide variety of tasks. In this part of the book, we describe the existing approaches to unsupervised learning and some of the popular thought about how we can make progress in this field.

A central cause of the difficulties with unsupervised learning is the high dimensionality of the random variables being modeled. This brings two distinct challenges: a statistical challenge and a computational challenge. The *statistical challenge* regards generalization: the number of configurations we may want to distinguish can grow exponentially with the number of dimensions of interest, and this quickly becomes much larger than the number of examples one can possibly have (or use with bounded computational resources). The *computational challenge* associated with high-dimensional distributions arises because many algorithms for learning or using a trained model (especially those based on estimating an explicit probability function) involve intractable computations that grow exponentially with the number of dimensions.

With probabilistic models, this computational challenge arises from the need to perform intractable inference or to normalize the distribution.

- *Intractable inference*: inference is discussed mostly in chapter 19. It regards the question of guessing the probable values of some variables a, given other variables b, with respect to a model that captures the joint distribution over a, b and c. In order to even compute such conditional probabilities, one needs to sum over the values of the variables c, as well as compute a normalization constant that sums over the values of a and c.

- *Intractable normalization constants (the partition function)*: the partition function is discussed mostly in chapter 18. Normalizing constants of probability functions come up in inference (above) as well as in learning. Many probabilistic models involve such a normalizing constant. Unfortunately, learning such a model often requires computing the gradient of the logarithm of the partition function with respect to the model parameters. That computation is generally as intractable as computing the partition function itself. Monte Carlo Markov chain (MCMC) methods (chapter 17) are often used to deal with the partition function (computing it or its gradient). Unfortunately, MCMC methods suffer when the modes of the model distribution are numerous and well separated, especially in high-dimensional spaces (section 17.5).

One way to confront these intractable computations is to approximate them, and many approaches have been proposed, as discussed in this third part of the book. Another interesting way, also discussed here, would be to avoid these intractable computations altogether by design, and methods that do not require such computations are thus very appealing. Several generative models have been proposed in recent years with that motivation. A wide variety of contemporary approaches to generative modeling are discussed in chapter 20.

Part III is the most important for a researcher—someone who wants to understand the breadth of perspectives that have been brought to the field of deep learning and push the field forward toward true artificial intelligence.

13

Linear Factor Models

Many of the research frontiers in deep learning involve building a probabilistic model of the input, $p_{\text{model}}(\boldsymbol{x})$. Such a model can, in principle, use probabilistic inference to predict any of the variables in its environment given any of the other variables. Many of these models also have latent variables $\boldsymbol{h}$, with $p_{\text{model}}(\boldsymbol{x}) = \mathbb{E}_{\boldsymbol{h}} p_{\text{model}}(\boldsymbol{x} \mid \boldsymbol{h})$. These latent variables provide another means of representing the data. Distributed representations based on latent variables can obtain all the advantages of representation learning that we have seen with deep feedforward and recurrent networks.

In this chapter, we describe some of the simplest probabilistic models with latent variables: linear factor models. These models are sometimes used as building blocks of mixture models (Hinton et al., 1995a; Ghahramani and Hinton, 1996; Roweis et al., 2002) or of larger, deep probabilistic models (Tang et al., 2012). They also show many of the basic approaches necessary to building generative models that the more advanced deep models will extend further.

A linear factor model is defined by the use of a stochastic linear decoder function that generates $\boldsymbol{x}$ by adding noise to a linear transformation of $\boldsymbol{h}$.

These models are interesting because they allow us to discover explanatory factors that have a simple joint distribution. The simplicity of using a linear decoder made these models some of the first latent variable models to be extensively studied.

A linear factor model describes the data-generation process as follows. First, we sample the explanatory factors $\boldsymbol{h}$ from a distribution

$$\mathbf{h} \sim p(\boldsymbol{h}), \tag{13.1}$$

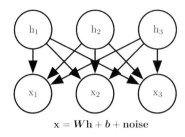

$$\mathbf{x} = \boldsymbol{W}\mathbf{h} + \boldsymbol{b} + \text{noise}$$

Figure 13.1: The directed graphical model describing the linear factor model family, in which we assume that an observed data vector $\boldsymbol{x}$ is obtained by a linear combination of independent latent factors $\boldsymbol{h}$, plus some noise. Different models, such as probabilistic PCA, factor analysis or ICA, make different choices about the form of the noise and of the prior $p(\boldsymbol{h})$.

where $p(\boldsymbol{h})$ is a factorial distribution, with $p(\boldsymbol{h}) = \prod_i p(h_i)$, so that it is easy to sample from. Next we sample the real-valued observable variables given the factors

$$\boldsymbol{x} = \boldsymbol{W}\boldsymbol{h} + \boldsymbol{b} + \text{noise}, \tag{13.2}$$

where the noise is typically Gaussian and diagonal (independent across dimensions). This is illustrated in figure 13.1.

13.1 Probabilistic PCA and Factor Analysis

Probabilistic PCA (principal components analysis), factor analysis and other linear factor models are special cases of the above equations (13.1 and 13.2) and only differ in the choices made for the noise distribution and the model's prior over latent variables $\boldsymbol{h}$ before observing $\boldsymbol{x}$.

In **factor analysis** (Bartholomew, 1987; Basilevsky, 1994), the latent variable prior is just the unit variance Gaussian

$$\mathbf{h} \sim \mathcal{N}(\boldsymbol{h}; \mathbf{0}, \boldsymbol{I}), \tag{13.3}$$

while the observed variables x_i are assumed to be **conditionally independent**, given $\boldsymbol{h}$. Specifically, the noise is assumed to be drawn from a diagonal covariance Gaussian distribution, with covariance matrix $\boldsymbol{\psi} = \text{diag}(\boldsymbol{\sigma}^2)$, with $\boldsymbol{\sigma}^2 = [\sigma_1^2, \sigma_2^2, \ldots, \sigma_n^2]^\top$ a vector of per-variable variances.

The role of the latent variables is thus to *capture the dependencies* between the different observed variables x_i. Indeed, it can easily be shown that $\boldsymbol{x}$ is just a multivariate normal random variable, with

$$\mathbf{x} \sim \mathcal{N}(\boldsymbol{x}; \boldsymbol{b}, \boldsymbol{W}\boldsymbol{W}^\top + \boldsymbol{\psi}). \tag{13.4}$$

To cast PCA in a probabilistic framework, we can make a slight modification to the factor analysis model, making the conditional variances σ_i^2 equal to each other. In that case the covariance of x is just $WW^\top + \sigma^2 I$, where σ^2 is now a scalar. This yields the conditional distribution

$$\mathbf{x} \sim \mathcal{N}(x; b, WW^\top + \sigma^2 I), \tag{13.5}$$

or equivalently

$$\mathbf{x} = W\mathbf{h} + b + \sigma\mathbf{z}, \tag{13.6}$$

where $\mathbf{z} \sim \mathcal{N}(z; 0, I)$ is Gaussian noise. Then, as Tipping and Bishop (1999) show, we can use an iterative EM algorithm for estimating the parameters W and σ^2.

This **probabilistic** PCA model takes advantage of the observation that most variations in the data can be captured by the latent variables h, up to some small residual **reconstruction error** σ^2. As shown by Tipping and Bishop (1999), probabilistic PCA becomes PCA as $\sigma \to 0$. In that case, the conditional expected value of h given x becomes an orthogonal projection of $x - b$ onto the space spanned by the d columns of W, as in PCA.

As $\sigma \to 0$, the density model defined by probabilistic PCA becomes very sharp around these d dimensions spanned by the columns of W. This can make the model assign very low likelihood to the data if the data do not actually cluster near a hyperplane.

13.2 Independent Component Analysis (ICA)

Independent component analysis (ICA) is among the oldest representation learning algorithms (Herault and Ans, 1984; Jutten and Herault, 1991; Comon, 1994; Hyvärinen, 1999; Hyvärinen et al., 2001a; Hinton et al., 2001; Teh et al., 2003). It is an approach to modeling linear factors that seeks to separate an observed signal into many underlying signals that are scaled and added together to form the observed data. These signals are intended to be fully independent, rather than merely decorrelated from each other.[1]

Many different specific methodologies are referred to as ICA. The variant that is most similar to the other generative models we have described here is a variant (Pham et al., 1992) that trains a fully parametric generative model. The prior distribution over the underlying factors, $p(h)$, must be fixed ahead of time by

---

[1]See section 3.8 for a discussion of the difference between uncorrelated variables and independent variables.

the user. The model then deterministically generates $\boldsymbol{x} = \boldsymbol{W}\boldsymbol{h}$. We can perform a nonlinear change of variables (using equation 3.47) to determine $p(\boldsymbol{x})$. Learning the model then proceeds as usual, using maximum likelihood.

The motivation for this approach is that by choosing $p(\boldsymbol{h})$ to be independent, we can recover underlying factors that are as close as possible to independent. This is commonly used, not to capture high-level abstract causal factors, but to recover low-level signals that have been mixed together. In this setting, each training example is one moment in time, each x_i is one sensor's observation of the mixed signals, and each h_i is one estimate of one of the original signals. For example, we might have n people speaking simultaneously. If we have n different microphones placed in different locations, ICA can detect the changes in the volume between each speaker as heard by each microphone and separate the signals so that each h_i contains only one person speaking clearly. This is commonly used in neuroscience for electroencephalography, a technology for recording electrical signals originating in the brain. Multiple electrode sensors placed on the subject's head are used to measure many electrical signals coming from the body. The experimenter is typically only interested in signals from the brain, but signals from the subject's heart and eyes are strong enough to confound measurements taken at the subject's scalp. The signals arrive at the electrodes mixed together, so ICA is necessary to separate the electrical signature of the heart from the signals originating in the brain, and to separate signals in different brain regions from each other.

As mentioned before, many variants of ICA are possible. Some add some noise in the generation of $\boldsymbol{x}$ rather than using a deterministic decoder. Most do not use the maximum likelihood criterion, but instead aim to make the elements of $\boldsymbol{h} = \boldsymbol{W}^{-1}\boldsymbol{x}$ independent from each other. Many criteria that accomplish this goal are possible. Equation 3.47 requires taking the determinant of $\boldsymbol{W}$, which can be an expensive and numerically unstable operation. Some variants of ICA avoid this problematic operation by constraining $\boldsymbol{W}$ to be orthogonal.

All variants of ICA require that $p(\boldsymbol{h})$ be non-Gaussian. This is because if $p(\boldsymbol{h})$ is an independent prior with Gaussian components, then $\boldsymbol{W}$ is not identifiable. We can obtain the same distribution over $p(\boldsymbol{x})$ for many values of $\boldsymbol{W}$. This is very different from other linear factor models like probabilistic PCA and factor analysis, which often require $p(\boldsymbol{h})$ to be Gaussian in order to make many operations on the model have closed form solutions. In the maximum likelihood approach, where the user explicitly specifies the distribution, a typical choice is to use $p(h_i) = \frac{d}{dh_i}\sigma(h_i)$. Typical choices of these non-Gaussian distributions have larger peaks near 0 than does the Gaussian distribution, so we can also see most implementations of ICA as learning sparse features.

Many variants of ICA are not generative models in the sense that we use the phrase. In this book, a generative model either represents $p(\boldsymbol{x})$ or can draw samples from it. Many variants of ICA only know how to transform between $\boldsymbol{x}$ and $\boldsymbol{h}$ but do not have any way of representing $p(\boldsymbol{h})$, and thus do not impose a distribution over $p(\boldsymbol{x})$. For example, many ICA variants aim to increase the sample kurtosis of $\boldsymbol{h} = \boldsymbol{W}^{-1}\boldsymbol{x}$, because high kurtosis indicates that $p(\boldsymbol{h})$ is non-Gaussian, but this is accomplished without explicitly representing $p(\boldsymbol{h})$. This is because ICA is more often used as an analysis tool for separating signals, rather than for generating data or estimating its density.

Just as PCA can be generalized to the nonlinear autoencoders described in chapter 14, ICA can be generalized to a nonlinear generative model, in which we use a nonlinear function f to generate the observed data. See Hyvärinen and Pajunen (1999) for the initial work on nonlinear ICA and its successful use with ensemble learning by Roberts and Everson (2001) and Lappalainen et al. (2000). Another nonlinear extension of ICA is the approach of **nonlinear independent components estimation**, or NICE (Dinh et al., 2014), which stacks a series of invertible transformations (encoder stages) with the property that the determinant of the Jacobian of each transformation can be computed efficiently. This makes it possible to compute the likelihood exactly, and like ICA, NICE attempts to transform the data into a space where it has a factorized marginal distribution, but it is more likely to succeed thanks to the nonlinear encoder. Because the encoder is associated with a decoder that is its perfect inverse, generating samples from the model is straightforward (by first sampling from $p(\boldsymbol{h})$ and then applying the decoder).

Another generalization of ICA is to learn groups of features, with statistical dependence allowed within a group but discouraged between groups (Hyvärinen and Hoyer, 1999; Hyvärinen et al., 2001b). When the groups of related units are chosen to be nonoverlapping, this is called **independent subspace analysis**. It is also possible to assign spatial coordinates to each hidden unit and form overlapping groups of spatially neighboring units. This encourages nearby units to learn similar features. When applied to natural images, this **topographic ICA** approach learns Gabor filters, such that neighboring features have similar orientation, location or frequency. Many different phase offsets of similar Gabor functions occur within each region, so that pooling over small regions yields translation invariance.

13.3   Slow Feature Analysis

Slow feature analysis (SFA) is a linear factor model that uses information from time signals to learn invariant features (Wiskott and Sejnowski, 2002).

Slow feature analysis is motivated by a general principle called the slowness principle. The idea is that the important characteristics of scenes change very slowly compared to the individual measurements that make up a description of a scene. For example, in computer vision, individual pixel values can change very rapidly. If a zebra moves from left to right across the image, an individual pixel will rapidly change from black to white and back again as the zebra's stripes pass over the pixel. By comparison, the feature indicating whether a zebra is in the image will not change at all, and the feature describing the zebra's position will change slowly. We therefore may wish to regularize our model to learn features that change slowly over time.

The slowness principle predates slow feature analysis and has been applied to a wide variety of models (Hinton, 1989; Földiák, 1989; Mobahi et al., 2009; Bergstra and Bengio, 2009). In general, we can apply the slowness principle to any differentiable model trained with gradient descent. The slowness principle may be introduced by adding a term to the cost function of the form

$$\lambda \sum_t L(f(\boldsymbol{x}^{(t+1)}), f(\boldsymbol{x}^{(t)})), \tag{13.7}$$

where λ is a hyperparameter determining the strength of the slowness regularization term, t is the index into a time sequence of examples, f is the feature extractor to be regularized, and L is a loss function measuring the distance between $f(\boldsymbol{x}^{(t)})$ and $f(\boldsymbol{x}^{(t+1)})$. A common choice for L is the mean squared difference.

Slow feature analysis is a particularly efficient application of the slowness principle. It is efficient because it is applied to a linear feature extractor and can thus be trained in closed form. Like some variants of ICA, SFA is not quite a generative model per se, in the sense that it defines a linear map between input space and feature space but does not define a prior over feature space and thus does not impose a distribution $p(\boldsymbol{x})$ on input space.

The SFA algorithm (Wiskott and Sejnowski, 2002) consists of defining $f(\boldsymbol{x}; \boldsymbol{\theta})$ to be a linear transformation, then solving the optimization problem

$$\min_{\boldsymbol{\theta}} \mathbb{E}_t (f(\boldsymbol{x}^{(t+1)})_i - f(\boldsymbol{x}^{(t)})_i)^2 \tag{13.8}$$

subject to the constraints

$$\mathbb{E}_t f(\boldsymbol{x}^{(t)})_i = 0 \tag{13.9}$$

and

$$\mathbb{E}_t[f(\boldsymbol{x}^{(t)})_i^2] = 1. \qquad (13.10)$$

The constraint that the learned feature have zero mean is necessary to make the problem have a unique solution; otherwise we could add a constant to all feature values and obtain a different solution with equal value of the slowness objective. The constraint that the features have unit variance is necessary to prevent the pathological solution where all features collapse to 0. Like PCA, the SFA features are ordered, with the first feature being the slowest. To learn multiple features, we must also add the constraint

$$\forall i < j, \mathbb{E}_t[f(\boldsymbol{x}^{(t)})_i f(\boldsymbol{x}^{(t)})_j] = 0. \qquad (13.11)$$

This specifies that the learned features must be linearly decorrelated from each other. Without this constraint, all the learned features would simply capture the one slowest signal. One could imagine using other mechanisms, such as minimizing reconstruction error, to force the features to diversify, but this decorrelation mechanism admits a simple solution due to the linearity of SFA features. The SFA problem may be solved in closed form by a linear algebra package.

SFA is typically used to learn nonlinear features by applying a nonlinear basis expansion to $\boldsymbol{x}$ before running SFA. For example, it is common to replace $\boldsymbol{x}$ with the quadratic basis expansion, a vector containing elements $x_i x_j$ for all i and j. Linear SFA modules may then be composed to learn deep nonlinear slow feature extractors by repeatedly learning a linear SFA feature extractor, applying a nonlinear basis expansion to its output, and then learning another linear SFA feature extractor on top of that expansion.

When trained on small spatial patches of videos of natural scenes, SFA with quadratic basis expansions learns features that share many characteristics with those of complex cells in V1 cortex (Berkes and Wiskott, 2005). When trained on videos of random motion within 3-D computer-rendered environments, deep SFA learns features that share many characteristics with the features represented by neurons in rat brains that are used for navigation (Franzius et al., 2007). SFA thus seems to be a reasonably biologically plausible model.

A major advantage of SFA is that it is possible to theoretically predict which features SFA will learn, even in the deep nonlinear setting. To make such theoretical predictions, one must know about the dynamics of the environment in terms of configuration space (e.g., in the case of random motion in the 3-D rendered environment, the theoretical analysis proceeds from knowledge of the probability distribution over position and velocity of the camera). Given the knowledge of how the underlying factors actually change, it is possible to analytically solve for the optimal functions expressing these factors. In practice, experiments with deep SFA applied to simulated data seem to recover the theoretically predicted functions. This is in comparison to other learning algorithms, where the cost function depends highly on specific pixel values, making it much more difficult to determine what features the model will learn.

Deep SFA has also been used to learn features for object recognition and pose estimation (Franzius et al., 2008). So far, the slowness principle has not become the basis for any state-of-the-art applications. It is unclear what factor has limited its performance. We speculate that perhaps the slowness prior is too strong, and that, rather than imposing a prior that features should be approximately constant, it would be better to impose a prior that features should be easy to predict from one time step to the next. The position of an object is a useful feature regardless of whether the object's velocity is high or low, but the slowness principle encourages the model to ignore the position of objects that have high velocity.

13.4 Sparse Coding

Sparse coding (Olshausen and Field, 1996) is a linear factor model that has been heavily studied as an unsupervised feature learning and feature extraction mechanism. Strictly speaking, the term "sparse coding" refers to the process of inferring the value of h in this model, while "sparse modeling" refers to the process of designing and learning the model, but the term "sparse coding" is often used to refer to both.

Like most other linear factor models, it uses a linear decoder plus noise to obtain reconstructions of x, as specified in equation 13.2. More specifically, sparse coding models typically assume that the linear factors have Gaussian noise with isotropic precision β:

$$p(x \mid h) = \mathcal{N}(x; Wh + b, \frac{1}{\beta}I).$$ (13.12)

The distribution $p(h)$ is chosen to be one with sharp peaks near 0 (Olshausen and Field, 1996). Common choices include factorized Laplace, Cauchy or factorized Student t-distributions. For example, the Laplace prior parametrized in terms of the sparsity penalty coefficient λ is given by

$$p(h_i) = \text{Laplace}(h_i; 0, \frac{2}{\lambda}) = \frac{\lambda}{4} e^{-\frac{1}{2}\lambda|h_i|},$$ (13.13)

and the Student t prior by

$$p(h_i) \propto \frac{1}{(1 + \frac{h_i^2}{\nu})^{\frac{\nu+1}{2}}}. \tag{13.14}$$

Training sparse coding with maximum likelihood is intractable. Instead, the training alternates between encoding the data and training the decoder to better reconstruct the data given the encoding. This approach will be justified further as a principled approximation to maximum likelihood later, in section 19.3.

For models such as PCA, we have seen the use of a parametric encoder function that predicts $\boldsymbol{h}$ and consists only of multiplication by a weight matrix. The encoder that we use with sparse coding is not a parametric encoder. Instead, the encoder is an optimization algorithm, which solves an optimization problem in which we seek the single most likely code value:

$$\boldsymbol{h}^* = f(\boldsymbol{x}) = \arg\max_{\boldsymbol{h}} p(\boldsymbol{h} \mid \boldsymbol{x}). \tag{13.15}$$

When combined with equation 13.13 and equation 13.12, this yields the following optimization problem:

$$\arg\max_{\boldsymbol{h}} p(\boldsymbol{h} \mid \boldsymbol{x}) \tag{13.16}$$

$$= \arg\max_{\boldsymbol{h}} \log p(\boldsymbol{h} \mid \boldsymbol{x}) \tag{13.17}$$

$$= \arg\min_{\boldsymbol{h}} \lambda ||\boldsymbol{h}||_1 + \beta ||\boldsymbol{x} - \boldsymbol{W}\boldsymbol{h}||_2^2, \tag{13.18}$$

where we have dropped terms not depending on $\boldsymbol{h}$ and divided by positive scaling factors to simplify the equation.

Due to the imposition of an L^1 norm on $\boldsymbol{h}$, this procedure will yield a sparse $\boldsymbol{h}^*$ (see section 7.1.2).

To train the model rather than just perform inference, we alternate between minimization with respect to $\boldsymbol{h}$ and minimization with respect to $\boldsymbol{W}$. In this presentation, we treat β as a hyperparameter. Typically it is set to 1 because its role in this optimization problem is shared with λ, and there is no need for both hyperparameters. In principle, we could also treat β as a parameter of the model and learn it. Our presentation here has discarded some terms that do not depend on $\boldsymbol{h}$ but do depend on β. To learn β, these terms must be included, or β will collapse to 0.

Not all approaches to sparse coding explicitly build a $p(\boldsymbol{h})$ and a $p(\boldsymbol{x} \mid \boldsymbol{h})$. Often we are just interested in learning a dictionary of features with activation values that will often be zero when extracted using this inference procedure.

If we sample $\boldsymbol{h}$ from a Laplace prior, it is in fact a zero probability event for an element of $\boldsymbol{h}$ to actually be zero. The generative model itself is not especially sparse; only the feature extractor is. Goodfellow et al. (2013d) describe approximate inference in a different model family, the spike and slab sparse coding model, for which samples from the prior usually contain true zeros.

The sparse coding approach combined with the use of the nonparametric encoder can in principle minimize the combination of reconstruction error and log-prior better than any specific parametric encoder. Another advantage is that there is no generalization error to the encoder. A parametric encoder must learn how to map $\boldsymbol{x}$ to $\boldsymbol{h}$ in a way that generalizes. For unusual $\boldsymbol{x}$ that do not resemble the training data, a learned parametric encoder may fail to find an $\boldsymbol{h}$ that results in accurate reconstruction or in a sparse code. For the vast majority of formulations of sparse coding models, where the inference problem is convex, the optimization procedure will always find the optimal code (unless degenerate cases such as replicated weight vectors occur). Obviously, the sparsity and reconstruction costs can still rise on unfamiliar points, but this is due to generalization error in the decoder weights, rather than to generalization error in the encoder. The lack of generalization error in sparse coding's optimization-based encoding process may result in better generalization when sparse coding is used as a feature extractor for a classifier than when a parametric function is used to predict the code. Coates and Ng (2011) demonstrated that sparse coding features generalize better for object recognition tasks than the features of a related model based on a parametric encoder, the linear-sigmoid autoencoder. Inspired by their work, Goodfellow et al. (2013d) showed that a variant of sparse coding generalizes better than other feature extractors in the regime where extremely few labels are available (twenty or fewer labels per class).

The primary disadvantage of the nonparametric encoder is that it requires greater time to compute $\boldsymbol{h}$ given $\boldsymbol{x}$ because the nonparametric approach requires running an iterative algorithm. The parametric autoencoder approach, developed in chapter 14, uses only a fixed number of layers, often only one. Another disadvantage is that it is not straightforward to back-propagate through the nonparametric encoder, which makes it difficult to pretrain a sparse coding model with an unsupervised criterion and then fine-tune it using a supervised criterion. Modified versions of sparse coding that permit approximate derivatives do exist but are not widely used (Bagnell and Bradley, 2009).

Sparse coding, like other linear factor models, often produces poor samples, as shown in figure 13.2. This happens even when the model is able to reconstruct the data well and provide useful features for a classifier. The reason is that each

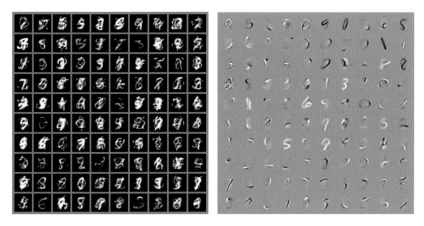

Figure 13.2: Example samples and weights from a spike and slab sparse coding model trained on the MNIST dataset. *(Left)* The samples from the model do not resemble the training examples. At first glance, one might assume the model is poorly fit. *(Right)* The weight vectors of the model have learned to represent penstrokes and sometimes complete digits. The model has thus learned useful features. The problem is that the factorial prior over features results in random subsets of features being combined. Few such subsets are appropriate to form a recognizable MNIST digit. This motivates the development of generative models that have more powerful distributions over their latent codes. Figure reproduced with permission from Goodfellow et al. (2013d).

individual feature may be learned well, but the factorial prior on the hidden code results in the model including random subsets of all the features in each generated sample. This motivates the development of deeper models that can impose a nonfactorial distribution on the deepest code layer, as well as the development of more sophisticated shallow models.

13.5 Manifold Interpretation of PCA

Linear factor models including PCA and factor analysis can be interpreted as learning a manifold (Hinton et al., 1997). We can view probabilistic PCA as defining a thin pancake-shaped region of high probability—a Gaussian distribution that is very narrow along some axes, just as a pancake is very flat along its vertical axis, but is elongated along other axes, just as a pancake is wide along its horizontal axes. This is illustrated in figure 13.3. PCA can be interpreted as aligning this pancake with a linear manifold in a higher-dimensional space. This interpretation applies not just to traditional PCA but also to any linear autoencoder that learns matrices W and V with the goal of making the reconstruction of x lie as close to x as possible.

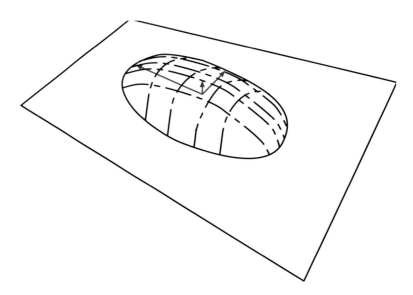

Figure 13.3: Flat Gaussian capturing probability concentration near a low-dimensional manifold. The figure shows the upper half of the "pancake" above the "manifold plane," which goes through its middle. The variance in the direction orthogonal to the manifold is very small (arrow pointing out of plane) and can be considered "noise," while the other variances are large (arrows in the plane) and correspond to "signal" and to a coordinate system for the reduced-dimension data.

Let the encoder be

$$\boldsymbol{h} = f(\boldsymbol{x}) = \boldsymbol{W}^\top (\boldsymbol{x} - \boldsymbol{\mu}). \tag{13.19}$$

The encoder computes a low-dimensional representation of h. With the autoencoder view, we have a decoder computing the reconstruction

$$\hat{\boldsymbol{x}} = g(\boldsymbol{h}) = \boldsymbol{b} + \boldsymbol{V}\boldsymbol{h}. \tag{13.20}$$

The choices of linear encoder and decoder that minimize reconstruction error

$$\mathbb{E}[||\boldsymbol{x} - \hat{\boldsymbol{x}}||^2] \tag{13.21}$$

correspond to $\boldsymbol{V} = \boldsymbol{W}$, $\boldsymbol{\mu} = \boldsymbol{b} = \mathbb{E}[\boldsymbol{x}]$ and the columns of $\boldsymbol{W}$ form an orthonormal basis, which spans the same subspace as the principal eigenvectors of the covariance matrix

$$\boldsymbol{C} = \mathbb{E}[(\boldsymbol{x} - \boldsymbol{\mu})(\boldsymbol{x} - \boldsymbol{\mu})^\top]. \tag{13.22}$$

In the case of PCA, the columns of $\boldsymbol{W}$ are these eigenvectors, ordered by the magnitude of the corresponding eigenvalues (which are all real and non-negative).

One can also show that eigenvalue λ_i of $\boldsymbol{C}$ corresponds to the variance of $\boldsymbol{x}$ in the direction of eigenvector $\boldsymbol{v}^{(i)}$. If $\boldsymbol{x} \in \mathbb{R}^D$ and $\boldsymbol{h} \in \mathbb{R}^d$ with $d < D$, then the optimal reconstruction error (choosing $\boldsymbol{\mu}$, $\boldsymbol{b}$, $\boldsymbol{V}$ and $\boldsymbol{W}$ as above) is

$$\min \mathbb{E}[||\boldsymbol{x} - \hat{\boldsymbol{x}}||^2] = \sum_{i=d+1}^{D} \lambda_i. \tag{13.23}$$

Hence, if the covariance has rank d, the eigenvalues λ_{d+1} to λ_D are 0 and reconstruction error is 0.

Furthermore, one can also show that the above solution can be obtained by maximizing the variances of the elements of $\boldsymbol{h}$, under orthogonal $\boldsymbol{W}$, instead of minimizing reconstruction error.

Linear factor models are some of the simplest generative models and some of the simplest models that learn a representation of data. Much as linear classifiers and linear regression models may be extended to deep feedforward networks, these linear factor models may be extended to autoencoder networks and deep probabilistic models that perform the same tasks but with a much more powerful and flexible model family.

14

Autoencoders

An **autoencoder** is a neural network that is trained to attempt to copy its input to its output. Internally, it has a hidden layer h that describes a **code** used to represent the input. The network may be viewed as consisting of two parts: an encoder function $h = f(x)$ and a decoder that produces a reconstruction $r = g(h)$. This architecture is presented in figure 14.1. If an autoencoder succeeds in simply learning to set $g(f(x)) = x$ everywhere, then it is not especially useful. Instead, autoencoders are designed to be unable to learn to copy perfectly. Usually they are restricted in ways that allow them to copy only approximately, and to copy only input that resembles the training data. Because the model is forced to prioritize which aspects of the input should be copied, it often learns useful properties of the data.

Modern autoencoders have generalized the idea of an encoder and a decoder beyond deterministic functions to stochastic mappings $p_{\text{encoder}}(h \mid x)$ and $p_{\text{decoder}}(x \mid h)$.

The idea of autoencoders has been part of the historical landscape of neural networks for decades (LeCun, 1987; Bourlard and Kamp, 1988; Hinton and Zemel, 1994). Traditionally, autoencoders were used for dimensionality reduction or feature learning. Recently, theoretical connections between autoencoders and latent variable models have brought autoencoders to the forefront of generative modeling, as we will see in chapter 20. Autoencoders may be thought of as being a special case of feedforward networks and may be trained with all the same techniques, typically minibatch gradient descent following gradients computed by back-propagation. Unlike general feedforward networks, autoencoders may also be trained using **recirculation** (Hinton and McClelland, 1988), a learning algorithm based on comparing the activations of the network on the original input to the activations

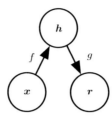

Figure 14.1: The general structure of an autoencoder, mapping an input x to an output (called reconstruction) r through an internal representation or code h. The autoencoder has two components: the encoder f (mapping x to h) and the decoder g (mapping h to r).

on the reconstructed input. Recirculation is regarded as more biologically plausible than back-propagation but is rarely used for machine learning applications.

14.1 Undercomplete Autoencoders

Copying the input to the output may sound useless, but we are typically not interested in the output of the decoder. Instead, we hope that training the autoencoder to perform the input copying task will result in h taking on useful properties.

One way to obtain useful features from the autoencoder is to constrain h to have a smaller dimension than x. An autoencoder whose code dimension is less than the input dimension is called **undercomplete**. Learning an undercomplete representation forces the autoencoder to capture the most salient features of the training data.

The learning process is described simply as minimizing a loss function

$$L(x, g(f(x))),\qquad(14.1)$$

where L is a loss function penalizing $g(f(x))$ for being dissimilar from x, such as the mean squared error.

When the decoder is linear and L is the mean squared error, an undercomplete autoencoder learns to span the same subspace as PCA. In this case, an autoencoder trained to perform the copying task has learned the principal subspace of the training data as a side effect.

Autoencoders with nonlinear encoder functions f and nonlinear decoder functions g can thus learn a more powerful nonlinear generalization of PCA. Unfortunately, if the encoder and decoder are allowed too much capacity, the autoencoder can learn to perform the copying task without extracting useful information about the distribution of the data. Theoretically, one could imagine that an autoencoder with a one-dimensional code but a very powerful nonlinear encoder could learn to represent each training example $x^{(i)}$ with the code i. The decoder could learn to map these integer indices back to the values of specific training examples. This specific scenario does not occur in practice, but it illustrates clearly that an autoencoder trained to perform the copying task can fail to learn anything useful about the dataset if the capacity of the autoencoder is allowed to become too great.

14.2 Regularized Autoencoders

Undercomplete autoencoders, with code dimension less than the input dimension, can learn the most salient features of the data distribution. We have seen that these autoencoders fail to learn anything useful if the encoder and decoder are given too much capacity.

A similar problem occurs if the hidden code is allowed to have dimension equal to the input, and in the **overcomplete** case in which the hidden code has dimension greater than the input. In these cases, even a linear encoder and a linear decoder can learn to copy the input to the output without learning anything useful about the data distribution.

Ideally, one could train any architecture of autoencoder successfully, choosing the code dimension and the capacity of the encoder and decoder based on the complexity of distribution to be modeled. Regularized autoencoders provide the ability to do so. Rather than limiting the model capacity by keeping the encoder and decoder shallow and the code size small, regularized autoencoders use a loss function that encourages the model to have other properties besides the ability to copy its input to its output. These other properties include sparsity of the representation, smallness of the derivative of the representation, and robustness to noise or to missing inputs. A regularized autoencoder can be nonlinear and overcomplete but still learn something useful about the data distribution, even if the model capacity is great enough to learn a trivial identity function.

In addition to the methods described here, which are most naturally interpreted as regularized autoencoders, nearly any generative model with latent variables and equipped with an inference procedure (for computing latent representations given input) may be viewed as a particular form of autoencoder. Two generative modeling approaches that emphasize this connection with autoencoders are the descendants of the Helmholtz machine (Hinton et al., 1995b), such as the variational autoencoder (section 20.10.3) and the generative stochastic networks (section 20.12). These models naturally learn high-capacity, overcomplete encodings of the input and do not require regularization for these encodings to be useful. Their encodings are naturally useful because the models were trained to approximately maximize the probability of the training data rather than to copy the input to the output.

14.2.1 Sparse Autoencoders

A sparse autoencoder is simply an autoencoder whose training criterion involves a sparsity penalty $\Omega(\boldsymbol{h})$ on the code layer $\boldsymbol{h}$, in addition to the reconstruction error:

$$L(\boldsymbol{x}, g(f(\boldsymbol{x}))) + \Omega(\boldsymbol{h}), \tag{14.2}$$

where $g(\boldsymbol{h})$ is the decoder output, and typically we have $\boldsymbol{h} = f(\boldsymbol{x})$, the encoder output.

Sparse autoencoders are typically used to learn features for another task, such as classification. An autoencoder that has been regularized to be sparse must respond to unique statistical features of the dataset it has been trained on, rather than simply acting as an identity function. In this way, training to perform the copying task with a sparsity penalty can yield a model that has learned useful features as a byproduct.

We can think of the penalty $\Omega(\boldsymbol{h})$ simply as a regularizer term added to a feedforward network whose primary task is to copy the input to the output (unsupervised learning objective) and possibly also perform some supervised task (with a supervised learning objective) that depends on these sparse features. Unlike other regularizers, such as weight decay, there is not a straightforward Bayesian interpretation to this regularizer. As described in section 5.6.1, training with weight decay and other regularization penalties can be interpreted as a MAP approximation to Bayesian inference, with the added regularizing penalty corresponding to a prior probability distribution over the model parameters. In this view, regularized maximum likelihood corresponds to maximizing $p(\boldsymbol{\theta} \mid \boldsymbol{x})$, which is equivalent to maximizing $\log p(\boldsymbol{x} \mid \boldsymbol{\theta}) + \log p(\boldsymbol{\theta})$. The $\log p(\boldsymbol{x} \mid \boldsymbol{\theta})$ term is the usual data log-likelihood term, and the $\log p(\boldsymbol{\theta})$ term, the log-prior over parameters, incorporates the preference over particular values of $\boldsymbol{\theta}$. This view is described in section 5.6. Regularized autoencoders defy such an interpretation because the regularizer depends on the data and is therefore by definition not a prior in the formal sense of the word. We can still think of these regularization terms as implicitly expressing a preference over functions.

Rather than thinking of the sparsity penalty as a regularizer for the copying task, we can think of the entire sparse autoencoder framework as approximating maximum likelihood training of a generative model that has latent variables. Suppose we have a model with visible variables x and latent variables h, with an explicit joint distribution $p_{\text{model}}(x, h) = p_{\text{model}}(h)p_{\text{model}}(x \mid h)$. We refer to $p_{\text{model}}(h)$ as the model's prior distribution over the latent variables, representing the model's beliefs prior to seeing x. This is different from the way we have previously used the word "prior," to refer to the distribution $p(\theta)$ encoding our beliefs about the model's parameters before we have seen the training data. The log-likelihood can be decomposed as

$$\log p_{\text{model}}(x) = \log \sum_{h} p_{\text{model}}(h, x). \tag{14.3}$$

We can think of the autoencoder as approximating this sum with a point estimate for just one highly likely value for h. This is similar to the sparse coding generative model (section 13.4), but with h being the output of the parametric encoder rather than the result of an optimization that infers the most likely h. From this point of view, with this chosen h, we are maximizing

$$\log p_{\text{model}}(h, x) = \log p_{\text{model}}(h) + \log p_{\text{model}}(x \mid h). \tag{14.4}$$

The $\log p_{\text{model}}(h)$ term can be sparsity inducing. For example, the Laplace prior,

$$p_{\text{model}}(h_i) = \frac{\lambda}{2} e^{-\lambda|h_i|}, \tag{14.5}$$

corresponds to an absolute value sparsity penalty. Expressing the log-prior as an absolute value penalty, we obtain

$$\Omega(h) = \lambda \sum_{i} |h_i|, \tag{14.6}$$

$$-\log p_{\text{model}}(h) = \sum_{i} \left(\lambda|h_i| - \log \frac{\lambda}{2} \right) = \Omega(h) + \text{const}, \tag{14.7}$$

where the constant term depends only on λ and not h. We typically treat λ as a hyperparameter and discard the constant term since it does not affect the parameter learning. Other priors, such as the Student t prior, can also induce sparsity. From this point of view of sparsity as resulting from the effect of $p_{\text{model}}(h)$ on approximate maximum likelihood learning, the sparsity penalty is not a regularization term at all. It is just a consequence of the model's distribution over its latent variables. This view provides a different motivation for training an autoencoder: it is a way of approximately training a generative model. It also provides a different reason for why the features learned by the autoencoder are useful: they describe the latent variables that explain the input.

Early work on sparse autoencoders (Ranzato et al., 2007a, 2008) explored various forms of sparsity and proposed a connection between the sparsity penalty and the $\log Z$ term that arises when applying maximum likelihood to an undirected probabilistic model $p(\boldsymbol{x}) = \frac{1}{Z}\tilde{p}(\boldsymbol{x})$. The idea is that minimizing $\log Z$ prevents a probabilistic model from having high probability everywhere, and imposing sparsity on an autoencoder prevents the autoencoder from having low reconstruction error everywhere. In this case, the connection is on the level of an intuitive understanding of a general mechanism rather than a mathematical correspondence. The interpretation of the sparsity penalty as corresponding to $\log p_{\text{model}}(\boldsymbol{h})$ in a directed model $p_{\text{model}}(\boldsymbol{h})p_{\text{model}}(\boldsymbol{x} \mid \boldsymbol{h})$ is more mathematically straightforward.

One way to achieve *actual zeros* in $\boldsymbol{h}$ for sparse (and denoising) autoencoders was introduced in Glorot et al. (2011b). The idea is to use rectified linear units to produce the code layer. With a prior that actually pushes the representations to zero (like the absolute value penalty), one can thus indirectly control the average number of zeros in the representation.

14.2.2 Denoising Autoencoders

Rather than adding a penalty Ω to the cost function, we can obtain an autoencoder that learns something useful by changing the reconstruction error term of the cost function.

Traditionally, autoencoders minimize some function

$$L(\boldsymbol{x}, g(f(\boldsymbol{x}))), \tag{14.8}$$

where L is a loss function penalizing $g(f(\boldsymbol{x}))$ for being dissimilar from $\boldsymbol{x}$, such as the L^2 norm of their difference. This encourages $g \circ f$ to learn to be merely an identity function if they have the capacity to do so.

A **denoising autoencoder** (DAE) instead minimizes

$$L(\boldsymbol{x}, g(f(\tilde{\boldsymbol{x}}))), \tag{14.9}$$

where $\tilde{\boldsymbol{x}}$ is a copy of $\boldsymbol{x}$ that has been corrupted by some form of noise. Denoising autoencoders must therefore undo this corruption rather than simply copying their input.

Denoising training forces f and g to implicitly learn the structure of $p_{\text{data}}(\boldsymbol{x})$, as shown by Alain and Bengio (2013) and Bengio et al. (2013c). Denoising autoencoders thus provide yet another example of how useful properties can emerge as a byproduct of minimizing reconstruction error. They are also an example of how overcomplete, high-capacity models may be used as autoencoders as long as care is taken to prevent them from learning the identity function. Denoising autoencoders are presented in more detail in section 14.5.

14.2.3 Regularizing by Penalizing Derivatives

Another strategy for regularizing an autoencoder is to use a penalty Ω, as in sparse autoencoders,

$$L(\boldsymbol{x}, g(f(\boldsymbol{x}))) + \Omega(\boldsymbol{h}, \boldsymbol{x}), \tag{14.10}$$

but with a different form of Ω:

$$\Omega(\boldsymbol{h}, \boldsymbol{x}) = \lambda \sum_i ||\nabla_{\boldsymbol{x}} h_i||^2. \tag{14.11}$$

This forces the model to learn a function that does not change much when $\boldsymbol{x}$ changes slightly. Because this penalty is applied only at training examples, it forces the autoencoder to learn features that capture information about the training distribution.

An autoencoder regularized in this way is called a **contractive autoencoder**, or CAE. This approach has theoretical connections to denoising autoencoders, manifold learning, and probabilistic modeling. The CAE is described in more detail in section 14.7.

14.3 Representational Power, Layer Size and Depth

Autoencoders are often trained with only a single layer encoder and a single layer decoder. However, this is not a requirement. In fact, using deep encoders and decoders offers many advantages.

Recall from section 6.4.1 that there are many advantages to depth in a feedforward network. Because autoencoders are feedforward networks, these advantages also apply to autoencoders. Moreover, the encoder is itself a feedforward network, as is the decoder, so each of these components of the autoencoder can individually benefit from depth.

One major advantage of nontrivial depth is that the universal approximator theorem guarantees that a feedforward neural network with at least one hidden layer can represent an approximation of any function (within a broad class) to an arbitrary degree of accuracy, provided that it has enough hidden units. This means that an autoencoder with a single hidden layer is able to represent the identity function along the domain of the data arbitrarily well. However, the mapping from input to code is shallow. This means that we are not able to enforce arbitrary constraints, such as that the code should be sparse. A deep autoencoder, with at least one additional hidden layer inside the encoder itself, can approximate any mapping from input to code arbitrarily well, given enough hidden units.

Depth can exponentially reduce the computational cost of representing some functions. Depth can also exponentially decrease the amount of training data needed to learn some functions. See section 6.4.1 for a review of the advantages of depth in feedforward networks.

Experimentally, deep autoencoders yield much better compression than corresponding shallow or linear autoencoders (Hinton and Salakhutdinov, 2006).

A common strategy for training a deep autoencoder is to greedily pretrain the deep architecture by training a stack of shallow autoencoders, so we often encounter shallow autoencoders, even when the ultimate goal is to train a deep autoencoder.

14.4 Stochastic Encoders and Decoders

Autoencoders are just feedforward networks. The same loss functions and output unit types that can be used for traditional feedforward networks are also used for autoencoders.

As described in section 6.2.2.4, a general strategy for designing the output units and the loss function of a feedforward network is to define an output distribution $p(\boldsymbol{y} \mid \boldsymbol{x})$ and minimize the negative log-likelihood $- \log p(\boldsymbol{y} \mid \boldsymbol{x})$. In that setting, $\boldsymbol{y}$ is a vector of targets, such as class labels.

In an autoencoder, $\boldsymbol{x}$ is now the target as well as the input. Yet we can still apply the same machinery as before. Given a hidden code $\boldsymbol{h}$, we may think of the decoder as providing a conditional distribution $p_{\text{decoder}}(\boldsymbol{x} \mid \boldsymbol{h})$. We may then train the autoencoder by minimizing $- \log p_{\text{decoder}}(\boldsymbol{x} \mid \boldsymbol{h})$. The exact form of this loss function will change depending on the form of p_{decoder}. As with traditional feedforward networks, we usually use linear output units to parametrize the mean of a Gaussian distribution if $\boldsymbol{x}$ is real valued. In that case, the negative log-likelihood yields a mean squared error criterion. Similarly, binary $\boldsymbol{x}$ values correspond to a Bernoulli distribution whose parameters are given by a sigmoid output unit, discrete $\boldsymbol{x}$ values correspond to a softmax distribution, and so on. Typically, the output variables are treated as being conditionally independent given

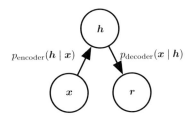

Figure 14.2: The structure of a stochastic autoencoder, in which both the encoder and the decoder are not simple functions but instead involve some noise injection, meaning that their output can be seen as sampled from a distribution, $p_{\text{encoder}}(h \mid x)$ for the encoder and $p_{\text{decoder}}(x \mid h)$ for the decoder.

h so that this probability distribution is inexpensive to evaluate, but some techniques, such as mixture density outputs, allow tractable modeling of outputs with correlations.

To make a more radical departure from the feedforward networks we have seen previously, we can also generalize the notion of an **encoding function** $f(x)$ to an **encoding distribution** $p_{\text{encoder}}(h \mid x)$, as illustrated in figure 14.2.

Any latent variable model $p_{\text{model}}(h, x)$ defines a stochastic encoder

$$p_{\text{encoder}}(h \mid x) = p_{\text{model}}(h \mid x) \tag{14.12}$$

and a stochastic decoder

$$p_{\text{decoder}}(x \mid h) = p_{\text{model}}(x \mid h). \tag{14.13}$$

In general, the encoder and decoder distributions are not necessarily conditional distributions compatible with a unique joint distribution $p_{\text{model}}(x, h)$. Alain et al. (2015) showed that training the encoder and decoder as a denoising autoencoder will tend to make them compatible asymptotically (with enough capacity and examples).

14.5   Denoising Autoencoders

The **denoising autoencoder** (DAE) is an autoencoder that receives a corrupted data point as input and is trained to predict the original, uncorrupted data point as its output.

The DAE training procedure is illustrated in figure 14.3. We introduce a corruption process $C(\tilde{\mathbf{x}} \mid \mathbf{x})$, which represents a conditional distribution over

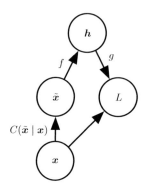

Figure 14.3: The computational graph of the cost function for a denoising autoencoder, which is trained to reconstruct the clean data point x from its corrupted version $\tilde{x}$. This is accomplished by minimizing the loss $L = -\log p_{\text{decoder}}(x \mid h = f(\tilde{x}))$, where $\tilde{x}$ is a corrupted version of the data example x, obtained through a given corruption process $C(\tilde{x} \mid x)$. Typically the distribution p_{decoder} is a factorial distribution whose mean parameters are emitted by a feedforward network g.

corrupted samples $\tilde{\mathbf{x}}$, given a data sample $\mathbf{x}$. The autoencoder then learns a **reconstruction distribution** $p_{\text{reconstruct}}(\mathbf{x} \mid \tilde{\mathbf{x}})$ estimated from training pairs $(x, \tilde{x})$ as follows:

1. Sample a training example x from the training data.

2. Sample a corrupted version $\tilde{x}$ from $C(\tilde{\mathbf{x}} \mid \mathbf{x} = x)$.

3. Use $(x, \tilde{x})$ as a training example for estimating the autoencoder reconstruction distribution $p_{\text{reconstruct}}(x \mid \tilde{x}) = p_{\text{decoder}}(x \mid h)$ with h the output of encoder $f(\tilde{x})$ and p_{decoder} typically defined by a decoder $g(h)$.

Typically we can simply perform gradient-based approximate minimization (such as minibatch gradient descent) on the negative log-likelihood $-\log p_{\text{decoder}}(x \mid h)$. As long as the encoder is deterministic, the denoising autoencoder is a feedforward network and may be trained with exactly the same techniques as any other feedforward network.

We can therefore view the DAE as performing stochastic gradient descent on the following expectation:

$$-\mathbb{E}_{\mathbf{x} \sim \hat{p}_{\text{data}}(\mathbf{x})} \mathbb{E}_{\tilde{\mathbf{x}} \sim C(\tilde{\mathbf{x}}|\mathbf{x})} \log p_{\text{decoder}}(x \mid h = f(\tilde{x})), \tag{14.14}$$

where $\hat{p}_{\text{data}}(\mathbf{x})$ is the training distribution.

14.5.1 Estimating the Score

Score matching (Hyvärinen, 2005) is an alternative to maximum likelihood. It provides a consistent estimator of probability distributions based on encouraging the model to have the same **score** as the data distribution at every training point x. In this context, the score is a particular gradient field:

$$\nabla_x \log p(x). \tag{14.15}$$

Score matching is discussed further in section 18.4. For the present discussion, regarding autoencoders, it is sufficient to understand that learning the gradient field of $\log p_{\text{data}}$ is one way to learn the structure of p_{data} itself.

A very important property of DAEs is that their training criterion (with conditionally Gaussian $p(x \mid h)$) makes the autoencoder learn a vector field $(g(f(x)) - x)$ that estimates the score of the data distribution. This is illustrated in figure 14.4.

Denoising training of a specific kind of autoencoder (sigmoidal hidden units, linear reconstruction units) using Gaussian noise and mean squared error as the reconstruction cost is equivalent (Vincent, 2011) to training a specific kind of undirected probabilistic model called an RBM with Gaussian visible units. This kind of model is described in detail in section 20.5.1; for the present discussion, it suffices to know that it is a model that provides an explicit $p_{\text{model}}(x; \theta)$. When the RBM is trained using **denoising score matching** (Kingma and LeCun, 2010), its learning algorithm is equivalent to denoising training in the corresponding autoencoder. With a fixed noise level, regularized score matching is not a consistent estimator; it instead recovers a blurred version of the distribution. If the noise level is chosen to approach 0 when the number of examples approaches infinity, however, then consistency is recovered. Denoising score matching is discussed in more detail in section 18.5.

Other connections between autoencoders and RBMs exist. Score matching applied to RBMs yields a cost function that is identical to reconstruction error combined with a regularization term similar to the contractive penalty of the CAE (Swersky et al., 2011). Bengio and Delalleau (2009) showed that an autoencoder gradient provides an approximation to contrastive divergence training of RBMs.

For continuous-valued x, the denoising criterion with Gaussian corruption and reconstruction distribution yields an estimator of the score that is applicable to general encoder and decoder parametrizations (Alain and Bengio, 2013). This means a generic encoder-decoder architecture may be made to estimate the score

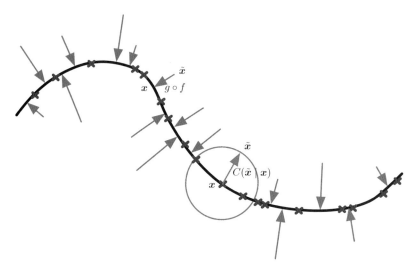

Figure 14.4: A denoising autoencoder is trained to map a corrupted data point $\tilde{x}$ back to the original data point x. We illustrate training examples x as red crosses lying near a low-dimensional manifold, illustrated with the bold black line. We illustrate the corruption process $C(\tilde{x} \mid x)$ with a gray circle of equiprobable corruptions. A gray arrow demonstrates how one training example is transformed into one sample from this corruption process. When the denoising autoencoder is trained to minimize the average of squared errors $||g(f(\tilde{x})) - x||^2$, the reconstruction $g(f(\tilde{x}))$ estimates $\mathbb{E}_{\mathbf{x}, \tilde{\mathbf{x}} \sim p_{\text{data}}(\mathbf{x})C(\tilde{\mathbf{x}}|\mathbf{x})}[\mathbf{x} \mid \tilde{x}]$. The vector $g(f(\tilde{x})) - \tilde{x}$ points approximately toward the nearest point on the manifold, since $g(f(\tilde{x}))$ estimates the center of mass of the clean points x that could have given rise to $\tilde{x}$. The autoencoder thus learns a vector field $g(f(x)) - x$ indicated by the green arrows. This vector field estimates the score $\nabla_x \log p_{\text{data}}(x)$ up to a multiplicative factor that is the average root mean square reconstruction error.

by training with the squared error criterion

$$||g(f(\tilde{x})) - x||^2 \tag{14.16}$$

and corruption

$$C(\tilde{\mathbf{x}} = \tilde{x}|x) = \mathcal{N}(\tilde{x}; \mu = x, \Sigma = \sigma^2 I) \tag{14.17}$$

with noise variance σ^2. See figure 14.5 for an illustration of how this works.

In general, there is no guarantee that the reconstruction $g(f(x))$ minus the input x corresponds to the gradient of any function, let alone to the score. That is why the early results (Vincent, 2011) are specialized to particular parametrizations, where $g(f(x)) - x$ may be obtained by taking the derivative of another function. Kamyshanska and Memisevic (2015) generalized the results of Vincent (2011) by identifying a family of shallow autoencoders such that $g(f(x)) - x$ corresponds to a score for all members of the family.

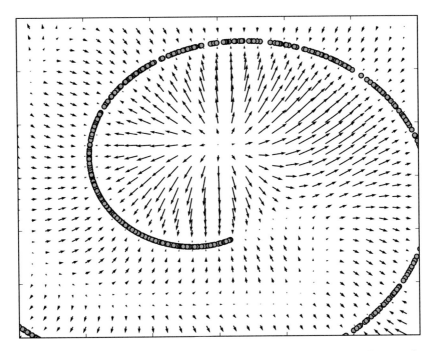

Figure 14.5: Vector field learned by a denoising autoencoder around a 1-D curved manifold near which the data concentrate in a 2-D space. Each arrow is proportional to the reconstruction minus input vector of the autoencoder and points towards higher probability according to the implicitly estimated probability distribution. The vector field has zeros at both maxima of the estimated density function (on the data manifolds) and at minima of that density function. For example, the spiral arm forms a 1-D manifold of local maxima that are connected to each other. Local minima appear near the middle of the gap between two arms. When the norm of reconstruction error (shown by the length of the arrows) is large, probability can be significantly increased by moving in the direction of the arrow, and that is mostly the case in places of low probability. The autoencoder maps these low probability points to higher probability reconstructions. Where probability is maximal, the arrows shrink because the reconstruction becomes more accurate. Figure reproduced with permission from Alain and Bengio (2013).

So far we have described only how the denoising autoencoder learns to represent a probability distribution. More generally, one may want to use the autoencoder as a generative model and draw samples from this distribution. This is described in section 20.11.

14.5.1.1 Historical Perspective

The idea of using MLPs for denoising dates back to the work of LeCun (1987) and Gallinari et al. (1987). Behnke (2001) also used recurrent networks to denoise images. Denoising autoencoders are, in some sense, just MLPs trained to denoise. The name "denoising autoencoder," however, refers to a model that is intended not merely to learn to denoise its input but to learn a good internal representation as a side effect of learning to denoise. This idea came much later (Vincent et al., 2008, 2010). The learned representation may then be used to pretrain a deeper unsupervised network or a supervised network. Like sparse autoencoders, sparse coding, contractive autoencoders, and other regularized autoencoders, the motivation for DAEs was to allow the learning of a very high-capacity encoder while preventing the encoder and decoder from learning a useless identity function.

Prior to the introduction of the modern DAE, Inayoshi and Kurita (2005) explored some of the same goals with some of the same methods. Their approach minimizes reconstruction error in addition to a supervised objective while injecting noise in the hidden layer of a supervised MLP, with the objective to improve generalization by introducing the reconstruction error and the injected noise. Their method was based on a linear encoder, however, and could not learn function families as powerful as the modern DAE can.

14.6   Learning Manifolds with Autoencoders

Like many other machine learning algorithms, autoencoders exploit the idea that data concentrates around a low-dimensional manifold or a small set of such manifolds, as described in section 5.11.3. Some machine learning algorithms exploit this idea only insofar as they learn a function that behaves correctly on the manifold but that may have unusual behavior if given an input that is off the manifold. Autoencoders take this idea further and aim to learn the structure of the manifold.

To understand how autoencoders do this, we must present some important characteristics of manifolds.

An important characterization of a manifold is the set of its **tangent planes**. At a point x on a d-dimensional manifold, the tangent plane is given by d basis vectors that span the local directions of variation allowed on the manifold. As illustrated in figure 14.6, these local directions specify how one can change x infinitesimally while staying on the manifold.

All autoencoder training procedures involve a compromise between two forces:

1. Learning a representation h of a training example x such that x can be approximately recovered from h through a decoder. The fact that x is drawn from the training data is crucial, because it means the autoencoder

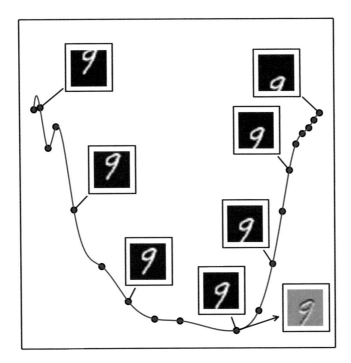

Figure 14.6: An illustration of the concept of a tangent hyperplane. Here we create a 1-D manifold in 784-D space. We take an MNIST image with 784 pixels and transform it by translating it vertically. The amount of vertical translation defines a coordinate along a 1-D manifold that traces out a curved path through image space. This plot shows a few points along this manifold. For visualization, we have projected the manifold into 2-D space using PCA. An n-dimensional manifold has an n-dimensional tangent plane at every point. This tangent plane touches the manifold exactly at that point and is oriented parallel to the surface at that point. It defines the space of directions in which it is possible to move while remaining on the manifold. This 1-D manifold has a single tangent line. We indicate an example tangent line at one point, with an image showing how this tangent direction appears in image space. Gray pixels indicate pixels that do not change as we move along the tangent line, white pixels indicate pixels that brighten, and black pixels indicate pixels that darken.

need not successfully reconstruct inputs that are not probable under the data-generating distribution.

2. Satisfying the constraint or regularization penalty. This can be an architectural constraint that limits the capacity of the autoencoder, or it can be a regularization term added to the reconstruction cost. These techniques generally prefer solutions that are less sensitive to the input.

Clearly, neither force alone would be useful—copying the input to the output is not useful on its own, nor is ignoring the input. Instead, the two forces together are useful because they force the hidden representation to capture information about the structure of the data-generating distribution. The important principle is that the autoencoder can afford to represent *only the variations that are needed to reconstruct training examples*. If the data-generating distribution concentrates near a low-dimensional manifold, this yields representations that implicitly capture a local coordinate system for this manifold: only the variations tangent to the manifold around x need to correspond to changes in $h = f(x)$. Hence the encoder learns a mapping from the input space x to a representation space, a mapping that is only sensitive to changes along the manifold directions, but that is insensitive to changes orthogonal to the manifold.

A one-dimensional example is illustrated in figure 14.7, showing that, by making the reconstruction function insensitive to perturbations of the input around the data points, we cause the autoencoder to recover the manifold structure.

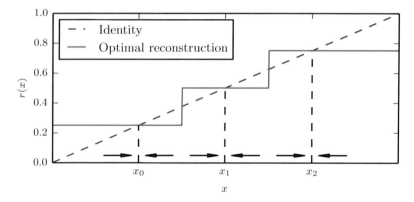

Figure 14.7: If the autoencoder learns a reconstruction function that is invariant to small perturbations near the data points, it captures the manifold structure of the data. Here the manifold structure is a collection of 0-dimensional manifolds. The dashed diagonal line indicates the identity function target for reconstruction. The optimal reconstruction function crosses the identity function wherever there is a data point. The horizontal arrows at the bottom of the plot indicate the $r(x) - x$ reconstruction direction vector at the base of the arrow, in input space, always pointing toward the nearest "manifold" (a single data point in the 1-D case). The denoising autoencoder explicitly tries to make the derivative of the reconstruction function $r(x)$ small around the data points. The contractive autoencoder does the same for the encoder. Although the derivative of $r(x)$ is asked to be small around the data points, it can be large between the data points. The space between the data points corresponds to the region between the manifolds, where the reconstruction function must have a large derivative to map corrupted points back onto the manifold.

To understand why autoencoders are useful for manifold learning, it is instructive to compare them to other approaches. What is most commonly learned to characterize a manifold is a **representation** of the data points on (or near) the manifold. Such a representation for a particular example is also called its embedding. It is typically given by a low-dimensional vector, with fewer dimensions than the "ambient" space of which the manifold is a low-dimensional subset. Some algorithms (nonparametric manifold learning algorithms, discussed below) directly learn an embedding for each training example, while others learn a more general mapping, sometimes called an encoder, or representation function, that maps any point in the ambient space (the input space) to its embedding.

Manifold learning has mostly focused on unsupervised learning procedures that attempt to capture these manifolds. Most of the initial machine learning research on learning nonlinear manifolds has focused on **nonparametric** methods based on the **nearest neighbor graph**. This graph has one node per training example and edges connecting near neighbors to each other. These methods (Schölkopf et al., 1998; Roweis and Saul, 2000; Tenenbaum et al., 2000; Brand, 2003; Belkin and Niyogi, 2003; Donoho and Grimes, 2003; Weinberger and Saul, 2004; Hinton and Roweis, 2003; van der Maaten and Hinton, 2008) associate each node with a tangent plane that spans the directions of variations associated with the difference vectors between the example and its neighbors, as illustrated in figure 14.8.

A global coordinate system can then be obtained through an optimization or by solving a linear system. Figure 14.9 illustrates how a manifold can be tiled by a large number of locally linear Gaussian-like patches (or "pancakes," because the Gaussians are flat in the tangent directions).

A fundamental difficulty with such local nonparametric approaches to manifold learning is raised in Bengio and Monperrus (2005): if the manifolds are not very smooth (they have many peaks and troughs and twists), one may need a very large number of training examples to cover each one of these variations, with no chance to generalize to unseen variations. Indeed, these methods can only generalize the shape of the manifold by interpolating between neighboring examples. Unfortunately, the manifolds involved in AI problems can have very complicated structures that can be difficult to capture from only local interpolation. Consider for example the manifold resulting from translation shown in figure 14.6. If we watch just one coordinate within the input vector, x_i, as the image is translated, we will observe that one coordinate encounters a peak or a trough in its value once for every peak or trough in brightness in the image. In other words, the complexity of the patterns of brightness in an underlying image template drives the complexity of the manifolds that are generated by performing simple image transformations. This

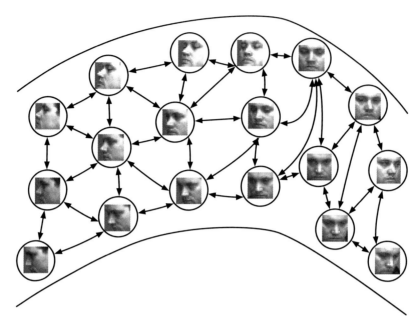

Figure 14.8: Nonparametric manifold learning procedures build a nearest neighbor graph in which nodes represent training examples a directed edges indicate nearest neighbor relationships. Various procedures can thus obtain the tangent plane associated with a neighborhood of the graph as well as a coordinate system that associates each training example with a real-valued vector position, or **embedding**. It is possible to generalize such a representation to new examples by a form of interpolation. As long as the number of examples is large enough to cover the curvature and twists of the manifold, these approaches work well. Images from the QMUL Multiview Face Dataset (Gong et al., 2000).

motivates the use of distributed representations and deep learning for capturing manifold structure.

14.7 Contractive Autoencoders

The contractive autoencoder (Rifai et al., 2011a,b) introduces an explicit regularizer on the code $\boldsymbol{h} = f(\boldsymbol{x})$, encouraging the derivatives of f to be as small as possible:

$$\Omega(\boldsymbol{h}) = \lambda \left\| \frac{\partial f(\boldsymbol{x})}{\partial \boldsymbol{x}} \right\|_F^2 . \tag{14.18}$$

The penalty $\Omega(\boldsymbol{h})$ is the squared Frobenius norm (sum of squared elements) of the Jacobian matrix of partial derivatives associated with the encoder function.

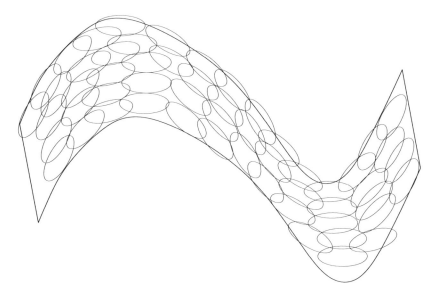

Figure 14.9: If the tangent planes (see figure 14.6) at each location are known, then they can be tiled to form a global coordinate system or a density function. Each local patch can be thought of as a local Euclidean coordinate system or as a locally flat Gaussian, or "pancake," with a very small variance in the directions orthogonal to the pancake and a very large variance in the directions defining the coordinate system on the pancake. A mixture of these Gaussians provides an estimated density function, as in the manifold Parzen window algorithm (Vincent and Bengio, 2003) or in its nonlocal neural-net-based variant (Bengio et al., 2006c).

There is a connection between the denoising autoencoder and the contractive autoencoder: Alain and Bengio (2013) showed that in the limit of small Gaussian input noise, the denoising reconstruction error is equivalent to a contractive penalty on the reconstruction function that maps $\boldsymbol{x}$ to $\boldsymbol{r} = g(f(\boldsymbol{x}))$. In other words, denoising autoencoders make the reconstruction function resist small but finite-sized perturbations of the input, while contractive autoencoders make the feature extraction function resist infinitesimal perturbations of the input. When using the Jacobian-based contractive penalty to pretrain features $f(\boldsymbol{x})$ for use with a classifier, the best classification accuracy usually results from applying the contractive penalty to $f(\boldsymbol{x})$ rather than to $g(f(\boldsymbol{x}))$. A contractive penalty on $f(\boldsymbol{x})$ also has close connections to score matching, as discussed in section 14.5.1.

The name **contractive** arises from the way that the CAE warps space. Specifically, because the CAE is trained to resist perturbations of its input, it is encouraged to map a neighborhood of input points to a smaller neighborhood of output points.

We can think of this as contracting the input neighborhood to a smaller output neighborhood.

To clarify, the CAE is contractive only locally—all perturbations of a training point x are mapped near to $f(x)$. Globally, two different points x and x' may be mapped to $f(x)$ and $f(x')$ points that are farther apart than the original points. It is plausible that f could be expanding in-between or far from the data manifolds (see, for example, what happens in the 1-D toy example of figure 14.7). When the $\Omega(h)$ penalty is applied to sigmoidal units, one easy way to shrink the Jacobian is to make the sigmoid units saturate to 0 or 1. This encourages the CAE to encode input points with extreme values of the sigmoid, which may be interpreted as a binary code. It also ensures that the CAE will spread its code values throughout most of the hypercube that its sigmoidal hidden units can span.

We can think of the Jacobian matrix J at a point x as approximating the nonlinear encoder $f(x)$ as being a linear operator. This allows us to use the word "contractive" more formally. In the theory of linear operators, a linear operator is said to be contractive if the norm of Jx remains less than or equal to 1 for all unit-norm x. In other words, J is contractive if it shrinks the unit sphere. We can think of the CAE as penalizing the Frobenius norm of the local linear approximation of $f(x)$ at every training point x in order to encourage each of these local linear operators to become a contraction.

As described in section 14.6, regularized autoencoders learn manifolds by balancing two opposing forces. In the case of the CAE, these two forces are reconstruction error and the contractive penalty $\Omega(h)$. Reconstruction error alone would encourage the CAE to learn an identity function. The contractive penalty alone would encourage the CAE to learn features that are constant with respect to x. The compromise between these two forces yields an autoencoder whose derivatives $\frac{\partial f(x)}{\partial x}$ are mostly tiny. Only a small number of hidden units, corresponding to a small number of directions in the input, may have significant derivatives.

The goal of the CAE is to learn the manifold structure of the data. Directions x with large Jx rapidly change h, so these are likely to be directions that approximate the tangent planes of the manifold. Experiments by Rifai et al. (2011a,b) show that training the CAE results in most singular values of J dropping below 1 in magnitude and therefore becoming contractive. Some singular values remain above 1, however, because the reconstruction error penalty encourages the CAE to encode the directions with the most local variance. The directions corresponding to the largest singular values are interpreted as the tangent directions that the contractive autoencoder has learned. Ideally, these tangent directions should correspond to real variations in the data. For example, a CAE applied to images should learn tangent vectors that show how the image changes as objects in the image gradually change pose, as shown in figure 14.6. Visualizations of the experimentally obtained singular vectors do seem to correspond to meaningful transformations of the input image, as shown in figure 14.10.

One practical issue with the CAE regularization criterion is that although it is cheap to compute in the case of a single hidden layer autoencoder, it becomes much more expensive in the case of deeper autoencoders. The strategy followed by Rifai et al. (2011a) is to separately train a series of single-layer autoencoders, each trained to reconstruct the previous autoencoder's hidden layer. The composition of these autoencoders then forms a deep autoencoder. Because each layer was separately trained to be locally contractive, the deep autoencoder is contractive as well. The result is not the same as what would be obtained by jointly training the entire architecture with a penalty on the Jacobian of the deep model, but it captures many of the desirable qualitative characteristics.

Another practical issue is that the contraction penalty can obtain useless results if we do not impose some sort of scale on the decoder. For example, the encoder could consist of multiplying the input by a small constant ϵ, and the decoder could consist of dividing the code by ϵ. As ϵ approaches 0, the encoder drives the contractive penalty $\Omega(\boldsymbol{h})$ to approach 0 without having learned anything about

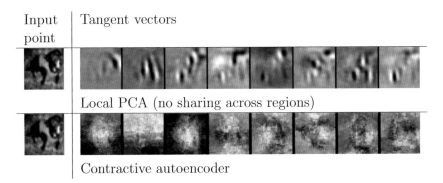

Figure 14.10: Illustration of tangent vectors of the manifold estimated by local PCA and by a contractive autoencoder. The location on the manifold is defined by the input image of a dog drawn from the CIFAR-10 dataset. The tangent vectors are estimated by the leading singular vectors of the Jacobian matrix $\frac{\partial \boldsymbol{h}}{\partial \boldsymbol{x}}$ of the input-to-code mapping. Although both local PCA and the CAE can capture local tangents, the CAE is able to form more accurate estimates from limited training data because it exploits parameter sharing across different locations that share a subset of active hidden units. The CAE tangent directions typically correspond to moving or changing parts of the object (such as the head or legs). Images reproduced with permission from Rifai et al. (2011c).

the distribution. Meanwhile, the decoder maintains perfect reconstruction. In Rifai et al. (2011a), this is prevented by tying the weights of f and g. Both f and g are standard neural network layers consisting of an affine transformation followed by an element-wise nonlinearity, so it is straightforward to set the weight matrix of g to be the transpose of the weight matrix of f.

14.8 Predictive Sparse Decomposition

Predictive sparse decomposition (PSD) is a model that is a hybrid of sparse coding and parametric autoencoders (Kavukcuoglu et al., 2008). A parametric encoder is trained to predict the output of iterative inference. PSD has been applied to unsupervised feature learning for object recognition in images and video (Kavukcuoglu et al., 2009, 2010; Jarrett et al., 2009; Farabet et al., 2011), as well as for audio (Henaff et al., 2011). The model consists of an encoder $f(\boldsymbol{x})$ and a decoder $g(\boldsymbol{h})$ that are both parametric. During training, $\boldsymbol{h}$ is controlled by the optimization algorithm. Training proceeds by minimizing

$$||\boldsymbol{x} - g(\boldsymbol{h})||^2 + \lambda|\boldsymbol{h}|_1 + \gamma||\boldsymbol{h} - f(\boldsymbol{x})||^2. \tag{14.19}$$

As in sparse coding, the training algorithm alternates between minimization with respect to $\boldsymbol{h}$ and minimization with respect to the model parameters. Minimization with respect to $\boldsymbol{h}$ is fast because $f(\boldsymbol{x})$ provides a good initial value of $\boldsymbol{h}$, and the cost function constrains $\boldsymbol{h}$ to remain near $f(\boldsymbol{x})$ anyway. Simple gradient descent can obtain reasonable values of $\boldsymbol{h}$ in as few as ten steps.

The training procedure used by PSD is different from first training a sparse coding model and then training $f(\boldsymbol{x})$ to predict the values of the sparse coding features. The PSD training procedure regularizes the decoder to use parameters for which $f(\boldsymbol{x})$ can infer good code values.

Predictive sparse coding is an example of **learned approximate inference**. In section 19.5, this topic is developed further. The tools presented in chapter 19 make it clear that PSD can be interpreted as training a directed sparse coding probabilistic model by maximizing a lower bound on the log-likelihood of the model.

In practical applications of PSD, the iterative optimization is used only during training. The parametric encoder f is used to compute the learned features when the model is deployed. Evaluating f is computationally inexpensive compared to inferring $\boldsymbol{h}$ via gradient descent. Because f is a differentiable parametric function, PSD models may be stacked and used to initialize a deep network to be trained with another criterion.

14.9 Applications of Autoencoders

Autoencoders have been successfully applied to dimensionality reduction and information retrieval tasks. Dimensionality reduction was one of the first applications of representation learning and deep learning. It was one of the early motivations for studying autoencoders. For example, Hinton and Salakhutdinov (2006) trained a stack of RBMs and then used their weights to initialize a deep autoencoder with gradually smaller hidden layers, culminating in a bottleneck of 30 units. The resulting code yielded less reconstruction error than PCA into 30 dimensions, and the learned representation was qualitatively easier to interpret and relate to the underlying categories, with these categories manifesting as well-separated clusters.

Lower-dimensional representations can improve performance on many tasks, such as classification. Models of smaller spaces consume less memory and runtime. Many forms of dimensionality reduction place semantically related examples near each other, as observed by Salakhutdinov and Hinton (2007b) and Torralba et al. (2008). The hints provided by the mapping to the lower-dimensional space aid generalization.

One task that benefits even more than usual from dimensionality reduction is **information retrieval**, the task of finding entries in a database that resemble a query entry. This task derives the usual benefits from dimensionality reduction that other tasks do, but also derives the additional benefit that search can become extremely efficient in certain kinds of low-dimensional spaces. Specifically, if we train the dimensionality reduction algorithm to produce a code that is low-dimensional and *binary*, then we can store all database entries in a hash table that maps binary code vectors to entries. This hash table allows us to perform information retrieval by returning all database entries that have the same binary code as the query. We can also search over slightly less similar entries very efficiently, just by flipping individual bits from the encoding of the query. This approach to information retrieval via dimensionality reduction and binarization is called **semantic hashing** (Salakhutdinov and Hinton, 2007b, 2009b) and has been applied to both textual input (Salakhutdinov and Hinton, 2007b, 2009b) and images (Torralba et al., 2008; Weiss et al., 2008; Krizhevsky and Hinton, 2011).

To produce binary codes for semantic hashing, one typically uses an encoding function with sigmoids on the final layer. The sigmoid units must be trained to be saturated to nearly 0 or nearly 1 for all input values. One trick that can accomplish this is simply to inject additive noise just before the sigmoid nonlinearity during training. The magnitude of the noise should increase over time. To fight that noise and preserve as much information as possible, the network must increase the magnitude of the inputs to the sigmoid function, until saturation occurs.

The idea of learning a hashing function has been further explored in several directions, including the idea of training the representations to optimize a loss more directly linked to the task of finding nearby examples in the hash table (Norouzi and Fleet, 2011).

15

Representation Learning

In this chapter, we first discuss what it means to learn representations and how the notion of representation can be useful to design deep architectures. We explore how learning algorithms share statistical strength across different tasks, including using information from unsupervised tasks to perform supervised tasks. Shared representations are useful to handle multiple modalities or domains, or to transfer learned knowledge to tasks for which few or no examples are given but a task representation exists. Finally, we step back and argue about the reasons for the success of representation learning, starting with the theoretical advantages of distributed representations (Hinton et al., 1986) and deep representations, ending with the more general idea of underlying assumptions about the data-generating process, in particular about underlying causes of the observed data.

Many information processing tasks can be very easy or very difficult depending on how the information is represented. This is a general principle applicable to daily life, to computer science in general, and to machine learning. For example, it is straightforward for a person to divide 210 by 6 using long division. The task becomes considerably less straightforward if it is instead posed using the Roman numeral representation of the numbers. Most modern people asked to divide CCX by VI would begin by converting the numbers to the Arabic numeral representation, permitting long division procedures that make use of the place value system. More concretely, we can quantify the asymptotic runtime of various operations using appropriate or inappropriate representations. For example, inserting a number into the correct position in a sorted list of numbers is an $O(n)$ operation if the list is represented as a linked list, but only $O(\log n)$ if the list is represented as a red-black tree.

In the context of machine learning, what makes one representation better than another? Generally speaking, a good representation is one that makes a subsequent learning task easier. The choice of representation will usually depend on the choice of the subsequent learning task.

We can think of feedforward networks trained by supervised learning as performing a kind of representation learning. Specifically, the last layer of the network is typically a linear classifier, such as a softmax regression classifier. The rest of the network learns to provide a representation to this classifier. Training with a supervised criterion naturally leads to the representation at every hidden layer (but more so near the top hidden layer) taking on properties that make the classification task easier. For example, classes that were not linearly separable in the input features may become linearly separable in the last hidden layer. In principle, the last layer could be another kind of model, such as a nearest neighbor classifier (Salakhutdinov and Hinton, 2007a). The features in the penultimate layer should learn different properties depending on the type of the last layer.

Supervised training of feedforward networks does not involve explicitly imposing any condition on the learned intermediate features. Other kinds of representation learning algorithms are often explicitly designed to shape the representation in some particular way. For example, suppose we want to learn a representation that makes density estimation easier. Distributions with more independences are easier to model, so we could design an objective function that encourages the elements of the representation vector $\boldsymbol{h}$ to be independent. Just like supervised networks, unsupervised deep learning algorithms have a main training objective but also learn a representation as a side effect. Regardless of how a representation was obtained, it can be used for another task. Alternatively, multiple tasks (some supervised, some unsupervised) can be learned together with some shared internal representation.

Most representation learning problems face a trade-off between preserving as much information about the input as possible and attaining nice properties (such as independence).

Representation learning is particularly interesting because it provides one way to perform unsupervised and semi-supervised learning. We often have very large amounts of unlabeled training data and relatively little labeled training data. Training with supervised learning techniques on the labeled subset often results in severe overfitting. Semi-supervised learning offers the chance to resolve this overfitting problem by also learning from the unlabeled data. Specifically, we can learn good representations for the unlabeled data, and then use these representations to solve the supervised learning task.

Humans and animals are able to learn from very few labeled examples. We do not yet know how this is possible. Many factors could explain improved human performance—for example, the brain may use very large ensembles of classifiers or

Bayesian inference techniques. One popular hypothesis is that the brain is able to leverage unsupervised or semi-supervised learning. There are many ways to leverage unlabeled data. In this chapter, we focus on the hypothesis that the unlabeled data can be used to learn a good representation.

15.1   Greedy Layer-Wise Unsupervised Pretraining

Unsupervised learning played a key historical role in the revival of deep neural networks, enabling researchers for the first time to train a deep supervised network without requiring architectural specializations like convolution or recurrence. We call this procedure **unsupervised pretraining**, or more precisely, **greedy layer-wise unsupervised pretraining**. This procedure is a canonical example of how a representation learned for one task (unsupervised learning, trying to capture the shape of the input distribution) can sometimes be useful for another task (supervised learning with the same input domain).

Greedy layer-wise unsupervised pretraining relies on a single-layer representation learning algorithm such as an RBM, a single-layer autoencoder, a sparse coding model, or another model that learns latent representations. Each layer is pretrained using unsupervised learning, taking the output of the previous layer and producing as output a new representation of the data, whose distribution (or its relation to other variables, such as categories to predict) is hopefully simpler. See algorithm 15.1 for a formal description.

Greedy layer-wise training procedures based on unsupervised criteria have long been used to sidestep the difficulty of jointly training the layers of a deep neural net for a supervised task. This approach dates back at least as far as the neocognitron (Fukushima, 1975). The deep learning renaissance of 2006 began with the discovery that this greedy learning procedure could be used to find a good initialization for a joint learning procedure over all the layers, and that this approach could be used to successfully train even fully connected architectures (Hinton et al., 2006; Hinton and Salakhutdinov, 2006; Hinton, 2006; Bengio et al., 2007; Ranzato et al., 2007a). Prior to this discovery, only convolutional deep networks or networks whose depth resulted from recurrence were regarded as feasible to train. Today, we now know that greedy layer-wise pretraining is not required to train fully connected deep architectures, but the unsupervised pretraining approach was the first method to succeed.

Greedy layer-wise pretraining is called **greedy** because it is a **greedy algorithm**, meaning that it optimizes each piece of the solution independently, one piece at a time, rather than jointly optimizing all pieces. It is called **layer-wise** because these independent pieces are the layers of the network. Specifically, greedy layer-wise pretraining proceeds one layer at a time, training the k-th layer while keeping the previous ones fixed. In particular, the lower layers (which are trained first) are not adapted after the upper layers are introduced. It is called **unsupervised** because each layer is trained with an unsupervised representation learning algorithm. However it is also called **pretraining** because it is supposed to be only a first step before a joint training algorithm is applied to **fine-tune** all the layers together. In the context of a supervised learning task, it can be viewed as a regularizer (in some experiments, pretraining decreases test error without decreasing training error) and a form of parameter initialization.

It is common to use the word "pretraining" to refer not only to the pretraining stage itself but to the entire two-phase protocol that combines the pretraining phase and a supervised learning phase. The supervised learning phase may involve training a simple classifier on top of the features learned in the pretraining phase, or it may involve supervised fine-tuning of the entire network learned in the pretraining phase. No matter what kind of unsupervised learning algorithm or what model type is employed, in most cases, the overall training scheme is nearly the same. While the choice of unsupervised learning algorithm will obviously affect the details, most applications of unsupervised pretraining follow this basic protocol.

Greedy layer-wise unsupervised pretraining can also be used as initialization for other unsupervised learning algorithms, such as deep autoencoders (Hinton and Salakhutdinov, 2006) and probabilistic models with many layers of latent variables. Such models include deep belief networks (Hinton et al., 2006) and deep Boltzmann machines (Salakhutdinov and Hinton, 2009a). These deep generative models are described in chapter 20.

As discussed in section 8.7.4, it is also possible to have greedy layer-wise *supervised* pretraining. This builds on the premise that training a shallow network is easier than training a deep one, which seems to have been validated in several contexts (Erhan et al., 2010).

15.1.1 When and Why Does Unsupervised Pretraining Work?

On many tasks, greedy layer-wise unsupervised pretraining can yield substantial improvements in test error for classification tasks. This observation was responsible for the renewed interested in deep neural networks starting in 2006 (Hinton et al., 2006; Bengio et al., 2007; Ranzato et al., 2007a). On many other tasks, however, unsupervised pretraining either does not confer a benefit or even causes noticeable

---

Algorithm 15.1 *Greedy layer-wise unsupervised pretraining protocol*

Given the following: Unsupervised feature learning algorithm $\mathcal{L}$, which takes a training set of examples and returns an encoder or feature function f. The raw input data is $\boldsymbol{X}$, with one row per example, and $f^{(1)}(\boldsymbol{X})$ is the output of the first stage encoder on $\boldsymbol{X}$. In the case where fine-tuning is performed, we use a learner $\mathcal{T}$, which takes an initial function f, input examples $\boldsymbol{X}$ (and in the supervised fine-tuning case, associated targets $\boldsymbol{Y}$), and returns a tuned function. The number of stages is m.

$f \leftarrow$ Identity function
$\tilde{\boldsymbol{X}} = \boldsymbol{X}$
for $k = 1, \ldots, m$ **do**
    $f^{(k)} = \mathcal{L}(\tilde{\boldsymbol{X}})$
    $f \leftarrow f^{(k)} \circ f$
    $\tilde{\boldsymbol{X}} \leftarrow f^{(k)}(\tilde{\boldsymbol{X}})$
end for
if *fine-tuning* **then**
    $f \leftarrow \mathcal{T}(f, \boldsymbol{X}, \boldsymbol{Y})$
end if
Return f

---

harm. Ma et al. (2015) studied the effect of pretraining on machine learning models for chemical activity prediction and found that, on average, pretraining was slightly harmful, but for many tasks was significantly helpful. Because unsupervised pretraining is sometimes helpful but often harmful, it is important to understand when and why it works in order to determine whether it is applicable to a particular task.

At the outset, it is important to clarify that most of this discussion is restricted to greedy unsupervised pretraining in particular. There are other, completely different paradigms for performing semi-supervised learning with neural networks, such as virtual adversarial training, described in section 7.13. It is also possible to train an autoencoder or generative model at the same time as the supervised model. Examples of this single-stage approach include the discriminative RBM (Larochelle and Bengio, 2008) and the ladder network (Rasmus et al., 2015), in which the total objective is an explicit sum of the two terms (one using the labels, and one only using the input).

Unsupervised pretraining combines two different ideas. First, it makes use of the idea that the choice of initial parameters for a deep neural network can have a significant regularizing effect on the model (and, to a lesser extent, that it can improve optimization). Second, it makes use of the more general idea that learning about the input distribution can help with learning about the mapping from inputs to outputs.

Both ideas involve many complicated interactions between several parts of the machine learning algorithm that are not entirely understood.

The first idea, that the choice of initial parameters for a deep neural network can have a strong regularizing effect on its performance, is the least understood. At the time that pretraining became popular, it was understood as initializing the model in a location that would cause it to approach one local minimum rather than another. Today, local minima are no longer considered to be a serious problem for neural network optimization. We now know that our standard neural network training procedures usually do not arrive at a critical point of any kind. It remains possible that pretraining initializes the model in a location that would otherwise be inaccessible—for example, a region that is surrounded by areas where the cost function varies so much from one example to another that minibatches give only a very noisy estimate of the gradient, or a region surrounded by areas where the Hessian matrix is so poorly conditioned that gradient descent methods must use very small steps. However, our ability to characterize exactly what aspects of the pretrained parameters are retained during the supervised training stage is limited. This is one reason that modern approaches typically use simultaneous unsupervised learning and supervised learning rather than two sequential stages. One may also avoid struggling with these complicated ideas about how optimization in the supervised learning stage preserves information from the unsupervised learning stage by simply freezing the parameters for the feature extractors and using supervised learning only to add a classifier on top of the learned features.

The other idea, that a learning algorithm can use information learned in the unsupervised phase to perform better in the supervised learning stage, is better understood. The basic idea is that some features that are useful for the unsupervised task may also be useful for the supervised learning task. For example, if we train a generative model of images of cars and motorcycles, it will need to know about wheels, and about how many wheels should be in an image. If we are fortunate, the representation of the wheels will take on a form that is easy for the supervised learner to access. This is not yet understood at a mathematical, theoretical level, so it is not always possible to predict which tasks will benefit from unsupervised learning in this way. Many aspects of this approach are highly dependent on the specific models used. For example, if we wish to add a linear classifier on top of pretrained features, the features must make the underlying classes linearly separable. These properties often occur naturally but do not always do so. This is another reason that simultaneous supervised and unsupervised learning can be preferable—the constraints imposed by the output layer are naturally included from the start.

From the point of view of unsupervised pretraining as learning a representation, we can expect unsupervised pretraining to be more effective when the initial representation is poor. One key example of this is the use of word embeddings. Words represented by one-hot vectors are not very informative because every two distinct one-hot vectors are the same distance from each other (squared L^2 distance of 2). Learned word embeddings naturally encode similarity between words by their distance from each other. Because of this, unsupervised pretraining is especially useful when processing words. It is less useful when processing images, perhaps because images already lie in a rich vector space where distances provide a low-quality similarity metric.

From the point of view of unsupervised pretraining as a regularizer, we can expect unsupervised pretraining to be most helpful when the number of labeled examples is very small. Because the source of information added by unsupervised pretraining is the unlabeled data, we may also expect unsupervised pretraining to perform best when the number of unlabeled examples is very large. The advantage of semi-supervised learning via unsupervised pretraining with many unlabeled examples and few labeled examples was made particularly clear in 2011 with unsupervised pretraining winning two international transfer learning competitions (Mesnil et al., 2011; Goodfellow et al., 2011), in settings where the number of labeled examples in the target task was small (from a handful to dozens of examples per class). These effects were also documented in carefully controlled experiments by Paine et al. (2014).

Other factors are likely to be involved. For example, unsupervised pretraining is likely to be most useful when the function to be learned is extremely complicated. Unsupervised learning differs from regularizers like weight decay because it does not bias the learner toward discovering a simple function but rather leads the learner toward discovering feature functions that are useful for the unsupervised learning task. If the true underlying functions are complicated and shaped by regularities of the input distribution, unsupervised learning can be a more appropriate regularizer.

These caveats aside, we now analyze some success cases where unsupervised pretraining is known to cause an improvement and explain what is known about why this improvement occurs. Unsupervised pretraining has usually been used to improve classifiers and is usually most interesting from the point of view of reducing test set error. Unsupervised pretraining can help tasks other than classification, however, and can act to improve optimization rather than being merely a regularizer. For example, it can improve both train and test reconstruction error for deep autoencoders (Hinton and Salakhutdinov, 2006).

Erhan et al. (2010) performed many experiments to explain several successes of unsupervised pretraining. Improvements to training error and improvements to test error may both be explained in terms of unsupervised pretraining taking the parameters into a region that would otherwise be inaccessible. Neural network training is nondeterministic and converges to a different function every time it is run. Training may halt at a point where the gradient becomes small, a point where early stopping ends training to prevent overfitting, or at a point where the gradient is large, but it is difficult to find a downhill step because of problems such as stochasticity or poor conditioning of the Hessian. Neural networks that receive unsupervised pretraining consistently halt in the same region of function space, while neural networks without pretraining consistently halt in another region. See figure 15.1 for a visualization of this phenomenon. The region where pretrained networks arrive is smaller, suggesting that pretraining reduces the variance of the estimation process, which can in turn reduce the risk of severe over fitting. In other words, unsupervised pretraining initializes neural network parameters into a region that they do not escape, and the results following this initialization are more consistent and less likely to be very bad than without this initialization.

Erhan et al. (2010) also provide some answers to *when* pretraining works best—the mean and variance of the test error were most reduced by pretraining for deeper networks. Keep in mind that these experiments were performed before the invention and popularization of modern techniques for training very deep networks (rectified linear units, dropout and batch normalization) so less is known about the effect of unsupervised pretraining in conjunction with contemporary approaches.

An important question is how unsupervised pretraining can act as a regularizer. One hypothesis is that pretraining encourages the learning algorithm to discover features that relate to the underlying causes that generate the observed data. This is an important idea motivating many other algorithms besides unsupervised pretraining and is described further in section 15.3.

Compared to other forms of unsupervised learning, unsupervised pretraining has the disadvantage of operating with two separate training phases. Many regularization strategies have the advantage of allowing the user to control the strength of the regularization by adjusting the value of a single hyperparameter. Unsupervised pretraining does not offer a clear way to adjust the the strength of the regularization arising from the unsupervised stage. Instead, there are very many hyperparameters, whose effect may be measured after the fact but is often difficult to predict ahead of time. When we perform unsupervised and supervised

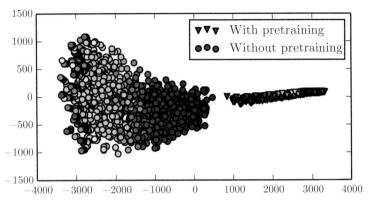

Figure 15.1: Visualization via nonlinear projection of the learning trajectories of different neural networks in *function space* (not parameter space, to avoid the issue of many-to-one mappings from parameter vectors to functions), with different random initializations and with or without unsupervised pretraining. Each point corresponds to a different neural network at a particular time during its training process. This figure is adapted with permission from Erhan et al. (2010). A coordinate in function space is an infinite-dimensional vector associating every input x with an output y. Erhan et al. (2010) made a linear projection to high-dimensional space by concatenating the y for many specific x points. They then made a further nonlinear projection to 2-D by Isomap (Tenenbaum et al., 2000). Color indicates time. All networks are initialized near the center of the plot (corresponding to the region of functions that produce approximately uniform distributions over the class y for most inputs). Over time, learning moves the function outward, to points that make strong predictions. Training consistently terminates in one region when using pretraining and in another, nonoverlapping region when not using pretraining. Isomap tries to preserve global relative distances (and hence volumes) so the small region corresponding to pretrained models may indicate that the pretraining-based estimator has reduced variance.

learning simultaneously, instead of using the pretraining strategy, there is a single hyperparameter, usually a coefficient attached to the unsupervised cost, that determines how strongly the unsupervised objective will regularize the supervised model. One can always predictably obtain less regularization by decreasing this coefficient. In unsupervised pretraining, there is not a way of flexibly adapting the strength of the regularization—either the supervised model is initialized to pretrained parameters, or it is not.

Another disadvantage of having two separate training phases is that each phase has its own hyperparameters. The performance of the second phase usually cannot be predicted during the first phase, so there is a long delay between proposing hyperparameters for the first phase and being able to update them using feedback from the second phase. The most principled approach is to use validation set error in the supervised phase to select the hyperparameters of the pretraining phase, as discussed in Larochelle et al. (2009). In practice, some hyperparameters, like the number of pretraining iterations, are more conveniently set during the pretraining phase, using early stopping on the unsupervised objective, which is not ideal but is computationally much cheaper than using the supervised objective.

Today, unsupervised pretraining has been largely abandoned, except in the field of natural language processing, where the natural representation of words as one-hot vectors conveys no similarity information and where very large unlabeled sets are available. In that case, the advantage of pretraining is that one can pretrain once on a huge unlabeled set (for example with a corpus containing billions of words), learn a good representation (typically of words, but also of sentences), and then use this representation or fine-tune it for a supervised task for which the training set contains substantially fewer examples. This approach was pioneered by Collobert and Weston (2008b), Turian et al. (2010), and Collobert et al. (2011a) and remains in common use today.

Deep learning techniques based on supervised learning, regularized with dropout or batch normalization, are able to achieve human-level performance on many tasks, but only with extremely large labeled datasets. These same techniques outperform unsupervised pretraining on medium-sized datasets such as CIFAR-10 and MNIST, which have roughly 5,000 labeled examples per class. On extremely small datasets, such as the alternative splicing dataset, Bayesian methods outperform methods based on unsupervised pretraining (Srivastava, 2013). For these reasons, the popularity of unsupervised pretraining has declined. Nevertheless, unsupervised pretraining remains an important milestone in the history of deep learning research and continues to influence contemporary approaches. The idea of pretraining has been generalized to **supervised pretraining**, discussed in section 8.7.4, as a very common approach for transfer learning. Supervised pretraining for transfer learning is popular (Oquab et al., 2014; Yosinski et al., 2014) for use with convolutional networks pretrained on the ImageNet dataset. Practitioners publish the parameters of these trained networks for this purpose, just as pretrained word vectors are published for natural language tasks (Collobert et al., 2011a; Mikolov et al., 2013a).

15.2   Transfer Learning and Domain Adaptation

Transfer learning and domain adaptation refer to the situation where what has been learned in one setting (e.g., distribution P_1) is exploited to improve generalization in another setting (say, distribution P_2). This generalizes the idea presented in the previous section, where we transferred representations between an unsupervised learning task and a supervised learning task.

In **transfer learning**, the learner must perform two or more different tasks, but we assume that many of the factors that explain the variations in P_1 are relevant to the variations that need to be captured for learning P_2. This is typically understood in a supervised learning context, where the input is the same but the target may be of a different nature. For example, we may learn about one set of visual categories, such as cats and dogs, in the first setting, then learn about a different set of visual categories, such as ants and wasps, in the second setting. If there is significantly more data in the first setting (sampled from P_1), then that may help to learn representations that are useful to quickly generalize from only very few examples drawn from P_2. Many visual categories *share* low-level notions of edges and visual shapes, the effects of geometric changes, changes in lighting, and so on. In general, transfer learning, multitask learning (section 7.7), and domain adaptation can be achieved via representation learning when there exist features that are useful for the different settings or tasks, corresponding to underlying factors that appear in more than one setting. This is illustrated in figure 7.2, with shared lower layers and task-dependent upper layers.

Sometimes, however, what is shared among the different tasks is not the semantics of the input but the semantics of the output. For example, a speech recognition system needs to produce valid sentences at the output layer, but the earlier layers near the input may need to recognize very different versions of the same phonemes or subphonemic vocalizations depending on which person is speaking. In cases like these, it makes more sense to share the upper layers (near the output) of the neural network and have a task-specific preprocessing, as illustrated in figure 15.2.

In the related case of **domain adaptation**, the task (and the optimal input-to-output mapping) remains the same between each setting, but the input distribution is slightly different. For example, consider the task of sentiment analysis, which consists of determining whether a comment expresses positive or negative sentiment. Comments posted on the web come from many categories. A domain adaptation scenario can arise when a sentiment predictor trained on customer reviews of media content, such as books, videos and music, is later used to analyze comments about consumer electronics, such as televisions or smartphones. One can imagine that there is an underlying function that tells whether any statement is positive, neutral, or negative, but of course the vocabulary and style may vary from one domain to another, making it more difficult to generalize across domains. Simple unsupervised pretraining (with denoising autoencoders) has been found to be very successful for sentiment analysis with domain adaptation (Glorot et al., 2011b).

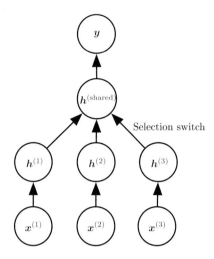

Figure 15.2: Example architecture for multitask or transfer learning when the output variable **y** has the same semantics for all tasks while the input variable **x** has a different meaning (and possibly even a different dimension) for each task (or, for example, each user), called $\mathbf{x}^{(1)}$, $\mathbf{x}^{(2)}$ and $\mathbf{x}^{(3)}$ for three tasks. The lower levels (up to the selection switch) are task-specific, while the upper levels are shared. The lower levels learn to translate their task-specific input into a generic set of features.

A related problem is that of **concept drift**, which we can view as a form of transfer learning due to gradual changes in the data distribution over time. Both concept drift and transfer learning can be viewed as particular forms of multitask learning. While the phrase "multitask learning" typically refers to supervised learning tasks, the more general notion of transfer learning is applicable to unsupervised learning and reinforcement learning as well.

In all these cases, the objective is to take advantage of data from the first setting to extract information that may be useful when learning or even when directly making predictions in the second setting. The core idea of representation learning is that the same representation may be useful in both settings. Using the same representation in both settings allows the representation to benefit from the training data that is available for both tasks.

As mentioned before, unsupervised deep learning for transfer learning has found success in some machine learning competitions (Mesnil et al., 2011; Goodfellow et al., 2011). In the first of these competitions, the experimental setup is the following. Each participant is first given a dataset from the first setting (from distribution P_1), illustrating examples of some set of categories. The participants must use this to learn a good feature space (mapping the raw input to some representation), such that when we apply this learned transformation to inputs from the transfer setting (distribution P_2), a linear classifier can be trained and generalize well from few labeled examples. One of the most striking results found in this competition is that as an architecture makes use of deeper and deeper representations (learned in a purely unsupervised way from data collected in the first setting, P_1), the learning curve on the new categories of the second (transfer) setting P_2 becomes much better. For deep representations, fewer labeled examples of the transfer tasks are necessary to achieve the apparently asymptotic generalization performance.

Two extreme forms of transfer learning are **one-shot learning** and **zero-shot learning**, sometimes also called **zero-data learning**. Only one labeled example of the transfer task is given for one-shot learning, while no labeled examples are given at all for the zero-shot learning task.

One-shot learning (Fei-Fei et al., 2006) is possible because the representation learns to cleanly separate the underlying classes during the first stage. During the transfer learning stage, only one labeled example is needed to infer the label of many possible test examples that all cluster around the same point in representation space. This works to the extent that the factors of variation corresponding to these invariances have been cleanly separated from the other factors, in the learned representation space, and that we have somehow learned which factors do and do not matter when discriminating objects of certain categories.

As an example of a zero-shot learning setting, consider the problem of having a learner read a large collection of text and then solve object recognition problems. It may be possible to recognize a specific object class even without having seen an image of that object if the text describes the object well enough. For example, having read that a cat has four legs and pointy ears, the learner might be able to guess that an image is a cat without having seen a cat before.

Zero-data learning (Larochelle et al., 2008) and zero-shot learning (Palatucci et al., 2009; Socher et al., 2013b) are only possible because additional information has been exploited during training. We can think of the zero-data learning scenario as including three random variables: the traditional inputs $\boldsymbol{x}$, the traditional outputs or targets $\boldsymbol{y}$, and an additional random variable describing the task, T. The model is trained to estimate the conditional distribution $p(\boldsymbol{y} \mid \boldsymbol{x}, T)$, where T is a description of the task we wish the model to perform.

In our example of recognizing cats after having read about cats, the output is a binary variable y with $y = 1$ indicating "yes" and $y = 0$ indicating "no." The task variable T then represents questions to be answered, such as "Is there a cat in this image?" If we have a training set containing unsupervised examples of objects that live in the same space as T, we may be able to infer the meaning of unseen instances of T. In our example of recognizing cats without having seen an image of the cat, it is important that we have had unlabeled text data containing sentences such as "cats have four legs" or "cats have pointy ears."

Zero-shot learning requires T to be represented in a way that allows some sort of generalization. For example, T cannot be just a one-hot code indicating an object category. Socher et al. (2013b) provide instead a distributed representation of object categories by using a learned word embedding for the word associated with each category.

A similar phenomenon happens in machine translation (Klementiev et al., 2012; Mikolov et al., 2013b; Gouws et al., 2014): we have words in one language, and the relationships between words can be learned from unilingual corpora; on the other hand, we have translated sentences that relate words in one language with words in the other. Even though we may not have labeled examples translating word A in language X to word B in language Y, we can generalize and guess a translation for word A because we have learned a distributed representation for words in language X and a distributed representation for words in language Y, then created a link (possibly two-way) relating the two spaces, via training examples consisting of matched pairs of sentences in both languages. This transfer will be most successful if all three ingredients (the two representations and the relations between them) are learned jointly.

Zero-shot learning is a particular form of transfer learning. The same principle explains how one can perform **multimodal learning**, capturing a representation in one modality, a representation in the other, and the relationship (in general a joint distribution) between pairs $(\boldsymbol{x}, \boldsymbol{y})$ consisting of one observation $\boldsymbol{x}$ in one modality and another observation $\boldsymbol{y}$ in the other modality (Srivastava and Salakhutdinov, 2012). By learning all three sets of parameters (from $\boldsymbol{x}$ to its representation, from $\boldsymbol{y}$ to its representation, and the relationship between the two representations), concepts in one representation are anchored in the other, and vice versa, allowing one to meaningfully generalize to new pairs. The procedure is illustrated in figure 15.3.

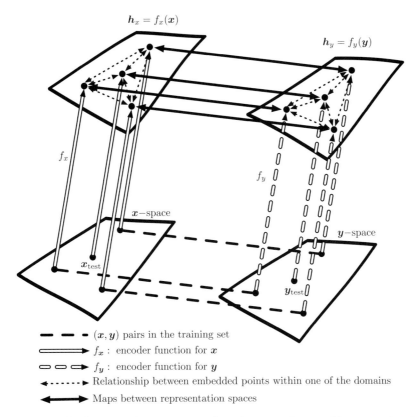

$$\boldsymbol{h}_x = f_x(\boldsymbol{x})$$

$$\boldsymbol{h}_y = f_y(\boldsymbol{y})$$

- - - - $(\boldsymbol{x}, \boldsymbol{y})$ pairs in the training set
⇒ f_x : encoder function for $\boldsymbol{x}$
⊂⊃⊃⇒ f_y : encoder function for $\boldsymbol{y}$
◄·······► Relationship between embedded points within one of the domains
◄━━━━► Maps between representation spaces

Figure 15.3: Transfer learning between two domains $\boldsymbol{x}$ and $\boldsymbol{y}$ enables zero-shot learning. Labeled or unlabeled examples of $\boldsymbol{x}$ allow one to learn a representation function f_x and similarly with examples of $\boldsymbol{y}$ to learn f_y. Each application of the f_x and f_y functions appears as an upward arrow, with the style of the arrows indicating which function is applied. Distance in $\boldsymbol{h}_x$ space provides a similarity metric between any pair of points in $\boldsymbol{x}$ space that may be more meaningful than distance in $\boldsymbol{x}$ space. Likewise, distance in $\boldsymbol{h}_y$ space provides a similarity metric between any pair of points in $\boldsymbol{y}$ space. Both of these similarity functions are indicated with dotted bidirectional arrows. Labeled examples (dashed horizontal lines) are pairs $(\boldsymbol{x}, \boldsymbol{y})$ that allow one to learn a one-way or two-way map (solid bidirectional arrow) between the representations $f_x(\boldsymbol{x})$ and the representations $f_y(\boldsymbol{y})$ and to anchor these representations to each other. Zero-data learning is then enabled as follows. One can associate an image $\boldsymbol{x}_{\text{test}}$ to a word $\boldsymbol{y}_{\text{test}}$, even if no image of that word was ever presented, simply because word representations $f_y(\boldsymbol{y}_{\text{test}})$ and image representations $f_x(\boldsymbol{x}_{\text{test}})$ can be related to each other via the maps between representation spaces. It works because, although that image and that word were never paired, their respective feature vectors $f_x(\boldsymbol{x}_{\text{test}})$ and $f_y(\boldsymbol{y}_{\text{test}})$ have been related to each other. Figure inspired from suggestion by Hrant Khachatrian.

15.3   Semi-Supervised Disentangling of Causal Factors

An important question about representation learning is: what makes one representation better than another? One hypothesis is that an ideal representation is one in which the features within the representation correspond to the underlying causes of the observed data, with separate features or directions in feature space corresponding to different causes, so that the representation disentangles the causes from one another. This hypothesis motivates approaches in which we first seek a good representation for $p(\boldsymbol{x})$. Such a representation may also be a good representation for computing $p(\boldsymbol{y} \mid \boldsymbol{x})$ if $\boldsymbol{y}$ is among the most salient causes of $\boldsymbol{x}$. This idea has guided a large amount of deep learning research since at least the 1990s (Becker and Hinton, 1992; Hinton and Sejnowski, 1999) in more detail. For other arguments about when semi-supervised learning can outperform pure supervised learning, we refer the reader to section 1.2 of Chapelle et al. (2006).

In other approaches to representation learning, we have often been concerned with a representation that is easy to model—for example, one whose entries are sparse or independent from each other. A representation that cleanly separates the underlying causal factors may not necessarily be one that is easy to model. However, a further part of the hypothesis motivating semi-supervised learning via unsupervised representation learning is that for many AI tasks, these two properties coincide: once we are able to obtain the underlying explanations for what we observe, it generally becomes easy to isolate individual attributes from the others. Specifically, if a representation $\boldsymbol{h}$ represents many of the underlying causes of the observed $\boldsymbol{x}$, and the outputs $\boldsymbol{y}$ are among the most salient causes, then it is easy to predict $\boldsymbol{y}$ from $\boldsymbol{h}$.

First, let us see how semi-supervised learning can fail because unsupervised learning of $p(\mathbf{x})$ is of no help to learning $p(\mathbf{y} \mid \mathbf{x})$. Consider, for example, the case where $p(\mathbf{x})$ is uniformly distributed and we want to learn $f(\boldsymbol{x}) = \mathbb{E}[\mathbf{y} \mid \boldsymbol{x}]$. Clearly, observing a training set of $\boldsymbol{x}$ values alone gives us no information about $p(\mathbf{y} \mid \mathbf{x})$.

Next, let us see a simple example of how semi-supervised learning can succeed. Consider the situation where $\mathbf{x}$ arises from a mixture, with one mixture component per value of $\mathbf{y}$, as illustrated in figure 15.4. If the mixture components are well separated, then modeling $p(\mathbf{x})$ reveals precisely where each component is, and a single labeled example of each class will then be enough to perfectly learn $p(\mathbf{y} \mid \mathbf{x})$. But more generally, what could tie $p(\mathbf{y} \mid \mathbf{x})$ and $p(\mathbf{x})$ together?

If $\mathbf{y}$ is closely associated with one of the causal factors of $\mathbf{x}$, then $p(\mathbf{x})$ and $p(\mathbf{y} \mid \mathbf{x})$ will be strongly tied, and unsupervised representation learning that tries to disentangle the underlying factors of variation is likely to be useful as a semi-supervised learning strategy.

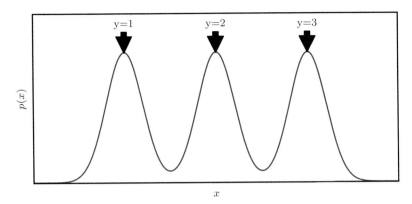

Figure 15.4: Mixture model. Example of a density over x that is a mixture over three components. The component identity is an underlying explanatory factor, y. Because the mixture components (e.g., natural object classes in image data) are statistically salient, just modeling $p(x)$ in an unsupervised way with no labeled example already reveals the factor y.

Consider the assumption that $\mathbf{y}$ is one of the causal factors of $\mathbf{x}$, and let $\mathbf{h}$ represent all those factors. The true generative process can be conceived as structured according to this directed graphical model, with $\mathbf{h}$ as the parent of $\mathbf{x}$:

$$p(\mathbf{h}, \mathbf{x}) = p(\mathbf{x} \mid \mathbf{h})p(\mathbf{h}). \tag{15.1}$$

As a consequence, the data has marginal probability

$$p(\boldsymbol{x}) = \mathbb{E}_{\mathbf{h}}p(\boldsymbol{x} \mid \boldsymbol{h}). \tag{15.2}$$

From this straightforward observation, we conclude that the best possible model of $\mathbf{x}$ (from a generalization point of view) is the one that uncovers the above "true" structure, with $\boldsymbol{h}$ as a latent variable that explains the observed variations in $\boldsymbol{x}$. The "ideal" representation learning discussed above should thus recover these latent factors. If $\mathbf{y}$ is one of these (or closely related to one of them), then it will be easy to learn to predict $\mathbf{y}$ from such a representation. We also see that the conditional distribution of $\mathbf{y}$ given $\mathbf{x}$ is tied by Bayes' rule to the components in the above equation:

$$p(\mathbf{y} \mid \mathbf{x}) = \frac{p(\mathbf{x} \mid \mathbf{y})p(\mathbf{y})}{p(\mathbf{x})}. \tag{15.3}$$

Thus the marginal $p(\mathbf{x})$ is intimately tied to the conditional $p(\mathbf{y} \mid \mathbf{x})$, and knowledge of the structure of the former should be helpful to learn the latter. Therefore, in situations respecting these assumptions, semi-supervised learning should improve performance.

An important research problem regards the fact that most observations are formed by an extremely large number of underlying causes. Suppose $\mathbf{y} = \mathrm{h}_i$, but the unsupervised learner does not know which h_i. The brute force solution is for an unsupervised learner to learn a representation that captures *all* the reasonably salient generative factors h_j and disentangles them from each other, thus making it easy to predict $\mathbf{y}$ from $\mathbf{h}$, regardless of which h_i is associated with $\mathbf{y}$.

In practice, the brute force solution is not feasible because it is not possible to capture all or most of the factors of variation that influence an observation. For example, in a visual scene, should the representation always encode all the smallest objects in the background? It is a well-documented psychological phenomenon that human beings fail to perceive changes in their environment that are not immediately relevant to the task they are performing—see, for example Simons and Levin (1998). An important research frontier in semi-supervised learning is determining *what* to encode in each situation. Currently, two of the main strategies for dealing with a large number of underlying causes are to use a supervised learning signal at the same time as the unsupervised learning signal so that the model will choose to capture the most relevant factors of variation, or to use much larger representations if using purely unsupervised learning.

An emerging strategy for unsupervised learning is to modify the definition of which underlying causes are most salient. Historically, autoencoders and generative models have been trained to optimize a fixed criterion, often similar to mean squared error. These fixed criteria determine which causes are considered salient. For example, mean squared error applied to the pixels of an image implicitly specifies that an underlying cause is only salient if it significantly changes the brightness of a large number of pixels. This can be problematic if the task we wish to solve involves interacting with small objects. See figure 15.5 for an example of a robotics task in which an autoencoder has failed to learn to encode a small ping pong ball. This same robot is capable of successfully interacting with larger objects, such as baseballs, which are more salient according to mean squared error.

Other definitions of salience are possible. For example, if a group of pixels follows a highly recognizable pattern, even if that pattern does not involve extreme brightness or darkness, then that pattern could be considered extremely salient. One way to implement such a definition of salience is to use a recently developed approach called **generative adversarial networks** (Goodfellow et al., 2014c). In this approach, a generative model is trained to fool a feedforward classifier. The feedforward classifier attempts to recognize all samples from the generative model as being fake and all samples from the training set as being real. In this framework, any structured pattern that the feedforward network can recognize is highly salient.

Input | Reconstruction

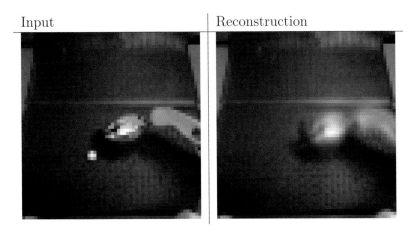

Figure 15.5: An autoencoder trained with mean squared error for a robotics task has failed to reconstruct a ping pong ball. The existence of the ping pong ball and all its spatial coordinates are important underlying causal factors that generate the image and are relevant to the robotics task. Unfortunately, the autoencoder has limited capacity, and the training with mean squared error did not identify the ping pong ball as being salient enough to encode. Images graciously provided by Chelsea Finn.

The generative adversarial network is described in more detail in section 20.10.4. For the purposes of the present discussion, it is sufficient to understand that the networks *learn* how to determine what is salient. Lotter et al. (2015) showed that models trained to generate images of human heads will often neglect to generate the ears when trained with mean squared error, but will successfully generate the ears when trained with the adversarial framework. Because the ears are not extremely bright or dark compared to the surrounding skin, they are not especially salient according to mean squared error loss, but their highly recognizable shape and consistent position means that a feedforward network can easily learn to detect them, making them highly salient under the generative adversarial framework. See figure 15.6 for example images. Generative adversarial networks are only one step toward determining which factors should be represented. We expect that future research will discover better ways of determining which factors to represent and develop mechanisms for representing different factors depending on the task.

A benefit of learning the underlying causal factors, as pointed out by Schölkopf et al. (2012), is that if the true generative process has $\mathbf{x}$ as an effect and $\mathbf{y}$ as a cause, then modeling $p(\mathbf{x} \mid \mathbf{y})$ is robust to changes in $p(\mathbf{y})$. If the cause-effect relationship were reversed, this would not be true, since by Bayes' rule, $p(\mathbf{x} \mid \mathbf{y})$ would be sensitive to changes in $p(\mathbf{y})$. Very often, when we consider changes in

Ground Truth   MSE   Adversarial

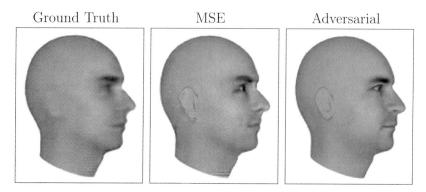

Figure 15.6: Predictive generative networks provide an example of the importance of learning which features are salient. In this example, the predictive generative network has been trained to predict the appearance of a 3-D model of a human head at a specific viewing angle. *(Left)*Ground truth. This is the correct image, which the network should emit. *(Center)*Image produced by a predictive generative network trained with mean squared error alone. Because the ears do not cause an extreme difference in brightness compared to the neighboring skin, they were not sufficiently salient for the model to learn to represent them. *(Right)*Image produced by a model trained with a combination of mean squared error and adversarial loss. Using this learned cost function, the ears are salient because they follow a predictable pattern. Learning which underlying causes are important and relevant enough to model is an important active area of research. Figures graciously provided by Lotter et al. (2015).

distribution due to different domains, temporal nonstationarity, or changes in the nature of the task, *the causal mechanisms remain invariant* ("the laws of the universe are constant"), while the marginal distribution over the underlying causes can change. Hence, better generalization and robustness to all kinds of changes can be expected via learning a generative model that attempts to recover the causal factors $\mathbf{h}$ and $p(\mathbf{x} \mid \mathbf{h})$.

15.4 Distributed Representation

Distributed representations of concepts—representations composed of many elements that can be set separately from each other—are one of the most important tools for representation learning. Distributed representations are powerful because they can use n features with k values to describe k^n different concepts. As we have seen throughout this book, neural networks with multiple hidden units and probabilistic models with multiple latent variables both make use of the strategy of distributed representation. We now introduce an additional observation. Many deep learning algorithms are motivated by the assumption that the hidden units can learn to represent the underlying causal factors that explain the data, as discussed in section 15.3. Distributed representations are natural for this approach, because each direction in representation space can correspond to the value of a different underlying configuration variable.

An example of a distributed representation is a vector of n binary features, which can take 2^n configurations, each potentially corresponding to a different region in input space, as illustrated in figure 15.7. This can be compared with a *symbolic representation*, where the input is associated with a single symbol or category. If there are n symbols in the dictionary, one can imagine n feature detectors, each corresponding to the detection of the presence of the associated category. In that case only n different configurations of the representation space are possible, carving n different regions in input space, as illustrated in figure 15.8. Such a symbolic representation is also called a one-hot representation, since it can be captured by a binary vector with n bits that are mutually exclusive (only one of them can be active). A symbolic representation is a specific example of the broader class of nondistributed representations, which are representations that may contain many entries but without significant meaningful separate control over each entry.

The following examples of learning algorithms are based on nondistributed representations:

- Clustering methods, including the k-means algorithm: each input point is assigned to exactly one cluster.

- k-nearest neighbors algorithms: one or a few templates or prototype examples are associated with a given input. In the case of $k > 1$, multiple values describe each input, but they cannot be controlled separately from each other, so this does not qualify as a true distributed representation.

- Decision trees: only one leaf (and the nodes on the path from root to leaf) is activated when an input is given.

- Gaussian mixtures and mixtures of experts: the templates (cluster centers) or experts are now associated with a *degree* of activation. As with the k-nearest neighbors algorithm, each input is represented with multiple values, but those values cannot readily be controlled separately from each other.

- Kernel machines with a Gaussian kernel (or other similarly local kernel): although the degree of activation of each "support vector" or template example is now continuous-valued, the same issue arises as with Gaussian mixtures.

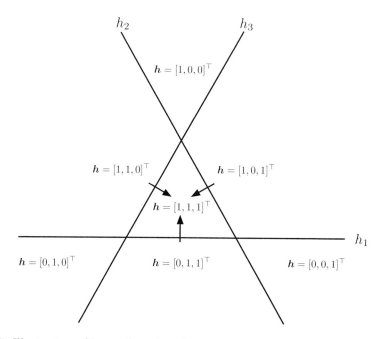

Figure 15.7: Illustration of how a learning algorithm based on a distributed representation breaks up the input space into regions. In this example, there are three binary features h_1, h_2, and h_3. Each feature is defined by thresholding the output of a learned linear transformation. Each feature divides $\mathbb{R}^2$ into two half-planes. Let h_i^+ be the set of input points for which $h_i = 1$, and h_i^- be the set of input points for which $h_i = 0$. In this illustration, each line represents the decision boundary for one h_i, with the corresponding arrow pointing to the h_i^+ side of the boundary. The representation as a whole takes on a unique value at each possible intersection of these half-planes. For example, the representation value $[1, 1, 1]^\top$ corresponds to the region $h_1^+ \cap h_2^+ \cap h_3^+$. Compare this to the non-distributed representations in figure 15.8. In the general case of d input dimensions, a distributed representation divides $\mathbb{R}^d$ by intersecting half-spaces rather than half-planes. The distributed representation with n features assigns unique codes to $O(n^d)$ different regions, while the nearest neighbor algorithm with n examples assigns unique codes to only n regions. The distributed representation is thus able to distinguish exponentially many more regions than the nondistributed one. Keep in mind that not all $\boldsymbol{h}$ values are feasible (there is no $\boldsymbol{h} = \boldsymbol{0}$ in this example), and that a linear classifier on top of the distributed representation is not able to assign different class identities to every neighboring region; even a deep linear-threshold network has a VC dimension of only $O(w \log w)$, where w is the number of weights (Sontag, 1998). The combination of a powerful representation layer and a weak classifier layer can be a strong regularizer; a classifier trying to learn the concept of "person" versus "not a person" does not need to assign a different class to an input represented as "woman with glasses" than it assigns to an input represented as "man without glasses." This capacity constraint encourages each classifier to focus on few h_i and encourages $\boldsymbol{h}$ to learn to represent the classes in a linearly separable way.

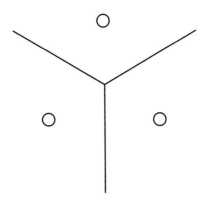

Figure 15.8: Illustration of how the nearest neighbor algorithm breaks up the input space into different regions. The nearest neighbor algorithm provides an example of a learning algorithm based on a nondistributed representation. Different non-distributed algorithms may have different geometry, but they typically break the input space into regions, *with a separate set of parameters for each region.* The advantage of a nondistributed approach is that, given enough parameters, it can fit the training set without solving a difficult optimization algorithm, because it is straightforward to choose a different output *independently* for each region. The disadvantage is that such nondistributed models generalize only locally via the smoothness prior, making it difficult to learn a complicated function with more peaks and troughs than the available number of examples. Contrast this with a distributed representation, figure 15.7.

- Language or translation models based on n-grams: the set of contexts (sequences of symbols) is partitioned according to a tree structure of suffixes. A leaf may correspond to the last two words being w_1 and w_2, for example. Separate parameters are estimated for each leaf of the tree (with some sharing being possible).

For some of these nondistributed algorithms, the output is not constant by parts but instead interpolates between neighboring regions. The relationship between the number of parameters (or examples) and the number of regions they can define remains linear.

An important related concept that distinguishes a distributed representation from a symbolic one is that *generalization arises due to shared attributes* between different concepts. As pure symbols, "cat" and "dog" are as far from each other as any other two symbols. However, if one associates them with a meaningful distributed representation, then many of the things that can be said about cats can generalize to dogs and vice versa. For example, our distributed representation may contain entries such as "has_fur" or "number_of_legs" that have the same value for the embedding of both "cat" and "dog." Neural language models that operate on distributed representations of words generalize much better than other models that operate directly on one-hot representations of words, as discussed in section 12.4. Distributed representations induce a rich *similarity space*, in which semantically close concepts (or inputs) are close in distance, a property that is absent from purely symbolic representations.

When and why can there be a statistical advantage from using a distributed representation as part of a learning algorithm? Distributed representations can have a statistical advantage when an apparently complicated structure can be compactly represented using a small number of parameters. Some traditional nondistributed learning algorithms generalize only due to the smoothness assumption, which states that if $u \approx v$, then the target function f to be learned has the property that $f(u) \approx f(v)$ in general. There are many ways of formalizing such an assumption, but the end result is that if we have an example (x, y) for which we know that $f(x) \approx y$, then we choose an estimator $\hat{f}$ that approximately satisfies these constraints while changing as little as possible when we move to a nearby input $x + \epsilon$. This assumption is clearly very useful, but it suffers from the curse of dimensionality: to learn a target function that increases and decreases many times in many different regions,[1] we may need a number of examples that is at least as large as the number of distinguishable regions. One can think of each of these regions as a category or symbol: by having a separate degree of freedom for each symbol (or region), we can learn an arbitrary decoder mapping from symbol to value. However, this does not allow us to generalize to new symbols for new regions.

If we are lucky, there may be some regularity in the target function, besides being smooth. For example, a convolutional network with max pooling can recognize an object regardless of its location in the image, even though spatial translation of the object may not correspond to smooth transformations in the input space.

Let us examine a special case of a distributed representation learning algorithm, which extracts binary features by thresholding linear functions of the input. Each binary feature in this representation divides $\mathbb{R}^d$ into a pair of half-spaces, as illustrated in figure 15.7. The exponentially large number of intersections of n of the corresponding half-spaces determines how many regions this distributed representation learner can distinguish. How many regions are generated by an arrangement of n hyperplanes in $\mathbb{R}^d$? By applying a general result concerning the

---

[1] Potentially, we may want to learn a function whose behavior is distinct in exponentially many regions: in a d-dimensional space with at least 2 different values to distinguish per dimension, we might want f to differ in 2^d different regions, requiring $O(2^d)$ training examples.

intersection of hyperplanes (Zaslavsky, 1975), one can show (Pascanu et al., 2014b) that the number of regions this binary feature representation can distinguish is

$$\sum_{j=0}^{d} \binom{n}{j} = O(n^d). \tag{15.4}$$

Therefore, we see a growth that is exponential in the input size and polynomial in the number of hidden units.

This provides a geometric argument to explain the generalization power of distributed representation: with $O(nd)$ parameters (for n linear threshold features in $\mathbb{R}^d$), we can distinctly represent $O(n^d)$ regions in input space. If instead we made no assumption at all about the data, and used a representation with one unique symbol for each region, and separate parameters for each symbol to recognize its corresponding portion of $\mathbb{R}^d$, then specifying $O(n^d)$ regions would require $O(n^d)$ examples. More generally, the argument in favor of the distributed representation could be extended to the case where instead of using linear threshold units we use nonlinear, possibly continuous, feature extractors for each of the attributes in the distributed representation. The argument in this case is that if a parametric transformation with k parameters can learn about r regions in input space, with $k \ll r$, and if obtaining such a representation was useful to the task of interest, then we could potentially generalize much better in this way than in a nondistributed setting, where we would need $O(r)$ examples to obtain the same features and associated partitioning of the input space into r regions. Using fewer parameters to represent the model means that we have fewer parameters to fit, and thus require far fewer training examples to generalize well.

A further part of the argument for why models based on distributed representations generalize well is that their capacity remains limited despite being able to distinctly encode so many different regions. For example, the VC dimension of a neural network of linear threshold units is only $O(w \log w)$, where w is the number of weights (Sontag, 1998). This limitation arises because, while we can assign very many unique codes to representation space, we cannot use absolutely all the code space, nor can we learn arbitrary functions mapping from the representation space $\boldsymbol{h}$ to the output $\boldsymbol{y}$ using a linear classifier. The use of a distributed representation combined with a linear classifier thus expresses a prior belief that the classes to be recognized are linearly separable as a function of the underlying causal factors captured by $\boldsymbol{h}$. We will typically want to learn categories such as the set of all images of all green objects or the set of all images of cars, but not categories that require nonlinear XOR logic. For example, we typically do not want to partition the data into the set of all red cars and green trucks as one class and the set of all green cars and red trucks as another class.

The ideas discussed so far have been abstract, but they may be experimentally validated. Zhou et al. (2015) find that hidden units in a deep convolutional network trained on the ImageNet and Places benchmark datasets learn features that are often interpretable, corresponding to a label that humans would naturally assign. In practice it is certainly not always the case that hidden units learn something that has a simple linguistic name, but it is interesting to see this emerge near the top levels of the best computer vision deep networks. What such features have in common is that one could imagine *learning about each of them without having to see all the configurations of all the others*. Radford et al. (2015) demonstrated that a generative model can learn a representation of images of faces, with separate directions in representation space capturing different underlying factors of variation. Figure 15.9 demonstrates that one direction in representation space corresponds to whether the person is male or female, while another corresponds to whether the person is wearing glasses. These features were discovered automatically, not fixed a priori. There is no need to have labels for the hidden unit classifiers: gradient descent on an objective function of interest naturally learns semantically interesting features, as long as the task requires such features. We can learn about

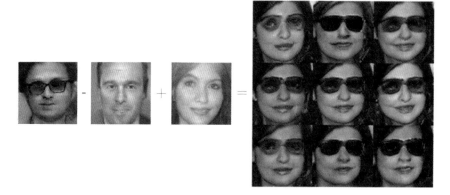

Figure 15.9: A generative model has learned a distributed representation that disentangles the concept of gender from the concept of wearing glasses. If we begin with the representation of the concept of a man with glasses, then subtract the vector representing the concept of a man without glasses, and finally add the vector representing the concept of a woman without glasses, we obtain the vector representing the concept of a woman with glasses. The generative model correctly decodes all these representation vectors to images that may be recognized as belonging to the correct class. Images reproduced with permission from Radford et al. (2015).

the distinction between male and female, or about the presence or absence of glasses, without having to characterize all the configurations of the $n - 1$ other features by examples covering all these combinations of values. This form of statistical separability is what allows one to generalize to new configurations of a person's features that have never been seen during training.

15.5 Exponential Gains from Depth

We have seen in section 6.4.1 that multilayer perceptrons are universal approximators, and that some functions can be represented by exponentially smaller deep networks compared to shallow networks. This decrease in model size leads to improved statistical efficiency. In this section, we describe how similar results apply more generally to other kinds of models with distributed hidden representations.

In section 15.4, we saw an example of a generative model that learned about the explanatory factors underlying images of faces, including the person's gender and whether they are wearing glasses. The generative model that accomplished this task was based on a deep neural network. It would not be reasonable to expect a shallow network, such as a linear network, to learn the complicated relationship between these abstract explanatory factors and the pixels in the image. In this and other AI tasks, the factors that can be chosen almost independently from each other yet still correspond to meaningful inputs are more likely to be very high level and related in highly nonlinear ways to the input. We argue that this demands *deep* distributed representations, where the higher level features (seen as functions of the input) or factors (seen as generative causes) are obtained through the composition of many nonlinearities.

It has been proved in many different settings that organizing computation through the composition of many nonlinearities and a hierarchy of reused features can give an exponential boost to statistical efficiency, on top of the exponential boost given by using a distributed representation. Many kinds of networks (e.g., with saturating nonlinearities, Boolean gates, sum/products, or RBF units) with a single hidden layer can be shown to be universal approximators. A model family that is a universal approximator can approximate a large class of functions (including all continuous functions) up to any nonzero tolerance level, given enough hidden units. However, the required number of hidden units may be very large. Theoretical results concerning the expressive power of deep architectures state that there are families of functions that can be represented efficiently by an architecture of depth k, but that would require an exponential number of hidden units (with respect to the input size) with insufficient depth (depth 2 or depth $k - 1$).

In section 6.4.1, we saw that deterministic feedforward networks are universal approximators of functions. Many structured probabilistic models with a single hidden layer of latent variables, including restricted Boltzmann machines and deep belief networks, are universal approximators of probability distributions (Le Roux and Bengio, 2008, 2010; Montúfar and Ay, 2011; Montúfar, 2014; Krause et al., 2013).

In section 6.4.1, we saw that a sufficiently deep feedforward network can have an exponential advantage over a network that is too shallow. Such results can also be obtained for other models such as probabilistic models. One such probabilistic model is the **sum-product network**, or SPN (Poon and Domingos, 2011). These models use polynomial circuits to compute the probability distribution over a set of random variables. Delalleau and Bengio (2011) showed that there exist probability distributions for which a minimum depth of SPN is required to avoid needing an exponentially large model. Later, Martens and Medabalimi (2014) showed that there are significant differences between every two finite depths of SPN, and that some of the constraints used to make SPNs tractable may limit their representational power.

Another interesting development is a set of theoretical results for the expressive power of families of deep circuits related to convolutional nets, highlighting an exponential advantage for the deep circuit even when the shallow circuit is allowed to only approximate the function computed by the deep circuit (Cohen et al., 2015). By comparison, previous theoretical work made claims regarding only the case where the shallow circuit must exactly replicate particular functions.

15.6 Providing Clues to Discover Underlying Causes

To close this chapter, we come back to one of our original questions: what makes one representation better than another? One answer, first introduced in section 15.3, is that an ideal representation is one that disentangles the underlying causal factors of variation that generated the data, especially those factors that are relevant to our applications. Most strategies for representation learning are based on introducing clues that help the learning find these underlying factors of variations. The clues can help the learner separate these observed factors from the others. Supervised learning provides a very strong clue: a label y, presented with each x, that usually specifies the value of at least one of the factors of variation directly. More generally, to make use of abundant unlabeled data, representation learning makes use of other, less direct hints about the underlying factors. These hints take the form of implicit prior beliefs that we, the designers of the learning algorithm, impose in order to guide the learner. Results such as the no free lunch theorem show that regularization strategies are necessary to obtain good generalization. While it is impossible to find a universally superior regularization strategy, one goal of deep learning is to find a set of fairly generic regularization strategies that are applicable to a wide variety of AI tasks, similar to the tasks that people and animals are able to solve.

We provide here a list of these generic regularization strategies. The list is clearly not exhaustive but gives some concrete examples of how learning algorithms can be encouraged to discover features that correspond to underlying factors. This list was introduced in section 3.1 of Bengio et al. (2013d) and has been partially expanded here.

- *Smoothness*: This is the assumption that $f(\boldsymbol{x}+\epsilon\boldsymbol{d}) \approx f(\boldsymbol{x})$ for unit $\boldsymbol{d}$ and small ϵ. This assumption allows the learner to generalize from training examples to nearby points in input space. Many machine learning algorithms leverage this idea, but it is insufficient to overcome the curse of dimensionality.

- *Linearity*: Many learning algorithms assume that relationships between some variables are linear. This allows the algorithm to make predictions even very far from the observed data, but can sometimes lead to overly extreme predictions. Most simple machine learning algorithms that do not make the smoothness assumption instead make the linearity assumption. These are in fact different assumptions—linear functions with large weights applied to high-dimensional spaces may not be very smooth. See Goodfellow et al. (2014b) for a further discussion of the limitations of the linearity assumption.

- *Multiple explanatory factors*: Many representation learning algorithms are motivated by the assumption that the data is generated by multiple underlying explanatory factors, and that most tasks can be solved easily given the state of each of these factors. Section 15.3 describes how this view motivates semi-supervised learning via representation learning. Learning the structure of $p(\boldsymbol{x})$ requires learning some of the same features that are useful for modeling $p(\boldsymbol{y} \mid \boldsymbol{x})$ because both refer to the same underlying explanatory factors. Section 15.4 describes how this view motivates the use of distributed representations, with separate directions in representation space corresponding to separate factors of variation.

- *Causal factors*: The model is constructed in such a way that it treats the factors of variation described by the learned representation $\boldsymbol{h}$ as the causes of the observed data $\boldsymbol{x}$, and not vice versa. As discussed in section 15.3, this is advantageous for semi-supervised learning and makes the learned model more robust when the distribution over the underlying causes changes or when we use the model for a new task.

- *Depth, or a hierarchical organization of explanatory factors*: High-level, abstract concepts can be defined in terms of simple concepts, forming a hierarchy. From another point of view, the use of a deep architecture expresses our belief that the task should be accomplished via a multistep program, with each step referring back to the output of the processing accomplished via previous steps.

- *Shared factors across tasks*: When we have many tasks corresponding to different y_i variables sharing the same input $\mathbf{x}$, or when each task is associated with a subset or a function $f^{(i)}(\mathbf{x})$ of a global input $\mathbf{x}$, the assumption is that each y_i is associated with a different subset from a common pool of relevant factors $\mathbf{h}$. Because these subsets overlap, learning all the $P(y_i \mid \mathbf{x})$ via a shared intermediate representation $P(\mathbf{h} \mid \mathbf{x})$ allows sharing of statistical strength between the tasks.

- *Manifolds*: Probability mass concentrates, and the regions in which it concentrates are locally connected and occupy a tiny volume. In the continuous case, these regions can be approximated by low-dimensional manifolds with a much smaller dimensionality than the original space where the data live. Many machine learning algorithms behave sensibly only on this manifold (Goodfellow et al., 2014b). Some machine learning algorithms, especially autoencoders, attempt to explicitly learn the structure of the manifold.

- *Natural clustering*: Many machine learning algorithms assume that each connected manifold in the input space may be assigned to a single class. The data may lie on many disconnected manifolds, but the class remains constant within each one of these. This assumption motivates a variety of learning algorithms, including tangent propagation, double backprop, the manifold tangent classifier and adversarial training.

- *Temporal and spatial coherence*: Slow feature analysis and related algorithms make the assumption that the most important explanatory factors change slowly over time, or at least that it is easier to predict the true underlying explanatory factors than to predict raw observations such as pixel values. See section 13.3 for further description of this approach.

- *Sparsity*: Most features should presumably not be relevant to describing most inputs—there is no need to use a feature that detects elephant trunks when representing an image of a cat. It is therefore reasonable to impose a prior that any feature that can be interpreted as "present" or "absent" should be absent most of the time.

- *Simplicity of factor dependencies*: In good high-level representations, the factors are related to each other through simple dependencies. The simplest possible is marginal independence, $P(\mathbf{h}) = \prod_i P(\mathbf{h}_i)$, but linear dependencies or those captured by a shallow autoencoder are also reasonable assumptions. This can be seen in many laws of physics and is assumed when plugging a linear predictor or a factorized prior on top of a learned representation.

The concept of representation learning ties together all the many forms of deep learning. Feedforward and recurrent networks, autoencoders and deep probabilistic models all learn and exploit representations. Learning the best possible representation remains an exciting avenue of research.

16

Structured Probabilistic Models for Deep Learning

Deep learning draws on many modeling formalisms that researchers can use to guide their design efforts and describe their algorithms. One of these formalisms is the idea of **structured probabilistic models**. We discuss structured probabilistic models briefly in section 3.14. That brief presentation is sufficient to understand how to use structured probabilistic models as a language to describe some of the algorithms in part II. Now, in part III, structured probabilistic models are a key ingredient of many of the most important research topics in deep learning. To prepare to discuss these research ideas, in this chapter, we describe structured probabilistic models in much greater detail. This chapter is intended to be self-contained; the reader does not need to review the earlier introduction before continuing with this chapter.

A structured probabilistic model is a way of describing a probability distribution, using a graph to describe which random variables in the probability distribution interact with each other directly. Here we use "graph" in the graph theory sense—a set of vertices connected to one another by a set of edges. Because the structure of the model is defined by a graph, these models are often also referred to as **graphical models**.

The graphical models research community is large and has developed many different models, training algorithms, and inference algorithms. In this chapter, we provide basic background on some of the most central ideas of graphical models, with an emphasis on the concepts that have proved most useful to the deep learning research community. If you already have a strong background in graphical models, you may wish to skip most of this chapter. However, even a graphical model expert may benefit from reading the final section of this chapter, section 16.7, in which we highlight some of the unique ways in which graphical models are used for deep learning algorithms. Deep learning practitioners tend to use very different model structures, learning algorithms and inference procedures than are commonly used by the rest of the graphical models research community. In this chapter, we identify these differences in preferences and explain the reasons for them.

We first describe the challenges of building large-scale probabilistic models. Next, we describe how to use a graph to describe the structure of a probability distribution. While this approach allows us to overcome many challenges, it is not without its own complications. One of the major difficulties in graphical modeling is understanding which variables need to be able to interact directly, that is, which graph structures are most suitable for a given problem. In section 16.5, we outline two approaches to resolving this difficulty by learning about the dependencies. Finally, we close with a discussion of the unique emphasis that deep learning practitioners place on specific approaches to graphical modeling, in section 16.7.

16.1 The Challenge of Unstructured Modeling

The goal of deep learning is to scale machine learning to the kinds of challenges needed to solve artificial intelligence. This means being able to understand high-dimensional data with rich structure. For example, we would like AI algorithms to be able to understand natural images,[1] audio waveforms representing speech, and documents containing multiple words and punctuation characters.

Classification algorithms can take an input from such a rich high-dimensional distribution and summarize it with a categorical label—what object is in a photo, what word is spoken in a recording, what topic a document is about. The process of classification discards most of the information in the input and produces a single output (or a probability distribution over values of that single output). The classifier is also often able to ignore many parts of the input. For example, when recognizing an object in a photo, it is usually possible to ignore the background of the photo.

It is possible to ask probabilistic models to do many other tasks. These tasks are often more expensive than classification. Some of them require producing multiple output values. Most require a complete understanding of the entire structure of the input, with no option to ignore sections of it. These tasks include the following:

- **Density estimation**: Given an input $\boldsymbol{x}$, the machine learning system returns an estimate of the true density $p(\boldsymbol{x})$ under the data-generating distribution.

---

[1] A **natural image** is an image that might be captured by a camera in a reasonably ordinary environment, as opposed to a synthetically rendered image, a screenshot of a web page, etc.

This requires only a single output, but it also requires a complete understanding of the entire input. If even one element of the vector is unusual, the system must assign it a low probability.

- **Denoising**: Given a damaged or incorrectly observed input $\tilde{\boldsymbol{x}}$, the machine learning system returns an estimate of the original or correct $\boldsymbol{x}$. For example, the machine learning system might be asked to remove dust or scratches from an old photograph. This requires multiple outputs (every element of the estimated clean example $\boldsymbol{x}$) and an understanding of the entire input (since even one damaged area will still reveal the final estimate as being damaged).

- **Missing value imputation**: Given the observations of some elements of $\boldsymbol{x}$, the model is asked to return estimates of or a probability distribution over some or all of the unobserved elements of $\boldsymbol{x}$. This requires multiple outputs. Because the model could be asked to restore any of the elements of $\boldsymbol{x}$, it must understand the entire input.

- **Sampling**: The model generates new samples from the distribution $p(\boldsymbol{x})$. Applications include speech synthesis, that is, producing new waveforms that sound like natural human speech. This requires multiple output values and a good model of the entire input. If the samples have even one element drawn from the wrong distribution, then the sampling process is wrong.

For an example of a sampling task using small natural images, see figure 16.1.

Modeling a rich distribution over thousands or millions of random variables is a challenging task, both computationally and statistically. Suppose we wanted to model only binary variables. This is the simplest possible case, and yet already it seems overwhelming. For a small 32×32 pixel color (RGB) image, there are 2^{3072} possible binary images of this form. This number is over 10^{800} times larger than the estimated number of atoms in the universe.

In general, if we wish to model a distribution over a random vector $\mathbf{x}$ containing n discrete variables capable of taking on k values each, then the naive approach of representing $P(\mathbf{x})$ by storing a lookup table with one probability value per possible outcome requires k^n parameters!

This is not feasible for several reasons:

- *Memory—the cost of storing the representation*: For all but very small values of n and k, representing the distribution as a table will require too many values to store.

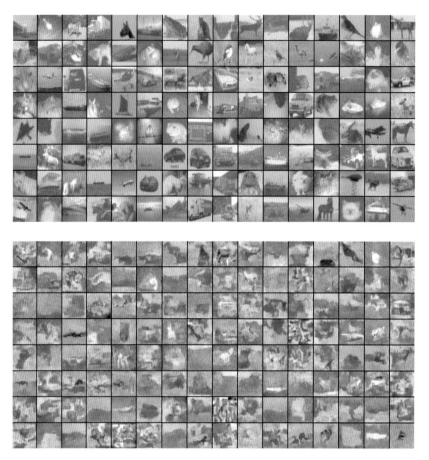

Figure 16.1: Probabilistic modeling of natural images. *(Top)* Example 32×32 pixel color images from the CIFAR-10 dataset (Krizhevsky and Hinton, 2009). *(Bottom)* Samples drawn from a structured probabilistic model trained on this dataset. Each sample appears at the same position in the grid as the training example that is closest to it in Euclidean space. This comparison allows us to see that the model is truly synthesizing new images, rather than memorizing the training data. Contrast of both sets of images has been adjusted for display. Figure reproduced with permission from Courville et al. (2011).

- *Statistical efficiency*: As the number of parameters in a model increases, so does the amount of training data needed to choose the values of those parameters using a statistical estimator. Because the table-based model has an astronomical number of parameters, it will require an astronomically large training set to fit accurately. Any such model will overfit the training set very badly unless additional assumptions are made linking the different entries in the table (as in back-off or smoothed n-gram models; section 12.4.1).

- *Runtime—the cost of inference*: Suppose we want to perform an inference task where we use our model of the joint distribution $P(\mathbf{x})$ to compute some other distribution, such as the marginal distribution $P(x_1)$ or the conditional distribution $P(x_2 \mid x_1)$. Computing these distributions will require summing across the entire table, so the runtime of these operations is as high as the intractable memory cost of storing the model.

- *Runtime—the cost of sampling*: Likewise, suppose we want to draw a sample from the model. The naive way to do this is to sample some value $u \sim U(0, 1)$, then iterate through the table, adding up the probability values until they exceed u and return the outcome corresponding to that position in the table. This requires reading through the whole table in the worst case, so it has the same exponential cost as the other operations.

The problem with the table-based approach is that we are explicitly modeling every possible kind of interaction between every possible subset of variables. The probability distributions we encounter in real tasks are much simpler than this. Usually, most variables influence each other only indirectly.

For example, consider modeling the finishing times of a team in a relay race. Suppose the team consists of three runners: Alice, Bob and Carol. At the start of the race, Alice carries a baton and begins running around a track. After completing her lap around the track, she hands the baton to Bob. Bob then runs his own lap and hands the baton to Carol, who runs the final lap. We can model each of their finishing times as a continuous random variable. Alice's finishing time does not depend on anyone else's, since she goes first. Bob's finishing time depends on Alice's, because Bob does not have the opportunity to start his lap until Alice has completed hers. If Alice finishes faster, Bob will finish faster, all else being equal. Finally, Carol's finishing time depends on both her teammates. If Alice is slow, Bob will probably finish late too. As a consequence, Carol will have quite a late starting time and thus is likely to have a late finishing time as well. However, Carol's finishing time depends only *indirectly* on Alice's finishing time via Bob's. If we already know Bob's finishing time, we will not be able to estimate Carol's finishing time better by finding out what Alice's finishing time was. This means we can model the relay race using only two interactions: Alice's effect on Bob and Bob's effect on Carol. We can omit the third, indirect interaction between Alice and Carol from our model.

Structured probabilistic models provide a formal framework for modeling only direct interactions between random variables. This allows the models to have significantly fewer parameters and therefore be estimated reliably from less data.

These smaller models also have dramatically reduced computational cost in terms of storing the model, performing inference in the model, and drawing samples from the model.

16.2 Using Graphs to Describe Model Structure

Structured probabilistic models use graphs (in the graph theory sense of "nodes" or "vertices" connected by edges) to represent interactions between random variables. Each node represents a random variable. Each edge represents a direct interaction. These direct interactions imply other, indirect interactions, but only the direct interactions need to be explicitly modeled.

There is more than one way to describe the interactions in a probability distribution using a graph. In the following sections, we describe some of the most popular and useful approaches. Graphical models can be largely divided into two categories: models based on directed acyclic graphs, and models based on undirected graphs.

16.2.1 Directed Models

One kind of structured probabilistic model is the **directed graphical model**, otherwise known as the **belief network** or **Bayesian network**[2] (Pearl, 1985).

Directed graphical models are called "directed" because their edges are directed, that is, they point from one vertex to another. This direction is represented in the drawing with an arrow. The direction of the arrow indicates which variable's probability distribution is defined in terms of the other's. Drawing an arrow from a to b means that we define the probability distribution over b via a conditional distribution, with a as one of the variables on the right side of the conditioning bar. In other words, the distribution over b depends on the value of a.

Continuing with the relay race example from section 16.1, suppose we name Alice's finishing time t_0, Bob's finishing time t_1, and Carol's finishing time t_2. As we saw earlier, our estimate of t_1 depends on t_0. Our estimate of t_2 depends directly on t_1 but only indirectly on t_0. We can draw this relationship in a directed graphical model, illustrated in figure 16.2.

---

[2] Judea Pearl suggested using the term "Bayesian network" when one wishes to "emphasize the judgmental" nature of the values computed by the network, i.e., to highlight that they usually represent degrees of belief rather than frequencies of events.

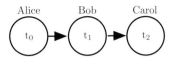

Figure 16.2: A directed graphical model depicting the relay race example. Alice's finishing time t_0 influences Bob's finishing time t_1, because Bob does not get to start running until Alice finishes. Likewise, Carol only gets to start running after Bob finishes, so Bob's finishing time t_1 directly influences Carol's finishing time t_2.

Formally, a directed graphical model defined on variables $\mathbf{x}$ is defined by a directed acyclic graph $\mathcal{G}$ whose vertices are the random variables in the model, and a set of **local conditional probability distributions** $p(x_i \mid Pa_{\mathcal{G}}(x_i))$, where $Pa_{\mathcal{G}}(x_i)$ gives the parents of x_i in $\mathcal{G}$. The probability distribution over $\mathbf{x}$ is given by

$$p(\mathbf{x}) = \Pi_i p(x_i \mid Pa_{\mathcal{G}}(x_i)). \qquad (16.1)$$

In our relay race example, this means that, using the graph drawn in figure 16.2,

$$p(t_0, t_1, t_2) = p(t_0)p(t_1 \mid t_0)p(t_2 \mid t_1). \qquad (16.2)$$

This is our first time seeing a structured probabilistic model in action. We can examine the cost of using it, to observe how structured modeling has many advantages relative to unstructured modeling.

Suppose we represented time by discretizing time ranging from minute 0 to minute 10 into 6-second chunks. This would make t_0, t_1 and t_2 each be a discrete variable with 100 possible values. If we attempted to represent $p(t_0, t_1, t_2)$ with a table, it would need to store 999,999 values (100 values of t_0 × 100 values of t_1 × 100 values of t_2, minus 1, since the probability of one of the configurations is made redundant by the constraint that the sum of the probabilities be 1). If instead, we make a table only for each of the conditional probability distributions, then the distribution over t_0 requires 99 values, the table defining t_1 given t_0 requires 9,900 values, and so does the table defining t_2 given t_1. This comes to a total of 19,899 values. This means that using the directed graphical model reduced our number of parameters by a factor of more than 50!

In general, to model n discrete variables each having k values, the cost of the single table approach scales like $O(k^n)$, as we have observed before. Now suppose we build a directed graphical model over these variables. If m is the maximum number of variables appearing (on either side of the conditioning bar) in a single conditional probability distribution, then the cost of the tables for the directed model scales like $O(k^m)$. As long as we can design a model such that $m << n$, we get very dramatic savings.

In other words, as long as each variable has few parents in the graph, the distribution can be represented with very few parameters. Some restrictions on the graph structure, such as requiring it to be a tree, can also guarantee that operations like computing marginal or conditional distributions over subsets of variables are efficient.

It is important to realize what kinds of information can and cannot be encoded in the graph. The graph encodes only simplifying assumptions about which variables are conditionally independent from each other. It is also possible to make other kinds of simplifying assumptions. For example, suppose we assume Bob always runs the same regardless of how Alice performs. (In reality, Alice's performance probably influences Bob's performance—depending on Bob's personality, if Alice runs especially fast in a given race, this might encourage Bob to push hard and match her exceptional performance, or it might make him overconfident and lazy). Then the only effect Alice has on Bob's finishing time is that we must add Alice's finishing time to the total amount of time we think Bob needs to run. This observation allows us to define a model with $O(k)$ parameters instead of $O(k^2)$. However, note that t_0 and t_1 are still directly dependent with this assumption, because t_1 represents the absolute time at which Bob finishes, not the total time he spends running. This means our graph must still contain an arrow from t_0 to t_1. The assumption that Bob's personal running time is independent from all other factors cannot be encoded in a graph over t_0, t_1, and t_2. Instead, we encode this information in the definition of the conditional distribution itself. The conditional distribution is no longer a $k \times k - 1$ element table indexed by t_0 and t_1 but is now a slightly more complicated formula using only $k - 1$ parameters. The directed graphical model syntax does not place any constraint on how we define our conditional distributions. It only defines which variables they are allowed to take in as arguments.

16.2.2 Undirected Models

Directed graphical models give us one language for describing structured probabilistic models. Another popular language is that of **undirected models**, otherwise known as **Markov random fields** (MRFs) or **Markov networks** (Kindermann, 1980). As their name implies, undirected models use graphs whose edges are undirected.

Directed models are most naturally applicable to situations where there is a clear reason to draw each arrow in one particular direction. Often these are situations where we understand the causality, and the causality flows in only one direction. One such situation is the relay race example. Earlier runners affect the finishing times of later runners; later runners do not affect the finishing times of earlier runners.

Not all situations we might want to model have such a clear direction to their interactions. When the interactions seem to have no intrinsic direction, or to operate in both directions, it may be more appropriate to use an undirected model.

As an example of such a situation, suppose we want to model a distribution over three binary variables: whether or not you are sick, whether or not your coworker is sick, and whether or not your roommate is sick. As in the relay race example, we can make simplifying assumptions about the kinds of interactions that take place. Assuming that your coworker and your roommate do not know each other, it is very unlikely that one of them will give the other an infection such as a cold directly. This event can be seen as so rare that it is acceptable not to model it. However, it is reasonably likely that either of them could give you a cold, and that you could pass it on to the other. We can model the indirect transmission of a cold from your coworker to your roommate by modeling the transmission of the cold from your coworker to you and the transmission of the cold from you to your roommate.

In this case, it is just as easy for you to cause your roommate to get sick as it is for your roommate to make you sick, so there is not a clean unidirectional narrative on which to base the model. This motivates using an undirected model. As with directed models, if two nodes in an undirected model are connected by an edge, then the random variables corresponding to those nodes interact with each other directly. Unlike directed models, the edge in an undirected model has no arrow and is not associated with a conditional probability distribution.

We denote the random variable representing your health as h_y, the random variable representing your roommate's health as h_r, and the random variable representing your colleague's health as h_c. See figure 16.3 for a drawing of the graph representing this scenario.

Figure 16.3: An undirected graph representing how your roommate's health h_r, your health h_y, and your work colleague's health h_c affect each other. You and your roommate might infect each other with a cold, and you and your work colleague might do the same, but assuming that your roommate and your colleague do not know each other, they can only infect each other indirectly via you.

Formally, an undirected graphical model is a structured probabilistic model defined on an undirected graph $\mathcal{G}$. For each clique $\mathcal{C}$ in the graph,[3] a **factor** $\phi(\mathcal{C})$ (also called a **clique potential**) measures the affinity of the variables in that clique for being in each of their possible joint states. The factors are constrained to be nonnegative. Together they define an **unnormalized probability distribution**

$$\tilde{p}(\mathbf{x}) = \Pi_{\mathcal{C} \in \mathcal{G}} \phi(\mathcal{C}). \tag{16.3}$$

The unnormalized probability distribution is efficient to work with so long as all the cliques are small. It encodes the idea that states with higher affinity are more likely. However, unlike in a Bayesian network, there is little structure to the definition of the cliques, so there is nothing to guarantee that multiplying them together will yield a valid probability distribution. See figure 16.4 for an example of reading factorization information from an undirected graph.

Our example of the cold spreading between you, your roommate, and your colleague contains two cliques. One clique contains h_y and h_c. The factor for this clique can be defined by a table and might have values resembling these:

	$h_y = 0$	$h_y = 1$
$h_c = 0$	2	1
$h_c = 1$	1	10

A state of 1 indicates good health, while a state of 0 indicates poor health (having been infected with a cold). Both of you are usually healthy, so the corresponding state has the highest affinity. The state where only one of you is sick has the lowest

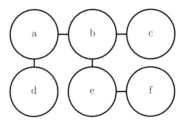

Figure 16.4: This graph implies that $p(a, b, c, d, e, f)$ can be written as $\frac{1}{Z}\phi_{a,b}(a, b)\phi_{b,c}(b, c)\phi_{a,d}(a, d)\phi_{b,e}(b, e)\phi_{e,f}(e, f)$ for an appropriate choice of the ϕ functions.

---

[3]A clique of the graph is a subset of nodes that are all connected to each other by an edge of the graph.

affinity, because this is a rare state. The state where both of you are sick (because one of you has infected the other) is a higher affinity state, though still not as common as the state where both are healthy.

To complete the model, we would need to also define a similar factor for the clique containing h_y and h_r.

16.2.3   The Partition Function

While the unnormalized probability distribution is guaranteed to be nonnegative everywhere, it is not guaranteed to sum or integrate to 1. To obtain a valid probability distribution, we must use the corresponding normalized probability distribution[4]

$$p(\mathbf{x}) = \frac{1}{Z}\tilde{p}(\mathbf{x}), \tag{16.4}$$

where Z is the value that results in the probability distribution summing or integrating to 1:

$$Z = \int \tilde{p}(\mathbf{x})d\mathbf{x}. \tag{16.5}$$

You can think of Z as a constant when the ϕ functions are held constant. Note that if the ϕ functions have parameters, then Z is a function of those parameters. It is common in the literature to write Z with its arguments omitted to save space. The normalizing constant Z is known as the **partition function**, a term borrowed from statistical physics.

Since Z is an integral or sum over all possible joint assignments of the state $\mathbf{x}$, it is often intractable to compute. To be able to obtain the normalized probability distribution of an undirected model, the model structure and the definitions of the ϕ functions must be conducive to computing Z efficiently. In the context of deep learning, Z is usually intractable. Because of the intractability of computing Z exactly, we must resort to approximations. Such approximate algorithms are the topic of chapter 18.

One important consideration to keep in mind when designing undirected models is that it is possible to specify the factors in such a way that Z does not exist. This happens if some of the variables in the model are continuous and the integral of $\tilde{p}$ over their domain diverges. For example, suppose we want to model a single scalar variable $x \in \mathbb{R}$ with a single clique potential $\phi(x) = x^2$. In this case,

$$Z = \int x^2 dx. \tag{16.6}$$

---

[4]A distribution defined by normalizing a product of clique potentials is also called a **Gibbs distribution**.

Since this integral diverges, there is no probability distribution corresponding to this choice of $\phi(x)$. Sometimes the choice of some parameter of the ϕ functions determines whether the probability distribution is defined. For example, for $\phi(x; \beta) = \exp\left(-\beta x^2\right)$, the β parameter determines whether Z exists. Positive β results in a Gaussian distribution over x, but all other values of β make ϕ impossible to normalize.

One key difference between directed modeling and undirected modeling is that directed models are defined directly in terms of probability distributions from the start, while undirected models are defined more loosely by ϕ functions that are then converted into probability distributions. This changes the intuitions one must develop to work with these models. One key idea to keep in mind while working with undirected models is that the domain of each of the variables has dramatic effect on the kind of probability distribution that a given set of ϕ functions corresponds to. For example, consider an n-dimensional vector valued random variable $\mathbf{x}$ and an undirected model parametrized by a vector of biases $\boldsymbol{b}$. Suppose we have one clique for each element of $\mathbf{x}$, $\phi^{(i)}(\mathrm{x}_i) = \exp(b_i \mathrm{x}_i)$. What kind of probability distribution does this result in? The answer is that we do not have enough information, because we have not yet specified the domain of $\mathbf{x}$. If $\mathbf{x} \in \mathbb{R}^n$, then the integral defining Z diverges, and no probability distribution exists. If $\mathbf{x} \in \{0, 1\}^n$, then $p(\mathbf{x})$ factorizes into n independent distributions, with $p(\mathrm{x}_i = 1) = \mathrm{sigmoid}\,(b_i)$. If the domain of $\mathbf{x}$ is the set of elementary basis vectors $(\{[1, 0, \ldots, 0], [0, 1, \ldots, 0], \ldots, [0, 0, \ldots, 1]\})$, then $p(\mathbf{x}) = \mathrm{softmax}(\boldsymbol{b})$, so a large value of b_i actually reduces $p(\mathrm{x}_j = 1)$ for $j \neq i$. Often, it is possible to leverage the effect of a carefully chosen domain of a variable to obtain complicated behavior from a relatively simple set of ϕ functions. We explore a practical application of this idea in section 20.6.

16.2.4 Energy-Based Models

Many interesting theoretical results about undirected models depend on the assumption that $\forall \mathbf{x}, \tilde{p}(\mathbf{x}) > 0$. A convenient way to enforce this condition is to use an **energy-based model** (EBM) where

$$\tilde{p}(\mathbf{x}) = \exp(-E(\mathbf{x})), \tag{16.7}$$

and $E(\mathbf{x})$ is known as the **energy function**. Because $\exp(z)$ is positive for all z, this guarantees that no energy function will result in a probability of zero for any state $\mathbf{x}$. Being completely free to choose the energy function makes learning simpler. If we learned the clique potentials directly, we would need to use constrained optimization to arbitrarily impose some specific minimal probability value. By learning the energy function, we can use unconstrained optimization.[5] The probabilities in an energy-based model can approach arbitrarily close to zero but never reach it.

Any distribution of the form given by equation 16.7 is an example of a **Boltzmann distribution**. For this reason, many energy-based models are called **Boltzmann machines** (Fahlman et al., 1983; Ackley et al., 1985; Hinton et al., 1984; Hinton and Sejnowski, 1986). There is no accepted guideline for when to call a model an energy-based model and when to call it a Boltzmann machine. The term Boltzmann machine was first introduced to describe a model with exclusively binary variables, but today many models such as the mean-covariance restricted Boltzmann machine incorporate real valued variables as well. While Boltzmann machines were originally defined to encompass both models with and without latent variables, the term Boltzmann machine is today most often used to designate models with latent variables, while Boltzmann machines without latent variables are more often called Markov random fields or log-linear models.

Cliques in an undirected graph correspond to factors of the unnormalized probability function. Because $\exp(a)\exp(b) = \exp(a + b)$, this means that different cliques in the undirected graph correspond to the different terms of the energy function. In other words, an energy-based model is just a special kind of Markov network: the exponentiation makes each term in the energy function correspond to a factor for a different clique. See figure 16.5 for an example of how to read the form of the energy function from an undirected graph structure. One can view an energy-based model with multiple terms in its energy function as being a **product of experts** (Hinton, 1999). Each term in the energy function corresponds to another factor in the probability distribution. Each term of the energy function can be thought of as an "expert" that determines whether a particular soft constraint is satisfied. Each expert may enforce only one constraint that concerns only a low-dimensional projection of the random variables, but when combined by multiplication of probabilities, the experts together enforce a complicated high-dimensional constraint.

One part of the definition of an energy-based model serves no functional purpose from a machine learning point of view: the $-$ sign in equation 16.7. This $-$ sign could be incorporated into the definition of E. For many choices of the function E, the learning algorithm is free to determine the sign of the energy anyway. The $-$ sign is present primarily to preserve compatibility between the machine learning literature and the physics literature. Many advances in probabilistic modeling were originally developed by statistical physicists, for whom E refers to actual physical energy and does not have arbitrary sign. Terminology such as "energy"

---

[5]For some models, we may still need to use constrained optimization to make sure Z exists.

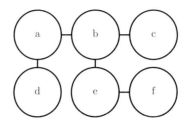

Figure 16.5: This graph implies that $E(\mathrm{a,b,c,d,e,f})$ can be written as $E_{\mathrm{a,b}}(\mathrm{a,b}) + E_{\mathrm{b,c}}(\mathrm{b,c}) + E_{\mathrm{a,d}}(\mathrm{a,d}) + E_{\mathrm{b,e}}(\mathrm{b,e}) + E_{\mathrm{e,f}}(\mathrm{e,f})$ for an appropriate choice of the per-clique energy functions. Note that we can obtain the ϕ functions in figure 16.4 by setting each ϕ to the exponential of the corresponding negative energy, e.g., $\phi_{\mathrm{a,b}}(\mathrm{a,b}) = \exp\left(-E(\mathrm{a,b})\right)$.

and "partition function" remains associated with these techniques, even though their mathematical applicability is broader than the physics context in which they were developed. Some machine learning researchers (e.g., Smolensky [1986], who referred to negative energy as **harmony**) have chosen to emit the negation, but this is not the standard convention.

Many algorithms that operate on probabilistic models need to compute not $p_{\mathrm{model}}(\boldsymbol{x})$ but only $\log \tilde{p}_{\mathrm{model}}(\boldsymbol{x})$. For energy-based models with latent variables $\boldsymbol{h}$, these algorithms are sometimes phrased in terms of the negative of this quantity, called the **free energy**:

$$\mathcal{F}(\boldsymbol{x}) = -\log \sum_{\boldsymbol{h}} \exp\left(-E(\boldsymbol{x}, \boldsymbol{h})\right). \tag{16.8}$$

In this book, we usually prefer the more general $\log \tilde{p}_{\mathrm{model}}(\boldsymbol{x})$ formulation.

16.2.5 Separation and D-Separation

The edges in a graphical model tell us which variables directly interact. We often need to know which variables *indirectly* interact. Some of these indirect interactions can be enabled or disabled by observing other variables. More formally, we would like to know which subsets of variables are conditionally independent from each other, given the values of other subsets of variables.

Identifying the conditional independences in a graph is simple for undirected models. In this case, conditional independence implied by the graph is called **separation**. We say that a set of variables $\mathbb{A}$ is **separated** from another set of variables $\mathbb{B}$ given a third set of variables $\mathbb{S}$ if the graph structure implies that $\mathbb{A}$ is independent from $\mathbb{B}$ given $\mathbb{S}$. If two variables a and b are connected by a path involving only unobserved variables, then those variables are not separated. If no path exists between them, or all paths contain an observed variable, then they are separated. We refer to paths involving only unobserved variables as "active" and paths including an observed variable as "inactive."

When we draw a graph, we can indicate observed variables by shading them in. See figure 16.6 for a depiction of how active and inactive paths in an undirected model look when drawn in this way. See figure 16.7 for an example of reading separation from an undirected graph.

Similar concepts apply to directed models, except that in the context of directed models, these concepts are referred to as **d-separation**. The "d" stands for "dependence." D-separation for directed graphs is defined the same as separation for undirected graphs: We say that a set of variables $\mathbb{A}$ is d-separated from another set of variables $\mathbb{B}$ given a third set of variables $\mathbb{S}$ if the graph structure implies that $\mathbb{A}$ is independent from $\mathbb{B}$ given $\mathbb{S}$.

As with undirected models, we can examine the independences implied by the graph by looking at what active paths exist in the graph. As before, two variables are dependent if there is an active path between them and d-separated if no such path exists. In directed nets, determining whether a path is active is somewhat

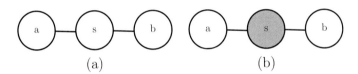

$$(a) \qquad\qquad (b)$$

Figure 16.6: (a) The path between random variable a and random variable b through s is active, because s is not observed. This means that a and b are not separated. (b) Here s is shaded in, to indicate that it is observed. Because the only path between a and b is through s, and that path is inactive, we can conclude that a and b are separated given s.

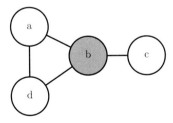

Figure 16.7: An example of reading separation properties from an undirected graph. Here b is shaded to indicate that it is observed. Because observing b blocks the only path from a to c, we say that a and c are separated from each other given b. The observation of b also blocks one path between a and d, but there is a second, active path between them. Therefore, a and d are not separated given b.

more complicated. See figure 16.8 for a guide to identifying active paths in a directed model. See figure 16.9 for an example of reading some properties from a graph.

It is important to remember that separation and d-separation tell us only about those conditional independences *that are implied by the graph*. There is no requirement that the graph imply all independences that are present. In particular, it is always legitimate to use the complete graph (the graph with all possible edges) to represent any distribution. In fact, some distributions contain independences that are not possible to represent with existing graphical notation. **Context-specific independences** are independences that are present dependent on the value of some variables in the network. For example, consider a model of three binary variables: a, b and c. Suppose that when a is 0, b and c are independent, but when a is 1, b is deterministically equal to c. Encoding the behavior when $a = 1$ requires an edge connecting b and c. The graph then fails to indicate that b and c are independent when $a = 0$.

In general, a graph will never imply that an independence exists when it does not. However, a graph may fail to encode an independence.

16.2.6   Converting between Undirected and Directed Graphs

We often refer to a specific machine learning model as being undirected or directed. For example, we typically refer to RBMs as undirected and sparse coding as directed. This choice of wording can be somewhat misleading, because no probabilistic model is inherently directed or undirected. Instead, some models are most easily *described* using a directed graph, or most easily described using an undirected graph.

Directed models and undirected models both have their advantages and disadvantages. Neither approach is clearly superior and universally preferred. Instead, we should choose which language to use for each task. This choice will partially depend on which probability distribution we wish to describe. We may choose to use either directed modeling or undirected modeling based on which approach can capture the most independences in the probability distribution or which approach uses the fewest edges to describe the distribution. Other factors can affect the decision of which language to use. Even while working with a single probability distribution, we may sometimes switch between different modeling languages. Sometimes a different language becomes more appropriate if we observe a certain subset of variables, or if we wish to perform a different computational task. For example, the directed model description often provides a straightforward approach to efficiently draw samples from the model (described in section 16.3), while the

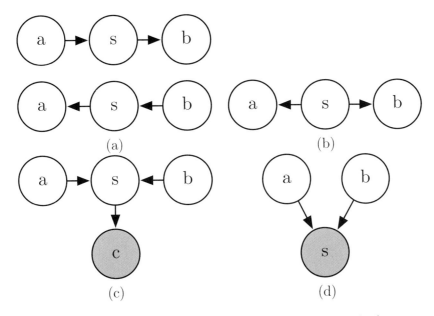

Figure 16.8: All the kinds of active paths of length two that can exist between random variables a and b. *(a)* Any path with arrows proceeding directly from a to b or vice versa. This kind of path becomes blocked if s is observed. We have already seen this kind of path in the relay race example. *(b)* Variables a and b are connected by a *common cause* s. For example, suppose s is a variable indicating whether or not there is a hurricane, and a and b measure the wind speed at two different nearby weather monitoring outposts. If we observe very high winds at station a, we might expect to also see high winds at b. This kind of path can be blocked by observing s. If we already know there is a hurricane, we expect to see high winds at b, regardless of what is observed at a. A lower than expected wind at a (for a hurricane) would not change our expectation of winds at b (knowing there is a hurricane). However, if s is not observed, then a and b are dependent, i.e., the path is active. *(c)* Variables a and b are both parents of s. This is called a **V-structure**, or **the collider case**. The V-structure causes a and b to be related by the **explaining away effect**. In this case, the path is actually active when s is observed. For example, suppose s is a variable indicating that your colleague is not at work. The variable a represents her being sick, while b represents her being on vacation. If you observe that she is not at work, you can presume she is probably sick or on vacation, but it is not especially likely that both have happened at the same time. If you find out that she is on vacation, this fact is sufficient to *explain* her absence. You can infer that she is probably not also sick. *(d)* The explaining away effect happens even if any descendant of s is observed! For example, suppose that c is a variable representing whether you have received a report from your colleague. If you notice that you have not received the report, this increases your estimate of the probability that she is not at work today, which in turn makes it more likely that she is either sick or on vacation. The only way to block a path through a V-structure is to observe none of the descendants of the shared child.

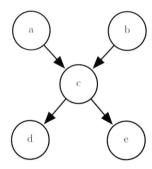

Figure 16.9: From this graph, we can read out several d-separation properties. Examples include:

- a and b are d-separated given the empty set
- a and e are d-separated given c
- d and e are d-separated given c

We can also see that some variables are no longer d-separated when we observe some variables:

- a and b are not d-separated given c
- a and b are not d-separated given d

undirected model formulation is often useful for deriving approximate inference procedures (as we will see in chapter 19, where the role of undirected models is highlighted in equation 19.56).

Every probability distribution can be represented by either a directed model or an undirected model. In the worst case, one can always represent any distribution by using a "complete graph." For a directed model, the complete graph is any directed acyclic graph in which we impose some ordering on the random variables, and each variable has all other variables that precede it in the ordering as its ancestors in the graph. For an undirected model, the complete graph is simply a graph containing a single clique encompassing all the variables. See figure 16.10 for an example.

Of course, the utility of a graphical model is that the graph implies that some variables do not interact directly. The complete graph is not very useful because it does not imply any independences.

When we represent a probability distribution with a graph, we want to choose a graph that implies as many independences as possible, without implying any independences that do not actually exist.

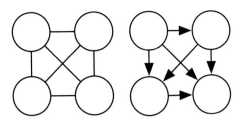

Figure 16.10: Examples of complete graphs, which can describe any probability distribution. Here we show examples with four random variables. *(Left)* The complete undirected graph. In the undirected case, the complete graph is unique. *(Right)* A complete directed graph. In the directed case, there is not a unique complete graph. We choose an ordering of the variables and draw an arc from each variable to every variable that comes after it in the ordering. There are thus a factorial number of complete graphs for every set of random variables. In this example, we order the variables from left to right, top to bottom.

From this point of view, some distributions can be represented more efficiently using directed models, while other distributions can be represented more efficiently using undirected models. In other words, directed models can encode some independences that undirected models cannot encode, and vice versa.

Directed models are able to use one specific kind of substructure that undirected models cannot represent perfectly. This substructure is called an **immorality**. The structure occurs when two random variables a and b are both parents of a third random variable c, and there is no edge directly connecting a and b in either direction. (The name "immorality" may seem strange; it was coined in the graphical models literature as a joke about unmarried parents.) To convert a directed model with graph $\mathcal{D}$ into an undirected model, we need to create a new graph $\mathcal{U}$. For every pair of variables x and y, we add an undirected edge connecting x and y to $\mathcal{U}$ if there is a directed edge (in either direction) connecting x and y in $\mathcal{D}$ or if x and y are both parents in $\mathcal{D}$ of a third variable z. The resulting $\mathcal{U}$ is known as a **moralized graph**. See figure 16.11 for examples of converting directed models to undirected models via moralization.

Likewise, undirected models can include substructures that no directed model can represent perfectly. Specifically, a directed graph $\mathcal{D}$ cannot capture all the conditional independences implied by an undirected graph $\mathcal{U}$ if $\mathcal{U}$ contains a **loop** of length greater than three, unless that loop also contains a **chord**. A loop is a sequence of variables connected by undirected edges, with the last variable in the sequence connected back to the first variable in the sequence. A chord is a connection between any two nonconsecutive variables in the sequence defining a loop. If $\mathcal{U}$ has loops of length four or greater and does not have chords for these

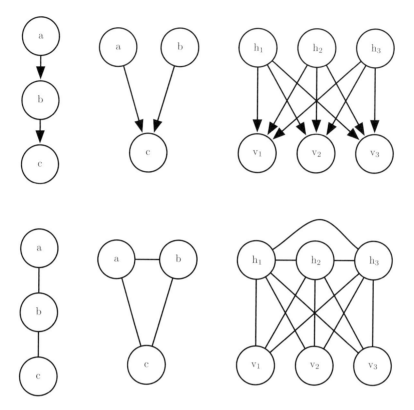

Figure 16.11: Examples of converting directed models (top row) to undirected models (bottom row) by constructing moralized graphs. *(Left)* This simple chain can be converted to a moralized graph merely by replacing its directed edges with undirected edges. The resulting undirected model implies exactly the same set of independences and conditional independences. *(Center)* This graph is the simplest directed model that cannot be converted to an undirected model without losing some independences. This graph consists entirely of a single immorality. Because a and b are parents of c, they are connected by an active path when c is observed. To capture this dependence, the undirected model must include a clique encompassing all three variables. This clique fails to encode the fact that a⊥b. *(Right)* In general, moralization may add many edges to the graph, thus losing many implied independences. For example, this sparse coding graph requires adding moralizing edges between every pair of hidden units, thus introducing a quadratic number of new direct dependences.

loops, we must add the chords before we can convert it to a directed model. Adding these chords discards some of the independence information that was encoded in $\mathcal{U}$. The graph formed by adding chords to $\mathcal{U}$ is known as a **chordal**, or **triangulated**, graph, because all the loops can now be described in terms of smaller, triangular

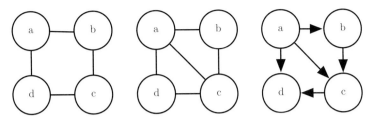

Figure 16.12: Converting an undirected model to a directed model. *(Left)* This undirected model cannot be converted to a directed model because it has a loop of length four with no chords. Specifically, the undirected model encodes two different independences that no directed model can capture simultaneously: a⊥c | {b, d} and b⊥d | {a, c}. *(Center)* To convert the undirected model to a directed model, we must triangulate the graph, by ensuring that all loops of greater than length three have a chord. To do so, we can either add an edge connecting a and c or we can add an edge connecting b and d. In this example, we choose to add the edge connecting a and c. *(Right)* To finish the conversion process, we must assign a direction to each edge. When doing so, we must not create any directed cycles. One way to avoid directed cycles is to impose an ordering over the nodes, and always point each edge from the node that comes earlier in the ordering to the node that comes later in the ordering. In this example, we use the variable names to impose alphabetical order.

loops. To build a directed graph $\mathcal{D}$ from the chordal graph, we need to also assign directions to the edges. When doing so, we must not create a directed cycle in $\mathcal{D}$, or the result will not define a valid directed probabilistic model. One way to assign directions to the edges in $\mathcal{D}$ is to impose an ordering on the random variables, then point each edge from the node that comes earlier in the ordering to the node that comes later in the ordering. See figure 16.12 for a demonstration.

16.2.7 Factor Graphs

Factor graphs are another way of drawing undirected models that resolve an ambiguity in the graphical representation of standard undirected model syntax. In an undirected model, the scope of every ϕ function must be a *subset* of some clique in the graph. Ambiguity arises because it is not clear if each clique actually has a corresponding factor whose scope encompasses the entire clique—for example, a clique containing three nodes may correspond to a factor over all three nodes, or may correspond to three factors that each contain only a pair of the nodes. Factor graphs resolve this ambiguity by explicitly representing the scope of each ϕ function. Specifically, a factor graph is a graphical representation of an undirected model that consists of a bipartite undirected graph. Some of the nodes are drawn as circles. These nodes correspond to random variables, as in a standard undirected

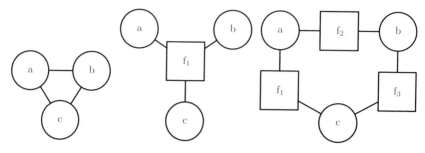

Figure 16.13: An example of how a factor graph can resolve ambiguity in the interpretation of undirected networks. *(Left)* An undirected network with a clique involving three variables: a, b and c. *(Center)* A factor graph corresponding to the same undirected model. This factor graph has one factor over all three variables. *(Right)* Another valid factor graph for the same undirected model. This factor graph has three factors, each over only two variables. Representation, inference, and learning are all asymptotically cheaper in this factor graph than in the factor graph depicted in the center, even though both require the same undirected graph to represent.

model. The rest of the nodes are drawn as squares. These nodes correspond to the factors ϕ of the unnormalized probability distribution. Variables and factors may be connected with undirected edges. A variable and a factor are connected in the graph if and only if the variable is one of the arguments to the factor in the unnormalized probability distribution. No factor may be connected to another factor in the graph, nor can a variable be connected to a variable. See figure 16.13 for an example of how factor graphs can resolve ambiguity in the interpretation of undirected networks.

16.3 Sampling from Graphical Models

Graphical models also facilitate the task of drawing samples from a model.

One advantage of directed graphical models is that a simple and efficient procedure called **ancestral sampling** can produce a sample from the joint distribution represented by the model.

The basic idea is to sort the variables x_i in the graph into a topological ordering, so that for all i and j, j is greater than i if x_i is a parent of x_j. The variables can then be sampled in this order. In other words, we first sample $x_1 \sim P(x_1)$, then sample $P(x_2 \mid Pa_{\mathcal{G}}(x_2))$, and so on, until finally we sample $P(x_n \mid Pa_{\mathcal{G}}(x_n))$. So long as each conditional distribution $p(x_i \mid Pa_{\mathcal{G}}(x_i))$ is easy to sample from, then the whole model is easy to sample from. The topological sorting operation guarantees that we can read the conditional distributions in equation 16.1 and sample from them in order. Without the topological sorting, we might attempt to sample a variable before its parents are available.

For some graphs, more than one topological ordering is possible. Ancestral sampling may be used with any of these topological orderings.

Ancestral sampling is generally very fast (assuming sampling from each conditional is easy) and convenient.

One drawback to ancestral sampling is that it only applies to directed graphical models. Another drawback is that it does not support every conditional sampling operation. When we wish to sample from a subset of the variables in a directed graphical model, given some other variables, we often require that all the conditioning variables come earlier than the variables to be sampled in the ordered graph. In this case, we can sample from the local conditional probability distributions specified by the model distribution. Otherwise, the conditional distributions we need to sample from are the posterior distributions given the observed variables. These posterior distributions are usually not explicitly specified and parametrized in the model. Inferring these posterior distributions can be costly. In models where this is the case, ancestral sampling is no longer efficient.

Unfortunately, ancestral sampling is applicable only to directed models. We can sample from undirected models by converting them to directed models, but this often requires solving intractable inference problems (to determine the marginal distribution over the root nodes of the new directed graph) or requires introducing so many edges that the resulting directed model becomes intractable. Sampling from an undirected model without first converting it to a directed model seems to require resolving cyclical dependencies. Every variable interacts with every other variable, so there is no clear beginning point for the sampling process. Unfortunately, drawing samples from an undirected graphical model is an expensive, multipass process. The conceptually simplest approach is **Gibbs sampling**. Suppose we have a graphical model over an n-dimensional vector of random variables $\mathbf{x}$. We iteratively visit each variable x_i and draw a sample conditioned on all the other variables, from $p(x_i \mid x_{-i})$. Due to the separation properties of the graphical model, we can equivalently condition on only the neighbors of x_i. Unfortunately, after we have made one pass through the graphical model and sampled all n variables, we still do not have a fair sample from $p(\mathbf{x})$. Instead, we must repeat the process and resample all n variables using the updated values of their neighbors. Asymptotically, after many repetitions, this process converges to sampling from the correct distribution. It can be difficult to determine when the samples have reached a sufficiently accurate approximation of the desired distribution. Sampling techniques for undirected models are an advanced topic, covered in more detail in chapter 17.

16.4 Advantages of Structured Modeling

The primary advantage of using structured probabilistic models is that they allow us to dramatically reduce the cost of representing probability distributions as well as learning and inference. Sampling is also accelerated in the case of directed models, while the situation can be complicated with undirected models. The primary mechanism that allows all these operations to use less runtime and memory is choosing to not model certain interactions. Graphical models convey information by leaving edges out. Anywhere there is not an edge, the model specifies the assumption that we do not need to model a direct interaction.

A less quantifiable benefit of using structured probabilistic models is that they allow us to explicitly separate representation of knowledge from learning of knowledge or inference given existing knowledge. This makes our models easier to develop and debug. We can design, analyze, and evaluate learning algorithms and inference algorithms that are applicable to broad classes of graphs. Independently, we can design models that capture the relationships we believe are important in our data. We can then combine these different algorithms and structures and obtain a Cartesian product of different possibilities. It would be much more difficult to design end-to-end algorithms for every possible situation.

16.5 Learning about Dependencies

A good generative model needs to accurately capture the distribution over the observed, or "visible," variables $\mathbf{v}$. Often the different elements of $\mathbf{v}$ are highly dependent on each other. In the context of deep learning, the approach most commonly used to model these dependencies is to introduce several latent or "hidden" variables, $\mathbf{h}$. The model can then capture dependencies between any pair of variables v_i and v_j indirectly, via direct dependencies between v_i and $\mathbf{h}$, and direct dependencies between $\mathbf{h}$ and v_j.

A good model of $\mathbf{v}$ which did not contain any latent variables would need to have very large numbers of parents per node in a Bayesian network or very large cliques in a Markov network. Just representing these higher-order interactions is costly—both in a computational sense, because the number of parameters that must be stored in memory scales exponentially with the number of members in a clique, but also in a statistical sense, because this exponential number of parameters requires a wealth of data to estimate accurately.

When the model is intended to capture dependencies between visible variables with direct connections, it is usually infeasible to connect all variables, so the graph must be designed to connect those variables that are tightly coupled and omit edges between other variables. An entire field of machine learning called **structure learning** is devoted to this problem. For a good reference on structure learning, see (Koller and Friedman, 2009). Most structure learning techniques are a form of greedy search. A structure is proposed and a model with that structure is trained, then given a score. The score rewards high training set accuracy and penalizes model complexity. Candidate structures with a small number of edges added or removed are then proposed as the next step of the search. The search proceeds to a new structure that is expected to increase the score.

Using latent variables instead of adaptive structure avoids the need to perform discrete searches and multiple rounds of training. A fixed structure over visible and hidden variables can use direct interactions between visible and hidden units to impose indirect interactions between visible units. Using simple parameter learning techniques, we can learn a model with a fixed structure that imputes the right structure on the marginal $p(\mathbf{v})$.

Latent variables have advantages beyond their role in efficiently capturing $p(\mathbf{v})$. The new variables $\mathbf{h}$ also provide an alternative representation for $\mathbf{v}$. For example, as discussed in section 3.9.6, the mixture of Gaussians model learns a latent variable that corresponds to the category of examples the input was drawn from. This means that the latent variable in a mixture of Gaussians model can be used to do classification. In chapter 14 we saw how simple probabilistic models like sparse coding learn latent variables that can be used as input features for a classifier, or as coordinates along a manifold. Other models can be used in this same way, but deeper models and models with different kinds of interactions can create even richer descriptions of the input. Many approaches accomplish feature learning by learning latent variables. Often, given some model of $\mathbf{v}$ and $\mathbf{h}$, experimental observations show that $\mathbb{E}[\mathbf{h} \mid \mathbf{v}]$ or $\mathrm{argmax}_h p(\boldsymbol{h}, \boldsymbol{v})$ is a good feature mapping for $\boldsymbol{v}$.

16.6 Inference and Approximate Inference

One of the main ways we can use a probabilistic model is to ask questions about how variables are related to each other. Given a set of medical tests, we can ask what disease a patient might have. In a latent variable model, we might want to extract features $\mathbb{E}[\mathbf{h} \mid \mathbf{v}]$ describing the observed variables $\mathbf{v}$. Sometimes we need to solve such problems in order to perform other tasks. We often train our models using the principle of maximum likelihood. Because

$$\log p(\boldsymbol{v}) = \mathbb{E}_{\mathbf{h} \sim p(\mathbf{h}|\mathbf{v})} \left[\log p(\boldsymbol{h}, \boldsymbol{v}) - \log p(\boldsymbol{h} \mid \boldsymbol{v})\right], \qquad (16.9)$$

we often want to compute $p(\mathbf{h} \mid \boldsymbol{v})$ in order to implement a learning rule. All these are examples of **inference** problems in which we must predict the value of some variables given other variables, or predict the probability distribution over some variables given the value of other variables.

Unfortunately, for most interesting deep models, these inference problems are intractable, even when we use a structured graphical model to simplify them. The graph structure allows us to represent complicated, high-dimensional distributions with a reasonable number of parameters, but the graphs used for deep learning are usually not restrictive enough to also allow efficient inference.

It is straightforward to see that computing the marginal probability of a general graphical model is #P hard. The complexity class #P is a generalization of the complexity class NP. Problems in NP require determining only whether a problem has a solution and finding a solution if one exists. Problems in #P require counting the number of solutions. To construct a worst-case graphical model, imagine that we define a graphical model over the binary variables in a 3-SAT problem. We can impose a uniform distribution over these variables. We can then add one binary latent variable per clause that indicates whether each clause is satisfied. We can then add another latent variable indicating whether all the clauses are satisfied. This can be done without making a large clique, by building a reduction tree of latent variables, with each node in the tree reporting whether two other variables are satisfied. The leaves of this tree are the variables for each clause. The root of the tree reports whether the entire problem is satisfied. Because of the uniform distribution over the literals, the marginal distribution over the root of the reduction tree specifies what fraction of assignments satisfy the problem. While this is a contrived worst-case example, NP hard graphs commonly arise in practical real-world scenarios.

This motivates the use of approximate inference. In the context of deep learning, this usually refers to variational inference, in which we approximate the true distribution $p(\mathbf{h} \mid \boldsymbol{v})$ by seeking an approximate distribution $q(\mathbf{h}|\mathbf{v})$ that is as close to the true one as possible. This and other techniques are described in depth in chapter 19.

16.7   The Deep Learning Approach to Structured Probabilistic Models

Deep learning practitioners generally use the same basic computational tools as other machine learning practitioners who work with structured probabilistic models. In the context of deep learning, however, we usually make different design decisions about how to combine these tools, resulting in overall algorithms and models that have a very different flavor from more traditional graphical models.

Deep learning does not always involve especially deep graphical models. In the context of graphical models, we can define the depth of a model in terms of the graphical model graph rather than the computational graph. We can think of a latent variable h_i as being at depth j if the shortest path from h_i to an observed variable is j steps. We usually describe the depth of the model as being the greatest depth of any such h_i. This kind of depth is different from the depth induced by the computational graph. Many generative models used for deep learning have no latent variables or only one layer of latent variables but use deep computational graphs to define the conditional distributions within a model.

Deep learning essentially always makes use of the idea of distributed representations. Even shallow models used for deep learning purposes (such as pretraining shallow models that will later be composed to form deep ones) nearly always have a single large layer of latent variables. Deep learning models typically have more latent variables than observed variables. Complicated nonlinear interactions between variables are accomplished via indirect connections that flow through multiple latent variables.

By contrast, traditional graphical models usually contain mostly variables that are at least occasionally observed, even if many of the variables are missing at random from some training examples. Traditional models mostly use higher-order terms and structure learning to capture complicated nonlinear interactions between variables. If there are latent variables, they are usually few in number.

The way that latent variables are designed also differs in deep learning. The deep learning practitioner typically does not intend for the latent variables to take on any specific semantics ahead of time—the training algorithm is free to invent the concepts it needs to model a particular dataset. The latent variables are usually not very easy for a human to interpret after the fact, though visualization techniques may allow some rough characterization of what they represent. When latent variables are used in the context of traditional graphical models, they are often designed with some specific semantics in mind—the topic of a document, the intelligence of a student, the disease causing a patient's symptoms, and so forth. These models are often much more interpretable by human practitioners and often have more theoretical guarantees, yet they are less able to scale to complex problems and are not reusable in as many different contexts as deep models are.

Another obvious difference is the kind of connectivity typically used in the deep learning approach. Deep graphical models typically have large groups of units that are all connected to other groups of units, so that the interactions between two groups may be described by a single matrix. Traditional graphical models have very few connections, and the choice of connections for each variable may be individually designed. The design of the model structure is tightly linked with the choice of inference algorithm. Traditional approaches to graphical models typically aim to maintain the tractability of exact inference. When this constraint is too limiting, a popular approximate inference algorithm is called **loopy belief propagation**. Both approaches often work well with sparsely connected graphs. By comparison, models used in deep learning tend to connect each visible unit v_i to many hidden units h_j, so that $\mathbf{h}$ can provide a distributed representation of v_i (and probably several other observed variables too). Distributed representations have many advantages, but from the point of view of graphical models and computational complexity, distributed representations have the disadvantage of usually yielding graphs that are not sparse enough for the traditional techniques of exact inference and loopy belief propagation to be relevant. As a consequence, one of the most striking differences between the larger graphical models community and the deep graphical models community is that loopy belief propagation is almost never used for deep learning. Most deep models are instead designed to make Gibbs sampling or variational inference algorithms efficient. Another consideration is that deep learning models contain a very large number of latent variables, making efficient numerical code essential. This provides an additional motivation, besides the choice of high-level inference algorithm, for grouping the units into layers with a matrix describing the interaction between two layers. This allows the individual steps of the algorithm to be implemented with efficient matrix product operations, or sparsely connected generalizations, like block diagonal matrix products or convolutions.

Finally, the deep learning approach to graphical modeling is characterized by a marked tolerance of the unknown. Rather than simplifying the model until all quantities we might want can be computed exactly, we increase the power of the model until it is just barely possible to train or use. We often use models whose marginal distributions cannot be computed and are satisfied simply to draw approximate samples from these models. We often train models with an intractable objective function that we cannot even approximate in a reasonable amount of time, but we are still able to approximately train the model if we can efficiently obtain an estimate of the gradient of such a function. The deep learning approach is often to figure out what the minimum amount of information we absolutely need is, and then to figure out how to get a reasonable approximation of that information as quickly as possible.

16.7.1 Example: The Restricted Boltzmann Machine

The **restricted Boltzmann machine** (RBM) (Smolensky, 1986), or **harmonium**, is the quintessential example of how graphical models are used for deep learning. The RBM is not itself a deep model. Instead, it has a single layer of latent variables that may be used to learn a representation for the input. In chapter 20, we will see how RBMs can be used to build many deeper models. Here, we show how the RBM exemplifies many of the practices used in a wide variety of deep graphical models: its units are organized into large groups called layers, the connectivity between layers is described by a matrix, the connectivity is relatively dense, the model is designed to allow efficient Gibbs sampling, and the emphasis of the model design is on freeing the training algorithm to learn latent variables whose semantics were not specified by the designer. In section 20.2, we revisit the RBM in more detail.

The canonical RBM is an energy-based model with binary visible and hidden units. Its energy function is

$$E(\boldsymbol{v}, \boldsymbol{h}) = -\boldsymbol{b}^\top \boldsymbol{v} - \boldsymbol{c}^\top \boldsymbol{h} - \boldsymbol{v}^\top \boldsymbol{W} \boldsymbol{h}, \tag{16.10}$$

where $\boldsymbol{b}$, $\boldsymbol{c}$, and $\boldsymbol{W}$ are unconstrained, real valued, learnable parameters. We can see that the model is divided into two groups of units: $\boldsymbol{v}$ and $\boldsymbol{h}$, and the interaction between them is described by a matrix $\boldsymbol{W}$. The model is depicted graphically in figure 16.14. As this figure makes clear, an important aspect of this model is that there are no direct interactions between any two visible units or between any two hidden units (hence "restricted"; a general Boltzmann machine may have arbitrary connections).

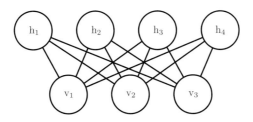

Figure 16.14: An RBM drawn as a Markov network.

The restrictions on the RBM structure yield the nice properties

$$p(\mathbf{h} \mid \mathbf{v}) = \Pi_i p(\mathrm{h}_i \mid \mathbf{v}) \qquad (16.11)$$

and

$$p(\mathbf{v} \mid \mathbf{h}) = \Pi_i p(\mathrm{v}_i \mid \mathbf{h}). \qquad (16.12)$$

The individual conditionals are simple to compute as well. For the binary RBM we obtain

$$P(\mathrm{h}_i = 1 \mid \mathbf{v}) = \sigma\left(\mathbf{v}^\top \boldsymbol{W}_{:,i} + b_i\right), \qquad (16.13)$$

$$P(\mathrm{h}_i = 0 \mid \mathbf{v}) = 1 - \sigma\left(\mathbf{v}^\top \boldsymbol{W}_{:,i} + b_i\right). \qquad (16.14)$$

Together these properties allow for efficient **block Gibbs sampling**, which alternates between sampling all of $\mathbf{h}$ simultaneously and sampling all of $\mathbf{v}$ simultaneously. Samples generated by Gibbs sampling from an RBM model are shown in figure 16.15.

Since the energy function itself is just a linear function of the parameters, it is easy to take its derivatives. For example,

$$\frac{\partial}{\partial W_{i,j}} E(\mathbf{v}, \mathbf{h}) = -\mathrm{v}_i \mathrm{h}_j. \qquad (16.15)$$

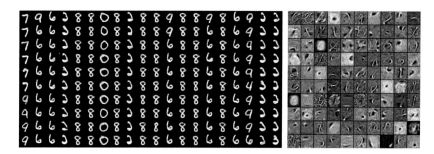

Figure 16.15: Samples from a trained RBM and its weights. *(Left)* Samples from a model trained on MNIST, drawn using Gibbs sampling. Each column is a separate Gibbs sampling process. Each row represents the output of another 1,000 steps of Gibbs sampling. Successive samples are highly correlated with one another. *(Right)* The corresponding weight vectors. Compare this to the samples and weights of a linear factor model, shown in figure 13.2. The samples here are much better because the RBM prior $p(\boldsymbol{h})$ is not constrained to be factorial. The RBM can learn which features should appear together when sampling. On the other hand, the RBM posterior $p(\boldsymbol{h} \mid \boldsymbol{v})$ is factorial, while the sparse coding posterior $p(\boldsymbol{h} \mid \boldsymbol{v})$ is not, so the sparse coding model may be better for feature extraction. Other models are able to have both a nonfactorial $p(\boldsymbol{h})$ and a nonfactorial $p(\boldsymbol{h} \mid \boldsymbol{v})$. Image reproduced with permission from LISA (2008).

These two properties—efficient Gibbs sampling and efficient derivatives—make training convenient. In chapter 18, we will see that undirected models may be trained by computing such derivatives applied to samples from the model.

Training the model induces a representation h of the data v. We can often use $\mathbb{E}_{h \sim p(h|v)}[h]$ as a set of features to describe v.

Overall, the RBM demonstrates the typical deep learning approach to graphical models: representation learning accomplished via layers of latent variables, combined with efficient interactions between layers parametrized by matrices.

The language of graphical models provides an elegant, flexible and clear language for describing probabilistic models. In the chapters ahead, we use this language, among other perspectives, to describe a wide variety of deep probabilistic models.

17

Monte Carlo Methods

Randomized algorithms fall into two rough categories: Las Vegas algorithms and Monte Carlo algorithms. Las Vegas algorithms always return precisely the correct answer (or report that they failed). These algorithms consume a random amount of resources, usually memory or time. In contrast, Monte Carlo algorithms return answers with a random amount of error. The amount of error can typically be reduced by expending more resources (usually running time and memory). For any fixed computational budget, a Monte Carlo algorithm can provide an approximate answer.

Many problems in machine learning are so difficult that we can never expect to obtain precise answers to them. This excludes precise deterministic algorithms and Las Vegas algorithms. Instead, we must use deterministic approximate algorithms or Monte Carlo approximations. Both approaches are ubiquitous in machine learning. In this chapter, we focus on Monte Carlo methods.

17.1 Sampling and Monte Carlo Methods

Many important technologies used to accomplish machine learning goals are based on drawing samples from some probability distribution and using these samples to form a Monte Carlo estimate of some desired quantity.

17.1.1 Why Sampling?

We may wish to draw samples from a probability distribution for many reasons. Sampling provides a flexible way to approximate many sums and integrals at reduced cost. Sometimes we use this to provide a significant speedup to a costly but tractable sum, as in the case when we subsample the full training cost with minibatches. In other cases, our learning algorithm requires us to approximate an intractable sum or integral, such as the gradient of the log partition function of an undirected model. In many other cases, sampling is actually our goal, in the sense that we want to train a model that can sample from the training distribution.

17.1.2 Basics of Monte Carlo Sampling

When a sum or an integral cannot be computed exactly (for example, the sum has an exponential number of terms, and no exact simplification is known), it is often possible to approximate it using Monte Carlo sampling. The idea is to view the sum or integral as if it were an expectation under some distribution and to *approximate the expectation by a corresponding average*. Let

$$s = \sum_{\boldsymbol{x}} p(\boldsymbol{x}) f(\boldsymbol{x}) = E_p[f(\mathbf{x})] \tag{17.1}$$

or

$$s = \int p(\boldsymbol{x}) f(\boldsymbol{x}) d\boldsymbol{x} = E_p[f(\mathbf{x})] \tag{17.2}$$

be the sum or integral to estimate, rewritten as an expectation, with the constraint that p is a probability distribution (for the sum) or a probability density (for the integral) over random variable $\mathbf{x}$.

We can approximate s by drawing n samples $\boldsymbol{x}^{(1)}, \ldots, \boldsymbol{x}^{(n)}$ from p and then forming the empirical average

$$\hat{s}_n = \frac{1}{n} \sum_{i=1}^{n} f(\boldsymbol{x}^{(i)}). \tag{17.3}$$

This approximation is justified by a few different properties. The first trivial observation is that the estimator $\hat{s}$ is unbiased, since

$$\mathbb{E}[\hat{s}_n] = \frac{1}{n} \sum_{i=1}^{n} \mathbb{E}[f(\boldsymbol{x}^{(i)})] = \frac{1}{n} \sum_{i=1}^{n} s = s. \tag{17.4}$$

But in addition, the **law of large numbers** states that if the samples $\boldsymbol{x}^{(i)}$ are i.i.d., then the average converges almost surely to the expected value:

$$\lim_{n \to \infty} \hat{s}_n = s, \tag{17.5}$$

provided that the variance of the individual terms, $\text{Var}[f(\boldsymbol{x}^{(i)})]$, is bounded. To see this more clearly, consider the variance of $\hat{s}_n$ as n increases. The variance $\text{Var}[\hat{s}_n]$ decreases and converges to 0, so long as $\text{Var}[f(\mathbf{x}^{(i)})] < \infty$:

$$\text{Var}[\hat{s}_n] = \frac{1}{n^2} \sum_{i=1}^{n} \text{Var}[f(\mathbf{x})] \tag{17.6}$$

$$= \frac{\text{Var}[f(\mathbf{x})]}{n}. \tag{17.7}$$

This convenient result also tells us how to estimate the uncertainty in a Monte Carlo average or equivalently the amount of expected error of the Monte Carlo approximation. We compute both the empirical average of the $f(\boldsymbol{x}^{(i)})$ and their empirical variance,[1] and then divide the estimated variance by the number of samples n to obtain an estimator of $\text{Var}[\hat{s}_n]$. The **central limit theorem** tells us that the distribution of the average, $\hat{s}_n$, converges to a normal distribution with mean s and variance $\frac{\text{Var}[f(\mathbf{x})]}{n}$. This allows us to estimate confidence intervals around the estimate $\hat{s}_n$, using the cumulative distribution of the normal density.

All this relies on our ability to easily sample from the base distribution $p(\mathbf{x})$, but doing so is not always possible. When it is not feasible to sample from p, an alternative is to use importance sampling, presented in section 17.2. A more general approach is to form a sequence of estimators that converge toward the distribution of interest. That is the approach of Monte Carlo Markov chains (section 17.3).

17.2 Importance Sampling

An important step in the decomposition of the integrand (or summand) used by the Monte Carlo method in equation 17.2 is deciding which part of the integrand should play the role of probability $p(\boldsymbol{x})$ and which part of the integrand should play the role of the quantity $f(\boldsymbol{x})$ whose expected value (under that probability distribution) is to be estimated. There is no unique decomposition because $p(\boldsymbol{x})f(\boldsymbol{x})$ can always be rewritten as

$$p(\boldsymbol{x})f(\boldsymbol{x}) = q(\boldsymbol{x})\frac{p(\boldsymbol{x})f(\boldsymbol{x})}{q(\boldsymbol{x})}, \tag{17.8}$$

where we now sample from q and average $\frac{pf}{q}$. In many cases, we wish to compute an expectation for a given p and an f, and the fact that the problem is specified from the start as an expectation suggests that this p and f would be a natural

---

[1]The unbiased estimator of the variance is often preferred, in which the sum of squared differences is divided by $n - 1$ instead of n.

choice of decomposition. However, the original specification of the problem may not be the the optimal choice in terms of the number of samples required to obtain a given level of accuracy. Fortunately, the form of the optimal choice q^* can be derived easily. The optimal q^* corresponds to what is called optimal importance sampling.

Because of the identity shown in equation 17.8, any Monte Carlo estimator

$$\hat{s}_p = \frac{1}{n} \sum_{i=1,\mathbf{x}^{(i)} \sim p}^{n} f(\boldsymbol{x}^{(i)}) \tag{17.9}$$

can be transformed into an importance sampling estimator

$$\hat{s}_q = \frac{1}{n} \sum_{i=1,\mathbf{x}^{(i)} \sim q}^{n} \frac{p(\boldsymbol{x}^{(i)}) f(\boldsymbol{x}^{(i)})}{q(\boldsymbol{x}^{(i)})}. \tag{17.10}$$

We see readily that the expected value of the estimator does not depend on q:

$$\mathbb{E}_q[\hat{s}_q] = \mathbb{E}_q[\hat{s}_p] = s. \tag{17.11}$$

The variance of an importance sampling estimator, however, can be greatly sensitive to the choice of q. The variance is given by

$$\mathrm{Var}[\hat{s}_q] = \mathrm{Var}[\frac{p(\mathbf{x})f(\mathbf{x})}{q(\mathbf{x})}]/n. \tag{17.12}$$

The minimum variance occurs when q is

$$q^*(\boldsymbol{x}) = \frac{p(\boldsymbol{x})|f(\boldsymbol{x})|}{Z}, \tag{17.13}$$

where Z is the normalization constant, chosen so that $q^*(\boldsymbol{x})$ sums or integrates to 1 as appropriate. Better importance sampling distributions put more weight where the integrand is larger. In fact, when $f(\boldsymbol{x})$ does not change sign, $\mathrm{Var}[\hat{s}_{q^*}] = 0$, meaning that *a single sample is sufficient* when the optimal distribution is used. Of course, this is only because the computation of q^* has essentially solved the original problem, so it is usually not practical to use this approach of drawing a single sample from the optimal distribution.

Any choice of sampling distribution q is valid (in the sense of yielding the correct expected value), and q^* is the optimal one (in the sense of yielding minimum variance). Sampling from q^* is usually infeasible, but other choices of q can be feasible while still reducing the variance somewhat.

Another approach is to use **biased importance sampling**, which has the advantage of not requiring normalized p or q. In the case of discrete variables, the biased importance sampling estimator is given by

$$\hat{s}_{BIS} = \frac{\sum_{i=1}^{n} \frac{p(\boldsymbol{x}^{(i)})}{q(\boldsymbol{x}^{(i)})} f(\boldsymbol{x}^{(i)})}{\sum_{i=1}^{n} \frac{p(\boldsymbol{x}^{(i)})}{q(\boldsymbol{x}^{(i)})}} \tag{17.14}$$

$$= \frac{\sum_{i=1}^{n} \frac{p(\boldsymbol{x}^{(i)})}{\tilde{q}(\boldsymbol{x}^{(i)})} f(\boldsymbol{x}^{(i)})}{\sum_{i=1}^{n} \frac{p(\boldsymbol{x}^{(i)})}{\tilde{q}(\boldsymbol{x}^{(i)})}} \tag{17.15}$$

$$= \frac{\sum_{i=1}^{n} \frac{\tilde{p}(\boldsymbol{x}^{(i)})}{\tilde{q}(\boldsymbol{x}^{(i)})} f(\boldsymbol{x}^{(i)})}{\sum_{i=1}^{n} \frac{\tilde{p}(\boldsymbol{x}^{(i)})}{\tilde{q}(\boldsymbol{x}^{(i)})}}, \tag{17.16}$$

where $\tilde{p}$ and $\tilde{q}$ are the unnormalized forms of p and q, and the $\boldsymbol{x}^{(i)}$ are the samples from q. This estimator is biased because $\mathbb{E}[\hat{s}_{BIS}] \neq s$, except asymptotically when $n \to \infty$ and the denominator of equation 17.14 converges to 1. Hence this estimator is called asymptotically unbiased.

Although a good choice of q can greatly improve the efficiency of Monte Carlo estimation, a poor choice of q can make the efficiency much worse. Going back to equation 17.12, we see that if there are samples of q for which $\frac{p(\boldsymbol{x})|f(\boldsymbol{x})|}{q(\boldsymbol{x})}$ is large, then the variance of the estimator can get very large. This may happen when $q(\boldsymbol{x})$ is tiny while neither $p(\boldsymbol{x})$ nor $f(\boldsymbol{x})$ are small enough to cancel it. The q distribution is usually chosen to be a simple distribution so that it is easy to sample from. When $\boldsymbol{x}$ is high dimensional, this simplicity in q causes it to match p or $p|f|$ poorly. When $q(\boldsymbol{x}^{(i)}) \gg p(\boldsymbol{x}^{(i)})|f(\boldsymbol{x}^{(i)})|$, importance sampling collects useless samples (summing tiny numbers or zeros). On the other hand, when $q(\boldsymbol{x}^{(i)}) \ll p(\boldsymbol{x}^{(i)})|f(\boldsymbol{x}^{(i)})|$, which will happen more rarely, the ratio can be huge. Because these latter events are rare, they may not show up in a typical sample, yielding typical underestimation of s, compensated rarely by gross overestimation. Such very large or very small numbers are typical when $\boldsymbol{x}$ is high dimensional, because in high dimension the dynamic range of joint probabilities can be very large.

In spite of this danger, importance sampling and its variants have been found very useful in many machine learning algorithms, including deep learning algorithms. For example, see the use of importance sampling to accelerate training in neural language models with a large vocabulary (section 12.4.3.3) or other neural nets with a large number of outputs. See also how importance sampling has been used to estimate a partition function (the normalization constant of a probability distribution) in section 18.7, and to estimate the log-likelihood in deep directed models, such as the variational autoencoder, in section 20.10.3. Importance sampling may also be used to improve the estimate of the gradient of the cost function used to train model parameters with stochastic gradient descent, particularly for models, such as classifiers, in which most of the total value of the cost function comes from a small number of misclassified examples. Sampling more difficult examples more frequently can reduce the variance of the gradient in such cases (Hinton, 2006).

17.3　Markov Chain Monte Carlo Methods

In many cases, we wish to use a Monte Carlo technique but there is no tractable method for drawing exact samples from the distribution $p_{\text{model}}(\mathbf{x})$ or from a good (low variance) importance sampling distribution $q(\mathbf{x})$. In the context of deep learning, this most often happens when $p_{\text{model}}(\mathbf{x})$ is represented by an undirected model. In these cases, we introduce a mathematical tool called a **Markov chain** to approximately sample from $p_{\text{model}}(\mathbf{x})$. The family of algorithms that use Markov chains to perform Monte Carlo estimates is called **Markov chain Monte Carlo methods** (MCMC). Markov chain Monte Carlo methods for machine learning are described at greater length in Koller and Friedman (2009). The most standard, generic guarantees for MCMC techniques are only applicable when the model does not assign zero probability to any state. Therefore, it is most convenient to present these techniques as sampling from an energy-based model (EBM) $p(\boldsymbol{x}) \propto \exp\left(-E(\boldsymbol{x})\right)$ as described in section 16.2.4. In the EBM formulation, every state is guaranteed to have nonzero probability. MCMC methods are in fact more broadly applicable and can be used with many probability distributions that contain zero probability states. However, the theoretical guarantees concerning the behavior of MCMC methods must be proved on a case-by-case basis for different families of such distributions. In the context of deep learning, it is most common to rely on the general theoretical guarantees that naturally apply to all energy-based models.

To understand why drawing samples from an energy-based model is difficult, consider an EBM over just two variables, defining a distribution $p(a, b)$. In order to sample a, we must draw a from $p(a \mid b)$, and in order to sample b, we must draw it from $p(b \mid a)$. It seems to be an intractable chicken-and-egg problem. Directed models avoid this because their graph is directed and acyclic. To perform **ancestral sampling**, one simply samples each of the variables in topological order, conditioning on each variable's parents, which are guaranteed to have already been sampled (section 16.3). Ancestral sampling defines an efficient, single-pass method of obtaining a sample.

In an EBM, we can avoid this chicken-and-egg problem by sampling using a Markov chain. The core idea of a Markov chain is to have a state $\boldsymbol{x}$ that begins as an arbitrary value. Over time, we randomly update $\boldsymbol{x}$ repeatedly. Eventually $\boldsymbol{x}$ becomes (very nearly) a fair sample from $p(\boldsymbol{x})$. Formally, a Markov chain is defined by a random state $\boldsymbol{x}$ and a transition distribution $T(\boldsymbol{x}' \mid \boldsymbol{x})$ specifying the probability that a random update will go to state $\boldsymbol{x}'$ if it starts in state $\boldsymbol{x}$. Running the Markov chain means repeatedly updating the state $\boldsymbol{x}$ to a value $\boldsymbol{x}'$ sampled from $T(\mathbf{x}' \mid \boldsymbol{x})$.

To gain some theoretical understanding of how MCMC methods work, it is useful to reparametrize the problem. First, we restrict our attention to the case where the random variable $\mathbf{x}$ has countably many states. We can then represent the state as just a positive integer x. Different integer values of x map back to different states $\boldsymbol{x}$ in the original problem.

Consider what happens when we run infinitely many Markov chains in parallel. All the states of the different Markov chains are drawn from some distribution $q^{(t)}(x)$, where t indicates the number of time steps that have elapsed. At the beginning, $q^{(0)}$ is some distribution that we used to arbitrarily initialize x for each Markov chain. Later, $q^{(t)}$ is influenced by all the Markov chain steps that have run so far. Our goal is for $q^{(t)}(x)$ to converge to $p(x)$.

Because we have reparametrized the problem in terms of positive integer x, we can describe the probability distribution q using a vector $\boldsymbol{v}$ with

$$q(\mathbf{x} = i) = v_i. \tag{17.17}$$

Consider what happens when we update a single Markov chain's state x to a new state x'. The probability of a single state landing in state x' is given by

$$q^{(t+1)}(x') = \sum_x q^{(t)}(x) T(x' \mid x). \tag{17.18}$$

Using our integer parametrization, we can represent the effect of the transition operator T using a matrix $\boldsymbol{A}$. We define $\boldsymbol{A}$ so that

$$A_{i,j} = T(\mathbf{x}' = i \mid \mathbf{x} = j). \tag{17.19}$$

Using this definition, we can now rewrite equation 17.18. Rather than writing it in terms of q and T to understand how a single state is updated, we may now use $\boldsymbol{v}$

and $\boldsymbol{A}$ to describe how the entire distribution over all the different Markov chains (running in parallel) shifts as we apply an update:

$$\boldsymbol{v}^{(t)} = \boldsymbol{A}\boldsymbol{v}^{(t-1)}. \tag{17.20}$$

Applying the Markov chain update repeatedly corresponds to multiplying by the matrix $\boldsymbol{A}$ repeatedly. In other words, we can think of the process as exponentiating the matrix $\boldsymbol{A}$:

$$\boldsymbol{v}^{(t)} = \boldsymbol{A}^t\boldsymbol{v}^{(0)}. \tag{17.21}$$

The matrix $\boldsymbol{A}$ has special structure because each of its columns represents a probability distribution. Such matrices are called **stochastic matrices**. If there is a nonzero probability of transitioning from any state x to any other state x' for some power t, then the Perron-Frobenius theorem (Perron, 1907; Frobenius, 1908) guarantees that the largest eigenvalue is real and equal to 1. Over time, we can see that all the eigenvalues are exponentiated:

$$\boldsymbol{v}^{(t)} = \left(\boldsymbol{V}\mathrm{diag}(\boldsymbol{\lambda})\boldsymbol{V}^{-1}\right)^t \boldsymbol{v}^{(0)} = \boldsymbol{V}\mathrm{diag}(\boldsymbol{\lambda})^t\boldsymbol{V}^{-1}\boldsymbol{v}^{(0)}. \tag{17.22}$$

This process causes all the eigenvalues that are not equal to 1 to decay to zero. Under some additional mild conditions, $\boldsymbol{A}$ is guaranteed to have only one eigenvector with eigenvalue 1. The process thus converges to a **stationary distribution**, sometimes also called the **equilibrium distribution**. At convergence,

$$\boldsymbol{v}' = \boldsymbol{A}\boldsymbol{v} = \boldsymbol{v}, \tag{17.23}$$

and this same condition holds for every additional step. This is an eigenvector equation. To be a stationary point, $\boldsymbol{v}$ must be an eigenvector with corresponding eigenvalue 1. This condition guarantees that once we have reached the stationary distribution, repeated applications of the transition sampling procedure do not change the *distribution* over the states of all the various Markov chains (although the transition operator does change each individual state, of course).

If we have chosen T correctly, then the stationary distribution q will be equal to the distribution p we wish to sample from. We describe how to choose T in section 17.4.

Most properties of Markov chains with countable states can be generalized to continuous variables. In this situation, some authors call the Markov chain a **Harris chain**, but we use the term Markov chain to describe both conditions. In general, a Markov chain with transition operator T will converge, under mild conditions, to a fixed point described by the equation

$$q'(\mathbf{x}') = \mathbb{E}_{\mathbf{x}\sim q}T(\mathbf{x}' \mid \mathbf{x}), \tag{17.24}$$

which in the discrete case is just rewriting equation 17.23. When $\mathbf{x}$ is discrete, the expectation corresponds to a sum, and when $\mathbf{x}$ is continuous, the expectation corresponds to an integral.

Regardless of whether the state is continuous or discrete, all Markov chain methods consist of repeatedly applying stochastic updates until eventually the state begins to yield samples from the equilibrium distribution. Running the Markov chain until it reaches its equilibrium distribution is called **burning in** the Markov chain. After the chain has reached equilibrium, a sequence of infinitely many samples may be drawn from the equilibrium distribution. They are identically distributed, but any two successive samples will be highly correlated with each other. A finite sequence of samples may thus not be very representative of the equilibrium distribution. One way to mitigate this problem is to return only every n successive samples, so that our estimate of the statistics of the equilibrium distribution is not as biased by the correlation between an MCMC sample and the next several samples. Markov chains are thus expensive to use because of the time required to burn in to the equilibrium distribution and the time required to transition from one sample to another reasonably decorrelated sample after reaching equilibrium. If one desires truly independent samples, one can run multiple Markov chains in parallel. This approach uses extra parallel computation to eliminate latency. The strategy of using only a single Markov chain to generate all samples and the strategy of using one Markov chain for each desired sample are two extremes; deep learning practitioners usually use a number of chains that is similar to the number of examples in a minibatch and then draw as many samples as are needed from this fixed set of Markov chains. A commonly used number of Markov chains is 100.

Another difficulty is that we do not know in advance how many steps the Markov chain must run before reaching its equilibrium distribution. This length of time is called the **mixing time**. Testing whether a Markov chain has reached equilibrium is also difficult. We do not have a precise enough theory for guiding us in answering this question. Theory tells us that the chain will converge, but not much more. If we analyze the Markov chain from the point of view of a matrix $\mathbf{A}$ acting on a vector of probabilities $\mathbf{v}$, then we know that the chain mixes when $\mathbf{A}^t$ has effectively lost all the eigenvalues from $\mathbf{A}$ besides the unique eigenvalue of 1. This means that the magnitude of the second-largest eigenvalue will determine the mixing time. In practice, though, we cannot actually represent our Markov chain in terms of a matrix. The number of states that our probabilistic model can visit is exponentially large in the number of variables, so it is infeasible to represent $\mathbf{v}$, $\mathbf{A}$, or the eigenvalues of $\mathbf{A}$. Because of these and other obstacles, we usually do not know whether a Markov chain has mixed. Instead, we simply run the Markov chain for an amount of time that we roughly estimate to be sufficient, and use heuristic methods to determine whether the chain has mixed. These heuristic methods include manually inspecting samples or measuring correlations between successive samples.

17.4 Gibbs Sampling

So far we have described how to draw samples from a distribution $q(\boldsymbol{x})$ by repeatedly updating $\boldsymbol{x} \leftarrow \boldsymbol{x}' \sim T(\boldsymbol{x}' \mid \boldsymbol{x})$. We have not described how to ensure that $q(\boldsymbol{x})$ is a useful distribution. Two basic approaches are considered in this book. The first one is to derive T from a given learned p_{model}, described below with the case of sampling from EBMs. The second one is to directly parametrize T and learn it, so that its stationary distribution implicitly defines the p_{model} of interest. Examples of this second approach are discussed in sections 20.12 and 20.13.

In the context of deep learning, we commonly use Markov chains to draw samples from an energy-based model defining a distribution $p_{\text{model}}(\boldsymbol{x})$. In this case, we want the $q(\boldsymbol{x})$ for the Markov chain to be $p_{\text{model}}(\boldsymbol{x})$. To obtain the desired $q(\boldsymbol{x})$, we must choose an appropriate $T(\boldsymbol{x}' \mid \boldsymbol{x})$.

A conceptually simple and effective approach to building a Markov chain that samples from $p_{\text{model}}(\boldsymbol{x})$ is to use **Gibbs sampling**, in which sampling from $T(\mathbf{x}' \mid \mathbf{x})$ is accomplished by selecting one variable $\mathbf{x}_i$ and sampling it from p_{model} conditioned on its neighbors in the undirected graph $\mathcal{G}$ defining the structure of the energy-based model. We can also sample several variables at the same time as long as they are conditionally independent given all their neighbors. As shown in the RBM example in section 16.7.1, all the hidden units of an RBM may be sampled simultaneously because they are conditionally independent from each other given all the visible units. Likewise, all the visible units may be sampled simultaneously because they are conditionally independent from each other given all the hidden units. Gibbs sampling approaches that update many variables simultaneously in this way are called **block Gibbs sampling**.

Alternate approaches to designing Markov chains to sample from p_{model} are possible. For example, the Metropolis-Hastings algorithm is widely used in other disciplines. In the context of the deep learning approach to undirected modeling, it is rare to use any approach other than Gibbs sampling. Improved sampling techniques are one possible research frontier.

17.5 The Challenge of Mixing between Separated Modes

The primary difficulty involved with MCMC methods is that they have a tendency to **mix** poorly. Ideally, successive samples from a Markov chain designed to sample from $p(\boldsymbol{x})$ would be completely independent from each other and would visit many different regions in $\boldsymbol{x}$ space proportional to their probability. Instead, especially in high-dimensional cases, MCMC samples become very correlated. We refer to such behavior as slow mixing or even failure to mix. MCMC methods with slow mixing can be seen as inadvertently performing something resembling noisy gradient descent on the energy function, or equivalently noisy hill climbing on the probability, with respect to the state of the chain (the random variables being sampled). The chain tends to take small steps (in the space of the state of the Markov chain), from a configuration $\boldsymbol{x}^{(t-1)}$ to a configuration $\boldsymbol{x}^{(t)}$, with the energy $E(\boldsymbol{x}^{(t)})$ generally lower or approximately equal to the energy $E(\boldsymbol{x}^{(t-1)})$, with a preference for moves that yield lower energy configurations. When starting from a rather improbable configuration (higher energy than the typical ones from $p(\mathbf{x})$), the chain tends to gradually reduce the energy of the state and only occasionally move to another mode. Once the chain has found a region of low energy (for example, if the variables are pixels in an image, a region of low energy might be a connected manifold of images of the same object), which we call a mode, the chain will tend to walk around that mode (following a kind of random walk). Once in a while it will step out of that mode and generally return to it or (if it finds an escape route) move toward another mode. The problem is that successful escape routes are rare for many interesting distributions, so the Markov chain will continue to sample the same mode longer than it should.

This is very clear when we consider the Gibbs sampling algorithm (section 17.4). In this context, consider the probability of going from one mode to a nearby mode within a given number of steps. What will determine that probability is the shape of the "energy barrier" between these modes. Transitions between two modes that are separated by a high energy barrier (a region of low probability) are exponentially less likely (in terms of the height of the energy barrier). This is illustrated in figure 17.1. The problem arises when there are multiple modes with high probability that are separated by regions of low probability, especially when each Gibbs sampling step must update only a small subset of variables whose values are largely determined by the other variables.

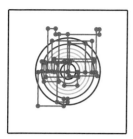 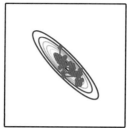 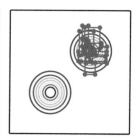

Figure 17.1: Paths followed by Gibbs sampling for three distributions, with the Markov chain initialized at the mode in both cases. *(Left)*A multivariate normal distribution with two independent variables. Gibbs sampling mixes well because the variables are independent. *(Center)*A multivariate normal distribution with highly correlated variables. The correlation between variables makes it difficult for the Markov chain to mix. Because the update for each variable must be conditioned on the other variable, the correlation reduces the rate at which the Markov chain can move away from the starting point. *(Right)*A mixture of Gaussians with widely separated modes that are not axis aligned. Gibbs sampling mixes very slowly because it is difficult to change modes while altering only one variable at a time.

As a simple example, consider an energy-based model over two variables a and b, which are both binary with a sign, taking on values -1 and 1. If $E(a, b) = -wab$ for some large positive number w, then the model expresses a strong belief that a and b have the same sign. Consider updating b using a Gibbs sampling step with a = 1. The conditional distribution over b is given by $P(b = 1 \mid a = 1) = \sigma(w)$. If w is large, the sigmoid saturates, and the probability of also assigning b to be 1 is close to 1. Likewise, if a = -1, the probability of assigning b to be -1 is close to 1. According to $P_{\text{model}}(a, b)$, both signs of both variables are equally likely. According to $P_{\text{model}}(a \mid b)$, both variables should have the same sign. This means that Gibbs sampling will only very rarely flip the signs of these variables.

In more practical scenarios, the challenge is even greater because we care about making transitions not only between two modes but more generally between all the many modes that a real model might contain. If several such transitions are difficult because of the difficulty of mixing between modes, then it becomes very expensive to obtain a reliable set of samples covering most of the modes, and convergence of the chain to its stationary distribution is very slow.

Sometimes this problem can be resolved by finding groups of highly dependent units and updating all of them simultaneously in a block. Unfortunately, when the dependencies are complicated, it can be computationally intractable to draw a sample from the group. After all, the problem that the Markov chain was originally introduced to solve is this problem of sampling from a large group of variables.

In the context of models with latent variables, which define a joint distribution $p_{\text{model}}(\boldsymbol{x}, \boldsymbol{h})$, we often draw samples of $\boldsymbol{x}$ by alternating between sampling from $p_{\text{model}}(\boldsymbol{x} \mid \boldsymbol{h})$ and sampling from $p_{\text{model}}(\boldsymbol{h} \mid \boldsymbol{x})$. From the point of view of mixing rapidly, we would like $p_{\text{model}}(\boldsymbol{h} \mid \boldsymbol{x})$ to have high entropy. From the point of view of learning a useful representation of $\boldsymbol{h}$, we would like $\boldsymbol{h}$ to encode enough information about $\boldsymbol{x}$ to reconstruct it well, which implies that $\boldsymbol{h}$ and $\boldsymbol{x}$ should have high mutual information. These two goals are at odds with each other. We often learn generative models that very precisely encode $\boldsymbol{x}$ into $\boldsymbol{h}$ but are not able to mix very well. This situation arises frequently with Boltzmann machines—the sharper the distribution a Boltzmann machine learns, the harder it is for a Markov chain sampling from the model distribution to mix well. This problem is illustrated in figure 17.2.

All this could make MCMC methods less useful when the distribution of interest has a manifold structure with a separate manifold for each class: the distribution is concentrated around many modes, and these modes are separated by vast regions of high energy. This type of distribution is what we expect in many classification problems, and it would make MCMC methods converge very slowly because of poor mixing between modes.

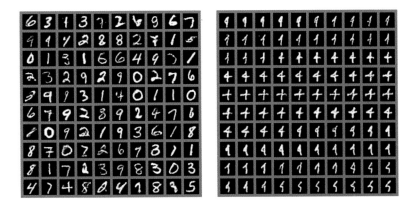

Figure 17.2: An illustration of the slow mixing problem in deep probabilistic models. Each panel should be read left to right, top to bottom. *(Left)*Consecutive samples from Gibbs sampling applied to a deep Boltzmann machine trained on the MNIST dataset. Consecutive samples are similar to each other. Because the Gibbs sampling is performed in a deep graphical model, this similarity is based more on semantic than raw visual features, but it is still difficult for the Gibbs chain to transition from one mode of the distribution to another, for example, by changing the digit identity. *(Right)*Consecutive ancestral samples from a generative adversarial network. Because ancestral sampling generates each sample independently from the others, there is no mixing problem.

17.5.1 Tempering to Mix between Modes

When a distribution has sharp peaks of high probability surrounded by regions of low probability, it is difficult to mix between the different modes of the distribution. Several techniques for faster mixing are based on constructing alternative versions of the target distribution in which the peaks are not as high and the surrounding valleys are not as low. Energy-based models provide a particularly simple way to do so. So far, we have described an energy-based model as defining a probability distribution

$$p(\boldsymbol{x}) \propto \exp\left(-E(\boldsymbol{x})\right). \tag{17.25}$$

Energy-based models may be augmented with an extra parameter β controlling how sharply peaked the distribution is:

$$p_\beta(\boldsymbol{x}) \propto \exp\left(-\beta E(\boldsymbol{x})\right). \tag{17.26}$$

The β parameter is often described as being the reciprocal of the **temperature**, reflecting the origin of energy-based models in statistical physics. When the temperature falls to zero, and β rises to infinity, the energy-based model becomes deterministic. When the temperature rises to infinity, and β falls to zero, the distribution (for discrete $\boldsymbol{x}$) becomes uniform.

Typically, a model is trained to be evaluated at $\beta = 1$. However, we can make use of other temperatures, particularly those where $\beta < 1$. **Tempering** is a general strategy of mixing between modes of p_1 rapidly by drawing samples with $\beta < 1$.

Markov chains based on **tempered transitions** (Neal, 1994) temporarily sample from higher-temperature distributions to mix to different modes, then resume sampling from the unit temperature distribution. These techniques have been applied to models such as RBMs (Salakhutdinov, 2010). Another approach is to use **parallel tempering** (Iba, 2001), in which the Markov chain simulates many different states in parallel, at different temperatures. The highest temperature states mix slowly, while the lowest temperature states, at temperature 1, provide accurate samples from the model. The transition operator includes stochastically swapping states between two different temperature levels, so that a sufficiently high-probability sample from a high-temperature slot can jump into a lower temperature slot. This approach has also been applied to RBMs (Desjardins et al., 2010; Cho et al., 2010). Although tempering is a promising approach, at this point it has not allowed researchers to make a strong advance in solving the challenge of sampling from complex EBMs. One possible reason is that there are **critical temperatures** around which the temperature transition must be very slow (as the temperature is gradually reduced) for tempering to be effective.

17.5.2   Depth May Help Mixing

When drawing samples from a latent variable model $p(\boldsymbol{h}, \boldsymbol{x})$, we have seen that if $p(\boldsymbol{h} \mid \boldsymbol{x})$ encodes $\boldsymbol{x}$ too well, then sampling from $p(\boldsymbol{x} \mid \boldsymbol{h})$ will not change $\boldsymbol{x}$ very much, and mixing will be poor. One way to resolve this problem is to make $\boldsymbol{h}$ a deep representation, encoding $\boldsymbol{x}$ into $\boldsymbol{h}$ in such a way that a Markov chain in the space of $\boldsymbol{h}$ can mix more easily. Many representation learning algorithms, such as autoencoders and RBMs, tend to yield a marginal distribution over $\boldsymbol{h}$ that is more uniform and more unimodal than the original data distribution over $\boldsymbol{x}$. It can be argued that this arises from trying to minimize reconstruction error while using all the available representation space, because minimizing reconstruction error over the training examples will be better achieved when different training examples are easily distinguishable from each other in $\boldsymbol{h}$-space, and thus well separated. Bengio et al. (2013a) observed that deeper stacks of regularized autoencoders or RBMs yield marginal distributions in the top-level $\boldsymbol{h}$-space that appeared more spread out and more uniform, with less of a gap between the regions corresponding to different modes (categories, in the experiments). Training an RBM in that higher-level space allowed Gibbs sampling to mix faster between modes. It remains unclear, however, how to exploit this observation to help better train and sample from deep generative models.

Despite the difficulty of mixing, Monte Carlo techniques are useful and are often the best tool available. Indeed, they are the primary tool used to confront the intractable partition function of undirected models, discussed next.

18

Confronting the Partition Function

In section 16.2.2 we saw that many probabilistic models (commonly known as undirected graphical models) are defined by an unnormalized probability distribution $\tilde{p}(\mathbf{x}; \theta)$. We must normalize $\tilde{p}$ by dividing by a partition function $Z(\boldsymbol{\theta})$ to obtain a valid probability distribution:

$$p(\mathbf{x}; \boldsymbol{\theta}) = \frac{1}{Z(\boldsymbol{\theta})} \tilde{p}(\mathbf{x}; \boldsymbol{\theta}). \tag{18.1}$$

The partition function is an integral (for continuous variables) or sum (for discrete variables) over the unnormalized probability of all states:

$$\int \tilde{p}(\boldsymbol{x}) d\boldsymbol{x} \tag{18.2}$$

or

$$\sum_{\boldsymbol{x}} \tilde{p}(\boldsymbol{x}). \tag{18.3}$$

This operation is intractable for many interesting models.

As we will see in chapter 20, several deep learning models are designed to have a tractable normalizing constant, or are designed to be used in ways that do not involve computing $p(\mathbf{x})$ at all. Yet, other models directly confront the challenge of intractable partition functions. In this chapter, we describe techniques used for training and evaluating models that have intractable partition functions.

18.1 The Log-Likelihood Gradient

What makes learning undirected models by maximum likelihood particularly difficult is that the partition function depends on the parameters. The gradient of the log-likelihood with respect to the parameters has a term corresponding to the gradient of the partition function:

$$\nabla_{\boldsymbol{\theta}} \log p(\mathbf{x}; \boldsymbol{\theta}) = \nabla_{\boldsymbol{\theta}} \log \tilde{p}(\mathbf{x}; \boldsymbol{\theta}) - \nabla_{\boldsymbol{\theta}} \log Z(\boldsymbol{\theta}). \tag{18.4}$$

This is a well-known decomposition into the **positive phase** and **negative phase** of learning.

For most undirected models of interest, the negative phase is difficult. Models with no latent variables or with few interactions between latent variables typically have a tractable positive phase. The quintessential example of a model with a straightforward positive phase and a difficult negative phase is the RBM, which has hidden units that are conditionally independent from each other given the visible units. The case where the positive phase is difficult, with complicated interactions between latent variables, is primarily covered in chapter 19. This chapter focuses on the difficulties of the negative phase.

Let us look more closely at the gradient of $\log Z$:

$$\nabla_{\boldsymbol{\theta}} \log Z \tag{18.5}$$

$$= \frac{\nabla_{\boldsymbol{\theta}} Z}{Z} \tag{18.6}$$

$$= \frac{\nabla_{\boldsymbol{\theta}} \sum_{\mathbf{x}} \tilde{p}(\mathbf{x})}{Z} \tag{18.7}$$

$$= \frac{\sum_{\mathbf{x}} \nabla_{\boldsymbol{\theta}} \tilde{p}(\mathbf{x})}{Z}. \tag{18.8}$$

For models that guarantee $p(\mathbf{x}) > 0$ for all $\mathbf{x}$, we can substitute $\exp(\log \tilde{p}(\mathbf{x}))$ for $\tilde{p}(\mathbf{x})$:

$$\frac{\sum_{\mathbf{x}} \nabla_{\boldsymbol{\theta}} \exp(\log \tilde{p}(\mathbf{x}))}{Z} \tag{18.9}$$

$$= \frac{\sum_{\mathbf{x}} \exp(\log \tilde{p}(\mathbf{x})) \nabla_{\boldsymbol{\theta}} \log \tilde{p}(\mathbf{x})}{Z} \tag{18.10}$$

$$= \frac{\sum_{\mathbf{x}} \tilde{p}(\mathbf{x}) \nabla_{\boldsymbol{\theta}} \log \tilde{p}(\mathbf{x})}{Z} \tag{18.11}$$

$$= \sum_{\mathbf{x}} p(\mathbf{x}) \nabla_{\boldsymbol{\theta}} \log \tilde{p}(\mathbf{x}) \tag{18.12}$$

$$= \mathbb{E}_{\mathbf{x} \sim p(\mathbf{x})} \nabla_{\boldsymbol{\theta}} \log \tilde{p}(\mathbf{x}). \tag{18.13}$$

This derivation made use of summation over discrete $\boldsymbol{x}$, but a similar result applies using integration over continuous $\boldsymbol{x}$. In the continuous version of the derivation, we use Leibniz's rule for differentiation under the integral sign to obtain the identity

$$\nabla_{\boldsymbol{\theta}} \int \tilde{p}(\mathbf{x}) d\boldsymbol{x} = \int \nabla_{\boldsymbol{\theta}} \tilde{p}(\mathbf{x}) d\boldsymbol{x}. \tag{18.14}$$

This identity is applicable only under certain regularity conditions on $\tilde{p}$ and $\nabla_{\boldsymbol{\theta}} \tilde{p}(\mathbf{x})$. In measure theoretic terms, the conditions are: (1) The unnormalized distribution $\tilde{p}$ must be a Lebesgue-integrable function of $\boldsymbol{x}$ for every value of $\boldsymbol{\theta}$. (2) The gradient $\nabla_{\boldsymbol{\theta}} \tilde{p}(\mathbf{x})$ must exist for all $\boldsymbol{\theta}$ and almost all $\boldsymbol{x}$. (3) There must exist an integrable function $R(\boldsymbol{x})$ that bounds $\nabla_{\boldsymbol{\theta}} \tilde{p}(\mathbf{x})$ in the sense that $\max_i |\frac{\partial}{\partial \theta_i} \tilde{p}(\mathbf{x})| \leq R(\boldsymbol{x})$ for all $\boldsymbol{\theta}$ and almost all $\boldsymbol{x}$. Fortunately, most machine learning models of interest have these properties.

This identity

$$\nabla_{\boldsymbol{\theta}} \log Z = \mathbb{E}_{\mathbf{x} \sim p(\mathbf{x})} \nabla_{\boldsymbol{\theta}} \log \tilde{p}(\mathbf{x}) \tag{18.15}$$

is the basis for a variety of Monte Carlo methods for approximately maximizing the likelihood of models with intractable partition functions.

The Monte Carlo approach to learning undirected models provides an intuitive framework in which we can think of both the positive phase and the negative phase. In the positive phase, we increase $\log \tilde{p}(\mathbf{x})$ for $\boldsymbol{x}$ drawn from the data. In the negative phase, we decrease the partition function by decreasing $\log \tilde{p}(\mathbf{x})$ drawn from the model distribution.

In the deep learning literature, it is common to parametrize $\log \tilde{p}$ in terms of an energy function (equation 16.7). In this case, we can interpret the positive phase as pushing down on the energy of training examples and the negative phase as pushing up on the energy of samples drawn from the model, as illustrated in figure 18.1.

18.2 Stochastic Maximum Likelihood and Contrastive Divergence

The naive way of implementing equation 18.15 is to compute it by burning in a set of Markov chains from a random initialization every time the gradient is needed. When learning is performed using stochastic gradient descent, this means the chains must be burned in once per gradient step. This approach leads to the training procedure presented in algorithm 18.1. The high cost of burning in the Markov chains in the inner loop makes this procedure computationally infeasible,

---

Algorithm 18.1 A naive MCMC algorithm for maximizing the log-likelihood with an intractable partition function using gradient ascent

---

Set ϵ, the step size, to a small positive number.

Set k, the number of Gibbs steps, high enough to allow burn in. Perhaps 100 to train an RBM on a small image patch.

while not converged **do**

    Sample a minibatch of m examples $\{\mathbf{x}^{(1)}, \dots, \mathbf{x}^{(m)}\}$ from the training set

    $\mathbf{g} \leftarrow \frac{1}{m} \sum_{i=1}^{m} \nabla_{\boldsymbol{\theta}} \log \tilde{p}(\mathbf{x}^{(i)}; \boldsymbol{\theta})$.

    Initialize a set of m samples $\{\tilde{\mathbf{x}}^{(1)}, \dots, \tilde{\mathbf{x}}^{(m)}\}$ to random values (e.g., from a uniform or normal distribution, or possibly a distribution with marginals matched to the model's marginals).

    for $i = 1$ to k **do**

        for $j = 1$ to m **do**

            $\tilde{\mathbf{x}}^{(j)} \leftarrow \text{gibbs\_update}(\tilde{\mathbf{x}}^{(j)})$.

        end for

    end for

    $\mathbf{g} \leftarrow \mathbf{g} - \frac{1}{m} \sum_{i=1}^{m} \nabla_{\boldsymbol{\theta}} \log \tilde{p}(\tilde{\mathbf{x}}^{(i)}; \boldsymbol{\theta})$.

    $\boldsymbol{\theta} \leftarrow \boldsymbol{\theta} + \epsilon \mathbf{g}$.

end while

---

but this procedure is the starting point that other more practical algorithms aim to approximate.

We can view the MCMC approach to maximum likelihood as trying to achieve balance between two forces, one pushing up on the model distribution where the data occurs, and another pushing down on the model distribution where the model samples occur. Figure 18.1 illustrates this process. The two forces correspond to maximizing $\log \tilde{p}$ and minimizing $\log Z$. Several approximations to the negative phase are possible. Each of these approximations can be understood as making the negative phase computationally cheaper but also making it push down in the wrong locations.

Because the negative phase involves drawing samples from the model's distribution, we can think of it as finding points that the model believes in strongly. Because the negative phase acts to reduce the probability of those points, they are generally considered to represent the model's incorrect beliefs about the world. They are frequently referred to in the literature as "hallucinations" or "fantasy particles." In fact, the negative phase has been proposed as a possible explanation for dreaming in humans and other animals (Crick and Mitchison, 1983), the idea being that the brain maintains a probabilistic model of the world and follows the

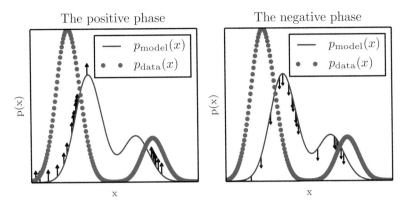

Figure 18.1: The view of algorithm 18.1 as having a "positive phase" and a "negative phase." *(Left)*In the positive phase, we sample points from the data distribution and push up on their unnormalized probability. This means points that are likely in the data get pushed up on more. *(Right)*In the negative phase, we sample points from the model distribution and push down on their unnormalized probability. This counteracts the positive phase's tendency to just add a large constant to the unnormalized probability everywhere. When the data distribution and the model distribution are equal, the positive phase has the same chance to push up at a point as the negative phase has to push down. When this occurs, there is no longer any gradient (in expectation), and training must terminate.

gradient of $\log \tilde{p}$ when experiencing real events while awake and follows the negative gradient of $\log \tilde{p}$ to minimize $\log Z$ while sleeping and experiencing events sampled from the current model. This view explains much of the language used to describe algorithms with a positive and a negative phase, but it has not been proved to be correct with neuroscientific experiments. In machine learning models, it is usually necessary to use the positive and negative phase simultaneously, rather than in separate periods of wakefulness and REM sleep. As we will see in section 19.5, other machine learning algorithms draw samples from the model distribution for other purposes, and such algorithms could also provide an account for the function of dream sleep.

Given this understanding of the role of the positive and the negative phase of learning, we can attempt to design a less expensive alternative to algorithm 18.1. The main cost of the naive MCMC algorithm is the cost of burning in the Markov chains from a random initialization at each step. A natural solution is to initialize the Markov chains from a distribution that is very close to the model distribution, so that the burn in operation does not take as many steps.

The **contrastive divergence** (CD, or CD-k to indicate CD with k Gibbs steps) algorithm initializes the Markov chain at each step with samples from the data

---

Algorithm 18.2 The contrastive divergence algorithm, using gradient ascent as the optimization procedure

---

Set ϵ, the step size, to a small positive number.
Set k, the number of Gibbs steps, high enough to allow a Markov chain sampling from $p(\mathbf{x}; \boldsymbol{\theta})$ to mix when initialized from p_{data}. Perhaps 1–20 to train an RBM on a small image patch.
while not converged **do**
    Sample a minibatch of m examples $\{\mathbf{x}^{(1)}, \ldots, \mathbf{x}^{(m)}\}$ from the training set
    $\mathbf{g} \leftarrow \frac{1}{m} \sum_{i=1}^{m} \nabla_{\boldsymbol{\theta}} \log \tilde{p}(\mathbf{x}^{(i)}; \boldsymbol{\theta})$.
    for $i = 1$ to m **do**
        $\tilde{\mathbf{x}}^{(i)} \leftarrow \mathbf{x}^{(i)}$.
    end for
    for $i = 1$ to k **do**
        for $j = 1$ to m **do**
            $\tilde{\mathbf{x}}^{(j)} \leftarrow \text{gibbs\_update}(\tilde{\mathbf{x}}^{(j)})$.
        end for
    end for
    $\mathbf{g} \leftarrow \mathbf{g} - \frac{1}{m} \sum_{i=1}^{m} \nabla_{\boldsymbol{\theta}} \log \tilde{p}(\tilde{\mathbf{x}}^{(i)}; \boldsymbol{\theta})$.
    $\boldsymbol{\theta} \leftarrow \boldsymbol{\theta} + \epsilon \mathbf{g}$.
end while

---

distribution (Hinton, 2000, 2010). This approach is presented as algorithm 18.2. Obtaining samples from the data distribution is free, because they are already available in the dataset. Initially, the data distribution is not close to the model distribution, so the negative phase is not very accurate. Fortunately, the positive phase can still accurately increase the model's probability of the data. After the positive phase has had some time to act, the model distribution is closer to the data distribution, and the negative phase starts to become accurate.

Of course, CD is still an approximation to the correct negative phase. The main way in which CD qualitatively fails to implement the correct negative phase is that it fails to suppress regions of high probability that are far from actual training examples. These regions that have high probability under the model but low probability under the data-generating distribution are called **spurious modes**. Figure 18.2 illustrates why this happens. Essentially, modes in the model distribution that are far from the data distribution will not be visited by Markov chains initialized at training points, unless k is very large.

Carreira-Perpiñan and Hinton (2005) showed experimentally that the CD estimator is biased for RBMs and fully visible Boltzmann machines, in that it

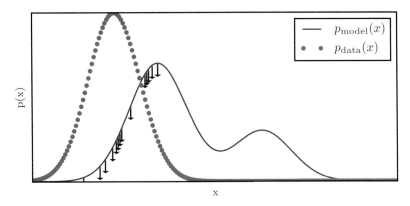

Figure 18.2: A spurious mode. An illustration of how the negative phase of contrastive divergence (algorithm 18.2) can fail to suppress spurious modes. A spurious mode is a mode that is present in the model distribution but absent in the data distribution. Because contrastive divergence initializes its Markov chains from data points and runs the Markov chain for only a few steps, it is unlikely to visit modes in the model that are far from the data points. This means that when sampling from the model, we will sometimes get samples that do not resemble the data. It also means that due to wasting some of its probability mass on these modes, the model will struggle to place highprobability mass on the correct modes. For the purpose of visualization, this figure uses a somewhat simplified concept of distance—the spurious mode is far from the correct mode along the number line in $\mathbb{R}$. This corresponds to a Markov chain based on making local moves with a single x variable in $\mathbb{R}$. For most deep probabilistic models, the Markov chains are based on Gibbs sampling and can make nonlocal moves of individual variables but cannot move all the variables simultaneously. For these problems, it is usually better to consider the edit distance between modes, rather than the Euclidean distance. However, edit distance in a high-dimensional space is difficult to depict in a 2-D plot.

converges to different points than the maximum likelihood estimator. They argue that because the bias is small, CD could be used as an inexpensive way to initialize a model that could later be fine-tuned via more expensive MCMC methods. Bengio and Delalleau (2009) show that CD can be interpreted as discarding the smallest terms of the correct MCMC update gradient, which explains the bias.

CD is useful for training shallow models like RBMs. These can in turn be stacked to initialize deeper models like DBNs or DBMs. But CD does not provide much help for training deeper models directly. This is because it is difficult to obtain samples of the hidden units given samples of the visible units. Since the hidden units are not included in the data, initializing from training points cannot solve the problem. Even if we initialize the visible units from the data, we will still need to burn in a Markov chain sampling from the distribution over the hidden units conditioned on those visible samples.

The CD algorithm can be thought of as penalizing the model for having a Markov chain that changes the input rapidly when the input comes from the data. This means training with CD somewhat resembles autoencoder training. Even though CD is more biased than some of the other training methods, it can be useful for pretraining shallow models that will later be stacked. This is because the earliest models in the stack are encouraged to copy more information up to their latent variables, thereby making it available to the later models. This should be thought of more of as an often-exploitable side effect of CD training rather than a principled design advantage.

Sutskever and Tieleman (2010) showed that the CD update direction is not the gradient of any function. This allows for situations where CD could cycle forever, but in practice this is not a serious problem.

A different strategy that resolves many of the problems with CD is to initialize the Markov chains at each gradient step with their states from the previous gradient step. This approach was first discovered under the name **stochastic maximum likelihood** (SML) in the applied mathematics and statistics community (Younes, 1998) and later independently rediscovered under the name **persistent contrastive divergence** (PCD, or PCD-k to indicate the use of k Gibbs steps per update) in the deep learning community (Tieleman, 2008). See algorithm 18.3. The basic idea of this approach is that, as long as the steps taken by the stochastic gradient algorithm are small, the model from the previous step will be similar to the model from the current step. It follows that the samples from the previous model's distribution will be very close to being fair samples from the current model's distribution, so a Markov chain initialized with these samples will not require much time to mix.

Because each Markov chain is continually updated throughout the learning process, rather than restarted at each gradient step, the chains are free to wander far enough to find all the model's modes. SML is thus considerably more resistant to forming models with spurious modes than CD is. Moreover, because it is possible to store the state of all the sampled variables, whether visible or latent, SML provides an initialization point for both the hidden and the visible units. CD is only able to provide an initialization for the visible units, and therefore requires burn-in for deep models. SML is able to train deep models efficiently. Marlin et al. (2010) compared SML to many other criteria presented in this chapter. They found that SML results in the best test set log-likelihood for an RBM, and that if the RBM's hidden units are used as features for an SVM classifier, SML results in the best classification accuracy.

Algorithm 18.3 The stochastic maximum likelihood / persistent contrastive divergence algorithm using gradient ascent as the optimization procedure

---

Set ϵ, the step size, to a small positive number.

Set k, the number of Gibbs steps, high enough to allow a Markov chain sampling from $p(\mathbf{x}; \boldsymbol{\theta} + \epsilon \mathbf{g})$ to burn in, starting from samples from $p(\mathbf{x}; \boldsymbol{\theta})$. Perhaps 1 for RBM on a small image patch, or 5–50 for a more complicated model like a DBM.

Initialize a set of m samples $\{\tilde{\mathbf{x}}^{(1)}, \ldots, \tilde{\mathbf{x}}^{(m)}\}$ to random values (e.g., from a uniform or normal distribution, or possibly a distribution with marginals matched to the model's marginals).

while not converged **do**

    Sample a minibatch of m examples $\{\mathbf{x}^{(1)}, \ldots, \mathbf{x}^{(m)}\}$ from the training set

    $\mathbf{g} \leftarrow \frac{1}{m} \sum_{i=1}^{m} \nabla_{\boldsymbol{\theta}} \log \tilde{p}(\mathbf{x}^{(i)}; \boldsymbol{\theta})$.

    for $i = 1$ to k **do**

        for $j = 1$ to m **do**

            $\tilde{\mathbf{x}}^{(j)} \leftarrow \text{gibbs\_update}(\tilde{\mathbf{x}}^{(j)})$.

        end for

    end for

    $\mathbf{g} \leftarrow \mathbf{g} - \frac{1}{m} \sum_{i=1}^{m} \nabla_{\boldsymbol{\theta}} \log \tilde{p}(\tilde{\mathbf{x}}^{(i)}; \boldsymbol{\theta})$.

    $\boldsymbol{\theta} \leftarrow \boldsymbol{\theta} + \epsilon \mathbf{g}$.

end while

SML is vulnerable to becoming inaccurate if the stochastic gradient algorithm can move the model faster than the Markov chain can mix between steps. This can happen if k is too small or ϵ is too large. The permissible range of values is unfortunately highly problem dependent. There is no known way to test formally whether the chain is successfully mixing between steps. Subjectively, if the learning rate is too high for the number of Gibbs steps, the human operator will be able to observe much more variance in the negative phase samples across gradient steps than across different Markov chains. For example, a model trained on MNIST might sample exclusively 7s on one step. The learning process will then push down strongly on the mode corresponding to 7s, and the model might sample exclusively 9s on the next step.

Care must be taken when evaluating the samples from a model trained with SML. It is necessary to draw the samples starting from a fresh Markov chain initialized from a random starting point after the model is done training. The samples present in the persistent negative chains used for training have been influenced by several recent versions of the model, and thus can make the model appear to have greater capacity than it actually does.

Berglund and Raiko (2013) performed experiments to examine the bias and variance in the estimate of the gradient provided by CD and SML. CD proves to have lower variance than the estimator based on exact sampling. SML has higher variance. The cause of CD's low variance is its use of the same training points in both the positive and negative phase. If the negative phase is initialized from different training points, the variance rises above that of the estimator based on exact sampling.

All these methods based on using MCMC to draw samples from the model can in principle be used with almost any variant of MCMC. This means that techniques such as SML can be improved by using any of the enhanced MCMC techniques described in chapter 17, such as parallel tempering (Desjardins et al., 2010; Cho et al., 2010).

One approach to accelerating mixing during learning relies not on changing the Monte Carlo sampling technology but rather on changing the parametrization of the model and the cost function. **Fast PCD**, or FPCD (Tieleman and Hinton, 2009) involves replacing the parameters $\boldsymbol{\theta}$ of a traditional model with an expression

$$\boldsymbol{\theta} = \boldsymbol{\theta}^{(\text{slow})} + \boldsymbol{\theta}^{(\text{fast})}. \tag{18.16}$$

There are now twice as many parameters as before, and they are added together element-wise to provide the parameters used by the original model definition. The fast copy of the parameters is trained with a much larger learning rate, allowing it to adapt rapidly in response to the negative phase of learning and push the Markov chain to new territory. This forces the Markov chain to mix rapidly, though this effect occurs only during learning while the fast weights are free to change. Typically one also applies significant weight decay to the fast weights, encouraging them to converge to small values, after only transiently taking on large values long enough to encourage the Markov chain to change modes.

One key benefit to the MCMC-based methods described in this section is that they provide an estimate of the gradient of $\log Z$, and thus we can essentially decompose the problem into the $\log \tilde{p}$ contribution and the $\log Z$ contribution. We can then use any other method to tackle $\log \tilde{p}(\mathbf{x})$ and just add our negative phase gradient onto the other method's gradient. In particular, this means that our positive phase can make use of methods that provide only a lower bound on $\tilde{p}$. Most of the other methods of dealing with $\log Z$ presented in this chapter are incompatible with bound-based positive phase methods.

18.3   Pseudolikelihood

Monte Carlo approximations to the partition function and its gradient directly confront the partition function. Other approaches sidestep the issue, by training the model without computing the partition function. Most of these approaches are based on the observation that it is easy to compute ratios of probabilities in an undirected probabilistic model. This is because the partition function appears in both the numerator and the denominator of the ratio and cancels out:

$$\frac{p(\mathbf{x})}{p(\mathbf{y})} = \frac{\frac{1}{Z}\tilde{p}(\mathbf{x})}{\frac{1}{Z}\tilde{p}(\mathbf{y})} = \frac{\tilde{p}(\mathbf{x})}{\tilde{p}(\mathbf{y})}. \tag{18.17}$$

The pseudolikelihood is based on the observation that conditional probabilities take this ratio-based form and thus can be computed without knowledge of the partition function. Suppose that we partition $\mathbf{x}$ into $\mathbf{a}$, $\mathbf{b}$ and $\mathbf{c}$, where $\mathbf{a}$ contains the variables we want to find the conditional distribution over, $\mathbf{b}$ contains the variables we want to condition on, and $\mathbf{c}$ contains the variables that are not part of our query:

$$p(\mathbf{a} \mid \mathbf{b}) = \frac{p(\mathbf{a}, \mathbf{b})}{p(\mathbf{b})} = \frac{p(\mathbf{a}, \mathbf{b})}{\sum_{\mathbf{a},\mathbf{c}} p(\mathbf{a}, \mathbf{b}, \mathbf{c})} = \frac{\tilde{p}(\mathbf{a}, \mathbf{b})}{\sum_{\mathbf{a},\mathbf{c}} \tilde{p}(\mathbf{a}, \mathbf{b}, \mathbf{c})}. \tag{18.18}$$

This quantity requires marginalizing out $\mathbf{a}$, which can be a very efficient operation provided that $\mathbf{a}$ and $\mathbf{c}$ do not contain many variables. In the extreme case, $\mathbf{a}$ can be a single variable and $\mathbf{c}$ can be empty, making this operation require only as many evaluations of $\tilde{p}$ as there are values of a single random variable.

Unfortunately, in order to compute the log-likelihood, we need to marginalize out large sets of variables. If there are n variables total, we must marginalize a set of size $n - 1$. By the chain rule of probability,

$$\log p(\mathbf{x}) = \log p(x_1) + \log p(x_2 \mid x_1) + \cdots + p(x_n \mid \mathbf{x}_{1:n-1}). \tag{18.19}$$

In this case, we have made $\mathbf{a}$ maximally small, but $\mathbf{c}$ can be as large as $\mathbf{x}_{2:n}$. What if we simply move $\mathbf{c}$ into $\mathbf{b}$ to reduce the computational cost? This yields the **pseudolikelihood** (Besag, 1975) objective function, based on predicting the value of feature x_i given all the other features $\boldsymbol{x}_{-i}$:

$$\sum_{i=1}^{n} \log p(x_i \mid \boldsymbol{x}_{-i}). \tag{18.20}$$

If each random variable has k different values, this requires only $k \times n$ evaluations of $\tilde{p}$ to compute, as opposed to the k^n evaluations needed to compute the partition function.

This may look like an unprincipled hack, but it can be proved that estimation by maximizing the pseudolikelihood is asymptotically consistent (Mase, 1995). Of course, in the case of datasets that do not approach the large sample limit, pseudolikelihood may display different behavior from the maximum likelihood estimator.

It is possible to trade computational complexity for deviation from maximum likelihood behavior by using the **generalized pseudolikelihood estimator** (Huang and Ogata, 2002). The generalized pseudolikelihood estimator uses m different sets $\mathbb{S}^{(i)}$, $i = 1, \dots, m$ of indices of variables that appear together on the left side of the conditioning bar. In the extreme case of $m = 1$ and $\mathbb{S}^{(1)} = 1, \dots, n$, the generalized pseudolikelihood recovers the log-likelihood. In the extreme case of $m = n$ and $\mathbb{S}^{(i)} = \{i\}$, the generalized pseudolikelihood recovers the pseudolikelihood. The generalized pseudolikelihood objective function is given by

$$\sum_{i=1}^{m} \log p(\mathbf{x}_{\mathbb{S}^{(i)}} \mid \mathbf{x}_{-\mathbb{S}^{(i)}}).$$ (18.21)

The performance of pseudolikelihood-based approaches depends largely on how the model will be used. Pseudolikelihood tends to perform poorly on tasks that require a good model of the full joint $p(\mathbf{x})$, such as density estimation and sampling. It can perform better than maximum likelihood for tasks that require only the conditional distributions used during training, such as filling in small amounts of missing values. Generalized pseudolikelihood techniques are especially powerful if the data has regular structure that allows the $\mathbb{S}$ index sets to be designed to capture the most important correlations while leaving out groups of variables that have only negligible correlation. For example, in natural images, pixels that are widely separated in space also have weak correlation, so the generalized pseudolikelihood can be applied with each $\mathbb{S}$ set being a small, spatially localized window.

One weakness of the pseudolikelihood estimator is that it cannot be used with other approximations that provide only a lower bound on $\tilde{p}(\mathbf{x})$, such as variational inference, which is covered in chapter 19. This is because $\tilde{p}$ appears in the denominator. A lower bound on the denominator provides only an upper bound on the expression as a whole, and there is no benefit to maximizing an upper bound. This makes it difficult to apply pseudolikelihood approaches to deep models such as deep Boltzmann machines, since variational methods are one of the dominant approaches to approximately marginalizing out the many layers of hidden variables that interact with each other. Nonetheless, pseudolikelihood is still useful for deep learning, because it can be used to train single-layer models or deep models using approximate inference methods that are not based on lower bounds.

Pseudolikelihood has a much greater cost per gradient step than SML, due to its explicit computation of all the conditionals. But generalized pseudolikelihood and similar criteria can still perform well if only one randomly selected conditional is computed per example (Goodfellow et al., 2013b), thereby bringing the computational cost down to match that of SML.

Though the pseudolikelihood estimator does not explicitly minimize $\log Z$, it can still be thought of as having something resembling a negative phase. The denominators of each conditional distribution result in the learning algorithm suppressing the probability of all states that have only one variable differing from a training example.

See Marlin and de Freitas (2011) for a theoretical analysis of the asymptotic efficiency of pseudolikelihood.

18.4 Score Matching and Ratio Matching

Score matching (Hyvärinen, 2005) provides another consistent means of training a model without estimating Z or its derivatives. The name *score matching* comes from terminology in which the derivatives of a log density with respect to its argument, $\nabla_{\boldsymbol{x}} \log p(\boldsymbol{x})$, are called its **score**. The strategy used by score matching is to minimize the expected squared difference between the derivatives of the model's log density with respect to the input and the derivatives of the data's log density with respect to the input:

$$L(\boldsymbol{x}, \boldsymbol{\theta}) = \frac{1}{2} || \nabla_{\boldsymbol{x}} \log p_{\text{model}}(\boldsymbol{x}; \boldsymbol{\theta}), -\nabla_{\boldsymbol{x}} \log p_{\text{data}}(\boldsymbol{x}) ||_2^2, \tag{18.22}$$

$$J(\boldsymbol{\theta}) = \frac{1}{2} \mathbb{E}_{p_{\text{data}}(\boldsymbol{x})} L(\boldsymbol{x}, \boldsymbol{\theta}), \tag{18.23}$$

$$\boldsymbol{\theta}^* = \min_{\boldsymbol{\theta}} J(\boldsymbol{\theta}). \tag{18.24}$$

This objective function avoids the difficulties associated with differentiating the partition function Z because Z is not a function of $\boldsymbol{x}$ and therefore $\nabla_{\mathbf{x}} Z = 0$. Initially, score matching appears to have a new difficulty: computing the score of the data distribution requires knowledge of the true distribution generating the training data, p_{data}. Fortunately, minimizing the expected value of $L(\boldsymbol{x}, \boldsymbol{\theta})$ is equivalent to minimizing the expected value of

$$\tilde{L}(\boldsymbol{x}, \boldsymbol{\theta}) = \sum_{j=1}^{n} \left(\frac{\partial^2}{\partial x_j^2} \log p_{\text{model}}(\boldsymbol{x}; \boldsymbol{\theta}) + \frac{1}{2} \left(\frac{\partial}{\partial x_j} \log p_{\text{model}}(\boldsymbol{x}; \boldsymbol{\theta}) \right)^2 \right), \tag{18.25}$$

where n is the dimensionality of $\boldsymbol{x}$.

Because score matching requires taking derivatives with respect to $\mathbf{x}$, it is not applicable to models of discrete data but the latent variables in the model may be discrete.

Like pseudolikelihood, score matching only works when we are able to evaluate $\log \tilde{p}(\mathbf{x})$ and its derivatives directly. It is not compatible with methods that provide only a lower bound on $\log \tilde{p}(\mathbf{x})$, because score matching requires the derivatives and second derivatives of $\log \tilde{p}(\mathbf{x})$, and a lower bound conveys no information about its derivatives. This means that score matching cannot be applied to estimating models with complicated interactions between the hidden units, such as sparse coding models or deep Boltzmann machines. While score matching can be used to pretrain the first hidden layer of a larger model, it has not been applied as a pretraining strategy for the deeper layers of a larger model. This is probably because the hidden layers of such models usually contain some discrete variables.

While score matching does not explicitly have a negative phase, it can be viewed as a version of contrastive divergence using a specific kind of Markov chain (Hyvärinen, 2007a). The Markov chain in this case is not Gibbs sampling, but rather a different approach that makes local moves guided by the gradient. Score matching is equivalent to CD with this type of Markov chain when the size of the local moves approaches zero.

Lyu (2009) generalized score matching to the discrete case (but made an error in the derivation that was corrected by Marlin et al. [2010]). Marlin et al. (2010) found that **generalized score matching** (GSM) does not work in high-dimensional discrete spaces where the observed probability of many events is 0.

A more successful approach to extending the basic ideas of score matching to discrete data is **ratio matching** (Hyvärinen, 2007b). Ratio matching applies specifically to binary data. Ratio matching consists of minimizing the average over examples of the following objective function:

$$L^{(\mathrm{RM})}(\boldsymbol{x}, \boldsymbol{\theta}) = \sum_{j=1}^{n} \left(\frac{1}{1 + \frac{p_{\mathrm{model}}(\boldsymbol{x};\boldsymbol{\theta})}{p_{\mathrm{model}}(f(\boldsymbol{x}),j);\boldsymbol{\theta})}} \right)^2, \tag{18.26}$$

where $f(\boldsymbol{x}, j)$ returns $\mathbf{x}$ with the bit at position j flipped. Ratio matching avoids the partition function using the same trick as the pseudolikelihood estimator: in a ratio of two probabilities, the partition function cancels out. Marlin et al. (2010) found that ratio matching outperforms SML, pseudolikelihood and GSM in terms of the ability of models trained with ratio matching to denoise test set images.

Like the pseudolikelihood estimator, ratio matching requires n evaluations of $\tilde{p}$ per data point, making its computational cost per update roughly n times higher than that of SML.

As with the pseudolikelihood estimator, ratio matching can be thought of as pushing down on all fantasy states that have only one variable different from a training example. Since ratio matching applies specifically to binary data, this means that it acts on all fantasy states within Hamming distance 1 of the data.

Ratio matching can also be useful as the basis for dealing with high-dimensional sparse data, such as word count vectors. This kind of data poses a challenge for MCMC-based methods because the data is extremely expensive to represent in dense format, yet the MCMC sampler does not yield sparse values until the model has learned to represent the sparsity in the data distribution. Dauphin and Bengio (2013) overcame this issue by designing an unbiased stochastic approximation to ratio matching. The approximation evaluates only a randomly selected subset of the terms of the objective and does not require the model to generate complete fantasy samples.

See Marlin and de Freitas (2011) for a theoretical analysis of the asymptotic efficiency of ratio matching.

18.5   Denoising Score Matching

In some cases we may wish to regularize score matching, by fitting a distribution

$$p_{\text{smoothed}}(\boldsymbol{x}) = \int p_{\text{data}}(\boldsymbol{y}) q(\boldsymbol{x} \mid \boldsymbol{y}) d\boldsymbol{y} \qquad (18.27)$$

rather than the true p_{data}. The distribution $q(\boldsymbol{x} \mid \boldsymbol{y})$ is a corruption process, usually one that forms $\boldsymbol{x}$ by adding a small amount of noise to $\boldsymbol{y}$.

Denoising score matching is especially useful because in practice, we usually do not have access to the true p_{data} but rather only an empirical distribution defined by samples from it. Any consistent estimator will, given enough capacity, make p_{model} into a set of Dirac distributions centered on the training points. Smoothing by q helps to reduce this problem, at the loss of the asymptotic consistency property described in section 5.4.5. Kingma and LeCun (2010) introduced a procedure for performing regularized score matching with the smoothing distribution q being normally distributed noise.

Recall from section 14.5.1 that several autoencoder training algorithms are equivalent to score matching or denoising score matching. These autoencoder training algorithms are therefore a way of overcoming the partition function problem.

18.6 Noise-Contrastive Estimation

Most techniques for estimating models with intractable partition functions do not provide an estimate of the partition function. SML and CD estimate only the gradient of the log partition function, rather than the partition function itself. Score matching and pseudolikelihood avoid computing quantities related to the partition function altogether.

Noise-contrastive estimation (NCE) (Gutmann and Hyvarinen, 2010) takes a different strategy. In this approach, the probability distribution estimated by the model is represented explicitly as

$$\log p_{\mathrm{model}}(\mathbf{x}) = \log \tilde{p}_{\mathrm{model}}(\mathbf{x}; \boldsymbol{\theta}) + c, \qquad (18.28)$$

where c is explicitly introduced as an approximation of $-\log Z(\boldsymbol{\theta})$. Rather than estimating only $\boldsymbol{\theta}$, the noise contrastive estimation procedure treats c as just another parameter and estimates $\boldsymbol{\theta}$ and c simultaneously, using the same algorithm for both. The resulting $\log p_{\mathrm{model}}(\mathbf{x})$ thus may not correspond exactly to a valid probability distribution, but it will become closer and closer to being valid as the estimate of c improves.[1]

Such an approach would not be possible using maximum likelihood as the criterion for the estimator. The maximum likelihood criterion would choose to set c arbitrarily high, rather than setting c to create a valid probability distribution.

NCE works by reducing the unsupervised learning problem of estimating $p(\mathbf{x})$ to that of learning a probabilistic binary classifier in which one of the categories corresponds to the data generated by the model. This supervised learning problem is constructed in such a way that maximum likelihood estimation defines an asymptotically consistent estimator of the original problem.

Specifically, we introduce a second distribution, the **noise distribution** $p_{\mathrm{noise}}(\mathbf{x})$. The noise distribution should be tractable to evaluate and to sample from. We can now construct a model over both $\mathbf{x}$ and a new, binary class variable y. In the new joint model, we specify that

$$p_{\mathrm{joint}}(y = 1) = \frac{1}{2}, \qquad (18.29)$$

$$p_{\mathrm{joint}}(\mathbf{x} \mid y = 1) = p_{\mathrm{model}}(\mathbf{x}), \qquad (18.30)$$

---

[1]NCE is also applicable to problems with a tractable partition function, where there is no need to introduce the extra parameter c. However, it has generated the most interest as a means of estimating models with difficult partition functions.

and

$$p_{\text{joint}}(\mathbf{x} \mid y = 0) = p_{\text{noise}}(\mathbf{x}). \tag{18.31}$$

In other words, y is a switch variable that determines whether we will generate $\mathbf{x}$ from the model or from the noise distribution.

We can construct a similar joint model of training data. In this case, the switch variable determines whether we draw $\mathbf{x}$ from the **data** or from the noise distribution. Formally, $p_{\text{train}}(y = 1) = \frac{1}{2}$, $p_{\text{train}}(\mathbf{x} \mid y = 1) = p_{\text{data}}(\mathbf{x})$, and $p_{\text{train}}(\mathbf{x} \mid y = 0) = p_{\text{noise}}(\mathbf{x})$.

We can now just use standard maximum likelihood learning on the **supervised** learning problem of fitting p_{joint} to p_{train}:

$$\boldsymbol{\theta}, c = \underset{\boldsymbol{\theta}, c}{\arg\max} \, \mathbb{E}_{\mathbf{x}, y \sim p_{\text{train}}} \log p_{\text{joint}}(y \mid \mathbf{x}). \tag{18.32}$$

The distribution p_{joint} is essentially a logistic regression model applied to the difference in log probabilities of the model and the noise distribution:

$$p_{\text{joint}}(y = 1 \mid \mathbf{x}) = \frac{p_{\text{model}}(\mathbf{x})}{p_{\text{model}}(\mathbf{x}) + p_{\text{noise}}(\mathbf{x})} \tag{18.33}$$

$$= \frac{1}{1 + \frac{p_{\text{noise}}(\mathbf{x})}{p_{\text{model}}(\mathbf{x})}} \tag{18.34}$$

$$= \frac{1}{1 + \exp\left(\log \frac{p_{\text{noise}}(\mathbf{x})}{p_{\text{model}}(\mathbf{x})}\right)} \tag{18.35}$$

$$= \sigma\left(-\log \frac{p_{\text{noise}}(\mathbf{x})}{p_{\text{model}}(\mathbf{x})}\right) \tag{18.36}$$

$$= \sigma\left(\log p_{\text{model}}(\mathbf{x}) - \log p_{\text{noise}}(\mathbf{x})\right). \tag{18.37}$$

NCE is thus simple to apply as long as $\log \tilde{p}_{\text{model}}$ is easy to back-propagate through, and, as specified above, p_{noise} is easy to evaluate (in order to evaluate p_{joint}) and sample from (to generate the training data).

NCE is most successful when applied to problems with few random variables, but it can work well even if those random variables can take on a high number of values. For example, it has been successfully applied to modeling the conditional distribution over a word given the context of the word (Mnih and Kavukcuoglu, 2013). Though the word may be drawn from a large vocabulary, there is only one word.

When NCE is applied to problems with many random variables, it becomes less efficient. The logistic regression classifier can reject a noise sample by identifying any one variable whose value is unlikely. This means that learning slows down greatly after p_{model} has learned the basic marginal statistics. Imagine learning a model of images of faces, using unstructured Gaussian noise as p_{noise}. If p_{model} learns about eyes, it can reject almost all unstructured noise samples without having learned anything about other facial features, such as mouths.

The constraint that p_{noise} must be easy to evaluate and easy to sample from can be overly restrictive. When p_{noise} is simple, most samples are likely to be too obviously distinct from the data to force p_{model} to improve noticeably.

Like score matching and pseudolikelihood, NCE does not work if only a lower bound on $\tilde{p}$ is available. Such a lower bound could be used to construct a lower bound on $p_{\text{joint}}(y = 1 \mid \mathbf{x})$, but it can only be used to construct an upper bound on $p_{\text{joint}}(y = 0 \mid \mathbf{x})$, which appears in half the terms of the NCE objective. Likewise, a lower bound on p_{noise} is not useful, because it provides only an upper bound on $p_{\text{joint}}(y = 1 \mid \mathbf{x})$.

When the model distribution is copied to define a new noise distribution before each gradient step, NCE defines a procedure called **self-contrastive estimation**, whose expected gradient is equivalent to the expected gradient of maximum likelihood (Goodfellow, 2014). The special case of NCE where the noise samples are those generated by the model suggests that maximum likelihood can be interpreted as a procedure that forces a model to constantly learn to distinguish reality from its own evolving beliefs, while noise contrastive estimation achieves some reduced computational cost by only forcing the model to distinguish reality from a fixed baseline (the noise model).

Using the supervised task of classifying between training samples and generated samples (with the model energy function used in defining the classifier) to provide a gradient on the model was introduced earlier in various forms (Welling et al., 2003b; Bengio, 2009).

Noise contrastive estimation is based on the idea that a good generative model should be able to distinguish data from noise. A closely related idea is that a good generative model should be able to generate samples that no classifier can distinguish from data. This idea yields generative adversarial networks (section 20.10.4).

18.7 Estimating the Partition Function

While much of this chapter is dedicated to describing methods that avoid needing to compute the intractable partition function $Z(\boldsymbol{\theta})$ associated with an undirected graphical model, in this section we discuss several methods for directly estimating the partition function.

Estimating the partition function can be important because we require it if we wish to compute the normalized likelihood of data. This is often important in *evaluating* the model, monitoring training performance, and comparing models to each other.

For example, imagine we have two models: model $\mathcal{M}_A$ defining a probability distribution $p_A(\mathbf{x}; \boldsymbol{\theta}_A) = \frac{1}{Z_A}\tilde{p}_A(\mathbf{x}; \boldsymbol{\theta}_A)$ and model $\mathcal{M}_B$ defining a probability distribution $p_B(\mathbf{x}; \boldsymbol{\theta}_B) = \frac{1}{Z_B}\tilde{p}_B(\mathbf{x}; \boldsymbol{\theta}_B)$. A common way to compare the models is to evaluate and compare the likelihood that both models assign to an i.i.d. test dataset. Suppose the test set consists of m examples $\{\boldsymbol{x}^{(1)}, \ldots, \boldsymbol{x}^{(m)}\}$. If $\prod_i p_A(\mathbf{x}^{(i)}; \boldsymbol{\theta}_A) > \prod_i p_B(\mathbf{x}^{(i)}; \boldsymbol{\theta}_B)$, or equivalently if

$$\sum_i \log p_A(\mathbf{x}^{(i)}; \boldsymbol{\theta}_A) - \sum_i \log p_B(\mathbf{x}^{(i)}; \boldsymbol{\theta}_B) > 0, \tag{18.38}$$

then we say that $\mathcal{M}_A$ is a better model than $\mathcal{M}_B$ (or, at least, it is a better model of the test set), in the sense that it has a better test log-likelihood. Unfortunately, testing whether this condition holds requires knowledge of the partition function. equation 18.38 seems to require evaluating the log-probability that the model assigns to each point, which in turn requires evaluating the partition function. We can simplify the situation slightly by rearranging equation 18.38 into a form in which we need to know only the **ratio** of the two model's partition functions:

$$\sum_i \log p_A(\mathbf{x}^{(i)}; \boldsymbol{\theta}_A) - \sum_i \log p_B(\mathbf{x}^{(i)}; \boldsymbol{\theta}_B) = \sum_i \left(\log \frac{\tilde{p}_A(\mathbf{x}^{(i)}; \boldsymbol{\theta}_A)}{\tilde{p}_B(\mathbf{x}^{(i)}; \boldsymbol{\theta}_B)}\right) - m \log \frac{Z(\boldsymbol{\theta}_A)}{Z(\boldsymbol{\theta}_B)}. \tag{18.39}$$

We can thus determine whether $\mathcal{M}_A$ is a better model than $\mathcal{M}_B$ without knowing the partition function of either model but only their ratio. As we will see shortly, we can estimate this ratio using importance sampling, provided that the two models are similar.

If, however, we wanted to compute the actual probability of the test data under either $\mathcal{M}_A$ or $\mathcal{M}_B$, we would need to compute the actual value of the partition functions. That said, if we knew the ratio of two partition functions, $r = \frac{Z(\boldsymbol{\theta}_B)}{Z(\boldsymbol{\theta}_A)}$, and we knew the actual value of just one of the two, say $Z(\boldsymbol{\theta}_A)$, we could compute the value of the other:

$$Z(\boldsymbol{\theta}_B) = rZ(\boldsymbol{\theta}_A) = \frac{Z(\boldsymbol{\theta}_B)}{Z(\boldsymbol{\theta}_A)} Z(\boldsymbol{\theta}_A). \tag{18.40}$$

A simple way to estimate the partition function is to use a Monte Carlo method such as simple importance sampling. We present the approach in terms of continuous variables using integrals, but it can be readily applied to discrete variables by replacing the integrals with summation. We use a proposal distribution $p_0(\mathbf{x}) = \frac{1}{Z_0}\tilde{p}_0(\mathbf{x})$, which supports tractable sampling and tractable evaluation of both the partition function Z_0 and the unnormalized distribution $\tilde{p}_0(\mathbf{x})$.

$$Z_1 = \int \tilde{p}_1(\mathbf{x}) \, d\mathbf{x} \tag{18.41}$$

$$= \int \frac{p_0(\mathbf{x})}{p_0(\mathbf{x})}\tilde{p}_1(\mathbf{x}) \, d\mathbf{x} \tag{18.42}$$

$$= Z_0 \int p_0(\mathbf{x})\frac{\tilde{p}_1(\mathbf{x})}{\tilde{p}_0(\mathbf{x})} \, d\mathbf{x} \tag{18.43}$$

$$\hat{Z}_1 = \frac{Z_0}{K} \sum_{k=1}^{K} \frac{\tilde{p}_1(\mathbf{x}^{(k)})}{\tilde{p}_0(\mathbf{x}^{(k)})} \quad \text{s.t.} : \mathbf{x}^{(k)} \sim p_0 \tag{18.44}$$

In the last line, we make a Monte Carlo estimator, $\hat{Z}_1$, of the integral using samples drawn from $p_0(\mathbf{x})$, and then weight each sample with the ratio of the unnormalized $\tilde{p}_1$ and the proposal p_0.

This approach also allows us to estimate the ratio between the partition functions as

$$\frac{1}{K} \sum_{k=1}^{K} \frac{\tilde{p}_1(\mathbf{x}^{(k)})}{\tilde{p}_0(\mathbf{x}^{(k)})} \quad \text{s.t.} : \mathbf{x}^{(k)} \sim p_0. \tag{18.45}$$

This value can then be used directly to compare two models as described in equation 18.39.

If the distribution p_0 is close to p_1, equation 18.44 can be an effective way of estimating the partition function (Minka, 2005). Unfortunately, most of the time p_1 is both complicated (usually multimodal) and defined over a high-dimensional space. It is difficult to find a tractable p_0 that is simple enough to evaluate while still being close enough to p_1 to result in a high-quality approximation. If p_0 and p_1 are not close, most samples from p_0 will have low probability under p_1 and therefore make (relatively) negligible contribution to the sum in equation 18.44.

Having few samples with significant weights in this sum will result in an estimator that is of poor quality because of high variance. This can be understood quantitatively through an estimate of the variance of our estimate $\hat{Z}_1$:

$$\hat{\text{Var}}\left(\hat{Z}_1\right) = \frac{Z_0}{K^2} \sum_{k=1}^{K} \left(\frac{\tilde{p}_1(\mathbf{x}^{(k)})}{\tilde{p}_0(\mathbf{x}^{(k)})} - \hat{Z}_1 \right)^2. \tag{18.46}$$

This quantity is largest when there is significant deviation in the values of the importance weights $\frac{\tilde{p}_1(\mathbf{x}^{(k)})}{\tilde{p}_0(\mathbf{x}^{(k)})}$.

We now turn to two related strategies developed to cope with the challenging task of estimating partition functions for complex distributions over high-dimensional spaces: annealed importance sampling and bridge sampling. Both start with the simple importance sampling strategy introduced above, and both attempt to overcome the problem of the proposal p_0 being too far from p_1 by introducing intermediate distributions that attempt to *bridge the gap* between p_0 and p_1.

18.7.1 Annealed Importance Sampling

In situations where $D_{\mathrm{KL}}(p_0\|p_1)$ is large (i.e., where there is little overlap between p_0 and p_1), a strategy called **annealed importance sampling** (AIS) attempts to bridge the gap by introducing intermediate distributions (Jarzynski, 1997; Neal, 2001). Consider a sequence of distributions $p_{\eta_0}, \ldots, p_{\eta_n}$, with $0 = \eta_0 < \eta_1 < \cdots < \eta_{n-1} < \eta_n = 1$ so that the first and last distributions in the sequence are p_0 and p_1, respectively.

This approach enables us to estimate the partition function of a multimodal distribution defined over a high-dimensional space (such as the distribution defined by a trained RBM). We begin with a simpler model with a known partition function (such as an RBM with zeros for weights) and estimate the ratio between the two model's partition functions. The estimate of this ratio is based on the estimate of the ratios of a sequence of many similar distributions, such as the sequence of RBMs with weights interpolating between zero and the learned weights.

We can now write the ratio $\frac{Z_1}{Z_0}$ as

$$\frac{Z_1}{Z_0} = \frac{Z_1}{Z_0} \frac{Z_{\eta_1}}{Z_{\eta_1}} \cdots \frac{Z_{\eta_{n-1}}}{Z_{\eta_{n-1}}} \tag{18.47}$$

$$= \frac{Z_{\eta_1}}{Z_0} \frac{Z_{\eta_2}}{Z_{\eta_1}} \cdots \frac{Z_{\eta_{n-1}}}{Z_{\eta_{n-2}}} \frac{Z_1}{Z_{\eta_{n-1}}} \tag{18.48}$$

$$= \prod_{j=0}^{n-1} \frac{Z_{\eta_{j+1}}}{Z_{\eta_j}}. \tag{18.49}$$

Provided the distributions p_{η_j} and $p_{\eta_{j+1}}$, for all $0 \leq j \leq n-1$, are sufficiently close, we can reliably estimate each of the factors $\frac{Z_{\eta_{j+1}}}{Z_{\eta_j}}$ using simple importance sampling and then use these to obtain an estimate of $\frac{Z_1}{Z_0}$.

Where do these intermediate distributions come from? Just as the original proposal distribution p_0 is a design choice, so is the sequence of distributions $p_{\eta_1} \ldots p_{\eta_{n-1}}$. That is, it can be specifically constructed to suit the problem domain. One general purpose and popular choice for the intermediate distributions is to use the weighted geometric average of the target distribution p_1 and the starting proposal distribution (for which the partition function is known) p_0:

$$p_{\eta_j} \propto p_1^{\eta_j} p_0^{1-\eta_j}. \tag{18.50}$$

In order to sample from these intermediate distributions, we define a series of Markov chain transition functions $T_{\eta_j}(\boldsymbol{x}' \mid \boldsymbol{x})$ that define the conditional probability distribution of transitioning to $\boldsymbol{x}'$ given we are currently at $\boldsymbol{x}$. The transition operator $T_{\eta_j}(\boldsymbol{x}' \mid \boldsymbol{x})$ is defined to leave $p_{\eta_j}(\boldsymbol{x})$ invariant:

$$p_{\eta_j}(\boldsymbol{x}) = \int p_{\eta_j}(\boldsymbol{x}') T_{\eta_j}(\boldsymbol{x} \mid \boldsymbol{x}') \, d\boldsymbol{x}'. \tag{18.51}$$

These transitions may be constructed as any Markov chain Monte Carlo method (e.g., Metropolis-Hastings, Gibbs), including methods involving multiple passes through all the random variables or other kinds of iterations.

The AIS sampling strategy is then to generate samples from p_0 and use the transition operators to sequentially generate samples from the intermediate distributions until we arrive at samples from the target distribution p_1:

- for $k = 1 \ldots K$

    - Sample $\boldsymbol{x}_{\eta_1}^{(k)} \sim p_0(\mathbf{x})$
    - Sample $\boldsymbol{x}_{\eta_2}^{(k)} \sim T_{\eta_1}(\mathbf{x}_{\eta_2}^{(k)} \mid \boldsymbol{x}_{\eta_1}^{(k)})$
    - $\ldots$
    - Sample $\boldsymbol{x}_{\eta_{n-1}}^{(k)} \sim T_{\eta_{n-2}}(\mathbf{x}_{\eta_{n-1}}^{(k)} \mid \boldsymbol{x}_{\eta_{n-2}}^{(k)})$
    - Sample $\boldsymbol{x}_{\eta_n}^{(k)} \sim T_{\eta_{n-1}}(\mathbf{x}_{\eta_n}^{(k)} \mid \boldsymbol{x}_{\eta_{n-1}}^{(k)})$

- end

For sample k, we can derive the importance weight by chaining together the importance weights for the jumps between the intermediate distributions given in equation 18.49:

$$w^{(k)} = \frac{\tilde{p}_{\eta_1}(\boldsymbol{x}_{\eta_1}^{(k)})}{\tilde{p}_0(\boldsymbol{x}_{\eta_1}^{(k)})} \frac{\tilde{p}_{\eta_2}(\boldsymbol{x}_{\eta_2}^{(k)})}{\tilde{p}_{\eta_1}(\boldsymbol{x}_{\eta_2}^{(k)})} \cdots \frac{\tilde{p}_1(\boldsymbol{x}_1^{(k)})}{\tilde{p}_{\eta_{n-1}}(\boldsymbol{x}_{\eta_n}^{(k)})}. \tag{18.52}$$

To avoid numerical issues such as overflow, it is probably best to compute $\log w^{(k)}$ by adding and subtracting log probabilities, rather than computing $w^{(k)}$ by multiplying and dividing probabilities.

With the sampling procedure thus defined and the importance weights given in equation 18.52, the estimate of the ratio of partition functions is given by:

$$\frac{Z_1}{Z_0} \approx \frac{1}{K} \sum_{k=1}^{K} w^{(k)} \tag{18.53}$$

To verify that this procedure defines a valid importance sampling scheme, we can show (Neal, 2001) that the AIS procedure corresponds to simple importance sampling on an extended state space, with points sampled over the product space $[\boldsymbol{x}_{\eta_1}, \ldots, \boldsymbol{x}_{\eta_{n-1}}, \boldsymbol{x}_1]$. To do this, we define the distribution over the extended space as

$$\tilde{p}(\boldsymbol{x}_{\eta_1}, \ldots, \boldsymbol{x}_{\eta_{n-1}}, \boldsymbol{x}_1) \tag{18.54}$$

$$= \tilde{p}_1(\boldsymbol{x}_1)\tilde{T}_{\eta_{n-1}}(\boldsymbol{x}_{\eta_{n-1}} \mid \boldsymbol{x}_1)\tilde{T}_{\eta_{n-2}}(\boldsymbol{x}_{\eta_{n-2}} \mid \boldsymbol{x}_{\eta_{n-1}}) \ldots \tilde{T}_{\eta_1}(\boldsymbol{x}_{\eta_1} \mid \boldsymbol{x}_{\eta_2}), \tag{18.55}$$

where $\tilde{T}_a$ is the reverse of the transition operator defined by T_a (via an application of Bayes' rule):

$$\tilde{T}_a(\boldsymbol{x}' \mid \boldsymbol{x}) = \frac{p_a(\boldsymbol{x}')}{p_a(\boldsymbol{x})}T_a(\boldsymbol{x} \mid \boldsymbol{x}') = \frac{\tilde{p}_a(\boldsymbol{x}')}{\tilde{p}_a(\boldsymbol{x})}T_a(\boldsymbol{x} \mid \boldsymbol{x}'). \tag{18.56}$$

Plugging the above into the expression for the joint distribution on the extended state space given in equation 18.55, we get:

$$\tilde{p}(\boldsymbol{x}_{\eta_1}, \ldots, \boldsymbol{x}_{\eta_{n-1}}, \boldsymbol{x}_1) \tag{18.57}$$

$$= \tilde{p}_1(\boldsymbol{x}_1)\frac{\tilde{p}_{\eta_{n-1}}(\boldsymbol{x}_{\eta_{n-1}})}{\tilde{p}_{\eta_{n-1}}(\boldsymbol{x}_1)}T_{\eta_{n-1}}(\boldsymbol{x}_1 \mid \boldsymbol{x}_{\eta_{n-1}}) \prod_{i=1}^{n-2} \frac{\tilde{p}_{\eta_i}(\boldsymbol{x}_{\eta_i})}{\tilde{p}_{\eta_i}(\boldsymbol{x}_{\eta_{i+1}})}T_{\eta_i}(\boldsymbol{x}_{\eta_{i+1}} \mid \boldsymbol{x}_{\eta_i}) \tag{18.58}$$

$$= \frac{\tilde{p}_1(\boldsymbol{x}_1)}{\tilde{p}_{\eta_{n-1}}(\boldsymbol{x}_1)}T_{\eta_{n-1}}(\boldsymbol{x}_1 \mid \boldsymbol{x}_{\eta_{n-1}}) \, \tilde{p}_{\eta_1}(\boldsymbol{x}_{\eta_1}) \prod_{i=1}^{n-2} \frac{\tilde{p}_{\eta_{i+1}}(\boldsymbol{x}_{\eta_{i+1}})}{\tilde{p}_{\eta_i}(\boldsymbol{x}_{\eta_{i+1}})}T_{\eta_i}(\boldsymbol{x}_{\eta_{i+1}} \mid \boldsymbol{x}_{\eta_i}). \tag{18.59}$$

We now have means of generating samples from the joint proposal distribution q over the extended sample via a sampling scheme given above, with the joint distribution given by

$$q(\boldsymbol{x}_{\eta_1}, \ldots, \boldsymbol{x}_{\eta_{n-1}}, \boldsymbol{x}_1) = p_0(\boldsymbol{x}_{\eta_1})T_{\eta_1}(\boldsymbol{x}_{\eta_2} \mid \boldsymbol{x}_{\eta_1}) \ldots T_{\eta_{n-1}}(\boldsymbol{x}_1 \mid \boldsymbol{x}_{\eta_{n-1}}). \tag{18.60}$$

We have a joint distribution on the extended space given by equation 18.59. Taking $q(\boldsymbol{x}_{\eta_1}, \ldots, \boldsymbol{x}_{\eta_{n-1}}, \boldsymbol{x}_1)$ as the proposal distribution on the extended state space from which we will draw samples, it remains to determine the importance weights:

$$w^{(k)} = \frac{\tilde{p}(\boldsymbol{x}_{\eta_1}, \ldots, \boldsymbol{x}_{\eta_{n-1}}, \boldsymbol{x}_1)}{q(\boldsymbol{x}_{\eta_1}, \ldots, \boldsymbol{x}_{\eta_{n-1}}, \boldsymbol{x}_1)} = \frac{\tilde{p}_1(\boldsymbol{x}_1^{(k)})}{\tilde{p}_{\eta_{n-1}}(\boldsymbol{x}_{\eta_{n-1}}^{(k)})} \cdots \frac{\tilde{p}_{\eta_2}(\boldsymbol{x}_{\eta_2}^{(k)})}{\tilde{p}_1(\boldsymbol{x}_{\eta_1}^{(k)})} \frac{\tilde{p}_{\eta_1}(\boldsymbol{x}_{\eta_1}^{(k)})}{\tilde{p}_0(\boldsymbol{x}_0^{(k)})}. \tag{18.61}$$

These weights are the same as proposed for AIS. Thus we can interpret AIS as simple importance sampling applied to an extended state, and its validity follows immediately from the validity of importance sampling.

Annealed importance sampling was first discovered by Jarzynski (1997) and then again, independently, by Neal (2001). It is currently the most common way of estimating the partition function for undirected probabilistic models. The reasons for this may have more to do with the publication of an influential paper (Salakhutdinov and Murray, 2008) describing its application to estimating the partition function of restricted Boltzmann machines and deep belief networks than with any inherent advantage the method has over the other method described below.

A discussion of the properties of the AIS estimator (e.g., its variance and efficiency) can be found in Neal (2001).

18.7.2 Bridge Sampling

Bridge sampling (Bennett, 1976) is another method that, like AIS, addresses the shortcomings of importance sampling. Rather than chaining together a series of intermediate distributions, bridge sampling relies on a single distribution p_*, known as the bridge, to interpolate between a distribution with known partition function, p_0, and a distribution p_1 for which we are trying to estimate the partition function Z_1.

Bridge sampling estimates the ratio Z_1/Z_0 as the ratio of the expected importance weights between $\tilde{p}_0$ and $\tilde{p}_*$ and between $\tilde{p}_1$ and $\tilde{p}_*$:

$$\frac{Z_1}{Z_0} \approx \sum_{k=1}^{K} \frac{\tilde{p}_*(\boldsymbol{x}_0^{(k)})}{\tilde{p}_0(\boldsymbol{x}_0^{(k)})} \Bigg/ \sum_{k=1}^{K} \frac{\tilde{p}_*(\boldsymbol{x}_1^{(k)})}{\tilde{p}_1(\boldsymbol{x}_1^{(k)})}. \tag{18.62}$$

If the bridge distribution p_* is chosen carefully to have a large overlap of support with both p_0 and p_1, then bridge sampling can allow the distance between two distributions (or more formally, $D_{\text{KL}}(p_0 \| p_1)$) to be much larger than with standard importance sampling.

It can be shown that the optimal bridging distribution is given by $p_*^{(opt)}(\mathbf{x}) \propto \frac{\tilde{p}_0(\boldsymbol{x})\tilde{p}_1(\boldsymbol{x})}{r\tilde{p}_0(\boldsymbol{x})+\tilde{p}_1(\boldsymbol{x})}$, where $r = Z_1/Z_0$. At first, this appears to be an unworkable solution as it would seem to require the very quantity we are trying to estimate, Z_1/Z_0. However, it is possible to start with a coarse estimate of r and use the resulting bridge distribution to refine our estimate iteratively (Neal, 2005). That is, we iteratively reestimate the ratio and use each iteration to update the value of r.

Linked importance sampling Both AIS and bridge sampling have their advantages. If $D_{\mathrm{KL}}(p_0\|p_1)$ is not too large (because p_0 and p_1 are sufficiently close), bridge sampling can be a more effective means of estimating the ratio of partition functions than AIS. If, however, the two distributions are too far apart for a single distribution p_* to bridge the gap, then one can at least use AIS with potentially many intermediate distributions to span the distance between p_0 and p_1. Neal (2005) showed how his linked importance sampling method leveraged the power of the bridge sampling strategy to bridge the intermediate distributions used in AIS and significantly improve the overall partition function estimates.

Estimating the partition function while training While AIS has become accepted as the standard method for estimating the partition function for many undirected models, it is sufficiently computationally intensive that it remains infeasible to use during training. Alternative strategies have been explored to maintain an estimate of the partition function throughout training.

Using a combination of bridge sampling, short-chain AIS and parallel tempering, Desjardins et al. (2011) devised a scheme to track the partition function of an RBM throughout the training process. The strategy is based on the maintenance of independent estimates of the partition functions of the RBM at every temperature operating in the parallel tempering scheme. The authors combined bridge sampling estimates of the ratios of partition functions of neighboring chains (i.e., from parallel tempering) with AIS estimates across time to come up with a low variance estimate of the partition functions at every iteration of learning.

The tools described in this chapter provide many different ways of overcoming the problem of intractable partition functions, but there can be several other difficulties involved in training and using generative models. Foremost among these is the problem of intractable inference, which we confront next.

19

Approximate Inference

Many probabilistic models are difficult to train because it is difficult to perform inference in them. In the context of deep learning, we usually have a set of visible variables $\boldsymbol{v}$ and a set of latent variables $\boldsymbol{h}$. The challenge of inference usually refers to the difficult problem of computing $p(\boldsymbol{h} \mid \boldsymbol{v})$ or taking expectations with respect to it. Such operations are often necessary for tasks like maximum likelihood learning.

Many simple graphical models with only one hidden layer, such as restricted Boltzmann machines and probabilistic PCA, are defined in a way that makes inference operations like computing $p(\boldsymbol{h} \mid \boldsymbol{v})$, or taking expectations with respect to it, simple. Unfortunately, most graphical models with multiple layers of hidden variables have intractable posterior distributions. Exact inference requires an exponential amount of time in these models. Even some models with only a single layer, such as sparse coding, have this problem.

In this chapter, we introduce several of the techniques for confronting these intractable inference problems. In chapter 20, we describe how to use these techniques to train probabilistic models that would otherwise be intractable, such as deep belief networks and deep Boltzmann machines.

Intractable inference problems in deep learning usually arise from interactions between latent variables in a structured graphical model. See figure 19.1 for some examples. These interactions may be due to direct interactions in undirected models or "explaining away" interactions between mutual ancestors of the same visible unit in directed models.

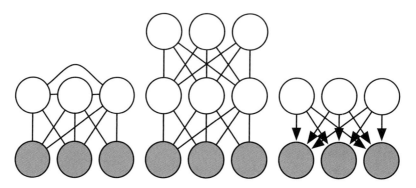

Figure 19.1: Intractable inference problems in deep learning are usually the result of interactions between latent variables in a structured graphical model. These interactions can be due to edges directly connecting one latent variable to another or longer paths that are activated when the child of a V-structure is observed. *(Left)*A **semi-restricted Boltzmann machine** (Osindero and Hinton, 2008) with connections between hidden units. These direct connections between latent variables make the posterior distribution intractable because of large cliques of latent variables. *(Center)*A deep Boltzmann machine, organized into layers of variables without intralayer connections, still has an intractable posterior distribution because of the connections between layers. *(Right)*This directed model has interactions between latent variables when the visible variables are observed, because every two latent variables are coparents. Some probabilistic models are able to provide tractable inference over the latent variables despite having one of the graph structures depicted above. This is possible if the conditional probability distributions are chosen to introduce additional independences beyond those described by the graph. For example, probabilistic PCA has the graph structure shown in the right yet still has simple inference because of special properties of the specific conditional distributions it uses (linear-Gaussian conditionals with mutually orthogonal basis vectors).

19.1 Inference as Optimization

Many approaches to confronting the problem of difficult inference make use of the observation that exact inference can be described as an optimization problem. Approximate inference algorithms may then be derived by approximating the underlying optimization problem.

To construct the optimization problem, assume we have a probabilistic model consisting of observed variables $\boldsymbol{v}$ and latent variables $\boldsymbol{h}$. We would like to compute the log-probability of the observed data, $\log p(\boldsymbol{v}; \boldsymbol{\theta})$. Sometimes it is too difficult to compute $\log p(\boldsymbol{v}; \boldsymbol{\theta})$ if it is costly to marginalize out $\boldsymbol{h}$. Instead, we can compute a lower bound $\mathcal{L}(\boldsymbol{v}, \boldsymbol{\theta}, q)$ on $\log p(\boldsymbol{v}; \boldsymbol{\theta})$. This bound is called the **evidence lower bound** (ELBO). Another commonly used name for this lower bound is the negative

variational free energy. Specifically, the evidence lower bound is defined to be

$$\mathcal{L}(\boldsymbol{v}, \boldsymbol{\theta}, q) = \log p(\boldsymbol{v}; \boldsymbol{\theta}) - D_{\mathrm{KL}}\left(q(\boldsymbol{h} \mid \boldsymbol{v}) \| p(\boldsymbol{h} \mid \boldsymbol{v}; \boldsymbol{\theta})\right), \tag{19.1}$$

where q is an arbitrary probability distribution over $\boldsymbol{h}$.

Because the difference between $\log p(\boldsymbol{v})$ and $\mathcal{L}(\boldsymbol{v}, \boldsymbol{\theta}, q)$ is given by the KL divergence, and because the KL divergence is always nonnegative, we can see that $\mathcal{L}$ always has at most the same value as the desired log-probability. The two are equal if and only if q is the same distribution as $p(\boldsymbol{h} \mid \boldsymbol{v})$.

Surprisingly, $\mathcal{L}$ can be considerably easier to compute for some distributions q. Simple algebra shows that we can rearrange $\mathcal{L}$ into a much more convenient form:

$$\mathcal{L}(\boldsymbol{v}, \boldsymbol{\theta}, q) = \log p(\boldsymbol{v}; \boldsymbol{\theta}) - D_{\mathrm{KL}}(q(\boldsymbol{h} \mid \boldsymbol{v}) \| p(\boldsymbol{h} \mid \boldsymbol{v}; \boldsymbol{\theta})) \tag{19.2}$$

$$= \log p(\boldsymbol{v}; \boldsymbol{\theta}) - \mathbb{E}_{\mathbf{h} \sim q} \log \frac{q(\boldsymbol{h} \mid \boldsymbol{v})}{p(\boldsymbol{h} \mid \boldsymbol{v})} \tag{19.3}$$

$$= \log p(\boldsymbol{v}; \boldsymbol{\theta}) - \mathbb{E}_{\mathbf{h} \sim q} \log \frac{q(\boldsymbol{h} \mid \boldsymbol{v})}{\frac{p(\boldsymbol{h}, \boldsymbol{v}; \boldsymbol{\theta})}{p(\boldsymbol{v}; \boldsymbol{\theta})}} \tag{19.4}$$

$$= \log p(\boldsymbol{v}; \boldsymbol{\theta}) - \mathbb{E}_{\mathbf{h} \sim q} \left[\log q(\boldsymbol{h} \mid \boldsymbol{v}) - \log p(\boldsymbol{h}, \boldsymbol{v}; \boldsymbol{\theta}) + \log p(\boldsymbol{v}; \boldsymbol{\theta})\right] \tag{19.5}$$

$$= -\mathbb{E}_{\mathbf{h} \sim q} \left[\log q(\boldsymbol{h} \mid \boldsymbol{v}) - \log p(\boldsymbol{h}, \boldsymbol{v}; \boldsymbol{\theta})\right]. \tag{19.6}$$

This yields the more canonical definition of the evidence lower bound,

$$\mathcal{L}(\boldsymbol{v}, \boldsymbol{\theta}, q) = \mathbb{E}_{\mathbf{h} \sim q} \left[\log p(\boldsymbol{h}, \boldsymbol{v})\right] + H(q). \tag{19.7}$$

For an appropriate choice of q, $\mathcal{L}$ is tractable to compute. For any choice of q, $\mathcal{L}$ provides a lower bound on the likelihood. For $q(\boldsymbol{h} \mid \boldsymbol{v})$ that are better approximations of $p(\boldsymbol{h} \mid \boldsymbol{v})$, the lower bound $\mathcal{L}$ will be tighter, in other words, closer to $\log p(\boldsymbol{v})$. When $q(\boldsymbol{h} \mid \boldsymbol{v}) = p(\boldsymbol{h} \mid \boldsymbol{v})$, the approximation is perfect, and $\mathcal{L}(\boldsymbol{v}, \boldsymbol{\theta}, q) = \log p(\boldsymbol{v}; \boldsymbol{\theta})$.

We can thus think of inference as the procedure for finding the q that maximizes $\mathcal{L}$. Exact inference maximizes $\mathcal{L}$ perfectly by searching over a family of functions q that includes $p(\boldsymbol{h} \mid \boldsymbol{v})$. Throughout this chapter, we show how to derive different forms of approximate inference by using approximate optimization to find q. We can make the optimization procedure less expensive but approximate by restricting the family of distributions q that the optimization is allowed to search over or by using an imperfect optimization procedure that may not completely maximize $\mathcal{L}$ but may merely increase it by a significant amount.

No matter what choice of q we use, $\mathcal{L}$ is a lower bound. We can get tighter or looser bounds that are cheaper or more expensive to compute depending on how we choose to approach this optimization problem. We can obtain a poorly matched q but reduce the computational cost by using an imperfect optimization procedure, or by using a perfect optimization procedure over a restricted family of q distributions.

19.2 Expectation Maximization

The first algorithm we introduce based on maximizing a lower bound $\mathcal{L}$ is the **expectation maximization** (EM) algorithm, a popular training algorithm for models with latent variables. We describe here a view on the EM algorithm developed by Neal and Hinton (1999). Unlike most of the other algorithms we describe in this chapter, EM is not an approach to approximate inference, but rather an approach to learning with an approximate posterior.

The EM algorithm consists of alternating between two steps until convergence:

- The **E-step** (expectation step): Let $\boldsymbol{\theta}^{(0)}$ denote the value of the parameters at the beginning of the step. Set $q(\boldsymbol{h}^{(i)} \mid \boldsymbol{v}) = p(\boldsymbol{h}^{(i)} \mid \boldsymbol{v}^{(i)}; \boldsymbol{\theta}^{(0)})$ for all indices i of the training examples $\boldsymbol{v}^{(i)}$ we want to train on (both batch and minibatch variants are valid). By this we mean q is defined in terms of the *current* parameter value of $\boldsymbol{\theta}^{(0)}$; if we vary $\boldsymbol{\theta}$, then $p(\boldsymbol{h} \mid \boldsymbol{v}; \boldsymbol{\theta})$ will change, but $q(\boldsymbol{h} \mid \boldsymbol{v})$ will remain equal to $p(\boldsymbol{h} \mid \boldsymbol{v}; \boldsymbol{\theta}^{(0)})$.

- The **M-step** (maximization step): Completely or partially maximize

$$\sum_i \mathcal{L}(\boldsymbol{v}^{(i)}, \boldsymbol{\theta}, q) \tag{19.8}$$

with respect to $\boldsymbol{\theta}$ using your optimization algorithm of choice.

This can be viewed as a coordinate ascent algorithm to maximize $\mathcal{L}$. On one step, we maximize $\mathcal{L}$ with respect to q, and on the other, we maximize $\mathcal{L}$ with respect to $\boldsymbol{\theta}$.

Stochastic gradient ascent on latent variable models can be seen as a special case of the EM algorithm where the M-step consists of taking a single gradient step. Other variants of the EM algorithm can make much larger steps. For some model families, the M-step can even be performed analytically, jumping all the way to the optimal solution for $\boldsymbol{\theta}$ given the current q.

Even though the E-step involves exact inference, we can think of the EM algorithm as using approximate inference in some sense. Specifically, the M-step assumes that the same value of q can be used for all values of $\boldsymbol{\theta}$. This will introduce a gap between $\mathcal{L}$ and the true $\log p(\boldsymbol{v})$ as the M-step moves further and further away from the value $\boldsymbol{\theta}^{(0)}$ used in the E-step. Fortunately, the E-step reduces the gap to zero again as we enter the loop for the next time.

The EM algorithm contains a few different insights. First, there is the basic structure of the learning process, in which we update the model parameters to improve the likelihood of a completed dataset, where all missing variables have their values provided by an estimate of the posterior distribution. This particular insight is not unique to the EM algorithm. For example, using gradient descent to maximize the log-likelihood also has this same property; the log-likelihood gradient computations require taking expectations with respect to the posterior distribution over the hidden units. Another key insight in the EM algorithm is that we can continue to use one value of q even after we have moved to a different value of $\boldsymbol{\theta}$. This particular insight is used throughout classical machine learning to derive large M-step updates. In the context of deep learning, most models are too complex to admit a tractable solution for an optimal large M-step update, so this second insight, which is more unique to the EM algorithm, is rarely used.

19.3 MAP Inference and Sparse Coding

We usually use the term *inference* to refer to computing the probability distribution over one set of variables given another. When training probabilistic models with latent variables, we are usually interested in computing $p(\boldsymbol{h} \mid \boldsymbol{v})$. An alternative form of inference is to compute the single most likely value of the missing variables, rather than to infer the entire distribution over their possible values. In the context of latent variable models, this means computing

$$\boldsymbol{h}^* = \arg\max_{\boldsymbol{h}} p(\boldsymbol{h} \mid \boldsymbol{v}). \tag{19.9}$$

This is known as **maximum a posteriori** inference, abbreviated as MAP inference.

MAP inference is usually not thought of as approximate inference—it does compute the exact most likely value of $\boldsymbol{h}^*$. However, if we wish to develop a learning process based on maximizing $\mathcal{L}(\boldsymbol{v}, \boldsymbol{h}, q)$, then it is helpful to think of MAP inference as a procedure that provides a value of q. In this sense, we can think of MAP inference as approximate inference, because it does not provide the optimal q.

Recall from section 19.1 that exact inference consists of maximizing

$$\mathcal{L}(\boldsymbol{v}, \boldsymbol{\theta}, q) = \mathbb{E}_{\mathbf{h} \sim q} \left[\log p(\boldsymbol{h}, \boldsymbol{v}) \right] + H(q) \tag{19.10}$$

with respect to q over an unrestricted family of probability distributions, using an exact optimization algorithm. We can derive MAP inference as a form of approximate inference by restricting the family of distributions q may be drawn from. Specifically, we require q to take on a Dirac distribution:

$$q(\boldsymbol{h} \mid \boldsymbol{v}) = \delta(\boldsymbol{h} - \boldsymbol{\mu}). \tag{19.11}$$

This means that we can now control q entirely via $\boldsymbol{\mu}$. Dropping terms of $\mathcal{L}$ that do not vary with $\boldsymbol{\mu}$, we are left with the optimization problem

$$\boldsymbol{\mu}^* = \arg\max_{\boldsymbol{\mu}} \log p(\boldsymbol{h} = \boldsymbol{\mu}, \boldsymbol{v}), \tag{19.12}$$

which is equivalent to the MAP inference problem

$$\boldsymbol{h}^* = \arg\max_{\boldsymbol{h}} p(\boldsymbol{h} \mid \boldsymbol{v}). \tag{19.13}$$

We can thus justify a learning procedure similar to EM, in which we alternate between performing MAP inference to infer $\boldsymbol{h}^*$ and then update $\boldsymbol{\theta}$ to increase $\log p(\boldsymbol{h}^*, \boldsymbol{v})$. As with EM, this is a form of coordinate ascent on $\mathcal{L}$, where we alternate between using inference to optimize $\mathcal{L}$ with respect to q and using parameter updates to optimize $\mathcal{L}$ with respect to $\boldsymbol{\theta}$. The procedure as a whole can be justified by the fact that $\mathcal{L}$ is a lower bound on $\log p(\boldsymbol{v})$. In the case of MAP inference, this justification is rather vacuous, because the bound is infinitely loose, due to the Dirac distribution's differential entropy of negative infinity. Adding noise to $\boldsymbol{\mu}$ would make the bound meaningful again.

MAP inference is commonly used in deep learning as both a feature extractor and a learning mechanism. It is primarily used for sparse coding models.

Recall from section 13.4 that sparse coding is a linear factor model that imposes a sparsity-inducing prior on its hidden units. A common choice is a factorial Laplace prior, with

$$p(h_i) = \frac{\lambda}{2} e^{-\lambda |h_i|}. \tag{19.14}$$

The visible units are then generated by performing a linear transformation and adding noise:

$$p(\boldsymbol{x} \mid \boldsymbol{h}) = \mathcal{N}(\boldsymbol{v}; \boldsymbol{W}\boldsymbol{h} + \boldsymbol{b}, \beta^{-1}\boldsymbol{I}). \tag{19.15}$$

Computing or even representing $p(\boldsymbol{h} \mid \boldsymbol{v})$ is difficult. Every pair of variables h_i and h_j are both parents of $\boldsymbol{v}$. This means that when $\boldsymbol{v}$ is observed, the graphical model contains an active path connecting h_i and h_j. All the hidden units thus participate in one massive clique in $p(\boldsymbol{h} \mid \boldsymbol{v})$. If the model were Gaussian, then these interactions could be modeled efficiently via the covariance matrix, but the sparse prior makes these interactions non-Gaussian.

Because $p(\boldsymbol{h} \mid \boldsymbol{v})$ is intractable, so is the computation of the log-likelihood and its gradient. We thus cannot use exact maximum likelihood learning. Instead, we use MAP inference and learn the parameters by maximizing the ELBO defined by the Dirac distribution around the MAP estimate of $\boldsymbol{h}$.

If we concatenate all the $\boldsymbol{h}$ vectors in the training set into a matrix $\boldsymbol{H}$, and concatenate all the $\boldsymbol{v}$ vectors into a matrix $\boldsymbol{V}$, then the sparse coding learning process consists of minimizing

$$J(\boldsymbol{H}, \boldsymbol{W}) = \sum_{i,j} |H_{i,j}| + \sum_{i,j} \left(\boldsymbol{V} - \boldsymbol{H}\boldsymbol{W}^\top \right)^2_{i,j}. \tag{19.16}$$

Most applications of sparse coding also involve weight decay or a constraint on the norms of the columns of $\boldsymbol{W}$, to prevent the pathological solution with extremely small $\boldsymbol{H}$ and large $\boldsymbol{W}$.

We can minimize J by alternating between minimization with respect to $\boldsymbol{H}$ and minimization with respect to $\boldsymbol{W}$. Both subproblems are convex. In fact, the minimization with respect to $\boldsymbol{W}$ is just a linear regression problem. Minimization of J with respect to both arguments, however, is usually not a convex problem.

Minimization with respect to $\boldsymbol{H}$ requires specialized algorithms such as the feature-sign search algorithm (Lee et al., 2007).

19.4   Variational Inference and Learning

We have seen how the evidence lower bound $\mathcal{L}(\boldsymbol{v}, \boldsymbol{\theta}, q)$ is a lower bound on $\log p(\boldsymbol{v}; \boldsymbol{\theta})$, how inference can be viewed as maximizing $\mathcal{L}$ with respect to q, and how learning can be viewed as maximizing $\mathcal{L}$ with respect to $\boldsymbol{\theta}$. We have seen that the EM algorithm enables us to make large learning steps with a fixed q and that learning algorithms based on MAP inference enable us to learn using a point estimate of $p(\boldsymbol{h} \mid \boldsymbol{v})$ rather than inferring the entire distribution. Now we develop the more general approach to variational learning.

The core idea behind variational learning is that we can maximize $\mathcal{L}$ over a restricted family of distributions q. This family should be chosen so that it is easy to compute $\mathbb{E}_q \log p(\boldsymbol{h}, \boldsymbol{v})$. A typical way to do this is to introduce assumptions about how q factorizes.

A common approach to variational learning is to impose the restriction that q is a factorial distribution:

$$q(\boldsymbol{h} \mid \boldsymbol{v}) = \prod_i q(h_i \mid \boldsymbol{v}). \tag{19.17}$$

This is called the **mean field** approach. More generally, we can impose any graphical model structure we choose on q, to flexibly determine how many interactions we want our approximation to capture. This fully general graphical model approach is called **structured variational inference** (Saul and Jordan, 1996).

The beauty of the variational approach is that we do not need to specify a specific parametric form for q. We specify how it should factorize, but then the optimization problem determines the optimal probability distribution within those factorization constraints. For discrete latent variables, this just means that we use traditional optimization techniques to optimize a finite number of variables describing the q distribution. For continuous latent variables, this means that we use a branch of mathematics called calculus of variations to perform optimization over a space of functions and actually determine which function should be used to represent q. Calculus of variations is the origin of the names "variational learning" and "variational inference," though these names apply even when the latent variables are discrete and calculus of variations is not needed. With continuous latent variables, calculus of variations is a powerful technique that removes much of the responsibility from the human designer of the model, who now must specify only how q factorizes, rather than needing to guess how to design a specific q that can accurately approximate the posterior.

Because $\mathcal{L}(\boldsymbol{v}, \boldsymbol{\theta}, q)$ is defined to be $\log p(\boldsymbol{v}; \boldsymbol{\theta}) - D_{\mathrm{KL}}(q(\boldsymbol{h} \mid \boldsymbol{v}) \| p(\boldsymbol{h} \mid \boldsymbol{v}; \boldsymbol{\theta}))$, we can think of maximizing $\mathcal{L}$ with respect to q as minimizing $D_{\mathrm{KL}}(q(\boldsymbol{h} \mid \boldsymbol{v}) \| p(\boldsymbol{h} \mid \boldsymbol{v}))$. In this sense, we are fitting q to p. However, we are doing so with the opposite direction of the KL divergence than we are used to using for fitting an approximation. When we use maximum likelihood learning to fit a model to data, we minimize $D_{\mathrm{KL}}(p_{\mathrm{data}} \| p_{\mathrm{model}})$. As illustrated in figure 3.6, this means that maximum likelihood encourages the model to have high probability everywhere that the data has high probability, while our optimization-based inference procedure encourages q to have low probability everywhere the true posterior has low probability. Both directions of the KL divergence can have desirable and undesirable properties. The choice of which to use depends on which properties are the highest priority for each application. In the inference optimization problem, we choose to use $D_{\mathrm{KL}}(q(\boldsymbol{h} \mid \boldsymbol{v}) \| p(\boldsymbol{h} \mid \boldsymbol{v}))$ for computational reasons. Specifically, computing $D_{\mathrm{KL}}(q(\boldsymbol{h} \mid \boldsymbol{v}) \| p(\boldsymbol{h} \mid \boldsymbol{v}))$

involves evaluating expectations with respect to q, so by designing q to be simple, we can simplify the required expectations. The opposite direction of the KL divergence would require computing expectations with respect to the true posterior. Because the form of the true posterior is determined by the choice of model, we cannot design a reduced-cost approach to computing $D_{\mathrm{KL}}(p(\boldsymbol{h} \mid \boldsymbol{v}) \| q(\boldsymbol{h} \mid \boldsymbol{v}))$ exactly.

19.4.1 Discrete Latent Variables

Variational inference with discrete latent variables is relatively straightforward. We define a distribution q, typically one where each factor of q is just defined by a lookup table over discrete states. In the simplest case, $\boldsymbol{h}$ is binary and we make the mean field assumption that q factorizes over each individual h_i. In this case we can parametrize q with a vector $\hat{\boldsymbol{h}}$ whose entries are probabilities. Then $q(h_i = 1 \mid \boldsymbol{v}) = \hat{h}_i$.

After determining how to represent q, we simply optimize its parameters. With discrete latent variables, this is just a standard optimization problem. In principle the selection of q could be done with any optimization algorithm, such as gradient descent.

Because this optimization must occur in the inner loop of a learning algorithm, it must be very fast. To achieve this speed, we typically use special optimization algorithms that are designed to solve comparatively small and simple problems in few iterations. A popular choice is to iterate fixed-point equations, in other words, to solve

$$\frac{\partial}{\partial \hat{h}_i} \mathcal{L} = 0 \tag{19.18}$$

for $\hat{h}_i$. We repeatedly update different elements of $\hat{\boldsymbol{h}}$ until we satisfy a convergence criterion.

To make this more concrete, we show how to apply variational inference to the **binary sparse coding model** (we present here the model developed by Henniges et al. [2010] but demonstrate traditional, generic mean field applied to the model, while they introduce a specialized algorithm). This derivation goes into considerable mathematical detail and is intended for the reader who wishes to fully resolve any ambiguity in the high-level conceptual description of variational inference and learning we have presented so far. Readers who do not plan to derive or implement variational learning algorithms may safely skip to the next section without missing any new high-level concepts. Readers who proceed with the binary sparse coding example are encouraged to review the list of useful properties of functions that commonly arise in probabilistic models in section 3.10. We use these properties liberally throughout the following derivations without highlighting exactly where we use each one.

In the binary sparse coding model, the input $\boldsymbol{v} \in \mathbb{R}^n$ is generated from the model by adding Gaussian noise to the sum of m different components, which can each be present or absent. Each component is switched on or off by the corresponding hidden unit in $\boldsymbol{h} \in \{0, 1\}^m$:

$$p(h_i = 1) = \sigma(b_i), \tag{19.19}$$

$$p(\boldsymbol{v} \mid \boldsymbol{h}) = \mathcal{N}(\boldsymbol{v}; \boldsymbol{W}\boldsymbol{h}, \boldsymbol{\beta}^{-1}), \tag{19.20}$$

where $\boldsymbol{b}$ is a learnable set of biases, $\boldsymbol{W}$ is a learnable weight matrix, and $\boldsymbol{\beta}$ is a learnable, diagonal precision matrix.

Training this model with maximum likelihood requires taking the derivative with respect to the parameters. Consider the derivative with respect to one of the biases:

$$\frac{\partial}{\partial b_i} \log p(\boldsymbol{v}) \tag{19.21}$$

$$= \frac{\frac{\partial}{\partial b_i} p(\boldsymbol{v})}{p(\boldsymbol{v})} \tag{19.22}$$

$$= \frac{\frac{\partial}{\partial b_i} \sum_{\boldsymbol{h}} p(\boldsymbol{h}, \boldsymbol{v})}{p(\boldsymbol{v})} \tag{19.23}$$

$$= \frac{\frac{\partial}{\partial b_i} \sum_{\boldsymbol{h}} p(\boldsymbol{h}) p(\boldsymbol{v} \mid \boldsymbol{h})}{p(\boldsymbol{v})} \tag{19.24}$$

$$= \frac{\sum_{\boldsymbol{h}} p(\boldsymbol{v} \mid \boldsymbol{h}) \frac{\partial}{\partial b_i} p(\boldsymbol{h})}{p(\boldsymbol{v})} \tag{19.25}$$

$$= \sum_{\boldsymbol{h}} p(\boldsymbol{h} \mid \boldsymbol{v}) \frac{\frac{\partial}{\partial b_i} p(\boldsymbol{h})}{p(\boldsymbol{h})} \tag{19.26}$$

$$= \mathbb{E}_{\mathbf{h} \sim p(\boldsymbol{h} \mid \boldsymbol{v})} \frac{\partial}{\partial b_i} \log p(\boldsymbol{h}). \tag{19.27}$$

This requires computing expectations with respect to $p(\boldsymbol{h} \mid \boldsymbol{v})$. Unfortunately, $p(\boldsymbol{h} \mid \boldsymbol{v})$ is a complicated distribution. See figure 19.2 for the graph structure of $p(\boldsymbol{h}, \boldsymbol{v})$ and $p(\boldsymbol{h} \mid \boldsymbol{v})$. The posterior distribution corresponds to the complete graph

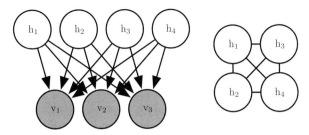

Figure 19.2: The graph structure of a binary sparse coding model with four hidden units. *(Left)*The graph structure of $p(\boldsymbol{h}, \boldsymbol{v})$. Note that the edges are directed, and that every two hidden units are coparents of every visible unit. *(Right)*The graph structure of $p(\boldsymbol{h} \mid \boldsymbol{v})$. To account for the active paths between coparents, the posterior distribution needs an edge between all the hidden units.

over the hidden units, so variable elimination algorithms do not help us to compute the required expectations any faster than brute force.

We can resolve this difficulty by using variational inference and variational learning instead.

We can make a mean field approximation:

$$q(\boldsymbol{h} \mid \boldsymbol{v}) = \prod_i q(h_i \mid \boldsymbol{v}). \tag{19.28}$$

The latent variables of the binary sparse coding model are binary, so to represent a factorial q we simply need to model m Bernoulli distributions $q(h_i \mid \boldsymbol{v})$. A natural way to represent the means of the Bernoulli distributions is with a vector $\hat{\boldsymbol{h}}$ of probabilities, with $q(h_i = 1 \mid \boldsymbol{v}) = \hat{h}_i$. We impose a restriction that $\hat{h}_i$ is never equal to 0 or to 1, in order to avoid errors when computing, for example, $\log \hat{h}_i$.

We will see that the variational inference equations never assign 0 or 1 to $\hat{h}_i$ analytically. In a software implementation, however, machine rounding error could result in 0 or 1 values. In software, we may wish to implement binary sparse coding using an unrestricted vector of variational parameters $\boldsymbol{z}$ and obtain $\hat{\boldsymbol{h}}$ via the relation $\hat{\boldsymbol{h}} = \sigma(\boldsymbol{z})$. We can thus safely compute $\log \hat{h}_i$ on a computer by using the identity $\log \sigma(z_i) = -\zeta(-z_i)$, relating the sigmoid and the softplus.

To begin our derivation of variational learning in the binary sparse coding model, we show that the use of this mean field approximation makes learning tractable.

The evidence lower bound is given by

$$\mathcal{L}(\boldsymbol{v}, \boldsymbol{\theta}, q) \tag{19.29}$$

$$= \mathbb{E}_{\mathbf{h} \sim q}[\log p(\boldsymbol{h}, \boldsymbol{v})] + H(q) \tag{19.30}$$

$$= \mathbb{E}_{\mathbf{h} \sim q}[\log p(\boldsymbol{h}) + \log p(\boldsymbol{v} \mid \boldsymbol{h}) - \log q(\boldsymbol{h} \mid \boldsymbol{v})] \tag{19.31}$$

$$= \mathbb{E}_{\mathbf{h} \sim q}\left[\sum_{i=1}^{m} \log p(h_i) + \sum_{i=1}^{n} \log p(v_i \mid \boldsymbol{h}) - \sum_{i=1}^{m} \log q(h_i \mid \boldsymbol{v})\right] \tag{19.32}$$

$$= \sum_{i=1}^{m}\left[\hat{h}_i(\log \sigma(b_i) - \log \hat{h}_i) + (1 - \hat{h}_i)(\log \sigma(-b_i) - \log(1 - \hat{h}_i))\right] \tag{19.33}$$

$$+ \mathbb{E}_{\mathbf{h} \sim q}\left[\sum_{i=1}^{n} \log \sqrt{\frac{\beta_i}{2\pi}} \exp\left(-\frac{\beta_i}{2}(v_i - \boldsymbol{W}_{i,:}\boldsymbol{h})^2\right)\right] \tag{19.34}$$

$$= \sum_{i=1}^{m}\left[\hat{h}_i(\log \sigma(b_i) - \log \hat{h}_i) + (1 - \hat{h}_i)(\log \sigma(-b_i) - \log(1 - \hat{h}_i))\right] \tag{19.35}$$

$$+ \frac{1}{2}\sum_{i=1}^{n}\left[\log\frac{\beta_i}{2\pi} - \beta_i\left(v_i^2 - 2v_i\boldsymbol{W}_{i,:}\hat{\boldsymbol{h}} + \sum_j\left[W_{i,j}^2\hat{h}_j + \sum_{k \neq j} W_{i,j}W_{i,k}\hat{h}_j\hat{h}_k\right]\right)\right]. \tag{19.36}$$

While these equations are somewhat unappealing aesthetically, they show that $\mathcal{L}$ can be expressed in a small number of simple arithmetic operations. The evidence lower bound $\mathcal{L}$ is therefore tractable. We can use $\mathcal{L}$ as a replacement for the intractable log-likelihood.

In principle, we could simply run gradient ascent on both $\boldsymbol{v}$ and $\boldsymbol{h}$, and this would make a perfectly acceptable combined inference and training algorithm. Usually, however, we do not do this, for two reasons. First, this would require storing $\hat{\boldsymbol{h}}$ for each $\boldsymbol{v}$. We typically prefer algorithms that do not require per example memory. It is difficult to scale learning algorithms to billions of examples if we must remember a dynamically updated vector associated with each example. Second, we would like to be able to extract the features $\hat{\boldsymbol{h}}$ very quickly, in order to recognize the content of $\boldsymbol{v}$. In a realistic deployed setting, we would need to be able to compute $\hat{\boldsymbol{h}}$ in real time.

For both these reasons, we typically do not use gradient descent to compute the mean field parameters $\hat{\boldsymbol{h}}$. Instead, we rapidly estimate them with fixed-point equations.

The idea behind fixed-point equations is that we are seeking a local maximum with respect to $\hat{\boldsymbol{h}}$, where $\nabla_{\boldsymbol{h}}\mathcal{L}(\boldsymbol{v}, \boldsymbol{\theta}, \hat{\boldsymbol{h}}) = \mathbf{0}$. We cannot efficiently solve this equation with respect to all of $\hat{\boldsymbol{h}}$ simultaneously. However, we can solve for a single variable:

$$\frac{\partial}{\partial \hat{h}_i}\mathcal{L}(\boldsymbol{v}, \boldsymbol{\theta}, \hat{\boldsymbol{h}}) = 0. \tag{19.37}$$

We can then iteratively apply the solution to the equation for $i = 1, \ldots, m$, and repeat the cycle until we satisfy a converge criterion. Common convergence criteria include stopping when a full cycle of updates does not improve $\mathcal{L}$ by more than some tolerance amount, or when the cycle does not change $\hat{\boldsymbol{h}}$ by more than some amount.

Iterating mean field fixed-point equations is a general technique that can provide fast variational inference in a broad variety of models. To make this more concrete, we show how to derive the updates for the binary sparse coding model in particular.

First, we must write an expression for the derivatives with respect to $\hat{h}_i$. To do so, we substitute equation 19.36 into the left side of equation 19.37:

$$\frac{\partial}{\partial \hat{h}_i} \mathcal{L}(\boldsymbol{v}, \boldsymbol{\theta}, \hat{\boldsymbol{h}}) \tag{19.38}$$

$$= \frac{\partial}{\partial \hat{h}_i} \left[\sum_{j=1}^{m} \left[\hat{h}_j (\log \sigma(b_j) - \log \hat{h}_j) + (1 - \hat{h}_j)(\log \sigma(-b_j) - \log(1 - \hat{h}_j)) \right] \right. \tag{19.39}$$

$$\left. + \frac{1}{2} \sum_{j=1}^{n} \left[\log \frac{\beta_j}{2\pi} - \beta_j \left(v_j^2 - 2 v_j \boldsymbol{W}_{j,:} \hat{\boldsymbol{h}} + \sum_k \left[W_{j,k}^2 \hat{h}_k + \sum_{l \neq k} W_{j,k} W_{j,l} \hat{h}_k \hat{h}_l \right] \right) \right] \right] \tag{19.40}$$

$$= \log \sigma(b_i) - \log \hat{h}_i - 1 + \log(1 - \hat{h}_i) + 1 - \log \sigma(-b_i) \tag{19.41}$$

$$+ \sum_{j=1}^{n} \left[\beta_j \left(v_j W_{j,i} - \frac{1}{2} W_{j,i}^2 - \sum_{k \neq i} \boldsymbol{W}_{j,k} \boldsymbol{W}_{j,i} \hat{h}_k \right) \right] \tag{19.42}$$

$$= b_i - \log \hat{h}_i + \log(1 - \hat{h}_i) + \boldsymbol{v}^\top \boldsymbol{\beta} \boldsymbol{W}_{:,i} - \frac{1}{2} \boldsymbol{W}_{:,i}^\top \boldsymbol{\beta} \boldsymbol{W}_{:,i} - \sum_{j \neq i} \boldsymbol{W}_{:,j}^\top \boldsymbol{\beta} \boldsymbol{W}_{:,i} \hat{h}_j. \tag{19.43}$$

To apply the fixed-point update inference rule, we solve for the $\hat{h}_i$ that sets equation 19.43 to 0:

$$\hat{h}_i = \sigma \left(b_i + \boldsymbol{v}^\top \boldsymbol{\beta} \boldsymbol{W}_{:,i} - \frac{1}{2} \boldsymbol{W}_{:,i}^\top \boldsymbol{\beta} \boldsymbol{W}_{:,i} - \sum_{j \neq i} \boldsymbol{W}_{:,j}^\top \boldsymbol{\beta} \boldsymbol{W}_{:,i} \hat{h}_j \right). \tag{19.44}$$

At this point, we can see that there is a close connection between recurrent neural networks and inference in graphical models. Specifically, the mean field fixed-point equations defined a recurrent neural network. The task of this network is to perform inference. We have described how to derive this network from a model description, but it is also possible to train the inference network directly. Several ideas based on this theme are described in chapter 20.

In the case of binary sparse coding, we can see that the recurrent network connection specified by equation 19.44 consists of repeatedly updating the hidden units based on the changing values of the neighboring hidden units. The input always sends a fixed message of $\boldsymbol{v}^\top \beta \boldsymbol{W}$ to the hidden units, but the hidden units constantly update the message they send to each other. Specifically, two units $\hat{h}_i$ and $\hat{h}_j$ inhibit each other when their weight vectors are aligned. This is a form of competition—between two hidden units that both explain the input, only the one that explains the input best will be allowed to remain active. This competition is the mean field approximation's attempt to capture the explaining away interactions in the binary sparse coding posterior. The explaining away effect actually should cause a multimodal posterior, so that if we draw samples from the posterior, some samples will have one unit active, other samples will have the other unit active, but very few samples will have both active. Unfortunately, explaining away interactions cannot be modeled by the factorial q used for mean field, so the mean field approximation is forced to choose one mode to model. This is an instance of the behavior illustrated in figure 3.6.

We can rewrite equation 19.44 into an equivalent form that reveals some further insights:

$$\hat{h}_i = \sigma \left(b_i + \left(\boldsymbol{v} - \sum_{j \neq i} \boldsymbol{W}_{:,j} \hat{h}_j \right)^\top \beta \boldsymbol{W}_{:,i} - \frac{1}{2} \boldsymbol{W}_{:,i}^\top \beta \boldsymbol{W}_{:,i} \right). \tag{19.45}$$

In this reformulation, we see the input at each step as consisting of $\boldsymbol{v} - \sum_{j \neq i} \boldsymbol{W}_{:,j} \hat{h}_j$ rather than $\boldsymbol{v}$. We can thus think of unit i as attempting to encode the residual error in $\boldsymbol{v}$ given the code of the other units. We can thus think of sparse coding as an iterative autoencoder, which repeatedly encodes and decodes its input, attempting to fix mistakes in the reconstruction after each iteration.

In this example, we have derived an update rule that updates a single unit at a time. It would be advantageous to be able to update more units simultaneously. Some graphical models, such as deep Boltzmann machines, are structured in such a way that we can solve for many entries of $\hat{\boldsymbol{h}}$ simultaneously. Unfortunately, binary sparse coding does not admit such block updates. Instead, we can use a heuristic technique called **damping** to perform block updates. In the damping approach, we solve for the individually optimal values of every element of $\hat{\boldsymbol{h}}$, then move all the values in a small step in that direction. This approach is no longer guaranteed to increase $\mathcal{L}$ at each step, but it works well in practice for many models. See Koller and Friedman (2009) for more information about choosing the degree of synchrony and damping strategies in message-passing algorithms.

19.4.2 Calculus of Variations

Before continuing with our presentation of variational learning, we must briefly introduce an important set of mathematical tools used in variational learning: **calculus of variations**.

Many machine learning techniques are based on minimizing a function $J(\boldsymbol{\theta})$ by finding the input vector $\boldsymbol{\theta} \in \mathbb{R}^n$ for which it takes on its minimal value. This can be accomplished with multivariate calculus and linear algebra, by solving for the critical points where $\nabla_{\boldsymbol{\theta}} J(\boldsymbol{\theta}) = \mathbf{0}$. In some cases, we actually want to solve for a function $f(\boldsymbol{x})$, such as when we want to find the probability density function over some random variable. This is what calculus of variations enables us to do.

A function of a function f is known as a **functional** $J[f]$. Much as we can take partial derivatives of a function with respect to elements of its vector-valued argument, we can take **functional derivatives**, also known as **variational derivatives**, of a functional $J[f]$ with respect to individual values of the function $f(\boldsymbol{x})$ at any specific value of $\boldsymbol{x}$. The functional derivative of the functional J with respect to the value of the function f at point $\boldsymbol{x}$ is denoted $\frac{\delta}{\delta f(\boldsymbol{x})} J$.

A complete formal development of functional derivatives is beyond the scope of this book. For our purposes, it is sufficient to state that for differentiable functions $f(\boldsymbol{x})$ and differentiable functions $g(y, \boldsymbol{x})$ with continuous derivatives, that

$$\frac{\delta}{\delta f(\boldsymbol{x})} \int g\left(f(\boldsymbol{x}), \boldsymbol{x}\right) d\boldsymbol{x} = \frac{\partial}{\partial y} g(f(\boldsymbol{x}), \boldsymbol{x}). \tag{19.46}$$

To gain some intuition for this identity, one can think of $f(\boldsymbol{x})$ as being a vector with uncountably many elements, indexed by a real vector $\boldsymbol{x}$. In this (somewhat incomplete) view, the identity providing the functional derivatives is the same as what we would obtain for a vector $\boldsymbol{\theta} \in \mathbb{R}^n$ indexed by positive integers:

$$\frac{\partial}{\partial \theta_i} \sum_j g(\theta_j, j) = \frac{\partial}{\partial \theta_i} g(\theta_i, i). \tag{19.47}$$

Many results in other machine learning publications are presented using the more general **Euler-Lagrange equation**, which allows g to depend on the derivatives of f as well as the value of f, but we do not need this fully general form for the results presented in this book.

To optimize a function with respect to a vector, we take the gradient of the function with respect to the vector and solve for the point where every element of the gradient is equal to zero. Likewise, we can optimize a functional by solving for the function where the functional derivative at every point is equal to zero.

As an example of how this process works, consider the problem of finding the probability distribution function over $x \in \mathbb{R}$ that has maximal differential entropy. Recall that the entropy of a probability distribution $p(x)$ is defined as

$$H[p] = -\mathbb{E}_x \log p(x). \tag{19.48}$$

For continuous values, the expectation is an integral:

$$H[p] = -\int p(x) \log p(x) dx. \tag{19.49}$$

We cannot simply maximize $H[p]$ with respect to the function $p(x)$, because the result might not be a probability distribution. Instead, we need to use Lagrange multipliers to add a constraint that $p(x)$ integrate to 1. Also, the entropy should increase without bound as the variance increases. This makes the question of which distribution has the greatest entropy uninteresting. Instead, we ask which distribution has maximal entropy for fixed variance σ^2. Finally, the problem is underdetermined because the distribution can be shifted arbitrarily without changing the entropy. To impose a unique solution, we add a constraint that the mean of the distribution be μ. The Lagrangian functional for this optimization problem is

$$\mathcal{L}[p] = \lambda_1 \left(\int p(x) dx - 1 \right) + \lambda_2 \left(\mathbb{E}[x] - \mu \right) + \lambda_3 \left(\mathbb{E}[(x-\mu)^2] - \sigma^2 \right) + H[p] \tag{19.50}$$

$$= \int \left(\lambda_1 p(x) + \lambda_2 p(x) x + \lambda_3 p(x)(x-\mu)^2 - p(x) \log p(x) \right) dx - \lambda_1 - \mu \lambda_2 - \sigma^2 \lambda_3. \tag{19.51}$$

To minimize the Lagrangian with respect to p, we set the functional derivatives equal to 0:

$$\forall x, \frac{\delta}{\delta p(x)} \mathcal{L} = \lambda_1 + \lambda_2 x + \lambda_3 (x-\mu)^2 - 1 - \log p(x) = 0. \tag{19.52}$$

This condition now tells us the functional form of $p(x)$. By algebraically rearranging the equation, we obtain

$$p(x) = \exp \left(\lambda_1 + \lambda_2 x + \lambda_3 (x-\mu)^2 - 1 \right). \tag{19.53}$$

We never assumed directly that $p(x)$ would take this functional form; we obtained the expression itself by analytically minimizing a functional. To finish the minimization problem, we must choose the λ values to ensure that all our constraints are satisfied. We are free to choose any λ values, because the gradient of the Lagrangian with respect to the λ variables is zero as long as the constraints are satisfied. To satisfy all the constraints, we may set $\lambda_1 = 1 - \log \sigma \sqrt{2\pi}$, $\lambda_2 = 0$, and $\lambda_3 = -\frac{1}{2\sigma^2}$ to obtain

$$p(x) = \mathcal{N}(x; \mu, \sigma^2). \tag{19.54}$$

This is one reason for using the normal distribution when we do not know the true distribution. Because the normal distribution has the maximum entropy, we impose the least possible amount of structure by making this assumption.

While examining the critical points of the Lagrangian functional for the entropy, we found only one critical point, corresponding to maximizing the entropy for fixed variance. What about the probability distribution function that *minimizes* the entropy? Why did we not find a second critical point corresponding to the minimum? The reason is that no specific function achieves minimal entropy. As functions place more probability density on the two points $x = \mu + \sigma$ and $x = \mu - \sigma$, and place less probability density on all other values of x, they lose entropy while maintaining the desired variance. However, any function placing exactly zero mass on all but two points does not integrate to one and is not a valid probability distribution. Thus there is no single minimal entropy probability distribution function, much as there is no single minimal positive real number. Instead, we can say that there is a sequence of probability distributions converging toward putting mass only on these two points. This degenerate scenario may be described as a mixture of Dirac distributions. Because Dirac distributions are not described by a single probability distribution function, no Dirac or mixture of Dirac distribution corresponds to a single specific point in function space. These distributions are thus invisible to our method of solving for a specific point where the functional derivatives are zero. This is a limitation of the method. Distributions such as the Dirac must be found by other methods, such as guessing the solution and then proving that it is correct.

19.4.3 Continuous Latent Variables

When our graphical model contains continuous latent variables, we can still perform variational inference and learning by maximizing $\mathcal{L}$. However, we must now use calculus of variations when maximizing $\mathcal{L}$ with respect to $q(\boldsymbol{h} \mid \boldsymbol{v})$.

In most cases, practitioners need not solve any calculus of variations problems themselves. Instead, there is a general equation for the mean field fixed-point updates. If we make the mean field approximation

$$q(\boldsymbol{h} \mid \boldsymbol{v}) = \prod_i q(h_i \mid \boldsymbol{v}), \tag{19.55}$$

and fix $q(h_j \mid \boldsymbol{v})$ for all $j \neq i$, then the optimal $q(h_i \mid \boldsymbol{v})$ may be obtained by normalizing the unnormalized distribution

$$\tilde{q}(h_i \mid \boldsymbol{v}) = \exp\left(\mathbb{E}_{\mathbf{h}_{-i} \sim q(\mathbf{h}_{-i} \mid \boldsymbol{v})} \log \tilde{p}(\boldsymbol{v}, \boldsymbol{h})\right), \tag{19.56}$$

as long as p does not assign 0 probability to any joint configuration of variables. Carrying out the expectation inside the equation will yield the correct functional form of $q(h_i \mid \boldsymbol{v})$. Deriving functional forms of q directly using calculus of variations is only necessary if one wishes to develop a new form of variational learning; equation 19.56 yields the mean field approximation for any probabilistic model.

Equation 19.56 is a fixed-point equation, designed to be iteratively applied for each value of i repeatedly until convergence. However, it also tells us more than that. It tells us the functional form that the optimal solution will take, whether we arrive there by fixed-point equations or not. This means we can take the functional form from that equation but regard some of the values that appear in it as parameters, which we can optimize with any optimization algorithm we like.

As an example, consider a simple probabilistic model, with latent variables $\boldsymbol{h} \in \mathbb{R}^2$ and just one visible variable, v. Suppose that $p(\boldsymbol{h}) = \mathcal{N}(\boldsymbol{h}; 0, \boldsymbol{I})$ and $p(v \mid \boldsymbol{h}) = \mathcal{N}(v; \boldsymbol{w}^\top \boldsymbol{h}; 1)$. We could actually simplify this model by integrating out $\boldsymbol{h}$; the result is just a Gaussian distribution over v. The model itself is not interesting; we have constructed it only to provide a simple demonstration of how calculus of variations can be applied to probabilistic modeling.

The true posterior is given, up to a normalizing constant, by

$$p(\boldsymbol{h} \mid \boldsymbol{v}) \tag{19.57}$$
$$\propto p(\boldsymbol{h}, \boldsymbol{v}) \tag{19.58}$$
$$= p(h_1)p(h_2)p(\boldsymbol{v} \mid \boldsymbol{h}) \tag{19.59}$$
$$\propto \exp\left(-\frac{1}{2}\left[h_1^2 + h_2^2 + (v - h_1 w_1 - h_2 w_2)^2\right]\right) \tag{19.60}$$
$$= \exp\left(-\frac{1}{2}\left[h_1^2 + h_2^2 + v^2 + h_1^2 w_1^2 + h_2^2 w_2^2 - 2vh_1 w_1 - 2vh_2 w_2 + 2h_1 w_1 h_2 w_2\right]\right). \tag{19.61}$$

Because of the presence of the terms multiplying h_1 and h_2 together, we can see that the true posterior does not factorize over h_1 and h_2.

Applying equation 19.56, we find that

$$\tilde{q}(h_1 \mid \boldsymbol{v}) \tag{19.62}$$

$$= \exp\left(\mathbb{E}_{h_2 \sim q(h_2|\boldsymbol{v})} \log \tilde{p}(\boldsymbol{v}, \boldsymbol{h})\right) \tag{19.63}$$

$$= \exp\left(-\frac{1}{2}\mathbb{E}_{h_2 \sim q(h_2|\boldsymbol{v})}\left[h_1^2 + h_2^2 + v^2 + h_1^2 w_1^2 + h_2^2 w_2^2\right.\right. \tag{19.64}$$

$$\left.\left. - 2vh_1 w_1 - 2vh_2 w_2 + 2h_1 w_1 h_2 w_2\right]\right). \tag{19.65}$$

From this, we can see that there are effectively only two values we need to obtain from $q(h_2 \mid \boldsymbol{v})$: $\mathbb{E}_{h_2 \sim q(h|\boldsymbol{v})}[h_2]$ and $\mathbb{E}_{h_2 \sim q(h|\boldsymbol{v})}[h_2^2]$. Writing these as $\langle h_2 \rangle$ and $\langle h_2^2 \rangle$, we obtain

$$\tilde{q}(h_1 \mid \boldsymbol{v}) = \exp\left(-\frac{1}{2}\left[h_1^2 + \langle h_2^2 \rangle + v^2 + h_1^2 w_1^2 + \langle h_2^2 \rangle w_2^2\right.\right. \tag{19.66}$$

$$\left.\left. - 2vh_1 w_1 - 2v\langle h_2 \rangle w_2 + 2h_1 w_1 \langle h_2 \rangle w_2\right]\right). \tag{19.67}$$

From this, we can see that $\tilde{q}$ has the functional form of a Gaussian. We can thus conclude $q(\boldsymbol{h} \mid \boldsymbol{v}) = \mathcal{N}(\boldsymbol{h}; \boldsymbol{\mu}, \boldsymbol{\beta}^{-1})$ where $\boldsymbol{\mu}$ and diagonal $\boldsymbol{\beta}$ are variational parameters, which we can optimize using any technique we choose. It is important to recall that we did not ever assume that q would be Gaussian; its Gaussian form was derived automatically by using calculus of variations to maximize q with respect to $\mathcal{L}$. Using the same approach on a different model could yield a different functional form of q.

This was, of course, just a small case constructed for demonstration purposes. For examples of real applications of variational learning with continuous variables in the context of deep learning, see Goodfellow et al. (2013d).

19.4.4   Interactions between Learning and Inference

Using approximate inference as part of a learning algorithm affects the learning process, and this in turn affects the accuracy of the inference algorithm.

Specifically, the training algorithm tends to adapt the model in a way that makes the approximating assumptions underlying the approximate inference algorithm become more true. When training the parameters, variational learning increases

$$\mathbb{E}_{\mathbf{h} \sim q} \log p(\boldsymbol{v}, \boldsymbol{h}). \tag{19.68}$$

For a specific $\boldsymbol{v}$, this increases $p(\boldsymbol{h} \mid \boldsymbol{v})$ for values of $\boldsymbol{h}$ that have high probability under $q(\boldsymbol{h} \mid \boldsymbol{v})$ and decreases $p(\boldsymbol{h} \mid \boldsymbol{v})$ for values of $\boldsymbol{h}$ that have low probability under $q(\boldsymbol{h} \mid \boldsymbol{v})$.

This behavior causes our approximating assumptions to become self-fulfilling prophecies. If we train the model with a unimodal approximate posterior, we will obtain a model with a true posterior that is far closer to unimodal than we would have obtained by training the model with exact inference.

Computing the true amount of harm imposed on a model by a variational approximation is thus very difficult. There exist several methods for estimating $\log p(\boldsymbol{v})$. We often estimate $\log p(\boldsymbol{v}; \boldsymbol{\theta})$ after training the model and find that the gap with $\mathcal{L}(\boldsymbol{v}, \boldsymbol{\theta}, q)$ is small. From this, we can conclude that our variational approximation is accurate for the specific value of $\boldsymbol{\theta}$ that we obtained from the learning process. We should not conclude that our variational approximation is accurate in general or that the variational approximation did little harm to the learning process. To measure the true amount of harm induced by the variational approximation, we would need to know $\boldsymbol{\theta}^* = \max_{\boldsymbol{\theta}} \log p(\boldsymbol{v}; \boldsymbol{\theta})$. It is possible for $\mathcal{L}(\boldsymbol{v}, \boldsymbol{\theta}, q) \approx \log p(\boldsymbol{v}; \boldsymbol{\theta})$ and $\log p(\boldsymbol{v}; \boldsymbol{\theta}) \ll \log p(\boldsymbol{v}; \boldsymbol{\theta}^*)$ to hold simultaneously. If $\max_q \mathcal{L}(\boldsymbol{v}, \boldsymbol{\theta}^*, q) \ll \log p(\boldsymbol{v}; \boldsymbol{\theta}^*)$, because $\boldsymbol{\theta}^*$ induces too complicated of a posterior distribution for our q family to capture, then the learning process will never approach $\boldsymbol{\theta}^*$. Such a problem is very difficult to detect, because we can only know for sure that it happened if we have a superior learning algorithm that can find $\boldsymbol{\theta}^*$ for comparison.

19.5 Learned Approximate Inference

We have seen that inference can be thought of as an optimization procedure that increases the value of a function $\mathcal{L}$. Explicitly performing optimization via iterative procedures such as fixed-point equations or gradient-based optimization is often very expensive and time consuming. Many approaches to inference avoid this expense by learning to perform approximate inference. Specifically, we can think of the optimization process as a function f that maps an input $\boldsymbol{v}$ to an approximate distribution $q^* = \arg\max_q \mathcal{L}(\boldsymbol{v}, q)$. Once we think of the multistep iterative optimization process as just being a function, we can approximate it with a neural network that implements an approximation $\hat{f}(\boldsymbol{v}; \boldsymbol{\theta})$.

19.5.1 Wake-Sleep

One of the main difficulties with training a model to infer h from v is that we do not have a supervised training set with which to train the model. Given a v, we do not know the appropriate h. The mapping from v to h depends on the choice of model family, and evolves throughout the learning process as θ changes. The wake-sleep algorithm (Hinton et al., 1995b; Frey et al., 1996) resolves this problem by drawing samples of both h and v from the model distribution. For example, in a directed model, this can be done cheaply by performing ancestral sampling beginning at h and ending at v. The inference network can then be trained to perform the reverse mapping: predicting which h caused the present v. The main drawback to this approach is that we will only be able to train the inference network on values of v that have high probability under the model. Early in learning, the model distribution will not resemble the data distribution, so the inference network will not have an opportunity to learn on samples that resemble data.

In section 18.2 we saw that one possible explanation for the role of dream sleep in human beings and animals is that dreams could provide the negative phase samples that Monte Carlo training algorithms use to approximate the negative gradient of the log partition function of undirected models. Another possible explanation for biological dreaming is that it is providing samples from $p(h, v)$ which can be used to train an inference network to predict h given v. In some senses, this explanation is more satisfying than the partition function explanation. Monte Carlo algorithms generally do not perform well if they are run using only the positive phase of the gradient for several steps then with only the negative phase of the gradient for several steps. Human beings and animals are usually awake for several consecutive hours then asleep for several consecutive hours. It is not readily apparent how this schedule could support Monte Carlo training of an undirected model. Learning algorithms based on maximizing $\mathcal{L}$ can be run with prolonged periods of improving q and prolonged periods of improving θ, however. If the role of biological dreaming is to train networks for predicting q, then this explains how animals are able to remain awake for several hours (the longer they are awake, the greater the gap between $\mathcal{L}$ and $\log p(v)$, but $\mathcal{L}$ will remain a lower bound) and to remain asleep for several hours (the generative model itself is not modified during sleep) without damaging their internal models. Of course, these ideas are purely speculative, and there is no hard evidence to suggest that dreaming accomplishes either of these goals. Dreaming may also serve reinforcement learning rather than probabilistic modeling, by sampling synthetic experiences from the animal's transition model, on which to train the animal's policy. Or sleep may serve some other purpose not yet anticipated by the machine learning community.

19.5.2   Other Forms of Learned Inference

This strategy of learned approximate inference has also been applied to other models. Salakhutdinov and Larochelle (2010) showed that a single pass in a learned inference network could yield faster inference than iterating the mean field fixed-point equations in a DBM. The training procedure is based on running the inference network, then applying one step of mean field to improve its estimates, and training the inference network to output this refined estimate instead of its original estimate.

We have already seen in section 14.8 that the predictive sparse decomposition model trains a shallow encoder network to predict a sparse code for the input. This can be seen as a hybrid between an autoencoder and sparse coding. It is possible to devise probabilistic semantics for the model, under which the encoder may be viewed as performing learned approximate MAP inference. Due to its shallow encoder, PSD is not able to implement the kind of competition between units that we have seen in mean field inference. However, that problem can be remedied by training a deep encoder to perform learned approximate inference, as in the ISTA technique (Gregor and LeCun, 2010b).

Learned approximate inference has recently become one of the dominant approaches to generative modeling, in the form of the variational autoencoder (Kingma, 2013; Rezende et al., 2014). In this elegant approach, there is no need to construct explicit targets for the inference network. Instead, the inference network is simply used to define $\mathcal{L}$, and then the parameters of the inference network are adapted to increase $\mathcal{L}$. This model is described in depth in section 20.10.3.

Using approximate inference, it is possible to train and use a wide variety of models. Many of these models are described in the next chapter.

20

Deep Generative Models

In this chapter, we present several of the specific kinds of generative models that can be built and trained using the techniques presented in chapters 16–19. All these models represent probability distributions over multiple variables in some way. Some allow the probability distribution function to be evaluated explicitly. Others do not allow the evaluation of the probability distribution function but support operations that implicitly require knowledge of it, such as drawing samples from the distribution. Some of these models are structured probabilistic models described in terms of graphs and factors, using the language of graphical models presented in chapter 16. Others cannot be easily described in terms of factors but represent probability distributions nonetheless.

20.1 Boltzmann Machines

Boltzmann machines were originally introduced as a general "connectionist" approach to learning arbitrary probability distributions over binary vectors (Fahlman et al., 1983; Ackley et al., 1985; Hinton et al., 1984; Hinton and Sejnowski, 1986). Variants of the Boltzmann machine that include other kinds of variables have long ago surpassed the popularity of the original. In this section we briefly introduce the binary Boltzmann machine and discuss the issues that come up when trying to train and perform inference in the model.

We define the Boltzmann machine over a d-dimensional binary random vector $\mathbf{x} \in \{0, 1\}^d$. The Boltzmann machine is an energy-based model (section 16.2.4), meaning we define the joint probability distribution using an energy function:

$$P(\boldsymbol{x}) = \frac{\exp\left(-E(\boldsymbol{x})\right)}{Z}, \tag{20.1}$$

where $E(\boldsymbol{x})$ is the energy function, and Z is the partition function that ensures that $\sum_{\boldsymbol{x}} P(\boldsymbol{x}) = 1$. The energy function of the Boltzmann machine is given by

$$E(\boldsymbol{x}) = -\boldsymbol{x}^\top \boldsymbol{U} \boldsymbol{x} - \boldsymbol{b}^\top \boldsymbol{x}, \tag{20.2}$$

where $\boldsymbol{U}$ is the "weight" matrix of model parameters and $\boldsymbol{b}$ is the vector of bias parameters.

In the general setting of the Boltzmann machine, we are given a set of training examples, each of which are n-dimensional. Equation 20.1 describes the joint probability distribution over the observed variables. While this scenario is certainly viable, it does limit the kinds of interactions between the observed variables to those described by the weight matrix. Specifically, it means that the probability of one unit being on is given by a linear model (logistic regression) from the values of the other units.

The Boltzmann machine becomes more powerful when not all the variables are observed. In this case, the latent variables can act similarly to hidden units in a multilayer perceptron and model higher-order interactions among the visible units. Just as the addition of hidden units to convert logistic regression into an MLP results in the MLP being a universal approximator of functions, a Boltzmann machine with hidden units is no longer limited to modeling linear relationships between variables. Instead, the Boltzmann machine becomes a universal approximator of probability mass functions over discrete variables (Le Roux and Bengio, 2008).

Formally, we decompose the units $\boldsymbol{x}$ into two subsets: the visible units $\boldsymbol{v}$ and the latent (or hidden) units $\boldsymbol{h}$. The energy function becomes

$$E(\boldsymbol{v}, \boldsymbol{h}) = -\boldsymbol{v}^\top \boldsymbol{R} \boldsymbol{v} - \boldsymbol{v}^\top \boldsymbol{W} \boldsymbol{h} - \boldsymbol{h}^\top \boldsymbol{S} \boldsymbol{h} - \boldsymbol{b}^\top \boldsymbol{v} - \boldsymbol{c}^\top \boldsymbol{h}. \tag{20.3}$$

Boltzmann Machine Learning   Learning algorithms for Boltzmann machines are usually based on maximum likelihood. All Boltzmann machines have an intractable partition function, so the maximum likelihood gradient must be approximated using the techniques described in chapter 18.

One interesting property of Boltzmann machines when trained with learning rules based on maximum likelihood is that the update for a particular weight connecting two units depends only on the statistics of those two units, collected under different distributions: $P_{\text{model}}(\boldsymbol{v})$ and $\hat{P}_{\text{data}}(\boldsymbol{v})P_{\text{model}}(\boldsymbol{h} \mid \boldsymbol{v})$. The rest of the network participates in shaping those statistics, but the weight can be updated without knowing anything about the rest of the network or how those statistics were produced. This means that the learning rule is "local," which makes Boltzmann machine learning somewhat biologically plausible. It is conceivable that if each neuron were a random variable in a Boltzmann machine, then the axons and dendrites connecting two random variables could learn only by observing the firing pattern of the cells that they actually physically touch. In particular, in the positive phase, two units that frequently activate together have their connection strengthened. This is an example of a Hebbian learning rule (Hebb, 1949) often summarized with the mnemonic "fire together, wire together." Hebbian learning rules are among the oldest hypothesized explanations for learning in biological systems and remain relevant today (Giudice et al., 2009).

Other learning algorithms that use more information than local statistics seem to require us to hypothesize the existence of more machinery than this. For example, for the brain to implement back-propagation in a multilayer perceptron, it seems necessary for the brain to maintain a secondary communication network for transmitting gradient information backward through the network. Proposals for biologically plausible implementations (and approximations) of back-propagation have been made (Hinton, 2007a; Bengio, 2015) but remain to be validated, and Bengio (2015) links back-propagation of gradients to inference in energy-based models similar to the Boltzmann machine (but with continuous latent variables).

The negative phase of Boltzmann machine learning is somewhat harder to explain from a biological point of view. As argued in section 18.2, dream sleep may be a form of negative phase sampling. This idea is more speculative though.

20.2 Restricted Boltzmann Machines

Invented under the name **harmonium** (Smolensky, 1986), restricted Boltzmann machines are some of the most common building blocks of deep probabilistic models. We briefly describe RBMs in section 16.7.1. Here we review the previous information and go into more detail. RBMs are undirected probabilistic graphical models containing a layer of observable variables and a single layer of latent variables. RBMs may be stacked (one on top of the other) to form deeper models. See figure 20.1 for some examples. In particular, figure 20.1a shows the graph structure of the RBM itself. It is a bipartite graph, with no connections permitted between any variables in the observed layer or between any units in the latent layer.

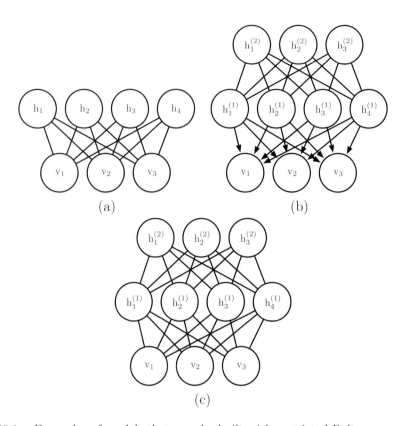

Figure 20.1: Examples of models that may be built with restricted Boltzmann machines. *(a)* The restricted Boltzmann machine itself is an undirected graphical model based on a bipartite graph, with visible units in one part of the graph and hidden units in the other part. There are no connections among the visible units, nor any connections among the hidden units. Typically every visible unit is connected to every hidden unit, but it is possible to construct sparsely connected RBMs such as convolutional RBMs. *(b)* A deep belief network is a hybrid graphical model involving both directed and undirected connections. Like an RBM, it has no intralayer connections. However, a DBN has multiple hidden layers, and thus connections between hidden units are in separate layers. All the local conditional probability distributions needed by the deep belief network are copied directly from the local conditional probability distributions of its constituent RBMs. Alternatively, we could also represent the deep belief network with a completely undirected graph, but it would need intralayer connections to capture the dependencies between parents. *(c)* A deep Boltzmann machine is an undirected graphical model with several layers of latent variables. Like RBMs and DBNs, DBMs lack intralayer connections. DBMs are less closely tied to RBMs than DBNs are. When initializing a DBM from a stack of RBMs, it is necessary to modify the RBM parameters slightly. Some kinds of DBMs may be trained without first training a set of RBMs.

We begin with the binary version of the restricted Boltzmann machine, but as we see later, there are extensions to other types of visible and hidden units.

More formally, let the observed layer consist of a set of n_v binary random variables, which we refer to collectively with the vector $\mathbf{v}$. We refer to the latent, or hidden, layer of n_h binary random variables as $\boldsymbol{h}$.

Like the general Boltzmann machine, the restricted Boltzmann machine is an energy-based model with the joint probability distribution specified by its energy function:

$$P(\mathbf{v} = \boldsymbol{v}, \mathbf{h} = \boldsymbol{h}) = \frac{1}{Z} \exp\left(-E(\boldsymbol{v}, \boldsymbol{h})\right). \tag{20.4}$$

The energy function for an RBM is given by

$$E(\boldsymbol{v}, \boldsymbol{h}) = -\boldsymbol{b}^\top \boldsymbol{v} - \boldsymbol{c}^\top \boldsymbol{h} - \boldsymbol{v}^\top \boldsymbol{W} \boldsymbol{h}, \tag{20.5}$$

and Z is the normalizing constant known as the partition function:

$$Z = \sum_{\boldsymbol{v}} \sum_{\boldsymbol{h}} \exp\left\{-E(\boldsymbol{v}, \boldsymbol{h})\right\}. \tag{20.6}$$

It is apparent from the definition of the partition function Z that the naive method of computing Z (exhaustively summing over all states) could be computationally intractable, unless a cleverly designed algorithm could exploit regularities in the probability distribution to compute Z faster. In the case of restricted Boltzmann machines, Long and Servedio (2010) formally proved that the partition function Z is intractable. The intractable partition function Z implies that the normalized joint probability distribution $P(\boldsymbol{v})$ is also intractable to evaluate.

20.2.1   Conditional Distributions

Though $P(\boldsymbol{v})$ is intractable, the bipartite graph structure of the RBM has the special property of its conditional distributions $P(\mathbf{h} \mid \mathbf{v})$ and $P(\mathbf{v} \mid \mathbf{h})$ being factorial and relatively simple to compute and sample from.

Deriving the conditional distributions from the joint distribution is straightforward:

$$P(\boldsymbol{h} \mid \boldsymbol{v}) = \frac{P(\boldsymbol{h}, \boldsymbol{v})}{P(\boldsymbol{v})} \tag{20.7}$$

$$= \frac{1}{P(\boldsymbol{v})} \frac{1}{Z} \exp\left\{\boldsymbol{b}^\top \boldsymbol{v} + \boldsymbol{c}^\top \boldsymbol{h} + \boldsymbol{v}^\top \boldsymbol{W} \boldsymbol{h}\right\} \tag{20.8}$$

$$= \frac{1}{Z'} \exp\left\{\boldsymbol{c}^\top \boldsymbol{h} + \boldsymbol{v}^\top \boldsymbol{W} \boldsymbol{h}\right\} \tag{20.9}$$

$$= \frac{1}{Z'} \exp \left\{ \sum_{j=1}^{n_h} c_j h_j + \sum_{j=1}^{n_h} \boldsymbol{v}^\top \boldsymbol{W}_{:,j} h_j \right\} \tag{20.10}$$

$$= \frac{1}{Z'} \prod_{j=1}^{n_h} \exp \left\{ c_j h_j + \boldsymbol{v}^\top \boldsymbol{W}_{:,j} h_j \right\}. \tag{20.11}$$

Since we are conditioning on the visible units $\mathbf{v}$, we can treat these as constant with respect to the distribution $P(\mathbf{h} \mid \mathbf{v})$. The factorial nature of the conditional $P(\mathbf{h} \mid \mathbf{v})$ follows immediately from our ability to write the joint probability over the vector $\boldsymbol{h}$ as the product of (unnormalized) distributions over the individual elements, h_j. It is now a simple matter of normalizing the distributions over the individual binary h_j.

$$P(h_j = 1 \mid \boldsymbol{v}) = \frac{\tilde{P}(h_j = 1 \mid \boldsymbol{v})}{\tilde{P}(h_j = 0 \mid \boldsymbol{v}) + \tilde{P}(h_j = 1 \mid \boldsymbol{v})} \tag{20.12}$$

$$= \frac{\exp \left\{ c_j + \boldsymbol{v}^\top \boldsymbol{W}_{:,j} \right\}}{\exp \left\{ 0 \right\} + \exp \left\{ c_j + \boldsymbol{v}^\top \boldsymbol{W}_{:,j} \right\}} \tag{20.13}$$

$$= \sigma \left(c_j + \boldsymbol{v}^\top \boldsymbol{W}_{:,j} \right). \tag{20.14}$$

We can now express the full conditional over the hidden layer as the factorial distribution:

$$P(\boldsymbol{h} \mid \boldsymbol{v}) = \prod_{j=1}^{n_h} \sigma \left((2\boldsymbol{h} - 1) \odot (\boldsymbol{c} + \boldsymbol{W}^\top \boldsymbol{v}) \right)_j. \tag{20.15}$$

A similar derivation will show that the other condition of interest to us, $P(\boldsymbol{v} \mid \boldsymbol{h})$, is also a factorial distribution:

$$P(\boldsymbol{v} \mid \boldsymbol{h}) = \prod_{i=1}^{n_v} \sigma \left((2\boldsymbol{v} - 1) \odot (\boldsymbol{b} + \boldsymbol{W}\boldsymbol{h}) \right)_i. \tag{20.16}$$

20.2.2 Training Restricted Boltzmann Machines

Because the RBM admits efficient evaluation and differentiation of $\tilde{P}(\boldsymbol{v})$ and efficient MCMC sampling in the form of block Gibbs sampling, it can readily be trained with any of the techniques described in chapter 18 for training models that have intractable partition functions. This includes CD, SML (PCD), ratio matching, and so on. Compared to other undirected models used in deep learning, the RBM is relatively straightforward to train because we can compute $P(\mathbf{h} \mid \boldsymbol{v})$

exactly in closed form. Some other deep models, such as the deep Boltzmann machine, combine both the difficulty of an intractable partition function and the difficulty of intractable inference.

20.3 Deep Belief Networks

Deep belief networks (DBNs) were one of the first nonconvolutional models to successfully admit training of deep architectures (Hinton et al., 2006; Hinton, 2007b). The introduction of deep belief networks in 2006 began the current deep learning renaissance. Prior to the introduction of deep belief networks, deep models were considered too difficult to optimize. Kernel machines with convex objective functions dominated the research landscape. Deep belief networks demonstrated that deep architectures can be successful by outperforming kernelized support vector machines on the MNIST dataset (Hinton et al., 2006). Today, deep belief networks have mostly fallen out of favor and are rarely used, even compared to other unsupervised or generative learning algorithms, but they are still deservedly recognized for their important role in deep learning history.

Deep belief networks are generative models with several layers of latent variables. The latent variables are typically binary, while the visible units may be binary or real. There are no intralayer connections. Usually, every unit in each layer is connected to every unit in each neighboring layer, though it is possible to construct more sparsely connected DBNs. The connections between the top two layers are undirected. The connections between all other layers are directed, with the arrows pointed toward the layer that is closest to the data. See figure 20.1b for an example.

A DBN with l hidden layers contains l weight matrices: $\boldsymbol{W}^{(1)}, \ldots, \boldsymbol{W}^{(l)}$. It also contains $l + 1$ bias vectors $\boldsymbol{b}^{(0)}, \ldots, \boldsymbol{b}^{(l)}$, with $\boldsymbol{b}^{(0)}$ providing the biases for the visible layer. The probability distribution represented by the DBN is given by

$$P(\boldsymbol{h}^{(l)}, \boldsymbol{h}^{(l-1)}) \propto \exp\left(\boldsymbol{b}^{(l)\top}\boldsymbol{h}^{(l)} + \boldsymbol{b}^{(l-1)\top}\boldsymbol{h}^{(l-1)} + \boldsymbol{h}^{(l-1)\top}\boldsymbol{W}^{(l)}\boldsymbol{h}^{(l)}\right), \quad (20.17)$$

$$P(h_i^{(k)} = 1 \mid \boldsymbol{h}^{(k+1)}) = \sigma\left(b_i^{(k)} + \boldsymbol{W}_{:,i}^{(k+1)\top}\boldsymbol{h}^{(k+1)}\right) \forall i, \forall k \in 1, \ldots, l-2, \quad (20.18)$$

$$P(v_i = 1 \mid \boldsymbol{h}^{(1)}) = \sigma\left(b_i^{(0)} + \boldsymbol{W}_{:,i}^{(1)\top}\boldsymbol{h}^{(1)}\right) \forall i. \quad (20.19)$$

In the case of real-valued visible units, substitute

$$\mathbf{v} \sim \mathcal{N}\left(\boldsymbol{v}; \boldsymbol{b}^{(0)} + \boldsymbol{W}^{(1)\top}\boldsymbol{h}^{(1)}, \boldsymbol{\beta}^{-1}\right) \quad (20.20)$$

with $\boldsymbol{\beta}$ diagonal for tractability. Generalizations to other exponential family visible units are straightforward, at least in theory. A DBN with only one hidden layer is just an RBM.

To generate a sample from a DBN, we first run several steps of Gibbs sampling on the top two hidden layers. This stage is essentially drawing a sample from the RBM defined by the top two hidden layers. We can then use a single pass of ancestral sampling through the rest of the model to draw a sample from the visible units.

Deep belief networks incur many of the problems associated with both directed models and undirected models.

Inference in a deep belief network is intractable because of the explaining away effect within each directed layer and the interaction between the two hidden layers that have undirected connections. Evaluating or maximizing the standard evidence lower bound on the log-likelihood is also intractable, because the evidence lower bound takes the expectation of cliques whose size is equal to the network width.

Evaluating or maximizing the log-likelihood requires confronting not just the problem of intractable inference to marginalize out the latent variables, but also the problem of an intractable partition function within the undirected model of the top two layers.

To train a deep belief network, one begins by training an RBM to maximize $\mathbb{E}_{\mathbf{v} \sim p_{\text{data}}} \log p(\boldsymbol{v})$ using contrastive divergence or stochastic maximum likelihood. The parameters of the RBM then define the parameters of the first layer of the DBN. Next, a second RBM is trained to approximately maximize

$$\mathbb{E}_{\mathbf{v} \sim p_{\text{data}}} \mathbb{E}_{\mathbf{h}^{(1)} \sim p^{(1)}(\boldsymbol{h}^{(1)} | \boldsymbol{v})} \log p^{(2)}(\boldsymbol{h}^{(1)}), \tag{20.21}$$

where $p^{(1)}$ is the probability distribution represented by the first RBM, and $p^{(2)}$ is the probability distribution represented by the second RBM. In other words, the second RBM is trained to model the distribution defined by sampling the hidden units of the first RBM, when the first RBM is driven by the data. This procedure can be repeated indefinitely, to add as many layers to the DBN as desired, with each new RBM modeling the samples of the previous one. Each RBM defines another layer of the DBN. This procedure can be justified as increasing a variational lower bound on the log-likelihood of the data under the DBN (Hinton et al., 2006).

In most applications, no effort is made to jointly train the DBN after the greedy layer-wise procedure is complete. However, it is possible to perform generative fine-tuning using the wake-sleep algorithm.

The trained DBN may be used directly as a generative model, but most of the interest in DBNs arose from their ability to improve classification models. We can take the weights from the DBN and use them to define an MLP:

$$\boldsymbol{h}^{(1)} = \sigma \left(b^{(1)} + \boldsymbol{v}^{\top} \boldsymbol{W}^{(1)} \right), \tag{20.22}$$

$$\boldsymbol{h}^{(l)} = \sigma \left(b_i^{(l)} + \boldsymbol{h}^{(l-1)\top} \boldsymbol{W}^{(l)} \right) \forall l \in 2, \ldots, m. \tag{20.23}$$

After initializing this MLP with the weights and biases learned via generative training of the DBN, we can train the MLP to perform a classification task. This additional training of the MLP is an example of discriminative fine-tuning.

This specific choice of MLP is somewhat arbitrary, compared to many of the inference equations in chapter 19 that are derived from first principles. This MLP is a heuristic choice that seems to work well in practice and is used consistently in the literature. Many approximate inference techniques are motivated by their ability to find a maximally *tight* variational lower bound on the log-likelihood under some set of constraints. One can construct a variational lower bound on the log-likelihood using the hidden unit expectations defined by the DBN's MLP, but this is true of *any* probability distribution over the hidden units, and there is no reason to believe that this MLP provides a particularly tight bound. In particular, the MLP ignores many important interactions in the DBN graphical model. The MLP propagates information upward from the visible units to the deepest hidden units, but does not propagate any information downward or sideways. The DBN graphical model has explaining away interactions between all the hidden units within the same layer as well as in top-down interactions between layers.

While the log-likelihood of a DBN is intractable, it may be approximated with AIS (Salakhutdinov and Murray, 2008). This permits evaluating its quality as a generative model.

The term "deep belief network" is commonly used incorrectly to refer to any kind of deep neural network, even networks without latent variable semantics. The term should refer specifically to models with undirected connections in the deepest layer and directed connections pointing downward between all other pairs of consecutive layers.

The term may also cause some confusion because "belief network" is sometimes used to refer to purely directed models, while deep belief networks contain an undirected layer. Deep belief networks also share the acronym DBN with dynamic Bayesian networks (Dean and Kanazawa, 1989), which are Bayesian networks for representing Markov chains.

20.4 Deep Boltzmann Machines

A **deep Boltzmann machine**, or DBM (Salakhutdinov and Hinton, 2009a) is another kind of deep generative model. Unlike the deep belief network (DBN), it is an entirely undirected model. Unlike the RBM, the DBM has several layers of latent variables (RBMs have just one). But like the RBM, within each layer, each of the variables are mutually independent, conditioned on the variables in the neighboring layers. See figure 20.2 for the graph structure. Deep Boltzmann machines have been applied to a variety of tasks, including document modeling (Srivastava et al., 2013).

Like RBMs and DBNs, DBMs typically contain only binary units—as we assume for simplicity of our presentation of the model—but it is straightforward to include real-valued visible units.

A DBM is an energy-based model, meaning that the joint probability distribution over the model variables is parametrized by an energy function E. In the case of a deep Boltzmann machine with one visible layer, $\boldsymbol{v}$, and three hidden layers, $\boldsymbol{h}^{(1)}$, $\boldsymbol{h}^{(2)}$, and $\boldsymbol{h}^{(3)}$, the joint probability is given by

$$P\left(\boldsymbol{v}, \boldsymbol{h}^{(1)}, \boldsymbol{h}^{(2)}, \boldsymbol{h}^{(3)}\right) = \frac{1}{Z(\boldsymbol{\theta})} \exp\left(-E(\boldsymbol{v}, \boldsymbol{h}^{(1)}, \boldsymbol{h}^{(2)}, \boldsymbol{h}^{(3)}; \boldsymbol{\theta})\right). \tag{20.24}$$

To simplify our presentation, we omit the bias parameters below. The DBM energy function is then defined as follows:

$$E(\boldsymbol{v}, \boldsymbol{h}^{(1)}, \boldsymbol{h}^{(2)}, \boldsymbol{h}^{(3)}; \boldsymbol{\theta}) = -\boldsymbol{v}^\top \boldsymbol{W}^{(1)} \boldsymbol{h}^{(1)} - \boldsymbol{h}^{(1)\top} \boldsymbol{W}^{(2)} \boldsymbol{h}^{(2)} - \boldsymbol{h}^{(2)\top} \boldsymbol{W}^{(3)} \boldsymbol{h}^{(3)}. \tag{20.25}$$

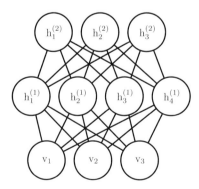

Figure 20.2: The graphical model for a deep Boltzmann machine with one visible layer (bottom) and two hidden layers. Connections are only between units in neighboring layers. There are no intralayer connections.

In comparison to the RBM energy function (equation 20.5), the DBM energy function includes connections between the hidden units (latent variables) in the form of the weight matrices ($\boldsymbol{W}^{(2)}$ and $\boldsymbol{W}^{(3)}$). As we will see, these connections have significant consequences for the model behavior as well as how we go about performing inference in the model.

In comparison to fully connected Boltzmann machines (with every unit connected to every other unit), the DBM offers some advantages that are similar to those offered by the RBM. Specifically, as illustrated in figure 20.3, the DBM layers can be organized into a bipartite graph, with odd layers on one side and even layers on the other. This immediately implies that when we condition on the variables in the even layer, the variables in the odd layers become conditionally independent. Of course, when we condition on the variables in the odd layers, the variables in the even layers also become conditionally independent.

The bipartite structure of the DBM means that we can apply the same equations we have previously used for the conditional distributions of an RBM to determine the conditional distributions in a DBM. The units within a layer are conditionally independent from each other given the values of the neighboring layers, so the distributions over binary variables can be fully described by the Bernoulli parameters, giving the probability of each unit being active. In our example with two hidden layers, the activation probabilities are given by

$$P(v_i = 1 \mid \boldsymbol{h}^{(1)}) = \sigma\left(\boldsymbol{W}_{i,:}^{(1)}\boldsymbol{h}^{(1)}\right), \qquad (20.26)$$

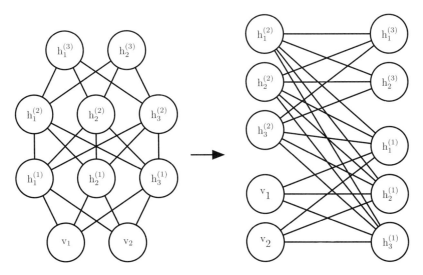

Figure 20.3: A deep Boltzmann machine, rearranged to reveal its bipartite graph structure.

$$P(h_i^{(1)} = 1 \mid \boldsymbol{v}, \boldsymbol{h}^{(2)}) = \sigma\left(\boldsymbol{v}^\top \boldsymbol{W}_{:,i}^{(1)} + \boldsymbol{W}_{i,:}^{(2)} \boldsymbol{h}^{(2)}\right), \tag{20.27}$$

and

$$P(h_k^{(2)} = 1 \mid \boldsymbol{h}^{(1)}) = \sigma\left(\boldsymbol{h}^{(1)\top} \boldsymbol{W}_{:,k}^{(2)}\right). \tag{20.28}$$

The bipartite structure makes Gibbs sampling in a deep Boltzmann machine efficient. The naive approach to Gibbs sampling is to update only one variable at a time. RBMs allow all the visible units to be updated in one block and all the hidden units to be updated in a second block. One might naively assume that a DBM with l layers requires $l + 1$ updates, with each iteration updating a block consisting of one layer of units. Instead, it is possible to update all the units in only two iterations. Gibbs sampling can be divided into two blocks of updates, one including all even layers (including the visible layer) and the other including all odd layers. Because of the bipartite DBM connection pattern, given the even layers, the distribution over the odd layers is factorial and thus can be sampled simultaneously and independently as a block. Likewise, given the odd layers, the even layers can be sampled simultaneously and independently as a block. Efficient sampling is especially important for training with the stochastic maximum likelihood algorithm.

20.4.1 Interesting Properties

Deep Boltzmann machines have many interesting properties.

DBMs were developed after DBNs. Compared to DBNs, the posterior distribution $P(\boldsymbol{h} \mid \boldsymbol{v})$ is simpler for DBMs. Somewhat counterintuitively, the simplicity of this posterior distribution allows richer approximations of the posterior. In the case of the DBN, we perform classification using a heuristically motivated approximate inference procedure, in which we guess that a reasonable value for the mean field expectation of the hidden units can be provided by an upward pass through the network in an MLP that uses sigmoid activation functions and the same weights as the original DBN. *Any* distribution $Q(\boldsymbol{h})$ can be used to obtain a variational lower bound on the log-likelihood. This heuristic procedure therefore enables us to obtain such a bound. Yet the bound is not explicitly optimized in any way, so it may be far from tight. In particular, the heuristic estimate of Q ignores interactions between hidden units within the same layer as well as the top-down feedback influence of hidden units in deeper layers on hidden units that are closer to the input. Because the heuristic MLP-based inference procedure in the DBN is not able to account for these interactions, the resulting Q is presumably far from optimal. In DBMs, all the hidden units within a layer are conditionally independent given the other layers. This lack of intralayer interaction makes it possible to use fixed-point equations to optimize the variational lower bound and find the true optimal mean field expectations (to within some numerical tolerance).

The use of proper mean field allows the approximate inference procedure for DBMs to capture the influence of top-down feedback interactions. This makes DBMs interesting from the point of view of neuroscience, because the human brain is known to use many top-down feedback connections. Because of this property, DBMs have been used as computational models of real neuroscientific phenomena (Series et al., 2010; Reichert et al., 2011).

One unfortunate property of DBMs is that sampling from them is relatively difficult. DBNs only need to use MCMC sampling in their top pair of layers. The other layers are used only at the end of the sampling process, in one efficient ancestral sampling pass. To generate a sample from a DBM, it is necessary to use MCMC across all layers, with every layer of the model participating in every Markov chain transition.

20.4.2 DBM Mean Field Inference

The conditional distribution over one DBM layer given the neighboring layers is factorial. In the example of the DBM with two hidden layers, these distributions are $P(\boldsymbol{v} \mid \boldsymbol{h}^{(1)})$, $P(\boldsymbol{h}^{(1)} \mid \boldsymbol{v}, \boldsymbol{h}^{(2)})$, and $P(\boldsymbol{h}^{(2)} \mid \boldsymbol{h}^{(1)})$. The distribution over *all* hidden layers generally does not factorize because of interactions between layers. In the example with two hidden layers, $P(\boldsymbol{h}^{(1)}, \boldsymbol{h}^{(2)} \mid \boldsymbol{v})$ does not factorize because of the interaction weights $\boldsymbol{W}^{(2)}$ between $\boldsymbol{h}^{(1)}$ and $\boldsymbol{h}^{(2)}$, which render these variables mutually dependent.

As was the case with the DBN, we are left to seek out methods to approximate the DBM posterior distribution. Unlike the DBN, however, the DBM posterior distribution over their hidden units—while complicated—is easy to approximate with a variational approximation (as discussed in section 19.4), specifically a mean field approximation. The mean field approximation is a simple form of variational inference, where we restrict the approximating distribution to fully factorial distributions. In the context of DBMs, the mean field equations capture the bidirectional interactions between layers. In this section we derive the iterative approximate inference procedure originally introduced in Salakhutdinov and Hinton (2009a).

In variational approximations to inference, we approach the task of approximating a particular target distribution—in our case, the posterior distribution over the hidden units given the visible units—by some reasonably simple family of distributions. In the case of the mean field approximation, the approximating family is the set of distributions where the hidden units are conditionally independent.

We now develop the mean field approach for the example with two hidden layers. Let $Q(\boldsymbol{h}^{(1)}, \boldsymbol{h}^{(2)} \mid \boldsymbol{v})$ be the approximation of $P(\boldsymbol{h}^{(1)}, \boldsymbol{h}^{(2)} \mid \boldsymbol{v})$. The mean field assumption implies that

$$Q(\boldsymbol{h}^{(1)}, \boldsymbol{h}^{(2)} \mid \boldsymbol{v}) = \prod_j Q(h_j^{(1)} \mid \boldsymbol{v}) \prod_k Q(h_k^{(2)} \mid \boldsymbol{v}). \qquad (20.29)$$

The mean field approximation attempts to find a member of this family of distributions that best fits the true posterior $P(\boldsymbol{h}^{(1)}, \boldsymbol{h}^{(2)} \mid \boldsymbol{v})$. Importantly, the inference process must be run again to find a different distribution Q every time we use a new value of $\boldsymbol{v}$.

One can conceive of many ways of measuring how well $Q(\boldsymbol{h} \mid \boldsymbol{v})$ fits $P(\boldsymbol{h} \mid \boldsymbol{v})$. The mean field approach is to minimize

$$\mathrm{KL}(Q\|P) = \sum_{\boldsymbol{h}} Q(\boldsymbol{h}^{(1)}, \boldsymbol{h}^{(2)} \mid \boldsymbol{v}) \log \left(\frac{Q(\boldsymbol{h}^{(1)}, \boldsymbol{h}^{(2)} \mid \boldsymbol{v})}{P(\boldsymbol{h}^{(1)}, \boldsymbol{h}^{(2)} \mid \boldsymbol{v})} \right). \qquad (20.30)$$

In general, we do not have to provide a parametric form of the approximating distribution beyond enforcing the independence assumptions. The variational approximation procedure is generally able to recover a functional form of the approximate distribution. However, in the case of a mean field assumption on binary hidden units (the case we are developing here) there is no loss of generality resulting from fixing a parametrization of the model in advance.

We parametrize Q as a product of Bernoulli distributions; that is, we associate the probability of each element of $\boldsymbol{h}^{(1)}$ with a parameter. Specifically, for each j, $\hat{h}_j^{(1)} = Q(h_j^{(1)} = 1 \mid \boldsymbol{v})$, where $\hat{h}_j^{(1)} \in [0, 1]$, and for each k, $\hat{h}_k^{(2)} = Q(h_k^{(2)} = 1 \mid \boldsymbol{v})$, where $\hat{h}_k^{(2)} \in [0, 1]$. Thus we have the following approximation to the posterior:

$$Q(\boldsymbol{h}^{(1)}, \boldsymbol{h}^{(2)} \mid \boldsymbol{v}) = \prod_j Q(h_j^{(1)} \mid \boldsymbol{v}) \prod_k Q(h_k^{(2)} \mid \boldsymbol{v}) \qquad (20.31)$$

$$= \prod_j (\hat{h}_j^{(1)})^{h_j^{(1)}} (1 - \hat{h}_j^{(1)})^{(1-h_j^{(1)})} \times \prod_k (\hat{h}_k^{(2)})^{h_k^{(2)}} (1 - \hat{h}_k^{(2)})^{(1-h_k^{(2)})}. \qquad (20.32)$$

Of course, for DBMs with more layers, the approximate posterior parametrization can be extended in the obvious way, exploiting the bipartite structure of the graph to update all the even layers simultaneously and then to update all the odd layers simultaneously, following the same schedule as Gibbs sampling.

Now that we have specified our family of approximating distributions Q, it remains to specify a procedure for choosing the member of this family that best fits P. The most straightforward way to do this is to use the mean field equations specified by equation 19.56. These equations were derived by solving for where the derivatives of the variational lower bound are zero. They describe in an abstract manner how to optimize the variational lower bound for any model, simply by taking expectations with respect to Q.

Applying these general equations, we obtain the update rules (again, ignoring bias terms):

$$\hat{h}_j^{(1)} = \sigma\left(\sum_i v_i W_{i,j}^{(1)} + \sum_{k'} W_{j,k'}^{(2)} \hat{h}_{k'}^{(2)}\right), \quad \forall j, \tag{20.33}$$

$$\hat{h}_k^{(2)} = \sigma\left(\sum_{j'} W_{j',k}^{(2)} \hat{h}_{j'}^{(1)}\right), \quad \forall k. \tag{20.34}$$

At a fixed point of this system of equations, we have a local maximum of the variational lower bound $\mathcal{L}(Q)$. Thus these fixed-point update equations define an iterative algorithm where we alternate updates of $\hat{h}_j^{(1)}$ (using equation 20.33) and updates of $\hat{h}_k^{(2)}$ (using equation 20.34). On small problems such as MNIST, as few as ten iterations can be sufficient to find an approximate positive phase gradient for learning, and fifty usually suffice to obtain a high-quality representation of a single specific example to be used for high-accuracy classification. Extending approximate variational inference to deeper DBMs is straightforward.

20.4.3 DBM Parameter Learning

Learning in the DBM must confront both the challenge of an intractable partition function, using the techniques from chapter 18, and the challenge of an intractable posterior distribution, using the techniques from chapter 19.

As described in section 20.4.2, variational inference allows the construction of a distribution $Q(\boldsymbol{h} \mid \boldsymbol{v})$ that approximates the intractable $P(\boldsymbol{h} \mid \boldsymbol{v})$. Learning then proceeds by maximizing $\mathcal{L}(\boldsymbol{v}, Q, \boldsymbol{\theta})$, the variational lower bound on the intractable log-likelihood, $\log P(\boldsymbol{v}; \boldsymbol{\theta})$.

For a deep Boltzmann machine with two hidden layers, $\mathcal{L}$ is given by

$$\mathcal{L}(Q, \boldsymbol{\theta}) = \sum_i \sum_{j'} v_i W_{i,j'}^{(1)} \hat{h}_{j'}^{(1)} + \sum_{j'} \sum_{k'} \hat{h}_{j'}^{(1)} W_{j',k'}^{(2)} \hat{h}_{k'}^{(2)} - \log Z(\boldsymbol{\theta}) + \mathcal{H}(Q). \quad (20.35)$$

This expression still contains the log partition function, $\log Z(\boldsymbol{\theta})$. Because a deep Boltzmann machine contains restricted Boltzmann machines as components, the hardness results for computing the partition function and sampling that apply to restricted Boltzmann machines also apply to deep Boltzmann machines. This means that evaluating the probability mass function of a Boltzmann machine requires approximate methods such as annealed importance sampling. Likewise, training the model requires approximations to the gradient of the log partition function. See chapter 18 for a general description of these methods. DBMs are typically trained using stochastic maximum likelihood. Many of the other techniques described in chapter 18 are not applicable. Techniques such as pseudolikelihood require the ability to evaluate the unnormalized probabilities, rather than merely obtain a variational lower bound on them. Contrastive divergence is slow for deep Boltzmann machines because they do not allow efficient sampling of the hidden units given the visible units—instead, contrastive divergence would require burning in a Markov chain every time a new negative phase sample is needed.

The nonvariational version of stochastic maximum likelihood algorithm is discussed in section 18.2. Variational stochastic maximum likelihood as applied to the DBM is given in algorithm 20.1. Recall that we describe a simplified variant of the DBM that lacks bias parameters; including them is trivial.

20.4.4 Layer-Wise Pretraining

Unfortunately, training a DBM using stochastic maximum likelihood (as described above) from a random initialization usually results in failure. In some cases, the model fails to learn to represent the distribution adequately. In other cases, the DBM may represent the distribution well, but with no higher likelihood than could be obtained with just an RBM. A DBM with very small weights in all but the first layer represents approximately the same distribution as an RBM.

Various techniques that permit joint training have been developed and are described in section 20.4.5. However, the original and most popular method for overcoming the joint training problem of DBMs is greedy layer-wise pretraining. In this method, each layer of the DBM is trained in isolation as an RBM. The first layer is trained to model the input data. Each subsequent RBM is trained to model samples from the previous RBM's posterior distribution. After all the

---

Algorithm 20.1 The variational stochastic maximum likelihood algorithm for training a DBM with two hidden layers

---

Set ϵ, the step size, to a small positive number

Set k, the number of Gibbs steps, high enough to allow a Markov chain of $p(\boldsymbol{v}, \boldsymbol{h}^{(1)}, \boldsymbol{h}^{(2)}; \boldsymbol{\theta} + \epsilon\Delta_{\boldsymbol{\theta}})$ to burn in, starting from samples from $p(\boldsymbol{v}, \boldsymbol{h}^{(1)}, \boldsymbol{h}^{(2)}; \boldsymbol{\theta})$.

Initialize three matrices, $\tilde{\boldsymbol{V}}$, $\tilde{\boldsymbol{H}}^{(1)}$, and $\tilde{\boldsymbol{H}}^{(2)}$ each with m rows set to random values (e.g., from Bernoulli distributions, possibly with marginals matched to the model's marginals).

while not converged (learning loop) **do**

    Sample a minibatch of m examples from the training data and arrange them as the rows of a design matrix $\boldsymbol{V}$.

    Initialize matrices $\hat{\boldsymbol{H}}^{(1)}$ and $\hat{\boldsymbol{H}}^{(2)}$, possibly to the model's marginals.

    while not converged (mean field inference loop) **do**

        $\hat{\boldsymbol{H}}^{(1)} \leftarrow \sigma\left(\boldsymbol{V}\boldsymbol{W}^{(1)} + \hat{\boldsymbol{H}}^{(2)}\boldsymbol{W}^{(2)\top}\right)$.

        $\hat{\boldsymbol{H}}^{(2)} \leftarrow \sigma\left(\hat{\boldsymbol{H}}^{(1)}\boldsymbol{W}^{(2)}\right)$.

    end while

    $\Delta_{\boldsymbol{W}^{(1)}} \leftarrow \frac{1}{m}\boldsymbol{V}^{\top}\hat{\boldsymbol{H}}^{(1)}$

    $\Delta_{\boldsymbol{W}^{(2)}} \leftarrow \frac{1}{m}\hat{\boldsymbol{H}}^{(1)\,\top}\hat{\boldsymbol{H}}^{(2)}$

    for $l = 1$ to k (Gibbs sampling) **do**

        Gibbs block 1:

        $\forall i, j, \tilde{V}_{i,j}$ sampled from $P(\tilde{V}_{i,j} = 1) = \sigma\left(\boldsymbol{W}^{(1)}_{j,:}\left(\tilde{\boldsymbol{H}}^{(1)}_{i,:}\right)^{\top}\right)$.

        $\forall i, j, \tilde{H}^{(2)}_{i,j}$ sampled from $P(\tilde{H}^{(2)}_{i,j} = 1) = \sigma\left(\tilde{\boldsymbol{H}}^{(1)}_{i,:}\boldsymbol{W}^{(2)}_{:,j}\right)$.

        Gibbs block 2:

        $\forall i, j, \tilde{H}^{(1)}_{i,j}$ sampled from $P(\tilde{H}^{(1)}_{i,j} = 1) = \sigma\left(\tilde{\boldsymbol{V}}_{i,:}\boldsymbol{W}^{(1)}_{:,j} + \tilde{\boldsymbol{H}}^{(2)}_{i,:}\boldsymbol{W}^{(2)\top}_{j,:}\right)$.

    end for

    $\Delta_{\boldsymbol{W}^{(1)}} \leftarrow \Delta_{\boldsymbol{W}^{(1)}} - \frac{1}{m}\boldsymbol{V}^{\top}\tilde{\boldsymbol{H}}^{(1)}$

    $\Delta_{\boldsymbol{W}^{(2)}} \leftarrow \Delta_{\boldsymbol{W}^{(2)}} - \frac{1}{m}\tilde{\boldsymbol{H}}^{(1)\top}\tilde{\boldsymbol{H}}^{(2)}$

    $\boldsymbol{W}^{(1)} \leftarrow \boldsymbol{W}^{(1)} + \epsilon\Delta_{\boldsymbol{W}^{(1)}}$ (this is a cartoon illustration, in practice use a more effective algorithm, such as momentum with a decaying learning rate)

    $\boldsymbol{W}^{(2)} \leftarrow \boldsymbol{W}^{(2)} + \epsilon\Delta_{\boldsymbol{W}^{(2)}}$

end while

RBMs have been trained in this way, they can be combined to form a DBM. The DBM may then be trained with PCD. Typically PCD training will make only a small change in the model's parameters and in its performance as measured by the log-likelihood it assigns to the data, or its ability to classify inputs. See figure 20.4 for an illustration of the training procedure.

This greedy layer-wise training procedure is not just coordinate ascent. It bears some passing resemblance to coordinate ascent because we optimize one subset of the parameters at each step. The two methods differ because the greedy layer-wise training procedure uses a different objective function at each step.

Greedy layer-wise pretraining of a DBM differs from greedy layer-wise pretraining of a DBN. The parameters of each individual RBM may be copied to the corresponding DBN directly. In the case of the DBM, the RBM parameters must be modified before inclusion in the DBM. A layer in the middle of the stack of RBMs is trained with only bottom-up input, but after the stack is combined to form the DBM, the layer will have both bottom-up and top-down input. To account for this effect, Salakhutdinov and Hinton (2009a) advocate dividing the weights of all but the top and bottom RBM in half before inserting them into the DBM. Additionally, the bottom RBM must be trained using two "copies" of each visible unit and the weights tied to be equal between the two copies. This means that the weights are effectively doubled during the upward pass. Similarly, the top RBM should be trained with two copies of the topmost layer.

Obtaining the state of the art results with the deep Boltzmann machine requires a modification of the standard SML algorithm, which is to use a small amount of mean field during the negative phase of the joint PCD training step (Salakhutdinov and Hinton, 2009a). Specifically, the expectation of the energy gradient should be computed with respect to the mean field distribution in which all the units are independent from each other. The parameters of this mean field distribution should be obtained by running the mean field fixed-point equations for just one step. See Goodfellow et al. (2013b) for a comparison of the performance of centered DBMs with and without the use of partial mean field in the negative phase.

20.4.5 Jointly Training Deep Boltzmann Machines

Classic DBMs require greedy unsupervised pretraining and, to perform classification well, require a separate MLP-based classifier on top of the hidden features they extract. This has some undesirable properties. It is hard to track performance during training because we cannot evaluate properties of the full DBM while training the first RBM. Thus, it is hard to tell how well our hyperparameters are working until quite late in the training process. Software implementations of DBMs need to have many different components for CD training of individual RBMs, PCD training of the full DBM, and training based on back-propagation through the MLP. Finally, the MLP on top of the Boltzmann machine loses many of the advantages of the Boltzmann machine probabilistic model, such as being able to perform inference when some input values are missing.

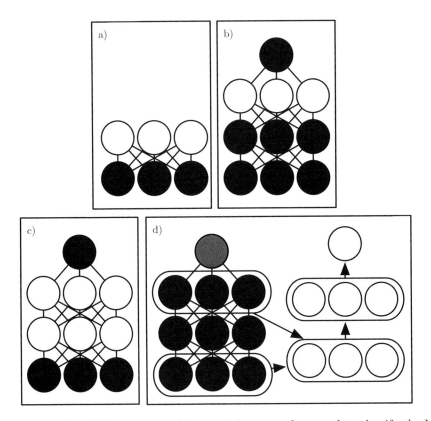

Figure 20.4: The deep Boltzmann machine training procedure used to classify the MNIST dataset (Salakhutdinov and Hinton, 2009a; Srivastava et al., 2014). *(a)*Train an RBM by using CD to approximately maximize $\log P(\boldsymbol{v})$. *(b)*Train a second RBM that models $\boldsymbol{h}^{(1)}$ and target class y by using CD-k to approximately maximize $\log P(\boldsymbol{h}^{(1)}, \mathrm{y})$, where $\boldsymbol{h}^{(1)}$ is drawn from the first RBM's posterior conditioned on the data. Increase k from 1 to 20 during learning. *(c)*Combine the two RBMs into a DBM. Train it to approximately maximize $\log P(\mathbf{v}, \mathrm{y})$ using stochastic maximum likelihood with $k = 5$. *(d)*Delete y from the model. Define a new set of features $\boldsymbol{h}^{(1)}$ and $\boldsymbol{h}^{(2)}$ that are obtained by running mean field inference in the model lacking y. Use these features as input to an MLP whose structure is the same as an additional pass of mean field, with an additional output layer for the estimate of y. Initialize the MLP's weights to be the same as the DBM's weights. Train the MLP to approximately maximize $\log P(\mathrm{y} \mid \mathbf{v})$ using stochastic gradient descent and dropout. Figure reprinted from Goodfellow et al. (2013b).

There are two main ways to resolve the joint training problem of the deep Boltzmann machine. The first is the **centered deep Boltzmann machine** (Montavon and Muller, 2012), which reparametrizes the model in order to make the Hessian of the cost function better conditioned at the beginning of the learning process. This yields a model that can be trained without a greedy layer-wise pretraining stage. The resulting model obtains excellent test set log-likelihood and produces high-quality samples. Unfortunately, it remains unable to compete with appropriately regularized MLPs as a classifier. The second way to jointly train a deep Boltzmann machine is to use a **multi-prediction deep Boltzmann machine** (Goodfellow et al., 2013b). This model uses an alternative training criterion that allows the use of the back-propagation algorithm to avoid the problems with MCMC estimates of the gradient. Unfortunately, the new criterion does not lead to good likelihood or samples, but, compared to the MCMC approach, it does lead to superior classification performance and ability to reason well about missing inputs.

The centering trick for the Boltzmann machine is easiest to describe if we return to the general view of a Boltzmann machine as consisting of a set of units $\boldsymbol{x}$ with a weight matrix $\boldsymbol{U}$ and biases $\boldsymbol{b}$. Recall from equation 20.2 that the energy function is given by

$$E(\boldsymbol{x}) = -\boldsymbol{x}^\top \boldsymbol{U} \boldsymbol{x} - \boldsymbol{b}^\top \boldsymbol{x}. \qquad (20.36)$$

Using different sparsity patterns in the weight matrix $\boldsymbol{U}$, we can implement structures of Boltzmann machines, such as RBMs or DBMs with different numbers of layers. This is accomplished by partitioning $\boldsymbol{x}$ into visible and hidden units and zeroing out elements of $\boldsymbol{U}$ for units that do not interact. The centered Boltzmann machine introduces a vector $\boldsymbol{\mu}$ that is subtracted from all the states:

$$E'(\boldsymbol{x}; \boldsymbol{U}, \boldsymbol{b}) = -(\boldsymbol{x} - \boldsymbol{\mu})^\top \boldsymbol{U} (\boldsymbol{x} - \boldsymbol{\mu}) - (\boldsymbol{x} - \boldsymbol{\mu})^\top \boldsymbol{b}. \qquad (20.37)$$

Typically $\boldsymbol{\mu}$ is a hyperparameter fixed at the beginning of training. It is usually chosen to make sure that $\boldsymbol{x} - \boldsymbol{\mu} \approx \boldsymbol{0}$ when the model is initialized. This reparametrization does not change the set of probability distributions that the model can represent, but it does change the dynamics of stochastic gradient descent applied to the likelihood. Specifically, in many cases, this reparametrization results in a Hessian matrix that is better conditioned. Melchior et al. (2013) experimentally confirmed that the conditioning of the Hessian matrix improves, and observed that the centering trick is equivalent to another Boltzmann machine learning technique, the **enhanced gradient** (Cho et al., 2011). The improved conditioning of the Hessian matrix enables learning to succeed, even in difficult cases like training a deep Boltzmann machine with multiple layers.

The other approach to jointly training deep Boltzmann machines is the multi-prediction deep Boltzmann machine (MP-DBM), which works by viewing the mean field equations as defining a family of recurrent networks for approximately solving every possible inference problem (Goodfellow et al., 2013b). Rather than training the model to maximize the likelihood, the model is trained to make each recurrent network obtain an accurate answer to the corresponding inference problem. The training process is illustrated in figure 20.5. It consists of randomly sampling a training example, randomly sampling a subset of inputs to the inference network, and then training the inference network to predict the values of the remaining units.

This general principle of back-propagating through the computational graph for approximate inference has been applied to other models (Stoyanov et al., 2011; Brakel et al., 2013). In these models and in the MP-DBM, the final loss is not the lower bound on the likelihood. Instead, the final loss is typically based on the approximate conditional distribution that the approximate inference network imposes over the missing values. This means that the training of these models is somewhat heuristically motivated. If we inspect the $p(\boldsymbol{v})$ represented by the Boltzmann machine learned by the MP-DBM, it tends to be somewhat defective, in the sense that Gibbs sampling yields poor samples.

Back-propagation through the inference graph has two main advantages. First, it trains the model as it is really used—with approximate inference. This means that approximate inference, for example, to fill in missing inputs or to perform classification despite the presence of missing inputs, is more accurate in the MP-DBM than in the original DBM. The original DBM does not make an accurate classifier on its own; the best classification results with the original DBM were based on training a separate classifier to use features extracted by the DBM, rather than by using inference in the DBM to compute the distribution over the class labels. Mean field inference in the MP-DBM performs well as a classifier without special modifications. The other advantage of back-propagating through approximate inference is that back-propagation computes the exact gradient of the loss. This is better for optimization than the approximate gradients of SML training, which suffer from both bias and variance. This probably explains why MP-DBMs may be trained jointly while DBMs require a greedy layer-wise pretraining. The disadvantage of back-propagating through the approximate inference graph is that it does not provide a way to optimize the log-likelihood, but rather gives a heuristic approximation of the generalized pseudolikelihood.

The MP-DBM inspired the NADE-k (Raiko et al., 2014) extension to the NADE framework, which is described in section 20.10.10.

The MP-DBM has some connections to dropout. Dropout shares the same parameters among many different computational graphs, with the difference between

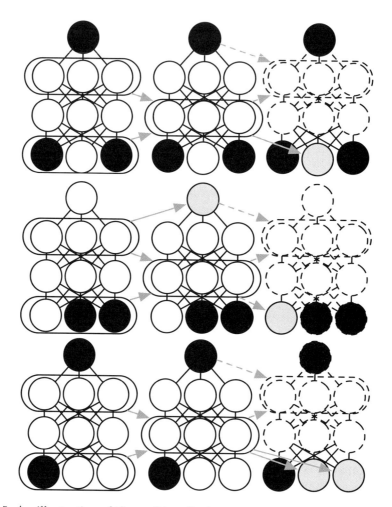

Figure 20.5: An illustration of the multiprediction training process for a deep Boltzmann machine. Each row indicates a different example within a minibatch for the same training step. Each column represents a time step within the mean field inference process. For each example, we sample a subset of the data variables to serve as inputs to the inference process. These variables are shaded black to indicate conditioning. We then run the mean field inference process, with arrows indicating which variables influence which other variables in the process. In practical applications, we unroll mean field for several steps. In this illustration, we unroll for only two steps. Dashed arrows indicate how the process could be unrolled for more steps. The data variables that were not used as inputs to the inference process become targets, shaded in gray. We can view the inference process for each example as a recurrent network. We use gradient descent and back-propagation to train these recurrent networks to produce the correct targets given their inputs. This trains the mean field process for the MP-DBM to produce accurate estimates. Figure adapted from Goodfellow et al. (2013b).

each graph being whether it includes or excludes each unit. The MP-DBM also shares parameters across many computational graphs. In the case of the MP-DBM, the difference between the graphs is whether each input unit is observed or not. When a unit is not observed, the MP-DBM does not delete it entirely as dropout does. Instead, the MP-DBM treats it as a latent variable to be inferred. One could imagine applying dropout to the MP-DBM by additionally removing some units rather than making them latent.

20.5 Boltzmann Machines for Real-Valued Data

While Boltzmann machines were originally developed for use with binary data, many applications such as image and audio modeling seem to require the ability to represent probability distributions over real values. In some cases, it is possible to treat real-valued data in the interval [0, 1] as representing the expectation of a binary variable. For example, Hinton (2000) treats grayscale images in the training set as defining [0,1] probability values. Each pixel defines the probability of a binary value being 1, and the binary pixels are all sampled independently from each other. This is a common procedure for evaluating binary models on grayscale image datasets. Nonetheless, it is not a particularly theoretically satisfying approach, and binary images sampled independently in this way have a noisy appearance. In this section, we present Boltzmann machines that define a probability density over real-valued data.

20.5.1 Gaussian-Bernoulli RBMs

Restricted Boltzmann machines may be developed for many exponential family conditional distributions (Welling et al., 2005). Of these, the most common is the RBM with binary hidden units and real-valued visible units, with the conditional distribution over the visible units being a Gaussian distribution whose mean is a function of the hidden units.

There are many ways of parametrizing Gaussian-Bernoulli RBMs. One choice is whether to use a covariance matrix or a precision matrix for the Gaussian distribution. Here we present the precision formulation. The modification to obtain the covariance formulation is straightforward. We wish to have the conditional distribution

$$p(\boldsymbol{v} \mid \boldsymbol{h}) = \mathcal{N}(\boldsymbol{v}; \boldsymbol{W}\boldsymbol{h}, \boldsymbol{\beta}^{-1}). \tag{20.38}$$

We can find the terms we need to add to the energy function by expanding the unnormalized log conditional distribution:

$$\log \mathcal{N}(\boldsymbol{v}; \boldsymbol{W}\boldsymbol{h}, \boldsymbol{\beta}^{-1}) = -\frac{1}{2}(\boldsymbol{v} - \boldsymbol{W}\boldsymbol{h})^\top \boldsymbol{\beta}(\boldsymbol{v} - \boldsymbol{W}\boldsymbol{h}) + f(\boldsymbol{\beta}). \quad (20.39)$$

Here f encapsulates all the terms that are a function only of the parameters and not the random variables in the model. We can discard f because its only role is to normalize the distribution, and the partition function of whatever energy function we choose will carry out that role.

If we include all the terms (with their sign flipped) involving $\boldsymbol{v}$ from equation 20.39 in our energy function and do not add any other terms involving $\boldsymbol{v}$, then our energy function will represent the desired conditional $p(\boldsymbol{v} \mid \boldsymbol{h})$.

We have some freedom regarding the other conditional distribution, $p(\boldsymbol{h} \mid \boldsymbol{v})$. Note that equation 20.39 contains a term

$$\frac{1}{2}\boldsymbol{h}^\top \boldsymbol{W}^\top \boldsymbol{\beta}\boldsymbol{W}\boldsymbol{h}. \quad (20.40)$$

This term cannot be included in its entirety because it includes $h_i h_j$ terms. These correspond to edges between the hidden units. If we included these terms, we would have a linear factor model instead of a restricted Boltzmann machine. When designing our Boltzmann machine, we simply omit these $h_i h_j$ cross terms. Omitting them does not change the conditional $p(\boldsymbol{v} \mid \boldsymbol{h})$, so equation 20.39 is still respected. We still have a choice, however, about whether to include the terms involving only a single h_i. If we assume a diagonal precision matrix, we find that for each hidden unit h_i, we have a term

$$\frac{1}{2}h_i \sum_j \beta_j W_{j,i}^2. \quad (20.41)$$

In the above, we used the fact that $h_i^2 = h_i$ because $h_i \in \{0, 1\}$. If we include this term (with its sign flipped) in the energy function, then it will naturally bias h_i to be turned off when the weights for that unit are large and connected to visible units with high precision. The choice of whether to include this bias term does not affect the family of distributions that the model can represent (assuming that we include bias parameters for the hidden units), but it does affect the learning dynamics of the model. Including the term may help the hidden unit activations remain reasonable even when the weights rapidly increase in magnitude.

One way to define the energy function on a Gaussian-Bernoulli RBM is thus:

$$E(\boldsymbol{v}, \boldsymbol{h}) = \frac{1}{2}\boldsymbol{v}^\top(\boldsymbol{\beta} \odot \boldsymbol{v}) - (\boldsymbol{v} \odot \boldsymbol{\beta})^\top \boldsymbol{W}\boldsymbol{h} - \boldsymbol{b}^\top \boldsymbol{h}, \quad (20.42)$$

but we may also add extra terms or parametrize the energy in terms of the variance rather than precision if we choose.

In this derivation, we have not included a bias term on the visible units, but one could easily be added. One final source of variability in the parametrization of a Gaussian-Bernoulli RBM is the choice of how to treat the precision matrix. It may be either fixed to a constant (perhaps estimated based on the marginal precision of the data) or learned. It may also be a scalar times the identity matrix, or it may be a diagonal matrix. Typically we do not allow the precision matrix to be nondiagonal in this context, because some operations on the Gaussian distribution require inverting the matrix, and a diagonal matrix can be inverted trivially. In the sections ahead, we will see that other forms of Boltzmann machines permit modeling the covariance structure, using various techniques to avoid inverting the precision matrix.

20.5.2 Undirected Models of Conditional Covariance

While the Gaussian RBM has been the canonical energy model for real-valued data, Ranzato et al. (2010a) argue that the Gaussian RBM inductive bias is not well suited to the statistical variations present in some types of real-valued data, especially natural images. The problem is that much of the information content present in natural images is embedded in the covariance between pixels rather than in the raw pixel values. In other words, it is the relationships between pixels and not their absolute values where most of the useful information in images resides. Since the Gaussian RBM only models the conditional mean of the input given the hidden units, it cannot capture conditional covariance information. In response to these criticisms, alternative models have been proposed that attempt to better account for the covariance of real-valued data. These models include the mean and covariance RBM (mcRBM[1]), the mean product of Student t-distribution (mPoT) model, and the spike and slab RBM (ssRBM).

Mean and Covariance RBM   The mcRBM uses its hidden units to independently encode the conditional mean and covariance of all observed units. The mcRBM hidden layer is divided into two groups of units: mean units and covariance units. The group that models the conditional mean is simply a Gaussian RBM. The other half is a covariance RBM (Ranzato et al., 2010a), also called a cRBM, whose components model the conditional covariance structure, as described below.

---

[1]The term "mcRBM" is pronounced by saying the name of the letters M-C-R-B-M; the "mc" is not pronounced like the "Mc" in "McDonald's."

Specifically, with binary mean units $\boldsymbol{h}^{(m)}$ and binary covariance units $\boldsymbol{h}^{(c)}$, the mcRBM model is defined as the combination of two energy functions:

$$E_{\mathrm{mc}}(\boldsymbol{x}, \boldsymbol{h}^{(m)}, \boldsymbol{h}^{(c)}) = E_{\mathrm{m}}(\boldsymbol{x}, \boldsymbol{h}^{(m)}) + E_{\mathrm{c}}(\boldsymbol{x}, \boldsymbol{h}^{(c)}), \tag{20.43}$$

where E_{m} is the standard Gaussian-Bernoulli RBM energy function,[2]

$$E_{\mathrm{m}}(\boldsymbol{x}, \boldsymbol{h}^{(m)}) = \frac{1}{2}\boldsymbol{x}^\top \boldsymbol{x} - \sum_j \boldsymbol{x}^\top \boldsymbol{W}_{:,j} h_j^{(m)} - \sum_j b_j^{(m)} h_j^{(m)}, \tag{20.44}$$

and E_{c} is the cRBM energy function that models the conditional covariance information:

$$E_{\mathrm{c}}(\boldsymbol{x}, \boldsymbol{h}^{(c)}) = \frac{1}{2}\sum_j h_j^{(c)} \left(\boldsymbol{x}^\top \boldsymbol{r}^{(j)}\right)^2 - \sum_j b_j^{(c)} h_j^{(c)}. \tag{20.45}$$

The parameter $\boldsymbol{r}^{(j)}$ corresponds to the covariance weight vector associated with $h_j^{(c)}$, and $\boldsymbol{b}^{(c)}$ is a vector of covariance offsets. The combined energy function defines a joint distribution,

$$p_{\mathrm{mc}}(\boldsymbol{x}, \boldsymbol{h}^{(m)}, \boldsymbol{h}^{(c)}) = \frac{1}{Z} \exp\left\{-E_{\mathrm{mc}}(\boldsymbol{x}, \boldsymbol{h}^{(m)}, \boldsymbol{h}^{(c)})\right\}, \tag{20.46}$$

and a corresponding conditional distribution over the observations given $\boldsymbol{h}^{(m)}$ and $\boldsymbol{h}^{(c)}$ as a multivariate Gaussian distribution:

$$p_{\mathrm{mc}}(\boldsymbol{x} \mid \boldsymbol{h}^{(m)}, \boldsymbol{h}^{(c)}) = \mathcal{N}\left(\boldsymbol{x}; \boldsymbol{C}_{\boldsymbol{x}\mid\boldsymbol{h}}^{\mathrm{mc}}\left(\sum_j \boldsymbol{W}_{:,j} h_j^{(m)}\right), \boldsymbol{C}_{\boldsymbol{x}\mid\boldsymbol{h}}^{\mathrm{mc}}\right). \tag{20.47}$$

Note that the covariance matrix $\boldsymbol{C}_{\boldsymbol{x}\mid\boldsymbol{h}}^{\mathrm{mc}} = \left(\sum_j h_j^{(c)} \boldsymbol{r}^{(j)} \boldsymbol{r}^{(j)\top} + \boldsymbol{I}\right)^{-1}$ is nondiagonal and that $\boldsymbol{W}$ is the weight matrix associated with the Gaussian RBM modeling the conditional means. It is difficult to train the mcRBM via contrastive divergence or persistent contrastive divergence because of its nondiagonal conditional covariance structure. CD and PCD require sampling from the joint distribution of $\boldsymbol{x}, \boldsymbol{h}^{(m)}, \boldsymbol{h}^{(c)}$, which, in a standard RBM, is accomplished by Gibbs sampling over the conditionals. However, in the mcRBM, sampling from $p_{\mathrm{mc}}(\boldsymbol{x} \mid \boldsymbol{h}^{(m)}, \boldsymbol{h}^{(c)})$ requires computing $(\boldsymbol{C}^{\mathrm{mc}})^{-1}$ at every iteration of learning. This can be an impractical computational burden for larger observations. Ranzato and Hinton (2010) avoid direct sampling from the conditional $p_{\mathrm{mc}}(\boldsymbol{x} \mid \boldsymbol{h}^{(m)}, \boldsymbol{h}^{(c)})$ by sampling directly from the marginal $p(\boldsymbol{x})$ using Hamiltonian (hybrid) Monte Carlo (Neal, 1993) on the mcRBM free energy.

---

[2]This version of the Gaussian-Bernoulli RBM energy function assumes the image data have zero mean per pixel. Pixel offsets can easily be added to the model to account for nonzero pixel means.

Mean Product of Student t-distributions The mean product of Student t-distribution (mPoT) model (Ranzato et al., 2010b) extends the PoT model (Welling et al., 2003a) in a manner similar to how the mcRBM extends the cRBM. This is achieved by including nonzero Gaussian means by the addition of Gaussian RBM-like hidden units. Like the mcRBM, the PoT conditional distribution over the observation is a multivariate Gaussian (with nondiagonal covariance) distribution; however, unlike the mcRBM, the complementary conditional distribution over the hidden variables is given by conditionally independent Gamma distributions. The Gamma distribution $\mathcal{G}(k, \theta)$ is a probability distribution over positive real numbers, with mean $k\theta$. It is not necessary to have a more detailed understanding of the Gamma distribution to understand the basic ideas underlying the mPoT model.

The mPoT energy function is

$$E_{\mathrm{mPoT}}(\boldsymbol{x}, \boldsymbol{h}^{(m)}, \boldsymbol{h}^{(c)}) \tag{20.48}$$

$$= E_m(\boldsymbol{x}, \boldsymbol{h}^{(m)}) + \sum_j \left(h_j^{(c)} \left(1 + \frac{1}{2} \left(\boldsymbol{r}^{(j)\top} \boldsymbol{x} \right)^2 \right) + (1 - \gamma_j) \log h_j^{(c)} \right), \tag{20.49}$$

where $\boldsymbol{r}^{(j)}$ is the covariance weight vector associated with unit $h_j^{(c)}$, and $E_m(\boldsymbol{x}, \boldsymbol{h}^{(m)})$ is as defined in equation 20.44.

Just as with the mcRBM, the mPoT model energy function specifies a multivariate Gaussian, with a conditional distribution over $\boldsymbol{x}$ that has nondiagonal covariance. Learning in the mPoT model—again, like the mcRBM—is complicated by the inability to sample from the nondiagonal Gaussian conditional $p_{\mathrm{mPoT}}(\boldsymbol{x} \mid \boldsymbol{h}^{(m)}, \boldsymbol{h}^{(c)})$, so Ranzato et al. (2010b) also advocate direct sampling of $p(\boldsymbol{x})$ via Hamiltonian (hybrid) Monte Carlo.

Spike and Slab Restricted Boltzmann Machines Spike and slab restricted Boltzmann machines (Courville et al., 2011) or ssRBMs provide another means of modeling the covariance structure of real-valued data. Compared to mcRBMs, ssRBMs have the advantage of requiring neither matrix inversion nor Hamiltonian Monte Carlo methods. Like the mcRBM and the mPoT model, the ssRBM's binary hidden units encode the conditional covariance across pixels through the use of auxiliary real-valued variables.

The spike and slab RBM has two sets of hidden units: binary **spike** units **h** and real-valued **slab** units **s**. The mean of the visible units conditioned on the hidden units is given by $(\boldsymbol{h} \odot \boldsymbol{s})\boldsymbol{W}^{\top}$. In other words, each column $\boldsymbol{W}_{:,i}$ defines a component that can appear in the input when $h_i = 1$. The corresponding spike variable h_i determines whether that component is present at all. The corresponding slab variable s_i determines the intensity of that component, if it is present. When a spike variable is active, the corresponding slab variable adds variance to the input along the axis defined by $\boldsymbol{W}_{:,i}$. This allows us to model the covariance of the inputs. Fortunately, contrastive divergence and persistent contrastive divergence with Gibbs sampling are still applicable. There is no need to invert any matrix.

Formally, the ssRBM model is defined via its energy function:

$$E_{\mathrm{ss}}(\boldsymbol{x}, \boldsymbol{s}, \boldsymbol{h}) = -\sum_i \boldsymbol{x}^\top \boldsymbol{W}_{:,i} s_i h_i + \frac{1}{2}\boldsymbol{x}^\top \left(\boldsymbol{\Lambda} + \sum_i \boldsymbol{\Phi}_i h_i\right)\boldsymbol{x} \tag{20.50}$$

$$+ \frac{1}{2}\sum_i \alpha_i s_i^2 - \sum_i \alpha_i \mu_i s_i h_i - \sum_i b_i h_i + \sum_i \alpha_i \mu_i^2 h_i, \tag{20.51}$$

where b_i is the offset of the spike h_i, and $\boldsymbol{\Lambda}$ is a diagonal precision matrix on the observations $\boldsymbol{x}$. The parameter $\alpha_i > 0$ is a scalar precision parameter for the real-valued slab variable $\boldsymbol{s}_i$. The parameter $\boldsymbol{\Phi}_i$ is a nonnegative diagonal matrix that defines an $\boldsymbol{h}$-modulated quadratic penalty on $\boldsymbol{x}$. Each μ_i is a mean parameter for the slab variable $\boldsymbol{s}_i$.

With the joint distribution defined via the energy function, deriving the ssRBM conditional distributions is relatively straightforward. For example, by marginalizing out the slab variables $\boldsymbol{s}$, the conditional distribution over the observations given the binary spike variables $\boldsymbol{h}$ is given by

$$p_{\mathrm{ss}}(\boldsymbol{x} \mid \boldsymbol{h}) = \frac{1}{P(\boldsymbol{h})}\frac{1}{Z}\int \exp\{-E(\boldsymbol{x}, \boldsymbol{s}, \boldsymbol{h})\} \; d\boldsymbol{s} \tag{20.52}$$

$$= \mathcal{N}\left(\boldsymbol{x}; \boldsymbol{C}_{\boldsymbol{x}|\boldsymbol{h}}^{\mathrm{ss}}\sum_i \boldsymbol{W}_{:,i}\mu_i h_i \, , \, \boldsymbol{C}_{\boldsymbol{x}|\boldsymbol{h}}^{\mathrm{ss}}\right) \tag{20.53}$$

where $\boldsymbol{C}_{\boldsymbol{x}|\boldsymbol{h}}^{\mathrm{ss}} = \left(\boldsymbol{\Lambda} + \sum_i \boldsymbol{\Phi}_i h_i - \sum_i \alpha_i^{-1} h_i \boldsymbol{W}_{:,i} \boldsymbol{W}_{:,i}^\top\right)^{-1}$. The last equality holds only if the covariance matrix $\boldsymbol{C}_{\boldsymbol{x}|\boldsymbol{h}}^{\mathrm{ss}}$ is positive definite.

Gating by the spike variables means that the true marginal distribution over $\mathbf{h} \odot \mathbf{s}$ is sparse. This is different from sparse coding, where samples from the model "almost never" (in the measure theoretic sense) contain zeros in the code, and MAP inference is required to impose sparsity.

Comparing the ssRBM to the mcRBM and the mPoT models, the ssRBM parametrizes the conditional covariance of the observation in a significantly different way. The mcRBM and mPoT both model the covariance structure of the observation as $\left(\sum_j h_j^{(c)} r^{(j)} r^{(j)\top} + I\right)^{-1}$, using the activation of the hidden units $h_j > 0$ to enforce constraints on the conditional covariance in the direction $r^{(j)}$. In contrast, the ssRBM specifies the conditional covariance of the observations using the hidden spike activations $h_i = 1$ to pinch the precision matrix along the direction specified by the corresponding weight vector. The ssRBM conditional covariance is similar to that given by a different model: the product of probabilistic principal components analysis (PoPPCA) (Williams and Agakov, 2002). In the overcomplete setting, sparse activations with the ssRBM parametrization permit significant variance (above the nominal variance given by Λ^{-1}) only in the selected directions of the sparsely activated h_i. In the mcRBM or mPoT models, an overcomplete representation would mean that to capture variation in a particular direction in the observation space would require removing potentially all constraints with positive projection in that direction. This would suggest that these models are less well suited to the overcomplete setting.

The primary disadvantage of the spike and slab restricted Boltzmann machine is that some settings of the parameters can correspond to a covariance matrix that is not positive definite. Such a covariance matrix places more unnormalized probability on values that are farther from the mean, causing the integral over all possible outcomes to diverge. Generally this issue can be avoided with simple heuristic tricks. There is not yet any theoretically satisfying solution. Using constrained optimization to explicitly avoid the regions where the probability is undefined is difficult to do without being overly conservative and also preventing the model from accessing high-performing regions of parameter space.

Qualitatively, convolutional variants of the ssRBM produce excellent samples of natural images. Some examples are shown in figure 16.1.

The ssRBM allows for several extensions. Including higher-order interactions and average-pooling of the slab variables (Courville et al., 2014) enables the model to learn excellent features for a classifier when labeled data is scarce. Adding a term to the energy function that prevents the partition function from becoming undefined results in a sparse coding model, spike and slab sparse coding (Goodfellow et al., 2013d), also known as S3C.

20.6 Convolutional Boltzmann Machines

As we discuss in chapter 9, extremely high-dimensional inputs such as images place great strain on the computation, memory and statistical requirements of machine learning models. Replacing matrix multiplication by discrete convolution with a small kernel is the standard way of solving these problems for inputs that have translation invariant spatial or temporal structure. Desjardins and Bengio (2008) showed that this approach works well when applied to RBMs.

Deep convolutional networks usually require a pooling operation so that the spatial size of each successive layer decreases. Feedforward convolutional networks often use a pooling function such as the maximum of the elements to be pooled. It is unclear how to generalize this to the setting of energy-based models. We could introduce a binary pooling unit p over n binary detector units $\mathbf{d}$ and enforce $p = \max_i d_i$ by setting the energy function to be ∞ whenever that constraint is violated. This does not scale well though, as it requires evaluating 2^n different energy configurations to compute the normalization constant. For a small 3×3 pooling region this requires $2^9 = 512$ energy function evaluations per pooling unit!

Lee et al. (2009) developed a solution to this problem called **probabilistic max pooling** (not to be confused with "stochastic pooling," which is a technique for implicitly constructing ensembles of convolutional feedforward networks). The strategy behind probabilistic max pooling is to constrain the detector units so at most one may be active at a time. This means there are only $n + 1$ total states (one state for each of the n detector units being on, and an additional state corresponding to all the detector units being off). The pooling unit is on if and only if one of the detector units is on. The state with all units off is assigned energy zero. We can think of this as describing a model with a single variable that has $n+1$ states, or equivalently as a model that has $n+1$ variables that assigns energy ∞ to all but $n+1$ joint assignments of variables.

While efficient, probabilistic max pooling does force the detector units to be mutually exclusive, which may be a useful regularizing constraint in some contexts or a harmful limit on model capacity in other contexts. It also does not support overlapping pooling regions. Overlapping pooling regions are usually required to obtain the best performance from feedforward convolutional networks, so this constraint probably greatly reduces the performance of convolutional Boltzmann machines.

Lee et al. (2009) demonstrated that probabilistic max pooling could be used to build convolutional deep Boltzmann machines.[3] This model is able to perform operations such as filling in missing portions of its input. While intellectually appealing, this model is challenging to make work in practice, and usually does not perform as well as a classifier as traditional convolutional networks trained with supervised learning.

---

[3]The publication describes the model as a "deep belief network," but because it can be described as a purely undirected model with tractable layer-wise mean field fixed-point updates, it best fits the definition of a deep Boltzmann machine.

Many convolutional models work equally well with inputs of many different spatial sizes. For Boltzmann machines, it is difficult to change the input size for various reasons. The partition function changes as the size of the input changes. Moreover, many convolutional networks achieve size invariance by scaling up the size of their pooling regions proportional to the size of the input, but scaling Boltzmann machine pooling regions is awkward. Traditional convolutional neural networks can use a fixed number of pooling units and dynamically increase the size of their pooling regions to obtain a fixed-size representation of a variably sized input. For Boltzmann machines, large pooling regions become too expensive for the naive approach. The approach of Lee et al. (2009) of making each of the detector units in the same pooling region mutually exclusive solves the computational problems but still does not allow variably size pooling regions. For example, suppose we learn a model with 2×2 probabilistic max pooling over detector units that learn edge detectors. This enforces the constraint that only one of these edges may appear in each 2×2 region. If we then increase the size of the input image by 50 percent in each direction, we would expect the number of edges to increase correspondingly. Instead, if we increase the size of the pooling regions by 50 percent in each direction to 3×3, then the mutual exclusivity constraint now specifies that each of these edges may appear only once in a 3×3 region. As we grow a model's input image in this way, the model generates edges with less density. Of course, these issues only arise when the model must use variable amounts of pooling in order to emit a fixed-size output vector. Models that use probabilistic max pooling may still accept variably sized input images as long as the output of the model is a feature map that can scale in size proportional to the input image.

Pixels at the boundary of the image also pose some difficulty, which is exacerbated by the fact that connections in a Boltzmann machine are symmetric. If we do not implicitly zero pad the input, there will be fewer hidden units than visible units, and the visible units at the boundary of the image will not be modeled well because they lie in the receptive field of fewer hidden units. However, if we do implicitly zero pad the input, then the hidden units at the boundary will be driven by fewer input pixels and may fail to activate when needed.

20.7 Boltzmann Machines for Structured or Sequential Outputs

In the structured output scenario, we wish to train a model that can map from some input x to some output y, and the different entries of y are related to each other and must obey some constraints. For example, in the speech synthesis task, $\boldsymbol{y}$ is a waveform, and the entire waveform must sound like a coherent utterance.

A natural way to represent the relationships between the entries in $\boldsymbol{y}$ is to use a probability distribution $p(\mathbf{y} \mid \boldsymbol{x})$. Boltzmann machines, extended to model conditional distributions, can supply this probabilistic model.

The same tool of conditional modeling with a Boltzmann machine can be used not just for structured output tasks, but also for sequence modeling. In the latter case, rather than mapping an input $\boldsymbol{x}$ to an output $\boldsymbol{y}$, the model must estimate a probability distribution over a sequence of variables, $p(\mathbf{x}^{(1)}, \dots, \mathbf{x}^{(\tau)})$. Conditional Boltzmann machines can represent factors of the form $p(\mathbf{x}^{(t)} \mid \mathbf{x}^{(1)}, \dots, \mathbf{x}^{(t-1)})$ in order to accomplish this task.

An important sequence modeling task for the video game and film industry is modeling sequences of joint angles of skeletons used to render 3-D characters. These sequences are often collected using motion capture systems to record the movements of actors. A probabilistic model of a character's movement allows the generation of new, previously unseen, but realistic animations. To solve this sequence modeling task, Taylor et al. (2007) introduced a conditional RBM modeling $p(\boldsymbol{x}^{(t)} \mid \boldsymbol{x}^{(t-1)}, \dots, \boldsymbol{x}^{(t-m)})$ for small m. The model is an RBM over $p(\boldsymbol{x}^{(t)})$ whose bias parameters are a linear function of the preceding m values of $\boldsymbol{x}$. When we condition on different values of $\boldsymbol{x}^{(t-1)}$ and earlier variables, we get a new RBM over $\mathbf{x}$. The weights in the RBM over $\mathbf{x}$ never change, but by conditioning on different past values, we can change the probability of different hidden units in the RBM being active. By activating and deactivating different subsets of hidden units, we can make large changes to the probability distribution induced on $\mathbf{x}$. Other variants of conditional RBM (Mnih et al., 2011) and other variants of sequence modeling using conditional RBMs are possible (Taylor and Hinton, 2009; Sutskever et al., 2009; Boulanger-Lewandowski et al., 2012).

Another sequence modeling task is to model the distribution over sequences of musical notes used to compose songs. Boulanger-Lewandowski et al. (2012) introduced the **RNN-RBM** sequence model and applied it to this task. The RNN-RBM is a generative model of a sequence of frames $\boldsymbol{x}^{(t)}$ consisting of an RNN that emits the RBM parameters for each time step. Unlike previous approaches in which only the bias parameters of the RBM varied from one time step to the next, the RNN-RBM uses the RNN to emit all the parameters of the RBM, including the weights. To train the model, we need to be able to back-propagate the gradient of the loss function through the RNN. The loss function is not applied directly to the RNN outputs. Instead, it is applied to the RBM. This means that we must approximately differentiate the loss with respect to the RBM parameters using contrastive divergence or a related algorithm. This approximate gradient may then be back-propagated through the RNN using the usual back-propagation through time algorithm.

20.8   Other Boltzmann Machines

Many other variants of Boltzmann machines are possible.

Boltzmann machines may be extended with different training criteria. We have focused on Boltzmann machines trained to approximately maximize the generative criterion $\log p(\boldsymbol{v})$. It is also possible to train discriminative RBMs that aim to maximize $\log p(y \mid \boldsymbol{v})$ instead (Larochelle and Bengio, 2008). This approach often performs the best when using a linear combination of both the generative and the discriminative criteria. Unfortunately, RBMs do not seem to be as powerful supervised learners as MLPs, at least using existing methodology.

Most Boltzmann machines used in practice have only second-order interactions in their energy functions, meaning that their energy functions are the sum of many terms, and each individual term includes only the product between two random variables. An example of such a term is $v_i W_{i,j} h_j$. It is also possible to train higher-order Boltzmann machines (Sejnowski, 1987) whose energy function terms involve the products between many variables. Three-way interactions between a hidden unit and two different images can model spatial transformations from one frame of video to the next (Memisevic and Hinton, 2007, 2010). Multiplication by a one-hot class variable can change the relationship between visible and hidden units depending on which class is present (Nair and Hinton, 2009). One recent example of the use of higher-order interactions is a Boltzmann machine with two groups of hidden units, one group that interacts with both the visible units $\boldsymbol{v}$ and the class label y, and another group that interacts only with the $\boldsymbol{v}$ input values (Luo et al., 2011). This can be interpreted as encouraging some hidden units to learn to model the input using features that are relevant to the class, but also to learn extra hidden units that explain nuisance details necessary for the samples of $\boldsymbol{v}$ to be realistic without determining the class of the example. Another use of higher-order interactions is to gate some features. Sohn et al. (2013) introduced a Boltzmann machine with third-order interactions and binary mask variables associated with each visible unit. When these masking variables are set to zero, they remove the influence of a visible unit on the hidden units. This allows visible units that are not relevant to the classification problem to be removed from the inference pathway that estimates the class.

More generally, the Boltzmann machine framework is a rich space of models permitting many more model structures than have been explored so far. Developing a new form of Boltzmann machine requires some more care and creativity than developing a new neural network layer, because it is often difficult to find an energy function that maintains tractability of all the different conditional distributions needed to use the Boltzmann machine. Despite this required effort, the field remains open to innovation.

20.9 Back-Propagation through Random Operations

Traditional neural networks implement a deterministic transformation of some input variables $\boldsymbol{x}$. When developing generative models, we often wish to extend neural networks to implement stochastic transformations of $\boldsymbol{x}$. One straightforward way to do this is to augment the neural network with extra inputs $\boldsymbol{z}$ that are sampled from some simple probability distribution, such as a uniform or Gaussian distribution. The neural network can then continue to perform deterministic computation internally, but the function $f(\boldsymbol{x}, \boldsymbol{z})$ will appear stochastic to an observer who does not have access to $\boldsymbol{z}$. Provided that f is continuous and differentiable, we can then compute the gradients necessary for training using back-propagation as usual.

As an example, let us consider the operation consisting of drawing samples y from a Gaussian distribution with mean μ and variance σ^2:

$$y \sim \mathcal{N}(\mu, \sigma^2). \tag{20.54}$$

Because an individual sample of y is produced not by a function, but rather by a sampling process whose output changes every time we query it, it may seem counterintuitive to take the derivatives of y with respect to the parameters of its distribution, μ and σ^2. However, we can rewrite the sampling process as transforming an underlying random value z $\sim \mathcal{N}(z; 0, 1)$ to obtain a sample from the desired distribution:

$$y = \mu + \sigma z. \tag{20.55}$$

We are now able to back-propagate through the sampling operation, by regarding it as a deterministic operation with an extra input z. Crucially, the extra input is a random variable whose distribution is not a function of any of the variables whose derivatives we want to calculate. The result tells us how an infinitesimal change in μ or σ would change the output if we could repeat the sampling operation again with the same value of z.

Being able to back-propagate through this sampling operation allows us to incorporate it into a larger graph. We can build elements of the graph on top of the output of the sampling distribution. For example, we can compute the derivatives of some loss function $J(y)$. We can also build elements of the graph whose outputs are the inputs or the parameters of the sampling operation. For example, we could build a larger graph with $\mu = f(\boldsymbol{x}; \boldsymbol{\theta})$ and $\sigma = g(\boldsymbol{x}; \boldsymbol{\theta})$. In this augmented graph, we can use back-propagation through these functions to derive $\nabla_{\boldsymbol{\theta}} J(y)$.

The principle used in this Gaussian sampling example is more generally applicable. We can express any probability distribution of the form $p(\mathbf{y}; \boldsymbol{\theta})$ or $p(\mathbf{y} \mid \boldsymbol{x}; \boldsymbol{\theta})$ as $p(\mathbf{y} \mid \boldsymbol{\omega})$, where $\boldsymbol{\omega}$ is a variable containing both parameters $\boldsymbol{\theta}$, and if applicable, the inputs $\boldsymbol{x}$. Given a value y sampled from distribution $p(\mathbf{y} \mid \boldsymbol{\omega})$, where $\boldsymbol{\omega}$ may in turn be a function of other variables, we can rewrite

$$\mathbf{y} \sim p(\mathbf{y} \mid \boldsymbol{\omega}) \tag{20.56}$$

as

$$\boldsymbol{y} = f(\boldsymbol{z}; \boldsymbol{\omega}), \tag{20.57}$$

where $\boldsymbol{z}$ is a source of randomness. We may then compute the derivatives of $\boldsymbol{y}$ with respect to $\boldsymbol{\omega}$ using traditional tools such as the back-propagation algorithm applied to f, as long as f is continuous and differentiable almost everywhere. Crucially, $\boldsymbol{\omega}$ must not be a function of $\boldsymbol{z}$, and $\boldsymbol{z}$ must not be a function of $\boldsymbol{\omega}$. This technique is often called the **reparametrization trick**, **stochastic back-propagation**, or **perturbation analysis**.

The requirement that f be continuous and differentiable of course requires $\boldsymbol{y}$ to be continuous. If we wish to back-propagate through a sampling process that produces discrete-valued samples, it may still be possible to estimate a gradient on $\boldsymbol{\omega}$, using reinforcement learning algorithms such as variants of the REINFORCE algorithm (Williams, 1992), discussed in section 20.9.1.

In neural network applications, we typically choose $\boldsymbol{z}$ to be drawn from some simple distribution, such as a unit uniform or unit Gaussian distribution, and achieve more complex distributions by allowing the deterministic portion of the network to reshape its input.

The idea of propagating gradients or optimizing through stochastic operations dates back to the mid-twentieth century (Price, 1958; Bonnet, 1964) and was first used for machine learning in the context of reinforcement learning (Williams, 1992). More recently, it has been applied to variational approximations (Opper and Archambeau, 2009) and stochastic and generative neural networks (Bengio et al., 2013b; Kingma, 2013; Kingma and Welling, 2014b,a; Rezende et al., 2014; Goodfellow et al., 2014c). Many networks, such as denoising autoencoders or networks regularized with dropout, are also naturally designed to take noise as an input without requiring any special reparametrization to make the noise independent from the model.

20.9.1 Back-Propagating through Discrete Stochastic Operations

When a model emits a discrete variable $\boldsymbol{y}$, the reparametrization trick is not applicable. Suppose that the model takes inputs $\boldsymbol{x}$ and parameters $\boldsymbol{\theta}$, both encapsulated in the vector $\boldsymbol{\omega}$, and combines them with random noise $\boldsymbol{z}$ to produce $\boldsymbol{y}$:

$$\boldsymbol{y} = f(\boldsymbol{z}; \boldsymbol{\omega}). \tag{20.58}$$

Because $\boldsymbol{y}$ is discrete, f must be a step function. The derivatives of a step function are not useful at any point. Right at each step boundary, the derivatives are undefined, but that is a small problem. The large problem is that the derivatives are zero almost everywhere on the regions between step boundaries. The derivatives of any cost function $J(\boldsymbol{y})$ therefore do not give any information for how to update the model parameters $\boldsymbol{\theta}$.

The REINFORCE algorithm (REward Increment = nonnegative Factor × Offset Reinforcement × Characteristic Eligibility) provides a framework defining a family of simple but powerful solutions (Williams, 1992). The core idea is that even though $J(f(\boldsymbol{z}; \boldsymbol{\omega}))$ is a step function with useless derivatives, the expected cost $\mathbb{E}_{\boldsymbol{z} \sim p(\boldsymbol{z})} J(f(\boldsymbol{z}; \boldsymbol{\omega}))$ is often a smooth function amenable to gradient descent. Although that expectation is typically not tractable when $\boldsymbol{y}$ is high-dimensional (or is the result of the composition of many discrete stochastic decisions), it can be estimated without bias using a Monte Carlo average. The stochastic estimate of the gradient can be used with SGD or other stochastic gradient-based optimization techniques.

The simplest version of REINFORCE can be derived by simply differentiating the expected cost:

$$\mathbb{E}_z[J(\boldsymbol{y})] = \sum_{\boldsymbol{y}} J(\boldsymbol{y})p(\boldsymbol{y}), \tag{20.59}$$

$$\frac{\partial \mathbb{E}[J(\boldsymbol{y})]}{\partial \boldsymbol{\omega}} = \sum_{\boldsymbol{y}} J(\boldsymbol{y})\frac{\partial p(\boldsymbol{y})}{\partial \boldsymbol{\omega}} \tag{20.60}$$

$$= \sum_{\boldsymbol{y}} J(\boldsymbol{y})p(\boldsymbol{y})\frac{\partial \log p(\boldsymbol{y})}{\partial \boldsymbol{\omega}} \tag{20.61}$$

$$\approx \frac{1}{m} \sum_{\boldsymbol{y}^{(i)} \sim p(\boldsymbol{y}),\ i=1}^{m} J(\boldsymbol{y}^{(i)})\frac{\partial \log p(\boldsymbol{y}^{(i)})}{\partial \boldsymbol{\omega}}. \tag{20.62}$$

Equation 20.60 relies on the assumption that J does not reference $\boldsymbol{\omega}$ directly. It is trivial to extend the approach to relax this assumption. Equation 20.61 exploits the derivative rule for the logarithm, $\frac{\partial \log p(\boldsymbol{y})}{\partial \boldsymbol{w}} = \frac{1}{p(\boldsymbol{y})} \frac{\partial p(\boldsymbol{y})}{\partial \boldsymbol{w}}$. Equation 20.62 gives an unbiased Monte Carlo estimator of the gradient.

Anywhere we write $p(\boldsymbol{y})$ in this section, one could equally write $p(\boldsymbol{y} \mid \boldsymbol{x})$. This is because $p(\boldsymbol{y})$ is parametrized by $\boldsymbol{w}$, and $\boldsymbol{w}$ contains both $\boldsymbol{\theta}$ and $\boldsymbol{x}$, if $\boldsymbol{x}$ is present.

One issue with the simple REINFORCE estimator is that it has a very high variance, so that many samples of $\boldsymbol{y}$ need to be drawn to obtain a good estimator of the gradient, or equivalently, if only one sample is drawn, SGD will converge very slowly and will require a smaller learning rate. It is possible to considerably reduce the variance of that estimator by using **variance reduction** methods (Wilson, 1984; L'Ecuyer, 1994). The idea is to modify the estimator so that its expected value remains unchanged but its variance gets reduced. In the context of REINFORCE, the proposed variance reduction methods involve the computation of a **baseline** that is used to offset $J(\boldsymbol{y})$. Note that any offset $b(\boldsymbol{w})$ that does not depend on $\boldsymbol{y}$ would not change the expectation of the estimated gradient because

$$E_{p(\boldsymbol{y})}\left[\frac{\partial \log p(\boldsymbol{y})}{\partial \boldsymbol{w}}\right] = \sum_{\boldsymbol{y}} p(\boldsymbol{y}) \frac{\partial \log p(\boldsymbol{y})}{\partial \boldsymbol{w}} \tag{20.63}$$

$$= \sum_{\boldsymbol{y}} \frac{\partial p(\boldsymbol{y})}{\partial \boldsymbol{w}} \tag{20.64}$$

$$= \frac{\partial}{\partial \boldsymbol{w}} \sum_{\boldsymbol{y}} p(\boldsymbol{y}) = \frac{\partial}{\partial \boldsymbol{w}} 1 = 0, \tag{20.65}$$

which means that

$$E_{p(\boldsymbol{y})}\left[(J(\boldsymbol{y}) - b(\boldsymbol{w})) \frac{\partial \log p(\boldsymbol{y})}{\partial \boldsymbol{w}}\right] = E_{p(\boldsymbol{y})}\left[J(\boldsymbol{y}) \frac{\partial \log p(\boldsymbol{y})}{\partial \boldsymbol{w}}\right] - b(\boldsymbol{w}) E_{p(\boldsymbol{y})}\left[\frac{\partial \log p(\boldsymbol{y})}{\partial \boldsymbol{w}}\right] \tag{20.66}$$

$$= E_{p(\boldsymbol{y})}\left[J(\boldsymbol{y}) \frac{\partial \log p(\boldsymbol{y})}{\partial \boldsymbol{w}}\right]. \tag{20.67}$$

Furthermore, we can obtain the optimal $b(\boldsymbol{w})$ by computing the variance of $(J(\boldsymbol{y}) - b(\boldsymbol{w})) \frac{\partial \log p(\boldsymbol{y})}{\partial \boldsymbol{w}}$ under $p(\boldsymbol{y})$ and minimizing with respect to $b(\boldsymbol{w})$. What we find is that this optimal baseline $b^*(\boldsymbol{w})_i$ is different for each element ω_i of the vector $\boldsymbol{w}$:

$$b^*(\boldsymbol{w})_i = \frac{E_{p(\boldsymbol{y})}\left[J(\boldsymbol{y}) \frac{\partial \log p(\boldsymbol{y})}{\partial \omega_i}^2\right]}{E_{p(\boldsymbol{y})}\left[\frac{\partial \log p(\boldsymbol{y})}{\partial \omega_i}^2\right]}. \tag{20.68}$$

The gradient estimator with respect to ω_i then becomes

$$(J(\boldsymbol{y}) - b(\boldsymbol{w})_i) \frac{\partial \log p(\boldsymbol{y})}{\partial \omega_i}, \tag{20.69}$$

where $b(\boldsymbol{\omega})_i$ estimates the above $b^*(\boldsymbol{\omega})_i$. The estimate b is usually obtained by adding extra outputs to the neural network and training the new outputs to estimate $E_{p(\boldsymbol{y})}[J(\boldsymbol{y})\frac{\partial \log p(\boldsymbol{y})}{\partial \omega_i}^2]$ and $E_{p(\boldsymbol{y})}\left[\frac{\partial \log p(\boldsymbol{y})}{\partial \omega_i}^2\right]$ for each element of $\boldsymbol{\omega}$. These extra outputs can be trained with the mean squared error objective, using respectively $J(\boldsymbol{y})\frac{\partial \log p(\boldsymbol{y})}{\partial \omega_i}^2$ and $\frac{\partial \log p(\boldsymbol{y})}{\partial \omega_i}^2$ as targets when $\boldsymbol{y}$ is sampled from $p(\boldsymbol{y})$, for a given $\boldsymbol{\omega}$. The estimate b may then be recovered by substituting these estimates into equation 20.68. Mnih and Gregor (2014) preferred to use a single shared output (across all elements i of $\boldsymbol{\omega}$) trained with the target $J(\boldsymbol{y})$, using as baseline $b(\boldsymbol{\omega}) \approx E_{p(\boldsymbol{y})}[J(\boldsymbol{y})]$.

Variance reduction methods have been introduced in the reinforcement learning context (Sutton et al., 2000; Weaver and Tao, 2001), generalizing previous work on the case of binary reward by Dayan (1990). See Bengio et al. (2013b), Mnih and Gregor (2014), Ba et al. (2014), Mnih et al. (2014), or Xu et al. (2015) for examples of modern uses of the REINFORCE algorithm with reduced variance in the context of deep learning. In addition to the use of an input-dependent baseline $b(\boldsymbol{\omega})$, Mnih and Gregor (2014) found that the scale of $(J(\boldsymbol{y}) - b(\boldsymbol{\omega}))$ could be adjusted during training by dividing it by its standard deviation estimated by a moving average during training, as a kind of adaptive learning rate, to counter the effect of important variations that occur during the course of training in the magnitude of this quantity. Mnih and Gregor (2014) called this heuristic **variance normalization**.

REINFORCE-based estimators can be understood as estimating the gradient by correlating choices of $\boldsymbol{y}$ with corresponding values of $J(\boldsymbol{y})$. If a good value of $\boldsymbol{y}$ is unlikely under the current parametrization, it might take a long time to obtain it by chance and get the required signal that this configuration should be reinforced.

20.10 Directed Generative Nets

As discussed in chapter 16, directed graphical models make up a prominent class of graphical models. While directed graphical models have been very popular within the greater machine learning community, within the smaller deep learning community they have until roughly 2013 been overshadowed by undirected models such as the RBM.

In this section we review some of the standard directed graphical models that have traditionally been associated with the deep learning community.

We have already described deep belief networks, which are a partially directed model. We have also already described sparse coding models, which can be thought of as shallow directed generative models. They are often used as feature learners in the context of deep learning, though they tend to perform poorly at sample generation and density estimation. We now describe a variety of deep, fully directed models.

20.10.1 Sigmoid Belief Networks

Sigmoid belief networks (Neal, 1990) are a simple form of directed graphical model with a specific kind of conditional probability distribution. In general, we can think of a sigmoid belief network as having a vector of binary states s, with each element of the state influenced by its ancestors:

$$p(s_i) = \sigma \left(\sum_{j<i} W_{j,i} s_j + b_i \right). \tag{20.70}$$

The most common structure of sigmoid belief network is one that is divided into many layers, with ancestral sampling proceeding through a series of many hidden layers and then ultimately generating the visible layer. This structure is very similar to the deep belief network, except that the units at the beginning of the sampling process are independent from each other, rather than sampled from a restricted Boltzmann machine. Such a structure is interesting for a variety of reasons. One is that the structure is a universal approximator of probability distributions over the visible units, in the sense that it can approximate any probability distribution over binary variables arbitrarily well, given enough depth, even if the width of the individual layers is restricted to the dimensionality of the visible layer (Sutskever and Hinton, 2008).

While generating a sample of the visible units is very efficient in a sigmoid belief network, most other operations are not. Inference over the hidden units given the visible units is intractable. Mean field inference is also intractable because the variational lower bound involves taking expectations of cliques that encompass entire layers. This problem has remained difficult enough to restrict the popularity of directed discrete networks.

One approach for performing inference in a sigmoid belief network is to construct a different lower bound that is specialized for sigmoid belief networks (Saul et al., 1996). This approach has only been applied to very small networks. Another approach is to use learned inference mechanisms as described in section 19.5. The Helmholtz machine (Dayan et al., 1995; Dayan and Hinton, 1996) is a sigmoid belief network combined with an inference network that predicts the parameters of the mean field distribution over the hidden units. Modern approaches

(Gregor et al., 2014; Mnih and Gregor, 2014) to sigmoid belief networks still use this inference network approach. These techniques remain difficult because of the discrete nature of the latent variables. One cannot simply back-propagate through the output of the inference network, but instead must use the relatively unreliable machinery for back-propagating through discrete sampling processes, as described in section 20.9.1. Recent approaches based on importance sampling, reweighted wake-sleep (Bornschein and Bengio, 2015) and bidirectional Helmholtz machines (Bornschein et al., 2015) make it possible to quickly train sigmoid belief networks and reach state-of-the-art performance on benchmark tasks.

A special case of sigmoid belief networks is the case where there are no latent variables. Learning in this case is efficient, because there is no need to marginalize latent variables out of the likelihood. A family of models called auto-regressive networks generalize this fully visible belief network to other kinds of variables besides binary variables and other structures of conditional distributions besides log-linear relationships. Auto-regressive networks are described in section 20.10.7.

20.10.2 Differentiable Generator Networks

Many generative models are based on the idea of using a differentiable **generator network**. The model transforms samples of latent variables z to samples x or to distributions over samples x using a differentiable function $g(z; \theta^{(g)})$, which is typically represented by a neural network. This model class includes variational autoencoders, which pair the generator net with an inference net; generative adversarial networks, which pair the generator network with a discriminator network; and techniques that train generator networks in isolation.

Generator networks are essentially just parametrized computational procedures for generating samples, where the architecture provides the family of possible distributions to sample from and the parameters select a distribution from within that family.

As an example, the standard procedure for drawing samples from a normal distribution with mean μ and covariance Σ is to feed samples z from a normal distribution with zero mean and identity covariance into a very simple generator network. This generator network contains just one affine layer:

$$x = g(z) = \mu + Lz, \tag{20.71}$$

where L is given by the Cholesky decomposition of Σ.

Pseudorandom number generators can also use nonlinear transformations of simple distributions. For example, **inverse transform sampling** (Devroye, 2013) draws a scalar z from $U(0,1)$ and applies a nonlinear transformation to a scalar x. In this case $g(z)$ is given by the inverse of the cumulative distribution function $F(x) = \int_{-\infty}^{x} p(v)dv$. If we are able to specify $p(x)$, integrate over x, and invert the resulting function, we can sample from $p(x)$ without using machine learning.

To generate samples from more complicated distributions that are difficult to specify directly, difficult to integrate over, or whose resulting integrals are difficult to invert, we use a feedforward network to represent a parametric family of nonlinear functions g, and use training data to infer the parameters selecting the desired function.

We can think of g as providing a nonlinear change of variables that transforms the distribution over $\mathbf{z}$ into the desired distribution over $\mathbf{x}$.

Recall from equation 3.47 that, for invertible, differentiable, continuous g,

$$p_z(\mathbf{z}) = p_x(g(\mathbf{z})) \left| \det\left(\frac{\partial g}{\partial \mathbf{z}}\right) \right|. \tag{20.72}$$

This implicitly imposes a probability distribution over $\mathbf{x}$:

$$p_x(\mathbf{x}) = \frac{p_z(g^{-1}(\mathbf{x}))}{\left| \det\left(\frac{\partial g}{\partial \mathbf{z}}\right) \right|}. \tag{20.73}$$

Of course, this formula may be difficult to evaluate, depending on the choice of g, so we often use indirect means of learning g, rather than trying to maximize $\log p(\mathbf{x})$ directly.

In some cases, rather than using g to provide a sample of $\mathbf{x}$ directly, we use g to define a conditional distribution over $\mathbf{x}$. For example, we could use a generator net whose final layer consists of sigmoid outputs to provide the mean parameters of Bernoulli distributions:

$$p(\mathrm{x}_i = 1 \mid \mathbf{z}) = g(\mathbf{z})_i. \tag{20.74}$$

In this case, when we use g to define $p(\mathbf{x} \mid \mathbf{z})$, we impose a distribution over $\mathbf{x}$ by marginalizing $\mathbf{z}$:

$$p(\mathbf{x}) = \mathbb{E}_{\mathbf{z}} p(\mathbf{x} \mid \mathbf{z}). \tag{20.75}$$

Both approaches define a distribution $p_g(\mathbf{x})$ and allow us to train various criteria of p_g using the reparametrization trick of section 20.9.

The two different approaches to formulating generator nets—emitting the parameters of a conditional distribution versus directly emitting samples—have complementary strengths and weaknesses. When the generator net defines a conditional distribution over $\boldsymbol{x}$, it is capable of generating discrete data as well as continuous data. When the generator net provides samples directly, it is capable of generating only continuous data (we could introduce discretization in the forward propagation, but doing so would mean the model could no longer be trained using back-propagation). The advantage to direct sampling is that we are no longer forced to use conditional distributions whose form can be easily written down and algebraically manipulated by a human designer.

Approaches based on differentiable generator networks are motivated by the success of gradient descent applied to differentiable feedforward networks for classification. In the context of supervised learning, deep feedforward networks trained with gradient-based learning seem practically guaranteed to succeed given enough hidden units and enough training data. Can this same recipe for success transfer to generative modeling?

Generative modeling seems to be more difficult than classification or regression because the learning process requires optimizing intractable criteria. In the context of differentiable generator nets, the criteria are intractable because the data does not specify both the inputs $\boldsymbol{z}$ and the outputs $\boldsymbol{x}$ of the generator net. In the case of supervised learning, both the inputs $\boldsymbol{x}$ and the outputs $\boldsymbol{y}$ were given, and the optimization procedure needs only to learn how to produce the specified mapping. In the case of generative modeling, the learning procedure needs to determine how to arrange $\boldsymbol{z}$ space in a useful way and additionally how to map from $\boldsymbol{z}$ to $\boldsymbol{x}$.

Dosovitskiy et al. (2015) studied a simplified problem, where the correspondence between $\boldsymbol{z}$ and $\boldsymbol{x}$ is given. Specifically, the training data is computer-rendered imagery of chairs. The latent variables $\boldsymbol{z}$ are parameters given to the rendering engine describing the choice of which chair model to use, the position of the chair, and other configuration details that affect the rendering of the image. Using this synthetically generated data, a convolutional network is able to learn to map $\boldsymbol{z}$ descriptions of the content of an image to $\boldsymbol{x}$ approximations of rendered images. This suggests that contemporary differentiable generator networks have sufficient model capacity to be good generative models, and that contemporary optimization algorithms have the ability to fit them. The difficulty lies in determining how to train generator networks when the value of $\boldsymbol{z}$ for each $\boldsymbol{x}$ is not fixed and known ahead of each time.

The following sections describe several approaches to training differentiable generator nets given only training samples of $\boldsymbol{x}$.

20.10.3　Variational Autoencoders

The **variational autoencoder**, or VAE (Kingma, 2013; Rezende et al., 2014), is a directed model that uses learned approximate inference and can be trained purely with gradient-based methods.

To generate a sample from the model, the VAE first draws a sample z from the code distribution $p_{\text{model}}(z)$. The sample is then run through a differentiable generator network $g(z)$. Finally, x is sampled from a distribution $p_{\text{model}}(x; g(z)) = p_{\text{model}}(x \mid z)$. During training, however, the approximate inference network (or encoder) $q(z \mid x)$ is used to obtain z, and $p_{\text{model}}(x \mid z)$ is then viewed as a decoder network.

The key insight behind variational autoencoders is that they can be trained by maximizing the variational lower bound $\mathcal{L}(q)$ associated with data point x:

$$\mathcal{L}(q) = \mathbb{E}_{z \sim q(z \mid x)} \log p_{\text{model}}(z, x) + \mathcal{H}(q(z \mid x)) \tag{20.76}$$

$$= \mathbb{E}_{z \sim q(z \mid x)} \log p_{\text{model}}(x \mid z) - D_{\text{KL}}(q(z \mid x) \| p_{\text{model}}(z)) \tag{20.77}$$

$$\leq \log p_{\text{model}}(x). \tag{20.78}$$

In equation 20.76, we recognize the first term as the joint log-likelihood of the visible and hidden variables under the approximate posterior over the latent variables (just as with EM, except that we use an approximate rather than the exact posterior). We recognize also a second term, the entropy of the approximate posterior. When q is chosen to be a Gaussian distribution, with noise added to a predicted mean value, maximizing this entropy term encourages increasing the standard deviation of this noise. More generally, this entropy term encourages the variational posterior to place high probability mass on many z values that could have generated x, rather than collapsing to a single point estimate of the most likely value. In equation 20.77, we recognize the first term as the reconstruction log-likelihood found in other autoencoders. The second term tries to make the approximate posterior distribution $q(z \mid x)$ and the model prior $p_{\text{model}}(z)$ approach each other.

Traditional approaches to variational inference and learning infer q via an optimization algorithm, typically iterated fixed-point equations (section 19.4). These approaches are slow and often require the ability to compute $\mathbb{E}_{z \sim q} \log p_{\text{model}}(z, x)$ in closed form. The main idea behind the variational autoencoder is to train a parametric encoder (also sometimes called an inference network or recognition model) that produces the parameters of q. As long as z is a continuous variable, we can then back-propagate through samples of z drawn from $q(z \mid x) = q(z; f(x; \theta))$ to obtain a gradient with respect to θ. Learning then consists solely of maximizing

$\mathcal{L}$ with respect to the parameters of the encoder and decoder. All the expectations in $\mathcal{L}$ may be approximated by Monte Carlo sampling.

The variational autoencoder approach is elegant, theoretically pleasing, and simple to implement. It also obtains excellent results and is among the state-of-the-art approaches to generative modeling. Its main drawback is that samples from variational autoencoders trained on images tend to be somewhat blurry. The causes of this phenomenon are not yet known. One possibility is that the blurriness is an intrinsic effect of maximum likelihood, which minimizes $D_{\mathrm{KL}}(p_{\mathrm{data}}\|p_{\mathrm{model}})$. As illustrated in figure 3.6, this means that the model will assign high probability to points that occur in the training set but may also assign high probability to other points. These other points may include blurry images. Part of the reason that the model would choose to put probability mass on blurry images rather than some other part of the space is that the variational autoencoders used in practice usually have a Gaussian distribution for $p_{\mathrm{model}}(\boldsymbol{x}; g(\boldsymbol{z}))$. Maximizing a lower bound on the likelihood of such a distribution is similar to training a traditional autoencoder with mean squared error, in the sense that it has a tendency to ignore features of the input that occupy few pixels or that cause only a small change in the brightness of the pixels that they occupy. This issue is not specific to VAEs and is shared with generative models that optimize a log-likelihood, or equivalently, $D_{\mathrm{KL}}(p_{\mathrm{data}}\|p_{\mathrm{model}})$, as argued by Theis et al. (2015) and by Huszar (2015). Another troubling issue with contemporary VAE models is that they tend to use only a small subset of the dimensions of $\boldsymbol{z}$, as if the encoder were not able to transform enough of the local directions in input space to a space where the marginal distribution matches the factorized prior.

The VAE framework is straightforward to extend to a wide range of model architectures. This is a key advantage over Boltzmann machines, which require extremely careful model design to maintain tractability. VAEs work very well with a diverse family of differentiable operators. One particularly sophisticated VAE is the **deep recurrent attention writer** (DRAW) model (Gregor et al., 2015). DRAW uses a recurrent encoder and recurrent decoder combined with an attention mechanism. The generation process for the DRAW model consists of sequentially visiting different small image patches and drawing the values of the pixels at those points. VAEs can also be extended to generate sequences by defining variational RNNs (Chung et al., 2015b) by using a recurrent encoder and decoder within the VAE framework. Generating a sample from a traditional RNN involves only nondeterministic operations at the output space. Variational RNNs also have random variability at the potentially more abstract level captured by the VAE latent variables.

The VAE framework has been extended to maximize not just the traditional variational lower bound, but also the **importance-weighted autoencoder** (Burda et al., 2015) objective:

$$\mathcal{L}_k(\boldsymbol{x}, q) = \mathbb{E}_{\mathbf{z}^{(1)},\dots,\mathbf{z}^{(k)} \sim q(\boldsymbol{z}|\boldsymbol{x})} \left[\log \frac{1}{k} \sum_{i=1}^{k} \frac{p_{\mathrm{model}}(\boldsymbol{x}, \boldsymbol{z}^{(i)})}{q(\boldsymbol{z}^{(i)} \mid \boldsymbol{x})} \right]. \tag{20.79}$$

This new objective is equivalent to the traditional lower bound $\mathcal{L}$ when $k = 1$. However, it may also be interpreted as forming an estimate of the true $\log p_{\mathrm{model}}(\boldsymbol{x})$ using importance sampling of $\boldsymbol{z}$ from proposal distribution $q(\boldsymbol{z} \mid \boldsymbol{x})$. The importance-weighted autoencoder objective is also a lower bound on $\log p_{\mathrm{model}}(\boldsymbol{x})$ and becomes tighter as k increases.

Variational autoencoders have some interesting connections to the MP-DBM and other approaches that involve back-propagation through the approximate inference graph (Goodfellow et al., 2013b; Stoyanov et al., 2011; Brakel et al., 2013). These previous approaches required an inference procedure such as mean field fixed-point equations to provide the computational graph. The variational autoencoder is defined for arbitrary computational graphs, which makes it applicable to a wider range of probabilistic model families because there is no need to restrict the choice of models to those with tractable mean field fixed-point equations. The variational autoencoder also has the advantage of increasing a bound on the log-likelihood of the model, while the criteria for the MP-DBM and related models are more heuristic and have little probabilistic interpretation beyond making the results of approximate inference accurate. One disadvantage of the variational autoencoder is that it learns an inference network for only one problem, inferring $\boldsymbol{z}$ given $\boldsymbol{x}$. The older methods are able to perform approximate inference over any subset of variables given any other subset of variables, because the mean field fixed-point equations specify how to share parameters between the computational graphs for all these different problems.

One very nice property of the variational autoencoder is that simultaneously training a parametric encoder in combination with the generator network forces the model to learn a predictable coordinate system that the encoder can capture. This makes it an excellent manifold learning algorithm. See figure 20.6 for examples of low-dimensional manifolds learned by the variational autoencoder. In one of the cases demonstrated in the figure, the algorithm discovered two independent factors of variation present in images of faces: angle of rotation and emotional expression.

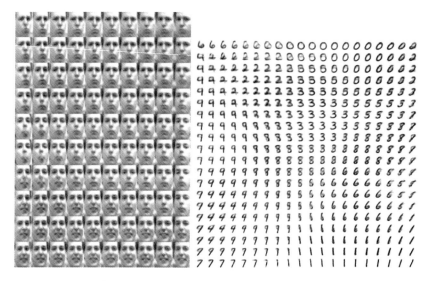

Figure 20.6: Examples of 2-D coordinate systems for high-dimensional manifolds, learned by a variational autoencoder (Kingma and Welling, 2014a). Two dimensions may be plotted directly on the page for visualization, so we can gain an understanding of how the model works by training a model with a 2-D latent code, even if we believe the intrinsic dimensionality of the data manifold is much higher. The images shown are not examples from the training set but images $\boldsymbol{x}$ actually generated by the model $p(\boldsymbol{x} \mid \boldsymbol{z})$, simply by changing the 2-D "code" $\boldsymbol{z}$ (each image corresponds to a different choice of "code" $\boldsymbol{z}$ on a 2-D uniform grid). *(Left)* The 2-D map of the Frey faces manifold. One dimension that has been discovered (horizontal) mostly corresponds to a rotation of the face, while the other (vertical) corresponds to the emotional expression. *(Right)* The 2-D map of the MNIST manifold.

20.10.4 Generative Adversarial Networks

Generative adversarial networks, or GANs (Goodfellow et al., 2014c), are another generative modeling approach based on differentiable generator networks.

Generative adversarial networks are based on a game theoretic scenario in which the generator network must compete against an adversary. The generator network directly produces samples $\boldsymbol{x} = g(\boldsymbol{z}; \boldsymbol{\theta}^{(g)})$. Its adversary, the **discriminator network**, attempts to distinguish between samples drawn from the training data and samples drawn from the generator. The discriminator emits a probability value given by $d(\boldsymbol{x}; \boldsymbol{\theta}^{(d)})$, indicating the probability that $\boldsymbol{x}$ is a real training example rather than a fake sample drawn from the model.

The simplest way to formulate learning in generative adversarial networks is as a zero-sum game, in which a function $v(\boldsymbol{\theta}^{(g)}, \boldsymbol{\theta}^{(d)})$ determines the payoff of the discriminator. The generator receives $-v(\boldsymbol{\theta}^{(g)}, \boldsymbol{\theta}^{(d)})$ as its own payoff. During learning, each player attempts to maximize its own payoff, so that at convergence

$$g^* = \arg\min_g \max_d v(g, d). \tag{20.80}$$

The default choice for v is

$$v(\boldsymbol{\theta}^{(g)}, \boldsymbol{\theta}^{(d)}) = \mathbb{E}_{\mathbf{x} \sim p_{\text{data}}} \log d(\boldsymbol{x}) + \mathbb{E}_{\boldsymbol{x} \sim p_{\text{model}}} \log\left(1 - d(\boldsymbol{x})\right). \tag{20.81}$$

This drives the discriminator to attempt to learn to correctly classify samples as real or fake. Simultaneously, the generator attempts to fool the classifier into believing its samples are real. At convergence, the generator's samples are indistinguishable from real data, and the discriminator outputs $\frac{1}{2}$ everywhere. The discriminator may then be discarded.

The main motivation for the design of GANs is that the learning process requires neither approximate inference nor approximation of a partition function gradient. When $\max_d v(g, d)$ is convex in $\boldsymbol{\theta}^{(g)}$ (such as the case where optimization is performed directly in the space of probability density functions), the procedure is guaranteed to converge and is asymptotically consistent.

Unfortunately, learning in GANs can be difficult in practice when g and d are represented by neural networks and $\max_d v(g, d)$ is not convex. Goodfellow (2014) identified nonconvergence as an issue that may cause GANs to underfit. In general, simultaneous gradient descent on two players' costs is not guaranteed to reach an equilibrium. Consider, for example, the value function $v(a, b) = ab$, where one player controls a and incurs cost ab, while the other player controls b and receives a cost $-ab$. If we model each player as making infinitesimally small gradient steps, each player reducing their own cost at the expense of the other player, then a and b go into a stable, circular orbit, rather than arriving at the equilibrium point at the origin. Note that the equilibria for a minimax game are not local minima of v. Instead, they are points that are simultaneously minima for both players' costs. This means that they are saddle points of v that are local minima with respect to the first player's parameters and local maxima with respect to the second player's parameters. It is possible for the two players to take turns increasing then decreasing v forever, rather than landing exactly on the saddle point, where neither player is capable of reducing its cost. It is not known to what extent this nonconvergence problem affects GANs.

Goodfellow (2014) identified an alternative formulation of the payoffs, in which the game is no longer zero-sum, that has the same expected gradient as maximum likelihood learning whenever the discriminator is optimal. Because maximum likelihood training converges, this reformulation of the GAN game should also converge, given enough samples. Unfortunately, this alternative formulation does not seem to improve convergence in practice, possibly because of suboptimality of the discriminator or high variance around the expected gradient.

In realistic experiments, the best-performing formulation of the GAN game is a different formulation that is neither zero-sum nor equivalent to maximum likelihood, introduced by Goodfellow et al. (2014c) with a heuristic motivation. In this best-performing formulation, the generator aims to increase the log-probability that the discriminator makes a mistake, rather than aiming to decrease the log-probability that the discriminator makes the correct prediction. This reformulation is motivated solely by the observation that it causes the derivative of the generator's cost function with respect to the discriminator's logits to remain large even in the situation when the discriminator confidently rejects all generator samples.

Stabilization of GAN learning remains an open problem. Fortunately, GAN learning performs well when the model architecture and hyperparameters are carefully selected. Radford et al. (2015) crafted a deep convolutional GAN (DCGAN) that performs very well for image synthesis tasks, and showed that its latent representation space captures important factors of variation, as shown in figure 15.9. See figure 20.7 for examples of images generated by a DCGAN generator.

The GAN learning problem can also be simplified by breaking the generation process into many levels of detail. It is possible to train conditional GANs (Mirza and Osindero, 2014) that learn to sample from a distribution $p(\boldsymbol{x} \mid \boldsymbol{y})$ rather than simply sampling from a marginal distribution $p(\boldsymbol{x})$. Denton et al. (2015) showed that a series of conditional GANs can be trained to first generate a very low-resolution version of an image, then incrementally add details to the image. This technique is called the LAPGAN model, due to the use of a Laplacian pyramid to generate the images containing varying levels of detail. LAPGAN generators are able to fool not only discriminator networks but also human observers, with experimental subjects identifying up to 40 percent of the outputs of the network as being real data. See figure 20.7 for examples of images generated by a LAPGAN generator.

One unusual capability of the GAN training procedure is that it can fit probability distributions that assign zero probability to the training points. Rather than maximizing the log-probability of specific points, the generator net learns to trace out a manifold whose points resemble training points in some way. Somewhat paradoxically, this means that the model may assign a log-likelihood of negative infinity to the test set, while still representing a manifold that a human observer judges to capture the essence of the generation task. This is not clearly an advantage or

Figure 20.7: Images generated by GANs trained on the LSUN dataset. *(Left)*Images of bedrooms generated by a DCGAN model, reproduced with permission from Radford et al. (2015). *(Right)*Images of churches generated by a LAPGAN model, reproduced with permission from Denton et al. (2015).

a disadvantage, and one may also guarantee that the generator network assigns nonzero probability to all points simply by making the last layer of the generator network add Gaussian noise to all the generated values. Generator networks that add Gaussian noise in this manner sample from the same distribution that one obtains by using the generator network to parametrize the mean of a conditional Gaussian distribution.

Dropout seems to be important in the discriminator network. In particular, units should be stochastically dropped while computing the gradient for the generator network to follow. Following the gradient of the deterministic version of the discriminator with its weights divided by two does not seem to be as effective. Likewise, never using dropout seems to yield poor results.

While the GAN framework is designed for differentiable generator networks, similar principles can be used to train other kinds of models. For example, **self-supervised boosting** can be used to train an RBM generator to fool a logistic regression discriminator (Welling et al., 2002).

20.10.5 Generative Moment Matching Networks

Generative moment matching networks (Li et al., 2015; Dziugaite et al., 2015) are another form of generative model based on differentiable generator networks. Unlike VAEs and GANs, they do not need to pair the generator network with any other network—neither an inference network, as used with VAEs, nor a discriminator network, as used with GANs.

Generative moment matching networks are trained with a technique called **moment matching**. The basic idea behind moment matching is to train the generator in such a way that many of the statistics of samples generated by the model are as similar as possible to those of the statistics of the examples in the training set. In this context, a **moment** is an expectation of different powers of a random variable. For example, the first moment is the mean, the second moment is the mean of the squared values, and so on. In multiple dimensions, each element of the random vector may be raised to different powers, so that a moment may be any quantity of the form

$$\mathbb{E}_{\boldsymbol{x}} \Pi_i x_i^{n_i}, \tag{20.82}$$

where $\boldsymbol{n} = [n_1, n_2, \ldots, n_d]^\top$ is a vector of nonnegative integers.

Upon first examination, this approach seems to be computationally infeasible. For example, if we want to match all the moments of the form $x_i x_j$, then we need to minimize the difference between a number of values that is quadratic in the dimension of $\boldsymbol{x}$. Moreover, even matching all the first and second moments would only be sufficient to fit a multivariate Gaussian distribution, which captures only linear relationships between values. Our ambitions for neural networks are to capture complex nonlinear relationships, which would require far more moments. GANs avoid this problem of exhaustively enumerating all moments by using a dynamically updated discriminator which automatically focuses its attention on whichever statistic the generator network is matching the least effectively.

Instead, generative moment matching networks can be trained by minimizing a cost function called **maximum mean discrepancy**, or MMD (Schölkopf and Smola, 2002; Gretton et al., 2012). This cost function measures the error in the first moments in an infinite-dimensional space, using an implicit mapping to feature space defined by a kernel function to make computations on infinite-dimensional vectors tractable. The MMD cost is zero if and only if the two distributions being compared are equal.

Visually, the samples from generative moment matching networks are somewhat disappointing. Fortunately, they can be improved by combining the generator network with an autoencoder. First, an autoencoder is trained to reconstruct the training set. Next, the encoder of the autoencoder is used to transform the entire training set into code space. The generator network is then trained to generate code samples, which may be mapped to visually pleasing samples via the decoder.

Unlike GANs, the cost function is defined only with respect to a batch of examples from both the training set and the generator network. It is not possible to make a training update as a function of only one training example or only one sample from the generator network. This is because the moments must be computed as an empirical average across many samples. When the batch size is too small, MMD can underestimate the true amount of variation in the distributions being sampled. No finite batch size is sufficiently large to eliminate this problem entirely, but larger batches reduce the amount of underestimation. When the batch size is too large, the training procedure becomes infeasibly slow, because many examples must be processed in order to compute a single small gradient step.

As with GANs, it is possible to train a generator net using MMD even if that generator net assigns zero probability to the training points.

20.10.6 Convolutional Generative Networks

When generating images, it is often useful to use a generator network that includes a convolutional structure (see, for example, Goodfellow et al. [2014c] or Dosovitskiy et al. [2015]). To do so, we use the "transpose" of the convolution operator, described in section 9.5. This approach often yields more realistic images and does so using fewer parameters than using fully connected layers without parameter sharing.

Convolutional networks for recognition tasks have information flow from the image to some summarization layer at the top of the network, often a class label. As this image flows upward through the network, information is discarded as the representation of the image becomes more invariant to nuisance transformations. In a generator network, the opposite is true. Rich details must be added as the representation of the image to be generated propagates through the network, culminating in the final representation of the image, which is of course the image itself, in all its detailed glory, with object positions and poses and textures and lighting. The primary mechanism for discarding information in a convolutional recognition network is the pooling layer. The generator network seems to need to add information. We cannot put the inverse of a pooling layer into the generator network because most pooling functions are not invertible. A simpler operation is to merely increase the spatial size of the representation. An approach that seems to perform acceptably is to use an "un-pooling" as introduced by Dosovitskiy et al. (2015). This layer corresponds to the inverse of the max-pooling operation under certain simplifying conditions. First, the stride of the max-pooling operation is constrained to be equal to the width of the pooling region. Second, the maximum input within each pooling region is assumed to be the input in the upper-left corner. Finally, all nonmaximal inputs within each pooling region are assumed to be zero. These are very strong and unrealistic assumptions, but they do allow the max-pooling operator to be inverted. The inverse un-pooling operation allocates a tensor of zeros, then copies each value from spatial coordinate i of the input to spatial coordinate $i \times k$ of the output. The integer value k defines the size of the pooling region. Even though the assumptions motivating the definition of the un-pooling operator are unrealistic, the subsequent layers are able to learn to compensate for its unusual output, so the samples generated by the model as a whole are visually pleasing.

20.10.7 Auto-Regressive Networks

Auto-regressive networks are directed probabilistic models with no latent random variables. The conditional probability distributions in these models are represented by neural networks (sometimes extremely simple neural networks, such as logistic regression). The graph structure of these models is the complete graph. They decompose a joint probability over the observed variables using the chain rule of probability to obtain a product of conditionals of the form $P(x_d \mid x_{d-1}, \ldots, x_1)$. Such models have been called **fully-visible Bayes networks** (FVBNs) and used successfully in many forms, first with logistic regression for each conditional distribution (Frey, 1998), and then with neural networks with hidden units (Bengio and Bengio, 2000b; Larochelle and Murray, 2011). In some forms of auto-regressive networks, such as NADE (Larochelle and Murray, 2011), described in section 20.10.10, we can introduce a form of parameter sharing that brings both a statistical advantage (fewer unique parameters) and a computational advantage (less computation). This is one more instance of the recurring deep learning motif of *reuse of features*.

20.10.8 Linear Auto-Regressive Networks

The simplest form of auto-regressive network has no hidden units and no sharing of parameters or features. Each $P(x_i \mid x_{i-1}, \ldots, x_1)$ is parametrized as a linear model (linear regression for real-valued data, logistic regression for binary data, softmax regression for discrete data). This model was introduced by Frey (1998) and has $O(d^2)$ parameters when there are d variables to model. It is illustrated in figure 20.8.

If the variables are continuous, a linear auto-regressive model is merely another way to formulate a multivariate Gaussian distribution, capturing linear pairwise interactions between the observed variables.

Linear auto-regressive networks are essentially the generalization of linear classification methods to generative modeling. They therefore have the same advantages and disadvantages as linear classifiers. Like linear classifiers, they may be trained with convex loss functions and sometimes admit closed form solutions

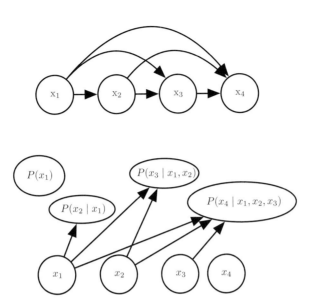

Figure 20.8: A fully visible belief network predicts the i-th variable from the $i - 1$ previous ones. *(Top)*The directed graphical model for an FVBN. *(Bottom)*Corresponding computational graph for the logistic FVBN, where each prediction is made by a linear predictor.

(as in the Gaussian case). Like linear classifiers, the model itself does not offer a way of increasing its capacity, so capacity must be raised using techniques like basis expansions of the input or the kernel trick.

20.10.9 Neural Auto-Regressive Networks

Neural auto-regressive networks (Bengio and Bengio, 2000a,b) have the same left-to-right graphical model as logistic auto-regressive networks (figure 20.8) but employ a different parametrization of the conditional distributions within that graphical model structure. The new parametrization is more powerful in the sense that its capacity can be increased as much as needed, allowing approximation of any joint distribution. The new parametrization can also improve generalization by introducing a parameter sharing and feature sharing principle common to deep learning in general. The models were motivated by the objective of avoiding the curse of dimensionality arising out of traditional tabular graphical models, sharing the same structure as figure 20.8. In tabular discrete probabilistic models, each conditional distribution is represented by a table of probabilities, with one entry and one parameter for each possible configuration of the variables involved. By using a neural network instead, two advantages are obtained:

1. The parametrization of each $P(x_i \mid x_{i-1}, \ldots, x_1)$ by a neural network with $(i - 1) \times k$ inputs and k outputs (if the variables are discrete and take k values, encoded one-hot) enables one to estimate the conditional probability without requiring an exponential number of parameters (and examples), yet still is able to capture high-order dependencies between the random variables.

2. Instead of having a different neural network for the prediction of each x_i, a *left-to-right* connectivity, illustrated in figure 20.9, allows one to merge all the neural networks into one. Equivalently, it means that the hidden layer features computed for predicting x_i can be reused for predicting x_{i+k} ($k > 0$). The hidden units are thus organized in *groups* that have the particularity that all the units in the i-th group only depend on the input values $x_1, \ldots, x_i$. The parameters used to compute these hidden units are jointly optimized to improve the prediction of all the variables in the sequence. This is an instance of the *reuse principle* that recurs throughout deep learning in scenarios ranging from recurrent and convolutional network architectures to multitask and transfer learning.

Each $P(x_i \mid x_{i-1}, \ldots, x_1)$ can represent a conditional distribution by having outputs of the neural network predict *parameters* of the conditional distribution

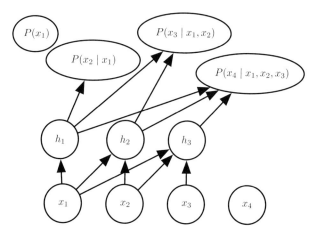

Figure 20.9: A neural auto-regressive network predicts the i-th variable x_i from the $i - 1$ previous ones, but is parametrized so that features (groups of hidden units denoted h_i) that are functions of $x_1, \ldots, x_i$ can be reused in predicting all the subsequent variables $x_{i+1}, x_{i+2}, \ldots, x_d$.

of x_i, as discussed in section 6.2.1.1. Although the original neural auto-regressive networks were initially evaluated in the context of purely discrete multivariate data (with a sigmoid output for a Bernoulli variable or softmax output for a multinoulli variable), it is natural to extend such models to continuous variables or joint distributions involving both discrete and continuous variables.

20.10.10 NADE

The **neural auto-regressive density estimator** (NADE) is a very successful recent form of neural auto-regressive network (Larochelle and Murray, 2011). The connectivity is the same as for the original neural auto-regressive network of Bengio and Bengio (2000b), but NADE introduces an additional parameter sharing scheme, as illustrated in figure 20.10. The parameters of the hidden units of different groups j are shared.

The weights $W'_{j,k,i}$ from the i-th input x_i to the k-th element of the j-th group of hidden unit $h_k^{(j)}$ ($j \geq i$) are shared among the groups:

$$W'_{j,k,i} = W_{k,i}. \tag{20.83}$$

The remaining weights, where $j < i$, are zero.

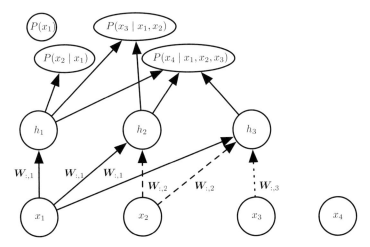

Figure 20.10: An illustration of the neural autoregressive density estimator (NADE). The hidden units are organized in groups $\boldsymbol{h}^{(j)}$ so that only the inputs $x_1, \dots, x_i$ participate in computing $\boldsymbol{h}^{(i)}$ and predicting $P(x_j \mid x_{j-1}, \dots, x_1)$, for $j > i$. NADE is differentiated from earlier neural auto-regressive networks by the use of a particular weight sharing pattern: $W'_{j,k,i} = W_{k,i}$ is shared (indicated in the figure by the use of the same line pattern for every instance of a replicated weight) for all the weights going out from x_i to the k-th unit of any group $j \geq i$. Recall that the vector $(W_{1,i}, W_{2,i}, \dots, W_{n,i})$ is denoted $\boldsymbol{W}_{:,i}$.

Larochelle and Murray (2011) chose this sharing scheme so that forward propagation in a NADE model would loosely resemble the computations performed in mean field inference to fill in missing inputs in an RBM. This mean field inference corresponds to running a recurrent network with shared weights, and the first step of that inference is the same as in NADE. The only difference is that with NADE, the output weights connecting the hidden units to the output are parametrized independently from the weights connecting the input units to the hidden units. In the RBM, the hidden-to-output weights are the transpose of the input-to-hidden weights. The NADE architecture can be extended to mimic not just one time step of the mean field recurrent inference but k steps. This approach is called NADE-k (Raiko et al., 2014).

As mentioned previously, auto-regressive networks may be extended to process continuous-valued data. A particularly powerful and generic way of parametrizing a continuous density is as a Gaussian mixture (introduced in section 3.9.6) with mixture weights α_i (the coefficient or prior probability for component i), per-component conditional mean μ_i and per-component conditional variance σ_i^2. A model called RNADE (Uria et al., 2013) uses this parametrization to extend NADE to real values. As with other mixture density networks, the parameters of this distribution are outputs of the network, with the mixture weight probabilities produced by a softmax unit, and the variances parametrized so that they are positive. Stochastic gradient descent can be numerically ill-behaved due to the interactions between the conditional means μ_i and the conditional variances σ_i^2. To reduce this difficulty, Uria et al. (2013) use a pseudogradient that replaces the gradient on the mean, in the back-propagation phase.

Another very interesting extension of the neural auto-regressive architectures gets rid of the need to choose an arbitrary order for the observed variables (Murray and Larochelle, 2014). In auto-regressive networks, the idea is to train the network to be able to cope with any order by randomly sampling orders and providing the information to hidden units specifying which of the inputs are observed (on the right side of the conditioning bar) and which are to be predicted and are thus considered missing (on the left side of the conditioning bar). This is nice because it allows one to use a trained auto-regressive network to *perform any inference problem* (i.e., predict or sample from the probability distribution over any subset of variables given any subset) extremely efficiently. Finally, since many orders of variables are possible ($n!$ for n variables) and each order o of variables yields a different $p(\mathbf{x} \mid o)$, we can form an ensemble of models for many values of o:

$$p_{\text{ensemble}}(\mathbf{x}) = \frac{1}{k} \sum_{i=1}^{k} p(\mathbf{x} \mid o^{(i)}). \tag{20.84}$$

This ensemble model usually generalizes better and assigns higher probability to the test set than does an individual model defined by a single ordering.

In the same paper, the authors propose deep versions of the architecture, but unfortunately that immediately makes computation as expensive as in the original neural auto-regressive network (Bengio and Bengio, 2000b). The first layer and the output layer can still be computed in $O(nh)$ multiply-add operations, as in the regular NADE, where h is the number of hidden units (the size of the groups h_i, in figures 20.10 and 20.9), whereas it is $O(n^2h)$ in Bengio and Bengio (2000b). For the other hidden layers, however, the computation is $O(n^2h^2)$ if every "previous" group at layer l participates in predicting the "next" group at layer $l + 1$, assuming n groups of h hidden units at each layer. Making the i-th group at layer $l + 1$ only depend on the i-th group, as in Murray and Larochelle (2014), at layer l reduces it to $O(nh^2)$, which is still h times worse than the regular NADE.

20.11 Drawing Samples from Autoencoders

In chapter 14, we saw that many kinds of autoencoders learn the data distribution. There are close connections between score matching, denoising autoencoders, and contractive autoencoders. These connections demonstrate that some kinds of autoencoders learn the data distribution in some way. We have not yet seen how to draw samples from such models.

Some kinds of autoencoders, such as the variational autoencoder, explicitly represent a probability distribution and admit straightforward ancestral sampling. Most other kinds of autoencoders require MCMC sampling.

Contractive autoencoders are designed to recover an estimate of the tangent plane of the data manifold. This means that repeated encoding and decoding with injected noise will induce a random walk along the surface of the manifold (Rifai et al., 2012; Mesnil et al., 2012). This manifold diffusion technique is a kind of Markov chain.

There is also a more general Markov chain that can sample from any denoising autoencoder.

20.11.1 Markov Chain Associated with Any Denoising Autoencoder

The above discussion left open the question of what noise to inject and where to obtain a Markov chain that would generate from the distribution estimated by the autoencoder. Bengio et al. (2013c) showed how to construct such a Markov chain for **generalized denoising autoencoders**. Generalized denoising autoencoders are specified by a denoising distribution for sampling an estimate of the clean input given the corrupted input.

Each step of the Markov chain that generates from the estimated distribution consists of the following substeps, illustrated in figure 20.11:

1. Starting from the previous state $\boldsymbol{x}$, inject corruption noise, sampling $\tilde{\boldsymbol{x}}$ from $C(\tilde{\boldsymbol{x}} \mid \boldsymbol{x})$.

2. Encode $\tilde{\boldsymbol{x}}$ into $\boldsymbol{h} = f(\tilde{\boldsymbol{x}})$.

3. Decode $\boldsymbol{h}$ to obtain the parameters $\boldsymbol{\omega} = g(\boldsymbol{h})$ of $p(\mathbf{x} \mid \boldsymbol{\omega} = g(\boldsymbol{h})) = p(\mathbf{x} \mid \tilde{\boldsymbol{x}})$.

4. Sample the next state $\boldsymbol{x}$ from $p(\mathbf{x} \mid \boldsymbol{\omega} = g(\boldsymbol{h})) = p(\mathbf{x} \mid \tilde{\boldsymbol{x}})$.

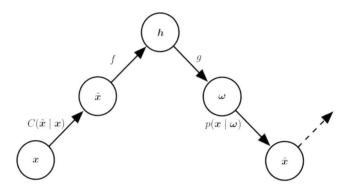

Figure 20.11: Each step of the Markov chain associated with a trained denoising autoencoder, which generates the samples from the probabilistic model implicitly trained by the denoising log-likelihood criterion. Each step consists in (a) injecting noise via corruption process C in state $\boldsymbol{x}$, yielding $\tilde{\boldsymbol{x}}$, (b) encoding it with function f, yielding $\boldsymbol{h} = f(\tilde{\boldsymbol{x}})$, (c) decoding the result with function g, yielding parameters $\boldsymbol{\omega}$ for the reconstruction distribution, and (d) given $\boldsymbol{\omega}$, sampling a new state from the reconstruction distribution $p(\mathbf{x} \mid \boldsymbol{\omega} = g(f(\tilde{\boldsymbol{x}})))$. In the typical squared reconstruction error case, $g(\boldsymbol{h}) = \hat{\boldsymbol{x}}$, which estimates $\mathbb{E}[\boldsymbol{x} \mid \tilde{\boldsymbol{x}}]$, corruption consists of adding Gaussian noise, and sampling from $p(\mathbf{x} \mid \boldsymbol{\omega})$ consists of adding Gaussian noise a second time to the reconstruction $\hat{\boldsymbol{x}}$. The latter noise level should correspond to the mean squared error of reconstructions, whereas the injected noise is a hyperparameter that controls the mixing speed as well as the extent to which the estimator smooths the empirical distribution (Vincent, 2011). In the example illustrated here, only the C and p conditionals are stochastic steps (f and g are deterministic computations), although noise can also be injected inside the autoencoder, as in generative stochastic networks (Bengio et al., 2014).

Bengio et al. (2014) showed that if the autoencoder $p(\mathbf{x} \mid \tilde{\mathbf{x}})$ forms a consistent estimator of the corresponding true conditional distribution, then the stationary distribution of the above Markov chain forms a consistent estimator (albeit an implicit one) of the data-generating distribution of $\mathbf{x}$.

20.11.2 Clamping and Conditional Sampling

Similarly to Boltzmann machines, denoising autoencoders and their generalizations (such as GSNs, described below) can be used to sample from a conditional distribution $p(\mathbf{x}_f \mid \mathbf{x}_o)$, simply by clamping the *observed* units $\mathbf{x}_f$ and only resampling the *free* units $\mathbf{x}_o$ given $\mathbf{x}_f$ and the sampled latent variables (if any). For example, MP-DBMs can be interpreted as a form of denoising autoencoder and are able to sample missing inputs. GSNs later generalized some of the ideas present in MP-DBMs to perform the same operation (Bengio et al., 2014). Alain et al. (2015) identified a missing condition from Proposition 1 of Bengio et al. (2014), which is that the transition operator (defined by the stochastic mapping going from one state of the chain to the next) should satisfy a property called **detailed balance**, which specifies that a Markov chain at equilibrium will remain in equilibrium whether the transition operator is run in forward or reverse.

An experiment in clamping half of the pixels (the right part of the image) and running the Markov chain on the other half is shown in figure 20.12.

20.11.3 Walk-Back Training Procedure

The walk-back training procedure was proposed by Bengio et al. (2013c) as a way to accelerate the convergence of generative training of denoising autoencoders. Instead of performing a one-step encode-decode reconstruction, this procedure consists of alternative multiple stochastic encode-decode steps (as in the generative Markov chain), initialized at a training example (just as with the contrastive divergence algorithm, described in section 18.2), and penalizing the last probabilistic reconstructions (or all the reconstructions along the way).

Training with k steps is equivalent (in the sense of achieving the same stationary distribution) as training with one step but practically has the advantage that spurious modes further from the data can be removed more efficiently.

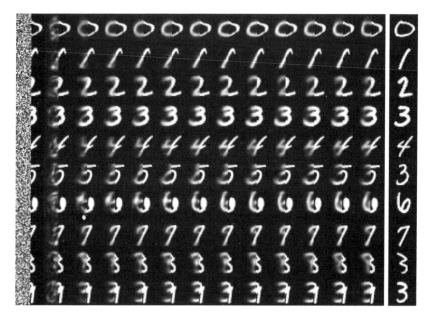

Figure 20.12: Illustration of clamping the right half of the image and running the Markov chain by resampling only the left half at each step. These samples come from a GSN trained to reconstruct MNIST digits at each time step using the walk-back procedure.

20.12 Generative Stochastic Networks

Generative stochastic networks, or GSNs (Bengio et al., 2014) are generalizations of denoising autoencoders that include latent variables $\mathbf{h}$ in the generative Markov chain, in addition to the visible variables (usually denoted $\mathbf{x}$).

A GSN is parametrized by two conditional probability distributions that specify one step of the Markov chain:

1. $p(\mathbf{x}^{(k)} \mid \mathbf{h}^{(k)})$ tells how to generate the next visible variable given the current latent state. Such a "reconstruction distribution" is also found in denoising autoencoders, RBMs, DBNs and DBMs.

2. $p(\mathbf{h}^{(k)} \mid \mathbf{h}^{(k-1)}, \mathbf{x}^{(k-1)})$ tells how to update the latent state variable, given the previous latent state and visible variable.

Denoising autoencoders and GSNs differ from classical probabilistic models (directed or undirected) in that they parametrize the generative process itself rather than the mathematical specification of the joint distribution of visible and latent variables. Instead, the latter is defined *implicitly, if it exists*, as the stationary distribution of the generative Markov chain. The conditions for existence of the stationary distribution are mild and are the same conditions required by standard MCMC methods (see section 17.3). These conditions are necessary to guarantee that the chain mixes, but they can be violated by some choices of the transition distributions (for example, if they are deterministic).

One could imagine different training criteria for GSNs. The one proposed and evaluated by Bengio et al. (2014) is simply reconstruction log-probability on the visible units, just as for denoising autoencoders. This is achieved by clamping $\mathbf{x}^{(0)} = \boldsymbol{x}$ to the observed example and maximizing the probability of generating $\boldsymbol{x}$ at some subsequent time steps, that is, maximizing $\log p(\mathbf{x}^{(k)} = \boldsymbol{x} \mid \mathbf{h}^{(k)})$, where $\mathbf{h}^{(k)}$ is sampled from the chain, given $\mathbf{x}^{(0)} = \boldsymbol{x}$. In order to estimate the gradient of $\log p(\mathbf{x}^{(k)} = \boldsymbol{x} \mid \mathbf{h}^{(k)})$ with respect to the other pieces of the model, Bengio et al. (2014) use the reparametrization trick, introduced in section 20.9.

The walk-back training procedure (described in section 20.11.3) was used (Bengio et al., 2014) to improve training convergence of GSNs.

20.12.1   Discriminant GSNs

The original formulation of GSNs (Bengio et al., 2014) was meant for unsupervised learning and implicitly modeling $p(\mathbf{x})$ for observed data $\mathbf{x}$, but it is possible to modify the framework to optimize $p(\mathbf{y} \mid \boldsymbol{x})$.

For example, Zhou and Troyanskaya (2014) generalize GSNs in this way, by only back-propagating the reconstruction log-probability over the output variables, keeping the input variables fixed. They applied this successfully to model sequences (protein secondary structure) and introduced a (one-dimensional) convolutional structure in the transition operator of the Markov chain. It is important to remember that, for each step of the Markov chain, one generates a new sequence for each layer, and that sequence is the input for computing other layer values (say the one below and the one above) at the next time step.

Hence, the Markov chain is really over the output variable (and associated higher-level hidden layers), and the input sequence only serves to condition that chain, with back-propagation enabling it to learn how the input sequence can condition the output distribution implicitly represented by the Markov chain. It is therefore a case of using the GSN in the context of structured outputs.

Zöhrer and Pernkopf (2014) introduced a hybrid model that combines a supervised objective (as in the above work) and an unsupervised objective (as in the original GSN work) by simply adding (with a different weight) the supervised and unsupervised costs, that is, the reconstruction log-probabilities of $\mathbf{y}$ and $\mathbf{x}$

respectively. Such a hybrid criterion had previously been introduced for RBMs by Larochelle and Bengio (2008). They show improved classification performance using this scheme.

20.13   Other Generation Schemes

The methods we have described so far use either MCMC sampling, ancestral sampling, or some mixture of the two to generate samples. While these are the most popular approaches to generative modeling, they are by no means the only approaches.

Sohl-Dickstein et al. (2015) developed a **diffusion inversion** training scheme for learning a generative model, based on nonequilibrium thermodynamics. The approach is based on the idea that the probability distributions we wish to sample from have structure. This structure can gradually be destroyed by a diffusion process that incrementally changes the probability distribution to have more entropy. To form a generative model, we can run the process in reverse, by training a model that gradually restores the structure to an unstructured distribution. By iteratively applying a process that brings a distribution closer to the target one, we can gradually approach that target distribution. This approach resembles MCMC methods in the sense that it involves many iterations to produce a sample. However, the model is defined to be the probability distribution produced by the final step of the chain. In this sense, there is no approximation induced by the iterative procedure. The approach introduced by Sohl-Dickstein et al. (2015) is also very close to the generative interpretation of the denoising autoencoder (section 20.11.1). As with the denoising autoencoder, diffusion inversion trains a transition operator that attempts to probabilistically undo the effect of adding some noise. The difference is that diffusion inversion requires undoing only one step of the diffusion process, rather than traveling all the way back to a clean data point. This addresses the following dilemma present with the ordinary reconstruction log-likelihood objective of denoising autoencoders: with small levels of noise the learner only sees configurations near the data points, while with large levels of noise it is asked to do an almost impossible job (because the denoising distribution is highly complex and multimodal). With the diffusion inversion objective, the learner can learn the shape of the density around the data points more precisely as well as remove spurious modes that could show up far from the data points.

Another approach to sample generation is the **approximate Bayesian computation** (ABC) framework (Rubin et al., 1984). In this approach, samples are rejected or modified to make the moments of selected functions of the samples match those of the desired distribution. While this idea uses the moments of the samples as in moment matching, it is different from moment matching because it modifies the samples themselves, rather than training the model to automatically emit samples with the correct moments. Bachman and Precup (2015) showed how to use ideas from ABC in the context of deep learning, by using ABC to shape the MCMC trajectories of GSNs.

We expect that many other possible approaches to generative modeling await discovery.

20.14   Evaluating Generative Models

Researchers studying generative models often need to compare one generative model to another, usually in order to demonstrate that a newly invented generative model is better at capturing some distribution than the pre-existing models.

This can be a difficult and subtle task. Often, we cannot actually evaluate the log-probability of the data under the model, but can evaluate only an approximation. In these cases, it is important to think and communicate clearly about what exactly is being measured. For example, suppose we can evaluate a stochastic estimate of the log-likelihood for model A, and a deterministic lower bound on the log-likelihood for model B. If model A gets a higher score than model B, which is better? If we care about determining which model has a better internal representation of the distribution, we actually cannot tell, unless we have some way of determining how loose the bound for model B is. However, if we care about how well we can use the model in practice, for example to perform anomaly detection, then it is fair to say that a model is preferable based on a criterion specific to the practical task of interest, for example, based on ranking test examples and ranking criteria such as precision and recall.

Another subtlety of evaluating generative models is that the evaluation metrics are often hard research problems in and of themselves. It can be very difficult to establish that models are being compared fairly. For example, suppose we use AIS to estimate $\log Z$ in order to compute $\log \tilde{p}(\boldsymbol{x}) - \log Z$ for a new model we have just invented. A computationally economical implementation of AIS may fail to find several modes of the model distribution and underestimate Z, which will result in us overestimating $\log p(\boldsymbol{x})$. It can thus be difficult to tell whether a high likelihood estimate is the result of a good model or a bad AIS implementation.

Other fields of machine learning usually allow for some variation in the pre-processing of the data. For example, when comparing the accuracy of object recognition algorithms, it is usually acceptable to preprocess the input images slightly differently for each algorithm based on what kind of input requirements it has. Generative modeling is different because changes in preprocessing, even very small and subtle ones, are completely unacceptable. Any change to the input data changes the distribution to be captured and fundamentally alters the task. For example, multiplying the input by 0.1 will artificially increase likelihood by a factor of 10.

Issues with preprocessing commonly arise when benchmarking generative models on the MNIST dataset, one of the more popular generative modeling benchmarks. MNIST consists of grayscale images. Some models treat MNIST images as points in a real vector space, while others treat them as binary. Yet others treat the grayscale values as probabilities for binary samples. It is essential to compare real-valued models only to other real-valued models and binary-valued models only to other binary-valued models. Otherwise the likelihoods measured are not on the same space. For binary-valued models, the log-likelihood can be at most zero, while for real-valued models, it can be arbitrarily high, since it is the measurement of a density. Among binary models, it is important to compare models using exactly the same kind of binarization. For example, we might binarize a gray pixel to 0 or 1 by thresholding at 0.5, or by drawing a random sample whose probability of being 1 is given by the gray pixel intensity. If we use the random binarization, we might binarize the whole dataset once, or we might draw a different random example for each step of training and then draw multiple samples for evaluation. Each of these three schemes yields wildly different likelihood numbers, and when comparing different models it is important that both models use the same binarization scheme for training and for evaluation. In fact, researchers who apply a single random binarization step share a file containing the results of the random binarization, so that there is no difference in results based on different outcomes of the binarization step.

Because being able to generate realistic samples from the data distribution is one of the goals of a generative model, practitioners often evaluate generative models by visually inspecting the samples. In the best case, this is done not by the researchers themselves, but by experimental subjects who do not know the source of the samples (Denton et al., 2015). Unfortunately, it is possible for a very poor probabilistic model to produce very good samples. A common practice to verify if the model only copies some of the training examples is illustrated in figure 16.1. The idea is to show for some of the generated samples their nearest neighbor in the training set, according to Euclidean distance in the space of x. This test is intended to detect the case where the model overfits the training set and just reproduces training instances. It is even possible to simultaneously underfit and overfit yet still produce samples that individually look good. Imagine a generative model trained on images of dogs and cats that simply learns to reproduce the training images of dogs. Such a model has clearly overfit, because it does not produces images that were not in the training set, but it has also underfit, because it assigns no probability to the training images of cats. Yet a human observer would judge each individual image of a dog to be high quality. In this simple example, it would be easy for a human observer who can inspect many samples to determine that the cats are absent. In more realistic settings, a generative model trained on data with tens of thousands of modes may ignore a small number of modes, and a human observer would not easily be able to inspect or remember enough images to detect the missing variation.

Since the visual quality of samples is not a reliable guide, we often also evaluate the log-likelihood that the model assigns to the test data, when this is computationally feasible. Unfortunately, in some cases the likelihood seems not to measure any attribute of the model that we really care about. For example, real-valued models of MNIST can obtain arbitrarily high likelihood by assigning arbitrarily low variance to background pixels that never change. Models and algorithms that detect these constant features can reap unlimited rewards, even though this is not a very useful thing to do. The potential to achieve a cost approaching negative infinity is present for any kind of maximum likelihood problem with real values, but it is especially problematic for generative models of MNIST because so many of the output values are trivial to predict. This strongly suggests a need for developing other ways of evaluating generative models.

Theis et al. (2015) review many of the issues involved in evaluating generative models, including many of the ideas described above. They highlight the fact that there are many different uses of generative models and that the choice of metric must match the intended use of the model. For example, some generative models are better at assigning high probability to most realistic points, while other generative models are better at rarely assigning high probability to unrealistic points. These differences can result from whether a generative model is designed to minimize $D_{\mathrm{KL}}(p_{\mathrm{data}}\|p_{\mathrm{model}})$ or $D_{\mathrm{KL}}(p_{\mathrm{model}}\|p_{\mathrm{data}})$, as illustrated in figure 3.6. Unfortunately, even when we restrict the use of each metric to the task it is most suited for, all the metrics currently in use continue to have serious weaknesses. One of the most important research topics in generative modeling is therefore not just how to improve generative models, but in fact, designing new techniques to measure our progress.

20.15   Conclusion

Training generative models with hidden units is a powerful way to make models understand the world represented in the given training data. By learning a model $p_{\text{model}}(\boldsymbol{x})$ and a representation $p_{\text{model}}(\boldsymbol{h} \mid \boldsymbol{x})$, a generative model can provide answers to many inference problems about the relationships between input variables in $\boldsymbol{x}$ and can offer many different ways of representing $\boldsymbol{x}$ by taking expectations of $\boldsymbol{h}$ at different layers of the hierarchy. Generative models hold the promise to provide AI systems with a framework for all the many different intuitive concepts they need to understand, giving them the ability to reason about these concepts in the face of uncertainty. We hope that our readers will find new ways to make these approaches more powerful and continue the journey to understanding the principles that underlie learning and intelligence.

Bibliography

Abadi, M., Agarwal, A., Barham, P., Brevdo, E., Chen, Z., Citro, C., Corrado, G. S., Davis, A., Dean, J., Devin, M., Ghemawat, S., Goodfellow, I., Harp, A., Irving, G., Isard, M., Jia, Y., Jozefowicz, R., Kaiser, L., Kudlur, M., Levenberg, J., Mané, D., Monga, R., Moore, S., Murray, D., Olah, C., Schuster, M., Shlens, J., Steiner, B., Sutskever, I., Talwar, K., Tucker, P., Vanhoucke, V., Vasudevan, V., Viégas, F., Vinyals, O., Warden, P., Wattenberg, M., Wicke, M., Yu, Y., and Zheng, X. (2015). TensorFlow: Large-scale machine learning on heterogeneous systems. Software available from tensorflow.org.

Ackley, D. H., Hinton, G. E., and Sejnowski, T. J. (1985). A learning algorithm for Boltzmann machines. *Cognitive Science*, **9**, 147–169.

Alain, G. and Bengio, Y. (2013). What regularized auto-encoders learn from the data generating distribution. In *ICLR'2013, arXiv:1211.4246*.

Alain, G., Bengio, Y., Yao, L., Éric Thibodeau-Laufer, Yosinski, J., and Vincent, P. (2015). GSNs: Generative stochastic networks. arXiv:1503.05571.

Allen, R. B. (1987). Several studies on natural language and back-propagation. In *IEEE First International Conference on Neural Networks*, volume 2, pages 335–341, San Diego. http://boballen.info/RBA/PAPERS/NL-BP/nl-bp.pdf.

Anderson, E. (1935). The Irises of the Gaspé Peninsula. *Bulletin of the American Iris Society*, **59**, 2–5.

Ba, J., Mnih, V., and Kavukcuoglu, K. (2014). Multiple object recognition with visual attention. *arXiv:1412.7755*.

Bachman, P. and Precup, D. (2015). Variational generative stochastic networks with collaborative shaping. In *Proceedings of the 32nd International Conference on Machine Learning, ICML 2015, Lille, France, 6-11 July 2015*, pages 1964–1972.

Bacon, P.-L., Bengio, E., Pineau, J., and Precup, D. (2015). Conditional computation in neural networks using a decision-theoretic approach. In *2nd Multidisciplinary Conference on Reinforcement Learning and Decision Making (RLDM 2015)*.

Bagnell, J. A. and Bradley, D. M. (2009). Differentiable sparse coding. In D. Koller, D. Schuurmans, Y. Bengio, and L. Bottou, editors, *Advances in Neural Information Processing Systems 21 (NIPS'08)*, pages 113–120.

Bahdanau, D., Cho, K., and Bengio, Y. (2015). Neural machine translation by jointly learning to align and translate. In *ICLR'2015, arXiv:1409.0473*.

Bahl, L. R., Brown, P., de Souza, P. V., and Mercer, R. L. (1987). Speech recognition with continuous-parameter hidden Markov models. *Computer, Speech and Language*, **2**, 219–234.

Baldi, P. and Hornik, K. (1989). Neural networks and principal component analysis: Learning from examples without local minima. *Neural Networks*, **2**, 53–58.

Baldi, P., Brunak, S., Frasconi, P., Soda, G., and Pollastri, G. (1999). Exploiting the past and the future in protein secondary structure prediction. *Bioinformatics*, **15**(11), 937–946.

Baldi, P., Sadowski, P., and Whiteson, D. (2014). Searching for exotic particles in high-energy physics with deep learning. *Nature communications*, **5**.

Ballard, D. H., Hinton, G. E., and Sejnowski, T. J. (1983). Parallel vision computation. *Nature*.

Barlow, H. B. (1989). Unsupervised learning. *Neural Computation*, **1**, 295–311.

Barron, A. E. (1993). Universal approximation bounds for superpositions of a sigmoidal function. *IEEE Trans. on Information Theory*, **39**, 930–945.

Bartholomew, D. J. (1987). *Latent variable models and factor analysis*. Oxford University Press.

Basilevsky, A. (1994). *Statistical Factor Analysis and Related Methods: Theory and Applications*. Wiley.

Bastien, F., Lamblin, P., Pascanu, R., Bergstra, J., Goodfellow, I. J., Bergeron, A., Bouchard, N., and Bengio, Y. (2012). Theano: new features and speed improvements. Deep Learning and Unsupervised Feature Learning NIPS 2012 Workshop.

Basu, S. and Christensen, J. (2013). Teaching classification boundaries to humans. In *AAAI'2013*.

Baxter, J. (1995). Learning internal representations. In *Proceedings of the 8th International Conference on Computational Learning Theory (COLT'95)*, pages 311–320, Santa Cruz, California. ACM Press.

Bayer, J. and Osendorfer, C. (2014). Learning stochastic recurrent networks. *ArXiv e-prints*.

Becker, S. and Hinton, G. (1992). A self-organizing neural network that discovers surfaces in random-dot stereograms. *Nature*, **355**, 161–163.

Behnke, S. (2001). Learning iterative image reconstruction in the neural abstraction pyramid. *Int. J. Computational Intelligence and Applications*, **1**(4), 427–438.

Beiu, V., Quintana, J. M., and Avedillo, M. J. (2003). VLSI implementations of threshold logic-a comprehensive survey. *Neural Networks, IEEE Transactions on*, **14**(5), 1217–1243.

Belkin, M. and Niyogi, P. (2002). Laplacian eigenmaps and spectral techniques for embedding and clustering. In T. Dietterich, S. Becker, and Z. Ghahramani, editors, *Advances in Neural Information Processing Systems 14 (NIPS'01)*, Cambridge, MA. MIT Press.

Belkin, M. and Niyogi, P. (2003). Laplacian eigenmaps for dimensionality reduction and data representation. *Neural Computation*, **15**(6), 1373–1396.

Bengio, E., Bacon, P.-L., Pineau, J., and Precup, D. (2015a). Conditional computation in neural networks for faster models. arXiv:1511.06297.

Bengio, S. and Bengio, Y. (2000a). Taking on the curse of dimensionality in joint distributions using neural networks. *IEEE Transactions on Neural Networks, special issue on Data Mining and Knowledge Discovery*, **11**(3), 550–557.

Bengio, S., Vinyals, O., Jaitly, N., and Shazeer, N. (2015b). Scheduled sampling for sequence prediction with recurrent neural networks. Technical report, arXiv:1506.03099.

Bengio, Y. (1991). *Artificial Neural Networks and their Application to Sequence Recognition*. Ph.D. thesis, McGill University, (Computer Science), Montreal, Canada.

Bengio, Y. (2000). Gradient-based optimization of hyperparameters. *Neural Computation*, **12**(8), 1889–1900.

Bengio, Y. (2002). New distributed probabilistic language models. Technical Report 1215, Dept. IRO, Université de Montréal.

Bengio, Y. (2009). *Learning deep architectures for AI*. Now Publishers.

Bengio, Y. (2013). Deep learning of representations: looking forward. In *Statistical Language and Speech Processing*, volume 7978 of *Lecture Notes in Computer Science*, pages 1–37. Springer, also in arXiv at http://arxiv.org/abs/1305.0445.

Bengio, Y. (2015). Early inference in energy-based models approximates back-propagation. Technical Report arXiv:1510.02777, Universite de Montreal.

Bengio, Y. and Bengio, S. (2000b). Modeling high-dimensional discrete data with multi-layer neural networks. In *NIPS 12*, pages 400–406. MIT Press.

Bengio, Y. and Delalleau, O. (2009). Justifying and generalizing contrastive divergence. *Neural Computation*, **21**(6), 1601–1621.

Bengio, Y. and Grandvalet, Y. (2004). No unbiased estimator of the variance of k-fold cross-validation. In S. Thrun, L. Saul, and B. Schölkopf, editors, *Advances in Neural Information Processing Systems 16 (NIPS'03)*, Cambridge, MA. MIT Press, Cambridge.

Bengio, Y. and LeCun, Y. (2007). Scaling learning algorithms towards AI. In *Large Scale Kernel Machines*.

Bengio, Y. and Monperrus, M. (2005). Non-local manifold tangent learning. In L. Saul, Y. Weiss, and L. Bottou, editors, *Advances in Neural Information Processing Systems 17 (NIPS'04)*, pages 129–136. MIT Press.

Bengio, Y. and Sénécal, J.-S. (2003). Quick training of probabilistic neural nets by importance sampling. In *Proceedings of AISTATS 2003*.

Bengio, Y. and Sénécal, J.-S. (2008). Adaptive importance sampling to accelerate training of a neural probabilistic language model. *IEEE Trans. Neural Networks*, **19**(4), 713–722.

Bengio, Y., De Mori, R., Flammia, G., and Kompe, R. (1991). Phonetically motivated acoustic parameters for continuous speech recognition using artificial neural networks. In *Proceedings of EuroSpeech'91*.

Bengio, Y., De Mori, R., Flammia, G., and Kompe, R. (1992). Neural network-Gaussian mixture hybrid for speech recognition or density estimation. In *NIPS 4*, pages 175–182. Morgan Kaufmann.

Bengio, Y., Frasconi, P., and Simard, P. (1993). The problem of learning long-term dependencies in recurrent networks. In *IEEE International Conference on Neural Networks*, pages 1183–1195, San Francisco. IEEE Press. (invited paper).

Bengio, Y., Simard, P., and Frasconi, P. (1994). Learning long-term dependencies with gradient descent is difficult. *IEEE Tr. Neural Nets*.

Bengio, Y., Latendresse, S., and Dugas, C. (1999). Gradient-based learning of hyperparameters. Learning Conference, Snowbird.

Bengio, Y., Ducharme, R., and Vincent, P. (2001). A neural probabilistic language model. In T. K. Leen, T. G. Dietterich, and V. Tresp, editors, *NIPS'2000*, pages 932–938. MIT Press.

Bengio, Y., Ducharme, R., Vincent, P., and Jauvin, C. (2003). A neural probabilistic language model. *JMLR*, **3**, 1137–1155.

Bengio, Y., Le Roux, N., Vincent, P., Delalleau, O., and Marcotte, P. (2006a). Convex neural networks. In *NIPS'2005*, pages 123–130.

Bengio, Y., Delalleau, O., and Le Roux, N. (2006b). The curse of highly variable functions for local kernel machines. In *NIPS'2005*.

Bengio, Y., Larochelle, H., and Vincent, P. (2006c). Non-local manifold Parzen windows. In *NIPS'2005*. MIT Press.

Bengio, Y., Lamblin, P., Popovici, D., and Larochelle, H. (2007). Greedy layer-wise training of deep networks. In *NIPS'2006*.

Bengio, Y., Louradour, J., Collobert, R., and Weston, J. (2009). Curriculum learning. In *ICML'09*.

Bengio, Y., Mesnil, G., Dauphin, Y., and Rifai, S. (2013a). Better mixing via deep representations. In *ICML'2013*.

Bengio, Y., Léonard, N., and Courville, A. (2013b). Estimating or propagating gradients through stochastic neurons for conditional computation. arXiv:1308.3432.

Bengio, Y., Yao, L., Alain, G., and Vincent, P. (2013c). Generalized denoising auto-encoders as generative models. In *NIPS'2013*.

Bengio, Y., Courville, A., and Vincent, P. (2013d). Representation learning: A review and new perspectives. *IEEE Trans. Pattern Analysis and Machine Intelligence (PAMI)*, **35**(8), 1798–1828.

Bengio, Y., Thibodeau-Laufer, E., Alain, G., and Yosinski, J. (2014). Deep generative stochastic networks trainable by backprop. In *ICML'2014*.

Bennett, C. (1976). Efficient estimation of free energy differences from Monte Carlo data. *Journal of Computational Physics*, **22**(2), 245–268.

Bennett, J. and Lanning, S. (2007). The Netflix prize.

Berger, A. L., Della Pietra, V. J., and Della Pietra, S. A. (1996). A maximum entropy approach to natural language processing. *Computational Linguistics*, **22**, 39–71.

Berglund, M. and Raiko, T. (2013). Stochastic gradient estimate variance in contrastive divergence and persistent contrastive divergence. *CoRR*, **abs/1312.6002**.

Bergstra, J. (2011). *Incorporating Complex Cells into Neural Networks for Pattern Classification*. Ph.D. thesis, Université de Montréal.

Bergstra, J. and Bengio, Y. (2009). Slow, decorrelated features for pretraining complex cell-like networks. In *NIPS'2009*.

Bergstra, J. and Bengio, Y. (2012). Random search for hyper-parameter optimization. *J. Machine Learning Res.*, **13**, 281–305.

Bergstra, J., Breuleux, O., Bastien, F., Lamblin, P., Pascanu, R., Desjardins, G., Turian, J., Warde-Farley, D., and Bengio, Y. (2010). Theano: a CPU and GPU math expression compiler. In *Proc. SciPy*.

Bergstra, J., Bardenet, R., Bengio, Y., and Kégl, B. (2011). Algorithms for hyper-parameter optimization. In *NIPS'2011*.

Berkes, P. and Wiskott, L. (2005). Slow feature analysis yields a rich repertoire of complex cell properties. *Journal of Vision*, **5**(6), 579–602.

Bertsekas, D. P. and Tsitsiklis, J. (1996). *Neuro-Dynamic Programming*. Athena Scientific.

Besag, J. (1975). Statistical analysis of non-lattice data. *The Statistician*, **24**(3), 179–195.

Bishop, C. M. (1994). Mixture density networks.

Bishop, C. M. (1995a). Regularization and complexity control in feed-forward networks. In *Proceedings International Conference on Artificial Neural Networks ICANN'95*, volume 1, page 141–148.

Bishop, C. M. (1995b). Training with noise is equivalent to Tikhonov regularization. *Neural Computation*, **7**(1), 108–116.

Bishop, C. M. (2006). *Pattern Recognition and Machine Learning*. Springer.

Blum, A. L. and Rivest, R. L. (1992). Training a 3-node neural network is NP-complete.

Blumer, A., Ehrenfeucht, A., Haussler, D., and Warmuth, M. K. (1989). Learnability and the Vapnik–Chervonenkis dimension. *Journal of the ACM*, **36**(4), 929—865.

Bonnet, G. (1964). Transformations des signaux aléatoires à travers les systèmes non linéaires sans mémoire. *Annales des Télécommunications*, **19**(9–10), 203–220.

Bordes, A., Weston, J., Collobert, R., and Bengio, Y. (2011). Learning structured embeddings of knowledge bases. In *AAAI 2011*.

Bordes, A., Glorot, X., Weston, J., and Bengio, Y. (2012). Joint learning of words and meaning representations for open-text semantic parsing. *AISTATS'2012*.

Bordes, A., Glorot, X., Weston, J., and Bengio, Y. (2013a). A semantic matching energy function for learning with multi-relational data. *Machine Learning: Special Issue on Learning Semantics*.

Bordes, A., Usunier, N., Garcia-Duran, A., Weston, J., and Yakhnenko, O. (2013b). Translating embeddings for modeling multi-relational data. In C. Burges, L. Bottou, M. Welling, Z. Ghahramani, and K. Weinberger, editors, *Advances in Neural Information Processing Systems 26*, pages 2787–2795. Curran Associates, Inc.

Bornschein, J. and Bengio, Y. (2015). Reweighted wake-sleep. In *ICLR'2015, arXiv:1406.2751*.

Bornschein, J., Shabanian, S., Fischer, A., and Bengio, Y. (2015). Training bidirectional Helmholtz machines. Technical report, arXiv:1506.03877.

Boser, B. E., Guyon, I. M., and Vapnik, V. N. (1992). A training algorithm for optimal margin classifiers. In *COLT '92: Proceedings of the fifth annual workshop on Computational learning theory*, pages 144–152, New York, NY, USA. ACM.

Bottou, L. (1998). Online algorithms and stochastic approximations. In D. Saad, editor, *Online Learning in Neural Networks*. Cambridge University Press, Cambridge, UK.

Bottou, L. (2011). From machine learning to machine reasoning. Technical report, arXiv.1102.1808.

Bottou, L. (2015). Multilayer neural networks. Deep Learning Summer School.

Bottou, L. and Bousquet, O. (2008). The tradeoffs of large scale learning. In *NIPS'2008*.

Boulanger-Lewandowski, N., Bengio, Y., and Vincent, P. (2012). Modeling temporal dependencies in high-dimensional sequences: Application to polyphonic music generation and transcription. In *ICML'12*.

Boureau, Y., Ponce, J., and LeCun, Y. (2010). A theoretical analysis of feature pooling in vision algorithms. In *Proc. International Conference on Machine learning (ICML'10)*.

Boureau, Y., Le Roux, N., Bach, F., Ponce, J., and LeCun, Y. (2011). Ask the locals: multi-way local pooling for image recognition. In *Proc. International Conference on Computer Vision (ICCV'11)*. IEEE.

Bourlard, H. and Kamp, Y. (1988). Auto-association by multilayer perceptrons and singular value decomposition. *Biological Cybernetics*, **59**, 291–294.

Bourlard, H. and Wellekens, C. (1989). Speech pattern discrimination and multi-layered perceptrons. *Computer Speech and Language*, **3**, 1–19.

Boyd, S. and Vandenberghe, L. (2004). *Convex Optimization*. Cambridge University Press, New York, NY, USA.

Brady, M. L., Raghavan, R., and Slawny, J. (1989). Back-propagation fails to separate where perceptrons succeed. *IEEE Transactions on Circuits and Systems*, **36**, 665–674.

Brakel, P., Stroobandt, D., and Schrauwen, B. (2013). Training energy-based models for time-series imputation. *Journal of Machine Learning Research*, **14**, 2771–2797.

Brand, M. (2003). Charting a manifold. In *NIPS'2002*, pages 961–968. MIT Press.

Breiman, L. (1994). Bagging predictors. *Machine Learning*, **24**(2), 123–140.

Breiman, L., Friedman, J. H., Olshen, R. A., and Stone, C. J. (1984). *Classification and Regression Trees*. Wadsworth International Group, Belmont, CA.

Bridle, J. S. (1990). Alphanets: a recurrent 'neural' network architecture with a hidden Markov model interpretation. *Speech Communication*, **9**(1), 83–92.

Briggman, K., Denk, W., Seung, S., Helmstaedter, M. N., and Turaga, S. C. (2009). Maximin affinity learning of image segmentation. In *NIPS'2009*, pages 1865–1873.

Brown, P. F., Cocke, J., Pietra, S. A. D., Pietra, V. J. D., Jelinek, F., Lafferty, J. D., Mercer, R. L., and Roossin, P. S. (1990). A statistical approach to machine translation. *Computational linguistics*, **16**(2), 79–85.

Brown, P. F., Pietra, V. J. D., DeSouza, P. V., Lai, J. C., and Mercer, R. L. (1992). Class-based *n*-gram models of natural language. *Computational Linguistics*, **18**, 467–479.

Bryson, A. and Ho, Y. (1969). *Applied optimal control: optimization, estimation, and control*. Blaisdell Pub. Co.

Bryson, Jr., A. E. and Denham, W. F. (1961). A steepest-ascent method for solving optimum programming problems. Technical Report BR-1303, Raytheon Company, Missle and Space Division.

Buciluă, C., Caruana, R., and Niculescu-Mizil, A. (2006). Model compression. In *Proceedings of the 12th ACM SIGKDD international conference on Knowledge discovery and data mining*, pages 535–541. ACM.

Burda, Y., Grosse, R., and Salakhutdinov, R. (2015). Importance weighted autoencoders. *arXiv preprint arXiv:1509.00519*.

Cai, M., Shi, Y., and Liu, J. (2013). Deep maxout neural networks for speech recognition. In *Automatic Speech Recognition and Understanding (ASRU), 2013 IEEE Workshop on*, pages 291–296. IEEE.

Carreira-Perpiñan, M. A. and Hinton, G. E. (2005). On contrastive divergence learning. In R. G. Cowell and Z. Ghahramani, editors, *Proceedings of the Tenth International Workshop on Artificial Intelligence and Statistics (AISTATS'05)*, pages 33–40. Society for Artificial Intelligence and Statistics.

Caruana, R. (1993). Multitask connectionist learning. In *Proc. 1993 Connectionist Models Summer School*, pages 372–379.

Cauchy, A. (1847). Méthode générale pour la résolution de systèmes d'équations simultanées. In *Compte rendu des séances de l'académie des sciences*, pages 536–538.

Cayton, L. (2005). Algorithms for manifold learning. Technical Report CS2008-0923, UCSD.

Chandola, V., Banerjee, A., and Kumar, V. (2009). Anomaly detection: A survey. *ACM computing surveys (CSUR)*, **41**(3), 15.

Chapelle, O., Weston, J., and Schölkopf, B. (2003). Cluster kernels for semi-supervised learning. In S. Becker, S. Thrun, and K. Obermayer, editors, *Advances in Neural Information Processing Systems 15 (NIPS'02)*, pages 585–592, Cambridge, MA. MIT Press.

Chapelle, O., Schölkopf, B., and Zien, A., editors (2006). *Semi-Supervised Learning*. MIT Press, Cambridge, MA.

Chellapilla, K., Puri, S., and Simard, P. (2006). High Performance Convolutional Neural Networks for Document Processing. In Guy Lorette, editor, *Tenth International Workshop on Frontiers in Handwriting Recognition*, La Baule (France). Université de Rennes 1, Suvisoft. http://www.suvisoft.com.

Chen, B., Ting, J.-A., Marlin, B. M., and de Freitas, N. (2010). Deep learning of invariant spatio-temporal features from video. NIPS*2010 Deep Learning and Unsupervised Feature Learning Workshop.

Chen, S. F. and Goodman, J. T. (1999). An empirical study of smoothing techniques for language modeling. *Computer, Speech and Language*, **13**(4), 359–393.

Chen, T., Du, Z., Sun, N., Wang, J., Wu, C., Chen, Y., and Temam, O. (2014a). DianNao: A small-footprint high-throughput accelerator for ubiquitous machine-learning. In *Proceedings of the 19th international conference on Architectural support for programming languages and operating systems*, pages 269–284. ACM.

Chen, T., Li, M., Li, Y., Lin, M., Wang, N., Wang, M., Xiao, T., Xu, B., Zhang, C., and Zhang, Z. (2015). MXNet: A flexible and efficient machine learning library for heterogeneous distributed systems. *arXiv preprint arXiv:1512.01274*.

Chen, Y., Luo, T., Liu, S., Zhang, S., He, L., Wang, J., Li, L., Chen, T., Xu, Z., Sun, N., et al. (2014b). DaDianNao: A machine-learning supercomputer. In *Microarchitecture (MICRO), 2014 47th Annual IEEE/ACM International Symposium on*, pages 609–622. IEEE.

Chilimbi, T., Suzue, Y., Apacible, J., and Kalyanaraman, K. (2014). Project Adam: Building an efficient and scalable deep learning training system. In *11th USENIX Symposium on Operating Systems Design and Implementation (OSDI'14)*.

Cho, K., Raiko, T., and Ilin, A. (2010). Parallel tempering is efficient for learning restricted Boltzmann machines. In *IJCNN'2010*.

Cho, K., Raiko, T., and Ilin, A. (2011). Enhanced gradient and adaptive learning rate for training restricted Boltzmann machines. In *ICML'2011*, pages 105–112.

Cho, K., van Merriënboer, B., Gulcehre, C., Bougares, F., Schwenk, H., and Bengio, Y. (2014a). Learning phrase representations using RNN encoder-decoder for statistical machine translation. In *Proceedings of the Empiricial Methods in Natural Language Processing (EMNLP 2014)*.

Cho, K., Van Merriënboer, B., Bahdanau, D., and Bengio, Y. (2014b). On the properties of neural machine translation: Encoder-decoder approaches. *ArXiv e-prints*, **abs/1409.1259**.

Choromanska, A., Henaff, M., Mathieu, M., Arous, G. B., and LeCun, Y. (2014). The loss surface of multilayer networks.

Chorowski, J., Bahdanau, D., Cho, K., and Bengio, Y. (2014). End-to-end continuous speech recognition using attention-based recurrent NN: First results. arXiv:1412.1602.

Chrisman, L. (1991). Learning recursive distributed representations for holistic computation. *Connection Science*, **3**(4), 345–366. http://repository.cmu.edu/cgi/viewcontent.cgi?article=3061&context=compsci.

Christianson, B. (1992). Automatic Hessians by reverse accumulation. *IMA Journal of Numerical Analysis*, **12**(2), 135–150.

Chrupala, G., Kadar, A., and Alishahi, A. (2015). Learning language through pictures. arXiv 1506.03694.

Chung, J., Gulcehre, C., Cho, K., and Bengio, Y. (2014). Empirical evaluation of gated recurrent neural networks on sequence modeling. NIPS'2014 Deep Learning workshop, arXiv 1412.3555.

Chung, J., Gülçehre, Ç., Cho, K., and Bengio, Y. (2015a). Gated feedback recurrent neural networks. In *ICML'15*.

Chung, J., Kastner, K., Dinh, L., Goel, K., Courville, A., and Bengio, Y. (2015b). A recurrent latent variable model for sequential data. In *NIPS'2015*.

Ciresan, D., Meier, U., Masci, J., and Schmidhuber, J. (2012). Multi-column deep neural network for traffic sign classification. *Neural Networks*, **32**, 333–338.

Ciresan, D. C., Meier, U., Gambardella, L. M., and Schmidhuber, J. (2010). Deep big simple neural nets for handwritten digit recognition. *Neural Computation*, **22**, 1–14.

Coates, A. and Ng, A. Y. (2011). The importance of encoding versus training with sparse coding and vector quantization. In *ICML'2011*.

Coates, A., Lee, H., and Ng, A. Y. (2011). An analysis of single-layer networks in unsupervised feature learning. In *Proceedings of the Thirteenth International Conference on Artificial Intelligence and Statistics (AISTATS 2011)*.

Coates, A., Huval, B., Wang, T., Wu, D., Catanzaro, B., and Andrew, N. (2013). Deep learning with COTS HPC systems. In S. Dasgupta and D. McAllester, editors, *Proceedings of the 30th International Conference on Machine Learning (ICML-13)*, volume 28 (3), pages 1337–1345. JMLR Workshop and Conference Proceedings.

Cohen, N., Sharir, O., and Shashua, A. (2015). On the expressive power of deep learning: A tensor analysis. arXiv:1509.05009.

Collobert, R. (2004). *Large Scale Machine Learning*. Ph.D. thesis, Université de Paris VI, LIP6.

Collobert, R. (2011). Deep learning for efficient discriminative parsing. In *AISTATS'2011*.

Collobert, R. and Weston, J. (2008a). A unified architecture for natural language processing: Deep neural networks with multitask learning. In *ICML'2008*.

Collobert, R. and Weston, J. (2008b). A unified architecture for natural language processing: Deep neural networks with multitask learning. In *ICML'2008*.

Collobert, R., Bengio, S., and Bengio, Y. (2001). A parallel mixture of SVMs for very large scale problems. Technical Report IDIAP-RR-01-12, IDIAP.

Collobert, R., Bengio, S., and Bengio, Y. (2002). Parallel mixture of SVMs for very large scale problems. *Neural Computation*, **14**(5), 1105–1114.

Collobert, R., Weston, J., Bottou, L., Karlen, M., Kavukcuoglu, K., and Kuksa, P. (2011a). Natural language processing (almost) from scratch. *The Journal of Machine Learning Research*, **12**, 2493–2537.

Collobert, R., Kavukcuoglu, K., and Farabet, C. (2011b). Torch7: A Matlab-like environment for machine learning. In *BigLearn, NIPS Workshop*.

Comon, P. (1994). Independent component analysis - a new concept? *Signal Processing*, **36**, 287–314.

Cortes, C. and Vapnik, V. (1995). Support vector networks. *Machine Learning*, **20**, 273–297.

Couprie, C., Farabet, C., Najman, L., and LeCun, Y. (2013). Indoor semantic segmentation using depth information. In *International Conference on Learning Representations (ICLR2013)*.

Courbariaux, M., Bengio, Y., and David, J.-P. (2015). Low precision arithmetic for deep learning. In *Arxiv:1412.7024, ICLR'2015 Workshop*.

Courville, A., Bergstra, J., and Bengio, Y. (2011). Unsupervised models of images by spike-and-slab RBMs. In *ICML'11*.

Courville, A., Desjardins, G., Bergstra, J., and Bengio, Y. (2014). The spike-and-slab RBM and extensions to discrete and sparse data distributions. *Pattern Analysis and Machine Intelligence, IEEE Transactions on*, **36**(9), 1874–1887.

Cover, T. M. and Thomas, J. A. (2006). *Elements of Information Theory, 2nd Edition*. Wiley-Interscience.

Cox, D. and Pinto, N. (2011). Beyond simple features: A large-scale feature search approach to unconstrained face recognition. In *Automatic Face & Gesture Recognition and Workshops (FG 2011), 2011 IEEE International Conference on*, pages 8–15. IEEE.

Cramér, H. (1946). *Mathematical methods of statistics*. Princeton University Press.

Crick, F. H. C. and Mitchison, G. (1983). The function of dream sleep. *Nature*, **304**, 111–114.

Cybenko, G. (1989). Approximation by superpositions of a sigmoidal function. *Mathematics of Control, Signals, and Systems*, **2**, 303–314.

Dahl, G. E., Ranzato, M., Mohamed, A., and Hinton, G. E. (2010). Phone recognition with the mean-covariance restricted Boltzmann machine. In *NIPS'2010*.

Dahl, G. E., Yu, D., Deng, L., and Acero, A. (2012). Context-dependent pre-trained deep neural networks for large vocabulary speech recognition. *IEEE Transactions on Audio, Speech, and Language Processing*, **20**(1), 33–42.

Dahl, G. E., Sainath, T. N., and Hinton, G. E. (2013). Improving deep neural networks for LVCSR using rectified linear units and dropout. In *ICASSP'2013*.

Dahl, G. E., Jaitly, N., and Salakhutdinov, R. (2014). Multi-task neural networks for QSAR predictions. arXiv:1406.1231.

Dauphin, Y. and Bengio, Y. (2013). Stochastic ratio matching of RBMs for sparse high-dimensional inputs. In *NIPS26*. NIPS Foundation.

Dauphin, Y., Glorot, X., and Bengio, Y. (2011). Large-scale learning of embeddings with reconstruction sampling. In *ICML'2011*.

Dauphin, Y., Pascanu, R., Gulcehre, C., Cho, K., Ganguli, S., and Bengio, Y. (2014). Identifying and attacking the saddle point problem in high-dimensional non-convex optimization. In *NIPS'2014*.

Davis, A., Rubinstein, M., Wadhwa, N., Mysore, G., Durand, F., and Freeman, W. T. (2014). The visual microphone: Passive recovery of sound from video. *ACM Transactions on Graphics (Proc. SIGGRAPH)*, **33**(4), 79:1–79:10.

Dayan, P. (1990). Reinforcement comparison. In *Connectionist Models: Proceedings of the 1990 Connectionist Summer School*, San Mateo, CA.

Dayan, P. and Hinton, G. E. (1996). Varieties of Helmholtz machine. *Neural Networks*, **9**(8), 1385–1403.

Dayan, P., Hinton, G. E., Neal, R. M., and Zemel, R. S. (1995). The Helmholtz machine. *Neural computation*, **7**(5), 889–904.

Dean, J., Corrado, G., Monga, R., Chen, K., Devin, M., Le, Q., Mao, M., Ranzato, M., Senior, A., Tucker, P., Yang, K., and Ng, A. Y. (2012). Large scale distributed deep networks. In *NIPS'2012*.

Dean, T. and Kanazawa, K. (1989). A model for reasoning about persistence and causation. *Computational Intelligence*, **5**(3), 142–150.

Deerwester, S., Dumais, S. T., Furnas, G. W., Landauer, T. K., and Harshman, R. (1990). Indexing by latent semantic analysis. *Journal of the American Society for Information Science*, **41**(6), 391–407.

Delalleau, O. and Bengio, Y. (2011). Shallow vs. deep sum-product networks. In *NIPS*.

Deng, J., Dong, W., Socher, R., Li, L.-J., Li, K., and Fei-Fei, L. (2009). ImageNet: A Large-Scale Hierarchical Image Database. In *CVPR09*.

Deng, J., Berg, A. C., Li, K., and Fei-Fei, L. (2010a). What does classifying more than 10,000 image categories tell us? In *Proceedings of the 11th European Conference on Computer Vision: Part V*, ECCV'10, pages 71–84, Berlin, Heidelberg. Springer-Verlag.

Deng, L. and Yu, D. (2014). Deep learning – methods and applications. *Foundations and Trends in Signal Processing*.

Deng, L., Seltzer, M., Yu, D., Acero, A., Mohamed, A., and Hinton, G. (2010b). Binary coding of speech spectrograms using a deep auto-encoder. In *Interspeech 2010*, Makuhari, Chiba, Japan.

Denil, M., Bazzani, L., Larochelle, H., and de Freitas, N. (2012). Learning where to attend with deep architectures for image tracking. *Neural Computation*, **24**(8), 2151–2184.

Denton, E., Chintala, S., Szlam, A., and Fergus, R. (2015). Deep generative image models using a Laplacian pyramid of adversarial networks. *NIPS*.

Desjardins, G. and Bengio, Y. (2008). Empirical evaluation of convolutional RBMs for vision. Technical Report 1327, Département d'Informatique et de Recherche Opérationnelle, Université de Montréal.

Desjardins, G., Courville, A. C., Bengio, Y., Vincent, P., and Delalleau, O. (2010). Tempered Markov chain Monte Carlo for training of restricted Boltzmann machines. In *International Conference on Artificial Intelligence and Statistics*, pages 145–152.

Desjardins, G., Courville, A., and Bengio, Y. (2011). On tracking the partition function. In *NIPS'2011*.

Desjardins, G., Simonyan, K., Pascanu, R., et al. (2015). Natural neural networks. In *Advances in Neural Information Processing Systems*, pages 2062–2070.

Devlin, J., Zbib, R., Huang, Z., Lamar, T., Schwartz, R., and Makhoul, J. (2014). Fast and robust neural network joint models for statistical machine translation. In *Proc. ACL'2014*.

Devroye, L. (2013). *Non-Uniform Random Variate Generation*. SpringerLink : Bücher. Springer New York.

DiCarlo, J. J. (2013). Mechanisms underlying visual object recognition: Humans vs. neurons vs. machines. NIPS Tutorial.

Dinh, L., Krueger, D., and Bengio, Y. (2014). NICE: Non-linear independent components estimation. arXiv:1410.8516.

Donahue, J., Hendricks, L. A., Guadarrama, S., Rohrbach, M., Venugopalan, S., Saenko, K., and Darrell, T. (2014). Long-term recurrent convolutional networks for visual recognition and description. arXiv:1411.4389.

Donoho, D. L. and Grimes, C. (2003). Hessian eigenmaps: new locally linear embedding techniques for high-dimensional data. Technical Report 2003-08, Dept. Statistics, Stanford University.

Dosovitskiy, A., Springenberg, J. T., and Brox, T. (2015). Learning to generate chairs with convolutional neural networks. In *Proceedings of the IEEE Conference on Computer Vision and Pattern Recognition*, pages 1538–1546.

Doya, K. (1993). Bifurcations of recurrent neural networks in gradient descent learning. *IEEE Transactions on Neural Networks*, **1**, 75–80.

Dreyfus, S. E. (1962). The numerical solution of variational problems. *Journal of Mathematical Analysis and Applications*, **5(1)**, 30–45.

Dreyfus, S. E. (1973). The computational solution of optimal control problems with time lag. *IEEE Transactions on Automatic Control*, **18(4)**, 383–385.

Drucker, H. and LeCun, Y. (1992). Improving generalisation performance using double back-propagation. *IEEE Transactions on Neural Networks*, **3**(6), 991–997.

Duchi, J., Hazan, E., and Singer, Y. (2011). Adaptive subgradient methods for online learning and stochastic optimization. *Journal of Machine Learning Research*.

Dudik, M., Langford, J., and Li, L. (2011). Doubly robust policy evaluation and learning. In *Proceedings of the 28th International Conference on Machine learning*, ICML '11.

Dugas, C., Bengio, Y., Bélisle, F., and Nadeau, C. (2001). Incorporating second-order functional knowledge for better option pricing. In T. Leen, T. Dietterich, and V. Tresp, editors, *Advances in Neural Information Processing Systems 13 (NIPS'00)*, pages 472–478. MIT Press.

Dziugaite, G. K., Roy, D. M., and Ghahramani, Z. (2015). Training generative neural networks via maximum mean discrepancy optimization. *arXiv preprint arXiv:1505.03906*.

El Hihi, S. and Bengio, Y. (1996). Hierarchical recurrent neural networks for long-term dependencies. In *NIPS'1995*.

Elkahky, A. M., Song, Y., and He, X. (2015). A multi-view deep learning approach for cross domain user modeling in recommendation systems. In *Proceedings of the 24th International Conference on World Wide Web*, pages 278–288.

Elman, J. L. (1993). Learning and development in neural networks: The importance of starting small. *Cognition*, **48**, 781–799.

Erhan, D., Manzagol, P.-A., Bengio, Y., Bengio, S., and Vincent, P. (2009). The difficulty of training deep architectures and the effect of unsupervised pre-training. In *Proceedings of AISTATS'2009*.

Erhan, D., Bengio, Y., Courville, A., Manzagol, P., Vincent, P., and Bengio, S. (2010). Why does unsupervised pre-training help deep learning? *J. Machine Learning Res.*

Fahlman, S. E., Hinton, G. E., and Sejnowski, T. J. (1983). Massively parallel architectures for AI: NETL, thistle, and Boltzmann machines. In *Proceedings of the National Conference on Artificial Intelligence AAAI-83*.

Fang, H., Gupta, S., Iandola, F., Srivastava, R., Deng, L., Dollár, P., Gao, J., He, X., Mitchell, M., Platt, J. C., Zitnick, C. L., and Zweig, G. (2015). From captions to visual concepts and back. arXiv:1411.4952.

Farabet, C., LeCun, Y., Kavukcuoglu, K., Culurciello, E., Martini, B., Akselrod, P., and Talay, S. (2011). Large-scale FPGA-based convolutional networks. In R. Bekkerman, M. Bilenko, and J. Langford, editors, *Scaling up Machine Learning: Parallel and Distributed Approaches*. Cambridge University Press.

Farabet, C., Couprie, C., Najman, L., and LeCun, Y. (2013). Learning hierarchical features for scene labeling. *IEEE Transactions on Pattern Analysis and Machine Intelligence*, **35**(8), 1915–1929.

Fei-Fei, L., Fergus, R., and Perona, P. (2006). One-shot learning of object categories. *IEEE Transactions on Pattern Analysis and Machine Intelligence*, **28**(4), 594–611.

Finn, C., Tan, X. Y., Duan, Y., Darrell, T., Levine, S., and Abbeel, P. (2015). Learning visual feature spaces for robotic manipulation with deep spatial autoencoders. *arXiv preprint arXiv:1509.06113*.

Fisher, R. A. (1936). The use of multiple measurements in taxonomic problems. *Annals of Eugenics*, **7**, 179–188.

Földiák, P. (1989). Adaptive network for optimal linear feature extraction. In *International Joint Conference on Neural Networks (IJCNN)*, volume 1, pages 401–405, Washington 1989. IEEE, New York.

Forcada, M., and Ñeco, R. (1997). Recursive hetero-associative memories for translation. In *Biological and Artificial Computation: From Neuroscience to Technology*, pages 453–462. http://citeseerx.ist.psu.edu/viewdoc/summary?doi=10.1.1.43.1968.

Franzius, M., Sprekeler, H., and Wiskott, L. (2007). Slowness and sparseness lead to place, head-direction, and spatial-view cells.

Franzius, M., Wilbert, N., and Wiskott, L. (2008). Invariant object recognition with slow feature analysis. In *Artificial Neural Networks-ICANN 2008*, pages 961–970. Springer.

Frasconi, P., Gori, M., and Sperduti, A. (1997). On the efficient classification of data structures by neural networks. In *Proc. Int. Joint Conf. on Artificial Intelligence*.

Frasconi, P., Gori, M., and Sperduti, A. (1998). A general framework for adaptive processing of data structures. *IEEE Transactions on Neural Networks*, **9**(5), 768–786.

Freund, Y. and Schapire, R. E. (1996a). Experiments with a new boosting algorithm. In *Machine Learning: Proceedings of Thirteenth International Conference*, pages 148–156, USA. ACM.

Freund, Y. and Schapire, R. E. (1996b). Game theory, on-line prediction and boosting. In *Proceedings of the Ninth Annual Conference on Computational Learning Theory*, pages 325–332.

Frey, B. J. (1998). *Graphical models for machine learning and digital communication*. MIT Press.

Frey, B. J., Hinton, G. E., and Dayan, P. (1996). Does the wake-sleep algorithm learn good density estimators? In D. Touretzky, M. Mozer, and M. Hasselmo, editors, *Advances in Neural Information Processing Systems 8 (NIPS'95)*, pages 661–670. MIT Press, Cambridge, MA.

Frobenius, G. (1908). Über matrizen aus positiven elementen, s. *B. Preuss. Akad. Wiss. Berlin, Germany*.

Fukushima, K. (1975). Cognitron: A self-organizing multilayered neural network. *Biological Cybernetics*, **20**, 121–136.

Fukushima, K. (1980). Neocognitron: A self-organizing neural network model for a mechanism of pattern recognition unaffected by shift in position. *Biological Cybernetics*, **36**, 193–202.

Gal, Y. and Ghahramani, Z. (2015). Bayesian convolutional neural networks with Bernoulli approximate variational inference. *arXiv preprint arXiv:1506.02158*.

Gallinari, P., LeCun, Y., Thiria, S., and Fogelman-Soulie, F. (1987). Memoires associatives distribuees. In *Proceedings of COGNITIVA 87*, Paris, La Villette.

Garcia-Duran, A., Bordes, A., Usunier, N., and Grandvalet, Y. (2015). Combining two and three-way embeddings models for link prediction in knowledge bases. *arXiv preprint arXiv:1506.00999*.

Garofolo, J. S., Lamel, L. F., Fisher, W. M., Fiscus, J. G., and Pallett, D. S. (1993). Darpa timit acoustic-phonetic continous speech corpus cd-rom. nist speech disc 1-1.1. *NASA STI/Recon Technical Report N*, **93**, 27403.

Garson, J. (1900). The metric system of identification of criminals, as used in Great Britain and Ireland. *The Journal of the Anthropological Institute of Great Britain and Ireland*, (2), 177–227.

Gers, F. A., Schmidhuber, J., and Cummins, F. (2000). Learning to forget: Continual prediction with LSTM. *Neural computation*, **12**(10), 2451–2471.

Ghahramani, Z. and Hinton, G. E. (1996). The EM algorithm for mixtures of factor analyzers. Technical Report CRG-TR-96-1, Dpt. of Comp. Sci., Univ. of Toronto.

Gillick, D., Brunk, C., Vinyals, O., and Subramanya, A. (2015). Multilingual language processing from bytes. *arXiv preprint arXiv:1512.00103*.

Girshick, R., Donahue, J., Darrell, T., and Malik, J. (2015). Region-based convolutional networks for accurate object detection and segmentation.

Giudice, M. D., Manera, V., and Keysers, C. (2009). Programmed to learn? The ontogeny of mirror neurons. *Dev. Sci.*, **12**(2), 350—363.

Glorot, X. and Bengio, Y. (2010). Understanding the difficulty of training deep feedforward neural networks. In *AISTATS'2010*.

Glorot, X., Bordes, A., and Bengio, Y. (2011a). Deep sparse rectifier neural networks. In *AISTATS'2011*.

Glorot, X., Bordes, A., and Bengio, Y. (2011b). Domain adaptation for large-scale sentiment classification: A deep learning approach. In *ICML'2011*.

Goldberger, J., Roweis, S., Hinton, G. E., and Salakhutdinov, R. (2005). Neighbourhood components analysis. In L. Saul, Y. Weiss, and L. Bottou, editors, *Advances in Neural Information Processing Systems 17 (NIPS'04)*. MIT Press.

Gong, S., McKenna, S., and Psarrou, A. (2000). *Dynamic Vision: From Images to Face Recognition*. Imperial College Press.

Goodfellow, I., Le, Q., Saxe, A., and Ng, A. (2009). Measuring invariances in deep networks. In *NIPS'2009*, pages 646–654.

Goodfellow, I., Koenig, N., Muja, M., Pantofaru, C., Sorokin, A., and Takayama, L. (2010). Help me help you: Interfaces for personal robots. In *Proc. of Human Robot Interaction (HRI)*, Osaka, Japan. ACM Press, ACM Press.

Goodfellow, I. J. (2010). Technical report: Multidimensional, downsampled convolution for autoencoders. Technical report, Université de Montréal.

Goodfellow, I. J. (2014). On distinguishability criteria for estimating generative models. In *International Conference on Learning Representations, Workshops Track*.

Goodfellow, I. J., Courville, A., and Bengio, Y. (2011). Spike-and-slab sparse coding for unsupervised feature discovery. In *NIPS Workshop on Challenges in Learning Hierarchical Models*.

Goodfellow, I. J., Warde-Farley, D., Mirza, M., Courville, A., and Bengio, Y. (2013a). Maxout networks. In S. Dasgupta and D. McAllester, editors, *ICML'13*, pages 1319–1327.

Goodfellow, I. J., Mirza, M., Courville, A., and Bengio, Y. (2013b). Multi-prediction deep Boltzmann machines. In *NIPS26*. NIPS Foundation.

Goodfellow, I. J., Warde-Farley, D., Lamblin, P., Dumoulin, V., Mirza, M., Pascanu, R., Bergstra, J., Bastien, F., and Bengio, Y. (2013c). Pylearn2: a machine learning research library. *arXiv preprint arXiv:1308.4214*.

Goodfellow, I. J., Courville, A., and Bengio, Y. (2013d). Scaling up spike-and-slab models for unsupervised feature learning. *IEEE Transactions on Pattern Analysis and Machine Intelligence*, **35**(8), 1902–1914.

Goodfellow, I. J., Mirza, M., Xiao, D., Courville, A., and Bengio, Y. (2014a). An empirical investigation of catastrophic forgetting in gradient-based neural networks. In *ICLR'2014*.

Goodfellow, I. J., Shlens, J., and Szegedy, C. (2014b). Explaining and harnessing adversarial examples. *CoRR*, **abs/1412.6572**.

Goodfellow, I. J., Pouget-Abadie, J., Mirza, M., Xu, B., Warde-Farley, D., Ozair, S., Courville, A., and Bengio, Y. (2014c). Generative adversarial networks. In *NIPS'2014*.

Goodfellow, I. J., Bulatov, Y., Ibarz, J., Arnoud, S., and Shet, V. (2014d). Multi-digit number recognition from Street View imagery using deep convolutional neural networks. In *International Conference on Learning Representations*.

Goodfellow, I. J., Vinyals, O., and Saxe, A. M. (2015). Qualitatively characterizing neural network optimization problems. In *International Conference on Learning Representations*.

Goodman, J. (2001). Classes for fast maximum entropy training. In *International Conference on Acoustics, Speech and Signal Processing (ICASSP)*, Utah.

Gori, M. and Tesi, A. (1992). On the problem of local minima in backpropagation. *IEEE Transactions on Pattern Analysis and Machine Intelligence*, **PAMI-14**(1), 76–86.

Gosset, W. S. (1908). The probable error of a mean. *Biometrika*, **6**(1), 1–25. Originally published under the pseudonym "Student".

Gouws, S., Bengio, Y., and Corrado, G. (2014). BilBOWA: Fast bilingual distributed representations without word alignments. Technical report, arXiv:1410.2455.

Graf, H. P. and Jackel, L. D. (1989). Analog electronic neural network circuits. *Circuits and Devices Magazine, IEEE*, **5**(4), 44–49.

Graves, A. (2011). Practical variational inference for neural networks. In *NIPS'2011*.

Graves, A. (2012). *Supervised Sequence Labelling with Recurrent Neural Networks*. Studies in Computational Intelligence. Springer.

Graves, A. (2013). Generating sequences with recurrent neural networks. Technical report, arXiv:1308.0850.

Graves, A. and Jaitly, N. (2014). Towards end-to-end speech recognition with recurrent neural networks. In *ICML'2014*.

Graves, A. and Schmidhuber, J. (2005). Framewise phoneme classification with bidirectional LSTM and other neural network architectures. *Neural Networks*, **18**(5), 602–610.

Graves, A. and Schmidhuber, J. (2009). Offline handwriting recognition with multidimensional recurrent neural networks. In D. Koller, D. Schuurmans, Y. Bengio, and L. Bottou, editors, *NIPS'2008*, pages 545–552.

Graves, A., Fernández, S., Gomez, F., and Schmidhuber, J. (2006). Connectionist temporal classification: Labelling unsegmented sequence data with recurrent neural networks. In *ICML'2006*, pages 369–376, Pittsburgh, USA.

Graves, A., Liwicki, M., Bunke, H., Schmidhuber, J., and Fernández, S. (2008). Unconstrained on-line handwriting recognition with recurrent neural networks. In J. Platt, D. Koller, Y. Singer, and S. Roweis, editors, *NIPS'2007*, pages 577–584.

Graves, A., Liwicki, M., Fernández, S., Bertolami, R., Bunke, H., and Schmidhuber, J. (2009). A novel connectionist system for unconstrained handwriting recognition. *Pattern Analysis and Machine Intelligence, IEEE Transactions on*, **31**(5), 855–868.

Graves, A., Mohamed, A., and Hinton, G. (2013). Speech recognition with deep recurrent neural networks. In *ICASSP'2013*, pages 6645–6649.

Graves, A., Wayne, G., and Danihelka, I. (2014a). Neural Turing machines. arXiv:1410.5401.

Graves, A., Wayne, G., and Danihelka, I. (2014b). Neural Turing machines. *arXiv preprint arXiv:1410.5401*.

Grefenstette, E., Hermann, K. M., Suleyman, M., and Blunsom, P. (2015). Learning to transduce with unbounded memory. In *NIPS'2015*.

Greff, K., Srivastava, R. K., Koutník, J., Steunebrink, B. R., and Schmidhuber, J. (2015). LSTM: a search space odyssey. *arXiv preprint arXiv:1503.04069*.

Gregor, K. and LeCun, Y. (2010a). Emergence of complex-like cells in a temporal product network with local receptive fields. Technical report, arXiv:1006.0448.

Gregor, K. and LeCun, Y. (2010b). Learning fast approximations of sparse coding. In L. Bottou and M. Littman, editors, *Proceedings of the Twenty-seventh International Conference on Machine Learning (ICML-10)*. ACM.

Gregor, K., Danihelka, I., Mnih, A., Blundell, C., and Wierstra, D. (2014). Deep autoregressive networks. In *International Conference on Machine Learning (ICML'2014)*.

Gregor, K., Danihelka, I., Graves, A., and Wierstra, D. (2015). DRAW: A recurrent neural network for image generation. *arXiv preprint arXiv:1502.04623*.

Gretton, A., Borgwardt, K. M., Rasch, M. J., Schölkopf, B., and Smola, A. (2012). A kernel two-sample test. *The Journal of Machine Learning Research*, **13**(1), 723–773.

Gülçehre, Ç. and Bengio, Y. (2013). Knowledge matters: Importance of prior information for optimization. In *International Conference on Learning Representations (ICLR'2013)*.

Guo, H. and Gelfand, S. B. (1992). Classification trees with neural network feature extraction. *Neural Networks, IEEE Transactions on*, **3**(6), 923–933.

Gupta, S., Agrawal, A., Gopalakrishnan, K., and Narayanan, P. (2015). Deep learning with limited numerical precision. *CoRR*, **abs/1502.02551**.

Gutmann, M. and Hyvarinen, A. (2010). Noise-contrastive estimation: A new estimation principle for unnormalized statistical models. In *Proceedings of The Thirteenth International Conference on Artificial Intelligence and Statistics (AISTATS'10)*.

Hadsell, R., Sermanet, P., Ben, J., Erkan, A., Han, J., Muller, U., and LeCun, Y. (2007). Online learning for offroad robots: Spatial label propagation to learn long-range traversability. In *Proceedings of Robotics: Science and Systems*, Atlanta, GA, USA.

Hajnal, A., Maass, W., Pudlak, P., Szegedy, M., and Turan, G. (1993). Threshold circuits of bounded depth. *J. Comput. System. Sci.*, **46**, 129–154.

Håstad, J. (1986). Almost optimal lower bounds for small depth circuits. In *Proceedings of the 18th annual ACM Symposium on Theory of Computing*, pages 6–20, Berkeley, California. ACM Press.

Håstad, J. and Goldmann, M. (1991). On the power of small-depth threshold circuits. *Computational Complexity*, **1**, 113–129.

Hastie, T., Tibshirani, R., and Friedman, J. (2001). *The elements of statistical learning: data mining, inference and prediction*. Springer Series in Statistics. Springer Verlag.

He, K., Zhang, X., Ren, S., and Sun, J. (2015). Delving deep into rectifiers: Surpassing human-level performance on ImageNet classification. *arXiv preprint arXiv:1502.01852*.

Hebb, D. O. (1949). *The Organization of Behavior*. Wiley, New York.

Henaff, M., Jarrett, K., Kavukcuoglu, K., and LeCun, Y. (2011). Unsupervised learning of sparse features for scalable audio classification. In *ISMIR'11*.

Henderson, J. (2003). Inducing history representations for broad coverage statistical parsing. In *HLT-NAACL*, pages 103–110.

Henderson, J. (2004). Discriminative training of a neural network statistical parser. In *Proceedings of the 42nd Annual Meeting on Association for Computational Linguistics*, page 95.

Henniges, M., Puertas, G., Bornschein, J., Eggert, J., and Lücke, J. (2010). Binary sparse coding. In *Latent Variable Analysis and Signal Separation*, pages 450–457. Springer.

Herault, J. and Ans, B. (1984). Circuits neuronaux à synapses modifiables: Décodage de messages composites par apprentissage non supervisé. *Comptes Rendus de l'Académie des Sciences*, **299(III-13)**, 525—528.

Hinton, G. (2012). Neural networks for machine learning. Coursera, video lectures.

Hinton, G., Deng, L., Dahl, G. E., Mohamed, A., Jaitly, N., Senior, A., Vanhoucke, V., Nguyen, P., Sainath, T., and Kingsbury, B. (2012a). Deep neural networks for acoustic modeling in speech recognition. *IEEE Signal Processing Magazine*, **29**(6), 82–97.

Hinton, G., Vinyals, O., and Dean, J. (2015). Distilling the knowledge in a neural network. *arXiv preprint arXiv:1503.02531*.

Hinton, G. E. (1989). Connectionist learning procedures. *Artificial Intelligence*, **40**, 185–234.

Hinton, G. E. (1990). Mapping part-whole hierarchies into connectionist networks. *Artificial Intelligence*, **46**(1), 47–75.

Hinton, G. E. (1999). Products of experts. In *ICANN'1999*.

Hinton, G. E. (2000). Training products of experts by minimizing contrastive divergence. Technical Report GCNU TR 2000-004, Gatsby Unit, University College London.

Hinton, G. E. (2006). To recognize shapes, first learn to generate images. Technical Report UTML TR 2006-003, University of Toronto.

Hinton, G. E. (2007a). How to do backpropagation in a brain. Invited talk at the NIPS'2007 Deep Learning Workshop.

Hinton, G. E. (2007b). Learning multiple layers of representation. *Trends in cognitive sciences*, **11**(10), 428–434.

Hinton, G. E. (2010). A practical guide to training restricted Boltzmann machines. Technical Report UTML TR 2010-003, Department of Computer Science, University of Toronto.

Hinton, G. E. and Ghahramani, Z. (1997). Generative models for discovering sparse distributed representations. *Philosophical Transactions of the Royal Society of London*.

Hinton, G. E. and McClelland, J. L. (1988). Learning representations by recirculation. In *NIPS'1987*, pages 358–366.

Hinton, G. E. and Roweis, S. (2003). Stochastic neighbor embedding. In *NIPS'2002*.

Hinton, G. E. and Salakhutdinov, R. (2006). Reducing the dimensionality of data with neural networks. *Science*, **313**(5786), 504–507.

Hinton, G. E. and Sejnowski, T. J. (1986). Learning and relearning in Boltzmann machines. In D. E. Rumelhart and J. L. McClelland, editors, *Parallel Distributed Processing*, volume 1, chapter 7, pages 282–317. MIT Press, Cambridge.

Hinton, G. E. and Sejnowski, T. J. (1999). *Unsupervised learning: foundations of neural computation*. MIT press.

Hinton, G. E. and Shallice, T. (1991). Lesioning an attractor network: investigations of acquired dyslexia. *Psychological review*, **98**(1), 74.

Hinton, G. E. and Zemel, R. S. (1994). Autoencoders, minimum description length, and Helmholtz free energy. In *NIPS'1993*.

Hinton, G. E., Sejnowski, T. J., and Ackley, D. H. (1984). Boltzmann machines: Constraint satisfaction networks that learn. Technical Report TR-CMU-CS-84-119, Carnegie-Mellon University, Dept. of Computer Science.

Hinton, G. E., McClelland, J., and Rumelhart, D. (1986). Distributed representations. In D. E. Rumelhart and J. L. McClelland, editors, *Parallel Distributed Processing: Explorations in the Microstructure of Cognition*, volume 1, pages 77–109. MIT Press, Cambridge.

Hinton, G. E., Revow, M., and Dayan, P. (1995a). Recognizing handwritten digits using mixtures of linear models. In G. Tesauro, D. Touretzky, and T. Leen, editors, *Advances in Neural Information Processing Systems 7 (NIPS'94)*, pages 1015–1022. MIT Press, Cambridge, MA.

Hinton, G. E., Dayan, P., Frey, B. J., and Neal, R. M. (1995b). The wake-sleep algorithm for unsupervised neural networks. *Science*, **268**, 1558–1161.

Hinton, G. E., Dayan, P., and Revow, M. (1997). Modelling the manifolds of images of handwritten digits. *IEEE Transactions on Neural Networks*, **8**, 65–74.

Hinton, G. E., Welling, M., Teh, Y. W., and Osindero, S. (2001). A new view of ICA. In *Proceedings of 3rd International Conference on Independent Component Analysis and Blind Signal Separation (ICA'01)*, pages 746–751, San Diego, CA.

Hinton, G. E., Osindero, S., and Teh, Y. (2006). A fast learning algorithm for deep belief nets. *Neural Computation*, **18**, 1527–1554.

Hinton, G. E., Deng, L., Yu, D., Dahl, G. E., Mohamed, A., Jaitly, N., Senior, A., Vanhoucke, V., Nguyen, P., Sainath, T. N., and Kingsbury, B. (2012b). Deep neural networks for acoustic modeling in speech recognition: The shared views of four research groups. *IEEE Signal Process. Mag.*, **29**(6), 82–97.

Hinton, G. E., Srivastava, N., Krizhevsky, A., Sutskever, I., and Salakhutdinov, R. (2012c). Improving neural networks by preventing co-adaptation of feature detectors. Technical report, arXiv:1207.0580.

Hinton, G. E., Vinyals, O., and Dean, J. (2014). Dark knowledge. Invited talk at the BayLearn Bay Area Machine Learning Symposium.

Hochreiter, S. (1991). Untersuchungen zu dynamischen neuronalen Netzen. Diploma thesis, T.U. München.

Hochreiter, S. and Schmidhuber, J. (1995). Simplifying neural nets by discovering flat minima. In *Advances in Neural Information Processing Systems 7*, pages 529–536. MIT Press.

Hochreiter, S. and Schmidhuber, J. (1997). Long short-term memory. *Neural Computation*, **9**(8), 1735–1780.

Hochreiter, S., Bengio, Y., and Frasconi, P. (2001). Gradient flow in recurrent nets: the difficulty of learning long-term dependencies. In J. Kolen and S. Kremer, editors, *Field Guide to Dynamical Recurrent Networks*. IEEE Press.

Holi, J. L. and Hwang, J.-N. (1993). Finite precision error analysis of neural network hardware implementations. *Computers, IEEE Transactions on*, **42**(3), 281–290.

Holt, J. L. and Baker, T. E. (1991). Back propagation simulations using limited precision calculations. In *Neural Networks, 1991., IJCNN-91-Seattle International Joint Conference on*, volume 2, pages 121–126. IEEE.

Hornik, K., Stinchcombe, M., and White, H. (1989). Multilayer feedforward networks are universal approximators. *Neural Networks*, **2**, 359–366.

Hornik, K., Stinchcombe, M., and White, H. (1990). Universal approximation of an unknown mapping and its derivatives using multilayer feedforward networks. *Neural networks*, **3**(5), 551–560.

Hsu, F.-H. (2002). *Behind Deep Blue: Building the Computer That Defeated the World Chess Champion*. Princeton University Press, Princeton, NJ, USA.

Huang, F. and Ogata, Y. (2002). Generalized pseudo-likelihood estimates for Markov random fields on lattice. *Annals of the Institute of Statistical Mathematics*, **54**(1), 1–18.

Huang, P.-S., He, X., Gao, J., Deng, L., Acero, A., and Heck, L. (2013). Learning deep structured semantic models for web search using clickthrough data. In *Proceedings of the 22nd ACM international conference on Conference on information & knowledge management*, pages 2333–2338. ACM.

Hubel, D. and Wiesel, T. (1968). Receptive fields and functional architecture of monkey striate cortex. *Journal of Physiology (London)*, **195**, 215–243.

Hubel, D. H. and Wiesel, T. N. (1959). Receptive fields of single neurons in the cat's striate cortex. *Journal of Physiology*, **148**, 574–591.

Hubel, D. H. and Wiesel, T. N. (1962). Receptive fields, binocular interaction, and functional architecture in the cat's visual cortex. *Journal of Physiology (London)*, **160**, 106–154.

Huszar, F. (2015). How (not) to train your generative model: schedule sampling, likelihood, adversary? *arXiv:1511.05101*.

Hutter, F., Hoos, H., and Leyton-Brown, K. (2011). Sequential model-based optimization for general algorithm configuration. In *LION-5*. Extended version as UBC Tech report TR-2010-10.

Hyotyniemi, H. (1996). Turing machines are recurrent neural networks. In *STeP'96*, pages 13–24.

Hyvärinen, A. (1999). Survey on independent component analysis. *Neural Computing Surveys*, **2**, 94–128.

Hyvärinen, A. (2005). Estimation of non-normalized statistical models using score matching. *Journal of Machine Learning Research*, **6**, 695–709.

Hyvärinen, A. (2007a). Connections between score matching, contrastive divergence, and pseudolikelihood for continuous-valued variables. *IEEE Transactions on Neural Networks*, **18**, 1529–1531.

Hyvärinen, A. (2007b). Some extensions of score matching. *Computational Statistics and Data Analysis*, **51**, 2499–2512.

Hyvärinen, A. and Hoyer, P. O. (1999). Emergence of topography and complex cell properties from natural images using extensions of ica. In *NIPS*, pages 827–833.

Hyvärinen, A. and Pajunen, P. (1999). Nonlinear independent component analysis: Existence and uniqueness results. *Neural Networks*, **12**(3), 429–439.

Hyvärinen, A., Karhunen, J., and Oja, E. (2001a). *Independent Component Analysis*. Wiley-Interscience.

Hyvärinen, A., Hoyer, P. O., and Inki, M. O. (2001b). Topographic independent component analysis. *Neural Computation*, **13**(7), 1527–1558.

Hyvärinen, A., Hurri, J., and Hoyer, P. O. (2009). *Natural Image Statistics: A probabilistic approach to early computational vision*. Springer-Verlag.

Iba, Y. (2001). Extended ensemble Monte Carlo. *International Journal of Modern Physics*, **C12**, 623–656.

Inayoshi, H. and Kurita, T. (2005). Improved generalization by adding both auto-association and hidden-layer noise to neural-network-based-classifiers. *IEEE Workshop on Machine Learning for Signal Processing*, pages 141–146.

Ioffe, S. and Szegedy, C. (2015). Batch normalization: Accelerating deep network training by reducing internal covariate shift.

Jacobs, R. A. (1988). Increased rates of convergence through learning rate adaptation. *Neural networks*, **1**(4), 295–307.

Jacobs, R. A., Jordan, M. I., Nowlan, S. J., and Hinton, G. E. (1991). Adaptive mixtures of local experts. *Neural Computation*, **3**, 79–87.

Jaeger, H. (2003). Adaptive nonlinear system identification with echo state networks. In *Advances in Neural Information Processing Systems 15*.

Jaeger, H. (2007a). Discovering multiscale dynamical features with hierarchical echo state networks. Technical report, Jacobs University.

Jaeger, H. (2007b). Echo state network. *Scholarpedia*, **2**(9), 2330.

Jaeger, H. (2012). Long short-term memory in echo state networks: Details of a simulation study. Technical report, Technical report, Jacobs University Bremen.

Jaeger, H. and Haas, H. (2004). Harnessing nonlinearity: Predicting chaotic systems and saving energy in wireless communication. *Science*, **304**(5667), 78–80.

Jaeger, H., Lukosevicius, M., Popovici, D., and Siewert, U. (2007). Optimization and applications of echo state networks with leaky- integrator neurons. *Neural Networks*, **20**(3), 335–352.

Jain, V., Murray, J. F., Roth, F., Turaga, S., Zhigulin, V., Briggman, K. L., Helmstaedter, M. N., Denk, W., and Seung, H. S. (2007). Supervised learning of image restoration with convolutional networks. In *Computer Vision, 2007. ICCV 2007. IEEE 11th International Conference on*, pages 1–8. IEEE.

Jaitly, N. and Hinton, G. (2011). Learning a better representation of speech soundwaves using restricted Boltzmann machines. In *Acoustics, Speech and Signal Processing (ICASSP), 2011 IEEE International Conference on*, pages 5884–5887. IEEE.

Jaitly, N. and Hinton, G. E. (2013). Vocal tract length perturbation (VTLP) improves speech recognition. In *ICML'2013*.

Jarrett, K., Kavukcuoglu, K., Ranzato, M., and LeCun, Y. (2009). What is the best multi-stage architecture for object recognition? In *ICCV'09*.

Jarzynski, C. (1997). Nonequilibrium equality for free energy differences. *Phys. Rev. Lett.*, **78**, 2690–2693.

Jaynes, E. T. (2003). *Probability Theory: The Logic of Science*. Cambridge University Press.

Jean, S., Cho, K., Memisevic, R., and Bengio, Y. (2014). On using very large target vocabulary for neural machine translation. arXiv:1412.2007.

Jelinek, F. and Mercer, R. L. (1980). Interpolated estimation of Markov source parameters from sparse data. In E. S. Gelsema and L. N. Kanal, editors, *Pattern Recognition in Practice*. North-Holland, Amsterdam.

Jia, Y. (2013). Caffe: An open source convolutional architecture for fast feature embedding. `http://caffe.berkeleyvision.org/`.

Jia, Y., Huang, C., and Darrell, T. (2012). Beyond spatial pyramids: Receptive field learning for pooled image features. In *Computer Vision and Pattern Recognition (CVPR), 2012 IEEE Conference on*, pages 3370–3377. IEEE.

Jim, K.-C., Giles, C. L., and Horne, B. G. (1996). An analysis of noise in recurrent neural networks: convergence and generalization. *IEEE Transactions on Neural Networks*, **7**(6), 1424–1438.

Jordan, M. I. (1998). *Learning in Graphical Models*. Kluwer, Dordrecht, Netherlands.

Joulin, A. and Mikolov, T. (2015). Inferring algorithmic patterns with stack-augmented recurrent nets. *arXiv preprint arXiv:1503.01007*.

Jozefowicz, R., Zaremba, W., and Sutskever, I. (2015). An empirical evaluation of recurrent network architectures. In *ICML'2015*.

Judd, J. S. (1989). *Neural Network Design and the Complexity of Learning*. MIT press.

Jutten, C. and Herault, J. (1991). Blind separation of sources, part I: an adaptive algorithm based on neuromimetic architecture. *Signal Processing*, **24**, 1–10.

Kahou, S. E., Pal, C., Bouthillier, X., Froumenty, P., Gülçehre, ç., Memisevic, R., Vincent, P., Courville, A., Bengio, Y., Ferrari, R. C., Mirza, M., Jean, S., Carrier, P. L., Dauphin, Y., Boulanger-Lewandowski, N., Aggarwal, A., Zumer, J., Lamblin, P., Raymond, J.-P., Desjardins, G., Pascanu, R., Warde-Farley, D., Torabi, A., Sharma, A., Bengio, E., Côté, M., Konda, K. R., and Wu, Z. (2013). Combining modality specific deep neural networks for emotion recognition in video. In *Proceedings of the 15th ACM on International Conference on Multimodal Interaction*.

Kalchbrenner, N. and Blunsom, P. (2013). Recurrent continuous translation models. In *EMNLP'2013*.

Kalchbrenner, N., Danihelka, I., and Graves, A. (2015). Grid long short-term memory. *arXiv preprint arXiv:1507.01526*.

Kamyshanska, H. and Memisevic, R. (2015). The potential energy of an autoencoder. *IEEE Transactions on Pattern Analysis and Machine Intelligence*.

Karpathy, A. and Li, F.-F. (2015). Deep visual-semantic alignments for generating image descriptions. In *CVPR'2015*. arXiv:1412.2306.

Karpathy, A., Toderici, G., Shetty, S., Leung, T., Sukthankar, R., and Fei-Fei, L. (2014). Large-scale video classification with convolutional neural networks. In *CVPR*.

Karush, W. (1939). *Minima of Functions of Several Variables with Inequalities as Side Constraints*. Master's thesis, Dept. of Mathematics, Univ. of Chicago.

Katz, S. M. (1987). Estimation of probabilities from sparse data for the language model component of a speech recognizer. *IEEE Transactions on Acoustics, Speech, and Signal Processing*, **ASSP-35**(3), 400–401.

Kavukcuoglu, K., Ranzato, M., and LeCun, Y. (2008). Fast inference in sparse coding algorithms with applications to object recognition. Technical report, Computational and Biological Learning Lab, Courant Institute, NYU. Tech Report CBLL-TR-2008-12-01.

Kavukcuoglu, K., Ranzato, M.-A., Fergus, R., and LeCun, Y. (2009). Learning invariant features through topographic filter maps. In *CVPR'2009*.

Kavukcuoglu, K., Sermanet, P., Boureau, Y.-L., Gregor, K., Mathieu, M., and LeCun, Y. (2010). Learning convolutional feature hierarchies for visual recognition. In *NIPS'2010*.

Kelley, H. J. (1960). Gradient theory of optimal flight paths. *ARS Journal*, **30**(10), 947–954.

Khan, F., Zhu, X., and Mutlu, B. (2011). How do humans teach: On curriculum learning and teaching dimension. In *Advances in Neural Information Processing Systems 24 (NIPS'11)*, pages 1449–1457.

Kim, S. K., McAfee, L. C., McMahon, P. L., and Olukotun, K. (2009). A highly scalable restricted Boltzmann machine FPGA implementation. In *Field Programmable Logic and Applications, 2009. FPL 2009. International Conference on*, pages 367–372. IEEE.

Kindermann, R. (1980). *Markov Random Fields and Their Applications (Contemporary Mathematics ; V. 1)*. American Mathematical Society.

Kingma, D. and Ba, J. (2014). Adam: A method for stochastic optimization. *arXiv preprint arXiv:1412.6980*.

Kingma, D. and LeCun, Y. (2010). Regularized estimation of image statistics by score matching. In *NIPS'2010*.

Kingma, D., Rezende, D., Mohamed, S., and Welling, M. (2014). Semi-supervised learning with deep generative models. In *NIPS'2014*.

Kingma, D. P. (2013). Fast gradient-based inference with continuous latent variable models in auxiliary form. Technical report, arxiv:1306.0733.

Kingma, D. P. and Welling, M. (2014a). Auto-encoding variational bayes. In *Proceedings of the International Conference on Learning Representations (ICLR)*.

Kingma, D. P. and Welling, M. (2014b). Efficient gradient-based inference through transformations between bayes nets and neural nets. Technical report, arxiv:1402.0480.

Kirkpatrick, S., Jr., C. D. G., , and Vecchi, M. P. (1983). Optimization by simulated annealing. *Science*, **220**, 671–680.

Kiros, R., Salakhutdinov, R., and Zemel, R. (2014a). Multimodal neural language models. In *ICML'2014*.

Kiros, R., Salakhutdinov, R., and Zemel, R. (2014b). Unifying visual-semantic embeddings with multimodal neural language models. *arXiv:1411.2539* [cs.LG].

Klementiev, A., Titov, I., and Bhattarai, B. (2012). Inducing crosslingual distributed representations of words. In *Proceedings of COLING 2012*.

Knowles-Barley, S., Jones, T. R., Morgan, J., Lee, D., Kasthuri, N., Lichtman, J. W., and Pfister, H. (2014). Deep learning for the connectome. *GPU Technology Conference*.

Koller, D. and Friedman, N. (2009). *Probabilistic Graphical Models: Principles and Techniques*. MIT Press.

Konig, Y., Bourlard, H., and Morgan, N. (1996). REMAP: Recursive estimation and maximization of a posteriori probabilities – application to transition-based connectionist speech recognition. In D. Touretzky, M. Mozer, and M. Hasselmo, editors, *Advances in Neural Information Processing Systems 8 (NIPS'95)*. MIT Press, Cambridge, MA.

Koren, Y. (2009). The BellKor solution to the Netflix grand prize.

Kotzias, D., Denil, M., de Freitas, N., and Smyth, P. (2015). From group to individual labels using deep features. In *ACM SIGKDD*.

Koutnik, J., Greff, K., Gomez, F., and Schmidhuber, J. (2014). A clockwork RNN. In *ICML'2014*.

Kočiský, T., Hermann, K. M., and Blunsom, P. (2014). Learning Bilingual Word Representations by Marginalizing Alignments. In *Proceedings of ACL*.

Krause, O., Fischer, A., Glasmachers, T., and Igel, C. (2013). Approximation properties of DBNs with binary hidden units and real-valued visible units. In *ICML'2013*.

Krizhevsky, A. (2010). Convolutional deep belief networks on CIFAR-10. Technical report, University of Toronto. Unpublished Manuscript: http://www.cs.utoronto.ca/ kriz/conv-cifar10-aug2010.pdf.

Krizhevsky, A. and Hinton, G. (2009). Learning multiple layers of features from tiny images. Technical report, University of Toronto.

Krizhevsky, A. and Hinton, G. E. (2011). Using very deep autoencoders for content-based image retrieval. In *ESANN*.

Krizhevsky, A., Sutskever, I., and Hinton, G. (2012). ImageNet classification with deep convolutional neural networks. In *NIPS'2012*.

Krueger, K. A. and Dayan, P. (2009). Flexible shaping: how learning in small steps helps. *Cognition*, **110**, 380–394.

Kuhn, H. W. and Tucker, A. W. (1951). Nonlinear programming. In *Proceedings of the Second Berkeley Symposium on Mathematical Statistics and Probability*, pages 481–492, Berkeley, Calif. University of California Press.

Kumar, A., Irsoy, O., Su, J., Bradbury, J., English, R., Pierce, B., Ondruska, P., Iyyer, M., Gulrajani, I., and Socher, R. (2015). Ask me anything: Dynamic memory networks for natural language processing. *arXiv:1506.07285*.

Kumar, M. P., Packer, B., and Koller, D. (2010). Self-paced learning for latent variable models. In *NIPS'2010*.

Lang, K. J. and Hinton, G. E. (1988). The development of the time-delay neural network architecture for speech recognition. Technical Report CMU-CS-88-152, Carnegie-Mellon University.

Lang, K. J., Waibel, A. H., and Hinton, G. E. (1990). A time-delay neural network architecture for isolated word recognition. *Neural networks*, **3**(1), 23–43.

Langford, J. and Zhang, T. (2008). The epoch-greedy algorithm for contextual multi-armed bandits. In *NIPS'2008*, pages 1096—1103.

Lappalainen, H., Giannakopoulos, X., Honkela, A., and Karhunen, J. (2000). Nonlinear independent component analysis using ensemble learning: Experiments and discussion. In *Proc. ICA*. Citeseer.

Larochelle, H. and Bengio, Y. (2008). Classification using discriminative restricted Boltzmann machines. In *ICML'2008*.

Larochelle, H. and Hinton, G. E. (2010). Learning to combine foveal glimpses with a third-order Boltzmann machine. In *Advances in Neural Information Processing Systems 23*, pages 1243–1251.

Larochelle, H. and Murray, I. (2011). The Neural Autoregressive Distribution Estimator. In *AISTATS'2011*.

Larochelle, H., Erhan, D., and Bengio, Y. (2008). Zero-data learning of new tasks. In *AAAI Conference on Artificial Intelligence*.

Larochelle, H., Bengio, Y., Louradour, J., and Lamblin, P. (2009). Exploring strategies for training deep neural networks. *Journal of Machine Learning Research*, **10**, 1–40.

Lasserre, J. A., Bishop, C. M., and Minka, T. P. (2006). Principled hybrids of generative and discriminative models. In *Proceedings of the Computer Vision and Pattern Recognition Conference (CVPR'06)*, pages 87–94, Washington, DC, USA. IEEE Computer Society.

Le, Q., Ngiam, J., Chen, Z., hao Chia, D. J., Koh, P. W., and Ng, A. (2010). Tiled convolutional neural networks. In J. Lafferty, C. K. I. Williams, J. Shawe-Taylor, R. Zemel, and A. Culotta, editors, *Advances in Neural Information Processing Systems 23 (NIPS'10)*, pages 1279–1287.

Le, Q., Ngiam, J., Coates, A., Lahiri, A., Prochnow, B., and Ng, A. (2011). On optimization methods for deep learning. In *Proc. ICML'2011*. ACM.

Le, Q., Ranzato, M., Monga, R., Devin, M., Corrado, G., Chen, K., Dean, J., and Ng, A. (2012). Building high-level features using large scale unsupervised learning. In *ICML'2012*.

Le Roux, N. and Bengio, Y. (2008). Representational power of restricted Boltzmann machines and deep belief networks. *Neural Computation*, **20**(6), 1631–1649.

Le Roux, N. and Bengio, Y. (2010). Deep belief networks are compact universal approximators. *Neural Computation*, **22**(8), 2192–2207.

LeCun, Y. (1985). Une procédure d'apprentissage pour Réseau à seuil assymétrique. In *Cognitiva 85: A la Frontière de l'Intelligence Artificielle, des Sciences de la Connaissance et des Neurosciences*, pages 599–604, Paris 1985. CESTA, Paris.

LeCun, Y. (1986). Learning processes in an asymmetric threshold network. In F. Fogelman-Soulié, E. Bienenstock, and G. Weisbuch, editors, *Disordered Systems and Biological Organization*, pages 233–240. Springer-Verlag, Les Houches, France.

LeCun, Y. (1987). *Modèles connexionistes de l'apprentissage*. Ph.D. thesis, Université de Paris VI.

LeCun, Y. (1989). Generalization and network design strategies. Technical Report CRG-TR-89-4, University of Toronto.

LeCun, Y., Jackel, L. D., Boser, B., Denker, J. S., Graf, H. P., Guyon, I., Henderson, D., Howard, R. E., and Hubbard, W. (1989). Handwritten digit recognition: Applications of neural network chips and automatic learning. *IEEE Communications Magazine*, **27**(11), 41–46.

LeCun, Y., Bottou, L., Orr, G. B., and Müller, K.-R. (1998a). Efficient backprop. In *Neural Networks, Tricks of the Trade*, Lecture Notes in Computer Science LNCS 1524. Springer Verlag.

LeCun, Y., Bottou, L., Bengio, Y., and Haffner, P. (1998b). Gradient based learning applied to document recognition. *Proc. IEEE*.

LeCun, Y., Kavukcuoglu, K., and Farabet, C. (2010). Convolutional networks and applications in vision. In *Circuits and Systems (ISCAS), Proceedings of 2010 IEEE International Symposium on*, pages 253–256. IEEE.

L'Ecuyer, P. (1994). Efficiency improvement and variance reduction. In *Proceedings of the 1994 Winter Simulation Conference*, pages 122—132.

Lee, C.-Y., Xie, S., Gallagher, P., Zhang, Z., and Tu, Z. (2014). Deeply-supervised nets. *arXiv preprint arXiv:1409.5185*.

Lee, H., Battle, A., Raina, R., and Ng, A. (2007). Efficient sparse coding algorithms. In B. Schölkopf, J. Platt, and T. Hoffman, editors, *Advances in Neural Information Processing Systems 19 (NIPS'06)*, pages 801–808. MIT Press.

Lee, H., Ekanadham, C., and Ng, A. (2008). Sparse deep belief net model for visual area V2. In *NIPS'07*.

Lee, H., Grosse, R., Ranganath, R., and Ng, A. Y. (2009). Convolutional deep belief networks for scalable unsupervised learning of hierarchical representations. In L. Bottou and M. Littman, editors, *Proceedings of the Twenty-sixth International Conference on Machine Learning (ICML'09)*. ACM, Montreal, Canada.

Lee, Y. J. and Grauman, K. (2011). Learning the easy things first: self-paced visual category discovery. In *CVPR'2011*.

Leibniz, G. W. (1676). Memoir using the chain rule. (Cited in TMME 7:2&3 p 321–332, 2010).

Lenat, D. B. and Guha, R. V. (1989). *Building large knowledge-based systems; representation and inference in the Cyc project*. Addison-Wesley Longman Publishing Co., Inc.

Leshno, M., Lin, V. Y., Pinkus, A., and Schocken, S. (1993). Multilayer feedforward networks with a nonpolynomial activation function can approximate any function. *Neural Networks*, **6**, 861–867.

Levenberg, K. (1944). A method for the solution of certain non-linear problems in least squares. *Quarterly Journal of Applied Mathematics*, **II**(2), 164–168.

L'Hôpital, G. F. A. (1696). *Analyse des infiniment petits, pour l'intelligence des lignes courbes*. Paris: L'Imprimerie Royale.

Li, Y., Swersky, K., and Zemel, R. S. (2015). Generative moment matching networks. *CoRR*, **abs/1502.02761**.

Lin, T., Horne, B. G., Tino, P., and Giles, C. L. (1996). Learning long-term dependencies is not as difficult with NARX recurrent neural networks. *IEEE Transactions on Neural Networks*, **7**(6), 1329–1338.

Lin, Y., Liu, Z., Sun, M., Liu, Y., and Zhu, X. (2015). Learning entity and relation embeddings for knowledge graph completion. In *Proc. AAAI'15*.

Linde, N. (1992). The machine that changed the world, episode 3. Documentary miniseries.

Lindsey, C. and Lindblad, T. (1994). Review of hardware neural networks: a user's perspective. In *Proc. Third Workshop on Neural Networks: From Biology to High Energy Physics*, pages 195–202, Isola d'Elba, Italy.

Linnainmaa, S. (1976). Taylor expansion of the accumulated rounding error. *BIT Numerical Mathematics*, **16**(2), 146–160.

LISA (2008). Deep learning tutorials: Restricted Boltzmann machines. Technical report, LISA Lab, Université de Montréal.

Long, P. M. and Servedio, R. A. (2010). Restricted Boltzmann machines are hard to approximately evaluate or simulate. In *Proceedings of the 27th International Conference on Machine Learning (ICML'10)*.

Lotter, W., Kreiman, G., and Cox, D. (2015). Unsupervised learning of visual structure using predictive generative networks. *arXiv preprint arXiv:1511.06380*.

Lovelace, A. (1842). Notes upon L. F. Menabrea's "Sketch of the Analytical Engine invented by Charles Babbage".

Lu, L., Zhang, X., Cho, K., and Renals, S. (2015). A study of the recurrent neural network encoder-decoder for large vocabulary speech recognition. In *Proc. Interspeech*.

Lu, T., Pál, D., and Pál, M. (2010). Contextual multi-armed bandits. In *International Conference on Artificial Intelligence and Statistics*, pages 485–492.

Luenberger, D. G. (1984). *Linear and Nonlinear Programming*. Addison Wesley.

Lukoševičius, M. and Jaeger, H. (2009). Reservoir computing approaches to recurrent neural network training. *Computer Science Review*, **3**(3), 127–149.

Luo, H., Shen, R., Niu, C., and Ullrich, C. (2011). Learning class-relevant features and class-irrelevant features via a hybrid third-order RBM. In *International Conference on Artificial Intelligence and Statistics*, pages 470–478.

Luo, H., Carrier, P. L., Courville, A., and Bengio, Y. (2013). Texture modeling with convolutional spike-and-slab RBMs and deep extensions. In *AISTATS'2013*.

Lyu, S. (2009). Interpretation and generalization of score matching. In *Proceedings of the Twenty-fifth Conference in Uncertainty in Artificial Intelligence (UAI'09)*.

Ma, J., Sheridan, R. P., Liaw, A., Dahl, G. E., and Svetnik, V. (2015). Deep neural nets as a method for quantitative structure – activity relationships. *J. Chemical information and modeling*.

Maas, A. L., Hannun, A. Y., and Ng, A. Y. (2013). Rectifier nonlinearities improve neural network acoustic models. In *ICML Workshop on Deep Learning for Audio, Speech, and Language Processing*.

Maass, W. (1992). Bounds for the computational power and learning complexity of analog neural nets (extended abstract). In *Proc. of the 25th ACM Symp. Theory of Computing*, pages 335–344.

Maass, W., Schnitger, G., and Sontag, E. D. (1994). A comparison of the computational power of sigmoid and Boolean threshold circuits. *Theoretical Advances in Neural Computation and Learning*, pages 127–151.

Maass, W., Natschlaeger, T., and Markram, H. (2002). Real-time computing without stable states: A new framework for neural computation based on perturbations. *Neural Computation*, **14**(11), 2531–2560.

MacKay, D. (2003). *Information Theory, Inference and Learning Algorithms*. Cambridge University Press.

Maclaurin, D., Duvenaud, D., and Adams, R. P. (2015). Gradient-based hyperparameter optimization through reversible learning. *arXiv preprint arXiv:1502.03492*.

Mao, J., Xu, W., Yang, Y., Wang, J., Huang, Z., and Yuille, A. L. (2015). Deep captioning with multimodal recurrent neural networks. In *ICLR'2015*. arXiv:1410.1090.

Marcotte, P. and Savard, G. (1992). Novel approaches to the discrimination problem. *Zeitschrift für Operations Research (Theory)*, **36**, 517–545.

Marlin, B. and de Freitas, N. (2011). Asymptotic efficiency of deterministic estimators for discrete energy-based models: Ratio matching and pseudolikelihood. In *UAI'2011*.

Marlin, B., Swersky, K., Chen, B., and de Freitas, N. (2010). Inductive principles for restricted Boltzmann machine learning. In *Proceedings of The Thirteenth International Conference on Artificial Intelligence and Statistics (AISTATS'10)*, volume 9, pages 509–516.

Marquardt, D. W. (1963). An algorithm for least-squares estimation of non-linear parameters. *Journal of the Society of Industrial and Applied Mathematics*, **11**(2), 431–441.

Marr, D. and Poggio, T. (1976). Cooperative computation of stereo disparity. *Science*, **194**.

Martens, J. (2010). Deep learning via Hessian-free optimization. In L. Bottou and M. Littman, editors, *Proceedings of the Twenty-seventh International Conference on Machine Learning (ICML-10)*, pages 735–742. ACM.

Martens, J. and Medabalimi, V. (2014). On the expressive efficiency of sum product networks. *arXiv:1411.7717*.

Martens, J. and Sutskever, I. (2011). Learning recurrent neural networks with Hessian-free optimization. In *Proc. ICML'2011*. ACM.

Mase, S. (1995). Consistency of the maximum pseudo-likelihood estimator of continuous state space Gibbsian processes. *The Annals of Applied Probability*, **5**(3), pp. 603–612.

McClelland, J., Rumelhart, D., and Hinton, G. (1995). The appeal of parallel distributed processing. In *Computation & intelligence*, pages 305–341. American Association for Artificial Intelligence.

McCulloch, W. S. and Pitts, W. (1943). A logical calculus of ideas immanent in nervous activity. *Bulletin of Mathematical Biophysics*, **5**, 115–133.

Mead, C. and Ismail, M. (2012). *Analog VLSI implementation of neural systems*, volume 80. Springer Science & Business Media.

Melchior, J., Fischer, A., and Wiskott, L. (2013). How to center binary deep Boltzmann machines. *arXiv preprint arXiv:1311.1354*.

Memisevic, R. and Hinton, G. E. (2007). Unsupervised learning of image transformations. In *Proceedings of the Computer Vision and Pattern Recognition Conference (CVPR'07)*.

Memisevic, R. and Hinton, G. E. (2010). Learning to represent spatial transformations with factored higher-order Boltzmann machines. *Neural Computation*, **22**(6), 1473–1492.

Mesnil, G., Dauphin, Y., Glorot, X., Rifai, S., Bengio, Y., Goodfellow, I., Lavoie, E., Muller, X., Desjardins, G., Warde-Farley, D., Vincent, P., Courville, A., and Bergstra, J. (2011). Unsupervised and transfer learning challenge: a deep learning approach. In *JMLR W&CP: Proc. Unsupervised and Transfer Learning*, volume 7.

Mesnil, G., Rifai, S., Dauphin, Y., Bengio, Y., and Vincent, P. (2012). Surfing on the manifold. Learning Workshop, Snowbird.

Miikkulainen, R. and Dyer, M. G. (1991). Natural language processing with modular PDP networks and distributed lexicon. *Cognitive Science*, **15**, 343–399.

Mikolov, T. (2012). *Statistical Language Models based on Neural Networks*. Ph.D. thesis, Brno University of Technology.

Mikolov, T., Deoras, A., Kombrink, S., Burget, L., and Cernocky, J. (2011a). Empirical evaluation and combination of advanced language modeling techniques. In *Proc. 12th annual conference of the international speech communication association (INTERSPEECH 2011)*.

Mikolov, T., Deoras, A., Povey, D., Burget, L., and Cernocky, J. (2011b). Strategies for training large scale neural network language models. In *Proc. ASRU'2011*.

Mikolov, T., Chen, K., Corrado, G., and Dean, J. (2013a). Efficient estimation of word representations in vector space. In *International Conference on Learning Representations: Workshops Track*.

Mikolov, T., Le, Q. V., and Sutskever, I. (2013b). Exploiting similarities among languages for machine translation. Technical report, arXiv:1309.4168.

Minka, T. (2005). Divergence measures and message passing. *Microsoft Research Cambridge UK Tech Rep MSRTR2005173*, **72**(TR-2005-173).

Minsky, M. L. and Papert, S. A. (1969). *Perceptrons*. MIT Press, Cambridge.

Mirza, M. and Osindero, S. (2014). Conditional generative adversarial nets. *arXiv preprint arXiv:1411.1784*.

Mishkin, D. and Matas, J. (2015). All you need is a good init. *arXiv preprint arXiv:1511.06422*.

Misra, J. and Saha, I. (2010). Artificial neural networks in hardware: A survey of two decades of progress. *Neurocomputing*, **74**(1), 239–255.

Mitchell, T. M. (1997). *Machine Learning*. McGraw-Hill, New York.

Miyato, T., Maeda, S., Koyama, M., Nakae, K., and Ishii, S. (2015). Distributional smoothing with virtual adversarial training. In *ICLR*. Preprint: arXiv:1507.00677.

Mnih, A. and Gregor, K. (2014). Neural variational inference and learning in belief networks. In *ICML'2014*.

Mnih, A. and Hinton, G. E. (2007). Three new graphical models for statistical language modelling. In Z. Ghahramani, editor, *Proceedings of the Twenty-fourth International Conference on Machine Learning (ICML'07)*, pages 641–648. ACM.

Mnih, A. and Hinton, G. E. (2009). A scalable hierarchical distributed language model. In D. Koller, D. Schuurmans, Y. Bengio, and L. Bottou, editors, *Advances in Neural Information Processing Systems 21 (NIPS'08)*, pages 1081–1088.

Mnih, A. and Kavukcuoglu, K. (2013). Learning word embeddings efficiently with noise-contrastive estimation. In C. Burges, L. Bottou, M. Welling, Z. Ghahramani, and K. Weinberger, editors, *Advances in Neural Information Processing Systems 26*, pages 2265–2273. Curran Associates, Inc.

Mnih, A. and Teh, Y. W. (2012). A fast and simple algorithm for training neural probabilistic language models. In *ICML'2012*, pages 1751–1758.

Mnih, V. and Hinton, G. (2010). Learning to detect roads in high-resolution aerial images. In *Proceedings of the 11th European Conference on Computer Vision (ECCV)*.

Mnih, V., Larochelle, H., and Hinton, G. (2011). Conditional restricted Boltzmann machines for structure output prediction. In *Proc. Conf. on Uncertainty in Artificial Intelligence (UAI)*.

Mnih, V., Kavukcuoglo, K., Silver, D., Graves, A., Antonoglou, I., and Wierstra, D. (2013). Playing Atari with deep reinforcement learning. Technical report, arXiv:1312.5602.

Mnih, V., Heess, N., Graves, A., and Kavukcuoglo, K. (2014). Recurrent models of visual attention. In Z. Ghahramani, M. Welling, C. Cortes, N. Lawrence, and K. Weinberger, editors, *NIPS'2014*, pages 2204–2212.

Mnih, V., Kavukcuoglo, K., Silver, D., Rusu, A. A., Veness, J., Bellemare, M. G., Graves, A., Riedmiller, M., Fidgeland, A. K., Ostrovski, G., Petersen, S., Beattie, C., Sadik, A., Antonoglou, I., King, H., Kumaran, D., Wierstra, D., Legg, S., and Hassabis, D. (2015). Human-level control through deep reinforcement learning. *Nature*, **518**, 529–533.

Mobahi, H. and Fisher, III, J. W. (2015). A theoretical analysis of optimization by Gaussian continuation. In *AAAI'2015*.

Mobahi, H., Collobert, R., and Weston, J. (2009). Deep learning from temporal coherence in video. In L. Bottou and M. Littman, editors, *Proceedings of the 26th International Conference on Machine Learning*, pages 737–744, Montreal. Omnipress.

Mohamed, A., Dahl, G., and Hinton, G. (2009). Deep belief networks for phone recognition.

Mohamed, A., Sainath, T. N., Dahl, G., Ramabhadran, B., Hinton, G. E., and Picheny, M. A. (2011). Deep belief networks using discriminative features for phone recognition. In *Acoustics, Speech and Signal Processing (ICASSP), 2011 IEEE International Conference on*, pages 5060–5063. IEEE.

Mohamed, A., Dahl, G., and Hinton, G. (2012a). Acoustic modeling using deep belief networks. *IEEE Trans. on Audio, Speech and Language Processing*, **20**(1), 14–22.

Mohamed, A., Hinton, G., and Penn, G. (2012b). Understanding how deep belief networks perform acoustic modelling. In *Acoustics, Speech and Signal Processing (ICASSP), 2012 IEEE International Conference on*, pages 4273–4276. IEEE.

Moller, M. F. (1993). A scaled conjugate gradient algorithm for fast supervised learning. *Neural Networks*, **6**, 525–533.

Montavon, G. and Muller, K.-R. (2012). Deep Boltzmann machines and the centering trick. In G. Montavon, G. Orr, and K.-R. Müller, editors, *Neural Networks: Tricks of the Trade*, volume 7700 of *Lecture Notes in Computer Science*, pages 621–637. Preprint: http://arxiv.org/abs/1203.3783.

Montúfar, G. (2014). Universal approximation depth and errors of narrow belief networks with discrete units. *Neural Computation*, **26**.

Montúfar, G. and Ay, N. (2011). Refinements of universal approximation results for deep belief networks and restricted Boltzmann machines. *Neural Computation*, **23**(5), 1306–1319.

Montufar, G. F., Pascanu, R., Cho, K., and Bengio, Y. (2014). On the number of linear regions of deep neural networks. In *NIPS'2014*.

Mor-Yosef, S., Samueloff, A., Modan, B., Navot, D., and Schenker, J. G. (1990). Ranking the risk factors for cesarean: logistic regression analysis of a nationwide study. *Obstet Gynecol*, **75**(6), 944–7.

Morin, F. and Bengio, Y. (2005). Hierarchical probabilistic neural network language model. In *AISTATS'2005*.

Mozer, M. C. (1992). The induction of multiscale temporal structure. In J. M. S. Hanson and R. Lippmann, editors, *Advances in Neural Information Processing Systems 4 (NIPS'91)*, pages 275–282, San Mateo, CA. Morgan Kaufmann.

Murphy, K. P. (2012). *Machine Learning: a Probabilistic Perspective*. MIT Press, Cambridge, MA, USA.

Murray, B. U. I. and Larochelle, H. (2014). A deep and tractable density estimator. In *ICML'2014*.

Nair, V. and Hinton, G. (2010). Rectified linear units improve restricted Boltzmann machines. In *ICML'2010*.

Nair, V. and Hinton, G. E. (2009). 3d object recognition with deep belief nets. In Y. Bengio, D. Schuurmans, J. D. Lafferty, C. K. I. Williams, and A. Culotta, editors, *Advances in Neural Information Processing Systems 22*, pages 1339–1347. Curran Associates, Inc.

Narayanan, H. and Mitter, S. (2010). Sample complexity of testing the manifold hypothesis. In *NIPS'2010*.

Naumann, U. (2008). Optimal Jacobian accumulation is NP-complete. *Mathematical Programming*, **112**(2), 427–441.

Navigli, R. and Velardi, P. (2005). Structural semantic interconnections: a knowledge-based approach to word sense disambiguation. *IEEE Trans. Pattern Analysis and Machine Intelligence*, **27**(7), 1075—1086.

Neal, R. and Hinton, G. (1999). A view of the EM algorithm that justifies incremental, sparse, and other variants. In M. I. Jordan, editor, *Learning in Graphical Models*. MIT Press, Cambridge, MA.

Neal, R. M. (1990). Learning stochastic feedforward networks. Technical report.

Neal, R. M. (1993). Probabilistic inference using Markov chain Monte-Carlo methods. Technical Report CRG-TR-93-1, Dept. of Computer Science, University of Toronto.

Neal, R. M. (1994). Sampling from multimodal distributions using tempered transitions. Technical Report 9421, Dept. of Statistics, University of Toronto.

Neal, R. M. (1996). *Bayesian Learning for Neural Networks*. Lecture Notes in Statistics. Springer.

Neal, R. M. (2001). Annealed importance sampling. *Statistics and Computing*, **11**(2), 125–139.

Neal, R. M. (2005). Estimating ratios of normalizing constants using linked importance sampling.

Nesterov, Y. (1983). A method of solving a convex programming problem with convergence rate $O(1/k^2)$. *Soviet Mathematics Doklady*, **27**, 372–376.

Nesterov, Y. (2004). *Introductory lectures on convex optimization : a basic course.* Applied optimization. Kluwer Academic Publ., Boston, Dordrecht, London.

Netzer, Y., Wang, T., Coates, A., Bissacco, A., Wu, B., and Ng, A. Y. (2011). Reading digits in natural images with unsupervised feature learning. Deep Learning and Unsupervised Feature Learning Workshop, NIPS.

Ney, H. and Kneser, R. (1993). Improved clustering techniques for class-based statistical language modelling. In *European Conference on Speech Communication and Technology (Eurospeech)*, pages 973–976, Berlin.

Ng, A. (2015). Advice for applying machine learning. `https://see.stanford.edu/materials/aimlcs229/ML-advice.pdf`.

Niesler, T. R., Whittaker, E. W. D., and Woodland, P. C. (1998). Comparison of part-of-speech and automatically derived category-based language models for speech recognition. In *International Conference on Acoustics, Speech and Signal Processing (ICASSP)*, pages 177–180.

Ning, F., Delhomme, D., LeCun, Y., Piano, F., Bottou, L., and Barbano, P. E. (2005). Toward automatic phenotyping of developing embryos from videos. *Image Processing, IEEE Transactions on,* **14**(9), 1360–1371.

Nocedal, J. and Wright, S. (2006). *Numerical Optimization.* Springer.

Norouzi, M. and Fleet, D. J. (2011). Minimal loss hashing for compact binary codes. In *ICML'2011.*

Nowlan, S. J. (1990). Competing experts: An experimental investigation of associative mixture models. Technical Report CRG-TR-90-5, University of Toronto.

Nowlan, S. J. and Hinton, G. E. (1992). Simplifying neural networks by soft weight-sharing. *Neural Computation,* **4**(4), 473–493.

Olshausen, B. and Field, D. J. (2005). How close are we to understanding V1? *Neural Computation,* **17**, 1665–1699.

Olshausen, B. A. and Field, D. J. (1996). Emergence of simple-cell receptive field properties by learning a sparse code for natural images. *Nature,* **381**, 607–609.

Olshausen, B. A., Anderson, C. H., and Van Essen, D. C. (1993). A neurobiological model of visual attention and invariant pattern recognition based on dynamic routing of information. *J. Neurosci.,* **13**(11), 4700–4719.

Opper, M. and Archambeau, C. (2009). The variational Gaussian approximation revisited. *Neural computation,* **21**(3), 786–792.

Oquab, M., Bottou, L., Laptev, I., and Sivic, J. (2014). Learning and transferring mid-level image representations using convolutional neural networks. In *Computer Vision and Pattern Recognition (CVPR), 2014 IEEE Conference on*, pages 1717–1724. IEEE.

Osindero, S. and Hinton, G. E. (2008). Modeling image patches with a directed hierarchy of Markov random fields. In J. Platt, D. Koller, Y. Singer, and S. Roweis, editors, *Advances in Neural Information Processing Systems 20 (NIPS'07)*, pages 1121–1128, Cambridge, MA. MIT Press.

Ovid and Martin, C. (2004). *Metamorphoses*. W.W. Norton.

Paccanaro, A. and Hinton, G. E. (2000). Extracting distributed representations of concepts and relations from positive and negative propositions. In *International Joint Conference on Neural Networks (IJCNN)*, Como, Italy. IEEE, New York.

Paine, T. L., Khorrami, P., Han, W., and Huang, T. S. (2014). An analysis of unsupervised pre-training in light of recent advances. *arXiv preprint arXiv:1412.6597*.

Palatucci, M., Pomerleau, D., Hinton, G. E., and Mitchell, T. M. (2009). Zero-shot learning with semantic output codes. In Y. Bengio, D. Schuurmans, J. D. Lafferty, C. K. I. Williams, and A. Culotta, editors, *Advances in Neural Information Processing Systems 22*, pages 1410–1418. Curran Associates, Inc.

Parker, D. B. (1985). Learning-logic. Technical Report TR-47, Center for Comp. Research in Economics and Management Sci., MIT.

Pascanu, R., Mikolov, T., and Bengio, Y. (2013). On the difficulty of training recurrent neural networks. In *ICML'2013*.

Pascanu, R., Gülçehre, Ç., Cho, K., and Bengio, Y. (2014a). How to construct deep recurrent neural networks. In *ICLR'2014*.

Pascanu, R., Montufar, G., and Bengio, Y. (2014b). On the number of inference regions of deep feed forward networks with piece-wise linear activations. In *ICLR'2014*.

Pati, Y., Rezaiifar, R., and Krishnaprasad, P. (1993). Orthogonal matching pursuit: Recursive function approximation with applications to wavelet decomposition. In *Proceedings of the 27 th Annual Asilomar Conference on Signals, Systems, and Computers*, pages 40–44.

Pearl, J. (1985). Bayesian networks: A model of self-activated memory for evidential reasoning. In *Proceedings of the 7th Conference of the Cognitive Science Society, University of California, Irvine*, pages 329–334.

Pearl, J. (1988). *Probabilistic Reasoning in Intelligent Systems: Networks of Plausible Inference*. Morgan Kaufmann.

Perron, O. (1907). Zur theorie der matrices. *Mathematische Annalen*, **64**(2), 248–263.

Petersen, K. B. and Pedersen, M. S. (2006). The matrix cookbook. Version 20051003.

Peterson, G. B. (2004). A day of great illumination: B. F. Skinner's discovery of shaping. *Journal of the Experimental Analysis of Behavior*, **82**(3), 317–328.

Pham, D.-T., Garat, P., and Jutten, C. (1992). Separation of a mixture of independent sources through a maximum likelihood approach. In *EUSIPCO*, pages 771–774.

Pham, P.-H., Jelaca, D., Farabet, C., Martini, B., LeCun, Y., and Culurciello, E. (2012). NeuFlow: dataflow vision processing system-on-a-chip. In *Circuits and Systems (MWS-CAS), 2012 IEEE 55th International Midwest Symposium on*, pages 1044–1047. IEEE.

Pinheiro, P. H. O. and Collobert, R. (2014). Recurrent convolutional neural networks for scene labeling. In *ICML'2014*.

Pinheiro, P. H. O. and Collobert, R. (2015). From image-level to pixel-level labeling with convolutional networks. In *Conference on Computer Vision and Pattern Recognition (CVPR)*.

Pinto, N., Cox, D. D., and DiCarlo, J. J. (2008). Why is real-world visual object recognition hard? *PLoS Comput Biol*, **4**.

Pinto, N., Stone, Z., Zickler, T., and Cox, D. (2011). Scaling up biologically-inspired computer vision: A case study in unconstrained face recognition on facebook. In *Computer Vision and Pattern Recognition Workshops (CVPRW), 2011 IEEE Computer Society Conference on*, pages 35–42. IEEE.

Pollack, J. B. (1990). Recursive distributed representations. *Artificial Intelligence*, **46**(1), 77–105.

Polyak, B. and Juditsky, A. (1992). Acceleration of stochastic approximation by averaging. *SIAM J. Control and Optimization*, **30(4)**, 838–855.

Polyak, B. T. (1964). Some methods of speeding up the convergence of iteration methods. *USSR Computational Mathematics and Mathematical Physics*, **4**(5), 1–17.

Poole, B., Sohl-Dickstein, J., and Ganguli, S. (2014). Analyzing noise in autoencoders and deep networks. *CoRR*, **abs/1406.1831**.

Poon, H. and Domingos, P. (2011). Sum-product networks: A new deep architecture. In *Proceedings of the Twenty-seventh Conference in Uncertainty in Artificial Intelligence (UAI)*, Barcelona, Spain.

Presley, R. K. and Haggard, R. L. (1994). A fixed point implementation of the backpropagation learning algorithm. In *Southeastcon'94. Creative Technology Transfer-A Global Affair., Proceedings of the 1994 IEEE*, pages 136–138. IEEE.

Price, R. (1958). A useful theorem for nonlinear devices having Gaussian inputs. *IEEE Transactions on Information Theory*, **4**(2), 69–72.

Quiroga, R. Q., Reddy, L., Kreiman, G., Koch, C., and Fried, I. (2005). Invariant visual representation by single neurons in the human brain. *Nature*, **435**(7045), 1102–1107.

Radford, A., Metz, L., and Chintala, S. (2015). Unsupervised representation learning with deep convolutional generative adversarial networks. *arXiv preprint arXiv:1511.06434*.

Raiko, T., Yao, L., Cho, K., and Bengio, Y. (2014). Iterative neural autoregressive distribution estimator (NADE-k). Technical report, arXiv:1406.1485.

Raina, R., Madhavan, A., and Ng, A. Y. (2009). Large-scale deep unsupervised learning using graphics processors. In L. Bottou and M. Littman, editors, *Proceedings of the Twenty-sixth International Conference on Machine Learning (ICML'09)*, pages 873–880, New York, NY, USA. ACM.

Ramsey, F. P. (1926). Truth and probability. In R. B. Braithwaite, editor, *The Foundations of Mathematics and other Logical Essays*, chapter 7, pages 156–198. McMaster University Archive for the History of Economic Thought.

Ranzato, M. and Hinton, G. H. (2010). Modeling pixel means and covariances using factorized third-order Boltzmann machines. In *CVPR'2010*, pages 2551–2558.

Ranzato, M., Poultney, C., Chopra, S., and LeCun, Y. (2007a). Efficient learning of sparse representations with an energy-based model. In *NIPS'2006*.

Ranzato, M., Huang, F., Boureau, Y., and LeCun, Y. (2007b). Unsupervised learning of invariant feature hierarchies with applications to object recognition. In *Proceedings of the Computer Vision and Pattern Recognition Conference (CVPR'07)*. IEEE Press.

Ranzato, M., Boureau, Y., and LeCun, Y. (2008). Sparse feature learning for deep belief networks. In *NIPS'2007*.

Ranzato, M., Krizhevsky, A., and Hinton, G. E. (2010a). Factored 3-way restricted Boltzmann machines for modeling natural images. In *Proceedings of AISTATS 2010*.

Ranzato, M., Mnih, V., and Hinton, G. (2010b). Generating more realistic images using gated MRFs. In *NIPS'2010*.

Rao, C. (1945). Information and the accuracy attainable in the estimation of statistical parameters. *Bulletin of the Calcutta Mathematical Society*, **37**, 81–89.

Rasmus, A., Valpola, H., Honkala, M., Berglund, M., and Raiko, T. (2015). Semi-supervised learning with ladder network. *arXiv preprint arXiv:1507.02672*.

Recht, B., Re, C., Wright, S., and Niu, F. (2011). Hogwild: A lock-free approach to parallelizing stochastic gradient descent. In *NIPS'2011*.

Reichert, D. P., Seriès, P., and Storkey, A. J. (2011). Neuronal adaptation for sampling-based probabilistic inference in perceptual bistability. In *Advances in Neural Information Processing Systems*, pages 2357–2365.

Rezende, D. J., Mohamed, S., and Wierstra, D. (2014). Stochastic backpropagation and approximate inference in deep generative models. In *ICML'2014*. Preprint: arXiv:1401.4082.

Rifai, S., Vincent, P., Muller, X., Glorot, X., and Bengio, Y. (2011a). Contractive auto-encoders: Explicit invariance during feature extraction. In *ICML'2011*.

Rifai, S., Mesnil, G., Vincent, P., Muller, X., Bengio, Y., Dauphin, Y., and Glorot, X. (2011b). Higher order contractive auto-encoder. In *ECML PKDD*.

Rifai, S., Dauphin, Y., Vincent, P., Bengio, Y., and Muller, X. (2011c). The manifold tangent classifier. In *NIPS'2011*.

Rifai, S., Bengio, Y., Dauphin, Y., and Vincent, P. (2012). A generative process for sampling contractive auto-encoders. In *ICML'2012*.

Ringach, D. and Shapley, R. (2004). Reverse correlation in neurophysiology. *Cognitive Science*, **28**(2), 147–166.

Roberts, S. and Everson, R. (2001). *Independent component analysis: principles and practice*. Cambridge University Press.

Robinson, A. J. and Fallside, F. (1991). A recurrent error propagation network speech recognition system. *Computer Speech and Language*, **5**(3), 259–274.

Rockafellar, R. T. (1997). Convex analysis. princeton landmarks in mathematics.

Romero, A., Ballas, N., Ebrahimi Kahou, S., Chassang, A., Gatta, C., and Bengio, Y. (2015). Fitnets: Hints for thin deep nets. In *ICLR'2015, arXiv:1412.6550*.

Rosen, J. B. (1960). The gradient projection method for nonlinear programming. part i. linear constraints. *Journal of the Society for Industrial and Applied Mathematics*, **8**(1), pp. 181–217.

Rosenblatt, F. (1958). The perceptron: A probabilistic model for information storage and organization in the brain. *Psychological Review*, **65**, 386–408.

Rosenblatt, F. (1962). *Principles of Neurodynamics*. Spartan, New York.

Roweis, S. and Saul, L. K. (2000). Nonlinear dimensionality reduction by locally linear embedding. *Science*, **290**(5500).

Roweis, S., Saul, L., and Hinton, G. (2002). Global coordination of local linear models. In T. Dietterich, S. Becker, and Z. Ghahramani, editors, *Advances in Neural Information Processing Systems 14 (NIPS'01)*, Cambridge, MA. MIT Press.

Rubin, D. B. et al. (1984). Bayesianly justifiable and relevant frequency calculations for the applied statistician. *The Annals of Statistics*, **12**(4), 1151–1172.

Rumelhart, D., Hinton, G., and Williams, R. (1986a). Learning representations by back-propagating errors. *Nature*, **323**, 533–536.

Rumelhart, D. E., Hinton, G. E., and Williams, R. J. (1986b). Learning internal representations by error propagation. In D. E. Rumelhart and J. L. McClelland, editors, *Parallel Distributed Processing*, volume 1, chapter 8, pages 318–362. MIT Press, Cambridge.

Rumelhart, D. E., McClelland, J. L., and the PDP Research Group (1986c). *Parallel Distributed Processing: Explorations in the Microstructure of Cognition*. MIT Press, Cambridge.

Russakovsky, O., Deng, J., Su, H., Krause, J., Satheesh, S., Ma, S., Huang, Z., Karpathy, A., Khosla, A., Bernstein, M., Berg, A. C., and Fei-Fei, L. (2014a). ImageNet Large Scale Visual Recognition Challenge.

Russakovsky, O., Deng, J., Su, H., Krause, J., Satheesh, S., Ma, S., Huang, Z., Karpathy, A., Khosla, A., Bernstein, M., et al. (2014b). Imagenet large scale visual recognition challenge. *arXiv preprint arXiv:1409.0575*.

Russel, S. J. and Norvig, P. (2003). *Artificial Intelligence: a Modern Approach*. Prentice Hall.

Rust, N., Schwartz, O., Movshon, J. A., and Simoncelli, E. (2005). Spatiotemporal elements of macaque V1 receptive fields. *Neuron*, **46**(6), 945–956.

Sainath, T., Mohamed, A., Kingsbury, B., and Ramabhadran, B. (2013). Deep convolutional neural networks for LVCSR. In *ICASSP 2013*.

Salakhutdinov, R. (2010). Learning in Markov random fields using tempered transitions. In Y. Bengio, D. Schuurmans, C. Williams, J. Lafferty, and A. Culotta, editors, *Advances in Neural Information Processing Systems 22 (NIPS'09)*.

Salakhutdinov, R. and Hinton, G. (2009a). Deep Boltzmann machines. In *Proceedings of the International Conference on Artificial Intelligence and Statistics*, volume 5, pages 448–455.

Salakhutdinov, R. and Hinton, G. (2009b). Semantic hashing. In *International Journal of Approximate Reasoning*.

Salakhutdinov, R. and Hinton, G. E. (2007a). Learning a nonlinear embedding by preserving class neighbourhood structure. In *Proceedings of the Eleventh International Conference on Artificial Intelligence and Statistics (AISTATS'07)*, San Juan, Porto Rico. Omnipress.

Salakhutdinov, R. and Hinton, G. E. (2007b). Semantic hashing. In *SIGIR'2007*.

Salakhutdinov, R. and Hinton, G. E. (2008). Using deep belief nets to learn covariance kernels for Gaussian processes. In J. Platt, D. Koller, Y. Singer, and S. Roweis, editors, *Advances in Neural Information Processing Systems 20 (NIPS'07)*, pages 1249–1256, Cambridge, MA. MIT Press.

Salakhutdinov, R. and Larochelle, H. (2010). Efficient learning of deep Boltzmann machines. In *Proceedings of the Thirteenth International Conference on Artificial Intelligence and Statistics (AISTATS 2010), JMLR W&CP*, volume 9, pages 693–700.

Salakhutdinov, R. and Mnih, A. (2008). Probabilistic matrix factorization. In *NIPS'2008*.

Salakhutdinov, R. and Murray, I. (2008). On the quantitative analysis of deep belief networks. In W. W. Cohen, A. McCallum, and S. T. Roweis, editors, *Proceedings of the Twenty-fifth International Conference on Machine Learning (ICML'08)*, volume 25, pages 872–879. ACM.

Salakhutdinov, R., Mnih, A., and Hinton, G. (2007). Restricted Boltzmann machines for collaborative filtering. In *ICML*.

Sanger, T. D. (1994). Neural network learning control of robot manipulators using gradually increasing task difficulty. *IEEE Transactions on Robotics and Automation*, **10**(3).

Saul, L. K. and Jordan, M. I. (1996). Exploiting tractable substructures in intractable networks. In D. Touretzky, M. Mozer, and M. Hasselmo, editors, *Advances in Neural Information Processing Systems 8 (NIPS'95)*. MIT Press, Cambridge, MA.

Saul, L. K., Jaakkola, T., and Jordan, M. I. (1996). Mean field theory for sigmoid belief networks. *Journal of Artificial Intelligence Research*, **4**, 61–76.

Savich, A. W., Moussa, M., and Areibi, S. (2007). The impact of arithmetic representation on implementing mlp-bp on fpgas: A study. *Neural Networks, IEEE Transactions on*, **18**(1), 240–252.

Saxe, A. M., Koh, P. W., Chen, Z., Bhand, M., Suresh, B., and Ng, A. (2011). On random weights and unsupervised feature learning. In *Proc. ICML'2011*. ACM.

Saxe, A. M., McClelland, J. L., and Ganguli, S. (2013). Exact solutions to the nonlinear dynamics of learning in deep linear neural networks. In *ICLR*.

Schaul, T., Antonoglou, I., and Silver, D. (2014). Unit tests for stochastic optimization. In *International Conference on Learning Representations*.

Schmidhuber, J. (1992). Learning complex, extended sequences using the principle of history compression. *Neural Computation*, **4**(2), 234–242.

Schmidhuber, J. (1996). Sequential neural text compression. *IEEE Transactions on Neural Networks*, **7**(1), 142–146.

Schmidhuber, J. (2012). Self-delimiting neural networks. *arXiv preprint arXiv:1210.0118*.

Schölkopf, B. and Smola, A. J. (2002). *Learning with kernels: Support vector machines, regularization, optimization, and beyond*. MIT Press.

Schölkopf, B., Smola, A., and Müller, K.-R. (1998). Nonlinear component analysis as a kernel eigenvalue problem. *Neural Computation*, **10**, 1299–1319.

Schölkopf, B., Burges, C. J. C., and Smola, A. J. (1999). *Advances in Kernel Methods — Support Vector Learning*. MIT Press, Cambridge, MA.

Schölkopf, B., Janzing, D., Peters, J., Sgouritsa, E., Zhang, K., and Mooij, J. (2012). On causal and anticausal learning. In *ICML'2012*, pages 1255–1262.

Schuster, M. (1999). On supervised learning from sequential data with applications for speech recognition.

Schuster, M. and Paliwal, K. (1997). Bidirectional recurrent neural networks. *IEEE Transactions on Signal Processing*, **45**(11), 2673–2681.

Schwenk, H. (2007). Continuous space language models. *Computer speech and language*, **21**, 492–518.

Schwenk, H. (2010). Continuous space language models for statistical machine translation. *The Prague Bulletin of Mathematical Linguistics*, **93**, 137–146.

Schwenk, H. (2014). Cleaned subset of WMT '14 dataset.

Schwenk, H. and Bengio, Y. (1998). Training methods for adaptive boosting of neural networks. In M. Jordan, M. Kearns, and S. Solla, editors, *Advances in Neural Information Processing Systems 10 (NIPS'97)*, pages 647–653. MIT Press.

Schwenk, H. and Gauvain, J.-L. (2002). Connectionist language modeling for large vocabulary continuous speech recognition. In *International Conference on Acoustics, Speech and Signal Processing (ICASSP)*, pages 765–768, Orlando, Florida.

Schwenk, H., Costa-jussà, M. R., and Fonollosa, J. A. R. (2006). Continuous space language models for the IWSLT 2006 task. In *International Workshop on Spoken Language Translation*, pages 166–173.

Seide, F., Li, G., and Yu, D. (2011). Conversational speech transcription using context-dependent deep neural networks. In *Interspeech 2011*, pages 437–440.

Sejnowski, T. (1987). Higher-order Boltzmann machines. In *AIP Conference Proceedings 151 on Neural Networks for Computing*, pages 398–403. American Institute of Physics Inc.

Series, P., Reichert, D. P., and Storkey, A. J. (2010). Hallucinations in Charles Bonnet syndrome induced by homeostasis: a deep Boltzmann machine model. In *Advances in Neural Information Processing Systems*, pages 2020–2028.

Sermanet, P., Chintala, S., and LeCun, Y. (2012). Convolutional neural networks applied to house numbers digit classification. *CoRR*, **abs/1204.3968**.

Sermanet, P., Kavukcuoglu, K., Chintala, S., and LeCun, Y. (2013). Pedestrian detection with unsupervised multi-stage feature learning. In *Proc. International Conference on Computer Vision and Pattern Recognition (CVPR'13)*. IEEE.

Shilov, G. (1977). *Linear Algebra*. Dover Books on Mathematics Series. Dover Publications.

Siegelmann, H. (1995). Computation beyond the Turing limit. *Science*, **268**(5210), 545–548.

Siegelmann, H. and Sontag, E. (1991). Turing computability with neural nets. *Applied Mathematics Letters*, **4**(6), 77–80.

Siegelmann, H. T. and Sontag, E. D. (1995). On the computational power of neural nets. *Journal of Computer and Systems Sciences*, **50**(1), 132–150.

Sietsma, J. and Dow, R. (1991). Creating artificial neural networks that generalize. *Neural Networks*, **4**(1), 67–79.

Simard, D., Steinkraus, P. Y., and Platt, J. C. (2003). Best practices for convolutional neural networks. In *ICDAR'2003*.

Simard, P. and Graf, H. P. (1994). Backpropagation without multiplication. In *Advances in Neural Information Processing Systems*, pages 232–239.

Simard, P., Victorri, B., LeCun, Y., and Denker, J. (1992). Tangent prop - A formalism for specifying selected invariances in an adaptive network. In *NIPS'1991*.

Simard, P. Y., LeCun, Y., and Denker, J. (1993). Efficient pattern recognition using a new transformation distance. In *NIPS'92*.

Simard, P. Y., LeCun, Y. A., Denker, J. S., and Victorri, B. (1998). Transformation invariance in pattern recognition — tangent distance and tangent propagation. *Lecture Notes in Computer Science*, **1524**.

Simons, D. J. and Levin, D. T. (1998). Failure to detect changes to people during a real-world interaction. *Psychonomic Bulletin & Review*, **5**(4), 644–649.

Simonyan, K. and Zisserman, A. (2015). Very deep convolutional networks for large-scale image recognition. In *ICLR*.

Sjöberg, J. and Ljung, L. (1995). Overtraining, regularization and searching for a minimum, with application to neural networks. *International Journal of Control*, **62**(6), 1391–1407.

Skinner, B. F. (1958). Reinforcement today. *American Psychologist*, **13**, 94–99.

Smolensky, P. (1986). Information processing in dynamical systems: Foundations of harmony theory. In D. E. Rumelhart and J. L. McClelland, editors, *Parallel Distributed Processing*, volume 1, chapter 6, pages 194–281. MIT Press, Cambridge.

Snoek, J., Larochelle, H., and Adams, R. P. (2012). Practical Bayesian optimization of machine learning algorithms. In *NIPS'2012*.

Socher, R., Huang, E. H., Pennington, J., Ng, A. Y., and Manning, C. D. (2011a). Dynamic pooling and unfolding recursive autoencoders for paraphrase detection. In *NIPS'2011*.

Socher, R., Manning, C., and Ng, A. Y. (2011b). Parsing natural scenes and natural language with recursive neural networks. In *Proceedings of the Twenty-Eighth International Conference on Machine Learning (ICML'2011)*.

Socher, R., Pennington, J., Huang, E. H., Ng, A. Y., and Manning, C. D. (2011c). Semi-supervised recursive autoencoders for predicting sentiment distributions. In *EMNLP'2011*.

Socher, R., Perelygin, A., Wu, J. Y., Chuang, J., Manning, C. D., Ng, A. Y., and Potts, C. (2013a). Recursive deep models for semantic compositionality over a sentiment treebank. In *EMNLP'2013*.

Socher, R., Ganjoo, M., Manning, C. D., and Ng, A. Y. (2013b). Zero-shot learning through cross-modal transfer. In *27th Annual Conference on Neural Information Processing Systems (NIPS 2013)*.

Sohl-Dickstein, J., Weiss, E. A., Maheswaranathan, N., and Ganguli, S. (2015). Deep unsupervised learning using nonequilibrium thermodynamics.

Sohn, K., Zhou, G., and Lee, H. (2013). Learning and selecting features jointly with point-wise gated Boltzmann machines. In *ICML'2013*.

Solomonoff, R. J. (1989). A system for incremental learning based on algorithmic probability.

Sontag, E. D. (1998). VC dimension of neural networks. *NATO ASI Series F Computer and Systems Sciences*, **168**, 69–96.

Sontag, E. D. and Sussman, H. J. (1989). Backpropagation can give rise to spurious local minima even for networks without hidden layers. *Complex Systems*, **3**, 91–106.

Sparkes, B. (1996). *The Red and the Black: Studies in Greek Pottery*. Routledge.

Spitkovsky, V. I., Alshawi, H., and Jurafsky, D. (2010). From baby steps to leapfrog: how "less is more" in unsupervised dependency parsing. In *HLT'10*.

Squire, W. and Trapp, G. (1998). Using complex variables to estimate derivatives of real functions. *SIAM Rev.*, **40**(1), 110—112.

Srebro, N. and Shraibman, A. (2005). Rank, trace-norm and max-norm. In *Proceedings of the 18th Annual Conference on Learning Theory*, pages 545–560. Springer-Verlag.

Srivastava, N. (2013). *Improving Neural Networks With Dropout*. Master's thesis, U. Toronto.

Srivastava, N. and Salakhutdinov, R. (2012). Multimodal learning with deep Boltzmann machines. In *NIPS'2012*.

Srivastava, N., Salakhutdinov, R. R., and Hinton, G. E. (2013). Modeling documents with deep Boltzmann machines. *arXiv preprint arXiv:1309.6865*.

Srivastava, N., Hinton, G., Krizhevsky, A., Sutskever, I., and Salakhutdinov, R. (2014). Dropout: A simple way to prevent neural networks from overfitting. *Journal of Machine Learning Research*, **15**, 1929–1958.

Srivastava, R. K., Greff, K., and Schmidhuber, J. (2015). Highway networks. *arXiv:1505.00387*.

Steinkrau, D., Simard, P. Y., and Buck, I. (2005). Using GPUs for machine learning algorithms. *2013 12th International Conference on Document Analysis and Recognition*, **0**, 1115–1119.

Stoyanov, V., Ropson, A., and Eisner, J. (2011). Empirical risk minimization of graphical model parameters given approximate inference, decoding, and model structure. In *Proceedings of the 14th International Conference on Artificial Intelligence and Statistics (AISTATS)*, volume 15 of *JMLR Workshop and Conference Proceedings*, pages 725–733, Fort Lauderdale. Supplementary material (4 pages) also available.

Sukhbaatar, S., Szlam, A., Weston, J., and Fergus, R. (2015). Weakly supervised memory networks. *arXiv preprint arXiv:1503.08895*.

Supancic, J. and Ramanan, D. (2013). Self-paced learning for long-term tracking. In *CVPR'2013*.

Sussillo, D. (2014). Random walks: Training very deep nonlinear feed-forward networks with smart initialization. *CoRR*, **abs/1412.6558**.

Sutskever, I. (2012). *Training Recurrent Neural Networks*. Ph.D. thesis, Department of computer science, University of Toronto.

Sutskever, I. and Hinton, G. E. (2008). Deep narrow sigmoid belief networks are universal approximators. *Neural Computation*, **20**(11), 2629–2636.

Sutskever, I. and Tieleman, T. (2010). On the Convergence Properties of Contrastive Divergence. In Y. W. Teh and M. Titterington, editors, *Proc. of the International Conference on Artificial Intelligence and Statistics (AISTATS)*, volume 9, pages 789–795.

Sutskever, I., Hinton, G., and Taylor, G. (2009). The recurrent temporal restricted Boltzmann machine. In *NIPS'2008*.

Sutskever, I., Martens, J., and Hinton, G. E. (2011). Generating text with recurrent neural networks. In *ICML'2011*, pages 1017–1024.

Sutskever, I., Martens, J., Dahl, G., and Hinton, G. (2013). On the importance of initialization and momentum in deep learning. In *ICML*.

Sutskever, I., Vinyals, O., and Le, Q. V. (2014). Sequence to sequence learning with neural networks. In *NIPS'2014, arXiv:1409.3215*.

Sutton, R. and Barto, A. (1998). *Reinforcement Learning: An Introduction*. MIT Press.

Sutton, R. S., Mcallester, D., Singh, S., and Mansour, Y. (2000). Policy gradient methods for reinforcement learning with function approximation. In *NIPS'1999*, pages 1057–1063. MIT Press.

Swersky, K., Ranzato, M., Buchman, D., Marlin, B., and de Freitas, N. (2011). On autoencoders and score matching for energy based models. In *ICML'2011*. ACM.

Swersky, K., Snoek, J., and Adams, R. P. (2014). Freeze-thaw Bayesian optimization. *arXiv preprint arXiv:1406.3896*.

Szegedy, C., Liu, W., Jia, Y., Sermanet, P., Reed, S., Anguelov, D., Erhan, D., Vanhoucke, V., and Rabinovich, A. (2014a). Going deeper with convolutions. Technical report, arXiv:1409.4842.

Szegedy, C., Zaremba, W., Sutskever, I., Bruna, J., Erhan, D., Goodfellow, I. J., and Fergus, R. (2014b). Intriguing properties of neural networks. *ICLR, **abs/1312.6199***.

Szegedy, C., Vanhoucke, V., Ioffe, S., Shlens, J., and Wojna, Z. (2015). Rethinking the Inception Architecture for Computer Vision. *ArXiv e-prints*.

Taigman, Y., Yang, M., Ranzato, M., and Wolf, L. (2014). DeepFace: Closing the gap to human-level performance in face verification. In *CVPR'2014*.

Tandy, D. W. (1997). *Works and Days: A Translation and Commentary for the Social Sciences*. University of California Press.

Tang, Y. and Eliasmith, C. (2010). Deep networks for robust visual recognition. In *Proceedings of the 27th International Conference on Machine Learning, June 21-24, 2010, Haifa, Israel*.

Tang, Y., Salakhutdinov, R., and Hinton, G. (2012). Deep mixtures of factor analysers. *arXiv preprint arXiv:1206.4635*.

Taylor, G. and Hinton, G. (2009). Factored conditional restricted Boltzmann machines for modeling motion style. In L. Bottou and M. Littman, editors, *Proceedings of the Twenty-sixth International Conference on Machine Learning (ICML'09)*, pages 1025–1032, Montreal, Quebec, Canada. ACM.

Taylor, G., Hinton, G. E., and Roweis, S. (2007). Modeling human motion using binary latent variables. In B. Schölkopf, J. Platt, and T. Hoffman, editors, *Advances in Neural Information Processing Systems 19 (NIPS'06)*, pages 1345–1352. MIT Press, Cambridge, MA.

Teh, Y., Welling, M., Osindero, S., and Hinton, G. E. (2003). Energy-based models for sparse overcomplete representations. *Journal of Machine Learning Research*, **4**, 1235–1260.

Tenenbaum, J., de Silva, V., and Langford, J. C. (2000). A global geometric framework for nonlinear dimensionality reduction. *Science*, **290**(5500), 2319–2323.

Theis, L., van den Oord, A., and Bethge, M. (2015). A note on the evaluation of generative models. arXiv:1511.01844.

Thompson, J., Jain, A., LeCun, Y., and Bregler, C. (2014). Joint training of a convolutional network and a graphical model for human pose estimation. In *NIPS'2014*.

Thrun, S. (1995). Learning to play the game of chess. In *NIPS'1994*.

Tibshirani, R. J. (1995). Regression shrinkage and selection via the lasso. *Journal of the Royal Statistical Society B*, **58**, 267–288.

Tieleman, T. (2008). Training restricted Boltzmann machines using approximations to the likelihood gradient. In W. W. Cohen, A. McCallum, and S. T. Roweis, editors, *Proceedings of the Twenty-fifth International Conference on Machine Learning (ICML'08)*, pages 1064–1071. ACM.

Tieleman, T. and Hinton, G. (2009). Using fast weights to improve persistent contrastive divergence. In L. Bottou and M. Littman, editors, *Proceedings of the Twenty-sixth International Conference on Machine Learning (ICML'09)*, pages 1033–1040. ACM.

Tipping, M. E. and Bishop, C. M. (1999). Probabilistic principal components analysis. *Journal of the Royal Statistical Society B*, **61**(3), 611–622.

Torralba, A., Fergus, R., and Weiss, Y. (2008). Small codes and large databases for recognition. In *Proceedings of the Computer Vision and Pattern Recognition Conference (CVPR'08)*, pages 1–8.

Touretzky, D. S. and Minton, G. E. (1985). Symbols among the neurons: Details of a connectionist inference architecture. In *Proceedings of the 9th International Joint Conference on Artificial Intelligence - Volume 1*, IJCAI'85, pages 238–243, San Francisco, CA, USA. Morgan Kaufmann Publishers Inc.

Töscher, A., Jahrer, M., and Bell, R. M. (2009). The BigChaos solution to the Netflix grand prize.

Tu, K. and Honavar, V. (2011). On the utility of curricula in unsupervised learning of probabilistic grammars. In *IJCAI'2011*.

Turaga, S. C., Murray, J. F., Jain, V., Roth, F., Helmstaedter, M., Briggman, K., Denk, W., and Seung, H. S. (2010). Convolutional networks can learn to generate affinity graphs for image segmentation. *Neural Computation*, **22**(2), 511–538.

Turian, J., Ratinov, L., and Bengio, Y. (2010). Word representations: A simple and general method for semi-supervised learning. In *Proc. ACL'2010*, pages 384–394.

Uria, B., Murray, I., and Larochelle, H. (2013). Rnade: The real-valued neural autoregressive density-estimator. In *NIPS'2013*.

van den Oörd, A., Dieleman, S., and Schrauwen, B. (2013). Deep content-based music recommendation. In *NIPS'2013*.

van der Maaten, L. and Hinton, G. E. (2008). Visualizing data using t-SNE. *J. Machine Learning Res.*, **9**.

Vanhoucke, V., Senior, A., and Mao, M. Z. (2011). Improving the speed of neural networks on CPUs. In *Proc. Deep Learning and Unsupervised Feature Learning NIPS Workshop*.

Vapnik, V. N. (1982). *Estimation of Dependences Based on Empirical Data*. Springer-Verlag, Berlin.

Vapnik, V. N. (1995). *The Nature of Statistical Learning Theory*. Springer, New York.

Vapnik, V. N. and Chervonenkis, A. Y. (1971). On the uniform convergence of relative frequencies of events to their probabilities. *Theory of Probability and Its Applications*, **16**, 264–280.

Vincent, P. (2011). A connection between score matching and denoising autoencoders. *Neural Computation*, **23**(7).

Vincent, P. and Bengio, Y. (2003). Manifold Parzen windows. In *NIPS'2002*. MIT Press.

Vincent, P., Larochelle, H., Bengio, Y., and Manzagol, P.-A. (2008). Extracting and composing robust features with denoising autoencoders. In *ICML 2008*.

Vincent, P., Larochelle, H., Lajoie, I., Bengio, Y., and Manzagol, P.-A. (2010). Stacked denoising autoencoders: Learning useful representations in a deep network with a local denoising criterion. *J. Machine Learning Res.*, **11**.

Vincent, P., de Brébisson, A., and Bouthillier, X. (2015). Efficient exact gradient update for training deep networks with very large sparse targets. In C. Cortes, N. D. Lawrence, D. D. Lee, M. Sugiyama, and R. Garnett, editors, *Advances in Neural Information Processing Systems 28*, pages 1108–1116. Curran Associates, Inc.

Vinyals, O., Kaiser, L., Koo, T., Petrov, S., Sutskever, I., and Hinton, G. (2014a). Grammar as a foreign language. Technical report, arXiv:1412.7449.

Vinyals, O., Toshev, A., Bengio, S., and Erhan, D. (2014b). Show and tell: a neural image caption generator. arXiv 1411.4555.

Vinyals, O., Fortunato, M., and Jaitly, N. (2015a). Pointer networks. *arXiv preprint arXiv:1506.03134*.

Vinyals, O., Toshev, A., Bengio, S., and Erhan, D. (2015b). Show and tell: a neural image caption generator. In *CVPR'2015*. arXiv:1411.4555.

Viola, P. and Jones, M. (2001). Robust real-time object detection. In *International Journal of Computer Vision*.

Visin, F., Kastner, K., Cho, K., Matteucci, M., Courville, A., and Bengio, Y. (2015). ReNet: A recurrent neural network based alternative to convolutional networks. *arXiv preprint arXiv:1505.00393*.

Von Melchner, L., Pallas, S. L., and Sur, M. (2000). Visual behaviour mediated by retinal projections directed to the auditory pathway. *Nature*, **404**(6780), 871–876.

Wager, S., Wang, S., and Liang, P. (2013). Dropout training as adaptive regularization. In *Advances in Neural Information Processing Systems 26*, pages 351–359.

Waibel, A., Hanazawa, T., Hinton, G. E., Shikano, K., and Lang, K. (1989). Phoneme recognition using time-delay neural networks. *IEEE Transactions on Acoustics, Speech, and Signal Processing*, **37**, 328–339.

Wan, L., Zeiler, M., Zhang, S., LeCun, Y., and Fergus, R. (2013). Regularization of neural networks using dropconnect. In *ICML'2013*.

Wang, S. and Manning, C. (2013). Fast dropout training. In *ICML'2013*.

Wang, Z., Zhang, J., Feng, J., and Chen, Z. (2014a). Knowledge graph and text jointly embedding. In *Proc. EMNLP'2014*.

Wang, Z., Zhang, J., Feng, J., and Chen, Z. (2014b). Knowledge graph embedding by translating on hyperplanes. In *Proc. AAAI'2014*.

Warde-Farley, D., Goodfellow, I. J., Courville, A., and Bengio, Y. (2014). An empirical analysis of dropout in piecewise linear networks. In *ICLR'2014*.

Wawrzynek, J., Asanovic, K., Kingsbury, B., Johnson, D., Beck, J., and Morgan, N. (1996). Spert-II: A vector microprocessor system. *Computer*, **29**(3), 79–86.

Weaver, L. and Tao, N. (2001). The optimal reward baseline for gradient-based reinforcement learning. In *Proc. UAI'2001*, pages 538–545.

Weinberger, K. Q. and Saul, L. K. (2004). Unsupervised learning of image manifolds by semidefinite programming. In *CVPR'2004*, pages 988–995.

Weiss, Y., Torralba, A., and Fergus, R. (2008). Spectral hashing. In *NIPS*, pages 1753–1760.

Welling, M., Zemel, R. S., and Hinton, G. E. (2002). Self supervised boosting. In *Advances in Neural Information Processing Systems*, pages 665–672.

Welling, M., Hinton, G. E., and Osindero, S. (2003a). Learning sparse topographic representations with products of Student t-distributions. In *NIPS'2002*.

Welling, M., Zemel, R., and Hinton, G. E. (2003b). Self-supervised boosting. In S. Becker, S. Thrun, and K. Obermayer, editors, *Advances in Neural Information Processing Systems 15 (NIPS'02)*, pages 665–672. MIT Press.

Welling, M., Rosen-Zvi, M., and Hinton, G. E. (2005). Exponential family harmoniums with an application to information retrieval. In L. Saul, Y. Weiss, and L. Bottou, editors, *Advances in Neural Information Processing Systems 17 (NIPS'04)*, volume 17, Cambridge, MA. MIT Press.

Werbos, P. J. (1981). Applications of advances in nonlinear sensitivity analysis. In *Proceedings of the 10th IFIP Conference, 31.8 - 4.9, NYC*, pages 762–770.

Weston, J., Bengio, S., and Usunier, N. (2010). Large scale image annotation: learning to rank with joint word-image embeddings. *Machine Learning*, **81**(1), 21–35.

Weston, J., Chopra, S., and Bordes, A. (2014). Memory networks. *arXiv preprint arXiv:1410.3916*.

Widrow, B. and Hoff, M. E. (1960). Adaptive switching circuits. In *1960 IRE WESCON Convention Record*, volume 4, pages 96–104. IRE, New York.

Wikipedia (2015). List of animals by number of neurons — Wikipedia, the free encyclopedia. [Online; accessed 4-March-2015].

Williams, C. K. I. and Agakov, F. V. (2002). Products of Gaussians and Probabilistic Minor Component Analysis. *Neural Computation*, **14**(5), 1169–1182.

Williams, C. K. I. and Rasmussen, C. E. (1996). Gaussian processes for regression. In D. Touretzky, M. Mozer, and M. Hasselmo, editors, *Advances in Neural Information Processing Systems 8 (NIPS'95)*, pages 514–520. MIT Press, Cambridge, MA.

Williams, R. J. (1992). Simple statistical gradient-following algorithms connectionist reinforcement learning. *Machine Learning*, **8**, 229–256.

Williams, R. J. and Zipser, D. (1989). A learning algorithm for continually running fully recurrent neural networks. *Neural Computation*, **1**, 270–280.

Wilson, D. R. and Martinez, T. R. (2003). The general inefficiency of batch training for gradient descent learning. *Neural Networks*, **16**(10), 1429–1451.

Wilson, J. R. (1984). Variance reduction techniques for digital simulation. *American Journal of Mathematical and Management Sciences*, **4**(3), 277—312.

Wiskott, L. and Sejnowski, T. J. (2002). Slow feature analysis: Unsupervised learning of invariances. *Neural Computation*, **14**(4), 715–770.

Wolpert, D. and MacReady, W. (1997). No free lunch theorems for optimization. *IEEE Transactions on Evolutionary Computation*, **1**, 67–82.

Wolpert, D. H. (1996). The lack of a priori distinction between learning algorithms. *Neural Computation*, **8**(7), 1341–1390.

Wu, R., Yan, S., Shan, Y., Dang, Q., and Sun, G. (2015). Deep image: Scaling up image recognition. arXiv:1501.02876.

Wu, Z. (1997). Global continuation for distance geometry problems. *SIAM Journal of Optimization*, **7**, 814–836.

Xiong, H. Y., Barash, Y., and Frey, B. J. (2011). Bayesian prediction of tissue-regulated splicing using RNA sequence and cellular context. *Bioinformatics*, **27**(18), 2554–2562.

Xu, K., Ba, J. L., Kiros, R., Cho, K., Courville, A., Salakhutdinov, R., Zemel, R. S., and Bengio, Y. (2015). Show, attend and tell: Neural image caption generation with visual attention. In *ICML'2015, arXiv:1502.03044*.

Yildiz, I. B., Jaeger, H., and Kiebel, S. J. (2012). Re-visiting the echo state property. *Neural networks*, **35**, 1–9.

Yosinski, J., Clune, J., Bengio, Y., and Lipson, H. (2014). How transferable are features in deep neural networks? In *NIPS'2014*.

Younes, L. (1998). On the convergence of Markovian stochastic algorithms with rapidly decreasing ergodicity rates. In *Stochastics and Stochastics Models*, pages 177–228.

Yu, D., Wang, S., and Deng, L. (2010). Sequential labeling using deep-structured conditional random fields. *IEEE Journal of Selected Topics in Signal Processing*.

Zaremba, W. and Sutskever, I. (2014). Learning to execute. arXiv 1410.4615.

Zaremba, W. and Sutskever, I. (2015). Reinforcement learning neural Turing machines. *arXiv:1505.00521*.

Zaslavsky, T. (1975). *Facing Up to Arrangements: Face-Count Formulas for Partitions of Space by Hyperplanes*. Number no. 154 in Memoirs of the American Mathematical Society. American Mathematical Society.

Zeiler, M. D. and Fergus, R. (2014). Visualizing and understanding convolutional networks. In *ECCV'14*.

Zeiler, M. D., Ranzato, M., Monga, R., Mao, M., Yang, K., Le, Q., Nguyen, P., Senior, A., Vanhoucke, V., Dean, J., and Hinton, G. E. (2013). On rectified linear units for speech processing. In *ICASSP 2013*.

Zhou, B., Khosla, A., Lapedriza, A., Oliva, A., and Torralba, A. (2015). Object detectors emerge in deep scene CNNs. ICLR'2015, arXiv:1412.6856.

Zhou, J. and Troyanskaya, O. G. (2014). Deep supervised and convolutional generative stochastic network for protein secondary structure prediction. In *ICML'2014*.

Zhou, Y. and Chellappa, R. (1988). Computation of optical flow using a neural network. In *Neural Networks, 1988., IEEE International Conference on*, pages 71–78. IEEE.

Zöhrer, M. and Pernkopf, F. (2014). General stochastic networks for classification. In *NIPS'2014*.

Index

Adaptive Computation and Machine Learning

Thomas Dietterich, Editor
Christopher Bishop, David Heckerman, Michael Jordan, and Michael Kearns, Associate Editors

Bioinformatics: The Machine Learning Approach, Pierre Baldi and Søren Brunak

Reinforcement Learning: An Introduction, Richard S. Sutton and Andrew G. Barto

Graphical Models for Machine Learning and Digital Communication, Brendan J. Frey

Learning in Graphical Models, Michael I. Jordan

Causation, Prediction, and Search, second edition, Peter Spirtes, Clark Glymour, and Richard Scheines

Principles of Data Mining, David Hand, Heikki Mannila, and Padhraic Smyth

Bioinformatics: The Machine Learning Approach, second edition, Pierre Baldi and Søren Brunak

Learning Kernel Classifiers: Theory and Algorithms, Ralf Herbrich

Learning with Kernels: Support Vector Machines, Regularization, Optimization, and Beyond, Bernhard Schölkopf and Alexander J. Smola

Introduction to Machine Learning, Ethem Alpaydin

Gaussian Processes for Machine Learning, Carl Edward Rasmussen and Christopher K.I. Williams

Semi-Supervised Learning, Olivier Chapelle, Bernhard Schölkopf, and Alexander Zien, Eds.

The Minimum Description Length Principle, Peter D. Grünwald

Introduction to Statistical Relational Learning, Lise Getoor and Ben Taskar, Eds.

Probabilistic Graphical Models: Principles and Techniques, Daphne Koller and Nir Friedman

Introduction to Machine Learning, second edition, Ethem Alpaydin

Machine Learning in Non-Stationary Environments: Introduction to Covariate Shift Adaptation, Masashi Sugiyama and Motoaki Kawanabe

Boosting: Foundations and Algorithms, Robert E. Schapire and Yoav Freund

Machine Learning: A Probabilistic Perspective, Kevin P. Murphy

Foundations of Machine Learning, Mehryar Mohri, Afshin Rostami, and Ameet Talwalker

Introduction to Machine Learning, third edition, Ethem Alpaydin

Deep Learning, Ian Goodfellow, Yoshua Bengio, and Aaron Courville